HANDBOOK OF THE PSYCHOLOGY OF RELIGION AND SPIRITUALITY

ALSO FROM CRYSTAL L. PARK

Handbook of Health Psychology and Aging
Edited by Carolyn M. Aldwin, Crystal L. Park, and Avron Spiro III

Handbook of
THE PSYCHOLOGY
OF RELIGION
AND SPIRITUALITY

SECOND EDITION

Edited by
RAYMOND F. PALOUTZIAN
CRYSTAL L. PARK

THE GUILFORD PRESS
New York   London

© 2013 The Guilford Press
A Division of Guilford Publications, Inc.
72 Spring Street, New York, NY 10012
www.guilford.com

Printed in the United States of America

This book is printed on acid-free paper.

Last digit is print number: 9 8 7 6 5 4 3 2 1

Library of Congress Cataloging-in-Publication Data is available from the Publisher.

ISBN 978-1-4625-1006-1

About the Editors

Raymond F. Paloutzian, PhD, is Professor Emeritus of Experimental and Social Psychology at Westmont College in Santa Barbara, California. He taught at Scripps College of The Claremont Colleges and has been a visiting professor at Stanford University and a guest professor and continuing visiting scholar at Katholieke Universiteit Leuven, Belgium. Dr. Paloutzian is Editor of *The International Journal for the Psychology of Religion*. A Fellow of the American Psychological Association (APA), the Association for Psychological Science, and the Western Psychological Association, he is a past president of APA Division 36 (Psychology of Religion and Spirituality).

Crystal L. Park, PhD, is Professor of Psychology at the University of Connecticut. She is Associate Editor of *Psychology and Health*, the *Journal of Consulting and Clinical Psychology, Psychology of Religion and Spirituality,* and *The International Journal for the Psychology of Religion.* Dr. Park is a past president and the current awards chair of APA Division 36, and the recipient of the Division's 2014 William James Award. Her research interests include the roles of religious beliefs and religious coping in response to stressful life events, the phenomenon of stress-related growth, and people's attempts to find meaning in or create meaning out of negative life events.

Contributors

Carolyn M. Aldwin, PhD, is Professor in Human Development and Family Sciences at Oregon State University, Corvallis, Oregon.

Gene G. Ano, PhD, is Professor in the Department of Psychology and Education at Mount San Antonio College, Walnut, California.

Justin L. Barrett, PhD, is the Thrive Professor of Developmental Science and Director of the Thrive Center for Human Development at Fuller Theological Seminary Graduate School of Psychology, Pasadena, California.

Roy F. Baumeister, PhD, is Eppes Eminent Professor in the Department of Psychology at Florida State University, Tallahassee, Florida.

Jacob A. Belzen, PhD, is Full Professor of Psychology of Religion at the University of Amsterdam, Amsterdam, The Netherlands.

P. Monroe Butler, MD, PhD, MTS, is completing medical studies at Boston University School of Medicine, Boston, Massachusetts.

Zhuo Chen, MS, is a PhD student in Psychology at the University of Oregon, Eugene, Oregon.

Adam B. Cohen, PhD, is Associate Professor, CARMA Lab, in the Department of Psychology at Arizona State University, Tempe, Arizona.

Jozef Corveleyn, PhD, is Professor in the Faculty of Psychology at Katholieke Universiteit, Leuven, Belgium, and part-time Professor of Clinical Psychology Religion in the Faculty of Psychology and Educational Sciences at the Free University of Amsterdam, The Netherlands.

Don E. Davis, PhD, is Assistant Professor of Psychology at Georgia State University, Atlanta, Georgia.

Jessie Dezutter, PhD, is a postdoctoral researcher at the Center for the Psychology of Religion, Faculty of Psychology at Katholieke Universiteit, Leuven, Belgium.

Michael J. Donahue, PhD, is Associate Professor and Director of Research Training at the Institute for the Psychological Sciences, Arlington, Virginia.

Robert A. Emmons, PhD, is Professor of Psychology at the University of California, Davis, Davis, California.

Julie J. Exline, PhD, is Associate Professor of Psychology at Case Western Reserve University, Cleveland, Ohio.

Melissa D. Falb, MA, is a PhD student in the Department of Psychology at Bowling Green State University, Bowling Green, Ohio.

Louis W. Fry, PhD, is in the Department of Management at Tarleton State University–Central Texas, Killeen, Texas.

Aubrey L. Gartner, PhD, is a postdoctoral fellow in Psychosocial Rehabilitation and Recovery Oriented Services at the Durham Veterans Affairs Medical Center, Durham, North Carolina.

Robert A. Giacalone, PhD, is Professor in the Department of Human Resource Management at the Fox School of Business and Management, Temple University, Philadelphia, Pennsylvania.

Alfredo Gonzalez, BA, is a Senior Helpline Supervisor at the Area Agency on Aging, Phoenix, Arizona.

Pehr Granqvist, PhD, is Associate Professor in the Department of Psychology at Stockholm University, Stockholm, Sweden.

Chelsea L. Greer, MS, is a PhD student in Counseling Psychology at Virginia Commonwealth University, Richmond, Virginia.

Arthur T. Hatton, BA, is an MS student in Psychology at Georgia Southern University, Statesboro, Georgia.

Peter C. Hill, PhD, is Professor of Social Psychology in the Rosemead School of Psychology at Biola University, La Mirada, California.

Ralph W. Hood, Jr., PhD, is Professor of Psychology at the University of Tennessee at Chattanooga, Chattanooga, Tennessee.

Joshua N. Hook, PhD, is Assistant Professor of Psychology at the University of North Texas, Denton, Texas.

Stephanie A. Hooker, MA, is a PhD student in Clinical Health Psychology at the University of Colorado Denver, Denver, Colorado.

Heidi Igarashi, MS, is a doctoral student in Human Development and Family Sciences at Oregon State University, Corvallis, Oregon.

David J. Jennings II, MS, is a PhD student in Counseling Psychology at Virginia Commonwealth University, Richmond, Virginia.

Carole L. Jurkiewicz, PhD, is John W. Dupuy Endowed Professor and Women's Hospital Distinguished Professor of Healthcare Management at Louisiana State University, Baton Rouge, Louisiana.

Lee A. Kirkpatrick, PhD, is Professor and Director of Graduate Studies in the Department of Psychology at the College of William and Mary, Williamsburg, Virginia.

Birgit Koopmann-Holm, MA, is a PhD candidate in Psychology at Stanford University, Stanford, California.

Jordan P. LaBouff, PhD, is Assistant Professor in the Department of Psychology and Honors College at the University of Maine, Orono, Maine.

Kevin L. Ladd, PhD, is Associate Professor in the Department of Psychology at Indiana University South Bend, South Bend, Indiana.

Michael R. Levenson, PhD, is Research Associate Professor in Human Development and Family Sciences at Oregon State University, Corvallis, Oregon.

Yin Lin, MS, is a PhD student in Counseling Psychology at Virginia Commonwealth University, Richmond, Virginia.

Karen Love, MA, lives in Arlington, Virginia.

Patrick Luyten, PhD, is Associate Professor of Clinical Psychology in the Faculty of Psychology at Katholieke Universiteit, Leuven, Belgium.

Kevin S. Masters, PhD, is Professor of Psychology and Program Director of Clinical Health Psychology at the University of Colorado Denver, Denver, Colorado.

Susan H. McFadden, PhD, is Professor Emerita of Psychology at the University of Wisconsin Oshkosh, Oshkosh, Wisconsin.

Patrick McNamara, PhD, is Associate Professor of Neurology and Psychiatry at Boston University School of Medicine, Boston, Massachusetts.

Masako Miyazaki, BFA, lives in Oakland, California.

Fathali M. Moghaddam, PhD, is Professor in the Department of Psychology and Director of the Conflict Resolution Program in the Department of Government, Georgetown University, Washington, DC.

Sebastian Murken, PhD, is a clinical psychologist in Germany and is Honorary Professor of Psychology of Religion at the University of Marburg, Marburg, Germany.

Michael E. Nielsen, PhD, is Professor and Chair of the Department of Psychology at Georgia Southern University, Statesboro, Georgia.

Camaron Ochs, BA, lives in Moraga, California.

Doug Oman, PhD, is Associate Adjunct Professor in the School of Public Health at the University of California, Berkeley, Berkeley, California.

Raymond F. Paloutzian, PhD, is Professor Emeritus of Experimental and Social Psychology at Westmont College, Santa Barbara, California.

Kenneth I. Pargament, PhD, is Professor of Psychology at Bowling Green State University, Bowling Green, Ohio.

Crystal L. Park, PhD, is Professor of Psychology at the University of Connecticut, Storrs, Connecticut.

Ralph L. Piedmont, PhD, is Professor of Pastoral Counseling at Loyola University Maryland, Columbia, Maryland.

Rebekah A. Richert, PhD, is Associate Professor in the Department of Psychology at the University of California, Riverside, Riverside, California.

Eric D. Rose, PhD, is a postdoctoral clinical fellow of Counseling and Psychological Services at Princeton University, Princeton, New Jersey.

Sussan Rößler-Namini, PhD, is a Research Associate of the Psychology of Religion Research Group at the University of Trier, Bad Kreuznach, Germany.

Wade C. Rowatt, PhD, is Associate Professor and Director of the PhD program in the Department of Psychology and Neuroscience at Baylor University, Waco, Texas.

Vassilis Saroglou, PhD, is Professor at the Centre for Psychology of Religion, Department of Psychology, at Université Catholique de Louvain, Louvain-la-Neuve, Belgium.

Sarah A. Schnitker, PhD, is Assistant Professor of Psychology at the Travis Research Institute at Fuller Theological Seminary, Pasadena, California.

Edward P. Shafranske, PhD, ABPP, is Professor of Psychology, Muriel Lipsey Endowed Chair for Counseling and Clinical Psychology, and Director of the PsyD program at Pepperdine University, Irvine, California; and lectures in the Psychiatry Residency Program at the University of California, Los Angeles, Los Angeles, California.

Megan Johnson Shen, PhD, is a postdoctoral fellow in the Department of Oncological Sciences at the Icahn School of Medicine at Mount Sinai, New York, New York.

Jeanne M. Slattery, PhD, is Professor of Psychology at Clarion University of Pennsylvania, Clarion, Pennsylvania.

Bernard Spilka, PhD, is Professor Emeritus in the Department of Psychology at the University of Denver, Denver, Colorado.

Heinz Streib, PhD, is Professor of Religious Education and Director at the Research Center for Biographical Studies in Contemporary Religion at Bielefeld University, Bielefeld, Germany.

Ann Taves, PhD, is Professor of Religious Studies at the University of California, Santa Barbara, Santa Barbara, California.

Jeanne L. Tsai, PhD, is Associate Professor of Psychology and Director of the Stanford Culture and Emotion Laboratory at Stanford University, Stanford, California.

Daryl R. Van Tongeren, PhD, is Assistant Professor of Psychology at Hope College, Holland, Michigan.

Amy B. Wachholtz, PhD, is Assistant Professor of Psychiatry at the University of Massachusetts Medical School and Director of Health Psychology at the University of Massachusetts Memorial Medical Center, Worcester, Massachusetts.

Zachary Warren, MA, MDiv, is a PhD student in Psychology at Georgetown University, Washington, DC.

Teresa A. Wilkins, MS, is a PhD student in the Pastoral Counseling Department at Loyola University Maryland, Columbia, Maryland.

Everett L. Worthington, Jr., PhD, is Professor of Psychology at Virginia Commonwealth University, Richmond, Virginia.

Anne L. Zell, PhD, is Assistant Professor in the Department of Psychology at Augustana College, Sioux Falls, South Dakota.

Preface

We were deeply gratified by the reception of the first edition of the *Handbook of the Psychology of Religion and Spirituality*. Widely cited, it has promoted and helped shape the subsequent proliferation of scholarship in this field. This proliferation, which we document in some depth in Chapter 1, has in turn prompted us to craft a second edition of the *Handbook*, allowing us to stay true to our mission of providing the most current theory and research in a single integrated and comprehensive volume. In this volume, we include the essential topics specific to the psychology of religion and spirituality (e.g., conversion, spiritual struggle, religious experience, ritual and prayer) and applications (e.g., clinical work, mental and physical health, work settings). We also include chapters on how the core topics of mainstream psychology (e.g., emotion, development, motivation, cognitive and social psychology, neuropsychology) are related to the psychology of religion and spirituality. These core chapters are essential to the *Handbook*, because we feel strongly that the psychology of religion and spirituality is central to all of human psychology, and these chapters provide linkages to the mainstream that we hope will promote more integration of this material into the rest of psychology.

We made sure that this book is not simply an update of the first edition, but also an extension of it. Most important, the changes are not merely cosmetic but are matters of substance. Of course, as a second edition, this volume contains many new citations on topics covered in the previous book. But this book goes much further: Most chapters are considerably redesigned and rethought but retain all essential elements from the first edition. The vast majority of chapters were completely or extensively rewritten. The number of chapters grew only slightly, by three, and thus the book remains a user-friendly size. Of the 33 chapters, 25 are completely new (five of which are on topics new to this second edition); 8 are significantly revised. We made a wish list of potential authors and our wishes were granted. We are deeply grateful to have many of the brightest and most knowledgeable writers in the psychology of religion and spirituality in this book.

In the first edition we set forth five integrative themes through which the research in this field can be understood: a multilevel interdisciplinary paradigm, religious meaning systems, theory and research, the role of the psychology of religion, and the path or trajectory of the psychology of religion. This edition carries those themes further than did the first edition, by more deeply integrating them into the chapters. Therefore, it is a foundational book whose core ideas are far reaching. We wanted it to convey a synthetic treatment of the varied topics in the field as a whole, and not be merely a collection of independent essays on topics in the psychology of religion. Because of its synthetic nature, we think this book has a wide range of uses for research and teaching, in both basic experimental and social psychological research and in clinical psychology, counseling, health, workplace, and other applied areas.

We took a major theoretical step forward in this second edition. Chapters 1 and 33 present an argument that the proper application of two pivotal themes—religious meaning systems and the multilevel interdisciplinary paradigm—allows us to recast how we conceptualize this field theoretically and expand the character and reach of our research. Doing so allows us to set aside the endless insistence on an unidentifiable and undefinable singularity as the central focus of research in the psychology of religion. In our own chapters and in those of many of our authors, we provide new ways to think about topics central to the psychology of religion and spirituality and explicit directions and considerations for future research. In this way, we hope to provide up-to-date theory and empirical findings to both new and established scholars, as well as to shape what we believe is the core area of inquiry into understanding human experience and behavior.

There are many people to thank, but we especially highlight our knowledgeable and talented authors. They did a wonderful job, as the users of this book will see. We also thank Mark Paloutzian and Rachel Wen-Paloutzian for preparation of the indices. As with the first edition of this handbook, we give a special thank you to our editor at The Guilford Press, Jim Nageotte. He gave us the guidance that we needed, the freedom to shape the book as we saw fit, and the correct amount of gentle extrinsic motivation to complete this big book, which we always wanted to complete by means of intrinsic motivation. Jim's wisdom was apparent in his original intellectual matchmaking; he separately approached each of us about coediting a handbook and created us as a team. In the 10 years we have worked together, we have developed a deep and delightful friendship and a style of collaboration that allows each of us to draw on our complementary strengths and balance out each other's excesses with joy and humor.

RAYMOND F. PALOUTZIAN
CRYSTAL L. PARK

Contents

I. FOUNDATIONS OF THE PSYCHOLOGY OF RELIGION

1. Recent Progress and Core Issues in the Science of the Psychology of Religion and Spirituality 3
Raymond F. Paloutzian and Crystal L. Park

2. Defining Religion and Spirituality 23
Doug Oman

3. Measurement Assessment and Issues in the Psychology of Religion and Spirituality 48
Peter C. Hill

4. Research Methods in the Psychology of Religion and Spirituality 75
Ralph W. Hood, Jr., and Jacob A. Belzen

5. Psychodynamic Psychology and Religion 94
Jozef Corveleyn, Patrick Luyten, and Jessie Dezutter

6. Evolutionary Psychology as a Foundation for the Psychology of Religion 118
Lee A. Kirkpatrick

7. Building Blocks of Sacralities: A New Basis for Comparison across Cultures and Religions 138
Ann Taves

II. RELIGION THROUGH THE DEVELOPMENTAL LENS

8. Religious and Spiritual Development in Childhood   165
Rebekah A. Richert and Pehr Granqvist

9. Religious Development from Adolescence to Middle Adulthood   183
*Michael R. Levenson, Carolyn M. Aldwin,
and Heidi Igarashi*

10. Old Persons, Old Age, Aging, and Religion   198
Susan H. McFadden

III. RELIGION AND BASIC PSYCHOLOGY SUBDISCIPLINES

11. The Neuropsychology of Religious Experience   215
Patrick McNamara and P. Monroe Butler

12. Exploring Religion's Basement: The Cognitive Science of Religion 234
Justin L. Barrett

13. Gods and Goals: Religion and Purposeful Action   256
Robert A. Emmons and Sarah A. Schnitker

14. The Religious Shaping of Feeling: Implications of Affect Valuation Theory 274
*Jeanne L. Tsai, Birgit Koopmann-Holm, Masako Miyazaki,
and Camaron Ochs*

15. The Role of Personality in Understanding Religious and Spiritual Constructs 292
Ralph L. Piedmont and Teresa A. Wilkins

16. Religiousness, Social Psychology, and Behavior   312
*Michael E. Nielsen, Arthur T. Hatton,
and Michael J. Donahue*

17. Cultural and Cross-Cultural Psychology of Religion   330
Vassilis Saroglou and Adam B. Cohen

IV. THE CONSTRUCTION AND EXPRESSION OF RELIGION AND SPIRITUALITY

18. Religion and Meaning   357
Crystal L. Park

19. Religious and Spiritual Struggles   380
   Julie J. Exline and Eric D. Rose

20. Conversion, Deconversion, and Spiritual Transformation: 399
   A Multilevel Interdisciplinary View
   Raymond F. Paloutzian, Sebastian Murken,
   Heinz Streib, and Sussan Rößler-Namini

21. Mystical, Spiritual, and Religious Experiences   422
   Ralph W. Hood, Jr., and Zhuo Chen

22. Ritual and Prayer: Forms, Functions, and Relationships   441
   Kevin L. Ladd and Bernard Spilka

23. Religious Fundamentalism, Right-Wing Authoritarianism, and Prejudice: 457
   Insights from Meta-Analyses, Implicit Social Cognition,
   and Social Neuroscience
   Wade C. Rowatt, Megan Johnson Shen,
   Jordan P. LaBouff, and Alfredo Gonzalez

24. Religion, Spirituality, and Forgiveness   476
   Everett L. Worthington, Jr., Don E. Davis, Joshua N. Hook,
   Daryl R. Van Tongeren, Aubrey L. Gartner,
   David J. Jennings II, Chelsea L. Greer, and Yin Lin

25. How Religion Can Support Self-Control and Moral Behavior   498
   Anne L. Zell and Roy F. Baumeister

V. THE PSYCHOLOGY
OF RELIGION AND APPLIED AREAS

26. Religion, Spirituality, and Health   519
   Kevin S. Masters and Stephanie A. Hooker

27. Religion, Spirituality, and Mental Health   540
   Crystal L. Park and Jeanne M. Slattery

28. The Religious Dimension of Coping: Advances in Theory, Research,   560
   and Practice
   Kenneth I. Pargament, Melissa D. Falb, Gene G. Ano,
   and Amy B. Wachholtz

29. Mindfulness in Psychology and Religion   580
   Michael R. Levenson and Carolyn M. Aldwin

30. Addressing Religiousness and Spirituality in Psychotherapy: 595
   Advancing Evidence-Based Practice
   Edward P. Shafranske

31. From Concept to Science: Continuing Steps in Workplace   617
   Spirituality Research
   *Peter C. Hill, Carole L. Jurkiewicz, Robert A. Giacalone,
   and Louis W. Fry*

32. Religion and the Staircase to Terrorism   632
   *Fathali M. Moghaddam, Zachary Warren,
   and Karen Love*

VI. CONCLUSION AND FUTURE DIRECTIONS

33. Directions for the Future of the Psychology of Religion and Spirituality: 651
   Research Advances in Methodology and Meaning Systems
   Crystal L. Park and Raymond F. Paloutzian

   Author Index   667

   Subject Index   686

HANDBOOK OF THE PSYCHOLOGY OF RELIGION AND SPIRITUALITY

Part I

FOUNDATIONS OF THE PSYCHOLOGY OF RELIGION

1

Recent Progress and Core Issues in the Science of the Psychology of Religion and Spirituality

Raymond F. Paloutzian and Crystal L. Park

In the 8 short years since the publication of the first edition of this handbook (Paloutzian & Park, 2005a), the science of the psychology of religion and spirituality has developed and expanded in many new and important ways. In this chapter, we convey the most pivotal and far-reaching of these recent developments. We do not elaborate on the central role of religiousness and spirituality in the history of human life or on the importance of psychological research on these topics today because these points were made in the 2005 *Handbook* and are amply confirmed by local and world events on a daily basis. Here, we review the professional and theoretical ideas that shaped the 2005 book and document and assess what has happened in the field since then in light of these ideas. In the companion chapter that closes the handbook, we examine the field's strengths and possible future contributions.

To show how the field has developed since 2005, we begin by documenting this progress in concrete terms. We document this progress because its magnitude, combined with the expanded audience engaged in it from other parts of psychology and allied disciplines, presents a compelling need for psychologists of religion to arrive at an unambiguous statement regarding what the central concern of this field is. It is important that the current generation of psychology of religion and spirituality scholars presents a more solid intellectual grounding to the next generation that is now emerging. These scholars need an intellectually clear and compelling framework through which to understand and integrate these recent advances and out of which their future research can flourish.

After illustrating this proliferation of information, we provide a framework based on the integrative themes (see Paloutzian & Park, 2005b) that structure both editions of the handbook to identify key issues that need to be resolved. We then elaborate on these issues in sections devoted to unresolved disagreements over what the foci of the psychology and spirituality are, developments in the model of religious meaning systems, and progress in integrating research across levels and between disciplines. We conclude with a brief look at a few of the paths the field has taken and roles it is playing. This chapter then paves the way for intellectually rich chapters that follow. We begin with a look some concrete indicators of progress in the field since 2005.

RECENT PROGRESS

A Snapshot of Evidence

Progress in the psychology of religion and spirituality can be documented in a number of ways. These include an increase in the number of books published on the topic, the establishment of new journals specifically for material on the psychology of religion and spirituality, a marked increase in articles in this area published in other special topic and mainstream psychology journals, a noticeable increase in presentations on this topic at professional meetings, an increase in the number of scholars who list this topic among their areas of expertise and interest, and the contents of this handbook. Let us briefly elaborate on each of these.

Handbooks

Since 2005, new handbooks and reference books dealing with the psychology of religion and spirituality have been published (de Souza, Francis, O'Higgins-Norman, & Scott (2009); Dowling & Scarlett, 2006; Miller, 2012; Pargament, Exline, & Jones, 2013; Pargament, Mahoney, & Shafranske, 2013; Roehlkepartain, King, Wagener, & Benson, 2006; Saroglou, in press). With the addition of these recent books to this second edition, a number of comprehensive resources with different emphases on the psychology of religion and spirituality are available to students and researchers. This is far beyond what anybody would have expected as recently as 10 years ago.

Journal Page Space

Research in the psychology of religion and spirituality has almost doubled within standard subdisciplinary journals. Within psychology of religion itself, for example, *The International Journal for the Psychology of Religion* increased in size; *Mental Health, Religion, and Culture* doubled its number of annual issues; the *Archives for the Psychology of Religion* changed from annual to quarterly publication; and four new periodicals were established: *Psychology of Religion and Spirituality, Journal of Muslim Mental Health, Journal for the Cognitive Science of Religion,* and *Religion, Brain, and Behavior.* These new journals significantly increased the number of primary publication outlets for research in this field and significantly added to the page space already devoted to the topic in existing journals,[1] such as *Journal for the Scientific Study of Religion, Review of Religious Research, Journal of Spirituality in Mental Health, Journal of Psychology and Theology,* and *Journal of Psychology and Christianity.*

Special Issues and Flagships

Research in the psychology of religion and spirituality began to appear more frequently in flagship and discipline-wide journals and in topical high-end journals.[2] The third-ever chapter concerned with the psychology of religion appeared in the *Annual Review of Psychology* (Bloom, 2012; Emmons & Paloutzian, 2003; Gorsuch, 1988). Special issues appeared on topics of the psychology of religion and spirituality in periodicals such as *Journal of Cross-Cultural Psychology* (Saroglou & Cohen, 2011), *Personality and Social Psychology Review* (Sedikides, 2010), and *Journal of Community & Applied Social Psychology* (Coyle & Lyons, 2011). Finally, publication of journal dialogues (i.e., a comprehensive lead paper followed by expert commentaries and then a reply to these commentaries by the authors of the lead paper) began to appear, such as that in *Psychological Bulletin* (Galen, 2012a, 2012b; Myers, 2012; Saroglou, 2012). As the above list illustrates, it has become more customary in this period to see research on the psychology of religion and spirituality treated within various subfields within psychology rather than as a separate topic segregated off unto itself.

Meetings

In addition to meetings designed to service the psychology of religion and spirituality (i.e., American Psychological Association [APA] Division 36 [Society for the Psychology of Religion and Spirituality] and the Society for the Scientific Study of Religion [SSSR]), other professional meetings have begun to devote more convention time to topics in the area. Also, the Society for Research in Child Development and the Society for Personality and Social Psychology began holding psychology of religion preconferences before their main meetings. The result has been an increase in cross-fertilization between the psychology of religion and spirituality and developmental and personality–social psychology researchers. In addition, scholarship in the area became more firmly established internationally through the biannual meetings of the International Association for the Psychology of Religion, whose 2011 meeting in Italy included participants from 27 nations and three continents (Scarpa, 2011–2012). Finally, one or more stand-alone conferences on various aspects of psychology of religion and spirituality were held in several countries, including Belgium, Canada, Czech Republic, Denmark, Italy, Iran, Mexico, the Netherlands, Poland, Scotland, Switzerland, and the United States. These meetings, added to the annual events of SSSR and APA Division 36, suggest a dramatic increase in interest and activity in a short period of time.

Critical Mass

Consistent with the professional activity just mentioned, much of this activity is occurring outside APA Division 36, which provided the associational home for most of the previous generation of scholars. There is a growing generation of scholars concerned with the psychology of religion and spirituality who seem less likely to identify only with this subfield, compared with past leaders, and instead list this topic as one among several in their portfolio of interests regardless of their general area of specialization.

This Book

Finally, this second edition reflects a wide range of new developments. New or greatly modified topics include research on the relation between religiousness and spirituality and mindfulness (Levenson & Aldwin, Chapter 29), cultural psychology (Saroglou &

Cohen, Chapter 17), cognitive science (Barrett, Chapter 12), neurology (McNamara & Butler, Chapter 11), affect valuation theory (Tsai, Koopmann-Holm, Miyazaki, & Ochs, Chapter 14), goals and purposeful action (Emmons & Schnitker, Chapter 13), and evidenced-based professional practice (Shafranske, Chapter 30). There are fully reconceptualized treatments of religion and terrorism (Moghaddam, Warren, & Love, Chapter 32), workplace spirituality (Hill, Jurkiewicz, Giacalone, & Fry, Chapter 31), and fundamentalism and authoritarianism (Rowatt, Johnson Shen, LaBouff, & Gonzalez, Chapter 23). The list of new developments extends to the humanities with the inclusion of a chapter on the building blocks of sacralities and problems inherent in cross-cultural comparisons by a scholar of religious studies (Taves, Chapter 7, this volume).

Summary

The combined evidence makes it clear that this field has come a long way. It is no longer a stand-alone area but rather an area whose research and theory are increasingly integrated into the parent discipline of psychology. It has matured to the point where it has a firm footing from which to say some compelling things to the rest of the scholarly world and beyond. For example, the model of meaning systems may begin to address basic issues of theory relevant to the rest of psychology; also, Part V of this book presents material applicable to clinically related areas (e.g., health, coping, mental health) and social-cultural areas (e.g., workplace policy, religious violence). In Chapter 33, we explain why we think the psychology of religion and spirituality will become more integrated within the rest of psychology while at the same time remaining a distinctive subfield that will not simply disappear into the whole.

Integrative Themes

In our 2005 book, we proposed that five themes could be used to cut across topics and help integrate this field, whose scope goes from the micro (e.g., neuroscientific) to the macro (e.g., social psychological, group, and cultural) levels. These themes are foundational to the arguments in this and the closing chapter and are applied throughout the book. We summarize them next,[3] slightly changed from their original presentation and applied to current issues.

1. *Theory in the psychology of religion and spirituality: Core multilevel issues.* An ideal goal in the psychology of religion and spirituality is to create a theory, based on evidence, that captures the range of phenomena subsumed by the topic and that has at its center a critical, correct statement and scientific assessment of its core elements and the psychological processes that connect them. Since processes can operate on multiple levels, from the neurological to the social, a comprehensive psychological theory of religion must address the phenomena at multiple levels, bearing in mind the fundamental rule of science that the validity or utility of a concept or process has to be capable of being evaluated by evidence. We need to apply this logic to the core notions used to define this area.

2. *Religious meaning systems* (RMS). In the first edition of the handbook, we argued that "religion" should be conceived in terms of religious meaning systems, that is, as a subset of meaning systems in general. Meaning systems (MSs), as we understand them psychologically, comprise mental processes that function together to enable a person (religious

or not) to live consciously and nonconsciously with a sense of relative continuity, evaluate incoming information relative to his or her guidelines, and regulate beliefs, affects, and actions accordingly. We did not spend much time in the last edition explaining what we mean by "religious" or how RMS might be distinguished from MS in general, other than to note the myriad definitional options of religion and spirituality (see Oman, Chapter 2, this volume; Zinnbauer & Pargament, 2005). In this edition, we confront that issue more directly. Thus, in the section on theory that follows, we argue that the term *religious* as an adjective modifying MS has no agreed-upon definition but instead designates a conceptually unstable subset of MSs that researchers operationalize in a number of different ways depending on the nature of their research. This instability will require that we talk not about religion in general but about particular religions or, better yet, about the particular aspects or features that have been operationalized. Even then, we need to realize that our operational definitions specify elements that are not necessarily present in all instances of religiousness, and that they may also be present outside in nonreligous realms.

3. *The multilevel interdisciplinary paradigm: Building theory by multiple-method data mapping.* Research on religiousness and spirituality needs to be conducted at all levels of analysis, the findings need to be related to each other, and the knowledge therefrom needs to be integrated. We need to move toward mapping evidence gained at one level with one method to its counterparts at the levels above and below. In this way, a multilevel interdisciplinary theory of religiousness and spirituality, anchored in the psychology of meaning making, can begin to take shape.

4. *Pathways of the psychology of religion and spirituality.* During the past 8 years, research in the psychology of religion and spirituality has been more fully integrated into research in psychology generally, and new research is reaching out to link additional subfields. We anticipate the expansion of this trend within psychology and its continued extension to allied disciplines as well.

5. *Roles of the psychology of religion and spirituality.* The psychology of religion and spirituality has various roles to play in service to psychology, scholarship generally, and human welfare. This means that the field has a role to play not only in the current so-called knowledge economy but also in the development of an applied psychology of religion. Both clinical and the nonclinical forms of such work would seem to be well positioned to make needed and worthwhile contributions.

These five themes,[4] which we offered in the first edition as a means of tying the handbook as a whole together, have been much more thoroughly woven into the individual chapters of the second edition, thus integrating the volume at a deeper level than the first edition. In preparing this second edition, however, we came to the realization that we could not refer to "religious meaning systems" without confronting the problem of defining religion more directly. We turn to this task in the next section.

THEORY: THE PSYCHOLOGY OF WHAT?

Although much of the scholarship in the psychology of religion and spirituality invokes a classical grand theory (e.g., Freud's psychoanalysis; see Corveleyn, Luyten, & Dezutter, Chapter 5, this volume, for updates) or one or more midlevel theories or mini-models such as attribution, attachment, intrinsic/extrinsic/quest, spiritual intelligence, or variations of developmental models, the form of these theories and models today is substantially as it was in 2005. So long as they stand the test of time and evidence, the concepts that emerge from them can be synthesized within a RMS model and fit within an evolutionary psychology metatheory (Kirkpatrick, Chapter 6, this volume). Moving toward this synthesis will require much testing of idea against idea and mapping results with analog results across levels, and such research can yield useful findings. However, we need a clear idea about what the central focus of this area of research is in order to succeed at synthesizing those concepts. The central focus depends on answers to the fundamental questions of definition and meaning that cut across all chapters in this book and every theoretical orientation or mini-model. Solving these fundamental questions goes to the root of this field, and thus takes priority over subjecting one of the existing notions to yet another test. Thus, we begin this section by tackling the problem of how to define, describe, or characterize this field. This is the pivotal element of the core issues—It has been a continuing dilemma and source of confusion. The future of theory and research in this field hinges on how it is resolved.

Core Issues

The centerpiece of the problem is evident in recurring issues that surface as psychologists of religion attempt to conceptualize religion and spirituality. The tendency to think and talk as if the field is or must be about a singularity is the most problematic. It surfaces in discussions of whether the psychology of religion is about one thing or essential element, whether it is self-evident (*sui generis*), and whether it is a particular kind of experience, belief, activity, emotion, or motive.

The consequences of leaving these matters unresolved become more apparent when we ask, for example, whether we should be trying to study religion in the singular versus religiousness expressed through religions in the plural; whether religion and spirituality can be said to rest upon a singular notion such as "the sacred"; whether humans have a specific need for religion or spirituality or transcendence; whether we are studying whatever the "it" is or the processes by which "it" works; and the degree to which religion or spirituality has psychologically unique properties that are regulated through processes not found elsewhere in human behavior.

In our view, the focus of the subfield of the psychology of religion is a hard-to-define, probably inherently unstable subset of the larger need to make meaning exhibited by humans and other animals, sometimes consciously and often not. Efforts to specify this subset in terms of a distinctive, unique feature, such as "the sacred," are, in our view, misguided. What scholars characterize as "the sacred" most likely refers to a cluster of attributes that need to be teased apart and specified more carefully. These different attributes most likely are not distinctively religious, spiritual, or sacred, but—in various combinations—may often be perceived as such. Thus, we think the field needs to abandon the quest for a singularity. We hope the following discussion clarifies why and how.

Religiousness and Uniqueness

The question of whether religion and spirituality reflect a unique psychological process, one that is not present in any other human behavior, is a recurring one (for careful examinations of this issue, see Baumeister, 2002; Paloutzian & Park, 2005b). Some definitions seem to presuppose the uniqueness of this process, thus unnecessarily or perhaps inadvertently protecting it from serious challenge (for a wide range of definitions, see Oman, Chapter 2, this volume; Zinnbauer & Pargament, 2005). If definitions stipulate or presuppose that religion and spirituality require their own special explanatory principles and cannot by definition be explained in terms of general psychological processes (Pargament, 2002), then we are simply asserting their uniqueness. (And seeing something as unique is but an easy psychological step away from seeing it as inherently set apart and, therefore, sacred; see later discussion.) However, if religion or spirituality is genuinely psychologically unique, it needs no protection; if it is not, this should be forthrightly acknowledged rather than implicitly shielded (Baumeister, 2002).

One variation of this issue invokes the notion of religion or the sacred as *sui generis,* that is, a thing unto itself that constitutes the core of "genuine religion." In fact, religious studies scholars have hunted for such an experiential singularity that would be the central element to all religions for about 100 years and have generally given up the hunt. Many would now agree that there is no experiential or other singularity that defines religion or spirituality, but instead that religions and spiritualities seem to be made up of elements from among a menu of possible ingredients (Burris, 2005; see also Taves, Chapter 7, this volume). This means that there is not likely to be one experience, meaning, practice, belief, motive, or other thing central to religion or spirituality but a range of them, from religion to religion, from spirituality to spirituality, and from individual to group, whose elements are not necessarily the same.

The Sacred

Some psychologists of religion argue that the distinctive feature of religion or spirituality lies in its connection with a singularity, such as "the sacred" (see, e.g., Pargament, 2007). If, however, any object, motivation, or kind of experience can be regarded as the sacred, as many definitions of the sacred tend to assume (Durkheim, 1912/1995; Pargament, 2007; Pargament & Mahoney, 2005), then there is no agreement on what the essential ingredients of the sacred are.

Psychologically, sacrality is a quality that people ascribe to or perceive in something. As such, it is based not on the thing but on the beliefs, values, and meanings that people attribute to it. We need to understand processes of sacralization as a subset of the more general processes of meaning making and assessment. Thus, psychological definitions of religion or spirituality that rely on notions such as "the sacred" create an obvious and glaring problem: By asserting the uniqueness of religion and spirituality by association with a presumed singularity, they define the singularity itself as outside the realm of psychological study and preclude explanations in terms of psychological processes. The psychological processes involved in religion or spirituality may be partly unique or not, but if so, the unique aspects are on weak ground if they depend on being true by definition.

Transcendence and Spirituality

Similar issues arise in relation to discussion of motives and needs related to religion. For example, let us consider the claim that people have a need for transcendence or a motive for spirituality for which they must strive (Pargament, 2007). How are we to understand these claims? Are these distinctive needs and motives or instances of more general needs and motives (see Park, Edmondson, & Hale-Smith, in press)? These claims lead us right back to definitions of transcendence and spirituality and whether they are going to be defined in ways that set them apart as unique from the outset or instances of more general needs and motives. If, as Kirkpatrick argues (Chapter 6, this volume), we want to situate the psychology of religion within a larger evolutionary framework, we would need to identify the underlying evolved needs and motives upon which proposed needs for transcendence or motives for spirituality rely. This would allow us to consider the role that proposed needs or motives might play from a broader evolutionary perspective, either as an adaptation that might, for example, heighten performance by focusing goal-directed action or reducing anxiety or as a spandrel built on, for example, the need to overdetect predators and, by extension, other unseen agents in order to survive.

We think that the common use of these terms in much of the psychology of religion literature does not go deep enough because it does not account for the fundamental psychological processes at their roots; common narrations about them sound as if they are self-evident givens, instead of stating a compelling theory and research-based reason why they might be there. Insofar as motives or needs for transcendence and spirituality rely on the built-in, automatic processes by which living creatures make meaning out of incomplete and ambiguous stimuli, they rely on processes that are not unique to religion and spirituality but are an essential aspect of all healthy human functioning (Park, 2010). Meaning making and assessment, not religion and spirituality, are the core psychological processes, although religion and spirituality may be among their most elaborated cultural expressions (Park, 2005a, 2005b; Park, Chapter 18, this volume). People and other animals make meaning whether they feel motivated to do so or not.

Implications

We now return to our earlier proposal that we conceive of the focus of the subfield as a hard-to-define, probably inherently unstable subset of the larger need to make meaning exhibited by humans and other animals, as discussed next. Although researchers may, by definition, set religion, spirituality, and/or the sacred apart as distinctive processes, we think the psychological grounds for doing so are weak. Despite the difficulties involved in defining the elusive, multifaceted phenomena we refer to as religions and spiritualities and the diversity of psychological motives, proclivities, and processes we presume are at work in them, we are quite certain that processes of meaning making and assessment are involved. An MS perspective, in short, provides a powerful framework for analyzing the myriad forms of religiousness and spirituality, both local and global, that humans have created.

In saying this, readers should remember that there are many types of MSs, classified in disparate ways by different cultures, not all of which distinguish among religion, spirituality, and other constructs. Moreover, while MSs are implicated in the most sophisticated of human cultural creations, they are also operative at less conscious, more automatic levels of processing—biological, psychological, and social—that are utilized by many species in addition to humans. It is to the complex, multifaceted nature of meaning systems to which we now turn.

DEVELOPMENTS IN THE MODEL OF RELIGIOUS MEANING SYSTEMS

Meaning, Meaning Making, and Meaning Systems

It is crucial at this point to distinguish the concepts at the heart of this chapter—the process of meaning making and the MSs that result from this process—from philosophical considerations of authentic or real meaning, which is not of concern in this discussion. We highlight up front, therefore, that we are *not* talking about essentialist notions of meaning. We make no claims regarding "the true meaning." The science of psychology is neutral with respect to religious or other truth claims. We neither accept nor reject them. With Kirkpatrick (2005), we think scientific knowledge about psychological processes is orthogonal with respect to the veridicality of religious truth claims.

Briefly, this chapter is about the operation of an MS within the human mind (see Park, 2005a, 2005b; Park, Chapter 18, this volume)—and by extrapolation counterparts at more macro (e.g., sociocultural) and micro (e.g., neurological) levels of analysis—that enables the person to make meanings and evaluate information in light of them as a key process by which he or she regulates behavior, perceptions, emotions, and memories throughout life. It is these psychological processes that we are trying to understand.

In our conceptualization of the psychology of religion and spirituality, and of psychology as a whole, the notion of meaning systems applies to psychological processes inherent in cognitive mechanisms and appraisal processes as discussed by clinical and social psychologists, but also to psychological processes at more macro and micro levels of analysis. Anthropologists, sociologists, and cultural psychologists have used the concept of MS with the particulars pitched at their level of analysis (e.g., Alexander, Smith, & Norton, 2011; Bruner, 1990; Geertz, 1973; Purzycki & Sosis, 2009). Also, some of the more micro-oriented neurocognitive researchers allude to analogous processes at the level of neurological functioning (e.g., Azari, 2006; Frith, 2007; Inzlicht, Tullett, & Good, 2011; McNamara, 2009; Schjødt, Stodkilde-Jørgensen, Geertz, & Roepstorff, 2009). So the idea of MSs, and in this case religion as an MS, is, we propose, a unifying idea.

The notion that humans are of necessity meaning makers is widely accepted in psychology and many other disciplines (see Baumeister, 1991; Proulx & Heine, 2006; Steger, 2009, for reviews). Frankl (1963) was an early proponent of this notion of a universal human "will to meaning." At the individual level, this process is generally described as a conscious or nonconscious need to make sense of one's experience and to feel that one's life has significance and purpose (Steger, 2009). Subsequent generations of researchers elaborated on this concept, expanding and broadening its reach (Newberg & Waldman, 2006; Stillman & Baumeister, 2009). At the cultural level, Geertz (1973) has made a compelling case that culture is not merely the sum of all of the variables that are operative; instead, those variables are all interactive in a complex web, and a culture and its meanings are understood through a process of "thick description" by the symbols within that web that constitutes the interconnected whole. Cultural meanings are found in the symbols in that web space, not in a mere algebraic weighting of the variables (see also Alexander et al., 2011), and there seems to be no developed human life without them.

Yet the specific understanding of what it means to say that humans have to make meaning is difficult to specify. For example, Baumeister (1991) described four needs that are met through meaning making—a sense of purpose, value/justification, efficacy or control, and self-worth (p. 29)—but this does not tell us how the process of meaning making works. It can best be understood in terms of two interrelated processes: meaning construction and meaning appraisal. Meaning construction, in its most basic form, is the process through which organisms (1) perceive wholes where the stimuli are actually parts; (2) make pattern, connection, or implication out of ambiguity; and (3) extrapolate continuity where it is unclear that there is any (Park & Folkman, 1997). Meaning appraisal, in its most basic form, is the process through which organisms assess new information in light of the way they have processed past information (i.e., their past experience and the implicit meaning system already in place) (Park, 2005a, 2005b). These interrelated processes are operative in perception, learning, development, social interaction, personality development, and all healthy human psychological functions, and also in the more highly elaborated beliefs, practices, values, and worldviews we associate with religiousness and spirituality.

A Deeper, Basic Psychological Process

Given the prior argument, we contend that the diverse array of human motives that others view as driving religion (e.g., the need for transcendence or spirituality) can be subsumed under the notion that people need to make meaning, though they do so through automatic, nonconscious processes more often than not. Our claim that people need to make meaning is based on the assumption that people need a *coherent and well-functioning meaning system at the biological and psychological levels* (Park et al., in press). At the biological and psychological levels, meaning systems are thus broad frameworks through which people attend to and perceive stimuli; organize their behavior; conceptualize themselves, others, and interpersonal relationships; remember their past; and anticipate their future. Because of its essential role in meeting a number of specific demands, including those for coherence, mastery and control, the reduction of uncertainty, identity, existential answers, and behavioral guidance, we posit that a well-functioning meaning system is necessary for healthy human functioning (Greenberg, Pyszczynski, & Solomon, 1986; Heine, Proulx, & Vohs, 2006) and, from an evolutionary perspective, has ultimate survival value (Kirkpatrick, Chapter 6, this volume).

From an MS perspective, religion and spirituality are more or less coherent, culturally elaborated meaning systems embedded in and acquired through social relationships and institutions situated in complex natural and built environments. As such, they are built upon and interact with meaning-making processes operating at the biological and psychological levels. As highly culturally elaborated systems, they are visible and distinctive when viewed cross-culturally and, at the same time, predictable in their ability to respond to cross-culturally recurrent matters of human concern. Because of this visibility and functionality, what we think of as religion and/or spirituality has a central role in the consciously articulated meaning systems of many people in virtually every culture. Given their versatility, religious/spiritual perspectives may be particularly capable of adapting to meet some of these demands, such as those for coherence, control, uncertainty reduction, and existential answers (Hood, Hill, & Spilka, 2009). Given its breadth, we propose that the model of meaning systems is capable of containing the whole span of research topics and dialogue within the psychology of religion. Although the point applies to an array of topics in psychology and to chapters in this book, we point to only a few examples as illustrations.

1. Take, for example, the processes that regulate goals and purposeful action (Emmons & Schnitker, Chapter 13, this volume). A human being does not have goals or purposeful motives, let alone more lofty spiritual strivings, in a non-meaning-laden vacuum. Even a goal defined in relatively immediate terms, such as caring for a sick loved one, depends on factors beyond itself, such as the degree of love shown to the caregiver by the sick person in past times, time conflicts, skill to perform the necessary tasks, and the availability of help, all of which contribute to the person's evaluation of the desirability, practicality, and possibility of performing the task at any given moment.

2. The same point can be made with respect to what may appear to us as more microlevel processes common to humans and other animals. Thus, for example, we can consider (a) the way other animals learn to respond to ambiguous stimuli and learn the location of food in a maze (or their natural habitat). In the first trial run in a T-maze, a rat is in a completely unknown environment and has no clue whether food is located down the left or the right arm of the maze. After several trials and errors, however, the rat has made the "correct" meaning out of the ambiguous stimulus series to which it has been exposed and has learned to turn left at the choice point to receive food reinforcement (i.e., it has "connected the dots" between running down the runway, seeing the choice point, executing one turn and not the other, and food in the goal box). Operant conditioning, thus, is an instance of meaning making. At a yet more microlevel, (b) we can consider the way neurons generate patterns out of an ambiguous barrage of bits and pieces of information, some of which apparently create consciousness. Similarly, (c) neurons in the retina of the eye receive certain wavelengths of the electromagnetic spectrum, called light, which set off neural impulses in the retinal receptors and from which the visual system eventually makes meaningful percepts. Finally, (d) even the phenomenon of human memory is based on meaning making. It is now known that a memory is not "retrieved" in the form in which it was initially stored, but is instead "reconstructed" (i.e., a meaning-making process) and can actually be changed by that very process, i.e., the meaning that was made and called a memory can be reconsolidated and stored in a new form (Debiec, LeDoux, & Nader, 2002). These are meaning assessment and meaning making processes, and it is hard to imagine human or animal functioning at an ordinary, healthy level without them.

3. A similar argument applies to religious conversion and spiritual transformation (Paloutzian, Murken, Streib, & Rößler-Namini, Chapter 20, this volume). A person does not accept a different belief or begin a new religious or spiritual practice without at some level—conscious or nonconscious—appraising his or her current needs and the degree to which they are being met and evaluating that appraisal in relation to the perceived alternatives and the anticipated effects of making a change. The person's final change or lack of it depends on his or her appraisal of the status quo in comparison to the perceived match, and benefits and costs, of sticking with what is or changing to something else. Technically, we can say that the person is responding to the meanings he or she makes of the options, not to the options as such.

4. Consider also the phenomenon of spiritual struggle (Exline & Rose, Chapter 19, this volume). Whether or not a person feels spiritual conflict between, for example, option *A* and option *B*, depends not on the two options as raw stimuli but on the person's perceptions, processing of those percepts, and evaluation of the consequences of his or

her possible choices in view of the higher order spiritual principles, purposes, or being(s) held in a superordinate position, possibly in a position of ultimate concern (Emmons, 1999). Thus, a person does not experience spiritual struggle or solve one by merely recognizing options but by working through a process of assessing what they might mean within his or her overarching meaning system.

5. Finally, the same argument applies to an idea called the Hyperactive Agency Detection Device (HADD; see Barrett, 2004; Barrett, Chapter 12, this volume), a clever concept that comes to us from the cognitive science of religion. This is the notion that the brain/mind is wired so that it is predisposed to detect agency in an object whether or not it is actually a property of that object—a process with survival value since it would prompt animals to flee when they encounter ambiguous stimuli that might possibly be preditors. However, the general idea that the mind detects agency needs clarification. Technically, the process is not "detection" but making meaning out of ambiguous stimuli. This seems straightforward when it is said that the HADD detects agency even if it is not there—something not possible. One can imagine it, hallucinate it, pretend it, have a sensory/perceptual illusion of it, but one cannot "detect" something that is not there. Insofar as we have no direct access to the minds of others, the general process is always inferential whether agency is present or not and, therefore, is one of meaning making via attribution of certain properties upon encountering an ambiguous stimulus complex.

Moreover, because meaning systems consist of much more than religion/spirituality, encompassing all the assumptions and goals that make up an individual's understanding of reality, we suggest that the meaning system concept is powerful enough to contain not only the psychological processes that regulate religiousness/spirituality but those that regulate much of human behavior.

Research on Religious Meaning Systems (RMSs)

Research interest in meaning has been proliferating in recent years. As of this writing, volumes on meaning edited by Markman, Proulx, and Lindberg and by Shaver and Mikulincer are forthcoming from APA, and the second edition of Wong's (2012) edited volume has recently been published. Research on meaning is being conducted in many domains of psychology—for example, including those concerned with trauma (e.g., Park, Mills, & Edmondson, 2012), health (e.g., Vehling et al., 2011), and terror management theory (e.g., Davis, Juhl, & Routledge, 2011)—and articles and books on many aspects of meaning are being published more broadly, including those concerned with philosophical matters (e.g., Flanagan, 2007; Hurford, 2007) and with meaning in culture (e.g., Alexander et al., 2011). Laboratory studies are also being conducted on meaning systems (e.g., Proulx & Heine, 2006). Some of this attention to meaning systems focuses specifically on religious/spiritual issues, but not much. For example, in Wong's (2012) edited book, only one chapter explicitly focuses on a religious component of meaning, within a Buddhist context. Further, with few exceptions, little research in the psychology of religion and spirituality has taken a meaning systems perspective. In Chapter 18 of this volume, Park reviews the research related to religious meaning systems, noting that most of this research was not explicitly conducted from this perspective.

MULTILEVEL INTERDISCIPLINARY PROGRESS

Why Multilevel and Interdisciplinary?

The multilevel interdisciplinary paradigm (MIP) was so named by Emmons and Paloutzian (2003) and elaborated by Paloutzian and Park (2005b) because the psychology of religion needed an idea to encourage researchers to operationalize their concepts at different levels of analysis within psychology and to compare their findings with those from other fields. If such comparisons are made and the findings are consistent, then the principles that connect them can be taken as more robust, and the eventual outcome has a greater chance of being a valid comprehensive theory of religiousness.

However, making progress toward a valid comprehensive theory of religiousness requires thinking in a new way, borrowing ideas from different fields, because in order to understand human behavior, especially a behavior so vast, rich, varied, and sometimes self-contradictory as human religiousness, research in psychology must be integrated with research from allied disciplines that study religion. Anthropologists, historians, neuroscientists, evolutionary biologists, sociologists, linguists, and religious studies scholars all study religiousness and spirituality in different ways, and all have specialized knowledge that they can share through collaboration. Thus, we think that expanding our reach under the umbrella of the MIP is essential, not optional, if we want to make progress toward genuine understanding.

We Challenge Us

We take seriously our own challenge to invoke the MIP. For example, in this second edition, we have expanded our scope to include far-reaching topics such as the cultural and cross-cultural psychology of religion (Saroglou & Cohen, Chapter 17) and religiousness and international terrorism (Moghaddam, Warren, & Love, Chapter 32). We widened our analytical reach from the cognitive psychology of religion in the first edition to the cognitive science of religion (Barrett, Chapter 12), an emerging area with a scope ranging from neuroscience to cultural anthropology. Noteworthy regarding this second edition is diversity of contributors, including a neurologist, coauthor of the chapter on the neuropsychology of religious experience (McNamara & Butler, Chapter 11); a scholar of public health, with an enlightening chapter on the meanings of religiousness and spirituality, bringing in historical as well as contemporary psychological and cross-cultural perspectives (Oman, Chapter 2); and a scholar in the field of government. Going into the humanities, we invited a past president of the American Academy of Religion to write about the most fundamental issues in the field through the eyes of a religious studies scholar (Taves, Chapter 7).

A leading psychological anthropologist commented that by itself psychological research on religiousness can be characterized as yielding knowledge that is good but "thin," because it tends to not account for the myriad complex cultural interactions that determine the phenomena "in vivo" (Luhrmann, personal communication, April, 2009). In light of this, we regard the integrative ideas in this book as showing great promise for contributing to the synthesis of knowledge about religiousness and spirituality.

Mapping Evidence to Adjacent Levels

It seems obvious that the lofty vision that we describe here can be accomplished only as data and concepts from one area of research map onto those from the levels of analysis immediately above and below it. In the ideal scenario, the multilayered maps of corresponding data and concepts would themselves be integrated with their counterparts at other levels. The eventual outcome would be comprehensive multilevel interdisciplinary theory.

To illustrate, we begin with some of the current research on brain processes in experiences that people deemed religious (see McNamara & Butler, Chapter 11, this volume, for a review). Unless one assumes that there are certain neural processes that are *sui generis* religious and to which no other meaning can possibly be attributed, a proposition for which there is no evidence, one must understand that our explanation of an experience about which a person makes a religious attribution cannot go directly from the behavior of neurons to a culturally defined meaning (e.g., "my mental experience was a real vision of the Virgin Mary") without also accounting for the attending psychological and social processes (see, e.g., Barrett, Chapter 12, this volume; Geertz, 2010). A complete explanation must be multilevel and interdisciplinary and requires that the evidence from various levels of analysis be consistent. Knowledge of the behavior of neurons cannot be mapped directly onto knowledge of cultural processes; the connection between them requires (at least) psychological and sociological knowledge as intermediate mapping steps. In general, the replication of findings across levels is the only way to confirm that the evidence is robust. Therefore, an explanation that works cannot skip essential levels of analysis that lay between those at the more micro and more macro levels.

By conducting research and developing theory that are collaborative, multilevel, and interdisciplinary, psychologists of religion will eventually be able to map knowledge among levels of analysis and invent more integrative theoretical concepts than are presently available. An explanation that works in a complete way will not skip levels of analysis but will instead show how they are interrelated. Meaning system processes are central to this endeavor because they connect what is happening at one level with what is happening at another. The model of religion as a meaning system, when properly applied to the formation and testing of research questions and to the interpretation of results from one level of analysis compared with its counterparts from adjacent levels, can yield a comprehensive, evidence-based theory capable of accounting for human religiousness.

Methodological Highlights and Directions

In Chapter 33, as we look to the future, we elaborate at length on a set of methodological highlights and offer suggestions and cite examples of how various kinds of research might proceed, the main points of which we now briefly introduce.

During the past 8 years, a number of methodological advances from the laboratory and the field have been used in search of valid psychological knowledge about religiousness (see Hood & Belzen, Chapter 4, this volume). The list of tools and techniques includes, but is not limited to, refinement in the use of questionnaires, priming in the laboratory and the field, so-called qualitative methods that involve in-depth interviews and validated methods to code the verbal transcripts to tap the deeper meaning of the person's thoughts, social neuroscientific techniques, and various methods (some used by nonpsychologists) of studying religiousness "in the wild," so to speak, which can involve adapting a laboratory technique to a field setting, testing ideas derived in humanities research in experimental ways, and going after unusual local manifestations of religiousness in contrast to those that reflect the more well-known world religions.

Used together, these techniques provide interesting alternative ways to vary the measures of constructs and offer variations in degree of external validity inherent in the findings. In combination with triangulation, they can yield robust multilevel findings. It is this combination that allows for comparison of results from research at different levels of analysis and that yields the mapping of findings with findings when a principle tested across levels demonstrates its robustness. The psychology of religion is ready for such integrated approaches in order to build theory at a level that has not yet been attained.

PATHS THE PSYCHOLOGY OF RELIGION IS TAKING: A SAMPLE

In what ways has this field evolved in the 8 years since the *Handbook* was first published? Although a detailed discussion is beyond the scope of this introductory chapter, it is important to at least briefly explore a few of the broader paths that the psychology of religion and spirituality has taken that affect the wide span of specific topics in the field.

1. Scholars have taken initial steps away from defining religion in only one way or only in a way that fixes its meaning for their particular study. The trend toward acknowledging the need to study religions and spiritualities that comprise groups of elements that are not necessarily homogeneous has begun, setting the stage for better cross-cultural research.

2. There have been some substantial theoretical advances especially within the orbit of midlevel theory. Most notable is attachment theory (see, e.g., Richert & Granqvist, Chapter 8, this volume).

3. Overlapping the domain of psychology, the cognitive science of religion (CSR; Barrett, Chapter 12, this volume) and the neuropsychology of religion (McNamara & Butler, Chapter 11, this volume) have emerged as distinct entities; the former with sufficient support to establish the International Association for the Cognitive Science of Religion (IACSR) and its *Journal for the Cognitive Science of Religion*. Scholars from the cognitive science and neuroscience of religion come from a variety of disciplines, although their concerns largely overlap the psychology of religion. Scholars in these three areas began to communicate to and collaborate with each other, creating rich grounds for cross-fertilization.

4. The cross-cultural and cultural psychology of religion and spirituality has been added to the plate (Belzen, 2010; Saroglou & Cohen, Chapter 17, this volume). Consistent with this, psychology of religion and spirituality journal editors are receiving a greater number of papers submitted from outside the United States and beyond European borders, including Middle Eastern and East Asian countries. This international activity creates the potential for a rich future for cross-cultural comparisons.

5. Scholars in the fields of anthropology and religious studies have begun to look seriously at modern empirical psychological research methods and to incorporate them

within their (inherently) interdisciplinary approaches to the topic (see, e.g., Slingerland, 2008; Taves, 2009; Taves, Chapter 7, this volume).

6. An interesting and potential-laden menu of methods for research in the psychology of religion and spirituality has developed that seems to create a wide open door for new research and theoretical thinking that can exploit the potential apparent in myriad combinations of methods, cultures and religions, and questions that go from the micro to the macro levels.

7. Substantial progress has been made on the model of meaning systems (Park, Chapter 18, this volume). The combination of methodological and broad area innovations sets the stage for serious posing of multilevel interdisciplinary theory in the psychology of religion and spirituality, whose subtopics are held together by the processes at the heart of the meaning system model.

This list reflects only those ideas and trends whose effects automatically reflect or would be reflected in developments across large swaths of the areas of research in the psychology of religion and spirituality. However, this field has shown remarkable developments across the board. A very short and perhaps particularly conspicuous list, with collateral chapters in the current volume, includes research work into mindfulness (Levenson & Aldwin, Chapter 29), cultural psychology (Saroglou & Cohen, Chapter 17), religious studies (Taves, Chapter 7), evidence-based practice (Shafranske, Chapter 30), and completely new treatments of religious violence and terrorism (Moghaddam, Warren, & Love, Chapter 32), workplace spirituality (Hill, Jurkiewicz, Giacalone, & Fry, Chapter 31), and religious conversion and deconversion (Paloutzian, Murken, Streib, & Rößler-Namini, Chapter 20). In truth, however, if the new paths traveled by specific areas were to be added to the list, it would, in effect, mean that the entire table of contents would be reproduced here because each topic shows many new advances. Taken as a whole, this is a lot of movement in a mere 8 years.

ROLES THE PSYCHOLOGY OF RELIGION IS PLAYING: A SAMPLE

There are two kinds of contributions that any field of scholarship should *want* to make: (1) applying the material to real human problems and (2) effecting the communications, dialogue, and developments in research and theory within one's own scholarly field and beyond. In other terms, these amount to helping others and advancing knowledge. We close this chapter with an exceedingly brief snapshot of a small number of ways the psychology of religion and spirituality has made such contributions in the recent past.

A prominent area of contribution is in clinical and counseling psychology and their role in mental and physical health care. It is now more common for psychologists to be prepared see any patient, at least on an initial basis, regardless of religious or spiritual orientation and to be sensitive to those variables in a manner similar to the way one would be sensitive to and take into account patient differences based on ethnic or racial group, national origin, or gender or sexual orientation. Concurrent with this, a greater number of professionals are being trained within various specialized population groups, thus making it easier for a person within a specialized group to receive competent mental health care treatment from a professional within that same group. Consistent with these and related applied trends, various chapters in the 2005 edition of the *Handbook* made important research-based contributions to the crafting of the *APA Resolution on Religious, Religion-Based, and/or Religion-Derived Prejudice* (American Psychological Association Presidential Working Group, 2008).

Scholarly evaluation of analogous research issues has not lagged behind. For example, the *Psychological Bulletin* recently published a journal dialogue on the issue of whether or not religion promotes prosociality (Galen, 2012a, 2012b; Myers, 2012; Saroglou, 2012; see also Nielsen, Hatton, & Donahue, Chapter 16, this volume). After centuries of debate in the proreligious/antireligious, philosophical, theological, and popular arenas about whether religion is good or bad, it is time to set aside rhetoric that protects one's own point of view and derogates the other. It is, instead, time to examine the empirical research on the question, draw whatever conclusions might emerge from that examination, and carry on the research in order to arrive at greater understanding of and applications to the problem. This is a genuine journal dialogue by three of the finest experts on the topic; it promises to be a milestone.

Looking back at the entire scene of the recent past, it is clear that the psychology of religion and spirituality has seen great change. This second edition of the *Handbook* documents this progress and offers a vision of what the future might hold..

ACKNOWLEDGMENTS

We wish to thank Ann Taves for her thorough critiques of previous drafts of this chapter and for her helpful contributions as a humanities scholar to crafting it.

NOTES

1. The *Journal of Psychology and Judaism* was published quarterly for about 20 years but ended early last decade.
2. Space constraints do not allow citation of every article in every journal, but a selective list of flagships and discipline-wide journals includes the *American Psychologist, Science, Psychological Science, Psychological Bulletin,* and *PloS ONE.* Topical high-end journals include, but are not limited to, the *Journal of Applied Social Psychology, Journal of Experimental Social Psychology, Journal of Personality, Journal of Personality and Social Psychology, Political Psychology, Journal of Happiness Studies, Psychotherapy and Psychosomatics, Journal of Cognition and Culture, Social Cognitive and Affective Neuroscience, Personality and Individual Differences, Journal of Clinical Psychology, Journal of Adult Psychological Development, Pain Medicine, Developmental Psychology, Attachment and Human Behavior, Journal of Psychopharmacology,* and *Health Psychology.*
3. These themes are more fully elaborated in Chapters 1 and 30 of the 2005 *Handbook.*
4. The themes are substantively identical to those presented in the 2005 *Handbook.* There is one slight rearrangement in that the discussion of methods is moved from its pairing with theory to the discussion of the multilevel interdisciplinary paradigm.

REFERENCES

Alexander, J. C., Smith, P., & Norton, M. (Eds.). (2011). *Interpreting Clifford Geertz: Cultural investigation in the social sciences*. Hants, UK: Palgrave Macmillan.

American Psychological Association Presidential Working Group. (2008). *Resolution on religious, religion-based, and/or religion-derived prejudice*. In B. S. Anton, Proceedings of the American Psychological Association for the legislative year 2007: Minutes of the annual meeting of the Council of Representatives and minutes of the meetings of the board of directors. *American Psychologist, 63*(5), 360–442.

Azari, N. P. (2006). Neuroimaging studies of religious experience: A critical review. In P. McNamara (Ed.), *The psychology of religious experience: Where God and science meet* (Vol. 3, pp. 33–54). Westport, CT: Praeger.

Barrett, J. L. (2004). *Why would anyone believe in God?* Lanham, MD: AltaMira Press.

Baumeister, R. F. (1991). *Meanings in life*. New York: Guilford Press.

Baumeister, R. F. (Ed.). (2002). Religion and psychology [Special issue]. *Psychological Inquiry, 13*(3).

Belzen, J. (2010). *Towards cultural psychology of religion: Principles, approaches, applications*. Heidelberg, Germany: Springer.

Bloom, P. (2012). Religion, morality, evolution. *Annual Review of Psychology, 63,* 179–199.

Bruner, J. (1990). *Acts of meaning*. Cambridge, MA: Harvard University Press.

Burris, J. P. (2005). Comparative-historical method [Further considerations]. In L. Jones (Ed.), *Encyclopedia of religion* (2nd ed., pp. 1871–1873). Detroit: Thomson Gale.

Coyle, A., & Lyons, E. (2011). The social psychology of religion: Current research themes. *Journal of Community & Applied Social Psychology, 21,* 461–540.

Davis, W., Juhl, J., & Routledge, C. (2011). Death and design: The terror management function of teleological beliefs. *Motivation and Emotion, 35,* 98–104.

Debiec, J., LeDoux, J. E., & Nader, K. (2002). Cellular and systems reconsolidation in the hippocampus. *Neuron, 36,* 527–538.

de Souza, M., Francis, L. J., O'Higgins-Norman, J., & Scott, D. G. (Eds.). (2009). *International handbook of education for spirituality, care and wellbeing*. New York: Springer.

Dowling, E. M., & Scarlett, G. W. (Eds.). (2006). *Encyclopedia of religious and spiritual development*. Thousand Oaks, CA: Sage.

Durkheim, E. (1995). *Elementary forms of the religious life* (K. Fields, Trans.). New York: Free Press. (Original work published 1912)

Emmons, R. A. (1999). *The psychology of ultimate concerns*. New York: Oxford University Press.

Emmons, R. A., & Paloutzian, R. F. (2003). The psychology of religion. *Annual Review of Psychology, 54,* 377–402.

Flanagan, O. (2007). *The really hard problem: Meaning in a material world*. Cambridge, MA: MIT Press.

Frankl, V. (1963). *Man's search for meaning*. New York: Washington Square Press.

Frith, C. (2007). *Making up the mind: How the brain creates our mental world*. Malden, MA: Blackwell.

Galen, L. W. (2012a). Does religious belief promote prosociality?: A critical examination. *Psychological Bulletin, 138,* 876–906.

Galen, L. W. (2012b). The complex and elusive nature of religious prosociality: Reply to Myers (2012) and Saroglou (2012). *Psychological Bulletin, 138,* 918–923.

Geertz, A. (2010). Brain, body, and culture: A biocultural theory of religion. *Method and Theory in the Study of Religion, 22,* 304–321.

Geertz, C. (1973). *The interpretation of cultures*. New York: Basic Books.

Gorsuch, R. L. (1988). Psychology of religion. *Annual Review of Psychology, 39,* 201–221.

Greenberg, J., Pyszcznski, T., & Solomon, S. (1986). The causes and consequences of a need for self-esteem: A terror management theory. In R. F. Baumeister (Ed.), *Self, efficacy, and agency* (pp. 189–212). New York: Plenum Press.

Heine, S. J., Proulx, T., & Vohs, K. D. (2006). The meaning maintenance model: On the coherence of social motivations. *Personality and Social Psychology Review, 10,* 88–110.

Hood, R. W., Jr., Hill, P. C., & Spilka, B. (2009). *The psychology of religion: An empirical approach* (4th ed.). New York: Guilford Press.

Hurford, J. R. (2007). *The origins of meaning: Language in the light of evolution.* Oxford, UK; Oxford University Press.

Inzlicht, M., Tullett, A. M., & Good, G. (2011). The need to believe: A neuroscience of religion as a motivated process. *Religion, Brain & Behavior, 1,* 192–212.

Kirkpatrick, L. A. (2005). *Attachment, evolution, and the psychology of religion.* New York: Guilford Press.

McNamara, P. (2009). *The neuroscience of religious experience.* New York: Cambridge University Press.

Miller, L. (2012). *Oxford handbook of psychology and spirituality.* New York: Oxford University Press.

Myers, D. (2012). Reflections on "religious belief and prosociality": Comment on Galen (2012). *Psychological Bulletin, 138,* 913–917.

Newberg, A., & Waldman, M. R. (2006). *Born to believe: God, science, and the origin of ordinary and extraordinary beliefs.* New York: Free Press.

Paloutzian, R. F., & Park, C. L. (Eds.). (2005a). *Handbook of the psychology of religion and spirituality.* New York: Guilford Press.

Paloutzian, R. F., & Park, C. L. (2005b). Integrative themes in the current science of the psychology of religion. In R. F. Paloutzian & C. L. Park (Eds.), *Handbook of the psychology of religion and spirituality* (pp. 3–20). New York: Guilford Press.

Pargament, K. I. (2002). Is religion nothing but . . . ?: Explaining religion versus explaining religion away. *Psychological Inquiry, 13,* 239–244.

Pargament, K. I. (2007). *Spiritually integrated psychotherapy: Understanding and addressing the sacred.* New York: Guilford Press.

Pargament, K., Exline, J., & Jones, J. (Eds.). (2013). *APA handbook of psychology, religion, and spirituality (Vol. 1): Context, theory, and research.* Washington, DC: American Psychological Association.

Pargament, K. I., & Mahoney, A. (2005). Sacred matters: Sanctification as a vital topic for the psychology of religion. *The International Journal for the Psychology of Religion, 15*(3), 179–198.

Pargament, K., Mahoney, A., & Shafranske, E. (Eds.). (2013). *APA handbook of psychology, religion, and spirituality (Vol. 2): An applied psychology of religion andspirituality.* Washington, DC: American Psychological Association.

Park, C. L. (2005a). Religion and meaning. In R. F. Paloutzian & C. L. Park (Eds.), *Handbook of the psychology of religion and spirituality* (pp. 295–314). New York: Guilford Press.

Park, C. L. (2005b). Religion as a meaning-making framework in coping with life stress. *Journal of Social Issues, 61,* 707–729.

Park, C. L. (2010). Making sense of the meaning literature: An integrative review of meaning making and its effects on adjustment to stressful life events. *Psychological Bulletin, 136,* 257–301.

Park, C. L., Edmondson, D., & Hale-Smith, A. (2013). Why religion?: Meaning as motivation. In K. I. Pargament, J. J. Exline, & J. Jones (Eds.), *APA handbook of psychology, religion, and spirituality (Vol. 1): Context, theory, and research* (pp. 157–171). Washington, DC: Amrican Psychological Association.

Park, C. L., & Folkman, S. (1997). Meaning in the context of stress and coping. *Review of General Psychology, 1,* 115–144.

Park, C. L., Mills, M., & Edmondson, D. (2012). PTSD as meaning violation: A test of a cognitive worldview perspective. *Psychological Trauma Theory, Research Practice, and Policy, 4,* 66–73.

Proulx, T., & Heine, S. J. (2006). Death and black diamonds: Meaning, mortality, and the meaning maintenance model. *Psychological Inquiry, 17,* 309–318.

Purzycki, B. G., & Sosis, R. (2009). The religious system as adaptive: Cognitive flexibility, public displays, and acceptance. In E. Voland & W. Schiefenhövel (Eds.), *The biological evolution of religious mind and behavior* (pp. 243–256). New York: Springer.

Roehlkepartain, E. C., King, P. E., Wagener, L. M., & Benson, P. L. (Eds.). (2006). *The handbook of spiritual development in childhood and adolescence.* Thousand Oaks, CA: Sage.

Saroglou, V. (2012). Is religion not prosocial at all?: Comment on Galen (2012). *Psychological Bulletin, 138,* 907–912.

Saroglou, V. (Ed.). (in press). *Religion, personality, and social behavior.* New York: Psychology Press.

Saroglou, V., & Cohen, A. B. (Eds.). (2011). Religion and culture: Perspectives from cultural and cross-cultural psychology [Special issue]. *Journal of Cross-Cultural Psychology, 42*(8).

Scarpa, C. (2011–2012). IAPR meeting, Bari, August 21–24, 2011. *Psicologia della Religione-news: Notiziario della Società Italiana di Psicologia della Religione, 16–17,* 3–5.

Schjødt, U., Stødkilde-Jørgensen, H., Geertz, A. W., & Roepstorff, A. (2009). Highly religious participants recruit areas of social cognition in personal prayer. *Social Cognitive and Affective Neuroscience, 4*(2), 199–207.

Sedikides, C. (Ed.). (2010). Religiosity: Perspectives from social and personality psychology [Special issue]. *Personality and Social Psychology Review, 14*(1).

Slingerland, E. (2008). *What science offers the humanities.* Cambridge: Cambridge.

Steger, M. F. (2009). Meaning in life. In S. J. Lopez (Ed.), *Oxford handbook of positive psychology* (2nd ed., pp. 679–687). Oxford, UK: Oxford University Press.

Stillman, T., & Baumeister, R. (2009). Uncertainty, belongingness, and four needs for meaning. *Psychological Inquiry, 20,* 249–251.

Taves, A. (2009). *Religious experience reconsidered: A building block approach to the study of religion and other special things.* Princeton, NJ: Princeton University Press.

Vehling, S., Lehmann, C., Oechsle, K., Bokemeyer, Krüll, A., Koch, U., & Mehnert, A. (2011). Global meaning and meaning-related life attitudes: Exploring their role in predicting depression, anxiety, and demoralization in cancer patients. *Supportive Care in Cancer, 19,* 513–520.

Wong, P. T. P. (Ed.). (2012). *Handbook of meaning* (2nd ed.). New York: Routledge.

Zinnbauer, B. J., & Pargament, K. I. (2005). Religiousness and spirituality. In R. F. Paloutzian & C. L. Park (Eds.), *Handbook of the psychology of religion and spirituality* (pp. 21–42). New York: Guilford Press.

2

Defining Religion and Spirituality

Doug Oman

In science . . . [w]e are always conscious that our terms are a little vague . . .
and we reach precision not by reducing their penumbra of vagueness, but
rather by keeping well within it, by carefully phrasing our sentences in such
a way that the possible shades of meaning of our terms do not matter.
— Karl Popper (1945/2006, pp. 21–22)

From a modern point of view, definitions of religion are not expected
to describe its 'essence' as such, but are considered as proposals to use the
term within a specific context.
— Arie L. Molendijk (1999, p. 9)

Religion and spirituality are topics of increasing interest in western culture, and
in psychological research and practice. Searches in PsycINFO show that both terms are
cited in the titles of an increasing proportion of professional publications in psychology.
Increased citations of religion have been modest, a doubling from the 1970s to the 2000s;
but the increased usage of terms related to *spirituality* has been dramatic, approximately
40-fold (see Figure 2.1).

Psychology does not employ these terms in a vacuum. Psychological findings and
perspectives are informed by larger cultural perspectives and, in turn, influence them.
Thus, while psychologists have much latitude in choosing operational definitions, they
must do so in view of the larger cultural discourse. Each psychologist is also a citizen
embedded in his or her own society and in the emerging global culture. It is within
this larger context that the present chapter seeks to view the task for psychologists of
understanding and defining the constructs of religion and spirituality. Encouraged by the
emerging multilevel interdisciplinary paradigm in the psychology of religion and spirituality, we draw on findings from multiple academic disciplines (Emmons & Paloutzian,
2003). We seek thereby to reverse the disciplinary and sometimes cultural insularity evident in many earlier psychological discussions of this topic.

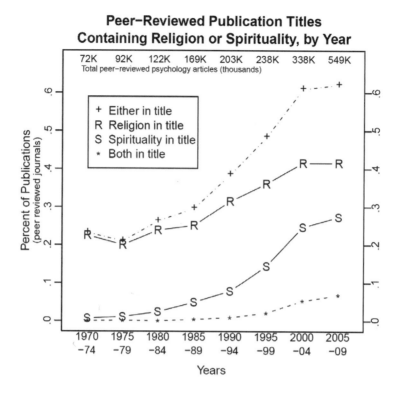

FIGURE 2.1. Growth of attention to "religion" and "spirituality" in professional psychology literature. Based on peer-reviewed journal articles indexed in PsycINFO on October 24, 2011. Title search terms were *religion, religious, religiousness* or *religiosity* (for religion), and *spirituality* or *spiritual* (for spirituality). Pooled across all years, about 7% of all titles that included spirituality or religion had both (760/10,486 peer reviewed; 1373/20,480 for all types of publications). From the 1970–1974 value of 0.007%, the proportion of peer-reviewed journal article titles containing spirituality grew 39-fold to 0.273% in 2005–2009.

In view of the burgeoning interest, one might imagine that the terms *religion* and *spirituality* are well defined and well understood—but the contrary is true. Many researchers espouse preferred definitions, but the field lacks an overall consensus. To some extent, a varied repertoire of definitions can reflect a healthy and rich diversity of scholarly approaches. Beyond a certain point, however, multiple definitions may undermine professional communication and scientific and scholarly progress.

This chapter's purpose is threefold: (1) to describe major issues and considerations related to selecting and using definitions of spirituality and religion; (2) to characterize some of the most influential current definitional approaches; and (3) to describe major strengths and weaknesses of each approach. We do not advocate for any single definition, usable on all occasions, that could be supposed to capture the "essence" of spirituality or religion. Instead, we urge that religion and spirituality be considered as likely *prototype* or *family resemblance* concepts, an influential perspective that has been largely neglected in the psychology of religion and spirituality (Rosch, 1973, 1975; Saler, 2000).

As explained later, if religion and spirituality display a prototype structure, then each may be definable by *clusters* of features (e.g., a belief in a higher being or a search for transcendence), but no single feature will be relevant in all contexts (see Taves, Chapter 7, this volume, for a detailed analysis of this issue). If this is correct, then a scholar's driving question when selecting a definition should not be "what is the correct definition?" but "what is the most helpful definition for my specific data, topic, and context?" (see chapter epigraph by Molendijk).

Accordingly, the bulk of this chapter offers what Molendijk (1999) calls a *pragmatics* of defining religion and spirituality. It discusses a series of criteria that may be relevant, in particular contexts, for evaluating the usefulness of a definition of religion and spirituality. As this chapter proceeds to describe these criteria and their justification, they set a context for introducing influential definitional approaches and explaining how each approach meets, or fails to meet, particular criteria. Many of the criteria we discuss (e.g., sensitivity and specificity) have long been familiar to psychologists of religion. Other criteria, such as those related to larger cultural impacts, have only recently been drawing sustained attention (see Saroglou & Cohen, Chapter 17, this volume).

In the next section, we sketch the history and major meanings carried by the terms *religion* and *spirituality*. The extensive third section offers a detailed pragmatics, surveying considerations for selecting definitions for particular purposes. The fourth section highlights three influential definitional approaches, and the fifth highlights emerging substantive topics. Major ideas are then summarized and final considerations offered.

HISTORIES OF MEANINGS

Terms and concepts for religion and spirituality (R/S) have co-evolved with the phenomena they have designated. Modern English meanings only emerged about two centuries ago, and are again in flux. Many of today's definitional approaches and R/S phenomena—even some disparaged as novel—possess ancient historical precedents. We, therefore, offer a brief and inevitably simplified historical sketch, along with citations to more detailed histories.

Prehistory

From Neolithic times, according to anthropologists, human cultures have recognized a world of powerful but invisible forces, and have sought to enlist aid or beneficially align themselves with potentially favorable forces. Concepts of a multilayered universe, generally containing an upperworld above and an underworld below, "appear to be universal in hunter-gatherer cosmology" (Guenther, 1999, p. 429). This earliest cultural form, called shamanism, can be viewed as a "substrate to all religion [that] has left its mythological and spiritual imprint on the many religious traditions over the world" (Guenther, 1999, p. 431). Shamans "everywhere" have entered altered states of consciousness for the sake of effecting healing cures or obtaining spiritual inspiration or guidance (Guenther, 1999, p. 427).

Over time, concepts of a spirit world remained, although shamanism was supplanted by other cultural forms. Different cultural zones have developed different vocabularies for discussing phenomena related to a spirit world. In South Asia, Hinduism speaks of a *sanatana dharma,* or timeless religion, as a universal common factor underlying all attempts to live in harmony with spiritual realities (Smith, 1991). Modern scholarly and scientific understandings have been primarily shaped by terms related to the Latin words *religio* and *spiritualitas.*

Religion

Platvoet (1999) has traced the meaning of terms related to the Latin *religio* from the third century B.C.E. to the mid-18th century C.E., when the English term *religion* acquired its major modern meanings. Beginning in the time of Cicero (106–46 B.C.E.), *religio* denoted piously and meticulously offered state-supervised acts of public worship of the Roman gods. Over the next 15 centuries, the term generally retained its core meaning of public ritual.

In English since the 16th century, *religion* has been widely understood as denoting (1) a particular system of faith and worship and/or (2) the human reverential recognition of a higher or unseen power. These meanings have been fairly stable since 1750, and appear to have clear parallels in other European languages (Byrne, 1999; Platvoet, 1999). However, people have not agreed on how to *define* religion. At the start of the 20th century, psychologist James Leuba (1901) identified 48 distinct definitions, and the profusion of definitions has abated neither in psychology nor in the larger culture (see history by Wulff, 1999, and R/S definition lists by Emmons, 1999, p. 93; Pargament, 1997, pp. 25–29; Zinnbauer & Pargament, 2005).

Toward the close of the 20th century, a new, more restricted meaning of religion emerged. In this new usage, which is increasingly common but far from universal, *religion* connotes especially the organized and institutional components of faith traditions, as opposed to the more inward and personal sides, often now referred to as *spirituality.* Table 2.1 shows several definitions of religion over the past century from diverse contexts, including theology, medicine, sociology, psychiatry, and psychology.

Spirituality

The word *spirituality* is traced by Schneiders (1989) to *pneumatikos,* a "Pauline neologism" (p. 680) used in 1 Corinthians 2:14–15 and elsewhere in the Apostle Paul's letters. He was not contrasting spiritual with material, or good with evil, but rather "the person under the influence of the Spirit of God" (*pneumatikos*) with the "merely natural human being" (*psychikos anthrôpos*) (p. 681). The contrast was essentially between "two ways of life or attitudes to life." Translated into Latin, this theological distinction persisted for centuries and gave rise to the adjective *spiritualis* and the noun *spiritualitas.* In the 12th and 13th centuries, a philosophical meaning emerged that opposed spirituality to materiality or corporeality. Thereafter, theories about progress and growth in Christian living became more and more dichotomous and conceived in terms of *ascent*, whereby the active life was viewed as a "lower way" and "merely a preparation" for the contemplative life (Sheldrake, 1998, pp. 49, 52).

In early English, *spirituality* was used positively to connote a personal and affective relationship with God. In the 17th and 18th centuries, spirituality was sometimes

TABLE 2.1. Past and Present Definitions of Religion (Selected), from Various Scholarly Contexts

Year	Author and Definition of Religion	Context
1902	James (1902/1961, p. 42): The feelings, acts, and experiences of individual men in their solitude, so far as they apprehend themselves to stand in relation to whatever they may consider the divine.	Psychology
1912	Durkheim (1912/1995, p. 44): A unified system of beliefs and practices relative to sacred things . . . which unite into one single moral community called a Church, all those who adhere to them	Sociology
1920	Pratt (1920, p. 2): The serious and social attitude of individuals or communities toward the power or powers which they conceive as having ultimate control over their interests and destinies.	Psychology
1970	Bellah (1970, p. 21): A set of symbolic forms and acts that relate man to the ultimate conditions of his existence.	Sociology
1975	Argyle and Beit-Hallahmi (1975, p. 1): A system of beliefs in a divine or superhuman power, and practices of worship or other rituals directed towards such a power.	Psychology
1991	O'Collins and Farrugia (1991, p. 203): Systems of belief in and response to the divine, including the sacred books, cultic rituals, and ethical practices of the adherents.	Theology
1993	Batson, Schoenrade, and Ventis (1993, p. 8): Whatever we as individuals do to come to grips personally with the questions that confront us because we are aware that we and others like us are alive and that we will die.	Psychology
1994	Peteet (1994, p. 237): Commitments to beliefs and practices characteristic of particular traditions.	Psychology
1997	Pargament (1992, p. 204; 1997, p. 32): A search for significance in ways related to the sacred.	Psychology
1998	Dollahite (1998, p. 5): A covenant faith community with teachings and narratives that enhance spirituality and encourage morality.	Interdisciplinary
2001	Highfield (2001, p. 328): Those values, beliefs, practices, and symbols that are adopted as a response to spiritual needs	Nursing
2008	Koenig (2008, p. 11): A system of beliefs and practices observed by a community, supported by rituals that acknowledge, worship, communicate with, or approach the Sacred, the Divine, God (in Western cultures), or Ultimate Truth, Reality, or nirvana (in Eastern cultures).	Medicine/ psychiatry

pejoratively contrasted with other similar terms such as *devotion, perfection,* and *piety,* because of its perceived association with heresies or excessive emotionalism (e.g., Quietism). Spirituality as a term then fell out of use in both Catholic and Protestant circles. It returned only in the early 20th century as a term preferred by those who saw continuities between the "ordinary" and "extraordinary" (i.e., mystical) dimensions of Christian living (Sheldrake, 1998, p. 44).

As the century progressed, the term *spirituality* became increasingly respectable, being used in titles for textbooks, scholarly book series, scholarly societies, and journals such as *Studies in Spirituality* (1991–) and *Spiritus* (2001–).[1] These journals serve an established scholarly discipline—largely overlooked in psychological scholarship—that is "descriptive-critical rather than prescriptive-normative," seeking not to apply unquestioned principles but to understand spiritual experience as it occurs (Schneiders, 1989, p.692; Sheldrake, 1998). Spirituality has also become a recognized and studied construct in fields ranging from psychology, psychiatry, and sociology to medicine, nursing, and gerontology. Yet no scholarly consensus has emerged on how to define spirituality. Table 2.2 shows several definitions from a variety of timepoints and disciplines.

Late in the 20th century, the word *spirituality* began to acquire an additional English usage as something that can be explicitly pursued not only within a formal religious tradition, but also *outside* of traditions. More than one-quarter of the U.S. adult

TABLE 2.2. Past and Present Definitions of Spirituality (Selected), from Various Scholarly Contexts

Year	Author and definition of spirituality	Context
1965	von Balthasar (1965, p. 7): That basic practical or existential attitude of man which is the consequence and expression of the way in which he understands his religious—or more generally, his ethically committed—existence.	Theology
1975	Tart (1975, p. 4): That vast realm of human potential dealing with ultimate purposes, with higher entities, with God, with love, with compassion, with purpose.	Psychology, transpersonal
1983	Wakefield (1983, p. 361): Those attitudes, beliefs, and practices, which animate people's lives and help them to reach out towards super-sensible realities.	Theology
1984	Shafranske and Gorsuch (1984, p. 231): A transcendent dimension within human experience . . . discovered in moments in which the individual questions the meaning of personal existence and attempts to place the self within a broader ontological context.	Psychology, transpersonal
1991	Fahlberg and Fahlberg (1991, p. 274): That which is involved in contacting the divine within the Self or self.	Health promotion
1991	Vaughan (1991, p. 105): A subjective experience of the sacred.	Psychology, transpersonal
1992	Doyle (1992, p. 302): The search for existential meaning	Medicine, palliative
1994	Hart (1994, p. 2): The way one lives out one's faith in daily life, the way a person relates to the ultimate conditions of existence.	Psychology
1998	Wuthnow (1998, p. viii): All the beliefs and activities by which individuals attempt to relate their lives to God or to a divine being or some other conception of a transcendent reality.	Sociology
2000	Hill et al. (2000, p. 66): The feelings, thoughts, experiences, and behaviors that arise from a search for the sacred.	Psychology
2003	Myers and Williard (2003, p. 149): The capacity and tendency present in all human beings to find and construct meaning about life and existence and to move toward personal growth, responsibility, and relationship with others.	Psychology
2006	Hufford and Bucklin (2006, p. 29): "Spirituality refers to the domain of spirit(s): God or gods, souls, angels, jinni, demons—and only by metaphorical extension to other intangible and invisible things . . . "	Medical humanities
2009	Puchalski et al. (2009, p. 887): The way individuals seek and express meaning and purpose and the way they experience their connectedness to the moment, to self, to others, to nature, and to the significant or sacred.	Medicine

population identifies itself as "spiritual but not religious," and nonorthodox spiritualities are also widespread in some parts of Europe (Oman & Thoresen, 2007; Sheldrake, 2011).

CHALLENGES AND ISSUES IN DEFINING R/S

The foregoing history shows how the terms *religion* and *spirituality* have carried many shifting and sometimes opposed connotations, underscoring the need to clarify their meanings. In psychology, as in other fields, clarification often means employing a context-specific definition. Yet, as Popper pointed out long ago (see chapter epigraph), such definitions are never completely adequate—they always leave a "penumbra of vagueness." A scholar or scientist must not only choose an *appropriate* definition for the problem at hand but also *use it well.* Accordingly, most research reports are accompanied by contextual detail that describes the precise measures used to assess R/S constructs as well as demographic and other participant characteristics that justify the application of the specific measures. This usage reflects one primary function of definitions: to facilitate clarity within individual research reports.

Definitions also facilitate *aggregation* of findings across multiple research studies, through vehicles such as reviews and meta-analyses. A field that uses too many different kinds of definitions and measures may undermine its capacity to detect broad patterns. In addition, definitions function to

- Facilitate interactions with other scholarly fields such as philosophy, theology, and law.
- Support communication with clients and patients of human service professionals.
- Influence relations with funders, the general public, and other important audiences.
- Evoke salient interpretive frameworks.[2]

Figure 2.2 illustrates the layered context of research by showing a broad range of groups that are all in some sense "stakeholders" in the research process. The importance of communicating with specific audiences varies across time and between research topics. All else being equal, the most successful definitions are those that support positive communication with the broadest range of audiences, especially those that directly influence or are influenced by the research process.

In an ideal world of perfect semantic stability, such as once seemed to exist in Newtonian physics, all scholars could employ a single definition that specifies universally necessary and sufficient criteria to identify a phenomenon of interest (e.g., religion or spirituality). Such definitions based on a "checklist of critical properties" are sometimes called "classical" or "monothetic" (Saler, 2000, pp. 79, 205). However, no such definitions have won acceptance regarding religion and spirituality, either in popular culture or in scholarship.

The absence of uniform classical definitions does not indicate that R/S terms are being used incoherently or illogically. Many concepts in everyday discourse conform to what is called a "prototype" or "family resemblance"[3] structure, as described in a series of influential experiments by psychologist Eleanor Rosch (1973, 1975). For natural-language

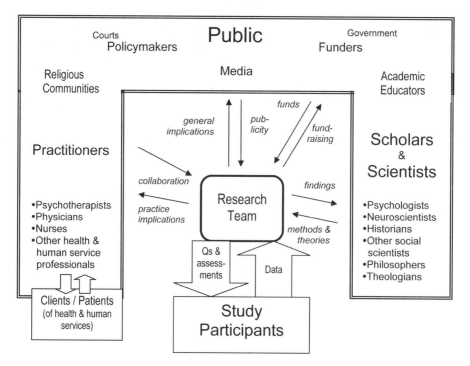

FIGURE 2.2. Communication context of research.

categories such as "fruit," "furniture," "bird," and "vehicle," Rosch reported strong evidence for what she called *prototype phenomena*: Some elements of a category were judged to be better examples of that category than others. With remarkable consistency, study participants judged the more prototypical elements as better examples, and recognized them more quickly and accurately in response tests. For example, cars and buses were among the most prototypical members of the category vehicle, while surfboards and blimps were among the least prototypical. Because membership exists on a continuum, prototype categories may lack sharp boundaries. And near its boundaries, a prototype category may provoke ongoing disagreement about whether particular objects qualify as instances.

In common discourse, do religion and spirituality conform to a prototype model? If true, this could help explain various ongoing debates in the psychology of R/S, such as whether highly individualized or New Age ways of living should qualify as religious or as spiritual.

In fact, both religion and spirituality appear to be strong candidates for prototype concepts, although their conformity to prototype structure is empirically unexamined. Evidence exists that related ideas, such as being a "spiritual person," exhibit a prototype structure (Walker & Pitts, 1998). Arguments have also been proffered for the prototype structure of concepts for the sacred (Anttonen, 2000), for meditation (Bond et al., 2009), for prayer (Lambert, Fincham, & Graham, 2011), and for forgiveness (Kearns & Fincham, 2004).

Most directly, Saler (2000), an anthropologist, has argued forcefully that *religion* is a prototype concept: "There are no sure, sharp, and universally accepted criteria for marking off religion from not-religion. . . . Religion . . . is a graded category the instantiations of which are linked by family resemblances" (p. xiv). As an element of the thinking process of scholars, he suggests, religion may be understood as a "folk category" (p. ix) that has been appropriated. For scholarly progress, Saler (2000) suggests:

> We can deal with religion in terms of a pool of elements that we deem *typical* of religion, without supposing that any one element is *necessary* for the existence of a religion. These elements or "typicality features" [such as theism] . . . are formally predicated of "religion," [but] not all of them will be found in all "religions." (p. xi)

Still, to foster necessary analytical clarity, well-constructed definitions of religion and/or spirituality are often required in specific contexts, such as research reports or systematic reviews. As Saler has noted, a definition that provides the needed context-specific clarity can be successful, even if it depends on *other* constructs that are in turn prototypical.[4] The crucial question is how a particular definition performs in a particular context. Accordingly, Platvoet (1999, p. 511) has issued a call to study the "pragmatics" of defining religion, a call that can be beneficially extended to spirituality:

> A pragmatics of defining "religion" should, therefore, be developed. It should analyse what kinds of definitions, or concepts, of "religion" have been, or might be, constructed in what contexts, for what purposes and with what results. It should review them to evaluate whether they are legitimate in view of the data to be studied; and whether they are adequate, or effective, in view of the purposes to be pursued and the analyses to be made . . . [and] to contest them if they happen to be inadequate for the task for which they have been developed. . . .

Such a pragmatics does not yet exist as an organized literature. To inaugurate such a literature, we now review considerations that could guide such a pragmatics. While a wide range of considerations is potentially relevant—we group them into no fewer than 10 subsections—only a fraction tend to be most urgent any particular context.

Sensitivity and Specificity

An optimal definition, like an optimal measurement instrument, should possess both *sensitivity* and *specificity*; that is, the definition should be neither too narrow nor too broad.

As awareness of multiple faith traditions has increased since the 1960s, some earlier definitions of religion have been recognized as lacking sensitivity: They failed to encompass important instances of the phenomenon. For example, Buddhism is widely recognized as a religion, but it lacks the conception of a creator God that is present in Christianity and Judaism. Consequently, since the 1950s, definitions of religion involving theism are much less common.

The converse problem is specificity, ensuring that religion and spirituality are not defined too broadly. Many purely functional definitions of religion and/or spirituality have been criticized on this account. For example, if spirituality is defined solely as a behavior or lifestyle that serves an integrative function in life, it might be possible for someone to say "I find my spirituality in gardening" or "Music is my spirituality" (Hill et al., 2000, p. 65). Such activities may be pursued apart from any larger framework that clearly connects them with more prototypical spiritual and religious concerns, such as ultimacy, sacredness, and transcendence. According to many scholars, categorizing such activities as intrinsically spiritual risks fostering conceptual confusion, the fragmentation of scholarly energies, and the inability to generalize from research findings (Hill et al., 2000; Koenig, 2008; Koenig, King, & Carson, 2012).

Distinctive Features of R/S

To provide an anchor, many scholars have suggested features to distinguish religion and spirituality from other phenomena. One influential approach seeks distinctiveness in the construct of the *sacred*. In Table 2.1, the sacred is mentioned in several definitions of religion, including by the early sociologist Emile Durkheim (1912/1995; Taves, Chapter 7, this volume).

In psychology, an approach first suggested by Pargament (1992, p. 204; 1997, p. 32) has become influential. Pargament defined religion as a "search for significance in ways related to the sacred." A commonly cited article by Hill and colleagues (2000) extended this approach into a rudimentary pragmatics. Hill et al. derived abstract criteria that can be used to evaluate concrete measures or operational definitions. Pargament's approach is mentioned at several points in this chapter as relevant to various definitional criteria. Although we do not endorse Pargament's approach as suitable for all occasions, this chapter concludes by highlighting it as one of several influential approaches meriting consideration.

A key issue in using Pargament's approach is the meaning and generalizability of the term *sacred* (itself perhaps a prototype category). An important strength is that the term *sacred* is readily understandable by adherents to Western traditions such as Christianity, where many linguistically related terms are used (e.g., *spiritus sancti* for Holy Spirit).

For Pargament (2007, p. 33), what is central (most prototypical) to the sacred is "God, divine beings, or a transcendent reality." However, other objects may also take on a sacred character if they have been "sanctified" by association with what Pargament calls "sacred qualities" (p. 39), qualities often used to describe the divine: transcendence, boundlessness, and ultimacy. Even people who lack belief in gods or divinities, he notes, may still perceive such qualities as present around them in their lives.

Can such conceptions of the "sacred" be applied cross-culturally? Several scholars have argued that premodern cultures and major faith traditions worldwide view life as existing within an ontological hierarchy, or "great chain of being" (Lovejoy, 1936; Smith, 1976/1992). Smith (1976/1992, p. 3) pointed out that if we reduce a multilevel ontological hierarchy to its minimum of two levels, we obtain a dichotomy between the sacred and the mundane.

Although many features of the sacred seem widely cross-culturally relevant, other specific features of Western notions of the sacred may be less generalizable. Major connotations of the sacred commonly mentioned in modern scholarship include something consecrated or "set apart" as well as something that is "numinous," reflecting divine or supernatural power (Otto, 1958; Zinnbauer, Pargament, & Scott, 1999). An additional third meaning includes reference to an action or ritual that *confers* sacred status (e.g., *sanctus* in Latin). While these meanings are fused into one word in English, and closely aligned in Latin, these qualities are most commonly denoted by separate terms, or not defined at all, in other Indo-European language groups. For example, for only one of these three meanings does Sanskrit contain a readily synonymous term (i.e., *yajati*, sacrifice, for the ritual meaning; see Lutzky, 1993).[5] Thus, scholars must be sensitive that what is fused in Western ideas of the sacred may be disaggregated elsewhere. The notion of the sacred may thus be a useful heuristic for identifying defining features of religion across cultures, but should not be used mechanically or blindly (see Taves, Chapter 7, this volume, for further discussion of this issue).

Importantly, what is perceived as sacred may vary over the course of an individual's spiritual development. For example, with regard to goals that are perceived as sacred, Hill et al. (2000), note that:

> Although some goals may appear non-sacred (e.g., personal wholeness or finding meaning in life), they may become of sacred importance or "sanctified" if they can legitimately assume sacred qualities or transcendent or ultimate significance . . . perhaps the most central part of the religious socialization process is the "sanctification" of seemingly non-religious goals. (p. 68)

Indeed, the topic of sanctification has received increasing empirical attention in the past decade (Pargament & Mahoney, 2005). Of course, goals may become desanctified as part of spiritual growth. What is viewed as prototypically sacred also varies to some extent across traditions and over time within traditions, as when new saints are canonized.

Multiple Dimensions

Most contemporary scholars agree that religion and spirituality are each multidimensional (Miller & Thoresen, 2003; Smart, 1996). Fully characterizing an individual's or group's religion or spirituality requires addressing not only beliefs but behavior, feeling, and experience. Zinnbauer and Pargament (2005) list psychologically relevant R/S dimensions that include biology, sensation, affect, cognition, behavior, identity, meaning, morality, relationships, roles, creativity, personality, self-awareness, and salience. Close inspection of any specific R/S dimension may reveal further levels of complexity, requiring increasingly fine-grained measures. For example, measures of dispositional tendencies to engage in R/S-motivated forgiveness commonly differentiate between self-forgiveness and other-forgiveness. However, other-forgiveness may itself require further disaggregation based upon whether an offender has shown remorse (Oman, 2009). Ultimately, each dimension—at whatever level of granularity—may over time also reciprocally influence other dimensions (Oman, 2013; Oman & Thoresen, 2007). In sum, unidimensional definitions of R/S risk producing highly truncated views of complex and dynamic phenomena.

Relation of Intrinsic and Extrinsic Dimensions

R/S definitions vary in their usefulness for articulating the relation between intrinsic and extrinsic dimensions of R/S engagement, widely studied constructs first enunciated in the 1950s by Gordon Allport. Pargament (1992) argued that Allport's distinction had misled the psychology of religion into excessively polarizing means-oriented religion from ends-oriented religion. In fact, he claimed, most people use religion as both a means and an end. Psychologists have set up

> a forced choice between two equally untenable alternatives: the hypocritical manipulation of a faith to achieve ends devoid of spiritual value (religion as used) or the devotion to spiritual values untainted by the nitty-gritty mechanisms it takes to realize them (religion as lived). (pp. 203–204)

In contrast to this caricature, Pargament argued that human and spiritual goals are often "intertwined" in the dynamics of everyday religious living (p. 210). That is, behavior in concrete situations reflects a complex interplay of both sacred and secular motives, pursued through both sacred and secular means (in Pargament's approach, the perceived sacred is the distinguishing feature of R/S). Further, in Pargament's view, because many traditions view the sacred (e.g., God) as taking an interest in human affairs, sacred and secular goals often overlap. Commonly, "because all people are [viewed as] 'children of God,' respect for oneself and compassion to others become religious goals" (p. 210).

To understand the dynamics of such "lived" religion, we must be alert to (1) how people use religion, (2) how they choose and pursue spiritual goals (e.g., those perceived as sacred), and (3) how previously secular goals may become "imbued" (p. 218) with sacred meaning and significance (e.g., sanctification; Pargament & Mahoney, 2005). Recognizing a complex of interacting means and ends

> adds some complexity to the task. [But by] conceptualizing and measuring the means and ends of religion in more of their richness . . . we may . . . be in a better position to appreciate the nature, roots, and results of [people's diverse] orientations to religious life. (Pargament, 1992, p. 218)

To study this dynamic means/ends interplay scientifically, we need both multidimensional measures and an adequate theoretical vocabulary. A set of definitions offered by Pargament has been helpful in this regard. One term *(spirituality)* is set aside to designate the seeking of something held sacred as an end. Another term *(religion)* designates the broader set of ways that sacredness may enter into a search—*as either means or as end*. The term *religion* thereby mostly *brackets* the precise position of whatever is sacred within the individual's goal system, implicitly acknowledging that a multiplicity of configurations is commonly at play in real life. The sacred may enter as means or "pathway" in many ways, all of which Pargament defines as part of religion:

> Attendance at religious congregations, religious beliefs, involvement in prayer and rituals, religious coping—these are just a few of the many sacred pathways taken to find, hold on to, or transform significance. . . . People involve themselves in religious activities for many reasons, not all of them spiritual. But if the sacred is a part of the pathway, the search qualifies as religious, regardless of where it leads. (Pargament, 1999, p. 12)

Consequently, one can recognize as religious many phenomena that are clearly related to sacrality, but do not qualify as spiritual, such as the proverbial soldier in a foxhole who is under attack and prays for his life but who is not seeking the sacred per se. Also classed as religious is the adoption of sacred pathways to seek typically nonsacred goals such as health, self-development, intimacy, or community participation (Zinnbauer & Pargament, 2005).[6]

In contrast, some other R/S definitions devote their terminological capital to other issues. An alternative approach described by Zinnbauer and Pargament (2005) defines religion and spirituality as two distinct types of search for the sacred. Religion is defined as taking place in an institutional context, whereas spirituality is unrestricted in its context. Interpreting these definitions literally seems to leave us without any term to designate a search for significance in ways merely *related* to the sacred: Seemingly, the prayers of the proverbial soldier in the foxhole would be classed as neither religious nor spiritual.

These diverging approaches show the difficulty of formulating a single definition for all occasions: Religion and spirituality—the two most familiar everyday terms—cannot easily absorb all the nuanced meanings that may at times be needed. As a remedy, one wonders whether on occasion a related term such as *religiousness* could be pressed into service, and given a technical meaning distinct from both "religion" and "spirituality."[7]

Inherent Capacity versus Manifest Characteristic

Some scholarly topics require distinguishing between a human *capacity* and its concrete *actualization*. The human capacity for spiritual and religious belief and engagement appears universal, but the exact nature and basis of this capacity holds much substantive interest (e.g., Bandura, 2003; Barrett, 2007).

Some scholars have defined *spirituality* itself as an inherent capacity or tendency. For example, Myers and Williard (2003) define *spirituality* as a "capacity and tendency present in all human beings to find and construct meaning" (see Table 2.2). In contrast, most approaches discussed earlier focus not on such a capacity but on ways that it is *actualized* (see Schneiders, 1986). An attraction of defining spirituality as a capacity is that one can affirm that all human beings possess spirituality. As Koenig (2008) points out, such affirmations may facilitate communicating with important audiences, such as patients and clients (Figure 2.2). However, a disadvantage is disconnection from prototypically distinctive features of R/S (e.g., the sacred or transcendent). Such capacity-focused definitions often provide little differentiation of spirituality from related constructs, such as meaning making.

Substantive versus Functional Approaches

Historically, many proffered definitions of religion have fallen into two major and widely cited categories: substantive and functional. Substantive approaches define religion through what is viewed as distinctive about its substance, which might be seen as a belief in an ultimate controller of destiny, a divine or superhuman power, or something else set apart and deemed to have sacred properties (e.g., in Table 1.1, definitions by Pratt, Argyle, and Koenig). Similarly, one may offer substantive definitions of spirituality (e.g., Hufford, Table 2.2). Substantive approaches are often useful in particular contexts, but have been criticized as failing to capture the dynamism of religion and spirituality.

In contrast, functional approaches emphasize the *purposes* served by religiousness (or spirituality) in an individual's life. Scholars have offered evidence that religious beliefs, emotions, practices, and experiences may provide meaning (see Park, Chapter 18, this volume) and facilitate dealing with fundamental existential issues such as death, suffering, and injustice, and may also help foster personal control and social cohesion. An illustrative example is Batson, Shoenrade, and Ventis's (Table 2.1) definition of religion as involving "whatever we . . . do to come to grips" with issues of death and dying. In defining spirituality, Doyle (Table 2.2) also uses a functional approach, based on "the search for existential meaning." Pargament, Koenig, and Perez (2000) observed that scholars have long debated the relative importance of various functions of religion. However, from their perspective, "there is no need to choose" (p. 521), since empirical findings have established that religion serves a variety of purposes in day-to-day living and in crisis.

Importantly, many definitions combine substantive and functional approaches. For example, in Table 2.1, Durkheim's definition refers both to the sacred (substance) and to social cohesion (function). Similarly, Pargament's definition of religion refers both to the sacred (substance) and to provision of meaning/significance (function). The definition of spirituality by Puchalski (Table 2.2) combines, or at least juxtaposes, a commonly used substantive criterion, sacrality, with the functional provision of meaning and connectedness.

Relation between Religion and Spirituality

Both religion and spirituality are mentioned in the titles of about 7% of psychology publications about these phenomena (see Figure 2.1, caption). Often, researchers must simultaneously define both of these constructs and articulate their interrelationship.

Miller and Thoresen (2003) point out that religion and spirituality may be viewed as complementary. Many people view religion as intended to foster spirituality. From that perspective, "the field of religion is to spirituality as the field of medicine is to health" (p. 28). Other professional literature (e.g., Highfield, 2001, p. 328) has also described the constructs as "complementary." In nursing literature, Emblen (1992) found only slight overlap in constructs of religion and spirituality, but both connoted a type of *need* that nurses can help address.

At the other extreme, the interconnections between religion and spirituality may be eclipsed by polarizing connotations. Zinnbauer and his colleagues (Zinnbauer & Pargament, 2005; Zinnbauer et al., 1999) have extensively documented the occurrence in professional and popular usage of at least five types of polarization:

1. Substantive religion versus functional spirituality.
2. Static religion versus dynamic spirituality.
3. Institutional objective religion versus personal subjective spirituality.
4. Belief-based religion versus emotional/experiential-based spirituality.
5. Negative religion versus positive spirituality.

For example, Zinnbauer and Pargament (2005) note that religion has at times been stripped of its functions and statically represented solely by what it *is* rather than by "what it does or how it works." In contrast, spirituality is "often used in modern discourse as a substitute for words such as *fulfilling, moving,* or *important*" (p. 25). Similarly, while "religiousness gets slapped with . . . mundane faith, outdated doctrine, or institutional hinderances to human potentials," spirituality is "credited with . . . the loftier side of life, the highest in human potential, and pleasurable affective states" (p. 26). These authors point out many drawbacks of framing the terms as rigid opposites, such as hindering inquiry and obscuring important features of the phenomena in question.

Both complementary and polarized usages of these terms by professionals may in part reflect appropriation of popular usage (Saler, 2000). To better understand popular usage, several studies have compared how samples of U.S. adults understand terms for religion and spirituality. Three findings are noteworthy. First, many surveys report that most US adults identify themselves as both spiritual and religious (Marler & Hadaway, 2002). Second, several studies indicate substantial overlap in how these constructs are understood (Marler & Hadaway, 2002). For example, in a survey of North American adults by Walker and Pitts (1998), respondents endorsed "belief in a higher power" and "has strong beliefs" as the two most prototypical descriptors of both religion and spirituality. Similarly, for both constructs, the sixth most prototypical descriptor was "devoted." Thus, there is little evidence that a majority views religion and spirituality as primarily representing opposing social identities. Nor are the terms recognized as designating intrinsically opposed ways of life.

A third finding is that religion and spirituality are usually not viewed as identical, and that their most commonly identified meanings in some ways do correspond with late-20th-century emphasis on religion as pertaining to organizations. For example, Walker and Pitts (1998) found that descriptors such as "church going" and "reads Bible" were rated by North American adults as highly prototypical of a "religious person" but were absent as descriptors of a "spiritual person" (pp. 418–419). Similar findings emerge from studies by Zinnbauer and Pargament (2005) and their colleagues. In contrast, proffered descriptions of spirituality place greater emphasis on feelings and experiences of connectedness to sacred beings or forces (Zinnbauer & Pargament, 2005).

Recognizing the Social Dimension of Spirituality

From a scientific perspective, religion and spirituality each possess a *social basis* and a *social dimension*. As researchers, we should not allow ourselves to be blinded to this fact by the individualistic language that sometimes accompanies spirituality. Many observers have noted that people who identify themselves as spiritual while rejecting the label "religious" often get together with other like-minded individuals. Over time, such relationships may coalesce into groups and become formalized. That is, people who reject membership in religious organizations may find themselves joining alternative organizations such as 12-step fellowships, yoga groups, or meditation centers that offer spiritual support. Some of these spiritual organizations may differ from religious organizations primarily in their novelty or the content of their beliefs or practices. Zinnbauer et al. (1999) noted that Neibuhr's church–sect theory suggests that sectarian movements that break from established churches tend over time to grow church like themselves. More broadly, Schneiders (2003) characterized the relation of religion with institutionalization as "dialectical," arguing that "institutionalization is a . . . paradoxical blessing [that] initiates people into an authentic tradition of spirituality, gives them companions on the journey and tested wisdom by which to live, and supports them in times of suffering and personal instability [but] . . . often undermines personal faith by its own infidelity to the tradition" (pp. 170, 172).

Wuthnow (1998, p. 181) argued that spiritual practices are "inevitably social" because of their ultimate reliance on resources provided by others, such as spiritual literature and instruction. Should spiritual organizations composed primarily of "spiritual but not religious" individuals be understood as alternative forms of religion, notwithstanding their members' nonreligious self-presentation? According to many definitions, both substantive and functional, such organizations are indeed religious (e.g., Highfield in Table 2.1).

Larger Cultural Impacts

Many groups in Figure 2.2 are well-recognized audiences for psychologists, such as research colleagues, study participants, medical patients, and psychotherapy clients. But R/S definitions possess wider cultural implications, and may be relevant to policymakers, courts, and educators. In U.S. publicly funded education, for example, the constitutional acceptability of teaching spiritual practices is likely to depend on the perceived relation between spirituality (which is not mentioned in the Constitution) and religion (which is) (Oman, Flinders, & Thoresen, 2008).

Parallel issues can arise in healthcare. For example, Warnock (2009, p. 470) has described a constitutionally based lawsuit against the U.S. Veterans Administration (VA) related to a "new ethical dilemma" regarding the provision of spiritual care. According to Warnock, "the most complicating aspect of spiritual care stems from its lack of a concise definition of faith, spirituality, and religion and their connection to organized religion" (p. 476). In order to "remove religious bias from spiritual assessment," she recommended that the VA might "eliminate the word 'religion' . . . from spiritual assessment" (p. 476). R/S definitions may also hold policy implications in various European countries, where "spirituality" has become an established concern in education, healthcare, or other fields (Sheldrake, 2011).

Derivative Constructs

A final consideration in formulating definitions of religion and spirituality is implications for derivative constructs such as religious coping (Pargament, 1997), religious conversion (Rambo, 1993), spiritual transformation (Hufford & Bucklin, 2006), spiritual development (Roehlkepartain, Benson, King, & Wagener, 2006), spiritual strivings (Emmons, 1999), and workplace spirituality (Giacalone & Jurkiewicz, 2003; Oman & Neuhauser, 2012), each of which has inspired book-length treatments. Other commonly studied related constructs include spiritual well-being (Paloutzian, Bufford, & Wildman, 2012), spiritual struggle (Exline & Rose, Chapter 19, this volume), spiritual modeling (Bandura, 2003; Oman, 2013), and sanctification (Pargament & Mahoney, 2005). More broadly, Wulff (1997) lists several dozen nouns that are modified by the adjective *spiritual* in contemporary literature, noting that virtually all could be (and many have been) "conjoined with religious as well, albeit with slight shifts in connotation" (p. 7).

Some of these R/S-related constructs, such as religious coping and spiritual strivings, might be regarded simply as dimensions of religion or spirituality—(e.g., as a component of religious or spiritual *practice*). Other constructs, however, describe processes of change over time, rendering them less easily comfortable to a dimensional model. Such change-focused constructs include spiritual development, spiritual modeling, and sanctification.

CHOOSING A DEFINITION: THREE APPROACHES

For readers who may be uncertain about where to begin, we now highlight and critique three definitional approaches for special attention. The first has been mentioned several times earlier. All three have many strengths, and each has been influential in different settings. For further details, readers are encouraged to consult the cited publications.

Religion and Spirituality as Search Processes

As mentioned earlier, several psychologists have defined religion and spirituality as search processes (Hill et al., 2000; Pargament, 1997, 2007; Zinnbauer & Pargament, 2005; see also Pargament in Table 2.1 and in Hill et al. in Table 2.2). Key elements of this approach are that:

- Spirituality and religion are each *search* processes, where "search" means "attempts to identify, articulate, maintain, or transform" the object of search (Hill et al., 2000, p. 66).
- Each search involves the *sacred*, most prototypically referring to "a divine being, divine object, Ultimate Reality, or Ultimate Truth as perceived by the individual" (Hill et al., 2000, p. 66) (see prior section on Distinctive Features of R/S).
- Spirituality is defined as a "search for the sacred," and religion (or religiousness) is defined more broadly as a "search for significance in ways related to the sacred" (Pargament, 1997, p. 32) (see prior section on Relation of Intrinsic and Extrinsic Dimensions).

Strengths of this approach include its blending of substantive and functional approaches; its ability to distinguish different degrees of internalization of a quest for the sacred; and its depolarization of religion as a means versus as an end. Limits of this approach include dissonance with the recent popular usage of religion as a narrower construct than spirituality and with self-understandings of those who identify themselves as "spiritual but not religious."

Spiritual Development as an Inherent Capacity for Self-Transcendence

Roehlkepartain et al. (2006) have offered a definition of spiritual development intended to guide and encourage the emerging research field of spiritual development in childhood and adolescence:

> Spiritual development is the process of growing the intrinsic human capacity for self-transcendence in which the self is embedded in something greater than the self, including the sacred. It is the developmental "engine" that propels the search for connectedness, meaning, purpose, and contribution. It is shaped both within and outside of religious traditions, beliefs and practices. (pp. 5–6)

Strengths of this approach include its theological flexibility and applicability both within and outside of religious traditions. It links spiritual development to both qualities (e.g., sacredness) and processes (self-transcendence). Limits include the absence of specificity of being "embedded in something greater," which seemingly could apply equally well to a civil community, a youth gang, or a multinational corporation.

One Religion, Multiple Spiritualities

Koenig (2008), a physician and leading research on religion and health, advocates multiple *diverging* approaches to defining spirituality. First, he offers a single substantively oriented definition of religion,[8] displayed in Table 2.1. Then, "for pragmatic reasons" (p. 12), Koenig proposes that spirituality should be defined using two general approaches: For patient care, spirituality should be defined "as broadly as possible so that all patients have an opportunity to have their spiritual needs addressed" (p. 18; e.g., Puchalski in Table 2.2). However, for research purposes, he advocates that we "return the definition of spirituality to its origins in religion, whether traditional or nontraditional. . . . If there is no connection with either religion or the supernatural, then I would not call a belief, practice, or experience spiritual. I would call it humanistic" (pp. 16–17). (A similar two-track approach is recommended by Koenig, et al., 2012.)

Strengths of Koenig's approach include (1) explicit recognition of the pragmatic aspect of defining spirituality; (2) recognition of the importance of social dimensions of spirituality; and (3) specificity in defining religion. Limits include the apparent construal of ritual as a *sin qua non* of religion rather than as a prototypical feature that may be reduced or absent in some cases.[9] It also gives little guidance for understanding the effects from "spiritual but not religious" ways of living (such as described by Wuthnow, 1998) that combine engagement with some prototypical features of religion with disengagement from others.

EMERGING SUBSTANTIVE TOPICS

In the past, our psychological definitions of religion and spirituality have been forged and tested most often through studies of phenomena close at hand, such as familiar Western traditions. In a rapidly changing and globalizing world, emerging phenomena may encourage new approaches. The most successful definitions, we suggested earlier, are often those that permit communication with multiple audiences. In closing, therefore, we offer a brief sample of emerging topics that might stretch, test, confirm, or force us to rethink our favorite definitions.

"Spiritual but Not Religious" Self-Identification

Approximately one in four U.S. adults identifies as "spiritual but not religious," but this population is not well understood. It almost surely is a very heterogeneous group that adheres to many different forms of spirituality (e.g., both "seeking" and "practice" spirituality; Wuthnow, 1998). Which definitions or typologies of spirituality are most helpful for understanding these individuals and the forces that shape them? Which definitions are best for studying health effects from their spirituality? Koenig (2008) has pointed out that very little is known about this group—even whether their health outcomes tend to be better or worse than those who identify themselves as neither spiritual nor religious.

Multiple Traditions

Recent surveys suggest that approximately 24% of U.S. adults attend services of at least one faith other than their own, and roughly 12% say they participate in the services of two or more faiths in addition to their own (Pew Forum, 2009). Far less commonly, but increasingly often, U.S. adults identify themselves as adhering to multiple traditions. Indeed, "in the wider history of religion, multiple religious belonging may have been the rule rather than the exception" (Cornille, 2010, p. 1). For example, in Japan, many people regulate different parts of life with different traditions. Not uncommonly, the same family may turn to a Buddhist priest to bury a deceased relative and to a Shinto priest to "confirm" a young child. The Japanese government reports that 93% of Japanese identify as Shinto, while 74% also practice Buddhism, implying at least two out of three adhere to both (Krause, Ingersoll-Dayton, Liang, & Sugisawa, 1999). Indeed, Gries, Su, and Schak (2012) recently argued that "zero-sum, forced-choice approaches to measuring religious belief do not work well outside of the Abrahamic world" (p. 623). In a sizeable Taiwanese sample, they reported many advantages from assessing religion based on degree of engagement questions such as "How much do you believe in the following religions?" (p. 635). Similarly, we must ask, what are the most useful definitional approaches to guide research on individuals and groups who adhere to multiple traditions, and for whom no single religious "community" can be said to exist?

Recovering the "Neglected Middle"

Sociologist Robert Wuthnow (1998) has suggested that in U.S. culture attending to spiritual practices represents a "way of retrieving the neglected middle in our understandings of religion" (p. 16). He documents what he calls a "practice-oriented spirituality," distinct from both the orthodox religious "dwelling spirituality" prevalent in the 1950s and the generally unsystematic "spiritual seeking" that became common in the 1960s. People who commit themselves to practice-oriented forms of spirituality may be deeply involved in religious communities or may be "sojourners whose lives exist on the edges of these communities" (p. 16). Even more than a comparatively passive dwelling spirituality, a practice spirituality "requires paying attention to some tradition or individual who has gone before . . . because there is a realization that tradition is not simply given, but interpreted, and that tradition is changeable rather than static" (p. 191).

If Wuthnow is correct, the study of such "practice spirituality" may clarify the sources and dynamics of intentional spiritual growth, but his ideas also pose many challenges. For example, how can psychologists best classify and assess such "practice-oriented" commitments (Oman, 2010)? How should such assessments inform psychological treatments? Should mindfulness-based interventions be regarded as forms of spiritual practice (Oman, 2012)?[10] Are our current definitions of religion and spirituality adequate for discussing the relevant professional choices?

SUMMARY AND CONCLUSION

Religiousness and spirituality have each been a part of human experience throughout human history, from Neolithic times to the present. In modern psychology, these phenomena have been investigated using concepts and terms inherited from Western discourse. In recent centuries, spirituality was commonly understood as a component of religion. Since the 1960s, popular connotations have shifted, and spirituality is now often viewed as the broader construct. These shifts in meaning offer both advantages and disadvantages, opportunities and dangers. At a minimum, they require psychologists and scholars in all fields to use these terms consciously and carefully, clarified with well-chosen definitions. More broadly, they underscore the need for a conscious and cumulative *pragmatics* of defining religion and spirituality in particular contexts, a task previously seldom if ever fully articulated in the psychology of religion and spirituality.

This chapter has embarked on the initial steps for such a pragmatics. We have examined several of the more influential psychological approaches to defining religion and spirituality, situating them within a wider context of cultural, historical, professional, and scholarly influences and concerns. We highlighted three approaches that we hope will provide useful reference points. The topic is far too broad and deep, however, for definitive coverage within a single chapter. Additional scholarly resources have been cited throughout. Where clear precedents are absent, the choice to employ particular concepts and definitions must often be justified through persuasive narratives (Kaplan, 1986). Ultimately, intuition and judgment are needed in each concrete situation.

Much recent progress is clearly evident in the psychological conceptualization of spirituality and religion. Such progress comes at an opportune time. Increasingly rigorous scientific studies have documented the importance of religion and spirituality for diverse areas of human functioning and well-being. Popular interest in religion and spirituality is strong across most of the world. Yet the social roles and concrete forms of religion and spirituality are shifting as a result of many factors, ranging from technological change to the globalization of culture. Perennial features of religion and spirituality are being rediscovered and reinvented in new contexts. Through the many thoughtful paradigms reviewed here, psychology holds great promise for discovering and disseminating wise approaches to religion and spirituality in the 21st century.

NOTES

1. Usages include textbooks such as Tanquerey's *The Spiritual Life: A Treatise on Ascetical and Mystical Theology* (1930), reference works such as the *Dictionnaire de Spiritualité* (begun in 1932), the book series *Classics of Western Spirituality* (begun in 1978), and the scholarly Society for the Study of Christian Spirituality (established in 1992).
2. Regardless of its precise structure (i.e., prototype vs. classical), a concept with rich associations may function in discourse as what Blumer (1954) called a "sensitizing" construct. Atchley (2009) used "spirituality" in this manner, arguing that "sensitizing concepts . . . do not point to something specific or concrete but instead deal with qualities to be sensitive to if we want to observe or communicate about a general field or region" (p. 5).
3. "Family resemblance" is a philosophical term from Ludwig Wittgenstein (1889–1951).
4. Saler (2000, p. 79) reports that "as Popper and others have noted, definitions, if we take them too seriously, can involve us in infinite regress. . . . Words given in the *definiens* are themselves

likely to be ambiguous or vague. A quest for precision might induce the definer to define them as well. . . . Any proffered definitions of categories such as religion . . . are likely to be problematic in one way or another [but] may nevertheless be useful in their own limited ways."

5. Lutzky (1993, p. 292) writes that "no single Proto-Indo-European [PIE] term for the concept 'sacred' can be posited, [perhaps] because the essence of the concept is not unitary, but it is rather a bipolar notion, with the general sense of 'separation-binding,' captured in a number of different PIE roots," and that "the Sanskrit word which most closely corresponds to the 'sacred,' *yajati*, refers to the ritual of sacrifice or to worship by means of sacrifice [but] no link to the polarity 'separation-binding' exists."

6. In contrast to Pargament (1999), Hill et al. (2000) appear to offer a narrower definition of what pathways count as "related to the sacred." Without further qualification, Pargament (1999) speaks of prayer, rituals, and religious coping as "just a few of the many sacred pathways." But Hill et al. (2000, p. 66) state that a pathway must occur in "a context that has as its primary goal the facilitation of [a search for the sacred]." Yet these authors neither define "context" nor clarify whether its definition should render as "religious" such common activities as private prayers offered outside of a house of worship.

7. For example, perhaps *spirituality* could be defined as a search for the sacred; *religion* as a social or cultural institution to foster spirituality; and *religiousness* as an individual's usage of religious resources or forms (such as prayers) for any type of goal.

8. Koenig's (2008, p. 11) definition is misleadingly polarizating if interpreted to imply that Eastern traditions lack strong personalized conceptions of the divine, such as Hindu avatars or Pure Land Buddhism's Amitabha Buddha (cosmic savior) (Smith & Novak, 2003).

9. For example, the Buddha "argued that 'belief in the efficacy of rites and ceremonies' is one of the Ten Fetters that bind the human spirit" (Smith & Novak, 2003, pp. 24–25). In some later Buddhism (e.g., American Vipassana) "ritual and ceremony are relatively absent" (p. 173).

10. Recently developed mindfulness self-report measures tap qualities fostered by spiritual practices within both Buddhism and other traditions (see Shapiro, Oman, Thoresen, Plante, & Flinders, 2008). Psychological definitions of mindfulness are ostensibly Buddhist derived. However, by abandoning the active distinguishing between "wholesome and unwholesome, beneficial and unbeneficial tendencies" as a key feature of mindfulness, they show what Wallace (2006, p. 61) called a "striking" contrast with the most widespread Buddhist understandings of mindfulness (see also a recent 18-article special issue on Buddhism and psychology, especially Dreyfus, 2011; also see Mikulas, 2011).

REFERENCES

Anttonen, V. (2000). What is it that we call 'religion'?: Analyzing the epistemological status of the sacred as a scholarly category in comparative religion. *Method & Theory in the Study of Religion, 12*, 195–206.

Argyle, M., & Beit-Hallahmi, B. (1975). *The social psychology of religion.* London: Routledge & Kegan Paul.

Atchley, R. C. (2009). *Spirituality and aging.* Baltimore, MD: Johns Hopkins University Press.

Bandura, A. (2003). On the psychosocial impact and mechanisms of spiritual modeling. *The International Journal for the Psychology of Religion, 13*, 167–174.

Barrett, J. L. (2007). Is the spell really broken?: Bio-psychological explanations of religion and theistic belief. *Theology and Science, 5*, 57–72.

Batson, C. D., Schoenrade, P., & Ventis, W. L. (1993). *Religion and the individual: A social-psychological perspective.* New York: Oxford University Press.

Bellah, R. N. (1970). *Beyond belief.* New York: Harper & Row.

Blumer, H. (1954). What is wrong with social theory? *American Sociological Review, 19*, 3–10.

Bond, K., Ospina, M. B., Hooton, N., Bialy, L., Dryden, D. M., Buscemi, N., et al. (2009). Defining a complex intervention: The development of demarcation criteria for "meditation." *Psychology of Religion and Spirituality, 1,* 129–137.

Byrne, P. (1999). The definition of religion: Squaring the circle. In J. Platvoet & A. L. Molendijk (Eds.), *The pragmatics of defining religion: Contexts, concepts, and contests* (pp. 379–396). Boston: Brill.

Cornille, C. (2010). Introduction: The dynamics of multiple belonging. In C. Cornille (Ed.), *Many mansions?: Multiple religious belonging and Christian identity* (pp. 1–6). Maryknoll, NY: Orbis.

Dollahite, D. C. (1998). Fathering, faith, and spirituality. *Journal of Men's Studies, 7,* 3–15.

Doyle, D. (1992). Have we looked beyond the physical and psychosocial? *Journal of Pain and Symptom Management, 7,* 302–311.

Dreyfus, G. (2011). Is mindfulness present-centred and non-judgmental?: A discussion of the cognitive dimensions of mindfulness. *Contemporary Buddhism, 12,* 41–54.

Durkheim, E. (1995). *The elementary forms of religious life* (K. E. Fields, Trans.). New York: Free Press. (Original work published 1912)

Emblen, J. D. (1992). Religion and spirituality defined according to current use in nursing literature. *Journal of Professional Nursing, 8,* 41–47.

Emmons, R. A. (1999). *The psychology of ultimate concerns: Motivation and spirituality in personality.* New York: Guilford Press.

Emmons, R. A., & Paloutzian, R. F. (2003). The psychology of religion. *Annual Review of Psychology, 54,* 377–402.

Fahlberg, L. L., & Fahlberg, L. A. (1991). Exploring spirituality and consciousness with an expanded science: Beyond the ego with empiricism, phenomenology, and contemplation. *American Journal of Health Promotion, 5,* 273–281.

Giacalone, R. A., & Jurkiewicz, C. L. (Eds.). (2003). *Handbook of workplace spirituality and organizational performance.* Armonk, NY: Sharpe.

Gries, P., Su, J., & Schak, D. (2012). Toward the scientific study of polytheism: Beyond forced-choice measures of religious belief. *Journal for the Scientific Study of Religion, 51,* 623–637.

Guenther, M. (1999). From totemism to shamanism: Hunter-gatherer contributions to world mythology and spirituality. In R. B. Lee & R. H. Daly (Eds.), *The Cambridge encyclopedia of hunters and gatherers* (pp. 426–433), Cambridge, UK: Cambridge University Press.

Hart, T. (1994). *Hidden spring: The spiritual dimension of therapy.* Mahwah, NJ: Paulist Press.

Highfield, M. E. F. (2001). Spiritual and religious care. In T. T. Fulmer, M. D. Foreman, & M. K. Walker (Eds.), *Critical care nursing of the elderly* (pp. 326–352). New York: Springer.

Hill, P. C., Pargament, K. I., Hood, R. W., Jr., McCullough, M. E., Swyers, J. P., Larson, D. B., et al. (2000). Conceptualizing religion and spirituality: Points of commonality, points of departure. *Journal for the Theory of Social Behaviour, 30,* 51–77.

Hufford, D. J., & Bucklin, M. A. (2006). The spirit of spiritual healing in the United States. In J. D. Koss-Chioino & P. Hefner (Eds.), *Spiritual transformation and healing* (pp. 25–42). Walnut Creek, CA: AltaMira Press.

James, W. (1961). *The varieties of religious experience.* New York: Collier. (Original work published 1902)

Kaplan, T. J. (1986). The narrative structure of policy analysis. *Journal of Policy Analysis and Management, 5,* 761–778.

Kearns, J. N., & Fincham, F. D. (2004). A prototype analysis of forgiveness. *Personality and Social Psychology Bulletin, 30,* 838–855.

Koenig, H. G. (2008). *Medicine, religion, and health: Where science and spirituality meet.* West Conshohocken, PA: Templeton Foundation Press.

Koenig, H. G., King, D. E., & Carson, V. B. (2012). *Handbook of religion and health, 2nd ed.* New York: Oxford University Press.

Krause, N., Ingersoll-Dayton, B., Liang, J., & Sugisawa, H. (1999). Religion, social support, and health among the Japanese elderly. *Journal of Health and Social Behavior, 40*, 405–421.

Lambert, N. M., Fincham, F. D., & Graham, S. M. (2011). Understanding the layperson's perception of prayer: A prototype analysis of prayer. *Psychology of Religion and Spirituality, 3*, 55–65.

Leuba, J. H. (1901). Introduction to a psychological study of religion. *Monist, 11*, 195–225.

Lovejoy, A. O. (1936). *The great chain of being: A study of the history of an idea.* Cambridge, MA: Harvard University Press.

Lutzky, H. (1993). On a concept underlying Indo-European terms for the sacred. *Journal of Indo-European Studies, 21*, 283–301.

Marler, P. L., & Hadaway, C. K. (2002). "Being religious" or "being spiritual" in America: A zero-sum proposition? *Journal for the Scientific Study of Religion, 41*, 289–300.

Mikulas, W. (2011). Mindfulness: Significant common confusions. *Mindfulness, 2*, 1–7.

Miller, W. R., & Thoresen, C. E. (2003). Spirituality, religion, and health: An emerging research field. *American Psychologist, 58*, 24–35.

Molendijk, A. L. (1999). In defense of pragmatism. In J. Platvoet & A. L. Molendijk (Eds.), *The pragmatics of defining religion: Contexts, concepts, and contests* (pp. 3–19). Boston: Brill.

Myers, J. E., & Williard, K. (2003). Integrating spirituality into counselor preparation: A developmental, wellness approach. *Counseling and Values, 47*, 142–155.

O'Collins, G., & Farrugia, E. G. (1991). *A concise dictionary of theology.* New York: Paulist Press.

Oman, D. (2009). Unique and common facets of religion and spirituality: Both are important. *Journal of Religion, Spirituality & Aging, 21*, 275–286.

Oman, D. (2010). Similarity in diversity? Four shared functions of integrative contemplative practice systems. In T. G. Plante (Ed.), *Contemplative practices in action: Spirituality, meditation, and health* (pp. 7–16). Santa Barbara, CA: Praeger.

Oman, D. (2012). Shall the twain meet?: Buddhist meditation, science, and diversity. *PsycCRITIQUES, 57*(Release 30), Article.

Oman, D. (2013). Spiritual modeling and the social learning of spirituality and religion. In K. I. Pargament, J. Exline, & J. Jones (Eds.), *APA handbook of psychology, religion, and spirituality (Vol. 1): Context, theory, and research* (pp. 187–204). Washington, DC: American Psychological Association.

Oman, D., Flinders, T., & Thoresen, C. E. (2008). Integrating spiritual modeling into education: A college course for stress management and spiritual growth. *The International Journal for the Psychology of Religion, 18*, 79–107.

Oman, D., & Neuhauser, L. (2012). Spiritual factors in occupational health and well-being: Opportunities for research translation. In P. C. Hill & B. Dik (Eds.), *Psychology of religion and workplace spirituality* (pp. 63–85). Greenwich, CT: Information Age.

Oman, D., & Thoresen, C. E. (2007). How does one learn to be spiritual? The neglected role of spiritual modeling in health. In T. G. Plante & C. E. Thoresen (Eds.), *Spirit, science and health: How the spiritual mind fuels physical wellness* (pp. 39–54). Westport, CT: Praeger.

Otto, R. (1958). *The idea of the holy: An inquiry into the non-rational factor in the idea of the divine and its relation to the rational.* New York: Oxford University Press.

Paloutzian, R. F., Bufford, R. K., & Wildman, A. J. (2012). Spiritual well-being scale: Mental and physical health relationships. In M. Cobb, C. Puchalski, & B. Rumbold (Eds.), *Spirituality in healthcare* (pp. 353–358). Oxford, UK: Oxford University Press.

Pargament, K. I. (1992). Of means and ends: Religion and the search for significance. *The International Journal for the Psychology of Religion, 2*, 201–229.

Pargament, K. I. (1997). *The psychology of religion and coping.* New York: Guilford Press.

Pargament, K. I. (1999). The psychology of religion and spirituality? Yes and no. *The International Journal for the Psychology of Religion 9*, 3–16.

Pargament, K. I. (2007). *Spiritually integrated psychotherapy.* New York: Guilford Press.

Pargament, K. I., Koenig, H. G., & Perez, L. M. (2000). The many methods of religious coping: Development and initial validation of the RCOPE. *Journal of Clinical Psychology, 56,* 519–543.

Pargament, K. I., & Mahoney, A. (2005). Sacred matters: Sanctification as a vital topic for the psychology of religion. *The International Journal for the Psychology of Religion, 15,* 179–198.

Pew Forum (2009). *Many Americans mix multiple faiths.* Retrieved December 13, 2009, from *http://pewforum.org/newassets/images/reports/multiplefaiths/multiplefaiths.pdf.*

Peteet, J. R. (1994). Approaching spiritual problems in psychotherapy: A conceptual framework. *Journal of Psychotherapy Practice & Research, 3,* 237–245.

Platvoet, J. (1999). Contexts, concepts and contests: Towards a pragmatics of defining 'religion.' In J. Platvoet & A. L. Molendijk (Eds.), *The pragmatics of defining religion: Contexts, concepts, and contests* (pp. 463–516). Boston: Brill.

Popper, K. R. (2006). *The open society and its enemies* (Vol. 2). New York: Routledge. (Original work published 1945)

Pratt, J. B. (1920). *The religious consciousness: A psychological study.* New York: MacMillan.

Puchalski, C., Ferrell, B., Virani, R., Otis-Green, S., Baird, P., Bull, J., et al. (2009). Improving the quality of spiritual care as a dimension of palliative care: The report of the consensus conference. *Journal of Palliative Medicine, 12,* 885–904.

Rambo, L. R. (1993). *Understanding religious conversion.* New Haven, CT: Yale University.

Roehlkepartain, E. C., Benson, P. L., King, P. E., & Wagener, L. M. (2006). Spiritual development in childhood and adolescence: Moving to the scientific mainstream. In E. C. Roehlkepartain, P. E. King, L. Wagener, & P. L. Benson (Eds.), *The handbook of spiritual development in childhood and adolescence* (pp. 1–15). Thousand Oaks, CA: Sage.

Rosch, E. (1975). Cognitive representations of semantic categories. *Journal of Experimental Psychology: General, 104,* 192–233.

Rosch, E. H. (1973). Natural categories. *Cognitive Psychology, 4,* 328–350.

Saler, B. (2000). *Conceptualizing religion: Immanent anthropologists, transcendent natives, and unbounded categories.* New York: Berghahn.

Schneiders, S. M. (1986). Theology and spirituality: Strangers, rivals or partners? *Horizons, 13,* 253–274.

Schneiders, S. M. (1989). Spirituality in the academy. *Theological Studies, 50,* 676–697.

Schneiders, S. M. (2003). Religion vs. spirituality: A contemporary conundrum. *Spiritus: A Journal of Christian Spirituality, 3,* 163–185.

Shafranske, E. P., & Gorsuch, R. L. (1984). Factors associated with the perception of spirituality in psychotherapy. *Journal of Transpersonal Psychology, 16,* 231–241.

Shapiro, S. L., Oman, D., Thoresen, C. E., Plante, T. G., & Flinders, T. (2008). Cultivating mindfulness: Effects on well-being. *Journal of Clinical Psychology, 64,* 840–862.

Sheldrake, P. (1998). *Spirituality and history: Questions of interpretation and method* (2nd ed.). Maryknoll, NY: Orbis Books.

Sheldrake, P. (2011). Spirituality in a European context. *Spiritus: A Journal of Christian Spirituality, 11,* 1–9.

Smart, N. (1996). *Dimensions of the sacred: An anatomy of the world's beliefs.* Berkeley: University of California Press.

Smith, H. (1991). *The world's religions.* New York: HarperCollins.

Smith, H. (1992). *Forgotten truth: The common vision of the world's religions.* New York: HarperCollins. (Original work published 1976)

Smith, H., & Novak, P. (2003). *Buddhism: A concise introduction.* New York: HarperCollins.

Tart, C. T. (1975). *Transpersonal psychologies.* New York: Harper & Row.

Vaughn, F. (1991). Spiritual issues in psychotherapy. *Journal of Transpersonal Psychology, 23,* 105–119.

von Balthasar, H. U. (1965). The gospel as norm and test of all spirituality in the church. *Concilium: Theology in the Age of Renewal* [English edition], *9*, 5–13.

Wakefield, G. S. (1983). Spirituality. In G. S. Wakefield (Ed.), *Westminster dictionary of Christian spirituality* (pp. 361–363). Philadelphia: Westminster Press.

Walker, L. J., & Pitts, R. C. (1998). Naturalistic conceptions of moral maturity. *Developmental Psychology, 34*, 403–419.

Wallace, B. A. (2006). *The attention revolution*. Boston: Wisdom.

Warnock, C. J. P. (2009). Who pays for providing spiritual care in healthcare settings?: The ethical dilemma of taxpayers funding holistic healthcare and the first amendment requirement for separation of church and state. *Journal of Religion and Health, 48*, 468–481.

Wulff, D. M. (1997). *Psychology of religion: Classic and contemporary*. New York: Wiley.

Wulff, D. M. (1999). Psychologists define religion: Patterns and prospects of a century-long quest. In J. Platvoet & A. L. Molendijk (Eds.), *The pragmatics of defining religion: Contexts, concepts, and contests* (pp. 207–224). Boston: Brill.

Wuthnow, R. (1998). *After heaven: Spirituality in America since the 1950s*. Berkeley: University of California Press.

Zinnbauer, B. J., & Pargament, K. I. (2005). Religiousness and spirituality. In R. F. Paloutzian & C. L. Park (Eds.), *The handbook of the psychology of religion and spirituality* (pp. 21–42). New York: Guilford Press.

Zinnbauer, B. J., Pargament, K. I., & Scott, A. B. (1999). The emerging meanings of religiousness and spirituality: Problems and prospects. *Journal of Personality, 67*, 889–919.

3

Measurement Assessment and Issues in the Psychology of Religion and Spirituality

Peter C. Hill

Imagine the dismay for runners in the 2005 Chicago Lakeshore Marathon when *every* runner who completed the course did so on average about 4% slower than what they expected. Was it just a bad day for everyone? Were the weather conditions *that* formidable? Not at all. The problem was one of measurement. It was later discovered that the course was wrongly charted and the runners ran 27.2 miles—a full mile further than the usual grueling marathon! In short, measurement matters—a lesson that psychologists of religion have long recognized. In fact, Gorsuch (1984), in a highly influential *American Psychologist* article, claimed that the then-current paradigm in the scientific study of religion was one of measurement. Given that paradigm change occurs only once an existing paradigm has successfully fulfilled its useful value (Kuhn, 1970), any paradigmatic change, such as the one suggested by Emmons and Paloutzian (2003) toward a *multilevel interdisciplinary paradigm* in the psychology of religion, testifies to the success of the previous paradigm. In fact, Gorsuch claimed that we now have measures that are "reasonably effective" and "available in sufficient variety for most any task in the psychology of religion" (p. 234). In a nutshell, the focus on measurement has been good for the psychology of religion.

The religious and spiritual landscape, however, has changed since Gorsuch's article was published in 1984, and it can be argued that the upsurge in social scientific interest in religiousness and spirituality has created the need for a continued focus on measurement. At the least, additional religious and spiritual measures functionally related to a particular research interest may be necessary (Hill & Pargament, 2003). Consider, for instance, the substantial literature linking religion and spirituality to health where separate measures are sometimes needed depending upon the population of interest (e.g., research on the relationship of religion and spirituality to alcohol dependency vs. surviving cancer). It is also true that new theories within the psychology of religiousness and spirituality have been developed and that testing these theories will require new measures. Furthermore, research in the psychology of religion and spirituality has expanded in recent years far beyond the Judeo-Christian tradition and contextually-sensitive measures are increasingly being developed. In fact, since Hill and Hood's (1999) edited volume reviewing 125 scales, it is conservatively estimated that at least another 100 measures have been developed, some of which are discussed in this chapter.

Still, however, researchers are encouraged to follow Gorsuch's (1984) advice and not construct new measures unless absolutely necessary. Instead, they should utilize and, when necessary, modify existing assessment instruments. As Miller (1998) stated when addressing the rarity of empirical research involving religious and spiritual constructs in addictions research, "It is not for lack of reliable instrumentation" (p. 980). To the extent that the ability to validly measure is a key indicator of a developing field's health and maturity, the psychology of religion and spirituality is alive and well as a science.

ASSESSING THE CURRENT STATE OF RELIGIOUS AND SPIRITUAL MEASUREMENT

If what has been said is indicative of measurement success, it is not uncritically so. Although it is true that the variety of scales do a respectable job of measuring religiousness, collectively they are not without limitations and deficiencies. Some of these limitations are due to the inherently complex nature of religious and spiritual constructs; other deficiencies are the responsibility of the scientific community. Fortunately, researchers are making systematic strides in addressing many of these shortcomings.

Measurement Hurdles and Advances

In the following sections I discuss a number of issues that have plagued the psychological study of religiousness and spirituality. With many new measures, however, researchers are aware of some of these issues and are attempting to address them when possible.

Lack of Conceptual Clarity

Measurement itself is barren; the key to good measurement is the sophistication and fertility of the theories and ideas within which the measuring instruments are grounded. A long-standing concern in the psychology of religion is that its empirical study has lacked coherence as a result of an absence of a guiding theoretical framework (Dittes, 1969). The disregard of theoretical development can be applied to even the foremost research framework in the psychology of religion to date: Allport's (1950) Intrinsic–Extrinsic (I-E) religious orientation model. What may have been a good theoretical beginning did not develop further, and after a few decades the I-E model was judged by some to be "theoretically impoverished and has really taught us little about the psychology of religion" (Kirkpatrick & Hood, 1990, p. 442). The alleged culprit was that much subsequent scientific effort was spent disproportionately on issues of measurement with an insufficiently developed theory to warrant the effort. Given that the I-E variable continues to be vitally important highlights even more the crucial significance of its solid theoretical grounding to the field's progress.

Sometimes our objects of study—religion and especially spirituality—are not clearly defined, including the literature that involves measurement development. Kapuscinski and Masters (2010) found tremendous diversity and lack of operational agreement among the 24 recent measures (19 of which were published after 1999) of spirituality they reviewed. Among many concerns listed, they emphasized three in particular: (1) the lack of emphasis on behavioral elements of spirituality despite the importance of behavior to the holistic understanding of psychological makeup; (2) the lack of consensus regarding language associated with traditional religious beliefs and behavior (they found that only about 33% of the measures included religious elements in their definition of spirituality, but 65% had individual items that contained traditional religious language), including in many studies an apparent disregard or even lack of awareness of the importance of this issue to their conceptualization of spirituality; and (3) the lack of a clearly defined psychologically based transcendent element (i.e., transcendence as perceived by the individual) as central to spirituality among a "significant minority" (p. 195) of researchers.

One cannot stress enough that solid theory is critical to good measurement. Despite the wide variety of research on religiousness and spirituality over the decades, until recently little has been drawn from well-established theoretical models in mainstream psychology. Fortunately, many of the chapters in this *Handbook* testify to the increased application to the religion and spirituality variable from such mainstream literature as the psychology of coping (see Pargament, Falb, Ano, & Wachholtz, Chapter 28), developmental psychology (Levenson, Aldwin, & Igarashi, Chapter 9; McFadden, Chapter 10; Richert & Granqvist, Chapter 8), motivation and goals (see Emmons & Schnitker, Chapter 13), personality theory (Piedmont & Wilkins, Chapter 15) and the study of both emotion (Tsai, Koopmann-Holm, Miyazaki, & Ochs, Chapter 14) and cognition (Barrett, Chapter 12).

It goes without saying that it is also important that the potential user of the scale have a clear conceptual understanding of the phenomena of interest before choosing a scale, and only then should a potential scale be considered *item by item*. This is especially important because some scales are not well named. For example, the Systems of Belief Inventory (SBI-15; Holland et al., 1998), which has reasonable strong psychometric properties, is not only a measure of beliefs but also a measure of practices (e.g., "I pray for help during bad times") and outcomes ("I have experienced peace of mind through my prayers and meditation"). The items are mixed on each of the scale's two factors. The SBI-15 is but one example of how cognitive, affective, and behavioral components are sometimes mixed together. At the very least, the potential user of the scale should consider whether such a mixed bag of items might interfere with efforts to untangle the various facets of spirituality from each other.

Sample Unrepresentativeness

Sampling in the psychology of religion is not immune to the problems associated with psychology's reliance on convenience samples of college students who are disproportionately Caucasian, younger, better educated, and from a higher socioeconomic status (four variables implicated in religious experience) than the population as a whole. For example, of the 24 measurement studies reviewed by Kapuscinski and Masters (2010), only one used a nationally representative sample (from the 1998 General Social Survey) and more than 50% relied on convenience samples of high school, undergraduate, or graduate students, which resulted in most of the samples containing at least 60% females (another variable implicated in religious experience).

The problem of representation is further complicated by the fact that Protestantism dominates the samples found in much of the literature investigating religiousness (Gorsuch, 1988; Hill & Hood, 1999). Although such dominance is understandable demographically (at least historically in the United States), it is nonetheless problematic when desiring to use a scale with a more pluralistic population. In contrast, if one is interested in developing measures of spirituality (especially nontheistic or transpersonal spirituality), it is important that the "traditionally" religious (e.g., people who identify with such designations as Protestants, Catholics, Jews, Evangelicals, Orthodox) not be *under*represented, which, if the researcher needs a scale representing a broad population (e.g., North Americans), is equally problematic as Protestant *over*representation. Regardless, it is important when considering an existing measure of spirituality to note the degree to which items involve religious language and to determine whether such usage, or lack thereof, is appropriate to the population being studied.

Cultural Insensitivity

Measures of religiousness and spirituality sometimes lack sensitivity to cultural variables (Chatters, Taylor, & Lincoln, 2002), a deficiency clearly related to the problem of adequate sample representation (for a review of cultural issues in testing, see Sandoval, Frisby, Geisinger, Ramos-Grenier, & Scheuneman, 1998). Of course, differences in religious and spiritual perspectives, affiliations, and practices are often related to cultural factors and, thus, the representation problem is not just one of Protestant overrepresentation but, as noted earlier, also one of Caucasian, American, educated, and middle-class overrepresentation as well. Hill and Pargament (2003) have noted that, even within American Protestantism, cultural insensitivity has been demonstrated when measuring African Americans—perhaps the most Protestant of all ethnic groups. Although some scale items may be directly offensive, perhaps a more common deficiency is either to emphasize irrelevant issues (or issues of secondary importance) or deemphasize issues of great importance (e.g., a strong ethos of community service [Ellison & Taylor, 1996] and the notion of reciprocal blessings with God [Black, 1999]) to the African American church.

Lack of Sustained Research Programs

A major problem in the area has been the failure to develop sustained research programs using standardized measures. Much research on religiousness and spirituality has been conducted within the context of other research agendas, often with religion, in particular, as an "add-on" variable only. As a result, measures of religion have often been imprecise, frequently involving single-item measures of general religious identification or church attendance. Of course, single-item measures are less reliable and contain more measurement error, are vulnerable to small wording changes, are especially problematic for cross-cultural adaptation or comparisons (Braithwaite & Scott, 1991), and should, therefore, be used only as a last resort.

Measurement in the psychology of religion has paid a price for this lack of systematic research. First, issues of scale validity are difficult to assess. Second, there is an absence and inutility of normative data for many of the scales. Although clearly defined norms are not necessary for scales used solely for research purposes, it is important to consider the samples upon which instruments have been used to establish psychometric adequacy. Many scales, especially those published before the 1980s, have not been used beyond their initial introduction (see Hill & Hood, 1999), so any validity assessment or normative data are usually based upon, in such cases, a single sample. Fortunately, however, given the recent proliferation of research, we are seeing more repeated usage of measures, especially those more recently developed.

Overreliance on Self-Report Measures

As in many other research domains, measures of religion and spirituality tend to rely primarily on paper-and-pencil self-reports. As Hill and Pargament (2003) point out, the well-documented limitations of self-reports in other domains of psychological study apply equally well to investigating religiousness: (1) Some aspects of religion and spirituality may be inadequately measured because they are difficult to articulate through closed-ended questions; (2) religion and spirituality may be especially susceptible to a social desirability bias (Batson, Schoenrade, & Ventis, 1993); (3) such scales may require reading levels beyond the ability of children, poorly educated adults, and some clinical populations; and (4) some paper-and-pencil measures may be boring or disengaging, thereby fostering a potential response set bias.

Although similar to self-report, one imaginative alternative that may circumvent some of the problems associated with self-reports has been developed by Nielsen and Webster (2011). Their Simultaneous Objective/Subjective Assessment technique allows the individual to indicate the relationship among people or constructs on a two-dimensional surface. The individual places a marker representing him- or herself and then places markers representing various religious groups, with close distances representing greater similarity among those markers. Software records the placement of markers and the timing of their movements. This technique has been used to measure people's schemas regarding world religions and among Christian denominations; preliminary results suggest that people scoring high on right-wing authoritarianism and Christian orthodoxy use more rigid group boundaries than do people scoring low on those measures (Nielsen & Webster, 2011).

Among alternative methodologies currently being explored are those that use implicit measures, such as an adaptation of the Implicit Association Test (Bassett et al., 2005; Ventis, Ball, & Viggiano, 2010). Some (e.g., Cohen, Shariff, & Hill, 2008; Hill, 1994; Wenger, 2004) have created an index of attitude accessibility (measured by response time) as an implicit indicator of the importance or centrality of religion. Others have attempted to use pictures to assess religious understandings (Bassett et al., 1990) or religious coping (Pendleton, Cavilli, Pargament, & Nasr, 2002). Physiological indicators such as computer tomography and positron-emission tomography scans have also been utilized (Newberg, d'Aquili, & Rause, 2001). As promising as some of these measures may be, they are likely incapable of capturing the complexity and richness of spiritual and religious experience and, therefore, will be most useful primarily as measures that supplement, and not replace, self-report instruments.

Measures Beyond the Judeo-Christian Tradition

Measures within Other Religious Traditions

Addressing the field's overreliance on the study of Protestants, psychologists of religion are increasingly studying people from other religious traditions and cultures, including those who report being spiritual but not religious. When attempting to create or modify existing measures to generalize research to non-Western religious traditions, the need for cultural sensitivity is magnified (Hill & Pargament, 2003). Researchers are encouraged to develop measures indigenous to the population or culture of interest. This will require that researchers put forth far greater effort than what empirically oriented psychological researchers typically do to understand the culture in general and, specifically, the religious and spiritual traditions of that culture. Creating indigenous measures provides an opportunity for psychologists to combine efforts with other social scientists (e.g., anthropologists, cross-cultural psychologists, empirically oriented theologians), thereby putting the *multilevel interdisciplinary paradigm* (Emmons & Paloutzian, 2003) into practice.

A number of such indigenous scales have been developed. Two examples within Islam, each with strong psychometric properties, include the Psychological Measure of Islamic Religiousness (Raiya, Pargament, Stein, & Mahoney, 2007) and The Religiosity of Islam Scale (RoIS; Jana-Masri & Priester, 2007). Of interest here are some of the items included in these measures. Although some items in the RoIS, for example, fit well with Western conceptions of religiousness or spirituality (e.g., "I believe that the Qur'an is the final word of Allah"), other items represent religious and cultural particularity (e.g., "I believe that men can shake hands with women," reverse-scored).

An example within the Hindu tradition is the Measures of Hindu Pathway Scales (Tarakeshwar, Pargament, & Mahoney, 2003), a 37-item measure of four religious pathways consistent with Hindu theology: devotion, ethical action, knowledge, and physical restraint/yoga. The four subscales, all of which are internally consistent, with alphas above .80, are moderately intercorrelated (.15–.44), showing that the four pathways are related but distinct. Of particular interest here, however, is the care with which the research team developed an indigenous measure. Only after 15 extensive interviews with Hindus living in the Uited States that were then coded and developed into a thematic framework that was reviewed by the Hindu participants were items generated and eventually selected based on traditional scale development procedures.

Sometimes simple translation of a scale to another language appears adequate, such as what Ai, Peterson, and Huang (2003) found with the RCOPE measure when used with Kosovar and Bosnian Muslim refugees in the United States. Similarly, Tapanya, Nicki, and Jarusawad (1997) found that the Age Universal I-E scale (Gorsuch & Venable, 1983) could, without modification beyond translation, be useful with Thai Buddhists. Furthermore, a relatively straightforward translation of the Spiritual Transcendence Scale (Piedmont, 1999) has now been validated on samples from India (Piedmont & Leach, 2002) and the Philippines (Piedmont, 2007). The Spiritual Well-Being Scale (Paloutzian & Ellison, 1982) has now been translated (and found to be reliable in the cultures represented) in Spanish, Portuguese, Chinese, Malay, and Arabic, and translation efforts are currently underway in at least seven other languages representing quite varied cultures (Paloutzian, Bufford, & Wildman, 2012).

However, it should not be assumed that simple translation is all that is necessary.

Some assumptions underlying a measure may not apply to other cultures. One must first be aware of and acknowledge religious and other cultural assumptions embedded within the scale and consider whether those assumptions apply to the culture to which the scale is being exported. Consider, for example, what the developers of the Chinese version of Underwood and Teresi's (2002) 16-item Daily Spiritual Experience Scale (DSES), which demonstrates high internal consistency and the same factor structure as the original scale developed in the States, had to say about the difficulties in the cross-cultural portability of the measure.

> While finding that all 16 items make sense and are common spiritual experiences to Chinese, the team encountered problems with the term "God." In Chinese, "God" can be a "human-ized" or "philosophical" higher power. Confucianism, Buddhism, and Daoism all have reli-gious rituals toward "humanized Gods." On the other hand, the term "God" can refer to spiritual transcendence, such as the notions of selfless social responsibility in Confucianism, enlightenment in Buddhism, and "merging with the way of nature" in Daoism. As such, the concept "God" had to be expanded to embrace both humanized and philosophical higher power in Chinese translation. To take care of this point, the team added an explanatory note to the term "God" while keeping the word "God" in translating the 16 items into Chinese. (Ng, Fong, Tsui, Au-Yeung, & Law, 2009, pp. 92–93)

Later in their article, the authors detailed in considerable length the steps they took to make sure that the DSES should even be applied to the religious and spiritual practices of Chinese. Such efforts are exemplary and should remind researchers of the necessary care in successfully transporting a measure to another culture (also see Ghorbani, Watson, & Khan, 2007).

Therefore, when exporting a current measure to another culture, the researcher should expect that such modifications beyond simple wording changes will be necessary. This has been found when exporting the Allport and Ross (1967) measure of religious orientation to Muslims, such as in the development of the Muslim-Christian Religious Orientation Scale (Ghorbani, Watson, Ghramaleki, Morris, & Hood, 2002) as well as a number of parallel versions for other cultures of Pargament's measure of religious cop-ing (RCOPE; Pargament, Smith, Koenig, & Perez, 1998): Jewish (Rosmarin, Pargament, Krumrei, & Flannelly, 2009), Hindu (Tarakeshwar, Pargament, & Mahoney, 2003), and Pakistani Muslim (Khan & Watson, 2006).

Whether or not a measure is applicable across cultures may depend on the aspect or component of religiousness or spirituality that is being investigated and measured. For example, there is now considerable evidence that Hood's (1975) Mysticism Scale, with perhaps small variations in wording, is useful in a variety of contexts: American Protestants, Tibetan Buddhists, Iranian Muslims, Israeli Jews, Indian Hindus, and Chi-nese Christians (see, e.g., Anthony, Hermans, & Sterkens, 2010; Chen, Yang, Hood, & Watson, 2011). The three factors of the scale have been replicated across these religious and cultural groups, thereby supporting Stace's (1960) common core thesis; that is, a common core set of components underlies mystical experiences regardless of cultural context, though some (e.g., Belzen, 2010) dismiss such findings as measurement artifact. The point here is that the question of universal versus diversity of religious experience remains unanswered, even for something as basic as mystical experience. However, even if such common core experiential components exist, communal and linguistic influences may structure such experiences in a culturally meaningful way that must be captured in measurement instruments (Hood & Chen, 2013).

Measures That Transcend Religious Traditions

Researchers sometimes attempt to develop a measure of spirituality that is not linked to specific religious traditions. Of course, the idea is that such a measure can be used across religious traditions and may also be of value in assessing those who see themselves as spiritual but not religious. Such an approach assumes that one can validly assess a generic spiritual experience without focusing on substantive and perhaps functional issues associated with specific traditions, and may thus demonstrate a pluralistic ignorance not unlike other cultural insensitivities. Cohen and Hill (2007) found, for example, differences in the relationship of intrinsic (I) and extrinsic (E) religious motivations between American Protestants, Catholics, and Jews, such that the oft-found negative relationship between I and E held only for Protestants. In fact, they found a moderately *positive* correlation between the I and E religious orientations for Jews. Such differences found within the Judeo-Christian tradition in North America should serve as a warning of the importance of religion as a cultural variable (Cohen, 2009; also see Saroglou & Cohen, Chapter 17, this volume).

Still, how religion and spirituality function in people's lives likely generalizes in many regards across traditions, and empirical findings of such generalized functions is of value to the field. One solution is to create, when possible, general (or tradition-specific) measures from which parallel tradition-specific (or general) measures are further developed.

APPROACH TO THE REVIEW OF INDIVIDUAL SCALES

A Hierarchical Approach

To discuss all available measures is beyond the scope of this chapter and would lend redundancy to other reviews (Hill & Hood, 1999; Hill & Edwards, 2013; Kapuscinski & Masters, 2010). Instead, a number of promising scales that demonstrate reasonably strong psychometric properties (based on four criteria identified and discussed shortly) are highlighted through use of a two-level hierarchical model to construct organization of religion and spirituality recommended by Tsang and McCullough (2003). The goal of Level I measures is "to assess broad dispositional differences in religious tendencies or traits so that one might draw conclusions about how 'religious' a person is" (p. 349). This superordinate dispositional level of organization (what they call Level I) can be used to measure a general religious factor that may predict many other variables (Gorsuch, 1984).

The subordinate Level II measures in Tsang and McCullough's (2003) hierarchy assess how people "experience religious (and spiritual) realities, their motivations for being religious, and their deployment of their religion to solve problems in the world" (pp. 349–350). This functional level of organization often assesses subdimensions of the general religiousness factor and is useful in predicting more specific variables to see a complete relationship. Tsang and McCullough recommend that before researchers explore Level II functional variables, they should first control for the more general Level

I religiousness factor to disentangle the functional variable from the more general trait-like quality.

Given that there is surely a finite number of ways to conceptualize general religiousness, it seems that Gorsuch's (1984) claim of a sufficient availability of measures is especially true for Level I measures. However, as we discover more ways in which religion is individually experienced, further precise measures at the functional Level II may yet need to be constructed.

Four Criteria

Four criteria for evaluating scales were used and are summarized in Table 3.1: theoretical structure, representative sampling/generalization, measures of reliability, and measures of validity. Four levels of each criterion ranging from "exemplary" to "none or minimal" are presented in the table. These levels are not meant to be absolute and could surely be refuted, especially when such descriptors as "exemplary" or "minimally acceptable" are

TABLE 3.1. General Rating Criteria for Evaluating Measures of Religion or Spirituality

Criterion	Criterion rating			
	Exemplary (rating = 3)	Good (2)	Acceptable (1)	Minimal or none (0)
Theoretical basis	Clearly grounded in well-established (perhaps dominant) theoretical framework	Clearly grounded in a plausible but not necessarily consensual theoretical framework	Only partially well connected to theory	Theory is posed but connection to theory is unclear or the theory is suspect; no theory discussed
Sample representativeness/ generalization	Clearly represents a broadly conceived population, not limited by a religious tradition or narrow spirituality	Clearly represents by design a less broadly conceived population (e.g., Christians, people in treatment)	Clearly represents by design a narrowly conceived population (e.g., Evangelicals, Mormons) or a less clear representation of a broader population	Limited to a restrictive sample in one study only; clearly not representative of population or sample not identified
Reliability (coefficient alpha or test–retest at minimum 2 weeks)	Excellent ($r > .80$) across two or more studies	Good ($r = .70–.80$) across 2 or more studies	Excellent ($r > .80$) or good ($r = .70–.80$) in one study only; moderate ($r = .60–.70$) in two or more studies	Moderate ($r = .60–.70$) or low ($r < .60$) in one study only; no reliability reported
Validity	High correlations across multiple (diverse) samples from different studies on at least two types of validity	Significant correlations across multiple samples (from one study or multiple studies) on at least two types of validity	Significant correlations on at least two types of validity on only one sample or one type of validity on multiple samples	Significant correlations on only one measure of validity on only one sample; no significant correlations found

used. The purpose here is not to grade each measure listed in the Appendix on each of the four criteria. Rather, the purpose is simply to demonstrate how measurement success is defined in the psychology of religion and also to communicate a basis for how the scales included for review here were selected. Specifically, only scales that would achieve at least minimally acceptable ratings on all four criteria were selected for review. Most of the scales reviewed here, however, clearly exceed the minimal acceptable rating on more than one criterion.

Theoretical Basis

Consideration of the theoretical basis of a measure involves two considerations: (1) The scale itself should have a theoretical underpinning and (2) the researcher should also have a clear theoretical basis for the research at hand. Unfortunately, for reasons already discussed (e.g., complex multidimensional constructs, religion or spirituality as an "add-on" variable only, lack of sustained research programs), empirical research on the religion variable, including that which has involved the development of instruments, has often lacked a strong theoretical basis. Preference for inclusion here was given to scales developed in the context of larger theoretical programs.

Representative Sampling and Generalization

As already discussed, deficiencies in sampling are common, and researchers are cautioned to recognize that, for example, measures of non-Protestant (especially non-Western) religion are quite rare, although such scales are beginning to be developed. Somewhat related is the subtle, but significant, problem that many measures of religion likely reflect Christian religious biases, even when not explicitly identified as measures of Christian religion.

Ideally, then, what we would have is a measure with items that clearly represents a broadly conceived population that is limited neither by a specific religious tradition (hence, a measure of religion that cuts across all religions) nor a narrow spirituality (e.g., one that is defined by only one dimension). At the opposite extreme is a nonrepresentative sample or a representative sample of such a narrow population (e.g., a specific denomination) that renders the instrument meaningless for research purposes. Thus, for the broader research community, there are two dimensions to consider: the representation of the sample to its population as well as the breadth of the population for generalization.

Reliability

Scale reliability when measuring religiousness or spirituality is typically assessed through two techniques: (1) internal consistency describing the internal structure of the scale and (2) test–retest reliability. The majority of scales rely on internal consistency reliability, the most common of which is Cronbach's (1951) *coefficient alpha,* while the test–retest measure of reliability is used less frequently. The use of parallel forms for reliability testing of instruments in psychology of religion research is exceedingly rare.

There is a practical issue to consider with regard to reliability. Although the statistical reliability of a scale suffers when there are relatively few items that makeup the scale, short scales are appealing because they are generally more feasible, especially when the measure of religion or spirituality is part of a larger battery of research or clinical instruments. Also, short scales are attractive and sometimes necessary for research involving large samples, which, in turn, allows researchers to retain the study's statistical power. Many of these same trade-offs are involved in validity issues as well.

Validity

Validity is the extent to which the instrument measures what it claims to be measuring. Issues regarding validity have been interspersed throughout this chapter and have usually been alluded to in the context of two concerns: problems of validity as a result of (1) nonrepresentative samples (usually where an American Protestant orientation is overrepresented) and (2) a lack of sustained research programs across different samples. Nevertheless, the scales reviewed here are not without some validity claims.

Whereas reliability of religiousness measures tends to be assessed primarily by internal consistency, validity assessment is more heterogeneous. At least one of the three following methods of determining validity is used in most scales (with each method well-represented among the scales discussed here): (1) convergent validity, (2) factorial validity, and (3) criterion-related validity (either "known groups" or discriminant validity).

DISCUSSION OF SELECTED SCALES

Representative scales from selected domains will now be briefly discussed. For each level of the hierarchy discussed previously, selected categories recommended by the Fetzer Institute/National Institute of Aging Working Group (1999) on religion and spirituality (with a few additional categories) are used. Space limitations preclude even a brief discussion of promising measures; instead, Appendix 3.1 provides a list of recommended measures of each domain.

Level I: Measures of Dispositional Religiousness or Spirituality

Scales That Assess General Religiousness or Spirituality

The attempt here is to assess religious or spiritual differences between people, perhaps as broadly as a personality trait that may be independent of the Big Five personality dimensions. Tsang and McCullough (2003) cite evidence from three sources that suggest indirect support for the existence of such a broad characteristic: (1) conceptually meaningful correlations among distinct aspects of religiousness (e.g., church attendance, engagement in private religious practices, self-rated importance of religion) found especially in homogenous cultural groups; (2) factors found within multiple-item measures that are frequently intercorrelated, suggesting some higher order factor; and (3) evidence that religiousness may be partially heritable (see D'Onofrio, Eaves, Murrelle, Maes, & Spilka, 1999). Piedmont's (1999) Spiritual Transcendence Scale and Hood's (1975) Mysticism Scale are examples that measure general spiritual orientations (transcendent or mystical orientations in these cases) without reference to a specific religious tradition. A recent measure also designed to cut across religious traditions but still containing religious language (e.g., such terms as God and prayer) is the 20-item Beliefs and Values

Scale (King et al., 2006). Designed specifically for use in clinical research and useful for both religious and nonreligious individuals, this two-factor scale demonstrated high reliability (both test–retest and internal consistency) and validity on two separate samples. Unfortunately, the two factors were unlabeled; however, the first factor (17 items) seems to assess a general spiritual orientation while the second factor (three items) appears to assess spiritual beliefs that are clearly outside of a religious context.

Scales That Assess Religious or Spiritual Well-Being

Paloutzian and Ellison's (1982) 20-item Spiritual Well-Being Scale (SWBS) has become a standard bearer in the religious and spiritual well-being literature and has been used in more than 300 published articles and chapters and almost 200 dissertations and master's theses (Paloutzian et al., 2012). The SWBS has three dimensions: religious well-being (RWB), existential well-being (EWB), and overall spiritual well-being (SWB), which is the combined RWB and EWB scores. The RWB items cluster together as one factor, thus suggesting a general religiousness well-being measure. Through its frequent use, the SWBS has established convergent and discriminant validity, although it is subject to ceiling effects among conservative religious populations (Ledbetter, Smith, Vosler-Hunter, & Fischer, 1991). An updated review of the measure (including its strengths and weaknesses), particularly as it relates to mental and physical health, is found in Paloutzian et al. (2012).

The Functional Assessment of Chronic Illness Therapy—Spiritual Well-Being Scale (FACIT-Sp: Peterman, Fitchett, Brady, Hernandez, & Cella, 2002) is a recommended measure designed to assess spiritual well-being and quality of life in chronically ill patients. Researchers are reminded that these are measures of spiritual well-being and not a general measure of spirituality or religiousness.

Scales That Assess Religious or Spiritual Commitment

One way of defining a general dispositional measure is to assess the degree to which a person is religiously or spiritually committed. Although some measures of religious commitment might better assess a functional element of religious experience (e.g., the motivating force of an intrinsic religious orientation), the measures listed here clearly assess a general religious or spiritual commitment.

The Religious Commitment Inventory (RCI-10; Worthington et al., 2003) is a 10-item measure of religious commitment that has been tested on individuals from a variety of religious traditions (Christians, Buddhists, Muslims, Hindus). Although a two-factor structure was supported, the two factors are highly intercorrelated, suggesting that this measure best be used as a full-scale assessment of general religious commitment. Worthington et al. report that the RCI-10 shows good internal consistency, 3-week and 5-month test–retest reliability, and construct as well as discriminant validity.

The Santa Clara Strength of Religious Faith Questionnaire (SCSRFQ; Plante & Boccaccini, 1997) is a 10-item scale designed to measure the strength of religious faith in the general population, not just among people who rate themselves as religious. If brevity of assessment is necessary, a five-item short form (SCSRFQ-SF) has also been developed (Plante, Vallaeys, Sherman, & Wallston, 2002), with a single-factor structure that includes all five items with good internal consistency and convergent validity (Storch et al., 2004).

Scales That Assess Religious or Spiritual Beliefs

Few measures of religious belief specifically—a topic of considerable interest to an earlier generation of psychologists of religion—have been developed in recent years. Most recent attempts have been measures of spiritual beliefs outside of a religious context. Examples of such measures include the SBI-15 (Holland et al., 1998), the Spiritual Belief Scale (Schaler, 1996), and the already discussed Beliefs and Values Scale (King et al., 2006).

Perhaps the most frequently used measure of Christian belief is the 24-item Christian Orthodoxy (Fullerton & Hunsberger, 1982) scale. Many of the items strongly correlate with each other, so Hunsberger (1989) later developed a shortened six-item measure that correlates well with the original measure. Measures of other religious traditions include the 11-item Buddhist Beliefs and Practices Scale (Emavardhana & Tori, 1997), which assesses agreement with Buddhist teachings regarding specific beliefs (e.g., the theory of karma and rebirth, the doctrine of anatta, or no soul) and practices (e.g., observing the five precepts, practice of meditation) and the *Student Religiosity Questionnaire* (Francis & Katz, 1992), which has been translated into Hebrew and has been shown to validly assess Jewish beliefs and practices on a population of Jewish high school students (Katz & Schmida, 1992) and Jewish teacher trainees (Francis & Katz, 1992). See Hill and Hood (1999) for a review of many other religious belief scales.

Scales That Assess Religious or Spiritual Development

The Faith Maturity Scale by Benson, Donahue, and Erickson (1993) is a 38-item scale designed to measure "the degree to which a person embodies the priorities, commitments, and perspectives characteristic of vibrant and life transforming faith, as these have been understood in 'mainline' Protestant traditions" (p. 3). Thus, this measure tends to emphasize values or behavioral manifestations of faith rather than belief content (Tisdale, 1999).

The Spiritual Assessment Inventory (Hall & Edwards, 1996) measures spiritual development or maturity from both an object relations and contemplative spirituality perspective. The scale is limited to a Western Christian context (e.g., stressing an individual relationship with God), and most of the initial testing of the scale has been conducted among religious college students. However, the scale has a strong theoretical base and is currently used in numerous research programs involving more general populations.

Leak and his colleagues have developed two promising measures of religious development. The first is a 59-item 5-point Likert Religious Maturity scale (Leak & Fish, 1999) based on Allport's (1950) conceptualization of mature religion as a combination of commitment and doubt. The second is an eight-item, forced-choice Faith Development Scale (Leak, Loucks, & Bowlin, 1999) rooted in Fowler's (1981) theory. Both measures are well grounded in theory, are reasonably reliable, and demonstrate strong content, predictive, and construct validity.

Scales That Assess Religious Attachment

A theoretical development that has generated much recent research explores spirituality within the context of attachment theory. Example measures include Kirkpatrick and Shaver's (1992) Attachment to God Scale. The scale utilizes three attachment style vignettes, one each describing avoidant attachment, anxious/ambivalent attachment, and secure attachment patterns. Participants are asked which vignette best describes their relationship with God. An alternative to this categorical measure is the nine-item Likert-style Attachment to God Scale developed by Rowatt and Kirkpatrick (2002). Another attachment measure with good psychometric properties is the 28-item Attachment to God Inventory (Beck & McDonald, 2004), although the measure assesses only the insecure patterns of avoidance and anxiety. Virtually all of the measures of religious attachment have been developed within a Judeo-Christian context.

Scales That Assess Religious Social Participation or Religious/Spiritual Support

Measures of social participation have typically utilized single items centering around church attendance or, less frequently, financial contributions. Multi-item measures of perceived social support from one's religion are rare and, when used, are frequently included as part of a larger measure. For example, the Religious Involvement Inventory (Hilty & Morgan, 1985) is a multidimensional measure that demonstrates reasonably good psychometric qualities and includes a 14-item church involvement subscale. The church involvement subscale maintains comparable psychometric qualities to the entire scale and appears to be a useful measure of church participation. Thurstone and Chave's (1929) Attitude toward the Church Scale, although with dated wording that may require modest revision, has been used in more than 30 studies (Wulff, 1999).

Research indicates that one of the benefits of religion is that it often provides a basis for support, whether social or otherwise. The 21-item Religious Support Scale (Fiala, Bjorck, & Gorsuch, 2002) contains three subscales assessing the perception of support from God, congregation members, and church leaders. They used this measure to provide evidence that religious support can provide unique resources beyond other forms of social support. Similarly, Genia's (1997) Spiritual Experience Index—Revised (SEI-R) contains a 13-item Spiritual Support subscale that consists primarily of items tapping a sense of support drawn through one's perceived relationship with God. Genia has found that the subscale correlates positively with measures of spiritual well-being, intrinsic religious orientation, and worship attendance.

Scales That Assess Religious or Spiritual Private Practices

Measures of private practices are well represented in multidimensional measures, including, for example, such subscales as the Religious Practice dimension of DeJong, Faulkner, and Warland's (1976) measure of religiosity, the Christian Behavior and Home Religious Observance subscales of the Dimensions of Religiosity Scale (Cornwall, Albrecht, Cunningham, & Pitcher, 1986), the Christian Walk subscale of Bassett's Shepherd Scale (Bassett et al., 1981), and the Jewish Religious Observance subscale of the Student Religiosity Questionnaire (Francis & Katz, 1992). Other subscales that tend to emphasize ritualistic behavior, prayer or meditation, or reading of sacred documents are fairly common as parts of larger multidimensional measures. Finally, the Religious Background and Behavior scale (Connors, Tonigan, & Miller, 1996) is a frequent measure of choice by researchers. It has good psychometric qualities, is devoted primarily to measuring private and spirituality (R/S) practices, is less exclusively Christian in focus than many other scales, and is developed for use with a clinical population.

One of the most common spiritual practices is prayer. Ladd and Spilka's (2002, 2006; see Ladd & Spilka, Chapter 22, this volume) 29-item Inward, Outward, Upward Prayer Scale has eight subscales that load on three second-order factors: *inward* prayers that focus on self-examination, *outward* prayers that stress relationship with others, and *upward* prayers that emphasize the human–divine connection. Although primarily restricted to Christian populations at this time, the subscales demonstrate adequate reliabilities and provide evidence for both convergent and divergent validity.

Level II: Measures of Functional Religiousness or Spirituality

Understanding the varieties of *how* a person's religious or spiritual life is experienced is often an issue of utmost importance to psychologists of religion, especially when trying to uncover the mechanisms that link religion to some other phenomena. For example, when discussing the relationship of religion to physical and mental health, Hill and Pargament (2003) identified recent advances in conceptualizing and measuring religion that may be functionally relevant: perceived closeness to God, religion and spirituality as orienting or motivating forces, religious support, and religious or spiritual struggle. Following is a brief discussion of representative measures of several key religious operations or functions.

Scales That Assess Religious or Spiritual Experiences

Many measures of religion and spirituality stress their experiential nature by assessing feelings and awareness associated with involvement with what the person deems to be transcendent. Underwood's (1999; Underwood & Teresi, 2002) Daily Spiritual Experience Scale (DSES) is "intended to measure the individual's perception of the transcendent (God, the divine) in daily life and the perception of interaction with, or involvement of, the transcendent in life . . . this domain makes spirituality its central focus and can be used effectively across many religious boundaries" (Underwood, 1999, p. 11). This scale has excellent psychometric properties and uses a language that is applicable across various religious traditions; in fact, according to its website *(www.dsescale.org)*, as of Fall 2010, the scale has been translated and tested in a number of languages (Spanish, Hebrew, Mandarin Chinese, French, German, Greek, Korean, Portuguese, and Vietnamese). However, findings from a Jewish sample suggest that the norms, originally established on a largely Christian sample, may not be the same for other religious groups (Kalkstein & Tower, 2009).

Scales That Assess Religion or Spirituality as a Motivating Force

Alhough measurement issues differentiating the "flagrantly utilitarian motivation" (Burris, 1999, p. 144) underlying the extrinsic religious orientation versus the "'otherly,' nonmundane, even self-denying quality" (p. 144) of the intrinsic religious orientation have been mired in methodological and theoretical debate, religious orientation remains a potentially important construct for the psychology of religion. Gorsuch and McPherson's (1989) Revised Religious Orientation Scale modifies the original Allport and Ross (1967) scale along the lines of Kirkpatrick's (1989) reanalysis of results from several studies of religious orientation, namely that the extrinsic scale subdivides into two categories (personally oriented and socially oriented extrinsicness). This brief 14-item scale, with its strong psychometric qualities, is probably the single best current measure of religious orientation, if for no other reason than its advantageous position of utilizing two decades of research findings on the I-E construct. There are a number of other measures of religious orientation (11 measures of religious orientation are reviewed in Hill & Hood, 1999), including three items from the five-item Duke Religion Index (Koenig, Patterson, & Meador, 1997), which, despite its brevity (an appeal if only a limited number of items can be afforded), maintains reasonably strong psychometric qualities.

However, an important challenge for I-E research was posed by Batson and his colleagues, who suggested that a thorough understanding of Allport's notion of a mature religious sentiment must include "the degree to which an individual's religion involves an open-ended, responsive dialogue with existential questions raised by the contradictions and tragedies of life" (Batson et al., 1993, p. 169). Batson and Schoenrade's (1991a, 1991b) Quest Scale is an operationalization of this approach to religion that emphasizes the positive role of doubt and an appreciation for the complexities of issues when approaching life through one's religious or spiritual framework. Another scale for consideration that moderately correlates with quest ($r = .55$) is the 10-item Spiritual Openness (SO) subscale of Genia's (1997) SEI-R.

Another orientation to religion that can be considered a motivating force is religious fundamentalism. Altemeyer and Hunsberger's (2004) 12-item Religious Fundamentalism Scale (RFS) is recommended over its earlier 20-item counterpart (Altemeyer & Hunsberger, 1992), not only because of its brevity but also because its strong psychometric properties match and even sometimes exceed the longer version. An alternative to Altemeyer and Hunsberger's conceptualization of fundamentalism in terms of right-wing militancy is Hood, Hill, and Williamson's (2005) view of fundamentalism as an allegiance solely to a sacred text, which may (or may not) be militantly held. The Intratextual Fundamentalism Scale (IFS; Williamson, Hood, Ahmad, Sadiq, & Hill, 2010) has demonstrated adequate psychometric properties on both a U.S. Christian and Pakistani Muslim sample. These two scales (RFS and IFS) represent clear conceptual differences of what it means to be a fundamentalist.

Scales That Assess Religious or Spiritual Coping with Adversity

People often turn to religious and spiritual resources to cope with life stressors. The extensive 105-item measure, 21-subscales of Religious Coping Scale (RCOPE; Pargament, Koenig, & Perez, 2000) and particularly its 14-item brief counterpart (Brief RCOPE; Pargament et al., 1998; see Pargament, Falb, Ano, & Wachholtz, Chapter 28, this volume) are the most frequently used general measures of religious and spiritual coping. The Brief RCOPE consists of two factors (each with seven items): positive religious coping and negative religious coping. Both the RCOPE and the Brief RCOPE have been tested among many samples and continue to exhibit excellent psychometric characteristics.

Of interest to many researchers is the extent to which religion and spirituality might influence psychosocial adjustment following trauma. The Spiritual Transformation Scale (Cole, Hopkins, Tisak, Steel, & Carr, 2008) assesses spiritual changes following trauma (specifically, a diagnosis of cancer), both growth and decline, across four domains (worldview, relationships with others, goals/priorities, and self of sense). This two-factor, 40-item scale has excellent psychometric properties. However, the scale will require small modification if used with a population other than cancer patients.

Scales That Assess Religious or Spiritual Struggle

Researchers are increasingly interested in documenting the liabilities that may accompany religious experience. For example, many religious or spiritual people report that they experience struggle in their spiritual life, such as with God, with other people (such as family members), or within themselves. Exline's Religious Comfort and Strain scale (Exline, Yali, & Sanderson, 2000) is recommended for consideration on this topic. Similarly, the nine-item Attitudes Toward God Scale (Wood, Worthington, Exline, Yali, Aten, & McMinn, 2010) contains a four-item Disappointment and Anger toward God factor in addition to a five-item factor of positive attitudes toward God (see Exline & Rose, Chapter 19, this volume). This measure is highly internally consistent and temporally stable and has been validated in ethnically and religiously diverse samples, including a sample of atheists.

Scales That Assess Religious or Spiritual Meaning and Values

Coping with adversity often involves finding meaning through what the threatening event or object poses. Of all of life's functions, religion, so claimed the eminent psychologist of religion Walter Houston Clark (1958), is best suited to meet the human need for meaning, thus prompting many psychologists of religion to promote this need as a unifying construct for the field (e.g., see in this volume Paloutzian & Park, Chapter 1; Park, Chapter 18).

Until recently, however, religion and spirituality as unique sources of meaning have been disregarded in the measurement literature. Rather, when measures of meaning have been used in the psychology of religion and spirituality research, they have largely been measures free of religious content in part because a sense of meaning has been construed primarily as a mediating or dependent variable. Examples of such measures include the Sense of Coherence scale (SOC; Antonovsky, 1987), the Purpose in Life scale (PIL; Crumbaugh & Maholick, 1964), and the Seeking of Noetic Goals scale (SONG; Crumbaugh, 1977) as well as the eight-item Meaning/Peace subscale of the FACIT-Sp (Peterman et al., 2002). Alhough these are excellent scales and may be useful for some investigations in the psychology of religion, they will not in and of themselves allow researchers to discriminate between individuals who ascribe their sense of life meaning to a religious or spiritual source and those who experience meaning from some other life source. The sole exception is Krause's (2008) single-factor six-item measure where a religious or spiritual component is explicitly identified (e.g., one item is "God put me in this life for a purpose").

Multidimensional Measures

Many measures attempt to tap the multidimensionality of the religious or spiritual experience. The Fetzer Institute/National Institute on Aging Working Group (1999) produced the Brief Multidimensional Measure of Religiousness/Spirituality, a 38-item multidimensional measure that cuts across 10 conceptual domains. This measure was embedded in the 1997–1998 General Social Survey (GSS), a random national survey of the National Data Program for the Social Sciences. Initial psychometric analyses from the GSS data "support the theoretical basis of the measure and indicate it has the appropriate reliability and validity to facilitate further research" (p. 89). Other validated multidimensional measures worth consideration include the four-subscale (Sense of Peace, Faith in God, Religious Behavior, and Compassionate View of Others), 25-item Ironson–Woods Spirituality/Religiosity Index (Ironson et al., 2002) and the seven-subscale (Personal Faith, Intolerance of Ambiguity, Orthodoxy, Social Conscience, Knowledge of Religious History, Life Purpose, and Church Involvement), 82-item Religious Involvement Inventory (Hilty & Morgan, 1985; Hilty, Morgan, & Burns, 1984).

CONCLUSION

The results of this analysis support Gorsuch's (1984) claim almost 30 years ago that the measurement paradigm in the scientific study of religion and spirituality has been largely successful and that we now have a sufficient arsenal of measurement instruments. The rise of interest among scientific researchers in religion and spirituality, much of which has occurred since Gorsuch's influential article, has triggered a further proliferation of measures—a source of concern given the complexity and conceptual confusion surrounding particularly the spirituality variable. Still, what has developed in this period of time is an impressive array of measures of religiousness and spirituality that should help move empirical research forward in the years ahead.

APPENDIX 3.1. SPECIFIC MEASURES OF RELIGION AND SPIRITUALITY BY 12 COMMON DOMAINS

Level I: Measures of Dispositional Religiousness or Spirituality

1. Scales That Assess General Religiousness or Spirituality
   - Mysticism Scale (Hood, 1975)
   - Religiosity Measure (Rohrbaugh & Jessor, 1975)
   - Spiritual Transcendence Scale (Piedmont, 1999)

2. Scales That Assess Religious or Spiritual Well-Being
   - Spiritual Well-Being Scale (Paloutzian & Ellison, 1982)
   - Functional Assessment of Chronic Illness Therapy—Spiritual Well-Being Scale (Peterman et al., 2002)

3. Scales That Assess Religious or Spiritual Commitment
   - Dimensions of Religious Commitment Scale (Glock & Stark, 1966)
   - Religious Commitment Scale (Pfeifer & Waelty, 1995)

- Religious Commitment Inventory—10 (Worthington et al., 2003)
- Santa Clara Strength of Religious Faith Questionnaire (Plante et al., 2002)

4. Scales That Assess Religious or Spiritual Beliefs
    - Beliefs and Values Scale (King et al., 2006)
    - Buddhist Beliefs and Practices Scale (Emavardhana & Tori, 1997)
    - Christian Orthodoxy Scale (Fullerton & Hunsberger, 1982; Hunsberger, 1989)
    - Love and Guilt Oriented Dimensions of Christian Belief (McConahay & Hough, 1973)
    - Loving and Controlling God Scale (Benson & Spilka, 1973)
    - Belief Inventory (Holland et al., 1998)
    - Spiritual Belief Scale (Schaler, 1996)
    - Student Religiosity Questionnaire (Francis & Katz, 1988)
    - Views of Suffering Scale (Hale-Smith, Park, & Edmondson, 2012)

5. Scales That Assess Religious or Spiritual Development
    - Faith Development Interview Guide (Fowler, 1981)
    - Faith Development Scale (Leak, Loucks, & Bowlin, 1999)
    - Faith Maturity Scale (Benson, Donahue, & Erickson, 1993)
    - Religious Maturity Scale (Leak & Fish, 1999)
    - Spiritual Assessment Inventory (Hall & Edwards, 1996)

6. Scales That Assess Religious Attachment
    - Attachment to God Inventory (Beck & McDonald, 2004)
    - Attachment to God Scale (Kirkpatrick & Shaver, 1992)
    - Attachment to God Scale (Rowatt & Kirkpatrick, 2002)

7. Scales That Assess Religious Social Participation or Religious/Spiritual Support
    - Attitude toward the Church Scale (Thurstone & Chave, 1929)
    - Attitude Toward Church and Religious Practices (Dynes, 1955)
    - Congregation Climate Scales (Pargament, Silverman, Johnson, Echemendia, & Snyder, 1983)
    - Congregation Satisfaction Questionnaire (Silverman, Pargament, Johnson, Echemendia, & Snyder, 1983)
    - Religious Involvement Inventory (Hilty & Morgan, 1985)
    - Religious Support Scale (Krause, 1999)
    - Religious Support Scale (Fiala, Bjorck, & Gorsuch, 2002)
    - Spiritual Experience Index—Revised (Genia, 1997)

8. Scales That Assess Religious or Spiritual Private Practices
    - Buddhist Beliefs and Practices Scale (Emavardhana & Tori, 1997)
    - Inward, Outward, Upward Prayer Scale (Ladd & Spilka, 2002, 2006)
    - Religious Background and Behavior (Connors, Tonigan, & Miller, 1996)
    - Types of Prayer Scale (Poloma & Pendleton, 1989)

9. Scales That Assess Religious or Spiritual History
    - The SPIRITual History (Maugans, 1996)
    - Spiritual History Scale (Hayes, Meador, Branch, & George, 2001)

Level II: Measures of Functional Religiousness or Spirituality

10. Scales That Assess Religious or Spiritual Experiences
    - Attitudes Toward God Scale (Wood et al., 2010)
    - Daily Spiritual Experience Scale (Underwood, 1999)
    - Index of Core Spiritual Experiences (INSPIRIT) (Kass, Friedman, Leserman, Zuttermeister, & Benson, 1991)
    - Religious Experiences Episode Measure (REEM) (Hood, 1970)
    - Religious Strain (Exline et al., 2000)
    - Spiritual Experience Index-Revised (Genia, 1997)
    - Spiritual Orientation Inventory (Elkins, Hedstrom, Hughes, Leaf, & Saunders, 1988)

11. Scales That Assess Religion or Spirituality as a Motivating Force
    - Duke Religion Index (Koenig et al., 1997)
    - Intratextual Fundamentalism Scale (Williamson et al., 2010)
    - Intrinsic-Extrinsic Scale - Revised (Gorsuch & McPherson, 1989)
    - Quest Scale (Batson et al., 1993)
    - Religious Orientation Scale (Allport & Ross, 1967)
    - Religious Internalization Scale (Ryan, Rigby, & King, 1993)
    - Religious Fundamentalism Scale (Altemeyer & Hunsberger, 1992, 2004)

12. Scales That Assess Religious or Spiritual Coping with Adversity
    - Attitudes Toward God Scale (Wood et al., 2010)
    - Religious Comfort and Strain Scale (Exline et al., 2000)
    - Religious Coping Scale (RCOPE) (Pargament et al., 2000)
    - Religious Coping Activities Scale (Pargament et al., 1990)
    - Religious Pressures Scale (Altemeyer, 1988)
    - Religious Problem-Solving Scale (Pargament, Kennell, Hathaway, Grevengoed, Newman, & Jones, 1988)
    - Spiritual Transformation Scale (Cole et al., 2008)

13. Scales That Assess Religious or Spiritual Meaning and Values
    - Functional Assessment of Chronic Illness Therapy—Spiritual Well-Being Scale (Peterman et al., 2002)
    - Meaning Scale (Krause, 2008)
    - Purpose in Life Scale (Crumbaugh & Maholick, 1964)
    - Seeking of Noetic Goals Scale (Crumbaugh, 1977)
    - Sense of Coherence Scale (Antonovsky, 1987)

REFERENCES

Ai, A. L., Peterson, C., & Huang, B. (2003). The effects of religious-spiritual coping on positive attitudes of adult Muslim refugees from Kosovo and Bosnia. *The International Journal for the Psychology of Religion, 13,* 29–47.

Allport, G. W. (1950). *The individual and his religion.* New York: Macmillan.

Allport, G. W., & Ross, J. M. (1967). Personal religious orientation and prejudice. *Journal of Personality and Social Psychology, 5,* 432–443.

Altemeyer, B. (1988). *Enemies of freedom: Understanding right-wing authoritarianism.* San Francisco: Jossey-Bass.

Altemeyer, B., & Hunsberger, B. (1992). Authoritarianism, religious fundamentalism, quest, and prejudice. *The International Journal for the Psychology of Religion, 2,* 113–133.

Altemeyer, B., & Hunsberger, B. (2004). A revised Religious Fundamentalism Scale: The short and sweet of it. *The International Journal of the Psychology of Religion, 14,* 47–54.

Anthony, F.-V., Hermans, C. A. M., & Sterkens, C. (2010). A comparative study of mystical experience among Christian, Muslim, and Hindu students in Tamil Nadu, India. *Journal for the Scientific Study of Religion, 49,* 264–277.

Antonovsky, A. (1987). *Unraveling the mystery of health.* San Francisco: Jossey-Bass.

Bassett, R. L., Miller, S., Anstey, K., Crafts, K., Harmon, J., Lee, Y., et al. (1990). Picturing God: A nonverbal measure of God concept for conservative protestants. *Journal of Psychology and Christianity, 9*(2), 73–81.

Bassett, R. L., Sadler, R. D., Kobischen, E. E., Skiff, D. M., Merrill, I. J., Atwater, B. J., et al. (1981). The Shepherd Scale: Separating the sheep from the goats. *Journal of Psychology and Theology, 9,* 335–351.

Bassett, R. L., Thrower, J., Barclay, J., Powers, C., Smith, A., Tindall, M., et al. (2005). One effort to measure implicit attitudes toward spirituality and religion. *Journal of Psychology and Christianity, 24,* 210–218.

Batson, C. D., & Schoenrade, P. A. (1991a). Measuring religion as quest: 1. Validity concerns. *Journal for the Scientific Study of Religion, 30,* 416–429.

Batson, C. D., & Schoenrade, P. A. (1991b). Measuring religion as quest: 2. Reliability concerns. *Journal for the Scientific Study of Religion, 30,* 430–447.

Batson, C. D., Schoenrade, P., & Ventis, W. L. (1993). *Religion and the individual: A social-psychological perspective* (rev. ed.). New York: Oxford University Press.

Beck, R., & McDonald, A. (2004). Attachment to God: The Attachment to God Inventory, tests of working model correspondence, and an exploration of faith group differences. *Journal of Psychology and Theology, 32,* 92–103.

Belzen, J. (2010). To read and to be read—the problematic nature of communication: Comment on comments. *Mental Health, Religion & Culture, 13,* 417–436.

Benson, P., & Spilka, B. (1973). God image as a function of self-esteem and locus of control. *Journal for the Scientific Study of Religion, 12,* 297–310.

Benson, P. L., Donahue, M. J., & Erickson, J. A. (1993). The Faith Maturity Scale: Conceptualization, measurement, and empirical validation. In M. L. Lynn & D. O. Moberg (Eds.), *Research in the social scientific study of religion* (Vol. 5, pp. 1–26). Greenwich, CT: JAI Press.

Black, H. K. (1999). Poverty and prayer: Spiritual narratives of elderly African-American women. *Review of Religious Research, 40,* 359–374.

Braithwaite, V. A., & Scott, W. A. (1991). Values. In J. P. Robinson, P. R. Shaver, & L. S. Wrightsman (Eds.), *Measures of personality and social psychological attitudes* (pp. 661–753). New York: Academic Press.

Burris, C. T. (1999). Religious Orientation Scale. In P. C. Hill & R. W. Hood, Jr. (Eds.), *Measures of religiosity* (pp. 144–154). Birmingham, AL: Religious Education Press.

Chatters, L. M., Taylor, R. J., & Lincoln, K. D. (2002). Advances in the measurement of religiosity among older African Americans: Implications for health and mental health researchers. In J. H. Skinner & J. A. Teresi (Eds.), *Multicultural measurement in older populations* (pp. 199–220). New York: Springer.

Chen, Z., Yang, L., Hood, R. W., Jr., & Watson, P. J. (2011). Mystical experience in Tibetan Buddhists: Common core thesis revisited. *Journal for the Scientific Study of Religion, 50,* 328–338.

Clark, W. H. (1958). *The psychology of religion: An introduction to religious experience and behavior.* Toronto: Macmillan.

Cohen, A. B. (2009). Many forms of culture. *American Psychologist, 64,* 194–204.

Cohen, A. B., & Hill, P. C. (2007). Religion as culture: Religious individualism and collectivism among American Catholics, Jews, and Protestants. *Journal of Personality, 75,* 709–742.

Cohen, A. B., Shariff, A. F., & Hill, P. C. (2008). The accessibility of religious beliefs. *Journal of Research in Personality, 42,* 1408–1417.

Cole, B. S., Hopkins, C. M., Tisak, J., Steel, J. L., & Carr, B. I. (2008). Assessing spiritual growth and spiritual decline following a diagnosis of cancer: Reliability and validity of the Spiritual Transformation Scale. *Psycho-Oncology, 17,* 112–121.

Connors, G. J., Tonigan, J. S., & Miller, W. R. (1996). A measure of religious background and behavior for use in behavior change research. *Psychology of Addictive Behaviors, 10,* 90–96.

Cornwall, M., Albrecht, S. L., Cunningham, P. H., & Pitcher, B. L. (1986). The dimensions of religiosity: A conceptual model with an empirical test. *Review of Religious Research, 27,* 226–244.

Cronbach, L. (1951). Coefficient alpha and the internal structure of tests. *Psychometrika, 31,* 93–96.

Crumbaugh, J. C. (1977). The Seeking of Noetic Goals test (SONG): A complementary scale to the Purpose in Life Test (PIL). *Journal of Clinical Psychology, 33,* 900–907.

Crumbaugh, J. C., & Maholick, L T. (1964). An experimental study in existentialism: The psychometric approach to Frankl's concept of noogenic neurosis. *Journal of Clinical Psychology, 20,* 200–207.

DeJong, G. F., Faulkner, J. E., & Warland, R. H. (1976). Dimensions of religiosity reconsidered: Evidence from a cross-cultural study. *Social Forces, 54,* 866–889.

Dittes, J. E. (1969). Psychology of religion. In G. Lindzey & E. Aronson (Eds.), *The handbook of social psychology* (2nd ed., Vol. 5, pp. 602–659). Reading, MA: Addison-Wesley.

D'Onofrio, B. M., Eaves, L. J., Murrelle, L., Maes, H. H., & Spilka, B. (1999). Understanding biological and social influences on religious affiliation, attitudes, and behaviors: A behavior genetic perspective. *Journal of Personality, 67,* 953–984.

Dynes, R. R. (1955). Church-sect typology and socio-economic status. *American Sociological Review, 20,* 555–660.

Elkins, D. N., Hedstrom, L. J., Hughes, L. L., Leaf, J. A., & Saunders, C. (1988). Toward phenomenological spirituality: Definition, description and measurement. *Journal of Humanistic Psychology, 28*(4), 5–18.

Ellison, C. G., & Taylor, R. J. (1996). Turning to prayer: Social and situational antecedents of religious coping among African-Americans. *Review of Religious Research, 38,* 111–131.

Emavardhana, T., & Tori, C. D. (1997). Changes in self-concept, ego defense mechanisms, and religiosity following seven-day Vipassana meditation retreats. *Journal for the Scientific Study of Religion, 36,* 194–206.

Emmons, R. A., & Paloutzian, R. F. (2003). The psychology of religion. *Annual Review of Psychology, 54,* 377–402.

Exline, J. J., Yali, A. M., & Sanderson, W. C. (2000). Guilt, discord, and alienation: The role of religious strain in depression and suicidality. *Journal of Clinical Psychology, 56,* 1481–1496.

Fetzer Institute/National Institute on Aging Working Group. (1999). *Multidimensional measurement of religiousness/spirituality for use in health research: A report of the Fetzer Institute/ National Institute on Aging Working Group.* Kalamazoo, MI: John E. Fetzer Institute.

Fiala, W. E., Bjorck, J. P., & Gorsuch, R. L. (2002). The Religious Support Scale: Construction, validation, and cross-validation. *American Journal of Community Psychology, 30,* 761–786.

Fowler, J. (1981). *Stages of faith.* San Francisco: Harper & Row.

Francis, L. J., & Katz, Y. J. (1992). The relationship between personality and religiosity in an Israeli sample. *Journal for the Scientific Study of Religion, 31,* 153–162.

Fullerton, J. T., & Hunsberger, B. (1982). A unidimensional measure of Christian orthodoxy. *Journal for the Scientific Study of Religion, 21,* 317–326.

Genia, V. (1997). The Spiritual Experience Index: Revision and reformulation. *Review of Religious Research, 38,* 344–361.

Ghorbani, N., Watson, P. J., Ghramaleki, A. F., Morris, R. J., & Hood, R. W., Jr. (2002). Muslim-Christian Religious Orientation Scales: Distinctions, correlations, and cross-cultural analysis in Iran and the United States. *The International Journal for the Psychology of Religion, 12,* 69–91.

Ghorbani, N., Watson, P. J., & Khan, Z. H. (2007). Theoretical, empirical, and potential ideological dimensions of using Western conceptualizations to measure Muslim religious commitments. *Journal of Muslim Mental Health, 2,* 113–131.

Glock, C., & Stark, R. (1966). *Christian beliefs and anti-Semitism.* New York: Harper & Row.

Gorsuch, R. L. (1984). Measurement: The boon and bane of investigating religion. *American Psychologist, 39,* 228–236.

Gorsuch, R. L. (1988). Psychology of religion. *Annual Review of Psychology, 39,* 201– 221.

Gorsuch, R. L., & McPherson, S. E. (1989). Intrinsic/extrinsic measurement: I/E-revised and single-item scales. *Journal for the Scientific Study of Religion, 28,* 348–354.

Gorsuch, R. L., & Venable, D. G. (1983). Development of an "Age Universal" I-E scale. *Journal for the Scientific Study of Religion, 22,* 181–187.

Hale-Smith, A., Park, C. L., & Edmondson, D. (2012). Measuring religious beliefs: Development of the Views of Suffering Scale. *Psychological Assessment.*

Hall, T. W., & Edwards, K. J. (1996). The initial development and factor analysis of the Spiritual Assessment Inventory. *Journal of Psychology and Theology, 24,* 233–246.

Hays, J. C., Meador, K. G., Branch, P. S., & George, L. K. (2001). The Spirituality History Scale in Four Dimensions (SHS-4): Validity and reliability. *Gerontologist, 41,* 239–249.

Hill, P. C. (1994). Toward an attitude process model of religious experience. *Journal for the Scientific Study of Religion, 33,* 303–314.

Hill, P. C., & Edwards, E. (2013). Measurement in the psychology of religiousness and spirituality: Existing measures and new frontiers. In K. Pargament, J. J. Exline, & J. W. Jones (Eds.), *APA handbook of psychology, religion, and spirituality (Vol. 1): Context, theory, and research* (pp. 51–77). Washington, DC: American Psychological Association.

Hill, P. C., & Hood, R. W., Jr. (Eds.). (1999). *Measures of religiosity.* Birmingham, AL: Religious Education Press.

Hill, P. C., & Pargament, K. I. (2003). Advances in the conceptualization and measurement of religion and spirituality. *American Psychologist, 58,* 64–74.

Hilty, D. M., & Morgan, R. L. (1985). Construct validation for the Religious Involvement Inventory: Replication. *Journal for the Scientific Study of Religion, 24,* 75–86.

Hilty, D. M., Morgan, R. L., & Burns, J. E. (1984). King and Hunt revisited: Dimensions of religious involvement. *Journal for the Scientific Study of Religion, 23,* 252–266.

Holland, J. C., Kash, K. M., Passik, S., Gronert, M. K., Sison, A., Lederberg, M., et al. (1998). A brief spiritual beliefs inventory for use in quality of life research in life-threatening illness. *Psycho-Oncology, 7,* 460–469.

Hood, R. W., Jr. (1970). Religious orientation and the report of religious experience. *Journal for the Scientific Study of Religion, 9,* 285–291.

Hood, R. W., Jr. (1975). The construction and preliminary validation of a measure of reported mystical experience. *Journal for the Scientific Study of Religion, 14,* 29–41.

Hood, R. W., Jr., & Chen, Z. (2013). The social scientific study of Christian mysticism. In J. Lamm (Ed.), *The Wiley-Blackwell companion to Christian mysticism* (pp. 577–591). London: Wiley-Blackwell.

Hood, R. W., Jr., Hill, P. C., & Williamson, W. P. (2005). *The psychology of religious fundamentalism.* New York: Guilford Press.

Hunsberger, B. (1989). A short version of the Christian Orthodoxy Scale. *Journal for the Scientific Study of Religion, 28,* 360–365.

Ironson, G., Solomon, G. F., Balbin, E. G., O'Cleirigh, C. O., George, A., Kumar, M., et al. (2002). The Ironson-Woods Spirituality/ Religiousness Index is associated with long survival, health behaviors, less distress, and low cortisol in people with HIV/AIDS. *Annals of Behavioral Medicine, 24*(1), 34–48.

Jana-Masri, A., & Priester, P. E. (2007). The development and validation of a Qur'an-based instrument to assess Islamic religiosity: The Religiosity of Islam Scale. *Journal of Muslim Mental Health, 2,* 177–188.

Kalkstein, S., & Tower, R. B. (2009). The Daily Spiritual Experiences Scale and well-being: Demographic comparisons and scale validation with older Jewish adults and a diverse Internet sample. *Journal of Religion and Health, 48,* 402–417.

Kapuscinski, A. N., & Masters, K. S. (2010). The current status of measures of spirituality: A critical review of scale development. *Psychology of Religion and Spirituality, 2,* 191–205.

Kass, J. D., Friedman, R., Leserman, J., Zuttermeister, P. C., & Benson, H. (1991). Health outcomes and a new index of spiritual experience. *Journal for the Scientific Study of Religion, 30,* 203–211.

Katz, Y. J., & Schmida, M. (1992). Validation of the Student Religiosity Questionnaire. *Educational and Psychological Measurement, 52,* 353–356.

Khan, Z. H., & Watson, P. J. (2006). Construction of the Pakistani Religious Coping Practices Scale: Correlations with religious coping, religious orientation, and reactions to stress among Muslim university students. *The International Journal for the Psychology of Religion, 16,* 101–112.

King, M., Jones, L., Barnes, K., Low, J., Walker, C., Wilkinson, S., et al. (2006). Measuring spiritual belief: Development and standardization of a Beliefs and Values Scale. *Psychological Medicine, 36,* 417–425.

Kirkpatrick, L. A. (1989). A psychometric analysis of the Allport-Ross and Feagin measures of intrinsic-extrinsic religious orientation. In D. O. Moberg & M. L. Lynn (Eds.), *Research in the social scientific study of religion* (Vol. 1, pp. 1–31). Greenwich, CT: JAI Press.

Kirkpatrick, L. A., & Hood, R. W., Jr. (1990). Intrinsic-extrinsic religious orientation: The boon or bane of contemporary psychology of religion. *Journal for the Scientific Study of Religion, 29,* 442–462.

Kirkpatrick, L. A., & Shaver, P. R. (1992). An attachment-theoretical approach to romantic love and religious belief. *Personality and Social Psychology Bulletin, 18,* 266–275.

Koenig, H., Patterson, G. R., & Meador, K. G. (1997). Religion index for psychiatric research: A 5–item measure for use in health outcome studies. *American Journal of Psychiatry, 154,* 885.

Krause, N. (1999). Religious support. In *Multidimensional measurement of religiousness/spirituality for use in health research: A report of the Fetzer Institute/National Institute on Aging Working Group* (pp. 57–64). Kalamazoo, MI: John E. Fetzer Institute.

Krause, N. (2008). The social foundations of religious meaning in life. *Research on Aging, 30,* 395–427.

Kuhn, T. S. (1970). *The structure of scientific revolutions* (2nd ed.). Chicago: University of Chicago Press.

Ladd, K. L., & Spilka, B. (2002). Inward, outward, and upward: Cognitive aspects of prayer. *Journal for the Scientific Study of Religion, 41,* 475–484.

Ladd, K. L., & Spilka, B. (2006). Inward, outward, upward prayer: Scale reliability and validation. *Journal for the Scientific Study of Religion, 45,* 233–251.

Leak, G. K., & Fish, S. B. (1999). Development and initial validation of a measure of religious maturity. *The International Journal for the Psychology of Religion, 9,* 83–103.

Leak, G. K., Loucks, A. A., & Bowlin, P. (1999). Development and initial validation of an objective measure of faith development. *The International Journal for the Psychology of Religion, 9,* 105–124.

Ledbetter, M. F., Smith, L. A., Vosler-Hunter, W. L., & Fischer, J. D. (1991). An evaluation of the research and clinical usefulness of the Spiritual Well-Being Scale. *Journal of Psychology and Theology, 19,* 49–55.

Maugans, T. A. (1996). The SPIRITual History. *Archives of Family Medicine, 5,* 11–16.

McConahay, J. B., & Hough, J. C., Jr. (1973). Love and guilt-oriented dimensions of Christian belief. *Journal for the Scientific Study of Religion, 12*, 53–64.

Miller, W. R. (1998). Researching the spiritual dimensions of alcohol and other drug problems. *Addiction, 93*, 979–990.

Newberg, A., d'Aquili, E. G., & Rause, V. (2001). *Why God won't go away: Brain science and the biology of belief.* New York: Ballantine Books.

Ng, S., Fong, T. C. T., Tsui, E. Y. L., Au-Yeung, F. S. W., & Law, S. K. W. (2009). Validation of the Chinese version of Underwood's Daily Spiritual Experience Scale—Transcending cultural boundaries? *International Journal of Behavioral Medicine, 16*, 91–97.

Nielsen, M. E., & Webster, D. G. (2011, August). *Christian orthodoxy and right wing authoritarianism predict group boundaries.* Paper presented at the annual meeting of the International Association for the Psychology of Religion, Bari, Italy.

Paloutzian, R. F., Bufford, R. K., & Wildman, A. J. (2012). Spiritual Well-Being Scale: Mental and physical health relationships. In M. Cobb, C. M. Puchalski, & B. Rumbold (Eds.), *Oxford textbook of spirituality in healthcare* (pp. 353–358). New York: Oxford University Press.

Paloutzian, R. F., & Ellison, C. W. (1982). Loneliness, spiritual well-being, and quality of life. In L. A. Peplau & D. Perlman (Eds.), *Loneliness: A sourcebook of current theory, research and therapy* (pp. 224–237). New York: Wiley Interscience.

Pargament, K. I., Ensing, D. S., Falgout, K., Olsen, H., Reilly, B., Van Haitsma, K., et al. (1990). God help me: I. Religious coping efforts as predictors of the outcomes to significant life events. *American Journal of Community Psychology, 18*, 793–824.

Pargament, K. I., Kennell, J., Hathaway, W., Grevengoed, N., Newman, J., & Jones, W. (1988). Religion and the problem-solving process: Three styles of coping. *Journal for the Scientific Study of Religion, 27*, 90–104.

Pargament, K. I., Koenig, H. G., & Perez, L. M. (2000). The many methods of religious coping: Development and initial validation of the RCOPE. *Journal of Clinical Psychology, 56*, 519–543.

Pargament, K. I., Silverman, W., Johnson, S., Echemendia, R., & Snyder, S. (1983). The psychosocial climate of religious congregations. *American Journal of Community Psychology, 11*, 351–381.

Pargament, K. I., Smith, B. W., Koenig, H. G., & Perez, L. (1998). Patterns of positive and negative religious coping with major life stressors. *Journal for the Scientific Study of Religion, 37*, 710–724.

Pendleton, S., Cavilli, K. S., Pargament, K. I., & Nasr, S. (2002). Spirituality in children with cystic fibrosis: A qualitative study. *Pediatrics, 109*, 1–11.

Peterman, A. H., Fitchett, G., Brady, M. J., Hernandez, L., & Cella, D. (2002). Measuring spiritual well-being in people with cancer: The Functional Assessment of Chronic Illness Therapy—Spiritual Well-Being Scale (FACIT-Sp). *Annals of Behavioral Medicine, 24*, 49–58.

Pfeifer, S., & Waelty, U. (1995). Psychopathology and religious commitment: A controlled study. *Psychopathology, 28*, 70–77.

Piedmont, R. L. (1999). Does spirituality represent the sixth factor of personality?: Spiritual transcendence and the Five-Factor Model. *Journal of Personality, 67*, 985–1013.

Piedmont, R. L. (2007). Cross-cultural generalizability of the Spiritual Transcendence Scale to the Philippines: Spirituality as a human universal. *Mental Health, Religion, and Culture, 10*. 89–107.

Piedmont, R. L., & Leach, M. M. (2002). Cross-cultural generalizability of the Spiritual Transcendence Scale in India: Spirituality as a universal aspect of human experience. *American Behavioral Scientist, 45*, 1888–1901.

Plante, T. G., & Boccaccini, M. T. (1997). The Santa Clara Strength of Religious Faith Questionnaire. *Pastoral Psychology, 45*, 375–387.

Plante, T. G., Vallaeys, C. L., Sherman, A. C., & Wallston, K. A. (2002). The development of a brief version of the Santa Clara Strength of Religious Faith Questionnaire. *Pastoral Psychology, 50,* 359–368.

Poloma, M. M., & Pendleton, B. F. (1989). Exploring types of prayer and quality of life: A research note. *Review of Religious Research, 31,* 46–53.

Raiya, H. A., Pargament, K. I., Stein, C., & Mahoney, A. (2007). Lessons learned and challenges faced in developing the Psychological Measure of Islamic Religiousness. *Journal of Muslim Mental Health, 2,* 133–154.

Rohrbaugh, J., & Jessor, R. (1975). Religiosity in youth: A personal control against deviant behavior. *Journal of Personality, 43,* 136–155.

Rosmarin, D. H., Pargament, K. I., Krumrei, E. J., & Flannelly, K. J. (2009). Religious coping among Jews: Development and initial validation of the JCOPE. *Journal of Clinical Psychology, 65,* 670–683.

Rowatt, W. C., & Kirkpatrick, L. A. (2002). Two dimensions of attachment to God and their relation to affect, religiosity, and personality constructs. *Journal for the Scientific Study of Religion, 41,* 637–651.

Ryan, R. M., Rigby, S., & King, K. (1993). Two types of religious internalization and their relations to religious orientations and mental health. *Journal of Personality and Social Psychology, 65,* 586–596.

Sandoval, J. H., Frisby, C. L., Geisinger, K. F., Ramos-Grenier, J., & Scheuneman, J. D. (1998). *Test interpretation and diversity: Achieving equity in assessment.* Washington, DC: American Psychological Association.

Schaler, J. A. (1996). Spiritual thinking in addiction-treatment providers: The Spiritual Belief Scale. *Alcoholism Treatment Quarterly, 14,* 7–33.

Silverman, W. H., Pargament, K. I., Johnson, S. M., Echemendia, R. J., & Snyder, S. (1983). Measuring member satisfaction with the church. *Journal of Applied Psychology, 68,* 664–677.

Stace, W. T. (1960). *Mysticism and philosophy.* New York: Lippincott.

Storch, E. A., Roberti, J. W., Bagner, D. M., Lewin, A. B., Baumeister, A. L., & Geffken, G. R. (2004). Further psychometric properties of the Santa Clara Strength of Religious Faith Questionnaire—Short-Form. *Journal of Psychology and Christianity, 23,* 51–53.

Tapanya, S., Nicki, R., & Jarusawad, O. (1997). Worry and intrinsic/extrinsic religious orientation among Buddhist (Thai) and Christian (Canadian) elderly persons. *The International Journal of Aging & Human Development, 44,* 73–83.

Tarakeshwar, N., Pargament, K. I., & Mahoney, A. (2003). Initial development of a measure of religious coping among Hindus. *Journal of Community Psychology, 31,* 607–628.

Thurstone, L. L., & Chave, E. J. (1929). *The measurement of attitude: A psychophysical method and some experiments with a scale for measuring attitude toward the church.* Chicago: University of Chicago Press.

Tisdale, T. C. (1999). Faith Maturity Scale. In P. C. Hill & R. W. Hood, Jr. (Eds.), *Measures of religiosity* (pp. 171–174). Birmingham, AL: Religious Education Press.

Tsang, J., & McCullough, M. E. (2003). Measuring religious constructs: A hierarchical approach to construct organization and scale selection. In S. J. Lopez & C. R. Snyder (Eds.), *Positive psychological assessment: A handbook of models and measures* (pp. 345–360). Washington, DC: American Psychological Association.

Underwood, L. G. (1999). Daily spiritual experiences. In *Multidimensional measurement of religiousness/spirituality for use in health research: A report of the Fetzer Institute/National Institute of Aging Working Group* (pp. 11–17). Kalamazoo, MI: John E. Fetzer Institute.

Underwood, L. G., & Teresi, J. A. (2002). The Daily Spiritual Experience Scale: Development, theoretical description, reliability, exploratory factor analysis, and preliminary construct validity using health-related data. *Annals of Behavioral Medicine, 24,* 22–33.

Ventis, W. L., Ball, C. T., & Viggiano, C. (2010). A Christian Humanist Implicit Association Test: Validity and test-retest reliability. *Psychology of Religion and Spirituality, 2,* 181–189.

Wenger, J. L. (2004). The automatic activation of religious concepts: Implications for religious orientations. *The International Journal for the Psychology of Religion, 14,* 109–123.

Williamson, W. P., Hood, R. W., Jr., Ahmad, A., Sadiq, M., & Hill, P. C. (2010). The Intratextual Fundamentalism Scale: Cross-cultural application, validity evidence, and relationship with religious orientation and the Big Five Factor markers. *Mental Health, Religion & Culture, 13,* 721–727.

Wood, B. T., Worthington, E. L., Jr., Exline, J. J., Yali, A. M., Aten, J. D., & McMinn, M. R. (2010). Development, refinement, and psychometric properties of the Attitudes Toward God Scale (ATGS-9). *Psychology of Religion and Spirituality, 2,* 148–167.

Worthington, E. L., Jr., Wade, N. G., Hight, T. L., Ripley, J. S., McCullough, M. E., Berry, J. W., et al. (2003). The Religious Commitment Inventory–10: Development, refinement, and validation of a brief scale for research and counseling. *Journal of Counseling Psychology, 50,* 84–96.

Wulff, D. M. (1999). Attitude Toward the Church Scale. In P. C. Hill & R. W. Hood, Jr. (Eds.), *Measures of religiosity* (pp. 467–471). Birmingham, AL: Religious Education Press.

4

Research Methods in the Psychology of Religion and Spirituality

Ralph W. Hood, Jr., and Jacob A. Belzen

The psychology of religion is in the process of broadening its methodological base. In two of the three articles on psychology and religion published in the *Annual Review of Psychology,* the emphasis was more upon the statistical treatment of measurement-based data than the hermeneutical analyses (Gorsuch, 1988; Emmons & Paloutzian, 2003). In this sense, numbers dominated over nouns. However, at the end of their review, Emmons and Paloutzian (2003, p. 395) called for a new *multilevel interdisciplinary paradigm* (MIP). This occasioned our own effort to suggest that hermeneutical aspects implicit in the call for the new paradigm be more explicitly acknowledged (Belzen & Hood, 2006).

In the two "bookend" chapters to the first and second editions of this handbook, the editors emphasized the role of meaning making as a possible integrative theme for the psychology of religion (Paloutzian & Park, 2005; Park & Paloutzian, 2005; see also Chapters 1 and 3 of this volume). The value of using data at multiple levels of analysis, hermeneutical as well as statistical, was welcomed and used to structure our review of research methods in the psychology of religion and spirituality. We continue to use this structure in this second edition with even greater attention to issues of meaning.

The first edition of this handbook also called for "meaning-sensitive" measures (Park & Paloutzian, 2005, pp. 553–554). This welcomed call is beginning to be heard. For instance, Kapuscinski and Masters (2010) reviewed 24 measures of spirituality and paid equal attention to the psychometric characteristics of various measures as well as the meaning issues implicit in each measure. They creatively advise the use of focus groups to explore individuals' evaluations of the meaning of otherwise merely adequate psychometric scale items (see Masters & Hooker, Chapter 26, this volume).

The enhanced concern with conceptual (meaning) issues in the psychology of religion places meaning making at the center of concern as researchers use a plurality of methods to steer between the Scylla of the statistical and the Charybdis of the hermeneutical analysis of data. As Machado and Silva (2007) have persuasively argued, mathematization and experimentation must be complemented by conceptual analysis to clarify the meaning of concepts, reveal unacknowledged assumptions, and evaluate the consistency of theoretical accounts in any scientific analysis. Insofar as the call for a new paradigm is multidimensional and nonreductive, experimental methods are but one valued approach in what must be a plurality of methods applied appropriately to the level and context within which questions regarding religion and spirituality are addressed (Belzen & Hood, 2006).

While we applaud the new paradigm as multilevel and interdisciplinary, the field is far from realizing this ideal. The value of experimental methods in terms of random assignment of subjects in contexts providing great control and precision, permitting causal inferences, is tempered by the limited generalizability of findings in what has been called a "loss of ecological validity" (Lawson, Graham, & Baker, 2007, p. 44). Likewise, Smith (2010) has emphasized that the issue in scientific research is less one of statistical significance and more one of what meaningful difference is actually accounted for in any study.

Our discussion of methodology in this chapter suggests areas in which multiple methods continue to be profitably used in the psychology of religion. In the process, we present how different methods—experiment, quasi-experiment, field research, natural manipulations, correlational studies, survey, narrative, and psychoanalysis—complement one another and provide a more complete understanding of religious and spiritual phenomena than can be achieved by any single method. In the spirit of a methodological agnosticism (Hood, in press), we do not deny the possibility of any higher order meaningfully integrative schemes but rather explore such schemes in terms of their empirical consequences. There is no single scientific method; rather, there are methods that, when sensitively employed, allow religion and spirituality to be studied both from the bottom up and from the outside in and, by so doing, provide many meaningful frames for the scientific study of religion and spirituality. The key here is that sciences and methodologies must respect the brute fact of plurality in the various meaningful frames that methodologies can suggest.

EXPERIMENTAL AND QUASI-EXPERIMENTAL DESIGN

Chemical Facilitation of Religious and Spiritual Experiences

Entheogen is becoming the preferred term replacing the older term *psychedelic* for those who believe chemicals can facilitate religious or spiritual experiences (Hood, Hill, & Spilka, 2009, pp. 323–329). Chemicals that have been widely recognized to facilitate religious and spiritual experiences have been variously framed in a long history as pathological ("psychotomimetic") mind manifesting ("psychedelic") to an experience of ultimate reality or God ("entheogen"). One of the earliest experimental studies in the psychology of religion became known as the Good Friday experiment. Pahnke (1969) administered either psilocybin or a placebo (nicotinic acid) to 20 volunteer graduate students at Andover-Newton Theological Seminary. Participants met in groups of four with two experimental and two control groups matched for compatibility. Each group had two leaders, one of whom had been given psilocybin. The participants met to hear a Good Friday service so that religious set and setting were maximized for all participants. Immediately after the service and in a 6-month follow-up all participants completed a questionnaire largely consisting of Stace's (1960) criteria of mysticism. Results for the immediate and long-term follow-up indicated that the controls responded to the criteria of mysticism at a significantly lower percentage than the experimental participants and that experimental participants found their experiences to be exceptionally meaningful.[1]

Nearly 25 years after their participation in the original Pahnke study, Doblin (1991) was able to locate nine participants of the original control group and seven of the original experimental group and readministered Pahnke's original questionnaire. The follow-up results indicated a similar difference between control and experimental groups found in the original study, again affirming the meaningfulness of the chemically triggered mystical experiences under appropriate set and setting conditions.

A recent study used psilocybin in a rigorously designed double-blind study in which set and setting were maximized to facilitate positive experiences, including mystical ones. Not only did the experimental group report higher rates on all aspects of mysticism as measured by a standard measure of mysticism, but they rated the experience as one of the most meaningful in their life (Griffiths, Richards, McCann, & Jesse, 2006). At approximately 1-year follow-up, the experimental group reaffirmed that their experience was among the most meaningful, if not *the* most meaningful, experience of their life (Griffiths, Richard, Johnson, McCann, & Jesse, 2008).

Experimental studies employing entheogens are significant for three reasons. First, they permit a true experimental design with participants randomly assigned to experimental and control conditions. Second, set and setting can be maximized to ensure positive experiences (religious setting in Pahnke's study; a pleasant aesthetic environment in Griffiths et al.'s study). Even negative experiences during a session, if properly handled by the guide, produce ultimately positive evaluations (Hood, 2008). Third, immediate posttest and longer term posttests ranging from approximately 1 year (Griffiths et al., 2008) to almost 25 years (Doblin, 1991) highlight that what is most important about these experiences is their meaningfulness. Furthermore, by replicating experimental studies using psilocybin, flaws in original studies can be methodologically resolved. For instance, in psilocybin studies, placebo controls are often readily identified so that the double-blind fails, but Griffiths et al. (2006) used a powerful placebo control and documented the effectiveness of the double-blind in their study. Also, Griffiths assessed participants on a variety of relevant measures, not simply Stace's (1960) criteria of mysticism.

While Pahnke's study is often cited as exemplary in the use of a true experimental design, Shanon's (2002) quasi-experimental study of ayahuasca provides a complementary methodological approach to the study of chemically triggered religious/spiritual experiences. Ayahuasca is a naturally occurring psychoactive brew widely used throughout the upper Amazon. Shanon, a cognitive psychologist, has extensively studied experiences elicited by ayahuasca in a variety of religious and nonreligious settings. He has also taken ayahuasca over 100 times across many years. Therefore, he is able to compare his own experiences with those of participants he has interviewed. Shanon's primary method is phenomenological, and he has provided the best cartography of mental states elicited by ayahuasca. He also provides quantitative analyses based on the first 67 of his own sessions and structured interviews with others who have taken ayahuasca for moderate or extensive periods of time in both religious and nonreligious settings. He then compares this material to reports in the anthropological literature. Shanon's work is exemplary in that it suggests an analogue to quasi-experimental methods. By carefully comparing the use of ayahuasca in various $N = 1$ studies as well as comparing his experiences with reports by others who concurrently drink this brew and with reports from anthropologists, Shanon can study the effects of dosage, experiences over time, and the effects of set and setting. The very subjectivity that some might suggest contaminate single person reports becomes a necessary source of objectivity in charting the phenomenology of the ayahuasca experience. This is consistent with Taves's (2009) call to focus upon how experiences come to be deemed religious. Both external and internal perspectives are needed to get complementary yet more complete understanding of how experiences can be variously framed.

A final example of a novel methodological twist is the use of multidimensional scaling on autobiographical material. Oxman, Rosenberg, Schnurr, Tucker, and Gala (1988) obtained 92 autobiographical accounts of personal experiences that fulfilled four criteria: The passage was (1) from a published source, (2) written in English, (3) at least several hundred words to provide data for textual analysis, and (4) written after an acute episode or important experience. The accounts were divided into four categories: 19 schizophrenic, 26 experiences triggered by psychoactive substances, 21 mystical/ecstatic experiences, and 26 autobiographical experiences. The researchers then used multidimensional scaling to provide cartography of the key words that differentiated these groups from one another. Results showed important differences between groups, such that experiences facilitated by psychoactive chemicals are dominated by words referring to "sense" while mystical/ecstatic experiences are associated with word referring to "ideal value" and life-altering "religious" encounters (see Hood & Chen, Chapter 21, this volume).

Research on entheogens is one of the best exemplars of the MIP. Another example is research on meditation (see McNamara & Butler, Chapter 11, this volume). The range of studies includes qualitative and quantitative work, longitudinal and $N = 1$ research, experimental, and quasi-experimental field analogies. It is instructive that researchers themselves serve as subjects despite breaking a cardinal rule of objectivity that obtains in true experimental designs, and the result is a strong plea for the objective nature of what is experienced. In this sense, research on psychoactive substances parallels early research in German and American psychology in which introspection was a respected method and the researcher was the subject (Danziger, 1990). Hood (2008) has referred to the dual role of researcher as studying both others from an objective stance and themselves from personal introspection as "confessional scholars" (p. 17).

Intercessory Prayer

Experimental designs have also been extensively employed in the assessment of the efficacy of intercessory prayer (see Ladd & Spilka, Chapter 22, this volume). Studies have documented that one of the most common requests in intercessory prayer is for medical healing either for self or others (Barnes, Powell-Griner, McFann, & Nahin, 2004). However, the debate on whether intercessory prayer can be studied through a true experimental design is confounded by ontological issues concerning the nature of God. As Gorsuch (2002) notes, the methodology of science would seem to be inert in the face of the claim that one has a control group for which they are certain God is not acting. Insofar as a divine being is assumed to mediate prayer requests, the notion that one can do a true double-blind study is paradoxical at best. How does one double-blind God? Thus, not surprisingly, there have been mixed results from studies using large Ns and double-blind procedures where the purpose of intercessory prayer is medically documented healing. Two major studies failed to find significant effects when differential medical outcome was assessed (Aviles et al., 2001; Benson et al., 2006). Other studies found small but statistically significant effects (e.g., Harris, Thoresen, McCullough, & Larson, 1999). These small but significant effects (typically $p < .02$) are consistent with Hodge's (2007) meta-analysis of 17 intercessory prayer studies using various sized samples and medical outcomes. However, to assess prayer for its medical effects is seen by some as a distortion of prayer's spiritual efficacy (Shuman & Meador, 2003).

Field studies of intercessory prayer try to avoid use of distal prayers as adopted in experimental studies and tend to use methodological controls more appropriate to assumptions of natural processes operating in diseases and their cures. Often prayers are not matched with the faith tradition of those prayed for, nor are the prayers assessed for their own religious motivations. Following this possibility, Lee and Poloma (2009) have collected extensive narratives of Pentecostal exemplars whose healing narratives play a significant role in their faith commitment. One project studied an exemplar interviewed by Lee and Poloma and used a pre–post measure design to document that, in field conditions in Mozambique, the proximate act of prayer (by laying on of hands) produced significant changes in vision and in auditory function for Mozambicans (Brown, Mory, Williams, & McClymond, 2010). However, the study lacked a comparison group, and it is likely that using visual or auditory thresholds that are variable simply documents well-known suggestive or placebo effects when medical functions as opposed to diseases are assessed. Even greater effects of prayer compared with other placebo possibilities such as hypnosis only document possible differential placebo, not real prayer effects. Further, as suggested in some of the narratives in the Lee and Poloma's (2009) interviews and in Hood and Williamson's (2008) study of Appalachian Pentecostal serpent handlers, often miracle narratives of healing are explicitly divorced from medical documentation as a concession to secular methods not needed by those who have the appropriate faith. Thus, studies of healing prayers in natural contexts are best viewed as healing deemed to be religious, as Taves (2009) would have it, and not as documented medical healings, and the focus is best placed upon how the healing experiences are meaningfully embedded in narrative and what consequences follow from this fact, rather than double-blind efforts in either laboratory or field studies to prove that prayer can be *medically* efficacious.

Other complementary approaches to the study of prayer have focused upon the structure of written prayers and their possible consequences for both the medical and spiritual well-being of the person praying rather than for the person prayed for. Using well-established procedures devised by Pennebaker (1993), researchers have begun to study the effects of written prayers offered in response to traumatic events that are hypothesized to have similar healing effects to other forms of emotional disclosure. In these studies, proximate prayer is not the physical laying on of hands but rather prayers addressed to God in writing. Using established methodologies such as Linguistic Inquiry and Word Count (LIWC) software devised by Pennebaker and his colleagues, written texts can be examined with a standardized computer program (Pennebaker, Francis, & Booth, 2008). Emotional words (both positive and negative), causal statements, and insight can be quantified and used to document positive effects of self-disclosure in the narration of emotional distress (Penebarker, Mayne, & Francis, 1997).

VandeCreek, Janus, Pennebaker, and Binau (2002) explored the effect of prayers for help with difficult personal experiences. Participants wrote either disclosures, letters to God, or extemporaneous disclosure prayers. Multivariate analysis of variance of the LIWC program results indicate that the frequency of causal expressions and negative emotionality were not significantly different across the three conditions. However, insightful and positive emotional expressions occurred more often in prayers than in disclosures. Results suggest that these prayers are linguistically similar to disclosures and may also be associated with personal benefits and positive health outcomes. However, Grossoehme et al. (2010) applied this technique to written prayers in a prayer book available in a pediatric hospital. The analysis of 800 prayers written over a 6-month period, primarily (81%) by parents, using LIWC did not share characteristics typically associated with written emotional disclosures and thus perhaps do not result in positive health outcomes for those who pray. These results are not conclusive and suggest that perhaps personal self-disclosure of difficult emotional conditions may have health benefits when the concern is for oneself but not when the primary concern is for the health of another, especially when it is a close relative, such as one's own child.

Parapsychological Studies

A parallel issue from survey research closely related to prayer research is the widely documented but ignored fact that one of the most consistent correlates of religious experience are paranormal experiences (see Hood et al., 2009, pp. 347–350). McDonald (2000) found paranormal beliefs to be one of the five dimensions that underlie 11 measures of spirituality. Like research on intercessory prayer, experimental and quasi-experimental studies can best identify the subjective consequences of the claim to have had paranormal experiences, and perhaps are useful to explore the phenomenology of such experiences. However, experimental psychology has no meaningful methods to falsify the occurrence of paranormal phenomenon. Instead, multiple methods reveal a strong relationship between belief in God and belief in paranormal phenomena and how both may have real effects in believers' lives. It is the perception of such effects that psychologists can study.

Parapsychological research approaches the same methodological dilemmas that have plagued intercessory prayer research with some of the same empirical outcomes. A serious confound ignored in intercessory prayer studies, whether distal or proximate, is the possibility of direct mental effects on human physiological processes (Henry, 2005). For instance, the issues raised by the apparent small but reliable effects obtained in ganzfeld studies have radical implications (Bem & Honorton, 1994). The empirical quality of ganzfeld research is impeccable and recognized even by its harshest critics (e.g., Milton & Wiseman, 1999). Meta-analyses, effect size, and file drawer analyses have long characterized this research and still are relatively rare in the psychology of religion. However, most significant is the theoretical advances that must be considered based upon studies where small but persistent effect sizes exist and yet seem conceptually incomprehensible. Likely researchers in intercessory prayer can lead the way to conceptual advancement in the psychology of religion and spirituality by following the lead of ganzfield researchers and agreeing on a set of methodological guidelines by which a broad range of investigators could produce data that would theoretically integrate psychology with other disciplines such as theology, medicine, and the radically intriguing claims of quantum physics (Hood, 2008). As Walach, Kohls, von Stillfried, Hinterberger, and Schmidt (2009) have argued, parapsychological research has morphed into the psychology of spirituality, which may be its lasting legacy.

FIELD RESEARCH AND NATURAL MANIPULATIONS

Cognitive Dissonance Following Religious Belief Disconfirmation

When participants cannot be randomly assigned to groups, one can use quasi-experimental designs that often exceed experimental designs in contextual realism and still allow internal validity. For example, Batson (1975) took advantage of a church retreat to divide junior high school girls into two groups: those who did and those who did not believe that Jesus was the Son of God. He then had these naturally occurring nonequivalent groups read a contrived newspaper article in which Christianity was presented as a hoax. While most in both groups did not believe the article, those who did (about one-third) indicated a greater intensity of religious belief if they were in the believers group. The apparently paradoxical finding was interpreted as supporting cognitive dissonance theory. Batson and his colleagues review other quasi-experimental studies on cognitive dissonance as well as historical and field studies to support the claim that faced with belief-disconfirming information, devout believers are likely to strengthen rather than abandon their beliefs (Batson, Schoenrade, & Ventis, 1993).

In light of the call for the MIP, it is worth noting that field research methods reveal a different pattern of results than laboratory-based experimental methods. Beliefs can rarely be readily disconfirmed in field studies, suggesting that cognitions operate in real-world contexts in ways often undetected in controlled laboratory work (Taves, 2009). The complexity and ambiguity of many prophecies shield them from the requirement of an "unequivocal and undeniable disconfirmation" (Festinger, Riecken & Schachter, 1956, p. 3). To understand why within religious groups prophecy is seldom perceived to fail requires researchers to move from laboratory studies to a consideration of field research.

Taves (in press) proposes an empirically testable model focusing upon group process by which what she terms a revelator is able to produce a revelation that is endorsed by an initial small group of followers and progressively by many more if successful. Her model significantly overlaps with Stark's (1999) theory of revelation, in which individual differences in the ability to experience revelations are linked with well-known social processes to develop a theory of both the acceptance of revelations (likely in an initial intense primary group) and the resistance to novel revelations by a group founded upon revelation. Similar models have been posed by James (1902/1985, p. 270) and LaBarre (1972, p. 265), suggesting that the call for the new paradigm has echoes in the past and perhaps are just now being empirically addressed. Interestingly, insofar as revelations require social acceptance, their study must be both historical and cultural, as both Belzen (2010) and Taves (in press) persuasively argue.

Using interview, ethnomethodological and phenomenological oriented methods to understand how participants rationalize within a real-life situation suggests that belief disconfirmation or failed prophecy are negotiated terms and cannot be operationalized easily by experimenters. Understanding that different methods yield differing views illustrates the value of the call for a new MIP. One common assumption, provided by laboratory research, is that people are driven by the need to reduce dissonance and hence refuse to accept disconfirmation by adjusting their beliefs to the changed framework. The laboratory context is itself a social construction in which dissonance reduction perhaps functions more precisely than in actual life contexts where individuals in prophetic groups seldom acknowledge that prophecy fails (Hood, 2011). Participant observation, interview, and ethnomethodological studies indicate that the most common response of members within groups is to deny the failure of prophecy and to seek an alternative interpretative frame within which their beliefs continue to make sense (Tumminia, 1998; Dein, 2001).

Conversion

Studies of religious conversion parallel many of the complementary findings of cognitive dissonance within and outside the lab. Like animal behavior, cognitive complexities and behaviors in the wild are seldom simple replications of those of animals confined in zoos. Judgment of the value of religious experience is socially complex and requires an assessment of the cultural context in order to identify an experience religious. Insofar as Belzen (2010) has emphasized a cultural level of analysis to religion, a psychology of religion narrowly confined within a particular discipline is impossible. Even the identification of religious leaders as pathological by purely psychological criteria is fraught with conceptual difficulties given that one can be both pathological and a spiritual leader (Storr, 1996).

Religion and psychopathology may be best viewed as orthogonal constructs. The *Diagnostic and Statistical Manual of Mental Disorders* (fourth edition, text revision) cautions that "a clinician who is unfamiliar with the nuances of an individual's cultural frame of reference may incorrectly judge as psychopathology those normal variations in behavior, belief, or experience that are particular to the individual's culture" (American Psychiatric Association, 2000, p. xxxiv). Even behaviors such as handling poisonous serpents and drinking poison can be seen as normal variations of beliefs if framed in such a way as to deem them legitimate religious practices (Hood & Williamson, 2008).

In an excellent exemplar of the call for a new paradigm, a medieval historian and a psychiatrist teamed up to study medieval saints. Kroll and Bachrach (2006) demonstrated that in an empirical assessment of 1,462 individuals elevated to sainthood in the years 450 to 1500, the vast majority were recognized for their positive social service. However, a minority were recognized for heroic acts of asceticism or mysticism (approximately 10% in each category), often facilitated by lacerations of the flesh, extreme fasting, or sleep deprivation. Nevertheless, they caution against the easy attribution of psychopathology to practices whose purpose is perhaps simply identified as the pursuit of spiritual excellence. Likewise, Belzen (2010) has noted the necessity of employing multiple perspectives in his narrative case study of an instance of manslaughter in the Netherlands. Clinical psychologists studying conversion to new religious movements tend to identify pathological characteristics of converts while social-psychologically oriented field researchers tend to focus upon the adaptive and meaningful transformations that converts find (see Paloutzian, Murken, Streib, and Rößler-Namini, Chapter 20, this volume).

Natural "Manipulations" in Field Studies

Neither experimental nor quasi-experimental designs need to be restricted to the laboratory (Aronson, Wilson, & Brewer, 1998). Field studies can have an advantage of being more consistent with "real life" and thus maximizing contextual realism while maintaining the internal validity of an experiment. Also, sometimes one can take advantage of naturally occurring events to approximate a "manipulation."

Illustrating the use of natural conditions as a "manipulation," researchers took advantage of a mandatory 5-day wilderness experience for seniors at an all-male private school (Hood, 1977b). The focus of the research was on the elicitation of mystical experiences, often reported in nature settings. Researchers predicted that anticipatory stress and activity stress incongruity would elicit reports of mystical experience. The researchers identified three high-stress activities: white water rafting, a solitary evening in the woods with minimal equipment, and rock climbing. A control condition, smooth water canoeing, was identified as a low-stress event. Immediately before each activity, participants were assessed for anticipatory stress on an objective measure. In all cases, those who had low anticipatory stress for high-stress activities reported higher mysticism scores than those anticipating high stress for the high-stress activities. In addition, because none anticipated the canoe activity as high stress, each individual could serve as his own control, indicating that anticipatory stress/setting stress incongruity accounted for the higher reports of mystical experience. However, within the field study, because no one anticipated a low-stress activity as highly stressful, researchers could not test the other possible incongruity: low anticipatory/high setting stress.

In a subsequent year, researchers used the same school and program to test the incongruity between anticipatory stress and setting stress hypothesis (Hood, 1978a). The researchers focused upon the solo experience in which small groups of individuals were led into the woods by the researcher. Each individual was dropped off at an isolated place that was not in view of anyone else. Just prior to being dropped off, each individual was assessed on an objective measure of anticipatory stress. Since different groups participated in the solo experience over five separate evenings, the researchers took advantage of the likelihood of thunderstorms occurring on at least some of the nights. (The researchers had informed consent to leave participants out even in storm conditions.) Fortunately, this potential storm situation occurred on three of the five nights. Storm versus no storm became the naturally occurring "manipulation" of setting stress. Given that the evening was spent alone without a tent (only a tarp was provided), the researchers identified the storm evenings as higher setting stress relative to the nonstorm evenings. (Unobtrusive measures provided confirmation of the stress when several individuals "broke solo" during the storm nights and returned to base camp unable or unwilling to complete the solo experience.) As predicted, both low anticipatory stress/high setting stress and high anticipatory stress/low setting stress elicited greater magnitude of religious experience than the stress congruity conditions. Thus, the anticipatory stress and setting stress incongruity hypothesis was replicated for both high-stress experiences and extended to support the incongruity hypothesis for low-stress experiences anticipated as stressful. These studies indicate the possibility of quasi-experimental studies in field situations as well as the possibility of using anticipated natural events as experimental "manipulations."

The extension of quasi-experimental studies to field conditions adds psychological realism to experimental realism while maintaining internal validity. In their review of quasi-experimental research in the social psychology of religion, Batson et al. (1993) bemoaned the paucity of studies: "We hope quasi-experimental designs will soon become the research method of choice in the social psychology of religion" (p. 385). The Emmons and Paloutzian (2003) review of the field indicates that this hope is being rapidly fulfilled. Quasi-experimental methods need not be restricted to the laboratory. Field research not only complements laboratory research but can be often done with assurance of both experimental realism and internal validity at minimal expense, especially if researchers can take advantage of existing programs with which to embed their research.

CORRELATIONAL AND SURVEY STUDIES

While correlation studies are far from useless, their limitations are obvious. Correlated variables are notoriously open to a variety of interpretations so that the adage "correlation is not causation" has become a mantra for the experimental psychologist. However, despite this fact, correlational studies remain common and complement experimental studies for a variety of reasons. Often they permit the study of noncollege populations. Sears (1986) noted that since the 1960s more than 80% of experimental laboratory studies have involved undergraduate college students, and little has changed in the last quarter of a century since this was noted. Survey studies, while correlational, can use random samples and thus study a range of persons more representative of the population of interest. Thus, surveys complement laboratory and field studies.

Authoritarianism, Dogmatism, and Religious Fundamentalism

Correlational studies can be especially useful in comparing sampling with college undergraduates with predictions made from real-life data. Since the days of the original authoritarian personality research (Adorno, Frenkel-Brunswik, Levinson, & Sanford, 1950), authoritarianism, first as a personality construct and then as a learned social behavior (Altemeyer, 1988), has been correlated with religious fundamentalism. Rokeach's (1960) dogmatism theory ranges across the entire political spectrum, while Altemeyer (1988) focuses only upon "right-wing authoritarianism" (RWA). However, both Rokeach (1960) and Altemeyer (1988) focus upon the process rather than the content of belief. The massive literature on authoritarianism and religious fundamentalism has led to the persistent claim of a relationship between these two constructs (Hood et al., 2009, pp. 420–422).

While this claim is supported by laboratory studies, field studies reveal a different assertion. It has been over a quarter of a century since one prominent empirical researcher noted that "the widespread belief that there is a strong relationship between religious orthodoxy and authoritarianism appears to be a prominent instance of [the] tendency to transform suspicions and speculations into certainties" (Stark, 1971, p. 172). Given that most measures of fundamentalism are belief oriented, orthodoxy is often but a synonym for fundamentalism in empirical studies so that strong correlations are built in between orthodoxy, authoritarianism, and RWA (Altemeyer, 1988), and thus Stark's (1971) criticism applies doubly. However, not only can fundamentalism as a *content* of belief be separated from orthodoxy as *process* of belief, but correlation statistical methods such as regression can be used to identify the differential relationship of authoritarianism and orthodoxy to measures of fundamentalism (Kirkpatrick, 1993). That field studies do not find the consistent relationships between authoritarianism and fundamentalism reported by laboratory studies suggests it would be useful for each to use the measures common to the other to see if it is the context (survey vs. questionnaire studies), the samples (college undergraduates vs. national samples), or the measures that reflect such startling differences. In addition, common measures of authoritarianism and fundamentalism can be included in interview studies comparing persons who deconvert from fundamentalist religions with controls in the same groups that stay (Streib, Hood, Keller, Csöff, & Silver, 2009). This permits the identification of individual differences that lead some persons within the same religious group to exit while others continue in the group. Identifying these differences within a real-life context of differential religious engagement and disengagement requires the use of complementary methods.

Mystical Experience

Survey data can be used to provide a backdrop for experimental and quasi-experimental studies. For instance, numerous surveys over the last decade in both America and Europe have assessed reports of mystical experiences (see Hood et al., 2009, pp. 343–347). The worry that self-reports of religious experience may not be truthful can be methodologically approached from a variety of means. For instance, Hood and Morris (1981a) demonstrated that, using criteria of mysticism common in the empirical literature, persons equally knowledgeable about these criteria differentially reported experiencing them. This suggests that persons refuse to report experiences they do not have and do not simply affirm having experiences about which they are knowledgeable.

In addition, Hood (1978b) used a voice stress analysis to measure micro tremors in the voice of persons reporting or denying they had mystical experiences. As predicted, intrinsic subjects reported mystical experience and extrinsic subjects denied having such experiences, and neither indicated stress in their voice response. However, indiscriminately proreligious subjects tended both to report mystical experiences and to indicate stress, suggesting they are false positives. Even more intriguing was the fact of indiscriminately antireligious subjects who denied having mystical experiences but showed stress patterns in their voice. This suggests false negative, or those denying experiences they might in fact have. Thus, self-report data can be approached in ways that allow some assessment of their veracity. Another approach not yet widely used in the psychology of religion is to identify the emotional states of respondents by distinctive facial expressions (Keltner, 1995). These various methods permit researchers to provide evidence regarding whether or not the assertion that one has had an experience is truthful.

Another use of survey data is to identify commonly reported triggers of religious and spiritual experiences that can then be studied in the laboratory. For instance, the nature and frequency of varieties of prayer is well documented in major surveys (Poloma & Gallup, 1991). Furthermore, independent factor analytic studies yield similar types of prayers. Suggestions from survey studies that indicated that meditative or contemplative prayer were especially significant in terms of subjective consequences led Hood and his colleagues to use an isolation tank in quasi-experimental studies of prayer.

In one study, Hood and Morris (1981b) used a double-blind procedure to have either intrinsic or extrinsic participants try to imagine either religious or cartoon figures while floating in a hydrated magnesium sulfate solution, heated to external body temperature, and totally sound-proofed and dark (isolation tank). As predicted, participants different in religious types did not differ in their ability to imagine figures (in the cartoon condition), but did differ in religious imagery, with the intrinsics reporting more religious imagery under the religious condition than extrinsics. Intrinsics even reported more religious imagery under the cartoon set than extrinsics did under the religious condition. This study relates to one discussed previously in which indiscriminately proreligious persons (but not intrinsics) exhibit stress while reporting religious experiences. Hood interpreted these studies to argue that indiscriminately proreligious types are conflicted with respect to religion and tend to attempt to appear religious under appropriate religious sets. Studies of this kind shows that quasi-experimental studies under laboratory conditions are not only possible but can, as in the case of isolation tanks, use laboratory environments that are especially relevant to religious traditions that seek solitude as a meaningful context for prayer.

Surveys and questionnaires can also be useful in longitudinal research. For instance, Kirkpatrick (1997) solicited responses from female readers of the *Denver Post* to a variety of measures of religiosity as well as indicators of attachment style. He was able to assess the same 146 women at a 4-year interval. When statistically controlling for religion at the first assessment, he found that insecure-anxious persons were more likely to report having had a religious experience or a religious conversion than either secure or ambivalent attachment types. He replicated these findings with a sample of college students in a much shorter (4 months) longitudinal study (Kirkpatrick, 1998). Thus, survey and questionnaire studies can yield meaningful data, even though they cannot establish causation directly.

NARRATIVE ANALYSIS AND PSYCHOANALYSIS

Narrative psychology has been useful in studies of conversion. The earlier paradigm of a sudden change elicited by a crisis situation leading to a permanent conversion has been overshadowed by the gradual seeker model. In this paradigm, the individual actively searches for meaning and is involved in a gradual process of spiritual transformation that may continue throughout one's life. How one narrates this transformation is part of the linguistic turn in psychology in which narrative history is more crucial than factual history. Narrative analysis focuses upon the means by which individuals utilize the language of their culture and tradition to construct the story of their own spiritual or religious transformation.

Another example is in the continuing concern over distinctions between religion and spirituality (see Oman, Chapter 2, this volume). In many instances, measures of spirituality function the same as religiosity measures. However, this is confounded by the fact that most people in the United States who identify themselves as "religious" also identify themselves as "spiritual" (Zinnbauer et al., 1997). However, a significant minority (typically less than one-third) identify themselves as "spiritual but not religious." Interview studies are useful in indicating that these individuals are often antireligious and opposed to not simply institutionalized practices but to dogmatic (in the positive religious sense) constructions or interpretations of religious experiences. Spirituality is constructed and clarified within the "religious and spiritual" types by their faith tradition.

As narrative studies revealed (e.g., Lindgren, 2004), spirituality, rather than being a "fuzzy" concept for those outside religion, is fluid and flexible and relates to what psychoanalytic theorists see as an expanded and mature use of illusion (Sorensen, 2004). However, insofar as an expanded theory of illusion in psychoanalysis focuses upon the psychological recollection and construction of events, ontological claims to objectivity are bracketed in the same way they are in narrative analyses.

Psychoanalytic theory continues to be a rich source for hypotheses that can be empirically studied by a variety of means (see Corveleyn, Luyten, & Dezutter, Chapter 5, this volume). One example is the provocative work by Carroll (1986) empirically testing psychological factors involved in historical apparitions (hallucinations) of the Virgin Mary. He suggests that Catholicism is particularly suited to classic psychoanalytic study because lay Catholics have the Catholic imagination. Thus, Carroll argues that the Catholic recourse to concrete metaphors drawn from daily life when thinking about religious issues allows the psychoanalysis easy access to unconscious determinants of religious imagery.

The focus on concrete imagery also emphasizes embodiment, allowing Catholics to utilize sexual imagery in describing their religious experiences, especially mystical ones (Carroll, 2010). The use of compatible terms to describe both sexual and mystical experiences was empirically demonstrated by Hood and Hall (1980), who documented that Christian women described both their religious and erotic experiences in congruent adjectives but Christian males did not. Likewise, Kripal (2001), himself a confessional mystic scholar, has identified the homosexual aspects of many religious traditions, suggesting the relevance of classical psychoanalytic theory not only to Catholicism, where it is perhaps most obvious, but to many other religious traditions (Eastern and Western) as well. These controversial researches are partially supported by neurophysiological studies in which data suggest that many of the same pathways involved in sexual experiences are also involved in religious experiences (Newberg, D'Aquihl, & Rause, 2001). Additional support for a relationship between mystical experiences and sex is found in surveys in which less traditionally religious individuals cite sex as a trigger of mystical experience (Hood, 1977a). Confidence of such relationships is enhanced by their support from such diverse methodologies.

An appropriate psychological method to explore psychoanalytic theories and psychological narrative is to use archive taped interviews so that other researchers can evaluate the original material from which such constructions are made. Examples are Hovi's (2004) study of the Word of Life congregation in Turku, Finland, and the studies by Hood and his colleagues of the serpent-handling sect of Appalachia (Hood–Williamson Archive for Serpent Handling Sects of Appalachia). In both, these investigators have their original videos archived at their respective universities. Thus, unlike the clinical psychoanalytic "couch," the taped or videotaped interview is open to public data.

Even non-psychoanalytic-oriented narrative psychologists have returned to $N = 1$ studies, as exemplified by Lindgren's (2004) study of the conversion of the former Swedish Ambassador Mohammed Knut Bernstrom to Islam at the age of 67. Narrative psychology also interfaces with reflexive ethnography in which the investigator's own commitment is acknowledged and involved in illustrating how narration plays a significant role in structuring our experience and life histories (e.g., Gergen & Gergen, 1988). Consistent with the call for a new paradigm, narrative analyses are nonreductive relative to the religions and spiritualities encoded in the narration.

SERPENT HANDLERS RESEARCH AND MIP

As a final example, it might be useful to look at a research example that fits well within the call for a new paradigm. Hood and his colleagues have focused upon the serpent-handling sect of Appalachia using a variety of methods. For a decade, Hood and his colleague have documented entire services and have archived this material for use by other researchers (Hood–Williamson Archive for Serpent Handling Sects). Williamson, Polio, and Hood (2000) employed an opened-ended interview process and used phenomenological methods to identify the experience of handling from the handler's perspective. Part of this technique was to articulate the phenomenology of handling and then have handlers who did not participate in the original interviews read the analysis and rate the extent to which it captured, as best that words can, the experience. The phenomenology of anointing complements electrophysiological data of an actual handler "under the anointing" recorded in a laboratory setting (Burton, 1993). These data, in turn, complement actual samples of data taken from handlers before service and immediately after handling a serpent in a regular church service that same evening (Schwartz, 1999).

The experience of anointing has been incorporated into explanatory models derived from psychoanalytic theory. Serpent handling sermons have been analyzed for their narrative form, and the social history of the movement has been empirically documented in terms of the Church of God's initial support and subsequent abandonment of the practice (Hood & Williamson, 2008). An oral history of the tradition by a handler has been compiled (Hood, 2005). Two quasi-experimental studies explored prejudice toward serpent handlers. In one study, researchers used a modified Solomon four-groups design to demonstrate that when viewing actual field tapes in which handlers express their faith in the ritual of serpent handling as opposed to viewing a tape of a Pentecostal service without handling, individuals in the experimental group changed prejudicial attitudes toward handlers without changing their rational rejection of the practice. Pre–post and posttest-only experimental groups came to see handling as a sincere expression of faith and a practice that ought not to be outlawed for consenting adults. However, they still rejected the practice for themselves (Hood, Williamson, & Morris, 2000). Finally, extensive taping of individuals and services over 10 years allows longitudinal studies of persons who were bitten by snakes and what effects this had on subsequent participation in the tradition. It also permits actual studies of persons who have been bit and sought medical aid versus those who were bit and suffered the bite, including maiming and even loss of life, all documented on archived video. Thus, the study of these sects has used a variety of methods—field and lab, quantitative and qualitative—to document a living tradition that many have stereotyped but whose dynamic history continues. No single method could capture the variety of interesting questions that can be asked of this unique American religious tradition.

CONCLUSION

The psychology of religion is enriched by the use of multiple methods and will profit from opening up to interdisciplinary approaches. Experimental and quasi-experimental paradigms will benefit from the use of additional complementary methods if a truly multilevel interdisciplinary paradigm is to be actualized. This is not only desirable, but can be empirically assessed. Here empirical psychology can take a lesson from psychoanalysis. A MIP will also make applications of psychology more attractive to researchers on religion from other disciplines. For example, this approach can enable fruitful collaboration with narrative, personality, and social psychology to broaden the psychohistorical approaches that have been employed in research on religious personalities and phenomena primarily from a psychoanalytically perspective (Belzen, 2010).

Hood, Hill, and Williamson (2005) have proposed an intratextual model of fundamentalism that can be applied to nonreligious, quasi-fundamentalist groups. Here *intratextual* refers to reliance upon a single sacred text, not multiple authoritative sources, which are what is more familiar to academics, an intertextual model for knowledge. Sorenson (2004) has suggested that intratextual model creates a cohesive group of isolated disciplines or schools. His interest as a relational psychoanalyst (and clinical psychologist) is to compare the literature citations of three psychoanalytic schools (Kleinian, Kohutian, and relational psychoanalysis). Using multidimensional scaling for the authors cited in the schools respective journals revealed that the more "fundamentalist" schools (Kleinian and Kohutian) each cited a very restrictive range of their own authorities while relational psychoanalysts cited a broader range (Sorenson, 2004, pp. 1–17). It would be useful to use a similar method to assess the progress toward a MIP for the psychology of religion. Insofar as one utilizes the new paradigm within the context of questions of meaning, then a marriage of the empirical psychologies associated with Ray Paloutzian and of the historical and contextual methods associated with Ann Taves seems to promise the most meaningful future for an interdisciplinary, multiple-level, and nonreductive psychology of religion. Fortunately, the marriage has occurred.

NOTE

1. In an indefensible breach of research ethics, a psychological disruptive experience that occurred to one of the experimental participants was not reported in any of the write-up of this widely cited study (see Doblin, 1991).

REFERENCES

Adorno, T. W., Frenkel-Brunswik, E., Levinson, D. J., & Sanford, R. N. (1950). *The authoritarian personality*. New York: Harper & Row.

Altemeyer, B. (1988). *Enemies of freedom: Understanding right-wing authoritarianism*. San Francisco: Jossey-Bass.

American Psychiatric Association. (2000). *Diagnostic and statistical manual of mental disorders* (4th ed., text rev.). Washington, DC: Author.

Aronson, E., Wilson, T. D., & Brewer, M. B. (1998). Experimentation in social psychology. In D.

T. Gilbert, S. T. Fiske, & G. Lindsey (Eds.), *The handbook of social psychology* (Vol. 1, pp. 99–142). New York: Oxford University Press.

Aviles, J., Whelan, E., Hernke, D., Williams, B., Kenny, K., O'Fallon, W., et al. (2001). Intercessory prayer and cardiovascular disease progression in a coronary care unit population: A randomized controlled trial. *Mayo Clinic Proceedings, 76*(12), 1192–1198.

Barnes, P. M., Powell-Griner, E., McFann, K., & Nahin, R. L. (2004). Complementary and alternative medicine use among adults: United States, 2002. *Advance Data, 343,* 1–19.

Batson, C. D. (1975). Rational processing or rationalization? The effect of disconfirming information on a stated religious belief. *Journal of Personality and Social Psychology, 32,* 176–184.

Batson, C. D., Schoenrade, P., & Ventis, W. L. (1993). *Religion and the individual: A social-psychological perspective.* New York: Oxford University Press.

Belzen, J. A. (2010). *Towards a cultural psychology of religion: Principles, approaches, applications.* New York: Springer.

Belzen, J. A., & Hood, R. W., Jr. (2006). Methodological issues in the psychology of religion: Toward another paradigm? *The Journal of Psychology, 140,* 5–28.

Bem, D. J., & Honorton, C. (1994). Does psi exist?: Replicable evidence for an anomalous process of information transfer. *Psychological Bulletin, 115,* 4–18.

Benson H., Dusek J. A., Sherwood, J. B., Lam, P., Bethea, C. F., Carpenter, W., et al. (2006). Study of the therapeutic effects of intercessory prayer (STEP) in cardiac bypass patients: A multicenter randomized trial of uncertainty and certainty of receiving intercessory prayer. *American Heart Journal, 151*(4), 934–942.

Brown, C. G., Mory, S. C., Williams, R., & McClymond, M. J. (2010). Study of the therapeutic effects of proximate intercessory prayer (STEPP) on auditory and visual impairments in rural Mozambique. *Southern Medical Journal, 103*(9), 864–869.

Burton, T. (1993). *Serpent-handling believers.* Knoxville: University of Tennessee Press.

Carroll, M. P. (1986). *The cult of the Virgin Mary: Psychological origins.* Princeton, NJ: Princeton University Press.

Carroll, M. P. (2010). Psychoanalytic theories of religion and the "Catholic problem." In B. Beit-Hallahmi (Ed.), *Psychoanalysis and theism: Critical reflections on the Grünbaum thesis* (pp. 81–98). Lanham, MD: Jason Aronson.

Danziger, K. (1990). *Constructing the subject: Historical origins of psychological research.* Cambridge, UK: Cambridge University Press.

Dein, S. (2001). What really happens when prophecy fails: The case of Lubavitch. *Sociology of Religion, 62,* 383–401.

Doblin, R. (1991). Pahnke's "Good Friday" experiment: A long-term follow-up and methodological critique. *Journal of Transpersonal Psychology, 23,* 1–28.

Emmons, R. A., & Paloutzian, R. F. (2003). The psychology of religion. *Annual Review of Psychology, 54,* 377–402.

Festinger, L., Riecken, H.W., & Schachter, S. (1956). *When prophecy fails.* Minneapolis: University of Minnesota Press.

Gergen, K. J., & Gergen, M. M. (1988). Narrative and the self as relationship. *Advances in Experimental Psychology, 21,* 17–56.

Gorsuch, R. L. (1988). The psychology of religion. *Annual Review of Psychology, 39,* 201–221.

Gorsuch, R. L. (2002). *Integrating psychology and spirituality.* Westport, CT: Praeger.

Griffiths, R. R., Richards, W. A., Johnson, M. W., McCann, U. D., & Jesse, R. (2008). Mystical-type experiences occasioned by psilocybin mediate the attribution of personal meaning and spiritual significance 14 months later. *Journal of Psychopharmacology, 22,* 621–632.

Griffiths, R. R., Richards, W. A., McCann, U. D., & Jesse, R. (2006). Psilocybin can occasion mystical experiences having substantial and sustained personal meaning and spiritual significance. *Psychopharmacology, 187,* 268–283.

Grossoehme, D. H., VanDyke, R., Jacobson, C., Cotton, S., Ragsdale, J. R., & Seid, M. (2010).

Written prayers in a pediatric hospital: Linguistic analysis. *Psychology of Religion and Spirituality, 2*(4), 227–233.

Harris, A. H., Thoresen, C. E., McCullough, M. E., & Larson, D. B. (1999). Spiritually and religiously-oriented health interventions. *Journal of Health Psychology, 4*(3), 413–434.

Henry, J. (2005). *Parapsychology: Research on exceptional experiences.* New York: Routledge.

Hodge, D. R. (2007). A systematic review of the empirical literature on intercessory prayer. *Research on Social Work Practice, 17,* 174–187.

Hood, R. W., Jr. (1977a). Differential triggering of mystical experience as a function of self-actualization. *Review of Religious Research, 18,* 264–270.

Hood, R. W., Jr. (1977b). Eliciting mystical states of consciousness with semi-structured nature experiences. *Journal for the Scientific Study of Religion, 15,* 155–163.

Hood, R. W., Jr. (1978a). Anticipatory set and setting stress incongruity as elicitors of mystical experience in solitary nature situations. *Journal for the Scientific Study of Religion, 17,* 278–287.

Hood, R. W., Jr. (1978b). The usefulness of the indiscriminately pro and anti categories of religious orientation. *Journal for the Scientific Study of Religion, 17,* 278–287.

Hood, R. W., Jr. (Ed). (2005). *Handling serpents: Pastor Jimmy Morrow's history of the Jesus' name tradition.* Mercer, GA: Mercer University Press.

Hood, R. W., Jr. (2008). Mysticism and the paranormal. In J. H. Ellens (Ed.), *Miracles: God, science, and psychology in the paranormal* (Vol. 3, pp. 16–37). Westport, CT: Praeger.

Hood, R. W., Jr. (2011). Where prophecy lives. Psychological and sociological studies of cognitive dissonance. In D. Tumminia & W. H. Swatos (Eds.), *How prophecy lives: The Festinger thesis and beyond* (pp. 21–40). Leiden, The Netherlands: Brill.

Hood, R. W., Jr. (in press). Methodological agnosticism for the social sciences?: Lessons from Sorokin's and James's allusions to psychoanalysis, mysticism and Godly love. In M. Lee & A. Yong (Eds), *Godly love: Theological, interdisciplinary, and methodological essays.* New York: New York University Press.

Hood, R. W., Jr., & Hall, J.R. (1980). Gender differences in the description of erotic and mystical experiences. *Review of Religious Research, 21,* 195–207.

Hood, R. W., Jr., Hill, P. C., & Spilka, B. (2009). *The psychology of religion: An empirical approach* (4th ed.). New York: Guilford Press.

Hood, R. W., Jr., Hill, P. C., & Williamson, W. P. (2005). *The psychology of religious fundamentalism: An intratextual model.* New York: Guilford Press.

Hood, R. W., Jr., & Morris, R. J. (1981a). Knowledge and experience criteria in the report of mystical experience. *Review of Religious Research, 23,* 76–84.

Hood, R. W., Jr., & Morris, R. J. (1981b). Sensory isolation and the differential elicitation of the report of visual imagery in intrinsic and extrinsic subjects. *Journal for the Scientific Study of Religion, 20,* 261–273.

Hood, R. W., Jr., & Williamson, W. P. (2008). *Them that believe: The power and meaning of the Christian serpent-handling tradition.* Berkeley: University of California Press.

Hood, R. W., Jr., Williamson, W. P., & Morris, R. J. (2000). Changing views of serpent handling: A quasi-experimental study. *Journal for the Scientific Study of Religion, 39,* 531–544.

Hovi, T. (2004). Religious conviction shaped and maintained by narration. *Archive for the Psychology of Religion, 26,* 35–73.

James, W. (1985). *The varieties of religious experience: A study in human nature.* Cambridge, MA: Harvard University Press. (Original work published 1902)

Kapuscinski, A. N., & Masters, K. S. (2010). The current status of measures of spirituality: A critical review of scale development. *Psychology of Religion and Spirituality, 2,* 1–20.

Keltner, D. (1995). Signs of appeasement: Evidence for the distinct displays embarrassment, amusement, & Shame. *Journal of Personality and Social Psychology, 68,* 441–454.

Kirkpatrick, L. A. (1993). Fundamentalism, Christian orthodoxy, and intrinsic religious orientation. *Journal for the Scientific Study of Religion, 32,* 256–268.

Kirkpatrick, L. A. (1997). A longitudinal study of changes in religious belief and behavior as a function of individual differences in adult attachment styles. *Journal for the Scientific Study of Religion, 36,* 207–217.

Kirkpatrick, L. A. (1998). God as substitute attachment figure: A longitudinal study of adult attachment style and religious changes in college. *Personality and Social Psychology Bulletin, 24,* 961–973.

Kripal, J. J. (2001). *Roads of excess, palaces of wisdom: Eroticism & reflexivity in the study of mysticism.* Chicago: University of Chicago Press.

Kroll, J., & Bachrach, B. (2006). *The mystic mind: The psychology of medieval mystics and ascetics.* New York: Routledge.

LaBarre, W. (1972). *The ghost dance: The origins of religion.* New York: Delta.

Lawson, R. B., Graham, J. E., & Baker, K. M. (2007). *A history of psychology: Globalization, ideas, and applications.* Upper Saddle River, NJ: Pearson.

Lee, M. T., & Poloma, M. M. (2009). *A sociological study of the great commandment in Pentecostalism: The practice of Godly love as benevolent servitude.* Lewiston, NY: Edwin Mellon Press.

Lindgren, T. (2004). The narrative construction of Muslim identity—A single case study. *Archive for the Psychology of Religion, 26,* 51–73.

Machado, A., & Silva, F. J. (2007). Toward a richer view of the scientific method. *American Psychologist, 62,* 671–681.

McDonald, D. A. (2000). Spirituality: Description and measurement, and relation to the five-factor model of personality. *Journal of Personality, 68,* 153–197.

Milton, J., & Wiseman, R. (1999). Does psi exist?: Lack of replication of anomalous process of information transfer. *Psychological Bulletin, 125,* 387–391.

Newberg, A., D'Aquihl, E., & Rause, V. (2001). *Why God won't go away: Brain science and the biology of belief.* New York: Ballantine.

Oxman, T. E., Rosenberg, S. D., Schnurr, P. P., Tucker, G. J., & Gala, G. G. (1988). The language of altered states. *Journal of Nervous and Mental Disease, 176,* 401–408.

Pahnke, W. N. (1969). Psychedelic drugs and mystical experience. In E. M. Pattison (Ed.), *Clinical psychiatry and religion* (pp. 149–162). Boston: Little, Brown.

Paloutzian, R. F., & Park, C. L. (2005). Integrative themes in the current science of the psychology of religion. In R. F. Paloutzian & C. L. Park (Eds.), *Handbook of the psychology of religion and spirituality* (pp. 3–20). New York: Guilford Press.

Park, C. L., & Paloutzian, R. F. (2005). One step toward integration and an expansive future. In R. F. Paloutzian & C. L. Park (Eds.), *Handbook of the psychology of religion and spirituality* (pp. 550–564). New York: Guilford Press.

Pennebaker, J. W. (1993). Putting stress into words: Health, linguistic and therapeutic implications. *Behavior Research and Therapy, 32,* 539–548.

Pennebaker, J. W., Francis, M. E., & Booth, R. J. (2008). *Linguistic and Word Count Inquiry* (Version 2008) [Computer software]. Mahwah, NJ: Erlbaum.

Pennebaker, J. W., Mayne, T. J., & Francis, M. E. (1997). Linguistic predictors of adaptive bereavement. *Journal of Personality and Social Psychology, 72,* 863–871.

Poloma, M. M., & Gallup, G. H., Jr. (1991). *Varieties of prayer: A survey report.* Philadelphia: Trinity Press International.

Rokeach, M. (1960). *The open and closed mind.* New York: Basic Books.

Schwartz, S. (1999). *Faith, serpents, and fire: Images of Kentucky holiness believers.* Jackson: University Press of Mississippi.

Sears, D. (1986). College sophomores in the laboratory: Influence of a narrow data base on social psychology's view of human nature. *Journal of Personality and Social Psychology, 51,* 515–530.

Shanon, B. (2002). *The antipodes of the mind.* New York: Oxford University Press.

Shuman, J., & Meador, K. G. (2003). *Heal thyself: Spirituality, medicine, and the distortion of Christianity.* New York: Oxford University Press.

Smith, C. (2010). Five proposals for reforming article publishing in the social scientific study of religion (especially quantitative): Improving the quality, values, and cumulativeness of our scholarship. *Journal for the Scientific Study of Religion, 49,* 583–595.

Sorenson, R. L. (2004). *Minding spirituality.* Hillsdale, NJ: Analytic Press.

Stace, W. T. (1960). *Mysticism and philosophical analysis.* Philadelphia: Lippincott.

Stark, R. (1971). Psychopathology and religious commitment. *Review of Religious Research, 12,* 165–176.

Stark, R. (1999). A theory of revelations. *Journal for the Scientific Study of Religion, 38,* 287–308.

Storr, A. (1996). *Feet of clay. Saint, sinners, and madmen: a study of Gurus.* New York: Free Press.

Streib, H., Hood, R. W., Jr., Keller, B., Csöff, R.-M., & Silver, C. (2009). *Deconversion: Qualitative and Quantitative results from cross-cultural research in Germany and the United States.* Göttingen, Germany: Vandenhoeck & Ruprecht.

Taves, A. (2009). *Religious experience reconsidered: A building-block approach to the study of religion and other special things.* Princeton, NJ: Princeton University Press.

Taves, A. (in press). *Revelatory events: Extra-ordinary experiences and new visionary movements.* New York: Oxford University Press.

Tumminia, D. (1998). How prophecy never fails: Interpretative reason in a flying saucer group. *Sociology of Religion, 59,* 157–170.

VandeCreek, L., Janus, M.-D., Pennebaker, J. W., & Binau, B. (2002). Praying about difficult experiences as self-disclosure to God. *The International Journal for the Psychology of Religion, 12,* 29–39.

Walach, H., Kohls, N., von Stillfried, N., Hinterberger, T., & Schmidt, S. (2009). Spirituality: The legacy of parapsychology. *Archive for the Psychology of Religion, 31,* 277–308.

Williamson, P. W., Polio, H. R., & Hood, R. W., Jr. (2000). A phenomenological analysis of anointing among serpent handlers. *Journal for the Scientific Study of Religion, 10,* 221–240.

Zinnbauer, B. J., Pargament, K. I., Cole, B., Rye, M. S., Butter, E. M., & Belavich, T. G. (1997). Religion and spirituality: Unfuzzying the fuzzy. *Journal for the Scientific Study of Religion, 36,* 549–564.

5

Psychodynamic Psychology and Religion

Jozef Corveleyn, Patrick Luyten, and Jessie Dezutter

Psychoanalytic[1] approaches to religion and spirituality are, to say the least, controversial and have provoked much discussion. Some critics are very positive toward the psychoanalytic contribution to the study of religion in general and to psychology of religion in particular (Beit-Hallahmi, 1996). Others are skeptical and judge the psychoanalytic approach as, although not without merit, overly simplistic, often reductionist, and generally not sufficiently empirically supported (e.g., Hood, Hill, & Spilka, 2009; Wulff, 1997). Hence, although the psychoanalytic literature on religion is vast, many contemporary overviews of the psychology of religion devote only a small and mostly historical sketch of psychoanalytic thinking concerning religion (e.g., Emmons & Paloutzian, 2003; Paloutzian, 1996; Hood, Hill, & Spilka, 2009).

It is not our intention in this chapter to give a complete overview of all psychoanalytic research efforts of the past century. This would be an almost impossible task. Moreover, several extensive older reviews exist (e.g., Beit-Hallahmi, 1996; Meissner, 1984; Saffady, 1976; Wulff, 1997). In the recent history of the psychoanalytic research community, one can distinguish a new era beginning in the 1970s, characterized by a clearly positive approach to religion and personal religiosity. This pioneering work of some psychoanalysts, working with an interpersonal and interactional model of personality, includes Meissner (1984, 1987, 2000), Rizzuto (1979, 1993, 1998), Malkwitz (2003), Jones (1991a, 1991b), and Sorensen (2004). Overviews of this new evolution can be found in, among others, Belzen (2009), Winer and Anderson (2007), Hall, (2007a, 2007b), and Heine (2005). A critical reflection on this "positive" tendency has been made by Blass (2006).

Rather than presenting a complete overview (see, e.g., Corveleyn & Luyten, 2005), we present an overview of recent developments and findings and clarify the strengths and limitations of psychoanalytically inspired approaches to religion. In order to provide a balanced review of strengths and limitations, following Freud (1923/1961, 1924/1961), we distinguish, as in our 2005 chapter, among psychoanalysis as (1) an encompassing theory of both "normal" and "pathological" psychological functioning, (2) a method of investigation, and (3) a form of treatment. To understand fully the psychoanalytic approach to religion, in the first section we make the necessary distinctions between religion as a cultural versus a personal phenomenon. This distinction enables us to situate the original contribution of Freud correctly. In the second section we provide a brief sketch of the developments in psychoanalytic theorizing since Freud and describe their contributions to the study of religion. In the third section we demonstrate the strengths and limitations of psychodynamically inspired empirical research concerning religion in the context of recent theoretical and methodological developments in psychoanalysis. In the fourth section we discuss clinical implications of the newest tendencies in the psychoanalytic approach to religion in the context of the debate concerning the integration of religion and spirituality in psychotherapy and counseling. We close the chapter with some conclusions and directions for future research.

THE TWO SIDES OF "RELIGION": RELIGION AS A CULTURAL PHENOMENON AND RELIGION AS A PERSONAL EXPERIENCE—THE BASICS OF FREUD'S APPROACH

Any psychoanalytic—and for that matter any psychological—approach to religion should distinguish between religion as a general *cultural* and *social* fact on the one hand and *personal* religion on the other hand. As a cultural phenomenon, religion is always a "given" that cannot be explained, let alone explained away, by psychology. Following Vergote (1996, 1998), who draws on Geertz (1973), religion can be described in part as a system of symbols that acts to establish powerful, pervasive, and long-lasting moods and motivations. Although religions in this sense of the term are subject to changes over time and within a particular culture, they nevertheless consist of rather stable theological principles and a more or less established and stable organization.[2] Hence, the term *religion* (or better, *religions*; see Taves, Chapter 7, this volume) refers in part to a number of organized forms of belief, as is illustrated in the so-called world religions (e.g., Christianity, Islam, Judaism) and in some so-called new religious movements. Personal religion, on the other hand, or religion as it is lived, is made up of a mix of these theological principles with psychological (personal) and sociological influences. Better yet, it is the result of a continuous confrontation and interaction of the individual with the preexisting culture, including religion, in which he or she is born and living. Personal religion is thus colored by one's own personal, idiosyncratic history in a cultural–religiosity mix.

This distinction between personal religion and religion as a cultural phenomenon finds an important parallel in psychoanalysis between psychoanalysis "proper" and so-called applied psychoanalysis. Although the distinction is to some extent artificial, the former is mainly concerned with explaining the psychological functioning of the individual, whereas the latter is broadly aimed at explaining sociocultural processes and phenomena. It was Freud (1927/1961) who initiated this latter approach in his analysis of religion. His purpose was not only to understand (*Verstehen*) personal religion but also to explain the cultural phenomenon (*Erklären*) in the perspective of the evolution of humankind. Despite the criticism of reductionism in this "psychoanalytic archeology" (Beit-Hallahmi, 1996, p. 11), the application of psychoanalytic theories and hypotheses to religion has been and continues to be popular among many philosophers, theologians, and sociologists (e.g., Devereux, 1953/1974; Devisch, 2009; Hart, 2011; Ortigues & Ortigues, 1966; see also Segal, 2011).

The distinction between religion as a personal and a cultural phenomenon overlaps with Freud's so-called ontogenetic and phylogenetic theories of religion (Wulff, 1997). Interestingly, whereas Freud did show interest in the development of personal religion (ontogenetic perspective) in his famous case study of the Wolf Man (Freud, 1918/1955), he was nevertheless mainly interested in the phylogenetic perspective—that is, in explaining the origin and development of religion as a sociocultural phenomenon (e.g., Freud, 1913/1953; 1939/1964) that inevitably affects the individual(s) in a community. In a nuanced way, Blass (2003, 2006) argues that Freud's main concern in focusing on the phylogenetic perspective was philosophical, namely to understand the truth claim (about the existence of God/god) of religions and their believers against empirical and scientific evidence.

It has only been relatively recently, with the growing popularity of object relations theory and self psychology, that personal religion has become the center of attention of psychoanalytic studies of religion (see Hall, 2007a, 2007b; Kernberg, 2000). Moreover, as Blass (2006) has convincingly argued, this growing attention within psychoanalysis for personal religion is also partly due to a shift in religions themselves, away from organized religion and religion as a quest for truth and toward religion as deeply held, personal beliefs and experiences that are not necessarily linked to organized forms (see Oman, Chapter 2, this volume).

Freud and Religion

From his early experiences with the Judaic faith and traditions of his family and the Catholic tradition of his nanny (Gay, 1987; Rice, 1990; Rizzuto, 1998) to his final work *Moses and Monotheism* (Freud, 1939/1964)—Freud's ultimate attempt to understand the historical origins of Jewish religion and (monotheistic) religion in general—religion was always an important aspect in Freud's life and in his scientific activity. Although often depicted as a rationalistic and atheistic thinker—and many of his works can be read from that perspective—Freud was not at all fundamentally or merely antireligious. For example, he did count religion, together with art, philosophy, and ethics, as one of the most impressive accomplishments of civilization (Freud, 1930/1961).

The only real opponent of Freud's perspective on religion as a cultural given, who did not become a dissident during his lifetime like Carl Gustav Jung and Alfred Adler, was the Lutheran pastor and psychoanalyst Oskar Pfister. In his virulent criticism *The Illusion of a Future* (Pfister, 1928)—the title being a variant of Freud's (1927/1961) *The Future of an Illusion*—Pfister argued that Freud's view of religion was itself tribute to the "belief" in rational progress and in the triumphs of rationalistic science and thus, according to Freud's own definition, an illusion. Pfister's critique can be seen as the starting point of a series of critiques on Freud's views on religion.

First and foremost is the criticism of reductionism, which concerns Freud's philosophical rationalistic background. According to this criticism, Freud completely reduces religion to an irrational prephase in the evolution of humankind toward a more realistic, rational, and scientific civilization (cf. Meissner, 2000; Vergote, 1998). This reductionism criticism is currently often the major and frequently the only criticism leveled at Freud and at older psychoanalytic approaches to religion in general. In fact, if it is not taken as a final judgment on Freud's approach to religion, one must say that this criticism is correct. Freud did consider religion to be essentially an illusion, a fulfillment of personal desires, such as a deep longing for protection against the perils of nature, preferably by an exalted father figure. With Vergote (1998), we agree that it is clear that Freud should not have made this attempt of *explaining* religion as such. His attempts to explain religion are not based on any detailed or systematic observations, clinical or otherwise. To the contrary, he seems to have been driven by a rationalistic Enlightenment philosophy, which pushed him to tackle religion in its entirety. Remarkably, this is in strong contrast with his repeated affirmation that psychoanalysis is not a worldview, not even a complete anthropology (Freud, 1933/1964). Psychoanalysis always should be, in his opinion, both as a science and as a method of treatment, neutral toward religion. It is also in contrast to his otherwise great effort to empirically observe (clinical evidence) and understand phenomena in great detail and depth (Vergote, 1998). Nevertheless, it would also be incorrect to reduce Freud's approach of religion as completely biased by a rationalistic ideology (see Vergote, 1998). His approach did raise fundamental psychological questions about religion and about individual religious faith. More concretely, Freud did ask important questions about the part that is played in personal religion by personal desires, fantasies, and conflicts linked to the individual's personal history and his/her encounters with significant others.

A second criticism on Freud's views of religion, which is mostly leveled by more "interpersonally" oriented authors, is that Freud reduces religion to a one-person motivational matter, and neglects the interpersonal and, more generally, sociocultural components of religion (e.g., Jones, 1991a, 1991b; Kakar, 1996, 2007; Saha, 2009). Indeed, many of his theories can be read from such a perspective, although it would be also too simplistic to reduce Freud's approach to religion as being completely a "one-person" psychology.

THERE IS MORE THAN ONE PSYCHOLOGY IN THE FAMILY OF PSYCHOANALYSIS

Psychoanalysis is not, as some critics often want us to believe, limited to the eternal rephrasing of Freud, nor is it limited to the exegetical rereading and rediscussion of the *n*th interpretation of some of his not-so-clear sentences. Freud's work is not the gold standard of a metric system. Psychoanalysis, and psychoanalytic approaches to religion in particular, did not stop to evolve after Freud's death—quite to the contrary. With Pine (1990; see also McWilliams, 2011, and Wallerstein, 1992), one can currently distinguish somewhat schematically "four psychologies of psychoanalysis": drive psychology, ego psychology, object relational psychology, and self psychology. These four psychologies represent different perspectives on psychological functioning, and must not be seen as competing perspectives but as complementary views of the same, complex, psychological reality. Mainly, the first three of these approaches have inspired psychodynamically oriented research in the psychology of religion (a major exception is the self psychology-inspired case study by Belzen, 2008). In addition, especially with the advent of object relational theories, psychoanalysis in general has become less reductionistic and less hostile toward religion (cultural and personal) than Freud's original formulations and those of many of his contemporaries (Blass, 2006).

Drive Psychology

This was Freud's primary approach to human behavior. It looks at human behavior from the perspective of personal motives or tendencies and wishes, which are formulated in terms of conflicting "pulsions" (drives) and their vicissitudes. It is hypothesized that some wishes give rise to inner conflicts because they are experienced as unacceptable by the inner moral and ethical standards of the individual and/or dangerous in relation to the requirements of the outside world. A central role is allocated to defense or transmutation mechanisms to deal with unacceptable wishes (drives). These defense mechanisms are, of course, largely influenced by social, cultural, and educational factors. In that sense, Freud was not an unrealistic one-person psychologist, as some of his critics pretend. This "classical" approach inspired much of the older psychoanalytic literature on religion (Capps, 2001), and focused, as Freud, mostly on the "hidden" personal desires and conflicts in religion and in personal religiosity. However, this "classical" approach is still inspiring researchers today.

According to Pine (1990), the work of the influential French psychoanalyst Jacques Lacan and his followers should also be situated in the drive psychology tradition. Although regularly referring to religion, Lacan never wrote an entire contribution about religion. His views, however, have inspired several important approaches to religion (e.g., Dolto & Séverin, 1977; Maître, 1997). Castel (2011) is, with his very profound and well-documented study on anxiety and obsessionality (scrupulosity) in the context of religion, a recent example of the fruitfulness of the (non-Lacanian) drive psychology approach. Vasse (1991) has applied Lacanian concepts and theories to study the main autobiographical works of the creative religious Theresa of Avila (see also the more recent study of Julia Kristeva, 2008). Michel de Certeau (1963, 1980), in turn, has provided interesting insights and hypotheses concerning the raise of mysticism in the 17th century in general and the possession of Sister Jeanne des Anges of Loudun (in relation to the psychoanalytic theory on hysteria) and her exorcist Surin (in relation to the problem of psychogenic psychosis) in particular (see also Lietaer & Corveleyn, 1995). Also, the seminal work of Vergote (1988, 1996, 1998) on religion has been heavily influenced by both "classical" Freudian as well as by Lacanian psychoanalysis. His research on topics such as the image of God in relation to the symbolic and imaginary parental images (Vergote & Tamayo, 1980), religious experience (Vergote, 1996), and pathological forms of religion (Vergote, 1988, 1996) testifies to this deep awareness of the reciprocity between individual desires and conflicts and given cultural environments. Finally, the studies of Moyaert (2009) on the adoration of the crucified and Corveleyn (2009) on the psychodynamics of the religious delusion in schizophrenia (as in the Schreber case) and in psychogenic (hysterical) psychosis are more recent examples of this classical approach.

Ego Psychology

Ego psychology mainly focuses on the "other side" of the psychic conflict, namely the capacity of the ego to defend against personal drives and to adapt to reality (Pine, 1990). Erik Erikson (e.g., 1958, 1968, 1969) is probably the most well-known representative of this perspective in the psychology of religion, not only because of his works on identity formation in great religious leaders, such as Martin Luther (Erikson, 1958) and Mahatma

Gandhi (Erikson, 1969), but also because of his seminal work in the area of developmental psychology, in which he mainly focuses the topics of identity formation and of the socioaffective developmental steps (Erikson, 1968; also see Zock, 1990, for an overview). Together with the structuralistic approach to child development by Jean Piaget, Erikson's developmental theories have heavily influenced research on religious development in childhood and adolescence as well as on religious education (see also in this volume Richert & Granqvist, Chapter 8, and Levenson, Aldwin, & Igarashi, Chapter 9).

Another good example of the ego psychological approach can be found in the work of Meissner (1992, 2003) on the founder of the Jesuits, Ignatius of Loyola (for another case study, see Meissner, 2009a). In his psychobiographical study, Meissner (1992) convincingly shows that Ignatius, despite considerable psychopathological problems in his young adulthood, was able to overcome these problems to a great extent, as is evidenced by his great creativity and religious leadership, even in religiously and politically very troubled times. In particular, Meissner shows that Ignatius was able successfully to mobilize constructive ego capacities and defense mechanisms to compensate for certain ego defects. Moreover, with this work, Meissner also shows that sanctity (in religious terms) or religious creativity is not the result of a "supernatural" transformation of personality, but is constructed with the ordinary building blocks of human personality, including pathological ones (see also Corveleyn, 1997).

Psychology of Object Relations

In this approach, the focus is on the individual's representations of self and others, the development of these representations, and the influence they exert on current perceptions, experiences, and (interpersonal) behaviors (see Jones, 1991a, 1991b, 1996; Meissner, 2009a).

Rizzuto's (1979, 1993) work on the representation of God has been groundbreaking in the object relational branch of the psychoanalytic family and still is influential in this whole area and in the broader field of empirical research in the psychology of religion (see, e.g., Hall, 2007a; Black, 2006; Belzen, 2009). Her work remains a good example of this approach. She mainly attempts to show how representations from significant others in early childhood influence and shape, in interaction with the sociocultural environment, an individual's later representation of God (see also McDargh, 1983; Spero, 1992). Empirical research on the influence of early childhood experiences and representations of parental figures has been conducted before the object relational approach tackled this question, namely, for example, by the drive psychology author Vergote and his group (see the overview in Vergote & Tamayo, 1980), in which it is made clear that the Christian image of God-Father is, in fact, a composite image. Specifically, this image is composed of both paternal and maternal characteristics, and this composite image or representation changes in relation with gender, personality characteristics, and intensity of belief. The specific contribution of the object relational approach to the representation of God research demonstrates in a more precise manner how the affective level or quality (e.g., symbiotic, distant, warm, severe) of the early object relational representation influences the later, adult representation of God. Object relational theories have also played an important role in broadening the scope of psychoanalytic studies of religion, in that they provided new theoretical tools to study the role of early object relations in particular religious phenomena, such as religious experiences, and eastern religions (Wulff, 1997), where "classical" drive and ego psychological theories seemed to be less applicable. Historically speaking, one can say that it has been the object relational movement that led to a breakthrough in the development of a more positive attitude toward religion in the psychoanalytic world in general (see Blass, 2006; Jones, 1991a, 1991b). This can to a large extent be ascribed to the great influence of Donald Winnicott's (1953) concept of transitional objects and of transitional space.

> In Winnicott's view, the transitional object represents the infant's first attempt to begin to separate from the mother and relate to the world outside the mother. It is a replacement for the mother and indicates the child's emerging capacity to separate from the mother and to make substitutions for her as the child grows into an individual in his or her own right. (Meissner, 2009b, p. 220)

In line with this first step of creating a transitional object, one can consider many human activities and experiences that happen simultaneously in both "atmospheres"—the inner world and the outer reality—as transitional *phenomena*. It is the "world" of interaction of the subjective and the objective, "an intermediate area of illusion within which the child can play out the drama of separation and attachment. But the need for a capacity for illusion, however modified or diminished by the growth of objectivity and realistic adaptation, is never completely eliminated" (Meissner, 2009b, p. 221). It is within this area of illusion that "Winnicott locates man's capacity for culture, creativity, and particularly of religion and religious experience" (Meissner, 2009b, p. 221). This is clearly an alternative way to situate religion and religious belief in the functioning of the psyche than Freud's way of confronting religion and religious belief with the rational scientific definition of reality and of truth. Winnicott's valuation of the world of illusion as a psychologically necessary step in individual development and in the maintenance of mental balance for the adolescent and adult person has facilitated the psychological study of religious belief and experiences in the psychoanalytic world. This is exemplified in the work of Pruyser (1968; see Malony & Spilka, 1991), Kakar (1991), Rizzuto (1979), and Jones (1991a, 1991b).

CURRENT EMPIRICAL RESEARCH IN PSYCHOANALYSIS AND ITS RELEVANCE FOR A PSYCHOANALYTIC PSYCHOLOGY OF RELIGION

Recent Developments within Psychoanalysis: A Growing Research Culture

Empirical research on personal religion from a psychodynamic perspective has mainly focused on the detailed study of individual lives, mostly by means of the traditional case study method. This research method has been until recently the preferred method of investigation in psychoanalysis, and has undeniably resulted in a wide variety of valuable insights and theoretical hypotheses about human beings, including their religious beliefs, experiences, and behaviors (e.g., Beit-Hallahmi, 1996; Meissner, 1984, 1987; Spilka, Hood, Hunsberger, & Gorsuch, 2003; Wulff, 1997). However, it has become increasingly clear that the traditional case study method has serious methodological flaws (e.g., Spence, 1994). One of the most important pitfalls is related to the selective release of data, which is typical of case studies. This makes it hard to judge the extent to which theoretical prejudices might have played a role in the selection and interpretation of material or to what extent alternative, and perhaps more parsimonious, explanations are possible. Because of this selective release and virtual absence of data, psychoanalysis has, not surprisingly, shown a remarkable resistance to falsification. This is also true for the psychoanalytic study of religion.

Although the influence of new trends and discoveries in current scientific research literature in psychology is obvious, there has been little progress in the empirical study of religion from a psychodynamic point of view because of an overreliance on anecdote, authority, and selectively released case material.[3] This has led to a proliferation of theories and hypotheses. Hence, "old" and "new" psychoanalytic theories concerning religion stand side by side, even if they contradict each other. Because psychoanalysis continued to rely on an outdated research methodology, which was no longer accepted as conforming to scientific standards by the larger scientific community, once its boon, the traditional case study method was rapidly becoming psychoanalysis's bane.

However, the waning influence of psychoanalysis in mainstream psychology and psychiatry in combination with the advent of evidence-based medicine and managed care finally led to a growing awareness in some psychoanalytic circles toward the end of the 1980s that if psychoanalysis was to survive, it had to use other research methods than the traditional case study method (Luyten, Blatt, & Corveleyn, 2006a, 2006b). The result was a boon not only to psychodynamically inspired empirical research but also to an increasing dialogue and integration between psychoanalysis and various branches of mainstream psychology as well as the development of new methods that are specifically designed to test often complex psychodynamic hypotheses (e.g., Westen, 1998; Westen, Novotny, & Thompson-Brenner, 2004; see also Holt, 2002, Huprich & Greenberg, 2003, & Luyten, Mayes, Fonagy, Target, & Blatt, 2009). This was paralleled by a growing move within mainstream psychology toward more idiographic research and toward the study of private experiences in general (e.g., Singer & Kolligian, 1987).

The Need for Good Theory and the Promise of Psychoanalysis

Even a quick perusal of the psychological literature in general and research in the psychology of religion in particular demonstrates the need for comprehensive theories. Empirical studies abound, but they are widely scattered, poorly integrated, and more often than not lacking an overarching theoretical framework (see Spence, 1994). This situation reinforces many in their belief that the systematic empirical study of religion does not have much to offer (see also Hood & Belzen, Chapter 4, this volume). However, we suspect that the poor quality of many of these studies appears to be due to the poor quality of the research questions asked rather than to the methods used as such. This only further highlights the need for good theory. In line with Batson (1997), we think that what the psychology of religion needs is not so much theory per se, because there are an abundance of them, but *good* theories: that is, theories that are not only capable of providing an overarching view of human nature, including humanity's relationship with religions, but also able to generate a coherent, theoretically based research program. Here, we are convinced that psychoanalytic theories, in conjunction with recent methodological developments both within psychoanalysis and within mainstream psychology, have much to offer.

From a theoretical point of view, psychoanalysis provides a wide variety of theories and hypotheses, which have been based on the detailed study of individual lives. As is the case in much research in mainstream psychology, research in the psychology of religion has shown an overreliance on broad and abstract notions, which tell us little about what role religions play in the concrete, daily life of people. Hence, most research has been unable to bridge the gap between nomothetic and idiographic levels (for an exception, see Emmons, 1999). This same dissatisfaction with "grand theories" can be observed in mainstream psychology, and has led to a rapidly increasing number of microlevel theories and subsequent studies of very concrete behaviours and attitudes. On a methodological level, this has resulted in a move away from more traditional methods, such as self-report questionnaires and cross-sectional designs, to the use of methods that are able to tap in more detail and more depth psychological processes in real life (e.g., experience sampling, diary methods). In addition, instead of relying on cross-sectional designs, which are of limited value to investigate causal relationships, longitudinal studies are increasingly used in combination with more sophisticated statistical methods such as structural equation modeling, growth curve modeling, and survival analysis (e.g., Willett, Singer, & Martin, 1998). These latter two statistical methods are particularly interesting, because they allow analyzing data on both idiographic and nomothetic levels. As stated earlier, these developments have also led to a growing methodological sophistication in empirical research in psychoanalysis. Psychoanalytically oriented researchers have adapted and adopted these methods that do more justice to the complexity of psychodynamic hypotheses, which often imply interactive, recursive models than more traditional methods and statistical methods (e.g., Westen & Shedler, 1999).

Yet these developments within psychoanalysis have, with very few exceptions, not been applied to the psychoanalytic study of religiousness. Here lies an important task for the future for psychodynamically oriented researchers. In this regard, we also make a strong plea for methodological pluralism because we believe that the existing divide within the psychology of religion between a hermeneutic, interpretive approach that focuses on understanding (*Verstehen*) and meaning on the one hand and a (neo-)positivistic approach that focuses on explanation (*Erklären*) and general laws on the other hand is not only to a large extent artificial but also unfruitful (Luyten et al., 2006b). Any scientific endeavor involves interpretation and meaning, just as all scientific research includes a process of systematic testing and falsification. There is no experimental and/or quasi-experimental research without previous theorizing and subsequent interpretation. Likewise, interpretations can and should be empirically tested. Hence, whereas (quasi-) experimental research in the psychology of religion should be more aware of the complexity and overdetermination of phenomena, interpretive approaches should develop (1) clear criteria to judge the probability of interpretations and, in general, (2) more rigorous research methodologies. Whereas it can be said that much (quasi-)experimental research in the psychology of religion concerns "impeccable studies of nothing very much" (Spence, 1994, p. 23), many interpretive studies are vulnerable to the critique that "anything goes" in such studies. Hence, instead of seeing these approaches as conflicting, they should rather be seen as completing each other, with much possibility of mutual enrichment.

We also believe that this does not mean that the case study method as such has outlived its usefulness. Controlled case study research, and more rigorous qualitative research in general (Denzin & Lincoln, 2002; Elliott, Fischer, & Rennie, 1999; Yin,

2009), involving a clear set of hypotheses, careful selection of cases, and explicit rules for analysis and interpretation of data is increasingly used in mainstream psychology (Camic, Rhodes, & Yardley, 2003). These new methodologies provide an excellent opportunity for psychoanalytically oriented scholars in the psychology of religion because they are, like the traditional "uncontrolled" case study method, able to capture the uniqueness of each individual, but this time in a methodologically rigorous manner.

In sum, the recent theoretical and methodological developments just reviewed, both within psychoanalysis and mainstream psychology, not only may lead to significant contributions to the psychoanalytic study of religion, but may also have much to offer to the psychology of religion in general. We now illustrate this with a short review of research on religious experience, the representation of God, and the relationship between mental health and religion.

Some Illustrations

Religious Experience

The topic of religious experience has attracted much research attention (see Hood & Chen, Chapter 21, this volume). In the psychoanalytic literature, this topic has been investigated mainly with the well-known case study method. Examples were already discussed in the description of the different currents in the psychoanalytic family. The most recent examples are the study on Teresa of Avily by Kristeva (2008) and Belzen's (2004, 2008) study on a psychiatric ego-documented case of melancholia, in which religion and personal religiosity played an important role. However, despite this attention devoted to religious experience, we are far from reaching consensus on the meaning of such terms as *religious, mystical,* and *spiritual* experience (see in this volume Oman, Chapter 2, and Taves, Chapter 7). In addition, comprehensive theories that are able to explain the wide variety of such experiences are lacking (Luyten & Corveleyn, 2003). Inspired by psychoanalytic theory, Vergote (1996) has convincingly shown in several studies that one must carefully distinguish between various forms of religious experience based on a thorough historical and sociocultural analysis as well as consider at least three interrelated factors that determine whether or not an experience is interpreted by an individual as religious: (1) the perception of an event or situation (e.g., standing on top of a mountain), (2) the affective endowment of this event by the individual, and (3) the preexisting religious/spiritual belief (or the absence of such beliefs) of the individual. For instance, Vergote and his associates found that only those subjects who were religious were likely to interpret certain experiences (e.g., concerning love, nature) as religious. This was further substantiated by their finding that those who believed in a personal God (religious individuals) believed that these experiences showed the hand of God, whereas those who believed in an impersonal higher power (spiritual individuals) saw a confirmation of their belief in a higher impersonal power in these experiences. Hence, people tend to interpret certain experiences congruent with their preexisting beliefs. For some, such experiences are "only" beautiful, "peak" experiences, for others they are the reflection of a higher power or a personal God. Thus, experiences as such are not religious, nor spiritual, nor mystical. They are endowed with such meanings by human beings (Park, Chapter 18, this volume).

Hence, these findings point to the importance of taking into account the preexisting personal belief structure of the individual, which, in turn, is intimately associated with the person's personal history. Traditionally, however, there is a tendency to study religious experiences in complete isolation, as if such experiences exist isolated from historical, sociocultural, and personal factors. However, as the differentiations between different forms and determinants of religious experiences show, it appears that such experiences are only one aspect or phase of a long—sometimes very long—process or history. For instance, religious experiences can be one phase in the process of mourning or in the search for meaning during or after a depressive episode (see Park, Chapter 18, this volume). Hence, carefully designed and detailed longitudinal studies are needed to investigate the complex and often recursive interactions between the life history of the individual, including his or her religious/spiritual socialization, personality factors, and recent life experiences. Measuring these factors, as is mostly the case in existing studies, appears to be a rather crude way to investigate a dynamic process that develops over time. As noted before, growth curve modeling could provide one tool to study such complex interactions over time at both idiographic and nomothetic levels. In this line, the upcoming psychoanalytic research on religious experience should be linked to, for example, the current psychological research on the possible role of religion and religious experiences in *chronic* life adversities or when confronted with traumatizing life events, as in the research of Park (2005) and Dezutter et al. (Dezutter, Krysinska, & Corveleyn, 2011; Dezutter, Wachholtz, & Corveleyn, 2011).

Representation of God

A second example where recent trends in the interface between psychoanalysis and mainstream psychology may lead to important advances in our understanding concerns research on the representation of God. By and large, most systematic empirical research from a psychodynamic point of view in the psychology of religion has focused on the representation of God and more particular on the relationship between this representation and representations of significant others (e.g., mother, father). These studies have undoubtedly led to significant insights in the development of religiosity in individuals. The studies of Rizzuto (1979) and McDargh (1983), mentioned earlier, are two cases in point. Both authors have made a compelling case for the complex interaction and interweaving of sociocultural images of God and the personal life history of individuals.

However, typically, these studies have been limited to very few subjects, rely heavily on reconstruction with all the difficulties associated with such an approach, and/or are for the most part cross-sectional in nature (e.g., Cecero, Marmon, Beitel, Hutz, & Jones, 2004; Dezutter et al., 2010; Gerard, Jobes, Cimbolic, Ritzler, & Montana, 2003; Schaap-Jonker, Eurelings-Bontekoe, Verhagen, & Zock, 2002). In addition, these studies have tended to focus on the actual representation of God. However, rigorous cross-cultural research by Vergote and collaborators with a specially constructed Semantic Differential Parental Scale (SDPS) has shown, in line with psychoanalytic theorizing, the importance of distinguishing between the symbolic and the actual representation of God. In contrast to the actual representation, which is based on the concrete developmental history of the individual, the symbolic representation refers to the more stable cultural representation of God. It was found that the symbolic representation of God is in general, across cultures, a function of both paternal and maternal qualities, with maternal qualities being more important. From this perspective, many interesting questions arise, such as: What is the relationship between the actual and symbolic representation of God? Have the large sociocultural changes in our Western society made maternal aspects more important in the actual and/or symbolic representation of God? If so, are these changes less clear in more patriarchal cultures and/or specific religious groups? Hence, because representations of God are not static entities, neither on an individual level nor on the cultural level (McDargh, 1983; Rizzuto, 1979), but rather dynamic concepts that continue to evolve over time, longitudinal research is needed to answer such questions (see also Granqvist, 2002; Granqvist & Kirkpatrick, 2008). Unfortunately, however, currently such research is virtually nonexistent, and most studies continue to focus on the actual representation of God using cross-sectional designs.

Yet the methodological tools for such studies are now available. Research methods such as growth curve modeling and controlled case study research appear to be particularly promising in this regard to investigate the complex and recursive interactions between symbolic and actual representations of God over time. A dozen or more reliable and valid measures of object relations are available that could be used in such studies (Huprich & Greenberg, 2003). Westen and his collaborators, for instance, developed the Social Cognition and Object Relations Scale (Westen, 2002), which includes scales for rating the complexity of representations of others, affective quality of representations, emotional investment in relationships, and understanding of social causality. Blatt and Auerbach (2003) developed several measures that tap various aspects of both content and structural characteristics of object representations. Some studies have used these instruments to investigate the representation of God (e.g., Brokaw & Edwards, 1994; Hall & Fletcher-Brokaw, 1995; Hall, Fletcher-Brokaw, Edwards, & Pike, 1998). Additionally, research inspired by object relational theories provides ample opportunity for integration between psychodynamic theory and research and developmental psychopathology (Fonagy & Target, 2002), social cognition (Westen, 1991), cognitive psychology (Blatt & Auerbach, 2003), attachment theory (Fonagy, 1999; Granqvist, 2002, 2006; Aletti, 2009), and schema theories (Cecero et al., 2004), and is immediately relevant for clinical practice (e.g., Blatt, Auerbach, & Levy, 1997).

Religion and Mental Health

A third and final area where psychoanalytic theory and research might lead to significant advances in our knowledge concerns the relationship between religion and mental health. Psychodynamic theory and research, in line with standard clinical psychology research, clearly suggests that religion and mental health are intrinsically interwoven (see Miller & Kelley, 2005; Dezutter et al., 2010; Dezutter, Krysinska, et al., 2011; Dezutter, Wachholtz, & Corveleyn, 2011). However, again, most research in this area is cross-sectional, thereby neglecting the fact that religion and mental health most probably reciprocally interact. Even longitudinal studies in this area assume that the relationship between religion and mental health is linear and nonrecursive. Notwithstanding this, often sweeping conclusions are made regarding the relationship between religion and mental health based on such studies. In addition, current research tends to reify the constructs of religiosity and mental health, as if they are completely independent things. Of course, theoretically and for research purposes, one can define and operationalize religiosity and mental health separately, but this does not mean that the individual should be seen as the "host" of two "guests": namely religiosity on the one hand and mental health on the other. If one takes the just-mentioned definition of personal religion seriously, it must be clear that personal religiosity and mental health are intrinsically interwoven. From infancy on, people are drawn toward certain aspects of religion or particular religions as a whole. Alternatively, depending on their personal history, they may become indifferent or may as well start to hate certain aspects of religion or religion in general, but nevertheless they are influenced by it (see Paloutzian, Murken, Streib, & Rößler-Namini, Chapter 20, this volume). The reason for this is that (particular aspects of) religion, as a symbolic system, appeals on certain—often universal—human issues. Hence, one should always consider two directions of causality, one going from religion to the individual psyche and the other from the individual psyche to religion (Vergote, 1996). Take, for instance, the example of Christian religion and the issue of sin, repentance, and forgiveness (see, e.g., Kalayjian & Paloutzian, 2009). Christian teachings concerning these issues attract many people precisely because these are almost universal issues that every human being sooner or later has to deal with. However, the other way around, it is well known that individuals in which obsessive–compulsive traits predominate are often particularly attracted to and occupied with these issues (and particular sin and punishment). Hence, unraveling the relationship between religiosity and mental health is often like the familiar "chicken and the egg" problem. Only longitudinal studies, including recursive influences, can do justice to the complexity of this relationship. Hence, although many have acknowledged, precisely because of the many possible interactions among religion and mental health, that religion may be an expression of a mental disorder, a socializing and suppressing agent, a haven for those under stress, or a risk factor for psychopathology or may have therapeutic value for some (Spilka et al., 2003), research tends to blur these essential distinctions. Moreover, there clearly is a lack of an encompassing theory to explain these various relationships.

In this context, we believe that the psychodynamic distinction between various levels of personality development and functioning may provide a starting point for such a comprehensive theory, and is especially useful for clinical practice when confronted with (alleged) religious psychopathology. From a psychodynamic point of view, one can distinguish between three levels of psychopathology: the psychotic, the borderline, and the neurotic (e.g., McWilliams, 2011). Somewhat schematically, it can be said that at the psychotic level individuals are mainly characterized by a severe disturbance in reality testing, which puts them at increased risk for manifest psychotic symptoms (e.g., delusions, hallucinations). The most characteristic disturbances at the borderline level concern low impulse control and identity diffusion, in combination with the use of primitive defense mechanisms (e.g., splitting). On these two levels of personality functioning, one often is able to make a more or less accurate distinction between pathological variants of religion (e.g., the individual who believes that he is God vs. someone whose representation of God is either very cruel or much idealized, or both) and "normal" religiosity. On the neurotic level, however, which is characterized by good reality testing, more differentiated images of self and other, and the use of more mature defense mechanisms (e.g., reaction formation, rationalization), the distinction between normal "lived religiosity" and religious psychopathology is often very difficult to make, precisely because religion at this level of personality functioning is deeply woven in and interwoven with the fabric of the individual's personality.

Other criteria than those traditionally used in research, such as the deviation of a cultural or statistical norm, are needed here to make a judgment concerning the nature of religiosity. Vergote (1988) proposes the following intrinsically psychological criteria: (1) the ability of someone to speak a common (religious) language, (2) the extent to which an individual is still able to work in the broad sense of the term (i.e., to actively exert an influence on his/her *umwelt*), (3) the extent to which someone is still able to love others in a way that recognizes their autonomy, and (4) the extent to which an individual can enjoy his or her activities. This is not to deny the importance of cultural norms. In fact, many studies of the relationship between religiosity and mental health appear to ignore in whole or in part the importance of cultural norms and only consider a statistical norm to distinguish between normal and "pathological" religiosity. Instead, we propose to speak of the *relative relativity* of the distinction between normal and pathological religiosity. This distinction is often relative because it is frequently difficult to judge the extent to which religion is normal or pathological, especially in individuals functioning at a neurotic level. However, at the same time, this relativity is itself relative, because in some instances individuals within a certain (sub)culture can easily make this distinction, particularly those functioning at the psychotic level. For instance, where there would be much disagreement in Western societies concerning the nature of the belief of a homemaker who somewhat neglects her other duties and others around her because she spends most of her day praying in front of an altar at home, most if not many would agree that an individual with a Messiah delusion who completely isolates him- or herself and is not able to communicate anymore with others shows signs of pathological religiosity.

The clinical implications of such a psychodynamic perspective often differ in important respects from clinical approaches inspired by other theoretical frameworks. First, there is no clear distinction between "normal" and "pathological" religiosity, particularly at the neurotic level. Meissner (1991) has provided in this context a very useful distinction between various religious modi depending on the underlying personality structure, such as the hysterical, the obsessional, the depressive–masochistic, the narcissistic, and the paranoid modus. Each of these modi reflects a particular religious faith that is the result of a particular developmental history in which religiosity, mental health, and personal history are intrinsically interwoven. A second clinical implication concerns the attitude toward religious issues in counseling and psychotherapy. This issue is part of a wider discussion, which we now address.

PSYCHOANALYSIS AND THE CURRENT DEBATE ON THE INTEGRATION OF PSYCHOTHERAPY AND RELIGION OR SPIRITUALITY

Corveleyn and Lietaer observed as early as 1994 a change in the attitudes of psychologists toward religiosity and spirituality in general and in their psychotherapeutic work more specifically (1994, p. 203). Their attitudes had been changing in the 1980s from "anti-" or "indifferent" toward religion to openness and positive attention (for more recent data about psychodynamic psychotherapists, see Bartoli, 2003; Graetz Simmons, 2004). However, these conclusions were based mainly, if not exclusively, on North

American research and review articles. In general, European psychologists and psychotherapists of all kinds of theoretical families have approached the problem of the relationship between psychotherapy and religiosity or spirituality in a different way than their North American colleagues in the past two decades. In several recent North American publications (see Miller & Kelley, 2005; Shafranske, Chapter 30, this volume), several, often far-reaching proposals have been made to integrate religion and/or spirituality and psychotherapy. These proposals range from the integration of traditional Christian (e.g., prayer, Bible exegesis) or Eastern (e.g., meditation, yoga) elements in existing forms of counseling and psychotherapy to the development of explicitly religious and/or spiritually inspired psychotherapy (see Kuchan, 2008; Tummala-Narra, 2009). The fact that religion and spirituality are often positive for (mental) health (see Part V, this volume), and the finding that integrating such religious and/or spiritual elements often leads to increased effectiveness of clinical interventions, especially among strongly religious clients (Worthington, Kurusu, McCullough, & Sandage, 1996), has convinced many, even ardent opponents of religion such as Ellis (Nielsen, Johnson, & Ellis, 2001), of the need and value of integrating religion and/or spirituality with psychotherapy. Hence, psychotherapists are encouraged to be more active in stimulating patients not only to explore but also to rediscover the religious and/or spiritual dimension in their patients' lives (see, e.g., Malkwitz, 2003; Gurney & Rogers, 2007; Goldstein, 2009; Shafranske, 2009). In Europe, in contrast, one hardly finds such standpoints in scientific publications. It is not our intention to speculate about the possible interpretations of this difference, nor do we try to develop a representative "European" standpoint. This is quite impossible, because there is not such a generalized integration movement, nor a general interest in spiritual matters in the European psychotherapy world. However, perhaps in Europe there is a much more keen awareness that the positive association between mental health and religion and/or spirituality does not as such and itself buttress such a "spiritual strategy." This would be a naïve functionalistic "use" of religion and spirituality as an "insurance" for better mental health. To use an analogy: we know that married people live longer: should we then advise all our patients to marry? (See Sloan, Bagiella, VandeCreek, Hover, & Casalona, 2000.)

In contrast to this spiritual strategy, we would like to argue in favor of a variant of the classical Freudian attitude of the psychotherapist toward the ethical and religious values of the patient, namely *benevolent neutrality* (Corveleyn, 2000). The classical Freudian standpoint is generally believed to be actively hostile toward religion or at least simply antireligious. In our view, this is based on a misinterpretation of Freud. Although he personally was atheistic, and his theoretical writings describe religion as an illusion, in his clinical writings he actively promoted benevolent neutrality toward religious issues. We believe that this benevolent or sympathetic neutrality can be considered to be the basic attitude of most European psychotherapists, not only those who have received psychoanalytic training but all therapists, regardless of theoretical orientation.

The term *neutrality* implies that the psychotherapist is not a pastoral worker whose task is to engage actively in a discussion on the truth or falsity of faith (beliefs, attitudes, and emotions). Of course, the psychotherapist must not be too cautious in refraining from directing the dialogue into the religious or spiritual domain. The therapist's tact (Poland, 1975) should not be the alibi for his or her personal resistance toward religion. The resistance of many clients to speak about religious and/or spiritual issues is often already high, because of the intimate character of these issues (Rümke, 1952). The therapist should thus not add his or her personal resistance to that of the client.

Traditionally, the "received view" of neutrality stresses the necessity of a *strict* neutrality (Strean, 1986). In that view, neutrality is defined as impersonal. Relying on some of Freud's rare technical writings, the attitude of the analyst is described in metaphors like "being a perfect mirror" or "being like an unemotional surgeon" (e.g., see Freud, 1912/1958, p. 115). Remarkably, in reference to this so-called classical standard, Freud himself was not a classical psychoanalyst. For instance, already in 1895, explaining what should, in his view, basically characterize the attitude of the analyst, Freud (1895/1955) explains how a therapist must counter the resistance of the patient with gentle attempts to *influence* him or her. The analyst must *elicit* the (intellectual) interest of the patient and try to *stimulate* therapist–patient collaboration. Only then, Freud asserts, does it become possible to overcome the affectively based resistance. He stresses that the therapist must try to do "something human" for the patient, based on real sympathy (Freud 1895/1955, pp. 282–283, 265). Thus, *neutrality is not indifference* and acting without human interest for the real concerns of the patient. It implies neutrality toward the *content* about which the patient speaks but sympathy and compassion for the *person* who is going through the therapeutic process.

However, is all this applicable to the domain of spirituality and religion? Freud's repeated negative judgments about religious matters are well known. Is Freud's critical position not automatically leading to the idea that psychoanalytic therapy only can aim at the deconstruction of the personal religious attitude of the patient? Because psychoanalysis is directed toward the demolition of the imaginary illusions of the patient insofar as they inhibit further personal development, psychoanalysis should also cure his or her "illusory" religious beliefs. This simple transposition of Freud's rationalistic explanation of religion as a cultural phenomenon to the level of therapeutic action has *de facto* seduced more than one psychoanalyst. In our opinion, this is not a correct transposition. Freud, as a person and as a psychotherapist, was much more humble in these matters. For example, in his correspondence with the Protestant pastor Oskar Pfister, Freud wrote, "In itself psycho-analysis is neither religious nor non-religious, but an impartial [*sans parti*] tool which both priest and layman can use in the service of the sufferer" (Meng & Freud, 1963, p. 17).

The psychotherapist must thus take a position *sans parti*. His or her only task is to pay attention to all kinds of things the patient says about him- or herself with the aim of obtaining a greater personal freedom toward inner inhibitions and deformations. It is the therapist's role to promote a greater freedom that enhances the patient's psychological well-being and in this way opens and improves his or her further personal development. This liberating action in therapy *can* possibly foster the development of a personal religious experience, or it can set the person free from oppressing religious representations or practices. However, intrinsically, this liberation "for" or "from" religion is not the primary goal of the therapeutic action. The psychotherapist should not hinder the (believing or nonbelieving) client's spiritual discovery by indicating to her or him the direction toward a prefabricated spiritual or religious pathway.

One thus could say that the prescription of neutrality mainly concerns the *content* aspect of the therapeutic process. The *relational* aspect that carries the therapeutic process is not well described by only referring to abstinence, the narrow interpretation of neutrality. Therefore, Freud spoke in relation to this aspect of the therapeutic commitment about "sympathy" and "interest," for which he coined the notion of "benevolent neutrality" *(wohlwollende Neutralität)*. With this interpretation of the concept of neutrality in relation to religion and spirituality, we feel in good company with the object relational and interpersonal approach of the group of psychoanalytic therapists headed by Rizzuto (1993; see also McDargh, 1993; Meissner, 2000; Shafranske, 2009).

CONCLUSIONS

Although not without limitations and pitfalls, the psychoanalytic study of religion has much to offer to the theoretician, researcher, and clinician. Not surprisingly, therefore, psychoanalysis had, and still has, an important impact on the field.

However, it appears to be imperative for the future of the psychoanalytic study of religion that more attention be devoted to the empirical testing of theories and hypotheses. In fact, as we suggested, instead of being described in the near future as a once-interesting, though long *passé*, approach, psychoanalysis could play an important role in furthering the field of the psychology of religion, both theoretically and methodologically. Theoretically, psychoanalysis has a wealth of insights and theories to offer, which are based on the detailed study of individual lives. The increasing dialogue between psychoanalysis and other social sciences as well as the neurosciences is likely to open up many interesting research vistas. Methodologically, these complex theories ask for complex designs and analysis methods—both quantitative and qualitative—and thus may lead not only to bridging the gap between "interpretive" and "positivistic" research traditions within the psychology of religion but ultimately also to a more complete understanding of what fascinates all researchers in the field: the relationship between humanity and what transcends it.

NOTES

1. With the term *psychoanalytic*, we refer to the original contribution of Freud and followers and to the current orthodox Freudian school. With the term 'psychodynamic' we refer to the broader 'family' of psychologies that have come into existence on the basis of major contributions of scholars who originally followed Freud's psychology (see further in the text). The actual 'psychodynamic' psychology is not only based on 'in treatment' empirical data, but mainly on empirical contributions made with empirical methods which are standard in academic psychology and which aim at 'testing' parts of the theoretical basis of psychoanalytic psychology.

2. Although the distinction is not always easy to make, this more or less stable theological and organizational component also distinguishes religion from less traditional forms of belief (e.g., some cults or sects) and from belief(s) in a higher power that transcends humanity, for which we like to reserve the term *spirituality*.

3. Readers may find this depiction of the empirical status of psychodynamic hypotheses concerning religion somewhat unfair. We partially agree with this critique. Indeed, much systematic empirical research in mainstream psychology of religion has been inspired, either implicitly or explicitly, by psychoanalytic theories and hypotheses (e.g., Corveleyn, 1996; Beit-Hallahmi & Argyle, 1997). However, our point is that psychoanalytic researchers themselves have, with few exceptions, barely used others methods than anecdote or case material. For instance, a

review of the more than 2,000 studies included in Beit-Hallahmi's (1996) authoritative over-view of psychoanalytic studies of religion shows that, even when liberal criteria are used, less than 5% used a methodology other than historical sources, anecdote, or traditional case stud-ies. In addition, with some important exceptions, a considerable number of these studies show a variety of theoretical and methodological flaws, such as the testing of clearly oversimplified psychoanalytic hypotheses and small samples sizes.

REFERENCES

Aletti, M. (2009). Psicoanalisi e teoria dell'attacamento: Due approcci a religion e spiritualità. [Psychoanalysis and attachment theory: Two approaches of religion and spirituality]. In M. Aletti & G. Rossi (Eds.), *Psicologia della relgione e teoria dell'attacamento* [Psychology of religion and attachment theory] (pp. 105–126). Roma: Aracne.

Bartoli, E. (2003). Psychoanalytic practice and the religious patient: A current perspective. *Bulletin of the Menninger Clinic, 67,* 347–366.

Batson, C. D. (1997). An agenda item for psychology of religion: Getting respect. In B. Spilka & D. N. McIntosh (Eds.), *The psychology of religion: Theoretical approaches* (pp. 3–8). Colorado: Westview Press.

Beit-Hallahmi, B. (1996). *Psychoanalytic studies of religion: A critical assessment and annotated bibliography.* Westport, CT: Greenwood Press.

Beit-Hallahmi, B., & Argyle, M. (1997). *The psychology of religious behaviour, belief and experience.* London: Routledge.

Belzen, J. A. (2004). *Religie, melancholie en zelf: Een historische en psychologische studie over een psychiatrisch ego-document uit de negentiende eeuw* (Studies op het terrein der gods-dienstpsychologie, deel 11) [Religion, melancholy and self: An historical and psychological study about a psychiatric ego-document from the 19th century (Studies in the domain of psychology of religion, volume 11)]. S.l.: Uitgeverij Kok.

Belzen, J. A. (2008). Autobiography, psychic functioning and mental health: The role of religion in personal life. In J. A. Belzen & A. Geels (Eds.), *Autobiography and the psychological study of religious lives* (pp. 117–157). Amsterdam: Rodopi.

Belzen, J. A. (Ed.). (2009). *Changing the scientific study of religion: Beyond Freud?: Theoretical, empirical and clinical studies from psychoanalytic perspectives.* Dordrecht, The Netherlands: Springer.

Black, D. M. (Ed.). (2006). *Psychoanalysis and religion in the 21st century: Competitors or collaborators?* London: Routledge.

Blass, R. B. (2003). The puzzle of Freud's puzzle analogy: Reviving a struggle with doubt and conviction in Freud's *Moses and monotheism. International Journal of Psycho-Analysis, 84,* 669–682.

Blass, R. B. (2006). Beyond illusion: Psychoanalysis and the question of religious truth. *International Journal of Psychoanalysis, 85,* 615–634. Reprinted in D. M. Black (Ed.), *Psychoanalysis and religion in the 21st century: Competitors or collaborators?* (pp. 23–43). London: Routledge. (Original work published 2004)

Blatt, S. J., & Auerbach, J. S. (2003). Psychodynamic measures of therapeutic change. *Psychoanalytic Inquiry, 23,* 268–307.

Blatt, S. J., Auerbach, J. S., & Levy, K. N. (1997). Mental representation in personality development, psychopathology, and the therapeutic process. *Review of General Psychology, 1,* 351–374.

Brokaw, B. F., & Edwards, K. J. (1994). The relationship of God image to level of object relations development. *Journal of Psychology and Theology, 22,* 352–371.

Camic, P. M., Rhodes, J. E., & Yardley, L. (Eds.). (2003). *Qualitative research in psychology: Expanding perspectives in methodology and design.* Washington, DC: American Psychological Association.

Capps, D. (Ed.). (2001). *Freud and Freudians on religion: A reader.* New Haven, CT: Yale University Press.

Castel, P.-H. (2011). *Ames scrupuleuses, vies d'angoisse, tristes obsédés. Obsessions et contrainte intérieure de l'antiquité à Freud. Volume 1* [Scrupulous souls, lives in anxiety, sad obsessed persons. Obsessions and the interior compulsion from Antiquity to Freud. Volume 1]. Paris: Les Editions d'Ithaque.

Cecero, J. C., Marmon, T. S., Beitel, M., Hutz, A., & Jones, C. (2004). Images of mother, self, and God as predictors of dysphoria in non-clinical samples. *Personality and Individual Differences, 36,* 1669–1680.

Corveleyn, J. (1996). The psychological explanation of religion as wish-fulfilment. A test-case: The belief in immortality. In H. Grzymala-Moszczynska & B. Beit-Hallahmi (Eds.), *Religion, psychopathology and coping* (pp. 57–70). Amsterdam: Rodopi.

Corveleyn, J. (1997). The obsessional episode in the conversion experience of Ignatius of Loyola. A psychobiographical contribution. In J. A. Belzen (Ed.), *Hermeneutical approaches in psychology of religion* (pp. 155–172). Amsterdam: Rodopi.

Corveleyn, J. (2000). In defense of benevolent neutrality: Against a 'spiritual strategy'. *Journal of Individual Psychology, 56,* 343–352.

Corveleyn, J. (2009). Religious delusion in psychosis and hysteria. In J. A. Belzen (Ed.), *Changing the scientific study of religion: Beyond Freud?: Theoretical, empirical and clinical studies from psychoanalytic perspectives* (pp. 85–109). Dordrecht, The Netherlands: Springer.

Corveleyn, J., & Lietaer, H. (1994). A critical review of current psychological research on the interaction between religion and mental health. In D. Hutsebaut & J. Corveleyn (Eds.), *Belief and unbelief: Psychological perspectives* (pp. 203–218). Amsterdam: Rodopi.

Corveleyn, J., & Luyten, P. (2005). Psychodynamic psychologies and religion. In R. F. Paloutzian & C. L. Park (Eds.), *Handbook of the psychology of religion and spirituality* (pp. 80–100). New York: Guilford Press.

de Certeau, M. (1963). *Surin: Guide spirituel pour la perfection* [Surin: Spiritual guide towards perfection]. Paris: Desclée De Brouwer.

de Certeau, M. (1980). *La possession de Loudun* [The possession of Loudun] (2nd ed.). Paris: Gallimard/Julliard.

Denzin, N. K., & Lincoln, Y. S. (Eds.). (2002). *Handbook of qualitative research* (2nd ed.). London: Sage.

Devereux, G. (Ed.). (1974). *Psychoanalysis and the occult.* London: Souvenir Press. (Original work published 1953)

Devisch, R. (2009). The paternal methaphor revisited in post-Freudian French religious psychoanalytic anthropology. In J. A. Belzen (Ed.), *Changing the scientific study of religion: Beyond Freud?: Theoretical, empirical and clinical studies from psychoanalytic perspectives* (pp. 243–274). Dordrecht, The Netherlands: Springer.

Dezutter, J., Luyckx, K., Schaap-Jonker, H., Büssing, A., Corveleyn, J., & Hutsebaut, D. (2010). God image and happiness in chronic pain patients: The mediating role of disease interpretation. *Pain Medicine, 11,* 765–773.

Dezutter, J., Krysinska, K., & Corveleyn, J. (2011), Religious factors in pain management: A psychological perspective. *Journal of Anesthesia & Clinical Research.*

Dezutter, J., Wachholtz, A., & Corveleyn, J. (2011). Prayer and pain: The mediating role of positive reappraisal. *Journal of Behavioral Medicine, 34,* 542–549.

Dolto, F., & Séverin, G. (1977). *L'évangile au risque de la psychanalyse* (Tome 1 et 2) [The New Testament in confrontation with psychoanalysis (Vol. 1 and 2)]. Paris: Jean-Pierre Delarge/Seuil.

Elliott, R., Fischer, C. T., & Rennie, D. L. (1999). Evolving guidelines for publication of qualitative research studies in psychology and related fields. *British Journal of Clinical Psychology, 38,* 215–229.

Emmons, R. A. (1999). *The psychology of ultimate concerns: Motivation and spirituality in personality.* New York: Guilford Press.

Emmons, R. A., & Paloutzian, R. (2003). The psychology of religion. *Annual Review of Psychology, 54,* 377–402.

Erikson, E. H. (1958). *Young man Luther: A study in psychoanalysis and history.* New York: Norton.

Erikson, E. H. (1968). *Identity: Youth and crisis.* London: Faber & Faber.

Erikson, E. H. (1969). *Gandhi's truth: On the origin of militant nonviolence.* New York: Norton.

Fonagy, P. (1999). Psychoanalytic theory from the viewpoint of attachment theory and research. In J. Cassidy & P. R. Shaver (Eds.), *Handbook of attachment: Theory, research, and clinical applications* (pp. 595–624). New York: Guilford Press.

Fonagy, P., & Target, M. (2002). *Psychoanalytic theories: Perspectives from developmental psychopathology.* London: Whurr.

Freud, S. (1953). Totem and taboo. In J. Strachey (Ed. & Trans.), *The standard edition of the complete psychological works of Sigmund Freud* (Vol. 13, pp. 1–161). London: Hogarth Press. (Original work published 1913)

Freud, S. (1955). From the history of an infantile neurosis. In J. Strachey (Ed. & Trans.), *The standard edition of the complete psychological works of Sigmund Freud* (Vol. 17, pp. 1–123). London: Hogarth Press. (Original work published 1918)

Freud, S. (1955). Studies on hysteria. In J. Strachey (Ed. & Trans.), *The standard edition of the complete psychological works of Sigmund Freud* (Vol. 2, pp. 1–319). London: Hogarth Press. (Original work published 1895)

Freud, S. (1958). Recommendations to physicians practising psycho-analysis. In J. Strachey (Ed. & Trans.), *The standard edition of the complete psychological works of Sigmund Freud* (Vol. 12, pp. 109–120). London: Hogarth Press. (Original work published 1912)

Freud, S. (1961). The ego and the id. In J. Strachey (Ed. & Trans.), *The standard edition of the complete psychological works of Sigmund Freud* (Vol. 19, pp. 1–66). London: Hogarth Press. (Original work published 1923)

Freud, S. (1961). Civilization and its discontents. In J. Strachey (Ed. & Trans.), *The standard edition of the complete psychological works of Sigmund Freud* (Vol. 21, pp. 64–145). London: Hogarth Press. (Original work published 1930)

Freud, S. (1961). The future of an illusion. In J. Strachey (Ed. & Trans.), *The standard edition of the complete psychological works of Sigmund Freud* (Vol. 21, pp. 5–56). London: Hogarth Press. (Original work published 1927)

Freud, S. (1961). A short account of psycho-analysis. In J. Strachey (Ed. & Trans.), *The standard edition of the complete psychological works of Sigmund Freud* (Vol. 19, pp. 191–209). London: Hogarth Press. (Original work published 1924)

Freud, S. (1964). *Moses and monotheism.* In J. Strachey (Ed. & Trans.), *The standard edition of the complete psychological works of Sigmund Freud* (Vol. 23, pp. 7–137). London: Hogarth Press. (Original work published 1939)

Freud, S. (1964). *New introductory lectures on psycho-analysis.* In J. Strachey (Ed. & Trans.), *The standard edition of the complete psychological works of Sigmund Freud* (Vol. 22, pp. 1–182). London: Hogarth Press. (Original work published 1933)

Gay, P. (1987). *A godless Jew: Freud, atheism, and the making of psychoanalysis.* New Haven, CT: Yale University Press/Hebrew Union College Press.

Geertz, C. (1973). *The interpretation of cultures.* New York: Basic Books.

Gerard, S. M., Jobes, D., Cimbolic, P., Ritzler, B. A., & Montana, S. (2003). A Rorschach study of interpersonal disturbance in priest child molesters. *Sexual Addiction & Compulsivity, 10,* 53–66.

Goldstein, S. (2009). The parallel paths of psychoanalysis and spirituality: Convergences, divergences, transformation. *Psychoanalytic Perspectives, 6,* 45–66.

Graetz Simmons, J. (2004). Heart and spirit: Research with psychoanalysts and psychoanalytic psychotherapists about spirituality. *International Journal of Psychoanalysis, 85,* 951–971.

Granqvist, P. (2002). *Attachment and religion: An integrative developmental framework.* Unpublished doctoral dissertation, University of Uppsala, Department of Psychology. Retrieved April 12, 2004, from *http://publications.uu.se/theses/abstract.xsql?dbid=1904.*

Granqvist, P. (2006). On the relation between secular and divine relationships: An emerging attachment perspective and a critique of the "depth" approaches. *The International Journal for the Psychology of Religion, 16,* 1–18.

Granqvist, P., & Kirkpatrick, L. A. (2008). Attachment and religious representations and behavior. In J. Cassidy & P. R. Shaver (Eds.), *Handbook of attachment: Theory, research, and clinical applications* (pp. 906–932). New York: Guilford Press.

Gurney, A. G., & Rogers, S. A. (2007). Object-relations and spirituality: Revisiting a clinical dialogue. *Journal of Clinical Psychology, 63,* 961–977.

Hall, T. W. (2007a). Psychoanalysis, attachment, and spirituality: Part I. The emergence of two relational traditions. *Journal of Psychology and Theology, 35,* 14–28.

Hall, T. W. (2007b). Psychoanalysis, attachment, and spirituality: Part II. The spiritual stories we live by. *Journal of Psychology and Theology, 35,* 29–42.

Hall, T. W., & Fletcher-Brokaw, B. (1995). The relationship of spiritual maturity to level of object relations development and God image. *Pastoral Psychology, 43,* 373–391.

Hall, T. W., Fletcher-Brokaw, B., Edwards, K. J., & Pike, P. (1998). An empirical exploration of psychoanalysis and religion: Spiritual maturity and object relations development. *Journal for the Scientific Study of Religion, 37,* 303–313.

Hart, C. W. (2011). Paul Tillich and psychoanalysis. *Journal of Religion and Health, 50,* 646–655.

Heine, S. (2005). *Grundlagen der religionspsychologie. Modelle und methoden* [Fundamentals of psychology of religion: Models and methods]. Göttingen, Germany: Vandenhoeke & Ruprecht.

Holt, R. R. (2002). Quantitative research on the primary process: Method and findings. *Journal of the American Psychoanalytic Association, 50,* 457–482.

Hood, R. W., Jr., Hill, P. C., & Spilka, B. (2009). *The psychology of religion: An empirical approach* (4th ed.). New York: Guilford Press.

Huprich, S. K., & Greenberg, R. P. (2003). Advances in the assessment of object relations in the 1990s. *Clinical Psychology Review, 23,* 665–698.

Jones, J. W. (1991a). *Contemporary psychoanalysis and religion. Transference and transcendence.* New Haven, CT: Yale University Press.

Jones, J. W. (1991b). The relational self: Contemporary psychoanalysis reconsiders religion. *Journal of the American Academy of Religion, LIX,* 119–135.

Jones, J. W. (1996). *Religion and psychology in transition: Psychoanalysis, feminism and theology.* New Haven, CT: Yale University Press.

Kakar, S. (1991). *The analyst and the mystic: Psychoanalytic reflections on religion and mysticism.* Chicago: University of Chicago Press.

Kakar, S. (1996). *The colors of violence: Cultural identities, religion, and conflict.* Chicago: University of Chicago Press.

Kakar, S. (2007). *The Indians: Portrait of a people.* Delhi: Penguin-Viking.

Kalayjian, A., & Paloutzian, R. F. (Eds.). (2009). *Forgiveness and reconciliation: Psychological pathways for conflict transformation and peace building.* New York: Springer.

Kernberg, O. F. (2000). Psychoanalytic perspectives on the religious experience. *American Journal of Psychotherapy, 54,* 452–476.

Kristeva, J. (2008). *Thérèse mon amour: Récit* [Teresa, my love: A story]. Paris: Fayard.

Kuchan, K. L. (2008). Prayer as therapeutic process toward aliveness within a spiritual direction relationship. *Journal of Religion and Health, 47,* 263–275.

Lietaer, H., & Corveleyn, J. (1995). Psychoanalytical interpretation of the demoniacal possession and the mystical development of Sister Jeanne des Anges from Loudun. *The International Journal for the Psychology of Religion, 5,* 259–276.

Luyten, P., Blatt, S. J., & Corveleyn, J. (2006a). Building a bridge over troubled water: Response to commentaries. *Journal of the American Psychoanalytic Association, 54*, 627–632.

Luyten, P., Blatt, S. J., & Corveleyn, J. (2006b). Minding the gap between positivism and hermeneutics in psychoanalytic research. *Journal of the American Psychoanalytic Association, 54*, 571–610.

Luyten, P., & Corveleyn, J. (2003). Mysticism, creativity, and psychoanalysis: Still crazy after all these years? *The International Journal for the Psychology of Religion, 13*, 97–109.

Luyten, P., Mayes, P., Fonagy, P., Target, M., & Blatt, S. (Eds.). (2009). *Handbook of contemporary psychodynamic approaches to psychopathology.* New York: Guilford Press.

Maître, J. (1997). *Mystique et féminité. Essai de psychanalyse sociohistorique* [Mysticism and femininity. A sociohistorical psychoanalytic essay]. Paris: Editions du Cerf.

Malkwitz, L. (2003). "Ich möchte an Sie glauben können!": Das Phänomen, Religiosität in der psychoanalytisch Praxis ["I would like to belief in you": The phenomenon "religiosity" in the psychoanalytic practice]. *Forum Psychoanalyse, 19*, 343–361.

Malony, H. N., & Spilka, B. (Eds.). (1991). *Religion in psychodynamic perspective: The contributions of Paul W. Pruyser.* New York: Oxford University Press.

McDargh, J. (1983). *Psychoanalytic object relations theory and the study of religion: On faith and the imaging of God.* Lanham, MD: University Press of America.

McDargh, J. (1993). On developing a psychotheological perspective. In M. L. Randour (Ed.), *Exploring sacred landscapes: Religious and spiritual experiences in psychotherapy* (pp. 172–193). New York: Columbia University Press.

McWilliams, N. (2011). *Psychoanalytic diagnosis. Understanding personality structure in the clinical process* (2nd ed.). New York: Guilford Press.

Meissner, W. W. (1984). *Psychoanalysis and religious experience.* New Haven, CT: Yale University Press.

Meissner, W. W. (1987). *Life and faith: Psychological perspectives on religious experience.* Washington, DC: Georgetown University Press.

Meissner, W. W. (1991). Religious psychopathology. *Bulletin of the Menninger Clinic, 55*, 281–298.

Meissner, W. W. (1992). *Ignatius of Loyola: The psychology of a saint.* New Haven, CT: Yale University Press.

Meissner, W. W. (2000). Psychoanalysis and religion: Current perspectives. In J. K. Boehnlein (Ed.), *Psychiatry and religion: The convergence of mind and spirit* (pp. 53–69). Washington, DC: American Psychiatric Press.

Meissner, W. W. (2003). Methodological issues in the psychohistory–psychobiography of religious figures. *Annual Review of Psychoanalysis, 31*, 181–196.

Meissner, W. W. (2009a). Religious conflicts in psychoanalysis—A case study. Changing views of the nature and meaning of religious beliefs in the analytic process. In J. A. Belzen (Ed.), *Changing the scientific study of religion: Beyond Freud?: Theoretical, empirical and clinical studies from psychoanalytic perspectives.* (pp. 57–83). Dordrecht, The Netherlands: Springer.

Meissner, W. W. (2009b). The God question in psychoanalysis. *Psychoanalytic Psychology, 26*, 210–233.

Meng, H., & Freud, E. L. (Eds.). (1963). *Psychoanalysis and faith: The letters of Sigmund Freud & Oskar Pfister.* New York: Basic Books.

Miller, L., & Kelley, B. S. (2005). Relationships of religiosity and spirituality with mental health and psychopathology. In R. F. Paloutzian & C. L. Park (Eds.), *Handbook of the psychology of religion and spirituality.* (pp. 460–478). New York: Guilford Press.

Moyaert, P. (2009). The adoration of the Crucified: What Freud and Post-Freudian psychoanalysis could have learned from this Christian prayer. In J. A. Belzen (Ed.), *Changing the scientific study of religion: Beyond Freud?: Theoretical, empirical and clinical studies from psychoanalytic perspectives* (pp. 141–159). Heidelberg, Germany: Springer.

Nielsen, S. L., Johnson, W. B., & Ellis, A. (2001). *Counseling and psychotherapy with religious persons: A rational emotive behavior therapy approach.* Mahwah, NJ: Erlbaum.

Ortigues, M.-C., & Ortigues, E. (1966). *L'œdipe africain* [The African oedipus]. Paris: Plon.

Paloutzian, R. F. (1996). *Invitation to the psychology of religion* (2nd ed.). Boston: Allyn & Bacon.

Park, C. L. (2005). Religion as a meaning-making framework in coping with life stress. *Journal of Social Issues, 61,* 707–729.

Pfister, O. (1928). Die Illusion einer Zukunft: Eine freundschaftliche Auseinandersetzung mit Sigmund Freud [The illusion of a future: A friendly discussion with Sigmund Freud]. *Imago, 14,* 149–184.

Pine, F. (1990). *Drive, ego, object and self: A synthesis for clinical work.* New York: Basic Books.

Poland, W. S. (1975). Tact as a psychoanalytic function. *International Journal of Psychoanalysis, 56,* 155–162.

Pruyser, P. W. (1968). *A dynamic psychology of religion.* New York: Harper & Row.

Rice, E. (1990). *Freud and Moses. The long journey home.* Albany: State University of New York Press.

Rizzuto, A.-M. (1979). *The birth of the living God: A psychoanalytic study.* Chicago: University of Chicago Press.

Rizzuto, A.-M. (1993). Exploring sacred landscapes. In M. L. Randour (Ed.), *Exploring sacred landscapes: Religious and spiritual experiences in psychotherapy* (pp. 16–33). New York: Columbia University Press.

Rizzuto, A.-M. (1998). *Why did Freud reject God?: A psychodynamic interpretation.* New Haven, CT: Yale University Press.

Rümke, H. C. (1952). *The psychology of unbelief: Character and temperament in relation to unbelief.* London: Rockliff.

Saffady, W. (1976). New developments in the psychoanalytic study of religion: A bibliographic survey of the literature since 1960. *Psychoanalytic Review, 63,* 291–299.

Saha, S. (2009). Sudhir Kakar and the socio-psychological explanation of Hindu-Muslim Communal riots in India. *Australian Journal of Politics and History, 55,* 565–583.

Schaap-Jonker, H., Eurelings-Bontekoe, E., Verhagen, P. J., & Zock, H. (2002). Image of God and personality pathology: An exploratory study among psychiatric patients. *Mental Health, Religion & Culture, 5,* 55–71.

Segal, R. A. (2011). Mysticism and psychoanalysis: Review essay. *Religious Studies Review, 37,* 1–18.

Shafranske, E. P. (2009). Spiritually oriented psychodynamic psychotherapy. *Journal of Clinical Psychology, 65,* 147–157.

Singer, J. L., & Kolligian, J. (1987). Personality: Developments in the study of private experience. *Annual Review of Psychology, 38,* 533–574.

Sloan, R., Bagiella, E., VandeCreek, L., Hover, M., & Casalone, C. (2000). Should physicians prescribe religious activities? *New England Journal of Medicine, 342,* 1913–1916.

Sorensen, R. L. (2004). *Minding spirituality.* Hillsdale, NJ: Analytic Press.

Spence, D. P. (1994). The failure to ask the hard questions. In P. F. Talley, H. H. Strupp, & S. F. Butler (Eds.), *Psychotherapy research and practice. Bridging the gap* (pp. 19–38). New York: Basic Books.

Spero, M. H. (1992). *Religious objects as psychological structures: A critical integration of object relations theory, psychotherapy, and Judaism.* Chicago: University of Chicago Press.

Spilka, B., Hood, R. W., Jr., Hunsberger, B., & Gorsuch, R. (2003). *The psychology of religion. An empirical approach* (3rd ed.). New York: Guilford Press.

Strean, H. S. (Ed.). (1986). *Countertransference: Current issues in psychoanalytic practice.* New York: Haworth Press.

Tummala-Narra, P. (2009). The relevance of a psychoanalytic perspective in exploring religious and spiritual identity in psychotherapy. *Psychoanalytic Psychology, 26,* 83–95.

Vasse, D. (1991). *L'autre du désir et le dieu de la foi: Lire aujourd'hui Thérèse d'Avila* [The other of desire and the god of faith: Reading Theresa of Avila today]. Paris: Seuil.

Vergote, A. (1988). *Guilt and desire: Religious attitudes and their pathological derivatives.* New Haven, CT: Yale University Press.

Vergote, A. (1996). *Religion, belief and unbelief: A psychological study*. Leuven, The Netherlands: Leuven University Press.

Vergote, A. (1998). Religion after the critique of psychoanalysis. In J. Corveleyn & D. Hutsebaut (Eds.), *Antoon Vergote: Psychoanalysis, phenomenological anthropology and religion* (pp. 17–37). Leuven, The Netherlands: Leuven University Press.

Vergote, A., & Tamayo, A. (1980). *The parental figures and the representation of God: A psychological and cross-cultural study*. The Hague, The Netherlands: Mouton.

Wallerstein, R. S. (1992). *The common ground of psychoanalysis*. Northvale, NJ: Jason Aronson.

Westen, D. (1991). Social cognition and object relations. *Psychological Bulletin, 109*, 429–455.

Westen, D. (1998). The scientific legacy of Sigmund Freud: Toward a psychodynamically informed psychological science. *Psychological Bulletin, 124*, 333–371.

Westen, D. (2002). *Manual for the Social Cognition and Object Relations Scales (SCORS)*. Atlanta, GA: Emory University.

Westen, D., Novotny, C. M., & Thompson-Brenner, H. (2004). The empirical status of empirically supported psychotherapies: Assumptions, findings, and reporting in controlled clinical trials. *Psychological Bulletin, 130*, 631–663.

Westen, D., & Shedler, J. (1999). Revising and assessing Axis II: Part II. Toward an empirically based and clinically useful classification of personality disorders. *American Journal of Psychiatry, 156*, 273–285.

Winer, J. A., & Anderson, J. W. (2007). *Spirituality and religion: Psychoanalytic perspectives*. Catskill, NY: Mental Health Resources.

Willett, J. B., Singer, J. D., & Martin, N. C. (1998). The design and analysis of longitudinal studies of development and psychopathology in context: Statistical models and methodological recommendations. *Development and Psychopathology, 10*, 395–426.

Winnicott, D. (1953). Transitional objects and transitional phenomena: A study of the first not-me possession. *International Journal of Psycho-Analysis, 34*, 89–97.

Worthington, E. L., Jr., Kurusu, T. A., McCullough, M. E., & Sandage, S. J. (1996). Empirical research on religion and psychotherapeutic processes and outcomes: A 10-year review and research prospectus. *Psychological Bulletin, 119*, 448–487.

Wulff, D. M. (1997). *Psychology of religion. Classic and contemporary* (2nd ed.). New York: Wiley.

Yin, R. (2009). *Case study research: Design and methods* (4th ed.). Thousand Oaks, CA: Sage.

Zock, H. (1990). *A psychology of ultimate concern: Erik H. Erikson's contribution to the psychology of religion*. Amsterdam, The Netherlands: Rodopi.

6

Evolutionary Psychology as a Foundation for the Psychology of Religion

Lee A. Kirkpatrick

Psychology, if not allowed to be contaminated with too much biology, can accommodate endless numbers of theoreticians in the future.

—EDWARD O. WILSON (1998, p. 42)

The typical chapter for a handbook provides an overview of a research area, allowing researchers to back away momentarily from their specialized niches to glimpse a bird's-eye view of their larger context. Because progress in science is measured not by any single study but rather the aggregate of many, such essays provide occasion to celebrate the accomplishments within a field or subfield over some period of time.

This is not such a chapter; if anything, its purpose is rather the opposite. I believe that the psychology of religion has made embarrassingly little progress since its inception more than a century ago. Countless data have been collected, measures developed, and constructs proposed, but the resulting movement has been almost entirely circular rather than progressive. I generally do not blame psychologists of religion for this state of affairs: The problems and weaknesses of the field have by and large been inherited from the field's parent discipline. Psychology generally and, consequentially, the psychology of religion specifically have been wandering aimlessly for decades without a rudder—that is, a paradigm that offers a coherent and powerful metatheory for organizing, integrating, and guiding research across otherwise disparate subdisciplines and theoretical models. Evolutionary psychology, as a broad perspective for conceptualizing and studying all areas of human psychology, offers a solution to this problem.

INTRODUCTION TO THE EVOLUTIONARY PSYCHOLOGY OF RELIGION

I begin this section by providing a brief overview of contemporary evolutionary psychology (EP) and its fundamental tenets. I then discuss how the EP perspective might be applied to psychology of religion, distinguishing between two distinct kinds of hypotheses about religion that emerge from this perspective: religion as an *adaptation* versus religion as an evolutionary *by-product*. I conclude by comparing and contrasting EP with another recently emerging interdisciplinary area of research: the cognitive science of religion (CSR; see Barrett, Chapter 12, this volume), with which it overlaps in some ways but differs significantly in others. Because both the adaptation–by-product and EP–CSR distinctions are crucial to a proper understanding of how EP might be applied to religion, these two themes recur throughout the remainder of the chapter.

Evolutionary Psychology

EP begins with the premise that because human beings, like all other living things, are the product of eons of evolution by natural selection, we can use our knowledge about how natural selection works as a basis for developing and testing hypotheses about human nature, including the design and functional organization of human psychology. (For general overviews of this perspective, see, e.g., Buss, 2004; Pinker, 1997; Tooby & Cosmides, 1992.)

Most people have little trouble seeing how natural selection works in "designing" physical traits of organisms: Eyes are useful for seeing, wings are useful for flying, beaks are useful for cracking seeds, and so forth, thereby enhancing the chances of survival to reproductive age (e.g., by acquiring adequate nutrition, avoiding predators) and mating and ensuring the survival of offspring. It is equally obvious how this reasoning applies to physiological traits of humans: For example, our digestive system, including components such as saliva and the stomach, is "designed" to process food in ways that create energy to drive the body's other processes and eliminate waste; the circulatory system, including the heart, arteries, and capillaries, is designed to move oxygen and digestive products to other parts of the body.[1] Less obvious, it seems, is that the same reasoning must apply equally to psychology and behavior. Hardware is useless without software: A digestive system, for example, is useless unless the right kinds of foods are identified, obtained, and put into it. Thus, each species must possess its own unique set of cognitive adaptations or psychological mechanisms, which have co-evolved with the physical structures required to implement adaptive behavioral strategies. All organisms possess species-specific psychologies for solving adaptive problems, such as identifying, evaluating, and obtaining appropriate foods; identifying, evaluating, and attracting quality mates; and avoiding predators and other environmental threats. In addition, many species (including humans) possess complex systems for negotiating numerous, functionally distinct kinds of relationships with conspecifics, including parental investment in offspring, other kin relations, and intrasexual competition for dominance or rank, to name just a few.

The EP perspective converges with that of such disparate fields as neuroscience, cognitive science, and artificial intelligence on the conclusion that the brain/mind comprises a very large number of functionally domain-specific psychological mechanisms and systems, in much the same way as the rest of the body comprises numerous organs and systems. Each psychological mechanism, like each body organ, has been designed to perform one or more adaptive functions; genes encoding recipes for organs designed in this way, rather than alternative ways, were over evolutionary time more successful in propagating themselves in future generations via the successful survival and reproduction of the individuals containing them. *Human nature*, a term that has become virtually extinct from the psychologist's lexicon, represents the totality of this species-universal psychological architecture (Tooby & Cosmides, 1992).

This conceptual model of human psychology contrasts markedly with the prevailing perspective in most of psychology and other social sciences—dubbed the standard social science model (SSSM) by Tooby and Cosmides (1992)—in which the brain/mind is conceptualized as a kind of general, all-purpose computer that operates by a small number of general principles (e.g., symbolic logic, operant conditioning) in the service of a similarly small number of broad motivations (e.g., seeking pleasure and avoiding pain, maintaining self-esteem). Despite lip service routinely paid to the notion that both nature and nurture are important—a debate most researchers claim to have put behind them—the SSSM perspective clearly emphasizes the nurture side of the equation by focusing almost exclusively on such processes as learning, socialization, and culture. The evolutionary history of the human mind, if acknowledged at all, is deemed irrelevant for understanding how we think and behave today. Once cultural evolution took off, it seems widely assumed, the millions of years of biological evolution that preceded and enabled it were relegated to a historical footnote.

However, brains/minds cannot be designed as "all-purpose information-processing devices" for the same reasons that computers are not. Computers are capable of performing a wide range of sophisticated tasks precisely because of the existence of numerous, functionally specific software programs that are well designed to produce desired outputs in response to particular inputs. A computer without specialized software cannot, in fact, do anything at all. One needs specialized word-processing programs to write and edit text, statistics programs to analyze data, and spreadsheet programs to organize arrays of information. To get a computer to behave in more and more complex ways, one needs to add more and more sophisticated, specialized software: As William James (1890) noted more than a century ago, the complexity of human behavior relative to that of other species requires the existence of more instincts, not fewer. Evolution cannot have designed the brain to be a general problem solver, because there is no such thing as a general problem in nature (Symons, 1992). The agenda for an EP approach to psychology thus involves identifying (1) the particular psychological mechanisms or cognitive adaptations that make up our evolved psychological architecture, (2) the adaptive functions for which these respective adaptations were designed; and (3) the design specifications of each of these (i.e., the inputs, information-processing algorithms, and outputs by which each mechanism interacts with environments to produce behavior).

Some Key Implications of an EP Approach

As noted, the idea that humans possess a species-universal psychological architecture comprising highly numerous, functionally domain-specific mechanisms or systems is not unique to EP; numerous disciplines have converged more or less independently on this conceptualization of human psychology. EP's crucial and unique contribution lies in (1) explaining *why* human psychology is organized in this way rather than some other way—as a consequence of evolution by natural selection—and (2) therefore bringing our knowledge of natural selection, and the processes by which it operates, to bear on the question of what these evolved cognitive mechanisms are and how they are designed. An evolutionary approach is both constraining and generative with respect to the development of plausible hypotheses about the content and function of our evolved psychology. To illustrate, I now sketch three kinds of insights that emerge uniquely from an EP perspective.

1. Natural selection ultimately operates according to one and only one strict criterion: the differential replication of genetic recipes. Adaptations, including cognitive ones, evolve not because they are necessarily beneficial to the individuals carrying them, nor to groups to which individuals belong. The survival, health, and happiness of an individual are consequential only to the extent that they lead ultimately to reproduction (and thus genetic replication). Moreover, many adaptations promote genetic replication at considerable costs to individuals. The process of kin selection (Hamilton, 1964) gives rise to adaptations designed to motivate individuals to invest in the welfare of close relatives (particularly offspring), often at great cost to themselves, because close kin are more likely than nonkin to carry the same genes. For example, although the attachment system is designed to promote the survival and welfare of helpless infants, it is adaptive only because of the existence of a caregiving system that motivates parents to be responsive to the infant's needs. Another selection process, sexual selection, involves the evolution of traits that contribute to genetic replication by enhancing an individual's ability to attract quality mates, again often at costs to the individual. The enormous and gaudy tails on peacocks are designed to impress and attract mates, despite (or even because of) the fact that such tails are metabolically expensive to construct and maintain and significantly increase the risk of predation. In short, an evolutionary perspective forces us into the realization that our evolved psychology is not necessarily designed to make us, as individuals, healthy or happy.

2. Although EP endeavors to explain behavior by tracing it to the evolved psychological adaptations that give rise to it (in response to particular environments), this is not to say that all behavior is the direct consequence of a mechanism designed for the purpose of producing that particular behavior. Many (or perhaps most) adaptations, both physiological and cognitive, also give rise to various kinds of by-products. One common type of by-product, dubbed "spandrels" by Gould and Lewontin (1979), are corollary effects of an adaptation that are not adaptive per se but that arise as a consequence of the adaptation's design, much like the "side effects" of a medication. A classic example of a spandrel is the navel (belly-button), which emerges as a by-product of the umbilical cords (which itself is an adaptation, as part of a reproductive system that involves internal gestation). Another common kind of by-product, dubbed "exaptations" by Gould (1991; but see Buss, Haselton, Shackelford, Bleske, & Wakefield, 1998, for clarification) involves the use of an adaptation for a purpose other than the adaptive function for which it was designed by natural selection. For example, the human nose is designed for inhaling oxygen and sensing olfactory stimuli in the atmosphere, but it can also be utilized for holding one's eyeglasses. It is widely assumed that our evolved psychology contains adaptations designed specifically for spoken language; however, the historically recent emergence of written language is a by-product of this in combination with other mechanisms. Indeed, much of our daily behavior in modern environments must be understood in terms of by-products of adaptations designed to solve much more ancient adaptive problems: We

surely do not possess adaptations designed for driving automobiles, computing prime numbers, or engaging in the academic study of religion from a scientific perspective. Attributing any behavior to a by-product rather than to an adaptation does not in any way render an evolutionary approach any less relevant, but it shifts the task from identifying the design and function of an adaptation to identifying the adaptations of which the behavior is a by-product and explaining how and why the by-product emerges from the adaptations (Buss et al., 1998). As I discuss in the following section, the question of whether religious belief and behavior reflects an adaptation designed for this purpose or is a by-product of adaptations designed by natural selection for other, non-religion-specific purposes is a central issue in the application of EP to religion.

3. A related and equally important insight that emerges uniquely from an EP perspective is that evolved traits reflect adaptation to past rather than present environments: Adaptations are evolved solutions to adaptive problems that were faced recurrently by our distant ancestors in the environments they inhabited. Because cultural change can be much more rapid than biological evolution, the environments in which we live today differ in many ways from that of our hunter–gatherer ancestors. Consequently, "mismatches" between current and past environments can often lead to behavior that appears maladaptive in modern environments. Our evolved preferences for sweet and fatty foods were adaptive in an environment in which ripe fruit and meat were scarce commodities, but too easily lead to obesity in modern environments in which sweets and fats are plentiful and cheap. An EP perspective is unique in forcing us to think in terms of adaptation in ancestral environments rather than contemporary ones.

Applying EP to the Psychology of Religion

In light of the preceding discussion, the central issue for an evolutionary psychology of religion (EPR) is that of identifying the (evolved) cognitive adaptations that give rise to those particular thoughts, beliefs, values, and behaviors that we categorize as "religious" and to explain how and why this occurs. This agenda immediately leads to the crucial question, Do humans possess cognitive adaptations specifically designed by natural selection to produce "religious" beliefs and behavior? Or does "religious" belief and behavior instead emerge as a by-product of (perhaps numerous) adaptations designed for other, non-religion-specific purposes?

Perhaps the most obvious application of evolutionary thinking to religion is the hypothesis that religion, or some particular aspect(s) of it, represents an *adaptation*—the product(s) of evolved psychological mechanisms or systems designed by natural selection as a solution to one or more adaptive problems. That is, if the mind is like a computer populated by specialized software programs, are one or more of those programs designed specifically to produce religion or some aspect(s) of it, because, over deep time, genes for constructing such cognitive mechanisms on average were more successful than those for alternative mechanisms? Scholars have long speculated that as *Homo religiosus*, we possess one or more religious "instincts" designed to produce religion for some adaptive purpose. Such claims, whether explicit or implicit, tend to be based on such observations as the apparent universality of religion across time and cultures, neurological evidence for "God modules" in the brain (see McNamara & Butler, Chapter 11, this volume, for a review), and the heritability of religiosity (i.e., "God genes"). Hypotheses about the *adaptive function* of such religious instincts have ranged from defense against fear of death or other forms of comfort and anxiety reduction to group-level benefits such as promoting group cohesion and solidarity or reducing conflict.

As I have argued elsewhere, however (Kirkpatrick, 2006, 2008), such arguments for an adaptive function of religion do not stand up to careful examination in light of modern evolutionary theory. Observations about universality, neurobiological correlates, and heritability of religion are equally consistent with both adaptationist and by-product views. Adaptationist hypotheses often fail to acknowledge that, for example, natural selection is blind to purely psychological benefits such as anxiety reduction, and it is not a simple matter to demonstrate how such feel-good effects translate into real differences in reproductive success. Simple models of *group selection*, in which natural selection is seen to shape traits in ways that benefit "the species" or groups within it, were rendered obsolete by crucial theoretical developments in the 1960s and 1970s, raising serious questions about the hypothesis that religion reflects adaptations designed to foster group cohesion and related functions that benefit "the species" or "the group."[2] Although it is easy to generate examples in which particular religious beliefs appear consistent with the promotion of reproductive fitness (e.g., "Go forth and multiply"), it is equally easy to generate examples to the contrary (e.g., vows of chastity). In short, the task of identifying a plausible adaptive function of religion, and then specifying the design by which a psychological system performs this function, is far more difficult than has often been appreciated.

My own view (Kirkpatrick, 1999, 2005) is that the diverse collection of phenomena we refer to as "religion" emerges from our evolved psychology as a collection of by-products of numerous other adaptations, none of which is specifically designed for "religion" purposes. Beliefs about the existence of supernatural forces and beings appear to emerge as a spandrel-like by-product of evolved systems dedicated to understanding the physical, biological, and interpersonal worlds (Boyer, 1994, 2001): For example, an evolved agency-detector mechanism, designed to distinguish animate from inanimate objects in the world, can be "fooled" readily to produce psychological animism and anthropomorphism (Atran, 2002; Barrett, 2004; Guthrie, 1993), in much the same way as find ourselves cursing our computer when it crashes. Once these spandrel-like effects enable ideas about gods and other supernatural beings, I suggest further, specific forms of religious belief emerge as by-products of psychological mechanisms dedicated to processing information about functionally distinct kinds of interpersonal relationships—for example, attachments, kinships, dominance and status competitions, social-exchange relationships, friendships, coalitions—which whir into action to shape specific beliefs and expectations about these beings and guide behavior toward them. Thus, for example, gods might be perceived as attachment figures, dominant or high-status individuals, or social-exchange partners, each leading to a different set of expectations and inferences about their behavior and decisions about how to best interact with them (Kirkpatrick, 1999, 2005).

Although I strongly favor the "religion as by-product" approach over religion as adaptation, I address throughout this chapter the implications for both. As will become readily apparent, the distinction is crucial in many ways with respect to the question of how religion can be understood from an EP perspective.

EP and Cognitive Science of Religion

Over the last decade or so, the scientific study of religion has seen the rise of another new approach to the topic, dubbed by Barrett (2007; see Barrett, Chapter 12, this volume) and others as the *cognitive science of religion*, which overlaps in many ways with the evolutionary psychology of religion as discussed here. Indeed, much of the research that might be reviewed under the latter rubric could equally well be classified as CSR. The similarities and differences between the two approaches, however, are both important and instructive.

First, CSR reflects an explicit attempt to develop an inherently interdisciplinary effort, aimed at a social–scientific understanding of religion at multiple levels of analysis. As such, it has a broader agenda than does EP (or any other approach to the *psychology* of religion per se), attempting to bridge the gap between psychological and anthropological/sociological approaches to religion by explaining how religions, as culturally shared sets of beliefs and practices, emerge from individual-level psychological processes. That is, CSR researchers aspire to integrate the psychological level of analysis (i.e., how and why individuals think, feel, and behave as they do) and a cultural level of analysis (i.e., the dynamic processes that emerge from individuals interacting and exchanging ideas with one another over time). The latter processes are often referred to as *cultural evolution* in recognition of important similarities to biological (genetic) evolution. As Barrett (2007) notes, much CSR research is "evolutionary" in this cultural sense, with the goal of understanding (in light of a given model of psychology) how and why particular sets of religious beliefs and practices come to be shared within group.

Of course, sociologists and anthropologists have been studying religion at this cultural level of analysis for many years, but for the most part in ways completely independent of the psychology of religion. What is new and promising in contemporary CSR approaches is that models of cultural processes are explicitly built upon models of human psychology. Moreover, most CSR researchers reject the traditional SSSM approach to psychology in favor of the assumptions that (1) there exists a species-universal "human nature" that (2) comprises numerous, functionally specialized mechanisms and systems. These assumptions are precisely in line with an EP approach. However, as Barrett (2007) notes, the majority of CSR approaches are not "evolutionary" at the psychological (i.e., EP) level of analysis despite being so at the cultural level of analysis. It is difficult to understand why this is the case, in light of the fact that natural selection is the only known (to science) process by which humans could come to possess the kind of universal, functional psychological architecture posited by CSR.

I suspect one important reason for this is because many researchers share the view articulated by Barrett (2007, p. 779) that the question of *why* we possess the particular psychological architecture we do "amounts to a secondary project"—an optional, extra question that one might or might not be interested in addressing. From an EP perspective, nothing could be further from the truth. Questions about why we have the particular "human nature" that we do, as opposed to all of the potential alternative human natures that we might otherwise have, are the starting point for EP, not an afterthought: The power of the EP view comes from the recognition that the task of figuring out how something works (in this case, the human brain/mind) is expedited tremendously by knowing what that something is *for* (in this case, to solve the vast diversity of adaptive problems faced recurrently by our distant ancestors). As I hope to make clear throughout the remainder of this chapter, adopting an EP perspective from the beginning changes the way we think about psychology—and consequently about the psychology of religion—in fundamental ways.

FUNDAMENTAL QUESTIONS REGARDING THE NATURE OF RELIGION

In keeping with the forward- rather than backward-looking approach that I have adopted here, the remainder of the chapter is not intended to present a summary of extant theories and empirical findings. Rather, my goal is to demonstrate some ways in which an EP offers a novel way of approaching many of the central, long-standing questions in the psychology of religion. Adopting an EP approach not only changes the kinds of answers (or hypotheses) one might offer to these questions; in many cases, it leads to entirely new questions, to fundamental reframing of old questions, or even to the dismissal of some questions entirely. In this section I address some implications of an EP perspective for thinking about fundamental questions regarding the definition and nature of religion itself.

Defining Religion

One of the most vexing problems in the history of psychology of religion is one of the most fundamental: How should religion be defined? Scholars have debated this issue for centuries with no hint of agreement on what criteria distinguish religion from nonreligion (see Oman, Chapter 2, and Taves, Chapter 7, this volume, for in-depth analyses of this issue). An EP approach to the topic cannot itself answer this question, but it does have important implications for how (or even whether) we approach the problem.

First, it is crucial to acknowledge the (previously discussed) difference between psychological and cultural levels of analysis. Strictly speaking, EP is an approach to understanding individual psychology; consequently, any definition of religion from this perspective should focus on identifying particular kinds of beliefs, behaviors, and experiences of an individual whom we choose to deem "religious." This in contrast to definitions of religion at a cultural level of analysis that focus on *shared* beliefs and activities. An evolutionary perspective is not necessary for justifying this distinction, but it underscores its importance and is essential for understanding the crucial differences between the processes operating at these different levels of analysis. Failure to distinguish clearly these two levels of analysis, and differences between the processes by which they respectively operate, has been the source of much confusion and unnecessary conflict in the emerging CSR literature (see Kirkpatrick, 2011, for discussion).

Second, an EP approach raises the more fundamental issue of whether it is important to unambiguously define religion in the first place, and it offers two distinct answers depending on which EP approach one chooses to adopt. If one wishes to argue that religion is an *adaptation* (i.e., that our evolved psychological architecture includes cognitive mechanisms and systems designed by natural selection specifically to produce "religious" beliefs, behaviors, or experiences), then it is absolutely incumbent upon the researcher to define precisely the particular beliefs and behaviors the mechanism is designed to produce. Because in this view religion is the result of a cognitive adaptation that evolved to solve a particular adaptive problem, a clear definition of religion is not optional; it is part-and-parcel of the theoretical explanation.

On the other hand, the "religion as by-product" view points in the opposite direction. To the extent that religion emerges from a variety of evolved psychological systems designed by natural selection for other (non-religion-specific) purposes, religion represents a category of phenomena invented by humans, not an external reality to be discovered. We can define it in whatever we like, but such definitions are only likely to get in the way of scientific progress. For example, it is difficult to articulate why belief in God is widely deemed "religious" but belief in ghosts is not, or why certain kinds of rituals are "religious" and others not. On virtually any dimension one might choose, "religion" tends to shade into "nonreligion" through many gradations of gray. This is precisely what we should expect if religion emerges as a by-product of numerous, functionally specific psychological systems. Squabbling over where these lines might (arbitrarily) be drawn, under these circumstances, is unlikely to contribute usefully to our efforts to explain why people hold particular beliefs or behave in particular ways.

Is Religion *Sui Generis?*

Another related, long-standing question in religious studies and the psychology of religion is that of whether religion is *sui generis* (see also Paloutzian & Park, Chapter 1, this volume). With respect to the psychology of religion—in contrast to, for example, religious studies or philosophy of religion—the question can be cast in terms of whether religion can ultimately be understood entirely as a function of mundane (non-religion-specific) psychological systems and processes, or whether it is necessary to postulate additional, religious-specific psychological systems and processes. On the one hand, the psychology of religion has seen a long tradition of attempting to explain religion in terms of more general motivations, personality traits, attribution processes, and so forth; on the other hand, numerous researchers have argued that such approaches will ultimately fall short without recourse to uniquely religious psychological phenomena (e.g., Emmons, 2000; Pargament, Magyar-Russell, & Murray-Swank, 2005; Piedmont, 1999). Again, an EP perspective does not necessarily answer the question, but offers a clear, and nonarbitrary way of clarifying the question in ways that render it more tractable.

As typically stated, the *sui generis* question is not a well-formed one. What exactly does it mean for religion to be "unique"? In some sense, religion is virtually unique by definition, or we would not have words like "religion" to describe it nor specialized academic disciplines to study it. In another sense, which seems to be the one adopted by the researchers cited previously, the question can be operationally defined in terms of whether all of the variance in religion-specific variables (as measured by psychologists) either loads on a unique factor in factor analyses of large variable sets or can be statistically predicted from other non-religion-specific variables in multiple regression analyses. This seems on first blush like a reasonable way to operationalize the question, until one realizes it would be a simple matter to create a set of questionnaire or behavioral measures concerning virtually any specific set of attitudes or behaviors that would, in the context of a larger personality or intelligence inventory, surely produce a separate factor in a factor analysis and predict unique variance in other carefully chosen dependent measures (i.e., variance above and beyond that predicted by general traits or intelligences).

From an EP perspective, the question can be meaningfully operationalized in a non-arbitrary way in terms of the adaptation versus by-product distinction: that is, whether our species' evolved psychological architecture does or does not contain one or more religion-specific cognitive adaptations. If it does, as the religion-as-adaptation perspective suggests, then religion "really is" *sui generis* in an unambiguous and nonarbitrary sense: There are aspects of human psychology that are, by design, uniquely religious, and we will never fully understand the psychology of religion without reference to these particular systems or processes. If instead religion emerges as a by-product of numerous cognitive adaptations that evolved for other nonreligion purposes, then (again, more or less by definition) religion is *not* sui generis, in which case it should be (in principle) possible to understand its underlying psychology entirely as a function of other non-religion-specific systems.

Parsing Religion into Types and Kinds

If there is one activity at which all academics excel, it is conceptually dividing up the world and its contents into categories, types, and dimensions. Psychologists parse their subject matter into emotion versus cognition versus motivation; sensation versus perception; individual/personal versus interpersonal; and the omnipresent positive versus negative. In psychology of religion we find these same distinctions as well as countless other category systems differentiating, for example, ritual, doctrine, emotion, knowledge, ethics, and community components (Verbit, 1970); ideological, ritualistic, experiential, intellectual, and consequential dimensions (Glock, 1962); and committed versus consensual religion (Allen & Spilka, 1967).

The principal problem with most such approaches is that they are essentially arbitrary. Analogously, the many parts of an automobile might be classified based on color, size and weight, substance or material from which they are constructed, or cost. Certain such systems might be adopted because they are useful for a particular purpose, such as color for painting or weight for choosing a shipping method, but none could claim a privileged status as superior in any broad sense. To humans who rely heavily on their sense of sight and who possess color vision, classification of things by color comes easily and naturally. However, there is no good reason to think that classifications based on what happens to be salient to our perceptual systems will necessarily be useful for other purposes. Consequently, an infinite number of such schemes are possible, and theorists can (and do) argue fruitlessly about which way is "best," with no possible way of resolving the dispute.

If one's goal, however, is to understand how and why automobiles work—and to provide a useful basis for diagnosing and fixing a problem when one is broken—a conceptual understanding based on *function* is inherently superior to the alternatives. A mechanic or engineer thinks about automobiles in terms of specific components organized into systems (e.g., fuel, electrical) that are designed to perform specific functions. The cause of a car failing to start could be, for example, in the electrical system or the fuel system, each of which consists of particular components designed to do particular things and that can malfunction in particular ways. Thinking in functional terms immediately leads directly to hypotheses about the possible causes of the problem and procedures for testing them. A function-based system enjoys privileged status because of all the ways in which it is possible to classify car parts, only one of these corresponds to an organization that "really" is inherent in an automobile, because it reflects the way in which the automobile "really is" designed to function. To the extent that we, as psychologists, endeavor to understand how and why human brain/minds work, we are in the position of the mechanic or engineer rather than the painter or shipping clerk. We need to carve nature at its joints, and an EP perspective provides crucial insights into how this might be done in the most useful manner. That is, an EP perspective offers the prospect of distinguishing types or kinds of religion in a functional, rather than merely descriptive, manner.

Consider, as an example, the problem of distinguishing types of prayer. The arbitrariness of prayer classification schemes is clearly illustrated by the varying numbers and definitions of prayer types proposed by different researchers: Foster (1992) discusses 21 different types; Poloma and Gallup (1991) at least six; Poloma and Pendleton (1989) and Hood, Morris, and Harvey (1993) each have proposed four-category typologies (which overlap considerably in some ways but not others). So how are we to decide which of these typologies is "best"? (See also Ladd & Spilka, Chapter 22, this volume.)

A functional EP perspective, in contrast, provides a nonarbitrary basis for making such determinations. And again, the adaptation–by-product issue is crucial. From an adaptationist perspective, the task would be to determine why one or more religion-specific cognitive adaptations reliably give rise to qualitatively distinct types or kinds of prayer, perhaps in response to different environments. I am not aware of any such extant theory, but in principle it is possible: Such a theory might specify, in functional terms, why prayer takes certain forms in particular environments but other forms in other environments.

In contrast, the "religion as by-product" perspective offers a variety of ways to analyze prayer into types or kinds that are functionally important. To the extent that one's beliefs about God emerge from the attachment system, for example, prayer should reflect efforts to gain proximity to God and to seek comfort and security in the face of stress or perceived danger, and God should not be viewed as expecting something in return. To the extent that one's beliefs about God emerge from a social-exchange (reciprocal altruism) system, it should involve asking for material things or specific forms of assistance, in exchange for which one would need to offer something to God in return. To the extent that beliefs about God emerge from a dominance-competition system, prayers should reflect expressions of fear and awe and requests for mercy and forgiveness. That is, different types of prayer can be distinguished theoretically in terms of the distinct psychological systems giving rise to them and the functions they serve. Such function-based distinctions should prove more useful empirically in examining the relationships between prayer types and other variables because they conform to real functional differences, much as the mechanic's functional approach to automobiles is more likely to lead to correct diagnosis when a car will not start.

FUNDAMENTAL QUESTIONS ABOUT THE PERVASIVENESS OF RELIGION

One of the central questions in all scientific approaches to religion, including psychology, is why religion is and has been so pervasive across all known human societies. (I deliberately avoid referring to religion as "universal," because it is confounded by the question of one's definitions of both "religion" and "universal.") Explaining the pervasiveness of religion is a central goal of CSR as well as EPR. Because both approaches share similar views of a species-universal psychological architecture (if not the details of its origin and specific content), this section of the chapter generally reflects the views of both perspectives.

Nature versus Nurture

This age-old question, often phrased alternatively in terms of genes versus environments, has as long a history in the psychology of religion as in psychology generally. However, it represents a false and misleading dichotomy, akin to the question of whether lungs or oxygen is more important for breathing. Just as breathing necessarily involves the interaction of specific physiological mechanisms (lungs) with oxygen-rich air, and cannot in principle be understood without reference to both, religion (or any other psychological or behavioral phenomenon) must be understood except in terms of the interaction of environmental factors with evolved psychological systems. For example, any attachment behavior (toward a human caregiver or toward God) cannot be explained without reference to perceptions about environmental dangers and the caregiver's proximity *and* an evolved attachment system designed to attend to, and process, these particular kinds of environmental inputs.

Relatedly, it is important to note that EP explanations are by no means contrary to or inconsistent with explanations in terms of learning, rationality, socialization, or culture. Such processes are, of course, very real, but they do not represent alternative explanations to biology or adaptation; indeed, they are themselves phenomena to be explained. Learning requires a brain/mind designed to enable it. The valiant attempt of radical behaviorism to establish universal learning principles failed when it was demonstrated in now-classic experiments that in any given species some associations were learned much more readily than others (e.g., Garcia, Ervin, & Koelling, 1966; Seligman & Hager, 1972), while Chomsky (1957) argued convincingly that the rate and manner in which children learn language could not be explained by simple reinforcement principles and required a dedicated "language organ" to enable and organize language learning. "Culture" not only influences individuals, it is created by and interpreted by them (see Saroglou & Cohen, Chapter 17, this volume). The effects of culture on individuals, and the processes by which cultures change over time, cannot be understood without reference to the evolved psychology of the individuals interacting with it (Boyd & Richerson, 1985; Sperber, 1996; Tooby & Cosmides, 1992).

With these points in mind, the straightforward answer to the question of why religion is so pervasive (if not universal) must include reference to both nature and nurture. On the one hand, regularities in belief and behavior across all societies result from the fact that all humans share the same psychological architecture, comprising the same set of functional mechanisms. This is true whether this evolved psychology includes mechanisms specifically designed to produce religious beliefs (adaptationist position) or not (by-product position); by-products of cognitive adaptations, like belly buttons, can be as universal as the adaptations that produce them. On the other hand, adaptations (or their by-products) produce universal belief and behavior only to the extent that the environments in which they operate are (functionally) universal as well. Calluses on the soles of the feet are pervasive across many cultures not only because skin contains a mechanism designed to produce them in response to repeated friction, but because people in those cultures walk barefoot. This point is important because, to the extent that environments differ in functionally important ways, universal cognitive adaptations will produce *variable* rather than uniform behavior in different environments—for the same reason that people who wear shoes do not have calluses on the soles of their feet. I take up this equally important question about individual differences in religion later in this chapter.

The age-old question of whether humans possess a "religious instinct," therefore must be reframed. The term *instinct* has largely disappeared from the lexicon of modern EP—in part because it reflects an outdated notion of behavior resulting from nature rather than nurture—replaced by a conceptualization of cognitive adaptations (or psychological mechanisms) designed to produce different behavioral outputs in response to different environmental inputs. Thus reframed, the question becomes whether any of the many cognitive adaptations that make up our evolved psychological architecture are designed to produce religion-specific beliefs, experiences, or behaviors: in other words, are religious beliefs and behavior "designed" products of adaptations, or are they by-products of adaptations designed by natural selection for other non-religion-specific purposes? Both views are capable of explaining why religion is pervasive, but, as discussed previously, there are many strong arguments to favor the by-product view over the adaptation view.

Religious Motivation

Psychologists of religion have long sought to explain the pervasiveness of religion in terms of religious motivation: that is, the idea that religion somehow satisfies one or more "fundamental" or "basic" human needs or motives. Such postulated religious motives have ranged from meaning, control, and self-esteem (Spilka, Shaver, & Kirkpatrick, 1985) to interpersonal relatedness or belongingness (Galanter, 1978) to the resolution of existential concerns (Batson, Schoenrade, & Ventis, 1993). However, there are a variety of problems with these traditional approaches when viewed from an EP perspective.

First, lists of such purported basic human motives tend to include a very small number of highly general motives. An EP perspective, in contrast, leads to the expectation that human motives should be far more numerous and functionally specific. For example, an evolved system motivating organisms to "control events" would have been of little value because, like a command line in a chess-playing computer program that says "make good moves," it provides no guidance as to how to achieve this goal. A broad motivation for "relatedness" conflates a variety of functionally distinct types of interpersonal relationship (e.g., kinship, mating, and coalitions) that pose very different kinds of adaptive problems and for which we, therefore, must possess functionally domain-specific solutions.

Second, many SSSM approaches to motivation conceptualize motivation in a manner similar to the outmoded view of "instincts" noted previously (i.e., as trait-like drives) that are constantly "on." In contrast, EP (and CSR) offers an alternative view of motives in the context of information-processing algorithms that are activated and deactivated by internal and external stimuli. We are not hungry (i.e., motivated to eat) all the time: Instead, an eating-regulation system motivates us to eat at certain times, contingent on both internal (stomach fullness, blood glucose levels) and external (aroma of a freshly baked pie) cues. Attachment behavior is motivated by perceptions of danger and of proximity of the attachment figure. Any motivational theory about religious belief and behavior, whether as adaptation or by-product, must include reference to the contextual cues that regulate motivation contingently.

Third, many of the particular fundamental motives posited by SSSM researchers are problematic in specific ways from an EP perspective. For example, self-esteem does not represent a motive or goal but rather an index or gauge designed to monitor success or failure with respect to relationship-specific adaptive problems (Leary & Downs, 1995; Kirkpatrick & Ellis, 2001). We are "motivated" to obtain and retain mates, friends, and allies (in some contexts more than others) and experience high "self-esteem" when we succeed.

Is Religion "Motivated"?

Finally, an EP (and/or CSR) approach to religion raises the question of whether the idea of religious motivation is useful or appropriate at all. Our evolved visual system gives rise to seeing, but it would seem odd to explain seeing as a consequence of "visual motivation" or a "motivation for seeing." The reason it seems odd is that explaining something in terms of a motivation for it implies that, in the absence of such motivation, something would not occur—in other words, that "not something" is the default state—which clearly is not ordinarily the case for vision. If religion similarly emerges "naturally" (i.e., spontaneously and cognitively effortlessly) from our evolved psychology, it might reasonably asked whether it makes sense to talk about religious "motivation" at all.

Would humans by default be atheists if not motivated to be religious? Much scholarship in CSR, beginning with Boyer (1994), supports what Barrett and Lanham (2008) refer to as the naturalness-of-religion thesis, according to which beliefs in supernatural agents, for example, emerge spontaneously and effortlessly from human psychology in much the same way that visual illusions emerge from the visual system (e.g., as a consequence of a hypersensitive agency detection system; Barrett, 2004). Such a system is hypersensitive because it has been calibrated by natural selection, like a fire alarm, to err on the side of caution in turn because the adaptive costs of false-positive and false-negative errors are asymmetrical: It is generally safer to mistake a stick for a snake than vice versa (Guthrie, 1993). From this perspective, then, we do not need to be motivated to believe in gods any more than we need to be motivated to see an optical illusion.

Indeed, this view suggests that what requires motivation is activation of alternative psychological systems that raise doubts about our initial perceptions, which, based on additional information, may (or may not) override them. You likely would continue to believe your visual system's perception that two lines are of unequal length until someone suggests otherwise, in which case you might check by using a ruler. You likely would then trust the ruler over your initial perception—the belief produced by one set of mechanisms would win out in your mind over the belief produced by your visual system, assuming you have had sufficient experience with rulers to know to trust them. Of course, there is no tool so simple as a ruler available for determining whether perceived supernatural agents are illusions or not. Consequently, in most contexts, it is much less likely (relative to the visual illusion example) that alternative psychological mechanisms will override initial perceptions about gods, consistent with the fact that considering the entire history of our species, the proportion of atheists likely has been vanishingly small.

I hasten to add that the visual–illusion analogy is not intended to assume or imply anything about the truth or falsity of religious beliefs. The questions addressed by EP about the psychological origins of beliefs are, as with any other scientific approach to such questions, entirely orthogonal to questions about whether or not those beliefs are ontologically true. In a sense, the fundamental independence of these two kinds of questions is even more apparent from an EP perspective than many SSSM perspectives because it assumes that our psychological architecture is designed to produce thinking and behavior that is *adaptive*, in the strict inclusive-fitness sense, rather than accurate or correct. Although having truthful knowledge about the world is, of course, often useful, an evolutionary perspective reveals there are many instances in which this is not the case (see Kurzban, 2010, for an engaging and insightful discussion).

FUNDAMENTAL QUESTIONS ABOUT VARIABILITY OF RELIGION

Another particularly important set of questions in the psychology of religion to which all of these arguments apply with force involves individual differences. In personality psychology generally, researchers have proposed hundreds if not thousands of dimensions and typologies by which to sort differences between people. Researchers eventually managed to determine that the bulk of the variance in all of these dimensions can be captured by five giant factors: the so-called Big Five model of individual differences (e.g., Digman, 1990). Unfortunately, this solution is reminiscent of the hilarious sci-fi novel *The Hitchhiker's Guide to the Galaxy* (Adams, 1979), in which an immense supercomputer crunches data for millions of years before it finally determines that the answer to "life, the universe, and everything" is precisely "42," at which time it becomes apparent that an even more immense supercomputer is needed to determine what exactly the question was. Why exactly five personality factors? Why these particular five? Nobody seems to know.

The psychology of religion has very much followed its parent discipline in its quest to determine the dimensionality of religion, with classic factor analysis studies producing large numbers of diverse dimensions (e.g., Broen, 1957; King & Hunt, 1969) and more recent studies focusing more narrowly on dimensions such as intrinsic and extrinsic religiosity (Allport & Ross, 1967), means, ends, and quest orientations (Batson et al., 1993), and fundamentalism (Hunsberger, 1995). A more recent addition to the list is spiritual intelligence (Emmons, 2000), which, like most other such constructs, is open to criticism for being either too broad or too narrow, glossing over or confounding important differences on one hand and failing to acknowledge others (e.g., Gardner, 2000). Again, the problem is one of arbitrariness: No one way of carving up individual differences can claim superiority over any other because there are no clear criteria for making such decisions.

The issue of individual differences raises interesting questions and problems for an evolutionary perspective: Given the existence of a species-universal psychology, how do stable individual differences emerge? Variability is, of course, a necessary ingredient for natural selection to occur; however, natural selection tends to reduce variability over time as less adaptive variants are eliminated and more adaptive ones become universal (Tooby & Cosmides, 1990). A discussion of the many ways in which individual differences emerge from this process is beyond the scope of the present article; the interested reader is referred to Buss and Greiling (1999) for details. Here I illustrate two general ways of approaching individual differences in religious belief from the perspective of a multiple by-products theory.

First, given that a diverse collection of numerous domain-specific psychological mechanisms are (hypothesized to be) responsible for religious belief and behavior, people vary in the degree to which different mechanisms underlie their personal religious thinking. Thus, for example, people for whom the attachment system largely drives their religious beliefs will conceptualize God as a personal being who loves them, cares for them, and watches over them. For others, God is conceptualized as a social-exchange partner whose provision of benefits is predicated on expectations of some kind of reciprocity. Thus, individual differences in beliefs may reflect the activation of different psychological systems.

Second, many psychological systems give rise to domain-specific patterns of individual differences as they interact with environments and experience across a person's lifetime. For example, a universal attachment system gives rise to well-studied individual differences with respect to the quality and nature of interactions between infants and their primary caregivers and the patterns of thinking and behaving arising from these (Ainsworth, Blehar, Waters, & Wall, 1978), with parallel styles of individual differences emerging in adulthood in the context of romantic relationships (Hazan & Shaver, 1987). Much research now demonstrates that individual differences in attachment are related empirically, both cross-sectionally and longitudinally, to individual differences in beliefs about God and other religion variables (see Granqvist & Kirkpatrick, 2008, for a review).

Because some evolved psychological systems are expected to differ between the sexes, particularly those closely related to mating and competition for mates, this line of thinking also provides a framework for examining the surprisingly understudied question of sex differences in religiosity. For example, men more than women compete with one another for status, prestige, and dominance and thus might be expected (more than women) to conceptualize God with respect to dimensions such as power and dominance. Results consistent with this hypothesis have been reported in both adolescents (Cox, 1967) and adults (Nelsen, Cheek, & Au, 1985).

Finally, these conceptualizations of individual differences can be applied equally well to differences between cultures. Some religions, including most variants of Christianity, appear to be strongly attachment based, whereas the gods in many other cultures seem to reflect the operation of other psychological systems such as social exchange (e.g., performing sacrifices and rituals in exchange for gods providing various benefits). Questions about cross-cultural variability in religion can be cast in terms of the ways in which particular historical and environmental contexts have led different cultures to develop religions that reflect different aspects of evolved psychology. Alternatively, such variability might be examined in terms of the kinds of domain-specific individual differences that emerge from a given psychological system. For example, predominant beliefs about the benevolence versus malevolence of gods across cultures are correlated empirically with differences in predominant childrearing styles in ways that are theoretically consistent with attachment theory (e.g., Rohner, 1975).

CONCLUSIONS

For most of human history, the field of medicine comprised a motley collection of attempts to understand and repair bodies based on intuition, superstition, and trial and error. Modern medicine did not emerge until it was finally appreciated that the body comprises numerous, functionally specific tissues, organs, and systems, each of which was "designed" to perform particular tasks in concert with other parts. This functional approach to anatomy and physiology not only made sense of the body's structure and organization, but led to testable and practical hypotheses about the kinds of things that can go wrong with bodies and how to fix them. Needless to say, this changed everything. (When was the last time you had a good bloodletting?)

To contemporary evolutionary psychologists, the history of psychology bears a disconcerting resemblance to that of medicine.[3] From this perspective, it seems highly unlikely, if not altogether impossible, to construct a comprehensive, accurate understanding of how the brain and mind work in the absence of a functional approach to its inherent design and organization. The human brain/mind is the product of natural selection processes that have designed it, like the remainder of the body, according to principles that are now well understood. If one wants to ascertain how something works, the most efficient path is to begin with knowledge—or at least strong hypotheses—regarding what it is designed to do. It is just a matter of time before the power and promise of this approach is acknowledged sufficiently widely to produce a paradigm shift in psychology and the social sciences generally.

The revolution, although in its infancy, has begun. The psychology of the future will be guided, shaped, and organized by an evolutionary perspective. The psychology of religion will do well to follow.

NOTES

1. Although I adopt a common convention by referring to adaptations as having been "designed" by natural selection, this should not be misinterpreted as implying that natural selection has any purpose, intent, or foresight.
2. A newer version of "group selection" has been revitalized in recent years by D.S. Wilson (2002; Sober & Wilson, 1998) in a new form that other evolutionary biologists acknowledge as valid and equivalent to traditional inclusive-fitness theory. However, evolutionary biologists remain critical about the conclusions that Wilson draws, based upon this model, with respect to human societies as "superorganisms" and the evolution of "group adaptations" such as religion (West, El Mouden, & Gardner, 2011). On the other hand, there is widespread agreement that group selection can and does operate in cultural evolution—that is, with respect to changes in beliefs, practices, and norms rather than to genetically transmitted adaptations (e.g., Boyd & Richerson, 1985; Richerson & Boyd 2005).
3. I do not intend to imply here that practicing clinicians are medieval barbers nor that their techniques are ineffective. However, I have no doubt—and I fully expect that most clinicians would agree—that psychological practice would be much more uniformly effective if based on a stronger, more comprehensive psychological science.

REFERENCES

Adams, D. (1979). *The hitchhiker's guide to the galaxy.* New York: Pocket Books.

Ainsworth, M. D. S., Blehar, M. C., Waters, E., & Wall, S. (1978). *Patterns of attachment: A psychological study of the strange situation.* Hillsdale, NJ: Erlbaum.

Allen, R. O., & Spilka, B. (1967). Committed and consensual religion: A specification of religion-prejudice relationships. *Journal for the Scientific Study of Religion, 6,* 191–206.

Allport, G. W., & Ross, J. M. (1967). Personal religious orientation and prejudice. *Journal of Personality and Social Psychology, 5*, 432–443.

Atran, S. (2002). *In gods we trust: The evolutionary landscape of religion.* Oxford, UK: Oxford University Press.

Barrett, J. L. (2004). *Why would anyone believe in God?* Walnut Creek, CA: AltaMira Press.

Barrett, J. L. (2007). Cognitive science of religion: What is it and why is it? *Religion Compass, 1*(6), 768–786.

Barrett, J. L., & Lanham, J. A. (2008). The science of religious beliefs. *Religion, 38*, 109–124.

Batson, C. D., Schoenrade, P., & Ventis, W. L. (1993). *Religion and the individual: A social-psychological perspective.* New York: Oxford University Press.

Boyd, R., & Richerson, P. J. (1985). *Culture and the evolutionary process.* Chicago: University of Chicago Press.

Boyer, P. (1994). *The naturalness of religious ideas: A cognitive theory of religion.* Berkeley: University of California Press.

Boyer, P. (2001). *Religion explained: The evolutionary origins of religious thought.* New York: Basic.

Broen, W. E., Jr. (1957). A factoranalytic study of religious attitudes. *Journal of Abnormal and Social Psychology, 54*, 176179.

Buss, D. M. (2004). *Evolutionary psychology: The new science of the mind* (2nd ed.). Boston: Pearson.

Buss, D. M., & Greiling, H. (1999). Adaptive individual differences. *Journal of Personality, 67*, 209–243.

Buss, D. M., Haselton, M. G., Shackelford, T. K. Bleske, A. L., & Wakefield, J. C. (1998). Adaptations, exaptations, and spandrels. *American Psychologist, 53*, 533–548.

Chomsky, N. (1957). *Syntactic structures.* The Hague, The Netherlands: Mouton.

Cox, E. (1967). *Sixth form religion.* London: SCM Press.

Digman, J. (1990). Personality structure: The emergence of the five-factor model. *Annual Review of Psychology, 41*, 417–440.

Emmons, R. A. (2000). Is spirituality an intelligence? Motivation, cognition, and the psychology of ultimate concern. *The International Journal for the Psychology of Religion, 10*, 3–26.

Foster, R. J. (1992). *Prayer: Find the heart's true home.* San Francisco: Harper & Row.

Galanter, M. (1978). The "relief effect": A sociobiological model for neurotic distress and large-group therapy. *American Journal of Psychiatry, 135*, 588.

Garcia, J., Ervin, F. R., & Koelling, R. A. (1966). Learning with prolonged delay of reinforcement. *Psychonomic Science, 5*, 121–122.

Gardner, H. (2000). A case against spiritual intelligence. *The International Journal for the Psychology of Religion, 10*, 27–34.

Glock, C. Y. (1962). On the study of religious commitment. *Religious Education, 57*, S98–S110.

Gould, S. J. (1991). Exaptation: A crucial tool for evolutionary psychology. *Journal of Social Issues, 47*, 43–65.

Gould, S. J., & Lewontin, R. C. (1979). The spandrels of San Marco and the Panglossian paradigm: A critique of the adaptationist programme. *Proceedings of the Royal Society of London B, 205*, 581–598.

Granqvist, P., & Kirkpatrick, L. A. (2008). Attachment and religious representations and behavior. In J. Cassidy & P. R. Shaver (Eds.), *Handbook of attachment: Theory, research, and clinical applications* (2nd ed.). New York: Guilford Press.

Guthrie, S. G. (1993). *Faces in the clouds: A new theory of religion.* New York: Oxford University Press.

Hamilton, W. D. (1964). The evolution of social behavior. *Journal of Theoretical Biology, 7*, 1–52.

Hazan, C., & Shaver, P. (1987). Romantic love conceptualized as an attachment process. *Journal of Personality and Social Psychology, 52*, 511–524.

Hood, R. W., Jr., Morris, R. J., & Harvey, D. K. (1993, October). *Religiosity, prayer, and their relationship to mystical experience.* Paper presented at the annual meeting of the Religious Research Association, Raleigh, NC.

Hunsberger, B. (1995). Religion and prejudice: The role of religious fundamentalism, quest and right wing authoritarianism. *Journal of Social Issues, 51*(2), 113–129.

James, W. (1890). *Principles of psychology.* New York: Henry Holt.

King, M. B., & Hunt, R. A. (1969). Measuring the religious variable: Amended findings. *Journal for the Scientific Study of Religion, 8,* 321–323.

Kirkpatrick, L. A. (1999). Toward an evolutionary psychology of religion. *Journal of Personality, 67,* 921–952.

Kirkpatrick, L. A. (2005). *Attachment, evolution, and the psychology of religion.* New York: Guilford Press.

Kirkpatrick, L. A. (2006). Religion is not an adaptation. In P. McNamara (Ed.), *Where God and science meet: How brain and evolutionary studies alter our understanding of religion* (Vol. 1, pp. 159–179). Westport, CT: Praeger.

Kirkpatrick, L. A. (2008). Religion is not an adaptation: Some fundamental issues and arguments. In R. Sosis et al. (Eds.), *The evolution of religion: Studies, theories, and critiques* (pp. 47–52). Santa Margarita, CA: Collins Foundation Press.

Kirkpatrick, L. A. (2011). The role of evolutionary psychology within an interdisciplinary science of religion. *Religion, 41,* 329–339.

Kirkpatrick, L. A., & Ellis, B. J. (2001). An evolutionary approach to self-esteem: Multiple domains and multiple functions. In G. J. O. Fletcher & M. S. Clark (Eds.), *The Blackwell handbook of social psychology: Vol. 2. Interpersonal processes* (pp. 411–436). Oxford, UK: Blackwell.

Kurzban, R. (2010). *Why everyone (else) is a hypocrite: Evolution and the modular mind.* Princeton, NJ: Princeton University Press.

Laythe, B., Finkel, D., Bringle, R., & Kirkpatrick, L. A. (2002). Religious fundamentalism as a predictor of prejudice: A two-component model. *Journal for the Scientific Study of Religion, 41,* 623–635.

Leary, M. R., & Downs, D. L. (1995). Interpersonal functions of the self-esteem motive: The self-esteem system as a sociometer. In M. H. Kernis (Ed.), *Efficacy, agency, and self-esteem* (pp. 123–144). New York: Plenum.

Nelsen, H. M., Cheek, N. H., Jr., & Au, P. (1985). Gender differences in images of God. *Journal for the Scientific Study of Religion, 24,* 396–402.

Pargament, K. I., Magyar-Russell, G. M., & Murray-Swank, N. A. (2005). The sacred and the search for significance: Religion as a unique process. *Journal of Social Issues, 61,* 665–687.

Piedmont, R.L. (1999). Does spirituality represent the sixth factor of personality? Spiritual transcendence and the five-factor model. *Journal of Personality, 67,* 985–1013.

Pinker, S. (1997). *How the mind works.* New York: Norton.

Poloma, M. M., & Gallup, G. H., Jr. (1991). *Varieties of prayer: A survey report.* Philadelphia: Trinity Press International.

Poloma, M. M., & Pendleton, B. F. (1989). Exploring types of prayer and quality of life research: A research note. *Review of Religious Research, 31,* 46–53.

Richerson, P. J., & Boyd, R. (2005). *Not by genes alone: How culture transformed human evolution.* Chicago: University of Chicago Press.

Rohner, R. P. (1975). *They love me, they love me not.* New Haven, CT: HRAF Press.

Seligman, M., & Hager, J. (1972). *Biological boundaries of learning.* New York: Appleton-Century-Crofts.

Sober, E., & Wilson, D. S. (1998). *Unto others: The evolution and psychology of unselfish behavior.* Cambridge, MA: Harvard University Press.

Sperber, D. (1996). *Explaining culture: A naturalistic approach.* Oxford, UK: Blackwell.

Spilka, B., Shaver, P. R., & Kirkpatrick, L. A. (1985). General attribution theory for the psychology of religion. *Journal for the Scientific Study of Religion, 24*(1), 120.

Symons, D. (1992). On the use and misuse of Darwinism in the study of behavior. In J. H. Barkow,

L. Cosmides, & J. Tooby (Eds.), *The adapted mind* (pp. 137–159). New York: Oxford University Press.

Tooby, J., & Cosmides, L. (1990). On the universality of human nature and the uniqueness of the individual: The role of genetics and adaptation. *Journal of Personality, 58*, 17–67.

Tooby, J., & Cosmides, L. (1992). The psychological foundations of culture. In J. H. Barkow, L. Cosmides, & J. Tooby (Eds.), *The adapted mind* (pp. 19–136). New York: Oxford University Press.

Verbit, M. F. (1970). The components and dimensions of religious behavior: Toward a reconceptualization of religiosity. In P. E. Hammond & B. Johnson (Eds.), *American mosaic* (pp. 24–39). New York: Random House.

West, S. A., El Mouden, C., & Gardner, A. (2011). Sixteen common misconceptions about the evolution of cooperation in humans. *Evolution and Human Behavior, 32*, 231–262.

Wilson, D. S. (2002). *Darwin's cathedral: Evolution, religion and the nature of society.* Chicago: University of Chicago Press.

Wilson, E. O. (1998). *Consilience: The unity of knowledge.* New York: Knopf.

7

Building Blocks of Sacralities

A New Basis for Comparison across Cultures and Religions

Ann Taves

Both the psychology of religion and religious studies focus on religion and, as a result, have struggled albeit in different ways with the problems inherent in specifying a definition of religion and, more recently, spirituality. Although neither field is homogeneous, both fields have a strong empirical orientation and a growing interest in developing multilevel interdisciplinary approaches. The methods employed in the two fields differ, however, with religious studies favoring historical and qualitative ethnographic methods and psychology favoring quantitative methods, whether experimental, survey, or ethnographic. Perhaps most crucially, as psychologists, psychologists of religion are primarily interested in identifying the psychological processes that mediate "religion and spirituality," while religious studies scholars have traditionally been concerned with the various ways that "religion and spirituality" are manifest across times, places, and cultures. Psychologists of religion, as a result, have been preoccupied with operationalizing "religion and spirituality" in order to pursue quantitative research, while religious studies scholars have been preoccupied with the question of whether the concept of religion translates across times, places, and cultures.

Although many scholars of religion would view a comparative-historical approach as constituting the traditional heart of the academic study of religion, skepticism about the translatability of the concept of religion across times, places, and cultures in recent decades has led scholars of religion to resist generalizations about "religion" (or by extension "spirituality") and to retreat from large-scale comparisons to more focused studies of particular topics and themes (Burris, 2005, p. 1871). Many in religious studies would agree with Burris when he states: "The very breadth of the discipline makes comparative statements of any depth tenuous, and this would appear to be a legacy with which the field is destined to grapple. As a softer discipline whose net is cast wide and which is poised between any number of epistemologies, a willingness to persist in asking the question of what religion is across daunting theoretical chasms may define the heart of its enterprise" (Burris, 2005, p. 1872).

While scholars of religion have retreated from large-scale comparisons, psychologists of religion have sought to make their subfield, which has traditionally focused on data from U.S. and European subjects, more genuinely cross-cultural (Saroglou & Cohen, Chapter 17, this volume; Saroglou & Cohen, 2011). Insofar as psychologists of religion aspire to a *cross- culturally viable* multilevel interdisciplinary approach to the psychology of religion, some awareness of what has been learned by scholars of religion and other comparativists may be helpful in considering how we might best study this elusive, multifaceted scholarly interest we call "religion and spirituality."

The central problem we face in setting up comparisons is that the general terms we use to depict our object of study (e.g., religion, spirituality) are abstractions implicated in webs of meaning (e.g., defined in relation to other concepts such as sacred, magic, superstition, the occult, folk beliefs) that do not map well from one culture or time period to another. Even within a single culture, the boundaries between linked terms (e.g., religion, spirituality, sacred, magic, superstition, the occult, folk beliefs) are unstable and highly contested, such that one person's religion may be another's superstition or folk belief. The traditional ways around this problem in religious studies and the psychology of religion are to stipulate a definition for the purposes of a given study, to risk overgeneralization based on selected cultures, and/or to avoid cross-cultural generalizations altogether. Although scholars in the humanities can choose to focus on particular cultures and avoid attempts at generalization, scientists seek to generalize wherever possible. Since overgeneralization is obviously not an ideal solution, stipulating definitions for a particular study tends to be the preferred option. Stipulated definitions, however, do not provide an adequate basis for generalization because they artificially stabilize our object of study. In so doing, they not only give the impression that we are all studying the same thing; they also obscure the processes whereby the things scholars loosely collect under the heading of religion and spirituality are generated and maintained on the ground (Taves, 2011).

If we consider the nature of comparisons, we can view the problem from another angle. All comparisons presuppose a point of analogy between two or more things that are being compared. When we use abstractions, such as "religion" or "spirituality," as our point of analogy, we run into difficulties translating the concepts across cultures and then either give up the attempt or artificially stabilize our object of study. Rather than attempt to characterize the abstract nouns religion or spirituality, some theorists—this author included—have argued for a building block approach that conceives of religions and spiritualities as disparate wholes made up of parts, such as beliefs and practices. These composite definitions often go on to specify the sacred as the distinctive feature, whether attached to a part or the whole, which makes the whole religious or spiritual.

Most scholars of religion, however, would question whether there is any one, agreed upon definition of the sacred that we can use to set up comparisons across times or cultures. In light of this, I argue here that we should adopt a building block approach to sacralities in which we identify more basic elements and processes, which, although not uniquely specifying "the sacred," are nonetheless typically mixed and matched by people to generate things they sometimes characterize as sacred. As will become apparent, the indeterminacy of that which people deem sacred is inherent in the processes of valuation that leads to the specification of sacrality in any particular instance. Insofar as individuals or groups embrace different systems of valuation, that which they deem sacred will differ as well. Still, identifying the basic elements and processes—building blocks of sacralities—will allow us to set up more precise comparisons across times and places, which will allow researchers to better understand how these basic elements and processes can be used to generate disparate cultural phenomena, some of which people view as sacred, and in some cases to elaborate the more complex systems that scholars and practitioners may characterize as religions and spiritualities.

The first of the following three parts uses the definitions proposed by Durkheim (1912/1995) and Pargament (1997) to illustrate the advantages of a building-block approach to religions and spiritualities and the difficulties inherent in specifying the sacred as the distinctive feature that makes them religious or spiritual. The second part identifies four basic elements and processes, which are not unique to religions or spiritualities, that people mix and match to generate phenomena they deem sacred. The third part concludes with suggestions for further research.

A BUILDING-BLOCK APPROACH TO RELIGIONS AND SPIRITUALITIES

Religions and Spiritualities as Composites

In both religious studies and the psychology of religion, some theorists have followed Durkheim in stressing the importance of viewing religions and spiritualities as wholes made up of parts, and identified a relationship with "sacred things" as the feature that sets religious and spiritual systems apart from others. Durkheim (1912/1995, p. 38) explicitly conceived of a religion (not "religion" in the abstract) as a "system that has a certain coherence." Such systems, in his view, were not constituted by a single idea or derived from a single principle, but were instead "whole[s] composed of separate and relatively distinct parts." Durkheim thus characterized "a religion [as] a unified system of beliefs and practices relative to sacred things, that is to say, things set apart and forbidden—beliefs and practices which unite into one single moral community called a Church, all those who adhere to them" (p. 44).

Leaving aside for the moment how Durkheim defined "sacred things," we can note that a sacred thing or cluster of similar sacred things serves as "an organizational center" around which "a set of beliefs and rites" typically cluster to form a "cult" (p. 38). A religion is typically "a system of cults," which may be "ranked and subordinated to some dominant cult" or "simply exist side by side in confederation" (p. 39). Durkheim's definition relies on a number of metaphors and image schemas (Johnson, 2007; Lakoff & Johnson, 1980/2003, 1999), including: A SYSTEM is a WHOLE made up of PARTS. Sacred things are CENTERS around which beliefs and rites cluster to form cults. Cults are the PARTS that make up the WHOLE. Religions as whole SYSTEMS organize their PARTS by means of SCALES (ranking and subordinating) or LINKS (confederating).[1]

Although Durkheim acknowledges that religious phenomena can exist apart from a religious system, a religion for Durkheim is more than "a unified system of beliefs and practices"; it is a system of beliefs and practices that "unite into one single moral community called a Church, all those who adhere to them" (Durkheim, 1912/1995, p. 44). While Durkheim acknowledged that magic typically involves beliefs and practices, even beliefs and practices relative to sacred things, he differentiated magic from religion on the grounds that "the magician has a clientele, not a Church" (p. 42). Durkheim's sociological theory of religion is thus built into his definition of religion in a way that allows him to distinguish between religion and magic.

Pargament and collaborators (Hill et al., 2000, pp. 65–72; Pargament, 1997, 1999a; Pargament, Magyar-Russell, & Murray-Swank, 2005; Pargament & Mahoney, 2005; Zinnbauer & Pargament, 2005) formulated definitions of religion and spirituality that have been highly influential within the psychology of religion. Pargament (1999a, pp. 11–12) defines religion as "a search for significance in ways related to the sacred," where "significance" refers to "whatever people value in their lives . . . good or bad," and "spirituality" simply as "a search for the sacred." "Searching" refers "not only to [efforts] to find significance but to conserve . . . or transform" it. Searches have two dimensions: "a pathway and a destination."

Where Durkheim relies on a PART–WHOLE image schema to conceptualize the relationship between the sacred and religion, Pargament relies on the CENTER–PERIPHERY image schema to position the sacred at the center ("the most central religious function") and religion at the periphery (1999a, p. 13). In his conception, spirituality is closer to the center than religion, which, as he points out, makes religion the broader construct (1999a, p. 13). The metaphor of a search relies on the PATH image schema, while significance, which implies greater or lesser value, draws on the SCALE image schema. The cognitive metaphors they use have different entailments. Durkheim's definition draws our attention to the way in which parts (cults; i.e., specific beliefs and practices related to sacred things) are prioritized and coordinated within an overarching system. Pargament's use of a CENTER–PERIPHERY schema draws our attention to the center and the means people use to get there (PATHS).

Because each definition draws upon image schemas (PART–WHOLE, CENTER–PERIPHERY, PATH, SCALE), both researchers and subjects can readily recognize systems, centers, paths, and scales relatively easily both within and between cultures (Slingerland, 2004). Thus, to take PATHS as an example, all paths, whether literal or metaphorical, have (1) a starting point, (2) a goal, and (3) a means of moving from the starting point to the goal (Johnson, 1987, pp. 113–117). Hindu and Buddhist practitioners explicitly use the path concept (*marga* or *pada* in Sanskrit) to characterize particular means of reaching tradition specific goals, and scholars of Buddhism (Buswell & Gimello, 1992) have encouraged the use of the path concept in the comparative study of religion. Even though use of the PATH schema is not as prominent in Western religious traditions, it is frequently invoked as a metaphor. As an image schema, both subjects and scholars can easily frame traditions of belief and practice in terms of a path concept (see, e.g., Lindahl, 2011; Taves, 2009, pp. 46–48, 64–66).

Conceptions of the Sacred

Although we can easily recognize systems, centers, and paths across times and cultures, we cannot distinguish specifically religious or spiritual systems, centers, paths, or scales, as these theorists are well aware, without some additional defining factor. For these theorists, the distinguishing feature of the systems, paths, and so on is the sacred. Here, however, things get more complicated. Although references to the sacred have the rhetorical effect of grounding religion and spirituality in something unique, such references tacitly suggest two further claims, both of them problematic: (1) that the sacred is the basic building block from which religions and spiritualities are constructed, and (2) that researchers can use the sacred as a means of identifying religions and spiritualities across cultures.

The problem, as suggested earlier, is that regardless of whether we focus on scholars or their subjects, we do not find an agreed-upon definition of the sacred that we can operationalize for the purposes of cross-cultural research. Among scholars, we see both focused definitions (e.g., Durkheim, 1912/1995; Eliade, 1957/1987; Otto, 1923/1976), which provide alternatives long debated by scholars (e.g., Idinopulos & Yonan, 1996), and catchall definitions (e.g., Zinnbauer & Pargament, 2005, p. 34), which include everything and thus are impossible to operationalize. We can use the definitions offered by Durkheim and Pargament, insofar as the latter can be specified, to illustrate the range of views. Thus, Durkheim defines the sacred as marked by prohibitions and taboos, while Pargament associates the sacred with the divine or divinity.

The Sacred as Marked by Prohibitions and Taboos

All religious systems, according to Durkheim (1912/1995, pp. 34–35), divide things into two classes that can be designated as sacred and profane. Because anything can be designated as sacred ("a rock, a tree, a spring, a pebble"), the distinction cannot be specified in terms of content, but only in terms of the absolute disjunction between the two classes. Thus, he says, "the sacred and the profane are always and everywhere conceived by the human intellect as separate genera, as two worlds with nothing in common." While the form of the contrast varies from one religion to the next, the basic opposition is present, he holds, in all religions. The opposition is always marked by "a visible sign that permits ready recognition of this very special classification" (p. 37), typically prohibitions and taboos against touching or mingling, whether literal or figurative. Thus, sacred things are "things set apart and forbidden" (p. 44). Crucially, according to Durkheim, people often nest other oppositions, such as pure–impure or good–evil, *within the realm of the sacred* (pp. 412–415, italics added). In doing so, Durkheim created a doubly dichotomized conception of the sacred in which worlds could be nested within worlds (Pickering, 1984, Chapters 7 and 8).

The Sacred as Divine

Pargament offers a catchall definition of the sacred that draws from many sources, including Durkheim's "things set apart" and Eliade's conception of the "real" (Pargament & Mahoney, 2005, pp. 180–182; Zinnbauer & Pargament, 2005, p. 34). Still, for Pargament and Mahoney (2005, p. 181), "the core of the sacred consists of concepts of God, the divine, and transcendence," although he is quick to add that "sacred matters . . . also encompass any object that takes on extraordinary character by virtue of its association with, or representation of, divinity." Pargament's definition turns on his understanding of "the divine," "divinity," and "divine-like qualities." Although he does not explicitly define these qualities, the divine or divinity is not limited to "beliefs in God" (Pargament, 1999b, pp. 38–39), but does apparently exclude the "demonic" (Pargament & Mahoney, 2005, p. 183). In excising the demonic, Pargament breaks with Durkheim and others who make room for negative conceptions within the sacred.[2] In so far as Pargament's definition is not simply circular, such that the sacred is the divine, the distinctive feature is the weight it gives to God, gods, and higher powers.

These are just two definitions of the sacred. We could also consider Eliade's definition of the sacred as "hierophany" or a powerful manifestation of "the real" (Eliade, 1957/1987, pp. 12–13), Rudolf Otto's definition of the holy as the "numinous" or "mysterium tremendum et facinans" (1923/1976), or Marcel Mauss's conception of the sacred as "a species of the genus *mana*," where *mana* is a force that infuses both "religion" and "magic" (Mauss, 1904/1972, 7–8, 119). If we expand our purview to include definitions of "religion" (i.e., non-building-block definitions of the abstract concept), we can add other even more distinctive features to our list of possibilities, including the British anthropologist Edmund Tylor's definition of religion in terms of "the belief in Spiritual Beings" (1873/1970, p. 8) or the American theologian Paul Tillich's (1957) definition of religion as "ultimate concern." In light of the diversity of definitions of the sacred and religion-in-the-abstract (see Oman, Chapter 2, this volume), our ability to work across cultures would be enhanced if we did not attempt to specify *the* distinctive feature of religions and spiritualities, but rather sought to identify the more basic elements and processes, which are not unique to religions or spiritualities, that people mix and match to create them.

BASIC ELEMENTS AND PROCESSES

If we abandon the quest for unique features and instead focus on basic elements and processes that people mix and match, the scholarly debates over the definition of religion(s) over the past century are remarkably suggestive. Taking our cue from Durkheim's definition of sacred things as "things set apart and forbidden," we can identify the most basic process as one of *setting things* (anything) *apart* from the ordinary or everyday. From the debates over defining the most elementary form of religion, we can identify two broad classes of things that people set apart: *nonordinary powers*, including deities, and *nonordinary realities or worlds*. Finally, building on Tillich's definition of religion as ultimate concern, we can identify *processes of valuation* as the means whereby people rank and order that which they set apart. I take up each in turn, considering how they might be mixed and matched.

Setting Things Apart

Building on Durkheim's definition of sacred things as "things set apart and forbidden," Kopytoff (1986, pp. 73–74) recasts sacralization as an example of a more general process of "singularization." Taves (2009, pp. 29–44; 2010, pp. 176–180) extends this point, suggesting that we consider "sacred things" as a subset of "special things," where specialness is understood to fall along a continuum from ordinary to singular. Specialness as a scalar quality partakes of more or less. People can consider things to be special without viewing them as full-blown singularities. In this view, singularities, whether people label them as sacred or not, are things that people claim are discontinuous, that they mark as such by setting them apart and protect as such by means of prohibitions against mixing or comparing them with other things.

This understanding of specialness is congruent with Dissanayake's (1990, pp. 92–101; 2008) understanding of art as a behavior, which she views, at its most basic, as an instance of "making special," that is, making "ordinary experience (e.g., ordinary objects, movements, sounds, utterances, surroundings) . . . *extra*ordinary" (2008, p. 252). We can transform psychologists Graham and Haidt's (2012) definition of sacredness, which they specify as "the human tendency to invest people, places, times, and ideas with importance *far beyond the utility they possess*," into a compatible understanding of specialness by reformulating it as "the human tendency to invest particular things with importance far beyond that of other—more ordinary—things in their class." Replacing "sacrality" with "specialness" is crucial, however, as it allows us to consider a wide range of things that are set apart (e.g., a mammalian mother's bond with her own particular infants, behaviors that set playing apart from "reality," tokens such as coins that we invest with exchange value, and objects that we designate as disgusting or as art) without worrying about whether scholars or anyone else considers them sacred.[3]

In identifying the most basic process as one of setting things apart from the ordinary or everyday, I am breaking with Durkheim in several important ways. First, and most crucially, "setting apart" is not a definition of the sacred; it is merely a process that people use to designate things that they perceive as nonordinary. Second, setting something apart need not entail prohibitions or radical breaks between the thing set apart and other things in its class. People may view things they set apart on a continuum, conceiving of things as more or less special depending on the context in which it is placed, the use to which they want to put it, its history, and their relationship to the thing in question (Taves, 2009, 2010). Third, we can distinguish between the basic process of setting things apart and Durkheim's idea of the sacred and profane as "two worlds with nothing in common." If we consider the latter as one particular way in which things can be set apart, we can consider other ways in which people set things apart that Durkheim subordinated or excluded in adopting a "two worlds" approach.[4] Specifically, we can also consider powers that people perceive as nonordinary and ascribe to various things—animate, inanimate, seen and unseen—that they may set apart in "this world" without necessarily postulating another one. The idea of nonordinary powers is central to the animistic and preanimistic approaches to defining religion that Durkheim rejected.

Nonordinary Powers

Insofar as Pargament's definition highlights deities and higher powers, it follows in the footsteps of Tylor's animistic definition of religion as "the belief in Spiritual Beings." The idea of "spiritual beings" as the distinctive feature of religion-in-the-abstract has a robust history, and many scholars in religious studies, anthropology, and sociology continue to adopt an animistic style definition, stipulating what they mean by religion in terms of spiritual beings or some variant thereof (Atran, 2002; Barrett, 1999, 2004; Boyer, 2001; Kirkpatrick, 2005; McCauley, 2011; Pyysiäinen, 2009; Spiro, 1966). Despite its continued popularity, the idea that religion at its most basic should be defined in terms of gods and higher powers was widely rejected by early twentieth-century anthropologists and sociologists who felt that Tylor's (1873/1970) minimal definition of religion as "the belief in Spiritual Beings" was not minimal enough. Thus, British anthropologist R. R. Marett (1914), French sociologists Henri Hubert and Marcel Mauss (Mauss, 1904/1972), German sociologist Max Weber (1922/1978), and Dutch phenomenologist Gerhard van der Leeuw (1937/1986) all argued that a belief in spiritual beings was premised on, and thus could be derived from, a more fundamental *preanimistic* belief in impersonal power, which they variously labeled as "Mana" (Marett, Hubert, Mauss), "charisma" (Weber), or simply "Power" (van der Leeuw). Although they recognized that this sort of impersonal power was often characterized as magical, they nonetheless argued that religion (Marett, Weber, van der Leeuw) or the sacred (Hubert, Mauss) in its most basic form was rooted in power of this sort.

As with Durkheim's conception of the sacred, they all thought that people could ascribe this power to anything, which suggests that it is not the thing to which the power is ascribed per se but that which the power adds to the thing that is crucial. Weber suggested that the belief in spirits, demons, and the soul was the result of a process of abstraction from this magicoreligious matrix that "crystallized in the notion that certain beings are concealed 'behind' and responsible for the activity of the charismatically endowed natural objects, artifacts, animals, or persons" (Weber, 1922/1978, p. 401). Van der Leeuw (1937/1986) provides an extended phenomenological description of the way conceptions of power have been elaborated across times and cultures, including how, by adding "will" and "form" to "power," people can generate a panoply of entities from souls, deceased ancestors, and spirits to deities.

Crucially, however, they all recognize that the power in question is not just ordinary power. Thus, Marett (1914), relying on an Anglican missionary's account of the beliefs of the Melanesians, describes "mana" as a power that is "*beyond the ordinary* power of men, *outside the common* processes of nature" (p. 104). Hubert and Mauss (Mauss, 1904/1972) view "the quality of mana — and of the sacred — [as] appertain[ing] to things . . . considered to exist *outside the normal* world and normal practices" (p. 119). Weber (1922/1978, pp. 400-401) characterizes charisma in terms of "*extra-ordinary*" powers and van der Leeuw (1937/1986, p. 28) indicates that people perceive the power in question as "extraordinary" or "markedly unusual." They all refer, in other words, to powers that people perceive as nonordinary, extraordinary, or special. These thinkers thus agreed on several key points: (1) what we think of as religion and magic are derived from a religiomagical matrix of impersonal power; (2) this power can be attributed to anything whether animate, inanimate, natural, or human-made; and (3) the power or powers in question are not ordinary powers, but powers that people perceive as nonordinary, extraordinary, or special and thus as adding something unusual to the thing in question.[5]

Across a wide range of fields—sociology, anthropology, and psychology—scholars have tended to shy away from the idea of a preanimistic religiomagical matrix, not wanting, I suspect, to conflate religion and magic. Thus, for example, in elaborating Weber's notion of charisma, most sociologists and anthropologists have focused their attention on charismatic agents, relegating the discussion of charismatic objects to the seemingly unrelated literature on "fetishes" and religious relics and amulets (Taves, in press), though Riesebrodt (2009, pp. 74–79) stands as a notable exception in this regard. As noted previously, many scholars identified with the cognitive science of religion have taken a Tylorian definition of religion as their starting point and concentrated on explaining the naturalness of beliefs in unseen agents, giving little or no attention to objects. Even Sorensen's (2007) cognitive theory of magic, which argues that "magic plays a pivotal role in the development of all religious institutions and traditions" (pp. 3–4), nonetheless argues for the value of the distinction between religion and magic.

Rather than shy away from the idea of an underlying magicoreligious matrix, I think we should embrace it. Following the lead of theorists who positioned "animism" within a larger framework of (preanimistic) impersonal powers, we can locate contemporary research on the detection of agency and the attribution of nonordinary powers to (unseen) animates within a larger field of powers (ordinary and nonordinary) that people attribute to objects, artifacts, animals, and persons. If we position the tendency to overattribute agency within the larger framework of detecting and evaluating the powers at play in a given field, we can view it not simply as a means of detecting threats but also as a means of identifying the resources at hand. This allows us to conceive of things to which persons attribute nonordinary powers not only as potential threats or signs of danger but also as potential *resources* (i.e., means of overcoming danger), whether in the form of "magical" objects, "sacred" places, or "supernatural" beings. This broader framework allows for a more integrated approach and raises new questions for research in at least three inter-related areas: the relationship between nonordinary powers and folk biological "kinds" (i.e., animates, objects, artifacts), the measurable (placebo-like) effects of believing in nonordinary powers, and the role of nonordinary powers in the emergence of new beliefs and novel practices.

Arguments for the naturalness of popular religion are premised on an animistic definition of religion, a cross-culturally reliable distinction between animates and non-animates, and an evolved tendency to overdetect and overattribute agency (Barrett, 2004; Boyer, 2001; McCauley, 2011). Research along this line has focused on the developing theory of mind in children and explored when and under what conditions they attribute qualities of mind to unseen agents (Barrett, Chapter 12, this volume). The animistic definition of religion employed in this body of research has obscured the intriguing over-lap between arguments for the naturalness of popular religion and arguments for the naturalness of magic (Bloom, 2010; Hood, 2008; Lindeman & Swedholm, 2012; Sub-botsky, 2010). Although research on popular religion focuses on animates and by exten-sion unseen agents and research on magic takes more account of objects (contaminated objects, transitional objects), there is a striking overlap in the way they conceptualize their object of study and the research they cite (e.g., on theory of mind, disgust and con-tamination).[6]

A more integrated approach to the things to which people attribute nonordinary power—whether persons, animates, artifacts, or objects—requires more nuanced dis-tinctions between types of power and the capacities that inform them. We can distinguish between at least three different kinds.

1. *The capacity to act intentionally*, which presupposes an awareness of awareness and thus the ability to give reasons for why one acts. Entities with the capacity to act intentionally do not always use it, however, and are responsible for many unintended actions for which they cannot give reasons.

2. *The capacity to act*, which presupposes at least some primitive level of awareness or animation on the part of the entity but not conscious intentionality.
3. *The capacity to produce an effect*, which does not require awareness or animation.

We need to know more about how these distinctions emerge developmentally and the degree to which they correlate with distinctions between (unseen) animates and nonanimates, whether natural objects, artifacts, or places, in different cultural contexts. What difference inheres, if any, in the attribution of nonordinary powers to unseen deities, statues that have been blessed (and thus "animated"), eucharistic wafers, sacred mountains, relics, and lucky charms? What, if any, difference does belief in these nonordinary powers make for people in the context of goal-directed action?[7]

A more integrated approach also allows us to consider the effects of calling upon things to which we ascribe nonordinary powers in the context of goal-directed action. Specifically, it allows us to compare the effects of calling upon the nonordinary powers that people ascribe to unseen agents, special places, and believed-in objects with the nonordinary powers that patients ascribe to placebos (i.e., fake drugs and simulated medical procedures). Clinical trials of drugs use placebos as controls in order to determine whether pharmacologically active ingredients are producing the desired effect as opposed the *belief* that such ingredients are present and having an effect.[8] Although clinical trials are designed to test the effects of pharmacologically active ingredients, the emerging interest in placebos (or simulated drugs) *as such* is leading researchers to examine the effect of "words and rituals, symbols, and meanings . . . in shaping the patient's brain" (Benedetti, Carlino, & Pollo, 2011). Following Moerman and Jones (2002), a number of studies have recast the placebo response as a "meaning response," including a study (Kohls, Sauer, Offenbächer, & Giordano, 2011) that examines "spirituality" as a predictor of placebo effects. Concluding that "meaningfulness seems to be both a hallmark of spirituality and placebo reactions," they suggest that "a research agenda addressing responses and effects of both placebo and spirituality could therefore be (1) synergistic, (2) valuable to each phenomenon on its own, and (3) contributory to an extended placebo paradigm that is centered around the concept of meaningfulness" (p. 1838).

Research across domains is becoming increasingly common in placebo research, most notably across the domains of medicine and sports performance (Beedie, 2007; Pollo, Carlino, & Benedetti, 2011) where, in the latter case, the goal of the procedure is not health but high performance. Researchers are also comparing modern biomedical treatment with alternative practices such as acupuncture and traditional healing rituals. Such comparisons allow researchers to identify the quasi-ritualized aspects of modern medicine that play a role in placebo effects and the role of placebo effects in traditional healing practices (Kaptchuk, 2011). Such research can be extended to religious healing in other contexts.

In light of the measurable effects of belief in the nonordinary powers of drugs when fake drugs are substituted for real ones, we can hypothesize that belief in nonordinary powers attributed to other things will have measurable effects as well. To test this, we can set up comparisons between real and fake drugs, acknowledged placebos, good-luck charms, and deities using subjects' belief in their nonordinary powers as the point of analogy. In setting up such studies, identification of subjects who attribute nonordi-nary powers to the thing in question is critical. Thus, in considering whether good-luck charms had a measurable effect on performance, Damisch, Stoberock, and Mussweiler (2010) preselected subjects who believed in the efficacy of good-luck charms. Such pro-cedures can also be used to test the effects of belief in the efficacy of a deity or any other entity to whom people attribute nonordinary powers.

In the end, this research will most likely allow us to consider a variety of powers, some more widely culturally sanctioned than others, that, when believed in, will produce measurable effects. In addition to simulated biomedical practices, these will most likely include alternative healing practices, beloved objects, occult powers, and supernatural deities, to name just a few. Recognition of this range of powers, ordinary and extraordi-nary, that can produce measurable effects will require us to locate them within a more environmentally oriented psychology in which such powers are conceived as affording (i.e., enabling) various goal-directed actions (Johnson, 2007, pp. 45–49; Taves, in press). Such actions could involve healing, coping, performing, or achieving in relation to either this worldly or otherworldly objectives.

Finally, while both psychologists and cognitive scientists have attended to the role of nonordinary powers in contexts where the claims regarding such powers are fairly well established (see, e.g., Pargament, Falb, Ano, & Wachholtz, Chapter 28, this volume, in the context of coping, and McCauley & Lawson, 2002; Sorensen, 2007; and White-house, 2004, in the context of ritual), far less attention has been devoted to contexts where new things are emerging and claims regarding nonordinary powers are highly contested. Additional focus on fields in flux where people are proposing new beliefs and novel practices would allow us to consider how people ascertain what powers are at play in a field, how they characterize them, and how they draw upon them in the context of goal directed action.

Nonordinary Worlds

Durkheim's conception of the sacred and profane as "two worlds with nothing in com-mon" highlights an alternative approach to defining religion that downplays the role of spiritual beings and nonordinary powers. In this definitional tradition, the distinc-tive feature is the presence of alternative, nonordinary, noneveryday worlds or realities. Although nonordinary worlds are frequently populated with spiritual beings, here I heighten the contrast between the two approaches by focusing on two lines of develop-ment that downplay the role of spiritual beings. The first, illustrated by anthropologists Robert Hertz and Louis Dumont, elaborates on Durkheim's doubly dichotomous concep-tion of the sacred in which worlds are nested within worlds. The second, illustrated by Clifford Geertz and Robert Bellah, illustrates the interaction between alternate, compet-ing cultural worlds within a given society.

Consideration of Hertz and Dumont allows us to see how Durkheim's conception of the sacred and profane as "distinct worlds" can generate oppositions within oppositions or, more graphically, worlds within worlds, where one is ranked higher or valued more than the other. Thus, almost in passing, Durkheim commented on the "ambiguity of the sacred," noting that oppositions, such as good–evil, auspicious–inauspicious, and pure–impure, were "religious forces," at once opposed to each other and to the profane. He thus located these oppositions within the realm of the sacred, because their existence and opposition were apparent only within that "world" or frame of reference. In Christianity, for example, God/Satan and heaven–hell are "religious oppositions" that make sense or are apparent only to those who have entered into a Christian theological cosmos. Hertz, a student of Durkheim's, elaborated on the negative or "darker" side of the sacred, which Durkheim left relatively untheorized. In a still widely cited paper, Hertz (1909/1973) argued that across a wide range of cultures, perhaps most cultures with Indo-European languages, the left hand was metaphorically linked with the "dark side" of the sacred, thus launching the discussion of what later scholars came to call "the left hand of the sacred" (Burnside, 1991; Parkin, 1996; Knott, 2005, 2006).

Picking up on Hertz's work later in the 20th century, Louis Dumont analyzed the pure–impure opposition that structured the the Hindu caste system, arguing that opposition and asymmetry were inherently connected within the system to generate what he referred to as "hierarchical oppositions" (Parkin, 1996, pp. 79–85). A closer look at how opposition and asymmetry were connected in this case illustrates the way in which substances with nonordinary power, in this case the power to defile, can structure an entire cultural system.

If we look at the pure–impure opposition, it is evident that this opposition is only inherently marked, if and when the negative pole—the impure—is marked through a connection to defilement and disgust. Purity, as the absence of any admixture, is in itself premised on the ontologically unmarked distinction between mixed–unmixed. As long as mixing is conceptualized neutrally, mixtures such as blends, alloys, and hybrids can be perceived as positive, negative, or neutral depending on the circumstances. If and when impurity is conceived as a blending of two oppositions—mixed–unmixed and defiled–undefiled—then impurity is marked because defilement is marked.

Defilement is an intriguing concept that is notoriously resistant to definition. Philosopher Paul Ricoeur (1967) characterized it phenomenologically as "a quasi-material something that infects as a sort of filth, that harms by invisible properties, and that nevertheless works *in the manner of a force in the field of our undividedly psychic and corporeal existence*" (pp. 25–26, italics added). Phenomenologically, defilement feels like a nonordinary power, which due to the close ties between defilement and disgust, generates a distinction between purity and impurity. The feeling of disgust, is an evolved food-related emotion that psychologists Rozin and Fallon (1987) define as revulsion toward the incorporation of offensive objects. They suggest it develops in childhood in relation to feces as a "universal disgust object" and generally follows the "laws of sympathetic magic," but varies both in intensity and type between individuals and cultural groups. The close association between defilement and disgust simultaneously sets things that are considered defiled apart as salient and ascribes to them a negative value.

While the opposition between purity and impurity plays a central role in both Hinduism and Judaism and an important role in many other traditions, research on purity–impurity in psychology has been carried out primarily by psychologists interested in morality (Rozin & Fallon, 1987; Haidt, Rozin, McCauley, & Imada, 1997; Rozin, Lowery, Imada, & Haidt, 1999; Haidt, Graham, & Joseph, 2009; Graham et al., 2011), not psychologists of religion. A building block approach that focuses on basic elements and processes allows us to analyze the way the pure–impure opposition structures worlds without having to characterize purity or defilement as moral emotions, (proto)-religious or sacred concepts, or magic.

We can use this analysis of hierarchical oppositions to deepen our analysis of things set apart and at the same time identify the mechanism required to distinguish nonordinary and ordinary powers. Linguistically, setting apart is a method of separating things by splitting or dividing them. Although we can separate things into two or more parts without marking them, referring to something as "set apart" draws our attention *to* the thing set apart and *away from* a larger whole from which it is being distinguished. In simultaneously implying and obscuring the larger whole, setting apart marks the thing set apart as salient or more colloquially as nonordinary. If the boundary between the thing set apart and the remainder is then protected by prohibitions against recombining them, the distinction between them is reinforced. This suggests two important points. First, setting things apart draws attention to the thing that is set apart rather than the class of things from which it is distinguished, thus marking the thing set apart as salient. Second, salience is a necessary but not sufficient basis for establishing value. Although in the case of evolved emotions, salience and valuation may be conflated, in other cases something may be noticed (i.e., salient) consciously or nonconsciously without being ascribed positive or negative value.

These distinctions allow us to distinguish two steps involved in generating what Dumont referred to as hierarchical oppositions (Dumont, 1966/1970). First, people must single out something (e.g., something perceived as disgusting), setting it apart from other things in its class and marking it as nonordinary. In doing so, people generate a distinction between ordinary–nonordinary, in which the nonordinary is marked in this case as both salient and negative. To generate what Dumont referred to as a hierarchical opposition, we have to take the further step of nesting a second opposition within one side of the first marked opposition. Thus, we can nest the opposition between pure–impure within the nonordinary portion of the ordinary–nonordinary opposition generated by the feeling of disgust to create a hierarchical opposition. Because the structure of a hierarchical opposition is parallel to Durkheim's doubly dichotomized conception of the sacred, many of Dumont's followers read Durkheim's concept of the sacred as exemplifying what Dumont meant by a hierarchical opposition (Parkin, 2003, pp. 70, 138–142).

In Dumont's conception, oppositions are subordinated to an ultimate value (or values) that informs the whole. This not only combines opposition and valuation, but places the emphasis on the latter. In the hierarchical opposition created by the marked opposition between purity and impurity, it is the opposition between purity and defilement that allows purity to be conceptualized as an ultimate or encompassing value rather than something inherent in purity alone. In this case, the difference in value between the two poles, which allows the pure to encompass the impure and ensures that we will value the pure over the impure, lies in the association between impurity, defilement, and disgust.

A focus on nonordinary worlds instead of nonordinary powers allows us to set up different comparisons for purposes of research. Although researchers sometimes make sharp distinctions between entering into religious and imaginary worlds based on the distinctions subjects make between them, there are obvious etic similarities. Entering into religious worlds via believed-in rituals and entering into imaginary worlds via play and other simulations (e.g., literature, drama, film, or computer) are all premised etically, if not emically, on the willing suspension of disbelief. If we set aside the question of the relationship between the imaginary and the real and (for now) the question of how subjects decide if something is real or imagined, we can consider the possibility that play has a foundational role in the generation of alternative realities or worlds, some of which people "believe in" more than others.

Two factors make this seem plausible. First, play has the structure of an alternate world. It, too, is premised on a distinction between two realms, one of which is marked as nonordinary. Though the boundaries of what counts as play are disputed, it is clear that a wide range of animal species are able to make a distinction between playing and regular, ordinary behavior. Animals signal to one another that their actions are "play" not "reality" by means of various cues, tail wagging, mock bows, and so on (Burghardt, 2005). Second, the distinction is expressed behaviorally, not linguistically. Animals do not need to "believe in" play, they just need to agree to play. The fact that many animal species learn to make this distinction suggests that this ability has deep evolutionary roots.

When we add in some more specifically human abilities, we get pretend play—that is, the ability to enter into a specially marked space in which we cocreate alternative realms and bind ourselves by agreed-upon rules specific to that space (Leslie, 1994). Some researchers speculate that pretend play is the context in which children first practice the skills that prepare them to negotiate complex cultural institutions (Rakoczy, 2008). In making up the rules that govern pretend play, young humans learn that specific rules govern particular spheres of activity and, by extension, how to play by the rules that govern particular cultural activities and institutions.[9]

If Rakoczy is right, then we can turn to developmental psychology to find out more about how children learn to distinguish fantasy from reality, pretend alternative worlds from "real," believed-in alternative worlds, and how under some circumstances pretending something is real (as–if) can lead to the belief that it really is (O'Connor & Aardema, 2005; Rosengren, Johnson, & Harris, 2000). In terms of measurable effects, we can then ask what difference the distinction between two realms (e.g., this world and another world) makes when (1) goal-directed actions are oriented toward ends valued in this realm or an alternative realm and (2) the alternative realm is considered real versus imaginary.

These questions point to an underlying issue that has been bedeviling renewed efforts to coordinate the insights of evolutionary theories of religion. Not only have most theorists been starting with definitions of religion, rather than the underlying elements and processes used to construct religion-like things, but they have been defining religion in terms of different elements—some starting with nonordinary powers and some with nonordinary worlds—and coming to very different conclusions. Thus, Atran (2002), Boyer (2001), and Kirkpatrick (2005) start with Tylorian spiritual beings (or counterintuitive agents), while Wilson (2002) starts with the Durkheimian social group. As discussions between theorists are starting to make clear (see Kirkpatrick, Chapter 6, this volume), theories of the first sort are grounded in biological theories of evolution and focus more on the survival of the individual, while Wilson's is grounded in cultural theories of evolution (or coevolution of genes and culture) and focuses more on the survival of the group. The most recent contribution to this discussion—Robert Bellah's *Religion in Human Evolution* (2011)—adopts an alternate-worlds approach to defining religion, which he derives from Durkheim as read through the work of Clifford Geertz and Alfred Schultz. He grounds the creation of alternate worlds in play, which as he indicates takes place in a "relaxed field"—offline as it were. He suggests that the capacity to go offline "may be one of our greatest capacities . . . and that religion, along with science and art, may be the result of that capacity to go offline" (Bellah, 2011, p. xx).

Bellah's work allows us to ask not only *what* is set apart but *where* it is set apart. Thus, we have considered the setting apart of nonordinary powers *within* the everyday world, the setting apart of alternative worlds *from* the everyday world, and the setting apart of nonordinary powers *within* alternative worlds. In grounding religion, defined in terms of the creation of alternative worlds, in the "relaxed field" of play, Bellah tacitly contrasts the alternate world of play with an everyday world that requires vigilance and the constant assessment of the threats and resources at hand. Evolutionary theories that focus on the detection of threats and resources, whether ordinary or nonordinary, in the everyday world highlight basic survival mechanisms, such as predator detection and attachment to caregivers, while evolutionary theories that focus on the creation and elaboration of alternate worlds highlight specifically human capacities for joint intentional action, symbolic representation, and abstract reflection. While theories of the first type generally argue that religion is a "spandrel" or by-product of evolved capacities with no particular survival benefit, research on the placebo effect suggests that the attribution of nonordinary powers to things may trigger capacities that are otherwise unavailable to people, thus providing an evolutionary advantage.

Finally, distinguishing approaches that focus on nonordinary powers in the everyday world from those that focus on the creation of alternative worlds raises the question of their relationship. Under what conditions, if any, can alternative worlds become the everyday world? When, if ever, does play become reality? The way people conceive of the relationship becomes most evident, I suggest, when matters of life and death are at stake. What people do at that point—which world they inhabit—can tell us a great deal about how they relate them. Do the powers and priorities that characterize alternative worlds recede in the face of threats in the everyday world or do people mobilize them in the everyday world to combat threats and reshape priorities? However the relationship is handled, it points to the need for processes of valuation.

Processes of Valuation

Theologians (Tillich, 1957), scholars of religion (Baird, 1971; Ferré, 1979; Rennie, 1996), and psychologists of religion (Leuba, 1912, pp. 45–52; Emmons, 1999) have all argued that religion is centrally concerned with matters of significance and value. Tillich's (1957) definition of religion in terms of "ultimate concern" is often viewed as emblematic of this approach. While scholars (Baird, 1971; Ferré, 1979) have adapted his definition for the study of religion, their efforts have been resisted within religious studies largely on the grounds of its generality (Smith, 1998, p. 281). In terms of basic elements and processes, however, we can locate claims regarding ultimate significance, meaning, and/or value within the context of more general processes of valuation.

This is not the first time we have alluded to processes of valuation. In the previous section, we analyzed the process of setting apart as a necessary but not sufficient basis for establishing value and thus as a fundamental component of larger systems of valuation. In examining the steps needed to generate a hierarchical opposition, in which oppositions are subordinated to values that govern the whole, we considered a more complex process of valuation. In this section, I suggest that religions, philosophies, ideologies, worldviews, and so on can be construed as systems of valuation. In their more highly elaborated instances, we can conceive of them as systems or frameworks for assessing, ranking, manipulating, and sometimes transcending things that matter. Whether people consider a special thing as, for example, religious, mystical, magical, superstitious, spiritual, ideological, or secular will depend in part on preexisting systems of belief and practice, the web of concepts related to specialness, and the way that people position themselves in a given context. Things that seem special may be caught up in preexisting systems of belief and practice and assessed in light of them. Relative to such systems people may decide that something is more or less special than they originally thought. Assessed in light of such a system, people may conclude that something that seemed special at first actually was not, such that the thing loses its specialness in their eyes and becomes ordinary. In other instances, a person may value the thing more highly than does the system of valuation, leading them to question or challenge the system's assessment. In such cases, individuals may position themselves in opposition to the extant system of valuation, challenging established beliefs and practices and perhaps generating new or modified ones.[10]

Within a system, the value ascribed to things can also be manipulated. In light of systemic rankings, people may attempt to subordinate their initial valuation of something (e.g., wealth, leisure, pleasure) to something deemed higher by the system (e.g., service to others, charity, compassion). Monotheistic traditions devalue "other gods" by labeling them as "idols." The biblical story of Abraham and Isaac ranks attachment to a deity over attachment to one's child. Finally, some systems culminate in a paradox that undercuts or calls on people to let go of (and in that sense transcend) that which the system itself taught them to value, as in the case of paths that wind up saying there is no path or paths that ask followers to sacrifice or abandon all that the path initially taught them to value.

Spiritualities, in so far as they partake of a PATH schema, mark routes through various systems, religious and otherwise. PATHS set apart some goals relative to other goals, thus marking them as special. They identify routes to goals, thus offering means or methods for achieving the goals. Following a path presupposes that we have chosen it as a means to a particular goal. Choosing it sets it apart from other paths, placing more value on it than the others and marking it as more or less special. Following a path, like setting things apart, presupposes someone — an actor — who chooses an option (a path) and, in choosing it, sets it apart from other options (other paths). Where systems express values through ranking and ordering them and paths chart routes through systems, choosing something not only sets it apart but also creates and enacts value.

Conceiving what we think of as religions as systems of valuation allows us to compare the ways in which various systems, whether deemed religious or not, assess, rank, and manipulate value. Considering spiritualities as PATHS allows us to compare the ways in which particular paths specify goals (and vice versa) and in so doing designate value, whether those paths are viewed as spiritual or not. Finally, and most basically, we can compare the setting apart of things as acts of choice and enactments of value, albeit not always conscious choices or enactments.

Although what we as scholars think of as religions, philosophies, and so on can be construed as more or less formalized, more or less coherent systems of valuation, they are not the only systems of valuation that people draw upon in making choices. Nor are highly elaborated, formalized, and coherent systems required for people to make choices.

Indeed, as discussions of "theological incorrectness" in the cognitive science of religion literature make evident (Barrett, 1999; Slone, 2004), the more formalized and coherent systems often stand in explicit tension with less coherent, but more pragmatic, more automatic, seemingly intuitive processes of valuation.[11]

While Durkheim, Eliade, and van der Leeuw all stress that anything can be set apart as special or singularized, this does not preclude the possibility that there are species-wide tendencies to set a few things apart as special, culturally specific tendencies with respect to others, and random or idiosyncratic variation with respect to the remainder. Indeed, researchers in the emergent field of neuroeconomics are developing a common lexicon to bridge natural and social science disciplines interested in a biologically grounded understanding of value-based decision-making. In a review of the literature in this area, Rangel, Camerer, and Montague (2008) provide a computational model of value-based decision making and discuss three different types of valuation systems, which they refer to as pavlovian, habit, and goal-directed systems.

If, as previously suggested, we consider the wide range of things that people set apart as special without limiting ourselves to those they explicitly characterize as sacred, we can consider the possibility that some processes of valuation are more deeply rooted in our evolutionary history than others and thus more automatic. We could hypothesize and test whether the level at which a behavior is rooted makes us statistically more likely to set some things apart than others (Taves, 2011, p. 305). Thus, for example, people might set apart their own infants, dangerous substances, and anomalous objects through mechanisms of attachment, disgust, or attention that are deeply rooted in our evolutionary history. If this is the case, then so far as religions and others systems of valuation attempt to subordinate deeply rooted valuations to what they posit as higher goals, we would expect that such systems would devalue the more deeply rooted valuations with terms such as "idolatrous," "superstitious," "illusory," or "unreal."

FURTHER RESEARCH

Focusing on the way people identify and engage nonordinary powers, create and enter into alternate worlds, and orient themselves in relation to what they think matters most does not allow us to clearly delimit the sacred, the religious, or the spiritual. Nonetheless, finding more generic ways to characterize the processes and elements that people mix and match to create sacralities does allow us to do two things: (1) to set up comparisons between particular processes and/or elements across historical, cultural, and intellectual divides based on specific points of analogy that we identify as researchers, regardless of how people characterize and evaluate them and (2) consider how people embed and mobilize these processes and elements within different cultural contexts and the meaning and value they attribute to them in those contexts. These are questions that both psychologists of religion and religious studies scholars can explore using their own distinctive methods.

The focus on basic processes and elements has allowed us to make a number of comparisons that cut across subspecialties and disciplines and has raised a number of questions for further research that can be addressed by both psychologists and scholars of religion.

1. *Setting things apart.* While acknowledging that anything can be set apart or singularized, we need to use cross-species and cross-cultural comparisons to investigate whether people are more likely to set some things apart than others. We also need to further integrate setting things apart with potentially related research on topics such as salience and the minimal group effect. In the latter case, for example, Tajfel, Billig, Bundy, and Flament's (1971) finding that subjects valorize groups to which they know they have been randomly assigned in an experimental context suggests a tendency to view "my group," however constituted, as special.

2. *Nonordinary powers.* We need to integrate the research on the naturalness of popular religiosity, magic, and superstition within a common framework (Lindeman & Swedholm, 2012). In so far as the powers associated with persons and other animates differ from those associated with objects, places, and artifacts, doing so will require a clearer understanding of how the capacities associated with folk biological "kinds" (persons, animates, objects, artifacts) interconnect developmentally with children's understanding of different types of power. We need not only a developmentally grounded theory of mind but also a developmentally grounded "theory of powers." We also need to integrate research on placebo effects with research on the effects of practices variously deemed religious, magical, and/or superstitious. In so doing, we arrive at a more comprehensive understanding of how words and rituals, symbols and meanings, influence neural processes and in some cases, under some circumstances, produce measurable behavioral effects.

3. *Nonordinary worlds.* We need to know more about how children learn to distinguish reality from fantasy—in particular, how they learn to distinguish "pretend" alternative worlds from "real" believed-in alternative worlds—and how these distinctions play out in cultural distinctions between, for example, the arts, sports, and religion. We need to know more about the interactions between everyday and alternative worlds under different kinds of conditions, including those that threaten life (e.g., war, conquest, disease, and famine) and those that may threaten cultures (e.g., contact, competition, and exchange).

4. *Processes of valuation.* Building on the research on "theological incorrectness," as well as research in disciplines such as neuroeconomics, we need to explore how, if at all, and under what conditions people use the more elaborated systems of valuation to prioritize alternative worlds and shape behavior in the world they view as everyday. At what point do people decide to break with such systems, either intentionally or in practice, and what happens if and when they do so?

It has also become evident that these basic processes and elements build upon one another. In considering the setting apart of nonordinary powers within the everyday world, the setting apart of alternative worlds from the everyday world, and the setting apart of nonordinary powers within nonordinary worlds, we have seen how people can use the process of setting things apart to construct increasingly complex formations and generate more formalized processes of valuation through systematic reflection on the whole. Moreover, people bring elements of these complex alternate worlds into relationship with the everyday world, in some cases privileging the alternate world over the everyday to the point where it becomes the everyday world. Investigating how individuals and groups assemble the basic elements and processes discussed here into larger complexes is a crucial task, albeit beyond the scope of this essay. For those who are interested, the following Coda provides a brief thought experiment to help readers envision how people can use these basic elements and processes to generate religions and spiritualities.

Coda: Generating Models from the Basic Building Blocks

We can extend the building-block metaphor quite literally to imagine a set of "kits" that designers could use to construct religions and other things. We could start two basic kits: a Powers Kit and an Alternative Worlds Kit. The Powers Kit would supply designers with methods for creating or discovering powers they can set apart and assign to various things (objects, people, places, abstractions) and then involve in experiences and events of their choosing. The Alternative Worlds Kit would allow designers to generate alternative realms or worlds, mark boundaries and control movement between the realms, and provide the realms with internal organization and structure. The two kits could be used separately or combined to create different effects.

While means of interacting with powers and moving between realms would emerge in conjunction with the two basic kits, a supplementary "Paths Kit" would allow designers to create formal routes, including "alternate," "higher," or "esoteric" paths. Designers could also use a more advanced "Codification Kit" to systematize the rules, procedures, and paths developed using the other kits. There is no "Values Kit," because values emerge in the process of setting apart powers, generating nonordinary realms, and constructing paths. Systematizing a design makes the valuation process more explicit. Values would become most apparent, however, if we added a "Meta Kit" that asked designers to compare what they have created from various standpoints and discuss whether what they have created could be captured under one rubric and, if not, what should be excluded and why.

ACKNOWLEDGMENTS

I thank Ralph Hood, Jared Lindahl, Bryan Rennie, and Ted Slingerland for their comments on the first draft and the members of the Southern California Working Group in Cognition, Culture, and Religion—especially Justin Barrett, Pete Hill, and Rebekah Richert—for precipitating a thoroughgoing revision more closely attuned to the target audience. Above all, I thank my husband (and editor), not only for reading every draft numerous times, but also for many more discussions of the content than a chapter author had any right to expect!

NOTES

1. Cognitive linguists use SMALL CAPS to denote image schemas and basic (or conceptual) metaphors. The analysis in this section is premised on the idea that comparisons grounded in image schemas and basic metaphors that emerge through the interaction of our bodies with the physical environment provide a promising basis for setting up comparisons across times and cultures (Slingerland, 2004).
2. Just as Durkheim's excision of magic (as noncongregational) reflected his interest in social explanations, so Pargament's excision of the demonic may reflect his interest in positive measurable effects. Both elisions seem arbitrary, however.

3. In saying this, I am not assuming that the underlying mechanisms are the same—they clearly are not—but rather that the observable behavior is similar.

4. In adopting a "two worlds" definition of the sacred, Durkheim (1912/1995) discounted spiritual beings (because, he argued, animism was not the most elementary form of religion [pp. 45–67]), magic (because he viewed magicians as having clients rather than generating a "moral community" [p. 42]), and individualistic forms of religiosity (because he did not view them as distinct and autonomous systems [p. 43]).

5. Minimally, what is added can be characterized in terms of the additional layers of meaning that Bellah (2011, p. 8) and others attribute to symbols, such that "even in the midst of daily life . . . something ordinary becomes extraordinary." In the context of Weber's action-oriented sociology, this added dimension also *affords* something beyond the ordinary in a behavioral sense. For an attempt to specify this in terms of an ecological psychology of affordances, see Taves (in press). Chris Morales (2012) characterized "extraordinary affordances [as] . . . affordances a thing has which are beyond what the thing can afford on the basis of its physical properties." Such affordances, he argues, do "metaphysical work" that is highly observer dependent but not bound by physical constraints.

6. Gelman's (2003, pp. 296–325) discussion of unresolved issues surrounding the human tendency to essentialize gets at a parallel issue. She notes (pp. 306–307) the difficulties surrounding the "folk biological" understanding of essences (which informs the "animist" view of religion) in so far as the "properties [that essences share] are [also] shared by a set of other phenomena quite distinct from the realm of biology, including contamination, fetishes, and blessings" and suggests an alternate approach that she thinks would account for a wider range of phenomena.

7. This section to this point is adapted from Taves (in press).

8. If, in an effort to avoid deception, patients are told they are being given a placebo, the placebo may still work if the patient is told there is scientific evidence to suggest that placebos are effective. In this case, the patient ascribes nonordinary power to an acknowledged placebo rather than ascribing nonordinary power to what is, in fact, a "fake drug" (Kaptchuk et al., 2010).

9. This paragraph is taken from Taves (2011, pp. 306–307).

10. This paragraph and the next are adapted from Taves (2010, pp. 181–182).

11. This paragraph and a portion of the next are taken from Taves (2011, p. 292).

REFERENCES

Atran, S. (2002). *In gods we trust: The evolutionary landscape of religion.* New York: Oxford University Press.

Baird, R. D. (1971). *Category formation and the history of religions.* New York: Mouton de Gruyter.

Barrett, J. L. (1999). Theological correctness: Cognitive constraints and the study of religion. *Method and Theory in the Study of Religion, 11*(4), 325–339.

Barrett, J. L. (2004). The naturalness of religious concepts: An emerging cognitive science of religion. In P. Antes, A. W. Geertz, & R. W. Warne (Eds.), *New approaches to the study of religion* (pp. 401–418). Berlin: Walter de Gruyter.

Beedie, C. J. (2007). Placebo effects in competitive sport: Qualitative data. *Journal of Sports Science and Medicine, 6*, 21–28.

Bellah, R. (2011). *Religion in human evolution.* Cambridge, MA: Harvard University Press.

Benedetti, F. (2008). *Placebo effects: Understanding the mechanisms in health and disease.* New York: Oxford University Press.

Benedetti, F., Carlino, E., & Pollo, A. (2011). How placebos change the patient's brain. *Neuropsychopharmacology, 36*(1), 339–354.

Bloom, P. (2010). *How pleasure works: The new science of why we like what we like.* New York: Norton.

Boyer, P. (2001). *Religion explained: The evolutionary origins of religious thought.* New York: Basic Books.

Brown, R. F. (1981). Eliade on archaic religions: Some old and new criticisms. *Sciences Religieuses, 10*(4), 429–449.

Burghardt, G. M. (2005). *The genesis of animal play.* Cambridge, MA: MIT Press.

Burnside, C. (1991). The left hand of the sacred. *Method and Theory in the Study of Religion, 3,* 3–9.

Burris, J. P. (2005). Comparative-historical method [Further considerations]. In L. Jones (Ed.), *Encyclopedia of religion* (2nd ed., pp. 1871–1873). Detroit: Thomson Gale.

Buswell, R. E., & Gimello, R. M. (1992). *Paths to liberation: The marga and its transformations in Buddhist thought.* Honolulu: University of Hawaii Press.

Damisch, L., Stoberock, B., & Mussweiler, T. (2010). Keep your fingers crossed!: How superstition improves performance. *Psychological Science, 21*(7), 1014–1020.

Dissanayake, E. (1990). *What is art for?* Seattle: University of Washington Press.

Dissanayake, E. (2008). The arts after Darwin: Does art have an origin and adaptive function? In K. Zijlmans & W. Damme (Eds.), *World art studies: Exploring concepts and approaches* (pp. 241–264). Amsterdam, The Netherlands: Valiz.

Dumont, L. (1970). *Homo hierarchicus: An essay on the caste system.* Chicago: University of Chicago Press. (Original work published 1966)

Durkheim, E. (1995). *Elementary forms of the religious life* (K. Fields, trans.). New York: Free Press. (Original work published 1912)

Eliade, M. (1987). *The sacred and the profane.* San Diego: Harcourt. (Original work published 1957)

Emmons, R. A. (1999). *The psychology of ultimate concerns.* New York: Oxford University Press.

Ferré, F. (1970). The definition of religion. *Journal of the American Academy of Religion, 38*(1), 3–16.

Gelman, S. A. (2003). *The essential child: Origins of essentialism in everyday thought.* New York: Oxford University Press.

Graham, J., & Haidt, J. (2012). Sacred values and evil adversaries: A moral foundations approach. In M. Mikulincer & P. R. Shaver (Eds.), *The social psychology of morality: Exploring the causes of good and evil* (pp. 11–31). Washington, DC: American Psychological Association.

Graham, J., Nosek, B. A., Haidt, J., Iyer, R., Koleva, S., & Ditto, P. H. (2011). Mapping the moral domain. *Journal of Personality and Social Psychology, 101*(2), 366–385.

Haidt, J., Graham, J., & Joseph, C. (2009). Above and below left–right: Ideological narratives and moral foundations. *Psychological Inquiry, 20,* 110–119.

Haidt, J., Rozin, P., McCauley, C., & Imada, S. (1997). Body, psyche, and culture: The relationship between disgust and morality. *Psychology & Developing Societies, 9*(1), 107–131.

Hertz, R. (1973). The pre-eminence of the right hand. In R. Needham (Ed.), *Right and left: Essays on dual symbolic classification* (pp. 3–31). Chicago: University of Chicago. (Original work published 1909)

Hill, P. C., Pargament, K. I., Hood, R. W., McCullough, M. E., Jr., Swyers, J. P., Larson, D. B., et al. (2000). Conceptualizing religion and spirituality: Points of commonality, points of departure. *Journal for the Theory of Social Behaviour, 30*(1), 51–77.

Hood, B. M. (2008). *Supersense: Why we believe the unbelievable.* San Francisco: HarperOne.

Idinopulos, T. A., & Yonan, E. A. (Eds.). (1996). *The sacred and its scholars.* Leiden, The Netherlands: Brill.

James, W. (1985). *The varieties of religious experience.* Cambridge, MA: Harvard University Press. (Original work published 1902)

Johnson, M. (1987). *The body in the mind.* Chicago: University of Chicago Press.

Johnson, M. (2007). *The meaning of the body.* Chicago: University of Chicago Press.

Kaptchuk, T. J. (2011). Placebo studies and ritual theory: A comparative analysis of Navajo, acupuncture and biomedical healing. *Philosophical Transactions of the Royal Society of London. Series B. Biological Sciences, 366*, 1849–1858.

Kaptchuk, T. J., Friedlander, E., Kelley, J. M., Sanchez, M. N., Kokkotou, E., Singer, J. P., et al. (2010). Placebos without deception: A randomized controlled trial in irritable bowel syndrome. *PLoS ONE 5*(12), e15591.

Kaptchuk, T. J., Kerr, C. E., & Zanger, A. (2009). Placebo controls, exorcisms, and the devil. *Lancet, 374*(9697), 1234–1235.

Kirkpatrick, L. A. (2005). *Attachment, evolution, and the psychology of religion.* New York: Guilford Press.

Knott, K. (2005). *The location of religion.* London: Equinox Press.

Knott, K. (2006). The case of the left hand: The location of religion in an everyday text. In E. Arweck & P. J. Collins (Eds.), *Reading religion in text and context* (pp. 169–184). Burlington, VT: Ashgate.

Kohls, N., Sauer, S., Offenbächer, M., & Giordano, J. (2011). Spirituality: An overlooked predictor of placebo effects? *Philosophical Transactions of the Royal Society of London, B. Biological Sciences, 366*, 1838–1848.

Kopytoff, I. (1986). The cultural biography of things: Commoditization as process. In A. Appadurai (Ed.), *The social life of things* (pp. 64–91). Cambridge, UK: Cambridge University Press.

Lakoff, G., & Johnson, M. (1999). *Philosophy in the flesh.* New York: Basic Books.

Lakoff, G., & Johnson, M. (2003). *Metaphors we live by.* Chicago: University of Chicago. (Original work published 1980)

Leslie, A. M. (1994). Pretending and believing: Issues in the theory of ToMM. *Cognition, 50*, 211–238.

Leuba, J. (1912). *A psychological study of religion.* New York: Macmillan.

Lindahl, J. (2011, November). *Grounding the comparative study of contemplative paths in experimental cognitive science.* Paper presented at the annual meeting of the American Academy of Religion, San Francisco.

Lindeman, M., & Swedholm, A. M. (2012). What's in a term?: Paranormal, superstitious, magical and supernatural beliefs by any other name would mean the same. *Review of General Psychology, 16*(3), 241–255.

Marett, R. R. (1914). *The threshold of religion* (3rd ed.). London: Methuen.

Mauss, M. (1972). *A general theory of magic.* New York: Norton. (Original work published 1904)

McCauley, R. N. (2011). *Why religion is natural and science is not.* New York: Oxford University Press.

McCauley, R. N., & Lawson, E. T. (2002). *Bringing ritual to mind: Psychological foundations of cultural forms.* Cambridge: Cambridge University Press.

Meissner, K. (2011). The placebo effect and the autonomic nervous system: Evidence for an intimate relationship. *Philosophical Transactions of the Royal Society of London: B. Biological Sciences, 366*, 1808–1817.

Moerman, D. E., & Jonas, W. B. (2002). Deconstructing the placebo effect and finding the meaning response. *Annals of Internal Medicine, 136*(6), 471–476.

Morales, C. (2012, November 12). *Encountering the sacred: Religious tools and worlds.* Paper presented at the annual meeting of the Society for the Scientific Study of Religion, Phoenix.

Oakley, T. (2010). Image schemas. In D. Geeraerts & H. Cuyckens (Eds.), *The Oxford handbook of cognitive linguistics* (pp. 214–235). New York: Oxford University Press.

O'Connor, K. P., & Aardema, F. (2005). The imagination: Cognitive, pre-cognitive, and meta-cognitive aspects. *Consciousness and Cognition, 14*, 233–256.

Otto, R. (1976). *The idea of the holy.* New York: Oxford University Press. (Original work published 1923)

Pargament, K. I. (1997). *The psychology of religion and coping.* New York: Guilford Press.

Pargament, K. I. (1999a). The psychology of religion and spirituality?: Yes and no. *The International Journal of the Psychology of Religion, 9*(1), 3–16.

Pargament, K I. (1999b). The psychology of religion and spirituality?: Response to Stifoss-Hanssen, Emmons, and Crumpler. *The International Journal for the Psychology of Religion, 9*(1), 35–43.

Pargament, K. I., Magyar-Russell, G. M., & Murray-Swank, N. A. (2005). The sacred and the search for significance: Religion as a unique process. *Journal of Social Issues, 61*(4), 665–687.

Pargament, K. I., & Mahoney, A. (2005). Sacred matters: Sanctification as a vital topic for the psychology of religion. *The International Journal for the Psychology of Religion, 15*(3), 179–198.

Parkin, R. (1996). *The dark side of humanity: The work of Robert Hertz and its legacy.* Amsterdam, The Netherlands: OPA.

Parkin, R. (2003). *Louis Dumont and hierarchical opposition.* New York: Berghahn.

Pickering, W. S. F. (1984). *Durkheim's sociology of religion.* London: Routledge & Kegan Paul.

Pollo, A., Carlino, E., & Benedetti, F. (2011). Placebo mechanisms across different conditions: From the clinical setting to physical performance. *Philosophical Transactions of the Royal Society of London: Series B. Biological Sciences, 366*(1572), 1790–1798.

Price, D. D., Finniss, D. G., & Benedetti, F. (2008). A comprehensive review of the placebo effect: Recent advances and current thought. *Annual Review of Psychology, 59*, 569–590.

Pyysiäinen, I. (2009). *Supernatural agents: Why we believe in souls, gods, and buddhas.* New York: Oxford University Press.

Rakoczy, H. (2008). Pretense as individual and collective intentionality. *Mind and Language, 23*(5), 499–517.

Rangel, A., Camerer, C., & Montague, P. R. (2008). A framework for studying the neurobiology of value-based decision making. *Nature Reviews. Neuroscience, 9*(7), 545–556.

Rennie, B. (1996). *Reconstructing Eliade: Making sense of religion.* New York: State University of New York Press.

Ricoeur, P. (1967). *The symbolism of evil.* New York: Harper & Row.

Riesebrodt, M. (2009). *The promise of salvation: A theory of religion* (S. Rendall, trans.). Chicago: University of Chicago Press.

Rosengren, K. S., Johnson, C. N., & Harris, P. L. (Eds.). (2000). *Imagining the impossible: Magical, scientific, and religious thinking in children.* New York: Cambridge University Press.

Rozin, P., & Fallon, A. E. (1987). A perspective on disgust. *Psychological Review, 94*(1), 23.

Rozin, P., Lowery, L., Imada, S., & Haidt, J. (1999). The CAD triad hypothesis: A mapping between three moral emotions (contempt, anger, disgust) and three moral codes (community, autonomy, divinity). *Journal of Personality and Social Psychology, 76*, 574–586.

Saroglou, V., & Cohen, A. B. (Eds.). (2011). Religion and culture: Perspectives from cross-cultural psychology [Special issue]. *Journal of Cross-Cultural Psychology, 42*(8).

Slingerland, E. (2004). Conceptual metaphor theory as methodology for comparative religion. *Journal of the American Academy of Religion, 72*(1), 1–31.

Slingerland, E. (2008). *What science offers the humanities.* Cambridge, UK: Cambridge University Press.

Slone, D. J. (2004). *Theological incorrectness: Why religious people believe what they shouldn't.* New York: Oxford University Press.

Smith, J. Z. (1998). Religion, religions, religious. In M. C. Taylor (Ed.), *Critical terms for religious studies* (pp. 269–284). Chicago: University of Chicago Press.

Sorensen, J. (2007). *A cognitive theory of magic.* London: Equinox.

Spiro, M. E. (1966). Religion: Problems of definition and explanation. In M. Banton (Ed.), *Anthropological approaches to the study of religion* (pp. 85–126). London: Tavistock.

Subbotsky, E. (2010). *Magic and the mind: Mechanisms, functions, and development of magical thinking and behavior.* New York: Oxford University Press.

Tajfel, H., Billig, M. G., Bundy, R. P., & Flament, C. (1971). Social categorization and intergroup behavior. *European Journal of Social Psychology, 1,* 149–178.

Taves, A. (2009). *Religious experience reconsidered: A building-block approach to the study of religion and other special things.* Princeton, NJ: Princeton University Press.

Taves, A. (2010). No field is an island: Fostering collaboration between the academic study of religion and the sciences. *Method and Theory in the Study of Religion, 22*(2–3), 177–188.

Taves, A. (2011). 2010 Presidential address: "Religion" in the humanities and the humanities in the university. *Journal of the American Academy of Religion, 79*(2), 287–314.

Taves, A. (in press). Non-ordinary powers: Charisma, special affordances and the study of religion. In D. Xygalatas & L. McCorkle (Eds.), *Mental culture: Towards a cognitive science of religion.* London: Equinox.

Thompson, J. J., Ritenbaugh, C., & Nichter, M. (2009). Reconsidering the placebo response from a broad anthropological perspective. *Culture, Medicine and Psychiatry, 33*(1), 112–152.

Tillich, P. (1957). *The dynamics of faith.* New York: Harper.

Turner, S. (2003). Charisma reconsidered. *Journal of Classical Sociology, 3,* 5–26.

Tylor, E. B. (1970). *Religion in primitive culture.* Gloucester, MA: P. Smith. (Original work published 1873)

Van der Leeuw, G. (1986). *Religion in essence and manifestation.* Princeton: Princeton University Press. (Original work published 1937)

Weber, M. (1978). *Economy and society.* Berkeley: University of California. (Original work published 1922)

Whitehouse, H. (2004). *Modes of religiosity: A cognitive theory of religious transmission.* Walnut Creek, CA: Altamira Press.

Wilson, D. S. (2002). *Darwin's cathedral: Evolution, religion, and the nature of society.* Chicago: University of Chicago Press.

Zinnbauer, B. J., & Pargament, K. I. (2005). Religiousness and spirituality. In R. F. Paloutzian & C. L. Park (Eds.), *Handbook of psychology of religion and spirituality* (pp. 21–42). New York: Guilford Press.

Part II

RELIGION THROUGH THE DEVELOPMENTAL LENS

8

Religious and Spiritual Development in Childhood

Rebekah A. Richert and Pehr Granqvist

As Boyatzis (2005) noted in this *Handbook*'s previous edition, there has been a surge of research in the past decade into religious and spiritual development. Although peer-review articles containing the key words "children" and "religion" in PsycINFO represent only 0.3% of all articles with the key word "children," there has been an almost 30% increase in the number of articles since 2005, when the previous edition of this book was published. The goal of this chapter is to provide an overview of research to date into the social, relational, and cognitive factors related to religious and spiritual development in childhood. We do not address the period of adolescence, as that period in development is outlined in the next chapter (see Levenson, Aldwin, & Igarashi, Chapter 9, this volume), and we focus on research conducted since the last publication of this *Handbook*. Moreover, although experiences encountered in infancy and toddlerhood are likely important for subsequent religious and spiritual development, we largely reserve our review to studies conducted on children who have reached the ages associated with symbolic and mentalizing capacities. In our view, such capacities may be a prerequisite for children's developing understanding of religious and spiritual concepts. Thus, the research we review is primarily with children from the preschool years through middle childhood.

We begin the chapter by defining the primary constructs of *religious, spiritual,* and *development* as they are used within the body of research we review. We then review cognitive research on children's understanding and elaboration of central religious concepts, such as God, origins, the soul, and the afterlife. We then present research on the development of religious relationships, drawing largely on studies informed by attachment theory. We end the chapter by suggesting future directions for research and theory development.

DEFINING THE CONSTRUCTS

What Is "Religious" and "Spiritual"?

There has been much debate regarding proper definitions of the terms "religious" and "spiritual" (see Oman, Chapter 2, this volume). In this chapter, we rely primarily on the definitions of *religious* and *spiritual* provided in the previous edition. "*Religious development* may be defined as the child's growth within an organized community that has shared narratives, practices, teachings, rituals, and symbols" (Boyatzis, 2005, p. 125), the purposes of which are to bring people closer to what they deem to be sacred. "*Spirituality* has been defined as the search for and relationship with whatever one takes to be a holy or sacred transcendent entity" (Boyatzis, 2005, p. 125). Thus, *spiritual development* represents the unfolding of that search process and relationship. Within the research we review in this chapter, most researchers describe their area of study as religious development.

What Is "Development"?

A common misconception about the study of development is that the purpose of developmental research is to examine the factors that lead to some kind of steady increase in an ability over time with the goal of achieving some idealized outcome by the end of childhood (Schaffer, 2006). However, as Schaffer noted, "The core of development is change over age—a change that is not haphazard, not temporary and not easily reversible" (p. 5). Thus, in this chapter on religious and spiritual development, we do not start with the assumption that religiousness and spirituality in childhood is merely an immature form of religiousness and spirituality in adulthood. The developmental process itself is a meaningful research pursuit.

RELIGIOUS CONCEPTS

As Boyatzis (2005) noted, early cognitive-developmental approaches (e.g., Elkind, 1970; Goldman, 1964) were based on Piagetian assumptions of the stage-like nature of cognitive development. By the early 2000s, much of the research in cognitive developmental approaches to religious development was specifically focused on the relationship between developing social cognition (e.g., theory of mind) and understanding religious concepts. This shift in focus was largely driven by hypotheses about the fundamental nature of social cognition to the representation of supernatural agents (e.g., Barrett, 2004; Boyer & Walker, 2000).

Much of the current research into the development of religious concepts has shifted to a different, but related, focus, namely to address the debate surrounding whether religious concepts have persisted as a by-product of the evolution of human cognition or as an adaptation in and of themselves (e.g., Atran, 2002; Bering, 2006; Boyer, 2001; Granqvist, 2006; Kirkpatrick, 2004; Richert & Smith, 2010; see review in Kirkpatrick, Chapter 6, this volume). This question is particularly relevant to a cognitive approach, given the existing framework for research into the development of folk theories and concepts (see Barrett, Chapter 12, this volume). One hypothesis has been that because of certain cognitive propensities with which we are born, the human mind may be cognitively "prepared" to receive religious concepts (Barrett & Richert, 2003). There have been criticisms of this hypothesis, particularly because it was originally framed as an alternative to an anthropomorphic account of the development of God concepts (e.g., Lane, Wellman, & Evans, 2010). In addition, this hypothesis has fallen victim to problems of semantics, with words like "innate," "intuitive," "cognitively optimal," "cognitive predispositions," "natural," and most recently, "maturationally natural," all operating for different theorists as essentially interchangeable synonyms. From a cognitive development perspective, these terms overlap conceptually with Vygotsky's (1986) description of the relationship between spontaneous and scientific concepts. This issue is revisited in the Future Directions section.

God

Research into developing concepts of God has primarily focused on using traditional tests of children's developing theory of mind. Within the theory of mind framework, researchers are interested in how children learn that human minds are fallible, that one person's perspective is different from another's, and that people have different knowledge about the world (Flavell, 2004). Children tend to come to this understanding between the ages of 4 and 5 (Wellman, Cross, & Watson, 2001), a finding that has been replicated in China (Sabbagh, Xu, Carlson, Moses, & Lee, 2006), as well as Canada, India, Peru, Samoa, and Thailand (Callaghan et al., 2005). In considering religious concepts specifically, researchers have examined what happens to children's concepts of God's knowledge, perspectives, and beliefs when childen are beginning to understand the limitations of the human mind. Using these methods, researchers have found that about the age children begin to associate limited beliefs, perspectives, and knowledge to humans, they do not attribute those same limitations to God (Barrett, Richert, & Dreisenga, 2001; Barrett, Newman, & Richert, 2003; Richert & Barrett, 2005). These findings have been replicated cross-culturally with Mayan children (Knight, Sousa, Barrett, & Atran, 2004), but should be viewed in the context of potentially conflicting findings.

Makris and Pnevmatikos (2007) found that 3- and 4-year-olds indicated that both humans and God would have ignorance about the contents of a box. In addition, Lane et al. (2010) found that 4½-year-olds attributed false beliefs to God but not to a superhero. Giménez Dasí, Guerrero, and Harris (2005) found that it was not until age 5 that children differentiated between the mortality and ignorance of a friend and the immortality and omniscience of God. Five-year-olds are also more likely than adults to attribute human-like psychological, physical, and biological properties to both fantasy characters and religious beings (Shtulman, 2008).

Origins

One area of religious belief that has received increasing attention is in children's undersanding of the origin of species and the world as it relates to children's belief in creation of evolution. When interviewed about the origins of a variety of natural things (i.e., plants, animals, the earth, the sky, large rocks), preschoolers are about seven times more likely to attribute reseponsibiity to God than to people (Petrovich, 1997). In addition, although

5- to 7-year-olds demonstrate mixed preference for creationist or spontaneous generationist (e.g., it just appeared) origin accounts, 8- to 10-year-olds tend to prefer creation as an explanation for the origins of species and the earth than evolution or spontaneous generationist explanations (Evans, 2000), even if the children attend a secular school that endorses an evolutionary explanation (Evans, 2001). Recent research with Chinese school children, however, has suggested this tendency toward creationist accounts of origins is not universal. In fact, regardless of age, 6- to 14-year-olds in China overwhelmingly endorsed evolutionary explanations for the origins of humans and animals (Smith & Richert, 2011).

It has been proposed that a reason children prefer creationist explanations for origins is because of two cognitive frameworks within which children (and many adults) reason about the world: teleological reasoning and essentialism. In a number of research studies, American and British children have preferred teleological explanations for biological properties (Kelemen, 1999, 2004). In these studies, children are presented with explanations for why a particular natural or biological property exists (e.g., rocks are pointy). In the teleological explanations, children are told the property exists for a particular purpose (e.g., rocks are pointy so animals can scratch their backs on them). In the nonteleological explanations, children are told that the property exists as the result of natural physical processes (e.g., rocks are pointy because bits of stuff have piled up over a long period of time). As young as 4 years, children demonstrated a preference for the teleological explanations, and this preference persists until approximately age 10. Interestingly, even adults will revert to teleological explanations of these kinds in conditions of cognitive load (Kelemen & Rossett, 2009).

A second explanation for the preference for a creationist explanation for origins is the tendency to essentialize categories and members of categories. For example, 4- to 9-year-olds have been found to deny within-species variation (Shtulman & Schulz, 2008), and such denial has been correlated with a poorer understanding of natural selection in adults (Shtulman, 2006). Relatedly, in a study conducted in Israel, both secular and orthodox Jewish 7- to 11-year-olds were asked to indicate the stability of category membership and the shared internal features of animals in the same category (Diesendruck & Haber, 2009). In this case, children's essentializing of social categories was related to the belief that God created those categories.

The Soul and the Afterlife

It is important to consider children's afterlife beliefs in the context of their understanding of death. In recent research, 4-year-olds claim that a person who is dead, but not a person who is asleep, no longer has agency (Barrett & Behne, 2005); and 4- to 9-year-olds understand that once something is dead, it cannot come alive again (Poling & Evans, 2004). Children also tend to attribute certain psychological states (e.g., emotions, desires, knowledge) as continuing after we die (Bering & Bjorklund, 2004; Bering, Blasi, & Bjorklund, 2005; Harris & Giménez, 2005).

However, the attribution of continued functioning is related to the context in which children are thinking about death. In a related study, 5- to 12-year-old children attending Catholic and secular schools were interviewed about whether a mouse would be able to continue functioning in various domains after being eaten by an alligator (Bering et al., 2005). Older children were more likely to claim processes ceased functioning after death. However, children in the Catholic school were more likely than children in the secular school to claim that processes, especially mental processes, continued after death. In research conducted with children in Madagascar, 5- to 7-year-olds claimed that most processes, including psychological processes, ceased at death. When these children did claim something continued after death, they were also most likely to attribute continued mental processes, but only within the context of a religious narrative (Astuti & Harris, 2008). Given these findings, researchers have argued that by age 11, children hold two conceptions of death in mind: one scientific and one religious (Harris & Gimémez, 2005). This issue is addressed further in the Future Directions section.

Related to developing a concept of the afterlife, children are developing a concept of the soul (Richert & Harris, 2006). In research examining how children think about the soul and whether children differentiate the soul from the mind and body, 6- to 12-year-olds claimed the soul has spiritual (but not cognitive or physical) functions and remains stable over a person's life. In attributing spiritual finctions, children claimed that the soul, and not the mind, was the aspect of a person that connected them to God and that went to heaven when they died. In addition, children as young as 4 years of age claimed that a religious ritual changes a person's soul but not mind or brain, a tendency also demonstrated in children as old as 12 (Richert & Harris, 2006).

Religious Rituals

To our knowledge, only one study has examined how children in early childhood view religious rituals. Richert (2006) interviewed 4- to 12-year-old Protestant American children about whether both familiar and unfamiliar rituals would remain effective if the person performing the rituals performed incorrect actions. By the age of 6, children claimed that it would be wrong to change the actions of a familiar ritual; however, 4- to 6-year-olds were more likely than older children to claim that the ritual would no longer be effective if mistakes were made during the ritual. Additionally, 4- to 6-year-olds were more likely to view the ritual acts as functional, whereas 7- to 12-year-olds were more likely to view ritual acts as symbolic (Richert, 2006).

RELIGIOUS RELATIONSHIPS: ATTACHMENT

Research into the development of perceived relationships with religious beings has focused on the ways in which these relationships reflect attachment processes. This research has nearly exclusively focused on developing relationships with God rather than other religious or spiritual entities. As reviewed in more detail later, research along these lines suggests that religious and spiritual relationships capitalize on the attachment system and that relationships with God may often be viewed as symbolic attachment relationships (Granqvist & Kirkpatrick, 2008, 2013). Before proceeding to a discussion of the research directly related to religious relationships, we provide a brief review of and introduction to attachment theory.

Attachment is defined as "a strong disposition on the part of offspring in many mammalian species to seek proximity to and contact with a specific figure (i.e., to display attachment behaviors), and to do so particularly in certain situations such as when he or she is frightened, ill, or tired" (Granqvist & Kirkpatrick, 2013, following Bowlby, 1969/1982). At the time of its inception, attachment theory represented a departure from traditional models of child development focused on the secondary drive hypothesis, which argued that all children's inborn, primary drives are physiological in nature (Schaffer, 2006). According to this hypothesis, the association between the mother (e.g., her breast) and physiological drive fulfillment provides the explanation for why children come to develop selective attachments to their mothers. In contrast to this position, Bowlby (1969/1982) argued that infants are equally powerfully motivated at birth to start to form a bond with their caregivers as to obtain nourishment. According to Bowlby (1969/1982), throughout mammalian evolution, such a bond has offered protection and enhanced the chances of offspring survival to reproductive age. In this sense, attachment behaviors have been naturally selected as a part of human (and mammalian) evolution.

It is important to the study of religious relationships to understand the role that different patterns of attachment play in the development of other relationships than the child–caregiver bond itself. Dyadic differences in attachment relationships, identifiable from late infancy onward, have been classified into four basic categories: secure, avoidant, resistant, and disorganized (Ainsworth, Blehar, Waters, & Wall, 1978; Main & Solomon, 1990). Based on repeated experiences from interacting with their caregivers (or "attachment figures"), children develop internal working models, defined as "a hypothetical internal structure whereby the child mentally represents the attachment relationship and the partners involved in it, self as well as other" (Schaffer, 2006, p. 164). According to this model, and presuming stability in important contextual factors (e.g., caregiver sensitivity to the child's needs and signals), early attachment relationships are internalized as attachment models, which become increasingly generalizing with maturation and come to guide the individual's expectations, interpretations, and behavioral inclinations in future relationships.

Most of the research on the connections between attachment and relationships with God has been conducted with adults (for recent reviews, see Granqvist & Kirkpatrick, 2008, 2013; Granqvist, Mikulincer, & Shaver, 2010). Here we review attachment-related research conducted with children, starting with normative apsects of attachment, followed by considerations of individual differences in attachment security.

Attachment Normative Considerations on the Development of Religious Relationships

Although Bowlby's theorizing about attachment focused largely on the evolutionary origins of the attachment system and its manifestation in infant–mother relationships, he believed that the processes and dynamics of attachment have broad implications for social development and psychological functioning across the life span. One purpose of this section is to demonstrate that, with increased cognitive maturation, people may even start to develop symbolic attachments to unseen figures (e.g., God). We argue here that the relationship with God develops in temporal conjunction with the maturation of the attachment system and the cognitive developments associated with this maturation. We also illustrate that, already in childhood, heightened attachment activation is associated with increased significance of the individual's relationship with God (see Granqvist & Dickie, 2006, for a more detailed developmental overview).

As noted previously, the biological function of the attachment system is to maintain proximity between an infant and a protective attachment figure. To accomplish this proximity, the infant's behavioral repertoire initially consists of a series of more or less reflexive behaviors (known as relatively fixed action patterns) that are necessary to obtain proximity/protection (in addition to nourishment). With increasing cognitive abilities, older children are often satisfied by visual or verbal contact with the attachment figure or even by just knowing the attachment figure's whereabouts (Bretherton, 1987). Similar observations led early attachment theorists Sroufe and Waters (1977) to suggest that "felt security" should be viewed as the set goal of the attachment system in older individuals. Similarly, a consideration of cognitive abilities was an important part of the so-called move to the level of representation (Main, Kaplan, & Cassidy, 1985) that has been influential in attachment research for a quarter of a century. In our view, this move also opened the door to the possibility of imagined attachments to unseen others.

As attachment to caregivers increasingly moves toward goal-corrected partnerships in the preschool period, and children increasingly acquire skills at symbolic thinking (Bowlby, 1969/1982; Piaget, 1952/1963), they typically tolerate longer separations, presumably because of an ability to represent their attachment figures symbolically. Already at this age, children develop a rudimentary concept of God that they typically describe or draw as a person (Heller, 1986). Additional common themes in Heller's (1986) study included a view of God as, on the one hand, omnipresent, a nurturant therapist-type figure, and an intimate and close companion. On the other hand, God was also described as inconsistent and distant by some children. As noted in the prior sections on religious concepts, preschool children also increasingly acquire social cognitive or "mentalizing" abilities; that is, they gain an increased appreciation of the fact that other people have intentions and goals that motivate their behavior (Wellman et al., 2001).

These two aspects of cognitive development—symbolic thought and mentalization—undoubtedly contribute to children's emerging elaboration of unseen others as relational partners; ultimately, even invisible agents may be viewed as having intentions and goals. Moreover, whereas toddlers would use a concrete object such as a teddybear or blanket as "attachment surrogates" (Ainsworth, 1985) or "transitional objects" (Winnicott, 1953), preschool children may now also start to direct their attachment-related thoughts and behaviors to abstract, symbolic others, which is, of course, particularly likely when their primary attachment figures are unavailable for one reason or the other. As an illustration, starting at these ages, children are prone to elaborate with imaginary companions, especially when experiencing low levels of psychological well-being (Hoff, 2005).

However, unlike other transitional objects, God has a very special developmental standing in that the idea of God is almost universally taken seriously also by adults, who may well encourage the child's emerging God-related thoughts while (however subtly) discouraging "relationships" with other unseen transitional objects (see also Rizzuto, 1979). Consequently, although most other transitional objects have passed their due dates by middle childhood, the representation of and perceived relationship with God often continues to flourish throughout life.

Although young children's God representations can be viewed as abstractions, they tend to be comparatively concrete and anthropomorphic by adult standards (cf. Piaget's,

1954, concepts of preoperational egocentrism and animism). For example, 4-year-olds are somewhat more likely to say that God is like their parents than 5- or 6-year-olds (De Roos, Iedema, & Miedema, 2003). Such a human-like representation of God naturally aids developmentally in making God viable as a symbolic attachment figure. In a related discussion, Rizzuto (1979) suggested that at the end of the preschool period/early school period, children develop a "living" God representation. In middle childhood, as children enter school and move even farther from their parents' immediate care, their God representations continue to become decreasingly anthropomorphic, although at the same time God is typically viewed as personally closer than in early childhood (Eshleman, Dickie, Merasco, Shepard, & Johnson, 1999; Tamminen, 1994).

From the late preschool period onward, empirical data indicate that God is perceived as an available safe haven in times of stress. For example, although not explicitly informed by attachment theory, according to Tamminen (1994), 40% of Finnish 7- to 12-year-olds reported that they felt close to God particularly during loneliness and emergencies (e.g., escaping or avoiding danger, dealing with death or sorrow). In addition, in a quasi-experimental and semiprojective setup, Eshleman et al. (1999) showed that American preschool and elementary school children placed a God symbol closer to a fictional child when the fictional child was in attachment-activating situations than when the fictional child was in situations that would be less clear-cut as activators of the attachment system. These findings have now been conceptually replicated across three additional studies: one conducted in Sweden with 5-to-7-year-old children from religious and nonreligious homes (Granqvist, Ljungdahl, & Dickie, 2007); one conducted in the United States with children of the same ages, most of whose parents were highly religious (Dickie, Charland, & Poll, 2005); and one conducted in Italy with 6- to 8-year-olds from lay Catholic homes (Cassibba, Granqvist, & Costantini, 2013).

Religious Relationships and Individual Differences in Attachment

In the adult literature, two general hypotheses have been suggested regarding links between religious relationships and individual differences in attachment security (Granqvist & Kirkpatrick, 2008). Each hypothesis describes a distinct developmental pathway to religion and to different modes of being religious and spiritual. One of these paths goes via a largely controlled (or effortful) regulation of distress following experiences with insensitive caregivers and insecure attachment (the compensation hypothesis). God and other religious figures are held to function here as surrogate attachment figures to whom these individuals direct their frustrated attachment systems when their particular insecure and fragile strategy for managing distress is crumbling under intense levels of stress (Granqvist & Kirkpatrick, 2013).

The other path goes via experiences with sensitive, religious caregivers and secure attachment (the correspondence hypothesis). Insofar as these caregivers have been observably religious during the offspring's years of immaturity, the offspring is thus likely to become similarly religious (i.e., social correspondence; cf. "socialization"). Moreover, the perceived relationship with God is likely to mirror that of a secure attachment (i.e., internal working model correspondence).

The empirical literature has suggested that it is not entirely straightforward to apply these ideas to young children's religious and spiritual development. Two caveats are worthy of special attention. First, it may take many years of development until the individual gains the capacity to employ a compensation strategy, as this is a controlled/ effortful strategy that runs counter to how the insecurely attached individual habitually and automatically deals with stress (e.g., to deny stress and avoid attachment figures or to maximize distress and remain preoccupied with the principal attachment figure). Consequently, direct support for the compensation hypothesis is virtually absent in the few extant child studies. However, Dickie, Eshleman, Merasco, VanderWilt, and Johnson (1997) have found that children whose fathers were absent from home imagined a more loving and powerful God than did children from intact homes. Relatedly, Eshleman et al. (1999) found that when parents spent less quality time with their children and had less identity in the parenting role, children viewed God as closer (even when controlling for the age of children). It appears that these children may start to direct some attachment-related bids to God, but whether they were actually insecurely attached cannot be determined from those studies.

Second, while still largely under the influence of parents and unaware of other possibilities, it may take additional years of autonomy development until secure and insecure children show differential susceptibility to adopt parental religious values and standards. Thus, support for the social aspect of the correspondence hypothesis is also virtually absent in the childhood studies (see Granqvist et al., 2007; De Roos, 2006).

Empirical research on children's religious and spiritual development has, though, yielded both inferential and direct support for the internal working model aspect of the correspondence hypothesis across some studies. A study with 4- to 11-year-old American Protestant children showed that those who perceived their parents as nurturing (cf. sensitive, a predictor of security) also perceived God as nurturing (Dickie et al., 1997). In an additional study, 5- to 7-year-old Swedish children indicated how similar God was to a fictional child by placing a God symbol at a chosen distance from a fictional child. Compared with insecure children, secure children placed the God symbol closer to the fictional child when the fictional child was in attachment-activating situations (e.g., sick and in hospital) and further from the fictional child when the fictional child was in attachment-neutral situations (e.g., bored, in bad mood; Granqvist et al., 2007). The authors suggested that secure, but not insecure, children's attention shifted to God when the attachment system was activated.

Moreover, Cassibba et al. (2011) have recently extended parts of these findings in an Italian sample. Their findings showed that just as attachment security tends to be transmitted from mother to child (van IJzendoorn, 1995), the mothers' security (assessed with the Adult Attachment Interview; Main, Goldwyn, & Hesse, 2003) predicted a higher degree of proximity in their children's placements of a God symbol vis-à-vis the fictional child. These findings are theoretically important because they suggest, possibly for the first time, that experiences with secure versus insecure mothers generalize to the offspring's sense of the availability of another (symbolic) figure than the mother herself.

Furthermore, a series of studies by De Roos and colleagues have examined connections between Dutch kindergarten-age children's representations of attachment and experiences with parental discipline on the one hand and their concepts of God (as assessed by questionnaires) on the other. These studies have revealed that different factors predict children's loving and punishing concepts of God. When parents use strict and power-assertive childrearing practices, children are more likely to perceive of God as angry, punishing, and powerful (De Roos, Iedema, & Miedema, 2004). Additionally, when parents emphasize the children's autonomy, children are less likely to view God as powerful (De Roos et al., 2004).

However, across two studies, children's attachment representations failed to predict their concepts of God as punishing (De Roos, Miedema, & Iedema, 2001) and as positive versus negative (De Roos, 2006). It should be noted in this context, though, that the Swedish study described previously (Granqvist et al., 2007) also failed to find an association between attachment representations and the children's explicit responses to some of the same God concept questionnaires that were developed and used by De Roos and her colleagues. It may be that more implicit assessments (e.g., semiprojective tests of God's closeness across theoretically relevant situations) are required in order to obtain support for the idea of internal working mocel (IWM) correspondence in relation to representational measures of attachment. We return to this issue in the Future Directions next.

FUTURE DIRECTIONS

We suggest four directions for future research. The first two recommendations are related to the need to determine the relationship between implicit and explicit processes in both cognitive and social approaches to religious and spiritual development. Although related, we discuss these future directions separately as each approach has unique potential for future research. The third future direction is related to one of the overarching themes of this volume: the need for research into the development of religion as a meaning-making system. The fourth future direction is a call for longitudinal research into the developmental processes underlying religious and spiritual development in early childhood.

Determining the Relationship between Intuitive and Explicit Religious Cognitions

A general assumption of the current cognitive approaches has been that we have natural cognitive predispositions (e.g., agency attribution, assumptions of causality) that allow for the relatively easy transmission of supernatural and religious concepts, both across ontogeny and phylogeny (Bering, 2006). Recent approaches to outlining the relationship between intuitive and explicit concepts have focused how early, intuitive concepts of agency provide the foundation for naïve metaphysical and theological cognitions, such as concepts of the soul (Bloom, 2004) and God and death (Wellman & Johnson, 2008). In this account, culture "fills in" those cognitions with specific religious content (Kelemen, 2004).

For scholars interested in the cultural influences on cognitive development more generally, this account is dissatisfying and reflects one of the themes of this volume: the need to conduct research within a multilevel interdisciplinary paradigm (Paloutzian & Park, Chapter 1, this volume). Within this paradigm, there would be no need to separate which aspects of religious and spiritual development are a part of behavior in general (e.g., intuitive) from the aspects that are unique (e.g., explicit) (i.e., Dittes, 1969, as cited in Paloutzian & Park, 2005). From a developmental perspective, social interaction plays a fundamental role in shaping not only the content but also the structure of children's cognition (Bruner, 1990; Gauvain, 2001; Vygotsky, 1978). According to a Vygotskian (1978) perspective of cognitive development, cognitions first happen between a child and a more advanced member of society before becoming internalized as cognitions. One area related to religious and spiritual development in early childhood that is ripe for future research is in the nature of the relationship between engaging in shared religious activities (e.g., rituals, prayer, conversations) and the development of intuitive and explicit religious cognitions.

Related to the development of religious cognitions, one example of this process is through observation of and participation in religious rituals. In the observation of religious rituals, children may be internalizing the intentions of the ritual actors (e.g., Tomasello, Kruger, & Ratner, 1993), which often include communication with an unseen, supernatural agent and assumptions of supernatural causality. As noted previously, by age 6, children distinguish ritual actions from other kinds of actions in terms of how rigidly a ritual actor must perform the ritual actions (Richert, 2006). Additionally, younger children tend to assume the ritual actions are functional in some way (Richert, 2006), even if the outcome of the actions is not externally apparent (Richert & Harris, 2006). Future research should consider how these assumptions about and understandings of rituals reflect the internalization of religious cognitions.

From an evolutionary perspective, given that religious concepts evolved within the social context of cultural evolution, the concepts themselves should not be considered outside of the social context in which they have evolved or in which they develop (Richert & Smith, 2010). Future research should consider the implications of the fact that cognitive development, as well as the evolution of human cognition, occurs in cultural environments that contain and transmit religious and spiritual concepts. This means that the study of religious cognitions can provide an interesting forum for scholars taking a cultural approach to understanding cognitive development and the relationship between domain-specific and domain-general adaptations.

Distinguishing between Implicit and Controlled/Effortful Processes

An aspect of correspondence and compensation processes that warrants future research is the distinction, noted previously, between implicit and controlled (or effortful) uses of religion. Our expectation, based on the conclusions drawn both from the larger adult literature on the attachment–religion connection and the childhood studies reviewed here, is that when attachment activation is implicit or subliminal and God is the only attachment figure available in the situation, activation of internal working models and associated neural networks leads individuals with secure attachment experiences to experience God as psychologically accessible. Thus, the internal working model aspect of correspondence may apply especially at an implicit level because of a coherent/singular representation (Bowlby, 1973; Main, 1991) of God. In contrast, when activation of the attachment system is supraliminal and causes such high levels of subjective distress that the habitual insecure strategy breaks down, individuals with insecure attachment experiences will, with increasing maturation, be inclined to regulate distress by turning to God. In other words, the compensation hypothesis refers to an effortful strategy of distress regulation through an attachment surrogate that actually runs counter to how the self and attachment figures are unconsciously/implicitly represented by the individual. Another way to phrase this is to say that the relationship with God is not functional at the implicit level because of an incoherent/multiple representation (Bowlby, 1973; Main, 1991) of God.

As to when the capacity for such a compensatory use of God matures is presently a matter of speculation, but our best guess is that adolescence is a key period (see Granqvist, 2012). With adolescence comes more autonomy vis-à-vis parents and the amplification of attachment transfer from parents to others, most often romantic partners and close friends. Insecure adolescents often have difficulties not only with their parents but also in establishing security-enhancing relationships with others. Partly for these reasons, insecure adolesecents are prone to experience emotional turmoil (e.g., serious loneliness and emotional isolation) at levels not previously encountered.

Religion as a Meaning System (RMS)

Related to another of the themes of this edited volume (see Paloutzian & Park, Chapter 1, this volume), one direction in which research into children's religious and spiritual development could expand is related to how religion and spirituality become a meaning system through which children interpret their lives (see Park, Chapter 18, this volume). Much of the research into religious and spiritual development has yet to incorporate the emotional and personal nature of spiritual and religious experiences. In some of the earliest research into children's spiritual development, Cole (1990) took a psychoanalytic approach to describing children's spiritual experiences. Through interviews and children's drawings, Cole provided a compelling ethnography of the spiritual lives of children and noted "how young we are when we start wondering about it all, the nature of the journey and of the final destination" (p. 335).

Johnson (2008) outlined spiritual development as "a distinct human capacity to become aware of what is truly vital in life" (p. 26). Johnson argued that in understanding spiritual development as the development of the spirit, we can follow a developmental trajectory from an intuitive understanding of a vitalized world and people in infancy to the ability to reflect on this vitalization in childhood. Related to this reflection, Harris (2000) analyzed the kinds of metaphysical questions children ask during the childhood years. On the basis of these questions, Harris suggested that by the time children are 3 or 4 they are capable of navigating among various mental spaces (e.g., real, imaginary, religious) and noting and seeking to resolve puzzles they encounter within these mental spaces.

Recent approaches have also considered the implications of the fact that children's concepts of God not only involve understanding God's mental states but also the utility of attributing intentionality to God (Bering & Parker, 2006). In particular, it may not be until approximately age 7 that children can be primed to attribute communicative intent to an invisible agent. In addition, children's belief in the efficacy of prayer increases from ages 3 to 8, and has an inverse relationship with children's belief in the efficacy of wishing (Woolley, 2000). However, the implications for the increased belief in prayer for children's use of prayer as a means of connecting with God are not at all understood. The implications of these studies are that during early and middle childhood children develop appropriately mature cognition for using religious and spiritual beliefs and experiences in the construct of a personal meaning system.

Recent reviews of the development of reasoning about various religious topics are also relevant to moving in the direction of how religion and spirituality develop as a meaning-making system (Evans & Lane, 2011; Evans, Legare, & Rosengren, 2011; Legare, Evans, Rosengren, & Harris, 2012). In a review of research into using creation and evolution as an explanation of origins, Evans and Lane (2011) built from dual-process models of cognition, which suggest that individuals process information at two levels: an intuitive/implicit/automatic level and an abstract/rational/hypothetical level. Related to the coexistence of both creationist and evolutionary accounts for origins, Evans and Lane note that both origin accounts incorporate both types of reasoning, and that people combine these types of reasoning in diverse ways to satisfy needs for meaning and systematicity. Further evidence for this dual-processing approach can be derived from research into reasoning about illness and death (Legare et al., 2012). In relation to children's religious and spiritual development, future research should examine when and under what circumstances children begin to question and reflect on their religious beliefs and the ways in which this reflection contributes to the development of religion as a meaning system.

The Need for Prospective Longitudinal Studies

In order to truly understand the *development* of any phenomenon, and especially the development of individual differences in that phenomenon, it is necessary to study processes and their directions. This requires longitudinal research designs. Cross-sectional studies can be a rich source for developmental hypotheses, but are in principle always fragile to cohort effects as well as unable to disentangle processes. Short-term experimental designs are very useful for establishing causal relations and in ruling out alternative interpretations to lab-triggered variation in a phenomenon of interest to development, but are in principle always fragile to external validity concerns and naturally fail to capture real-life maturation over extended periods of time. With true disappointment, we note that long-term prospective longitudinal studies are, to the best of our knowledge, virtually absent in the literature on religious and spiritual development in childhood (see Tamminen, 1994, for a rare exception). Developmental psychology as a general field has gained tremendously by not putting a blind eye to this time-consuming and (quite frankly) often frustrating design requirement. For example, how else would we know about stability and change in developmental constructs such as temperament and attachment, and how would we know of their implications for later socioemotional development? We strongly encourage developmental psychologists of religion and spirituality to open their eyes to the possibility of similar gains from studying religious and spiritual development longitudinally.

CONCLUDING REMARKS

Since the previous publication of this *Handbook*, there has been a marked increase in research into religious and spiritual development in childhood. The current research has largely been split in focus between the development of religious cognitions and attachment bonds with God. Although we noted a number of future directions for researchers interested in early religious and spiritual development, we are hopeful that this favorable trend will continue, especially because the study of the developmental processes involved in religiousness and spirituality can be informative both to scholars interested in the psychology of religion as well as scholars interested more generally in developmental psychology.

REFERENCES

Ainsworth, M. D. S. (1985). Attachments across the life span. *Bulletin of the New York Academy of Medicine, 61,* 792–812.

Ainsworth, M. D. S., Blehar, M. C., Waters, E., & Wall, S. (1978). *Patterns of attachment.* Hillsdale, NJ: Erlbaum.

Astuti, R., & Harris, P. L. (2008). Understanding mortality and the life of the ancestors in rural Madagascar. *Cognitive Science, 32,* 713–740.

Atran, S. (2002). *In Gods we trust: The evolutionary landscape of religion.* New York: Oxford University Press.

Barrett, H. C., & Behne, T. (2005). Children's understanding of death as the cessation of agency: A test using sleep versus death. *Cognition, 96*(2), 93–108.

Barrett, J. L. (2004). *Why would anyone believe in God?* Walnut Creek, CA: AltaMira.

Barrett, J. L., Newman, R., & Richert, R. A. (2003). When seeing is not believing: Children's understanding of humans' and non-humans' use of background knowledge in interpreting visual displays. *Journal of Cognition and Culture, 3,* 91–108.

Barrett, J. L., & Richert, R. A. (2003). Anthropomorphism or preparedness? Exploring children's God concepts. *Review of Religious Research, 44,* 300–312.

Barrett, J. L., Richert, R. A., & Dreisenga, A. (2001). God's beliefs vs. mom's: The development of natural and non-natural agent concepts. *Child Development, 71*(1), 50–65.

Bering, J. M. (2006). The folk psychology of souls. *Behavioral and Brain Sciences, 29,* 453–498.

Bering, J. M., & Bjorklund, D. F. (2004). The natural emergence of reasoning about the afterlife as a developmental regularity. *Developmental Psychology, 40,* 217–233.

Bering, J. M., Blasi, C. H., & Bjorklund, D. (2005). The development of 'afterlife' beliefs in religiously and secularly schooled children. *British Journal of Developmental Psychology, 23,* 587–607.

Bering, J. M., & Parker, B. D. (2006). Children's attributions of intentions to an invisible agent. *Developmental Psychology, 42*(2), 253–262.

Bloom, P. (2004). *Descartes's baby: How the science of child development explains what makes us human.* New York: Basic Books.

Bowlby, J. (1973). *Attachment and loss: Vol. 2. Separation.* New York: Basic Books.

Bowlby, J. (1982). *Attachment and loss: Vol. 1. Attachment* (2nd ed.). New York: Basic Books. (Original work published 1969)

Boyatzis, C. J. (2005). Religious and spiritual development in childhood. In R. F. Paloutzian & C. L. Park (Eds.), *Handbook of the psychology or religion and spirituality* (pp. 123–143). New York: Guilford Press.

Boyer, P. (2001). *Religion explained: The evolutionary origins of religious thought.* New York: Basic Books.

Boyer, P., & Walker, S. (2000). Intuitive ontology and cultural input in the acquisition of religious concepts. In K. S. Rosengren, C. N. Johnson, & P. L. Harris (Eds.), *Imagining the impossible: Magical, scientific, and religious thinking in children* (pp. 130–156). Cambridge, UK: Cambridge University Press.

Bretherton, I. (1987). New perspectives on attachment relations: Security, communication, and internal working models. In J. D. Osofsky (Ed.), *Handbook of infant development* (2nd ed., pp. 1061–1100). New York: Wiley.

Bruner, J. (1990). *Acts of meaning.* Cambridge, MA: Harvard University Press.

Callaghan, T., Rochat, P., Lillard, A., Claux, M. L., Odden, H., Itakura, S., et al. (2005).

Synchrony in the onset of mental state reasoning: Evidence from five cultures. *Psychological Science, 16*(5), 378–384.

Cassibba, R., Granqvist, P., & Costantini, A. (2013). Mothers' attachment security predicts their children's sense of God's closeness. *Attachment and Human Development, 15*, 51–64.

Cole, R. (1990). *The spiritual life of children.* Boston: Houghton Mifflin.

De Roos, S. A. (2006). Young children's God concepts: Influences of attachment and religious socialization in a family and school context. *Religious Education, 101*(1), 84–103.

De Roos, S. A., Iedema, J., & Miedema, S. (2003). Effects of mothers' and schools' religious denomination on preschool children's God concepts. *Journal of Beliefs and Values, 24*(2), 165–181.

De Roos, S. A., Iedema, J., & Miedema, S. (2004). Influence of maternal denomination, God concepts, and childrearing practices on young children's God concepts. *Journal for the Scientific Study of Religion, 43*(4), 519–535.

De Roos, S. A., Miedema, S., & Iedema, J. (2001). Attachment, working models of self and others, and God concept in kindergarten. *Journal for the Scientific Study of Religion, 40*, 607–618.

Dickie, J. R., Charland, K., & Poll, E. (2005). *Attachment and children's concepts of God.* Unpublished manuscript, Hope College, Holland, MI.

Dickie, J. R., Eshleman, A. K., Merasco, D. M., VanderWilt, M., & Johnson, M. (1997). Parent–child relationships and children's images of God. *Journal for the Scientific Study of Religion, 36*, 25–43.

Diesendruck, G., & Haber, L. (2009). God's categories: The effect of religiosity on children's teleological and essentialist beliefs about categories. *Cognition, 110*, 100–114.

Elkind, D. (1970). The origins of religion in the child. *Review of Religious Research, 12*(1), 35–42.

Eshleman, A. K., Dickie, J. R., Merasco, D. M., Shepard, A., & Johnson, M. (1999). Mother God, father God: Children's perceptions of God's distance. *The International Journal for the Psychology of Religion, 9*, 139–146.

Evans, E. M. (2000). The emergence of beliefs about the origins of species in school-age children. *Merrill-Palmer Quarterly, 46*, 221–254.

Evans, E. M. (2001). Cognitive and contextual factors in the emergence of diverse belief systems: Creation versus evolution. *Cognitive Psychology, 42*, 217–266.

Evans, E. M., & Lane, J. D. (2011). Contradictory or complementary?: Creationist and evolutionist explanations of the origin(s) of species. *Human Development, 54*, 144–159.

Evans, E. M., Legare, C. H., & Rosengren, K. S. (2011). Engaging multiple epistemologies: Implications for science education. In R. Taylor & M. Ferrari (Eds.), *Epistemology and science education: Understanding the evolution vs. intelligent design controversy* (pp. 111–140). New York: Routledge.

Flavell, J. H. (2004). Theory-of-mind development: Retrospect and prospect. *Merrill–Palmer Quarterly, 50*, 274–290.

Gauvain, M. (2001). *The social context of cognitive development.* New York: Guilford Press.

Giménez Dasí, M., Guerrero, S., & Harris, P. L. (2005). Intimations of immortality and omniscience in early childhood. *European Journal of Developmental Psychology, 2*, 285–297.

Goldman, R. G. (1964). *Religious thinking from childhood to adolescence.* London: Routledge & Kegan Paul.

Granqvist, P. (2006). Religion as a by-product of evolved psychology: The case of attachment and implications for brain and religion research. In P. McNamara (Ed.), *Where God and science meet: Vol. 2. The neurology of religious experience* (pp. 105–150). Westport, CT: Praeger/Greenwood.

Granqvist, P. (2012). Attachment and religious development in adolescence: The implications of culture. In G. Trommsdorff & X. Chen (Eds.), *Values, religion, and culture in adolescent development* (pp. 315–340). Cambridge, UK: Cambridge University Press.

Granqvist, P., & Dickie, J. R. (2006). Attachment theory and spiritual development in childhood and adolescence. In P. L. Benson, E. C. Roehlkepartain, P. E. King, & L. Wageners (Eds.),

The handbook of spiritual development in childhood and adolescence (pp. 197–210). Thousand Oaks, CA: Sage.

Granqvist, P., & Kirkpatrick, L. A. (2008). Attachment and religious representations and behavior. In J. Cassidy & P. R. Shaver (Eds.), *Handbook of attachment: Theory, research, and clinical applications* (2nd ed., pp. 906–933). New York: Guilford Press.

Granqvist, P., & Kirkpatrick, L. A. (2013). Religion, spirituality, and attachment. In K. Pargament (Ed.), *APA handbook for the psychology of religion and spirituality (Vol. 1): Context, theory, and research* (pp. 129–155). Washington, DC: American Psychological Association.

Granqvist, P., Ljungdahl, C., & Dickie, J. R. (2007). God is nowhere, God is now here: Attachment activation, security of attachment (SAT), and God proximity among 5–7-year-old children. *Attachment & Human Development, 9,* 55–71.

Granqvist, P., Mikulincer, M., & Shaver, P. R. (2010). Religion as attachment: Normative processes and individual differences. *Personality and Social Psychology Review, 14,* 49–59.

Harris, P. L. (2000). On not falling down to earth: Children's metaphysical questions. In K. S. Rosengren, C. N. Johnson, & P. L. Harris (Eds.), *Imagining the impossible: Magical, scientific, and religious thinking in children* (pp. 157–178). Cambridge, UK: Cambridge University Press.

Harris, P. L., & Giménez, M. (2005). Children's acceptance of conflicting testimony: The case of death. *Journal of Cognition and Culture, 5,* 143–164.

Heller, D. (1986). *The children's God.* Chicago: University of Chicago Press.

Hoff, E. V. (2005). Imaginary companions, creativity, and self-image in middle childhood. *Creativity Research Journal, 17,* 167–180.

Johnson, C. (2008). The spirit of spiritual development. In R. Lerner, R. Roeser, & E. Phelps (Eds.), *Positive youth development and spirituality: From theory to research* (pp. 25–41). West Conshohocken, PA: Templeton Foundation Press.

Kelemen, D. (1999). Why are rocks pointy?: Children's preference for teleological explanations of the natural world. *Developmental Psychology, 35,* 1440–1452.

Kelemen, D. (2004). Are children "intuitive theists"?: Reasoning about purpose and design in nature. *Psychological Science, 15,* 295–301.

Kelemen, D., & Rosset, E. (2009). The human function compunction: Teleological explanation in adults. *Cognition, 111,* 138–143.

Kirkpatrick, L. A. (2004). *Attachment, evolution, and the psychology of religion.* New York: Guilford Press.

Knight, N., Sousa, P., Barrett, J. L., & Atran, S. (2004). Children's attributions of beliefs to humans and God: Cross-cultural evidence. *Cognitive Science, 28,* 117–126.

Lane, J. D., Wellman, H. M., & Evans, E. M. (2010). Children's understanding of ordinary and extraordinary minds. *Child Development, 81*(5), 1475–1489.

Legare, C. H., Evans, E. M., Rosengren, K. S., & Harris, P. L. (2012). The coexistence of natural and supernatural explanations across cultures and development. *Child Development, 83*(3), 779–793.

Main, M. (1991). Metacognitive knowledge, metacognitive monitoring, and singular (coherent) vs. multiple (incoherent) models of attachment: Findings and directions for future research. In C. M. Parkes & J. Stevenson-Hinde (Eds.), *Attachment across the life cycle* (pp. 127–159). London: Tavistock/Routledge.

Main, M., Goldwyn, R., & Hesse, E. (2003). *Adult attachment scoring and classification systems.* Unpublished manuscript, University of California at Berkeley.

Main, M., Kaplan, N., & Cassidy, J. (1985). Security in infancy, childhood, and adulthood: A move to the level of representation. In I. Bretherton & E. Waters (Eds.), Growing points of attachment theory and research. *Monographs of the Society for Research in Child Development, 50* (1–2, Serial No. 209), 66–104.

Main, M., & Solomon, J. (1990). Procedures for identifying infants as disorganized/disoriented during the Ainsworth Strange Situation. In M. T. Greenberg, D. Cicchetti, & E. M.

Cummings (Eds.), *Attachment in preschool years: Theory, research, and intervention* (pp. 121–160). Chicago: University of Chicago.

Makris, N., & Pnevmatikos, D. (2007). Children's understanding of human and super-natural minds. *Cognitive Development, 22*(3), 365–375.

Paloutzian, R. F., & Park, C. L. (2005). Integrative themes in the current science of the psychology of religion. In R. F. Paloutzian & C. L. Park (Eds.), *Handbook of the psychology of religion and spirituality* (pp. 3–20). New York: Guilford Press.

Petrovich, O. (1997). Understanding of non-natural causality in children and adults: A case against artificialism. *Psyche en Geloof, 8,* 151–165.

Piaget, J. (1954). *The construction of reality in the child.* New York: Basic Books.

Piaget, J. (1963). *The origins of intelligence in children.* New York: Norton. (Original work published 1952)

Poling, D. A., & Evans, E. M. (2004). Are dinosaurs the rule or the exception? Developing concepts of death and extinction. *Cognitive Development, 19,* 363–383.

Richert, R. A. (2006). The ability to distinguish ritual actions in children. *Method & Theory in the Study of Religion, 18,* 144–165.

Richert, R. A., & Barrett, J. L. (2005). Do you see what I see? Young children's assumptions about God's perceptual abilities. *The International Journal for the Psychology of Religion, 15,* 283–295.

Richert, R. A., & Harris, P. L. (2006). The ghost in my body: Children's developing concept of the soul. *Journal of Cognition and Culture, 6,* 409–427.

Richert, R. A., & Smith, E. I. (2010). The role of religious concepts in the evolution of human cognition. In U. Frey (Ed.), *The nature of God: Evolution and religion* (pp. 93–110). Antwerp, Belgium: Tectum.

Rizzuto, A. M. (1979). *The birth of the living God: A psychoanalytical study.* Chicago: Chicago University Press.

Sabbagh, M. A., Xu, F., Carlson, S. M., Moses, L. J., & Lee, K. (2006). The development of executive functioning and theory of mind: A comparison of Chinese and U.S. preschoolers. *Psychological Science, 17,* 74–81.

Schaffer, H. R. (2006). *Key concepts in developmental psychology.* Los Angeles: Sage.

Shtulman, A. (2006). Qualitative differences between naïve and scientific theories of evolution. *Cognitive Psychology, 52,* 170–194.

Shtulman, A. (2008). Variation in the anthropomorphization of supernatural beings and its implications for cognitive theories of religion. *Journal of Experimental Psychology: Learning, Memory, and Cognition, 34*(5), 1123–1138.

Shtulman, A., & Schulz, L. (2008). The relation between essentialist beliefs and evolutionary reasoning. *Cognitive Science, 32,* 1049–1062.

Smith, E. I., & Richert, R. A. (2011, April). *The creation of belief: Chinese children's use of evolution to explain the origin of species.* Poster presented at the biennial meeting of the Society for Research in Child Development, Montreal, Canada.

Sroufe, L. A., & Waters, E. (1977). Attachment as an organizational construct. *Child Development, 48,* 1184–1199.

Tamminen, K. (1994). Religious experiences in childhood and adolescence: A viewpoint of religious development between the ages of 7 and 20. *The International Journal for the Psychology of Religion, 4,* 61–85.

Tomasello, M., Kruger, A. C., & Ratner, H. H. (1993). Cultural learning. *Behavioral and Brain Sciences, 16,* 495–552.

van IJzendoorn, M. H. (1995). Adult attachment representations, parental responsiveness, and infant attachment: A meta-analysis on the predictive validity of the Adult Attachment Interview. *Psychological Bulletin, 117,* 387–403.

Vygotsky, L. S. (1978). *Mind in society: The development of higher psychological processes.* Cambridge, MA: Harvard University Press.

Vygotsky, L. S. (1986). *Thought and language.* Cambridge, MA: Massachusetts Institute of Technology.

Wellman, H., Cross, D., & Watson, J. (2001). Meta-analysis of theory of mind development: The truth about false-belief. *Child Development, 72,* 655–684.

Wellman, H. M., & Johnson, C. N. (2008). Developing dualism: From intuitive understanding to transcendental ideas. In A. Antonietti, A. Corradini, & J. Lowe (Eds.), *Psycho-physical dualism today: An interdisciplinary approach* (pp. 3–35). Lanham, MD: Lexington Books.

Winnicott, D. W. (1953). Transitional objects and transitional phenomena—A study of the first not-me possession. *The International Journal of Psychoanalysis, 34,* 89–97.

Woolley, J. D. (2000). The development of beliefs about mental-physical causality in imagination, magic, and religion. In K. Rosengren, C. Johnson, & P. L. Harris (Eds.), *Imagining the impossible: Magical, scientific, and religious thinking in children* (pp. 99–129). Cambridge, MA: Cambridge University Press.

9

Religious Development from Adolescence to Middle Adulthood

Michael R. Levenson, Carolyn M. Aldwin,
and Heidi Igarashi

In postmodern cultures such as those of North America and western Europe, many traditions, including religious ones, are no longer passed largely unaltered from one generation to the next. Some observers have concluded that religion itself is diminishing in influence with each successive generation, based primarily on declines in religious attendance in the United States (Wuthnow, 2007). However, observation of campus life at American universities leaves little doubt that interest in religion among some students is strong (Cherry, DeBerg, & Porterfield, 2001). The percentage of emerging adults who declare themselves to be religious is quite high (Smith, Snell, & Longest, 2009; Wuthnow, 2007). However, the longitudinal National Survey of Youth and Religion (Smith et al., 2009) showed a downward trend in religious affiliation. Does this mean that the religious impulse is fading away in younger people or that spiritual experience is of diminishing importance to them? It may mean that there is increased diversity in religiousness precisely because of perceived freedom of choice and expression.

Social structure and psychological meaning are inextricably intertwined (Elder & Shanahan, 2006). This suggests that secular trends in changes in religiousness and spirituality ultimately affect individuals' religious and spiritual experiences, which in turn affect changes at the social structural level. Thus, in this chapter, we first review the secular trends in religiousness and spirituality and then discuss how these trends affect religious meaning and development in young adulthood and midlife.

SECULAR TRENDS IN RELIGIOUSNESS AND SPIRITUALITY

There are several pathways involved in the relationship between social structure and psychological meaning. This section begins with a review of changes in religious socialization and source of religious influence. We then examine changes in religiousness among young adults in the United States as well as other countries. These changes in religiousness are in some ways mirrored by age differences in spirituality, which in turn has led to the current major debate as to whether individuals can be spiritual in the absence of an affirmation of religiousness. Indeed, there is some question concerning what the two terms actually mean in the minds of those who avow either or both of them.

Changes in Religious Socialization

As we shall see in the following section, the picture of religiousness and spirituality in adolescents and younger adults is complex and somewhat confusing, with various researchers finding both increases and decreases in religious behavior. One conclusion we can draw is that there is increasing diversity among younger Americans who are entering and moving through young adulthood, as well as increasing diversity among nations. The diversity observed in the United States may reflect the way young people now define what it means to become an adult. Arnett (2004), who coined the term "emerging adulthood," has noted the very strong emphasis on independence—being one's own person. This may be much more pronounced in the United States today than in other countries, but may well be a path that others will soon follow.

As Smith and Snell (2009) noted, parental religious socialization in childhood is very important in sustaining their children's religiousness from early adolescence through late adolescence and very early adulthood. However, Arnett pointed out a pronounced difference in the influence of parental religious socialization on adolescents and very young adults, on the one hand and emerging adults (ages 20–30), on the other. In his sample of 300 regionally diverse U.S. emerging adults, Arnett (2004) found that childhood religious socialization by parents had *no* influence on emerging adults' religiousness. Arnett observed that this anomalous finding fits perfectly with his observation that American young people define adulthood as making their own choices. It may be that children and adolescents do what they are told, to the extent that their actions can be observed by parents (such as "go to church"), and acknowledge beliefs that their parents insist upon without actually holding those beliefs or even knowing what they mean. They may mark their self-definition as adults, in part, by divorcing themselves from their parents' religious beliefs regardless of whether the parents are religious or not.

Changes in Sources of Religious Influence

Although parental influence wanes in emerging adulthood in favor of "independent choice," it would be naïve to take independence at face value. Independent choice is an ideology; influence is the reality. Peers and education are also important (cf. Hood, Hill, & Spilka, 2009, for an exhaustive review). However, there are social and cultural factors that can strongly influence religious socialization and spiritual experience that may vary by cohort. In the late 1960s and 1970s, the exposure of many young adults to entheogens (psychedelic substances used in religious, spiritual, and/or shamanic contexts) led to altered states of consciousness that many regarded as spiritual (Forte, 1997; Hood, 2005; Smith, 2000). There can be little doubt that these experiences profoundly changed the religious lives of many. For the current cohort of young adults, the most pronounced influence is the advent of the Internet.

The Internet is a technology that has radically shaped the experience of emerging adults and post-Baby Boomers. Google has become the new library. If Google isn't enough, one can choose from millions of books that can be ordered from Amazon.com to be delivered to one's doorstep (or to one's e-book reader). No doubt the Internet is supplementing brick-and-mortar places for meeting others, communicating with one's friends, going to the movies, and shopping. It facilitates "in-person" social interaction, as well as political movements. This cultural development strongly suggests that the Internet will have major implications for religious congregations, including what the composition and conduct of such congregations will look like in the future.

Analyses of data from the General Social Surveys (GSS; 2000–2002) found that, although its rate is on the rise, visiting religious websites, even for information, does not occupy much of the time spent on the Internet by younger Americans, although it appears to be on the rise (Wuthnow, 2007). Importantly, websites show no sign, thus far, of becoming "virtual congregations" (Wuthnow, 2007). However, Wuthnow did suggest that the Internet affects the practices of religious on-line "surfers." They practiced more meditation and were more likely to volunteer than to emphasize group study or prayer. They were far more likely to talk to their friends about spiritual matters than to religious professionals. They were as likely to spend time in nature as "to talk with a member of the clergy" (Wuthnow, 2007, p. 210). Wuthnow concluded that this "profiles" them as "spiritual tinkerers." Some may be "tinkering," by taking a little of several religions and combining them, with a large dash of interpretation, in an individualized belief system (cf. Arnett, 2004). However, they are also using cohort-specific means of seeking information.

Wuthnow argued that the Internet is much like television, radio, and religious bookstores in providing information and is, therefore, no big deal in the development of religious consciousness. We believe that he overlooked one important difference between these media and the Internet: The latter sites are *interactive*. Indeed, they are more interactive by far than a religious service presided over by an authority that produces one-way communication to his or her flock. For all of its flaws, the Internet does provide the opportunity to "talk back" to authority as well as for individuals to talk to each other, thus leveling the hierarchy. We believe that religion on the Internet will develop further and contribute to the decline of authoritarian religion. In light of history (recent as well as ancient), the clergy do not seem to have a monopoly on spiritual truth after all. It may be wise to avoid confusing religion with human hierarchy.

Dawson (2004) examined whether virtual communities are even possible, and found evidence from large-scale surveys (cf. DiMaggio, 2001) that the Internet at least does not impede social interaction. Internet users have other forms of human contact that are at least as extensive as those of nonusers, including greater involvement in the arts and politics.

At present, Internet use for religious purposes is largely informational. However, Dawson sees reason to believe that this may change. Religion is closely tied to identity formation and "religion is coming adrift from its conventional social moorings, just as our identity constructing processes are" (Dawson, 2004, p. 86). He went on to remark that "throughout human history and in most parts of the world, religious praxis has not been an exclusive affiliation to a specific institution or place like a church" (Dawson, 2004, p. 86). As a virtual meeting place, we believe that the Internet is a key to future religious socialization and holds promise for the cultivation of spiritual development.

These changes in both socialization and sources of influence have had a profound impact on religiousness and spirituality, both in the United States and around the world.

Changes in Religiousness in Young Adults in the United States

Studies of changes in religiousness and spirituality among young adults yield a complex picture. Findings on change and stability in religiousness vary as a function of method—more precisely, of how questions are asked. People's self-attributions of religiousness show different trends than participation in formal religious ceremonies, which in turn show different trends from private religious practice. Further complicating the picture is the often ill-defined difference between religiousness and spirituality (see Oman, Chapter 2, this volume, for an in-depth discussion). We first address changes in religiousness, defined loosely as the affirmation of affiliation with one specific religion—more specifically, attendance at religious services or observations—both in the United States and then in other countries. Following this, we address changes in spirituality, or religious experience.

Overall, religious attendance has declined in the United States among young adults. Analyses of the GSS found that those 21–45 years of age who report never attending religious services has increased from 14 to 20% in the 25 years ending in 2002 (Wuthnow, 2007). Further, analyses of the longitudinal National Survey of Youth and Religion (NSYR) found that, in 2007–2008, 35% of those in the United States between ages 18 and 23 never attend services, an increase of 18% in 5 years (Smith & Snell, 2009). Over that period, there was a decline in every index of religious practice in the NSYR with the exception of meditation practice (excluding prayer), which increased from 11 to 16%.

However, there may be individual differences in those secular trends. Wuthnow (2007) reported an increase in weekly attendance among those 18–25 years between 1990 and 2000, perhaps reflecting an increase in evangelical religion among the young. Further, religious attendance in the United States increased as a function of age, at least in the GSS data collected from 1998–2002. In part, this may result from the tendency to increase religious attendance after having children. The number of children in the family is also associated with greater parental attendance (although this may be due to the more religious having more children). However, the analyses of the GSS also reported a decline in attendance for parents after the children have left home.

Beyond attendance of religious services, Smith et al. (2009) endeavored to assess strength of religious commitment and change in commitment using a composite measure of data collected from a U.S. representative sample surveyed at three times: 2003, 2005, and 2007–2008. At first measurement, participants were between 13 and 17 years old; at the third wave, they were 18–23 years old. Besides frequency of attendance, the measure included reported importance of faith and the frequency with which respondents prayed on their own. These indices were then combined to form a measure of religious strength ranging from lowest through minimal and moderate to highest. This measure was then compared across Waves 1 and 3.

The basic result was that all "levels of religiousness" declined between Waves 1 and 3, except the "lowest," which increased. For example, those who scored highest at Wave 1 decreased 12% by Wave 3. This was the overall pattern for all levels, with "moderate" also declining, except for "minimal" and "lowest," which increased by 11%, regardless of religious denomination.

Simple zero-order correlations suggested that religious commitment was related to attendance at services, attributing high importance to faith, frequency of solitary prayer, frequency of religious experiences, and having very religious parents. Frequency of scripture reading was most strongly associated with retention of a belief in the importance of faith from Waves 1 to 3. Logistic regression showed that strong parental religious involvement, frequency of individual prayer, high importance attributed to religious faith, and frequency of reading scripture at Wave 1 were the strongest influences on religious strength at Wave 3.

There was stability in some subgroups. The religiously "devoted" at Wave 1 were by far the most likely to be at the highest level of religious strength at Wave 3. Other categories ranged from the "regular" at Time 1, who were somewhat religious at Wave 3, through the "sporadic" and the "disengaged," who were not at all likely to be at the highest level at Wave 3. However, Smith and Snell (2009) noted that *within* each group at Wave 1, there were some mavericks who did exhibit different trajectories.

Qualitative analyses traced six pathways to the higher levels of religiousness. Four of these pathways included strong parental involvement and one involved the strong involvement of other adults. The sixth was more independent, emphasizing the individual's faith and personal religious experiences. In all six, the teenager at Wave 1 had no doubt about their religious faith. Four pathways to lower religiousness over 5 years all began with low parental religious service attendance. It is regrettable that quantitative pathways to sustained or diminished religiousness were not computed.

The Pew Forum report, *Religion among the Millennials* (2010), documented a steady decline in the most widely used indices of religiousness over the past 40 years in each of the five generations that emerged into adulthood in the 20th century, as assessed most recently near the end of the first decade of the 21st. For example, religion was important to 75% of the oldest of the generations (the "Greatest") at the most recent assessment but to only 40% of the Millennials. However, 53% of the Millennials expressed certainty in their belief in God compared to 61% of Generation X and 65% of Boomers. Interestingly, in the late 1990's, 59% of Generation X expressed certainty of God's existence. In the late 1980s, 59% of Boomers were certain. Perhaps not too much should be made of this, but there is a hint of an increase in certainty with age and a suggestion that not everyone perceives the importance of religious institutions as equivalent to a certain belief in God.

Looking at the apparently declining religiousness among young adults, Wuthnow (2007, p. 214) remarked that if he were a religious leader, he would be troubled by the data describing the religious lives of young Americans. Although most data for older young adults point to a story of decline in religiousness, the GSS revealed some interesting exceptions. First, there has been an increase in belief in life after death among those ages 21–45 years. Moreover, the percentages are very high, reaching 87% of women who were 40–45 years of age in 1998–2002 (Wuthnow, 2007). There is also a strong belief in the United States in the existence of angels. Fifty-six percent of the U.S. longitudinal sample believed in the existence of angels, including 36% of those who considered themselves to be nonreligious. Twenty-five percent of this group also believed in demons and evil spirits, 37% in miracles from God, 24% in life after death, and 36% in God's judgment on judgment day (Smith & Snell, 2009, p. 124). Although a larger percentage of the religious affiliates believed in these things, the fact that a quarter to a third of *nonreligious* emerging adults did as well is not trivial. It at least makes one wonder what "nonreligious" means among these people. Could nonreligious mean "spiritual" but not attracted to a specific religion among some of them? Or could there be a loss of connection between specific beliefs on the one hand and knowledge of the contexts in which they developed on the other? In other words, is religious belief increasingly disconnected from religious education?

Changes in Religiousness among Young Adults in Other Countries

Looking around the world, there is remarkable diversity in religiousness. This is especially striking in the former Soviet Bloc, where, for example, 75% of Poles but only 12% of Czechs were found to pray daily (Smith, 2009). Sorting through the ocean of data provided by Smith's report for the Templeton Foundation, derived from the World Values Survey and the International Social Survey Program, we found that the percentage of those younger than 30 who considered themselves to be religious persons generally was somewhat smaller than among those who were 30–39 years of age. However, the differences between countries eclipsed age and period effects.

Argentina and Brazil provide interesting examples of cross-national differences. In Argentina in 1984, 59% of those younger than 30 considered themselves to be religious compared with about 61% of those 30–39 years old. In 1999, 79% of those younger than 30 reported being religious compared with 86.7% of those aged 30–39. In contrast, in neighboring Brazil, in 1991 82.5% of those younger than 30 considered themselves to be religious compared to 81.3% in 1997. In Bulgaria, adults under 30 were much more religious in 1999 (43%) than in 1990 (29%), but there is a similar relationship with age, with 42% of 30- to 39-year-olds regarding themselves as religious in 1999 as compared to 31% in 1990.

The message is quite clear that religion is not in decline in all places and among all peoples. In some countries, such as (East) Germany and Estonia, religiousness appears to be at a low ebb. In China, on the other hand, religiousness is steadily increasing (Chau, 2001, 2011; Dillon, 1994; Lee, 2007). Moreover, as these authors documented, religious participation is increasing in Christianity and Islam, as well as more traditional religions of China.

The national differences reported by Smith (2009) were certainly large and dramatic. They also reflected ongoing change. Smith addressed secularization theory, which holds that economically more developed societies are increasingly secular and that more educated people are less religious. There is some evidence for secularization theory, but the evidence is mixed and shows wide variability. Scandinavian countries and Japan are increasingly secular, but China, the United States, and Argentina are not. It will be interesting to observe the effects of rapid economic development in Brazil and India, especially among adolescents and young adults. Some formerly communist countries remain nonreligious while others have experienced a reemergence of religion.

Age Differences in Spiritual Practice

Despite the decline in religious attendance in the United States, Smith's survey also found that 76.3% of those younger than age 30 reported being a religious person in 1982, and in 1999, 76.7% did so. What, then, does being a religious person mean? Perhaps personal spirituality may be supplanting allegiance to specific religions. Unfortunately, longitudinal data on changes in spirituality do not appear to exist, but the existing cross-sectional studies may prove illustrative.

In response to a question concerning how best to understand God (Wuthnow, 2007), a national sample of adults, ranging in age from 21 to 97 years, generally endorsed personal experience in preference to "church doctrine" (theology). The difference in endorsement is modest for the oldest respondents, substantial (three to two) for middle-aged adults, but very large (three to one) for younger adults, ages 21–39. The latter finding is also consistent with Arnett's 2004 report of his in-depth interviews with 20- to 29-year-olds in four U.S. cities.

In this vein, it is interesting that more than half (58%) of biblical literalists and nearly 70% of nonliteralists in the Religion and Diversity Survey endorsed the idea that "God can only be known as people empty their minds and look inside themselves" (Wuthnow, 2007, p. 105). This is a statement about spiritual practice and experience and expresses a method shared across diverse religious traditions from Sufism to Zen. Authentic religious experience is only available to those who have emptied their minds of "the world," including self-consciousness. In Zen this is literally called "mindlessness" (Kapleau, 1989).

Wuthnow (2007) correctly distinguished spiritual seeking from spiritual practice. The former is more superficial while the latter requires a commitment to make one's self present to the transcendent dimension. Formal prayer, meditation, and mantra are forms of spiritual practice. People in their 20s were much less likely than those who were middle aged or older to report daily prayer (47 vs. 72%) or meditation (8 vs. 37%). It is possible that 8% is on the low side (cf. Smith & Snell, 2009). However, as Wuthnow (2007) suggested, based on the Arts and Religion Survey (Wuthnow, 2003), the young who do pray or meditate may take the method more seriously. They may integrate their prayer and meditation with music and art in a way that supports the devotional attitude. We might add that the gospel music tradition in the African American Protestant church is an example of this aspect of practice. Sacred art has long been a part of contemplative practice, including, for example, Gregorian chant in the Catholic Church and mandala art in Buddhist and Hindu traditions. Such attention to context may serve to increase the emptying of the mind of mundane concerns and facilitate experience interpreted as sacred.

Spiritual but Not Religious?

These prior observations coincide with the finding that many young adults consider themselves to be spiritual but not religious. As Wuthnow (2007) pointed out, it is certainly the case that religious young people are more likely than those who are not involved in religion to be concerned with spirituality. However, the declining religious affiliations and church attendance among the young, combined with the "significant minority"

(Wuthnow, 2007, p. 134) who report being spiritual but not religious, again raises the question of what "being religious" truly means. As Wuthnow remarked, it is a curious idea because religion and spirituality have been so tightly linked in the past. In contrast, Smith and Snell found little evidence for a combination of "low external" and "high internal" religion—that is, spiritual but not religious—with only 7% of the NSYR reporting this pattern. Thus, they would appear to be skeptical that there is even a significant minority of "spiritual but not religious."

We do not speculate about why this difference might appear between the two studies, but it certainly calls for further research. We should note that Smith and Snell (2009) also found that 11 to 20% (by denomination) of the NSYR sample considered themselves to be "spiritual but not religious," including 17% of the nonreligious, compared to 11% of those who identified themselves as Roman Catholic. Interestingly, they also found virtually no one who was religious but not spiritual (.2%). Oser, Scarlett, and Bucher (2006) remarked that the relatively small percentage of exclusively spiritual young people may have a resource for spiritual development that is powerful. Indeed, the "spiritual but not religious" may have devoted more thought to such issues than those who report being both or neither. Oser et al. went on to consider the observations of W. C. Smith (1998) on the differences between faith and belief. They took Smith's point that faith is action, not merely the endorsement of dogma. We would express this as religion as practice in contrast to religion as belief.

Evidence that spirituality and religiousness may be distinct, though related, constructs can be found in their independent relationships with well-being, established in the National Survey of Midlife Development in the United States (MIDUS). Spiritual experience accounted for independent variance in positive affect, personal growth, purpose in life, self-acceptance, and positive interpersonal relationships. These effects were more pronounced among women. Formal religious participation was a much weaker predictor of well-being (Greenfield, Vaillant, & Marks, 2009). These effects may be more salient to emerging adulthood through midlife than now well-established health protective effects of participation (cf. Oman & Thoresen, 2005).

Summary

Thus, there is considerable evidence in the literature for both stability and change in religiousness and spirituality among young adults. On the one hand, formal religious attendance has declined over the past few decades, especially in parts of Europe. On the other hand, there is evidence that spiritual practices such as meditation have increased, at least among U.S. youths. Further, there is a remarkable consistency in the percentage of young adults over two decades who describe themselves as religious persons (76%). It is likely that the sources of socialization and social influences on religiousness and spirituality are changing, and that the Internet is becoming an increasingly important source of religious/spiritual information for today's youth. Thus, it is likely that the form of religiousness/spirituality is altering, but it would be incorrect to say that that current cohorts are less religious/spiritual than earlier ones. As suggested by Templeton and Eccles (2008), the possibility of religion and spirituality fueling a growth in a universal rather than parochial morality based on compassion for all is very real.

PSYCHOLOGICAL CONSEQUENCES OF CHANGES IN RELIGION AND SPIRITUALITY

Both Smith and Snell (2009) and Wuthnow (2007) expressed concerns about a cultural crisis in young adults in the United States. They were especially careful in their consideration of increasing religious tolerance that has no doubt grown from the cultural relativism cultivated by mid-20th-century social sciences. However, Smith and Snell suspected, probably correctly, that this tolerance is not carefully thought out by most of the young but arises in a context of moral apathy and the distractions of postmodern life. Rather than humility and openness based on a recognition of the value of religious diversity, cultural relativism and religious tolerance may emerge from an atmosphere of "whatever" and frank ignorance and "intellectual disengagement" fostered by universities that increasingly deemphasize liberal arts and general intellectual development in favor of marketable skills (Uecker, Regnerus, & Vaaler, 2007, p. 1683). Probably religious tolerance in young people has diverse sources ranging from parental influence through differential levels of exposure to simple indifference.

This section examines the psychological consequences of this change in religious attitudes, in terms of meaning and experience, theories of religious development, and, finally, the moral implications of this change.

Religion, Meaning, and Experience

Religion and spirituality are unique in that they are centrally concerned with the meaning of our lives. One way of distinguishing spirituality from simply endorsing the usual measures of religiousness is by understanding spirituality as striving to understand that meaning. While attendance at religious services has generally been declining, at least in the United States, there is evidence that spirituality is relatively constant, and younger adults are more likely to distinguish between religiousness and spirituality in their lives.

Such spiritual striving reflects *ultimate concern* (Emmons, 1999). Ultimate concern engages all psychological domains, including, emotion, cognition, and motivation. In all religions, there are those who engage in contemplative practice, which includes many forms of meditation, reading for divine inspiration (rather than for mere information), and, indeed, any practice that elevates one's consciousness beyond selfish concerns, liberates one from conditioned habits, and enhances mindfulness (cf. Easwaran, 2008; Goldstein, 1993; Keating, 1999; Shah, 1964). Many, if not most, people who have spiritual practices receive some form of guidance from *spiritual models,* who may teach more by example than by pedagogy (Oman & Thoresen, 2007). People who identify themselves as spiritual may rely on experience rather than dogma. Spiritual experience can take many forms regardless of the practice involved. Dreams, experience in the wilderness, self-transcendence in meditation, and art can all be sources of spiritual experience. Thus, spiritual meaning continues to be important for young adults, even if explicit religiousness, at least among some groups, is decreasing.

On the basis of his experiences as a Sufi teacher, Shah (2000) argued that considerable cognitive and emotional development are prerequisites for spiritual development. The latter he considered to be distinct from intellectual and affective development. It follows that young adulthood is the time when an attraction to spiritual development is likely to emerge. Perhaps the limitations of intellect and emotion as ways of approaching life's meaning become more apparent when we become mature enough to perceive that "something is missing."

Psychological Theories of Religious Development

In contrast to the quantification of religiousness, and distinctions between religiousness and spirituality, it is possible to think of religiousness and/or spirituality as outcomes of a developmental process. For example, contemporary scholars such as Fowler (1981) and Oser and Gmunder (1991) have argued for the possibility of religious development rather than the mere choice of a static belief system.

There have been several theories of the religious development in adults, perhaps most famously Fowler's stages of faith (Fowler, 1981). Oser and Gmunder's (1991) stage theory of religious judgment has also attracted wide attention. Such stage theories are structural in the Piagetian sense of depicting universal, transformational changes from a teleological point of view. Because of their origins in the overarching structural model, they tend to emphasize cognition. However, Erikson's stage theory (1963) exemplifies the same model in the context of social and emotional development, and it may therefore be useful to think of such theories as ontogenetic, as did Erikson (cf. Levenson & Crumpler, 1996). Such theories in their cognitive incarnations tend to move from simple to more complex thinking. Fowler's theory appears to have an additional dimension because it moves from simple-mindedness *through* complexity to simplicity. The adolescent to adult stages include the synthetic-conventional stage, in which self-identity and faith are tied to significant others; the individual-reflective stage, which involves self-reflection and meaning making, often involving differentiating from earlier faith; conjunctive faith, which is thought to develop in midlife and entails further reflection in an attempt to bridge contradictions in faith; and finally universalizing faith, which involves increased inclusiveness while holding universalizable principles. This is an excellent structural model for developmental theory and is not restricted to cognition.

Fowler (1981) found that about half of the adolescents he interviewed were at the synthetic-conventional stage of faith. In contrast, only 18% of young adults were still at this stage, while 40% had an individual-reflective type of faith, supporting our observation of individuation in young adulthood. Only adults older than 40 had conjunctive faith, and only one subject had a universalizing-type faith. This suggests an interesting developmental trend toward more complex faith conceptualizations with age. Althoygh there have been several attempts to develop both qualitative and quantitative measures to test Fowler's theory (for reviews, see Oser et al., 2006), unfortunately none of these articles examined age differences in types of faith.

Nelson (2010) contrasted childhood with adult religiousness in terms of spiritual maturity that involved a degree of self-transcendence essential for the development of compassion. He suggested that, rather than stages of development as in Fowler's theory, such development may be better described as a spiral wherein the basic issues of religion remain the same but are dealt with at increasingly deeper levels. This is similar to Erikson's description of stages of development, in which each stage can be revisited and each dialectic better resolved as each succeeding crisis of developmental transition is negotiated. It also retains the "universalizing faith" that forms the final stage in Fowler's theory and certainly entails self-transcendence and compassion.

Oser et al. (2006) regarded Fowler's work as more of a theory of socioemotional development, while Oser and Gmunder's (1991) is more obviously related to cognitive development, following both Piaget and Kohlberg (Feldman, 2008). Oser and Gmunder presented a theory of religious (or spiritual) judgment organized in a system of seven polar opposites representing ways in which people think about contingencies that result in conflicts. They employed vignettes, reminiscent of those found in Kohlberg's justice reasoning interview, to examine how people at different ages or developmental levels make judgments in such conflict. The "Paul" vignette, for example, involves a newly graduated medical doctor who is in a plane crash. Just before the plane crashes, Paul promises God that, if he is saved from death, he will go to a poor country to serve the needy rather than have the lucrative career that is available to him. To complicate matters further, Paul has a fiancée, so he promises to forego that relationship if the fiancée declines to go along. Paul survives and the interview concerns what Paul is to do.

The polar opposites involved in coding the responses are "freedom versus dependence, transcendence versus immanence, hope versus absurdity, transparency versus opacity, eternal versus ephemeral, trust versus mistrust, and holy versus profane" (Oser et al., 2006, p. 961). These are regarded as defining "some issue that may be brought to bear when interpreting a contingency situation" (Oser et al., 2006, p. 961). Their coding scheme revealed a set of stages that proceeded from the consideration of only one of a set of polar opposites at earlier developmental stages to consideration of both simultaneously. The stages proceed through God's punishment for breaking the promise (stage one) to trying to discern God's will throughout life whether that involves the specific promised service or not (stage five). This is an interesting dilemma for Paul because at the time of the promise he is acting from fear, not discernment (see Levenson et al., 2011).

On the basis of interview data from 112 church members, Oser and Gmunder (1991) hypothesized that, until age 25, the level of religious judgement increases with age. However, in adulthood, stages were fairly consistent and did not appear to regress in late life. To our knowledge, there have been no attempts in the literature to confirm these age-related hypotheses.

Indeed, while several new theories of religiosity have emerged (see Oser et al., 2006), it is very surprising that none really take an adult developmental perspective. Our search of PsychINFO showed that nearly all of the studies of religious development are focused on childhood and adolescence. In his critique of this literature, Feldman (2008) observed that an important distinction can be made between universal stages and those that can be universalizable. In other words, in adult development, not everyone goes through stages—or even developmental stages—but among some individuals, universalizable stages can occur.

Nonetheless, there is a dearth of empirical studies on whether religious development occurs in young adulthood and midlife and what that development may entail.

Does Spirituality Have Moral Consequences?

A positive take on the apparent change from religiousness to spirituality in young adulthood is its potential consequences for moral development. Templeton and Eccles (2008) pointed to another approach to spirituality in positive youth development. "Expanding circle morality" (ECM) broadens an individual's horizon of concern beyond self and family ultimately to include all people or even all beings in their "self-concept." This could quite legitimately be regarded as a process of spiritual development that is by no means limited to youth. We believe that the window opened by the Internet, for all of its needless distractions, provides an opportunity to literally expand one's horizons.

Armstrong (2006) argued that contemporary religions originated in the elevation of the value of compassion, which is consistent with ECM, as an approach to spirituality. Many younger (as well as older) adults avail themselves of opportunities to volunteer in service to others both in response to ongoing local needs as well as to natural disasters. The Dalai Lama (1999), in Tibetan Buddhist theory, is the present incarnation of Avalokiteshvara, the Bodhisattva of compassion, who emphasized that his basic religion is compassion. If the Internet provides an endless variety of experiential junk food, it also provides a reminder of the scope of human problems and indeed the precarious and fragile status of much of life on Earth. This could be a powerful stimulus for ECM.

The research by Templeton and Eccles indicated that identifying oneself as spiritual was more strongly related to ECM that identifying with a specific religion alone. The expansion of one's domain of moral concern might be expected to be strongly related to the expansion of one's consciousness. This was expressed in different terms by Levenson and Crumpler (1996) in their liberative model of development. The liberative model posits the possibility of reducing one's biosocial conditioning in ways that have been practiced for millennia by the contemplative psychologies that are present, if not widely recognized, in all religions. Contemplative practices such as meditation, studying teaching stories, and many other practices form the spiritual core of religions. There is much to be learned from observing relationships between liberation from a conditioned self and the attendant expansion of consciousness, on the one hand, and the expansion of one's scope of moral concern on the other. The recent collection of articles edited by Wayment and Bauer (2008) addresses this point in terms of "quieting the ego."

SUMMARY

The question of religiousness and spirituality in young adulthood and midlife is complex. Despite the decline in religious attendance, at least in the United States and much of Europe, religiousness and spirituality are clearly an important part of young adults' identity. For some, this religious identity may progress throughout the life span, in either linear or nonlinear patterns, while for others, it may decrease. There are also complex patterns of changes across cohorts in religiousness and spirituality, with clear cross-national differences. However, these large, empirical studies tend to ask fairly simple questions, which do not reflect the complexities of religious and spiritual development, theories of which were reviewed in the second half of this chapter.

However, there is relatively little empirical substantiation of the applicability of these theories in adulthood. Given the current focus simply on the development of measures, it is not surprising that, to our knowledge, no longitudinal studies of religious development in adulthood exist. However, there is a surprising lack even of cross-sectional studies of religious development in young adulthood and midlife, which we hope future studies will address.

ACKNOWLEDGMENT

Preparation of this chapter was supported by Grant No. 21733 from the John Templeton Foundation.

REFERENCES

Armstrong, K. (2006). *The great transformation: The beginning of our religious traditions.* New York: Alfred A. Knopf.

Arnett, J. (2004). *Emerging adulthood: The winding road from the late teens through the twenties.* Oxford, UK: Oxford University Press.

Chau, A. Y. (2001). *Miraculous response: Popular religion in contemporary China.* Stanford, CA: Stanford University Press.

Chau, A. Y. (2011). *Religion in contemporary China: Revitalization and innovation.* New York: Routledge.

Cherry, C., DeBerg, B. A., & Porterfield, A. (2001). *Religion on campus.* Chapel Hill: University of North Carolina Press.

Curnow, T. (1999). *Wisdom, intuition, and ethics.* Brookfield, VT: Ashgate.

Dalai Lama. (1999). *Ethics for the new millennium.* New York: Riverhead Books.

Dawson, L.L. (2004). Religion and the quest for virtual community. In L. L. Dawson & D. E. Cowan (Eds.), *Religion online: Finding faith on the internet* (pp. 75–89). New York: Routledge.

Dillon, M. (1994). Muslim communities in contemporary China: The resurgence of Islam after the Cultural Revolution. *Journal of Islamic Studies, 5,* 70–101.

DiMaggio, P. (2001). Doing religion in cyberspace: The promise and the perils. *Council of Societies for the Study of Religion Bulletin, 30,* 3–9.

Easwaran, E. (2008). *The mantram handbook* (5th ed.). Tomales, CA: Nilgiri Press.

Elder, G. H., & Shanahan, M. J. (2006). The life course and human development. In R. M. Lerner & W. Damon (Eds.), *Handbook of child psychology: Vol. 1. Theoretical models of human development* (6th ed., pp. 665–715). Hoboken, NJ: Wiley.

Emmons, R. A. (1999). *The psychology of ultimate concerns: Motivation and spirituality in personality.* New York: Guilford Press.

Erikson, E.H. (1963). *Childhood and society.* New York: Norton.

Feldman, D. H. (2008). The role of developmental change in spiritual development. In R. M. Lerner, R. W. Roeser, & E. Phelps (Eds.), *Positive youth development and spirituality: From theory to research* (pp. 167–196). West Conshohocken, PA: Templeton Foundation Press.

Forte, R. (Ed.). (1997). *Entheogens and the future of religion.* San Francisco, CA: Council on Spiritual Practices.

Fowler, J. (1981). *Stages of faith: The psychology of human development and the quest for meaning.* New York: HarperCollins.

Goldstein, J. (1993). *Insight meditation: The practice of freedom.* Boston: Shambhala.

Greenfield, E. A., Vaillant, G. E., & Marks, N. E. (2009). Do formal religious participation and spiritual perceptions have independent linkages with diverse dimensions of psychological well-being? *Journal of Health and Social Behavior, 50,* 196–212.

Hood, R. W., Jr. (2005). Mystical, spiritual, and religious experiences. In R. F. Paloutzian & C. L. Park (Eds.), *Handbook of the psychology of religion and spirituality* (pp. 348–364). New York: Guilford Press.

Hood, R. W., Jr., Hill, P. C., & Spilka, B. (2009). *The psychology of religion: An empirical approach* (4th ed.). New York: Guilford Press.

Jung, C. G. (1968). *The archtypes and the collective unconscious* (R. F. C. Hull, Trans). Princeton, NJ: Princeton University Press.

Kapleau, P. (1989). *The three pillars of Zen: Teaching, practice, and enlightenment.* New York: Anchor Books.

Keating, T. (1999). *The human condition: Contemplation and transformation.* Mahwah, NJ: Paulist Press.

Lau, M. A., Bishop, S. R., Segal, Z. V., Buis, T., Anderson, N. D., Carlson, L., et al. (2006). The Toronto Mindfulness Scale: Development and validation. *Journal of Clinical Psychology, 62,* 1445–1467.

Lee, T. L. (2007). Christianity in contemporary China: An update. *Journal of Church and State, 49,* 277–304.

Levenson, M. R., Aldwin, C., Beyer, D. J., Dieker, A., Niedermeyer, M., Porkorny, J., et al. (2011). The contemplative life as freedom: The liberative model of human development. *Noetic Now, 8.*

Levenson, M. R., & Crumpler, C. A. (1996). Three models of adult development. *Human Development, 39,* 135–149.

Mrazek, M. D., Smallwood, J. & Schooler, J. W. (2012). Mindfulness and mind-wandering: Finding convergence through opposing constructs. *Emotuion, 12*(3), 442–448.

Nelson, J. M. (2010). *Psychology, religion, and spirituality.* New York: Springer.

Oman, D., & Thoresen, D. E. (2005). Do religion and spirituality influence health? In R. F. Paloutzian & C. L. Park (Eds.), *Handbook of the psychology of religion and spirituality* (pp. 435–459). New York: Guilford Press.

Oman, D., & Thoresen, C. E. (2007). How does one learn to be spiritual? The neglected role of spiritual modeling in health. In T. G. Plante & C. E. Thoresen (Eds.), *Spirit, science, and health: How the spiritual mind fuels physical wellness* (pp. 39–56). Westport, CT: Praeger.

Oser, F., & Gmunder, P. (1991). *Religious judgement: A developmental approach.* Birmingham, AL: Religious Education Press.

Oser, F., Scarlett, W. G., & Bucher, A. (2006). Religious and spiritual development throughout the life span. In W. Daemon & R. M. Lerner (Eds.), *Handbook of child psychology: Vol. 2. Theoretical models of human development,* (6th ed., pp. 942–998). Hoboken, NJ: Wiley.

Pew Research Center, Pew Forum on Religion and Public Life. (2010). *Religion among the millennials.* Retrieved from *http://pewforum.org/Age/Religion-Among-the-Millennials.aspx.*

Shah, I. (1964). *The Sufis.* New York: Doubleday.

Shah, I. (2000). *Knowing how to know: A practical philosophy in the Sufi tradition.* Los Altos, CA: ISHK Book Service.

Smith, H. (2000). *Cleansing the doors of perception: The religious significance of entheogenic plants and chemicals.* New York: Tarcher.

Smith, C., & Snell, P. (2009). *Souls in transition: The religious and spiritual lives of emerging adults.* Oxford, UK: Oxford University Press.

Smith, C., Snell, P., & Longest, K. (2009). Religious trajectories from the teenage years. In C. Smith & P. Snell (Eds.), *Souls in transition: The religious and spiritual lives of emerging adults* (pp. 211–256). Oxford, UK: Oxford University Press.

Smith, T. W. (2009). *Religious change around the world.* Retrieved from *http://news.uchicago. edu/files/religionsurvey_20091023.pdf.*

Smith, W. C. (1998). *Faith and belief: The difference between them.* Oxford, UK: Oneworld Publications.

Templeton, J. L., & Eccles, J. S. (2008). Spirituality, "expanding circle morality," and positive youth development. In R. M. Lerner, R. W. Roeser, & E. Phelps (Eds.), *Positive youth development and spirituality: From theory to research* (pp. 197–209). West Conshohocken, PA: Templeton Foundation Press.

Trumble, W. R. (2007). *Shorter Oxford English dictionary* (6th ed.). Oxford, UK: Oxford University Press.

Uecker, J. E., Regnerus, M. D., & Vaaler, M. L. (2007). Losing my religion: The social sources of religious decline in early adulthood. *Social Forces, 85,* 1667–1692.

Wayment, H. A., & Bauer, J. (2008). *Transcending self-interest: Psychological explorations of the quiet ego.* Washington, DC: American Psychological Association.

Wuthnow, R. (2003). *All in synch: How music and art are revitalizing American religion.* Berkeley: University of California Press.

Wuthnow, R. (2007). *After the baby boomers: How twenty- and thirty-somethings are shaping the future of American religion.* Princeton, NJ: Princeton University Press.

10

Old Persons, Old Age, Aging, and Religion

Susan H. McFadden

Since the first volume of the *Handbook of the Psychology of Religion and Spirituality* appeared, wars, economic recession, and natural disasters have plagued persons of all ages. The worldwide events of the early years of the 21st century presented historians with opportunities to reflect on their meaning and impact, and compare them with the wars, recessions, and disasters of the past. In contrast, a quieter and less disruptive event early in 2004 could not be as easily traced through history: The social networking site Facebook was launched. It joined other online communities enabling a global, nearly instant capacity for communication, unrivaled by any modern invention in its effects on human communication except perhaps for the telephone.

Admittedly, putting what some believe to be an adolescent preoccupation with narcissistic, insipid comments that can be mean and/or unintelligible in the same paragraph with complex sources of human suffering may seem to be insensitive as well as historically suspect. However, as I reviewed the gerontological literature on religion and aging published since late 2003, when I completed my chapter for the *Handbook*'s first volume (McFadden, 2005), one of the most consistent themes I observed was an emphasis on social connectedness that had not been so obvious in the works reviewed previously. Although I can claim no causal relation with the rapid spread of Internet-based social connections, nevertheless this new form of communication represents a technological expression of relationality and the desire for community that is reflected in much recent research and scholarship on the psychology of religion and spirituality in old age.

In addition to disapproval of placing what can be a trivial waste of time alongside major disruptions in human life, readers may object because this is supposed to be a chapter about old people. Do they even know what Facebook is? In fact, many do, and those who have access to computers are some of the most avid users of online social media. A review of 151 articles cited in 11 different databases between 1990 and 2008 found a steady increase in publications on older adult use of computers. The authors concluded that "the most common use of computers and the Internet for older adults appears to be for communication and social support" (Wagner, Hassanein, & Head, 2010, p. 873).

Some of these persons have been diagnosed with dementia. Researchers in Wales surveyed online members of a self-help network called DASNI (Dementia Advocacy and Support Network International) and found that DASNI participation gave people an important sense of belonging, identity, purpose, and value (Clare, Rowlands, & Quin, 2008).

Faith communities have begun to employ digital connectivity to support their mission by making information more widely available and by promoting opportunities for interaction afforded by the Web 2.0 world (Lytle, 2009). Farrell's (2011) review of the websites of 600 congregations representing nine Christian denominations in the United States found an "age divide" not in terms of computer use but in the fact that the denominations with the highest percentage of older persons had the least sophisticated and interactive websites. However, as more old people use the Internet for social interactions, they may insist that their congregations replace static, brochure-like web pages with what Farrell calls "portals for actual church activity" (p. 85).

Along with the theme of social connectivity, another recurrent message in the literature on the psychology of religion and aging can be identified with a phrase commonly found on Facebook: "It's complicated." This statement usually appears when someone needs to explain relationship dilemmas (e.g., dating without being divorced) but the statement "It's complicated" applies in a scholarly way to the way researchers have been evaluating the definitions, measures, and methods employed in the psychological study of old people's religiousness and spirituality. In the first volume of this *Handbook*, editors Paloutzian and Park (2005) encouraged this by calling for a multilevel interdisciplinary paradigm that acknowledges the dynamic, reciprocal determinism of human beings and their environments. Other chapters, particularly on definitions of religiousness and spirituality (Zinnbauer & Pargament, 2005), measurement (Hill, 2005), and research methods (Hood & Belzen, 2005), supported the editors' paradigm and are cited in many of the studies reviewed here.

In the first section of this chapter, I revisit topics addressed in the gerontology chapter of the first volume of the *Handbook*. The theme "It's complicated" is reinforced by a review of current thinking about defining and measuring religiousness and spirituality among old persons. In addition, the section describes the debate over how psychologists and other social scientists studying religion and aging should balance attention to common factors found among religions with the study of unique attributes of particular religious traditions. It concludes by adding the complicating factor of time and the effort to identify sources and types of stability and change in religiousness and spirituality.

The chapter on gerontology in the first *Handbook* suggested possibilities for intellectual cross-fertilization between gerontology and the psychology of religion, particularly in terms of these disciplines' studies of cognition and emotion. There has been little movement toward the development of conceptual models that address the interaction between religion and old people's social cognition and moral reasoning. In contrast, the growth of positive psychology and its call for more research on topics like gratitude, forgiveness, and hope has contributed to progress in connecting the psychology of late-life emotion with the psychology of religion. For example, Krause and Ellison (2009b) found that old people's feelings of gratitude toward God reflect their level and type of participation in faith communities. Also, the need for greater study of religious emotions in later life has begun to be addressed, most notably in the development of a multidimensional measure of the experience of worship, including the emotions it evokes (Idler et al., 2009). The second section of the current chapter touches on some of the issues presented in the first volume, but places them more firmly within a social context by considering issues of relationality and belongingness within faith communities.

Before moving to the discussion of new developments in research on religion and aging, we need to pause to consider the language employed to refer to this chapter's focal persons and period of life. A paper published in one of the premier research journals for gerontology (*Journal of Gerontology: Social Sciences*) influenced the terminology used here. Richard Settersten argued that gerontologists resist talking about "old people" and "old age" because "these terms leave us feeling unsettled or uneasy" (2005, p. S174). Ever sensitive to both subtle and obvious indicators of cultural ageism, most gerontologists reject the label "seniors" and instead speak of "older adults" in "later life." Settersten claimed that this language results in "an ideology of 'agelessness,' itself a kind of ageism, in which old age is viewed as something that can be transcended. . . . In taking steps to confront and even embrace these taboo terms the visibility and value of old people and old age in science and society might be promoted and raised rather than avoided and low-ered" (p. S174). He continued by stating that although gerontologists talk about aging, a process that begins at conception, they usually only study old age "in ways that knife it off from the past" (p. S174).

In line with the argument about complexity presented in the next section, Settersten (2005) asserted that gerontologists need to work within the creative tension between commonness and difference across the life span instead of defaulting automatically to the assumption of increasing variability with age. The shared characteristics of all old people reflect the kinds of existential and spiritual issues that make the study of the psychology of religion so salient for this age group. For example, Settersten's list of commonalities includes normative declines in physical and mental health, loss of close friends and fam-ily members to death, awareness of personal mortality, deeper desire for meaning, and "greater acceptance of things that cannot be controlled in life, coupled with greater fear of losing control over one's life" (p. S175). These are among the many reasons that old age evokes fear and stigmatization of those whose very existence reminds the not-yet-old of human vulnerability, dependency, and mortality.

The acknowledgment of commonalities among the old does not mean that geron-tologists should return to the stage theories of the 20th century that in some simplistic interpretations had everyone marching in lockstep to the end of life. Rather, Settersten says, "We must be as open to things that are shared within and between groups of old people as we are to the things that fracture the coherence of 'old age' or 'old people' as categories" (p. S175). The same might be said of the commonalities and differences among religions, a topic explored in the next section.

REVISITING FACTORS AFFECTING RESEARCH ON RELIGION AND AGING

A study published in 2005 examined the quality of research on religion and spirituality in four major gerontology journals between 1985 and 2002. The authors divided the research into two groups: studies with religion and/or spirituality as the primary focus and stud-ies that dealt with religion and/or spirituality tangentially. They read 66 published works and rated them on the multidimensionality of their measures and on internal validity (reliable measure(s), inferential statistics, and multivariate statistics for studies with more than one independent variable). External validity ratings assessed the use of a random sample, specification of response rate, and repeated measures. The researchers also evaluated theoretical sophistication by coding for whether the study offered (1) a rationale for the questions it addressed about religion, (2) hypotheses about religion, and (3) an explanatory model of religion's mediation or moderation of outcomes (Weaver, Flannelly, Strock, Krause, & Flannelly, 2005). Results showed that studies focused specifically on religion used multidimensional measures, and the number of studies using these measures increased over the period examined. Similarly, ratings of internal and external validity and of theoretical sophistication increased across time.

One disappointment from findings of this study is that despite the use of multidimensional scales, most research measured just a few of the dimensions. Thus, only a slice of a whole, complex, multidetermined religious life in old age is being captured in this research. More heartening is the authors' conclusion that methodological sophistication has improved significantly. However, that conclusion needs to be tempered by their observation that "less than 80% of major studies tested specific hypotheses, and only half presented explanatory models" (Weaver et al., 2005, p. 132). In other words, despite progress in the development of multidimensional scales, more work is needed to ensure that they fully capture the ways religion affects the lives of old people (see Hill, Chapter 3, this volume). This will be challenging given the ongoing debate how these constructs should be defined. In particular, the issue of "unmoored spirituality" (unconnected to religious beliefs or traditions) remains thorny. In addition, some researchers are calling for the end of "generic" measures of religiousness and spirituality that have no grounding in the particularities of faith traditions (e.g., Glicksman, 2009).

Definitional Issues

As noted in the earlier *Handbook* volume, during the 1990s, controversies erupted over whether spirituality should be defined and measured apart from religiousness (McFadden, 2005; Zinnbauer & Pargament, 2005). Although most researchers treat religiousness and spirituality as separate but related constructs, they continue to debate the extent of their overlap (see Oman, Chapter 2, this volume). For example, in a review of *Spirituality and Aging*, a book written by noted social gerontologist Robert Atchley (2009), Stephen Sapp (2010) claimed that Atchley embraced "unmoored spirituality." While praising Atchley's courage in addressing a topic that is the object of scorn from some scientists, Sapp also stated that Atchley's definition of spirituality risks alienating some religious old persons by implying that "their traditional religion is lacking in some way" (Sapp, 2010, p. 275).

Harold Koenig, whose research has been a major influence on the study of religion, spirituality, and aging since the 1980s, questions whether researchers who follow Atchley's model are conflating elders' spirituality with their ability to continue to feel that life is meaningful through their appreciation of beauty, feelings of gratitude and hope, and humor in the midst of age-related difficulties. One could argue that all of these reflect people's "search for the sacred," as implied by positive psychologists who list these responses in the category of "transcendence," which they consider to be one of six human virtues (Peterson & Seligman, 2004). Koenig disagrees. He contends that spirituality measures are "contaminated with questions assessing positive character traits or mental health: optimism, forgiveness, gratitude, meaning and purpose in life, peacefulness, harmony, and general well-being" (Koenig, 2008, p. 349). Koenig apparently wants to put the spiritual genie back into the religion bottle, saying that "the term spirituality should be measured using questions about public and private religious beliefs, practices, rituals, ceremonies, attitudes, degree of commitment, and level of motivation, that are appropriate to the faith traditions of the subjects under study" (p. 354). Despite his leadership in this domain of scholarship and research, Koenig's opinion appears to be a minority position at this time.

Peter Coleman, a British gerontologist, argues that it is impossible today to avoid ambiguity when using the term "spiritual." Moreover, although researchers may distinguish the domain of the religious from that of the spiritual, Coleman notes that the persons in their 70s, 80s, and 90s who have participated in his research rarely use the terms "spiritual" and "spirituality." Beginning in the 1970s, Coleman encouraged his research participants to speak about their beliefs, whether tethered to a specific religious tradition or more generally associated with existential meaning. This enabled him to observe that "many of the salient elements in current discourses about belief, religion and spirituality were already present in some older people's thoughts and conversations in the 1970s: in particular the foregrounding of personal experience (and personal interpretation of that experience) rather than the authority of church teaching" (2011, p. 25).

One pathway out of the definitional morass would be for psychologists of religion to heed Paloutzian and Park's (2005; Chapter 1, this volume) call for interdisciplinary collaborations, particularly with philosophers, theologians, and religious studies scholars. The knowledge base of these persons can assist psychologists in conceptualizing unique and common ways of being religious and spiritual. The psychologists, in turn, can identify and study the processes that influence how old persons come to view certain beliefs and practices as sacred or as meaningful and the outcomes of holding fast to these beliefs, especially in times of trouble. A model of research teams comprising psychologists and theologians is found in some European universities, where psychologists of religion regularly collaborate with theologians on research (e.g., Noth, Morgenthaler, & Greider, 2011).

Unique and Common Ways of Being Religious and Spiritual

Although it seems unlikely at this time that many gerontologists will heed Koenig's insistence that spirituality measures should focus on expressions of religious faith, they are embracing the postmodern "critical stance toward universalism in religious studies" (Nelson, 2009, p. 199). Taking this position, Glicksman (2009) argues that gerontologists have failed to note how definitions and measures of religiousness and spirituality reflect unacknowledged American Protestant ideals and values, which make certain items inapplicable to persons from other faith traditions because of their emphasis on individualistic, private religious behaviors (see also Cohen, Hall, Koenig, & Meador, 2005). Oman (2009; Chapter 2, this volume) counters that it is possible, and necessary, to study both unique and common facets of religion and spirituality, and that researchers can empirically test how specific religious traditions function as moderators on the associations of various measured dimensions of religiousness and spirituality with the outcomes of interest (e.g., physical or mental health).

A study by Krause (2004) illustrates Oman's point. Krause wanted to know whether one could identify commonalities among religious old people as well as particular attributes unique to African Americans, a group well known among gerontologists for their high levels of measured religiousness (e.g., Taylor, Chatters, & Jackson, 2007). Krause developed and tested a conceptual model that included church attendance and church-based social support as common factors shared by persons of faith. Gerontologists have repeatedly demonstrated that these common factors contribute to well-being among old persons regardless of race (see Krause, 2008, for a review). However, unique to elder African-Americans is the function of the church in addressing racial injustice and giving them a theological basis for coping with it. Krause's model proposed that an increase in the proportion of African-Americans in a congregation would be associated with greater attendance and thus more opportunities for emotional support coping with injustice. This, he hypothesized, would produce greater life satisfaction. Results of his national study of 752 African-Americans, age 66 and older, showed that their satisfaction with life comes both from the factors common to faith-community participation and the particularities of African-Americans churches' traditions and theological support for confronting and resisting racism.

Krause's (2004) attention to the theology articulated in African-Americans churches is an example of an emerging recognition of the need for social scientists studying religion and spirituality to know more about particularities of various faith traditions. However, his willingness to account for both unique and common aspects of religiousness is not shared by all. For example, Hall, Koenig, and Meador (2004) claim that learning about religious particularities is like learning to be fluent in a language; they call for a "cultural-linguistic" approach to understanding different religious worldviews. Less inclined toward identifying commonalities, and strongly opposed to what they view as "generic" approaches to religion and spirituality, they assert that those who would study religion and spirituality need to make their measures more theologically grounded and reflective of the beliefs associated with particular faith traditions (Hall, Meador, & Koenig, 2008).

Hall, Koenig, and Meadow (2010) illustrated their "cultural-linguistic" approach to the unique factors of religion in a pilot study of members of one Christian denomination: Episcopalians. They wanted see if "native speakers" (i.e., those very familiar with the Episcopalian worldview) could differentiate people nominated by their priests as "well-formed" and "unformed" Episcopalians using a method of narrative content analysis. The former were members "who were both identified with the denomination and deeply formed by its distinct theological context" (p. 167), while the latter were "members who, despite identification with the denomination, were not recognizably formed by the distinct theological context of that denomination" (p. 167). The groups scored similarly on standard measures of spirituality, forgiveness, and religious attendance, and yet experts (Episcopal priests) doing blind reviews of their responses to open-ended questions (e.g., "Who or what is God for you?" "Please describe your practice or prayer, if any") correctly classified 20 of the 23 participants. The authors claimed the experts' "fluency" enabled them to detect differences that were not captured by standard measures of religiousness and spirituality.

Glicksman (2009) agrees with the goal of conducting more finely tuned, theologically sensitive studies of old people. In particular, he objects to general measures of religiousness that include items that contradict tenets of traditional Judaism. For example, he notes that some scales categorize reading and study of sacred literature as private religious activities. However, "Judaism encourages study with at least one other person (called "chevruta") and in general study is a social activity" (Glicksman, 2009, p. 253). Like Hall et al. (2010), Glicksman wants to understand differences within a specific faith group. He and a colleague studied denominationally affiliated "core Jews," nonaffiliated "core Jews" (both groups comprising persons who identified their religion as Judaism) and "noncore" Jews, who stated they were Jewish but identified with another faith (usually Christianity) (Glicksman & Koropeckyj-Cox, 2009). In some surveys, all of these people would be grouped together as "Jews," but Glicksman and Koropeckyj-Cox believe that examining meaningful distinctions among Jews can promote a better understanding of the interplay between religion and ethnicity (see Saroglou & Cohen, Chapter 17, this volume). They compared data from the 2000–2001 National Jewish Population Survey (NJPS) and data collected by the NJPS in 1990. In one decade, the percentage of older Jews who identified with a denomination fell from 87 to 72%, as did the percentage who observed Jewish rituals like the Passover seder. These changes were true both of the affiliated and the nonaffiliated core Jews.

Further study is required to determine whether the three categories of Jews identified by Glicksman and Koropeckyj-Cox, as well as the "formed" and "unformed" Episcopalians studied by Hall, Koenig and Meador, are associated with differences in the variables studied by psychologists of religion. For example, do formed Episcopalians or affiliated core Jews show less prejudice, more effective coping, better health, or a greater sense of life meaning than unformed Episcopalians or nonaffiliated core Jews and noncore Jews? Psychologists of religion who pay attention to development would also want to know whether people shift from one category to another as they mature through adulthood.

It's About Time

One of the key challenges for gerontologists is to understand the dynamics of stability and change in individuals and in cohorts, but these dynamics cannot be captured without repeated data collection. The importance of examining change and stability is illustrated in a report on a 2-year longitudinal study of religious coping by hospitalized persons age 55 and older. The study used the Brief RCOPE and showed that positive religious coping (e.g., seeking spiritual support, collaborative religious coping, benevolent religious reappraisals) was associated with "increases in stress-related growth, spiritual outcomes and cognitive functioning," while negative religious coping (punishing God reappraisal, demonic reappraisal, interpersonal religious discontent) predicted "declines in spiritual outcome and quality of life, increases in depressed mood, and declines in independence in daily activities" (Pargament, Koenig, Tarakeshwar, & Hahn, 2004, p. 726). These differences were strongest in people who had scored consistently with positive or negative coping both at baseline and follow-up.

The effects of positive and negative religious coping have been well documented, but this study offered several important new insights. One relates to the previous discussion about the importance of accounting for varying theological perspectives that do not necessarily align with psychological assumptions about well-being. For example, although psychologists often assume that psychological well-being depends on an internal locus of control, some religious persons, particularly African-American Christians, show better outcomes in well-being when they embrace the idea of God-mediated control (Krause, 2005). Similarly, Pargament et al. (2004) observed that some of the persons in their study demonstrated "religious passivity" (a kind of external locus of control), but they also experienced positive spiritual outcomes, such as the sense of growing closer to God and the church and spiritual growth. These spiritual outcomes can coexist with a negative turn in health and well-being. That is, persons might be very ill and close to death and yet experience a different kind of well-being associated with their belief that God's promises of love and comfort abide through suffering and loss.

A second important observation from the Pargament et al. (2004) study of medically ill old people is that negative religious coping is not necessarily a chronic condition. The persons who showed negative coping at only baseline or at follow-up 2 years later did not show the health disadvantages of the group with negative religious coping at both times. Analyses did not show differences in outcomes when the change went from positive to negative or vice versa.

One weakness of the Pargament et al. (2004) study is that it does not report the range of ages of participants. Thus, we cannot know how many birth cohorts were included. As Dannefer and Kelley-Moore note, "Without the ability to compare multiple birth cohorts, we are unable to determine whether change or stability with age is cohort specific or universal across cohorts" (2009, p. 394). In recent years, gerontologists have gathered more multiple-cohort longitudinal data, and have begun to get a clearer understanding of the complexities of integrating levels of analysis, from examination of population trends to study of rates of within-person change (Hofer & Piccinin, 2010). Unfortunately, such data usually do not include multidimensional measures of religiousness and spirituality. Overall, there are few longitudinal studies of religiousness and spirituality across the life span, although it is heartening to see that Weaver et al.'s analysis of gerontological research found an increase in the "use of repeated-measured designs, in which participants were surveyed two or more times over a period of a year or more (2005, p. 133).

A notable exception to the observation about the paucity of longitudinal studies spanning many years is found in research by Wink and Dillon (2003) using data from the Institute of Human Development (IHD) longitudinal study. The IHD research began in the 1920s when the participants were very young and followed them through old age, with interviews conducted four times in adulthood. These interviews included several standard questions about religiousness (e.g., frequency of religious participation and prayer, belief in God and the afterlife), but spirituality was not directly addressed. Thus, Wink and Dillon deduced participants' spirituality from ratings of their statements about "the importance of noninstitutionalized religion or non-tradition-centered beliefs and practices" (2003, p. 918). They found religious stability across adulthood, particularly in those who had been more religious as young adults. On the other hand, spirituality appeared to become more important from midlife on, although, as they observed, it is impossible to disentangle the influences of psychological development from the cultural changes of the post-1960s.

One of the most pervasive cultural changes in the last half-century has been overall decline in religious participation in certain faith communities. Coleman (2011), who has studied old persons' religious beliefs and behaviors in the United Kingdom for more than 40 years, notes that, like elders in the United States, British old people "continue to appear substantially more religious in attitude and interest" than younger members of the population (p. 29). They are more likely to attend religious services regularly and be socially engaged with the faith community, although Coleman also found that his more recent studies show more "heterodoxy of belief" (p. 30) compared with the more clearly articulated Christian beliefs he found in his earlier research with old people.

SOCIAL RELATIONSHIPS AND FAITH COMMUNITIES

Numerous examples of attention to the significance of social relationships and community for understanding religiousness and spirituality appeared in the first volume of the *Handbook*. For example, writing about religious and spiritual development in childhood, Boyatzis (2005) called on psychologists to pay attention to the "sociocultural embeddedness of religious and spiritual growth and to study interpersonal and cultural mediators that develop a *relational consciousness* [italics added]" (p. 138). Piedmont's (2005) chapter on personality reviewed two important midrange theories about human relationships—object relations theory and attachment theory—that in their recent "rapprochement" have been shown to have "far-reaching implications for our understanding of spirituality" (Hall, 2007, p. 14). In addressing religion, morality, and self-control, Geyer and Baumeister (2005) adopted a social-functionalist perspective to argue that religions provide pathways to human virtue which in turn "promotes healthy, harmonious society" (p. 413).

Papers published after the *Handbook* also employ a social-functionalist perspective. For example, Graham and Haidt state that psychological studies of religiousness need to be "relentlessly social" (2010, p. 140). Another recent study criticizes the individualistic focus of most research on religiousness, spirituality, and psychology by saying that "the chasm within these studies is their sole focus on intrapersonal indices of religion and spirituality" (Brelsford, Marinelli, Ciarrocchi, & Dy-Liacco, 2009, p. 151).

As shown in the work of Neal Krause, the emphasis on relationality and social connectedness is particularly significant for the effort to understand the dynamics of religiousness and spirituality in old age. Krause has developed a conceptual model that turns on the idea that religions bind people together in social relationships that have important implications for psychosocial functioning. His model asserts that more frequent church attendance creates more cohesive congregations. Old people participating in these congregations receive more spiritual and emotional support from fellow congregants, and feel a closer spiritual connection to others. These social connections are associated with greater gratitude toward God (Krause & Ellison, 2009b), more satisfaction with health (Krause & Wulff, 2005), a deeper sense of meaning in life (Krause, 2007), support for coping with financial strain (Krause, 2006), and adoption of religious coping responses (Krause, 2010b). In addition, among very old people (age 85 and older), having a close friend in church is associated with fewer physician visits (Krause, 2010a).

Despite all these apparently positive outcomes from old people's involvement in faith communities, we should not forget that congregational life can also be fraught with controversy and riddled with meanness. Working with longitudinal data, Krause and Ellison (2009a) found that negative interactions with fellow church members produce greater religious doubt in old people—doubt that they suppress out of concern that it will potentiate the negativity they experience. When they do this, they become less satisfied with their health. Nevertheless, Linda George, a gerontologist who has studied religion, spirituality, and aging for many years recently concluded that most old people are "still happy after all these years" (George, 2010). She notes that one important reason for their subjective well-being is the emotional and spiritual resilience that flows from their religious behaviors.

Resilience, sometimes described as the "bounce-back" response from adversity to adaptive, competent functioning, is attracting increasing attention from developmental psychologists (e.g., Ciccetti & Blender, 2006). Ramsey and Blieszner's (1999, 2013) narrative analyses of interviews with old people in Germany and the United States have revealed a number of important insights into the spiritual resilience nurtured in religious communities and reinforced by religious beliefs. Nominated by the pastors of their Lutheran congregations as the people the pastors would turn to for emotional and spiritual comfort, the old people in Ramsey and Blieszner's studies told hopeful yet realistic stories about their ability to deal with the exigencies of aging. They accepted the limitations wrought by old age, but maintained a strong sense of hopefulness about the ultimate outcomes of their lives. Ramsey and Blieszer also described these spiritually resilient elders as secure in their sense of individual identity while also being securely connected to their communities, particularly their faith communities. Finally, the stories of these old people revealed that the conundrum for developmentalists over what remains stable and what changes in life is not an either/or proposition. Old people of deep and long-enduring faith understand that their lives are a complex mixture of growth and transformation along with centeredness and stability. Ramsey and Blieszer concluded that their interviewees had gained these perspectives through individual life experiences viewed through the lens of Lutheran theology and religious practice.

None of the persons Ramsey and Blieszner interviewed had been diagnosed with a form of dementia. All were still living independently and, though slowed by age, they could still participate in their faith communities. Nevertheless, it is important to extend these themes of relationality, social connectedness, and resilience to persons with progressive forgetfulness. Some research has even shown that social ties within religious communities may slow the rate of cognitive loss (Hill, Burdette, Angel, & Angle, 2006). Moreover, spirituality can moderate the negative effects of frailty (which, for many old people, involves memory loss) on psychological well-being (Kirby, Coleman, & Daley, 2004).

These studies argue for the continuing importance of faith communities for their members experiencing cognitive decline. However, congregations can be ageist, particularly in their exclusion of elders with dementia. Some religious organizations are working to remedy this. A good example is the Dementia Group of the Christian Council on Aging (*www.ccoa.org.uk*) in Great Britain, which publishes an online newsletter with advice and support for congregations seeking to strengthen their ministries with elders with dementia and those who care for them. Faith communities can become schools for friendship with persons with dementia by providing guidance grounded in their theological understandings of personhood and relationality; they also offer opportunities for people to form meaningful relationships regardless of cognitive status (McFadden & McFadden, 2011).

THE FUTURE: IN THE CLOUD?

In the last decade, many important components of personal and social life have moved into "the cloud," a metaphor describing the location in cyberspace of everything from personal photo albums and financial transactions to college courses, retail outlets, and information about nearly everything a human being might want to know. As stated at the outset of this chapter, old people make up a growing segment of the users of online resources for information and interpersonal interaction. All forms of "senior housing," including nursing homes, are recognizing the need to provide wireless Internet access. The question this chapter raises about life in the cloud concerns the extent to which it will replace regular, personal contact with people who share beliefs about what is most meaningful in life and about how to live in answer to the call of religious faith. For isolated old people, frequent online contacts with clergy and fellow congregants could be a great blessing. With video connections, they could participate in worship services in "real time." They could also interact with much younger people, perhaps taking on the role of a "spiritual model" (Oman & Thoresen, 2003). Undoubtedly, some faith communities will find creative ways of moving into the cloud, where persons of all ages can discover rich new interpersonal connections for the kind of emotional and spiritual support Krause (2010a) has found to be so important to well-being.

But, of course, "it's complicated." Sociologists report that in the United States social networks are shrinking and people have fewer persons to whom they can turn to discuss important personal matters. In a study comparing national data collected in 1985 and in 2004, McPherson, Smith-Lovin, and Brashears (2006) found that mean network sizes had been reduced by about one-third. The one demographic group that proved the exception to this conclusion was the old: "The elderly have been more stable than most other groups in their core social connections" (p. 371). Although the study did not measure religious participation, the research reported in this chapter suggests that many of those connections occurred within faith communities. The question for the future is whether people will continue to form meaningful relationships—whether in the cloud or in person—with others who share their religious beliefs and with whom they participate in religious life.

Sociologist Robert Wuthnow has concluded that since the 1950s many Americans have rejected a spirituality of "dwelling" (inhabiting a sacred space defined by religious traditions) in favor of a spirituality of "seeking." Spiritual seeking has been embraced because "people have been losing faith in a metaphysic that can make them feel at home in the universe and . . . they increasingly negotiate among competing glimpses of the sacred, seeking partial knowledge and practical wisdom" (1998, p. 3). This is true not only in the United States but also in Europe. A study by Storm (2009) conducted in 10 European countries identified four subtypes of what she called "fuzzy fidelity"—people who are "neither very religious nor specifically non religious" (p. 702): moderately religious, passively religious, belonging without believing, and believing without belonging. In the United States, Baker and Smith (2009) parsed the category of "not religious" and concluded it comprises three groups: atheists, agnostics, and unchurched believers.

Will people in these categories cope differently with the physical, social, and mental changes of aging compared with the old people studied by gerontologists for the past three decades, people who often had lifelong associations with faith communities and deeply held religious beliefs? In the United States, 76 million baby boomers are moving into old age, and tracking their sense of life meaning as the challenges of old age mount will keep psychologists of religion and aging busy for years to come. For example, it will be important to address the meaning new cohorts of elders derive from their stance toward religiousness and spirituality and how it affects their decision making, especially around the kinds of life and death issues regularly encountered in old age. As noted by many persons who study religion, spirituality, and aging, this work will need to expand beyond the limited purview of so many of the studies reviewed here that included only American Christians and Jews. For example, Coleman states, "Although current generations of older people still tend to see themselves as religious and Christian, this is likely to change in the near future with the ageing of the baby boomers" (2011, p. 154).

For the present, it is good to be reminded once again of the strengths and resilience of today's old people. This chapter has largely relied on a review of research documenting the physical and psychosocial benefits accruing to old persons with long-time personal connections to faith communities. Most of this research employed multidimensional measures of religiousness and spirituality, measures that people completed on paper, in the cloud, or in response to a structured telephone call. As valid and reliable as these measures are, however, sometimes one can learn as much or more from spending time with old people and listening to their stories. For example, on a pleasant summer evening, I sat on the deck of a small cabin "up north," talking with a 93-year-old man and his 89-year-old wife. As we chatted about life on the lake over the last 70 years, they reflected on their involvement with a local church. The congregation originally reached out to the man in the late 1930s, when he and his buddies came to the area for deer hunting. A few years later, when he married and introduced his wife to the woods and lakes of Michigan's Upper Peninsula, they continued to participate in the congregation. The day before our talk, they visited a fellow church member who was homebound and close to death. They knew they would never see their long-time friend again, and that regrettably this would be their last visit to the lake. As I watched them later, sitting on the bench on their dock after sunset, I thought about their stories, struggles, and strengths and the faith and faith communities that had been so important in their long lives. We have much more to learn from persons like them. We also have much to learn from persons now moving into later life who will bring different religious and spiritual resources to bear upon the existential challenges of old age.

REFERENCES

Atchley, R. C. (2009). *Spirituality and aging*. Baltimore, MD: Johns Hopkins University Press.

Baker, J. O., & Smith, B. (2009). None too simple: Examining issues of religious nonbelief and nonbelonging in the United States. *Journal for the Scientific Study of Religion, 48,* 719–733.

Boyatzis, C. J. (2005). Religious and spiritual development in childhood. In R. F. Paloutzian & C. L. Park (Eds.), *Handbook of the psychology of religion and spirituality* (pp. 123–143). New York: Guilford Press.

Brelsford, G. M., Marinelli, S., Ciarrocchi, J. W., & Dy-Liacco, G. S. (2009). Generativity and spiritual disclosure in close relationships. *Psychology of Religion and Spirituality, 1,* 150–161.

Ciarrocchi, D., & Blender, J. A. (2006). A multiple-levels-of-analysis perspective on resilience: Implications for the developing brain, neural plasticity, and preventive interventions. *Annals of the New York Academy of Science, 1094,* 248–258.

Clare, L., Rowlands, J. M., & Quin, R. (2008). Collective strength: The impact of developing a shared social identity in early-stage dementia. *Dementia, 7,* 9–30.

Cohen, A. B., Hall, D. E., Koenig, H. G., & Meador, K. G. (2005). Social versus individual motivation: Implications for normative definitions of religious orientation. *Personality and Social Psychology Review, 9,* 48–61.

Coleman, P. G. (2011). *Belief and ageing: Spiritual pathways in later life.* Portland, OR: Policy Press.

Dannefer, D., & Kelley-Moore, J. A. (2009). Theorizing the life course: New twists in the paths. In V. L. Bengtson, D. Gans, N. Putney, & M. Silverstein (Eds.), *Handbook of theories of aging* (2nd ed., pp. 389–411). New York: Springer.

Farrell, J. (2011). The divide online: Civic organizing, identity building, and Internet fluency among different religious groups. *Journal of Media and Religion, 10,* 73–90.

George, L. K. (2010). Still happy after all these years: Research frontiers on subjective well-being in later life. *Journal of Gerontology: Social Sciences, 65B,* 331–339.

Geyer, A. L., & Baumeister, R. F. (2005). Religion, morality, and self-control: Values, virtues, and vices. In R. F. Paloutzian & C. L. Park (Eds.), *Handbook of the psychology of religion and spirituality* (pp. 412–432). New York: Guilford Press.

Glicksman, A. (2009). The contemporary study of religion and spirituality among the elderly: A critique. *Journal of Religion, Spirituality, and Aging, 21,* 244–258.

Glicksman, A., & Koropeckyj-Cox, T. (2009). Aging among Jewish Americans: Implications for understanding religion, ethnicity, and service needs. *The Gerontologist, 49,* 817–827.

Graham, J., & Haidt, J. (2010). Beyond beliefs: Religions bind individuals into moral communities. *Personality and Social Psychology Review, 14,* 140–150.

Hall, D. E., Koenig, H. G., & Meador, K. G. (2004). Conceptualizing "religion": How languages shapes and constrains knowledge in the study of religion and health. *Perspectives in Biology and Medicine, 47,* 386–401.

Hall, D. E., Koenig, H. G., & Meador, K. G. (2010). Episcopal measure of faith tradition: A context-specific approach to measuring religiousness. *Journal of Religion and Health, 49,* 164–178.

Hall, D. E., Meador, K. G., & Koenig, H. G. (2008). Measuring religiousness in health research: Review and critique. *Journal of Religion and Health, 47,* 134–163.

Hall, T. W. (2007). Psychoanalysis, attachment, and spirituality: Part I. The emergence of two relational traditions. *Journal of Psychology and Theology, 35,* 14–28.

Hill, P. C. (2005). Measurement in the psychology of religion and spirituality: Current status and evaluation. In R. F. Paloutzian & C. L. Park (Eds.), *Handbook of the psychology of religion and spirituality* (pp. 43–61). New York: Guilford Press.

Hill, T. D., Burdette, A. M., Angel, J. L., & Angel, R. J. (2006). Religious attendance and cognitive functioning among older Mexican Americans. *Journal of Gerontology: Psychological Sciences, 61B,* P3–P9.

Hofer, S. M., & Piccinin, A. M. (2010). Toward an integrative science of life-span development and aging. *Journal of Gerontology: Psychological Sciences, 65B,* 269–278.

Hood, R. W., Jr., & Belzen, J. A. (2005). Research methods in the psychology of religion. In R. F. Paloutzian & C. L. Park (Eds.), *Handbook of the psychology of religion and spirituality* (pp. 62–79). New York: Guilford Press.

Idler, E. L., Boulifard, D. A., Labouvie, E., Chen, Y. Y., Krause, T. J., & Contrada, R. J. (2009). Looking inside the black box of "attendance at services": New measures for exploring an old dimension in religion and health research. *The International Journal for the Psychology of Religion, 19,* 1–20.

Kirby, S. E., Coleman, P. G., & Daley, D. (2004). Spirituality and well-being in frail and nonfrail older adults. *Journal of Gerontology: Psychological Sciences, 59B,* P123–P129.

Koenig, H. G. (2008). Concerns about measuring "spirituality" in research. *Journal of Nervous and Mental Disease, 196,* 349–355.

Krause, N. (2004). Common facets of religion, unique facets of religion, and life satisfaction among older African Americans. *Journal of Gerontology: Social Sciences, 59B,* S109–S117.

Krause, N. (2005). God-mediated control and psychological well-being in late life. *Research on Aging, 27,* 136–164.

Krause, N. (2006). Exploring the stress-buffering effects of church-based and secular social support on self-rated health in late life. *Journal of Gerontology: Social Sciences, 61B,* S35–S43.

Krause, N. (2007). Longitudinal study of social support and meaning in life. *Psychology and Aging, 23,* 456–469.

Krause, N. (2008). *Aging in the church: How social relationships affect health.* West Conshohocken, PA: Templeton Foundation Press.

Krause, N. (2010a). Close companions at church, health and health care use in late life. *Journal of Aging and Health, 22,* 434–451.

Krause, N. (2010b). The social milieu of the church and religious coping responses: A longitudinal investigation of older whites and older blacks. *The International Journal for the Psychology of Religion, 20,* 109–129.

Krause, N., & Ellison, C. G. (2009a). The doubting process: A longitudinal study of the precipants and consequences of religious doubt in older adults. *Journal for the Scientific Study of Religion, 48,* 293–312.

Krause, N., & Ellison, C. G. (2009b). Social environment of the church and feelings of gratitude toward God. *Psychology of Religion and Spirituality, 1,* 191–205.

Krause, N., & Wulff, K. M. (2005). Church-based social ties, a sense of belonging in a congregation, and physical health status. *The International Journal for the Psychology of Religion, 15,* 73–93.

Lytle, J. A. (2009). One hour on Sunday is not enough: The power of the Internet to inform, form, and transform people of faith. *Congregations, 18*(3), 18–21.

McFadden, S. H. (2005). Points of connection: Gerontology and the psychology of religion. In R. F. Paloutzian & C. L. Park (Eds.), *Handbook of the psychology of religion and spirituality* (pp. 162–176). New York: Guilford Press.

McFadden, S. H., & McFadden, J. T. (2011). *Aging together: Dementia, friendship, and flourishing communities.* Baltimore, MD: Johns Hopkins University Press.

McPherson, M., Smith-Lovin, L., & Brashears, M. E. (2006). Social isolation in America: Changes in core discussion networks over two decades. *American Sociological Review, 71,* 353–375.

Nelson, J. M. (2009). *Psychology, religion, and spirituality.* New York: Springer.

Noth, I., Morgenthaler, C., & Greider, K. J. (2011). *Pastoralpsychologie und Religionpsychologie im Dialog* [Pastoral psychology and psychology of religion in dialogue]. Stuttgart, Germany: Verlag W. Kohlhammer.

Oman, D. (2009). Unique and common facets of religion and spirituality: Both are important. *Journal of Religion, Spirituality, and Aging, 21,* 275–286.

Oman, D., & Thoresen, C. E. (2003). Spiritual modeling: A key to spiritual and religious growth? *The International Journal for the Psychology of Religion, 13,* 149–165.

Paloutzian, R. F., & Park, C. L. (2005). Integrative themes in the current science of the psychology of religion. In R. F. Paloutzian & C. L. Park (Eds.), *Handbook of the psychology of religion and spirituality* (pp. 3–20). New York: Guilford Press.

Pargament, K. I., Koenig, H. G., Tarakeshwar, N., & Hahn, J. (2004). Religious coping methods as predictors of psychological, physical and spiritual outcomes among medically ill elderly patients: A two-year longitudinal study. *Journal of Health Psychology, 9,* 713–730.

Peterson, C., & Seligman, M. E. P. (2004). *Character strengths and virtues: A handbook and classification.* Washington, DC: American Psychological Association.

Piedmont, R. L. (2005). The role of personality in understanding religious and spiritual constructs. In R. F. Paloutzian & C. L. Park (Eds.), *Handbook of the psychology of religion and spirituality* (pp. 253–273). New York: Guilford Press.

Ramsey, J. L., & Blieszner, R. (1999). *Spiritual resilience in older women: Models of strength for challenges through the life span.* Thousand Oaks, CA: Sage.

Ramsey, J. L., & Blieszner, R. (2013). *Aging and spirituality: Hope, relationality, and the creative self.* Amityville, NY: Baywood.

Sapp, S. (2010). What have religion and spirituality to do with aging? Three approaches. *The Gerontologist, 50,* 271–279.

Settersten, R. A., Jr. (2005). Linking the two ends of life: What gerontology can learn from childhood studies. *Journal of Gerontology: Social Sciences, 60B,* S173–S180.

Storm, I. (2009). Halfway to heaven: Four types of fuzzy fidelity in Europe. *Journal for the Scientific Study of Religion, 48,* 702–718.

Taylor, R. J., Chatters, L. M., & Jackson, J. S. (2007). Religious and spiritual involvement among older African Americans, Caribbean Blacks, and non-Hispanic Whites: Findings from the National Survey of American Life. *Journal of Gerontology: Social Sciences, 62B,* S238–S250.

Wagner, N., Hassanein, K., & Head, M. (2010). Computer use by older adults: A multi-disciplinary review. *Computers in Human Behavior, 26,* 870–882.

Weaver, A. J., Flannelly, L. T., Strock, A. L., Krause, N., & Flannelly, K. J. (2005). The quantity and quality of research on religion and spirituality in four major gerontology journals between 1985 and 2002. *Research on Aging, 27,* 119–135.

Wink, P., & Dillon, M. (2003). Religiousness, spirituality, and psychosocial functioning in late adulthood: Findings from a longitudinal study. *Psychology and Aging, 18,* 916–924.

Wuthnow, R. (1998). *After heaven: Spirituality in America since the 1950s.* Berkeley: University of California Press.

Zinnbauer, B. J., & Pargament, K. I. (2005). Religiousness and spirituality. In R. F. Paloutzian & C. L. Park (Eds.), *Handbook of the psychology of religion and spirituality* (pp. 21–42). New York: Guilford Press.

Part III

RELIGION AND BASIC PSYCHOLOGY SUBDISCIPLINES

11

The Neuropsychology of Religious Experience

Patrick McNamara and P. Monroe Butler

BIRTH OF THE NEUROLOGY OF RELIGIOSITY

Neuroscientists, psychologists, and behavioral neurologists have long been interested in changes in religiosity following circumscribed brain lesions or generalized brain dysfunction. Connections among epilepsy, psychiatric illness, and alterations in religious ideation have been noted since antiquity, but little else could be ascertained about the nature of the brain pathology until the rise of modern medicine in the 19th and 20th centuries, which provided the tools of microscopy, gross neuropathology, neuroanatomy, and electroencephalography. In the 1970s, a series of reports (Bear & Fedio, 1977; Dewhurst & Beard, 1970; Geschwind, 1979; Waxman & Geschwind, 1975) ignited interest in brain–religion relationships. These early investigators described patients with intense religious obsessions and preoccupations. Dewhurst and Beard (1970) reported that some patients with temporal lobe epilepsy (TLE)—an epilepsy in which the seizure focus is in the temporal lobes, a region of the brain that controls memory, emotion, and aspects of language—were prone to intense religious conversions. Advances in neuroimaging in the latter half of the 20th century have added *in vivo* assessments of brain activity to these classic lesion-correlational approaches in the attempt to understand alterations in religious cognition due to brain dysfunction. Understanding brain correlates of religious beliefs, behaviors, and experiences can deepen our understanding of religion itself—certainly, a neurology of religiosity is crucial for developing a complete theory of the neuropsychology of religion more generally.

In this chapter, we briefly review the current methods and technologies available to the clinician-scientist to study the brain correlates of religiosity. This leads to a discussion of current findings on altered religious belief and behaviors in neurologically dysfunctional patients. Conditions discussed include our own research on patients with Parkinson's disease, in addition to patients with TLE, schizophrenia, or obsessive–compulsive disorder, stroke and neurosurgery patients, and patients with autism spectrum disorder. Next, we summarize what little is known about the neurochemistry of religiosity and brain activity correlates of religious cognition in neurologically intact healthy adults. We conclude with a tentative synthesis of the data on brain correlates of religious cognition and behavior.

We acknowledge that religion is difficult to define. Most of the data to date from the neurology of religion is from Western countries and draws primarily from Judeo-Christian traditions. Not all religions as meaning systems focus on supernatural-god concepts. Nevertheless, the practice of religious rituals and belief in supernatural agents occurs in virtually all human cultures (Brown, 1991; Murdock, 1965). We suggest that these basic components of religiousness (self, ritual, supernatural agent) can be studied profitably in the neurological arena. We fully realize that reducing the focus of study to these basic component processes carries with it the danger of not doing full justice to the the rich complexity of religious phenomena. We fully agree and endorse this sentiment. We do not advocate cessation of studies on the full array of religiousness across history, cultures, and individuals. The neurologist and neuropsychologist, however, have to begin with psychological processes whose component processes stand some chance of being reliably correlated with specific brain activity patterns.

Suppose we find that there are consistent brain activity patterns or correlates of religious beliefs and behaviors? What would that tell us about religion or the psychology of religion more generally? In one sense, it would be a banal discovery. After all, *all* beliefs and behaviors have some basis in brain activity patterns, because that is how we human beings operate. In addition, all kinds of distinctive forms of cognition have been correlated with distinctive patterns of brain activity. There is nothing surprising in that. So, for example, imagination, pretense and play, counterfactual ruminations, sexual desire, mathematical problem solving, planning, hand tool construction, action identification, person perception, theory of mind processing (ToM), dreaming, empathy, creativity, and many other forms of cognition have all been associated with more or less distinctive patterns of brain activity that are specific to each of those forms of cognition. Of course, there is never one spot in the brain that handles any particular cognitive function. Instead, the brain seems to prefer recruitment of similar neuronal networks when "handling" a given species of cognition. When engaging in ToM processing, for example, various sites in the orbitofrontal cortex are consistently recruited during such tasks. In addition, various other brain networks are also recruited during ToM tasks, but there is always at least some recruitment of orbitofrontal networks during ToM tasks. So identifying consistent brain activity patterns when persons are engaged in religious behaviors will not be surprising.

What will be surprising and theoretically important in the study of brain correlates of religious beliefs and behaviors is that once the brain networks that consistently engage or activate when religious cognition is occurring are reliably identified, certain questions immediately emerge:

- Are these networks associated with any other, less complex forms of cognition such as "agency detection" or ToM processing? If so, then the neurology data would support theories of religious cognition that invoke these primary forms of cognition as important in the evolution of religious belief.
- Are these networks associated with any particular genetic loci? If so, how strong are the associations and what, if any, is the pattern of inheritance?

- Are these networks associated with any specific neuromodulators or neurotransmitters that regulate their activation patterns? If so, are these the transmitters that are targeted by or affected in any sort of specific way by the so-called enthcogens that people have been using for centuries to induce religious experiences?
- Do these networks come online in any sort of ordered developmental sequence? Is the emergence of religious cognition in children linked to the emergence of these brain systems in any meaningful way?
- Can lesions in these networks induce loss of religiosity? If so, can restoration of these networks facilitate religiosity in any meaningful way?

METHODS USED IN THE NEUROLOGICAL STUDY OF RELIGIOSITY

Neuropsychological Assessment

Direct assessments (i.e., self-report) of religiosity are virtually always valuable tools for assessing baseline levels of religiosity (see Hill, Chapter 3, this volume). Several well-validated and often used self-report measures include Brief Multidimensional Measure of Religiousness/Spirituality (BMMRS; Fetzer Institute and National Institute on Aging Working Group, 1999), the Extrinsic/Intrinsic Religiosity Scale (Gorsuch & McPherson, 1989), and the Duke University Religion Index (Koenig, Meador, & Parkerson, 1997). We have used the BMMRS and Extrinsic/Intrinsic Religiosity Survey with patients with Parkinson's disease (Butler, McNamara, & Durso, 2010; Butler, McNamara, Ghofrani, & Durso, 2011), and we found that these neurological patients had no difficulty completing the scales. Results from self-report measures provide important information about varied aspects of religious cognition by way of conscious self-appraisal of one's religiosity. Results are correlated with other neuropsychological functions, quality of life, patient adherence, and/or mood regulation.

We recommend that these self-report scales of religiosity be supplemented with standard neuropsychological assessment tools (e.g., the Wechsler Adult Intelligence Scale battery or the Delis–Kaplan Executive Function System battery of executive functions) whenever possible so that a database can be built up over time concerning cognitive neuropsychological correlates of various subdimensions of religiosity. A database of this sort would position researchers to address important outstanding questions of relevance to human health and clinical outcomes, such as:

- Does participation in religious activity correlate with slowed cognitive aging? If so, what dimensions of religiosity predict positive clinical outcomes?
- Do aspects of religiosity enhance "executive functioning" in children, young adults, or aged adults?
- What is the relationship between religiosity and temporal discounting, regulation of the self, mood, and prosocial behavior modeling?

Neuroimaging and Modeling

A wealth of neuroimaging studies on religious cognition emerged within the past 15 years. The most commonly used techniques are functional magnetic resonance imaging (fMRI), positron emission tomography (PET), and single photon emission computed tomography (SPECT). They are not the same. Because of this, it is necessary to understand exactly what each technique does and does not do.

fMRI was developed in the 1990s and represents a special form of MRI scanning to measure hemodynamic change in blood. Blood-oxygen-level dependence (BOLD) signals reflect transient change in oxyhemoglobin and deoxyhemoglobin levels, which exhibit differing magnetic properties detectable as magnetic resonance. Neural activity is inferred from local fluctuations in deoxyhemoglobin. Interpretation of results from fMRI studies must be interpreted with caution because the precise neurophysiological basis of BOLD signals is uncertain (for reviews, see Arthurs & Boniface, 2002; Ekstrom, 2010; Viswanathan & Freeman, 2007). Images are typically obtained every 1–5 seconds (temporal resolution) and mapped onto 2–5 mm^3 voxels (spatial resolution). Recent technological advances afford even greater spatial resolution. The advantages of fMRI imaging are that it is noninvasive, exhibits high spatial resolution, and images all areas (cortical and subcortical) of the brain.

PET scanning is an invasive procedure that involves injecting a radioactive isotope into the bloodstream of a patient followed by brain imaging via computation reconstruction methods. This nuclear imaging technique generates three-dimensional pictures of functional brain processing by reconstituting information obtained by the scanner. Essentially, a radioactive substance with brief half-life circulates through the body (imaging can be for brain or body), the radioactive traces concentrate in biologically active tissue, the tracer beta decays over time, emitting positrons (electron antiparticle), which in turn collide with nearby electrons, producing gamma particles that travel in opposite directions. The circular detecting device in a PET scanner surrounding the individual's head or body gathers these gamma photons in a scintillator. Normalized data and computational measures are applied to information regarding time and location of gamma photoemission couplets. The result transforms data streams into three-dimensional brain activation patterns as a function of time. PET is primarily a clinical diagnostic tool used in oncology, cardiology, pharmacology, and neurology. Numerous research programs use PET scanning (but only a few for religious cognition). The technology is a powerful tool, but production of radioactive isotopes is expensive and time consuming and must be coordinated within hours of testing. Exposing an individual to varying levels of radioactive substance and injection procedures comes with significant health and safety risks. PET is an incredibly valuable procedure, though, because of its functional specificity—radionuclides can be prepared as ligands to very specific biochemical substrates, such as dopamine receptors or enzymes, serotonin transporters, or amyloid deposits. In contrast to fMRI, PET can localize brain activation patterns both generally (glucose uptake) or with high neurochemical specificity (e.g., dopamine transporter activity).

SPECT, like PET, is a nuclear imaging technique dependent on use of radionuclides and photon emission. In contrast, SPECT furnishes actual three-dimensional information of tissue activity. A gamma camera captures photon emission patterns and maps the activity onto cross-sectional slices through patient tissue. Radionuclides can be neurochemically specific to target substrates, and the radiopharmaceuticals are injected in a patient's bloodstream. The gamma camera records images approximately every 15 seconds with spatial resolution of about 1 cm. The health risks to patients and cost to perform the procedure are the major drawbacks to this technique.

A newer technique, quantitative electroencephalography (EEG), holds promise for imaging nonconscious cognitive processes that occur continuously on the order of milliseconds. Since the discovery and advent of EEG by Hans Berger (1929, cited in Harmon-Jones & Peterson, 2009), bioengineering advancement in the past few decades has given rise to source localization techniques with high-density electrode signals (e.g., 64, 128, and 256 electrodes). Scalp-recorded EEG is a relatively noninvasive method to record microvoltage potentials at various locations on the cortical surface. Signal processing transformations estimate current sources inside the brain. Spatial and temporal accuracy is approximated at 5 mm and 5 ms, respectively (Baillet & Garnero, 1997). EEG source localization is a powerful tool to both confirm and extend fMRI research. The increased temporal resolution of EEG will help to elucidate brain activation patterns of quick, subtle, and dynamic cognitive processing. Some benefits of this approach compared with other imaging techniques are the relatively low cost, portability of equipment for use in varied environments, higher temporal resolution, tolerability of movement, and lack of aggravating noises or tightly enclosed testing space. The disadvantages include poor spatial resolution compared with fMRI and limited capture of subcortical brain activity. While EEG records *actual* neural activity (instead of presumed proxies such as BOLD signals), the data are usually limited to a particular subset of neuronal populations: postsynaptic extracellular field potentials in large pyramidal neurons in neocortical tissue close to the scalp surface. Neuronal activity in other neocortical layers, cells positioned deep in sulci, and subcortical structures are not readily imaged with the quantitative EEG approach.

Psychophysics

Psychophysics investigates the potential relationship between a given stimulus (e.g., visual, auditory) and subjective perceptional response. A commonly used visual psychophysics approach is semantic priming. Information processing in semantic networks is quickened when lexical decisions are made following exposure to semantically related concepts compared with those unrelated. For instance, asking a participant to respond to whether a given stimulus is a word or not would yield faster response times for the word "doctor" when preceded briefly by the word "nurse" compared with "purse" or "nursery." Many neuroimaging techniques use block-design or event-related tasks based on priming procedures. Psychophysics is an investigative tool in its own right, but when coupled with neuroimaging it serves as a powerful method to identify the neural correlates of a given cognitive task.

In the following section, we review the findings from the burgeoning field of the neuroscientific study of religion. Most or all of the research draws from use of the discussed methods and techniques: neuropsychological correlates of self-reported changes in religiosity after brain damage, neuroimaging and modeling, and psychophysics.

INCREASES IN RELIGIOSITY DUE TO BRAIN DYSFUNCTION

Temporal Lobe Epilepsy

Links between epilepsy and religiousness have been noted for centuries. Patients with TLE are prone to intense religious experiences, conversions, and perseverative concern over religious/philosophical topics (Bear & Fedio, 1977; Dewhurst & Beard, 1970;

Geschwind, 1979; Waxman & Geschwind, 1975). Religious experiences have been reported during partial seizure foci activation (ictal), in postictal times during the hours to days following a seizure, and during interictal periods. Ictal case reports document mystical experiences, intense emotions of God's presence, the sense of being connected to the infinite, hallucinations of God's voice, visual hallucinations of a religious figure, clairvoyance, telepathy, or perseverance on religious phrases. Four of the five well-documented cases of ictal religious experiences during partial seizure implicate right frontotemporal regions as mediating foci (Devinsky & Lai, 2008). We could find no instance where removal of the left temporal lobe, in the context of unilateral foci, resulted in *loss* or reduction of religiosity (Cirignotta, Todesco, & Lugaresi, 1980).

The crucial role of the right temporal cortex is underlined by the rare phenomenon of ecstatic seizures. These are seizures that are associated with religious ecstasy. Dostoyevsky may have experienced these sorts of seizures (Hughes, 2005). However, let us look at a case that has been studied more recently.

> The patient is a 30-year-old unmarried man who had a normal birth and gives no history of familial epilepsy, severe illness, or cranial injury. He attended secondary school and is currently employed full-time. A self-contained, suspicious, unsociable person, he is prone to lonely meditation. His only intellectual concerns, music and travel, are in harmony with his need to establish rarefied contacts with the environment. He has a taciturn nature and expresses himself slowly and with difficulty. At the age of 13 he began to have attacks of short duration (20–30 sec) characterized by psychomotor arrest, slight lapse of consciousness, and, above all, an ineffable sensation of "joy." The episodes had a frequency of 1 or 2 per month but have become almost daily in recent years. In January, 1979, he was referred to us after a tonic-clonic nocturnal seizure. He had never seen a physician before, as he did not consider his small attacks as negative events.
>
> Seizures generally come on when he is relaxed or drowsy. The subjective symptoms are defined by the patient himself as "indescribable," words seeming to him inadequate to express what he perceives in those instants. However, he says that the pleasure he feels is so intense that he cannot find its match in reality. Qualitatively, these sensations can only be compared with those evoked by music. All disagreeable feelings, emotions, and thoughts are absent during the attacks. His mind, his whole being is pervaded by a sense of total bliss. All attention to his surroundings is suspended: he almost feels as if this estrangement from the environment were a sine qua non for the onset of seizures. He insists that the only comparable pleasure is that conveyed by music. Sexual pleasure is completely different: once he happened to have an attack during sexual intercourse, which he carried on mechanically, being totally absorbed in his utterly mental enjoyment. The neurological examination was negative. The EEG in the waking state is normal. A focus of spike activity appears in the right temporal zone during sleep. During a 24-hr polygraphic recording, a psychomotor seizure was observed, at the end of which the patient said he had experienced one of his short and sudden states of ecstasy. (Dewhurst & Beard, 1970, pp. 705–706)

This case is remarkable in that the description of the experience associated with the seizures could have been taken to be a description by a religious mystic of a mystical experience. Interestingly enough, the patient himself asserted that the joy was more of a conative, spiritual-cognitive experience rather than a bodily or emotional experience per se.

Despite impressive reports of dramatic alterations in religiosity in patients with TLE, rates of heightened religiosity in these patients may not exceed 5% (Devinsky & Lai, 2008; Ogata & Miyakawa, 1998). Trimble and Freeman (2006) demonstrated that hyperreligious patients with TLE more frequently had bilateral seizure foci than unilateral (right or left) foci and more frequently reported episodes of postictal psychoses. Compared with a healthy churchgoer group, hyperreligious patients with TLE more often reported actual experiences of some great spiritual figure or supernatural being, either an evil presence or a benign spiritual presence.

The mechanistic question of just how seizure activity in the temporal lobe could give rise to religious experience is important to address. Geschwind (1979) identified a subset or phenotype of patients with TLE with hyperreligiosity, termed Geschwind syndrome (also called Waxman–Geschwind or Gastaut–Geschwind; Gastaut, 1954). Patients with TLE of this ilk exhibited a constellation of symptoms, including hypergraphia for philosophical/religious topics, hyposexuality, intensified mental life, and proneness to irritable outbursts. This behavioral profile contrasts with that seen in Klüver–Bucy syndrome, which involves bilateral removal of the temporal lobes. The classical symptoms of Klüver–Bucy syndrome are flattened affect, fluctuating attention, and hypersexuality. In TLE, overexcitation or hyperconnectivity between limbic and temporal sites leads to the TLE behaviors where everything but sex is significant and requires attention.

These partly reciprocal patterns in behavior are likely explainable through understanding the connectivity between frontotemporal and parietal cortices and subcortical limbic structures in inhibitory balance with hypothalamic drives. In Klüver–Bucy syndrome, prefrontal and temporal sites that remain after resection are underactive, while limbic-related sexual drives are disinhibited and behavior is controlled by posterior parietal cortex. Contrarily, prefrontal and temporal sites are released from inhibition in patients with TLE while limbic sites are inhibited. In TLE, the amygdala is overstimulated while in Klüver–Bucy it is absent or underactivated. Sexual drive depends on hypothalamic sites, which are regulated in turn by the amygdala. Without any top-down inhibitory control of amygdalar efferents that project onto hypothalamic sites, hypersexuality results. With overstimulation of the amygdala, inhibition of hypothalamic sites occurs and hyposexuality results.

In order to derive a complete neurocognitive model of hyperreligosity in TLE and related disorders, we have to bring in the self and its neuroanatomy. Although we cannot review the literature on neural correlates of the self, it is reasonable to suggest that right-sided prefrontal and anterior temporal networks are key nodes in mediation of the self construct (see McNamara, 2009, for a discussion on religion and the self). If we assume that right anterior temporal and prefrontal networks are hyperstimulated by limbic and amygdalar seizure foci and spikes in TLE, and further that right prefrontal anterior temporal networks mediate the executive self (Ochsner et al., 2005), then something about the executive self allows one to "perceive" religious stimuli (e.g., supernatural agents) with greater intensity than is normally the case. Bear and Fedio (1977), in fact, argued that heightened religiosity was due to a greater number or density of connections between cortical sites handling the senses and the limbic system, including the amygdala, so that patients with TLE experienced a greater number of sensory events as "significant" relative to healthy persons with fewer such connections. Ramachandran and Blakeslee (1998) later assessed this theory by measuring subconscious reactions to religious, sexual, and violent imagery via skin conductance responses (SCR) in individuals with temporal lobe epilepsy with religious preoccupations, normal "very religious" people, and normal "nonreligious" people. For individuals with temporal lobe epilepsy, SCRs were enhanced for religious words and images to about the level found in the religious controls. This result is consistent with Bear and Fedio's model of hyperconnectivity. Hypersynchronized (Hebbian theory: "neurons that fire together wire together") and discharging neurons in the amygdala would have the effect of chronically overstimulating the structure. Connections from the amygdala to the cortex would be excitatory, while impulses from the amygdala to the hypothalamus would be inhibitory. Increasing impulses from the amygdala to the cortex then would be interpreted at the cortical level as greater numbers and frequencies of significant emotional events, while impulses from the amygdala to the hypothalamus would result in prolonged inhibitory pressure on the hypothalamus.

All of the TLE-related data, including the striking phenomenon of ecstatic seizures, suggests that heightened religiosity is associated primarily with bilateral temporal lobe foci or with right-sided temporal lobe foci. Devinsky and Lai (2008) came to similar conclusions in their review of the literature. Heightened spike activity in the amygdala, particularly on the right side, stimulates both temporal and prefrontal sites such that heightened significance is attached to everyday events and complex ideations occur in response to chronic emotional stimulation as a result of amygdala overactivity. In short, the literature on TLE-related religiosity gives us an initial clue as to the brain circuits that normally handle religious material, namely the right-sided temporal and prefrontal networks, as it is these networks that attach religious concepts to the impulses originating in the amygdala or mesial temporal lobe. Interestingly, we later see that these links between right-sided prefrontal and anterior temporal networks and heightened religiosity can be identified reliably in several other neurocognitive disorders that are associated with changes in religiousness.

Schizophrenia

Reports of religious experiences are more frequent among the schizophrenia population than the general population, especially in those patients with positive symptoms (Huguelet, Mohr, Borras, Gilliéron, & Brandt, 2006; Mohr, Brandt, Borras, Gilliéron, & Huguelet, 2006; Siddle, Haddock, Tarrier, & Garagher, 2002). In a sample of 193 patients admitted to a community hospital for schizophrenia, 24% had religious delusions (Siddle et al., 2002). Huguelet et al. (2006) found that 16% of their sample of schizophrenic patients had positive psychotic symptoms involving religious content, but that the majority of the patients reported that religion was an important aspect of their lives. On the basis of semistructured interviews about religious coping conducted with a sample of 115 outpatient schizophrenics, Mohr et al. (2006) found that 71% of patients reported religion instilled hope, purpose, and meaning in their lives, whereas for others it induced spiritual despair (14%). Patients also reported that religion lessened (54%) or increased (10%) psychotic and general symptoms. Positive delusions with religious content appear to be linked with specific sites of neural dysfunction. Gearing et al. (2011), in a review of the literature on religiosity and schizophrenia, largely confirmed Mohr et al.'s (2006) claims regarding positive and negative effects of religiosity on symptomology.

SPECT neuroimaging on an individual with schizophrenia who was actively experiencing religious delusions revealed increased uptake in the left temporal region as well as reduced uptake in the occipital cortex, especially on the left (Puri, Lekh, Nijran, Bagary, & Richardson, 2001). The authors note, however, that these results in a single patient are difficult to interpret because increased/decreased uptake could mean either hyper/hypodysfunction in the left temporal lobe.

As in the case of temporal lobe epilepsy, the anatomical sites of dysfunction in schizophrenia include limbic networks, the amygdala, the hippocampus, the left temporal lobe, and dorsolateral prefrontal cortex. In addition to these TLE-related sites of pathology, schizophrenia is also associated with catecholamine overactivity in the limbic system and in the nucleus accumbens circuit (NAC). In sum, there is evidence for overactivity in limbic sites (such as the amygdala and NAC) and underactivity or dysfunction in cortical sites, including the left temporal and prefrontal lobes. The right temporal lobe and the parietal lobes appear to be relatively spared in schizophrenia.

Obsessive–Compulsive Disorder

Obsessive–compulsive disorder (OCD) is characterized by intrusive and unwanted ideas, thoughts, urges, and images known as obsessions, together with repetitive ritualistic cognitive and physical activities that make up compulsions. The frequency of religious obsessions in populations with OCD in the United States has been estimated at between 10% (Eisen et al., 1999) and 30% (Mataix-Cols, Rauch, Manzo, Jenike, & Baer, 1999; Steketee, Quay, & White, 1991). The clinicopathological functional and structural imaging studies of OCD suggest a consistent finding: abnormally increased activity in orbitofrontal cortex and in subcortical basal ganglia (particularly in the caudate) and limbic circuits (Fontaine, Mattei, & Roberts, 2007). These areas show increased metabolic and functional activity when OCD symptoms are provoked. When patients are treated with selective serotonin reuptake inhibitors, the functional activity in the orbitofrontal cortex and caudate nucleus resolves toward normal (Fontaine et al., 2007). Given the elevated rates of hyperreligousness in some patients with OCD, these data indicate that the overactivation of the orbitofrontal cortex and the caudate nucleus, which projects to the frontal lobes, may be implicated in hyperreligiousness. In both TLE and schizophrenia, the orbitofrontal cortex is also likely overactivated, and so the OCD data are consistent with the TLE and schizophrenia data.

One subtype of OCD, scrupulosity is particularly relevant to hyperreligosity (Greenberg & Huppert, 2010). Consider the following case:

> Thirty-three-year-old married man with three children. Following his marriage when 20, he became preoccupied with the thought that he had not had sufficient concentration during his wedding ceremony, rendering the marriage invalid. He went to see rabbis about it until a second ceremony was arranged. After this, he became preoccupied with his wife's menstrual cleanliness. The thoughts filled his mind all day, although he tried to dismiss them. Although he was aware that this preoccupation was excessive, he would question his wife many times a day as to whether she had become menstrually unclean. If she dismissed his question, he would decide that she was not taking the matter seriously and he would remain tense. He consulted rabbis very frequently as to whether—given his doubts—he was permitted to be with his wife, and they always permitted it. Nevertheless, he avoided touching his wife whenever possible, and intercourse was very infrequent. He only agreed to intercourse because of the commandment 'Be fruitful and multiply', but on occasion his wife 'forced' intercourse on him.
>
> In addition, he took a long time to complete the portions of daily prayer that are considered to be especially important and requiring particular devotion, every such line adding

an extra 10 minutes to his prayer. . . . Three years ago he became increasingly depressed, and responded to electroconvulsive therapy (ECT). The intensive thoughts were unaffected until he was given clomipramine. Since then his mental state has been kept relatively stable on regular clomipramine (up to 200 mg) . . . There are no psychotic features" (Greenberg, Witztum, & Pisante, 1987, pp. 32–35)

Note the similarities between this case and the TLE interictal behavioral syndrome. In both disorders there is hyperreligousness and hyposexuality. Unlike many patients with TLE, there is no evidence of ragefulness or irritability in this patient with OCD. Nor is there any evidence for hypergraphia.

Parietal Lobe Excision

Frontotemporal brain networks are in constant cross-talk with parietal cortical sites—namely, each communicate to orchestrate a mutual excitatory/inhibitory balance. If frontotemporal networks are important to religious cognition, then one might expect that a disruption in the frontal-parietal circuit control would alter religiosity. A recent article by Urgesi, Aglioti, Skrap, and Fabbro (2010) demonstrates that selective damage to left and right inferior posterior parietal regions induces an increase in scores on the Self-transcendence (ST) scale of the Temperament and Character Inventory (TCI; Cloninger, 1994). ST refers to one's degree of interest in searching for something metaphysical, divine, or beyond human existence. Twin studies have shown that the ST scale is associated with heritability estimates of 0.37 and 0.41 for male and female individuals, respectively (Kirk, Eaves, & Martin, 1999). The researchers tested 24 with high-grade glioma, 24 with low-grade glioma, 20 with recurrent gliomas, and 20 patients with brain meningiomas (control group). The recurrent glioma group allowed the authors to ascertain whether long-term changes in ST were induced by previous ablations of cortex after surgery. Within each patient group, half of the patients had lesions involving the frontotemporal cortex (anterior patients) and the other half had lesions involving the occipito-temporoparietal cortex (posterior patients). The main question was whether anterior versus posterior ablations or both would cause changes in ST. The results showed that both anterior and posterior lesions had effects and those effects were opposite, with anterior lesions decreasing ST and posterior lesions increasing ST; however, the posterior lesions had the most pronounced effects. ST scores in patients with meningioma involving the anterior or posterior areas revealed no significant effect. The analysis of patients with recurrent glioma who had undergone previous operations several months before testing showed that enhanced ST induced by posterior cortical ablation persisted. In sum, these results demonstrate clearly that ablation of two sites within posterior cortical regions (the inferior parietal lobe and the angular gyrus) has an enhancing effect on the subjective experience of self-transcendence. This seminal finding supports the idea that a disruption in frontal-parietal circuit control leads to alterations in religiosity. More specifically, frontotemporal gain of function compared with parietal loss of function engenders increase in religiousness/self-transcendence.

Summary of Neurological Data on Increased Religiousness

Taken together, the clinical data suggest that the limbic system (particularly the amygdala), portions of the basal ganglia, the right temporal lobe (particularly the anterior portion of the medial and superior temporal lobe), and the dorsomedial, orbitofrontal, and right dorsolateral prefrontal cortex are the crucial nodes in a brain circuit to orchestrate biobehavioral heightening in religiosity. When this circuit is stimulated in the right way, religious ecstasy results. When the circuit is overactivated, various forms of religiously tinged aberrations result. When cortical sites (right temporal and frontal) play the leading role, ideational changes in belief systems and outright delusional states are produced. When limbic and basal ganglia sites play the leading role, obesessional ideation and changes in ritual behaviors as well as increased interest in religious practices such as prayer and other rituals result. Beyond this meager summation, little more can be said with any degree of confidence.

REDUCTION IN RELIGIOSITY DUE TO BRAIN DAMAGE

Parkinson's Disease

Several studies from our research group (McNamara, Durso, & Brown, 2006; Butler et al., 2010; Butler, McNamara, Ghofrani, et al., 2011; Butler, McNamara, & Durso, 2011) revealed that a subtype of patients with Parkinson's disease (namely right forebrain damaged) exhibit reduced interest in religiosity (e.g., self-reported conscious religious cognition) and deficits in the automatic activation of religious concepts (nonconscious religious cognition). Parkinson's disease (PD) is a progressive neurodegenerative disorder that disrupts proper functioning of neostriatal and mesocortical catecholaminergic systems (Lotharius & Brundin, 2002; Olanow & Tatton, 2002). Neurobehavioral features of PD include mood, social cognitive, and executive function deficits (McNamara, Durso, & Harris, 2007, 2008; Williams-Gray, Foltynie, Brayne, Robbins, & Barker, 2007; Huang et al., 2007). A shift in personality has also been noted with patients with PD, characterized as harm avoidant, overly conscientious, moralistic, ambitious, and low on novelty-seeking behaviors (McNamara et al., 2007, 2008). The pathological features of PD result primarily from the loss of dopaminergic neurons in the ventral-lateral substantia nigra (Dauer & Przedborski, 2003).

In a cohort of 71 patients with PD and 75 age-matched neurologically intact controls, we administered a battery of neuropsychological tests, including two separate self-report measures of religious behavior: the BMMRS and Extrinsic/Intrinsic Religiosity Scale. BMMRS results demonstrated that individuals with PD, compared with age-matched controls with chronic health conditions, participate significantly less in private spiritual practices, experience less divine forgiveness, and report lower positive spiritual experience. Likewise, individuals with PD scored significantly lower in intrinsic religiosity. Covariate analysis revealed that patients with LPD with further progression of dopaminergic loss were most severely affected. On–off levodopa (dopamine precursor) drug testing confirmed that the findings were not drug-induced phenomena (Butler, McNamara, Ghofrani, & Durso, 2011).

Alterations in religiosity in PD is presumably related to this loss of right-sided frontostriatal dopaminergic function. In a series of studies (Butler et al., 2010; Butler, McNamara, Ghofrani, & Durso, 2011), we assessed semantic memory in individuals with PD and controls based on concept priming using religious and control categories. Religious concept activation was tested by use of computer-based visual priming tasks and response time measurements. In our experiments, after viewing religious and civic theme words, patients and controls responded to tasks to measure their semantic processing. Patients with PD (left onset > right onset) were selectively delayed in semantic processing of religious concepts only. Subjects were asked to respond *yes* or *no* on a button box as quickly as possible to a two-word phrase as it appeared on the screen: *yes* if the action could possibly be performed and *no* if not possible. Half of the two-word phrases were sensical and possible, while the other half were impossible tasks. Examples of religious and civic control concepts include *pray quietly, worship God, pay taxes,* and *serve jury*. Examples of impossible action phrases are *swim hills, open sand,* and *float town*. Immediately prior to the presentation of these action phrases was a religious ("sacred"), civic ("citizen"), or neutral ("housetop") prime word. All possible combinations of prime and target action phrases were presented in multiple trials. As expected, when controls were primed with the religious word and a semantically related religious action, then response times were significantly faster than when civic or neutral prime words preceded religious action phrases. Likewise, when the civic prime flashed, response times from control subjects were fastest for civic action phrases compared with religious or neutral word priming. Patients with PD displayed the predicted priming effect for civic concepts, but selective delays emerged in the religious prime and target pairs.

Autism Spectrum Disorders

Investigations comparing religiosity in individuals with autism spectrum disorders and nonautistic controls are virtually nonexistent. Autobiographical instances document a few cases in which the religious mind/brain is different in autism (Bering, 2002; Bittner, 2009; Dubin & Graetz, 2009). Preliminary reports from Caldwell-Harris (2009) suggest that individuals with Asperger syndrome compared with neurotypical adult controls exhibit reductions in religiosity with greater frequency of atheistic worldviews and fixation on physical causation as explanatory for all religious phenomena.

NEUROCHEMISTRY OF RELIGIOSITY

Evidence from neuropsychiatric and neurodegenerative disease implicate dopamine and serotonin in religious cognition (reviewed in McNamara, 2009; Previc, 2006). Subtle change in neurochemical function of both transmitters is associated with religiosity in neurologically intact individuals. Borg, Andrée, Soderstrom, and Farde (2003) used PET scan in 15 normal male adult subjects to investigate the role of serotonin and religious experience. Using a radioligand specific to serotonin 5-HT_{1a} receptors, they showed that increased binding density to 5-HT_{1a} receptors correlated inversely with ST scores (in particular, Spiritual Acceptance) on the TCI self-report personality dimensions. Interindividual variability in receptor density and function correlated with relative openness to religious experience. The serotonin transporter gene 5-HT_{1a} and 5-HT_6 gene polymorphisms are all correlated with personality characteristics high in religiosity (Ham et al., 2004; Lorenzi et al., 2005; Nillson et al., 2007). This is not surprising given that spiritual experiences are frequently reported following ingestion of drugs that act on the serotonin system such as lysergic acid diethylamide (LSD), psilocybin, N,N-dimethyltryptamine, mescaline, and 3,4 methylene-dioxymethamphetamine (see Hood & Chen, Chapter 21, this volume). On a behavioral level, these drugs elicit perceptual distortions, changes in the sense of self, a sense of insight, spiritual awareness, mystical experiences, and religious ecstasy. They do so by decreasing firing in the raphe system, which then removes the ability of the person to screen out large amounts of incoming sensory information. The person is then inundated with meaningful and vivid images. A decrease in serotonin also leads to an increase in firing of dopamine neurons in the circuit. Dopamine is the other neurotransmitter repeatedly implicated in religious experiences. Relatively high levels of dopamine in the circuit create a pleasurable and positive mood. When low serotonin is combined with high dopamine levels in the circuit, the feeling of being inundated with meaningful images and impressions is associated with positive affect, and one is much more likely to have religious experiences.

STUDIES OF HEALTHY POPULATIONS

Newberg et al. (2001) pioneered the use of functional imaging approaches to religion and brain issues. He and his colleagues have used PET and SPECT methods to study the brain states of experienced meditators during meditation and of nuns in prayer. They found in both cases decreased activation levels in the parietal lobes and increased activation levels in frontal lobes. There was also increased activation in the cingulate gyrus bilaterally and the thalami. They suggest that because the parietal region has been implicated in somesthesis, body schema disturbances, and the sense of self, the hypoperfusion in the parietal regions results in dissolution of the boundaries of the self and a more intense religious experience. Note that this formulation of the religious experience is consistent with some accounts from mystics who claim that they felt closer to God when they forgot themselves. Note also, however, that although some workers in the field point to the sense of presence as important for the religious experience, Newberg and colleagues seem to be arguing the opposite.

Azari et al. (2001) used PET scans to compare regional cerebral blood flow (brain activation) in six self-described religious (Christian) subjects with six nonreligious subjects reciting a biblical text (Psalms 23), a happy nursery rhyme, and a resting state while under PET scan. In the religious subjects during religious recitation, compared with baseline the right and left dorsolateral prefrontal, presupplementary motor area ([SMA] dorsomedial frontal), right medial parietal (precuneus), and left cerebellum were significantly activated. When comparing religious and happy recitation, religious subjects exhibited activation in the right dorsolateral prefrontal cortex, pre-SMA, right precuneus, and left cerebellum. When comparing religious recitation between believers and nonbelievers, the religious group selectively activated right dorsolateral and pre-SMA cortices.

Newberg, Wintering, Morgan, and Waldman (2006) measured regional cerebral blood flow using SPECT in a group of five Christian women who had practiced *glossolalia* for at least 5 years. *Glossolalia* is also known as "speaking in tongues" within Christian communities (see Hood & Belzen, Chapter 4, this volume). There is a reduction in volitional control, and then the individual begins to emit vocalizations that sound like a different language. Both the target individual and his or her community attribute religious meanings to these vocalizations. The researchers observed decreased activity in the left caudate and in the prefrontal lobes, and a trend toward increased activity in the right amygdala.

Beauregard and Paquette (2006) and Beauregard and O'Leary (2007) reported on two studies of Carmelite nuns in mystical states associated with their contemplative prayer practices. The first study involved fMRI scans of 15 nuns scanned in three different states. In one state the subject was restful and quiescent, instructed not to intentionally think about anything. In another state, the subjects were asked to recall the emotions of a memory of their most intense union with another human being. Finally, the experimental state involved participants recalling and reliving their most significant mystical experience. Self-induction methods were used to produce the control and mystical conditions. The second study used quantitative EEG to measure brain waves of the same nuns in the same three conditions, with subjects sitting in an isolation chamber. The results from the first study showed that many areas of the brain were involved in the nuns' recalling and reliving their most significant mystical experience, including especially the inferior parietal lobule, visual cortex, caudate nucleus, and left brainstem. The results from the second study showed significant theta activity increase during the mystical condition relative to the baseline condition in diverse brain sites, including the insula, right inferior parietal lobule and superior parietal lobule, right inferior and middle temporal cortices, anterior cingulate, and medial prefrontal cortices.

Schjødt and colleagues used fMRI to investigate brain activation patterns associated with overlearned forms of religious incantation (e.g., Lord's Prayer) and spontaneous forms of prayer (impromptu) in a group of Danish Christians (Schjødt, Geertz, Stødkild-Jørgensen, & Roepstorff, 2009; Schjødt, Stødkild-Jørgensen, Geertz, & Roepstorff, 2009). Recitation of the Lord's Prayer was associated with strong activation in the right caudate nucleus. Given that this nucleus is known to be a central node in an ascending network of dopaminergic systems that support reward and approach behaviors, among other things, the authors hypothesized that religious prayer was capable of stimulating the dopaminergic system of the dorsal striatum in religious people. Improvised prayer, on the other hand, elicited a strong response in the temporopolar region, the medial prefrontal cortex, the temporoparietal junction, and precuneus. All of these structures participate in mediation of the sense of self. The authors pointed out that praying to God appeared to activate areas of the brain known to be involved in social cognition and ToM processing.

Harris, Sheth, and Cohen (2008) imaged the brains of 14 healthy young adults while subjects made true–false decisions about statements with varying content: mathematics, geography, semantics, factual, autobiographical, ethical, and religious. Across statement type, belief compared with disbelief states generated BOLD signal increases during fMRI scan in ventromedial prefrontal cortex (left > right) and disbelief compared with belief states caused increased activity in the left inferior frontal gyrus, bilateral insula, dorsal anterior cingulated, and superior parietal lobe. Uncertainty compared with both belief and disbelief engaged the anterior cingulate cortex and decreased caudate activity. Unfortunately, the presentation of results did not include a difference in brain activation patterns by statement type (e.g., religious, ethical), so conclusions about the specificity of belief states in religious cognition compared with other belief states was not appreciable.

Kapogiannis et al. (2009) utilized a factor analytic technique from self-report data on religiosity in attempting to reveal underlying psychological structures inherent to religious cognition. The multidimensional scaling approach revealed three core dimensions: (D1) God's perceived level of involvement in the world, (D2) God's perceived emotions toward humankind, and (D3) doctrinal/experiential knowledge sources. In the same report, Kapogiannis et al. also scanned 20 religious and 20 nonreligious individuals under fMRI while subjects made decisions about statements to reflect the positive and negative ends of the three core psychological dimensions of religious cognition. Statements implying God's lack of involvement in the world (+D1) activated two right-sided anterior–posterior brain networks: one lateral system comprising the right inferior frontal gyrus, right middle temporal gyrus, and right middle occipital gyrus, and one medial system consisting of the right superior medial frontal gyrus and right precuneus. Statements regarding God's involvement in the world (-D1) did not produce a reliable pattern of activation. Positive D2 belief (God's love) modulated activity in the right middle frontal gyrus, and negative D2 statements (God's anger) increased left middle temporal activity. On the gradient of religious knowledge, abstract theological statements (+D3) activated the right inferior temporal gyrus and the left superior temporal gyrus, and negative D3 experiential religious knowledge modulated activity in a broad range of brain regions, including bilateral occipital lobes, the left precentral gyrus, and the left inferior frontal gyrus. The authors interpreted these findings generally as evidence for religious cognition as integrated into other cognitive processes, such as social cognition, ToM processing, semantic content decoding, intent-related, emotional processing, and imagery networks.

A TENTATIVE SYNTHESIS OF THE NEUROLOGICAL DATA

These results and similar ones from other investigative teams suggest there is a network of brain regions that consistently are activated when a person performs a religious act. The most important regions of the brain for studies of religious expression appear to be a circuit linking up the orbital and dorsomedial prefrontal cortex, the right dorsolateral prefrontal cortex, the ascending serotonergic systems, the mesocortical dopaminergic system, the amygdala/hippocampus, and the right anterior temporal lobes.

There is a huge literature on the connectivity patterns of each of these anatomical sites (reviewed in Gashghaei, Hilgetag, & Barbas, 2007). They are all interconnected, one with another. The posterior orbitofrontal cortex appears to regulate the limbic system and is densely interconnected with the insular, temporal polar, and parahippocampal cortices as well as with basal forebrain structures like the ventral striatum, nucleus basalis of Meynert, and amygdala (Nauta, 1962; Van Hoesen, 1981). The medial orbitofrontal cortex is reciprocally connected to the rostral portion of the insula, the medial basal amygdala, ventromedial temporal pole area 38, and medial subcallosal cingulate areas 24, 25, and 32. The anterior entorhinal area 36 is interconnected with the hippocampal formation. The lateral orbitofrontal region is interconnected to dorsal and caudal portions of the basal amygdala, which is a source of projections of emotional information to the visual processing centers in inferior temporal cortex: supracallosal areas 24 and 32, the auditory association cortex area 38 in the temporal lobe, inferior temporal cortex area 20, and prefrontal dorsal area 6. The latter area is interesting as it involves supplementary eye fields as well as Exner's area, which is thought to mediate cognitive functions involved in writing. Hypergraphia may be associated with hyperreligiosity in TLE and other neurological conditions (Waxman & Geschwind, 1975).

In summary, key nodes to modulate religious cognition appear to involve primarily limbic, temporal, and frontal cortices on the right. This proposal is congruent with those of other authors who have studied potential brain correlates of religiosity (e.g., Bear & Fedio, 1977; d'Aquili & Newberg, 1993; Devinsky & Lai, 2008; Persinger, 1987; Ramachandran, Hirstein, Armel, Tecoma, & Iragui, 1997; Trimble, 2007). Most of these authors, however, emphasize the role of the temporal lobes in religious experience presumably because of the impressive clinical data on temporal lobe epileptics. d'Aquili and Newberg (1993), more than any other scholars, have explored possible neuropsychological models of religious experience. They very sensibly assume that all the major association areas of the cortex generate some aspect of the total religious experience. They assume, for example, that the temporal lobes attach meaning and significance to events and thus are central to eliciting the profound adherence to religious frameworks. They argue that the parietal lobes undergo a deactivation during profound religious experience and this deactivation is related to a diminution in sense of self or ego.

No systematic efforts to document relationships between particular brain regions and particular aspects of religious cognition have yet been attempted or accomplished. We have no way of knowing, therefore, whether the clinical and neuroimaging data are giving us a biased picture of the true state of affairs with respect to brain mediation of religiosity. Despite these shortcomings of the existing data set on religion and brain, it is nevertheless striking, at least to us, that the picture is relatively consistent. There is a consistent set of brain structures that modulate religiosity up or down. When those structures are impaired, religiosity declines. When those structures are stimulated, religiosity heightens. We must conclude that those structures are crucially important for expression of religiosity.

REFERENCES

Arthurs, O. J., & Boniface, S. (2002). How well do we understand the neural origins of the fMRI BOLD signal? *Trends in Neuroscience, 25*(1), 27–31.

Azari, N. P., Nickel, J. P., Wunderlich, G., Niedeggen, M., Hefter, H., Tellmann, L., et al. (2001). Neural correlates of religious experience. *European Journal of Neuroscience, 13,* 1649–1652.

Baillet, S., & Garnero, L. (1997). A Bayesian approach to introducing anatomo-functional priors in the EEG/MEG inverse problem. *IEEE Transactions on Biomedical Engineering, 44,* 374–385.

Bear, D. M., & Fedio, P. (1977). Quantitative analysis of interictal behavior in temporal lobe epilepsy. *Archives of Neurology, 34,* 454–467.

Beauregard, M., & O'Leary, D. (2007). *The spiritual brain: A neuroscientist's case for the existence of the soul.* San Francisco: HarperCollins.

Beauregard, M., & Paquette, V. (2006). Neural correlates of a mystical experience in Carmelite nuns. *Neuroscience Letters, 405,* 186–190.

Bering, J. M. (2002). The existential theory of mind. *Review of General Psychology, 6,* 3–24.

Bittner, D. (2009). The old book switcheroo: Or anatomy of a delusion. *Journal of Religion and Health, 49,* 262–273.

Borg, J., Andrée, B., Soderstrom, H., & Farde, L. (2003). The serotonin system and spiritual experience. *American Journal of Psychiatry, 160,* 1965–1969.

Brown, D. E. (1991). *Human universals.* New York: McGraw-Hill.

Butler, P. M., McNamara, P., & Durso, R. (2010). Deficits in the automatic activation of religious concepts in patients with Parkinson's disease. *Journal of the International Neuropsychological Society, 16*, 252–261.

Butler, P. M., McNamara, P., & Durso, R. (2011). Side of onset in Parkinson's disease and alterations in religiosity: Novel behavioral phenotypes. *Behavioral Neurology, 24*, 133–141.

Butler, P. M., McNamara, P., Ghofrani, J., & Durso, R. (2012). Disease-associated alterations in religious cognition in patients with Parkinson's disease. *Journal of Clinical & Experimental Neuropsychology, 33*, 917–928.

Caldwell-Harris, C. (2009, March 13). *Born on the wrong planet?: Using forum postings to test hypotheses about special interests and religious beliefs of autistic spectrum young adults.* Cambridge, UK: Autism Research Center, Cambridge University.

Cirignotta, F., Todesco, C. V., & Lugaresi, E. (1980). Temporal lobe epilepsy with ecstatic seizures (so-called Dostoevsky epilepsy). *Epilepsia, 21*, 705–710.

Cloninger, C. R. (1994). *The Temperament and Character Inventory (TCI): A guide to its development and use.* St. Louis, MO: Centre for Psychobiology of Personality, Washington University.

d'Aquili, E., & Newberg, A. (1993). Religious and mystical states: A neuropsychological model. *Zygon, 28*, 177–200.

Dauer, W., & Przedborski, S. (2003). Parkinson's disease: Mechanisms and models. *Neuron, 39*, 889–909.

Devinsky, O., & Lai, G. (2008). Spirituality and religion in epilepsy. *Epilepsy and Behavior, 12*, 636–643.

Dewhurst, K., & Beard, A.W. (1970). Sudden religious conversions in temporal lobe epilepsy. *British Journal of Psychiatry: Journal of Mental Science, 117*, 497–507.

Dubin, N., & Graetz, J.E. (2009). Through a different lens: Spirituality in the lives of individuals with Asperger's syndrome. *Journal of Religion, Disability, & Health, 13*, 29–39.

Eisen, J. L., Goodman, W. K., Keller, M. B., Warshaw, M. G., DeMarco, L. M., Luce, D. D., et al. (1999). Patterns of remission and relapse in obsessive-compulsive disorder: A 2–year prospective study. *Journal of Clinical Psychiatry, 60*, 346–351.

Ekstrom, A. (2010). How and when the fMRI BOLD signal relates to underlying neural activity: The danger in dissociation. *Brain Research Review, 62*, 233–244.

Fetzer Institute and National Institute on Aging Working Group. (1999). *Multidimensional measurement of religiousness/spirituality for use in health research.* Kalamazoo, MI: Fetzer Institute.

Fontaine, D., Mattei, V., & Roberts, P. H. (2007). Obsessive-compulsive disorder and the frontal lobes. In B. L. Miller & J. L. Cummings (Eds.), *The human frontal lobes: Functions and disorders* (2nd ed., pp. 621–635). New York: Guilford Press.

Gashghaei, H. T., Hilgetag, C. C., & Barbas, H. (2007). Sequence of information processing for emotions based on the anatomical dialogue between prefrontal cortex and amygdala. *NeuroImage, 34*, 905–923.

Gastaut, H. (1954). *Epilepsies.* Springfield, IL: Charles C Thomas.

Gearing, R. E., Alonzo, D., Smolak, A., McHugh, K., Harmon, S., & Baldwin, S. (2011). Association of religion with delusions and hallucinations in the context of schizophrenia: Implications for engagement and adherence. *Schizophrenia Research, 126*, 150–163.

Geschwind, N. (1979). Behavioural changes in temporal lobe epilepsy. *Psychological Medicine, 9*, 217–219.

Gorsuch, R. L., & McPherson, S. E. (1989). Intrinsic/extrinsic measurement: I/E Revised and single item scales. *Journal for the Scientific Study of Religion, 28*, 348–354.

Greenberg, D., & Huppert, J. D. (2010). Scrupulosity: A unique subtype of obsessive-compulsive disorder. *Current Psychiatry Reports, 12*, 282–289.

Greenberg, D., Witztum, E., & Pisante, J. (1987). Scrupulosity: Religious attitudes and clinical presentations. *British Journal of Medical Psychology, 60*, 29–37.

Ham, B.-J., Kim, Y.-H., Choi, M.-J., Cha, J.-H., Choi, Y.-K., & Lee, M.-S. (2004). Serotonergic genes and personality traits in the Korean population. *Neuroscience Letters, 354*, 2–5.

Harmon-Jones, E., & Peterson, C. K. (2009). Electroencephalographic methods in social and personality psychology. In E. Harmon-Jones & J. S. Beer (Eds.), *Methods in social neuroscience* (pp. 170–196). New York: Guilford Press.

Harris, S., Sheth, S. A., & Cohen, M. S. (2008). Functional neuroimaging of belief, disbelief, and uncertainty. *Annals of Neurology, 63,* 141–147.

Huang, H. S., Matevossian, A., Whittle, C., Kim, S. Y., Schumacher, A., Baker, S. P., et al. (2007). Prefrontal dysfunction in schizophrenia involves mixed-lineage leukemia 1 regulated histone methylation at GABAergic gene promoters. *Neurobiology of Disease, 27,* 11254–11262.

Hughes, J. R. (2005). The idiosyncratic aspects of the epilepsy of Fyodor Dostoevsky. *Epilepsy & Behavior, 7,* 531–538.

Huguelet, P., Mohr, S., Borras, L., Gilliéron, C., & Brandt, P. Y. (2006). Spirituality and religious practices among outpatients with schizophrenia and their clinicians. *Psychiatric Services, 57,* 366–372.

Kapogiannis, D., Barbey, A. K., Su, M., Zamboni, G., Krueger, F., & Grafman, J. (2009). Cognitive and neural foundations of religious belief. *Proceedings of the National Academy of Science, 106,* 4876–4881.

Kirk, K. M., Eaves, L. J., & Martin, N. G. (1999). Self-transcendence as a measure of spirituality in a sample of older Australian twins. *Twins Research and Human Genetics, 2,* 81–87.

Koenig, H. G., Meador, K., & Parkerson, G. (1997). Religion Index for Psychiatric Research: A 5 item measure for use in health outcome studies. *American Journal of Psychiatry, 154,* 885–886.

Lorenzi, C., Serretti, A., Mandelli, L., Tubazio, V., Ploia, C., & Smeraldi, E. (2005). 5–HT1A polymorphism and self-transcendence in mood disorders. *American Journal of Medical Genetics: Part B (Neuropychiatric Genetics), 137B,* 33–35.

Lotharius, J., & Brundin, P. (2002). Impaired dopamine storage resulting from alpha-synuclein mutations may contribute to the pathogenesis of Parkinson's disease. *Human Molecular Genetics, 11,* 2395–2407.

Mataix-Cols, D., Rauch, S. L., Manzo, P. A., Jenike, M. A., & Baer, L. (1999). Use of factor-analyzed symptom dimensions to predict outcome with serotonin reuptake inhibitors and placebo in the treatment of obsessive-compulsive disorder. *American Journal of Psychiatry, 156,* 1409–1416.

McNamara, P. (2009). *The neuroscience of religious experience.* Cambridge, UK: Cambridge University Press.

McNamara, P., Durso, R., & Brown, A. (2006). Religiosity in patients with Parkinson's disease. *Neuropsychiatric Disease and Treatment, 2,* 341–348.

McNamara, P., Durso, R., & Harris, E. (2007). 'Machiavellianism' and frontal dysfunction: Evidence from Parkinson's disease (PD). *Cognitive Neuropsychiatry, 12,* 285–300.

McNamara, P., Durso, R., & Harris, E. (2008). Alterations of the sense of self and personality in Parkinson's disease. *International Journal of Geriatric Psychiatry, 23,* 79–84.

Mohr, S., Brandt, P. Y., Borras, L., Gilliéron, C., & Huguelet, P. (2006). Toward an integration of spirituality and religiousness into the psychosocial dimension of schizophrenia. *American Journal of Psychiatry, 163,* 1952–1959.

Murdock, G. P. (1965). *Culture and society: Twenty-four essays.* Pittsburgh: University of Pittsburgh Press.

Nauta, W. J. (1962). Neural associations of the amygdaloid complex in the monkey. *Brain, 122,* 61–73.

Newberg, A., Alavi, A., Baime, M., Pourdehnad, M., Santanna, J., & d'Aquili, E. (2001). The measurement of regional cerebral blood flow during the complex cognitive task of meditation: A preliminary SPECT study. *Psychiatry Research, 106,* 113–122.

Newberg, A. B., Wintering, N. A., Morgan, D., & Waldman, M. R. (2006). The measurement of regional cerebral blood flow during glossolalia: A preliminary SPECT study. *Psychiatry Research: Neuroimaging, 148,* 67–71.

Nillson, K. W., Damberg, M., Öhrvik, J., Leppert, J., Lindstrom, L., Anckarsäter, H., et al. (2007). Genes encoding for AP-2ß and the serotonin transporter are associated with the personality character spiritual acceptance. *Neuroscience Letters, 411*, 233–237.

Ochsner, K. N., Beer, J. S., Robertson, E. R., Cooper, J. C., Gabrieli, J. D. E., Kihsltrom, J. F., et al. (2005). The neural correlates of direct and reflected self-knowledge. *NeuroImage, 28*, 797–814.

Ogata, A., & Miyakawa, T. (1998). Religious experiences in epileptic patients with a focus on ictus-related episodes. *Psychiatry and Clinical Neurosciences, 52*, 321–325.

Olanow, C. W., & Tatton, W. G. (2002). Etiology and pathogenesis of Parkinson's disease. *Annual Review of Neuroscience, 22*, 123–144.

Persinger, M. A. (1987). *Neuropsychological bases of God beliefs*. New York: Praeger.

Previc, F. H. (2006). The role of the extrapersonal brain systems in religious activity. *Consciousness and Cognition, 15*, 500–539.

Puri, B. K., Lekh, S. K., Nijran, K. S., Bagary, M. S., & Richardson, A. J. (2001). Spect neuroimaging in schizophrenia with religious delusions. *International Journal of Psychophysiology, 40*, 143–148.

Ramachandran, V. S., & Blakeslee, S. (1998). *Phantoms in the brain: Probing the mysteries of the human mind*. New York: William Morrow.

Ramachandran, V. S., Hirstein, W. S., Armel, K. C., Tecoma, E., & Iragui, V. (1997, October 25). The neural basis of religious experience. *Society for Neuroscience Abstracts, 23*, 519.

Schjødt, U., Geertz, A., Stødkild-Jørgensen, H., & Roepstorff, A. (2009). Highly religious participants recruit areas of social cognition in personal prayer. *Social Cognitive and Affective Neuroscience, 4*, 199–207.

Schjødt, U., Stødkild-Jørgensen, H., Geertz, A. W., & Roepstorff, A. (2008). Rewarding prayers. *Neuroscience Letters, 443*(3), 165–168.

Siddle, R., Haddock, G., Tarrier, N., & Garagher, E. B. (2002). Religious delusions in patients admitted to hospital with schizophrenia. *Social Psychiatry and Psychiatric Epidemiology, 37*(3), 130–138.

Steketee, G., Quay, S., & White, K. (1991). Religion and guilt in OCD patients. *Journal of Anxiety Disorders, 5*, 359–367.

Trimble, M., & Freeman, A. (2006). An investigation of religiosity and the Gastaut–Geschwind syndrome in patients with temporal lobe epilepsy. *Epilepsy and Behavior, 9*, 407–414.

Trimble, M. R. (2007). *The soul in the brain: The cerebral basis of language, art, and belief*. Baltimore, MD: Johns Hopkins University Press.

Urgesi, C., Aglioti, S. M., Skrap, M., & Fabbro, F. (2010). The spiritual brain: Selective cortical lesions modulate human self-transcendence. *Neuron, 65*, 309–319.

Van Hoesen, G. W. (1981). The differential distribution, diversity, and sprouting of cortical projections to the amygdale in the rhesus monkey. In Y. Ben-Ari (Ed.), *The amygdaloid complex: INSERM symposium no. 20* (pp. 77–90). New York: Elsevier/North Holland Biomedical Press.

Viswanathan, A., & Freeman, R. D. (2007). Neurometabolic coupling in cerebral cortex reflects synaptic more than spiking activity. *Nature Neuroscience, 10*, 1308–1312.

Waxman, S. G., & Geschwind, N. (1975). The interictal behavior syndrome of temporal lobe epilepsy. *Archives of General Psychiatry, 32*, 1580–1586.

Williams-Gray, C. H., Foltynie, T., Brayne, C. E. G., Robbins, T. W., & Barker, R. A. (2007). Evolution of cognitive dysfunction in an incident Parkinson's disease cohort. *Brain, 130*, 1787–1798.

12

Exploring Religion's Basement

The Cognitive Science of Religion

Justin L. Barrett

If you have ever toured an architectural marvel such as a medieval cathedral or palace, you may remember being awed by the pleasing play on symmetries, the intricacies of the adornments, or the artistry of decorations. Harder to notice and appreciate may have been the role that particular building materials and techniques, the affordances of the natural space, and the practical constraints of the navigability, heating, and foundations played in making the building what it was. Upon reflection, we can recognize that, sure, you need a foundation and properly supported walls and roofs for a building, but still not recognize that the particulars of these hidden constraints importantly shape some of the aesthetically appealing features such as arches, buttresses, and spandrels.

Similarly, the stunning and moving edifices that we see as expressions of religion and spirituality often have hidden structural components that make them possible and give them particular shape. For the life-changing mystical experience, there is a psycho-cultural context that helps make the experience interpretable as "religious" (or not) and meaningful enough to be life changing. For every conversion that bears fruit in terms of community adoption and virtue cultivation, there is a faith tradition that was already there. For every experience of being cherished or abandoned by a personal god, there is the presumption that this god is an agent with attributes that support relational feelings and attributions. In the walls and under the floor of the exciting aspects of religion and spirituality that occupy most psychologists of religion lies another set of structures that we may profitably seek to understand. These are the structures that primarily occupy cognitive scientists of religion. Welcome to the basement.

My primary aim in this chapter is to introduce psychologists interested in the study of religion and spirituality to the cognitive science of religion (CSR) in hope that many topics of concern in the psychology of religion and spirituality would be enriched by investigations that concern CSR. One may appreciate a great house without knowledge of the foundation and structural support plans, but that appreciation is enhanced by knowledge of the necessary, hidden structures.

Comparison with Ozorak's chapter "Cognitive Approaches to Religion" in the first edition of this *Handbook* (2005) reveals that cognitive approaches flying under the CSR banner have seen considerable development and elaboration over the past decade. It is no longer responsible to present CSR research as a subtype of cognitive approaches to the psychology of religion, including those focused on religious schemata, language, judgments, and identity. Likewise, the importance of cognition, including memory dynamics, decision making, and social cognition, has become integral to psychology of religion generally and cannot be portioned off from specific topical studies any more than social psychology or personality psychology approaches might be. Hence, this chapter is not merely an updating of Ozorak's chapter but a reworking of how cognitive science is informing the study of religion.

WHAT IS CSR?

CSR is a loose constellation of approaches to the study of religious expression (including thoughts and actions) that share the principle that ordinary human pan-cultural psychological dynamics (cognition) inform and constrain cultural expressions, including those we might deem religious. Studies in CSR, then, seek to identify how particular cognitive dynamics inform particular forms of religious expression. In doing so, CSR purports to offer at least partial explanations for the recurrence of religious expression across cultures.

One peculiarity of CSR as an area of study within the psychology of religion and spirituality is that it was largely invented by nonpsychologists, and the bulk of those writing and researching in the area are not psychologists. The first formative publications in the area were all by nonpsychologists. These include anthropologist Stewart Guthrie's work on anthropomorphism (Guthrie, 1980, 1993), comparative religionist E. Thomas Lawson and philosopher Robert McCauley's treatment of religious ritual (Lawson & McCauley, 1990), anthropologist Pascal Boyer's hypotheses concerning the spread of religious ideas (Boyer, 1993, 1994), and anthropologist Harvey Whitehouse's observations concerning the role of different memory systems in different classes of rituals (Whitehouse, 1995, 1996). The area was foreshadowed by anthropologist Dan Sperber's novel rethinking of symbolism (Sperber, 1975).

What unified these early efforts, and continues to feature prominently in the field, is an emphasis on explaining cultural-level phenomena by appealing to the underlying *ordinary* psychological processes of individuals, particularly information-processing dynamics typically labeled *cognitive* (including affective dimensions of processing). From the beginning then, CSR has been characterized by an interdisciplinary and multilevel approach to phenomena deemed religious or spiritual: The cultural level is explained in part by psychological-level dynamics, and these dynamics are situated by cultural-level dynamics. Note, too, that with the exception of McCauley, all of the early contributors had expertise in non-Western religions and developed their theories to account for features of these traditional religions.

Emphasis on Ordinary Psychology

CSR scholars observe that the vast majority of humans throughout history, across cultures, and throughout life spans have entertained beliefs and engaged in practices that loosely look religious. As scholars with expertise in traditional religions, they are also aware that so-called religious thought, identification, social organization, and actions are typically inextricable from ordinary day-to-day thought, identification, social organization, and actions. These facts suggest that religion and spirituality appear to be closely knit to human nature. We should not, then, appeal to special economic conditions, social dynamics, pathologies, and the like to explain something so ordinary.[1] As much as CSR appeals to psychology to explain religious phenomena, then, it typically appeals to ordinary psychology as it generally operates in human environments. The scholars engaged in doing CSR rely on basic psychology as their explanatory inspiration for cultural-level phenomena.

Two-System Assumption

One of the tacit assumptions regarding ordinary psychology in much of CSR and central to a few topical areas (e.g., theological correctness–incorrectness) is that human thought can be characterized by a two-systems or dual-processing approach (Kahneman, 2003; Stanovich & West, 2000). One system we might call "intuitive" or "nonreflective" is characterized by rapid, automatic, reflexive, seemingly effortless, and often relatively emotional processing. The reflective reasoning system is slower, deliberate, effortful, and relatively affect-free. Importantly, the automatic deliverances of the intuitive system serve as default presumptions for the reflective system (Barrett, 2004b; Boyer, 2001; Sperber, 1997). As Kahneman explains, "Highly accessible impressions produced by System 1 [the intuitive system] control judgments and preferences, unless modified or overridden by the deliberate operations of System 2 [the reflective system]" (2003, p. 716). Unless sufficient reason exists for the reflective system to modify or override the intuitive system, intuition drives our thinking. The lesson for the study of religion is that our understanding of the psychology of religion will be enhanced by understanding the sorts of deliverances (i.e., intuitions or impressions in Kahneman's terms) that our intuitive, nonreflective system tends to grant and how these inform and constrain reflective thought and consequent behaviors.

Piecemeal Approach

Throughout the history of the study of religion, scholars have tried to find the magic-bullet explanation for religion, that special something that prompts people to be religious, without which we would all be nonreligious. Much ink has been spilled over what religion is or is not such that it might be "explained" by some kind of coherent, well-integrated causal explanation. However, perhaps the assumption that religion is a unitary thing that can be explained by a magic bullet is mistaken. Consider the category *tree*. *Tree* is a useful folk category for talking about some things in the world and maybe even for some applied purposes (such as landscaping), but it turns out to be not very useful for the scientific study of plants because it does not ultimately map onto a causally meaningful grouping of things, any more so than "large aquatic animals" or "furry things about the size of a breadbox" or even "white things" does. Perhaps *religion* is like *tree*—a useful folk category but not a useful explanatory category. If this is right, what then would scholars purporting to study religion actually do? The strategy adopted by most in CSR is to focus on particular categories that appear to be causally meaningful groupings, often using familiar labels in novel ways depending on what appear to be theoretically defensible groupings. For instance, McCauley and Lawson's (2002) category of *religious rituals* leaves out much of what many scholars would like to include under that heading, but they are willing to accept this restrictiveness for the sake of explanatory precision:

> With everything from Theravada Buddhism to Marxism to football in mind, various scholars in theology, religious studies, the humanities, and even the social sciences maintain that presumptions about CPS-agents [culturally postulated superhuman agents] are not critically important to religious phenomena. On this view cheering at football games or marching at May Day is just as much a religious ritual as is sacrificing pigs to the ancestors. Perhaps this is so. In that case what we have, then, may not be a theory of religious ritual. Instead, it is only a theory about actions that individuals and groups perform within organized communities of people who possess conceptual schemes that include presumptions about those actions' connections with the actions of agents who exhibit various counter-intuitive properties. (pp. 8–9)

If these more narrowly circumscribed phenomena turn out to extend beyond what is often meant by "religion" or to fall far short of capturing everything that might be "religion," so be it. A meaningful phenomenon has still been identified and considered. This piecemeal approach allows research to move forward without having the end state in sight, and liberates scholars from the assumption that all religious phenomena must have a single causal nexus. Provocative book titles aside,[2] CSR scholars have not tried to explain religion as a single thing out there to be explained.[3]

It does not follow from this piecemeal approach that these various phenomena (e.g., belief in superhuman agents, belief in the afterlife, religious rituals, prayer, spirit possession) do not interact to produce new complexes with different characteristics or consequences. As does psychology of religion generally, CSR leaves such a possibility open, and some programs of study have begun exploring these possibilities (Whitehouse, 2004).

EXEMPLARY RESEARCH AREAS IN CSR

Space limitations preclude an exhaustive overview of this still-young area. In the following, I sketch those areas that have generated the most theoretical and empirical attention, but these should not be regarded as representing any borders of CSR. CSR really amounts to a particular strategy for studying religion that can blend with other approaches in psychological and social sciences of religion.

Cognition and Gods[4]

Anthropomorphism and Agency Detection

Arguably the earliest published cognitive treatment of religion is anthropologist Stewart Guthrie's revival of the anthropomorphism theory of why belief in superhuman agents—gods—is so prevalent (Guthrie, 1980, 1993). Rather than a psychoanalytic stress on relational dynamics driving anthropomorphism, Guthrie's account emphasizes humans' ordinary perceptual and cognitive tendencies endowed through evolutionary dynamics. Guthrie argues that humans have a perceptual bias to attend to human-like forms or other information that might be caused by human-like beings. He casts the arguments in terms of an evolved tendency to overdetect agents for the sake of survival. It was better to "detect" agents with only fragmentary or ambiguous information than to miss their presence. Better to assume the rustling in the brush is an intentional agent such as a tiger than to become its lunch by assuming it is just the wind. Humans in particular represented our greatest threats and promises for survival and reproduction in our evolutionary environment. Guthrie argues that we evolved a bias to overdetect evidence of human-like agency around us and so we attribute natural forces and events to human-like beings or gods. Under this account, the special cultural elaborations that we call religion are the upshot of an ordinary, pan-human information-processing tendency that can be seen in many different domains of cultural expression.

To distinguish this tendency to find intentional agency around us from other treatments of anthropomorphism and to remain neutral with regard to whether the bias is to pick out human agency or intentional agency generally, I (clumsily) dubbed the cognitive system responsible for detection intentional agency the hypersensitive agency detection device (HADD; Barrett, 2004b). Although determining whether HADD delivers *false* positives when this processing allegedly detects spirits, ghosts, and gods is not easily done, HADD is often hypersensitive in at least two respects. First, it does not require a human or animal form or very much information for HADD to (at least temporarily) detect something as an agent. Experiments with infants suggest HADD is active in the first 5 months of life and only requires self-propelled and purposeful-looking movement for it to identify colored disks as agents (Rochat, Morgan, & Carpenter, 1997). This easy activation persists into adulthood, as demonstrated by numerous laboratory experiments (Scholl & Tremoulet, 2000). HADD is also hypersensitive in that frequently we override its outputs, assuring ourselves that the creak on the stairs was not a home intruder but the groaning of an old house on a windy night. Of course, this overriding of HADD's outputs is a symptom of a two-system mind.

That HADD's outputs are easily overridden has led some scholars in the field to question its centrality in generating beliefs in gods (Atran, 2002; Boyer, 2001). After all, if we readily override HADD's mistakes, why do we regard some experiences as evidence of superhuman agency rather than mistakes? Do HADD experiences really generate god concepts whole-cloth or only provide experiences that might be used in affirming already existing beliefs? For example, people who regard a form in the graveyard mist as a ghost already have a concept of ghosts consonant with the experience. Even though these concerns challenge the sufficiency of HADD for explaining why people believe in gods, undoubtedly HADD may play a role in encouraging the spread of ideas about or belief in gods. As Guthrie suggests, occasionally a HADD experience might be pondered later and not overridden and perhaps combined with others' experiences when postulating a suitable agent. Alternatively, people with a god concept may have a HADD experience that either strengthens their belief or motivates them to transmit the concept. Either way, occasionally HADD experiences may add emotional motivation to generate or transmit god concepts.

Future research providing more evidence that HADD experiences generate or encourage belief in gods would be valuable. Further, research is needed determining whether HADD is instrumental in all gods or just some subset. For instance, it may be that HADD encourages belief in forest spirits and ghosts but not in cosmic deities. Research is needed to firmly connect HADD to beliefs in particular religious agents.

Promiscuous Teleology and Attribution of Agency

One reputed activity of HADD is registering states of affairs as the result of agency. Supporting evidence that such attributions take place regularly with regard to the natural world comes from cognitive developmental research concerning children's understanding of natural kinds. Through numerous experiments, Deborah Kelemen and colleagues have produced considerable evidence that children exercise what she calls *promiscuous teleology*—*teleology* referring to a tendency to find design and purpose and *promiscuous* because it far exceeds what parents authorize (Kelemen, 1999a). For instance, children are inclined to say rocks are pointy not because of some physical processes but because being pointy keeps them from being sat upon (Kelemen, 1999b). Using teleological reasoning to account for the origins or causes of things extends to living things such as plants and animals and nonliving natural things such as rocks and rivers, but is less applicable to natural events such as thunderstorms (DiYanni & Kelemen, 2005). Perhaps not surprisingly, this teleological reasoning often finds a comfortable fit with the idea that the purpose was brought about by an intentional agent or creator (Kelemen & DiYanni, 2005). This assumption that some*one* brings about natural purpose and order may make it difficult to teach evolution by natural selection as an alternative to direct creation. Margaret Evans (2001) has found that even children from families and schools that endorse evolutionary accounts for features of animals do not begin endorsing such accounts at rates comparable to their parents until after age 10. It seems, then, that children have a strong bias to see the world as purposefully designed by someone. This conceptual space seems to invite a god or gods to fill the gap (Kelemen, 2004). Interestingly, Kelemen has produced evidence that adults who have not been formally educated show similar preference for teleological explanations (Casler & Kelemen, 2008), as do even scientifically educated adults under hurried response conditions (Kelemen & Rosset, 2009). These results suggest that promiscuous teleology is not simply outgrown but is only tamped down in some cultural contexts.

Psychologist Jesse Bering (2011) has argued that Kelemen's findings and Guthrie's observations are subtypes of a broader tendency for humans to try to make meaning of their experiences, particularly by appealing to intentional purposes lying behind them. People try to understand how the various aspects of their life experiences and understanding of the world join up, but not all attempts to synthesize meaning are equally appealing to human cognitive systems (see also Park, Chapter 18, this volume). Bering argues that our theory of mind system, which reasons in terms of beliefs and desires of other intentional beings, is eager for deployment in meaning making.

Given Kelemen's experimental findings, it would not be at all surprising that people would readily latch onto the notion of a being or beings that bring about conditions in the natural world or even are responsible for its origins. If these beings are deemed (or inferred to be or thought to be) responsible for conditions in the natural world—conditions that either facilitate or impinge upon human surviving and thriving—we might expect humans to attempt to interact with or propitiate these beings and thereby invent rituals and other practices.

Many of these inferred nonhuman beings that have some role in arranging the furniture of the world tend to be seen as having other properties that make them superhuman such as being superknowing or superperceiving. Might people be especially receptive to these ideas about intentional agents?

The Freudian, object relations, and Piagetian approaches to the development of god concepts all assume anthropomorphism to be the best characterization of young children's ideas: Gods are just human beings that might live in the clouds or something similar (Elkind, 1970; Goldman, 1965; Piaget, 1929). More recent cognitive developmental research, however, at least raises the possibility that by age 5 (or earlier) children can discriminate the properties of gods from other agents (such as dogs or mother) (Barrett, Newman, & Richert, 2003), and that their early development of intentional agent concepts might better be characterized as theomorphism. That is, on some dimensions at least, children attribute superproperties to humans and gods and then pare back those properties through development until they arrive at adult-like understandings of humans and gods (Barrett & Richert, 2003).[5]

Across a series of experiments using tasks adapted from standard work in cognitive development, Barrett and his collaborators replicated previous findings that children presume others' beliefs and perceptions are reliable reflections of what the child knows to be the case, even in contexts when an adult would recognize the fallibility of thought and perception. For instance, once children were told the meaning of a secret code or rules of a novel game, 3- and 4-year-olds assumed their mother, a dog, and God would all know the meaning of the code or the rules of the game at first presentation (Barrett et al., 2003). By age 5 they understood that the dog and their mother would not understand a secret code or the game. These children from Protestant homes did regard God as likely to understand these displays at all ages. Indeed, even the 3-year-olds were significantly more likely to attribute understanding to God than a dog. Similarly, if a 3-year-old knows that a cracker box contains rocks, he answers that his mother, a bear, God, or anyone else would know about the surprising contents as well (Barrett, Richert, & Driesenga, 2001). By age 5, children generally know that beliefs are fallible and, for instance, mother would likely believe a cracker box contains crackers even if the child knows that there are rocks in the box. Nicola Knight replicated this finding with Yukatek-speaking Maya children living in Mexico (Knight, Sousa, Barrett, & Atran, 2004). Knight also found that once they understood the fallibility of beliefs, these 4- to 7-year-olds differentiated among various deities in a way similar to adults, more frequently attributing accurate knowledge to the Catholic God than the forest spirits or sun god and these more frequently than animals, people, or household spooks (Knight, 2008). Importantly, the youngest children tended to treat all of these agents similarly: as superknowing. Richert, Barrett, and colleagues also investigated whether children thought God, a human, and a variety of animals would be able to see an object in the dark, hear a currently inaudible sound, or smell something not currently detected (Richert & Barrett, 2005). As in the other tasks, 5-year-olds successfully discriminated various agents' properties once they outgrow the tendency to overattribute perceptual access to all. These studies suggest that it may be the limitations of natural minds that take children longer to learn. Theological ideas about superknowing and superperceiving gods may be closer to the early-developing default assumptions (Barrett & Richert, 2003).

It may be that such developmental biases—part of the automated, largely unconscious and intuitive system—make the ideas of superknowing, superperceiving, beings that account for at least some of the apparent design and purpose in the natural world largely intuitive. Culturally supplied candidates that fit the conceptual space relatively well may be more likely to be generated, entertained, communicated, remembered, and affirmed as existent. The intuitive ring makes them seem right. The repeated exposure to such ideas means they are highly accessible, enhancing their intuitiveness and attractiveness. Concepts that resonate with intuitive biases—those that just seem right—will more likely win the battle for our attention and affirmation than more deviant ones, all else being equal.

Minimal Counterintuitiveness

Although concepts that enjoy good fit with intuitions are easy to understand and communicate, they might not always be all that interesting because they may seem commonplace. Ideas with just one or two tweaks, on the other hand, may enjoy the benefits of good intuitive fit but have additional attention-grabbing potential, leading to more investment and deeper processing. This suggestion, that being just a bit counterintuitive or "minimally counterintuitive" may actually make a concept more likely to be remembered and transmitted, forms a critical part of Pascal Boyer's cognitive-evolutionary account of why religious ideas spread so successfully: Religious ideas (among other successful cultural ideas) are not radically counterintuitive or wholly intuitive, but minimally counterintuitive and hence spread well (Boyer, 1993, 1994, 1998). Counterintuitiveness and its alleged mnemonic dynamics are slightly different from the more familiar psychological research concerning schemata and memory. Whereas schemata may vary across individuals and cultures, the anchoring intuitions to which Boyer appeals are regarded as largely stable in humans, a normal outcome of development (McCauley, 2011).

Boyer's predictions were supported by initial experimental studies that showed minimally counterintuitive ideas were remembered and transmitted more effectively than either intuitive (Barrett & Nyhof, 2001; Boyer & Ramble, 2001), more massively counterintuitive (Boyer & Ramble, 2001), or intuitive but bizarre (Barrett & Nyhof, 2001) concepts. Subsequent studies, however, provided more mixed results (Gonce, Upal, Slone, & Tweney, 2006; Norenzayan, Atran, Faulkner, & Schaller, 2006; Tweney, Upal, Gonce, Slone, & Edwards, 2006; Upal, Owsianiecki, Slone, & Tweney, 2007). Barrett (2008a) has suggested that these alleged failures to replicate were the result of poor construct validity due to ambiguities in how to operationalize counterintutiveness. To address this problem, Barrett (2008a) developed a formal scheme for coding and quantifying counterintuitive concepts, and then demonstrated the utility of this scheme in analyzing folktales from around the world (Barrett, Burdett, & Porter, 2009). True to Boyer's predictions, when these tales—the products of oral traditions—had counterintuitive objects in them, they tended to include only one counterintuitive feature, as previous text-coding studies had likewise found (Lisdorf, 2001).

Nevertheless, the first published experimental study using Barrett's coding scheme did not yield simple confirming or disconfirming evidence (Gregory & Barrett, 2009).

Justin Gregory generated intuitive (e.g., "A cat that is alive") and minimally counterintuitive (MCI) (e.g., "A fly that is immortal") test items using Barrett's coding scheme as well as analytically true (e.g., "A circle that is round") and analytically false (e.g., "A bachelor who is married") items. Through preratings, intuitive and counterintuitive items were matched for how thought provoking they were and how readily they could be imagined. Twenty-four items were presented in random order for 7 seconds each and then after a 3-minute distractor task, participants recalled as many items as they could. One week later they were asked to recall the items again. Under these conditions, the advantage for MCI items did not realize, but post hoc analyses revealed a potentially important result: Participants younger than 25 years did significantly remember MCI items better than intuitive items, whereas those older than 25 years significantly remembered MCI items worse than intuitive items.

Results to date indicate three directions for future research. First, although Gregory and Barrett may have found a mnemonic advantage for MCI concepts among younger participants, it may be that once extracted from a narrative context, MCI concepts are not as readily remembered because they require more elaboration than ordinary concepts. The role of narratives as vehicles for communicating MCI concepts certainly would benefit from more attention (Upal, 2010). Second, perhaps being counterintuitive by itself is not enough to be attention demanding and thus more memorable and likely to be transmitted. It may be that the ability to readily generate inferences, predictions, and explanations in domains broadly meaningful and important to humans—what Boyer has termed "inferential potential"—is the key to MCI mnemonic success (Boyer, 2001), and Gregory and Barrett (and perhaps others) have effectively neutralized this factor by controlling for how "thought provoking" items were. Third, and most intriguingly, it may be that Boyer's hypothesized transmission advantage for MCI concepts interacts with age such that MCI concepts are the province of the young and quite forgettable for older people.

MCI theory is applicable to a host of cultural concepts, not just those that might be considered religious and certainly not only to concepts of gods, but it does afford a theoretically and empirically motivated way to avoid difficulties with identifying gods with supernatural or superhuman agents. They can, instead, be identified as MCI intentional agents. Boyer notes, however, that those MCI agents that we typically call "gods" and that become central players in religious systems tend to have additional distinguishing factors, such as having access to morally relevant information, possessing the ability to act in the world, and motivating actions such as ritual and prayer (Barrett, 2008b; Boyer, 2001, 2003). Agents that can act in the world and have concerns about trespasses against themselves and others may be worth communicating with or ritually propitiating in order to avoid their wrath or garner their favor. Once such religious acts are begun, evidence exists that they are culturally adaptive and may thereby enjoy a selective advantage (Bulbulia, 2009; Sosis, 2004).

Theological Correctness

One potential consequence of a two-system mind—one fast and automatic and the other slow, reflective, and deliberate—is that we can have contradictory representations of the same thing. In many religious contexts, this means that we could have explicit, doctrinal beliefs that produce certain types of inferences in the offline, reflective mode and different inferences in the online, nonreflective mode. Notions of karma, for instance, may be (mis)represented online as some*one* punishing or rewarding or instead as something akin to dumb luck (Slone, 2004). Likewise, we might hear Christians, Muslims, or Jews talk about the utter transcendence of the Divine, but in the next moment confess thinking of God as having beliefs, desires, and attention much like a human. The gap between the stated, reflective beliefs and the online, automatic representation has been termed "theological correctness," or the TC effect: Analogous to political correctness, people know the right thing to say even if their thoughts are not consistently in line with it.

Through a series of experiments with religious believers and nonbelievers in the United States and in India, Barrett and colleagues demonstrated that adults' god concepts can function in markedly divergent ways depending on the conceptual demands of the context (Barrett, 1998, 1999; Barrett & Keil, 1996; Barrett & VanOrman, 1996). These studies capitalized on a well-established finding from research on schemata that, for any narrative, conceptual gaps are automatically filled by the audience's relevant expectations, resulting, in many cases, in intrusion errors in which something is remembered to having been in the narrative that was not actually there (Bransford & McCarrell, 1974). These TC studies presented participants with narratives that included God (or Vishnu, Krishna, etc. for Indian participants) but also included many inferential gaps. Comprehension questions or participant-generated paraphrases were scored for intrusion errors reflective of anthropomorphic divine attributes that were denied by participants when asked directly by questionnaire. For instance, participants who regarded God as capable of attending to any number of things at the same time erroneously remembered stories saying that God was interrupted, distracted, or completed one task before turning to another task. Control conditions ruled out that these results were only an artifact of the narratives or the comprehension questions. It appears that some divine attributes are too difficult or counterintuitive to easily generate inferences in online tasks.

Although these studies concerned god concepts, the general TC effect may extend to other areas of religious thought. Religion scholar Jason Slone has argued that the relative counterintuitiveness of some theological ideas entails that individual believers will frequently fail to understand and apply them correctly during automatic processing: A religious term or practice may have very different meanings across contexts. But further, because the reflective and nonreflective modes are not independent—the nonreflective mode outputs inform and constrain the reflective mode outputs—we might also expect many theological concepts to be distorted and misunderstood by the masses even during cool reflection. Slone calls this problem "theological incorrectness" and offers examples from Eastern and Western religious traditions (Slone, 2004).

Religious Practices

Religious Rituals

Although much attention in CSR has centered on how ordinary cognition might encourage the not-as-ordinary ideas that tend to characterize traditional religious beliefs, some of the earliest work in the area actually concerned religious practices such as ritual. Already in the 1970s, E. Thomas Lawson began wondering if the emerging accounts from Chomskian linguistics—particularly the idea that pan-cultural human cognition provides something like a universal grammar for languages—might have an analogue for religious rituals. Could pan-cultural cognition provide intuitions that anchor how religious rituals are conceptualized and executed? Lawson teamed up with Robert McCauley to answer this question affirmatively (Lawson & McCauley, 1990; McCauley & Lawson, 2002).

Lawson and McCauley's ritual form theory begins by circumscribing its focus as those actions that change the status of participants and represent culturally postulated superhuman (or MCI) agents in the action structure. That is, people act in some observable way upon some object or patient to prompt the gods to bring about some sort of change in state.[6] As actions, these religious rituals are conceptualized using the same cognitive equipment as is used for any other action. Consequently, across religious traditions and cultures, some commonalities in how religious rituals are understood would be expected.

Specifically, Lawson and McCauley predict that the particular form of the ritual—independent of reputed meanings—will generate judgments regarding whether participants and observers of the religious rituals will tend to regard substitutions of different elements to be permissible, will regard a given religious ritual as ritually reversible or repeatable, and will tend to perform the ritual with high levels of sounds, smells, sights, and other stimulation to excite the senses and emotions, what they call "sensory pageantry." Perhaps surprisingly, they also predict that having appropriately qualified and motivated agents involved in the execution of the ritual will matter more to observers than precise execution of a specified action sequence, and some preliminary findings appear to support this prediction (Barrett & Lawson, 2001).

Capturing so many performance-related features of religious rituals without appeal to cultural particulars (including theological meaning or social function) would be a major explanatory achievement. To date, little empirical research investigating its claims has been published, but initial experimental and ethnographic results are generally supportive (Barrett, 2002b; Barrett & Lawson, 2001; Malley & Barrett, 2003). Malley and Barrett (2003) report evidence from structured interviews that the ritual form theory's various predictions are largely consistent with intuitions regarding religious rituals in Hinduism, Judaism, and Islam, but numerous empirical gaps have likewise been identified (Barrett, 2004a).

Ritualized Behaviors

Resonant with Lee Kirkpatrick's efforts to stimulate a full-bodied evolutionary psychology of religion (Kirkpatrick, 1999, 2005; Chapter 6, this volume), Boyer and anthropologist Pierre Liénard have developed a cognitive-evolutionary account of ritualized cultural actions (religious or otherwise) (Boyer, 2003; Boyer & Liénard, 2006; Liénard & Boyer, 2006). They note that many (but not all) rituals are similar to personal "rituals" found in mothers-to-be and mothers of young children, children at different stages of development, and people with obsessive–compulsive disorder. Features include repetition, concern for action precision, and heightened affect surrounding the need to perform (or failure to perform) correctly. Boyer and Liénard argue that underlying all of these personal rituals (pathological or not) is an evolved hazard precaution system that has been selected for its ability to keep people away from unseen potential harms such as predators, pathogens, and contaminants. Cultural rituals piggyback on this system as is evinced by both the common features of such ritualized actions but also the recurrent themes surrounding these rituals such as cleanliness and purification, establishing sacred spaces, and fending off unseen threats.

Prayer

Verbally communicating with gods, spirits, and ancestors is a cross-culturally recurrent phenomenon but has received very little attention so far by cognitive scientists of religion. Following on the idea that nonreflective, online god concepts may be more anthropomorphic than explicit theologies profess, Barrett investigated how nonreflective representations of God might shape petitionary prayer practices among American Protestants (Barrett, 2001, 2002a). Although taught to make requests of God, they are not often instructed regarding the mode of causation to ask God to operate through. When I lose my keys, I could ask God to act psychologically (e.g., remind me where I left them or help me see where they are), or I could ask God to act physically (e.g., having them materialize on my desk). Either course of action is possible for an all-powerful God, but the theological correctness/incorrectness findings—for instance, that God may be tacitly assumed to have a distant location and must be immediately present to act mechanistically—predict an intuitive preference to ask a psychosocial being to act psychologically or socially. Through analyses of prayer journals and by asking young adults to judge their most likely prayer strategy in a number of hypothetical situations (controlling for, e.g., gravity of the situation, goodness of the solution), Barrett found a tendency for young adult participants to pray for God to act through psychological or social causation more than through biological or physical causation.

Sociopolitical Arrangements: Modes of Religiosity

Anthropologist Harvey Whitehouse was trained in standard social anthropology and did extended field work in Melanesia, where he witnessed most of the life cycle of an end-times splinter group, including its failure to bring about the return of the ancestors through a series of rituals (Whitehouse, 1995). Whitehouse was fascinated by the psychological research in the 1980s and 1990s concerning "flashbulb" and related episodic memories in contrast with semantic memory dynamics. He has cited the dynamics of these different memory systems as a core cause of what anthropologists and religion scholars have long noted about religions: they seem to come in two primary, divergent varieties. He dubbed these two "modes of religiosity" (Whitehouse, 2000, 2004).

In the *imagistic mode*, the more ancient of the two, the transmission of central theological insights is principally through highly emotional but rarely performed events such as brutal initiation rites or rites of terror (Whitehouse, 1996). Whitehouse argues that these events create emotion-laden memories of the events and one's coparticipants and generate individual exegetical reflection and feelings of relational connectedness with coparticipants. Because of these psychological dynamics, religious systems in this mode will tend to have relatively local, egalitarian political structures, be light on orthodoxy controls, and be slow to expand in terms of membership.

The *doctrinal mode*, in contrast, springs from frequently performed, relatively low-arousal theological transmission events such as weekly church or synagogue. Such events are suited to transmit complex theological ideas without any necessary emotional connection with coparticipants. Whitehouse argues that religions of the doctrinal mode tend to involve relatively hierarchical political structures for enforcing doctrinal orthodoxy, the potential for large imagined communities of fellow participants, and the potential for rapid expansion.

The modes theory not only helps account for why various social, political, and religious factors tend to cluster, but also how it is that religious ideas that are more than minimally counterintuitive may successfully spread. Each of the two modes offers some "cultural scaffolding" that helps in the transmission of ideas that are not otherwise optimal for memory and transmission (Whitehouse, 2004).[7]

Because of the account's breadth and apparent ability to address cultural development in many times and places, Whitehouse's modes theory has enjoyed attention from anthropologists, historians, archeologists, psychologists, and other cognitive scientists (Whitehouse & Laidlaw, 2004; Whitehouse & Martin, 2004; Whitehouse & McCauley, 2005). Nevertheless, empirical gaps still exist (Barrett, 2005), such as whether high-arousal rites really do generate complex exegetical reflection more than comparable low-arousal events, produce long-lasting memories and sense of solidarity with coparticipants, and serve as poor vehicles for verbal instruction.

Bodies and Spirits

One area in which CSR is breaking new ground in the study of religious phenomena as well as raising new issues for psychology generally is how the physical and nonphysical aspects of personhood are conceptualized and how these conceptualizations underpin such widespread cultural ideas as belief in some kind of afterlife and ideas about ghosts, ancestor-spirits, and spirit possession (Cohen & Barrett, 2011).

Intuitive Dualism

Psychologist Paul Bloom has argued that humans are naturally "intuitive dualists," regarding minds and bodies as separable entities because of representational conflicts between two conceptual systems that generate inferences regarding the properties of humans (Bloom, 2004).[8] One system, variously termed naïve or folk physics or mechanics, deals with solid, bounded physical objects and is present in the first few months of life (Spelke & Kinzler, 2007). This system registers human bodies as objects with certain physical properties, such as having to be contacted to be moved, moving continuously through space, and the like. The second system, dealing with minded agents, allows considerably more latitude. Agents, after all, can act at a distance. Bloom argues that these two systems, with their different developmental schedules, different evolutionary histories, and different input–output conditions, are only ever tenuously united in reasoning about humans. For this reason, they easily accommodate thinking about disembodied minds and something of us persisting after death (such as souls or spirits) (Bloom, 2007, 2009).

Afterlife Beliefs

What happens after biological death is culturally elaborated in various ways around the world. Ideas range from an afterworld that mirrors the present world, to vague spirit realms, to reincarnation in this world, to ghosts and spirits that continue to act in this world, to eternal paradise or damnation. Sometimes ideas about the afterlife feature prominently in religious systems, and sometimes they are afforded little importance. Absolute universal annihilation, however—simply the end—is unusual. Why so? On this question, it is hard to determine a consensus position among CSR scholars. Researchers debate whether such beliefs are intuitive versus counterintuitive (and how counterintuitive) and just which cognitive predilections undergird such beliefs.

For instance, Bloom sees some kind of afterlife as a natural extension of intuitive dualism and, as such, intuitive (Bloom, 2004). Jesse Bering likewise suggests that the impossibility of imagining no longer having certain classes of mental states makes it natural to assume that minds continue at least some operations after death (Bering, 2002). Add to this "simulation constraint" the natural human tendency to seek existential meaning in events, and subtle events after the death of a loved one (such as surprising sights or sounds or dreams), may be taken as evidence of the persistence of the other after death (Bering, 2006). In support of his position, in one set of experiments, Bering and collaborators showed that American children have stronger commitments to an afterlife earlier in childhood (Bering & Bjorkland, 2004; Bering, Hernández-Blasi, & Bjorkland, 2005). Bering further argues that such a strong predisposition to have afterlife beliefs was encouraged in the course of evolution by selective pressure because holding such a belief can promote reputation-enhancing behavior. If you believe ghosts or ancestor spirits might be around and watching, you are more inclined to behave in ways good for your social reputation, thereby making you a more attractive exchange partner (Bering, McLeod, & Shackelford, 2005).

Other scholars hold that while ordinary cognition may be configured in such a way as to make afterlife reasoning easy and attractive, it still is not fully intuitive. Boyer suggests that our "person file" for well-known others works with our theory of mind to generate ideas about the thoughts, feelings, and desires of the recently deceased, thereby providing some impetus for believing in some kind of afterlife if the idea comes up (Boyer, 2001). Consonant with the idea that afterlife beliefs may be slightly counterintuitive rather than fully intuitive, anthropologist Rita Astuti and psychologist Paul Harris found (contra Bering) that in Madagascar the degree of affirming continuation of mental states after death increased during childhood, suggesting the importance of testimony (Astuti & Harris, 2008). The contrast between Bering's and Astuti's findings is difficult to interpret because of numerous methodological differences, including the use of an anthropomorphized mouse (Bering) versus a human target (Astuti and Harris). Cohen, Burdett, Knight, and Barrett (2011) have produced cross-cultural data raising concerns about the trait categories used in these previous studies about afterlife beliefs. Disambiguating evidence on this topic would be helpful.

Spirit Possession

The idea that spirits (evil or benign) can enter bodies and exert control over them is common across cultures and presents some interesting conceptual challenges for observers of such events (Cohen, 2007). Who is doing the acting during possession? What happens to the agency of the possessed person? Given these difficulties, why is spirit possession cross-culturally pervasive in recognizably similar forms? Emma Cohen's cognitive engagement on the subject has already provided promising directions of study. Perhaps conceptualizing spirit possession capitalizes on an already-present conceptual arrangement that favors dualistic thinking and further imports a one-mind/one-body principle that governs normal mind–body reasoning. Through ethnographic and experimental work, Cohen has provided some preliminary evidence that even in the face of contrary theological teaching, spirit possession is most readily construed by observers and participants as a displacement of the mind from the body, and that something like a one-mind/one-body principle seems to be a cross-culturally recurrent assumption (Cohen & Barrett, 2008a, 2008b).

CONCLUSION

Although decidedly psychological in its theoretical resources, CSR models a genuinely multilevel, interdisciplinary, and methodologically pluralistic area of study. The majority of scholars working in the area cannot claim psychology as a home discipline but hail from anthropology, archeology, history, philosophy, religious studies, theology, and zoology. Regardless of their background, the unifying research strategy is to consider empirical evidence for how regular aspects of human psychology importantly inform and/or constrain religious expression and experience of various sorts, thereby rendering a particular phenomenon more or less likely. Relevant evidence may be experimental, correlational, ethnographic, material, or textual. Generally, the level of the phenomena to be explained is the group/cultural level as in: "Why do Afro-Brazilian spiritualists in community X uniformly conceptualize spirit possession as a full displacement of identity instead of a fusion of identities as they are taught?" (Cohen & Barrett, 2008a). Sometimes the level of the explanadum is broadened to cross-cultural comparisons ("Why is a displacement model of spirit possession the most common model across western Africa, the Caribbean, and Latin America?") or even to global concerns ("Why are beliefs in disembodied intentional beings essentially universal features of human cultures?"). Other times the questions pertain to individual thought and expression, as in "Do individuals use the same representation of their god across various contexts?" (Barrett, 1999). Because the answers to these questions are cast in terms of psychological dynamics of individuals (that impact individual- or group-level phenomena), frequently experiments and correlational studies that use individuals as the unit of analysis are performed, much as in psychology of religion generally. Pinning down cultural-level recurrences, however, is done through ethnographic, textual, or other methods common in cultural and historical studies.

Future Directions

The summary presented here certainly does not exhaust the range of concerns that occupy cognitive scientists of religion, but is only illustrative of what this approach has focused on and the theoretical strategies it characteristically uses. As our understanding of psychology advances, CSR should follow suit and not remain locked into unnecessarily restricted or misleading construals of how the mind works. Similarly, as this is a young area of study, many topics have not yet been addressed that would prove fruitful. I now highlight just three classes of investigation: empirically establishing conceptual anchors, further exploring diversity of religious expression, and understanding when and how religious phenomena congeal as meaning systems.

Empirically Establishing Conceptual "Anchors"

A pervasive theme in CSR is that cultural expression is anchored by underlying conceptual structures, biases, or predilections. Much work in the area draws upon cross-cultural, evolutionary, and cognitive developmental research to identify these anchors: what their properties are, where they come from, and how much flexibility they allow. The intuitions that underlie MCI effects, promiscuous teleology, intuitive dualism, HADD, and Lawson and McCauley's *action representation system* are all examples of conceptual anchors that may shape religious expression. To date, speculations about the conditions under which HADD is more or less sensitive to activation, its characteristic outputs, and even whether registering objects as agents versus identifying states of affairs as caused by agency are the function of the same system, for instance, are all empirically undersupported. The potential of such anchors to inform learning and cultural transmission of all sorts—not just in those domains deemed religious—makes research on these anchors a potential contribution to psychology generally.

Exploring Variability

Although CSR scholars occasionally attempt to explain very particular changes or practices in a specific cultural setting (Cohen, 2007; Malley, 2004; McCauley & Lawson, 2002), even these specific applications tend to cite context-general psychological dynamics as the primary causal factors. Once the conceptual anchors are more firmly determined and the ways in which they inform and constrain cultural expression is better established, then we will be in a better position to appreciate how additional factors serve to move individuals and groups away from these anchors. What accounts for individual and cultural diversity in religious expression apart from differential activation of general psychological factors? How do specific natural and cultural environmental factors push religious thought, experience, and action away from the anchors?

Religion as a Meaning System?

CSR's roots in the study of traditional religions that focus on ancestors, forest-spirits, fertility rituals, and healing through spirit-possession rather than morally interested cosmic deities with large literate guilds of theological experts has distanced CSR from treating religions as meaning systems in any interesting sense (see Park, Chapter 18, this volume). Surely research on promiscuous teleology and agency detection identifies the conceptual resources available to people for making sense of events and states of affairs in the world. But the expectation that the various beliefs and practices that contemporary Westerners identify with "religion" might cohere to produce an integrated existential meaning system is not obviously recurrent across cultures. A program for future work in the area would be to identify the conditions under which notions of counterintuitive causation or agency become elaborated into full-blown meaning systems. Are some ideas about the transcendent more favorable to such elaborations? Are some ecological conditions?

CSR was developed primarily by nonpsychologists to answer nonpsychological questions, but in seeking answers to these religious studies questions by appealing to psychological mechanisms, research in this area is encouraging advances in basic psychology. Four areas mentioned previously nicely illustrate how CSR (and other activities in psychology of religion) can "feed back" into psychology generally. First, ample research has explored the role of culture-derived and idiosyncratic schemata on memory: The content of what we know already impacts what we perceive and remember. But it has been the cognitive study of culture—and particularly the cognitive study of religion— that has heightened the potential importance of pan-human conceptual content biases in influencing memory dynamics, as illustrated by MCI theory.[9] Second, Kelemen and others' investigations into how children and adults naturally construe the type of causation behind things and events in the natural world readily bear upon religious cosmologies, invocation of gods to explain, and propitiating gods to change things but also constitutes basic psychological research concerning causal cognition and conceptual development. How we make sense of the world we are born into is surely a basic psychological question. Third, similarly, a basic psychological competence that supports all of our social interactions is our ability to reason about others as minded beings with beliefs, desires, percepts, and emotional states that predict and explain behaviors. The study of theory of mind has been a huge industry within psychology, but it has rarely considered how people reason about nonhuman minds. Cognitive-developmental research on god concepts has provided impetus for just such a broadening to consider the development of reasoning about various animals' mental properties as well as gods'. Fourth, although mind–body conceptions bear upon our judgments about whether someone is culpable for their actions (did he bump into me on purpose or was it just momentum?) as well as how we learn and think about the biological causes or effects of our mental states (as in psychosomatic illnesses), it has been explaining afterlife beliefs, spirit possession, and similar "religious" ideas that has been the greatest engine driving interest in how people conceptualize the relationship between minds and bodies.

I suggested that the topics of study in CSR are analogous to the seemingly boring basement and girders of a mansion. CSR is not foundational in the sense of necessary or primary for doing the study of religious and spiritual thought, experience, and behavior. Exciting findings have long been made before CSR and continue to be made entirely independently. But perhaps like understanding the boring parts of a grand structure, CSR can add depth to the study of religion and provide insights that otherwise would go unnoticed.

ACKNOWLEDGMENTS

I thank Miguel Farias for comments and Tenelle Porter and Rebecca Sok for assistance in preparing the manuscript.

NOTES

1. Of course, exceptional religious practices, experiences, arrangements, and the like may require exceptional explanations, but CSR has tended to focus on the ordinary—the basic foundations and supports of whatever religion and spirituality might be.
2. Boyer's *Religion Explained* (2001) in some ways parallel's Daniel Dennett's *Consciousness Explained* (1991) by actually reframing the phenomena under consideration rather than explaining it. Pyysiäinen's title *How Religion Works* (2003) is surely meant to bring to mind Steven Pinker's *How the Mind Works* (1997) while borrowing its cheeky overstatement. Neither Boyer nor Pyysiäinen claim that religion is one unified thing that they have explained.
3. An exception is when authors redefine "religion" in a narrow sense that might, in fact, be causally meaningful and then purport to have offered an explanation of religion. If the critic complains, "You have explained Y but you haven't explained X and X is part of religion," the reply is likely to be something akin to McCauley and Lawson's.
4. Ilkka Pyysiäinen has provided a synthetic treatment of cognitive and evolutionary approaches to beliefs in gods across cultures (2009).
5. In fairness, Piaget too observed that children seem to attribute some god-like properties to adults and then pared them back by about age 8 or 9; but among these properties was accounting for the natural features of the world, a property not supported by contemporary research with much younger children (Gelman & Kremer, 1991; Petrovich, 1997, 1999).
6. Thus, circumscribed many religious activities such as prayer, spirit possession, or participation in worship services are not counted as religious rituals for this theory.
7. The idea of cultural scaffolding—special cultural conditions or supports that encourage the spread of otherwise difficult or poor candidates for cultural success—appears in McCauley and Lawson (2002) and elsewhere in the CSR literature. Whitehouse illustrates how different psychological factors may be integrated with local conditions to provide a fuller account of particular cultural expression (Whitehouse, 2007).
8. The term "intuitive dualism" may be misleading in a certain sense. Bloom's account leaves open whether thinking that "I have a separable mind and body that are different substances" is an intuitive idea as opposed to it being a reflective idea that is strongly informed by the dynamics of intuitive reasoning about minds and bodies and is thus an idea we find very intuitive once it is suggested. Or perhaps we tend to reason as if we are dualists without necessarily recognizing that we are.
9. Dan Sperber has developed a general perspective of how "content biases" impact memory and acquisition of ideas that has inspired many working in CSR (Sperber, 1996).

REFERENCES

Astuti, R., & Harris, P. L. (2008). Understanding mortality and the life of the ancestors in rural Madagascar. *Cognitive Science, 32*, 713–740.

Atran, S. (2002). *In gods we trust: The evolutionary landscape of religion.* Oxford, UK: Oxford University Press.

Barrett, J. L. (1998). Cognitive constraints on Hindu concepts of the divine. *Journal for the Scientific Study of Religion, 37*, 608–619.

Barrett, J. L. (1999). Theological correctness: Cognitive constraint and the study of religion. *Method and Theory in the Study of Religion, 11*, 325–339.

Barrett, J. L. (2001). How ordinary cognition informs petitionary prayer. *Journal of Cognition and Culture, 1*(3), 259–269.

Barrett, J. L. (2002a). Dumb gods, petitionary prayer, and the cognitive science of religion. In I. Pyysiäinen & V. Anttonen (Eds.), *Current approaches in the cognitive study of religion* (pp. 93–109). London, UK: Continuum.

Barrett, J. L. (2002b). Smart gods, dumb gods, and the role of social cognition in structuring ritual intuitions. *Journal of Cognition and Culture, 2*, 183–194.

Barrett, J. L. (2004a). Bringing data to mind: Empirical claims of Lawson and McCauley's theory of religious ritual. In B. C. Wilson & T. Light (Eds.), *Religion as a human capacity: A festschrift in honor of E. Thomas Lawson* (pp. 265–288). Leiden, The Netherlands: Brill.

Barrett, J. L. (2004b). *Why would anyone believe in God?* Lanham, MD: AltaMira Press.

Barrett, J. L. (2005). In the empirical mode: Evidence needed for the modes of religiosity theory. In H. Whitehouse & R. N. McCauley (Eds.), *Mind and religion* (pp. 109–126). Lanham, MD: Alta Mira Press.

Barrett, J. L. (2008a). Coding and quantifying counterintuitiveness in religious concepts: Theoretical and methodological Reflections. *Method and Theory in the Study of Religion, 20,* 308–338.

Barrett, J. L. (2008b). Why Santa Claus is not a god. *Journal of Cognition and Culture, 8,* 149–161.

Barrett, J. L., Burdett, E. R., & Porter, T. J. (2009). Counterintuitiveness in folktales: Finding the cognitive optimum. *Journal of Cognition and Culture, 9,* 271–287.

Barrett, J. L., & Keil, F. C. (1996). Anthropomorphism and God concepts: Conceptualizing a non-natural entity. *Cognitive Psychology, 31,* 219–247.

Barrett, J. L., & Lawson, E. T. (2001). Ritual intuitions: cognitive contributions to judgments of ritual efficacy. *Journal of Cognition and Culture, 1,* 183–201.

Barrett, J. L., Newman, R. M., & Richert, R. A. (2003). When seeing does not lead to believing: Children's understanding of the importance of background knowledge for interpreting visual displays. *Journal of Cognition and Culture, 3,* 91–108.

Barrett, J. L., & Nyhof, M. (2001). Spreading non-natural concepts: The role of intuitive conceptual structures in memory and transmission of cultural materials. *Journal of Cognition and Culture, 1,* 69–100.

Barrett, J. L., & Richert, R. A. (2003). Anthropomorphism or preparedness?: Exploring children's God concepts. *Review of Religious Research, 44,* 300–312.

Barrett, J. L., Richert, R. A., & Driesenga, A. (2001). God's beliefs versus Mom's: The development of natural and non-natural agent concepts. *Child Development, 72,* 50–65.

Barrett, J. L., & VanOrman, B. (1996). The effects of image use in worship on God concepts. *Journal of Psychology and Christianity, 15,* 38–45.

Bering, J. M. (2002). Intuitive conceptions of dead agents' minds: The natural foundations of afterlife beliefs as phenomenological boundary. *Journal of Cognition and Culture, 2,* 263–308.

Bering, J. M. (2006). The folk psychology of souls. *Behavioral and Brain Sciences, 29,* 453–462.

Bering, J. M. (2011). *The belief instinct: The psychology of souls, destiny, and the meaning of life.* New York: Norton.

Bering, J. M., & Bjorkland, D. F. (2004). The natural emergence of reasoning about the afterlife as a developmental regularity. *Developmental Psychology, 40,* 217–233.

Bering, J. M., Hernández-Blasi, C., & Bjorkland, D. F. (2005). The development of 'afterlife' beliefs in secularly and religiously schooled children. *British Journal of Developmental Psychology, 23,* 587–607.

Bering, J. M., McLeod, K., & Shackelford, T. K. (2005). Reasoning about dead agents reveals possible adaptive trends. *Human Nature, 16,* 360–381.

Bloom, P. (2004). *Descartes' baby: How child development explains what makes us human.* London, UK: William Heinemann.

Bloom, P. (2007). Religion is natural. *Developmental Science, 10,* 147–151.

Bloom, P. (Ed.). (2009). *Religious belief as an evolutionary accident.* New York: Oxford University Press.

Boyer, P. (1993). Cognitive aspects of religious symbolism. In P. Boyer (Ed.), *Cognitive aspects of religious symbolism* (pp. 4–47). Cambridge, UK: Cambridge University Press.

Boyer, P. (1994). *The naturalness of religious ideas: A cognitive theory of religion.* Berkeley, CA: University of California Press.

Boyer, P. (1998). Cognitive tracks of cultural inheritance: How evolved intuitive ontology governs cultural transmission. *American Anthropologist, 100,* 876–889.

Boyer, P. (2001). *Religion explained: The evolutionary origins of religious thought.* New York: Basic Books.

Boyer, P. (2003). Religious thought and behavior as by-products of brain function. *Trends in Cognitive Sciences, 7,* 119–124.

Boyer, P., & Liénard, P. (2006). Why ritualized behavior?: Precaution systems and action-parsing in developmental, pathological, and cultural rituals. *Brain and Behavioral Sciences, 29*(6), 595–613.

Boyer, P., & Ramble, C. (2001). Cognitive templates for religious concepts: Cross-cultural evidence for recall of counter-intuitive representations. *Cognitive Science, 25,* 535–564.

Bransford, J. D., & McCarrell, N. S. (1974). A sketch of a cognitive approach to comprehension: Some thoughts about understanding what it means to comprehend. In W. B. Weimer & D. S. Palermo (Eds.), *Cognition and the symbolic processes* (pp. 189–229). Hillsdale, NJ: Erlbaum.

Bulbulia, J. (2009). Charismatic signaling. *Journal of Religion and Culture, 3*(4), 518–551.

Casler, K., & Kelemen, D. (2008). Developmental continuity in teleo-functional explanation: Reasoning about nature among Romanian Romani adults. *Journal of Cognition and Development, 9*(3), 340–362.

Cohen, E. (2007). *The mind possessed: The cognition of spirit possession in an Afro-Brazilian religious tradition.* New York: Oxford University Press.

Cohen, E., & Barrett, J. L. (2008a). Conceptualising possession trance: Ethnographic and experimental evidence. *Ethos, 36*(2), 246–267.

Cohen, E., & Barrett, J. L. (2008b). When minds migrate: conceptualising spirit possession. *Journal of Cognition and Culture, 8*(1–2), 23–48.

Cohen, E., & Barrett, J. L. (2011). In search of "folk anthropology": The cognitive anthropology of the person. In W. vanHuyssteen & E. Wiebe (Eds.), *In search of self: Interdisciplinary perspectives on personhood* (pp. 104–122). Grand Rapids, MI: Eerdmans.

Cohen, E., Burdett, E. R., Knight, N., & Barrett, J. L. (2011). Cross-cultural similarities and differences in person-body reasoning: Experimental evidence from the UK and Brazilian Amazon. *Cognitive Science, 35*(7), 1282–1304.

Dennett, D. C. (1991). *Consciousness explained.* New York: Little, Brown.

DiYanni, C., & Kelemen, D. (2005). Time to get a new mountain? The role of function in children's conceptions of natural kinds. *Cognition, 97,* 327–335.

Elkind, D. (1970). The origins of religion in the child. *Review of Religious Research, 12,* 35–42.

Evans, E. M. (2001). Cognitive and contextual factors in the emergence of diverse belief systems: Creation versus evolution. *Cognitive Psychology, 42,* 217–266.

Gelman, S. A., & Kremer, K. E. (1991). Understanding natural cause: Children's explanations of how objects and their properties originate. *Child Development, 62,* 396–414.

Goldman, R. G. (1965). *Readiness for religion.* London, UK: Routledge & Kegan Paul.

Gonce, L. O., Upal, M. A., Slone, D. J., & Tweney, R. D. (2006). Role of context in the recall of counterintuitive concepts. *Journal of Cognition and Culture, 6,* 521–547.

Gregory, J., & Barrett, J. L. (2009). Epistemology and counterintuitiveness: Role and relationship in epidemiology of cultural representation. *Journal of Cognition and Culture, 9*(3), 289–314.

Guthrie, S. E. (1980). A cognitive theory of religion. *Current Anthropology, 21,* 181–194.

Guthrie, S. E. (1993). *Faces in the clouds: A new theory of religion.* New York: Oxford University Press.

Kahneman, D. (2003). A perspective on judgment and choice: Mapping bounded rationality. *American Psychologist, 58*(9), 697–720.

Kelemen, D. (1999a). The scope of teleological thinking in preschool children. *Cognition, 70,* 241–272.

Kelemen, D. (1999b). Why are rocks pointy?: Children's preference for teleological explanations of the natural world. *Developmental Psychology, 35,* 1440–1453.

Kelemen, D. (2004). Are children "intuitive theists"?: Reasoning about purpose and design in nature. *Psychological Science, 15,* 295–301.

Kelemen, D., & DiYanni, C. (2005). Intuitions about origins: Purpose and intelligent design in children's reasoning about nature. *Journal of Cognition and Development, 6,* 3–31.

Kelemen, D., & Rosset, E. (2009). The human function compunction: Teleological explanation in adults. *Cognition, 111,* 138–143.

Kirkpatrick, L. A. (1999). Toward an evolutionary psychology of religion. *Journal of Personality, 67,* 921–952.

Kirkpatrick, L. A. (2005). *Attachment, evolution, and the psychology of religion.* New York: Guilford Press.

Knight, N. (2008). Yukatek Maya children's attributions of beliefs to natural and non-natural entitites. *Journal of Cognition and Culture, 8,* 235–243.

Knight, N., Sousa, P., Barrett, J. L., & Atran, S. (2004). Children's attributions of beliefs to humans and God: Cross-cultural evidence. *Cognitive Science, 28,* 117–126.

Lawson, E. T., & McCauley, R. N. (1990). *Rethinking religion: Connecting cognition and culture.* Cambridge, UK: Cambridge University Press.

Liénard, P., & Boyer, P. (2006). Whence collective ritual?: A cultural selection model of ritualized behavior. *American Anthropologist, 108,* 814–827.

Lisdorf, A. (2001). The spread of non-natural concepts. *Journal of Cognition and Culture, 4,* 151–174.

Malley, B. (2004). *How the Bible works: An anthropological study of evangelical biblicism.* Walnut Creek, CA: AltaMira Press.

Malley, B., & Barrett, J. L. (2003). Does myth inform ritual?: A test of the Lawson-McCauley hypothesis. *Journal of Ritual Studies, 17*(2), 1–14.

McCauley, R. N. (2011). *Why religion is natural and science is not.* New York: Oxford University Press.

McCauley, R. N., & Lawson, E. T. (2002). *Bringing ritual to mind: Psychological foundations of cultural forms.* Cambridge, UK: Cambridge University Press.

Norenzayan, A., Atran, S., Faulkner, J., & Schaller, M. (2006). Memory and mystery: The cultural selection of minimally counterintuitive narratives. *Cognitive Science, 30,* 531–553.

Ozorak, E. W. (2005). Cognitive approaches to religion. In R. F. Paloutzian & C. L. Park (Eds.), *Handbook of the psychology of religion and spirituality* (pp. 216–234). New York: Giuilford Press.

Petrovich, O. (1997). Understanding of non-natural causality in children and adults: A case against artificialism. *Psyche en Geloof, 8,* 151–165.

Petrovich, O. (1999). Preschool children's understanding of the dichotomy between the natural and the artificial. *Psychological Reports, 84,* 3–27.

Piaget, J. (1929). *The child's conception of the world.* New York: Harcourt Brace.

Pinker, S. (1997). *How the mind works.* New York: Norton.

Pyysiäinen, I. (2003). *How religion works: Towards a new cognitive science of religion and culture.* Leiden, The Netherlands: Brill.

Pyysiäinen, I. (2009). *Supernatural agents: Why we believe in souls, gods, and Buddhas.* New York: Oxford University Press.

Richert, R. A., & Barrett, J. L. (2005). Do you see what I see?: Young children's assumptions about God's perceptual abilities. *The International Journal for the Psychology of Religion, 15,* 283–295.

Rochat, P., Morgan, R., & Carpenter, M. (1997). Young infants' sensitivity to movement information specifying social causality. *Cognitive Development, 12,* 537–561.

Scholl, B., & Tremoulet, P. D. (2000). Perceptual causality and animacy. *Trends in Cognitive Sciences, 4,* 299–308.

Slone, D. J. (2004). *Theological incorrectness: Why religious people believe what they shouldn't.* New York: Oxford University Press.

Sosis, R. (2004). The adaptive value of religious ritual: Rituals promote group cohesion by requiring members to engage in behavior that is too costly to fake. *American Scientists, 92,* 166 174.

Spelke, E. S., & Kinzler, K. D. (2007). Core knowledge. *Developmental Science, 11,* 89–96.

Sperber, D. (1975). *Rethinking symbolism.* Cambridge, UK: Cambridge University Press.

Sperber, D. (1996). *Explaining culture: A naturalistic approach.* Oxford, UK: Blackwell.

Sperber, D. (1997). Intuitive and reflective beliefs. *Mind and Language, 12,* 67–83.

Stanovich, K. E., & West, R. F. (2000). Individual differences in reasoning: Implications for the rationality debate. *Behavioral and Brain Sciences, 23,* 645–665.

Tweney, R. D., Upal, M. A., Gonce, L. O., Slone, D. J., & Edwards, K. (2006). The creative structuring of counterintuitive worlds. *Journal of Cognition and Culture, 6,* 483–498.

Upal, M. A. (2010). An alternative account of the minimal counterintuitiveness effect. *Cognitive Systems Research, 11,* 194–203.

Upal, M. A., Owsianiecki, L., Slone, D. J., & Tweney, R. D. (2007). Contextualizing counterintuitiveness: How context affects comprehension and memorability of counterintuitive concepts. *Cognitive Science, 31,* 1–25.

Whitehouse, H. (1995). *Inside the cult: Religious innovation and transmission in Papua New Guinea.* Oxford, UK: Clarendon Press.

Whitehouse, H. (1996). Rites of terror: Emotion, metaphor, and memory in Melanesian initiation cults. *Journal of the Royal Anthropological Institute, 2,* 703–715.

Whitehouse, H. (2000). *Arguments and icons: Divergent modes of religiosity.* Oxford, UK: Oxford University Press.

Whitehouse, H. (2004). *Modes of religiosity: A cognitive theory of religious transmission.* Walnut Creek, CA: AltaMira Press.

Whitehouse, H. (2007). Towards an integration of ethnography, history, and the cognitive science of religion. In H. Whitehouse & J. A. Laidlaw (Eds.), *Religion, anthropology, and cognitive science* (pp. 247–280). Durham, NC: University of North Carolina Press.

Whitehouse, H., & Laidlaw, J. A. (Eds.). (2004). *Ritual and memory: Towards a comparative anthropology of religion.* Walnut Creek, CA: AltaMira Press.

Whitehouse, H., & Martin, L. H. (Eds.). (2004). *Theorizing religions past: Archaeology, history, and cognition.* Walnut Creek, CA: AltaMira Press.

Whitehouse, H., & McCauley, R. N. (Eds.). (2005). *Mind and religion: Psychological and cognitive foundations of religiosity.* Walnut Creek, CA: AltaMira Press.

13

Gods and Goals
Religion and Purposeful Action

Robert A. Emmons and Sarah A. Schnitker

Motivation encompasses the energization and direction of behavior. Motivation is an expansive topic and is not one that can be done complete justice in the context of a relatively brief exposition. We choose, therefore, to focus our efforts on goal theories of motivation and their relevance for the psychology of religion and spirituality. The goals construct is central in motivational science (Elliot & Fryer, 2008), as there is perhaps no characteristic more fundamentally human than the capacity to imagine future outcomes and to devise means to attain these outcomes. Because goals lie at the heart of motivation, our concern in this chapter is with goals rather than with other motivational constructs such as values or motives. The capacity to articulate specific goals in life and to develop effective ways to reach them is a critical aspect of human functioning (Emmons, 1986; Karoly, 1993).

The goals concept has both clinical utility and theoretically integrative potential, and thus is a particularly promising unit of analysis for widening and expanding theory, research, and practice in the psychology of religion (Park & Paloutzian, 2005). Park and Paloutzian champion meaning-based approaches to the psychology of religion and advocate that "future work should explicitly focus on the ways that meaning informs all aspects of religious experience" (p. 556). We do not necessarily disagree, but we recommend stepping back for a moment and asking the question, From where does meaning originate? It is our contention that goals provide a source of meaning, and that a proper understanding of religion as a meaning system cannot ignore the centrality of goals in the generation of meaning. In this sense, we are following Park (2005), who proposed that religion provides global meaning in life by prioritizing life goals and delineating pathways for achieving.

A number of major volumes on goals and human behavior have been published (Elliot, 2008; Moskowitz & Grant, 2009; Shah & Gardner, 2008). These volumes summarize the substantial advances that have been made in the scientific understanding of human beings as active, intentional, goal-directed agents. Curiously, though, the topic of religion is rarely mentioned in any of these otherwise authoritative compendiums on motivational science. Only a lone citation to religion in over 1,100 pages between the Moskowitz and Grant (2009) and Shah and Gardner (2008) edited books could be found. One goal of this chapter is to bring mainstream motivational science into a fruitful dialogue with the psychology of religion and to show what each field has to gain from such a relationship.

Goal theories can be considered midlevel theories in the psychology of religion. We define a goal as an imagined or envisioned state or condition toward which a person aspires and which drives voluntary activity. When a goal is active for a person, it directs and organizes their behavior toward accomplishing that goal. In terms of religion, religious behavior is directed toward obtaining goals, and can be understood primarily in terms of its role in goal acquisition. Goal theories share the following assumptions:

1. Behavior is organized around the pursuit of goals, with goals being defined as objectives toward which a person strives to obtain or avoid.
2. Goals influence ongoing thought and emotional reactions in addition to behavior.
3. Goals exist within a system of hierarchically organized superordinate and subordinate goals where functioning in one aspect of the system has ramifications for other parts of the system.
4. Goals are accessible to conscious awareness, though there is no requirement that the goal be represented in consciousness while the person is in active pursuit of it.

A goals approach to motivation assumes that (1) people seek purpose by setting and striving for goals; (2) these goals include the psychological, social, and spiritual; (3) goals have cognitive, affective, and behavioral significance; and (4) goal content (the "what" of goals), goal structure (the "how" of goals), and goal orientation (the "why" of goals) predict important life outcomes, such as well-being and performance. Over the past two decades, psychologists have learned how goals, as key integrative and analytic units in the study of human motivation, contribute to effective life functioning and to overall emotional, physical, and relational well-being. Our concern in this chapter is what goals reveal about the religious strivings of individuals.

The goal-directed nature of human religious striving was first documented by David Trout (1931) in his textbook, *Religious Behavior*. Trout noted the teleonomic quality of religious behavior, in that it is often purposive or goal directed. He coined the term "transcendental religious ultimates" to describe these religious goals. This was an anti-instinct and antiradical behaviorism movement that instead favored purposive or "telic" accounts of religious behavior. Intensity and perseveration of responses characterize religious behavior, according to Trout. But it was Gordon Allport, considered by most the founding father of personality psychology, who actually noted that the intentional nature of religious behavior was what made it distinctive. The field of personality has always had as its goal a scientific account of what a person is like, in his or her entirety. Whatever else it includes, this account, for Allport, must involve both *intention* and *religion*. In his book *Pattern and Growth in Personality* (1961), Allport wrote, "Intention refers to what the person is trying to do . . . it tells us what sort of future a person is trying to bring about, and this is the most important question we can ask of any mortal" (p. 223). All-port also made significant contributions to the psychology of religion. Most psychologists of religion are familiar with the intrinsic–extrinsic religious orientations (Tix & Frazier, 2005), but many of them forget that this distinction originated with Allport. For Allport, religion involves a response of the total self, and religious attitudes (or "sentiments," the term that he preferred) differ chiefly from other aspects of personality in their compre-hensiveness and centrality to the person (Allport, 1950).

PERSONAL STRIVINGS AND THE SACRED

To empirically study goals, and to differentiate them from other units of analysis, the term "personal strivings" was adopted (Emmons, 1999). Personal strivings are con-sciously accessible and personally meaningful objectives that people pursue in their daily lives. Personal strivings refer to the typical goals that a person characteristically is trying to accomplish. As individualized and cognitively elaborated representations, they are the concretized expression of future orientation and life purpose. Several points need to be made with respect to personal strivings and their conceptual nature. First, an empha-sis on the concept of striving implies an action-oriented perspective on human religious motivation. It stresses the behavioral movement toward identifiable end points, as evident in the definition of goals as "an imagined or envisaged state condition toward which a person aspires and which drives voluntary activity" (Karoly, 1993, p. 274). Second, striv-ings provide information not only on what a person is trying to do but also on whom a person is trying to be—the relatively high-level goals that are central aspects of a person's identity. Third, goals are highly personal; they reflect subjective experience, values, and commitments as uniquely identified by the person. Fourth, these goals represent poten-tialities rather than actualities in that they are never fully satisfied. They reflect what a person is *trying* to do, not necessarily what they are *actually* doing. To strive also implies that meaning comes from the "journey" and not just arriving at the "destination." How-ever, one can also strive toward particular modes of being without necessarily making a strenuous effort, for instance, in Eastern philosophies, which emphasize a cessation of goal cravings and nonattachment to goals (e.g., being at peace with oneself, being at one with the universe). Certainly, the notion of strivings (as a noun) would include these lat-ter examples, in that they reflect desired end points or objectives to be realized. Spiritual concerns are reflected in both "doing" as well as in "being" goals; indeed, perhaps that is an important distinction between the types of goals that different religious systems encourage their adherents to aspire toward.

Personal strivings can be thought of as superordinate abstracting qualities that ren-der a cluster of goals functionally equivalent for an individual. In this sense, a striving is similar to the traditional definition of a motive disposition, such as the achievement motive or the power motive (McAdams, 2009). However, the critical difference lies in the idiographic nature of the personal striving. Each person's strivings are uniquely his or hers; no two people share the same exact configuration of strivings. A personal striving is a unifying construct: It unites what may be phenotypically different goals or actions around a common quality or theme. A given striving can be achieved in a variety of ways and satisfied via any one of a number of concrete goals.

The use of goal language in discussions of spirituality and religion may seem unorthodox. Isn't religion about beliefs and doctrine, feelings and emotions, perceptions and experiences of what a person takes to be the sacred? Yes, but religion is also about goals. Spirituality is a motivational force that energizes and directs the goal-striving process. One of the basic functions of a religious belief system and a religious worldview is that it provides "an ultimate vision of what people should be striving for in their lives" (Pargament & Park, 1995, p. 15) and the strategies to reach those ends.

In their theoretical model of religion and self-regulatory processes, McCullough and Willoughby (2009) describe two ways in which religion influences goal *content*, or those specific spiritual ends toward which people strive. First, specific religions encourage specific goals and prescribed states by which adherents are supposed to organize their behavior. The unique goals prescribed by each religion probably arise from the special emphases in the written scriptures of each religion, the social and physical ecology in which the religion emerged (e.g., the surrounding cultural alternatives from which supporters of various religions wish to distinguish themselves, along with the resources available), and the changing physical and social circumstances to which specific religions must continually adapt (McCullough & Willoughby, 2009). Second, religion may promote virtuous, "being" goals related to being respectful, polite, forgiving, compassionate, and otherwise concerned for the welfare of one's interpersonal relationship partners and community. Conversely, religion may promote the rejection of self-enhancing goals related to independence, individuality, and personal gratification. In addition to the prescriptive nature of religion, there is also a long history of using goal language metaphorically to depict spiritual growth. In devotional writings and in sacred scriptures, spiritual growth and spiritual maturity are viewed as a process of goal attainment, with the ultimate goal being intimacy with the divine. In Islam, for example, spiritual growth involves specific goals of giving up personal independence, seeking obedience, and manifesting of one's faith in Allah in daily life.

If spirituality is the search for the sacred (Hill et al., 2000), then spiritual strivings represent unique, individually tailored ways in which the person negotiates his or her search for the sacred. Spiritual strivings include personal goals that are concerned with ultimate purpose, ethics, commitment to a higher power, and a seeking of the divine in daily experience (Emmons, 1999). By identifying and committing themselves to spiritual goals, people strive to develop and maintain a relationship to what is taken to be the sacred. In other words, spiritual strivings are strivings that reflect a desire to transcend the self, that reflect an integration of the individual with larger and more complex units, or that reflect deepening or maintaining a relationship with a higher power. Strivings are considered spiritual if they reflect concern for an integration of the person with larger and more complex units: with humanity, nature, with the cosmos ("to achieve union with the totality of existence," "to merge my will with God's will"; "to live my life at all times for God," "to approach life with mystery and awe"). As implied, spiritual strivings contain both conventional religious themes as well as more personalized expressions of spiritual concern. Martos, Kézdy, and Horvath-Szabo (2011) made a similar distinction between transcendental religious motivation and normative religious motivation and found a different pattern of correlates for these two types of spirituality.

Some other examples of spiritual goals or "ultimate concerns" are "trying hard not to expect God to answer all my prayers," "trying to become a more enlightened person," "trying to bring others closer to God," "trying to be a good Bahá'í," "trying to spend some time each day in meditation,", and "trying to be open to God's will," and "trying to develop my spirituality to survive the pain and physical downgrading of disease in my life." Notice that these goals are phrased in terms of what the person is trying to do, implying striving toward some future state that the person may or may not successfully achieve. An assessment of strivings offers a more idiographically sensitive description of individuals than traits but also reveals a more immediate and self-contained picture of personality than complex narratives that people construct of their entire life spans (McAdams, 2009).

One of the assumptions of goal theories of motivation is that goals are accessible to conscious awareness. However, there is no requirement that the striving be consciously represented as the person goes about their daily business. Some goals may be clearly explicit, whereas others may be automatic and nonconscious. In the latter case, the spiritual motivational system operates effortlessly without deliberative commitment. John Bargh (Bargh & Ferguson, 2000) has developed and tested a model of how personal goals can become automatized and nonconscious. According to this model, the repeated activation of a goal in a particular situation leads to an association between that goal and situational cues. Situational features can then trigger the goal and goal-relevant behaviors. For example, the goal to "get closer to God" might be triggered automatically by seeing a cross or by driving past a church. The activation of the goal might lead to the behavior of pulling over to the shoulder of the road to pray or entering the sanctuary to light a candle without becoming consciously aware of wanting to "get closer to God." The model proposes that the goal of "getting closer to God" does not need to be continuously conscious for it to activate and guide behavior. The activation differences between automatic and deliberate spiritual goals may be an interesting research topic for future inquiry. Experimental research could prime religious goals and the effect of activation of these goals on outcomes such as racial prejudice (Johnson, Rowatt, & LaBouff, 2010), aggression (Bushman, Ridge, Das, Key, & Busath, 2007), or forgiveness (Brown, Barnes, & Campbell, 2007).

Evidence suggests that spiritual strivings have positive implications. Consistent with the bulk of research in the psychology of religion, Emmons's (1999) approach to spiritual strivings emphasized an individual's relationship with a higher power or personified divine being (i.e., God) and assumes that desirable behavior patterns promoted by monotheistic religious traditions reflect spirituality. But it is not only having spiritual strivings that bodes well for functioning. These goals are appraised in ways that have been shown to facilitate positive experiential and performance outcomes. These goals were rated as more important, requiring more effort, and engaged in for more intrinsic reasons than were nonspiritual strivings. In addition, the underlying motives served by goals are linked to superior outcomes: for example, the degree to which personal strivings focused on intimacy in social relationships overlap with a spiritual focus and are linked to greater personal happiness and well-being (Emmons, 1999; Kasser & Ryan, 2001). In contrast, a higher proportion of strivings focused on having power over others and extrinsically oriented values (e.g., status, image, money) is tied to poorer adjustment (Emmons, 2008; Kasser & Ryan, 2001). Pargament and Sweeney (2011) suggest that spiritual strivings can be a benchmark for examining the effectiveness of spiritual resilience programs in the military.

In another relevant study, Roberts and Robins (2000) analyzed the life goals of nearly 700 undergraduates. These goals were clustered into the factor analytically derived categories of economic, aesthetic, social, political, hedonistic, and religious domains. Students who pursued religious life goals (e.g., "participating in religious activities" and "devoting attention to my spiritual life") also placed a relatively high value on (1) social goals (e.g., "working to promote the welfare of others"; $r = .32$); (2) relationship goals (e.g., "having a satisfying marriage/relationship" and "having harmonious relationships with my parents and siblings"; $r = .19$); and (c) political goals (e.g., "being influential in public affairs" and "becoming a community leader"; $r = .15$). Pursuing religious goals was not significantly associated with the extent to which people pursued economic goals (e.g., "having a high standard of living and wealth"), aesthetic goals (e.g., "producing good artistic work," "becoming accomplished in one of the performing arts"), or hedonistic goals (e.g., "having new and different experiences," "having fun").

Sanctifying Personal Goals

In measuring spirituality through goals, a persistent issue has been whether to rely on researchers' own classification of strivings as spiritual or to let participants define for themselves whether a particular goal serves a spiritual purpose. Goals that, on the surface, may appear to have little to do with spiritual needs may, in fact, be perceived as highly spiritual by individuals. Mahoney and Pargament (2005) refer to this process as "sanctification." Sanctification is a psychological process through which aspects of life are perceived by people as having spiritual character and significance. Striving sanctification is assessed by having people evaluate each goal on the following items:

- God played a role in the development of this striving.
- God is present in this striving.
- This striving is a reflection of God's will.
- I experience God through this striving.
- This striving may be characterized as holy.
- This striving reflects what I think God wants for me.
- This striving enables me to get closer to God.

Each statement is answered on a 1–5 scale, where 1 = strongly disagree and 5 = strongly agree. An average sanctification score is then derived for each separate goal, as well as an overall sanctification score for each person, summed across their individual goals. With this approach, one is able to identify sacred goals that, on the surface, appear to have little to do with spirituality. For example, goals rated high on sanctification include "not to dwell on my disability," "remain as independent as possible as long as I can," "be considerate of others," "help others in any way I can," and "remain helpful." Interpersonal strivings such as these last three examples, more so than other types of strivings, tend to be viewed as having a sacred significance. Therefore, strivings need not be overtly spiritual to be imbued with sacred qualities. Strivings that are sanctified are rated as more meaningful and as being supported more by others and are related to greater commitment to others than are less sanctified strivings.

In their sample of 150 community adults, Mahoney and Pargament (2005) found that people tended to place a high priority on strivings that they viewed as sacred. They invested more time and energy into spiritual strivings and derived greater satisfaction and sense of meaning from them relative to strivings that were more self-focused and materially oriented. Sanctification was correlated with conventional measures of religiousness such as church attendance and self-rated religiousness, but was also related to investment and important characteristics of the goals themselves. These included perceived support from others and higher expectations of success. Moreover, the bivariate links between sanctification of strivings and desirable attributes remained significant after taking into account general religiousness. Both forms of sanctification were associated with self-reports of a greater sense of meaning and purpose in life. Contrary to expectations, greater sanctification of strivings was not consistently related to better psychological or physical health. The only exception was that lower alcohol use was associated with greater degree of belief that God was expressed through or experienced in strivings. Not all strivings are likely to be sanctified. Strivings focused on altruistic activities, family life, and existential concerns were more highly sanctified than all other strivings, except for overtly religious objectives. In contrast, strivings focused on self-development and work or financial affairs were sanctified to a lesser degree than family life and other strivings. Health-related strivings were also perceived as less sacred than other strivings. Overall, it appears that adults are generally less likely to imbue self-focused or materially oriented strivings with spiritual meaning or significance. Instead, personal strivings that take an individual beyond oneself are more likely to be perceived to involve God's presence, will, or actions as well as to be characterized in sacred, transcendent terms.

Tix and Frazier (2005) found that striving sanctification was associated with less anxiety, depression, and hostility and with greater intrinsic religiousness. In their study, they asked participants to rate each of the strivings they listed according to the extent to which they were pursued "because of religious or spiritual reasons." This measure of nontheistic sanctification has some advantages over the theistic measure that we have used, although it is subject to various idiosyncratic interpretations of the terms religious and spiritual. They found a correlation of $r = .64$ between intrinsic religious motivation and participants' average rating of the extent to which they pursued their 10 most important goals for "religious or spiritual reasons." Thus, intrinsic religiousness may cause people's goals to become imbued with religious meaning. On the other hand, sanctification of goals could possibly influence intrinsic religiousness. Tix and Frazier also conducted mediational analyses in which they found that sanctification of strivings mediated the relationship between intrinsic religiousness and hostility. The authors suggest that having religious and/or spiritual motives for pursuing daily tasks may lessen hostility because such motives may encourage a reframing of problems (that otherwise may provoke hostility) through connection with a higher "purpose" for engaging in such tasks.

In research conducted with inpatients at an alcoholism treatment center, Hart (2007) found that a stronger intention to seek a sacred experience of connectedness/oneness with Divinity is associated with higher rates of abstention from alcohol, a stronger sense that one's life has meaning, purpose, and significance, and greater involvement in the active ingredients of recovery available through affiliation with Alcoholics Anonymous (AA). These findings suggest that the pursuit of sacred goals may help sustain long-term abstinence from alcohol and enhance quality of life during the aftercare phase of overcoming an addictive disorder. A spiritual striving orientation is associated with more a more favorable profile of recovery processes and outcomes, importantly extending the work on spiritual striving and well-being in nonclinical samples.

The Power of Sacred Strivings

What accounts for the unique ability of sacred strivings to predict well-being outcomes? As Pargament (2002) has argued, identifying what is sacred and striving to protect and preserve the sacred lends deep significance to human existence, a significance that is difficult to explain through more basic psychological or social levels of description. Spiritual strivings may have a unique empowering function; people are more likely to persevere in these strivings, even under difficult circumstances. This empowering function may be stronger in groups that have limited access to other resources, such as racial minorities, the elderly, and the chronically ill (Pargament, 2002). These are groups that typically score higher on conventional measures of religious involvement. People are more likely to take measures to protect and preserve strivings that focus on the sacred and to devote time and effort toward their realization. Spiritual strivings are also likely to provide stability and support in times of crisis by reorienting people to what is ultimately important in life (Emmons, Colby, & Kaiser, 1998). Investing goals with a sense of sacredness confers upon them a power to organize experience and to promote well-being that is absent in nonsacred strivings (Mahoney & Pargament, 2005). People admit that in today's Westernized secular culture, whether their spiritual strivings are socially accepted or socially sanctioned, they derive tremendous meaning and purpose from them. Hart (2007) suggested that the observed correlation of spiritual motivation to AA adherence may be due, in part, to a greater tendency of spiritual strivers to sanctify the processes involved in AA's planned program of recovery. A number of studies support the supposition that goal sanctification promotes effective goal striving.

The unique ability of spiritual strivings to promote well-being may be partially explained by the ability of religion to provide a unifying philosophy of life and to serve as an integrating force (Allport, 1950; Tillich, 1957). Goals, be they religious or not, are not adopted and pursued in isolation from other goals. Rather, they exist within a hierarchical system in which the pursuit of one goal has an impact upon other goals within the system. These intergoal relations can be inhibitory or facilitative. Inhibitory goals are those that are conflictual in nature. A structural dynamic approach (Shah & Kruglanski, 2008) suggests that both lateral and vertical associations between goals exist, and that the nature of these associations bears on effective goal pursuit. Vertical coherence of strivings is the degree to which subordinate strivings (e.g., "striving to go to church every week") contribute to the completion of superordinate strivings (e.g., "striving to develop a deep and meaningful relationship with my Creator"). Horizontal coherence refers to how success and progress of strivings contribute to the completion of other strivings at the same level. Congruence, on the other hand, represents the degree to which strivings promote relationships and intimacy with others, are personally chosen, and are inherently satisfying. Conflict or fragmentation is a source of stress that can undermine purposeful striving and thus well-being. Research has documented the deleterious effect of goal conflict on well-being (Emmons & King, 1988). Although purpose is forged out of the many possibilities that life presents, these same choices can be experienced as paralyzing (see also Schwartz, 2000). Johnson (1959) describes this predicament:

Out of the very contradictions that provide freedom come the distresses of conflict. Life can never be simple or easy for a conscious person. He must forever contend with the competing demands of a complicated world that give him no rest. Like Adam, the prototype of every man, he is lured by the unknown, tempted by untasted possibilities, seduced by the one he loves, forbidden by highest authority, caught in conflicts of desire, overcome with guilty remorse and driven forth to wrestle and sweat in a world of contradiction and uncertainty. (p. 104)

Some support for the integrative role of religious striving comes from research of ours (Emmons, Cheung, & Tehrani, 1998). Participants completed a goal instrumentality matrix in which they were asked to judge the degree to which each of their 15 personal strivings had a helpful effect (instrumental), harmful effect (conflictual), or no effect on each of their other strivings. We found that the presence of theistic spiritual strivings (strivings that explicitly refer to God) in particular were related to low levels of intergoal conflict and to greater levels of goal integration. To generate the data for this measure of goal conflict, the researchers asked participants to indicate the extent to which pursuing each of the goals on their list impeded or facilitated progress in pursuing each of their other goals. The proportion of spiritual goals was strongly negatively correlated with the amount of goal conflict participants experienced ($r = -.52$, $p < .01$). The proportion of goals in which God was explicitly mentioned (theistic strivings) was also negatively correlated with the goal conflict measure ($r = -.39$, $p < .01$). Furthermore, spiritual strivings were uniquely associated with overall goal integration. No other striving content category was associated with our measures of integration. William James stated, "But to find religion is only one out of many ways of reaching unity; and the process of remedying inner incompleteness and reducing inner discord is a general psychological process, which may take place with any sort of mental material, and need not necessarily assume the religious form" (1902/1985, p. 175). Greater levels of spiritual strivings, whether measured at relatively broad or narrower levels, tended to be associated with less overall conflict within a person's goal system, and thus a greater degree of integration.

Cast in the language of motivational science, spiritual strivings appeared to have a greater number of positive, excitatory connections with other goals, and fewer negative, inhibitory connections within people's overall goal systems. Spiritual strivings (e.g., "to praise God in action and thought") tend to show a greater number of positive, lateral associations with other goals in a person's goal network. In accordance with the view that religion represents ultimate concern, in theistic traditions, people experience God not only as Creator and Redeemer but also as "Integrator." In a related finding, Zinnbauer and Pargament (1998) found that recent converts were more likely to report a positive life transformation as reflected in a more unified sense of self and a belief that their goals had become more significant and meaningful compared with nonconverts who increased in their religious faith gradually and with religious individuals who had not experienced a recent change in their faith.

Religious goals also can serve as "compensatory convictions" (McGregor, 2007), providing clarity and conviction of purpose. The ability of religion to ignite, for better or for worse, passionate convictions is well documented historically and globally in contemporary life. This by itself may account for the powerful organizing force of spiritual motivation. There now appears to be sufficient evidence to support Allport's (1950) thesis that "the religious sentiment . . . is the portion of personality that arises at the core and that has the longest range intentions, and for this reason is capable of conferring marked integration upon personality . . . it is man's ultimate attempt to enlarge and to complete his own personality" (p. 142).

At the same time, not all religious or spiritual goals facilitate other goals or even one another. There is no guarantee that spiritual strivings will be well integrated within the overall self-system. Sincerely held beliefs may be held with a degree of ambivalence because they prove costly in the person's social environment. In our research, we found that desires to share one's faith with others were often not consonant with other goals in the person's hierarchy. One research participant possessed the striving to "share my faith with others," which she rated as having a very harmful effect on other goals within her goal system, including "treat others with love" and "keep in contact with my family." She perceived this striving to be highly important and worthy of commitment, yet the discomfort her spiritual striving was causing in her relationships left her with an uncomfortable sacred internal conflict. This brief example suggests that there might be therapeutic utility in assessing spiritual goal strivings and analyzing potential intergoal interference. Additionally, fundamentalist religious mind-sets might enhance internal consistency at the cost of interpersonal disharmony. Cognitive processing associated with fundamentalist thinking is likely to lead to the person's inability to tolerate healthy skepticism or doubt. Dogmatically held beliefs can bring about a forced unity at a surface level that might obscure conflicts that still persist at a deeper, less accessible level. Last, religious strivings might make people aware of discrepancies between what they believe and what they actually do. Although ideally such discrepancies can be motivating and lead to enhanced striving and ultimately to deeper faith, discrepancies between belief and action can also engender powerful feelings of inappropriate guilt, depression, and self-flagellation. Spiritual maturity or spiritual intelligence may be the critical factor influencing the integration of spiritual concerns into a well-functioning, coherent self-system.

The Spiritual Striving Questionnaire

Spiritual strivings are generally assessed through a series of interlocking assessment modules that can require anywhere from 2 to 4 hours to complete. Although significant clinical information can be gleaned from such assessments (Pargament, 2007; Singer, 2005) an alternative, briefer form of striving assessment is also desirable. Toward that end, a rating scale version of the strivings assessment procedure, known as the Spiritual Striving Questionnaire (SSQ; Emmons, 2008) has been developed.

The SSQ was adapted from the Personal Striving Coding Manual (Emmons, 1999) and the self-report survey of goal strivings developed by Leak, DeNeve, and Greteman (2007). Approximately two-thirds of the items reflect explicit religious and spiritual concerns ("discern and follow God's will for my life," "have a closer relationship to God"). In addition to these spiritual and religious goals, items were chosen to represent the major motive categories of achievement, affiliation–intimacy, and power. The final version of the SSQ consisted of 48 items (Cronbach's alpha = .93), for which participants rated the extent of agreement with the statement "I see myself as someone who is typically trying to _____" on a 1–5 scale, where 1 = disagree strongly and 5 = agree strongly. High scores indicate greater commitment to goal striving and can be taken as a general indicator of overall motivation to set and pursue goals.

Preliminary results using the SSQ have been promising. The SSQ has good psychometric properties. In a sample of adolescents attending an evangelical summer camp for youth, scores on the SSQ were positively and significantly associated with meaning in life, life satisfaction, vitality, and religious commitment, and were uncorrelated with self-esteem and depression. Demonstrating incremental validity, scores on the SSQ contributed to additional variance in predicting the mental health outcomes of life satisfaction and vitality above and beyond the Big Five personality traits. Furthermore, participants who indicated they had a recent spiritual transformation (had made a new personal commitment to God) scored significantly higher on the SSQ than those who had not undergone such a transformation. Results suggest that spiritual strivings can be assessed in a more direct and efficient manner than the more time-consuming original striving assessment methodology developed by Emmons (1999). Of course, there are trade-offs involved in sacrificing the amount of information obtained with ease of administration. For some purposes (and if time permits), the original open-ended methodology may be preferred.

APPROACH AND AVOIDANCE MOTIVATION AND SPIRITUAL GOALS

Goal-directed behavior may be motivated by a positive incentive or possibility or by a negative incentive or possibility. Every day, people move toward desired outcomes and avoid or move away from undesired outcomes. These respective tendencies are referred to as approach and avoidance motivation (Elliot, 2008). People who are pursuing an approach goal strive toward a positive goal outcome and regulate their behavior by moving or working toward the desired goal outcome, while those who have adopted an avoidance striving are focused on preventing or moving away from a negative outcome. A person may be trying to "get closer to God" or "avoid God's displeasure." One might strive to give thanks to God for the blessings in one's life, or one might strive not to be ungrateful to God for these gifts. Although the content of the two strivings is similar, the first striving is approach oriented, meaning that the individual strives to attain and maintain a grateful spirit for one's blessings; the second striving is avoidant, meaning that the individual strives to avoid or move away from an ungrateful attitude toward one's gifts from God. Negative goals provide an undesired outcome that evokes avoidant motivation as opposed to the presence of a positive outcome that potentially satisfies more basic needs or motives and is, therefore, intrinsically rewarding.

The motivational literature documents the negative effects of pursuing avoidance goals relative to approach goals. A focus on negative, avoidant goals represents inefficient and problematic regulatory processing that tends to result in more deleterious personal outcomes for the individual (Elliot & Friedman, 2007; Kashdan, Breen, & Julian, 2010). Avoidance goal adoption is related to lower levels of subjective well-being and poorer physical health (Elliot, 2008; Emmons, 1999). This focus on negative outcomes to be avoided is associated with a number of ineffective cognitive, perceptual, emotional, and behavioral processes, including threat appraisal, biased recall of negative information, and anxiety and worry (Elliot & Friedman, 2007).

Ryan and Fiorito (2003) found that avoidance spiritual goals were associated with low levels of well-being (lower self-esteem, less identity integration, and more negative affect). Avoidance goals predicted lower levels of well-being, and were moderated by approach goals, such that high levels of approach goals reduced the negative association between avoidance goals and well-being. Kneezel (2005) found that approach spiritual strivings were more likely to be sanctified compared with avoidance spiritual strivings, indicating that approach strivings are appraised in a more spiritually satisfying manner. Because the research was correlational, however, it was unclear whether viewing one's strivings as spiritually significant leads to more approach strivings, or whether approach-oriented individuals are more apt to be spiritual and thus sanctify their strivings. What we do know is that people most often endorse spiritual strivings that are approach oriented, perhaps testifying to the unique positive nature of spirituality. Unlike other types of strivings, spirituality seems immune to the avoidance motivational orientation. The large discrepancy between the percentage of avoidance spiritual and nonspiritual strivings speaks to the distinctiveness of spirituality from other domains in life. Only 2.73% of spiritual strivings, compared with 14.82% of nonspiritual strivings, were avoidant oriented. It is not clear whether sanctification leads to the setting of approach-oriented strivings or whether approach strivings and the sanctification of strivings both affect one another.

The mechanisms underlying approach and avoidance motivation in spirituality need to be delineated. These are unlikely to be the same as in other areas of motivation, such as achievement. Two possible mechanisms are a fear of lack of meaning or a need for transcendence and meaning. One who has a fear of meaningless may strive to avoid negative spiritual outcomes, as these may be threatening to one's meaning in daily life and even one's beliefs for life after death. On the other hand, individuals who are motivated by a need to transcend the self and have a sense of deep meaning in life pursuits should strive for positive spiritual outcomes that will enable them to deepen their relationship or connection to what they perceive to be sacred. They do not feel anxious that they will be unable to move toward their spiritual goals; instead, they feel competent that they can achieve increased spiritual maturity and satisfy their need for transcendence and meaning.

ADDITIONAL SPIRITUAL GOAL UNITS: PERSONAL PROJECTS

Recent work on religious goals has broadened the unit of goal analysis beyond strivings to include personal projects. A personal project is defined as "a set of interrelated acts extending over time, which are intended to maintain or attain a state of affairs foreseen by the individual" (Little, 1983, p. 278; 1989). Similar to strivings, personal projects reflect cognitive, affective, and behavioral aspects of goals. Projects differ from strivings in that they are a more contextualized unit of analysis and are more strongly derived from the sociocultural tasks facing a person within a specific life stage. Projects primarily focus on *what* a person is trying *to do,* whereas strivings have an added emphasis on *whom* a person is trying *to be.*

In a recent study (Schnitker, 2012), we asked participants to list 10 personal projects they were working on over the 10-week academic term. Projects with spiritual or religious content composed about 2% of the personal projects listed by participants, which is typical for a sample of college undergraduates. Examples of these spiritual projects include "Try to clarify my religious beliefs," "Read the Bible," "Get closer to God," and "Be not 'guilty' by taking off a religious headcovering."

We sought to replicate the positive relation between spiritual goals and well-being that was originally established with personal strivings research in our personal projects data. We did not find significant relations between the proportion of spiritual projects a person listed and well-being variables (i.e., life satisfaction, positive and negative affect, and depression). However, there was a positive relation between project sanctification and well-being. People who imbued their projects with more spiritual meaning ("How much does this project bring you closer to God or some spiritual reality?") reported higher levels of positive affect ($r = .14$, $p < .05$). They also rated themselves as more highly committed to their projects ($r = .20$, $p < .01$), as exerting more effort in the pursuit of their projects ($r = .20$, $p < .01$), as experiencing more progress on their projects ($r = .13$, $p < .05$), and as having more meaningful projects ($r = .24$, $p < .01$). Taken together, these findings indicate that the sanctification of personal projects may provide the same well-being benefits as does imbuing personal strivings with sacred meaning.

McGregor, Nash, and colleagues have examined personal projects in regard to religious motivation (McGregor, Nash, Mann, & Phills, 2010; McGregor, Nash, & Prentice, 2010). Their work replicates findings from the strivings literature that spiritual strivings have an approach (rather than avoidance) focus, and that spiritual strivings can serve as a unifying force to reduce intergoal conflict. According to their theory of reactive approach motivation (RAM), when people face an approach–avoidance conflict, the anxious arousal resulting from the conflict can be ameliorated by approaching a different, unimpeded goal. Even though the new goal is unrelated to the original source of anxiety, the RAM "may provide relief by constraining attention to information relevant to the [new] focal goal" (McGregor, Nash, & Prentice, 2010, p. 148). Specifically, a focus on idealistic and transcendent goals, such as those provided by religious belief, can provide a means for relieving uncertainty arousal arising from goal conflict. As people turn their attention to information relevant to an idealistic/transcendent goal, they experience a strong approach motivation toward this goal and ignore nonrelevant information, effectively blocking anxiety-inducing information. Religious and idealistic goals are particularly effective for activating RAM because they can be promoted in the privacy of a person's own thoughts, require few resources, and are resistant to obstacles in the temporal realm.

When participants were experimentally induced to experience goal-conflict anxiety, they subsequently rated their personal projects higher in idealism (which is conceptualized as inclusive of sacred and transcendent meaning) and higher in approach motivation (McGregor, Nash, Mann, & Phills, 2010). Consistent with the theory that people turn to religious ideals to activate approach motivation and relieve motivational conflict, increased idealism completely mediated the relation between the goal-conflict manipulation and increased approach motivation ratings of personal projects. Moreover, people who find uncertainty highly aversive exhibited higher idealism and religious zeal when induced to experience motivational conflict (McGregor, Nash, & Prentice, 2010).

WHERE DO SPIRITUAL GOALS COME FROM?

Why do people have spiritual strivings? What functions or purposes do spiritual strivings serve? Motivation deals not only with the content of behavior but also in understanding the distal and proximal wellsprings that influence individual's day-to-day actions. In accounting for religious motivation, there are two primary schools of thought. The first, which might be called the "global motive" approach, emphasizes specific motivational needs (either a few or many). The second approach is organized around psychological systems designed to solve adaptive problems faced by our ancestors.

That religion serves to satisfy a small number of fundamental motives has been postulated by a number of different psychologists of religion. These would include basic, fundamental motives such as meaning, control, self-esteem, and relatedness or belong-ingness (Kirkpatrick, Chapter 6, this volume; Spilka, Hood, Hunsberger, & Gorsuch, 2003). In contrast, others have proposed a much larger number of needs. For example, Reiss (2004) proposed a multifactorial theory in which people turn to religion for 15 different motives: status, acceptance, social contact, tranquility, eating, curiosity, exer-cise, independence, power, honor, family, vengeance, order, romance, and idealism. This global motive approach, while intuitively appealing, has been criticized on the grounds that is does not conform to innate psychological architecture (Kirkpatrick, 2005).

An approach that better reflects designed human psychology is the discrete domain-specific systems approach (Kirkpatrick, Chapter 6, this volume). According to contem-porary evolutionary psychology, the brain/mind comprises a host of domain-specific mechanisms designed by natural selection to solve adaptive problems faced recurrently by our ancestors in their environments. These mechanisms then serve to organize and direct behavior through a series of inputs and outputs. The adaptive problems include problems related to mating (e.g., selection, attraction, and retention of mates), problems related to competition for resources (e.g., the negotiation of status hierarchies, formation and main-tenance of alliances), problems related to acquiring assistance and support from others (e.g., selection and maintenance of friendships), and problems related to intergroup con-flict. The functional organization of these different systems must differ qualitatively from one another because the adaptive problems and their solutions vary widely across differ-ent domains (Kirkpatrick, 2005). Therefore, strivings reflecting these different systems are likely to be quite distinct from each other. Evolved systems that solve the problems just presented are the attachment system, coalitional psychology, kinship psychology, intrasexual competition, and social exchange (Kirkpatrick, 2005).

Perhaps then, spiritual strivings solve adaptive problems in these five domains of status, attachment, coalition formation, kinship, and social exchange. For example, strivings could be mapped in the following manner: status ("Let God take control and not think I can do better," "Let go and let God," "Follow God's plan for my life, "Sub-mit my will to Allah"), attachment ("Get closer to God," "Improve my relationship with God," "Work on things that separate me from God"), coalition formation ("Help people meet God," "Meet with believers," "Communicate my faith with others), kin-ship ("Make our home a place that models the love of Christ," "Honor and grow my child's spirituality," "Pray with wife"), and social exchange ("Thank God for blessings," "Worship God on a regular basis," "Be more thankful for what God has given to me"). The fit between individual strivings and psychological systems is a good one for these spiritual strivings

On the other hand, consider these strivings: "Knowing God," "Live my life at all times for God," "Glorifying God," "Have fun and enjoy life because God gave me this life," "Be faithful to God," "Remember what God has done for me," "Incorporate God into my daily life," "Practice the presence of God in daily activities." These strivings do not appear to map readily onto the psychological systems. Which adaptive problems do they offer solutions to? It is not clear.

So then, do spiritual or theistic strivings solve particular adaptive problems? We think the answer at this early stage of research is, mostly we don't know. Perhaps spiritual projects better fit the goals as solving adaptive problems theory since they are more context specific. On the other hand, striving for the sacred may be a unique motivation that does not easily fit the domain-specific psychological mechanism hypothesis. With this conclusion, we echo the sentiments of Pargament (2002), who persuasively argued that the unique functions of religion cannot be reduced to a more familiar, naturalistic set of human motivations. Nor are spiritual strivings mere epiphenomena with no descriptive or explanatory power. Rather, the sacred component of religion sets it aside from other human phenomena and requires that religious motivation, and the psychological study of religion more generally, needs to be appreciated more fully and on its own terms.

CONCLUSION

Empirical research on religious goals and their place in the pantheon of human experience is still in its early stages and has not kept up with advances in motivational science. Conceptualizing spiritual and religious motivation in terms of goals and goal processes can lead to advances that surpass a conventional focus on religious beliefs, behaviors, and attitudes. We believe that by drawing upon the concepts, theories, and methodologies from motivational science, substantial progress can be achieved in addressing how basic spiritual and religious needs and motives are translated into concrete goals, strivings, and daily projects. Beyond that initial question, a number of more specific issues in the realm of self-regulation and spiritual goal pursuit could be approached. Many of these issues involve the structural dynamics of goal systems, but there are others that could form the agenda for future research programs. For example, how are spiritual and religious goals effectively shielded, or protected, from competing goals? To what degree are spiritual goals substitutable, or perceived as fulfilling the same underlying motive? How are a person's spiritual goals supported by or hindered by significant others, and what are the implications of positive and negative interpersonal goal impact for psychological, spiritual, and physical well-being? Is the effect of spiritual strivings on well-being different for goals that are freely chosen and autonomously endorsed compared with those that are adopted out of pressure to please others or God (Kneezel & Emmons, 2006)? Given the heightened importance and centrality of spiritual goals within the overall goal system, relative to other goals, does disengagement from unattainable spiritual goals work in a similar fashion to nonspiritual goals? How is it possible to monitor goal progress when those goals by their very nature involve invisible objects (e.g., "Get closer to God"?) What sources of information are relied upon to make judgments about progress toward spiritual goals? Are spiritual goals pursued in an automatic, proceduralized manner, or are they more effortful and conscious? How do spiritual strivings shape the way people categorize others in the social environment (Fitzsimmons & Shah, 2009)? Can goal approaches to spiritual motivation shed new light on spiritual pathologies such as spiritual hypocrisy, spiritual discord, or spiritual inflexibility (Pargament, 2007)? These are just a few of the intriguing questions that await future scientific inquiry.

Emmons and Paloutzian (2003) concluded their *Annual Review of Psychology* chapter by advocating a multilevel interdisciplinary paradigm, a framework that was then enthusiastically adopted by the editors of the first edition of this handbook. The intersection of motivational science and the psychology of religion described in this chapter is a compelling illustration of this multilevel interdisciplinary framework, as it seems particularly well suited to addressing the issues and questions emerging from a consideration of the roots and fruits of religious motivation.

ACKNOWLEDGMENTS

Preparation of this chapter was supported by a generous grant from the John Templeton Foundation.

REFERENCES

Allport, G. W. (1950). *The individual and his religion.* New York: Macmillan.

Allport, G. W. (1961). *Pattern and growth in personality.* New York: Holt.

Bargh, J. A., & Ferguson, M. J. (2000). Beyond behaviorism: On the automaticity of higher mental processes. *Psychological Bulletin, 126,* 925–945.

Brown, W. P., Barnes, C. D., & Campbell, N. J. (2007). Fundamentalism and forgiveness. *Personality and Individual Differences, 43,* 1437–1447.

Bushman, B. J., Ridge, R. D., Das, E., Key, C. W., & Busath, G. L. (2007). When God sanctions killing: Effect of scriptural violence on aggression. *Psychological Science, 18,* 204–207.

Elliot, A. J. (Ed.). (2008). *Handbook of approach and avoidance motivation.* New York: Psychology Press.

Elliot, A. J., & Friedman, R. (2007). Approach–avoidance: A central characteristic of personal goals. In B. R. Little, K. Salmela-Aro, & S. D. Phillips (Eds.), *Personal project pursuit: Goals, action, and human flourishing* (pp. 97–118). Mahwah, NJ: Erlbaum.

Elliot, A. J., & Fryer, J. W. (2008). The goal construct in psychology. In J. Y. Shah & W. L. Gardner (Eds.), *Handbook of motivation science* (pp. 235–250). New York: Guilford Press.

Emmons, R. A. (1986). Personal strivings: An approach to personality and subjective wellbeing. *Journal of Personality and Social Psychology, 51,* 1058–1068.

Emmons, R. A. (1999). *The psychology of ultimate concerns: Motivation and spirituality in personality.* New York: Guilford Press.

Emmons, R. A. (2008, August). *Validating the Spiritual Striving Questionnaire in a young life population.* Poster presented at the 116th annual convention of the American Psychological Association, Boston.

Emmons, R. A., Cheung, C., & Tehrani, K. (1998). Assessing spirituality through personal goals: Implications for research on religion and SWB. *Social Indicators Research, 45,* 391–422.

Emmons, R. A., Colby, P. M., & Kaiser, H. A. (1998). When losses lead to gains: Personal goals and the recovery of meaning. In P. T. P. Wong & P. S. Fry (Eds.), *The human quest for meaning* (pp. 163–178). Hillsdale, NJ: Erlbaum.

Emmons, R. A., & King, L. A. (1988). Conflict among personal strivings: Immediate and long-term implications for psychological and physical wellbeing. *Journal of Personality and Social Psychology, 54,* 1040–1048.

Emmons, R. A., & Paloutzian, R. F. (2003). The psychology of religion. *Annual Review of Psychology, 54,* 377–402.

Fitzsimmons, G. M., & Shah, J. Y. (2009). Confusing one instrumental other for another: Goal effects on social categorization. *Psychological Science, 20,* 1468–1472.

Hart, K. H. (2007, August). *Correlates of spiritual striving among alcoholics in stage 2 recovery.* Paper presented at the annual convention of the American Psychological Association, San Francisco.

Hill, P. C., Pargament, K. I., Hood, R. W., Jr., McCullough, M. E., Swyers, J. P., Larson, D. B., et al. (2000). Conceptualizing religion and spirituality: Points of commonality, points of departure. *Journal for the Theory of Social Behaviour, 30,* 51–77.

James, W. (1985). *The varieties of religious experience.* New York: Penguin Classics. (Original work published 1902)

Johnson, M. K., Rowatt, W. C., & LaBouff, J. (2010). Priming Christian religious concepts increases religious prejudice. *Social Psychological and Personality Science, 1,* 119–126.

Johnson, P. E. (1959). *The psychology of religion.* New York: Abington Press.

Karoly, P. (1993). Goal systems: An organizational framework for clinical assessment and treatment planning. *Psychological Assessment, 3,* 273–280.

Kashdan, J. B., Breen, W. E., & Julian, T. (2010). Everyday strivings in war veterans with posttraumatic stress disorder: Suffering from a hyper-focus on avoidance and emotion regulation. *Behavior Therapy, 41,* 350–363.

Kasser, T., & Ryan, R. M. (2001). Be careful what you wish for: Optimal functioning and the relative attainment of intrinsic and extrinsic goals. In P. Schmuck & K. M. Sheldon (Eds.), *Life goals and well-being: Towards a positive psychology of human striving* (pp. 116–131). Göttingen, Germany: Hogrefe & Huber.

Kirkpatrick, L. (2005). *Attachment, evolution, and the psychology of religion.* New York: Guilford Press.

Kneezel, T. T. (2005). *Approach and avoidance spiritual striving.* Unpublished master's thesis, University of California, Davis.

Kneezel, T. T., & Emmons, R. A. (2006). Personality and spiritual development. In E. C. Roehlkepartain, P. E. King, L. Wagener, & P. L. Benson (Eds.), *The handbook of spiritual development in childhood and adolescence* (pp. 266–278). Thousand Oaks, CA: Sage.

Leak, G. K., DeNeve, K., & Greteman, A. J. (2007). The relationship between spirituality assessed through self-transcendent goal strivings, and positive psychological attributes. *Research in the Social Scientific Study of Religion, 18,* 263–279.

Little, B. R. (1983). Personal projects: A rational and method for investigation. *Environment and Behavior, 15,* 273–309.

Little, B. R. (1989). Personal projects analysis: Trivial pursuits, magnificent obsessions and the search for coherence. In D. M. Buss & N. Cantor (Eds.), *Personality psychology: Recent trends and emerging directions* (pp. 15–31). New York: Springer-Verlag.

Mahoney, A., & Pargament, K. I. (2005). A higher purpose: The sanctification of strivings in a community sample. *The International Journal for the Psychology of Religion, 15,* 239–262.

Martos, T., Kézdy, A., & Horváth-Szabó, K. (2011). Religious motivations for everyday goals: Their religious context and potential consequences. *Motivation and Emotion, 35,* 75–88.

McAdams, D. P. (2009). *The person: An introduction to the science of personality psychology* (5th ed.). New York: Wiley.

McCullough, M. E., & Willoughby, L. B. (2009). Religion, self-regulation, and self-control: Associations, explanations, and implications. *Psychological Bulletin, 135,* 69–93.

McGregor, I. (2007). Personal projects as compensatory convictions: Passionate pursuit and the fugitive self. In B. R. Little, K. Salmela-Aro, & S. D. Phillips (Eds.), *Personal project pursuit: Goals, action, and human flourishing* (pp. 171–195). Mahwah, NJ: Erlbaum.

McGregor, I., Nash, K., Mann, N., & Phills, C. E. (2010). Anxious uncertainty and reactive approach motivation (RAM). *Journal of Personality and Social Psychology, 99,* 133–147.

McGregor, I., Nash, K., & Prentice, M. (2010). Reactive approach motivation (RAM) for religion. *Journal of Personality and Social Psychology, 99,* 148–161.

Moskowitz, G. B., & Grant H. (Eds.). (2009). *The psychology of goals.* New York: Guilford Press.

Pargament, K. I. (2002). Is religion nothing but . . . ?: Explaining religion versus explaining religion away. *Psychological Inquiry, 13,* 239–244.

Pargament, K. I. (2007). *Spiritually integrated psychotherapy: Understanding and addressing the sacred.* New York: Guilford Press.

Pargament, K. I., & Park, C. L. (1995). Merely a defense?: The variety of religious means and ends. *Journal of Social Issues, 51,* 13–32.

Pargament, K. I., & Sweeney, P. J. (2011). Building spiritual fitness in the Army: An innovative approach to a vital aspect of human development. *American Psychologist, 66,* 58–64.

Park, C. L. (2005). Religion and meaning. In R. F. Paloutzian & C. L. Park (Eds.), *Handbook of the psychology of religion and spirituality* (pp. 295–314). New York: Guilford Press.

Park, C. L., & Paloutzian, R. F. (2005). One step toward integration and an expansive future. In R. F. Paloutzian & C. L. Park (Eds.), *Handbook of the psychology of religion and spirituality* (pp. 550–564). New York: Guilford Press.

Reiss, S. (2004). The sixteen strivings for God. *Zygon, 39,* 303–320.

Roberts, B. W., & Robins, R. W. (2000). Broad dispositions, broad aspirations: The intersection of personality traits and major life goal. *Personality and Social Psychology Bulletin, 26,* 1284–1296.

Ryan, K. R., & Fiorito, B. (2003). Means-Ends Spirituality Questionnaire: Reliability, validity, and relationship to psychological well-being. *Review of Religious Research, 45,* 130–154.

Schnitker, S. A. (2012). An examination of patience and well-being. *The Journal of Positive Psychology, 7,* 263–280.

Schwartz, B. (2000). Self-determination: The tyranny of freedom. *American Psychologist, 55,* 79–88.

Shah, J. Y., & Gardner, W. L. (Eds.). (2008). *Handbook of motivation science.* New York: Guilford Press.

Shah, J. Y., & Kruglanski, A. W. (2008). Structural dynamics: The challenge of change in goal systems. In J. Y. Shah & W. L. Gardner (Eds.), *Handbook of motivation science* (pp. 217–234). New York: Guilford Press.

Singer, J. A. (2005). *Personality and psychotherapy: Treating the whole person.* New York: Guilford Press.

Spilka, B., Hood, R. W., Jr., Hunsberger, B., & Gorsuch, R. (2003). *The psychology of religion: An empirical approach* (3rd ed.). New York: Guilford Press.

Tillich, P. (1957). *Dynamics of faith.* New York: Harper & Row.

Tix, A. P., & Frazier, P. A. (2005). Mediation and moderation of the relationship between intrinsic religiousness and mental health. *Personality and Social Psychology Bulletin, 31,* 295–306.

Trout, D. (1931). *Religious behavior: An introduction to the psychological study of religion.* New York: Macmillan.

Zinnbauer, B. J., & Pargament, K. I. (1998). Spiritual conversion: A study of religious change among college students. *Journal for the Scientific Study of Religion, 37,* 161–180.

14

The Religious Shaping of Feeling
Implications of Affect Valuation Theory

Jeanne L. Tsai, Birgit Koopmann-Holm,
Masako Miyazaki, and Camaron Ochs

O ver 80% of the world population identifies with a specific religion (Adherents. com, 2007; Central Intelligence Agency, 2011). For some individuals, this religion structures and shapes every dimension of their daily lives: what they wear, with whom they spend time, where they go, and what they eat. As important, but perhaps less overt, is how religion shapes people's psyches. Indeed, one of the major functions of religion is to provide followers with a way of understanding and coping with their life circumstances (see Pargament, Falb, Ano, & Wachholtz, Chapter 28, this volume; Park, 2005). Another is to provide a guide or map for how to lead a good life (in this volume, see Donahue & Nielsen, Chapter 16, and Park, Chapter 18). A central part of coping with life and leading a good life is regulating one's emotions. Indeed, several religious scholars have written about the centrality of emotion in religious experience (see Emmons, 2005a, for an excellent history of religion and emotion). For instance, two fundamental "truths" or tenets of Buddhism are that life is full of suffering, sorrow, and grief, and that the way to end this suffering is to relinquish one's attachments to the material world and achieve "enlightenment" (Smith, 1991). In this chapter, we explore several ways in which religion may shape people's *emotional* lives, specifically their emotional goals, using the framework of affect valuation theory (AVT; Tsai, 2007). But first, we discuss our approach to religion.

RELIGION AS A CULTURAL SYSTEM

According to Pargament and his colleagues (Pargament, Magyar-Russell, & Murray-Swank, 2005), religion is the "search for significance in ways related to the sacred"

(p. 667). By "sacred," these authors refer to things that are perceived as "holy, 'set apart' from the ordinary, and worthy of veneration and respect" (p. 668).

Following the footsteps of Geertz (1973) and other scholars (Cohen & Hall, 2009; Cohen & Hill, 2007), we assume a "religious culture perspective" (Cohen, 2009; Cohen, Malka, Rozin, & Cherfas, 2006; see Saroglou & Cohen, Chapter 17, this volume). In other words, we view religions as cultural systems (Kroeber & Kluckhohn, 1952) because they comprise historically derived and socially transmitted ideas (specifically related to "the sacred" or supernatural) that are instantiated in rituals (e.g., services and ceremonies), practices (e.g., prayer and meditation, singing), and products (e.g., texts, icons). Religious cultures are both products and producers of human action: Religious experts write texts that reflect that religion's core beliefs, and these texts in turn influence practitioners who read those texts. Religious ideas and practices provide meaning, or a way of understanding one's own and others' actions, thoughts, and feelings (Emmons, 2005b; Park, 2005). This view of religion is somewhat different from (but not opposed to) an approach that focuses more on the psychological and social functions of religious institutions in general (e.g., religious communities as sources of social support).

Religious cultures resemble national cultures in several ways. First, they contain smaller subcultures (e.g., sects and denominations) that exist within the larger dominant culture. Second, individuals within the same national or religious culture may vary in their responses to the dominant ideas and practices of their culture. For example, whereas one Buddhist practitioner may approach the Four Noble Truths with skepticism and doubt, another practitioner may approach them with unquestioning acceptance. As a result, any one religious group (e.g., Buddhists) may be simultaneously homogeneous (i.e., individuals are all exposed to the same set of religious ideas) *and* heterogeneous (i.e., individuals may respond to the same set of religious ideas in different ways). Third, religious cultures encompass multiple domains of daily life (e.g., home, work). Fourth, religious and national cultural ideas and practices are transmitted through similar paths, including parental and peer socialization, media representations, and engagement in rituals and practices. Finally, like national cultures, although there are core ideas and practices that remain intact over time, religious ideas and practices are also dynamic and changing (e.g., Wolfe, 2003).

Religious cultures, however, also differ from national cultures in important ways. Whereas national cultures typically involve a variety of ideas and practices that may or may not cohere with each other, religious ideas and practices are usually unified by fundamental themes related to death and suffering (Atran & Norenzayan, 2004) and to balancing one's own needs against others' needs (Shariff & Norenzayan, 2007). Religions also include beliefs about supernatural agents who "transcend death, deception, and illusion" and provide comfort during times when people feel uncertain, anxious (Atran & Norenzayan, 2004; Kay, Gaucher, McGregor, & Nash, 2010), and other culturally undesirable states. Third, and perhaps most importantly, religious cultures speak specifically to what people perceive to be "sacred" and "divine" and, therefore, refer to phenomena that are, from an empirical perspective, largely unknowable (McCullough & Willoughby, 2009).

Although several scholars have argued that the religious culture perspective is an important part of understanding what impact religion has on psychological functioning (Cohen & Hill, 2007), few have actually used this approach to understand the influence of religion on *emotional* functioning. By viewing religions as cultural systems, scholars can begin to address two main limitations of the existing literature on religion and emotion: (1) the focus on Christian contexts and (2) the lack of theory regarding how religion shapes feeling. In this chapter, we illustrate how AVT (Tsai, 2007)—a theory that directly predicts how culture shapes emotion—-not only addresses these gaps in the literature but raises new questions about the religious shaping of feeling.

AFFECT VALUATION THEORY

AVT is a theoretical framework that attempts to integrate people's affective ideals and goals into current models of emotion. Its main argument is that people's emotional experiences not only involve what people "actually" feel in the moment but also what people ideally want to feel in the moment and more generally in life. We focus on "affect," or feeling states that can be described in terms of two dimensions: (1) arousal and (2) valence (Barrett & Russell, 1999; Larsen & Diener, 1992; Thayer, 1989; Watson & Tellegen, 1985). For example, enthusiastic, excited, and elated are emotional states that differ from each other, but they are all high-arousal, positive states (what we refer to as "HAP" states). Similarly, calm, relaxed, and peaceful are emotional states that differ from each other in various ways, but they are all low-arousal positive states (what we refer to as "LAP" states). Affective states involve multiple components, including subjective experience (e.g., "I feel good"), physiological responses (e.g., increases in heart rate), and behavioral responses (e.g., smiling) (Barrett, Mesquita, Ochsner, & Gross, 2007; Levenson, 1994).

We began our work on affect because research suggests that across different languages and cultures, emotional states are classified in terms of the arousal and valence dimensions, suggesting that affect can be compared across cultures (Russell, Lewicka, & Nitt, 1989). AVT, however, can also be applied to discrete emotional states such as anger, sadness, and disgust as well as more complex emotional states that have been associated with religion, such as compassion, forgiveness, and hope.

AVT was first developed as a way of reconciling the mixed findings regarding cultural similarities and differences in emotion. On the one hand, a body of literature—mostly but not exclusively anthropological—suggested more differences than similarities in emotion across cultures (e.g., Kleinman & Good, 1985; Lutz, 1988). For example, in her ethnography of the Ifaluk, Lutz (1988) described the emotion of *fago*, a combination of sadness, pity, love, and compassion, which she argues does not exist in American culture. On the other hand, another body of literature—mostly but not exclusively psychological—suggested more similarities than differences in emotion across cultures (e.g., Breugelmans et al., 2005; Scherer, 1997). For example, in one of our own studies, we compared the autonomic (e.g., electrodermal activity) and subjective responses of European Americans and Hmong Americans when they were reliving different emotional episodes from their lives. Although we found some differences in expressive behavior (e.g., Hmong Americans smiled less than European Americans while reliving positive emotions), European Americans and Hmong Americans showed strikingly similar electrodermal responses and reported experiencing various positive and negative emotions at similar levels of intensity (Tsai, Chentsova-Dutton, Friere-Bebau, & Przymus, 2002).

Ideal Affect Differs from Actual Affect

In order to reconcile these different literatures, we began to consider the possibility that they were describing *different* affective phenomena. One literature seemed to be examining more the affective states that people actually feel ("actual affect"), whereas the other seemed to be examining more the affective states that people ideally want to feel ("ideal affect"). Whereas actual affect is a response to an event, ideal affect is a goal and a desired outcome. Both are important in emotional life but serve different functions: Actual affect tells the individual how he or she is doing, while ideal affect provides a way of interpreting that feeling (e.g., "Am I feeling how I want to feel?," "Is this a good feeling that I am having?"). In addition, ideal affect serves motivational functions: People engage in specific behaviors in order to feel how they ideally want to feel (e.g., drinking coffee to feel alert and energized, getting a massage to feel relaxed and calm). The distinction between actual and ideal affect is the first premise of AVT.

Consistent with this premise, when we ask people to rate how much they *actually* feel a variety of feelings and then how much they *ideally want to* feel those same states on average, we find that participants can easily differentiate between the two. More specifically, people report wanting to feel more positive than negative emotions, and wanting to feel *more* positive and *less* negative than they actually feel. This pattern holds across a variety of North American and East Asian (Tsai, Knutson, & Fung, 2006) as well as Christian and Buddhist (Tsai, Miao, & Seppala, 2007) contexts. Current research in our lab suggests that ideal affect and actual affect can be distinguished in terms of neural activity as well (Chim, Sims, Samanez-Larkin, Tsai, & Knutson, 2011).

The bulk of the research on emotion in general and on religion and emotion more specifically, however, has focused on actual affect (Emmons, 2005a). For example, in the religion and emotion literature, common questions include:

1. Does being religious improve emotional health and well-being?
2. Are religious people more likely to experience compassion, gratitude, and other prosocial emotions?
3. Are there "religious emotions," or emotions that only religious people experience?

On the basis of AVT, we argue that in order to answer any of these questions about religion and actual affect, we have to first understand how religion shapes ideal affect.

Culture Shapes Ideal Affect More Than Actual Affect

"I'm excited about my future!" Start speaking those kinds of words, and before long, you will rise to a new level of well-being, success, and victory.
—Joel Osteen (2004, p. 123)

[The 14th Dalai Lama] . . . has pointed out that a happy life is built on a foundation of a calm, stable state of mind.
—His Holiness the Dalai Lama and Howard C. Cutler (1998, p. 311)

The second premise of AVT is that cultural ideas and practices shape how people ideally want to feel. As demonstrated by studies that document cross-national differences in values (Schwartz, 1992), culture teaches people what is good, moral, and virtuous (Shweder, 2003). In AVT, this idea is applied to emotions and other feeling states. Cross-religion differences in values have also been documented (Saroglou & Dupuis, 2006; Schwartz & Huismans, 1995). For example, in a comparison of Jewish, Protestant, Catholic, and Greek Orthodox practitioners, Schwartz and Huismans (1995) observed similarities across the four religions in practitioners' endorsement of benevolence (caring about the welfare of close others), tradition (respect for norms and practices), conformity (restraint of actions), and security (safety) values. However, the degree to which religiosity was correlated with these values varied across religious traditions. Only a handful of studies, however, have examined how religion shapes *emotional* values, despite the fact that religious cultures teach people which *feelings* are good, virtuous, moral, and desirable to feel (Emmons, 2005a; Silberman, 2005; Snibbe & Markus, 2002).

We tested this hypothesis in two studies (Tsai et al., 2007) by comparing the affective states that readers are encouraged to feel by Christian and Buddhist texts. We were specifically interested in high-arousal positive (HAP) states such as excitement and enthusiasm, and low-arousal positive (LAP) states such as calm and peacefulness, because our previous work found that North American culture values HAP states more and LAP states less than East Asian cultures, and Christianity and Buddhism are dominant religions in these two contexts, respectively. In one study, we compared different translations of the Gospels of the New Testament with different translations of popular Buddhist sutras (e.g., Diamond Sutra, Heart Sutra). We used the Linguistic Inquiry and Word Count program (Pennebaker, Francis, & Booth, 2001) to identify the HAP and LAP words in each text, and then trained coders to read the passages in which the words appeared and determine whether readers were being (1) encouraged to feel the state, (2) discouraged from feeling the state, or (3) neither encouraged to nor discouraged from feeling the state. Interestingly, there were no differences in the frequency of HAP and LAP terms in the Christian and Buddhist classical texts. However, Christian texts endorsed HAP more than Buddhist texts did.

To look at more contemporary texts, we compared the frequency and endorsement of HAP and LAP states in best selling Christian and Buddhist self-help books, using a method similar to the one just described. Again, consistent with findings for the classical texts, there were no differences in the frequency of HAP words. Buddhist contemporary self-help books, however, had a greater frequency of LAP words than did Christian ones. Also consistent with our hypotheses, Christian best selling self-help books endorsed HAP states more and LAP states less than did Buddhist best selling self-help books, as illustrated by the prior quotes, even when controlling for differences in the frequency of LAP words. Although texts are just one form of codified religion, these findings provide evidence that religious cultures differ in their ideal affect, or the states that they teach their practitioners to want to feel.

More recently, Kim-Prieto and Diener (2009) reported religious differences in the desirability of various discrete emotions. For example, Christians reported viewing love as more desirable than did Muslims and Buddhists, whereas Muslims reported viewing sadness and shame as more desirable than did Christians and Buddhists.

Several studies have found that people place higher priority on goals that are deemed "sacred" (Emmons, 2005b) and that sanctified goals generate greater commitment, confidence, and investment of time and energy than do nonsanctified goals (Mahoney et al., 2005). Other research suggests that people who are religious score higher on social desirability, suggesting that being a good person or meeting religious ideals may be particularly important and motivating (Sedikides & Gebauer, 2010). Thus, affective ideals may play an even greater role in people's lives if they are sanctioned by their religious traditions, especially during times of anxiety and uncertainty (Kay et al., 2010).

Religions also identify undesirable feelings and acts that should be avoided, such as betrayal and deception, and other forms of "sinful" behavior. For example, in Schwartz and Huismans (1995), the more religious that Jews, Protestants, Catholics, and Greek Orthodox were, the less they valued hedonism (pursuing pleasure in life), achievement (personal accomplishment), stimulation (novelty and change in life), and self-direction (being independent). Saroglou, Delpierre, and Dernelle (2004) observed similar patterns among Muslims as well.

Since our first work describing the distinction between actual and ideal affect, we have also begun to examine cultural variation in how people want to avoid feeling ("avoided affect") (Koopmann-Holm & Tsai, 2013b). Although related, avoided affect is different from ideal affect and from actual affect. Not surprisingly, people want to avoid feeling negative states more than positive states, and they want to avoid feeling more negative and less positive than they actually feel (Koopmann-Holm & Tsai, 2013a). Although we have only begun to examine religious differences in avoided affect, our preliminary findings suggest that Catholics want to avoid high arousal negative states (e.g. fearfulness, hostility, nervousness) more than do Protestants and Buddhists. This is in line with what Hutchinson, Patock-Peckham, Cheong, and Nagoshi (1998) propose, namely that Catholicism is driven more by guilt (which is often associated with anxiety) than Protestantism. Thus, religious ideas and practices may also shape "affective anti-goals."

As suggested previously, religions teach us how to feel (or not feel) through religious *products*: texts, icons, and relics. Although no empirical work has yet compared religious relics in terms of their emotional content, Kieschnick (2008) argues that religious statues, paintings, art, and architecture are designed to trigger emotion. We believe that they may play an even greater role in modeling ideal affective states. For example, as much as the image of Buddha may elicit calm, it may also remind Buddhists that calm is the ideal way to feel. Indeed, practitioners may turn to religious relics and icons to remind themselves about how they should feel, especially during times of deep anxiety and uncertainty (McCullough & Willoughby, 2009).

AVT also predicts that whereas cultural ideas and practices shape how people actually feel, they shape how people want to feel even more. Whether or not people are able to achieve their ideal states depends on a host of factors, such as temperament, ability to regulate emotions, cultural engagement, or a combination of these factors. This may seem obvious, but in everyday life people are often surprised when a clergyman, monk, or any other devoutly religious person is accused or convicted of some morally reprehensible crime. This may be because we expect devoutly religious people, especially religious leaders, to think, behave, and *feel* in ways that are consistent with their religious ideals. However, as predicted by AVT, religious cultures may shape how people want to feel more than how they actually feel.

We recently conducted a series of studies in the United States to test this hypothesis with Buddhist-inspired meditation (Koopmann-Holm, Sze, Ochs, & Tsai, 2013a). In one study, Buddhist meditators who had been meditating for approximately 4 years reported wanting to feel LAP states more and HAP states less than nonmeditators. Consistent with AVT, there were no differences in how much Buddhist meditators and nonmeditators actually felt those states. To rule out the possibility that these findings were due to selection effects (i.e., people who value LAP states more and HAP states less may be more likely to practice meditation), we conducted another study in which we randomly assigned participants to an 8-week Buddhist-inspired meditation class (mindfulness or compassion), an 8-week improvisational theater class (class-control), and a no-class control. After 8 weeks, participants in both meditation classes showed greater increases in ideal LAP than did participants in the two control classes. There were no changes in ideal HAP across any of the conditions, perhaps because ideal HAP (i.e., mainstream American culture) is difficult to change in a culture that values HAP. Again, there were no significant changes in actual HAP or LAP, suggesting that although short engagement in a religious practice changes how people want to feel, much more religious practice may be needed to change how people actually feel. In another study, we demonstrated that these changes in ideal affect were not due to experimenter demand. Although more studies are needed, this work supports our prediction that meditation as a religious practice shapes how calm people ideally want to feel, perhaps even more than how calm they actually feel, at least initially.

If culture shapes ideal more than actual affect, are there factors that shape actual more than ideal affect? AVT predicts that *temperamental* factors shape actual affect more than they do ideal affect. By temperamental factors, we are referring to genetic predispositions to experience specific feelings. This premise is based on decades of research demonstrating that temperament accounts for up to 50% of the variance in actual affect (Diener & Lucas, 1999; Lykken & Tellegen, 1996). For example, extraversion is highly correlated with the experience of high-arousal positive states, and neuroticism is highly correlated with the experience of high-arousal negative states (Costa & McCrae, 1980; Gross, Sutton, & Ketelaar, 1998; Schimmack, Radhakrishnan, Oishi, Dzokoto, & Ahadi, 2002). Indeed, in both college and community samples, we have found that cultural variables account for a greater percentage of the variance in ideal affect compared with actual affect, whereas temperamental variables account for a greater percentage of the variance in actual affect compared with ideal affect (Tsai et al., 2006).

Are we saying that people never experience their ideal states? No. Indeed, there may be particular circumstances when people's actual affect is in line with how they want to feel, and specific religious settings (e.g., religious services, rituals, and ceremonies) and practices may increase the likelihood that people attain their ideal feelings. In addition, there may be particular people who are better able to reach their ideals than others. For example, it may be that less neurotic (or more emotionally stable) individuals benefit more from meditation in terms of increasing their actual LAP. Similarly, a review by Saroglou (2010) suggests that people who are more agreeable and conscientious are more likely to be religious. Being agreeable and conscientious may not only make people more likely to seek religion, but may make them more likely to comply with religious practices and traditions and, therefore, more likely to benefit from them. And this may help them achieve their ideal affect.

Manifestations of Ideal Affect in Daily Life

The third premise of AVT is that people's ideal affect has various psychological, social, and behavioral consequences. Ideal affect acts as a "measuring stick," or a reference point for people's emotions, as well as a guide for future behavior (Tsai, 2007). Indeed, in our current research, we find that above and beyond actual affect, ideal affect influences how people present themselves and perceive others (Moon, Chim, Tsai, Ho, & Fung, 2011), how people conceive of mental health and illness (Hong, Moon, & Tsai, 2013), what types of things they do to feel good (and stop feeling bad) (Tsai, Knutson, & Rothman, 2013), and even what kinds of consumer decisions they make (Sims, Tsai, Koopmann-Holm, Thomas, & Goldstein, 2013). For example, the more people value HAP, the more likely they are to perceive an excited (vs. calm) person as friendly, the more likely they are to define well-being in terms of excitement, and the more likely they are to choose exciting and energizing (vs. calm and soothing) gums and lotions. Again, these findings held after we controlled for actual affect, suggesting that ideal affect exerts an independent influence on these processes. Although we have not collected data specifically on different religious groups, based on our previous work, we predict that religious differences in ideal affect would result in religious differences in each of these domains. In other words, through ideal affect, religious orientation may shape aspects of people's lives that may not be overtly or explicitly religious (e.g., choice of consumer products).

It is through the lenses of AVT and the religious culture perspective that we now discuss the existing literature on religion and emotion.

IMPLICATIONS FOR RESEARCH ON RELIGION AND EMOTIONAL WELL-BEING

Dear Father in Heaven, I'm not a praying man, but if you're up there and you can hear me . . . show me the way . . . show me the way.
—GEORGE BAILEY, in *It's a Wonderful Life* (Capra, 1946)

As this quote from the Frank Capra (1946) film *It's a Wonderful Life* illustrates, a popular trope in American movies is that of the agnostic or atheist praying to God as a last hope. Norenzayan and Hansen (2006) observed that when people were primed with death cues, they were more likely to believe in a supernatural agent, even if they were not religious. One of the primary roles of most religions is to provide comfort during times of deep anxiety, despair, and desperation (Atran & Norenzayan, 2004; Kay et al., 2010). Therefore, it should not be surprising that one of the major scientific questions has been whether people who are religious actually experience *more* positive affect (e.g., joy, happiness, comfort, contentment) and *less* negative affect (e.g., sadness, anger, fear) than those who are not. One of the main assumptions of this literature is that people experience a variety of ups and downs in life, and therefore, individuals who are religious should be happier (and less unhappy) on average than those who are not because their religious affiliations afford them social, material, and psychological resources to cope with life's challenges (McCullough & Willoughby, 2009).

Although mixed, most of the existing literature *does* suggest a positive association between being religious (in the traditions studied) and being emotionally healthy. Overall, the more individuals report being religious (i.e., having religious beliefs and engaging in religious practices), the more satisfied they report being with their lives, the happier they report being overall, and the more positive feelings they report experiencing on a daily basis (e.g., Koenig, 2001; Koenig, George, & Titus, 2004). Religious individuals also report being more hopeful and optimistic and having greater purpose and meaning in life. Conversely, the more religious people report being, the *less* likely they are to experience a depressive episode, the fewer depressive symptoms they report having, and the less anxiety they report feeling (Koenig, 2001; Koenig et al., 2004; see also in this volume Masters & Hooker, Chapter 26; Park & Slattery, Chapter 27; Shafranske, Chapter 30).

Although most studies of religion and well-being use self-report measures, which are vulnerable to various biases (e.g., social desirability), several have employed physiological measures to overcome this limitation. For example, in a recently published study (Inzlicht & Tullett, 2010), the authors examined levels of defensive arousal in response to making an error by using event-related potentials (ERPs). They found that when Christian believers were primed with religious icons, they showed less defensive arousal when they made errors than did nonbelievers. These findings suggest that when believers are thinking about their religion, they are less anxious during threat than nonbelievers. Other studies using physiological measures suggest that people who have undergone meditation interventions show neural changes related to the increased experience of positive, approach-related emotions compared with wait-list controls (Davidson et al., 2003). These studies suggest that even when assessed by physiological measures, religious practice may promote well-being.

One of the main implications of AVT and findings from our own work, however, is that because self-reports of actual and ideal affect are moderately correlated, researchers should distinguish between actual and ideal affect in order to ensure that differences in actual affect are not due to differences in ideal affect and vice versa. A second implication is that the links between religion and well-being may be due to temperamental, self-regulatory, or other factors rather than religion per se. For instance, research suggests that agreeableness in adolescence and adulthood and extraversion in adulthood are positively correlated with religiosity (Saroglou, 2010), and other work suggests that both agreeableness and extraversion are directly and indirectly related to higher well-being. For example, agreeableness is associated with higher relationship satisfaction and peer acceptance, and extraversion is associated with greater experience of positive emotions (Ozer & Benet-Martinez, 2006). Higher relationship satisfaction, greater peer acceptance, and greater experience of positive emotions are all associated with higher well-being (Oishi & Schimmack, 2010).

The links among religiosity, temperamental factors, and well-being may also vary as a function of national context. For example, Sasaki, Kim, and Xu (2011) observed that for individuals with the G/G genotype of the oxytocin receptor gene (associated with being more socially oriented) religiosity was positively associated with well-being in Korea (where religion involves social affiliation more), but was negatively associated with well-being in North American contexts (where religion involves social affiliation less). Thus, in addition to including a broader variety of affective states, and a broader variety of religions, studies of religion and emotion need to consider other factors related to emotion to examine how they may interact with religious ideas and practices to shape emotional experience.

The third and perhaps most important implication of AVT is that not all religions have the same ideal affect; therefore, what it means to "be well" should vary across religious cultures. In other words, before asking "How does religion impact emotional health?" one has to ask how a particular religion *defines* emotional health. This becomes particularly important when researchers broaden their studies to include other religions and other national cultures, which may have different ideal or desired states. For example, based on the work described earlier, excitement, enthusiasm, and other HAP states may be more appropriate measurements of emotional well-being in Christian than in Buddhist contexts.

IMPLICATIONS FOR RESEARCH ON RELIGION AND PROSOCIAL EMOTIONS

In affective science, there has been a resurgence of interest in prosocial or interpersonally oriented emotions such as compassion, sympathy, empathy, forgiveness, and gratitude (Bartlett & DeSteno, 2006; Condon & DeSteno, 2010; Decety & Chaminade, 2003). As stated above, because one of the unique characteristics of religion is its explicit focus on treating others well, it should come as no surprise that many of these emotions are well-elaborated in religious texts (Watts, Dutton, & Guilliford, 2006). But do religious people actually experience more pro-social emotions?

Despite the emphasis on pro-social emotions in many religions, evidence for the link between religion and the experience of pro-social emotions is surprisingly weak (Mullet et al., 2003). For example, Duriez (2004) found that religiosity among Flemish students was not significantly related to empathy. Although religiosity is associated with self-reported forgiveness in general (McCullough & Worthington, 1999; Poloma & Gallup, 1991; see also Worthington et al., Chapter 24, this volume), when asked about specific transgressions, depth of religiosity (among a primarily Christian and Jewish sample) was not related to forgiveness (McCullough & Worthington, 1999; Tsang, McCullough, & Hoyt, 2005). One reason for the weak link between religion and prosocial emotions may be that religion is also associated with antisocial emotions. For example, Bushman, Ridge, Das, Key, and Busath (2007) found when subjects read biblical passages of God condoning violence, their aggression against another participant increased. In another study, certain religious primes (e.g., heaven, spirituality) increased aggression toward another participant when participants were encouraged to act in a vengeful way by the experimenter (Saroglou, Corneille, & Van Cappellen, 2009).

Gratitude, however, seems to be one feeling that *is* associated with religiosity. On the basis of both self- and peer ratings, McCullough, Emmons, and Tsang (2002) found that religiosity was associated with a grateful disposition. Indeed, different religions such as Judaism, Christianity, and Islam value gratitude and view it as important for living a good life (Emmons & Crumpler, 2000). For example, one sample of Catholic nuns and priests reported that gratitude was one of the emotions they most commonly felt toward God (Samuels & Lester, 1985). Similarly, Kim-Prieto and Diener (2009) found no differences in the desirability of gratitude among Christians, Muslims, Buddhists, Hindus, and Jews. However, as mentioned previously, the direction of this relationship remains unclear; it is possible that people with more grateful dispositions are more likely to become religious.

Researchers have begun to examine whether engagement in specific religious practices increases the experience of prosocial emotions. Although much more work is needed in this area, several studies have linked the practice of meditation to increased empathy (Lutz, Brefczynski-Lewis, Johnstone, & Davidson, 2008; Shapiro, Schwartz, & Bonner, 1998), social connectedness (Hutcherson, Seppala, & Gross, 2008), and hope and optimism for another (Koopmann-Holm, Sze, Ochs, & Tsai, 2013b). For example, we examined whether Buddhist-inspired meditation would increase feelings toward and about a convicted murderer (Koopmann-Holm et al., in press). Participants were randomly assigned to an 8-week mindfulness meditation class, an 8-week compassion meditation class, a class control condition (i.e., an improvisational theater class), or a no-class control condition. At the end of the 8 weeks, participants were presented with a letter by a convicted murderer, who admitted to killing his friend in a "blind fit of rage." In the letter, the murderer describes his life in prison and asks readers to write him. Participants were asked questions about the letter, and then told that the study was over. They were then given the opportunity to write a letter to the prisoner, even though "they were under no obligation to do so." Among participants who wrote, participants in the compassion meditation class did not differ from those in the other conditions in terms of how empathetic or forgiving their letters were. However, they wrote more hopeful and encouraging letters (e.g., "It's going to be okay"), suggesting that compassion meditation does have an effect on how people feel about and affectively respond to others.

Despite suggestions that religion might alter the actual experience of prosocial emotions, we propose that religion may shape the desirability of prosocial emotions even more. Consistent with this idea, across different religions, scholars have found that religious people valued being forgiving more than nonreligious people (Rokeach, 1973), and Cohen and colleagues (2006) found that Jews and Protestants differed in their beliefs about forgiveness but not in their actual experience of forgiveness. Similarly, we would argue that religion cultivates a value placed on gratitude. Interestingly, in their discussions of gratitude, McCullough, Kilpatrick, Emmons, and Larson (2001) argue that gratitude functions as a "barometer" and has "motivational value," which is very similar to our argument that ideal affect is a "measuring stick" and a "guide for future behavior" (Tsai, 2007).

AVT also asks what a desirable "prosocial" response is, and raises the possibility that religions (like national cultures) differ in what constitutes an ideal "prosocial" response. For example, although there are clearly common elements across religious traditions, compassion is described differently by Christian and Buddhist perspectives. From a Buddhist perspective, in order to feel compassion toward others, one must not only have the insight that all people are suffering but also the desire to reduce that suffering (Davidson & Harrington, 2002). Ideally, this compassion is felt as strongly for one's mother as for someone who has committed heinous crimes. These notions are less central in the Christian view of compassion and, therefore, are missing in studies of compassion conducted in Christian contexts. However, when examining whether Buddhist-inspired meditation (and other practices) actually produces more compassionate responses, these elements must be included in assessments of compassion.

Similarly, the meaning of forgiveness also shows some religious variation (Cohen et al., 2006). In a series of studies, Cohen and colleagues demonstrate differences between Jewish and Protestant views of unforgivable offenses that directly stem from differences between these two religious traditions. More specifically, Jews are more likely to believe that certain offenses (e.g., rape and murder, plagiarism) are unforgivable than are Protestant Christians. These religious group differences are mediated by specific beliefs about whether some offenses are too severe to forgive and whether an individual has a right to forgive.

In addition, religious contexts may differ in terms of what constitutes an appropriate affective response to someone's suffering. Here, too, there appear to be important national cultural differences. In a comparison of American and German sympathy cards (Koopmann-Holm & Tsai, 2013b), we find that whereas American sympathy cards are more positive and optimistic than German cards (e.g., "May you find comfort"), German sympathy cards are more negative than American cards (e.g., "I hope these words show how much I share your pain"), perhaps reflecting cultural differences in beliefs about how one should respond affectively to death, loss, and other negative events. Indeed, we find that Americans want to avoid negative emotion more than Germans do. Furthermore, the more people want to avoid negative emotion, the less comfortable they report being with expressions of sympathy that only mention negative feelings. Although preliminary, these findings suggest that whereas in American contexts an appropriate response to suffering is to find a "silver lining" to that suffering, in German contexts an appropriate response is to acknowledge the experience of pain and suffering. It is possible that religious differences in responses to suffering exist along these lines as well. For example, one of the tenets of Buddhism is that life is suffering; this acceptance of suffering may influence how people respond to their own and others' suffering.

IMPLICATIONS FOR RESEARCH ON "RELIGIOUS EMOTIONS"

A third, but less studied, question in the religion and emotion literature is whether there exist religious emotions, or emotions that only occur in the context of religion. Whereas some scholars argue that "religious emotions" are ordinary emotions that simply occur in religious contexts (e.g., shame expressed during Catholic confession is the same as shame expressed at a grocery store), other scholars have argued that emotions that are linked to the divine and sacred (i.e., emotions that occur in religious contexts) are fundamentally different from emotions that are not (Pargament et al., 2005; Watts et al., 2006). Emmons and colleagues (2005a) identify several emotions that are attached to the sacred such as awe/reverence, love, and hope, but empirical studies of the uniqueness of these states to religion are just beginning. For example, awe/reverence is "central to the experience of religion" (Keltner & Haidt, 2003, p. 297), and occurs when a person has perceived vastness but cannot easily integrate this experience into his or her existing knowledge base and, therefore, has to expend effort to do so. To examine whether awe induced by spiritual transformations and awe induced by experiences of profound beauty differed, Cohen, Gruber, and Keltner (2010) asked participants to retrospectively describe examples of such experiences from their own lives. Whereas both contained positive affect, spiritual transformations were associated with greater uncertainty and more negative affect than experiences of profound beauty. Furthermore, spiritual transformations produced longer lasting changes than did experiences of profound beauty. Thus, although much more work is needed, these findings support the notion that there may be something unique about emotions that occur in religious contexts.

However, rather than ask whether some emotions are religious or not, another approach would be to ask what aspects of the larger emotional experience are more or less shaped by religious beliefs. From the perspective of AVT, ideal affect influences the meaning of an emotional event, and this meaning is created before and after as well as during the emotional event itself. One of the reasons that emotions are so powerful is that they often influence people long before and long after they occur. Indeed, emotions themselves last on the order of seconds, but memories of emotions can last on the order of years, as can the anticipation of an emotional event. Two people, for example, may spend more time feeling excited about their wedding before and after their wedding than they did during it.

We propose that "actual affect" (or how people feel during an event) exists in the larger context of "ideal affect." Specifically, how people ideally want to feel should shape their predictions of how they will feel during an emotional event and how they remember or recall feeling after the emotional event, perhaps even more than how they actually feel during the event (Chim, Tsai, Lowdermilk, & Fung, 2013). In the prior example, people who value excitement may predict they will experience intense excitement, and will primarily remember the moments of intense excitement during the wedding, even if there were only a few of these moments during the wedding itself. Therefore, although the actual momentary response itself may be the same (e.g., physiology, behavioral expression, even certain levels of subjective experience), there should be religious differences in how the emotional experience is interpreted (and the consequences of that interpretation) as a function of ideal affect. Thus, our prediction is that the anticipation and recall of an emotional event will vary significantly as a function of religion, whereas the online experience may vary less. Work by Scollon, Howard, Caldwell, and Ito (2009) support this prediction. We are currently collecting data to test these predictions.

REMAINING QUESTIONS

This brief review of the literature illustrates that although compelling work has been conducted examining the intersection of religion and emotion, much more work is needed. In addition to the issues raised in this chapter, there are several topics that we believe would be important to explore further. First, it would be important to examine specifically how people use religious ideas, products, and practices to attain their ideal states. Second, future research should examine how religion shapes emotion across the life span. Are religious practices more effective in regulating emotion after years, even decades, of religious faith? Third, although we have talked about similarities between national and religious cultures, we have not discussed how the two intersect (Saroglou & Cohen, 2011). The same religion may be experienced in different ways depending upon the larger national cultural context in which it resides; for example, one study found that European American Christians described Jesus in primarily positive terms (e.g., benevolence, love, amazement), whereas Korean Christians described Jesus in both positive and negative terms (e.g., love, sin, crucified, benevolence) (Oishi, Seol, Koo, & Miao, 2011). These findings suggest that the practice of particular religions varies as a function of the national cultural context; future research should also examine how national cultures are shaped by dominant religious traditions (Sanchez-Burks, 2002). Fourth, given the considerable literature on the temperamental precursors to religion, it would be important to examine how religion and temperament interact to shape emotional functioning. Fifth, because affective responses involve multiple components ranging from neural activity and autonomic responses to subjective experience and complex behavior, a multilevel interdisciplinary approach to the religious shaping of emotion is severely needed. Last but certainly not least, more research should focus on the specific mechanisms by which specific religious ideas and practices shape affective phenomena.

SUMMARY

Despite the prevalence of religion and its powerful influence on daily life, surprisingly little empirical research has examined how religion shapes the psyche. Given the centrality of emotion to both psychological and religious experience, it is not surprising that much of the work that does exist focuses on religion and emotion. However, to date, the majority of this work has been limited to one religious tradition (Christianity), and has focused primarily on "actual affect" (the feelings that people actually experience). The aim of this chapter has been to illustrate how broadening this work to other religious cultures and to "ideal affect" (the feelings that people ideally want to feel) can significantly advance our understanding of the religious shaping of feeling.

REFERENCES

Adherents.com. (2007). *Major religions of the world ranked by number of adherents.* Retrieved from *www.adherents.com/Religions_By_Adherents.html.*

Atran, S., & Norenzayan, A. (2004). Religion's evolutionary landscape: Counterintuition, commitment, compassion, communion. *Behavioral and Brain Sciences, 27,* 713–770.

Barrett, L., Mesquita, B., Ochsner, K. N., & Gross, J. J. (2007). The experience of emotion. *Annual Review of Psychology, 58,* 373–403.

Barrett, L., & Russell, J. A. (1999). The structure of current affect: Controversies and emerging consensus. *Psychological Science, 8,* 10–14.

Bartlett, M. Y., & DeSteno, D. (2006). Gratitude and prosocial behavior: Helping when it costs you. *Psychological Science, 17,* 319–325.

Breugelmans, S. M., Ambadar, Z., Vaca, J. B., Poortinga, Y. H., Setiadi, B., Widiyanto, P., et al. (2005). Body sensations associated with emotions in Raramuri Indians, rural Javanese, and three student samples. *Emotion, 5,* 166–174.

Bushman, B. J., Ridge, R. D., Das, E., Key, C. W., & Busath, G. W. (2007). When God sanctions killing: Effect of scriptural violence on aggression. *Psychological Science, 18,* 204–207.

Capra, F. (Producer). (1946). *It's a wonderful life* [Motion picture]. Los Angeles: Liberty Films.

Central Intelligence Agency. (2011). *The world factbook.* Retrieved from *www.cia.gov/library/publications/the-world-factbook/geos/xx.html.*

Chim, L., Sims, T., Samanez-Larkin, G., Tsai, J., & Knutson, B. (2013). *Affect valuation alters anticipatory and consummatory responses to monetary rewards in the ventromedial prefrontal cortex.* Manuscript in preparation.

Chim, L., Tsai, J. L., Lowdermilk, C., & Fung, H. H. (2013). *To want to not·want to feel: The influence of ideal affect on affective response.* Manuscript in preparation.

Cohen, A. B. (2009). Many forms of culture. *American Psychologist, 64,* 194–204.

Cohen, A. B., Gruber, J., & Keltner, D. (2010). Comparing spiritual transformations and experiences of profound beauty. *Psychology of Religion and Spirituality, 2,* 127–135.

Cohen, A. B., & Hall, D. E. (2009). Existential beliefs, social satisfaction, and well-being among Catholic, Jewish, and Protestant older adults. *The International Journal for the Psychology of Religion, 19,* 39–54.

Cohen, A. B., & Hill, P. C. (2007). Religion as culture: Religious individualism and collectivism among American Catholics, Jews, and Protestants. *Journal of Personality and Social Psychology, 75,* 709–742.

Cohen, A. B., Malka, A., Rozin, P., & Cherfas, L. (2006). Religion and unforgivable offenses. *Journal of Personality, 74,* 85–118.

Condon, P., & DeSteno, D. (2011). Compassion for one reduces punishment for another. *Journal of Experimental Social Psychology, 47,* 698–701.

Costa, P. T., & McCrae, R. R. (1980). Influence of extraversion and neuroticism on subjective well-being: Happy and unhappy people. *Journal of Personality and Social Psychology, 38,* 668–678.

Dalai Lama, H. H., the, & Cutler, H. C. (1998). *The art of happiness: A handbook for living.* New York: Riverhead.

Davidson, R. J., & Harrington, A. (2002). *Visions of compassion: Western scientists and Tibetan Buddhists examine human nature.* New York: Oxford University Press.

Davidson, R. J., Kabat-Zinn, J., Schumacher, J., Rosenkranz, M., Muller, D., Santorelli, S., et al. (2003). Alterations in brain and immune function produced by mindfulness meditation. *Psychosomatic Medicine, 65,* 564–570.

Decety, J., & Chaminade, T. (2003). Neural correlates of feeling sympathy. *Neuropsychologia, 41,* 127–138.

Diener, E., & Lucas, R. E. (1999). Personality and subjective well-being. In D. Kahneman, E. Diener, & N. Schwarz (Eds.), *Well-being: Foundations of hedonic psychology* (pp. 213–229). New York: Russell Sage Foundation.

Duriez, B. (2004). Are religious people nicer people? Taking a closer look at the religion-empathy relationship. *Mental Health, Religion & Culture, 7,* 249–254.

Emmons, R. A. (2005a). Emotion and religion. In R. F. Paloutzian & C. L. Park (Eds.), *Handbook of the psychology of religion and spirituality* (pp. 235–252). New York: Guilford Press.

Emmons, R. A. (2005b). Striving for the sacred: Personal goals, life meaning, and religion. *Journal of Social Issues, 61,* 731–745.

Emmons, R. A., & Crumpler, C. A. (2000). Gratitude as a human strength: Appraising the evidence. *Journal of Social and Clinical Psychology, 19,* 56–69.

Geertz, C. (1973). *The interpretation of cultures.* New York: Basic Books.

Gross, J. J., Sutton, S., & Ketelaar, T. (1998). Relations between affect and personality: Support for the affect-level and affective reactivity views. *Personality and Social Psychology Bulletin, 24,* 279–288.

Hong, J., Moon, A., & Tsai, J. L. (2013). *Cultural differences in conceptions of mental health: The role of ideal affect.* Manuscript in preparation.

Hutcherson, C. A., Seppala, E. M., & Gross, J. J. (2008). Loving-kindness meditation increases social connectedness. *Emotion, 8,* 720–724.

Hutchinson, G. T., Patock-Peckham, J. A., Cheong, J. W., & Nagoshi, C. T. (1998). Personality predictors of religious orientation among Protestant, Catholic, and non-religious college students. *Personality and Individual Differences, 24,* 145–151.

Inzlicht, M., & Tullett, A. M. (2010). Reflecting on God: Religious primes can reduce neurophysiological response to errors. *Psychological Science, 21,* 1184–1190.

Kay, A. C., Gaucher, D., McGregor, I., & Nash, K. (2010). Religious belief as compensatory control. *Personality and Social Psychology Review, 14,* 37–48.

Keltner, D., & Haidt, J. (2003). Approaching awe: A moral, spiritual, and aesthetic emotion. *Cognition & Emotion, 17,* 297–314.

Kieschnick, J. (2008). Material culture. In J. Corrigan (Ed.), *The Oxford handbook of religion and emotion* (pp. 223–237). New York: Oxford University Press.

Kim-Prieto, C., & Diener, E. (2009). Religion as a source of variation in the experience of positive and negative emotions. *Journal of Positive Psychology, 4,* 447–460.

Kleinman, A., & Good, B. J. (1985). *Culture and depression: Studies in the anthropology and cross-cultural psychiatry of affect and disorder.* Berkeley: University of California Press.

Koenig, H. G. (2001). Religion and medicine II: Religion, mental health, and related behaviors. *International Journal of Psychiatry in Medicine, 31,* 97–109.

Koenig, H. G., George, L. K., & Titus, P. (2004). Religion, spirituality, and health in medically ill hospitalized older patients. *Journal of the American Geriatrics Society, 52,* 554–562.

Koopmann-Holm, B., Sze, J., Ochs, C., & Tsai, J. L. (2013a). Buddhist-inspired meditation increases the value of calm. *Emotion.* Advance online publication.

Koopmann-Holm, B., Sze, J., Ochs, C., & Tsai, J. L. (2013b). *Does meditation make people more compassionate?* Manuscript in preparation.

Koopmann-Holm, B., & Tsai, J. L. (2013a). *Avoided affect: Extending affect valuation theory to negative states.* Manuscript in preparation.

Koopmann-Holm, B., & Tsai, J. L. (2013b). *Cultural variation in avoided affect: Implications for responses to suffering.* Manuscript in preparation.

Kroeber, A. L., & Kluckhohn, C. (1952). Culture: A critical review of concepts and definitions. *Papers of the Peabody Museum of Archeaology and Ethnology* (Vol. 47). Cambridge, MA: Harvard University Press.

Larsen, R. J., & Diener, E. (1992). Promises and problems with the circumplex model of emotion. In M. S. Clark (Ed.), *Review of personality and social psychology: Emotion* (pp. 25–59). Newbury Park, CA: Sage.

Levenson, R. W. (1994). Human emotion: A functional view. In P. Ekman & R. J. Davidson (Eds.), *The nature of emotion: Fundamental questions* (pp. 123–126). New York: Oxford University Press.

Lutz, A., Brefczynski-Lewis, J., Johnstone, T., & Davidson, R. J. (2008). Regulation of the neural circuitry of emotion by compassion meditation: Effects of meditative expertise. *PLoS ONE, 3,* e1897.

Lutz, C. (1988). *Unnatural emotions: Everyday sentiments on a Micronesian atoll and their challenge to Western theory.* Chicago: University of Chicago Press.

Lykken, D., & Tellegen, A. (1996). Happiness is a stochastic phenomenon. *Psychological Science, 7,* 186–189.

Mahoney, A., Pargament, K. I., Cole, B., Jewell, T., Magyar, G. M., Tarakeshwar, N., et al. (2005). A higher purpose: The sanctification of strivings. *International Journal for the Psychology of Religion, 15,* 239–262.

McCullough, M. E., Emmons, R. A., & Tsang, J. (2002). The grateful disposition: A conceptual and empirical topography. *Journal of Personality and Social Psychology, 82,* 112–127.

McCullough, M. E., Kilpatrick, S. D., Emmons, R. A., & Larson, D. B. (2001). Is gratitude a moral affect? *Psychological Bulletin, 127,* 249–266.

McCullough, M. E., & Willoughby, B. L. B. (2009). Religion, self-regulation, and self-control: Associations, explanations, and implications. *Psychological Bulletin, 135,* 69–93.

McCullough, M. E., & Worthington, Jr., E. L. (1999). Religion and the forgiving personality. *Journal of Personality, 67,* 1141–1164.

Moon, A., Chim, L., Tsai, J. L., Ho, Y., & Fung, H. L. (2011, January). *The influence of cultural differences in ideal affect on self-presentation and other-perception of Facebook profiles.* Paper presented at the 12th annual meeting of the Society for Personality and Social Psychology, San Antonio, TX.

Mullet, E., Barros, J., Frongia, L., Usaï, V., Neto, F., & Shafighi, S. R. (2003). Religious involvement and the forgiving personality. *Journal of Personality, 71,* 1–19.

Norenzayan, A., & Hansen, I. G. (2006). Belief in supernatural agents in the face of death. *Personality and Social Psychology Bulletin, 32,* 174–187.

Oishi, S., & Schimmack, U. (2010). Culture and well-being: A new inquiry into the psychological wealth of nations. *Perspectives on Psychological Science, 5,* 463–471.

Oishi, S., Seol, K. O., Koo, M., & Miao, F. F. (2011). Was he happy? Cultural difference in conceptions of Jesus. *Journal of Research in Personality, 45,* 84–91.

Osteen, J. (2004). *Your best life now: 7 steps to living at your full potential.* New York: Time Warner.

Ozer, D. J., & Benet-Martinez, V. (2006). Personality and the prediction of consequential outcomes. *Annual Review of Psychology, 57,* 401–421.

Pargament, K. I., Magyar-Russell, G. M., & Murray-Swank, N. A. (2005). The sacred and the search for significance: Religion as a unique process. *Journal of Social Issues, 61,* 665–687.

Park, C. L. (2005). Religion and meaning. In R. F. Paloutzian & C. L. Park (Eds.), *Handbook of the psychology of religion and spirituality* (pp. 295–314). New York: Guilford Press.

Pennebaker, J. W., Francis, M. E., & Booth, R. J. (2001). *Linguistic inquiry and word count: LIWC* [Computer software]. Mahwah, NJ: Erlbaum.

Poloma, M. M., & Gallup, G. H. (1991). *Varieties of prayer: A survey report.* Philadephia: Trinity Press International.

Rokeach, M. (1973). *The nature of human values.* New York: Free Press.

Russell, J. A., Lewicka, M., & Nitt, T. (1989). A cross-cultural study of a circumplex model of affect. *Journal of Personality and Social Psychology, 57,* 848–856.

Samuels, P. A., & Lester, D. (1985). A preliminary investigation of emotions experienced toward God by Catholic nuns and priests. *Psychological Reports, 56,* 706.

Sanchez-Burks, J. (2002). Protestant relational ideology and (in)attention to relational cues in work settings. *Journal of Personality and Social Psychology, 83,* 919–929.

Saroglou, V. (2010). Religiousness as a cultural adaptation of basic traits: A five-factor model perspective. *Personality and Social Psychology Review, 14,* 108–125.

Saroglou, V., & Cohen, A. B. (2011). Psychology of culture and religion: Introduction to the JCCP special issue. *Journal of Cross-Cultural Psychology, 42,* 1309–1319.

Saroglou, V., Corneille, O., & Van Cappellen, P. (2009). Speak, lord, your servant is listening: Religious priming activities submissive thoughts and behaviors. *The International Journal for the Psychology of Religion, 19,* 143–154.

Saroglou, V., Delpierre, V., & Dernelle, R. (2004). Values and religiosity: A meta-analysis of studies using Schwartz's model. *Personality and Individual Differences, 37,* 721–734.

Saroglou, V., & Dupuis, J. (2006). Being Buddhist in Western Europe: Cognitive needs, prosocial character, and values. *The International Journal for the Psychology of Religion, 16,* 163–179.

Sasaki, J. Y., Kim, H. S., & Xu, J. (2011). Religion and well-being: The moderating role of culture and the oxytocin receptor (OXTR) gene. *Journal of Cross-Cultural Psychology, 42,* 1394–1405.

Scherer, K. (1997). The role of culture in emotion-antecedent appraisal. *Journal of Personality and Social Psychology, 73,* 902–922.

Schimmack, U., Radhakrishnan, P., Oishi, S., Dzokoto, V., & Ahadi, S. (2002). Culture, personality, and subjective well-being: Integrating process models of life satisfaction. *Journal of Personality and Social Psychology, 82,* 582–593.

Schwartz, S. H. (1992). Universals in the content and structure of values: Theoretical advances and empirical tests in 20 countries. In M. P. Zanna (Ed.), *Advances in experimental social psychology* (Vol. 25, pp. 1–65). San Diego: Academic Press.

Schwartz, S. H., & Huismans, S. (1995). Value priorities and religiosity in four Western religions. *Social Psychology Quaterly, 58,* 88–107.

Scollon, C. N., Howard, A. H., Caldwell, A. E., & Ito, S. (2009). The role of ideal affect in the experienced memory of emotions. *Journal of Happiness Studies, 10,* 257–269.

Sedikides, C., & Gebauer, J. E. (2010). Religiosity as self-enhancement: A meta-analysis of the relation between socially desirable responding and religiosity. *Personality and Social Psychology Review, 14,* 17–36.

Shapiro, S. L., Schwartz, G. E., & Bonner, G. (1998). Effects of mindfulness-based stress reduction on medical and premedical students. *Journal of Behavioral Medicine, 21,* 581–599.

Shariff, A. F., & Norenzayan, A. (2007). God is watching you: Priming God concepts increases prosocial behavior in an anonymous economic game. *Psychological Science, 18,* 803–809.

Shweder, R. (2003). *Why do men barbecue?: Recipes for cultural psychology.* Cambridge, MA: Harvard University Press.

Silberman, I. (2005). Religion as a meaning system: Implications for the new millennium. *Journal of Social Issues, 61,* 641–663.

Sims, T., Tsai, J. L., Thomas, E., & Goldstein, M. (2013). *Ideal affect shapes medical choices.* Manuscript in preparation.

Smith, H. (1991). *The world's religions: Our great wisdom traditions.* New York: HarperCollins.

Snibbe, A. C., & Markus, H. R. (2002). The psychology of religion and the religion of psychology. *Psychological Inquiry, 13,* 229–234.

Thayer, R. E. (1989). *The biopsychology of mood and arousal.* New York: Oxford University Press.

Tsai, J. L. (2007). Ideal affect: Cultural causes and behavioral consequences. *Perspectives on Psychological Science, 2,* 242–259.

Tsai, J. L., Chentsova-Dutton, Y., Friere-Bebau, L. H., & Przymus, D. (2002). Emotional expression and physiology in European Americans and Hmong Americans. *Emotion, 2,* 380–397.

Tsai, J. L., Knutson, B., & Fung, H. H. (2006). Cultural variation in affect valuation. *Journal of Personality and Social Psychology, 90,* 288–307.

Tsai, J. L., Knutson, B., & Rothman, A. (2013). *The pursuit of ideal affect.* Manuscript in preparation.

Tsai, J. L., Miao, F. F., & Seppala, E. (2007). Good feelings in Christianity and Buddhism: Religious differences in ideal affect. *Personality and Social Psychology Bulletin, 33,* 409–421.

Tsang, J. A., McCullough, M. E., & Hoyt, W. T. (2005). Psychometric and rationalization accounts of the religion-forgiveness discrepancy. *Journal of Social Issues, 61,* 785–805.

Watson, D., & Tellegen, A. (1985). Toward a consensual structure of mood. *Psychological Bulletin, 98,* 219–235.

Watts, F., Dutton, K., & Guilliford, L. (2006). Human spiritual qualities: Integrating psychology and religion. *Mental Health, Religion & Culture, 9,* 277–289.

Wolfe, A. (2003). *The transformation of American religion: How we actually live our faith.* New York: Free Press.

15

The Role of Personality in Understanding Religious and Spiritual Constructs

Ralph L. Piedmont and Teresa A. Wilkins

From the very beginning of American psychology in the latter part of the 19th century, spirituality and religiousness have been seen as having important implications for personality and psychological functioning. Over the years, many theorists outlined how and why our search for the sacred through both personal and organizational efforts was so influential in terms of directing behavior, organizing the sense of self, and contributing to ongoing growth and development. Although interest in these variables has ebbed and flowed over the years, there is no doubt that spirituality and religiousness have experienced a scientific renaissance in the past 20 years (Emmons & Paloutzian, 2003). One reason for this renewed interest is that research has shown that these constructs have numerous behavioral, cognitive, social, emotional, genetic, and neurobiological correlates, underscoring their value as key psychological qualities and shoring up the rationale for utilizing the multilevel interdisciplinary paradigm.

The purpose of this chapter is threefold. First, we argue why religious and spiritual (R/S) constructs should be considered of interest to personality psychologists. Second, we demonstrate how the Five-Factor Model of personality (FFM) can be a useful empirical framework for understanding what are and are not such constructs. Finally, we overview research demonstrating the added empirical and conceptual value that religiousness and spirituality have for the field and the potential contribution they can make to improving existing psychosocial models.

WHY SPIRITUALITY AND RELIGIOUSNESS SHOULD BE OF INTEREST TO PERSONALITY PSYCHOLOGISTS

Within the field of psychology, the term "numinous" has had a narrow focus, such as Otto's (1923/1958) examination of the holy, which he deemed at the center of all religions, or the virtue that emerges from Erikson's (1997) first stage of psychosocial development. Within the popular culture, the term has a broader connotation (utilized in this chapter) and refers to images that an individual perceives to be sacred, hallowed, and awe inspiring and that promote ultimate meaning, personal coherence, and emotional security. Religiousness and spirituality are two elements of this domain. Science has long been reluctant to consider such variables as proper scientific material because the concepts would often conjure up images of metaphysical whimsy and theological orthodoxy. Their inclusion would present a serious violation of scientific principles: One cannot use nonphysical (and hence not falsifiable) constructs as explanatory variables in scientific models. However, the psychology of religion is not grounded in esoteric cosmology but rather is focused on the physical implications of spiritual and religious phenomena on the psychological health and stability of the individual. It is important to realize that R/S constructs are not aimed at examining the nature of God or at whether or not God exists. Instead, the focus is on how *perceptions* of the transcendent impact the texture, tenor, direction, and quality of people's inner lives. As a component to how people organize and frame their sense of selfhood, numinous-type constructs can certainly be empirically validated and their value within larger psychological models clearly tested. Despite their suitability for scientific analysis, the larger question arises: Why should such constructs be studied in relation to personality characteristics? There are four compelling reasons why the field of personality should seriously consider them.

First, spirituality and religiousness are qualities that are present in every culture, age, and civilization (see also Saroglou & Cohen, Chapter 17, and Taves, Chapter 7, this volume). Spiritual understandings and motivations have influenced all aspects of a society: its law, philosophy, medicine, science, technology, architecture, and art to name a few. Such a powerful and profound influence on the human condition warrants significant attention from psychologists. To ignore it is to blind ourselves to a major psychological process, rendering all our theories and models incomplete and interpretively inadequate. Second, spirituality is no doubt a uniquely human experience. No other species shares the depth of thinking and expansiveness of awareness that the numinous affords humanity (Frankl, 1969; Maslow, 1970; Piedmont, 1999a; Sperry, 2001). There is little doubt that these cognitive capacities are an epiphenomenon of our own advanced cortical development. As Baumeister, Bauer, and Lloyd (2010, p. 76) noted: "The capacity to think about the future and orient behavior toward it . . . is arguably one of the most important advances in human cognition, and it may be an essential step in making culture and civilization possible." Piedmont (1999a) defined spiritual transcendence as an individual's innate capacity to construe a broad sense of personal meaning within an eschatological context, which underscores the awareness of one's own mortality. Thus, the study of religion and spirituality examines the expressions of psychological issues that are unique to the human experience and that construct a meaning-making system.

Third, and perhaps most compelling, is that R/S constructs are related to so many outcomes that are of interest to psychologists. Some of the outcomes to which spirituality and religiousness have been linked include mental and physical health, well-being, life satisfaction, psychological maturity, self-esteem, interpersonal style, worldview, sexual attitudes/behaviors, and marital satisfaction. Consequently, if any model of these phenomena is to be inclusive and complete, it needs to include such constructs. Further, as psychological variables, well-developed numinous scales have demonstrated that scores on these dimensions generalize validly across religious denominations, cultures, and languages.

A final reason why R/S constructs should be considered important to personologists is that while such variables may have been overlooked in the mainstream research literature, theoretical psychologists have long realized that spirituality and religiousness are appropriate objects of analysis for the field and need to be included when studying the human mind (see Piedmont's [2005] chapter in the first edition of this *Handbook* for a more detailed review of these approaches). Consequently, an extensive body of literature links personality with spirituality and religiousness, as we have discussed elsewhere (Piedmont & Wilkins, 2013). Beginning with James (1902/1982), psychologists have contemplated the aspects of a religious temperament. James scrutinized religious experiences from multiple perspectives and declared that "to the psychologist, the religious propensities of man must be at least as interesting as any other of the facts pertaining to his mental constitution" (p. 2). Freud (1913/1950, 1927/1961), an atheist, dismissed elements of religion as guilt inducing. However, more recent psychoanalytic work takes a distinctly favorable view of religiousness (see Corveleyn, Dezutter, & Luyten, Chapter 5, this volume). For example, Rizzuto (1979) asserted that the image of God is a transitional object that sustains people throughout their lives. Jung (1938/1966) viewed religion as the "fruit and the culmination of the completeness of life" (p. 50). He emphasized the religious nature of the human psyche (Jung, 1921/1971) and stressed that Freud had failed to see that, instead of being regressive, the symbolization of parental figures into God images was healthy and indicated psychological maturity. Finally, Adler (1927/1998) examined conduits for personality development and noted that *social interest* served as a vital element of a healthy lifestyle. While he thought engagement in some religious activities had value, he cautioned against imbalance and recommended involvement in community activities.

Interest in the numinous finds a home in the newer humanistic and existential approaches as well. Maslow (1970) was interested in the cultivation of humanity's higher nature through the process of self-actualization. An essential component to this move toward Being values was a religious/spiritual orientation. Maslow asserted that spiritual values "do not need supernatural concepts to validate them, they are well within the jurisdiction of a suitably enlarged science" (1970, p. 4). Frankl's (1959, 1969) logotherapeutic approach emphasized the importance of spiritual resources, which he labeled the "nöological dimension—in contradistinction to the biological and psychological ones. It is that dimension in which the uniquely human phenomena are located" (1969, p. 17). He insisted that people have an innate yearning for finding meaning and stressed that the will to find meaning undergirds their capability to suffer and to endure life's negative experiences.

Perhaps the most dominant of personality theories today are those that are trait based, arising out of Allport's (1950) pioneering work. Allport asserted that the religious aspects of the individual represented an organizing praxis of the personality that had implications for all other aspects of psychological functioning. For Allport, R/S served as a cardinal trait, a quality by which the operation of one's personality system is guided and directed. It enjoys this important status because of its seemingly singular place within the psychic system.

The current articulation of Allport's trait approach is found in the FFM, a comprehensive and robust taxonomy of personality traits (Costa & McCrae, 1995; McCrae &

Costa, 1997). The empirical strength of this model makes it an important framework for examining the value of R/S constructs. In the next section, we provide an overview of the FFM and its value for understanding and developing R/S constructs.

THE ROLE AND VALUE OF THE FFM FOR UNDERSTANDING R/S CONSTRUCTS

Over the past 30 years, researchers have converged on the existence of five orthogonal trait dimensions—known as the FFM—that constitute an adequate taxonomy of personality characteristics (Digman, 1990; Goldberg, 1993): neuroticism (N), the tendency to experience negative emotions such as anxiety, depression, and hostility; extraversion (E), the quantity and intensity of one's interpersonal interactions; openness (O), the proactive seeking and appreciation of new experiences; agreeableness (A), the quality of one's interpersonal interactions along a continuum from compassion to antagonism; and finally conscientiousness (C), the persistence, organization, and motivation exhibited in goal-directed behaviors (Costa & McCrae, 1992). Research has found strong cross-observer, cross-instrument convergence, indicating that these dimensions are not a product of any self-distortion or rater bias (e.g., Piedmont, 1994). These dimensions were also found to be extremely stable over the adult life span; 25-year stability coefficients indicate that 80% of the variance in these traits is unchanging, and 60% is estimated to remain constant over a 50-year adult life span (Costa & McCrae, 1994). Finally, these dimensions have a strong genetic basis (Heath, Neale, Kessler, Eaves, & Kendler, 1992), indicating that they are not mere summary descriptions of behavior but rather genotypic tendencies of individuals to think, act, and feel in consistent ways. The value of this model is twofold. Empirically, this model is well defined and robust, emerging even cross-culturally (McCrae & Costa, 1997). Conceptually, these domains are well validated and provide clear definitions of very circumscribed constructs. Therefore, the FFM can serve as a useful reference point for developing and evaluating religious variables (see Piedmont, 1999b, 2005, for a more detailed discussion).

Piedmont (1999b) outlined four ways that the FFM could be fruitfully applied to research on R/S constructs. One recommendation was to correlate such scales with the FFM domains in order to "illuminate the larger motivations and anticipated outcomes of [such] scales" (p. 344). In his chapter in the first edition of this *Handbook*, Piedmont (2005) presented a selection of findings collated from across several different studies that have linked spiritually related scales to the FFM personality domains. Two observations emerged from these data. First, all five personality domains significantly correlated with these various measures. In fact, many of these scales correlated with multiple FFM domains. The associations with the FFM can help anticipate the kinds of personological criteria scores they should predict. Second, the magnitude of these associations was small to moderate in strength, indicating that while R/S constructs have some common ground with personality, they are not redundant with, or reducible to, these dimensions. Piedmont concluded, "Scores on these religious scales contain much information about people that is not accounted for by the FFM . . . it is ultimately what religious constructs do *not* have in common with the FFM that is of the most importance" (1999b, p. 346).

Providing a more systematic evaluation, Saroglou (2010) conducted a meta-analysis of over 70 studies linking personality to the religious constructs. This international sample of more than 21,000 subjects replicated earlier findings (e.g., Saroglou, 2002) and clearly noted the role of A and C as central correlates of R/S constructs. Two important conclusions were drawn from these data. First, the linkage with A and C helps to put into context many observed findings using R/S constructs, such as the effects of religiousness on physical and mental health (outcomes also linked to C) and relations with social support and prosocial behavior (correlates of A). Second, Saroglou argued, these associations also suggested that R/S motivations represent characteristic adaptations of A and C. In other words, religious motivations may be culturally conditioned phenomena that develop from people high on A and C who also live in an environment where religion is present. Being caring, compassionate, and dutiful was hypothesized to predispose individuals to turn to religion and spirituality because of their natural appeal to such motivations. The support for this assertion was based on findings from longitudinal studies that provided evidence of how personality at one point in development predicted R/S experience at a later period. A review of this literature does provide important insights into how the quality and importance of spirituality unfolds over the life course.

SPIRITUALITY AND RELIGIOUSNESS ACROSS THE LIFE SPAN

Wink, Ciciolla, Dillon, and Tracy (2007) stated that "personality plays an important role in shaping religious and spiritual engagement, and, therefore, personality needs to be considered in any effort to understand how religion affects psychological functioning over the life course" (pp. 1067–1068). Addressing that issue has been problematic as a result of several factors such as the lack of a clear and consistent definition of spirituality and of religiousness and the absence in longitudinal research of reliable, valid, and standardized measures. While some evidence indicates that spirituality increases over the life span, conflicting results have emerged when examining religiousness.

Boyatzis (2003, 2005) noted the dearth of research addressing spirituality and religiousness in children and in adolescents. He emphasized the importance of examining the experiential component: "The core of spirituality is a sense of self-transcendence and the core of religion is seeking or being in relationship with the sacred" (2005, p. 136). While children "experience themselves as spiritual beings" (Houskamp, Fisher, & Stuber, 2004, p. 228), gathering quantitative data has been impeded by such elements as their inability to read and write. However, qualitative data have been accruing. Champagne (2003) discussed *sensitive*, *relational*, and *existential* modes of spirituality in preschoolers. On the basis of ethnographic research and clinical work, Mercer (2006) identified four avenues for spiritual expression in children: as mystics, activists, sages, and holy fools. She noted a darker element as well, when they struggle with imaginary monsters and/or real-life stressors. See Richert and Granqvist (Chapter 8, this volume) for an expanded examination of religious and spiritual development in children and Levenson, Aldwin, and Igarashi (Chapter 9, this volume) for their exploration of religious development from adolescence to middle adulthood.

In a study of Australian teens, Heaven and Ciarrocchi (2007) examined the impact of personality on religious values over a 3-year period. Using a measure of Eysenck's Psychoticism scale, which combines both low A and low C, and a marker scale of C, they investigated how changes in levels of those personality variables from the first year to the second year in high school were related to religious values in the third year. Results indicated that for boys there was a negative relationship between psychoticism and levels of religious values, whereas for girls there was a positive relationship between C and religiousness. While some elements of C appeared to predict religious values in later adolescence, the authors stated that among males, the Psychoticism scale was much more related to masculinity, with high scores associated with criminal behavior. Consequently, decreases on psychoticism for boys were related to higher religious values. Although that dimension contains elements of both A and C, the marker scale for C did not significantly predict changes in religious values, which suggested that A may be a key component for boys. Thus, gender could be an important moderator for understanding how personality impacts religious values.

McCullough, Tsang, and Brion (2003) examined the relationships of personality factors measured in adolescence with levels of adult religiousness. Using data from the Terman Longitudinal Study of high-ability children, they demonstrated that parental observer ratings of C, obtained when children were between 12 and 18 years old, correlated significantly with self-ratings of religiousness during adulthood (in 1940–1941). Only C was a significant personality predictor.

Utilizing the same data, McCullough, Enders, Brion, and Jain (2005) identified three reliable types of religious individuals. Each type carved out an arc over time. The first type scored low on religiousness in youth and remained low throughout the life span. The second type scored high on religiousness in youth, and remained so over time. The last type had a moderate level of religiousness in youth which increased into middle age and then decreased again in old age. In being positively related to levels of religiousness, A was the only personality factor to emerge as a variable that predicted membership in the three groups.

Wink and Dillon (2002, 2008) studied longitudinal data investigating spirituality and religiousness over the life span. They examined the development of the constructs in a cohort of over 200 people born in the 1920s, concentrating on a 60-year span from young adulthood until old age. They noted that over the course of adulthood spirituality increased significantly, with the period of middle to late adulthood being particularly impacted, especially for women. In addition, they found a relationship between the amount of negative life events in middle adulthood, such as financial troubles and conflicts within close relationships, and increases in women's spirituality in later adulthood. In contrast, the period from early to middle adulthood was important for the increase in men's spirituality. In this same sample, Wink et al. (2007) examined personality as a predictor of adult religiousness. They noted that levels of A, C, and O in adolescence predicted spiritual seeking and religiousness in old age.

There are several limitations to the longitudinal studies by Wink et al. and McCullough et al. First, because hybrid indices have been developed from available surveys and interview data at different assessment periods, no consistent index was used throughout the studies. Although the personality dimensions of A and C appear to have the highest associations with the R/S variables, the meaning of the relationships across time cannot be patently determined because no clear validity has been established for scores on the measures. Second, for all of the longitudinal studies conducted, the effect sizes linking the religiousness measures and the personality scales have been low to moderate (e.g., beta weights < .25). Finally, because Time 1 spirituality was not partialed from these correlations, it is possible that these cross-time associations merely reflect the artifactual covariance among all these measures present at Time 1. For a complete examination of personality's effect on spirituality, a full cross-lagged design would need to be implemented where the overlap between Time 1 personality and spirituality could be partialed from their cross-lagged Time 2 counterparts (see Marmor & Montemayor, 1977; Oud, 2007, for reviews of this type of design).

Despite limitations in the research to date, three important issues can be discerned from this review. First, psychological theorists have been formulating the role and importance of R/S constructs within the psychic system from the beginning of the field. For these individuals, whether existentialists, humanists, or trait psychologists, religious and spiritual variables serve important psychological functions that promote growth and resiliency. Second, correlations with trait models reveal some essential linkages that help to expand our understanding of how R/S constructs are experienced by individuals, and they partially explain why these variables correlate with outcomes such as prosocial behavior, mental and physical health, and psychological maturity. Third, the causal role of spirituality and religiousness in the mental life of the individual has not been clearly delineated. Some theorists (e.g., Allport) see these constructs as being central to the entire psychic system, impacting all other motivations. Some (e.g., Maslow or Frankl) see R/S variables as operating only at specific levels of development or in concert with other processes of adaptation. The empirical results found with the trait approach have some researchers (e.g., Wink and Saroglou) interpreting the findings as indicating that spirituality and religiousness are outcomes, or adaptations, of these basic trait dimensions. We, however, believe that religiousness and spirituality represent independent psychological dimensions not contained by other constructs, such as those represented in the FFM. As basic motivational constructs, religiousness and spirituality have their own causal influence on behavior. In the next sections, we outline the rationale and data that support this contention.

WHY SPIRITUALITY AND RELIGIOUSNESS ARE NOT PRODUCTS OF OTHER PERSONALITY DIMENSIONS

Given that spirituality and religiousness are individual difference variables, it is appropriate to correlate them with other measures of personality and with the domains of the FFM. From a personological perspective, such associations help to identify the larger psychological qualities that these constructs represent. However, it would be inaccurate to conclude from these relations that spirituality and religiousness are mere by-products or adaptations of these other personality domains. There are four reasons for this.

First, correlations between spirituality and religiousness with the FFM show association but not direction. After all, correlation does not imply causation. Although the direction of association is an essential question to be addressed (which we touch on below), the data presented so far are not able to address this issue. Second, the magnitude of correlations between personality and spirituality/religiousness, although consistent across multiple samples, is relatively small. From individual studies through meta-analyses, the linkages between measures of the FFM and spirituality/religiousness are consistently found to be less than $r = .25$. Such low values are hardly informative interpretively, and they are even less useful when presented as evidence for spirituality and religiousness being products of personality. Associations of this low magnitude may reflect methodological artifacts (e.g., singular reliance on self-report questionnaires) or error (e.g., there is no correction being made for the natural overlap among the FFM domains themselves). With personality explaining less than 7% of the variance in religiousness and spirituality, the larger question is, "What is contributing the other 93%?"

Third, while viewing spirituality and religiousness as outcomes of the FFM domains of A, O, and C may reflect individuals' perceptions of "spiritual" and "religious" people, those qualities do not always match well with the personality styles of individuals who are orthodox or conservative in their religious beliefs. Further, any quick perusal through the Bible presents numerous spiritual people who do not follow this pattern of personality styles. For example, the prophet Jonah, with his insistent prejudiced attitude toward the Ninevites, seems not to reflect the high O and A found in the research. Additional examples suggest themselves, such as Kings Saul and David, Eli the High Priest, and many others. Although variously lacking in the qualities of O, A, and C, those individuals nonetheless are purported to have had strong, direct relationships with God. Clearly, some other personal quality needs to account for this high level of spirituality. Perhaps this is why the stories of these individuals stand out so distinctly: Their ability to connect with God is not correlated to qualities we think someone high on the dimensions of O, A, and C should possess. Judeo-Christian scripture itself proclaims that spirituality is an innate quality all its own endowed to us directly from God: "For the truth about God is known to them instinctively; God has put that knowledge in their hearts" (Romans 1: 19–20; see also Ecclesiastes 3:10). Rather than being a by-product of some other process, our desire to strive to feel connected with something beyond ourselves that we deem sacred may well be a nonreducible aspect of our humanity.

Finally, from a philosophical perspective, if spirituality and religiousness are cultural adaptations working out of one's personality structure, what interest do they hold for psychology? Why study these constructs if they are simply the by-products or outcomes of other processes? Would it not be of greater interest to study those processes that are causing them? Ultimately, the field of psychology is concerned with identifying those psychological qualities, processes, and mechanisms that drive our behavior and direct the course of our lives. Without any causal precedence, spirituality and religiousness have less relevance and value as scientific constructs. In the next section, we provide a different perspective on religiousness and spirituality, seeing both as unique sources of motivation.

UNDERSTANDING SPIRITUALITY AND RELIGIOUSNESS AS INDEPENDENT SOURCES OF MOTIVATION

Rather than relying on simple zero-order correlations, the case for religiousness and spirituality as individual difference dimensions independent of the FFM begins with the factor analysis of trait descriptions adjectives. Goldberg (1990) encountered across multiple samples a factor he labeled "Religiosity," which was defined by terms such as "religious versus nonreligious" and "reverent versus irreverent." Saucier and Goldberg (1998) noted that this dimension has a moderately strong presence in the lexicon and may qualify as an individual difference dimension of some value beyond the traditional FFM domains. Ashton, Lee, and Goldberg (2004) also found evidence for religiosity being an additional, independent factor beyond the FFM. Finally, Saucier and Skrzypinska (2006) provided an extensive and systematic analysis of spiritual and religious constructs and noted that both (1) are independent of the FFM; (2) represent two distinct, nonreducible dimensions having different correlates; and (3) fall within the domain of personality, broadly construed.

Research using questionnaire-based measures of spirituality and religion has shown similar results. For example, MacDonald (2000) factor analyzed a number of spiritually based inventories and derived a measure that captured the resulting dimensions. When this new scale was jointly factor analyzed along with a measure of the FFM domains, he found that the spirituality measure formed an independent dimension from the FFM.

Piedmont (1999a, 2001) used the FFM as an empirical reference point for developing measures of spirituality and religiousness that were independent of the FFM. This research led to the development of the Assessment of Spirituality and Religious Sentiments (ASPIRES) scale (Piedmont, 2010, 2012). The ASPIRES provides measures of spirituality across three correlated facets: Prayer Fulfillment, Universality, and Connectedness. There are also two measures of religiousness: Religious Involvement and Religious Crisis.

Spirituality is hypothesized to represent a fundamental, inherent quality of the individual. Such a construct is referred to as a *motive*. As an intrinsic source of motivation, motives influence the basic adaptive orientation of individuals to their environments. Motives represent universal aspects of human behavior and are found in all human cultures. Religiousness, on the other hand, represents what we will term a "sentiment." A sentiment reflects emotional tendencies that develop out of social traditions and educational experiences (Ruckmick, 1920; Woodworth, 1940), including those related to religion. Sentiments can be very powerful motivators for individuals and have very direct effects on behavior. However, sentiments such as love, gratitude, and patriotism do not represent innate, genotypic qualities such as spirituality. Rather, sentiments create meaning systems for individuals by reflecting integrative themes that help knit coherence to their life processes. That is why the expressions of sentiments can and do vary across cultures and time periods. Sentiments may also be more amenable to change and modification. Thus, spirituality, as an evolved motivation, makes people sensitive to certain experiences, while religiousness helps to structure and gratify the expression of spiritual drives.

The ASPIRES subscales were designed to operationalize aspects of spirituality that are nondenominational and universal. A growing research literature documents the independence of these two dimensions from the domains of the FFM, and demonstrates the incremental validity of the ASPIRES scales to predict a wide range of psychosocially and clinically salient outcomes across samples, cultures, languages, and religious affiliations (see Piedmont, 2010, for an overview of this research). The ASPIRES scale provides empirically sustainable, trait-based definitions of spirituality and religiousness that are generalizable across cultures and religions (e.g., Piedmont, 2007; Piedmont & Leach, 2002; Rican & Janosova, 2010). When factor analysis is employed to cluster variables sharing substantive common variance, religiousness and spirituality consistently form an independent sixth factor from the FFM domains (Piedmont, 1999a; Piedmont, Mapa, & Williams, 2006; Rican & Janosova, 2010).

Understanding religiousness and spirituality as a separate dimension of personality has important implications. For example, decoupling spirituality and religiousness from personality is conceptually consistent with how spiritual growth and transformation is thought to occur, especially in adulthood. If spirituality were an outcome of personality, then any spiritual growth would need to be predicated on changes in the underlying levels of personality (e.g., O, A, and C). However, those personality dimensions have been shown to be very stable in adulthood (e.g., Costa & McCrae, 1994), thus making changes in spirituality unlikely. But spiritual change does happen, and there are theoretical and empirical models that indicate individuals do experience systematic changes in their spiritual levels over the life span (e.g., Dalby, 2006; Wink & Dillon, 2002, 2008). Because adult spirituality does change, and adult personality does not, this implies that spirituality reflects a separate psychological process.

The FFM provides useful empirical scaffolding for developing, defining, and validating spiritual and religious constructs. The value of the FFM is threefold. First, by empirically identifying spiritual qualities that are independent of the FFM, researchers can more objectively articulate those elements that do and do not constitute the R/S domain. Second, while finding a rational consensus on the nature of spiritual constructs may be elusive, a data-driven approach transcends partisanship (theoretical and theological) by virtue of its ability to describe events objectively and the presence of established standards for assessing empirical adequacy. Finally, the FFM also provides a foundation for linking R/S constructs to existing psychological models of functioning.

KEY ISSUES IN RESEARCH

In the previous edition of the *Handbook,* Piedmont (2005) identified five key empirical issues that confronted the field at that time: Since that writing, it seems appropriate to examine what progress has occurred. (1) understanding the personological content of R/S scales; (2) establishing the incremental validity of R/S scales; (3) the structural nature of religious and spiritual constructs; (4) the causal relationships between the numinous and the psychological; and (5) spirituality and religiosity as human universals. Each of these topics are addressed in turn.

Understanding the Personological Content of R/S Scales

What exactly do measures of spirituality and religiousness capture about individuals? The first step in any scientific enterprise is the accurate description of the phenomenon of interest. Without a coherent, accurate, and consensual definition of what it is that is being evaluated, it is impossible to create a cohesive, cumulative database. This was, and continues to be, a significant problem for the field. Kapuscinski and Masters (2010), in their recent review of measures of spirituality, noted, "The findings of the present review confirm the lack of agreement regarding the operationalization of spirituality" (p. 195). The range of definitions for R/S measures is quite broad, leading to potential problems concerning discriminant validity of the constructs. This has led to some serious empirical criticisms of the field, such as numinous-type constructs being merely the "religification" of already existing personality variables (van Wicklin, 1990). Buss (2002) flatly stated that spiritual and religious constructs "may simply parasitize existing evolved mechanisms or represent by-products of them" (p. 203). Without clear definitions, it will be impossible to demonstrate the scientific potency of R/S constructs. One place to begin to outline what spiritual scales capture is to relate them to larger models of personality.

As we have argued, the FFM provides a fitting place to begin to seek answers to questions relating to the personological content of R/S scales. It is encouraging to see more researchers using the FFM as an empirical and conceptual reference point to their work. Saroglou (2010) provided the most ambitious and comprehensive assessment of how spiritual and religious scales overlap with the FFM. Those points of contact provide interpretively useful insights into R/S scales. The use of trait-based personality models for evaluating such scales helps to build bridges with the larger psychological sciences, demonstrating not only the relevance of such constructs for understanding psychological dynamics but also helping researchers to better define, and refine, their constructs.

Ultimately, however, we believe that what will be of most interest to researchers will be what religious and spiritual scales *do not* share in common with other personality constructs. This nonoverlapping variance is what contains the value of R/S constructs: what they add to our understanding of individuals over and above any contribution of existing psychological constructs. As such, we believe that the FFM can be used as part of an *empirical* process for defining what is and is not a numinous-type variable.

We would suggest that any set of potential items for an R/S scale first be correlated with markers of the FFM, with those having substantial relationships being deleted from further consideration. This will have the result of leaving only items that are assessing content that reflects something new personologically (see Piedmont, 2010, on the development of the ASPIRES). Because these items were selected originally because of their theoretical relationship to numinous qualities, the items would represent appropriate, empirical prototypes for spiritual and religious qualities. Identifying a pool of such items would help to define the breadth of the domain. Then, analyses of these items can be used to develop a definition(s) of what religiousness and spirituality appear to represent.

Another way to define that domain would be to factor analyze a number of spiritual and religious scales jointly with markers of the FFM. In this manner, it would be possible to identify R/S qualities that are independent of the FFM. For example, Piedmont et al. (2006) jointly factor analyzed the Fetzer/National Institute of Health Brief Multidimensional Measure of Religiousness/Spirituality (BMMRS) with markers of the FFM. Because the BMMRS contains short forms of 12 different R/S measures, it was seen as an ideal measure for capturing a broad range of numinous phenomena. Four dimensions emerged. The first contained the five personality dimensions as well as measures reflecting forgiveness. The second dimension captured spiritual-type issues (e.g., "I look to God for strength"); the third dimension captured religious-type themes (e.g., "I frequently read the Bible or other religious literature"); and the fourth factor reflected issues of religious crisis (e.g., "I feel that God has abandoned me"). Because the FFM dimensions did not correlate at all with these other three factors, Piedmont et al. (2006) argued that these qualities represent essential elements of R/S functioning. Forgiveness would be considered outside the content domain of spirituality because of its significant overlap with the FFM domains. While some may object to this conclusion, we believe that relying on the FFM as the objective, empirical arbiter for defining content will result in the accumulation of a set of items (scales) that represent a new category of personality motivations. An examination of the content of these identified items (scales) will provide the foundation for defining what spirituality is.

Establishing the Incremental Validity of R/S Scales

The ultimate value of any construct is determined by what it can contribute to our understanding of a phenomenon over and above what is currently known. Science dislikes redundancy and seeks to identify the fewest elements necessary to explain an outcome. Sechrest (1963) proposed the term "incremental validity" to identify the process by which one determines whether a test does, in fact, result in an increase in the accuracy of some prediction over a baseline model. More information does not always result in improved understanding, and the incremental validity process provides a true test of the scientific value of a construct by discerning which information is complementary and which is redundant. While we noted previously those critics of the field who question the nature of numinous-type constructs, others question their usefulness for understanding psychological processes. Funder (2002) argued that the psychology of religion should not even exist as a subfield, positing that the "lack of internal coherence" only serves to further "Balkanize" (pp. 213–214) the social science of psychology. R/S constructs add only unnecessary information.

The only response to such criticisms is to demonstrate the incremental validity of such constructs. While some disagree with the incremental validity approach (see McCrae, 2010), others have echoed Piedmont's (1999b, 2005) call for demonstrating the unique, substantive value of spirituality and religiousness over and above the contribution of other variables. For example, Kapuscinski and Masters (2010) noted that "for spiritual and religious concepts to become prominent within mainstream psychology, studies will need to demonstrate that they are empirically and conceptually distinct from other constructs, and add predictive power for important psychosocial outcomes" (p. 200). In the past few years, there have been several studies utilizing methods such as hierarchical multiple regression, structural equation modeling, and mediation analyses, which examined the incremental predictive power of spirituality and religiousness. Froehlich, Fialkowski, Scheers, Wilcox, and Lawrence (2006) found spiritual maturity to be a significant predictor of total social support and of life satisfaction after controlling for universal and religious demographics and personality factors. Murray and Ciarrocchi (2007) discovered that both spirituality and religiousness predicted positive affect after controlling for personality. Piedmont, Ciarrocchi, Dy-Liacco, and Williams (2009) reported that together spirituality and religiousness demonstrated incremental validity over personality for a number of psychosocial outcomes, such as attitude toward abortion, individualism, interpersonal orientation, total materialism, and prosocial behavior (see Dy-Liacco, Piedmont, Murray-Swank, Rodgerson, & Sherman, 2009; Piedmont, 2007; Rican & Janosova, 2010, for additional examples employing cross cultural and cross denominational samples).

Because these studies employed a number of different measures, the findings reinforce the fact that many current R/S scales are capturing qualities of individuals not contained by traditional personality dimensions (see Kapuscinski & Masters, 2010, for an excellent overview of current measures). There is no doubt that such constructs provide new insights into individuals and how they create meaning and purpose in their lives, and studies such as these are the empirical justification for this perspective. The increasing recognition of the need for more incremental validity research is an encouraging barometer for the field, and the growing body of such findings counters the notion that spirituality and/or religion can be reduced to "nothing more than" (see Pargament, 2002) some other psychological process.

The Structural Nature of R/S Constructs

In his chapter on personality in the first edition of this *Handbook,* Piedmont (2005) argued for the need to clarify the relationship between spirituality and religiousness (Piedmont, 2005). Research has shown that most individuals see the two constructs as being quite similar (Musick, Traphagan, Koenig, & Larson, 2000; Zinnbauer & Pargament, 2005). Musick et al. questioned whether there is a meaningful distinction between these two constructs or if any disparities are "simply an artifact of the wishes of researchers hoping to find such differences" (p. 80). To use different terms would necessitate both the development of a conceptual model that makes significant differences between the two concepts and the presence of data that evidences the predictive value of making such a distinction.

While current research has become consistent in defining spirituality as a more personal, private quality and religiousness as more of an involvement in specific faith-based rituals and practices, little research has examined their empirical differences. As noted earlier, the ASPIRES scale distinguishes between spirituality (an intrinsic, universal motivation that drives, directs, and selects behavior) and religiousness (representing a sentiment: a learned value, belief, or attitude). This model views spirituality and religiousness as related constructs but having different psychological implications that support their separate usage. Because the ASPIRES scale contains measures of both types of constructs, empirical tests of these assumptions are possible.

Piedmont et al. (2009) examined these theoretical issues with two sets of conceptually important models using structural equation modeling (SEM). SEM is a multivariate technique that examines the value of causal models by testing the extent to which the correlations implied by the model are found in actual data. SEM also allows one to compare several different competing models and to determine which is superior. The first series of models examined how spirituality and religiousness related to each other: Were they independent predictors of psychological growth (Model 1) or were they correlated predictors of growth (Model 2)? If they were correlated, should they be collapsed to form a single predictor dimension (Model 3)? The results showed that Model 2 was superior; spirituality and religiousness were highly correlated (phi = .71) but not redundant. Each retained sufficient unique variance to warrant separate interpretation.

The next series of analyses evaluated models that examined whether spirituality and religiousness were predictors or consequences of psychological growth and, if predictors, which of the two was more fundamental. Were spirituality and religiousness the products of psychological growth (Model 4)? If not, was spirituality the predictor of both growth and religiousness (Model 5), or was religiousness the predictor of both growth and spirituality (Model 6)? Model 5 was found to be superior to the others. This model presented spirituality, the underlying motivation, as a cause of both religiousness and psychological growth. This is an important finding for two reasons. First, if this model is correct, it suggests that a perceived relationship with a transcendent reality could have positive consequences for a person's emotional health and stability. Second, it supports the ASPIRES model in that spirituality represents the more basic motivating dimension.

Levels of spirituality motivate individuals to seek out opportunities to gratify this need. Religion and its attendant rituals provide one such outlet for individuals to express and fulfill their spiritual needs. There may well be other outlets.

Although these findings have been replicated cross-culturally using a different measure of spirituality (e.g., Dy-Liacco et al., 2009), clearly more research is needed in this area. Of particular interest is identifying the underlying factor structure of spirituality and religiousness. Are they multidimensional or multifaceted qualities? A multidimensional scale is one that contains several, independent dimensions. Scores on one of these dimensions do not correlate with scores on any other, and information contained across these dimensions is nonredundant. A multifaceted scale, on the other hand, is one that contains multiple dimensions that are all correlated to some degree. This overlap exists because the dimensions are all emerging from a common latent construct. Multidimensional scales provide breadth of coverage, while multifaceted scales provide greater fidelity of assessment for a single domain. R/S constructs are frequently conceived of as being multidimensional in nature (e.g., Hill et al., 2000), although few data exist to support this contention. The best method to accomplish this analysis would be to jointly factor analyze measures of spirituality and religiousness along with measures of the FFM. Such a joint analysis would enable an evaluation of the dimensionality of the R/S scales within a factor space defined by personality. If multiple dimensions do exist within the scales, their redundancy with personality can be determined. Continuing our rationale from the first point discussed in this section, a numinous dimension would be considered multidimensional if it contained multiple factors that were *independent* of personality and each other.

The Causal Relationships between the Numinous and the Psychological

Of all the issues confronting the field today, this is perhaps the most important. Ultimately, this issue will determine the scientific value of R/S constructs. We have outlined our position earlier in this chapter, believing that spirituality and religiousness represent, ultimately, causal agents that impact our mental world. Given the correlational nature of all the data pertinent to this question, no resolution is yet possible. While researchers are becoming more aware of this issue of causality, to provide more concrete answers will require a reliance on more sophisticated technology in the field. As Kapuscinski and Masters (2010) have noted, better scales are needed if the field is going to be integrated into mainstream psychology. Such scales will need to employ more sophisticated psychometric techniques (e.g., use of observer ratings and the incremental validity paradigm, replication across varied samples). The data obtained from these scales will need to be analyzed with more advanced analytic techniques, such as SEM and time series analyses. No longer can the field rely on simple cross-sectional, correlational designs relating single-item measures to an outcome without controlling for any relevant covariates.

Longitudinal and experimental designs are necessary for providing stronger tests of our models and measures. The field needs to demonstrate how, and under what conditions, R/S constructs impact human functioning. In our opinion, the field must begin to rely more on empirically based procedures for defining the basic qualities that define the domain. There need to be clear, empirically verifiable criteria that must be met before an instrument can be seen as being a valid measure of spirituality or religiousness. Then the field will be ready to address this most challenging of issues: the relevance and importance of spirituality as a construct for describing psychological functioning. Perhaps the next edition of this *Handbook* will be able to report on the achievements in this area.

Spirituality and Religiousness as Human Universals

In the last 6 years, there has been promising, albeit limited, research examining the cross-cultural implications of the R/S dimensions, some of which has utilized the ASPIRES scales. The elimination of the emphasis on Christianity exhibited by some of the other available measurements in the field of the psychology of religion makes the ASPIRES instrument particularly appealing. Rican and Janosova (2010) found Piedmont's model to generalize to an atheistic culture. They developed the *Prague Spirituality Questionnaire* (PSQ), and using a sample of 323 secularized Czech college students, they replicated Piedmont's findings of spirituality as a separate personality factor. Tomcsányi, Ittzés, Horváth-Szabó, Martos, and Szabó (2010) were able to validate the Hungarian version of ASPIRES, using over 580 questionnaires. Via SEM, Chen (2011) successfully replicated the factor structures of both the Spiritual Transcendence Scale and the Religious Sentiments Scale in a sample of 547 native Chinese in Mainland China.

Current research in other countries has examined the impact of spirituality and of religiousness while utilizing additional scales. In a sample of 90 Polish students, Rózycka (2011) employed the Lexical Decision Task (Meyer & Schvaneveldt, 1971), and found a significant difference in response times between the control and experimental groups in recognizing what she termed "transcendental" words, compared with neutral words and nonsense words. While conducting research with university students from 37 different countries, she also discovered a strong negative correlation between spirituality and those believing in life as a zero-sum game (rho = −.78, N = 6138). She concluded that spirituality appears to be a pan-cultural, psychological dimension.

van Dierendonck, Rodríguez-Carvajal, Moreno-Jiménez, and Dijkstra (2009) defined inner resources as an element of spirituality. They noted, "To understand inner resources as a spiritual nonspecific personal resource, it is important to realize that they presuppose a universal capacity through which strength and support can be uncovered" (p. 751). van Dierendonc et al. studied the relationship between personality integration and individual well-being in two undergraduate samples: one from the Netherlands and one from Spain. They measured personality integration by focusing on goal integration, active–passive thinking, and inner resources; they examined well-being via a measure of vitality. They found that inner resources had a buffering effect on vitality, especially when goals conflicted.

Coleman et al. (2011) used the Royal Free Interview for Religious and Spiritual Beliefs and the Hospital Anxiety and Depression–Depression scale to analyze the impact of spirituality and religiousness on health issues among the elderly. The authors conducted interviews with samples of elderly residents of villages in Bulgaria and Romania (N = 160), and also performed a 1-year follow-up analysis of the Bulgarian sample. Results revealed an association between spiritual and religious belief and practice and the ability to cope with physical and mental health problems.

Unfortunately, the lack of clear definitions for the variables (e.g., spirituality, religiousness, personality factors, inner resources, purpose in life, and resilience) across many of the studies noted previously underscores the persistent need for consistency in labeling the terms. On a more positive note, the successful utilization of those variables across so many different cultures demonstrates that the concepts are not limited to Western perspectives and Judeo-Christian faiths. When R/S constructs are properly measured, their value as universal elements of personality may be substantiated.

CONCLUSIONS

Interest in the psychology of religion continues unabated. Professionals from both the social and physical sciences are coming to recognize the value of R/S constructs in their work. This sustained and growing interest is supported by the increasing number of research studies being published that continue to document the value of R/S constructs. In our opinion, it is the empirical value of this work that supports the continuing interest in this field. There have been some important new studies that attempt to highlight the universal robustness of R/S constructs for predicting a broad array of psychosocially relevant outcomes. Increasingly, these empirical findings are being replicated across cultures, religions, and samples. These results will continue to fuel interest in this area.

It is hoped that this chapter has provided three points of interest to the reader: (1) a compelling rationale for understanding R/S constructs as psychologically important constructs; (2) data supporting the predictive and interpretive utility of spiritual and religious measures; and (3) an empirical framework for evaluating and conducting future research in this field. We believe that the use of more sophisticated empirical techniques will help the field better define its constructs and assess the value of its research.

ACKNOWLEDGMENTS

We would like to thank Rose Piedmont for her efforts at proofreading and copyediting earlier versions of this chapter.

REFERENCES

Adler, A. (1998). *Understanding human nature: The psychology of personality.* Center City, MN: Hazelden. (Original work published 1927)

Allport, G. W. (1950). *The individual and his religion.* New York: Macmillan.

Ashton, M. C., Lee, K., & Goldberg, L. R. (2004). A hierarchical analysis of 1,710 English personality-descriptive adjectives. *Journal of Personality and Social Psychology, 87,* 707–721.

Baumeister, R. F., Bauer, I. M., & Lloyd, S. A. (2010). Choice, free will, and religion. *Psychology of Religion and Spirituality, 2,* 67–82.

Boyatzis, C. J. (2003). Religious and spiritual development: An introduction. *Review of Religious Research, 44*(3), 213–219.

Boyatzis, C. J. (2005). Religious and spiritual development in childhood. In R. F. Paloutzian & C. L. Park (Eds.), *The handbook of the psychology of religion and spirituality* (pp. 123–143). New York: Guilford Press.

Buss, D. M. (2002). Sex, marriage, and religion: What adaptive problems do religious phenomena solve? *Psychological Inquiry, 13,* 201–203.

Champagne, E. (2003). Being a child, a spiritual child. *The International Journal of Children's Spirituality, 8,* 43–53.

Chen, T. P. (2011). *Cross-cultural psychometric evaluation of the ASPIRES in mainland China.* Unpublished doctoral dissertation, Loyola University.

Coleman, P. G., Carare, R. O., Petrov, I., Forbes, E., Saigal, A., Spreadbury, J. H., et al. (2011). Spiritual belief, social support, physical functioning and depression among older people in Bulgaria and Romania. *Aging & Mental Health, 15*(3), 327–333.

Costa, P. T., Jr., & McCrae, R. R. (1992). *The NEO PI-R professional manual.* Odessa, FL: Psychological Assessment Resources.

Costa, P. T., Jr., & McCrae, R. R. (1994). "Set like plaster"?: Evidence for the stability of adult personality. In T. F. Heatherton, & J. L. Weinberger (Eds.), *Can personality change?* (pp. 21–40). Washington, DC: American Psychological Association.

Costa, P. T., Jr., & McCrae, R. R. (1995). Primary traits of Eysenck's P-E-N system: Three- and five-factor solutions. *The Journal of Personality and Social Psychology, 690,* 308–317.

Dalby, P. (2006). Is there a process of spiritual change or development associated with ageing?: A critical review of research. *Aging & Mental Health, 10,* 4–12.

Digman, J. M. (1990). Personality structure: Emergence of the five-factor model. *Annual Review of Psychology, 41,* 417–440.

Dy-Liacco, G. S., Piedmont, R. L., Murray-Swank, N. A., Rodgerson, T. E., & Sherman, M. F. (2009). Spirituality and religiosity as cross-cultural aspects of human experience. *Psychology of Religion and Spirituality, 1,* 35–52.

Emmons, R. A., & Paloutzian, R. F. (2003). The psychology of religion. *Annual Review of Psychology, 54,* 377–402.

Erikson, E. H. (1997). *The life cycle completed. Extended version with new chapters on the ninth stage of development by Joan M. Erikson.* New York: Norton.

Frankl, V. (1959). *Man's search for meaning.* Boston: Beacon.

Frankl, V. (1969). *The will to meaning: Foundations and applications of logotherapy.* New York: Meridian.

Freud, S. (1950). *Totem and taboo.* New York: Norton. (Original work published 1913)

Freud, S. (1961). *The future of an illusion.* New York: Norton. (Original work published 1927)

Froehlich, J. P., Fialkowski, G. M., Scheers, N. J., Wilcox, P. C., & Lawrence, R. T. (2006). Spiritual maturity and social support in a national study of a male religious order. *Pastoral Psychology, 54*(5), 465–478.

Funder, D. C. (2002). Why study religion? *Psychological Inquiry, 13,* 213–214.

Goldberg, L. R. (1990). An alternative "description of personality": The Big Five structure. *Journal of Personality and Social Psychology, 59,* 1216–1229.

Goldberg, L. R. (1993). The structure of phenotypic personality traits. *American Psychologist, 48,* 26–34. doi:10. 1037/0003–066X. 48. 1. 26

Heath, A. C., Neale, M. C., Kessler, R. C., Eaves, L. J., & Kendler, K. S. (1992). Evidence for genetic influences on personality from self-reports and informant ratings. *Journal of Personality and Social Psychology, 63,* 85–96.

Heaven, P. C. L., & Ciarrocchi, J. (2007). Personality and religious values among adolescents: A three-wave longitudinal analysis. *British Journal of Psychology, 98,* 681–694.

Hill, P. C., Pargament, K. I., Hood, R. W., McCullough, M. E., Swyers, J. P., Larson, D. B., et al. (2000). Conceptualizing religion and spirituality: Points of commonality, points of departure. *Journal for the Theory of Social Behavior, 30,* 51–77.

Houskamp, B. M., Fisher, L. A., & Stuber, M. L. (2004). Spirituality in children and adolescents: Research findings and implications for clinicians and researchers. *Child and Adolescent Psychiatric Clinics of North America, 13,* 221–230.

James, W. (1982). *The varieties of religious experience.* New York: Penguin Books. (Original work published 1902)

Jung, C. G. (1966). *Psychology and religion.* New Haven, CT: Yale University Press. (Original work published 1938)

Jung, C. G. (1971). *Psychological types.* Princeton, NJ: Princeton University Press. (Original work published 1921)

Kapuscinski, A. N., & Masters, K. S. (2010). The current status of measures of spirituality: A critical review of scale development. *Psychology of Religion and Spirituality, 2,* 191–205.

MacDonald, D. A. (2000). Spirituality: Description, measurement and relation to the Five-Factor Model of personality. *Journal of Personality, 68,* 153–197.

Marmor, G. S., & Montemayor, R. (1977). The cross-lagged panel design: A review. *Perceptual and Motor Skills, 45,* 883–893.

Maslow, A. H. (1970). *Religions, values, and peak-experiences.* New York: Penguin Books.

McCrae, R. R. (2010). The place of the FFM in personality psychology. *Psychological Inquiry, 21*(1), 57–64.

McCrae, R. R., & Costa, P. T., Jr. (1997). Personality trait structure as a human universal. *American Psychologist, 52,* 509–516.

McCullough, M. E., Enders, C. K., Brion, S. L., & Jain, A. R. (2005). The varieties of religious development in adulthood: A longitudinal investigation of religion and rational choice. *Journal of Personality and Social Psychology, 89,* 78–89.

McCullough, M. E., Tsang, J., & Brion, S. (2003). Personality traits in adolescence as predictors of religiousness in early adulthood: Findings from the Terman longitudinal study. *Personality and Social Psychology Bulletin, 29,* 980–991.

Mercer, J. A. (2006). Children as mystics, activists, sages, and holy fools: Understanding the spirituality of children and its significance for clinical work. *Pastoral Psychology, 54,* 497–515.

Meyer, D. E. & Schvaneveldt, R. W. (1971). Facilitation in recognizing pairs of words: Evidence of a dependence between retrieval operations. *Journal of Experimental Psychology, 90*(2), 227–234.

Murray, K., & Ciarrocchi, J. W. (2007). The dark side of religion, spirituality, and the moral emotions: Shame, guilt, and negative religiosity as markers for life dissatisfaction. *Journal of Pastoral Counseling, 42,* 22–41.

Musick, M. A., Traphagan, J. W., Koenig, H. G., & Larson, D. B. (2000). Spirituality in physical health and aging. *Journal of Adult Development, 7*(2), 73–86.

Otto, R. (1958). *The idea of the holy.* Oxford, UK: Oxford University Press. (Original work published 1923)

Oud, J. H. L. (2007). Continuous time modeling of reciprocal relationships in the cross-lagged panel design. In S. Boker & M. Wenger (Eds.), *Data analytic techniques for dynamical systems* (pp. 87–129). Mahwah, NJ: Erlbaum.

Pargament, K. I. (2002). Is religion nothing but . . . ? Explaining religion versus explaining religion away. *Psychological Inquiry, 13,* 239–244.

Piedmont, R. L. (1994). Validation of the NEO-PIR observer form for college students: Toward a paradigm for studying personality development. *Assessment, 1,* 259–268.

Piedmont, R. L. (1999a). Does spirituality represent the sixth factor of personality?: Spiritual transcendence and the five-factor model. *Journal of Personality, 67,* 983–1013.

Piedmont, R. L. (1999b). Strategies for using the Five-Factor Model of personality in religious research. *Journal of Psychology and Theology, 27*(4), 338–350.

Piedmont, R. L. (2001). Spiritual transcendence and the scientific study of spirituality. *Journal of Rehabilitation, 67,* 4–14.

Piedmont, R. L. (2005). The role of personality in understanding religious and spiritual constructs. In R. F. Paloutzian & C. L. Park (Eds.), *The handbook of the psychology of religion and spirituality* (pp. 253–273). New York: Guilford Press.

Piedmont, R. L. (2007). Cross-cultural generalizability of the Spiritual Transcendence Scale to the

Philippines: Spirituality as a human universal. *Mental Health, Religion & Culture, 10*(2), 89–107.

Piedmont, R. L. (2010). *Assessment of spirituality and religious sentiments, technical manual* (2nd ed.). Timonium, MD; Author.

Piedmont, R. L. (2012). Overview and development of a trait-based measure of numinous constructs: The Assessment of Spirituality and Religious Sentiments (ASPIRES) scale. In L. Miller (Ed.), *The Oxford handbook of the psychology of spirituality and consciousness* (pp. 104–122). New York: Oxford University Press.

Piedmont, R. L., Ciarrocchi, J. W., Dy-Liacco, G. S., & Williams, J. E. G. (2009). The empirical and conceptual value of the Spiritual Transcendence and Religious Involvement scales for personality research. *Psychology of Religion and Spirituality, 1,* 162–179.

Piedmont, R. L., & Leach, M. (2002). Cross-cultural generalizability of the Spiritual Transcendence Scale in India: Spirituality as a universal aspect of human experience. *American Behavioral Scientist, 45*(12), 1888–1901.

Piedmont, R. L., Mapa, A. T., & Williams, J. E. G. (2006). A factor analysis of the Fetzer/NIA Brief Multidimensional Measure of Religiousness/Spirituality (MMRS). *Research in the Social Scientific Study of Religion, 17,* 177–196.

Piedmont, R. L., & Wilkins, T. A. (2013). Spirituality, religiousness, and personality: Theoretical foundations and empirical applications. In K. Pargament, J. Exline, et al. (Eds.), *APA handbook of psychology, religion, and spirituality* (pp. 173–186). Washington, DC: American Psychological Association.

Rican, P., & Janosova, P. (2010). Spirituality as a basic aspect of personality: A cross-cultural verification of Piedmont's model. *The International Journal for the Psychology of Religion, 20,* 2–13.

Rizzuto, A. (1979). *The birth of the living God: A psychoanalytic study.* Chicago: University of Chicago Press.

Rózycka, J. (2011, April). *Spirituality as a cultural and individual dimension.* Paper presented at the 9th Mid-Year Conference on Religion & Spirituality, Columbia, MD.

Ruckmick, C. A. (1920). *The Brevity book on psychology.* Chicago: Brevity.

Saroglou, V. (2002). Religion and the five-factors of personality: A meta-analytic review. *Personality and Individual Differences, 32,* 15–25.

Saroglou, V. (2010). Religiousness as a cultural adaptation of basic traits: A five-factor model perspective. *Personality and Social Psychology Review, 14*(1), 108–125.

Saucier, G., & Goldberg, L. R. (1998). What is beyond the Big Five? *Journal of Personality, 66,* 495–524.

Saucier, G., & Skrzypinska, K. (2006). Spiritual but not religious?: Evidence for two independent dimensions. *Journal of Personality, 74,* 1257–1292.

Sechrest, L. (1963). Incremental validity: A recommendation. *Educational and Psychological Measurement, 23,* 153–158.

Sperry, L. (2001). *Spirituality in clinical practice: Incorporating the spiritual dimension in psychotherapy and counseling.* New York: Routledge.

Tomcsányi, T., Ittzés, A., Horváth-Szabó, K., Martos, T., & Szabó, T. (2010). Key issues in researching spirituality and religiosity in the light of the ASPIRES instrument (Assessment of Spirituality and Religious Sentiments) developed by Ralph Piedmont. *Psychiatria Hungarica: A Magyar Pszichiátriai Társaság Tudományos Folyóirata, 25*(2), 110–120.

van Dierendonck, D., Rodríguez-Carvajal, R., Moreno-Jiménez, B., & Dijkstra, M. (2009). Goal integration and well-being: Self-regulation through inner resources in the Netherlands and Spain. *Journal of Cross-Cultural Psychology, 40,* 746–760.

van Wicklin, J. F. (1990). Conceiving and measuring ways of being religious. *Journal of Psychology and Christianity, 9,* 27–40.

Wink, P., Ciciolla, L., Dillon, M., & Tracy, A. (2007). Religiousness, spiritual seeking, and personality: Findings from a longitudinal study. *Journal of Personality, 75,* 1051–1070.

Wink, P., & Dillon, M. (2002). Spiritual development across the adult life course: Findings from a longitudinal study. *Journal of Adult Development, 9*(1), 79–94.

Wink, P., & Dillon, M. (2008). Religiousness, spirituality, and psychosocial functioning in late adulthood: Findings from a longitudinal study. *Psychology of Religion and Spirituality, 1,* 102–115.

Woodworth, R. S. (1940). *Psychology* (4th ed.). New York: Henry Holt.

Zinnbauer, B. J., & Pargament, K. I. (2005). Religiousness and spirituality. In R. F. Paloutzian & C. L. Park (Eds.), *The handbook of the psychology of religion and spirituality* (pp. 21–42). New York: Guilford Press.

16

Religiousness, Social Psychology, and Behavior

Michael E. Nielsen, Arthur T. Hatton,
and Michael J. Donahue

Do people's thoughts about religious issues actually impact their behavior? Social psychology's concern with the broad range of human functioning, from the social stimuli that influence cognitive, emotional, motivational, and behavioral outcomes, to its work on persuasion and group interaction, brings with it the potential to shed light on the practical effects of people's religiousness. By this, we are not merely concerned with whether Catholics attend mass more than Methodists do, or other questions that are not very psychologically interesting. Much more meaningful are questions such as, Are people who are reminded of God more likely to be honest? Do religious involvement and spirituality predict differences in premarital sexuality? When does religiousness predict helping, and when does it predict discrimination toward others? Religions are social enterprises, and if religious beliefs and thoughts are meaningful, they should be expected to have behavioral consequences.

Because much of the research in the social psychology of religion was shaped by Allport's classic research on religious orientation, we begin with an overview of that work. The remainder of the chapter follows the common divisions of a social psychology text: social thought, social influence, and social relations. Space precludes this chapter from being expansive, but in some cases there is sufficient depth in the research literature that topics one might expect to find here are discussed in their own chapters, especially Chapters 17 on cultural issues, Chapter 23 on fundamentalism and authoritarianism, Chapter 25 on morality and self-control, and Chapter 32 on religious violence and terrorism.

DIFFERENT WAYS OF BEING RELIGIOUS: INTRINSIC, EXTRINSIC, AND QUEST

Intrinsic and Extrinsic

Allport's method of describing religion as either intrinsic or extrinsic continues to hold considerable sway in the social-psychological literature on psychology of religion, but as with most major measures in psychology, it has both proponents and detractors. Some people swear by it; some people swear at it. The story of its development is well known (see Donahue, 1985). Originally, the concept was proposed as a bipolar continuum between (1) the intrinsically religious, for whom religion is an end, the guiding force in life, and (2) the extrinsically religious, for whom religion is a source and relief and protection, just one of many affiliations. But when data began to be collected, instead of the expected strong negative correlation between the two subscales, the correlation was rather low (–.21), and so it was proposed that the two should be treated as separate and orthogonal constructs, in light of the weak relationship and the finding that people scoring high on both the intrinsic (I) and extrinsic (E) tended to be among the most prejudiced, and those scoring high only on I tended to be the least prejudiced (Allport & Ross, 1967). Although criticized very quickly, the scale and its underlying constructs remain prominent in social psychological work on religiousness.

Several revisions have been offered for the I and E scales, summarized in the first edition of this chapter (Donahue & Nielsen, 2005) and Hill and Hood's (1999) compendium of scales. Hoge's (1972) Intrinsic Religious Motivation Scale, based on a more bipolar model of the concepts, remains popular among those examining topics in mental and physical health, as does the Duke University Religion Index (Koenig, Meador, & Parkerson, 1997). Gorsuch and his colleagues offered two revisions of the scale: first an "age-universal" version, which reduced the reading level of the items (Gorsuch & Venable, 1983), and then a revised scale and suggested single-item measures (Gorsuch & McPherson, 1989). This latter version took into account research by Kirkpatrick (1989) indicating that E is best described as a two-dimensional construct: a "personal" E and a "social" E. Most recently, Francis (2007) has proposed the New Indices of Religious Orientation (NIRO). It presents scales with equal numbers of items measuring I, E, and Quest (Q, discussed later), with scales intended to correct problems with other scales in terms of their length, the weight accorded to components in each construct, and language accessibility. It is not yet widely used but appears promising.

Current Research

Donahue (in press) has assembled a database of articles for a meta-analysis of research using I, E, and Q over a 5-year period (2006–2010) in order to describe the current state of research that employs the I-E typology, using scales that have more or less direct descent from those proposed by Allport and Ross (1967): for example, the Age-Universal I/E scale (Gorsuch & Venable, 1983), the I/E-Revised (Gorsuch & McPherson, 1989), the Religious Life Inventory (Batson & Ventis, 1982), and the NIRO. At least 283 empirical I-E studies were reported during the 5-year period, including journal articles, books, and dissertations. The most popular operationalization of I and E was the Gorsuch and McPherson (1989) I/E-Revised, with one third of the studies using it. Twenty-four percent of the studies were said simply to use the Allport and Ross (1967) scales, but what this means is unclear, because the original scales had a unique, stem-specific response format (e.g., for frequency of church attendance), which was a 4-point scale without a neutral point, and most of the research reports indicated that the I-E scale they used had a 5-point Likert response format. Next most popular was the I/E-R's "predecessor": the Age-Universal scale (Gorsuch & Venable, 1983) with 15%.

I-E scales have proven quite robust in their application. In contrast to some assertions that they reflect a "conservative Protestant" theological presumption (Hall, Meador, & Koenig, 2008), they have been translated into Urdu for use with Pakistani Muslims (Khan, Watson, & Cothran, 2008), employed with Muslims in Bosnia–Herzegovina (Flere, Edwards, & Klanjšek, 2008), and with Israeli Jews (Musgrave & McFarlane, 2004). I and E have been used with a very wide range of topics (cf. Francis, 2007), but there remains too little research connecting I and E to people's actual behavior, focusing instead on their responses to other questionnaire scales or self-reports of behavior. Research using I and E also tends to be simple, relying more on correlational methods than on experimental approaches.

Sample sizes in these studies, although not exemplary, are generally sufficient to allow a reasonable amount of statistical power. The range was from 12 to over 11,000 (the later case being analyses from the Valuegenesis Project; Gillespie, Donahue, Boyatt, & Gane, 2004); the median was 180.

The Fourfold Approach

In his 1985 meta-analysis of IEQ research, Donahue recommended that future researchers using I and E use median splits on the scales, dividing respondents into people who score high versus low on I and high versus low on E, and then analyze the results using a 2 (I: high vs. low) × 2 (E: high vs. low) analysis of variance in order to explore the possibility of an I × E interaction, especially when nonreligious dependent variables are measured. In reviewing the literature, we did uncover four examples using the "fourfold" approach, but in each case the four I-E categories were submitted to a 4 × 1 analysis rather than the intended 2 × 2 in order to examine for the possibility of an interaction.

Perhaps this is for the best. Maxwell and Delaney (1993) have demonstrated that median splits are inappropriate for variables with an underlying continuous distribution and can even produce spurious significance. Of course, this does not eliminate the possibility of examining interactions. Current software allows calculation of interactions in regression models; future researchers are encouraged to employ such analyses. In his 1985 meta-analysis, Donahue noted 70 studies using I and E; that number has now increased to 1,200 studies. As part of the immense increase in studies, the relationship between I and E appears to be changing. Whereas the average correlation between I and E in 1985 was –.21, studies now show large, positive correlations (Donahue, 2012). This may reflect the broader use of the scales and other issues related to sampling.

Quest

Batson (1976) posited a third dimension of religiousness, which he called Quest (Q), to complement (although some would contend supplant) the I and E concepts (see Hood & Morris, 1985, and Batson and Ventis's 1985 reply). The argument was that the I concept, while tapping a concept of religious devotion and commitment, failed to include a maturing, continuing development, and thus might reflect a religious dogmatism. Repeated factor analyses have demonstrated that Q is independent of I and E, but beyond that, exactly what the scale is measuring has been the subject of some debate. Because of an emphasis on doubt in the actual scale items, and its failure to correlate with doctrinal orthodoxy, some contended that it did not actually measure religiousness, but instead tapped an attitude toward religion characterized by continuous seekership without concern for closure.

In most research, Q has been combined with I and E to examine the relationship among the three. In general, Q has been found to be more strongly associated with open-mindedness, openness to experience, and lack of prejudice. In Donahue's forthcoming meta-analysis, 64 studies employed some version of Q. Approximately one-third of the studies have employed Q in the absence of I and E, generally in the context of unpacking the concept of "questing" itself or in conjunction with the study of spiritualities not dependent on religion. Research in this area may be facilitated by a new measure of existential quest that appears largely uncorrelated with religiousness (Van Pachterbeke, Keller, & Saroglou, 2012).

Summary

Research with the I, E, and Q scales continues, with I being employed as a multi-item unidimensional measure of religiousness. Controversy over the measures continues (cf. Hall et al., 2008). But as Kirkpatrick and Hood (1990) have noted, it is time to move past the stage of simply correlating I and E with everything under the sun. Theory has long been among the desiderata of psychology of religion; perhaps, having established measures of important aspects of religiousness, they can be used to move us on toward broader and deeper questions.

SOCIAL THOUGHT

The Self

A guiding idea behind much of the social-psychological research on religion is the notion that people seek meaning about their place in the social world through connections to others and social roles (Hood, Hill, & Spilka, 2009; Park, Chapter 18, this volume). We validate our worth by means of social comparison processes and social judgments, often using religion to anchor our sense of self and to make meaning in the social world. Religion shapes what is viewed as good versus bad and, by implication, judgments about whether individuals are good or bad.

People use outward signs, such as religious dress or grooming, to signify religious identity, group membership, and status (Nielsen & White, 2008). Doing so can lessen feelings of uncertainty about one's identity (Hogg, Adelman, & Blagg, 2010). Identity processes appear to function at a very basic level. For example, theists and atheists exhibit quite different physiological reactions to religious primes, with theists showing little activity at the anterior cingulate cortex relative to atheists, suggesting that atheists' meaning systems were being challenged (Inzlicht & Tullett, 2010; cf. McNamara & Butler, Chapter 11, this volume).

Individuals carry multiple, potentially conflicting, identities, as when conservative Christians who are homosexual are faced with reconciling their religious views with their sexuality. In their nuanced analysis, Gaanzevoort, van der Laan, and Olsman (2011) illustrate this process and the forms it can take, either with identities being integrated or with one identity dominating the other. A comparable examination of racial and religious identities is found in White and White's (1995) study of blacks who joined the Mormon Church in spite of its racial policies at the time. Studies such as these illustrate the impact of identity on religious belief and behavior.

Social Attitudes and Behavior

How do religious attitudes relate to behaviors? As might be inferred from the preceding section, religion's impact on social issues can be complex. We briefly examine three areas that have garnered attention: abortion and stem cell issues, capital punishment, and voting.

Abortion and Stem Cell Research

On politically volatile issues such as abortion and stem cell research, religion weighs heavily in opinion making. In general, as religious involvement increases, opposition to abortion also increases (Hess & Rueb, 2005). Research also shows a distinction being made between elective abortions and abortions performed as a result of trauma such as rape, incest, or health problems of the mother. Over the past 40 years, opposition to elective abortions has intensified among Evangelical Christians, rising from 55 to 75%; and among liberal Protestants, from 15 to over 40%. Catholic opposition, however, has remained relatively stable at about 55% (Hoffmann & Johnson, 2005). A similar pattern emerges among American Hispanics (Ellison, Echevarría, & Smith, 2005).

Religiousness also is associated with views regarding embryonic stem cell research, which uses embryos harvested from unsuccessful fertility treatments to develop new treatments for various illnesses. Those with literalistic and intrinsic approaches to religion are more likely to have moral qualms with embryonic stem cell research than those with a more open, questioning stance toward religion (Nielsen, Williams, & Randolph-Seng, 2009).

Capital Punishment

In jury selection, attorneys often query prospective jurors about their religious beliefs. Having a strong belief in a personal, loving God is associated with less support for the death penalty, whereas jurors who support the death penalty are more likely than others to view the Bible literalistically and to believe that God requires the death penalty for murder (Unnever, Cullen, & Bartkowski, 2006). When such trials reach the sentencing stage, defendants who have declared dramatic conversion experiences enjoyed less severe sentences when the defense attorneys portrayed the offenders as changed and potentially reformable (Miller & Bornstein, 2006). Nevertheless, the effect of religious belief is inconsistent. Although literalism is associated with support for the death penalty, death penalty observers and doubters do not differ in their religious devotion, fundamentalism, or their beliefs about God's mercy toward criminals (Miller & Hayward, 2008).

Voting

Religions also may influence democratic voting and, therefore, the law. While demographic research focuses on denominational affiliation and political participation, social-psychological research has examined differences in voting behavior among people within denominations. For instance, people who believe that God is a frequent, active agent on the world stage are less likely to be personally involved in politics; that is, because they believe that God is taking care of things, there is no reason to be involved personally (Driskell, Embry, & Lyon, 2008).

A cautionary note is in order here. Researchers should not assume that religious attitudes correspond to behaviors. Data from the 2006 Panel Study of American Religion and Ethnicity indicate that this is not the case, as religious identity is one of several important identities, copresent with racial, gender, and other identities. Read and Eagle (2011) demonstrate that among black females, having a personal relationship with God is a better predictor of religious identity, whereas for black males it is weekly church attendance that is a better predictor of religious identity. Among whites, however, these items function similarly for women and for men. Because individuals hold multiple identities, which sometimes conflict with one another, religious identity may be more predictive of attitude–behavior correspondence in some situations, but racial or gender identity may predict more effectively in other situations.

SOCIAL INFLUENCE

Gender

Gender differences in engagement among Christians and people of other religions have been noted for decades, with a general and reliable pattern showing males to be less likely than females to attend services or to declare a religious affiliation (Smith, Denton, Faris & Regnerus, 2002). Although longitudinal data show that as gender roles have changed rates of religiousness are declining (Voicu, 2009), this is not universal. Muslim women in Burkina Faso who consider female genital circumcision a marker of their identity appear to be holding firm to that identity in the face of cultural forces threatening their group (Hayford & Trinitapoli, 2011). Beit-Hallahmi (2003) offers an excellent summary of gender differences in religiousness, noting that theoretical explanations ranging from individual differences and personality to socialization and the structural effects of society all have been applied with some degree of success. In short, gender-related religious differences are multiply determined, and offer a rich area for investigation.

Persuasion

How do people persuade one another in religious matters? In an interpersonal context, research suggests that messages conveying intimacy are more effective than those conveying dominance and formality, as were messages from people considered to be similar to the recipient (Mikkelson & Hesse, 2009). On a broader scale, a study of religious advertising in Hong Kong asked Christian clergy, churchgoers, and non-Christians about their views toward Christian church advertising (Au, 2000). All three groups considered advertising to be helpful in improving understanding about Christianity, but neither Christians nor non-Christians expected ads to result in conversions.

Perhaps the most thorough investigation of religious persuasion in recent years is that of Wright (2008), who examined the relative impact of dispositional, motivational, and situational factors on people's receptivity to a religious message. Wright's data clearly showed that dispositional and motivational factors better predicted interest in a religious message than did situational variables. Loneliness was the single strongest predictor of interest. Consistent with work on attachment (see Kirkpatrick, Chapter 6, this volume, and Richert & Granqvist, Chapter 8, this volume), insecure childhood attachment was associated with interest in the message when the childhood caregiver was nonreligious.

Groups and Religion

In a world that continues to grow in interconnectedness and access to information, how do religious groups try to achieve and maintain influence in the host society? Finke and Stark (2001) consider the competition between religious groups in pluralistic societies such as the United States as similar to a free market economy. In this view, religions compete with one another by tailoring their "products" to recruit or retain adherents. One might assume that this is done by reducing tension with the surrounding culture in order to appeal to the widest "customer base" possible. However, Finke and Stark found that very liberal religions can actually increase their market share by increasing in strictness and tension with the surrounding culture. Religious pluralism and competition also increase religious participation across the board (Finke, Guest, & Stark, 1996).

These results illustrate interesting mechanisms at work. A religious marketplace with intense competition between religions, as in the United States, fosters a culture that emphasizes religious identity, making it more difficult for people to stand on the sidelines without choosing (McGuire, 2002). This "supply side" view of the religious marketplace, which draws on classic sociological (Finke & Stark, 1992) and economic (Iannaccone, 1997) models of religion, suggests that individual motivation and other personal factors are less important than psychologists typically consider them to be.

In such a marketplace, what happens to religious minorities? Americans endorse religious pluralism but this is limited to interdenominational acceptance among Christian groups and does not extend to non-Christians, especially Muslims (Merino, 2010). Although, as Merino points out, those with more contact with non-Christians are more supportive of religious diversity, polls show that atheists are among the least liked people in America (Gervais, Shariff, & Norenzayan, 2011). American Muslims who integrate into American society report higher levels of religious discrimination against them than those who have not integrated into American society (Awad, 2010). Likewise, consider the question of whether Mormons are Christian. Among Protestants and Catholics, intrinsic and personal extrinsic religious orientation scores are negatively correlated with the opinion that Mormons are Christian. Among Mormons, however, the reverse pattern was found (Nielsen & Cragun, 2010).

Why, then, do religious minorities maintain their status in the face of majority pressure? If we ask them, answers point to the conviction that they are forgoing immediate rewards in favor of future rewards, and that their identity places a premium on their group membership (Cragun & Nielsen, 2011).

SOCIAL RELATIONS

Attraction and Intimacy

Many researchers have examined the roles that religious belief may play in bringing people together, with a focus on mate selection and sexuality. Viewed as a basic demographic variable, religious group membership helps to shape relationship patterns. For example, ultra-orthodox Jews use religious networks to determine whom they can date (Milevsky, Nimen, Raab, & Gross, 2011). This is true of other religious groups; Catholics are six times more likely to marry another Catholic than to marry outside the faith (Blackwell & Lichter, 2004). Such homogamy in terms of religion and other basic sociological variables (education, race) appears to be an enduring feature of relationship patterns.

Religiousness also influences sexual activity in relationships. Meier's (2003) analysis of national survey data finds that when religion reduces teenage sexuality rates, it does so by shaping parents' attitudes about sex, which affect teens' attitudes. Of course, attitudes do not always predict behavior; about 56% of U.S. teens who participate in the "pledge" movement to abstain from sex until marriage break their vow (Regnerus, 2007), and they are less likely to use contraception and just as likely as "non-pledgers" to contract sexually transmitted diseases (Brückner & Bearman, 2005).

Data concerning specific sexual practices indicate significant effects of religion. For example, when teens do become sexually active, religiousness is associated with lower rates of oral sex (Vazsonyi & Jenkins, 2010), although they also are at greater risk for unwanted pregnancy because they are less likely to use contraception when they do have sex (Zaleski & Schiaffino, 2000). Not all sexual behavior condemned by religious groups involves a partner. In a study of males at Brigham Young University, men who used pornography showed lower levels of religious involvement as well as lower levels of self-worth and higher levels of depression (Nelson, Padilla-Walker, & Carroll, 2010).

Religiousness is associated with more conservative attitudes about sexual intimacy, but spirituality appears to function differently. Among college men, but not college women, spirituality predicts more permissive attitudes toward sexuality (Brelsford, Luquis, & Murray-Swank, 2011). Additional research such as this would help us to understand not only people's attitudes about social issues but also the constructs of religion versus spirituality (see Oman, Chapter 2, this volume).

Finally, it is important to note that relationships can lead people away from religious involvement. Interviews with ex-Buddhist monks revealed that the desire for relationships and intimacy was a dominant reason for leaving the monastery (Mapel, 2007). A representative sample of more than 11,000 respondents found that, when parents divorce, children are more likely either to change religions or to leave religion altogether (Lawton & Bures, 2001). This was especially true for Catholics and conservative Protestants compared with moderate or liberal Protestants.

Prejudice and Discrimination

How readily to people embrace those who are different? Prejudice is a topic of enduring interest among social psychologists, and examples of prejudice impacting people's behaviors abound. Consider, for instance, how religions are viewed by the electorate. Exit polls measuring support for U.S. political candidates show born-again or Evangelical Christians admitting less support for Romney, a Mormon, and Mormons showing overwhelming support for Romney (Pew Research Center, 2012). Still, Romney overcame weak support among that core group of Republicans to become the Republican nominee. Such an outcome would be much more startling if a Muslim were to run for national office, as 43% of Americans admit to feeling some degree of prejudice toward Muslims, a figure more than double that for Christians, Jews, and Buddhists (Gallup Center for Muslim

Studies, 2010). Whether one considers such examples as illustrating prejudice or simply identity politics, the bottom line is that beliefs can and do affect behaviors.

One consistent theme in prejudice research is the finding that people who represent a threat to one's values are more likely to be the objects of prejudice. This has been found in the case of prejudice directed toward homosexuals (Kazyak, 2011) or toward the irreligious, who are considered untrustworthy by religious believers (Gervais, Shariff, & Norenzayan, 2011). This is confirmed in a nationally representative study of belief, which found that the single greatest factor predicting discrimination against religious "nones" is self-identifying as atheists (Cragun, Kosmin, Keysar, Hammer, & Nielsen, 2012). A different approach to the question offers ethnocentrism as a common link between bias against both atheists and religious conservatives (Yancey, 2010). In this model, people across the political spectrum direct animosity toward outgroup members. Thus, religious fundamentalists find themselves to be the object of animosity from religious liberals and atheists, and atheists find themselves to be the object of animosity from religious believers.

Not surprisingly, far more research has documented the existence of religious prejudice than its reduction. Allport's (1954) classic contact theory is one promising option, and continues to account for the results in some studies of opinions toward religious minorities (e.g., Nielsen, 2009). Still, there is great need for more work examining how to reduce prejudice in religious contexts. Readers interested in prejudice are referred to Rowatt et al. (Chapter 23, this volume) for more relevant work.

Prosocial Behavior

Helping

Do religious injunctions to follow a variant of the "golden rule" result in more helping and cooperation? As summarized in the first edition of this *Handbook*, research typically finds that religion is associated with increases in self-reported helping or prosocial behavior but more limited effects on actual behavior. Several studies in recent years are revealing effects consistent with a *limited prosociality* view, which finds that religiousness predicts prosocial acts directed toward proximal targets (e.g., family members, or ingroup members) but not toward distal targets (Saroglou, 2006).

This line of research is represented well by Saroglou, Pichon, Trompette, Verschueren, and Dernelle (2005), who showed that religiousness is associated with behavioral effects on prosocial behavior, including reductions in aggression and increased levels of helping others, effects confirmed by peers. Similar effects are seen in studies with priming of positive religious words on helping, which increase helping directed toward ingroup members but not toward outgroup members. Researchers in this area should use caution in order to avoid overinterpreting results based on I, E, and Q religious orientation measures, as they reflect differences in other cognitive capacities (Saroglou, 2006).

Other researchers using cognitive priming manipulations augment Saroglou's programmatic work. In a study of Facebook users, a religious context (synagogue attendees) elicited greater levels of trust and helping than did a fitness class or a music performance (Ruffle & Sosis, 2010). In studies such as this, the fact that participants' own religiousness did not affect levels of trust and helping points to the importance of contextual effects, which can be viewed as social modeling or conformity. It is worth noting that the limited prosociality effect mirrors the findings of forgiveness literature, that one's sense of betrayal is greater, and forgiveness more difficult, when an offense comes from an ingroup member (Rowatt et al., Chapter 23, this volume). Both one's helping and one's sense of betrayal are enhanced when the relationship with the other individual is proximal rather than distal.

Honesty

In the first edition of this *Handbook*, we noted that there was little empirical work in the area of religion and honesty. Fortunately, we see progress. Evidence now indicates that honesty appears to be increased—or cheating decreased—when participants are cognitively primed with religious words (Randolph-Seng & Nielsen, 2007; Shariff & Norenzayan, 2007). One promising approach here investigates how one's view of deity affects honesty. People having a more punitive view of God were found to cheat less than those with more benevolent views of God (Shariff & Norenzayan, 2011). This is noteworthy in that it finds a connection between honesty and a measure of religious belief, which has been somewhat elusive in previous investigations.

In a related vein, research employing cognitive priming also shows that exposure to religious words can increase cooperation in people in both a dictator game and a prisoner's dilemma game (Ahmed & Salas, 2011). Players of these games showed more cooperative behavior, and were more generous toward other players of the games, when they had completed scrambled sentence tasks involving religious words rather than nonreligious words. For example, 43.8% of participants who were primed with religious words cooperated in the prisoner's dilemma game versus 26.8% of participants who were primed with the control words.

In his significant new review of the relevant literature, Galen (2012) notes that religious individuals report they are more honest or they help others with greater frequency in a manner consistent with the limited prosociality explanation (Saroglou, 2006). He observes that studies involving priming tend to show effects regardless of the individual's personal religious involvement. Galen also argues that the prosocial effects often attributed to religion are better accounted for by general psychological processes, and research in this area suffers methodological problems, such as inappropriately combining people low in religiousness with those who are nonreligious, obscuring potential curvilinear effects.

In response, Myers (2012) agrees on several of Galen's points and offers eight questions that merit further research, on issues ranging from the value of self-reports and the merits of ingroup giving to the religiousness of people who adopt children or volunteer following a natural disaster. One of Myers's more intriguing suggestions is that we need to better understand the paradox presented by the fact that states with higher levels of religiosity show higher crime rates, but that individuals who are more religious are less likely to have been arrested for a crime. This hints at the role cultural context plays in social-psychological studies of religious attitudes and behavior, an issue that merits further examination. Saroglou (2012) challenges the claim that prosocial effects are a result of social desirability bias in self-reports or are reducible to ingroup favoritism. He also notes research showing that atheists report lower rates of charitable, nonreligious contributions than do churchgoers (Altemeyer, 2010).

Since the publication of the first edition of the *Handbook*, we have seen vigorous research and strong debate in our understanding of the connection between religion and helping or prosocial behavior. This is a rich area for further research as we address questions of causality, motivational effects, and more.

Religion and Aggression

In recent years, intergroup violence and aggression has taken center stage in popular discourse. Are indicators of religiousness, such as belief in God, associated with aggression? Researchers generally have taken either a descriptive (Juergensmeyer, 2003) or correlational (Delamontagne, 2010) approach to the question, making it difficult to answer questions of causality. What such studies do reveal is that rules regarding aggression can vary from one culture to another (Cohen, Nisbett, Bowdle, & Schwarz, 1996), and that religious violence appears to be influenced by individuals seeking groups that offer identity and behavioral parameters, qualities that religion fills quite well. This common thread unites research from India, investigating the status of Sikh or Muslim status in a predominantly Hindu country (Gaur, 2004), and Germany, which found that strong religious ingroup identification mediates Muslim acceptance of religious violence enacted by other Muslims (Fischer, Greitemeyer, & Kastenmuller, 2007). A general conclusion of this research is that violence frequently involves a small group that believes its core, sacred values are threatened by another, larger group (Ginges, Atran, Sachdeva, & Medin, 2011).

Experimental studies of religion-related aggression have been infrequently employed in the past, but are now becoming more prevalent, often using cognitive priming of religion. For example, exposure to religiously sanctioned violence increases levels of aggression among religious believers, as shown in a particularly an experiment involving U.S. and Dutch students (Bushman, Ridge, Das, Key, & Busath, 2007). Participants who believed in God and in the Bible showed more aggressive behavior after they read a Bible passage that depicted God commanding violent acts compared with people who did not read the Bible passage or who were nonbelievers. Cognitive priming research also suggests that actions such as these are nonrational, and that the actors in these situations are acting not necessarily in their own self-interest but, instead, by a sense of moral commitment to what they consider sacred (Ginges & Atran, 2009). In coming years, we expect to see more research using priming to test the roles religiousness plays in aggression and violence.

In the first edition of the *Handbook*, we summarized research on religion-related abuse, indicating that when victims of physical abuse characterized the aggressors as being motivated by religious justifications (e.g., as an interpretation of "spare the rod, spoil the child"), victims suffered more severe mental health symptoms years later (Bottoms, Nielsen, Murray, & Filipas, 2004). There is little more to report in this area of research, other than a finding that Christians scoring high on measures of extrinsic religious orientation and biblical literalism also scored higher on measures of child abuse potential (Rodriguez & Henderson, 2010). This is a topic that deserves more attention from researchers.

Conflict and Politics

Related to classic social-psychological concerns about aggression are those about broader scale conflict and peacemaking. Unfortunately, except for the areas of terrorism (Moghaddam, Warren, & Love, Chapter 32, this volume) and forgiveness (Farhadian & Emmons, 2009; Worthington et al., Chapter 24, this volume), these have received relatively little attention from researchers in the psychology of religion. We refer readers to our chapter in the first edition of the *Handbook* for a good theoretical background for these issues.

Psychologists have devoted little attention to the interaction of politics and religion; the same is true of political scientists (Kettell, 2012). Fortunately, this is beginning to change. Recent research finds that intrinsic religious orientation scores predict Protestant work ethic scores, even after controlling for conservatism (Jones, Furnham, & Deile, 2010). Religiousness simultaneously encourages and discourages support for social welfare (Malka, Soto, Cohen, & Miller, 2011), a finding amplified by Ross, Lelkes, and Russell's (2012) study of Christians' acknowledgment that Jesus might hold views differing from their own on social issues. Given research showing complex effects of religious beliefs on behavior (Driskel & Lyon, 2011), religion and politics seems an area ripe for additional study, both at the individual level as well as the broader, societal level. Collaborations with political scientists may well benefit both disciplines.

RECOMMENDATIONS

In this brief summary, we have seen that people's thoughts about religious issues do impact their behavior. Thinking about God increases honesty and prosocial behavior. Involvement in religious groups reduces the likelihood that teens will engage in sex, but those who do are less likely to use contraception. The broad range of human functioning that social psychologists study, from social cognition to group membership, offers a rich opportunity to better understand people and their beliefs and behavior.

Having surveyed the recent literature, we encourage researchers to consider how they might contribute to this knowledge base. In the area of social thought, the field could use more research dealing with multiple identities. What situational and cognitive factors lead to religious identity being more strongly predictive of behavior than other important identities, such as race or gender? Also worth further examination are "hot button" issues. We have some research on topics such as abortion, but do indicators of religiousness show similar relationships with opinions regarding illegal immigration, war, or social welfare programs? How do these views combine to predict voting behavior, and under what circumstances does one topic overwhelm others in predicting votes? Cognitive priming is becoming more common in social-psychological studies, and it might be a useful vehicle to examine these issues as well.

The topic of social influence strikes us as being most in need of new research. One area worth examining is how one person who is disaffected with his or her religious affiliation might influence another person. What processes occur in such an interaction, and how does one effectively "persuade" in this manner? Additional topics in social influence would include connecting the more sociological work on groups, summarized in this chapter, with psychological research on identity. In other words, can the rational choice model of religious group membership benefit from social identity theory or other perspectives? Also needing attention is conformity in religious groups. How are religious group norms used to shape or control adherents' behaviors? When an individual joins a congregation, how are its norms transmitted? If the new group member does not respond to social pressure, what formal and informal processes are used to instill compliance? Questions such as these are not examined with very great frequency in social psychology in general, and even less so in social-psychological studies of religiousness, but they once were of great interest to researchers. It is time to revisit them.

Topics in social relations that deserve more attention include the relative importance of information about someone's religiousness in determining attraction to that person. For example, for whom do religious similarities matter most, and at what point in a budding relationship do these similarities come to bear most strongly on the question of whether the relationship should continue or end? Questions such as these not only would tell us about attraction but would also be of interest to religious institutions. Relationship research also could benefit from drawing on a greater variety of research methods. An example here would be that a study of prejudice might employ the "lost letter" technique, as we suggested in the first edition of the *Handbook*, and thereby move beyond traditional survey techniques. Finally, the field needs more research on religion and family violence as well as cooperation with political scientists. Such research has the potential to have important practical benefits as well as provide light on issues of theoretical import.

A common theme among many of these recommendations is the role(s) of identity in religious belief and behavior. Religious groups offer an important avenue by which individuals can deal with uncertainty and gain meaning (Hogg et al., 2010; Park, Chapter 18, this volume). This might come by applying social identity theory (Ysseldyk, Matheson, & Anisman, 2010) to investigate how religiousness helps meet needs for affiliation and group membership or how it may exacerbate conflicts between groups. A better understanding of identity in religiousness may also help us better understand large data sets such as the General Social Survey, as implied by Brenner's (2011) finding that although self-reports of religious service attendance overestimate actual behavior, they may serve as a good indicator of individual religious identity. Such an interpretation could help researchers reevaluate a large body of research results, and might be particularly useful in reexamining old data sets using attendance measures in meta-analyses.

Social-psychological perspectives contribute a great deal to our understanding of people's religiousness, but we have significant room to improve the state of knowledge in the field (Donahue, 2005). Creative application of research techniques and continued development of social-psychological theories will help us understand not only why people do the religious things that they do but also the effects of those acts. People are social beings, and our effort to connect and interact with one another has helped to make people's religious acts and behaviors among the most fascinating for psychologists to study.

REFERENCES

Ahmed, A., & Salas, O. (2011). Implicit influences of Christian religious representations on dictator and prisoner's dilemma game decisions *Journal of Socio-Economics, 40*, 242–246.

Allport, G. W. (1954). *The nature of prejudice.* Reading, MA: Addison-Wesley.

Allport, G. W., & Ross, M. J. (1967). Personal religious orientation and prejudice. *Journal of Personality and Social Psychology, 5*, 432–443.

Altemeyer, B. (2010). Atheism and secularity in North America. In P. Zuckerman (Ed.), *Atheism and secularity: Vol. 2. Global experiences* (pp. 1–21). Santa Barbara, CA: Praeger.

Au, A. K. M. (2000). Attitudes toward church advertising in Hong Kong, *Marketing Intelligence and Planning, 18*(1), 39–44.

Awad, G. H. (2010). The impact of acculturation and religious identification on perceived discrimination for Arab/Middle Eastern Americans. *Cultural Diversity and Ethnic Minority Psychology, 16*(1), 59–67.

Batson, C. D. (1976). Religion as prosocial agent or double agent. *Journal for the Scientific Study of Religion, 15*, 29–45.

Batson, C. D., & Ventis, W. L. (1982). *The religious experience: A social-psychological perspective.* New York: Oxford University Press.

Batson, C. D., & Ventis, W. L. (1985). Misconception of quest: A reply to Hood and Morris. *Review of Religious Research, 26*, 398–407.

Beit-Hallahmi, B. (2003). Religion, religiosity, and gender. In C. Ember & M. Ember (Eds.), *The encyclopedia of sex and gender: Men and women in the world's cultures* (Vol. 1, pp. 117–127). Boston: Springer Science.

Blackwell, D. L., & Lichter, D. L. (2004). Homogamy among dating, cohabiting, and married couples. *The Sociological Quarterly, 45*(4), 719–737.

Bottoms, B., Nielsen, M. E., Murray, R., & Filipas, H. (2004). Religion related child physical abuse: Characteristics and psychological outcome. *Journal of Aggression, Maltreatment and Trauma, 8*, 87–114.

Brelsford, G. M., Luquis, R., & Murray-Swank, N. A. (2011). College students' permissive sexual attitudes: Links to religiousness and spirituality. *The International Journal for the Psychology of Religion, 21*(2), 127–136.

Brenner, P. S. (2011). Identity importance and overreporting of religious service attendance: Multiple imputation of religious attendance in the American Time Use Study and the General Social Survey. *Journal for the Scientific Study of Religion, 50*, 103–115.

Brückner, H., & Bearman, P. (2005). After the promise: The STD consequences of adolescent virginity pledges. *Journal of Adolescent Health, 36*, 271–278.

Bushman, B. J., Ridge, R. D., Das, E., Key, C. W., & Busath, G. L. (2007). When God sanctions killing: Effect of scriptural violence on aggression. *Psychological Science, 18*(3), 204–207.

Cohen, D., Nisbett, R. E., Bowdle, B. F., & Schwarz, N. (1996). Insult, aggression, and the southern culture of honor: An "experimental ethnography." *Journal of Personality and Social Psychology, 70*(5), 945–959.

Cragun, R. T., Kosmin, B., Keysar, A., Hammer, J. H., & Nielsen, M. E. (2012). On the receiving end: Discrimination toward the non-religious in the U.S. *Journal of Contemporary Religion, 27*, 105–127.

Cragun, R. T., & Nielsen, M. E. (2011). Social scientific perspectives on the FLDS raid and the corresponding media coverage. In C. K. Jacobson & L. Burton (Eds.), *Modern polygamy in the United States: Historical, cultural, and legal issues* (pp. 209–235). New York: Oxford University Press.

Delamontagne, R. G. (2010). Religiosity and hate groups: An exploratory and descriptive correlational study. *Journal of Religion and Society, 12*, 1–16.

Donahue, M. J. (1985). Intrinsic and extrinsic religiousness: Review and meta-analysis. *Journal of Personality and Social Psychology, 48*, 400–419.

Donahue, M. J. (2005). Disregarding (and disrespecting?) religion in social psychology: The case of the Handbook of Social Psychology (4th ed.). *Archive for the Psychology of Religion, 27*, 45–67.

Donahue, M. J., & Nielsen, M. E. (2005). Religion, attitudes and social behavior. In R. F. Paloutzian & C. L. Park (Eds.), *Handbook of the psychology of religion and spirituality* (pp. 274–291). New York: Guilford Press.

Driskell, R., Embry, E., & Lyon, L. (2008). Faith and politics: The influence of religious beliefs on political participation. *Social Science Quarterly, 82*, 294–314.

Driskel, R. L., & Lyon, L. (2011). Assessing the role of religious beliefs on secular and spiritual behaviors. *Review of Religious Research, 52*(4), 386–404.

Ellison, C. G., Echevarria, S., & Smith, B. (2005). Religion and abortion attitudes among U.S. Hispanics: Findings from the 1990 Latino National Political Survey. *Social Science Quarterly, 85,* 192–208.

Farhadian, C., & Emmons, R. A. (2009). The psychology of forgiveness in the world religions. In A. Kalayjian & R. F. Paloutzian (Eds.), *Forgiveness and reconciliation: Psychological pathways to conflict transformation and peace building* (pp. 55–70). New York: Springer.

Finke, R., Guest, A. M., & Stark, R. (1996). Mobilizing local religious markets: Religious pluralism in the empire state, 1855–1865. *American Sociological Review, 61*(2), 203–218.

Finke, R., & Stark, R. (1992). *The churching of America: Winners and losers in our religious economy, 1776–1990.* New Brunswick, NJ: Rutgers.

Finke, R., & Stark, R. (2001). The new holy clubs: Testing church-to-sect propositions. *Sociology of Religion, 62*(2), 175–189.

Fischer, P., Greitemeyer, T., & Kastenmuller, A. (2007). What do we think about Muslims?: The validity of Westerners' implicit theories about the associations between Muslims' religiosity, religious identity, aggression potential, and attitudes towards terrorism. *Group Processes and Intergroup Relations, 10,* 373–382.

Flere, S., Edwards, K. J., & Klanjšek, R. (2008). Religious orientation in three central European environments: Quest, intrinsic, and extrinsic dimensions. *The International Journal for the Psychology of Religion, 18,* 1–21.

Francis, L. J. (2007). Introducing the New Indices of Religious Orientation (NIRO): Conceptualization and measurement. *Mental Health, Religion & Culture, 10,* 585–602.

Gaanzevoort, R. R., van der Laan, M., & Olsman, E. (2011). Growing up gay and religious: Conflict, dialogue, and religious identity strategies. *Mental Health, Religion & Culture, 14* (3), 209–222.

Galen, L. (2012). Does religious belief promote prosociality?: A critical examination. *Psychological Bulletin, 138,* 876–906.

Gallup Center for Muslim Studies. (2010). *In U.S., prejudice stronger against muslims.* Retrieved from *www.gallup.com/poll/125312/religious-prejudice-stronger-against-muslims.aspx.*

Gaur, S. D. (2004). Aggression amongst majority-minority communities in India. *Psychological Studies, 49,* 245–255.

Gervais, W. M., Shariff, A. F., & Norenzayan, A. (2011). Do you believe in atheists?: Distrust is central to anti-atheist prejudice. *Journal of Personality and Social Psychology, 101*(6), 1189–1206.

Gillespie, V. B., Donahue, M. J., Boyatt, E., & Gane, B. (2004). *Valuegenesis: Ten years later: A study of two generations.* Riverside, CA: Hancock Center.

Ginges, J., & Atran, S. (2009). What motivates participation in violent political action: Selective incentives or parochial altruism? *Annals of the New York Academy of Sciences, 1167,* 115–123.

Ginges, J., Atran, S., Sachdeva, S., & Medin, D. (2011). Psychology out of the laboratory: The challenge of violent extremism. *American Psychologist, 66,* 507–519.

Gorsuch, R. L., & McPherson, S. E. (1989). Intrinsic/extrinsic measurement: I/E Revised and single-item scales. *Journal for the Scientific Study of Religion, 28,* 348–354.

Gorsuch, R. L., & Venable, G. D. (1983). Development of an "age universal" I-E scale. *Journal for the Scientific Study of Religion, 22,* 181–187.

Hall, D. E., Meador, K. G., & Koenig, H. G. (2008). Measuring religiousness in health research: Review and critique. *Journal of Religion and Health, 47,* 134–163.

Hayford, S. R., & Trinitapoli, J. (2011). Religious differences in female genital cutting: A case study from Burkina Faso. *Journal for the Scientific Study of Religion, 50*(2), 252–271.

Hess, J. A., & Rueb, J. D. (2005). Attitudes toward abortion, religion, and party affiliation among college students. *Current Psychology, 24,* 24–42.

Hill, P. C., & Hood, R. W., Jr. (1999). *Measures of religiosity*. Birmingham, AL: Religious Education Press.

Hoffmann, J. P., & Johnson, S. (2005). Attitudes toward abortion among religious traditions in the United States: Change or continuity? *Sociology of Religion, 66*, 161–182.

Hoge, D. R. (1972). A validated intrinsic religious motivation scale. *Journal for the Scientific Study of Religion, 11*, 369–376.

Hogg, M. A., Adelman, J. R., & Blagg, R. D. (2010). Religion in the face of uncertainty: An uncertainty-identity theory account of religiousness. *Personality and Social Psychology Review, 14*, 72–83.

Hood, R. W., Jr., Hill, P. C., & Spilka, B. (2009). *The psychology of religion: An empirical approach* (4th ed.). New York: Guilford Press.

Hood, R. W., Jr., & Morris, R. J. (1985). Conceptualization of quest: A critical rejoinder to Batson. *Review of Religious Research, 26*, 391–397.

Iannaccone, L. R. (1997). Rational choice: Framework for the scientific study of religion. In L. A. Young (Ed.), *Rational choice theory and religion: Summary and assessment* (pp. 25–45). New York: Routledge.

Inzlicht, M., & Tullett, A. M. (2010). Reflecting on God: Religious primes can reduce neurophysiological response to errors. *Psychological Science, 21*, 1184–1190.

Jones, H. B., Furnham, A., & Deile, A. J. (2010). Religious orientation and the Protestant work ethic. *Meantal Health, Religion & Culture, 13*, 697–706.

Juergensmeyer, M. (2003). *Terror in the mind of God: The global rise of religious violence*. Berkeley: University of California Press.

Kazyak, E. (2011). Same-sex marriage in a welcoming world: Rights consciousness of heterosexuals in liberal religious institutions. *Sexuality Research & Social Policy, 8*, 192–203.

Kettell, S. (2012). Has political science ignored religion? *PS: Political Science & Politics, 45*, 93–100.

Khan, Z. H., Watson, P. J., & Cothran, D. L. (2008). Self-control in Pakistani Muslims: Relationships with religious orientation, depression and anxiety. *Journal of Beliefs & Values, 29*, 213–216.

Kirkpatrick, L. A. (1989). A psychometric analysis of the Allport-Ross and Feagin measures of intrinsic-extrinsic religious orientation. *Research in the Social Scientific Study of Religion, 1*, 1–31.

Kirkpatrick, L. A., & Hood, R. W., Jr. (1990). Intrinsic–extrinsic religious orientation: The boon or bane of contemporary psychology of religion? *Journal for the Scientific Study of Religion, 29*, 442–462.

Koenig, H. G., Meador, K. G., & Parkerson, G. (1997). Religion index for psychiatric research. *American Journal of Psychiatry, 154*, 885–886.

Lawton, L., & Bures, R. (2001). Parental divorce and the switching of religious identity. *Journal for the Scientific Study of Religion, 40*, 99–111.

Malka, A., Soto, C. J., Cohen, A. B., & Miller, D. T. (2011). Religiosity and social welfare: Competing influences of cultural conservatism and prosocial value orientation. *Journal of Personality, 79*, 763–792.

Mapel, T. (2007). The adjustment process of ex-Buddhist monks to life after the monastery. *Journal of Religion and Health, 46*, 19–34.

Maxwell, S. E., & Delaney, H. D. (1993). Bivariate median splits and spurious statistical significance. *Psychological Bulletin, 113*, 181–190.

McGuire, M. B. (2002). *Religion: The social context* (5th ed.). Long Grove, IL: Waveland.

Meier, A. M. (2003). Adolescents' transition to first intercourse, religiosity, and attitudes about sex. *Social Forces, 81*, 1031–1052.

Merino, S. M. (2010). Religious diversity in a "Christian nation": The effects of theological exclusivity and interreligious contact on the acceptance of religious diversity. *Journal for the Scientific Study of Religion, 49*, 231–246.

Mikkelson, A. C., & Hesse, C. (2009). Discussions of religion and relational messages: Differences between comfortable and uncomfortable interactions. *Southern Communication Journal, 74*, 40–56.

Milevsky, A., Nimen, D. S., Raab, A., & Gross, R. (2011). A phenomenological examination of dating attitudes in ultra-orthodox Jewish emerging adult women. *Mental Health, Religion & Culture, 14*, 311–322.

Miller, M. K., & Bornstein, B. H. (2006). The use of religion in death penalty sentencing trials. *Law and Human Behavior, 30*, 675–684.

Miller, M. K., & Hayward, R. (2008). Religious characteristics and the death penalty. *Law and Human Behavior, 32*, 113–123.

Musgrave, C. F., & McFarlane, E. A. (2004). Israeli oncology nurses' religiosity, spiritual well-being, and attitudes toward spiritual care: A path analysis. *Oncology Nursing Forum, 31*, 321–327.

Myers, D. G. (2012). Reflections on "Does religious belief promote prosociality?" *Psychological Bulletin, 138*, 913–917.

Nelson, L. J., Padilla-Walker, L. M., & Carroll, J. S. (2010). "I believe it is wrong but I still do it": A comparison of religious young men who do versus do not use pornography. *Psychology of Religion and Spirituality, 2*, 136–147.

Nielsen, M. E. (2009). Opinions regarding polygamy among LDS church members: Demographic predictors. *Archive for the Psychology of Religion, 31*, 261–270.

Nielsen, M. E., & Cragun, R. T. (2010). Religious orientation, religious affiliation, and boundary maintenance: The case of polygamy. *Mental Health, Religion & Culture, 13*, 761–770.

Nielsen, M. E, Williams, J., & Randolph-Seng, B. (2009). Religious orientation, personality, and attitudes about human stem cell research. *The International Journal for the Psychology of Religion, 19*, 81–91.

Nielsen, M. E., & White, D. (2008). Men's grooming in the LDS Church: A qualitative study of norm violation. *Mental Health, Religion & Culture, 11*, 807–825.

Pew Research Center. (2012, February 29). *Religion and the 2012 Republican primaries: Arizona and Michigan.* Retrieved from *www.pewforum.org/Politics-and-Elections/Religion-and-the-2012-Republican-Primaries—Arizona-and-Michigan.aspx.*

Randolph-Seng, B., & Nielsen, M. E. (2007). Honesty: One effect of primed religious representations. *The International Journal for the Psychology of Religion, 17*, 303–315.

Read, J. G., & Eagle, D. E. (2011). Intersecting identities as a source of religious incongruence. *Journal for the Scientific Study of Religion, 50*, 116–132.

Regnerus, M. D. (2007). *Forbidden fruit: Sex and religion in the lives of American teenagers.* New York: Oxford University Press.

Rodriguez, C. M., & Henderson, R. C. (2010). Who spares the rod?: Religious orientation, social conformity, and child abuse potential. *Child Abuse & Neglect, 34*, 84–94.

Ross, L. D., Lelkes, Y., & Russell, A. G. (2012). How Christians reconcile their personal political views and the teachings of their faith: Projection as a means of dissonance reduction. *Proceedings of the National Academy of Sciences USA, 109*, 3616–3622.

Ruffle, B. J., & Sosis, R. H. (2010). *Do religious contexts elicit more trust and altruism?: An experiment on Facebook.* Retrieved from *http://papers.ssrn.com/sol3/papers.cfm?abstract_id=1566123.*

Saroglou, V. (2006, spring). Religion's role in prosocial behavior: Myth or reality? *Psychology of Religion Newsletter, American Psychological Association Division 36, 31*, 1–8.

Saroglou, V. (2012). Is religion not prosocial at all?: Comment on Galen (2012). *Psychological Bulletin, 138*, 907–912.

Saroglou, V., Pichon, I., Trompette, L., Verschueren, M., & Dernelle, R. (2005). Prosocial behavior and religion: New evidence based on projective measures and peer ratings. *Journal for the Scientific Study of Religion, 44*, 323–348.

Shariff, A. F., & Norenzayan, A. (2007). God is watching you: Supernatural agent concepts increase prosocial behavior in an anonymous economic game. *Psychological Science, 18,* 803–809.

Shariff, A. F., & Norenzayan, A. (2011). Mean gods make good people: Different views of God predict cheating behavior. *The International Journal for the Psychology of Religion, 21,* 85–96.

Smith, C., Denton, M. L., Faris, R., & Regnerus, M. (2002). Mapping American adolescent religious participation. *Journal for the Scientific Study of Religion, 41,* 597–612.

Unnever, J. D., Cullen, F. T., & Bartkowski, J. P. (2006). Images of God and public support for capital punishment: Does a close relationship with a loving God matter? *Criminology, 44,* 835–866.

Van Pachterbeke, M., Keller, J., & Saroglou, V. (2012). Flexibility in existential beliefs and worldviews: Introducing and measuring existential quest. *Journal of Individual Differences, 33,* 2–16.

Vazsonyi, A. T., & Jenkins, D. D. (2010). Religiosity, self-criticism and virginity status in college students. *Journal for the Scientific Study of Religion, 49,* 561–568.

Voicu, M. (2009). Religion and gender across Europe. *Social Compass, 56,* 144–162.

White, D., & White, O. K. (1995). Integrating religious and racial identities: An analysis of LDS African American explanations of the priesthood ban. *Review of Religious Research, 36,* 295–311.

Wright, P. J. (2008). Predicting reaction to a message of ministry: An audience analysis. *Journal for the Scientific Study of Religion, 47,* 63–81.

Yancey, G. (2010). Who has religious prejudice?: Differing sources of anti-religious animosity in the United States. *Review of Religious Research, 52,* 159–171.

Ysseldyk, R., Matheson, K., & Anisman, H. (2010). Religiosity as identity: Toward an understanding of religion from a social identity perspective. *Personality and Social Psychology Review, 14,* 60–71.

Zaleski, E. M., & Schiaffino, K. M. (2000). Religiosity and sexual risk-taking behavior during the transition to college. *Journal of Adolescence, 23,* 223–227.

17

Cultural and Cross-Cultural Psychology of Religion

Vassilis Saroglou and Adam B. Cohen

It is a fascinating and tremendous task to provide an integrated review of psychological research on religion and culture. As far as we know, no such effort has been made at least in the last 30 years (but see for previous steps of theorizing or reviewing Saroglou, 2003; Saroglou & Cohen, 2011a; Tarakeshwar, Stanton, & Pargament, 2003). Systematic research on this field is only emerging, and past and current work comes from various research traditions: cultural psychology (often adopting social experimental methods; see Atran, 2007; Cohen, 2009), cross-cultural psychology (often based on multicountry and multiethnic data; see Saroglou & Cohen, 2011b), comparative psychology of religion (questions and methods of psychology of religion are applied to non-Christian populations; see Saroglou, 2003; Abu-Raiya & Pargament, 2011), and qualitative idiographic approaches on religion and culture (see Belzen, 2010).

In the present chapter, after a short introduction on the theoretical links between religion and culture, we review empirical research, organized in three sections. In the first section, we examine psychological similarities and differences between religions, with a focus on the major components of religion and dimensions of religiosity as well as on the ways religion relates to personality, values, social behavior, and mental health. In the second section, we examine how a vast array of cultural factors shape religion and its outcomes and can, at least partially, explain interreligious differences. These cultural factors include socioeconomic and sociocultural factors; cultural psychological differences in the cognitive, emotional, social, and moral domains; different theologies; and broad cultural dimensions such as collectivism versus individualism. The third section deals with the interplay between religion and another major dimension of culture: ethnicity. We look at the role religion plays with respect to ethnic identity and interethnic relations in general as well as with respect to the mutual process of acculturation between immigrants and members of the host majority. In the conclusion, we further consider the main lines of research, highlight key methodological issues, and suggest future research directions.

RELIGION AND CULTURE: FOUR WAYS OF CONCEIVING THEIR INTERRELATIONS

Cultures and religions might relate to each other in four ways (see also Saroglou & Cohen, 2011a). First, religions can be considered to be cultures. Religions certainly contain all of the key elements of cultures, such as shared values, norms, symbols, and practices (Cohen, 2009; Fiske, 2002). Of course, religions have features that make them stand out from other forms of cultures; they typically include notions of transcendence and sacredness (Saroglou, 2011). Taking this view of religion and culture is consistent with the theme of this volume, highlighting religion as a meaning system, with meanings imbedded from the subindividual to the macro level (see Park, Chapter 18, this volume).

Second, religions and ethnic or national cultures may be empirically and theoretically confounded and inseparable. When one compares Americans and Japanese, one is often comparing Christians with members of Eastern religions. Thus, cross-cultural differences (e.g., Easterners are collectivist, Westerners are individualist) might be interpreted as religious differences (e.g., Buddhists are collectivist, Protestants are individualist). One reason that national or ethnic cultures and religious cultures can be so highly intertwined is that religion is in many cases historically responsible for national patterns of cultural parameters (Norris & Inglehart, 2004). Of course, the process going from religions to national cultures is extremely complex and is far from constituting a straightforward relation.

Third, religion can be seen as the result of other cultural influences—for example, country-level culture can cause a religion to develop in a certain way. Here, religions might be considered subcultures (e.g., Hinduism can be thought of as a subculture of the broader culture of the Indian subcontinent). In addition, religions may be mediating mechanisms of other cultural differences. For example, one could say that Scandinavian cultures (ecological, economic, social, historical factors) cause individuals to become Protestant, which in turn pushes them to often be more tolerant than Catholics in other European countries (see later discussion).

Finally, religions may moderate (interact with) other cultural influences. Even the nominally same religion takes vastly different forms when it encounters other aspects of culture. For example, in the United States, for Blacks and Latinos, religiousness is not associated with conservative politics, but it is among Whites and Asians (Cohen et al., 2009).

RELIGIOUS SIMILARITIES AND DIFFERENCES ACROSS RELIGIOUS AND CULTURAL GROUPS

For historical reasons (socioeconomic and scientific development in Western countries) as well as theological developments (valorization of the faith–science dialogue), psychology of religion has mostly been developed in and studied Protestant and Catholic contexts. Only very recently has there been an increasing number of studies on other religions, and cross-religious comparative psychological studies are emerging (but see Taves, Chapter 7, this volume, for a discussion).

From a comparative, cross-cultural/religious perspective, this is a fascinating area of investigation. Are the psychological characteristics of religion (main components and dimensions, predictors, and outcomes) basically the same, or do they differ across the various religious and cultural contexts? A fully universalistic attitude would consider that, beyond differences resulting from different religious orientations, the motives, expressions, and effects of religion are mainly universal across religions and cultures. The opposite attitude (i.e., excessive relativism) focuses too much on the variety of religious expressions and related psychological findings, thus quickly concluding that the unique way of fully understanding psychologically religious phenomena is to consider the role of cultural context (e.g., Belzen, 2010; see also Belzen & Lewis, 2010).

Research from cross-cultural psychology suggests the existence of both universals and cultural specifics if one has to understand human thoughts, emotions, and behaviors in general (Berry, Poortinga, Breugelmans, Chasiotis, & Sam, 2011; Norenzayan & Heine, 2005). As shown later in this chapter, the same is true for the psychological aspects of religion.

Of course, the intriguing and intellectually fascinating questions are, What are the "universals" of religion? What may be the explanatory factors of both universality and differences across religious expressions? May these universals be explained by some universality in human psychology? In parallel, do religions differ, not only in their theology and history but also in the psychological aspects (e.g., predictors, characteristics, or outcomes) of religious phenomena? Do such differences originate at the early theology/ anthropology and later historical and spiritual developments of the respective religious traditions, or are they due to other cultural dimensions, such as ethnic/country-level differences and socioeconomic and sociocultural factors at the individual and at the group/ country levels?

In this first section of the chapter, we review existing research that is in favor of both psychological universals and specifics of religion across various religious and cultural contexts. We focus here on the following key issues: basic components of religion and dimensions of religiousness as well as the relationship of religiousness to personality, values, social behavior, and mental health. (For an introduction to these topics and the way they are related to religion, see in this volume Piedmont & Wilkins, Chapter 15; Nielsen, Hatton, & Donahue, Chapter 16; and Park & Slattery, Chapter 27; see also Saroglou, in press; for culturally sensitive approaches to religion and human development, see Holden & Vittrup, 2010; Trommsdorff & Chen, 2012).

Religious Components and Dimensions

Throughout the last 50 years, theorists from both psychology and sociology of religion seem to have achieved a consensus that religions can be defined as integrating four major components: (1) beliefs and cognitions in relation to what people perceive as a transcendence, (2) specific moral rules and practices, (3) collective and individual rituals and emotions that bond people with each other and with (what they perceive to be a) transcendence, and (4) identification with highly valuable and supposedly eternal groups (Saroglou, 2011). These four components—believing, behaving, bonding, and belonging—reflect distinct psychological processes (cognitive, moral, emotional, and social) explaining religion and its effects. They are very likely present in all religions across history, even in nontheistic religions. However, across cultural and religious groups, there is important variability: These dimensions may differ in content (e.g., specific beliefs and rituals), salience (mean importance), and the ways in which they are interconnected or emphasized, leading, for instance, to intellectual, ritualistic, emotional, moralistic, or identity-based religiousness (Saroglou, 2011).

There is also some evidence that the major dimensions/forms of religiousness can be identified across many religious denominations and religions, although cultural differences may exist in the expression of these forms. For instance, *fundamentalist* and *orthodox* versus *questing* expressions of religious beliefs and practices seem to be present and predict similar outcomes among Christians, Hindus, Jews, and Muslims (Hood, Hill, & Gorsuch, 2009; Hunsberger & Jackson, 2005). However, it may be that what is perceived as the expression of fundamentalism in one cultural context (e.g., religious homophobia in the United States) can simply reflect average religiosity elsewhere (e.g., Mediterranean countries). The classic distinction between *intrinsic* and *extrinsic* religious orientations can be identified among Protestants, Catholics, Orthodox, Jews, and Muslims (e.g., Cohen & Hill, 2007; Flere, Edwards, & Klanjsek, 2008). There is, though, important variability across religious groups on the normative character (e.g., positive for Jews, negative for Protestants) and the content of extrinsic religiosity (Cohen, Hall, Koenig, & Meador, 2005). Similarly, the distinction between organized traditional *religiousness* and modern individual *spirituality*, potentially independent from religious traditions and groups, can presumably be found in many cultural contexts (e.g., Dy-Liacco, Piedmont, Murray-Swank, Rodgerson, & Sherman, 2009; Saroglou & Muñoz-García, 2008). However, there may again be important variability between religious–cultural groups on the mean levels on each of these dimensions, the degree of their interrelation, the specific components that define them, and their respective external outcomes. Finally, there is a common assumption that religions become very similar when one focuses on the *mystical dimension* of religion and the spirituality of the great mystics. Initial evidence suggests common dimensions on mystic experiences between American Christians and Iranian Muslims (Hood et al., 2001) as well as Israeli Jews (Lazar & Kravetz, 2005), Indian Hindus (Anthony, Hermans, & Sterkens, 2010), and Tibetan Buddhists (Chen, Hood, Yang, & Watson, 2011).

Relations of Religion with Personality, Social Behavior, and Mental Health

Similarities

Personality characteristics—more precisely predispositions—of individual religiosity (i.e., agreeableness, conscientiousness, and low impulsivity) seem to be similar for Catholic, Protestant, and Orthodox Christians as well as Jews, Muslims, and Buddhists (Saroglou, 2010, for a meta-analysis). Similarly, in all three major monotheistic traditions (i.e., Christianity, Islam, and Judaism), high religiosity consistently predicts preference of values reflecting conservation of personal and social order over values reflecting openness to change (autonomy) and hedonistic self-enhancement (see Saroglou, Delpierre, & Dernelle, 2004, for a meta-analysis). Religious people, especially fundamentalists, are prejudiced against people who are seen as threatening religious values, such as homosexuals, members of other religions, and atheists (see Rowatt, Johnson, LaBouff, & Gonzalez, Chapter 23, this volume). This has been found in studies with Christian, Hindu, Jewish, and Muslim participants. In parallel, specific forms of religion are related to prosocial intentions and behaviors, and this has been found in studies with participants from all the major religious traditions (Saroglou, 2013). Moreover, the links between religion and self-control-related behaviors such as low alcohol and drug use and restrictive sexuality seem to constitute additional "universals" across the major religions (McCullough & Willoughby, 2009).

Some features of religion have similar relationships with health across religious groups or across countries. Most religions help in finding meaning, provide social integration, and encourage healthy lifestyles, all promoting health (see in this volume Masters & Hooker, Chapter 26; Park & Slattery, Chapter 27). Empirical evidence does point to religions having positive health effects across cultures. For example, measures of religious beliefs and/or practice predict life satisfaction and related health constructs not only among U.S. Christians of different ethnic origins (e.g., Markides, 1983) but also among Buddhists (Ariyabuddhiphongs, 2009) and Muslims in various national contexts (e.g., Abdel-Khalek, 2007; Amer & Hood, 2007; Leach, 2009).

Differences

Beyond these striking similarities across different religions in the way religiosity expresses major psychological needs, attitudes, and behavioral tendencies, one can find interesting differences when comparing mean levels or strength of associations. These differences can be found between religious groups within the same country or across countries. As shown later, they may to some extent reflect socioeconomic and sociocultural differences at the group level, but they often persist even when controlling for such variables.

For instance, in a comparative study of 27 nations around the world, Georgas, Berry, van de Vijver, Kagitçibasi, and Poortinga (2006) found that Islamic countries, followed by Christian Orthodox countries, tend to show stronger family orientation by highly endorsing both hierarchical and emotionally supportive roles of parents within the family, in comparison with Protestant and Catholic countries.

There is a longer research tradition comparing Protestants and Catholics. Some evidence exists that religiosity in the United States (mostly Protestant participants in the studies) reflects more positive emotionality in personality traits (high extraversion, low neuroticism) and less discomfort with openness to experience than in Europe (mostly Catholic participants) (Saroglou, 2010). Sheldon (2006) found some evidence that Catholics are higher than Protestants of certain denominations (Unitarians, but not Baptists) in religious introspection. Religious introspection can be thought of, among other possibilities, as a measure, to some extent, of guilt (Ryan, 1982). Other differences can be interpreted in light of the classic distinction between the strong social dimension of Catholicism and the more individual, liberal, and achievement-oriented character of (at least mainstream) Protestant faith and ethic. For instance, for individuals raised as either moderate Protestant, conservative Protestant, or Catholic, parental divorce increases the likelihood of both switching to another religion and apostasy. However, the impact of divorce is particularly strong for Catholics and conservative Protestants, who are, in general, less likely to be religiously mobile (Lawton & Bures, 2001). Note also that for Catholic couples divorce has more negative effects on their well-being than for Protestant couples (Clark & Lelkes, 2005). The orientation toward work ethic seems to be higher among Protestants (Hayward & Kemmelmeier, 2011). In an experimental study,

Sanchez-Burks (2002) found that the activation, through priming, of the work context made American Calvinists (compared with non-Calvinists) restrict relational, social-emotional concerns, presumed to conflict, in Calvinism, with work imperatives. Similarly, in Germany, although both Catholics and Protestants are higher in social trust (an attitude important for the economy) than nonreligious individuals, Protestants tend to be more trusting; and the Protestant, but not Catholic, context (region) is also associated with trust regardless of individual religious beliefs (Traunmüller, 2011). Finally, Protestants tend to endorse internal attributions to a greater extent than do Catholics (Li, Johnson, Cohen, Williams, Knowles, & Chen, 2012).

As far as (mental) health is concerned, different religious groups may have different health outcomes, because of relevant differences in theology or other cultural parameters across the groups. Perhaps the earliest example of this is Durkheim's (1951/1897) finding that Jews and Catholics were less likely to commit suicide than Protestants, which he explained by group differences in collectivism. On the other hand, Jews report less life satisfaction and higher levels of depression and anxiety disorders than members of other Judeo-Christian religions, a finding that is clear even if the mechanism is not (Cohen, 2002; Cohen & Hall, 2009). Theological differences could be responsible, as could differences in willingness to report mental illness (Cohen, Gorvine, & Gorvine, 2013; Loewenthal, MacLeod, Lee, Cook, & Goldblatt, 2002).

Some evidence points to different rates of certain illnesses in certain groups, apparently because of different lifestyles. Jewish attorneys in Cleveland and Detroit were less likely to have a family history of stroke than non-Jews (Friedman & Hellerstein, 1968). Mormons may be less susceptible to cerebrovascular disease than non-Mormons (Jarvis, 1977; Lyon, Bishop, & Nielsen, 1981). Mennonites and Hutterites had the lowest incidence of new strokes in a 1½-year-long study (Abu-Zeid, Choi, Maini, & Nelson, 1975). In their 12-year prospective study of 112,000 Californians, Phillips, Kuzma, Beeson, and Lotz (1980) found that Seventh-Day Adventists were less likely to die from cerebrovascular disease. Differences in health behaviors (such as smoking rates) were theorized to explain these differences.

CULTURAL FACTORS AS MODERATING AND EXPLAINING RELIGION AND ITS OUTCOMES

Religion, in its expressions and outcomes, seems to be shaped by a large number of cultural factors. These factors often interact with religion in predicting human behavior. Furthermore, they seem to be, at least partially, responsible for cross-religious differences.

Moderation by Contextual–Cultural Factors

Differences between religious denominations seem to decrease, if not disappear, when the religious groups live in secularized societies—they are then similarly different from the nonreligious—and/or in countries in which they equally coexist. This is the case, for instance, regarding the way religiosity relates to various values among Catholics and Protestants living in countries such as Germany, the Netherlands, and Switzerland (Bréchon, 2003; Devos, Spini, & Schwartz, 2002; Halman & Riis, 2003). However, within a country, the minority versus majority status of a specific religious denomination makes a difference. For instance, Procter and Hornsby-Smith (2003), using European Values Study (EVS) data, found that Catholics living in countries with a Protestant tradition tend to accentuate a restrictive sexual morality or the importance of collectivistic values. Those authors interpret these findings as confirming the hypothesis of a "cultural defense." Guiso, Sapienza, and Zingales (2003), analyzing World Values Study (WVS) data, also found that when Catholics or Protestants are a minority group living within, respectively, a predominantly Protestant or Catholic country, they do not show the same intolerance that characterizes them when they are a majority group in a given country. Finally, political context may also play a role. For instance, Western European Catholics' religiosity was weakly but positively associated with the importance attributed to the value of security, but for Catholics living in Eastern European countries during the Communist antireligious regimes, the relationship was inverse (Roccas & Schwartz, 1997).

Cross-religious differences may be related to, but do not simply reflect, socioeconomic differences at the group level. Indeed, Inglehart and Baker (2000), analyzing WVS data from 60 countries representing 75% of the global population, found that the socioeconomic development of a country predicts a move from (1) traditional to secular and rational values and (2) values emphasizing survival to "postmaterialist" values emphasizing self-expression (participation, confidence, tolerance, subjective well-being, and concern for the quality of life). However, beyond the role of socioeconomic factors, differences in values were still observable depending on whether countries have been historically Catholic, Protestant, Orthodox, communist, Islamic, or Confucian. The Protestant cultural heritage is associated with a high appreciation of postmaterialist self-expression values, whereas low appreciation of these values is present in countries with Orthodox or communist heritage.

Similarly, an analysis of psychological variables from more than 100 countries (Georgas, van de Vijver, & Berry, 2004) showed that, beyond the role of economic factors, Protestant countries differ from Muslim ones on individualism, subjective well-being (high vs. low), and power distance (hierarchical relations: low vs. high). Protestant countries also differed from Catholic countries on secular authority (high versus low) and uncertainty avoidance (low vs. high). Catholic countries, in addition, tended to be high on harmony and uncertainty avoidance. Another analysis of the WVS data (Guiso et al., 2003) showed that when socioeconomic differences between countries are controlled, a number of associations between religiosity and values are similar among Catholics, Protestants, Muslims, and Hindus (e.g., low tolerance, conservative attitudes toward women, trust of the government, legitimization of poverty by attributing the responsibility to the poor people). However, for other values, some differences remained. For instance, Catholics and Protestants have a positive attitude toward the value of private property, whereas Muslims and Hindus have a negative attitude toward economic competition.

In sum, contextual-cultural factors at the group level such as degree of secularization, minority versus majority status, and socioeconomic development moderate expressions and social outcomes of religion. The domain of mental health provides an additional interesting case of illustration of how such cultural factors at the collective level interact with religion in predicting relevant outcomes.

Religion may have stronger effects on health or well-being in groups and societies in which religion is particularly important (Gebauer, Sedikides, & Neberich, 2012).

Religiosity correlates more positively with life satisfaction, and more negatively with depression, among African Americans compared with Caucasian Americans (Husaini, Blasi, & Miller, 1999; Musick, Koenig, Hays, & Cohen, 1998). Features of the national environment may also influence the relationship between religion and health or well-being. Religiousness is associated with slightly higher subjective well-being across four major world religions, but the effect is present only in nations with difficult life conditions and not in nations with favorable life conditions (Diener, Tay, & Myers, 2011). Elliott and Hayward (2009) found in the WVS, which included 65 countries, that while salience of personal religious identity was associated with life satisfaction everywhere, the magnitude of that association depended on the role of government regulation of individual liberties, including but not limited to religious liberty—the more government regulation, the lower the association.

There may be a triple interaction among culture, religion, and biology in predicting mental health. In comparing European Americans with Koreans, Sasaki, Kim, and Xu (2011) found that among people who were more genetically predisposed toward social sensitivity, Koreans, but not European Americans, had greater psychological well-being if they were more religious. As those authors suggest, religion may benefit well-being for those who are genetically predisposed to be socially sensitive but only to the extent that the cultural context provides adequate opportunities for social affiliation.

Note that the cultural factors go further than a mere interaction with religion in predicting health. They raise the question of how one should distinguish normative (i.e., religiously appropriate) behaviors from pathology (Abramowitz, Huppert, Cohen, Cahill, & Tolin, 2002; Loewenthal, 2007; O'Connor & Vandenberg, 2005). Drawing this distinction can be especially challenging given religious and cultural differences in norms for behavior. For example, obsessive–compulsive disorder (OCD) commonly involves excessive scrupulosity to religious demands, but there may be a fine line between being devoutly observant and being compulsive. Is an observant Jew showing signs of OCD or appropriate adherence to Jewish dietary laws if he or she refuses to eat a meat soup into which a drop of milk has accidentally fallen (Nemeroff & Rozin, 1992)? If a person worries whether his or her thoughts about having an affair are the exact moral equivalent of adultery, is this person showing thought–action fusion (sometimes a component of OCD) or devoutly following Jesus's teaching in the Sermon on the Mount (Cohen & Rozin, 2001; Siev & Cohen, 2007)? Several scholars have advocated for the need to integrate culture and religious sensitivity into clinical practice (Loewenthal, 2007; Richards & Bergin, 2000; see Shafranske, Chapter 30, this volume).

Theological or Broad Cultural Differences?

Differences within Monotheistic Traditions

Psychological differences between religious groups thus exist and are not pure artifacts of socioeconomic factors. Can these differences be attributed to strictly theological differences between religions (different teachings about humans, the world, and the divine)? Or should these be explained by other factors such as cultural differences on personality, cognitions, emotions, morality, and social behavior? It is too early, in terms of the existing empirical research, to make a conclusion on this issue, and, as mentioned early in this chapter, the two processes may mirror one another. Nevertheless, initial evidence confirms the pertinence of both kinds of explanatory processes.

A series of studies has compared Jews with members of Christian denominations, especially Protestants. Religion for Jews is as much about community and biological descent as it is belief, whereas for Protestants personal beliefs trump community and biological descent (Cohen & Hill, 2007). Practice better characterizes Jews' religiousness, whereas beliefs better characterizes Protestants' religiousness (Cohen, Siegel, & Rozin, 2003). Protestants judge more negatively than Jews the presence of immoral thoughts, perhaps because of the Protestant view that thoughts are the moral equivalent of actions (Cohen & Rozin, 2001). Also, Protestants, but not Jews, consider a selfish motivation to invalidate the moral quality of a moral action (Cohen & Rankin, 2004). Cohen, Malka, Rozin, and Cherfas (2006) also found that Protestants' religiousness reflects more strongly the importance to forgive even "unforgivable" (for Jews) offenses compared with that of Jews. Muslims too seem to differ from Christians on forgiveness: They are particularly sensitive to the offender's apologies and demonstration of repentance and thus less strongly endorse unconditional forgiveness (Mullet & Azar, 2009).

Psychological differences may even be due to theological traditions that are specific to particular religious denominations rather than a broad religion. In a series of cognitive experiments in three countries and comparing religious with nonreligious participants, Colzato et al. (2010) found that Dutch Calvinists have a detail-focused perception (they see first the several small rectangles within the big rectangle), whereas Italian Catholics and Israeli Jews have an holistic perception (they see first the "big picture," i.e., the big rectangle). According to those authors, Calvinism emphasizes individual responsibility, whereas Catholicism and Judaism place more emphasis on social responsibility.

Differences between Western and Eastern Religions

An interesting case in understanding differences in the psychological aspects of religion as being a function of theological (e.g., Buddhism, Confucianism, Hinduism) and/or broad cultural differences is the comparison between West and East. Series of recent studies in (cross-)cultural psychology identified many domains where Western culture(s) differ from Eastern culture(s). This applies to Easterners', compared with Westerners', perceptions of the self (less egocentrism and positivity about the self), cognitions (weaker motivation for consistency) and reasoning (higher use of holistic thinking and of context-based rather person-based attributions), emotions (more control and less expressiveness of emotions), morality (principles of loyalty and authority, in addition to care- and justice-based morality), and social relations marked by higher social conformity (Heine, 2010; Henrich, Heine, & Norenzayan, 2010; Kitayama & Cohen, 2007).

It is very likely, then, that religious experience, cognitions, emotions, morality, and social behavior differs when one compares religiosity in Christianity, or possibly in all the three monotheistic religions, with religiosity in Eastern cultures. This is a fascinating area for future investigation. The existing sporadic and initial empirical evidence suggests that several psychological processes involved in Western religiosity do not seem to be paralleled in Eastern religions. For instance, Miller (2000; but see Liu, 2010) found that being religious represents a risk-avoiding behavioral tendency in Western societies (Christians and Muslims, in Italy, the United States, and Turkey) but not in Eastern societies (Hindus and Buddhists, in India and Japan). In a similar line, Sasaki and Kim (2011) found through three studies that priming religion influenced acts of personal control for European Americans but not Asian Americans; religious coping was associated with personal control for European Americans but not East Asians; and themes of personal agency (e.g., spiritual growth, inclusion of diverse members) were more prevalent on American church websites while themes of relationships (e.g., close relationships within the church, social activities with other church members) were more prevalent on Korean church websites. Analyzing data from dozens of countries, and comparing especially Eastern countries (Japan, India, China) with Western ones, Stark (2001) found that religion has an effect in sustaining moral order only insofar as religion is based on belief in powerful, active, conscious, morally concerned gods, which is less typical of Eastern religions or cultures. Finally, both Christians and Hindus tend to make fatalistic interpretations of their life events, but there are important qualitative differences on the underlying processes (Young, Morris, Burrus, Krishnan, & Regmi, 2011).

Note that differences in religious aspects reflecting other cultural differences between the East and the West may be stable and pervasive across centuries. For instance, Tsai, Miao, and Seppala (2007) found that high-arousal positive states (e.g., excitement) are valued less, and low-arousal positive states (e.g., calm) more, in Buddhism than in Christianity, and these differences were consistent across old fundamental texts (Gospels and Lotus Sutra), contemporary self-help books, and reports of practitioners from the two religions.

However, religious and nonreligious cultural factors may not be in parallel but may have independent or even diverging influences. Analyzing data from the International Social Survey Program 2008, Clobert and Saroglou (2011b) found that religious Koreans, independently of their religious affiliation (Buddhists, Catholics, and Protestants) report high trust of science, whereas Western religious Catholics (Austria) and Protestants (Denmark) do the opposite. These results could be attributed to the higher presence of holistic and interdependent thought in Eastern cultures. Regarding another domain (i.e., interreligious prejudice), it was religious affiliation that made the difference. Among religious people from various Asian countries, Catholics and Protestants express high interreligious prejudice, whereas the opposite is the case for Buddhists and Taoists (Clobert & Saroglou, 2011a).

Individualism versus Collectivism

One can scarcely talk about culture in psychology, and thus differences between religious groups, without discussing individualism and collectivism. In individualistic cultures, people are socialized to be independent and to prioritize their own goals and to value self-expression. In collectivistic cultures, people are socialized to be interdependent and to prioritize their group's goals over their own (Markus & Kitayama, 1991; Triandis, 1995). Can we talk about religions as individualistic or collectivistic? It does seem fair to consider a religion that emphasizes intrinsic faith and personal relationship with God as individualistic, or a religion that emphasizes community integration as collectivistic (Cohen et al., 2005; Cohen & Hill, 2007). One reason that groups might differ in individualism or collectivism is that some religions base membership on internal faith (assent religions), whereas other religions base membership on birth (descent religions; Morris, 1996).

Cohen and Hill (2007) found that for intrinsic religiosity, Protestants scored highest, followed by Catholics; Jews had the lowest scores. On extrinsic religiosity, Catholics were higher than were Protestants, and Jews did not differ significantly from Catholics or Protestants. Further, extrinsic religiosity and intrinsic religiosity were correlated negatively among Protestants, nonsignificantly and close to zero among Catholics, but highly and positively among Jews. Individualism and collectivism may also have an influence on religious groups' coping strategies. Reviewing series of studies, Fischer, Ai, Aydin, Frey, and Haslam (2010) concluded that Muslims tend to use an interpersonally oriented (collective) coping style when dealing with adversity, whereas Christians are more likely to employ intrapersonally oriented (individualistic) strategies when facing comparable scenarios.

Interestingly, beyond differences between religious groups, there exists similarity when focusing on the way individual religiosity (general religiosity, beliefs, or practice) functions. Several investigators have found that religiosity is related to interdependence and collectivism, and this relationship occurs across religions and countries that may be either individualistic or collectivistic. This was found for Jews and Protestants in the United States (Cohen & Rozin, 2001), for Catholics in the Philippines, and for Muslims in Turkey (Cukur, de Guzman, & Carlo, 2004; Dy-Liacco et al., 2009). Nevertheless, communal individuals (who seek assimilation with their ambient culture) are most religious in religious cultures, whereas agentic individuals (who seek differentiation from their ambient culture) are most religious in nonreligious cultures (Gebauer, Paulhus, & Neberich, in press).

RELIGION, ETHNICITY, AND ACCULTURATION

A key domain in the interrelations between religion and culture is the one of ethnic identity in general and among immigrants in particular. Ethnic identity, acculturation, and intercultural relations constitute a major subfield in cross-cultural psychology. Theory and research on the role of religion on these issues have been accumulated in the last years.

Religion and Ethnicity

Ethnicity and Ethnic Identity

Ethnicity is a major dimension of culture that leads humans to form different groups on the basis of descent and corresponding physical characteristics, language, geographical proximity, and often religion. The extent of the overlap between religion and ethnicity may vary from total to null, and the mechanisms explaining their interconnection are multiple (Hvithamar, Warburg, & Jacobsen, 2009; Kivisto, 2007). Hammond and Warner (1993) distinguish between cultural groups (1) with religion serving as the major foundation of ethnicity (e.g., Amish, Jews); (2) with ethnicity reinforcing religion (e.g., Greek or Serbian Orthodox, Church of England); and (3) with religion shaping ethnicity (e.g., Irish, Italian, or Polish Catholic).

At the same time, several religions, especially those with numeric success (Christianity, Islam, Eastern religions), have evolved since their beginnings toward transethnic, global religious communities. They have developed theologies, beliefs, rituals, and organizations that emphasize the importance for their believers of transcending ethnic and national barriers and pursuing common, pan-human objectives and goals.

What are the connections between individual religiosity and attachment to ethnicity? Large international studies show that, across countries, religiosity is still today related, to a certain extent, to high ethnic and national identity and pride. People with frequent religious attendance tend to prefer an ethnic (ancestry- and descent-based) over a civic (citizenship- and respect-based) conception of national identity (Kunovich, 2009; data from 31 countries from the International Social Survey Program 2003). Young Europeans (18–29 years old) who identify strongly with their religion (Catholics and Protestants) have a stronger national pride (Campiche, 1997: EVS data 1990), stronger feelings of belonging to their region and country, and weaker feelings of belonging to Europe and the world, compared to their nonreligious peers (Belot, 2005: EVS data 1999; see also Bréchon, 2003). There is also evidence that marriage boundaries between certain ethnic groups are, in part, the result of differences with respect to religion: Intermarriage is more common between ethnic groups who have the same faith (Kalmjin, 1998).

Interethnic Relations

Does this religious attachment to ethnic ingroup translate into outgroup derogative attitudes, such as xenophobia and ethnic prejudice/discrimination? Studies suggest a complex picture, with interesting moderators such as religious denomination, country's cultural context, and religious dimension measured. For instance, religiousness is overall rather unrelated to the value of universalism, but is negatively related to it in countries with mono-religious tradition such as the Mediterranean ones, of Catholic (Italy, Portugal, Spain), Orthodox (Greece), Jewish (Israel), and Muslim (Turkey) tradition (Saroglou et al., 2004). In European multicountry studies, ethnocentrism or xenophobic attitudes are found to (1) overall be rather unrelated to religiosity, especially among young people, (2) sometimes be high among Catholics and Orthodox, and (3) be low among atheists and, in some countries, among Protestants (see Bréchon, 2003, and Strabac & Listhaug, 2008, for EVS data; Billiet & Meuleman, 2008, and Hooghe & Reeskens, 2006, for ESS data).

Not surprisingly, links of religion with xenophobic attitudes and racism become clearly positive when one uses measures of orthodox religious thinking and fundamentalism (Rowatt et al., Chapter 23, this volume). In contrast, spirituality implies high importance attributed to universalism (Saroglou & Muñoz-García, 2008) and strong identification as a citizen of the world among adolescents of various cultural backgrounds: natives of Christian tradition, Muslims, Jews, and Christians born of immigration, all living at the same country (Saroglou & Galand, 2004; Saroglou & Hanique, 2006; Saroglou & Mathijsen, 2007).

Understanding the Relations between Ethnicity and Religion

Several questions remain unanswered. Do people in general perceive ethnic identity to be more important than religious identity? It may also be that strongly religious people prioritize their religious identity over their ethnic one. Moreover, from a developmental perspective, what are the relations between the emergence in childhood of ethnic awareness

(Quintana & McKown, 2008) and the emergence and development of the awareness to belong to a religious group? Initial research on Christian and Muslim children in Belgium suggests that religious awareness emerges later than the ethnic one (Van der Straten & Roskam, 2012).

How are we to understand the links between religion and ethnicity? It is a shortcut to interpret these links as being (only) due to the exploitation of religion for ethnic and political reasons. The opposite causal direction may also be true. For instance, in a country with a strong ethnoreligious tradition (such as Greece), exposure to the securitizing religious discourse in churches was found to immunize natives' anti-immigrant attitudes from the political message that encourages tolerance and desecuritization (Karyotis & Patrikios, 2010).

Indeed, from a psychological perspective, religions may have their own reasons to embrace ethnic identity and related attitudes. First, investment in ethnic and national groups—and even transnational entities in the case of spirituality—may simply be one among other expressions of the social function of religion. Need to belong, collective identities and corresponding self-esteem, social sharing of emotions, trust, large cooperation and altruism not based on direct reciprocity can be satisfied in large groups that are in genetic, geographical, and cultural proximity with the religious ones. Second, nationalism and religious orthodoxy share some common values (Duriez, Luyten, Snauwaert, & Hutsebaut, 2002). Ethnic/national groups and religions are invested in by people who value social cohesion and stability as well as personal and social order and security. Third, both religions and nations have historically constituted large entities that symbolize, if not instantiate, feelings of integration, unity, and wholeness that overcome the many human divisions, especially the one between past, present, and future (Saroglou, 2006, 2011). This points to the mystic dimension of religiousness. The affinity between modern spirituality and attachment to the world as a whole may thus be a new, more symbolic expression of the same psychological process but within broader entities.

Religion and Immigrants' Acculturation

Immigrants' Acculturation

Acculturation refers to immigrants' attitudes, values, identities, and behaviors relative to both new and heritage cultures. Sociological studies suggest that religion's roles in the immigration process and consequences are important, complex, and dynamic, given increasing globalization (Cadge & Ecklund, 2007; Kivisto, 2007; Plüss, 2009). However, systematic quantitative studies on the psychology of acculturation and religiousness are only in their beginnings.

A key task for immigrants is to negotiate between at least two cultural identities: the heritage and the new one. A variety of processes and outcomes are possible (Hong, Wan, No, & Chiu, 2007). Recent research confirms, consistently across studies, that religiosity or religious identity of (first- and second-generation) immigrants is positively related to the origin ethnic identity and attachment to the heritage culture, while mostly unrelated or sometimes negatively related to the identity, attachment, or acculturation to the new, host culture. This is the case for Asian Americans and African Americans in the United States (Ghorpade, Lackritz, & Singh, 2006), Christian European women married to Muslim Arabs in Israel (Abu-Rayya, 2007), Christians from various countries, Arab and Turkish Muslims, as well as Jews living in Belgium (Friedman & Saroglou, 2010; Saroglou & Galand, 2004; Saroglou & Hanique, 2006; Saroglou & Mathijsen, 2007), Turkish Muslims in the Netherlands (Verkuyten & Yildiz, 2007), and Muslims from various countries in the US (Sirin et al., 2008). In other words, the evidence suggests that religiosity does not lead to strategies (especially integration) that include valorization of the adopted culture and are known to be successful for the acculturation process. Interestingly, whereas both the ethnic and religious identities seem to decrease when moving from the first to the second generation of immigrants, the interrelation between the two identities becomes stronger (Maliepaard, Lubbers, & Gijsberts, 2010).

The fact that immigrants' religiosity implies attachment to the origin identity can be explained by the general pattern of the religion/ethnicity-positive relations, presented in the previous section. Moreover, it expresses the importance for immigrants (including the second and third generation) of being integrated into networks and communities that allow them to easily maintain links and develop helpful and profitable exchanges (social, cultural, linguistic, economic, marital, and professional) with others similar in religion and ethnic origin (Kivisto, 2007; Plüss, 2009). However, the possible negative association between religiosity and acculturation to the adoptive culture is intriguing. Perhaps the religion emphasizes the (perception of) distinctiveness of the origin culture, religion, and values from those of the adoptive country, which, in turn increases disidentification with the new culture (Friedman & Saroglou, 2010). The origin ethnoreligious identity may thus become, in some cases, an oppositional identity (see Ogbu, 2008). It may also be that perception of discrimination leads to increased religious identification as a way to find refuge, which in turn, decreases the identification with the adoption country (Verkuyten & Yildiz, 2007).

Immigrants' Mental Health

These recent studies question, directly or indirectly, previous research suggesting a positive role of religion in immigrants' acculturation, especially with regard to mental health indicators. This research had suggested that, like for majority members, religious beliefs and practices play a positive role in mental health of ethnic and immigrant minority members, often through individual and social processes such as social support, constructive religious coping, healthy lifestyles, and beliefs and practices that enhance meaning, self-esteem, and self-control (Viladrich & Abraído-Lanza, 2009, for review). In the United States, the results seem clearer for African Americans among whom religious attendance and the degree of guidance received from religious beliefs appear to buffer the effects of perceived discrimination on psychological distress (Bierman, 2006; Ellison, Musick, & Henderson, 2008).

However, a large study of Mexican Americans suggests that, rather than buffering, religiousness exacerbates the deleterious effects of discrimination and acculturative stress on depressive symptoms (Ellison, Finch, Ryan, & Salinas, 2009). Another study of Belgian Muslims born of immigrants found that intrinsic religiosity was indirectly related to decreased self-esteem and increased depressive symptoms through perceived religious intolerance from the majority and feelings of anger toward the majority (Friedman & Saroglou, 2010). In fact, religion may exert complex, even conflicting, influences on minorities' mental health. Verkuyten (2008) observed that life satisfaction of ethnic minority members seems to decrease because of perceived discrimination, but also to increase because of high identification with the origin culture. As we described earlier, religion—or at least different aspects of it—does both.

The Host Majority's Attitudes

Acculturation is a double, reciprocal, process involving not only newcomers and their offspring but also majority members. The latter may have various attitudes toward immigrants and multiculturalism. Existing empirical research on religiosity and multiculturalism suggests that there are moderator effects of country (majority), target (minority), and religious dimension studied. For instance, Burris, Branscombe, and Jackson (2000) found that intrinsic religiosity is positively related to multiculturalism in Canada but unrelated to it in the United States. Anti-immigrant, ethnic, and anti-Muslim prejudice is unrelated to individual religiosity across 30 European countries, but religious attendance is related to anti-Muslim prejudice in eastern Europe (Strabac & Listhaug, 2008). In some countries, religiosity or spirituality of the majority is found to predict positive attitudes toward Muslim immigrants (Abu-Rayya & White, 2010: Australia) or clear separation in perceptions between terrorism and Islam as religion (Saroglou & Galand, 2004: Belgium).

Given the strong interconnection between ethnicity and religion in Jewish identity as well as the quasi-fusion in Westerners' perception of ethnic and religious elements when they refer to Western Muslims born of immigrant parents, it is difficult to classify anti-Semitism and Islamophobia as religious versus ethnic prejudice. Nevertheless, with respect to this issue, some recent studies provide interesting information on anti-Muslim attitudes. We review these next, since the West–Islam dialogue has become a hot issue in the post-9/11 world.

Anti-Muslim prejudice in Western countries seems to be stronger than typical ethnic prejudice. This is found, for instance, in a recent analysis of data from 30 European countries (Strabac & Listhaug, 2008). Similarly, religious English Canadians were found to endorse, toward Arab Muslim immigrants but not British immigrants, negative acculturation orientations such as assimilation and segregation (Safdar, Dupuis, Lewis, El-Geledi, & Bourhis, 2008). Muslim Arabs in the United States, compared with Christian Arabs, experience higher discrimination (Awad, 2010) and tend to use more separation and less integration and assimilation as acculturation strategies (Amer & Hovey, 2007). Interestingly, the psychological processes (e.g., value orientations, sociocognitive orientations) and sociodemographic factors seem to be similar for ethnic prejudice and anti-Muslim attitudes (Saroglou, Lamkaddem, Van Pachterbeke, & Buxant, 2009; Strabac & Listhaug, 2008). An analysis of U.S. newspaper articles (2002–2003) suggested that Muslim religious identity has come to mimic the inequality of race identity (Byng, 2008). Political scientists have suggested that, given the high fertility of religious immigrants in secularized Europe, in the future, ethnic cleavage between native and immigrant may come to be replaced by a transethnic religious divide between traditionalists and secularists (Kaufmann, 2007). Nevertheless, there is a way to distinguish between ethnic and religious components in Islamophobia. In a study on the native Belgians' attitudes toward the Islamic headscarf, it was found that (general) ethnic prejudice and antireligious sentiments, beyond their common overlap, predict, uniquely and additively, discomfort with this symbol and willingness to ban it (Saroglou et al., 2009).

CONCLUSION: STUDYING RELIGIOUS UNIVERSALS, VARIATION, AND THEIR MECHANICS

The present review of cultural, comparative, and international studies on personality, values, social behavior, mental health, ethnic identity, and acculturation suggests the importance of avoiding both an excessive universalistic and an excessive relativistic stand when trying to understand the psychological aspects of religion.

Overall, religions' major psychological functions seem to be universal, across religious and other cultural groups. Religion, including more contemporary forms of spirituality, provides, very likely universally, beliefs and worldviews, moral norms, rituals and emotions, and sense of community that, together, although in different combinations or with different intensity across cultures (see Saroglou, 2011), are used by many humans in order to face basic universal human needs. These are (1) the need for personal stability and order at the cognitive and/or emotional level; (2) the need for relational security in trusting others and the world (what is manifest even in nontheistic religions such as Buddhism; see Granqvist, Mikulincer, & Shaver, 2010); (3) the need to belong to larger groups—from ethnic to pan-human—and to promote social cohesion, in both individualistic and collectivistic cultures, even if it is at the detriment of other groups; and (4) the need for self-transcendence, which, in the case of religion, implies the connection with a transcendent entity that is external and superior to humans (see Demoulin, Saroglou, & Van Pachterbeke, 2008).

The possibly universal character of these psychological dimensions of religion manifests itself better when one focuses on the "big picture," that is, (1) broad psychological constructs such as large personality traits, big values priorities, global indicators of well-being, and general social attitudes and behaviors and (2) predictors, correlates, or outcomes of general individual religiosity within cultural groups or when comparing various religious groups with nonreligious peers. Psychological aspects of religion may then show, to some extent, universality, since (1) several human needs and psychological mechanisms to answer them are universal (Norenzayan & Heine, 2005), (2) religion may have been a by-product of broad evolutionary adaptation processes for humans as species in general (Atran, 2007; Kirkpatrick, Chapter 6, this volume), and (3) no other cultural phenomenon than religion seems to have succeeded, at least until today, in integrating *into one set* various mechanisms to face the just-mentioned diverse psychological needs (Saroglou, 2006, in press). We are, though, cautious not to yet affirm universality, since clearly comparative studies, using methodology typical of cross-cultural psychological research, and especially psychological studies comparing Eastern religions and cultures with Western monotheistic traditions, are only in their beginnings.

However, the specific ways of experiencing religion and the specific psychological processes involved in the realization of the religion-related goals seem to vary importantly across groups differing in ethnicity, socioeconomic status, sociocultural group-level factors, theological traditions, and broad cultural dimensions involving culture-specific personality, cognitions, emotions, social relations, and morality. There is a tremendous need to carry out systematic, theory-based, and methodologically rigorous cross-religious psychological research. The causal pathways are multiple, and there is a huge need to clarify them through psychological, but also interdisciplinary (historical, sociological, anthropological), research, including research adopting hermeneutical approaches (in this volume, see Hood & Belzen, Chapter 4; also Paloutzian & Park, Chapter 1, and Park & Paloutzian, Chapter 33, for a multilevel interdisciplinary paradigm). Religious phenomena, similarities, and differences may cause, or result from, other cultural dimensions; and religion's effects on external outcomes may be moderated or mediated by such nonreligious cultural factors; or, inversely, the effects of the latter on external outcomes may be moderated or mediated by religious factors.

Note also that we usually think of religious differences as *corresponding* with other cultural differences. For instance, Eastern religions should emphasize controlled emotions in collectivistic cultures, whereas Protestant Christianity should emphasize emotional expressiveness in individualistic cultures. However, an alternative, *compensatory model* (between religion and culture) is also plausible. For instance, in collectivistic Eastern cultures, meditation may help people to increase feelings of personal autonomy. In individualistic Western cultures, religious attendance may help people to solidify fragile social bonds.

To advance significantly in cross-religious psychological research, it is important to be inspired by recent methodological advances in cultural and cross-cultural psychology (Cohen, 2007; Matsumoto & van de Vijver, 2010). Three issues, in particular, seem to be of primary importance. The first is the benefits of carrying out experimental studies and using behavioral measures rather than drawing conclusions only from the comparison of scores obtained through self-report measures. Indeed, as noted by Heine (2010), when an independent variable is manipulated within cultures, comparisons across conditions are often not affected by issues such as the *reference group effect* (i.e., people's tendency to compare themselves with their group's norms and standards, which makes cross-cultural comparisons of mean scores unreliable) because the conditions within each culture share similar response styles and reference groups.

The second issue concerns the cross-religious applicability of measures of religiosity and different religious dimensions. If one wants to show that some dimension of religion has the same or a different role across cultures, it becomes necessary to show that the construct being measured is indeed the same. One would thus attempt to document *measurement invariance* to show that the measurement properties of the relevant scale are the same across groups (see Matsumoto & van de Vijver, 2010; Hill, Chapter 3, this volume). There are several issues to be taken into consideration: dimensional invariance (does the same religiosity scale have two factors in each religious-cultural group?), configural invariance (does an item load to the same factor in all groups?), metric invariance (do the common factors have the same meanings across groups?), strong factorial invariance (are the means and variances of scale items the same across groups?), and strict factorial invariance (are the items of a religiosity scale equally internally reliable across groups?). An alternative, complementary issue is to achieve *measurement equivalence:* Different items (e.g., belief in Jesus's divinity vs. belief that Mohammed is the prophet) may be equivalent in tapping religious orthodoxy for Christians versus Muslims, respectively.

A third issue is the importance of including a large number of psychological and social variables, at both the individual and the group level, and subsequently applying multilevel analyses when carrying out multigroup and/or multicountry studies. This is also important in order to consider the multiple possible confounds at play. For instance, many factors may be hidden beside the influence of socioeconomic variables (at the individual or the collective level) on the religion–mental health relation. But it is also important in order to disentangle religion's effects at the individual level from those at the collective level. Sometimes there exists *isomorphism* between the two levels: For instance, a multilevel analysis of international data showed that high endorsement of Protestant work ethic is typical of both individuals who are culturally Protestant and nations with dominantly Protestant history (Hayward & Kemmelmeier, 2011). However, in other domains, there may be *nonisomorphism*, which asks for further explanation. For instance, at the individual level, within societies, there often exists a positive association between religiosity and many indicators of life quality. Conversely, at the collective level, the more a country is religious, the more it may be characterized by dysfunctional psychosocial conditions, such as murder and suicide rates, mortality, abortions, alcohol consumption, and unemployment (Paul, 2009).

We close this chapter by proposing an additional research agenda, which may be of common interest for (cross-) cultural psychologists and cultural-comparative psychologists of religion. Where do long-term, persistent cultural, including religious, differences come from? Beyond the role of different historical and contextual experiences, human groups have differed between each other for centuries, for reasons probably related to ecological and environmental factors such as temperature, luminosity, climate, geology, and geography (Van de Vliert, 2008). It may be that some differences between religious groups are less dependent on the respective theologies and historical evolutions than on very basic factors having to do with the physical environment: Mediterranean people (Israeli Jews, Greek Christian Orthodox, and Turkish Muslims) may be more similar in their way of experiencing religion compared with Scandinavian and German Protestants and Catholics. Nature may precede both culture and religion.

REFERENCES

Abdel-Khalek, A. M. (2007). Religiosity, happiness, health, and psychopathology in a probability sample of Muslim adolescents. *Mental Health, Religion, and Culture, 10,* 571–583.

Abramowitz, J., Huppert, J., Cohen, A. B., Cahill, S. P., & Tolin, D. F. (2002). Religious obsessions and compulsions in a non-clinical sample: The Penn Inventory of Scrupulosity. *Behaviour Research and Therapy, 40,* 825–838.

Abu Raiya, H., & Pargament, K. I. (2011). Empirically based psychology of Islam: Summary and critique of the literature. *Mental Health, Religion & Culture, 14,* 93–115.

Abu-Rayya, H. M. (2007). Acculturation, Christian religiosity, and psychological and marital well-being among the European wives of Arabs in Israel. *Mental Health, Religion & Culture, 10,* 171–190.

Abu-Rayya, H. M., & White, F. A. (2010). Acculturation orientations and religious identity as predictors of Anglo-Australians' attitudes towards Australian Muslims. *International Journal of Intercultural Relations, 34,* 592–599.

Abu-Zeid, H. A. H., Choi, N. W., Maini, K. K., & Nelson, N. A. (1975). Incidence and epidemiologic features of cerebrovascular disease (stroke) in Manitoba, Canada. *Preventive Medicine, 4,* 567–578.

Amer, M. M., & Hood, R. W., Jr. (2007). Introduction to thematic issues on "Islamic religiosity: Measures and mental health." *Journal of Muslim Mental Health, 2,* 109–111.

Amer, M. M., & Hovey, J. D. (2007). Socio-demographic differences in acculturation and mental health for a sample of 2nd generation/early immigrant Arab Americans. *Journal of Immigrant and Minority Health, 9,* 335–347.

Anthony, F.-V., Hermans, C. A. M., & Sterkens, C. (2010). A comparative study of mystical experience among Christian, Muslim, and Hindu students in Tamil Nadu, India. *Journal for the Scientific Study of Religion, 49,* 264–277.

Ariyabuddhiphongs, V. (2009). Buddhist belief in merit (punña), Buddhist religiousness and life satisfaction among Thai Buddhists in Bangkok, Thailand. *Archive for the Psychology of Religion, 31,* 191–213.

Atran, S. (2007). Religion's social and cognitive landscape. In S. Kitayama & D. Cohen (Eds.), *Handbook of cultural psychology* (pp. 417–453). New York: Guilford Press.

Awad, J. H. (2010). The impact of acculturation and religious identification on perceived discrimination for Arab/Middle Eastern Americans. *Cultural Diversity and Ethnic Minority Psychology, 16,* 59–67.

Belot, C. (2005). Du local au mondial: Les espaces d'appartenance des jeunes Européens [From the local to the world: Belonging spaces among young Europeans]. In O. Galand & B. Roudet (Eds.), *Les jeunes Européens et leurs valeurs* [Young Europeans and their values] (pp. 177–203). Paris: La Découverte.

Belzen, J. A. (2010). *Towards cultural psychology of religion: Principles, approaches, applications.* New York: Springer.

Belzen, J. A., & Lewis, C. A. (Eds.). (2010). Cultural psychology of religion [Special issue]. *Mental Health, Religion, and Culture, 13*(4).

Berry, J. W., Poortinga, Y. H., Breugelmans, S. M., Chasiotis, A., & Sam, D. (2011). *Cross-cultural psychology: Theory and applications* (3rd ed.). Cambridge, UK: Cambridge University Press.

Bierman, A. (2006). Does religion buffer the effects of discrimination on mental health?: Differing effects by race. *Journal for the Scientific Study of Religion, 45,* 551–566.

Billiet, J., & Meuleman, B. (2008). *Religious diversity in Europe and its relation to social attitudes and value orientation.* Proceedings of the 3MC Conference, Berlin, Germany. Retrieved from *www.csdiworkshop.org/pdf/3mc2008_proceedings/session_32/Billiet_sept08.pdf.*

Bréchon, P. (2003). Integration into Catholicism and Protestantism in Europe: The impact on moral and political values. In L. Halman & O. Riis (Eds.), *Religion and secularizing society: The Europeans' religion at the end of the 20th century* (pp. 114–161). Leiden, The Netherlands: Brill.

Burris, C. T., Branscombe, N. R., & Jackson, L. M. (2000). "For God and country": Religion and the endorsement of national self-stereotypes. *Journal of Cross-Cultural Psychology, 31,* 517–527.

Byng, M. D. (2008). Complex inequalities: The case of Muslim Americans after 9/11. *American Behavioral Scientist, 51,* 659–674.

Cadge, W., & Ecklund, E. H. (2007). Immigration and religion. *Annual Review of Sociology, 33,* 359–379.

Campiche, R. J. (Ed.). (1997). *Cultures jeunes et religions en Europe* [Youth cultures and religions in Europe]. Paris: Cerf.

Chen, Z., Hood, R. W., Jr., Yang, L., & Watson, P. J. (2011). Mystical experience among Tibetan Buddhists: The common core thesis revisited. *Journal for the Scientific Study of Religion, 50,* 328–338.

Clark, A., & Lelkes, O. (2005). Deliver us from evil: Religion as insurance. *Papers on Economics of Religion, 6*(3). Retrieved from *www.ugr.es/~teoriahe/RePEc/gra/paoner/per06_03.pdf.*

Clobert, M., & Saroglou, V. (2011a, July). *Religion and prejudice in Eastern culture: An analysis of ISSP data.* Paper presented at the International Association for Cross-Cultural Psychology Conference, Istanbul, Turkey.

Clobert, M., & Saroglou, V. (2011b, August). *Religion, magical thinking and trust in science: Comparing East versus West.* Paper presented at the International Association for the Psychology of Religion Conference, Bari, Italy.

Cohen, A. B. (2002). The importance of spirituality in well-being for Jews and Christians. *Journal of Happiness Studies, 3,* 287–310.

Cohen, A. B. (2009). Many forms of culture. *American Psychologist, 64,* 194–204.

Cohen, A. B., Gorvine, B. J., & Gorvine, H. (2013). The religion, spirituality, and psychology of

Jews. In K. I. Pargament, J. J. Exline, & J. W. Jones (Eds.), *APA handbook of psychology, religion, and spirituality (Vol. 1): Context, theory, and research* (pp. 665–679). Washington, DC: American Psychological Association.

Cohen, A. B., & Hall, D. E. (2009). Existential beliefs, social satisfaction, and well-being among Catholic, Jewish, and Protestant older adults. *The International Journal for the Psychology of Religion, 19,* 39–54.

Cohen, A. B., Hall, D. E., Koenig, H. G., & Meador, K. G. (2005). Social versus individual motivation: Implications for normative definitions of religious orientation. *Personality and Social Psychology Review, 9,* 48–61.

Cohen, A. B., & Hill, P. C. (2007). Religion as culture: Religious individualism and collectivism among American Catholics, Jews, and Protestants. *Journal of Personality, 75,* 709–742.

Cohen, A. B., Malka, A., Hill, E. D., Thoemmes, F., Hill, P. C., & Sundie, J. M. (2009). Race as a moderator of the relationship between religiosity and political alignment. *Personality and Social Psychology Bulletin, 35,* 271–282.

Cohen, A. B., Malka, A., Rozin, P., & Cherfas, L. (2006). Religion and unforgivable offenses. *Journal of Personality, 74,* 85–118.

Cohen, A. B., & Rankin, A. (2004). Religion and the morality of positive mentality. *Basic and Applied Social Psychology, 26,* 45–57.

Cohen, A. B., & Rozin, P. (2001). Religion and the morality of mentality. *Journal of Personality and Social Psychology, 81,* 697–710.

Cohen, A. B., Siegel, J. I., & Rozin, P. (2003). Faith versus practice: Different bases for religiosity judgments by Jews and Protestants. *European Journal of Social Psychology, 33,* 287–295.

Cohen, D. (2007). Methods in cultural psychology. In S. Kitayama & D. Cohen (Eds.), *Handbook of cultural psychology* (pp. 196–236). New York: Guilford Press.

Colzato, L. S., van Beest, I., van den Wildenberg, W. P. M., Scorolli, C., Dorchin, S., Meiran, N., et al. (2010). God: Do I have your attention? *Cognition, 117,* 87–94.

Cukur, C. S., de Guzman, M. R. T., & Carlo, G. (2004). Religiosity, values, and horizontal and vertical individualism-collectivism: A study of Turkey, the United States, and the Philippines. *Journal of Social Psychology, 144,* 613–634.

Demoulin, S., Saroglou, V., & Van Pachterbeke, M. (2008). Infra-humanizing others, supra-humanizing gods: The emotional hierarchy. *Social Cognition, 26,* 235–247.

Devos, T., Spini, D., & Schwartz, S. H. (2002). Conflicts among human values and trust in institutions. *British Journal of Social Psychology, 41,* 481–494.

Diener, E., Tay, L., & Myers, D. G. (2011). The religion paradox: If religion makes people happy, why are so many dropping out? *Journal of Personality and Social Psychology, 101,* 1278–1290.

Duriez, B., Luyten, P., Snauwaert, B., & Hutsebaut, D. (2002). The importance of religiosity and values in predicting political attitudes: Evidence for the continuing importance of religiosity in Flanders (Belgium). *Mental Health, Religion & Culture, 5,* 35–54.

Durkheim, E. (1951). *Suicide: A study in sociology* (J. A. Spaulding & G. Simpson, Trans.). New York: Free Press. (Original work published 1897)

Dy-Liacco, G. S., Piedmont, R. L., Murray-Swank, N. A., Rodgerson, T. E., & Sherman, M. F. (2009). Spirituality and religiosity as cross-cultural aspects of human experience. *Psychology of Religion and Spirituality, 1,* 35–52.

Elliott, M., & Hayward, R. D. (2009). Religion and life satisfaction worldwide: The role of government regulation. *Sociology of Religion, 70,* 285–310.

Ellison, C. G., Finch, B. K., Ryan, D. N., & Salinas, J. J. (2009). Religious involvement and depressive symptoms among Mexican-origin adults in California. *Journal of Community Psychology, 37,* 171–193.

Ellison, C. G., Musick, M. A., & Henderson, A. K. (2008). Balm in Gilead: Racism, religious involvement, and psychological distress among African American adults. *Journal for the Scientific Study of Religion, 47,* 291–309.

Fischer, P., Ai, A. L., Aydin, N., Frey, D., & Haslam, S. A. (2010). The relationship between religious identity and preferred coping strategies: An examination of the relative importance of interpersonal and intrapersonal coping in Muslim and Christian faiths. *Review of General Psychology, 14,* 365–381.

Fiske, A. P. (2002). Using individualism and collectivism to compare cultures—A critique of the validity and measurement of the constructs: Comment on Oyserman et al. (2002). *Psychological Bulletin, 128,* 78–88.

Flere, S., Edwards, K. J., & Klanjsek, R. (2008). Religious orientation in three central European environments: Quest, intrinsic, and extrinsic dimensions. *The International Journal for the Psychology of Religion, 18,* 1–21.

Friedman, E. H., & Hellerstein, H. K. (1968). Occupational stress, law school hierarchy, and coronary artery disease in Cleveland attorneys. *Psychosomatic Medicine, 30,* 72–86.

Friedman, M., & Saroglou, V. (2010). Religiosity, psychological acculturation to the host culture, self-esteem and depressive symptoms among stigmatized and nonstigmatized religious immigrant groups in Western Europe. *Basic and Applied Social Psychology, 32,* 185–195.

Gebauer, J. E., Paulhus, D. L., & Neberich, W. (in press). Big Two personality and religiosity across cultures: Communals as religious conformists and agentics as religious contrarians. *Social Psychological and Personality Science.*

Gebauer, J. E., Sedikides, C., & Neberich, W. (2012). Religiosity, social self-esteem, and psychological adjustment: On the cross-cultural specificity of the psychological benefits of religiosity. *Psychological Science, 23,* 158–160.

Georgas, J., Berry, J. W., van de Vijver, F. J. R., Kagitçibasi, C., & Poortinga, Y. H. (Eds.). (2006). *Families across cultures: A 30-nation psychological study.* New York: Cambridge University Press.

Georgas, J., van de Vijver, F. J. R., & Berry, J. W. (2004). The ecocultural framework, ecosocial indices, and psychological variables in cross-cultural research. *Journal of Cross-Cultural Psychology, 35,* 74–96.

Ghorpade, J., Lackritz, J. R., & Singh, G. (2006). Intrinsic religious orientation among minorities in the United States: A research note. *The International Journal for the Psychology of Religion, 16,* 51–62.

Granqvist, P., Mikulincer, M., & Shaver, P. (2010). Religion as attachment: Normative processes and individual differences. *Personality and Social Psychology Review, 14,* 49–59.

Guiso, L., Sapienza, P., & Zingales, L. (2003). People's opium?: Religion and economic attitudes. *Journal of Monetary Economics, 50,* 225–282.

Halman, L., & Riis, O. (Eds.). (2003). *Religion and secularizing society: The Europeans' religion at the end of the 20th century.* Leiden, The Netherlands: Brill.

Hammond, P. E., & Warner, K. (1993). Religion and ethnicity in late-twentieth century America. *Annals of the American Academy of Political and Social Science, 527,* 55–56.

Hayward, R. D., & Kemmelmeier, M. (2011). Weber revisited: A cross-national analysis of religiosity, religious culture and economic attitudes. *Journal of Cross-Cultural Psychology, 42,* 1309–1319.

Heine, S. I. (2010). Cultural psychology. In S. T. Fiske, D. T. Gilbert, & G. Lindzey (Eds.), *Handbook of social psychology* (5th ed., Vol. 2, pp. 1423–1464). New York: Wiley.

Henrich, J., Heine, S. J., & Norenzayan, A. (2010). The weirdest people in the world? *Behavioral and Brain Sciences, 33,* 61–83.

Holden, G. W., & Vittrup, B. (2010). Religion. In M. H. Bornstein (Ed.), *Handbook of cultural developmental science* (pp. 279–295). New York: Psychology Press.

Hong, Y., Wan, C., No, S., & Chiu, C. (2007). Multicultural identities. In S. Kitayama & D. Cohen (Eds.), *Handbook of cultural psychology* (pp. 323–345). New York: Guilford Press.

Hood, R. W., Jr., Ghorbani, N., Watson, P. J., Ghramaleki, A. F., Bing, M. N., Davison, H. K., et al. (2001). Dimensions of the Mysticism Scale: Confirming the three-factor structure in the United States and Iran. *Journal for the Scientific Study of Religion, 40,* 691–705.

Hood, R. W., Jr., Hill, P. C., & Gorsuch, R. (2009). *The psychology of religion: An empirical approach* (4th ed.). New York: Guilford Press.

Hooghe, M., & Reeskens, T. (2006). Kerkelijke betrokkenheid, vertrouwen en etnocentrisme: Een vergelijkende studie onder christelijke gelovigen in Europa [Religious involvement, generalized trust and ethnocentrism in Europe: Comparative study among Christian denominations]. *Tijdschrift voor Sociologie, 27*, 263–284.

Hunsberger, B., & Jackson, L. M. (2005). Religion, meaning, and prejudice. *Journal of Social Issues, 61*, 807–826.

Husaini, B. A., Blasi, A. J., & Miller, O. (1999). Does public and private religiosity have a moderating effect on depression?: A bi-racial study of elders in the American South. *International Journal of Aging and Human Development, 48*, 63–72.

Hvithamar, A., Warburg, M., & Jacobsen, B. A. (Eds.). (2009). *Holy nations and global identities: Civil religion, nationalism, and globalization*. Leiden, The Netherlands: Brill.

Inglehart, R., & Baker, W. E. (2000). Modernization, cultural change, and the persistence of traditional values. *American Sociological Review, 65*, 19–51.

Jarvis, G. K. (1977). Mormon mortality rates in Canada. *Social Biology, 24*, 294–302.

Kalmijn, M. (1998). Intermarriage and homogamy: Causes, patterns, trends. *Annual Review of Sociology, 24*, 395–421.

Karyotis, G., & Patrikios, S. (2010). Religion, securitization and anti-immigration attitudes: The case of Greece. *Journal of Peace Research, 47*, 43–57.

Kaufmann, E. (2007). *Sacralization by stealth: Demography, religion and politics in Europe*. London: Institute for Jewish Policy Research. Retrieved from *www.jpr.org.uk/publications/ publication,php?id=197*.

Kitayama, S., & Cohen, D. (Eds.). (2007). *Handbook of cultural psychology*. New York: Guilford Press.

Kivisto, P. (2007). Rethinking the relationship between ethnicity and religion. In J. A. Beckford & N. J. Demerath III (Eds.), *The SAGE handbook of the sociology of religion* (pp. 490–510). London: Sage.

Kunovich, R. M. (2009). The sources and consequences of national identification. *American Sociological Review, 74*, 573–593.

Lawton, L. E., & Bures, R. (2001). Parental divorce and the "switching" of religious identity. *Journal for the Scientific Study of Religion, 40*, 99–111.

Lazar, A., & Kravetz, S. (2005). Responses to the Mystical Scale by religious Jewish persons: A comparison of structural models of mystical experience. *The International Journal for the Psychology of Religion, 15*, 51–62.

Leach, M. M. (2009). Introduction to special section: Islam and mental health: Fertile ground for research. *Research in the Social Scientific Study of Religion, 20*, 147–149.

Li, Y. J., Johnson, K. A., Cohen, A. B., Williams, M. J., Knowles, E. D., & Chen, Z. (2012). Fundamental(ist) attribution error: Protestants are dispositionally focused. *Journal of Personality and Social Psychology, 102*, 281–290.

Liu, E. Y. (2010). Are risk-taking persons less religious?: Risk preference, religious affiliation, and religious participation in Taiwan. *Journal for the Scientific Study of Religion, 49*, 172–178.

Loewenthal, K. M. (2007). *Religion, culture, and mental health*. Cambridge, UK: Cambridge University Press.

Loewenthal, K. M., MacLeod, A. K., Lee, M., Cook, S., & Goldblatt, V. (2002). Tolerance for depression: Are there cultural and gender differences? *Journal of Psychiatric and Mental Health Nursing, 9*, 681–688.

Lyon, J. L., Bishop, C. T., & Nielsen, N. S. (1981). Cerebrovascular disease in Utah, 1968–1971. *Stroke, 12*, 564–566.

Maliepaard, M., Lubbers, M., & Gijsberts, M. (2010). Generational differences in ethnic and religious attachment and their interrelation: A study among Muslim minorities in the Netherlands. *Ethnic and Racial Studies, 33*, 451–472.

Markides, K. S. (1983). Aging, religiosity, and adjustment: A longitudinal analysis. *Journal of Gerontology, 38*, 621–625.

Markus, H. R., & Kitayama, S. (1991). Culture and the self: Implications for cognition, emotion and motivation. *Psychological Review, 98,* 224–253.

Matsumoto, D., & van de Vijver, F. J. (Eds.). (2010). *Cross-cultural research methods in psychology.* New York: Cambridge University Press.

McCullough, M. E., & Willoughby, B. L. B. (2009). Religion, self-regulation, and self-control: Associations, explanations, and implications. *Psychological Bulletin, 135,* 69–93.

Miller, A. S. (2000). Going to hell in Asia: The relationship between risk and religion in a cross cultural setting. *Review of Religious Research, 42,* 5–18.

Morris, P. (1996). Community beyond tradition. In P. Heelas, S. Lash, & P. Morris (Eds.), *Detraditionalization: Critical reflections on authority and identity* (pp. 222–249). Cambridge, UK: Blackwell.

Mullet, E., & Azar, F. (2009). Apologies, repentance, and forgiveness: A Muslim-Christian comparison. *The International Journal for the Psychology of Religion, 19,* 275–285.

Musick, M. A., Koenig, H. G., Hays, J. C., & Cohen, H. J. (1998). Religious activity and depression among community-dwelling elderly persons with cancer: The moderating effect of race. *Journal of Gerontology: Social Sciences, 53B,* S218–S227.

Nemeroff, C., & Rozin, P. (1992). Sympathetic magical beliefs and *kosher* dietary practice: The interaction of rules and feelings. *Ethos, 20,* 96–115.

Norenzayan, A., & Heine, S. J. (2005). Psychological universals: What are they and how can we know? *Psychological Bulletin, 135,* 763–784.

Norris, P., & Inglehart, R. (2004). *Sacred and secular: Religion and politics worldwide.* New York: Cambridge University Press.

O'Connor, S., & Vandenberg, B. (2005). Psychosis or faith?: Clinicians' assessment of religious beliefs. *Journal of Consulting and Clinical Psychology, 73,* 610–616.

Ogbu, J. H. (Ed.). (2008). *Minority status, oppositional culture, and schooling.* New York: Routledge.

Paul, G. (2009). The chronic dependence of popular religiosity upon dysfunctional psychosociological conditions. *Evolutionary Psychology, 7,* 398–441.

Phillips, R. L., Kuzma, J. W., Beeson, W. L., & Lotz, T. (1980). Influence of selection versus lifestyle on risk of fatal cancer and cardiovascular disease among Seventh-Day Adventists. *American Journal of Epidemiology, 112,* 296–314.

Plüss, C. (2009). Migration and the globalization of religion. In P. B. Clarke (Ed.), *The Oxford handbook of the sociology of religion* (pp. 491–506). New York: Oxford University Press.

Procter, M., & Hornsby-Smith, P. (2003). Individual religiosity, religious context and values in Europe and North America. In L. Halman & O. Riis (Eds.), *Religion and secularizing society: The Europeans' religion at the end of the 20th century* (pp. 92–113). Leiden, The Netherlands: Brill.

Quintana, S. M., & McKown, C. (Eds.). (2008). *Handbook of race, racism, and the developing child.* New York: Wiley.

Richards, P. S., & Bergin, A. E. (Eds.). (2000). *Handbook of psychotherapy and religious diversity.* Washington, DC: American Psychological Association.

Roccas, S., & Schwartz, S. H. (1997). Church-state relations and the association of religiosity with values: A study of Catholics in six countries. *Cross-Cultural Research, 31,* 356–375.

Ryan, R. M. (1982). Control and information in the intrapersonal sphere: An extension of cognitive evaluation theory. *Journal of Personality and Social Psychology, 43,* 450–461.

Safdar, S., Dupuis, D. R., Lewis, R. J., El-Geledi, S., & Bourhis, R. Y. (2008). Social axioms and acculturation orientations of English Canadians toward British and Arab Muslim immigrants. *International Journal of Intercultural Relations, 32,* 415–426.

Sanchez-Burks, J. (2002). Protestant relational ideology and (in)attention to relational cues in work settings. *Journal of Personality and Social Psychology, 83,* 919–929.

Saroglou, V. (2003). Trans-cultural/religious constants vs. cross-cultural/religious differences in psychological aspects of religion. *Archive for the Psychology of Religion, 25,* 71–87.

Saroglou, V. (2006). Quête d'unité: Spécificité religieuse d'une fonction non nécessairement reli-gieuse [Quest for unity: Religious specifics of a universal psychological function]. *Archives de Psychologie, 72,* 161–181.

Saroglou, V. (2010). Religiousness as a cultural adaptation of basic traits: A five factor model per-spective. *Personality and Social Psychology Review, 14,* 108–125.

Saroglou, V. (2011). Believing, bonding, behaving, and belonging: The big four religious dimen-sions and cultural variation. *Journal of Cross-Cultural Psychology, 42,* 1320–1340.

Saroglou, V. (2013). Religion, spirituality, and altruism. In K. I. Pargament, J. J. Exline, & J. W. Jones (Eds.), *APA handbook of psychology, religion, and spirituality (Vol. 1): Context, theory, and research* (pp. 439–457). Washington, DC: American Psychological Association.

Saroglou, V. (Ed.). (in press). *Religion, personality, and social behavior.* New York: Psychology Press.

Saroglou, V., & Cohen, A. B. (2011a). Psychology of culture and religion: Introduction to the JCCP special issue. *Journal of Cross-Cultural Psychology, 42,* 1309–1319.

Saroglou, V., & Cohen, A. B. (Eds.). (2011b). Religion and culture: Perspectives from cross-cul-tural psychology [Special issue]. *Journal of Cross-Cultural Psychology, 42*(8).

Saroglou, V., Delpierre, V., & Dernelle, R. (2004). Values and religiosity: A meta-analysis of stud-ies using Schwartz's model. *Personality and Individual Differences, 37,* 721–734.

Saroglou, V., & Galand, P. (2004). Identities, values, and religion: A study among Muslim, other immigrant, and native Belgian young adults after the 9/11 attacks. *Identity: An International Journal of Theory and Research, 4,* 97–132.

Saroglou, V., & Hanique, B. (2006). Jewish identity, values, and religion in a globalized world: A study of late adolescents. *Identity: An International Journal of Theory and Research, 6,* 231–249.

Saroglou, V., Lamkaddem, B., Van Pachterbeke, M., & Buxant, C. (2009). Host society's dislike of the Islamic veil: The role of subtle prejudice, values, and religion. *International Journal for Intercultural Relations, 33,* 419–428.

Saroglou, V., & Mathijsen, F. (2007). Religion, multiple identities, and acculturation: A study of Muslim immigrants in Belgium. *Archive for the Psychology of Religion, 29,* 177–198.

Saroglou, V., & Muñoz-García, A. (2008). Individual differences in religion and spirituality: An issue of personality traits and/or values. *Journal for the Scientific Study of Religion, 47,* 83–101.

Sasaki, J. Y., & Kim, H. S. (2011). At the intersection of culture and religion: A cultural analysis of religion's implications for secondary control and social affiliation. *Journal of Personality and Social Psychology, 101,* 401–414.

Sasaki, J. Y., Kim, H. S., & Xu, J. (2011). Religion and well-being: The moderating role of cul-ture and an oxytocin receptor polymorphism. *Journal of Cross-Cultural Psychology, 42,* 1394–1405.

Sheldon, K. M. (2006). Catholic guilt?: Comparing Catholics' and Protestants' religious motiva-tions. *The International Journal for the Psychology of Religion, 16,* 209–223.

Siev, J., & Cohen, A. B. (2007). Is thought-action fusion related to religiosity?: Group differences between Jews and Christians. *Behaviour Research and Therapy, 45,* 829–837.

Sirin, S. R., Bikmen, N., Mir, M., Fine, M., Zaal, M., & Katsiaficas, D. (2008). Exploring dual identification among Muslim-American emerging adults: A mixed methods study. *Journal of Adolescence, 31,* 259–279.

Stark, R. (2001). Gods, rituals, and the moral order. *Journal for the Scientific Study of Religion, 40,* 619–636.

Strabac, Z., & Listhaug, O. (2008). Anti-Muslim prejudice in Europe: A multilevel analysis of survey data from 30 countries. *Social Science Research, 37,* 268–286.

Tarakeshwar, N., Stanton, J., & Pargament, K. I. (2003). Religion: An overlooked dimension in cross-cultural psychology. *Journal of Cross-Cultural Psychology, 34,* 377–394.

Traunmüller, R. (2011). Moral communities?: Religion as a source of social trust in a multilevel analysis of 97 German regions. *European Sociological Review, 27,* 346–363.

Triandis, H. C. (1995). *Individualism and collectivism.* Boulder, CO: Westview.

Trommsdorff, G., & Chen, X. (Eds.). (2012). *Values, religion, and culture in adolescent development.* Cambridge, UK: Cambridge University Press.

Tsai, J. L., Miao, F., & Seppala, E. (2007). Good feelings in Christianity and Buddhism: Religious differences in ideal affect. *Personality and Social Psychology Bulletin, 33,* 409–421.

Van de Vliert, E. (2008). *Climate, affluence, and culture.* New York: Cambridge University Press.

Van der Straten Waillet, N., & Roskam, I. (2012). Developmental and social determinants of religious social categorization. *Journal of Genetic Psychology, 173,* 208–220.

Verkuyten, M. (2008). Life satisfaction among ethnic minorities: The role of discrimination and group identification. *Social Indicators Research, 89,* 391–404.

Verkuyten, M., & Yildiz, A. A. (2007). National (dis)identification, and ethnic and religious identity: A study among Turkish-Dutch Muslims. *Personality and Social Psychology Bulletin, 33,* 1448–1462.

Viladrich, A., & Abraído-Lanza, A. F. (2009). Religion and mental health among minorities and immigrants in the U.S. In S. Loue & M. Sajatovic (Eds.), *Determinants of minority mental health and wellness* (pp. 149–174). New York: Springer.

Young, M. J., Morris, M. W., Burrus, J., Krishnan, L., & Regmi M. P. (2011). Deity and destiny: Patterns of fatalistic thinking in Christian and Hindu cultures. *Journal of Cross-Cultural Psychology, 42,* 1030–1053.

Part IV

THE CONSTRUCTION AND EXPRESSION OF RELIGION AND SPIRITUALITY

18

Religion and Meaning

Crystal L. Park

Meaning is widely regarded as central to human experience. Frankl (1969) considered "will to meaning" the primary human motive, arguing that the main goal in life is not to gain pleasure or power but to find meaning and value in life. Further, he posited that meaning is not inherent in life but rather must be actively created by each individual. Expanding on Frankl's ideas, Baumeister (1991) noted that people actively construct the meaning of their lives on a daily basis and that meaning is part of every action and thought. He described the human need for meaning as a craving, a desire—even an addiction, complete with tolerance and withdrawal effects (Baumeister, 1991).

Unpacking the notion of the "need for meaning," Park, Edmondson, and Hale-Smith (2013) asserted that this need may be better understood as the need for a functional meaning system. Although more cumbersome, this phrase more clearly describes the complex role of meaning in meeting myriad meaning-related needs. People require a system of meaning to comprehend the world and to navigate and organize the infinite stimuli they encounter, from basic perceptions of their environment to broad existential questions. In this sense, humans possess the most extreme example of a cognitive framework that provides prediction and explanation; other animals also have cognitive systems, albeit less complex (e.g., Shettleworth, 2010). However, humans go far beyond biological imperatives in the functions of their meaning systems. Humans desire a sense of purpose and direction, a feeling that what they are doing has some ultimate purpose, a view of their daily endeavors in the context of a bigger picture, transcendence; these are the demands placed upon their meaning systems.

A host of specific meaning-related needs has been identified, including self-regulation (Koole, McCullough, Kuhl, & Roelofsma, 2010), agency (Gray & Wegner, 2010), control (Kay, Gaucher, McGregor, & Nash, 2010), certainty (Hogg, Adelman, & Blagg, 2010), identity (Ysseldyk, Matheson, & Anisman, 2010), social validation and integration, comprehension, security (Park et al., 2013), purpose, efficacy, values, self-worth (Baumeister, 1991), and the need to cope with trauma and awareness of our own mortality (Vail et al., 2010).

Religion has been proposed as one way in which humans may meet these existential, meaning-related needs (e.g., Koltko-Rivera, 2006–2007; Park et al., 2013). In fact, Batson and Stocks (2004) went so far as to define religion as "whatever a person does to deal with existential questions" (p. 141). They further described the meaning-related existential basis of all of the needs identified by Maslow (1970) and how religion can address all of them. For example, safety needs raise the existential questions, "What can and should I do to protect myself? Are there powerful forces that I can and should appeal to for safety? How can I control the future?," all of which religion can satisfactorily answer (Batson & Stocks, 2004). Similarly, the construct of implicit religion has been put forward to describe how human endeavors that are not overtly religious in nature may be seen as inherently religious by the functions they serve (Bailey, 2010).

This chapter describes current theories and empirical findings regarding religion and meaning. To provide a framework for this review, a model of meaning is first presented that distinguishes global and situational meaning. This model is then used to describe how religion is often involved in both levels: global meaning in terms of beliefs, goals, and the subjective sense of meaningfulness, and situational meaning in both ordinary and stressful life circumstances. The chapter concludes with suggestions regarding future research on religion and meaning.

THE MEANING-MAKING MODEL

Humans strive to create and maintain order, certainty, and value in light of challenges and abruptions in their endeavours to do so.
    —STEVEN J. HEINE, TRAVIS PROULX, AND KATHLEEN D. VOHS (2006, p. 89)

Developed to integrate the various predominant strands of theory and research on meaning, the meaning-making model posits that there are two important aspects of meaning, global and situational meaning (Park, 2010; see Figure 18.1). Global meaning is an overarching system that provides the general framework through which people structure their lives and assign meanings to specific encounters with their environment (situational meaning). Global meaning comprises three aspects: beliefs, goals, and feelings (Park & Folkman, 1997). Global beliefs are broadly encompassing assumptions that inform people's views of their own nature as well as their understanding of other people and the world (Janoff-Bulman, 1992; Koltko-Rivera, 2004). Global goals refer to people's motivation/purpose for living, choice of goals, standards for judging behavior, and basis for self-esteem. Global goals are high-level ideals, states, or objects toward which people work to achieve or maintain (Karoly, 1999; Klinger, 1998). The emotional aspect of global meaning refers to experiencing a sense of meaning or purpose in life or as being connected to causes greater than oneself (Reker & Wong, 1988; Klinger, 1977). This sense of meaningfulness may be derived, in part, from seeing one's actions as oriented or making progress toward desired future goals (Baumeister, 1991; McGregor & Little, 1998).

Global meaning influences individuals' interpretations of both ordinary encounters and highly stressful events (appraised meaning). In everyday life, global meaning informs individuals' understanding of themselves and their lives and directs their personal projects and, through them, their general sense of well-being and life satisfaction (e.g.,

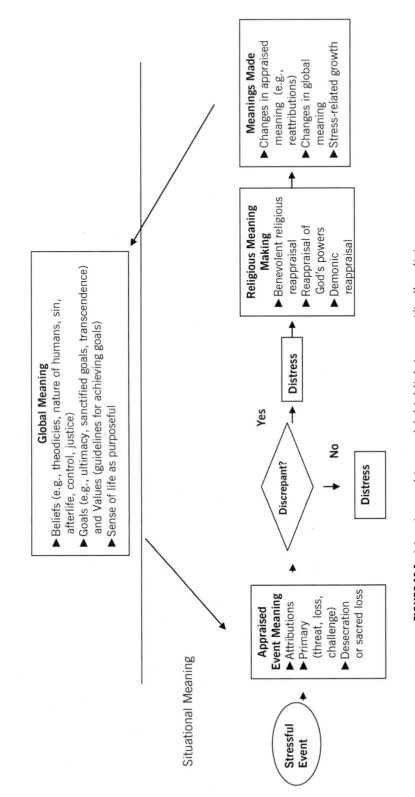

FIGURE 18.1. Meaning-making model, highlighting specifically religious aspects.

Emmons, 1999). Further, when individuals encounter potentially stressful or traumatic events, they assign a meaning to them. Appraised meanings are compared with global meaning, and stress or trauma is thought to occur when appraised meanings "shatter" or violate aspects of one's global meaning system (Janoff-Bulman, 1992; Koss & Figueredo, 2004). For example, experiencing a brutal assault by a stranger may violate one's global beliefs that the world is fair or that people are benevolent. Global goals are violated when an event is appraised as discrepant with what one wants. Thus, a brutal assault may also violate one's goals of staying healthy, safe, and intact.

Determining that an appraised event violates one's global meaning can lead to a loss of a sense of control or a sense that the world is predictable and comprehensible, creating distress. The meaning-making model posits that the extent of discrepancy between individuals' global beliefs and goals and their appraised situational meaning of the event determines their level of distress (Park & Folkman, 1997; Park, 2008). This distress, in turn, initiates meaning making, a search for restoration of coherence among aspects of global meaning and the appraised meaning assigned to the event (Park, Mills, & Edmondson, 2010).

Meaning making refers to attempts to restore global meaning when it has been disrupted or violated. Meaning making involves coming to see or understand the situation in a different way and reviewing and reforming one's beliefs and goals in order to regain consistency among them (Davis, Wortman, Lehman, & Silver, 2000). When situational meaning is discrepant with their global meaning, people typically attempt to change or distort their views of events to incorporate them into their global meaning (i.e., assimilation). However, when the discrepancy is too great, people may change their global meaning to incorporate events (i.e., accommodation). The meaning-making process helps people reduce their sense of discrepancy between appraised and global meanings and restore a sense that the world is comprehensible and that their own lives are worthwhile.

Meaning making is generally considered adaptive to the extent that satisfactory meanings are produced (Harper et al., 2007; Michael & Snyder, 2005). However, an inability to reduce discrepancies between situational and global meaning leads to rumination, intrusive thoughts, and depression (Gray, Maguen, & Litz, 2007). Meaning making can lead to many outcomes, referred to as *meanings made*. Many different meanings can be made through the process of meaning making, including changes in one's appraisal of a stressful event (e.g., coming to see it as less damaging or perhaps even fortuitous), changes in one's global meaning (e.g., viewing the world as less controllable), and stress-related growth (e.g., experiencing increased appreciation for life, stronger connections with family and friends, or greater self-awareness of one's strengths).

RELIGION AND GLOBAL MEANING

No other system of meaning is so bold in its proclaimed ability to provide a sense of significance. Meaning is embedded within religion's sacred character, so that it points to humanity's ultimate purpose—in the Judeo-Christian tradition, for example, to love and worship God.
—RALPH W. HOOD, JR., PETER C. HILL, AND BERNARD SPILKA (2009, p. 16)

Religion is a common basis for global meaning systems, but it is not the only one. For example, some researchers have discussed alternatives, such as science or naturalistic materialism (e.g., Fales, 2007; Preston & Epley, 2009). However, the extent to which nonreligious, nonmetaphysical frameworks can address issues of ultimate purpose and existence may be limited (Vail et al., 2010), and people often find such nonmetaphysical viewpoints unsatisfactory (Edmondson & Hale-Smith, 2013; Carvalho, 2006). Religious meaning systems, on the contrary, appear well suited to provide global meaning. For example, Hood, Hill, and Williamson (2005) identified four criteria by which religion is uniquely capable of providing global meaning: comprehensiveness, accessibility, transcendence, and direct claims.

Comprehensiveness refers to the vast scope of issues that religion can subsume, including beliefs about the world (e.g., human nature, social and natural environment, the afterlife), contingencies and expectations (rewards for righteousness and punishment for doing evil), goals (e.g., benevolence, altruism, supremacy), actions (e.g., compassion, charity, violence) and emotions (e.g., love, joy, peace) (Hood et al., 2009; Silberman, 2005). Religion is accessible in that it is widely promoted and comes in many forms, so that people can usually find a way of being religious or spiritual that suits them (Hood et al., 2005). Religions provide opportunities for transcending their own concerns or experience and connecting with something greater. Finally, religions make bold and authoritative claims regarding their ability to provide a sense of significance. All of these characteristics lead to the unmatched ability of religion to serve as the source of global meaning systems (Hood et al., 2009).

Religion and Global Beliefs

Systems of religious concepts tend to (1) be comprehensive and well integrated, (2) emphasize the orderliness of the universe, and (3) portray the world as "just" (or at least as not morally arbitrary). Religion provides answers to questions that otherwise might seem unanswerable. In short, religion is a major source of meaning.
    —BERNARD SPILKA, PHILLIP SHAVER, AND LEE A. KIRKPATRICK (1997, p. 159)

When religion is incorporated into people's global meaning systems, their understanding of God or of the divine (e.g., as loving and benevolent, wrathful, or distant) will inform their beliefs about the nature of people (e.g., inherent goodness, made in God's image, sinful human nature) and this world (e.g., the coming apocalypse, the illusory nature of reality) as well as, perhaps, the next (e.g., heaven, reincarnation) (McIntosh, 1995; Silberman, 2005).

Religion also forms the core of many individuals' identities in terms of how they understand themselves as a religious or spiritual being (e.g., as unworthy of God, as chosen; Pargament, 1997; Slattery & Park, 2011) as well as their social identification with a religious group (Ysseyldyk et al., 2010). Religious identity can also provide a source of self-esteem and moral superiority (Sedikides & Gebauer, 2010), although perceiving discrepancies between one's current and ideal spiritual selves has been related to poorer psychological functioning (e.g., Saunders, Lucas, & Kuras, 2007).

In addition to explicitly religious beliefs, religion can inform and influence other global beliefs, such as in fairness, control, coherence, benevolence of the world and other people, and vulnerability (Koltko-Rivera, 2006–2007). For example, in describing the just world theory (Lerner, 1980), Janoff-Bulman and Frantz (1997) noted, "Theories of deservingness generally encompass many religious perspectives, which enable believers to perceive meaning through the expectations of rewards and punishments that may be considerably delayed, such as one's fate after death" (p. 93).

A large body of research has established links between religiousness and beliefs regarding control, both through direct or primary means and secondary means, such as through intercessory prayer (Rothbaum, Weisz, & Snyder, 1982; Young & Morris, 2004). Some forms of religiousness explicitly encourage a surrender of control and a handing over of control to powerful others (Exline, 2002). Experimental research has demonstrated that following manipulations that lower a sense of personal control, people report higher levels of belief in a God who has control over events (Kay et al., 2010), consistent with the view that religion can serve as an important way to maintain a sense of control.

The concept of theodicy, while seldom investigated by psychologists of religion, appears to hold great promise for understanding how people come to withstand life's difficulties, even severely traumatic events. Theodicy refers to the explanations for human suffering: "philosophical/theological attempts to reconcile the presence of evil and suffering in the world with the idea of an all-powerful and good creator God" (Hall & Johnson, 2001, p. 5). Hall and Johnson discussed how individuals can hold only two of the following three propositions simultaneously: God is omnipotent, God is all good, and evil exists. They noted that people struggle to find some way to believe that these three statements are not logically incompatible or defend the plausibility of God's existence in the light of these seemingly contradictory propositions. Such struggle to make meaning or hold onto one's beliefs in a powerful and loving God when one has personally experienced evil or severe negative trauma can be great (Pargament, 1997; Kushner, 1981).

A variety of solutions to this dilemma lead to a variety of theodicy beliefs. Hall and Johnson (2001) note that one influential Christian viewpoint holds that goodness can occur only in a world where evil also exists, particularly those virtues that an individual comes to practice only through suffering because of evil, such as patience, mercy, forgiveness, endurance, faith, courage, and compassion (Hall & Johnson, 2001). In this meaning system, one can come to see one's traumatic or stressful experience as an opportunity to grow through one's suffering (e.g., to build one's soul, to become more Christ-like, to grow in agape love; Hall & Johnson, 2001). Another solution may be to view suffering as necessary for reaching future events, such as the ultimate goal of salvation (Baumeister, 1991).

Research has recently begun to focus on theodicies. One research group has published a measure purporting to measure theodicy, although it actually measures general beliefs in God's involvement in the world (Daugherty, West, Williams, & Brockman, 2009). However, a measure more explicitly assessing theodicies has recently been developed. This measure, the Views of Suffering Scale, taps a variety of different theodicies, including those of karma, randomness, and views of suffering as retribution and as soul building, along with beliefs that God has limited knowledge and that God suffers along with the sufferers (Hale-Smith, Park, & Edmondson, 2012). This new measure will allow researchers to examine a host of questions regarding theodicies and their roles in human functioning.

Although religiousness and spirituality have generally been found to influence global beliefs in positive ways, some types of religious beliefs can be negative in their content or influence on the believer as well. For example, some religious cognitions, such as religious extremism or rigidity as well as beliefs about an angry, uncaring, or punitive God can have powerfully destructive implications for personal and social functioning (see Exline & Rose, Chapter 19, and Moghaddam, Warren, & Love, Chapter 32, this volume). In terms of influences on the believer, some research has suggested that although a sense of secondary control is often helpful, it also poses the risk of religious fatalism, by which people may abdicate responsibility to take direct actions to alleviate problems (e.g., Franklin, Schlundt, & Wallston, 2008; Norenzayan & Lee, 2010). For example, one study of people with HIV found that those who believed God/higher power controlled their health were nearly five times more likely to refuse antiretroviral medication than were those without those beliefs (Kremer, Ironson, & Porr, 2009).

Religion and Global Goals

People who vary in their religiosity are guided by different value priorities—those who are more committed to religion attribute relatively high importance to values that express the motivation to avoid uncertainty, and relatively low importance to values that express the motivations to follow one's sensuous hedonistic desires, and the motivation to be independent in thought and action. This pattern of correlations has been found in many monotheisitic religious groups that varied in their economic strength, as well as in their ethnic and cultural composition and history.
—SONIA ROCCAS (2005, p. 757)

Religion is central to the life purposes of many people, providing their ultimate motivation and primary goals for living as well as prescriptions and guidelines for achieving those goals (e.g., Baumeister, 1991; Pargament, 1997). Ultimate goals can include connecting or adhering to what one regards as sacred; living a life full of benevolence, forgiveness, or altruism; achieving enlightenment; finding salvation; knowing God; or experiencing transcendence (Emmons, 1999; Pargament, Magyar-Russell, & Murray-Swank, 2005). Other goals can be derived from these superordinate ones, such as having peace of mind, working for peace and justice in the world, devoting oneself to one's family, or creating a strong sense of community with other believers. Of course, it must be noted, people often embrace negative goals, such as supremacy and destruction, in the name of religion as well (see Moghaddam et al., Chapter 32, this volume). While some goals are explicitly religious or spiritual, each and every goal that an individual holds may become connected to what he or she holds as sacred through the process of sanctification (e.g., Mahoney et al., 2005). Sanctification involves assigning spiritual significance and character to secular objects (Mahoney et al., 1999). Therefore, any goal can take on religious value if the individual ties it to his or her conceptualization of the sacred (Pargament et al., 2005). People sacralize everyday goals with different types of religious motivation (e.g., transcendent, culturally normative; Martos, Kézdy, & Horváth-Szabó, 2011).

Related to goals are values, broad preferences about the worth of ultimate goals and the appropriate courses of action to achieve those goals. Values are the guidelines that individuals use to determine worth, importance, or correctness (Schwartz & Bilsky, 1990) and reflect a person's sense of right and wrong. Values guide decision making regarding one's behavior in the course of achieving goals. Religion is an extremely potent source of values for individuals as well as for entire cultures, supplying a framework for determining what is right and good and to be pursued and what is wrong and bad and to be avoided (Baumeister, 1991). Divine will can be considered the ultimate arbiter of right and wrong (Baumeister, 1991; Emmons, 1999). Religions are in an unusually esteemed position to determine or establish these criteria of right and wrong and good and bad; they may, in fact, be the most powerful source of values in many cultures (Baumeister, 1991; see Saroglou & Cohen, Chapter 17, this volume).

Research examining values cross-culturally has found that in countries where people reported highly valuing certainty, self-restraint, and submission over superior external truths, the people were generally more religious, while citizens in countries valuing openness to change and free self-expression were less religious (Schwartz & Huismans, 1995). More recent research has extended this line of inquiry by focusing specifically on measures of religiousness, finding that religion/spirituality was associated with greater emphasis on values of benevolence and lower emphasis on self-direction, self-development, and hedonism (Saroglou & Muñoz-García, 2008).

Religious motivations have been a topic of considerable research (see Emmons & Schnitker, Chapter 13, this volume). These motivations can be quite revealing regarding global meaning—what religious ends do people pursue and by what means? Are people drawn to engage in religion as a rewarding endeavor or driven to engage in it out of fear (Jackson & Francis, 2004)? Although the lion's share of this research has used some variant of the intrinsic–extrinsic distinction (e.g., Francis, Lewis, & Robins, 2010; see Nielsen, Hatton, & Donahue, Chapter 16, this volume), there are other ways to conceptualize motivation that may have important implications for global religious goals (e.g., Ryan & Deci, 2000) that await integration into the psychology of religion (e.g., Neyrinck, Lens, Vansteenkiste, & Soenens, 2010; see Emmons & Schnitker, Chapter 13, this volume, for a review).

Religion and the Subjective Sense of Meaning in Life

Our framework suggests that the cognitive, motivational, and social aspects of finding meaning in life offer us the directions necessary for a rather "grand" psychological theory of understanding the role of religion in human life.

—RALPH W. HOOD, JR., ET AL. (2009, p. 12)

Although religion and meaning in life may seem obviously linked, surprisingly few studies have specifically documented these links, and most of the research has examined bivariate relations of fairly simplistic measures of both religion and sense of purpose. Results of these studies indicate that religiousness is related to a sense of meaning in life (Donahue, 1985; Tomer & Eliason, 2000). For example, a series of studies among college students produced moderate-size correlations (rs = approximately .40; Steger & Frazier, 2005).

The relationship between religiousness and meaning may be moderated by demographic factors. For example, religiousness appears to be more strongly related to a sense of life meaning in the elderly (Ardelt, 2003; Krause, 2008) and for older black adults compared with older white adults (Krause, 2008). Further, different aspects of religiousness and spirituality may be differentially related to a sense of meaning in life. Intrinsic religiousness has been found to be more strongly positively related to meaning in life than extrinsic religiousness in studies of both undergraduates (Francis & Hills, 2008;

Steger, Frazier, Oishi, & Kaler, 2006) and community-dwelling elders (Ardelt, 2003); some studies have found that extrinsic religiousness was unrelated (e.g., Francis, Jewell, & Robbins, 2010) or inversely related (e.g., Ardelt, 2003) to a sense of meaning in life.

Recent research suggests that the connections between religiousness or spirituality and a sense of meaning in life may be even more complex in that religiousness may change the very basis of meaning in life, by shifting people's focus away from hedonic concerns about the pursuit of pleasure toward eudemonic concerns about living according to one's core values or authentic self (Koole et al., 2010; Saroglou, Delpierre, & Dernelle, 2004; also see Ryan & Deci, 2001). Consistent with this notion, studies of undergraduates indicate that positive affect predicts meaning in life more strongly among students with lower religious involvement or students who were not primed with positive religious words relative to those who were primed or those with higher religious involvement (Hicks & King, 2008).

RELIGION AND SITUATIONAL MEANING

A religion provides individuals with something to believe in—typically a set of doctrines about natural and supernatural reality that enable people to understand their broader, ultimate context. . . . Religion guarantees that whatever happens to the individual, no matter how good or bad, will make sense.

—ROY F. BAUMEISTER (1991, pp. 183–184)

Religion can provide individuals with comprehensive and integrated frameworks of meaning that are able to explain many worldly events, experiences, and situations in highly satisfactory ways (Spilka, Hood, Hunsberger, & Gorsuch, 2003). Religious meaning systems provide ways to understand mundane, day-to-day occurrences as well as extraordinary ones (e.g., Zell & Baumeister, Chapter 25, this volume; Spilka et al., 2003). Research linking religion to meaning in day-to-day experiences and highly stressful events are reviewed next.

Religion and Meaning in Day-to-Day Experiences

In attempting to answer questions such as "Does life have any real meaning?" or "Is there any ultimate purpose to human existence?" implicit worldview beliefs give rise to goal concerns that reflect how people "walk with ultimacy" in daily life.

—ROBERT A. EMMONS (2005, p. 737)

Global religious beliefs can pervasively and continuously influence perceptions and interpretations by functioning as schemas (Silberman, 2005). Through basic cognitive processes of perception, language, and memory, religious beliefs, as schemas, influence what people notice, experience, and remember (Ozorak, 2005; Barrett, Chapter 12, this volume). The extent to which religious beliefs are salient and available determines the extent to which they are drawn upon to form perceptions and attributions (Ozorak, 2005). For example, a study of attention to visual stimuli found that, regardless of current religious affiliation, those who were raised as Calvinist (emphasizing individual responsibility) compared with those raised as Catholic or Jewish (emphasizing social solidarity) exhibited the global precedence effect (greater attention to global than to local features).

Further, the size of the effect varied as a function of the amount and strictness of religious practices (Colzato et al., 2010).

Although the effects of schemas are particularly powerful in ambiguous situations, people tend to consistently structure their perceptions and interpretations in ways that confirm their preexisting expectations (Ozorak, 2005). Global religious beliefs allow "top-down" or concept-driven processing, perception that is preceded by and shaped by expectation, in which people go beyond the information given and rely on their schematic information (i.e., beliefs and expectations) to fill in the gaps. Religious schemas have been shown to influence the speed, type, and extent of cognitive processing in which people engage (McIntosh, 1995; Ozorak, 2005).

Religion often prescribes goals and the appropriate behaviors to achieve these goals (see Emmons & Schnitker, Chapter 13, this volume). Global goals are pursued through a variety of lower level, more concrete goals. Personal strivings refer to the recurrent or ongoing goals that a person characteristically tries to attain or maintain. According to Emmons (2005), spiritual strivings refer to goals that involve self-transcendence and that concern ultimate questions of meaning and existence. Prototypic of these types of strivings are those that reflect increasing knowledge of God or a higher power (e.g., reading the Bible on a daily basis) or concern tending to one's ongoing relationship with God or a higher power (e.g., saying daily prayers).

Religion often underlies a broader span of strivings than those that are explicitly religious or spiritual. In fact, people can imbue virtually any personal striving as having spiritual significance and character (Mahoney et al., 2005). In a study of a community sample, people reported considering many of their strivings as sacred even when they were not explicitly spiritual or religious. However, they rated strivings that explicitly involved religious and spiritual issues as more sanctified than their other strivings (Mahoney et al., 2005). These authors concluded that personal strivings that are concerned with things beyond the self are more likely to be characterized in sacred, transcendent terms than are strivings that are focused on the self or on material possessions.

Religion and Meaning in Stressful Life Circumstances

Religion fills in the blanks in our knowledge of life and the world, and offers us a sense of security. This is especially true when we are confronted with crisis and death. Religion is therefore a normal, natural, functional development whereby "persons are prepared intellectually and emotionally to meet the non-manipulable aspects of existence positively by means of a reinterpretation of the total situation" (Bernhardt, 1958, p. 157).
                                            —RALPH W. HOOD, JR., ET AL. (2009, p. 13)

According to the meaning-making model, crises trigger processes of meaning making, through which individuals struggle to reduce discrepancies between their appraised meaning of a particular stressful event and their global beliefs and goals (Park, 2010; Baumeister & Vohs, 2002; Filipp, 1992). Religion is often an integral part of this meaning-making process. In fact, religion may exert its most pronounced influence in times of greatest stress (McIntosh, Silver, & Wortman, 1993; Pargament, 1997) for at least two reasons: (1) For most people, religion is part of their global beliefs and goals, which may be threatened or violated by traumatic events, and (2) most religions provide ways of understanding, reinterpreting, and adding value to difficulties and suffering as well as ways to see the work of a loving God (Pargament, 1997; Park, 2005). For people experiencing injustice, suffering, or trauma, a religious belief system and its associated goals may be the most unfailing way to make meaning from their experiences.

Religion as a framework of meaning can strongly influence individuals' initial appraisals, or understanding, of particular events. Following events experienced as highly stressful, individuals have a number of ways of making meaning, which generally involve changing the appraised meaning of events by understanding them in a different and less stressful way (e.g., by understanding the suffering as having redeeming value, or by searching for positive aspects of the event; Baumeister, 1991) or by changing the global beliefs and goals that were violated, to bring them more in line with their current understanding of what has happened (Pargament, 1997; Park, 2010). Finally, religion can be highly involved in the products of these processes, including the positive changes that individuals report following stressful experiences (Park, 2004). The following sections describe how religion is involved in meaning making through the processes of initial appraisals, appraisals of discrepancy, meaning-making coping (efforts at changing both appraised meaning and changing global meaning), and outcomes of the meaning-making process (meanings made).

Initial Appraisals

That God may be both the cause and the cure of hardship suggests another reason why harm leads us to God more strongly than help—with help people may thank Him, but with harm people both curse and embrace Him.
                                                    —KURT GRAY AND DANIEL M. WEGNER (2010, p. 12)

Any specific event can be experienced and understood in very different ways, depending on individuals' specific views, including their religious beliefs. Religious beliefs provide many alternatives for interpreting an event. For example, notions that there is a larger plan, that events are not random, or that personal growth can arise from struggle can inform the specific meaning of an event. Some individuals may believe that God would not harm them or visit upon them more than they could handle, whereas others may believe that God is trying to communicate something important through the event, or that the event is a punishment from God (Furnham & Brown, 1992). One study of hospice caregivers found that some caregivers appraised their situation as part of God's plan or as a way to gain strength or understanding from God, while others viewed their situation as a punishment from or desertion by God; the former was related to better adjustment to the loss, while the latter was related to greater distress (Mickley, Pargament, Brandt, & Hipp, 1998). Another study found that chronic pain patients who held a positive God image were more likely to appraise their illness as an opportunity to change their life or to re?ect upon what is essential in life, which predicted happiness in life, while chronic pain patients with an angry God image were less likely to appraise their illness in this way, leading to lower levels of happiness (Dezutter et al., 2010).

Religiousness can influence how people understand and respond to specific traumatic events. For example, in a study of students who were strongly adversely affected by the 2005 hurricanes along the Gulf Coast, higher religiousness was related to greater appraisal of the hurricanes as threatening and as more of a loss and less of a challenge.

Further, those who were more religious were more likely to perceive God as responsible for the hurricanes (Newton & McIntosh, 2009). Religious beliefs are clearly implicated in how people understand the afterlife and respond to bereavement (Benore & Park, 2004; Park & Halifax, 2011). For example, some people believe that the deceased continue to exist, that they will be reunited with the deceased after death, and even that they can continue to interact with the deceased currently, albeit in a different way, while others believe that there is no afterlife or that it is unpleasant or even painful (Flannelly, Ellison, Galek, & Koenig, 2008).

Causal attributions, people's understandings of why a given event occurred, are another important type of event appraisal; attributions can be naturalistic or religious (Spilka et al., 2003). For example, naturalistic explanations for illnesses can include stress, injury, pathogens, and weakened immune systems, while religious attributions can include God's efforts to teach, challenge, or punish the afflicted or to teach a lesson to others (Spilka et al., 2003). It is quite common for individuals to make naturalistic attributions for the immediate or proximal cause of the event but also invoke religious or metaphysical explanations for the more distal attributions (see Park & Folkman, 1997). Religious attributions appear to be particularly likely for aversive or harmful events (Gray & Wegner, 2010) and those of high ambiguity and threat (Spilka et al., 2003). The likelihood that an individual will make religious or nonreligious attributions for particular experiences or encounters also depends, in large part, on the relative availability of global religious and naturalistic beliefs (Gray & Wegner, 2010; Spilka et al., 2003) as well as the extent to which the explanatory power of each type of attribution is satisfactory (Spilka et al., 2003).

Another type of event appraisal based on religious meaning systems is that of sacred loss and desecration. These appraisals involve perception of the dissolution of a point of connection with transcendent reality. These appraisals can be of the event as a sacred loss, the perception of the loss of something viewed as a manifestation of God or something invested with sacred qualities. They can also be an appraisal of the event as desecration, perceiving sacred aspects of life as having been violated. One study of students whose parents divorced found that general religiousness predicted greater appraisals of sacred loss and desecration; these types of appraisals were highly distressing (Warner, Mahoney, & Krumrei, 2009).

Determinations of Discrepancy/Distress

Traumatic events undermine the belief systems that give meaning to human experience. They violate the victim's faith in a natural or divine order and cast the victim into a state of existential crisis.

—JUDITH L. HERMAN (1997, p. 51)

After appraising the initial meaning of an event, individuals must determine the extent to which that meaning is congruent with their general views of the world and their desires and goals. Although the meaning-making model is widely discussed in research on stressful life events (e.g., Gillies & Neimeyer, 2006; Skaggs & Barron, 2006), surprisingly little research has explicitly focused on how people evaluate the discrepancies between their global meaning and their appraisals of potentially traumatic events (Park et al., 2012). Several studies have provided indirect evidence that people higher in religiousness may perceive traumatic events as more discrepant with their global meaning systems, suggesting that sudden and inexplicable aversive events are highly challenging to the devout individual's positive global meaning (Park, 2005; Park & Cohen, 1993). For example, a study of college students coping with the death of a significant other found that religiousness was related to higher levels of disruption of both global beliefs and goals (Park, 2005). Similarly, in a study of bereaved parents of Sudden Infant Death Syndrome infants, parents' rating of the importance of religion was *positively* related to their reports of engaging in searching for meaning shortly after the death (McIntosh et al., 1993), suggesting a positive link between religiousness and violation of global meaning.

Religion and Meaning-Making Coping

Though the event may hurt or threaten, there is another and more important dimension to it. Beneath the surface of the situation, we can find God working his will; we can find a spiritual companion who makes the trauma more manageable; and we can find opportunities and challenges for spiritual growth. This is a powerful coping strategy.
—KENNETH I. PARGAMENT (1997, p. 223)

According to the meaning-making model, discrepancy produces distress and drives efforts to restore congruency through meaning making. People make meaning in many different ways, attempting to change their appraised meaning of the stressor to make it less aversive or minimize its impact, or change their global beliefs and goals to accommodate this new and unwelcome experience. Some of these processes are deliberate coping efforts, while others may be less effortful and experienced more as intrusive thoughts (see Park, 2010, for a review). Many of these meaning-making efforts have a religious aspect, and, in fact, much of religious coping comprises efforts to make meaning from the stressful situation. For example, the RCOPE (Pargament, Smith, Koenig, & Perez, 1998), a widely used measure of religious coping, includes a number of subscales explicitly tapping into religious reappraisals of the event or reconfiguring one's global meaning system. For example, coping through *benevolent religious reappraisal* refers to using religion to redefine the stressor as benevolent and potentially beneficial while *reappraisal of God's powers* refers to redefining God's ability to influence the stressful situation.

These types of religious reappraisals of both the meaning of the stressful event and one's global meaning are fairly common and may facilitate changes in meaning as well as powerfully influence adjustment to stressful events (see Pargament, Falb, Ano, & Wachholtz, Chapter 28, this volume, for a review of religious coping). For example, a study of college students coping with loss found that coping through religious reappraisal, particularly questioning God's power or seeing the loss as a punishment from God, were related to more stress-related growth but also more distress; reappraising the loss as more consistent with a benevolent God was also related to more stress-related growth but unrelated to distress (Stein et al., 2009).

Religion and Meanings Made

When the sacred is seen working its will in life's events, what first seems random, nonsensical and tragic is changed into something else—an opportunity to appreciate life more fully, a chance to be with God, a challenge to help others grow, or a loving act meant to prevent something worse from taking place.

—KENNETH I. PARGAMENT (1997, p. 223)

The eventual products or outcomes of meaning making are changes in appraised meaning of the stressful event and, sometimes, changes in global meaning. Because religious beliefs, like other basic beliefs, tend to be relatively stable, people confronting crises are thought to be more likely to reappraise their perceptions of situations to fit their preexisting beliefs than to change their religious beliefs (Pargament, 1997). Religion can be involved in both meanings made that involve changes in appraised meaning and those that involve changes in global meaning.

Changes in Appraised Meaning. In changing the meaning of a stressful situation, religiousness can be drawn upon to offer additional possibilities for causal attributions and to illuminate other aspects of the situation. Although reappraisals can be either positively or negatively toned, the motivation to reduce distress generally leads to reappraising stressful situations in a more positive light by giving them a more acceptable meaning, one more consistent with global beliefs and goals.

One of the most commonly studied changes in situational meaning made is reattributions. As noted earlier, people typically assign a causal understanding to a highly stressful event fairly shortly after its occurrence. Over time, through processes of meaning making, this attribution is often revised (Davis, Nolen-Hoeksema, & Larson, 1998). People tend to make reattributions that help to alleviate their distress. For example, people may initially feel that God neglected to care for them or even deliberately and unjustly caused their trauma. Over time, however, people may come to see the stressful event as the will of a loving or purposeful God, even if it is a God who is inscrutable and beyond human understanding (Spilka et al., 2003).

Religion offers many avenues for making positive reattributions, and is frequently invoked in the search for a more acceptable reason for an event's occurrence than what one may have originally made. For example, people can come to see the stressful event as a spiritual opportunity, as the punishment of an angry God, or as the product of human sinfulness (Pargament, 1997). Baumeister (1991) wrote of the "attributional blank check" that many religions provide, the possibility of believing that God may have higher purposes that humans cannot understand, so that one may remain convinced that events that seem highly aversive may, in fact, be serving desirable ends, even if a person does not know what these ends might be. Thus, religious explanations can permit religious individuals to trust that every event, regardless of its overt appearance and painfulness, is part of God's plan (Baumeister, 1991).

Reattributions for stressful encounters that help to sustain global religious beliefs may be derived through somewhat convoluted reasoning. For example, in a study examining the attributions that bereaved college students made for their friend's death, which occurred approximately 7 months earlier, one participant explained that her friend, who had been killed by a drunken driver who ran over the curb and struck her on the sidewalk, was entirely responsible for her own death and that God was not at all responsible. Another student explained that her friend, who had been severely disabled, was not at all responsible for her own death, a suicide, because God had made her the way she was and had given her no other options (Park & Cohen, 1992, cited in Park 2005). These reattributions illustrate some of the powerful ways that people can manipulate their understandings of events in the service of sustaining their religious beliefs when facing events that challenge them.

Although religion commonly facilitates the making of more positive meanings, these reinterpretations are not always positive. For example, people sometimes come to believe that God harmed them, either through deliberate action or through passivity and neglect. These negative results of the making-meaning process can lead to mistrust, anger, hurt, and disappointment toward God or even doubt regarding God's existence (Exline & Rose, Chapter 19, this volume). One study of elderly medical inpatients dramatically illustrates the possibility of negative outcomes of religious meaning-making coping. Negative religious interpretations of their illness (e.g., seeing their illness as the work of the devil or a result of God's abandonment) were related to higher rates of subsequent mortality, even after controlling for sociodemographic variables and physical and mental health (Pargament, Koenig, Tarakeshwar, & Hahn, 2001).

Changes in Global Meaning. Traumatic events expose people to the darker sides of life, including human vulnerability and evil (Garbarino & Bedard, 1996; Gray et al., 2007). These events are sometimes so discrepant with global meaning that no amount of situational reappraisal will restore a sense of congruence with the individual's preexisting global meaning. In these instances, individuals may reduce the discrepancy between their understanding of an event and their global meaning by changing their fundamental global beliefs or goals, including, perhaps, their understanding of themselves, others, and the world; their views of good and evil; the importance of forgiveness; their sense of meaning in life; and their relationships with family, community, and God (McCullough, Bono, & Root, 2005). For example, sometimes those with faith come to view God as less powerful (Kushner, 1981) or cease to believe in God altogether. Others may come to believe that they are unable to comprehend everything that happens in the world or God's reasoning for it, while others may become convinced of their own sinful nature (see Exline & Rose, Chapter 19, this volume). Individuals may change or reprioritize their global goals by, for example, rededicating themselves to their religious commitments or pledging to be more devout (Emmons, Colby, & Kaiser, 1998).

Periods of extreme stress and subsequent difficulties in making meaning from them sometimes lead to radical religious transformation (Spilka et al., 2003). Often, spiritual transformation involves conversion. Within their new denomination or religion, converts may find alternative systems of global beliefs and goals that help them answer their difficult questions and solve their life problems (Zinnbauer & Pargament, 1998). Importantly, spiritual transformations may be deconversions as well, such as losing one's faith or connection to a particular religion (see Paloutzian, Murken, Streib, & Roßler-Namini, Chapter 20, this volume for a review).

Stress-Related Growth. One outcome of meaning making that often straddles the global–situational meaning divide is stress-related growth. Stress-related growth refers to coming to see a negative event as the catalyst for positive life changes. Some of these changes are profound, such as reorienting one's life and rededicating oneself to reordered ultimate goals, while others involve smaller changes such as being more intimate with loved ones, handling stress more effectively, taking better care of oneself, seeing one's own identity more clearly, feeling closer to God, being more appreciative of the everyday aspects of life, and having the courage to try new things (Park, 2009). Growth appears to come from looking for positive aspects of negative events and identifying some redeeming features of the experience, which may involve changes in both situational and global meaning (Park & Fenster, 2004).

Many religious traditions, including Buddhism, Judaism, and Christianity, contend that spiritual growth occurs primarily during times of suffering (Aldwin, 2007). Through suffering, humans develop character, coping skills, and a base of life experience that may enable them to manage future struggles more successfully. Many religions also attempt to cultivate virtues such as compassion, which render people more attuned to the suffering of others (Exline, 2002). One revealing study of older Mexican Americans demonstrated how those who are highly religious can utilize their pain and suffering as a modality for deepening their faith. These elders viewed their suffering in various ways, including as a way to "suffer like Jesus," to become more compassionate toward others, or even to redeem oneself for previous sins (Krause & Bastida, 2009).

In fact, one of the most consistent findings regarding predictors of positive life change following life stressors or trauma is that religiousness, measured variously as intrinsic religiousness, religious attributions, and religious coping, is a strong predictor of reports of growth (Shaw, Joseph, & Linley, 2005). Religiousness has been shown to predict growth in individuals dealing with a variety of stressful life events, including bereavement and loss (Park, 2006), sexual assault (Frazier, Tashiro, Berman, Steger, & Long, 2004), interpersonal transgressions (Schultz, Tallman, & Altmaier, 2010), exposure to terrorism (Laufer, Solomon, & Levine, 2010), and cancer (Park, Edmondson, & Blank, 2009).

Further, this growth is often of a religious nature. Growth following stressful encounters generally involves increased coping skills, increased social support and relationships, and deepened or renewed perspectives and life philosophies (Park, 2009), and religion can be an element of each of these. Research has found, for example, that following a stressful encounter, many people report feeling closer to God, more sure in their faith, and more religious; they often report using more religious coping and increasing their commitment to their religion and their involvement in their religious community (e.g., Cole, Hopkins, Tisak, Steel, & Carr, 2008).

FUTURE RESEARCH DIRECTIONS

Although the need for meaning, and the natural role of religion in life meaning, have long formed psychologists' approaches to these topics, empirical approaches have suffered from a lack of clarity regarding meaning. Framing the "need for meaning" as the "need for a functional meaning system" helps to anchor the issues of meaning and religiousness/spirituality in ways that allow delineation of many contexts, processes, and specific types of meaning, allowing for more sophisticated empirical research. As this chapter makes clear, progress is being made in many areas, yet because this approach is fairly new, much remains to be learned.

In general, future research in this area should be longitudinal and, ideally, prospective (i.e., measuring meaning systems prior to as well as following stressful encounters). Religious and nonreligious meaning making and meanings made must be assessed at different times, and processes of meaning making should be assessed carefully, examining both deliberate meaning-making attempts and more automatic types of processing (see Park, 2010, for an overview of methodological issues).

Some of the topics that seem to be particularly promising include:

- *Interplay of intrapersonal and interpersonal processes.* Meaning is always mediated through one's own internal experience, yet much individual meaning is acquired through social processes, and meaning making often occurs in social situations, such as discussing one's understanding and suffering with another person, who may provide new insights or reinforce one's interpretations (Krause, 2008; Ysseldyk et al., 2010). How do these intra- and interpersonal processes inform and influence one another?

- *Centrality of religion to one's meaning system.* People may vary greatly in the extent to which religion informs different aspects of their global meaning (e.g., to identity or behavior in daily life; Dezutter et al., 2010). Such individual differences should be more closely examined, along with the ways that they influence how people function in ordinary life (e.g., appraising daily events) and in situations of crisis.

- *Religion versus secular influences on meaning.* Very little is understood about how religious and secular meanings interact in influencing either global or situational meaning. Intriguing research suggests that even people who do not profess a belief in God often report anger at God (see Exline & Rose, Chapter 19, this volume). When do secular influences predominate and when do they give way to religious influences?

- *Perceptions of discrepancy.* As noted in this chapter, sometimes individuals' religious meaning systems are strong enough to protect them from experiencing violations (e.g., a belief that, although beyond human understanding, there is a plan). Yet research has also demonstrated that stronger religiousness is related to more violations and more cognitive processing, at least following bereavement (e.g., McIntosh et al., 1993). Under what conditions do individuals experience violations of their global religious meaning? And how do individuals repair these violations? What happens when they are irreparable?

- *Life span/life course issues.* Religiousness typically changes across the life span through both normative and highly stressful processes (see Levenson, Aldwin, & Igarashi, Chapter 9, and Paloutzian et al., Chapter 20, this volume). More documentation of which specific aspects of religious meaning change and under what conditions would provide a much richer understanding of the interplay of life experiences and religious meaning across the life span.

- *Attention to content of beliefs.* A focus on meaning systems naturally homes in on the content of global beliefs. As noted earlier, a recent focus on theodicies is a welcome development in research in the psychology of religion. However, many other beliefs have received minimal attention, in spite of their obvious importance within religious meaning systems. Kahoe's (1987) call for increased attention to specific religious beliefs has largely gone unanswered. The psychology of religious meaning will be greatly advanced with increased focus on the specific beliefs that form individuals' religious meaning systems.

REFERENCES

Aldwin, C. M. (2007). *Stress, coping, and development: An integrative perspective* (2nd ed.). New York: Guilford Press.

Ardelt, M. (2003). Effects of religion and purpose in life on elders' subjective well-being and attitudes toward death. *Journal of Religious Gerontology, 14,* 55–77.

Bailey, E. (2010). Implicit religion. *Religion, 40,* 271–278.

Batson, C. D., & Stocks, E. L. (2004). Religion: Its core psychological functions. In J. Greenberg, S. L. Koole, & T. Pyszczynski (Eds.), *Handbook of experimental existential psychology* (pp. 141–155). New York: Guilford Press.

Baumeister, R. F. (1991). *Meanings of life.* New York: Guilford Press.

Baumeister, R. F., & Vohs, K. D. (2002). The pursuit of meaningfulness in life. In C. R. Snyder & S. J. Lopez (Eds.), *The handbook of positive psychology* (pp. 608–618). New York: Oxford University Press.

Benore, E. R., & Park, C. L. (2004). Death-specific religious beliefs and bereavement: Belief in an afterlife and continued attachment. *The International Journal for the Psychology of Religion, 14,* 1–22.

Bernhardt, W. H. (1958). *A functional philosophy of religion.* Denver, CO: Criterion.

Carvalho J. J., IV (2006). Overview of the structure of a scientific worldview. *Zygon: Journal of Religion & Science, 41,* 113–124.

Cole, B. S., Hopkins, C. M., Tisak, J., Steel, J. L., & Carr, B. I. (2008). Assessing spiritual growth and spiritual decline following a diagnosis of cancer: Reliability and validity of the spiritual transformation scale. *Psycho-Oncology, 17,* 112–121.

Colzato, L. S., van Beest, I., van den Wildenberg, W. P. M., Scorolli, C., Dorchin, S., Meiran, N., et al. (2010). God: Do I have your attention? *Cognition, 117,* 87–94.

Daugherty, T. K., West, A. M., Williams, M. C., & Brockman, J. M. (2009). Measuring theodicy: Individual differences in the perception of divine intervention. *Pastoral Psychology, 58,* 43–47.

Davis, C. G., Nolen-Hoeksema, S., & Larson, J. (1998). Making sense of loss and benefiting from the experience: Two construals of meaning. *Journal of Personality and Social Psychology, 75,* 561–574.

Davis, C. G., Wortman, C. B., Lehman, D. R., & Silver, R. C. (2000). Searching for meaning in loss: Are clinical assumptions correct. *Death Studies, 24,* 497–540.

Dezutter, J., Luyckx, K., Schaap-Jonker, H., Büssing, A., Corveleyn, J., & Hutsebaut, D. (2010). God image and happiness in chronic pain patients: The mediating role of disease interpretation. *Pain Medicine, 11,* 765–773.

Donahue, M. J. (1985). Intrinsic and extrinsic religiousness: Review and meta-analysis. *Journal of Personality and Social Psychology, 48,* 400–419.

Emmons, R. A. (1999). *The psychology of ultimate concerns.* New York: Guilford Press.

Emmons, R. A. (2005). Striving for the sacred: Personal goals, life meaning, and religion. *Journal of Social Issues, 61,* 731–745.

Emmons, R. A., Colby, P. M., & Kaiser, H. A. (1998). When losses lead to gains: Personal goals and the recovery of meaning. In P. T. P. Wong & P. S. Fry (Eds.), *The human quest for meaning: A handbook of psychological research and clinical applications* (pp. 163–178). Mahwah, NJ: Erlbaum.

Exline, J. J. (2002). Stumbling blocks on the religious road: Fractured relationships, nagging vices, and the inner struggle to believe. *Psychological Inquiry, 13,* 182–189.

Fales, E. (2007). Naturalism and physicalism. In M. Martin (Ed.), *The Cambridge companion to atheism* (pp. 118–134). Cambridge, UK: Cambridge University Press.

Filipp, S.-H. (1992). Could it be worse? The diagnosis of cancer as a prototype of traumatic life events. In L. Montada, S.-H. Filipp, & M. J. Lerner (Eds.), *Life crises and experiences of loss in adulthood* (pp. 23–56). Hillsdale, NJ: Erlbaum.

Flannelly, K. J., Ellison, C. G., Galek, K., & Koenig, H. G. (2008). Beliefs about life-after-death, psychiatric symptomatology and cognitive theories of psychopathology. *Journal of Psychology and Theology, 36,* 94–103.

Francis, L. J., & Hills, P. R. (2008). The development of the Meaning in Life Index (MILI) and its relationship with personality and religious behaviours and beliefs among UK undergraduate students. *Mental Health, Religion & Culture, 11,* 211–220.

Francis, L. J., Jewell, A., & Robbins, M. (2010). The relationship between religious orientation, personality, and purpose in life among an older Methodist sample. *Mental Health, Religion & Culture, 13,* 777–791.

Francis, L. J., Lewis, C. A., & Robbins, M. (2010). Religious orientation, mental health and culture: Conceptual and empirical perspectives. *Mental Health, Religion & Culture, 13,* 659–666.

Frankl, V. E. (1969). *The will to meaning.* New York: New American Library.

Franklin, M. D., Schlundt, D. G., & Wallston, K. A. (2008). Development and validation of a religious health fatalism measure for the African-American faith community. *Journal of Health Psychology, 13,* 323–335.

Frazier, P., Tashiro, T., Berman, M., Steger, M., & Long, J. (2004). Correlates of levels and patterns of positive life changes following sexual assault. *Journal of Consulting and Clinical Psychology, 72,* 19–30.

Furnham, A., & Brown, L. B. (1992). Theodicy: A neglected aspect of the psychology of religion. *The International Journal for the Psychology of Religion, 2,* 37–45.

Garbarino, J., & Bedard, C. (1996). Spiritual challenges to children facing violent trauma. *Childhood, 3,* 467–478.

Gillies, J., & Neimeyer, R. A. (2006). Loss, grief, and the search for significance: Toward a model of meaning reconstruction in bereavement. *Journal of Constructivist Psychology, 19,* 31–65.

Gray, K., & Wegner, D. M. (2010). Blaming god for our pain: Human suffering and the divine mind. *Personality and Social Psychology Review, 14,* 7–16.

Gray, M. J., Maguen, S., & Litz, B. T. (2007). Schema constructs and cognitive models of posttraumatic stress disorder. In L. P. Riso, P. L. du Toit, D. J. Stein, & J. E. Young (Eds.), *Cognitive schemas and core beliefs in psychological problems: A scientist-practitioner guide* (pp. 59–92). Washington, DC: American Psychological Association.

Hale-Smith, A., Park, C. L., & Edmondson, D. (2012). Measuring religious beliefs about suffering: Development of the Views of Suffering Scale. *Psychological Assessment, 24,* 855–866.

Hall, M. E. L., & Johnson, E. L. (2001). Theodicy and therapy: Philosophical/theological contributions to the problem of suffering. *Journal of Psychology and Christianity, 20,* 5–17.

Harper, F. W. K., Schmidt, J. E., Beacham, A. O., Salsman, J. M., Averill, A. J., Graves, K. D., et al. (2007). The role of social cognitive processing theory and optimism in positive psychosocial and physical behavior change after cancer diagnosis and treatment. *Psycho-Oncology, 16,* 79–91.

Heine, S. J., Proulx, T., & Vohs, K. D. (2006). Meaning maintenance model: On the coherence of human motivations. *Personality and Social Psychology Review, 10,* 88–110.

Herman, J. L. (1997). *Trauma and recovery.* New York: Basic Books.

Hicks, J. A., & King, L. A. (2008). Religious commitment and positive mood as information about meaning in life. *Journal of Research in Personality, 42,* 43–57.

Hogg, M. A., Adelman, J. R., & Blagg, R. D. (2010). Religion in the face of uncertainty: An uncertainty-identity theory account of religiousness. *Personality and Social Psychology Review, 14,* 72–83.

Hood, R. W., Jr., Hill, P. C., & Spilka, B. (2009). *The psychology of religion: An empirical approach* (4th ed.). New York: Guilford Press.

Hood, R. W., Jr., Hill, P. C., & Williamson, W. P. (2005). *The psychology of religious fundamentalism.* New York: Guilford Press.

Jackson, C. J., & Francis, L. J. (2004). Are interactions in Gray's reinforcement sensitivity theory proximal or distal in the prediction of religiosity: A test of the joint subsystems hypothesis. *Personality and Individual Differences, 36*, 1197–1209.

Janoff-Bulman, R. (1992). *Shattered assumptions: Towards a new psychology of trauma.* New York: Free Press.

Janoff-Bulman, R., & Frantz, C. M. (1997). The impact of trauma on meaning: From meaningless world to meaningful life. In M. Power & C. R. Brewin (Eds.), *The transformation of meaning in psychological therapies* (pp. 91–106). New York: Wiley.

Kahoe, R. D. (1987). Toward a radical psychotheology. *Psychologists Interested in Religious Issues Newsletter, 12*, 2–6.

Karoly, P. (1999). A goal systems-self-regulatory perspective on personality, psychopathology, and change. *Review of General Psychology, 3*, 264–291.

Kay, A. C., Gaucher, D., McGregor, I., & Nash, K. (2010). Religious belief as compensatory control. *Personality and Social Psychology Review, 14*, 37–48.

Klinger, E. (1977). *Meaning and void.* Minneapolis: University of Minnesota Press.

Klinger, E. (1998). The search for meaning in evolutionary perspective and its clinical implications. In P. T. P. Wong & P. S. Fry (Eds.), *The human quest for meaning: A handbook of psychological research and clinical applications* (pp. 27–50). Mahwah, NJ: Routledge.

Koltko-Rivera, M. E. (2004). The psychology of worldviews. *Review of General Psychology, 8*, 3–58.

Koltko-Rivera, M. E. (2006–2007, Winter). Religions influence worldviews; worldviews influence behavior: A model with research agenda. *Psychology of Religion Newsletter, 32*, 1–10.

Koole, S. L., McCullough, M. E., Kuhl, J., & Roelofsma, P. H. M. P. (2010). Why religion's burdens are light: From religiosity to implicit self-regulation. *Personality and Social Psychology Review, 14*, 95–107.

Koss, M. P., & Figueredo, A. J. (2004). Change in cognitive mediators of rape's impact on psychosocial health across 2 years of recovery. *Journal of Consulting and Clinical Psychology, 72*, 1063–1072.

Krause, N. (2008). The social foundation of religious meaning in life. *Research on Aging, 30*, 395–427.

Krause, N., & Bastida, E. (2009). Religion, suffering, and health among older Mexican Americans. *Journal of Aging Studies, 23*, 114–123.

Kremer, H., Ironson, G., & Porr, M. (2009). Spiritual and mind-body beliefs as barriers and motivators to HIV-treatment decision-making and medication adherence?: A qualitative study. *AIDS Patient Care and STDs, 23*, 127–134.

Kushner, H. S. (1981). *When bad things happen to good people.* New York: Schocken Books.

Laufer, A., Solomon, Z., & Levine, S. Z. (2010). Elaboration on posttraumatic growth in youth exposed to terror: The role of religiosity and political ideology. *Social Psychiatry and Psychiatric Epidemiology, 45*, 647–653.

Lerner, M. J. (1980). *The belief in a just world: A fundamental delusion.* New York: Plenum Press.

Mahoney, A., Pargament, K. I., Cole, B., Jewell, T., Magyar, G. M., Tarakeshwar, N., et al. (2005). A higher purpose: The sanctification of strivings in a community sample. *The International Journal for the Psychology of Religion, 15*, 239–262.

Mahoney, A., Pargament, K. I., Jewell, T., Swank, A. B., Scott, E., Emery, E., et al. (1999). Marriage and the spiritual realm: The role of proximal and distal religious constructs in marital functioning. *Journal of Family Psychology, 13*, 321–338.

Martos, T., Kézdy, A., & Horváth-Szabó, K. (2011). Religious motivations for everyday goals: Their religious context and potential consequences. *Motivation and Emotion, 35*, 75–88.

Maslow, A. H. (1970). *Motivation and personality* (2nd ed.). New York: Harper & Row.

McCullough, M. E., Bono, G., & Root, L. M. (2005). Religion and forgiveness. In R. F. Paloutzian & C. L. Park (Eds.), *Handbook of the psychology of religion and spirituality* (pp. 394–411). New York: Guilford Press.

McGregor, I., & Little, B. R. (1998). Personal projects, happiness, and meaning: On doing well and being yourself. *Journal of Personality and Social Psychology, 74,* 494–512.

McIntosh, D. N. (1995). Religion-as-schema, with implications for the relation between religion and coping. *The International Journal for the Psychology of Religion, 5,* 1–16.

McIntosh, D. N., Silver, R. C., & Wortman, C. B. (1993). Religion's role in adjustment to a negative life event: Coping with the loss of a child. *Journal of Personality and Social Psychology, 65,* 812–821.

Michael, S. T., & Snyder, C. R. (2005). Getting unstuck: The roles of hope, finding meaning, and rumination in the adjustment to bereavement among college students. *Death Studies, 29,* 435–458.

Mickley, J. R., Pargament, K. I., Brant, C. R., & Hipp, K. M. (1998). God and the search for meaning among hospice caregivers. *Hospice Journal, 13,* 1–18.

Newton, A. T., & McIntosh, D. (2009). Associations of general religiousness and specific religious beliefs with coping appraisals in response to Hurricanes Katrina and Rita. *Mental Health, Religion & Culture, 12,* 129–146.

Neyrinck, B., Lens, W., Vansteenkiste, M., & Soenens, B. (2010). Updating Allport's and Batson's framework of religious orientations: A reevaluation from the perspective of self-determination theory and Wulff's social cognitive model. *Journal for the Scientific Study of Religion, 49,* 425–438.

Norenzayan, A., & Lee, A. (2010). It was meant to happen: Explaining cultural variations in fate attributions. *Journal of Personality and Social Psychology, 98,* 702–720.

Ozorak, E. W. (2005). Cognitive approaches to religion. In R. F. Paloutzian & C. L. Park (Eds.), *Handbook of the psychology of religion and spirituality* (pp. 216–234). New York: Guilford Press.

Pargament, K. I. (1997). *The psychology of religion and coping: Theory, research, practice.* New York: Guilford Press.

Pargament, K. I., Koenig, H. G., Tarakeshwar, N., & Hahn, J. (2001). Religious struggle as a predictor of mortality among medically ill elderly patients: A 2-year longitudinal study. *Archives of Internal Medicine, 161,* 1881–1885.

Pargament, K. I., Magyar-Russell, G. M., & Murray-Swank, N. A. (2005). The sacred and the search for significance: Religion as a unique process. *Journal of Social Issues, 61,* 665–687.

Pargament, K. I., Smith, B. W., Koenig, H. G., & Perez, L. (1998). Patterns of positive and negative religious coping with major life stressors. *Journal for the Scientific Study of Religion, 37,* 710.

Park, C. L. (2004). The notion of growth following stressful life experiences: Problems and prospects. *Psychological Inquiry, 15,* 69–76.

Park, C. L. (2005). Religion as a meaning-making framework in coping with life stress. *Journal of Social Issues, 61,* 707–729.

Park, C. L. (2006). Exploring relations among religiousness, meaning, and adjustment to lifetime and current stressful encounters in later life. *Anxiety, Stress & Coping, 19,* 33–45.

Park, C. L. (2008). Testing the meaning making model of coping with loss. *Journal of Social and Clinical Psychology, 27,* 970–994.

Park, C. L. (2009). Overview of theoretical perspectives. *Medical illness and positive life change: Can crisis lead to personal transformation?* (pp. 11–30). Washington, DC: American Psychological Association.

Park, C. L. (2010). Making sense of the meaning literature: An integrative review of meaning making and its effects on adjustment to stressful life events. *Psychological Bulletin, 136,* 257–301.

Park, C. L., & Cohen, L. H. (1992). Religious beliefs and practices and the coping process. In B. Carpenter (Ed.), *Personal coping: Theory, research, and application* (pp. 185–189). New York: Praeger.

Park, C. L., & Cohen, L. H. (1993). Religious and non-religious coping with the death of a friend. *Cognitive Therapy and Research, 17,* 561–577.

Park, C. L., Edmondson, D., & Blank, T. O. (2009). Religious and non-religious pathways to stress-related growth in cancer survivors. *Applied Psychology: Health and Well-Being, 1,* 321–335.

Park, C. L., Edmondson, D., & Hale-Smith, A. (2013). Why religion?: Meaning as the motivation. In K. I. Pargament, J. J. Exline, J. Jones, & A. Mahoney (Eds.), *APA handbook of psychology, religion, and spirituality (Vol.1): Context, theory, and research* (pp. 157–171). Washington, DC: American Psychological Association.

Park, C. L., & Fenster, J. R. (2004). Stress-related growth: Predictors of occurrence and correlates with psychological adjustment. *Journal of Social and Clinical Psychology, 23,* 195–215.

Park, C. L., & Folkman, S. (1997). Meaning in the context of stress and coping. *Review of General Psychology, 1,* 115–144.

Park, C. L., & Halifax, R. J. (2011). Religion and spirituality in adjusting to bereavement: Grief as burden, grief as gift. In R. A. Neimeyer, D. L. Harris, H. R. Winokuer, & G. F. Thornton (Eds.), *Grief and bereavement in contemporary society: Bridging research and practice* (pp. 355–364). London: Routledge.

Park, C. L., Mills, M. A., & Edmondson, D. (2012). PTSD as meaning violation: Testing a cognitive worldview perspective. *Psychological Trauma: Theory, Research, Practice, and Policy, 4,* 66–73.

Preston, J., & Epley, N. (2009). Science and god: An automatic opposition between ultimate explanations. *Journal of Experimental Social Psychology, 45,* 238–241.

Reker, G. T., & Wong, P. T. P. (1988). Aging as an individual process: Toward a theory of personal meaning. In J. E. Birren & V. L. Bengston (Eds.), *Emergent theories of aging* (pp. 214–246). New York: Springer.

Roccas, S. (2005). Religion and value systems. *Journal of Social Issues, 61,* 747–759.

Rothbaum, F., Weisz, J. R., & Snyder, S. S. (1982). Changing the world and changing the self: A two-process model of perceived control. *Journal of Personality and Social Psychology, 42,* 5–37.

Ryan, R. M., & Deci, E. L. (2000). Self-determination theory and the facilitation of intrinsic motivation, social development, and well-being. *American Psychologist, 55,* 68–78.

Ryan, R. M., & Deci, E. L. (2001). On happiness and human potentials: A review of research on hedonic and eudaimonic well-being. *Annual Review of Psychology, 52,* 141–166.

Saroglou, V., Delpierre, V., & Dernelle, R. (2004). Values and religiosity: A meta-analysis of studies using Schwartz's model. *Personality and Individual Differences, 37,* 721–734.

Saroglou, V., & Muñoz-García, A. (2008). Individual differences in religion and spirituality: An issue of personality traits and/or values. *Journal for the Scientific Study of Religion, 47,* 83–101.

Saunders, S. M., Lucas, V., & Kuras, L. (2007). Measuring the discrepancy between current and ideal spiritual and religious functioning in problem drinkers. *Psychology of Addictive Behaviors, 21,* 404–408.

Schultz, J. M., Tallman, B. A., & Altmaier, E. M. (2010). Pathways to posttraumatic growth: The contributions of forgiveness and importance of religion and spirituality. *Psychology of Religion and Spirituality, 2,* 104–114.

Schwartz, S. H., & Bilsky, W. (1990). Toward a theory of the universal content and structure of values: Extensions and cross-cultural replications. *Journal of Personality and Social Psychology, 58,* 878–891.

Schwartz, S. H., & Huismans, S. (1995). Value priorities and religiosity in four Western religions. *Social Psychology Quarterly, 58,* 88–107.

Sedikides, C., & Gebauer, J. E. (2010). Religiosity as self-enhancement: A meta-analysis of the relation between socially desirable responding and religiosity. *Personality and Social Psychology Review, 14,* 17–36.

Shaw, A., Joseph, S., & Linley, P. A. (2005). Religion, spirituality, and posttraumatic growth: A systematic review. *Mental Health, Religion & Culture, 8,* 1–11.

Shettleworth, S. J. (2010). *Cognition, evolution, and behavior.* New York: Oxford University Press.

Silberman, I. (2005). Religion as a meaning system: Implications for the new millennium. *Journal of Social Issues, 61,* 641–663.

Skaggs, B. G., & Barron, C. R. (2006). Searching for meaning in negative events: Concept analysis. *Journal of Advanced Nursing, 53,* 559–570.

Slattery, J. M., & Park, C. L. (2011). Meaning making and spiritually oriented interventions. In J. D. Aten, M. R. McMinn, & E. L. Worthington, Jr. (Eds.), *Spiritually oriented interventions for counseling and psychotherapy* (pp. 15–40). Washington, DC: American Psychological Association.

Spilka, B., Hood, R. W., Jr., Hunsberger, B., & Gorsuch, R. (2003). *The psychology of religion: An empirical approach* (3rd ed.). New York: Guilford Press.

Spilka, B., Shaver, P. R., & Kirkpatrick, L. A. (1997). A general attribution theory for the psychology of religion. In B. Spilka & D. N. McIntosh (Eds.), *The psychology of religion: Theoretical approaches* (pp. 153–170). Boulder, CO: Westview.

Steger, M. F., & Frazier, P. (2005). Meaning in life: One link in the chain from religiousness to well-being. *Journal of Counseling Psychology, 52,* 574–582.

Steger, M. F., Frazier, P., Oishi, S., & Kaler, M. (2006). The Meaning in Life questionnaire: Assessing the presence of and search for meaning in life. *Journal of Counseling Psychology, 53,* 80–93.

Stein, C. H., Abraham, K. M., Bonar, E. E., McAuliffe, C. E., Fogo, W. R., Faigin, D. A., et al. (2009). Making meaning from personal loss: Religious, benefit finding, and goal-oriented attributions. *Journal of Loss and Trauma, 14,* 83–100.

Tomer, A., & Eliason, G. (2000). Beliefs about self, life, and death: Testing aspects of a comprehensive model of death anxiety and death attitudes. In A. Tomer (Ed.), *Death attitudes and the older adult* (pp. 137–153). Philadephia: Brunner-Routledge.

Vail, K. E., Rothschild, Z. K., Weise, D. R., Solomon, S., Pyszczynski, T., & Greenberg, J. (2010). A terror management analysis of the psychological functions of religion. *Personality and Social Psychology Review, 14,* 84–94.

Warner, H. L., Mahoney, A., & Krumrei, E. J. (2009). When parents break sacred vows: The role of spiritual appraisals, coping, and struggles in young adults' adjustment to parental divorce. *Psychology of Religion and Spirituality, 1,* 233–248.

Young, M. J., & Morris, M. W. (2004). Existential meanings and cultural models: The interplay of personal and supernatural agency in American and Hindu ways of responding to uncertainty. In J. Greenberg, S. L. Koole, & T. Pyszczynski (Eds.), *Handbook of experimental existential psychology* (pp. 215–230). New York: Guilford Press.

Ysseldyk, R., Matheson, K., & Anisman, H. (2010). Religiosity as identity: Toward an understanding of religion from a social identity perspective. *Personality and Social Psychology Review, 14,* 60–71.

Zinnbauer, B. J., & Pargament, K. I. (1998). Spiritual conversion: A study of religious change among college students. *Journal for the Scientific Study of Religion, 37,* 161–180.

19

Religious and Spiritual Struggles

Julie J. Exline and Eric D. Rose

Although religious and spiritual beliefs can provide a sense of security (e.g., Kirkpatrick, 2005) and meaning (Park, 2005, Chapter 18, this volume), they can also be a locus of struggle (for reviews, see Exline, 2002, 2013; Exline & Rose, 2005; Pargament, 2002, 2007; Pargament, Murray-Swank, Magyar, & Ano, 2005). Some struggles focus on the *spiritual* domain, which we define broadly as any belief, practice, relationship, or experience associated with whatever someone deems sacred (e.g., Hill & Pargament, 2003). Other problems center on *religion*, in which beliefs, practices, relationships, or experiences seen as sacred are associated with a shared (and sometimes institutional) system. Of course, these brief, partial definitions of religion and spirituality cannot fully capture these complex and multifaceted constructs; religion and spirituality have proven notoriously difficult to define (e.g., Zinnbauer & Pargament, 2005). Boundaries between religion and spirituality often blur, as many people pursue and experience spirituality in the context of specific religious traditions (e.g., Oman, Chapter 2, this volume; Zinnbauer et al., 1997).

In this chapter we frame *religious and spiritual struggles* (sometimes shortened to *struggles*) as experiences of conflict or distress that center on religious or spiritual issues. To maintain a tight focus, we attend primarily to struggles that people experience on the individual level. However, it is important to note, consistent with the multilevel interdisciplinary paradigm (Emmons & Paloutzian, 2003), that struggle could also be analyzed at the level of dyads, groups, organizations, or cultures. Some of the struggles we consider here can be termed "divine struggles" (Pargament, 2007): They focus specifically on people's beliefs, perceptions, or emotions involving God or a higher power. For example, people may fear punishment if they believe that they have offended God (e.g., Pargament, Koenig, & Perez, 2000), and they may experience anger if they hold God responsible for unjust suffering (e.g., Exline, Park, Smyth, & Carey, 2011). Although the religious/ spiritual domain often focuses on beliefs about a deity or transcendent force, it may also be seen as having a dark side: forces of supernatural evil. For example, people may be troubled by events attributed to the devil (e.g., Pargament et al., 2000). Other struggles are *intrapersonal*, as when people face their own moral failures, and *interpersonal*, when disagreements or offenses arise in a religious context (Pargament, 2007).

CHAPTER SCOPE AND AIMS

Researchers have shown a surge of interest in religious and spiritual struggle in recent years. In fact, the volume of empirical literature has more than doubled since our review in the first edition of this *Handbook* (Exline & Rose, 2005), making it virtually impossible to cover all of the relevant work in one chapter. Accordingly, we focus on developments that have occurred in the years since the first edition of the *Handbook*. Readers interested in work prior to 2005 should see one of the earlier reviews on struggle (e.g., Ano & Vasconcelles, 2005; Exline, 2002; Exline & Rose, 2005; Pargament, 2002; Pargament, Murray-Swank, et al., 2005; Thuné-Boyle, Stygall, Keshtgar, & Newman, 2006). Note that some of the articles relevant to religious/spiritual struggle use the term "negative religious coping" (e.g., Pargament, Falb, Ano, & Wachholtz, Chapter 28, this volume; Pargament et al., 2000; Pargament, Smith, Koenig, & Perez, 1998), in which religious and spiritual struggles are framed as ways of coping with stress.

This chapter emphasizes situations in which individuals subjectively experience a sense of struggle associated with religion or spirituality. We are not attempting to describe the dark side of religious/spiritual life in its entirety, a vast domain incorporating topics ranging from religious delusions to holy wars. Although in this volume our chapter may overlap with others on religious coping (Pargament et al., Chapter 28, this volume), mental health (Park & Slattery, Chapter 27, this volume), meaning (Park, Chapter 18, this volume), and religious violence (Moghaddam, Warren, & Love, Chapter 32, this volume), we maintain a tight focus on the struggle concept.

Most recent studies of religious/spiritual struggle have emphasized its links with indicators of emotional and physical well-being. The first section of our chapter provides a brief, selective overview of this work along with a critical evaluation. The second section uses a similar structure to our 2005 chapter, describing new research on four categories of struggle: anger toward God as a response to suffering, perceptions of supernatural evil, human limitation and sin, and interpersonal struggles surrounding religion. We emphasize basic research and ideas for future study. Space constraints, combined with the growth of the literature, prevent us from speculating about intervention strategies as we did in our 2005 *Handbook* chapter. Readers interested in interventions are referred to the chapter in the first edition of the *Handbook* along with other recent reviews of struggle interventions (e.g., Murray-Swank, 2013).

LINKS BETWEEN RELIGIOUS AND SPIRITUAL STRUGGLE AND INDICATORS OF WELL-BEING: EMOTIONAL DISTRESS, PHYSICAL SYMPTOMS, AND THE POSSIBILITY OF GROWTH

This section provides a snapshot of recent studies and lines of research on religious/spiritual struggle and distress. For a more thorough list of citations, greater detail on measures, and more information about specific samples in which spiritual struggle has been studied, see Exline (2013).

Emotional Distress

Overview of Recent Findings

Since religious and spiritual struggle imply some degree of internal conflict, it seems intuitive that they would correlate positively with other indicators of emotional distress. Many studies support this point. For example, Ano and Vasconcelles (2005) conducted a meta-analysis on religious coping that included 22 effect sizes related to struggle (framed as negative religious coping). Struggle showed a moderate association (effect size of .22) with other indicators of emotional distress such as depression, anxiety, and anger. Parallel results emerged from a meta-analysis on religiosity and depression by Smith, McCullough and Pohl (2003) and a national survey by McConnell, Pargament, Ellison, and Flannelly (2006). Many studies in medical and psychiatric settings, as well as studies focusing on a wide range of life stressors, have yielded similar patterns of results (see Exline, 2013, for a review).

Links between struggle and distress have emerged from studies using a wide variety of measures, including the RCOPE (Pargament et al., 2000) and Brief RCOPE (Pargament et al., 1998), a measure of "red flags" in religious coping (Pargament, Zinnbauer, Scott, Butter, Zerowin, et al., 1998), the Spiritual Assessment Inventory (Hall & Edwards, 1996, 2002), the Religious Comfort and Strain scale (Exline, Yali, & Sanderson, 2000), the Attitudes toward God Scale–9 (Wood et al., 2010), measures tailored specifically for Jews (Rosmarin, Pargament, Krumrei, & Flannelly, 2009; see also Rosmarin, Pargament, & Flannelly, 2009; Rosmarin, Pargament, & Mahoney, 2009) and Muslims (Raiya, Pargament, Mahoney, & Stein, 2008), and measures designed specifically for use in medical settings (e.g., Bowman, Beitman, Palesh, Prez, & Koopman, 2009; Cole, Hopkins, Tisak, Steel, & Carr, 2008; Fitchett & Risk, 2009). In addition, spiritual crisis scores on the Assessment for Spirituality and Religious Sentiments (ASPIRES) scale have been shown to predict Axis II psychopathology (Piedmont et al., 2007).

Although most of the studies examining struggle and emotional distress have been cross-sectional, recent longitudinal studies suggest that spiritual struggle may predict declines in mental health. For instance, Dew and colleagues (2010) found that in a group of 145 depressed adolescents, loss of faith predicted less improvement in depression scores over 6 months. Similarly, in a sample of patients with congestive heart failure, spiritual struggle at baseline predicted positive shifts in depression and negative shifts in self-efficacy 6 months later (Park, Brooks, & Sussman, 2009). A study of myeloma patients awaiting stem cell transplants revealed that greater spiritual struggle before the transplant predicted greater posttransplant anxiety, depression, and transplant-related concerns along with lower levels of emotional well-being (Sherman, Plante, Simonton, Latif, & Anaissie, 2009).

In terms of predicting long-term distress, the key question may be not whether people experience struggle but whether they become stuck in a chronic mode of struggle. Several longitudinal studies offer support for this view. In a study of elderly, medically ill individuals (Pargament, Koenig, Tarakeshwar, & Hahn, 2004), participants were sorted into four groups: nonstrugglers, transitory strugglers (struggle at baseline only), acute strugglers (follow-up only), and chronic strugglers (both timepoints). Chronic strugglers were the only ones showing declines in physical and mental health over 2 years. Similar patterns emerged from a longitudinal study of cancer patients (Exline et al., 2011, Study 5): Those who reported anger toward God at both time points showed the poorest mental and physical well-being at the 1-year follow-up.

Studies have also begun to identify mediators and third-variable explanations for the links between spiritual struggle and mental health symptoms, although there has been little consistency in the variables examined across studies. For example, a prospective study of cardiac surgery patients (Ai, Park, Huang, Rodgers, & Tice, 2007) revealed that the link between preoperative spiritual struggle and postoperative distress could be partly explained by problems in social support. A cross-sectional study of terminally ill cancer patients also identified social support, along with optimism and self-efficacy, as possible mediators (or third-variable explanations) of the struggle–adjustment link (Pearce, Singer, & Prigerson, 2006). Among terminally ill patients with end-stage congestive heart failure, death concerns fully mediated the link between religious struggle and depression (Edmondson, Park, Chaudoir, & Wortmann, 2008), whereas depressive coping mediated the link between negative religious coping and depression in a study of German breast cancer patients (Zwingmann, Wirtz, Müller, Körber, & Murken, 2006). A common thread across these studies may be that religious and spiritual struggles are linked with other nonreligious variables that indicate problems in coping (e.g., fearful or depressive thinking, a lack of self-efficacy, and problems with social support), any of which could partly explain the link between religious/spiritual struggle and emotional distress.

Summary and Evaluation

There seems to be little doubt that a link exists between emotional distress and religious/ spiritual struggle. At this stage, it would be useful to continue the use of longitudinal designs, preferably multiwave studies that could identify different trajectories over time. Experimental designs have also been underused in this area; brief exercises or laboratory-based manipulations could help to illuminate the short-term effects of struggle-related thoughts on mood or mental states. It will also be crucial to systematically test religious/ spiritual struggle interventions to see whether they have the power to reduce psychological distress. Several interventions have shown promise in initial, small-scale studies (e.g., Ano, 2005; Gear, Krumrei, & Pargament, 2009; Murray-Swank & Pargament, 2008; see Murray-Swank, 2013, for a review). As the field progresses, researchers should move toward systematic, large-scale evaluations of struggle interventions.

Our reading of the literature also suggests an implicit assumption that may be problematic: The framing of results often seems to imply that spiritual struggle causes psychological distress. Granted, there is evidence to support this point; however for maximum scientific integrity and rigor, more attention is needed to the possibility of other causal pathways. For example, studies using mediational analyses suggest that negative religious coping can be framed as a result of stress (Ai et al., 2007) or trauma (Bradley, Schwartz, & Kaslow, 2005). It is also possible that the relationship between religious/ spiritual struggle and distress is bidirectional: Struggle could create emotional distress, which in turn could perpetuate struggle.

To evaluate causal connections more systematically, longitudinal studies will be of some help, but experimental work will be critical. For example, a study might determine whether inducing a negative mood prompts people to see God (or a religious group) more negatively. Another way to examine whether distress causes spiritual struggle, one that would also build bridges with the broader mental health field, would be to add struggle measures to ongoing clinical trials for psychological disorders: If depression, anxiety, anger, or posttraumatic stress decrease in response to a secular intervention, do spiritual struggles subside as well?

Physical Symptoms and Mortality

Several early studies suggested that spiritual struggle might predict subsequent decreases in physical health. For example, a study of 96 medical rehabilitation inpatients demonstrated that spiritual struggle at admission (in particular, anger toward God) predicted poorer rehabilitation outcomes at a 4-month follow-up (Fitchett, Rybarczyk, DeMarco, & Nicholas, 1999). Several studies of medically ill, hospitalized older adults also offered provocative findings. For example, a widely cited study by Pargament, Koenig, Tarakeshwar, and Hahn (2001) showed that spiritual struggle predicted higher mortality rates over a 2-year period.

Overview of Recent Findings

Over the past 5 years, other studies have continued to reveal connections between spiritual struggle and physical and physiological indicators of stress and illness. For example, studies have shown that spiritual struggle was linked with higher levels of interleukin-6, an inflammatory cytokine, in patients facing cardiac surgery (Ai, Pargament, Kronfol, Tice, & Appel, 2010; Ai, Seymour, Tice, Qatar, & Bolling, 2009). In the longitudinal study of myeloma patients mentioned earlier (Sherman et al., 2009), those who showed increases in negative religious coping reported lower functional and physical well-being after receiving stem cell transplants. Another study of HIV/AIDS patients (Trevino et al., 2010) revealed that spiritual struggle predicted more severe physical symptoms 12 to 18 months later. These effects were shown not only on self-reported symptoms but also on a biomarker: CD4 counts.

Summary and Evaluation

Although small in comparison to the literature emphasizing emotional distress, a growing body of research shows links between religious/spiritual struggle and physical health. Furthermore, studies are beginning to use the hard physical evidence supplied by biomarkers rather than relying only on self-reports of symptoms. Longitudinal studies suggest that struggle early on can predict poorer health—and even higher rates of mortality—in the future. However, as with the literature on mental health, it will be important to examine assumptions about causal mechanisms thoughtfully and critically. It is possible that bidirectional relationships exist. For example, physical problems might create emotional distress and religious/spiritual struggle, which in turn perpetuate or worsen the health problems.

In future work, it would be useful (though costly) to attempt long-term prospective studies with healthy populations rather than focusing exclusively on people who are already facing physical illness. Experimental studies, which would not require samples of physically ill persons, could also yield useful information. For example, an experiment might randomly assign participants to reflect on spiritual struggles as opposed to other topics, and then look at effects of this manipulation on cortisol levels, brain activity, or indicators of stress in the sympathetic nervous system. Experiments could also frame the question in the opposite direction: Do specific brain states (or physiological states more generally) affect the odds or intensity of struggle?

The Potential for Growth

It seems intuitive to predict that religious and spiritual struggle would be linked with other indicators of distress; struggle, by definition, is painful. But might struggle also carry the potential for posttraumatic growth (e.g., Calhoun & Tedeschi, 2006) or other benefits? This possibility fits with the model presented by Pargament (2007): Spiritual crises represent a choice point, one that could lead to conservation of existing beliefs or major shifts in belief. Shifts in belief take many forms. For example, some individuals increase their devotion to a previously held belief system, whereas others discard or revise their beliefs or adopt elements of a different belief system. Depending on the context, any of these types of changes could represent growth.

Overview of Recent Findings

The possibility that spiritual struggle might lead to eventual growth has been understudied. Findings to date, most from cross-sectional studies, have been mixed (see Pargament, Desai, & McConnell, 2006, for a review and discussion). Although some studies suggest a positive link between struggle and growth (e.g., Pargament, Magyar, Benore, & Mahoney, 2005; Pargament, Smith et al., 1998; Pargament et al., 2000), others suggest no such connection (e.g., Krumrei, Mahoney, & Pargament, 2009; Phillips & Stein, 2007; see Ano & Vasconcelles, 2005, for a review). A longitudinal study of patients with congestive heart failure (Park, Brooks, & Sussman, 2009) actually suggested a negative link between struggle and growth: Baseline struggle predicted negative shifts in stress-related growth 6 months later.

Summary and Evaluation

At this point, the body of work that exists on struggle and growth is not sufficiently large or robust to allow firm conclusions. It may be that in terms of predicting growth, the key is not in the presence of spiritual struggle but how people deal with struggle once it arises. The Spiritual Assessment Inventory (SAI; Hall & Edwards, 1996, 2002) provides a useful model of how to assess both the presence of struggle and how people cope with it. In addition to evaluating whether participants experience negative feelings such as disappointment or anger with God, the SAI includes additional questions focusing on how people handle such feelings in the context of the relationship. We have been using similar strategies in our own recent work on anger toward God. We first evaluate the presence of struggle such as anger toward God, and then we examine the extent to which people use approach or avoidance strategies in response to this struggle. Other measures such as the RCOPE (Pargament, Smith, Koenig, & Perez, 1998) or Brief RCOPE (Pargament et al., 1998) could yield additional findings related to growth if they are analyzed in novel ways. For example, it could be useful to compare participants who show no signs of struggle with two groups of strugglers—those who respond with positive religious coping strategies versus those who do not.

Regardless of the analytic strategy, longitudinal studies will be important in identifying developmental shifts or character changes suggesting growth. It may also be useful to supplement self-report measures of growth with assessments of virtuous behaviors, perhaps giving participants in-the-moment opportunities to show generosity or compassion.

FOUR BROAD CATEGORIES OF RELIGIOUS AND SPIRITUAL STRUGGLE: A CLOSER LOOK

Much of the literature in the last 5 years has focused on religious/spiritual struggle as a general concept. Although this approach has been fruitful, it can also be informative to take a closer look at specific types of struggle. As in our earlier review (Exline & Rose, 2005), we now briefly (and selectively) review research related to four categories of struggle. To minimize redundancy with earlier work, we emphasize studies from 2005 and later.

Is God to Blame?: The Challenge of Suffering

Although the terms "spiritual struggle" and "negative religious coping" have been used in a broad sense in much of the existing literature, much of the research to date has emphasized divine struggles—those involving thoughts or feelings about God. For example, on the widely used Brief RCOPE (Pargament, Smith, et al., 1998), five of the seven items used to assess negative religious coping focus on God. These negative feelings can be focused toward God, as in the form of anger or protest (see Exline & Martin, 2005, for a review of early work), or they may reflect concern about God's disapproval, abandonment, or punishing attitudes toward the self (e.g., Exline et al., 2000; Pargament, Smith, et al., 1998, 2000). Studies of God images (for reviews, Hall & Fujikawa, 2013; Moriarty & Hoffman, 2007) and attachment to God (e.g., Beck & McDonald, 2004; Kirkpatrick, 2005; Rowatt & Kirkpatrick, 2002) are also relevant here.

Overview of Recent Findings

Several important advances in the past 5 years have been in the development of measures. For example, new scales designed to assess religious coping among Muslims (Raiya et al., 2008) and Jews (Rosmarin, Pargament, Krumrei, et al., 2009) include struggle items related to God. Also new are the Cancer and Deity Questionnaire (Bowman et al., 2009) and the Attitudes toward God Scale (Wood et al., 2010), which contains a four-item subscale on anger and disappointment toward God. Situation-specific items related to negative attributions and anger toward God have also been developed (Exline et al., 2011), as have items on whether anger and protest toward God are seen as morally acceptable (Exline, Kaplan, & Grubbs, 2012).

Anger toward God is one form of divine struggle that has received some focused attention in the past 5 years. We recently completed a five-study project focused specifically on anger toward God, drawing from groups of undergraduates, bereaved persons, and cancer patients as well as a national U.S. sample (Exline et al., 2011). Anger toward God showed consistent links with emotional distress and physical symptoms, in line with the broad struggle literature and other recent studies of anger toward God (e.g., Gall, Kristjansson, Charbonneau, & Florack, 2009; Strelan, Acton, & Patrick, 2009; Wood et al., 2010). We found that people become angry toward God for many of the same reasons they become angry toward other people—when they see God as being clearly responsible for causing severe harm, when they see God's intentions as cruel rather than kind, and when there is no close prior relationship with God to buffer against the anger (see Hall & Edwards, 1996, 2002, for an object relations perspective).

Although positive feelings toward God tend to predominate over negative feelings such as anger and disappointment, positive feelings do not rule out the possibility of negative feelings; the factors are largely independent (Beck, 2006; Exline et al., 2011; Wood et al., 2010). As Beck (2007) describes, some people may protest or complain to God while remaining closely engaged in the relationship, showing a "winter" form of faith as opposed to a sunny "summer" faith. In fact, several recent studies suggest that positive, resilient relationships with God often include some tolerance for protest in the form of anger, questioning, and complaint—just so long as exiting the relationship is not seen as a viable option (Exline, Kaplan, & Grubbs, 2012). Perhaps, as Allport said in 1950 (p. 73), "the mature religious sentiment is ordinarily fashioned in the workshop of doubt." In fact, an ability to tolerate a certain degree of relational friction without walking away may be seen as a healthy sign of realistic acceptance (Hall & Edwards, 1996, 2002) or spiritual integration (Pargament, 2007). Of course, perceived relationships with God sometimes take forms that are hostile, abusive, or otherwise destructive. In such cases, exiting the relationship (perhaps by revising one's beliefs about God or image of God) could be a sensible and healthy course of action. This possibility warrants more empirical attention.

One provocative finding that has emerged from several of our studies (e.g., Exline, Yali, & Lobel, 1999; Exline et al., 2011) is that some individuals who do not believe in God report anger around the idea of God. This pattern was found using retrospective reports (e.g., Study 1 of Exline et al., 2011), ratings of current anger (Study 4), lifetime frequency measures (Study 2), and hypothetical images of God (Study 2). Although only preliminary, these findings are consistent with the possibility that a history of anger toward God may be one route to nonbelief (along these lines, see Novotni & Petersen, 2001, for their discussion of emotional atheism). In ongoing studies, we are trying to gain deeper understanding of the link between anger toward God and doubt or nonbelief regarding God's existence, an approach that may provide opportunities for integration with existing research on religious doubt (e.g., Altemeyer & Hunsberger, 1997; Hunsberger, Pratt, & Pancer, 2002) and Batson and Schoenrade's (1991a, 1991b) concept of a quest orientation toward religion.

Summary and Evaluation

Evaluation of the literature that focuses specifically on divine struggles is rather difficult, because so much of the work framed in terms of general struggle actually emphasizes struggles involving God. At this stage it is clear that divine struggles are linked with distress. What may be helpful next is a deeper understanding of divine struggles at a conceptual level, which should include better integration with the literature on God images (e.g., Hall & Fujikawa, 2013; Moriarty & Hoffman, 2007). For example, to what extent do people see God as a personal being, one with whom the idea of a relationship makes sense? Is God all powerful or limited, kind or cruel, reliable or unworthy of trust? Does God intervene in people's daily lives? These questions are likely to be important in predicting whether divine struggles will arise and what form they will take. It will also be important to integrate new work on divine struggles with existing research that uses well-established frameworks such as object relations (Hall & Edwards, 1996, 2002) and attachment theory (Beck & McDonald, 2004; Kirkpatrick, 2005; Rowatt & Kirkpatrick, 2002) to conceptualize how people frame their bonds with God. In addition, it would be interesting to consider the leader–follower dynamics of people's perceived relationships with God, separate from the idea of a parental relationship.

There is a clear monotheism bias in literature on divine struggles to date, leaving many unanswered questions about how people from other traditions struggle with the sacred domain. Polytheism would be fascinating to study, as people may see themselves as having distinct relationships with different gods. Suffering may also be seen as the result of a higher power such as fate, karma, or a natural force rather than a personal deity. In nontheistic systems, people could experience a sense of disconnection, imbalance, or alienation in relation to the universe. They might also sense that the vital force that energizes life is being blocked somehow, as conceptualized in traditional Chinese medicine (see Anderson, 2001, for a discussion). These neglected forms of spiritual struggle represent a wide-open area for new research and conceptual development.

Perceived Attacks from the Spiritual Realm: The Challenge of Supernatural Evil

Another type of struggle can arise when people see themselves or others as being affected by forces seen as supernatural and powerful but evil in origin, such as the devil, demons, or evil spirits. This topic, which has received much less attention in the research literature than divine struggles, is often referenced in historical terms, in discussions of how people explained psychological disorders in the past (e.g., Davis, 2008; Frankfurter, 2006). Yet literal beliefs in supernatural evil are very much alive throughout much of the world today.

Overview of Recent Findings

Many of the writings about demonic forces within psychology still take the form of ethnographic and clinical case studies, as was the case prior to 2005 (see Exline & Rose, 2005, for a review). Recent papers have documented belief in demonic forces and spirit possession within Tibetan Buddhism (e.g., Plakun, 2008) and among indigenous populations in Bangladesh (Blum et al., 2009), to name just a few examples. Although many of the case studies are from outside the United States, vivid examples have also been presented in a book by popular writer M. Scott Peck (2005) and in clinical case studies from the United States (Reichbart, 2006; Ruskin, 2007; see also Bull, 2001).

In terms of empirical attention, it is important to note that both the RCOPE

(Paragment, Smith, et al., 2000) and the Brief RCOPE (Pargament et al., 1998) include items on demonic appraisal—in other words, seeing the devil as responsible for negative events. Demonic appraisal is framed in these measures as a form of negative religious coping or struggle, one that correlates positively with other struggles and negatively with other indicators of well-being. Thus, any data set that includes these items can provide some information about people's perceptions of "the demonic." Several religious coping studies have made special mention of demonic appraisals. For example, in the longitudinal study of religious coping and mortality mentioned earlier (Pargament et al., 2001), demonic appraisal was found to predict higher mortality rates. More recently, Krumrei (2011) looked specifically at the role of demonic appraisals in terms of adjustment to divorce. She found that such appraisals, though linked with poor adjustment, were common among individuals facing divorce. Among the 100 participants, 36% saw the devil as being at work in the divorce itself, 43% believed that their spouse was being influenced by demonic forces, and 31% viewed themselves as being influenced by demonic forces.

Other recent research has focused specifically on demonic appraisals about mental illness. For example, an analysis of Christian self-help books revealed that demonic influence was the most frequently cited reason for depression (Webb, Stetz, & Hedden, 2008). Another study revealed that among a sample of American Pentecostals, demonic influence was the most widely cited cause for schizophrenia (Harley, 2007). Another study of Pentecostals from Australia revealed comparable patterns, with many participants seeing the demonic as a source of both depression and schizophrenia (Hartog & Gow, 2005). Demonic appraisals for mental illness have also been documented in a Kuwaiti sample (Eid & Alzayed, 2005). Demonic appraisals are often framed as a treatment concern. For example, some argue that people holding these beliefs might not receive needed treatment or might even be harmed through the process of deliverance—that is, procedures designed to release or deliver people from evil spirits (e.g., Ganzevoort, 2006). Other writings suggest that psychotherapists should hold a more cooperative, open stance toward deliverance ministries (e.g., Filius, 2009).

Interest in the demonic is not limited to clinical psychology. For example, experimental work from a cognitive perspective has examined how people conceptualize the devil, often in contrast to God (Jensen, 2009; Meier, Hauser, Robinson, Friesen, & Schjeldahl, 2007; Shtulman, 2008). Other cognitive studies have examined ideas related to spirit possession: What happens when one person's mind transfers to the body of another? (Cohen & Barrett, 2008).

Other recent projects have considered the psychological functions that beliefs in Satan might serve. For example, Beck and Taylor (2008) found that robust notions of Satan predicted more positive experiences associated with God and were less likely to blame God for pain and suffering. In the same vein, Rose and Exline (2008) found that beliefs in Satan and in evil spirits were linked with lower levels of religious doubt. These findings raise the possibility that attributing negative events to evil forces might actually serve a defensive function, helping people maintain faith by protecting their positive images of God. Another fascinating idea about the possible functions of demonic beliefs was described in the 12th-century case of Christina the Astonishing (Baxendale, 2008). This woman, who is believed to have suffered from epilepsy, saw her seizures as the result of demonic torment. However, this demonic torment had a clear purpose in Christina's view: Through her own suffering, she believed that she was providing relief for those who were suffering in purgatory.

Summary and Evaluation

Empirical work on perceptions of supernatural evil is still in its infancy, although some interesting advances have been made in the past 5 years. From a diversity perspective, it seems prudent to learn more about people's perceptions of supernatural evil, because such beliefs seem to be common throughout the world. Psychologists are understandably wary about trying to prove the existence or nonexistence of supernatural forces, including evil ones. Yet it seems well within the domain of psychology to learn more about people's perceptions and beliefs regarding the demonic, and this remains a wide-open area.

Sin and Self-Forgiveness: The Challenge of Cultivating Virtue

One function of religion is to help people behave in morally upright ways, and there is some evidence that spiritually based interventions can help people to cultivate virtue (e.g., Ano, 2005). Yet, as we have described in earlier reviews (Exline, 2002; Exline & Rose, 2005), people often struggle spiritually when they must face their own human limitations. Although almost any personal failure or flaw might be viewed through a spiritual lens, sins—failures in the moral domain—seem particularly relevant here.

Overview of Recent Findings

Some of the most provocative new work in this area has been on problems related to scrupulosity and unwanted thoughts. In a recent project, we asked undergraduate participants to recall unwanted thoughts of interpersonal aggression and rate the level of distress these thoughts engendered (Rose, 2010). Results showed that distress about these unwanted thoughts was positively correlated with frequency of religious behavior for women but not for men. This gender-specific link between religious activity and distress was explained by two factors. First, for both genders, engagement in religious activity was positively linked with a bias to overattribute meaning and importance to thought content. Second, among women only, engagement in religious activity predicted greater belief that an unwanted thought of aggression represented a challenge to a valued nonaggressive self image. Greater distress was, in turn, predicted by the bias to overvalue thoughts and by the belief that an unwanted thought of aggression challenged a nonaggressive notion of self.

In our 2005 cross-sectional study, the direction of cause and effect was unclear. One possibility is that frequent engagement in religious behavior predisposed women to experience greater distress in the face of an unwanted thought of aggression. Alternatively, the results may reflect the use of religious activity by women as a means of coping with the presence of unwanted mental phenomena. The latter possibility has a clinical analogue in scrupulosity, a subtype of obsessive–compulsive disorder in which sufferers are plagued by persistent thoughts of sin and fear of punishment. Sufferers feel compelled to counter these thoughts and feelings via excessive religious behavior (see Miller & Hedges, 2008; Park & Slattery, Chapter 27, this volume). Scrupulosity research is still fairly sparse; however, recent work has made advances by highlighting factors that predict greater scrupulosity. Within clinical samples, potential predictors include biases in metacognition and a general tendency to obsess (Nelson, Abramowitz, Whiteside, & Deacon, 2006). Within a nonclinical sample, Olatunji, Tolin, Huppert and Lohr (2005) found that scrupulosity scores were predicted by fearful and disgusted emotional reactions to stimuli with moral relevance.

Sin-related struggles are likely to overlap with divine struggles involving God's disapproval or punishment. Along these lines, several recent studies have examined people's perceptions of feeling forgiven by God. For example, Lawler-Row (2010) found that in a sample of older adults, feeling forgiven by God was positively associated with self-forgiveness, religiosity, and successful aging and negatively associated with depression. In a national probability sample of adults in the United States, Toussaint, Williams, Musick, and Everson-Rose (2008) found that feeling forgiven by God was linked with lower depression levels, but only among women. Martin (2008) found that feeling forgiven by God was closely linked with self-forgiveness and religiosity in an undergraduate sample and a more broad-based adult sample. This project also included initial development of a measure, the Divine Forgiveness Scale, to assess perceptions of God's response to a specific offense as forgiving or punitive. A scenario-based experimental study revealed that participants saw seeking forgiveness from God as likely to promote positive outcomes such as psychological and spiritual growth (Bassett et al., 2008).

Summary and Evaluation

In the past 5 years, there have been substantial advances in research on scrupulosity, unwanted thoughts, and forgiveness from God. Most studies have been correlational and cross-sectional and have focused on links with other measures of religiosity or mental health. In the future, researchers should incorporate longitudinal and experimental work and pursue greater integration with theory and research on psychological topics such as self-regulation, self-perception, and qualities associated with the "quiet ego," including self-compassion, mindfulness, and humility (see Wayment & Bauer, 2008, for a review).

Challenges of Religious Community

In several other reviews (Exline, 2002, 2013; Exline & Rose, 2005), we have elaborated on interpersonal conflicts and disagreements that occur in a religious context. This is a very large category of struggle, with topics ranging from interfaith marriage to religiously motivated violence. Given the breadth of the topic and space constraints here, we can mention only a few key studies conducted on this topic in the years since the first version of the *Handbook*.

Overview of Recent Findings

Over the past few years, there has been continued attention to the topic of negative social interactions in religious congregations (e.g., Ellison, Krause, Shepherd, & Chaves, 2009; Krause & Ellison, 2009). Other studies have focused on ways in which beliefs about the sacred can fuel aggression. For example, laboratory experiments have shown that when people are primed with the idea that violence has been sanctioned by God, they behave more aggressively (e.g., Bushman, Ridge, Das, Key, & Busath, 2006). In addition, new research on the concept of desecration suggests that people often become outraged when they believe that their sanctified beliefs or practices are being disrespected by others (e.g., Pargament, Magyar, et al., 2005). They may even begin to see the perpetrators of these offenses as evil through a process of demonization (e.g., Pargament, Trevino, Mahoney, & Silberman, 2007). Findings such as these lead naturally into topics related to religiously oriented prejudice and violence, group-level struggles that are of tremendous social importance but fall outside the scope of this chapter (see Moghaddam et al., Chapter 32, this volume).

Summary and Evaluation

One challenge with earlier research on interpersonal religious conflicts was that it was difficult to discern whether the religious dimension added anything unique to our knowledge of the problem: People disagree about many topics, and members of all groups commit offenses, so what is unique about the religious domain? Recent studies have identified several important factors: the role of sacrilege and the belief that certain actions, including aggression, have been sanctioned by God. Empirical work on these concepts has added a new dimension to our understanding of religious struggles in the interpersonal domain.

CONCLUDING THOUGHTS

Our aim for this chapter was to provide an overview of research on religious and spiritual struggle, particularly studies published since the first version of the *Handbook*. Most of the recent studies have framed religious/spiritual struggle as a general construct (i.e., negative religious coping). This strategy has been effective when the goal is to examine how struggle, broadly speaking, correlates with variables such as well-being or health. Many studies now document links among struggle, emotional distress, and poor physical health across a variety of populations. These studies demonstrate that religious/spiritual struggle is an important problem for many people, one that does not exist in isolation but is intimately connected with other facets of well-being. From here, major advances may require long-term longitudinal and prospective studies, experimental designs, and systematic attention to biomarkers and mediating variables. Fortunately, a solid empirical foundation now exists to support such endeavors.

At the same time, conceptual and theoretical limitations arise when many different types of problems are covered by the umbrella concept of religious/spiritual struggle. Deeper understanding and better integration with other literatures will require more research on specific struggles. Knowledge of specific struggles will also be crucial when considering practical applications: How can we help people work through religious and spiritual struggles? Although we have not addressed intervention strategies in detail here (see Exline & Rose, 2005; Murray-Swank, 2013), it seems clear that a person dealing with rage toward God would require different forms of help than someone facing self-forgiveness problems or fears about supernatural evil. To make major strides in our knowledge about specific struggles, psychologists will benefit by learning from—and collaborating with—professionals who specialize in religious and spiritual issues, such as theologians, clergy, pastoral counselors, chaplains, and spiritual directors.

REFERENCES

Ai, A. L., Pargament, K., Kronfol, Z., Tice, T. N., & Appel, H. (2010). Pathways to postoperative hostility in cardiac patients: Mediation of coping, spiritual struggle and interleukin-6. *Journal of Health Psychology, 15*, 186–195.

Ai, A. L., Park, C. L., Huang, B., Rodgers, W., & Tice, T. N. (2007). Psychosocial mediation of religious coping styles: A study of short-term psychological distress following cardiac surgery. *Personality and Social Psychology Bulletin, 33*, 867–882.

Ai, A. L., Seymour, E. M., Tice, T. N., Qatar, K. Z., & Bolling, S. F. (2009). Spiritual struggle related to plasma interleukin-6 prior to cardiac surgery. *Psychology of Religion and Spirituality, 1*, 112–128.

Allport, G. W. (1950). *The individual and his religion.* New York: Macmillan.

Altemeyer, B., & Hunsberger, B. (1997). *Amazing conversions: Why some turn to faith and others abandon religion.* Amherst, NY: Prometheus.

Anderson, E. Z. (2001). Energy therapies for physical and occupational therapists working with older adults. *Physical & Occupational Therapy in Geriatrics, 18*, 35–49.

Ano, G. G. (2005). *Spiritual struggles between vice and virtue: A brief psychospiritual intervention.* Unpublished doctoral dissertation, Bowling Green State University.

Ano, G. G., & Vasconcelles, E. B. (2005). Religious coping and psychological adjustment to stress: A meta-analysis. *Journal of Clinical Psychology, 61*, 461–480.

Bassett, R. L., Edgerton, M., Johnson, J., Lill, C., Russo, G., Ardella, L., et al. (2008). Seeking forgiveness: The view from an experimental paradigm. *Journal of Psychology and Christianity, 27*, 140–149.

Batson, C. D., & Schoenrade, P. A. (1991a). Measuring religion as Quest: I. Validity concerns. *Journal for the Scientific Study of Religion, 30*, 416–429.

Batson, C. D., & Schoenrade, P. A. (1991b). Measuring religion as Quest: II. Reliability concerns. *Journal for the Scientific Study of Religion, 30*, 430–447.

Baxendale, S. (2008). The intriguing case of Christina the Astonishing. *Neurology, 70*, 2004–2007.

Beck, R. (2006). Communion and complaint: Attachment, object-relations, and triangular love perspectives on relationship with God. *Journal of Psychology and Theology, 34*, 43–52.

Beck, R. (2007). The winter experience of faith: Empirical, theological, and theoretical perspectives. *Journal of Psychology and Christianity, 26*, 68–78.

Beck, R., & McDonald, A. (2004). Attachment to God: The Attachment to God Inventory, tests of working model correspondence, and an exploration of faith group differences. *Journal of Psychology and Theology, 32*, 92–103.

Beck, R., & Taylor, S. (2008). The emotional burden of monotheism: Satan, theodicy, and relationship with God. *Journal of Psychology and Theology, 36*, 151–160.

Blum, L. S., Khan, R., Hyder, A. A., Shahanaj, S., El Arifeen, S., & Baqui, A. (2009). Childhood drowning in Matlab, Bangladesh: An in-depth exploration of community perceptions and practices. *Social Science & Medicine, 68*, 1720–1727.

Bowman, E. S., Beitman, J. A., Palesh, O., Prez, J. E., & Koopman, C. (2009). The Cancer and Deity Questionnaire: A new religion and cancer measure. *Journal of Psychosocial Oncology, 27*, 435–453.

Bradley, R., Schwartz, A. C., & Kaslow, N. J. (2005). Posttraumatic stress disorder symptoms among low-income, African American women with a history of intimate partner violence and suicidal behaviors: Self-esteem, social support, and religious coping. *Journal of Traumatic Stress, 18,* 685–696.

Bull, D. L. (2001). A phenomenological model of therapeutic exorcism for dissociative identity disorder. *Journal of Psychology & Theology, 29,* 131–139.

Bushman, B. J., Ridge, R. D., Das, E., Key, C. W., & Busath, G. L. (2006). When God sanctions killing: Effects of scriptural violence on aggression. *Psychological Science, 18,* 204–207.

Calhoun, L. G., & Tedeschi, R. G. (Eds.). (2006). *Handbook of posttraumatic growth: Research & practice.* Mahwah, NJ: Erlbaum.

Cohen, E., & Barrett, J. (2008). When minds migrate: Conceptualizing spirit possession. *Journal of Cognition and Culture, 8,* 23–48.

Cole, B. S., Hopkins, C. M., Tisak, J., Steel, J. L., & Carr, B. I. (2008). Assessing spiritual growth and spiritual decline following a diagnosis of cancer: Reliability and validity of the Spiritual Transformation Scale. *Psycho-Oncology, 17,* 112–121.

Davis, L. J. (2008). *Obsession: A history.* Chicago: University of Chicago Press.

Dew, R. E., Daniel, S. S., Goldston, D. B, McCall, W. V., Kuchibhatla, M., Schleifer, C., et al. (2010). A prospective study of religion/spirituality and depressive symptoms among adolescent psychiatric patients. *Journal of Affective Disorders, 120,* 149–157.

Edmondson, D., Park, C. L., Chaudoir, S. R., & Wortmann, J. H. (2008). Death without God: Religious struggle, death concerns, and depression in the terminally ill. *Psychological Science, 19,* 754–758.

Eid, S., & Alzayed, A. (2005). Knowledge of symptoms and treatment of schizophrenia and depression among Kuwaiti population. *Arab Journal of Psychiatry, 16,* 62–77.

Ellison, C. G., Krause, N. M., Shepherd, B. C., & Chaves, M. A. (2009). Size, conflict, and opportunities for interaction: Congregational effects on members' anticipated support and negative interaction. *Journal for the Scientific Study of Religion, 48,* 1–15.

Emmons, R. A., & Paloutzian, R. F. (2003). The psychology of religion. *Annual Review of Psychology, 54,* 377–402.

Exline, J. J. (2002). Stumbling blocks on the religious road: Fractured relationships, nagging vices, and the inner struggle to believe. *Psychological Inquiry, 13,* 182–189.

Exline, J. J. (2013). Religious and spiritual struggles. In K. I. Pargament, J. J. Exline, & J. W. Jones (Eds.), *APA handbook of psychology, religion, and spirituality (Vol. 1): Context, theory, and research* (pp. 459–475). Washington, DC: American Psychological Association.

Exline, J. J., Kaplan, K. J., & Grubbs, J. B. (2012). Anger, exit, and assertion: Do people see protest toward God as morally acceptable? *Psychology of Religion and Spirituality, 4*(4), 264–277.

Exline, J. J., & Martin, A. (2005). Anger toward God: A new frontier in forgiveness research. In E. L. Worthington, Jr. (Ed.), *Handbook of forgiveness* (pp. 73–88). New York: Routledge.

Exline, J. J., Park, C. L., Smyth, J. M., & Carey, M. P. (2011). Anger toward God: Social-cognitive predictors, prevalence, and links with adjustment to bereavement and cancer. *Journal of Personality and Social Psychology, 100,* 129–148.

Exline, J. J., & Rose, E. (2005). Religious and spiritual struggles. In R. F. Paloutzian & C. L. Park (Eds.), *Handbook of the psychology of religion and spirituality* (pp. 315–330). New York: Guilford Press.

Exline, J. J., Yali, A. M., & Lobel, M. (1999). When God disappoints: Difficulty forgiving God and its role in negative emotion. *Journal of Health Psychology, 4,* 365–379.

Exline, J. J., Yali, A. M., & Sanderson, W. C. (2000). Guilt, discord, and alienation: The role of religious strain in depression and suicidality. *Journal of Clinical Psychology, 56,* 1481–1496.

Filius, R. (2009). Psychotherapy and deliverance ministry. *Psyche en Geloof, 20,* 30–40.

Fitchett, G., & Risk, J. L. (2009). Screening for spiritual struggle. *Journal of Pastoral Care & Counseling, 63,* 1–2.

Fitchett, G., Rybarczyk, B. D., DeMarco, G. A., & Nicholas, J. J. (1999). The role of religion in medical rehabilitation outcomes: A longitudinal study. *Rehabilitation Psychology, 44,* 1–22.

Frankfurter, D. (2006). *Evil incarnate: Rumors of demonic conspiracy and satanic abuse in history*. Princeton, NJ: Princeton University Press.

Gall, T. L., Kristjansson, E., Charbonneau, C., & Florack, P. (2009). A longitudinal study on the role of spirituality in response to the diagnosis and treatment of breast cancer. *Journal of Behavioral Medicine, 32,* 174–186.

Ganzevoort, R. R. (2006). Deliverance as oppression: A violent aspect of evangelical congregations? *Psyche en Geloof, 17,* 112–120.

Gear, M. R., Krumrei, E. J., & Pargament, K. I. (2009). Development of a spiritually-sensitive intervention for college students experiencing spiritual struggles: Winding road. *Journal of College and Character, 10*(4), 1–5.

Hall, T. W., & Edwards, K. J. (1996). The initial development and factor analysis of the spiritual assessment inventory. *Journal of Psychology and Theology, 24,* 233–246.

Hall, T. W., & Edwards, K. J. (2002). The Spiritual Assessment Inventory: A theistic model and measure for assessing spiritual development. *Journal for the Scientific Study of Religion, 41,* 341–357.

Hall, T. W., & Fujikawa, A. (2013). *God images and the sacred*. In K. I. Pargament, J. J. Exline, & J. W. Jones (Eds.), *APA handbook of psychology, religion, and spirituality (Vol. 1): Context, theory, and research* (pp. 277–292). Washington, DC: American Psychological Association.

Harley, J. L. (2007). *Pentecostal Christian view toward causes and treatment of mental health disorders*. Unpublished doctoral dissertation, Regent University.

Hartog, K., & Gow, K. M. (2005). Religious attributions pertaining to the causes and cures of mental illness. *Mental Health, Religion & Culture, 8,* 263–276.

Hill, P. C., & Pargament, K. I. (2003). Advances in the conceptualization and measurement of religion and spirituality: Implications for physical and mental health research. *American Psychologist, 58,* 64–74.

Hunsberger, B., Pratt, M., & Pancer, S. M. (2002). A longitudinal study of religious doubts in high school and beyond: Relationships, stability, and searching for answers. *Journal for the Scientific Study of Religion, 41,* 255–266.

Jensen, L. A. (2009). Conceptions of God and the devil across the lifespan: A cultural-developmental study of religious liberals and conservatives. *Journal for the Scientific Study of Religion, 48,* 121–145.

Kirkpatrick, L. A. (2005). *Attachment, evolution, and the psychology of religion*. New York: Guilford Press.

Krause, N., & Ellison, C. G. (2009). The doubting process: A longitudinal study of the precipitants and consequences of religious doubt in older adults. *Journal for the Scientific Study of Religion, 48,* 293–312.

Krumrei, E. J. (2011). Demonization as a spiritual struggle with divorce: Prevalence rates and links to post-divorce adjustment. *Family Relations, 60,* 90–103.

Krumrei, E. J., Mahoney, A., & Pargament, K. I. (2009). Divorce and the divine: The role of spirituality in adjustment to divorce. *Journal of Marriage and Family, 71,* 373–383.

Lawler-Row, K. A. (2010). Forgiveness as a mediator of the religiosity-health relationship. *Psychology of Religion and Spirituality, 2,* 1–16.

Martin, A. M. (2008). *Exploring forgiveness: The relationship between feeling forgiven by God and self-forgiveness for an interpersonal offense*. Unpublished doctoral dissertation, Case Western Reserve University.

McConnell, K. M., Pargament, K. I., Ellison, C. G., & Flannelly, K. J. (2006). Examining the links between spiritual struggles and symptoms of psychopathology in a national sample. *Journal of Clinical Psychology, 62,* 1469–1484.

Meier, B. P., Hauser, D. J., Robinson, M. D., Friesen, C. K., & Schjeldahl, K. (2007). What's "up" with God?: Vertical space as a representation of the divine. *Journal of Personality and Social Psychology, 93,* 699–710.

Miller, C. H., & Hedges, D.W. (2008). Scrupulosity disorder: An overview and introductory analysis. *Journal of Anxiety Disorders, 22,* 1042–1058.

Moriarty, G., & Hoffman, M. (Eds.). (2007). *God image handbook for spiritual counseling and psychotherapy: Research, theory, and practice.* Philadelphia, PA: Haworth Press.

Murray-Swank, N. A., (2013). Religious and spiritual problems: Integrating theory and clinial practice. In K. I. Pargament, A. Mahoney, & E. Shafranske (Eds.), *APA handbook of psychology, religion, and spirituality* (Vol. 2). Washington, DC: American Psychological Association.

Murray-Swank, N. A., & Pargament, K. I. (2008). Solace for the soul: Evaluating a spiritually-integrated counseling intervention for sexual abuse. *Counseling and Spirituality, 27,* 157–174.

Nelson, E. A., Abramowitz, J. S., Whiteside, S. P., & Deacon, B. J. (2006). Scrupulosity in patients with obsessive-compulsive disorder: Relationship to clinical and cognitive phenomena. *Anxiety Disorders, 20,* 1071–1086.

Novotni, M., & Petersen, R. (2001). *Angry with God.* Colorado Springs, CO: Piñon.

Olatunji, B. O., Tolin, D. F., Huppert, J. D., & Lohr, J. M. (2005). The relation between fearfulness, disgust sensitivity and religious obsessions in a non-clinical sample. *Personality and Individual Differences, 38,* 891–902.

Pargament, K. I. (2002). The bitter and the sweet: An evaluation of the costs and benefits of religiousness. *Psychological Inquiry, 13,* 168–181.

Pargament, K. I. (2007). *Spiritually integrated psychotherapy: Understanding and addressing the sacred.* New York: Guilford Press.

Pargament, K. I., Desai, K. M., & McConnell, K. M. (2006). Spirituality: A pathway to posttraumatic growth or decline? In L. G. Calhoun & R. G. Tedeschi (Eds.), *Handbook of posttraumatic growth: Research & practice* (pp. 121–137). Mahwah, NJ: Erlbaum.

Pargament, K. I., Koenig, H. G., & Perez, L. M. (2000). The many methods of religious coping: Development and initial validation of the RCOPE. *Journal of Clinical Psychology, 56,* 519–543.

Pargament, K. I., Koenig, H. G., Tarakeshwar, N., & Hahn, J. (2001). Religious struggle as a predictor of mortality among medically ill elderly patients: A two-year longitudinal study. *Archives of Internal Medicine, 161,* 1881–1885.

Pargament, K. I., Koenig, H. G., Tarakeshwar, N., & Hahn, J. (2004). Religious coping methods as predictors of psychological, physical and spiritual outcomes among medically ill elderly patients: A two-year longitudinal study. *Journal of Health Psychology, 9,* 713–730.

Pargament, K. I., Magyar, G. M., Benore, E., & Mahoney, A. (2005). Sacrilege: A study of sacred loss and desecration and their implications for health and well-being in a community sample. *Journal for the Scientific Study of Religion, 44,* 59–78.

Pargament, K. I., Murray-Swank, N., Magyar, G. M., & Ano, G. G. (2005). Spiritual struggle: A phenomenon of interest to psychology and religion. In W. R. Miller & H. Delaney (Eds.), *Judeo-Christian perspectives on psychology: Human nature, motivation, and change* (pp. 245–268). Washington, DC: American Psychological Association.

Pargament, K. I., Smith, B. W., Koenig, H. G., & Perez, L. (1998). Patterns of positive and negative religious coping with major life stressors. *Journal for the Scientific Study of Religion, 37,* 710–724.

Pargament, K. I., Trevino, K., Mahoney, A., & Silberman, I. (2007). They killed our Lord: The perception of Jews as desecrators of Christianity as a predictor of anti-Semitism. *Journal for the Scientific Study of Religion, 46,* 143–158.

Pargament, K. I., Zinnbauer, B. J., Scott, A. B., Butter, E. M., Zerowin, J., & Stanik, P. (1998). Red flags and religious coping: Identifying some religious warning signs among people in crisis. *Journal of Clinical Psychology, 54,* 77–89.

Park, C. L. (2005). Religion and meaning. In R. F. Paloutzian & C. L. Park (Eds.), *Handbook of the psychology of religion and spirituality* (pp. 295–314). New York: Guilford Press.

Park, C. L., Brooks, M. A., & Sussman, J. (2009). Dimensions of religion and spirituality in psychological adjustment of older adults living with congestive heart failure. In A. L. Ai & M. Ardelt (Eds.), *Faith and well-being in later life* (pp. 41–58). Hauppauge, NY: Nova Science.

Pearce, M. J., Singer, J. L., & Prigerson, H. G. (2006). Religious coping among caregivers of terminally ill cancer patients: Main effects and psychosocial mediators. *Journal of Health Psychology, 11,* 743–759.

Peck, M. S. (2005). *Glimpses of the devil: A psychiatrist's personal accounts of possession, exorcism, and redemption.* New York: Free Press.

Phillips, R. E., III, & Stein, C. H. (2007). God's will, God's punishment, or God's limitations?: Religious coping strategies reported by young adults living with serious mental illness. *Journal of Clinical Psychology, 63,* 529–540.

Piedmont, R. L., Hassinger, C. J., Rhorer, J., Sherman, M. F., Sherman, N. C., & Williams, J. E. G. (2007). The relations among spirituality and religiosity and axis II functioning in two college samples. *Research in the Social Scientific Study of Religion, 18,* 53–73.

Plakun, E. M. (2008). Psychiatry in Tibetan Buddhism: Madness and its cure seen through the lens of religious and national history. *Journal of the American Academy of Psychoanalysis & Dynamic Psychiatry, 36,* 415–430.

Raiya, H. A., Pargament, K. I., Mahoney, A., & Stein, C. (2008). A psychological measure of Islamic religiousness: Development and evidence for reliability and validity. *The International Journal for the Psychology of Religion, 18,* 291–315.

Reichbart, R. (2006). On the convergence of folk belief and psychopathology: A demon as introject in a 12-year-old African American boy. *Journal of Infant, Child & Adolescent Psychotherapy, 5,* 459–485.

Rose, E. D. (2010). *Why is it more distressing to have unwanted thoughts of aggression when you are religious?* Unpublished doctoral dissertation, Case Western Reserve University.

Rose, E. D., & Exline, J. J. (2008, March). *The defensive function of belief in the devil and supernatural evil spirits.* Poster presented at the annual Mid-Year Conference on Religion and Spirituality, Columbia, MD.

Rosmarin, D. H., Pargament, K. I., & Flannelly, K. J. (2009). Do spiritual struggles predict poorer physical/mental health among Jews? *The International Journal for the Psychology of Religion, 19,* 244–258.

Rosmarin, D. H., Pargament, K. I., Krumrei, E. J., & Flannelly, K. J. (2009). Religious coping among Jews: Development and initial validation of the JCOPE. *Journal of Clinical Psychology, 65,* 670–683.

Rosmarin, D. H., Pargament, K. I., & Mahoney, A. (2009). The role of religiousness in anxiety, depression, and happiness in a Jewish community sample: A preliminary investigation. *Mental Health, Religion and Culture, 12,* 97–113.

Rowatt, W. C., & Kirkpatrick, L. A. (2002). Two dimensions of attachment to God and their relation to affect, religiosity, and personality constructs. *Journal for the Scientific Study of Religion, 41,* 637–651.

Ruskin, R. (2007). Possession. *American Journal of Psychiatry, 164,* 1014–1015.

Sherman, A. C., Plante, T. G., Simonton, S., Latif, U., & Anaissie, E. J. (2009). Prospective study of religious coping among patients undergoing autologous stem cell transplantation. *Journal of Behavioral Medicine, 32,* 118–128.

Shtulman, A. (2008). Variation in the anthropomorphization of supernatural beings and its implications for cognitive theories of religion. *Journal of Experimental Psychology: Learning, Memory, and Cognition, 34,* 1123–1138.

Smith, T. B., McCullough, M. E., & Poll, J. (2003). Religiousness and depression: Evidence for a main effect and the moderating influence of stressful life events. *Psychological Bulletin, 129,* 614–636.

Strelan, P., Acton, C., & Patrick, K. (2009). Disappointment with God and well-being: The mediating influence of relationship quality and dispositional forgiveness. *Counseling and Values, 53,* 202–213.

Thuné-Boyle, I. C., Stygall, J. A., Keshtgar, M. R., & Newman, S. P. (2006). Do religious/spiritual coping strategies affect illness adjustment in patients with cancer?: A systematic review of the literature. *Social Science and Medicine, 63,* 151–164.

Toussaint, L. L., Williams, D. R., Musick, M. A., & Everson-Rose, S. A. (2008). The association of forgiveness and 12-month prevalence of major depressive episode: Gender differences in a probability sample of U.S. adults. *Mental Health, Religion & Culture, 11,* 485–500.

Trevino, K. M., Pargament, K. I., Cotton, S., Leonard, A. C., Hahn, J., Caprini-Faigin, C. A., et al. (2010). Religious coping and physiological, psychological, social, and spiritual outcomes in patients with HIV/AIDS: Cross-sectional and longitudinal findings. *Aids and Behavior, 14,* 379–389.

Wayment, H. A., & Bauer, J. A. (Eds.). (2008). *Transcending self-interest: Psychological explorations of the quiet ego.* Washington, DC: American Psychological Association.

Webb, M., Stetz, K., & Hedden, K. (2008). Representation of mental illness in Christian self-help bestsellers. *Mental Health, Religion and Culture, 11,* 697–717.

Wood, B. T., Worthington, E. L., Jr., Exline, J. J., Yali, A. M., Aten, J. D., & McMinn, M. R. (2010). Development, refinement, and psychometric properties of the Attitudes toward God Scale (ATGS-9). *Psychology of Religion and Spirituality, 2,* 148–167.

Zinnbauer, B. J., & Pargament, K. I. (2005). Religiousness and spirituality. In R. F. Paloutzian & C. L. Park (Eds.), *Handbook of the psychology of religion and spirituality* (pp. 21–42). New York: Guilford Press.

Zinnbauer, B. J., Pargament, K. I., Cole, B. C., Rye, M. S., Butter, E. M., Belavich, T. C., et al. (1997). Religion and spirituality: Unfuzzying the fuzzy. *Journal for the Scientific Study of Religion, 36,* 549–564.

Zwingmann, C., Wirtz, M., Müller, C., Körber, J., & Murken, S. (2006). Positive and negative religious coping in German breast cancer patients. *Journal of Behavioral Medicine, 29,* 533–547.

20

Conversion, Deconversion, and Spiritual Transformation

A Multilevel Interdisciplinary View

Raymond F. Paloutzian, Sebastian Murken,
Heinz Streib, and Sussan Rößler-Namini

This chapter summarizes recent research on religious conversion[1] and deconversion, both part of the larger category called "spiritual transformation." In particular, it highlights two important research programs conducted since the publication of the first edition of this *Handbook* (Paloutzian & Park, 2005) and provides an overview of other studies published since then. Thus, this chapter is a follow-up, extension, and companion to the previous chapter (Paloutzian, 2005) rather than a simple update of it. The information presented and connections made then still stand as authoritative for the scope of literature examined and the meaning system components on which the findings from that literature were mapped. Thus, there is no reason to repeat it. In order to enrich one's understanding with the most complete picture of the longer history of past research on conversion and spiritual transformation and, therefore, put the present chapter in the best conceptual context, the interested reader is advised to examine the chapter on conversion in the first edition of the *Handbook* as companion reading to the present chapter. See also the extensive summaries of research on this topic in a comprehensive review article (Paloutzian, Richardson, & Rambo, 1999) and in two companion handbook chapters on conversion and spiritual transformation (Paloutzian, in press; Paloutzian & Lowe, 2012). In this chapter, we present the most recent research that adds to and illuminates, and perhaps begins to answer, some of the questions raised by the previous lines of research. In the process, we summarize research conducted in Europe in order to accent the increasing international scope of the research and to document similar and dissimilar trends in converting to and from a religious group in a major European country, Germany, and the United States. Doing this is in keeping with current awareness that cross-cultural comparisons are increasingly important (see Saroglou & Cohen, Chapter 17, this volume).

Among the key integrative themes that are intended to help knit the topics in this handbook together, the two pivotal ones are the multilevel interdisciplinary paradigm (MIP; Emmons & Paloutzian, 2003) and the model of religion as a meaning system (Park, 2005, Chapter 18, this volume; Silberman, 2005) (see also Paloutzian & Park, Chapter 1, this volume). In this chapter, we conceptualize and integrate research within an MIP and illustrate how the probability that a transformation will occur is influenced by an optimal and interdependent fit between what converting (or deconverting) might mean to the individual and to the group.

After a brief synopsis of the past research on the psychology of conversion and spiritual transformation just described, we present a recent body of research whose intellectual roots combine ideas from psychology with ideas from sociology, the outcome of which is a picture of conversion not as a function of the person, or of only social pressures, but of an optimal fit between the needs and wants of a person and whatever the environment, group, or ideology has to offer. The conclusion emphasizes the interaction between person and context, not the personality, mental states, emotions, or cognitions of the convert per se. Following that, we present research on a topic mostly new to scholarship on the psychology of conversion and spiritual transformation: research on deconversion. Deconversion *from* a religion is as much a change—a spiritual transformation—as conversion *to* a religion is. However, except for a few pieces of past research on allied topics such as atheism (Hunsberger & Altemeyer, 2006) and apostasy (Altemeyer & Hunsberger, 1997), the topic has only recently been examined in a comprehensive research program (Streib, Hood, Keller, Csöff, & Silver, 2009). Finally, we document a set of recent studies, noting the theoretical context of each, in order to provide an up-to-date, user-friendly *Handbook* chapter capable of facilitating future research.

We believe the data are compelling that (1) applying knowledge from multiple levels of analysis is essential for a complete understanding of spiritual transformations (whether conversion to a religion or deconversion from one), and that (2) combining evidence from multiple methods can yield insights that cannot be gained by use of any one method alone. Thus, quantitative, qualitative, and other companion methods are essential to blend together in order to lead to a more complete understanding of transformative processes that explain how a human undergoes such a major change.

SYNOPSIS OF RECENT HIGHLIGHTS

A brief sketch of recent comprehensive overviews provides a context for appreciating the main lines of research that will follow. First, Paloutzian et al. (1999) examined the varied lines of research on conversion (e.g., psychoanalytic, social-cognitive, sociological) around the question of whether a religious conversion causes someone's personality to change. The overall pattern of evidence led to the conclusion that when personality is understood at the level of basic traits or temperaments, there is little to indicate that an individual's personality is different after he or she is converted. Converts may feel as if everything about them, including their basic traits, is different, but there was little evidence to support that conclusion. On the other hand, other aspects of personality such as midlevel functions, goals, purposes, and strivings, and aspects of the more overarching level of personality such as purpose, meaning, and worldview often become different after a religious conversion. Thus, "what the person is about" may be substantially altered after a spiritual transformation, although the particular trait-based style with which the person lives out the change may not be appreciably different.

The scope of Paloutzian et al.'s (1999) review on personality as the main factor in the conversion process was incomplete because it placed all the attention on personal aspects of the individual convert, with the primary question being whether conversion caused change. However, some of the studies reviewed suggested that a person's personality might predict the type of group that he or she would convert to, rather than the type of group causing a change in the individual's personality after the person was in the group. Thus, a subsidiary finding emerged such that a particular personality might be drawn to a particular type of group.

Going beyond personality (trait) questions, however, Rambo (1993) laid out a comprehensive conceptual map of all the factors that have to be taken into account in order to have a complete understanding of the conversion process. The individual's personality was only one of them. His model made it clear that the combined and interactive effects of a vast array of factors, personalistic and contextual, need to be accounted for. These include demographic, mental, emotional, group, circumstantial, sequential, temporal, social, environmental, cultural, and other factors, with subcategories of each one. Thus, the long history of research that looked primarily at the individual convert seems inadequate. Because of this, Paloutzian (2005, in press) put spiritual transformation processes in the larger context of a meaning system model (Park, 2005; Chapter 18, this volume; Silberman, 2005; see Park, 2010, for comprehensive review) that includes components of a meaning system (beliefs and attitudes, values, goals, overall purposes, identity, and worldview and ultimate concern) that can be put under pressure to change by various means, and that can show outcomes that are evidence of internal change if the pressure on the system reaches some threshold. The specific empirical and theoretical question guiding the movement from the 1999 review focusing on personality factors to the 2005 chapter centered on whether the data on all the raw variables in the myriad studies of conversion would map clearly and straight-forwardly onto the components of a meaning system model. They did. This suggests that religious conversion is not mediated by psychological processes unique to it, but that it is instead is one instance of a larger category of human change processes: the spiritual transformation of a meaning system. Spiritual transformation can be seen as an overall process of change, which can occur in gradations from smaller to larger amounts and in parts or as a whole, within a meaning system. When that change is large enough and is about certain categories of content,[2] we call it a religious conversion.

The movement from seeing religious conversion as a personality process to seeing it as a change in a meaning system helped carry our conceptualization of the processes involved to a more complex level, one that is amenable to generating hypotheses and doing research within an MIP as a guiding idea. That movement allowed us to cast the notion in broader conceptual terms, with the hope that it might be possible within its framework to begin to integrate research from allied disciplines. Consistent with this, we believe this approach addresses human change more generally. That is, we want to understand all human change, not only religious conversions as if they were unique and mediated by processes unlike those that are involved in other kinds of human change. Fundamentally, we see whatever we learn about spiritual transformation as one instance of human change in general. The principles involved are part of and applicable to general psychology as a whole, not narrowly or singularly applicable to religiousness only.

This chapter expands our picture of spiritual transformation processes by including research on person–group fit, and deconversion, and other recent studies. The first highlights the importance of interactive processes in addition to personality processes in human change; the second highlights that the decision to leave a religion is just as central to questions about human change as is the decision to believe in and practice one. Spiritual transformations happen in both directions; people are drawn to and repelled from religions. The person–context fit approach integrates ideas and research from both psychological and sociological traditions. The deconversion research does the same. Combining these recent lines of research is in keeping with our efforts to take one step toward explaining spiritual transformations within a MIP (see also Paloutzian & Park, Chapter 1, this volume).

A FIT MODEL

The Notion of Fit

In addition to individuals who convert to specific religions differing in their personality structures, experiences, and biographical backgrounds, the existence of myriad religions means that the individuals also face an enormous religious marketplace (Gooren, 2006; Rambo & Farhadian, in press). Various churches, religious groups, and new religious movements (NRMs) cannot be conceptualized as being one category ("religion") because the differences among them are so great (see Oman, Chapter 2, and Taves, Chapter 7, this volume, for inherent difficulties with the single generic category "religion"). Thus, if one wants to understand the dynamics of religious conversion, a central question to investigate becomes: "*Which* person joins *which* religious group and why?" As already mentioned, research on conversion has to assume that the answer to this question depends on the interaction between individual characteristics and the environment provided by the specific religious group to which the convert turns. That is, personal factors drive the individual's tendency to change, while the nature of the group welcomes the changed one. In line with this consideration, recent conversion research has focused on the aspect of *fit* between different psychosocial patterns and specific religions as a key factor in religious change.

It postulates that specific individual needs may be fulfilled particularly well by particular religious groups, and that the fit between the needs of the person and what the religious group has to offer is a major determinant of entry into or exit from the group as well as the consequences arising from association with it. Thus, the concept of a *person–religion fit* can enhance our explanations of at least three phenomena: (1) mechanisms of conversion to a religious group, (2) the course of membership in the group (continuance vs. deconversion), and (3) psychosocial consequences of conversion (positive vs. negative). Relevant individual variables from which specific needs may arise include religious and biographical background, actual life situation/problems, and personality structure, whereas relevant religious group variables include teachings, rituals, hierarchy or social structure, and norms and rules. Neither the characteristics of the person nor the features of the religious group is alone sufficient to explain the membership process, but the interaction—more precisely, the fit—between the person and the group is assumed to increase explanatory power significantly. To quote Rambo (1993), "What makes any voluntary conversion process possible is a complex confluence of the 'right' potential convert coming into contact, under proper circumstances at the proper time, with the 'right' advocate and religious option" (p. 87).

Past research supports this line of thought. Although some authors—mainly in the context of research on NRMs—came to the conclusion that there was one clear profile of the "typical convert" regardless of the particular religious group that the person joined (e.g., Richardson, 1985a, pp. 209–210), an increasing number of cases that were exceptions to the profile were postulated (see Barker, 1989, pp. 14–15; Beckford & Levasseur, 1986, pp. 39–41; Hunt, 2003, pp. 96–98). Thus, generalizations about the characteristics of converts seemed to be oversimplified. Implicit or explicit references to a fit approach began to emerge (e.g., Klosinski, 1996, pp. 85–86; Poling & Kenney, 1986). Already by the late 1970s, Richardson and colleagues (Richardson & Stewart, 1977; Richardson, Stewart, & Simmonds, 1979) sketched a conversion process model that assumed that, in addition to affective bonding, ideological congruence between what the person was seeking or needed and what the group or ideology offered was pivotal to the process. The conceptualization of congruency is close to that of fit because it suggests that the individual chooses a religion by taking into account the degree to which a specific group addresses his or her general orientations, perspectives, and ideologies.

During the past decade, Murken, Namini, and colleagues conducted a comprehensive research program in which they applied the idea of fit to the study of self-chosen membership in religious groups (Murken & Namini, 2007; Murken, 2009; Namini & Murken, 2008; Namini, 2009; Namini, Appel, Jürgensen, & Murken, 2010). Within the framework of a longitudinal and comparative study design, they collected data from converts to three religious groups—a Pentecostal parish (PP), the New Apostolic Church (NAC), and Jehovah's Witnesses (JW)—in Germany between 2003 and 2006. Before reporting findings from their research, a look at two key examples of past studies consistent with a fit approach will provide some empirical background and context and set the stage for examining this recent research.

First, Klosinski (1983, 1985) compared members of two NRMs—the Neo-Sannyas movement (NSM; Bhagwan Shree Rajneesh) and the Society for Transcendental Meditation (TM; Maharishi Mahesh Yogi)—via biographical interviews and personality tests. He examined the psychodynamic aspects of conversion and assumed that specific features of each religious movement would prompt the conversion of a person whose personality and inner conflicts would make for a proper fit. He reported that the NSM group had a greater number of women with symptoms of hysteria, which he related to the sexual and erotic features of the Bhagwan ideology. On the other hand, the TM sample had proportionately more obsessive men, who he concluded would have the characteristics that would lead them to find the constant repetition of the TM mantra appealing. Similarly, the NSM group orientation was such that there was much emphasis placed on the figure of the spiritual leader and the group members' relationship with him. Thus, Klosinski found that converts to the group tended to be high in the need for a sense of group cohesion and to perceive a special relationship with a leader. In contrast, the TM group put more emphasis on its teachings and ideology, which Klosinski interpreted as basis for a better match with the cognitive structure of the TM followers.

Second, Kuner (1983) examined data from members of the Children of God (CoG), the Unification Church (UC), Ananda Marga (AM), and a student control group on the nature of their familial socialization and life circumstances shortly before their encounter with the religious group. He focused especially on the specific needs an individual developed through his or her life experiences. The results identified some general patterns that differentiated members of the three NRMs compared with those not in an NRM; there were also small differences between members of the three NRMs in loss of parents, birth order, and degree of preconversion religious quest, although there was no clear overall fit patterns to distinguish members from among these three NRMs. Converts to all three NRMs tended to come from families with many siblings in which the mother was dominant and the father was weak; these converts also characterized their personal situation prior to contact with the group as one of alienation. More specific results showed that conversion to the UC seemed to occur gradually and tended to include a theological quest, whereas conversion to the AM and CoG had stronger roots in a sense of deprivation of emotional needs and human contact, which were quickly met by the characteristics of these two groups.

Childhood and Familial Experiences

As the prior examples of studies indicate, an important domain to which a person–religion fit approach may apply is the biographical background and childhood familial experiences of the convert (see Murken & Namini, 2007, for review of findings summarized below). Mainstream psychology can provide empirical and theoretical frameworks such as (1) child developmental models, (2) psychoanalysis, (3) attachment theory, and (4) knowledge of birth order effects. For example, as a generality, early developmental influences such as traumatic events (e.g., divorce of parents, death of a parent, child abuse) and specific childrearing patterns (e.g., dominant mother and weak father) were repeatedly reported to facilitate conversion to religious groups. Members of NRMs often report that their fathers have been either absent, passive-unavailable, or actively rejecting, and they, more than nonconverts, perceive their relationships with their mothers as having been problematic (see also Cowan, in press; Yang & Abel, in press). Similarly, individuals interested or involved in new forms of religiosity tend to show insecure attachment histories (Buxant, Saroglou, Casalfiore, & Christians, 2007; Granqvist & Kirkpatrick, 2004). They typically come from relatively large families with several siblings.

Similarities in findings are not surprising if one considers that many of the groups studied share structural and theological characteristics. However, a closer look at single studies, especially those with comparative designs (e.g., Kuner, 1983; van der Lans & Derks, 1986), again indicates that differing family backgrounds route persons to involvement in certain groups. Thus, an application of a fit approach extends further. For example, thinking within a psychodynamic approach, the concept of person–religion fit may help illuminate possible connections between a specific pattern of familial experiences and the specific religious group to which the individual turns. Some individuals with difficult family backgrounds may find a solution for the resulting conflicts in a group that offers some kind of ideal family, whereas others may prefer groups that provide therapeutic experiences or that emphasize individualism. Some may choose a group that offers an emotional relationship with a religious figure or an especially personal father-like God concept as a substitute for deficits in their early relationships. Others whose needs are primarily intellectual may choose a faith that claims to have a compelling rational argument that theirs is the true religion.

Some findings from Namini and Murken's (2008) comparison of the family backgrounds of converts to a PP, the NAC, or JW further illustrate this point. Regarding loss of a parent, the authors found a significant difference in whether a person lost a parent before she or he was 15 years of age: Only 10% of the PP group reported such a loss, whereas 23% of the JW and 43% of the NAC groups did. The rate for the PP group was comparable to that for the general German population, whereas the rate for the NAC was more than four times higher. The extraordinarily high proportion of NAC converts who grew up without their biological father can be seen in the context that one of the church's primary provisions is a father-oriented theology and a hierarchy with a chief apostle—a presumedly strong father figure—at the top. On number of siblings, the authors found a trend: 68% of the JW group had two or more siblings, whereas 64% of those in the NAC grew up as a single child. This difference again seems consistent with the theologies and practices of the two religious groups. For example, in the JW theology the group is emphasized over the individual, which, moreover, is subordinated to a strict theology and weekly schedule that combines activities with others, properties consistent with having grown up in a group.

Person–Environment Fit

Research in the psychology of religion can profit from invoking theories established in general psychology. For example, the notion of a person–environment (P–E) fit model (see, e.g., Caplan, 1983, and Van Harrison, 1978) can be helpful to further our understanding of religious fit processes. The P–E fit approach has early intellectual and theoretical roots in the Gestalt psychology of the 1930s as expressed in the social psychological writings of Kurt Lewin (1936). Lewin's way of accounting for behavior was captured in his famous equation $B=f(P,E)$, where behavior is a function of the person and the environment. The dynamic interaction between personal and environmental variables to which Lewin points is also at the heart of P–E fit models. The theory states that strain or stress develops when there is a discrepancy between the motives or needs of the person and the supplies of the environment, or between the demands of the environment and the abilities of the person to meet those demands. Crucial for the well-being of the individual is the subjective fit between needs and supplies *(needs–supplies fit)* or between demands and abilities *(demands–abilities fit)*, whereby a perception by the individual that there is either "too much" or "too little" in the way of supplies or demands can have negative psychosocial consequences. Also, a perfect fit is not necessarily optimal since it can lead to understimulation and stagnation, because if what is needed and what is supplied are always exactly the same, then the growth that comes from new information, learning, and challenges is less likely.

Although P-E fit theory originated in the context of the psychology of work, some researchers have suggested that it can be used to understand stress in all life domains (Edwards & Rothbard, 1999). As applied to the psychological study of religious conversion, the concept of *person–religion fit* can be especially helpful to understand the psychosocial consequences of conversion and shed light upon the observation that religious conversions can offer benefits as well as pose risks. An early attempt to apply a P-E fit notion to the context of religion was made by Pargament and colleagues (Pargament, Johnson, Echemendia, & Silverman, 1985; Pargament, Tyler, & Steele, 1979), who examined Roman Catholic, Protestant, and Jewish communities on the psychosocial consequences of the degree to which what the individual wanted or needed matched what the religion provided. Individuals whose needs and wants corresponded with those the group provided showed higher psychosocial competencies but lower self-efficacy and less active coping strategies compared with individuals for whom the degree of correspondence was lower. They also found that in churches with an open atmosphere and more possibilities for individual autonomy, the degree to which the members tolerated ambiguity was positively related to various measures of psychosocial competence. Apparently, the more the atmosphere was one of openness, the more individuals who wanted to do so could explore, express themselves, and attempt to apply their skills. These results are consistent with a person–religion fit approach. One general conclusion is that the degree of fit between individuals and the religious environment depends on the relative weight of positive and negative trade-offs—psychosocial costs and benefits—that accrue to each member of the transaction.

In the just-mentioned recent research program, Murken, Namini, and colleagues (Namini, 2009; Namini et al., 2010) applied P–E fit theory to investigate the relation between needs–supplies fit and well-being in the context of conversions to the religious groups studied (PP, NAC, JW). Regression analysis indicated that the degree to which a person's needs for autonomy and relatedness could be met by the group was related to well-being and mental health. Further analysis for autonomy and relatedness showed that well-being and mental health measures tended to decrease when the amount of the need supplied exceeded what was needed. These results suggest that if a group "overdoes it" and floods the convert with more than he or she needs or wants, conflicts can be created that are detrimental to the convert's well-being. They also indicate that it is as suboptimal for a group to provide too much as it is for it to provide too little, insofar as the well-being of its participants is concerned.

Another exploratory analysis (Namini, 2009) investigated differences in the demands–abilities fit of members of different NRMs. It studied how members of the PP, NAC, and JW assessed potential demands–requirements of the group they converted to and their own abilities to fulfill them. Results indicated that the NAC group sensed fewer demands—couched in terms of "living up to God's commandments" and "knowing the Bible and its meaning"—than converts to the other two groups. The highest degree of perceived demands was consistently reported by JW converts. With respect to how converts perceived their own abilities, those in the JW had a higher belief that they could meet the demands of the group than those in either the PP or the NAC. Interestingly, however, those in the JW assessed their own abilities as slightly lower than the demands placed upon them. Thus, it seems that they always had something to strive for—neither too much nor too little, but, at least in their perceptions, enough to provide a continual sense of achievement and accomplishment to sustain their membership. Members of the PP also assessed their abilities as slightly lower than the demands of their religious community, whereas those in the NAC saw their abilities and the NAC's demands as almost equal. These observations suggest that examination of what specific religious groups require of new members compared with the self-perceived abilities of individuals turning toward these groups can help us identify potential costs and benefits of their involvement with a group.

Implications

The empirical findings suggest that research on conversion has to take into account the fit between characteristics of the individual and specifics of the religious groups. Generally, a fit between a person and the religious group to which the person turns can be assumed to facilitate a conversion, encourage continuance of membership, and lead to positive psychosocial consequences. In terms of the RMS model (cf. also Park, 2005, Chapter 18, this volume; Silberman, 2005; Paloutzian, 2005, in press), a person will more likely turn to a new religion or belief system if he or she can find meaning in it on a cognitive, affective, or social level. As the distinction between various forms of conversion (sudden vs. gradual) suggests, the degree to which a person's meaning system changes in the course of conversion may vary. From an RMS perspective, it can be assumed that people in general will try to maintain their overarching meaning system (i.e., look for a theology and group that fits and only change the appraisal of a situation or event when necessary). Independent of the details of the conversion process, it can be assumed that as long as the overarching meaning conveyed by a religious group fits an individual's experiences (i.e., can be successfully translated into daily life), he or she is likely to continue membership in a group. A sense of meaningfulness through religion can account for psychosocial adjustment in a similar way as a subjective person–religion fit, since the processes by which meaningfulness and its appraisal and by which a subjective sense of person–religion fit operates would seem to mesh well with each other. They may also reciprocally influence each other; for example, the subjective importance of certain personal beliefs, goals, and values may influence the effect of the person–religion fit in the conversion process.

Thinking in terms of a larger MIP, findings from neurophysiology (e.g., that new information that can connect to already available information or that is of special emotional relevance to a person is more easily stored; Goldstein, 2011) support the assumption that a particular religion may seem especially attractive when what it can provide fits individual needs, and can thus be perceived as more meaningful to the person.

However, personal and religious variables are so numerous and their interactions so complex that a simple or clear picture of whether a specific person fits a specific group is difficult to construct. As an example from attachment theory, which assumes that a person's religious search has its roots in experiences related to early attachment figures (see Richert & Granqvist, Chapter 8, this volume), one individual characteristic (here, childhood attachment representations) can work in different ways: An individual can search for a God image that matches his or her early attachment figure *(correspondence),* or do the opposite and search for a God image that compensates for the attachment qualities that the individual did not receive from his or her primary attachment figure *(compensation)* (Kirkpatrick, 1992, 2005). In the context of P-E fit theory, these two concepts are equivalent to the ideas of *supplementary fit* and *complementary fit* (Cable & Edwards, 2004), respectively. While the latter indicates that the needs of the individual and of the environment are fulfilled by the opposite resources of each other, the former describes how the characteristics of both sides are similar.

Moreover, with every additional variable that has to be taken into account, the number of possible fit patterns increases exponentially, and other moderating factors like crises, close relationships, availability of alternatives, and chance have to be considered as well (cf. Namini, 2009). Because of this, there is little support for the idea that there is a one-to-one correspondence between various aspects of the individual and various aspects of religions. To the contrary, research findings, some of which were summarized previously, illustrate how complex the relationships are and that more investigation into the association between (subjective) fit and meaning is needed.

CONVERSION AND DECONVERSION

We now include a section on deconversion for two reasons. First, theoretically, we believe that both conversion and deconversion are, at least in part, subsets of the broader category of spiritual transformation and that the psychological processes that mediate conversion and deconversion overlap, even if they may not be identical. Second, multiple conversions (and, therefore, deconversions) are more likely in the multicultural and multireligious environments of our modern world. Multiple conversions, however, often involve deconversion(s).[3] Also, in cultures with many nonaffiliates, nontheists, atheists, and agnostics, the term "deconversion" seems big enough to include processes of disaffiliation *without* a replacement belief or reaffiliation (Streib & Klein, 2013). Therefore, although related to conversion, the processes of changing to disbelief and/or disaffiliation are not identical to it and may constitute an independent but overlapping field of study (Streib, 2013). The term "deconversion" may connote the depth and intensity of biographical change that can be associated with disbelief and/or disaffiliation. Theoretically, also, if a P-E fit model increases our understanding of the processes involved in religious conversion, then it would likely show the same benefit for our efforts to account for deconversion. Among the reasons for this are that both religious conversion and deconversion are (1) consequences of the interaction between multilevel individual and group processes and (2) manifestations of one or more changes among the components of the person's meaning system.

In this section we devote primary attention to presenting the recent and extensive research program of Streib et al. (2009), with some attention to others as well. Streib et al.'s study is foremost because of its comprehensiveness and multinationality, and because it is the first large-scale study of its kind to apply both the so-called qualitative and quantitative techniques to data from the same research participants. For researchers who wish to apply so-called qualitative methods to gain certain kinds of insights, this project is a fine example of how also to invoke quantitative techniques in order to test hypotheses with same data set. The combination of techniques helps to strengthen the validity of our psychological theorizing. Therefore, we believe it is sufficiently important, for these methodological reasons, to highlight this point here. We follow this section with a summary of other empirical studies published in recent years.

Conceptualizing Deconversion

In their initial exploration of the concept of deconversion, Streib and Keller (2004) examined Barbour's (1994) work, which presents an analysis of autobiographies of leading theologians, philosophers, and other writers who were undergoing deconversion. Barbour interprets the rise of and interest in deconversion as due to increased individualism and religious pluralism present in modern society. He identified four criteria of deconversion that are present in most cases: (1) intellectual doubt or denial of the truth of a system of beliefs; (2) moral criticism, including the rejection of the entire way of life of a religious group; (3) emotional suffering that consists of grief, guilt, loneliness, and despair; and (4) disaffiliation from the religious community. However, evaluating Barbour's (1994) conceptualization of deconversion in light of Glock's (1962) five dimensions of religious commitment reveals that Barbour's list of criteria does not explicitly include Glock's experiential dimension. Nevertheless, it may be important to feel the loss of (sometimes very specific) religious experiences as part of a deconversion process. Because of this, Streib and Keller (2004) include the experiential dimension in their list of elements of deconversion. They are: (1) loss of specific religious experiences; (2) intellectual doubt, denial, or disagreement with specific beliefs; (3) moral criticism; (4) emotional suffering; and (5) disaffiliation from the community. Using these five characteristics prevents the reduction of deconversion to merely disaffiliation from the group.[4]

In addition to defining deconversion, we need to identify potential outcomes of the process. Although deconversion can be inferred when a person changes from one religious organization to another (but stays within the orbit of organized religions), it can also be manifest as an exit from the religious field altogether, which can itself be expressed in a number of ways. Streib et al. (2009) suggest the six possible deconversion trajectories summarized in Table 20.1. All of such trajectories can be viewed as migrations in the religious field, except "secularizing exit." Overall, deconversion is conceptualized as an intense biographical change that includes individual and social aspects: experiential, emotional, intellectual-ideological, social-environmental, moral, as well as changes or termination of group membership.

This characterization of deconversion can be easily mapped onto components of a meaning system, as summarized by Park (2005, 2010) or Paloutzian (2005, in press), and be interpreted in such terms. Intellectual doubt and moral criticism (two of the five criteria for deconversion) reflect beliefs, attitudes, and values—components of meaning systems. Disaffiliation and the final outcome of deconversion reflect new goals and purpose. The experiential and emotional aspects are implicit and inherent in meaning system change because the process involves stresses and pressures that may be experienced as various kinds of unease, affective depletion, lowering of resistance to change, feelings of dissatisfaction with the status quo for any number of reasons, and because much of the process of appraising incoming information occurs at an affective level. Finally, departing from a religion almost automatically involves a transformation, or at least a modification, of ultimate concern and worldview. Thus, it seems that the descriptive characteristics of deconversion summarized previously map reasonably well to the social-cognitive processes that comprise a shift in a meaning system, a change that constitutes some degree of spiritual transformation.

Empirical Studies on Deconversion

The history of research on deconversion shows that it is relatively recent and used to be done only occasionally and somewhat unsystematically (see Streib et al., 2009, Chapter

TABLE 20.1. The Six Possible Deconversion Trajectories According to Streib et al. (2009)

Type of trajectory	Characteristics
Secularizing exit	Termination of (concern with) religious belief and praxis and, eventually, disaffiliation from organized religion
Oppositional exit	Adopting a different system of beliefs and engaging in different ritual practices, while affiliating with a higher tension, more oppositional religious organization, which could mean, for example, conversion into a fundamentalist group
Religious switching	Migration to a religious organization with a similar system of beliefs and rituals and with no, or only marginal, difference in terms of integration in the surrounding culture
Integrating exit	Adopting a different system of beliefs and engaging in different ritual practices, while affiliating with an integrated or more accommodated religious organization
Privatizing exit	Disaffiliating from a religious organization, eventually including termination of membership, but continuation of private religious belief and private religious praxis
Heretical exit	Disaffiliating from a religious organization, eventually including termination of membership, and individual heretical appropriation of new belief system(s) or engagement in different religious praxis but without new organizational affiliation

2, for a review). Three developments contribute to its recent progress. First, discussion in the 1980s and 1990s about NRMs and public concern about "cults" triggered research, mostly interview studies, about apostates or defectors from the most controversial new religious groups (Jacobs, 1989; Levine, 1984; Skonovd, 1981; Streib 1999, 2000; Wright, 1987, in press). Second, studies of people who had left churches and secular apostates in Europe and the United States indicated a shift of research focus in the 1990s to mainstream religions and the religious landscape as a whole (Altemeyer & Hunsberger, 1997; Hunsberger, 2000; Jamieson, 2002; Richter & Francis, 1998). This research continues with a special interest in atheist and agnostic individuals or groups (Burris & Petrican, 2011; Burris & Redden, 2012), especially in the United States (Hunsberger & Altemeyer, 2006; Kosmin & Keysar, 2007). Third, large-scale surveys, such as the International Social Survey Programme (Leibniz Institute for the Social Sciences, 2010) and the General Social Survey (National Opinion Research Center, 2009), ask respondents to indicate their and their parent's religious affiliations and participation during the respondent's late childhood years. These data allow some inferences about deconversion, even though based on limited information (Streib, 2013).

Descriptive information such as that just described is useful, but psychology of religion must go beyond the descriptive level in order to understand the processes involved in various sorts of spiritual transformations. For example, questions about psychological processes include whether deconversion is related to personality, whether the well-being, growth, or development of deconverts differs from that of converts, whether deconversion is related to faith development, and how motivational, attitudinal, cognitive, and similar factors might lead to or follow such a change. This would include learning about factors that lead to an optimal versus nonoptimal fit between what the person wants and needs and what the religion was and was not able to supply.

The results of the Bielefeld cross-cultural study of deconversion (Streib et al., 2009) begins to address some of these issues. The research was conducted between 2002 and 2005 and included a total of 129 deconverts in Germany and the United States. Narrative and faith development interviews were conducted with 99 of these deconverts. In addition, an extensive questionnaire was completed by all deconverts as well as by in-tradition religious members. The goal was to survey approximately 10 in-tradition members for each deconvert. Thus, the quantitative database includes questionnaire responses from 1,067 in-tradition members and 129 deconverts. The questionnaire assessed spiritual/religious self-identification, personality traits, psychological well-being and growth, religious fundamentalism, right-wing authoritarianism, and religious styles. Also, faith development interviews were conducted with 177 in-tradition members.

As is apparent, the research program not only was based on an innovative design that included both quantitative and qualitative data, but was also aimed at comparing deconverts to in-tradition members in two nations. The biographical interview information allowed the researchers to identify the deconversion trajectories of the 99 cases. Various types of trajectories were found: 29 secular exiters, 24 privatizing exiters, nine heretical exiters, 13 religious switchers, 16 integrating exiters, and eight oppositional exiters. On the basis of the quantitative data, the deconverts could be profiled and contrasted with in-tradition members. This allowed questions about personality, well-being, and faith development to be addressed.

Deconversion and Personality

Regarding the relation of Big Five personality dimensions to deconversion, overall, the trait *openness to experience* was a key identifier of a deconvert. However, there were also some cross-cultural differences between Germany and the United States. For example, in Germany, deconverts scored significantly higher in *openness to experience* than in-tradition members, but this effect was magnified in the United States such that deconverts had even higher scores on this trait. Also, in Germany, in contrast to the United States, all Big Five subscales showed significant differences between in-tradition members and deconverts, but all of the relationships except for *openness to experience* were inverse for the German participants. This pattern of results suggests that deconversion in Germany may be associated with some kind of (mild) crisis.

Psychological Well-Being

The importance of this characteristic in German deconverts is apparent upon a close look at the results of Ryff's *psychological well-being* assessment (Ryff & Singer, 1996, 1998). There are cross-cultural differences. In the United States, deconverts increase in *autonomy* and *personal growth* and show no significant differences in the rest of the subscales. However, the opposite is the case in Germany. In Germany, *environmental mastery, positive relations with others, purpose in life,* and *self-acceptance* are all significantly lower for deconverts compared with in-tradition members. These results suggest that United States deconverts tend to associate personal gains with their transformation, whereas German deconverts are more likely to report losses and perhaps a (mild) crisis.

Deconversion and Spirituality

Overall, deconverts had an extraordinary increase in self-identification as "spiritual." In the United States, the proportion who self-identified as "more spiritual than religious" was almost twice as high as for in-tradition members. In both U.S. and German cultures, deconversion was associated with a reluctance to identify with "religion" and instead to identify with "spirituality." This is consistent with the notion that deconversion is an instance of the larger category of spiritual transformation of a meaning system, which leads to considerably higher self-identification with "spirituality" than represented in the general population (Streib, 2008).

Deconversion and Religious Schemas and Styles

Deconversion is also associated with changes in religious styles—whether we assess these using the faith development interview or the Religious Schema Scale (RSS; Streib, Hood, & Klein, 2010). Results of faith development interviews showed that between 70% (Germany) and 80% (United States) of in-tradition members scored at Stage 3,[5] while the majority of deconverts in both countries scored at Stage 4 (Germany: 53.1%; United States: 49%) and less at Stage 3 (Germany: 42.9%; United States: 45.1%). Cognitive developmentally, this suggests that people may be more likely to operate at an individuative–reflective religious style when they deconvert. However, when religious style was assessed by the RSS, deconverts in both countries showed a significant decrease in scores on the RSS Truth of Texts and Teachings subscale. This suggests that deconverts are reluctant to insist on the truth of their own religion and that they are open to the possible truths of other religions and to interreligious dialog. In sum, deconverts have a greater amount of individuative–reflective faith style than synthetic–conventional style. They also have higher scores on the RSS Fairness, Tolerance and Rational Choice, and Interreligious Dialog subscales and lower scores on the Truth of Text and Teachings subscale. This combination of interview and questionnaire data suggests that higher levels of faith development, religious styles, and religious schemata are characteristic features of the deconversion process.

A Typology of Deconversion Narratives

The analysis of narrative and faith development interviews triangulated[6] with the questionnaire data led to a typology of four kinds of deconversion narratives: pursuit of autonomy, debarred from paradise, finding a new frame of reference, lifelong quests—late revisions.

The *pursuit of autonomy* is a long-term gradual process of stepping out of the previously taken-for-granted religious environment that one was born into or raised in. It involves a search for individuation and the development of a critical new perspective, which most often leads to a secular or heretical exit. This type is generally associated with the individuative–reflective religious faith style (i.e., Stage 4) and with low scores on the RSS Truth of Text and Teachings subscale. There is a cross-cultural difference for deconverts of this type such that scores on psychological well-being tend to be high for those in the United States but moderate or low for those in Germany. In general, deconverts of this type are persons who either were born into a faith tradition or were brought by their parents into a community at a very young age, which they leave during adolescence or early adulthood, orient toward an open and sometimes insecure future, and insist on their personal independence and on making their own choices.

The *debarred from paradise* deconversion is characterized by an emotionally deep attachment to a religious tradition that is supposed to heal early trauma and protect from personal loss, a rather deep affiliation that does not normally develop before adolescence or early adulthood. Thus, many of these cases are midlife converts with all the expectation and affection of a once-for-a-lifetime decision. The deconversion process for such persons tends to include disappointment as a result of unfulfilled high expectations, abandonment of hopes, and withdrawal of affection by religious leaders, along with a wish to give testimony of these traumatic experiences. Deconverts of this type may become secular, adopt a private religious practice, or continue to search, but they seldom affiliate with another religious organization. In Streib et al.'s (2009) study, they almost always leave organized religions. This is the most intense and dramatic type of deconversion, and, with rare exceptions, is associated with very low scores on the religious fundamentalism scale combined with high scores in faith development, including individuative–reflective and conjunctive styles (i.e., Stages 4 and 5). This combination suggests strong rejection of the former belief system coupled with a more open, questioning, or exploring mind.

The third type of deconversion, *finding a new frame of reference,* is characterized by searching for and finding more intensity, guidance, and structure in religious life. This category includes many people who left the mainline churches in which they grew up. These deconversions are, therefore, mostly oppositional exits; they tend to include a change to a higher tension group. They involve a conversion experience that can be seen as reconversion. In the German cases in particular, an intense personal experience (e.g., feeling a deep personal relation with Jesus) often leads to a new kind of personal religiosity. Before the (re-)conversion, there may have been a hesitancy or moratorium toward religiousness that would involve orientations such as atheism, interest in other world religions, depression, or perhaps taking drugs. Thus, the new religiosity is manifest as a complete change of life and morality.

The *lifelong quests—late revisions* type of deconversion is characterized by leaving a religious environment once or many times because it fails to meet one's needs and expectations (i.e., a nonoptimal person–religion fit). In this type, the seeker's religious quest typically emerged in adolescence or young adulthood and led to conversion, typically into a religious group with higher tension. This type of deconvert has parallels with the second type who is "debarred from paradise." However, deconverts of this fourth type are not "debarred." They instead typically leave on their own in order to look for something better. There may even be a subsequent series of deconversions, usually as an integrating exit but occasionally as a private or heretical exit. Some cases of this type can be characterized as being on a lifelong journey in pursuit of an individual project, such as coming to terms with a traumatized childhood, finding the "fitting" mystical or spiritual environment, or finding inner peace.

Summary Picture

This pattern of findings suggests that deconversion may be a step toward freedom, autonomy, and personal growth. The pursuit of autonomy and the lifelong quests— late revision types illustrate this. However, if we reconsider the predefined criteria for deconversion, a new picture may be emerging that is based upon combined data from psychometric scales and analyses of biographical material. Briefly, the deconversion criteria reflect some kind of crisis; they focus on the individual's negations inherent in the deconversion process. However, if we add to this the positive accent apparent in the quantitative data in the Bielefeld study, we can begin to see how a crisis can be a turning point to something better.

This can be demonstrated by examining the deconversion criteria one by one. Loss of religious experience corresponds to *openness to experience* (a Big Five element), which emerged from the quantitative analyses as a key characteristic of deconversion. The crisis of deconversion could lead to a new cognitive structure, with a new interpretation of heaven and earth and a preference for a different religious schema. Moral criticism could function as the advent of the sense of *autonomy,* which also is shown in the quantitative data to be a key characteristic of deconversion. Emotional suffering can be exchanged for a sense of *personal growth,* especially for the deconvert who feels "debarred from paradise." In some cases the biographical interviews show evidence of posttraumatic growth. Finally, leaving a religious community constitutes a loss, and deconverts may struggle to compensate for this loss. Indeed, positive relations with others after deconversion seem to decline for those in Germany and remain about the same for those in the United States. However, there are also gains in a sense of connectedness for the lucky ones who immediately find a new community and a new identity with a self-identification as "spiritual person," also a key characteristic of deconversion.

Exceptions notwithstanding, the portrait of deconversion that emerges from these analyses, which combine questionnaire "quantitative" data and biographical interview "qualitative" data, is that of an active deconvert resembling the active convert described by Richardson (1978, 1985a, 1985b, 1995), a landmark turning point in conversion research. This active deconvert seems to have higher openness to experience, a preference for individuative–reflective faith style, lower religious fundamentalism, and a higher preference for a spiritual self-identification. Also, one's culture makes a difference. For example, the prior analyses reveal a higher sense of autonomy and personal growth in U.S. deconverts compared with those in Germany, whereas in Germany a deconvert, although experiencing some gains, also feels losses such as a lower sense of environmental mastery, lower positive relations with others, lower purpose in life, and lower self-acceptance. Such findings reveal examples of a nonoptimal fit between the needs and wants of the individual and his or her current religion. Moreover, almost all of the prior analyses can be understood in the framework of religion as meaning system, which, in turn, supports the structural parallel between conversion and deconversion.

ADDITIONAL RECENT STUDIES

Let us round out this presentation of recent research in order to provide the most up-to-date and useful summary possible. In addition to the two half-decade-long research programs summarized previously, there have been a number of individual studies of conversion. Space constraints allow only brief mention of each; yet an overview of this material opens many questions and can lead to rich resources for future research. Importantly and to the field's benefit, the religious and national contexts in which conversion has been studied have expanded well beyond its relatively narrow origins in Protestant Christianity in the United States (Paloutzian, in press). As a start, data from the International Social Survey Program and the World Values Survey have been used to examine broad trends in religious conversion in 40 countries (Barro, Hwang, & McCleary, 2010). Fortunately, there are psychological studies on certain samples.

For example, several studies examined conversion to Islam. Lakhdar, Vinsonneau, Apter, and Mullet (2007) explored the motivations for adults and adolescents in France converting to Islam. Köse and Loewenthal (2000) focused on similar factors among British converts to Islam, and Maslim and Bjorck (2009) did the same for women in the United States. An examination of these three studies offers a picture of cross-cultural similarities and differences that may be explored in future research.

Studies of conversion to variations of Judaism have likewise appeared. Bockian, Glenwick, and Bernstein (2005) examined the degree to which conversion to Judaism followed a specific stages of change model, with some evidence for it. This model could be extrapolated and explored in the context of conversion to other standard religions and/or NRMs. Beit-Hallahmi and Nevo (1987) focused on Israeli Jews who converted to Orthodox Judaism; interestingly, they used the term "born again" (a term typically used among Evangelical Christians) as a way of capturing the change in identity of these persons. More recently, attachment insecurity has been examined in relation to conversion among Orthodox Jews (Pirutinsky, 2009).

Jindra (2008) studied converts to JW and Unitarian Universalists in order to document their stages of religious development; her study is a good example of the combined use of so-called qualitative and quantitative methods. Hunsberger and Altemeyer (2006) did pioneering research on why people who were raised in a religion might depart altogether and adopt atheism. Less extreme but related "departure" phenomena have recently been explored by Diener, Tay, and Myers (2011), who ask plainly, "If religion makes people happy, why are so many dropping out?" (p. 1278). In contrast, to understand the draw that a religion can have, Hogg, Adelman, and Blagg (2010) propose an uncertainty-identity theory to account for the attraction that a religion can have to pull certain people in and to especially transform them into zealots. A different perspective on how a religion might have a hold on someone is found in Granqvist and Kirkpatrick's (2004) comprehensive meta-analysis of their research program on attachment and conversion. In the Netherlands, the transmission of religion as a function of authoritative parenting style has been supported by a panel study (Vermeer, Janssen, & Scheepers, 2012). Also internationally, in Slovakia and in the Czech Republic, Halama and Lacna (2011) reexamined the question of conversion and personality change in the wake of the review by Paloutzian et al. (1999), and found that converts' retrospective self-perceptions of change and similar perceptions by close others suggest a retrospective bias. Finally, Brandt and

Fournier (2009) published the results of an international conference on conversion with presentations from Russia, France, Switzerland, and the United States.

PUTTING IT ALL TOGETHER

We arrive at a set of conclusions that can be summarized as follows. First, we know now that in order to understand spiritual transformation of any sort, focusing only on the individual is incomplete. Second, we know that transformations happen both to and from a religion; thus, understanding the processes involved in deconversion is of equal importance to understanding those that mediate conversion. Third, people involved in spiritual transformations do not necessarily prefer the terms of traditional religions to express their developments and changes. A strong preference for the semantics of "spirituality" can be observed in conversion and deconversion, even though the research summarized here has clearly used the conceptual framework of religious conversion and deconversion. Fourth, efforts to learn about conversion and deconversion at a descriptive or categorical level and those that aim for explanations at the level of psychological processes, such as a social-cognitive meaning system approach, are complementary and each needs the other. This again argues for a multilevel interdisciplinary approach. Fifth, psychological research and theory about conversion, as a fundamental category of human change generally, have come a long way since its spotty trajectory began slightly over 100 years ago. Now seems like the most interesting questions may be on the edges of the discipline, where psychological ideas and methods bump up against and are combined with the ideas and methods of companion disciplines. We predict that the most intellectually rich research in the future will occur at those boundaries.

NOTES

1. As made clear in Oman (Chapter 2, this volume), there are myriad definitions of "religion," which implies an equal or greater list of would-be definitions of "religious conversion," some of which invoke the God concept and some of which do not. In this chapter, in order to connect our psychological ideas about the processes involved in conversion and deconversion with the larger category called "spiritual transformation," it is most useful to adopt the characterization of conversion used in Paloutzian (2005): "Conversion is a more distinct process by which a person goes from believing, adhering to, and/or practicing one set of religious teachings or spiritual values to believing, adhering to, and/or practicing a different set. The transformative process in conversion may take variable amounts of time, ranging from a few moments to several years, but it is the distinctiveness of the change that is its central identifying element. . . . In contrast to someone arriving at a point of belief through the process of socialization and other developmental mechanisms, the convert can identify a time before which the religion was not accepted and after which it was accepted" (p. 331).
2. The concept of spiritual transformation, which at its core is a change in a person's meaning system, goes far beyond the particular type called religious conversion. However, space limitations preclude us from discussing all variations. As illustrations, however, transformation may be manifest as change or growth in the context of life stress, grief and berevement, various identity or worldview life confrontations, and so forth, and may appear in both religious and nonreligious forms. Our analyses of the psychological processes that mediate religious conversions can be extrapolated to apply to other forms of transformation, and future research can

document where the changes in these variations of spiritual transformations map well onto each other and where they do not.

3. The concept of deconversion may not apply to every instance of adopting a new belief system, however. There is, for example, the phenomenon of what Streib (1999, 2000) calls the "accumulative heretic." Examples for a simultaneous accumulative heretic are the woman who is both a practicing Methodist minister and a practicing Johrei minister or the person who claims to simultaneously be Buddhist and Roman Catholic. Although rare, it is apparently possible to affiliate with and adopt a different religion while not deconverting from the previous one. There is little research on this kind of blending of meaning systems.

4. Conversely, even disaffiliation from a community does not necessarily mean termination of membership. For example, it can instead consist of total withdrawal from participation without formal termination of membership. This is especially important in the context of a religion that does not include formal membership as one of its key elements, such as Islam.

5. The faith development interview technique (Fowler, Streib, & Keller, 2004) yields a "stage" score from 1–6; the RSS allows the identification of "styles" that correspond to Fowler's stages. The results reported here are based on the evaluation of the faith development interviews.

6. "Triangulation" is the term for procedures of relating quantitative and qualitative data about one and the same research object (see, e.g., Denzin, 1989; Tashakkori & Teddlie, 2003), In the construction of case studies in the Bielefeld Deconversion Study, triangulation involved relating the scores of the single case to the mean differences between deconverts and in-tradition members on various scales in the quantitative data set.

REFERENCES

Altemeyer, B., & Hunsberger, B. (1997). *Amazing conversions: Why some turn to faith and others abandon religion.* New York: Prometheus.

Barbour, J. D. (1994). *Versions of deconversion: Autobiography and the loss of faith.* Charlottesville: University Press of Virginia.

Barker, E. (1989). *New religious movements: A practical introduction.* London: Her Majesty's Stationery Office.

Barro, R., Hwang, J., & McCleary, R. (2010). Religious conversion in 40 countries. *Journal for the Scientific Study of Religion, 49*(1), 15–36.

Beckford, J. A., & Levasseur, M. (1986). New religious movements in western Europe. In J. A. Beckford (Ed.), *New religious movements and rapid social change* (pp. 29–54). London: Sage.

BeitHallahmi, B., & Nevo, B. (1987). 'Born again' Jews in Israel: The dynamics of an identity change." *International Journal of Psychology, 22*, 75–81.

Bockian, M. J., Glenwick, D. S., & Bernstein, D. P. (2005). The applicability of the stages of change model to Jewish conversion. *The International Journal for the Psychology of Religion, 15*, 35–50.

Brandt, P.-Y., & Fournier, C.-A. (Eds.). (2009). *La conversion religieuse: Analyses psychologiques, anthropologiques et sociologiques* [The religious conversion: Psychological, anthropological, and sociological analyses]. Geneva: Labor et Fides.

Burris, C. T., & Petrican, R. (2011). Hearts strangely warmed (and cooled): Emotional experience in religious and atheistic individuals. *The International Journal for the Psychology of Religion, 21*(3), 183–197.

Burris, C. T., & Redden, E. K. (2012). No other gods before Mario?: Game preferences among atheistic and religious individuals. *The International Journal for the Psychology of Religion, 22*(4), 243–251.

Buxant, C., Saroglou, V., Casalfiore, S., & Christians, L.-L. (2007). Cognitive and emotional characteristics of New Religious Movements members: New questions and data on the mental health issue. *Mental Health, Religion & Culture, 10*, 219–238.

Cable, D. M., & Edwards, J. R. (2004). Complementary and supplementary fit: A theoretical and empirical integration. *Journal of Applied Psychology, 89*, 822–834.

Caplan, R. D. (1983). Person-environment fit: Past, present, and future. In C. L. Cooper (Ed.), *Stress research: Issues for the eighties* (pp. 35–78). Chichester, UK: Wiley.

Cowan, D. E. (in press). Beyond brainwashing: Conversion to new religious movements. In. L. Rambo & C. Farhadian (Eds.), *Oxford handbook of religious conversion.* Oxford, UK: Oxford University Press.

Denzin, N. K. (1989). *The research act: A theoretical introduction to sociological methods.* New York: McGraw-Hill.

Diener, E., Tay, L., & Myers, D. G. (2011). The religion paradox: If religion makes people happy, why are so many dropping out? *Journal of Personality and Social Psychology, 101*, 1278–1290.

Edwards, J. R., & Rothbard, N. P. (1999). Work and family stress and well-being: An examination of person-environment fit in the work and family domains. *Organizational Behavior and Human Decision Process, 77*, 85–129.

Emmons, R. A., & Paloutzian, R. F. (2003). *The research act: A theoretical introduction to sociological methods.* New York: McGraw-Hill.

Fowler, J. W., Streib, H., & Keller, B. (2004). *Manual for faith development research* (3rd ed.) Atlanta: Center for Research in Faith and Moral Development, Emory University.

Glock, C. Y. (1962). On the study of religious commitment. In J. Matthes (Ed.), *Kirche und Gesellschaft. Einführung in die Religionssoziologie* (pp. 98–110). Reinbek, Germany: Rowohlt, 1969.

Goldstein, E. B. (2011). *Cognitive psychology: Connecting mind, research and everyday experience* (3rd ed.). Belmont, CA: Wadsworth.

Gooren, H. (2006). The religious market model and conversion: Towards a new approach. *Exchange, 35*, 39–60.

Granqvist, P., & Kirkpatrick, L. A. (2004). Religious conversion and perceived childhood attachment: A meta-analysis. *The International Journal for the Psychology of Religion, 14*, 223–250.

Halama, P., & Lacna, M. (2011). Personality change following religious conversion: Perceptions of converts and their close acquaintances. *Mental Health, Religion & Culture, 14*, 757–768.

Hogg, M. A., Adelman, J. R., & Blagg, R. D. (2010). Religion in the face of uncertainty: An uncertainty-identity theory account of religiousness. *Personality and Social Psychology Review, 14*(1), 72–83.

Hunsberger, B. (2000). Swimming against the current: Exceptional cases of apostates and converts. In L. J. Francis & Y. J. Katz (Eds.), *Joining and leaving religion: Research perspectives* (pp. 233–248). Leominster, UK: Gracewing.

Hunsberger, B., & Altemeyer, B. (2006). *Atheists: A groundbreaking study of America's nonbelievers.* Amherst, MA: Prometheus Books.

Hunt, S. J. (2003). *Alternative religions: A sociological introduction.* Hamshire, UK: Ashgate.

Jacobs, J. L. (1989). *Divine disenchantment. Deconverting from new religions.* Bloomington: Indiana University Press.

Jamieson, A. (2002). *A churchless faith. Faith journeys beyond the churches.* London: Society for Promoting Christian Knowledge.

Jindra, I. W. (2008). Religious stage development among converts to different religious groups. *The International Journal for the Psychology of Religion, 18*, 195–215.

Kirkpatrick, L. A. (1992). Two dimensions of attachment to God and their relation to affect, religiosity, and personality constructs. *Journal for the Scientific Study of Religion, 41*, 637–651.

Kirkpatrick, L. A. (2005). *Attachment, evolution, and the psychology of religion.* New York: Guilford Press.

Klosinski, G. (1983). *Psychologische und psychodynamische Aspekte religiöser Konversion zu neureligiösen Bewegungen am Beispiel der Neo-Sannyas-Bewegung: Eine Vergleichsstudie bei der Neo-Sannyas-Bewegung und der Gesellschaft für Transzendentale Meditation mittels biographischer Interviews.* Tübingen, Germany: Nichtveröffentlichte Habilitationsschrift, Eberhardt-Karls-Universität Tübingen.

Klosinski, G. (1985). *Warum Bhagwan?: Auf der Suche nach Heimat, Geborgenheit und Liebe.* München, Germany: Kösel.

Klosinski, G. (1996). *Psychokulte: Was Sekten für Jugendliche so attraktiv macht.* München, Germany: Beck.

Köse, A., & Loewenthal, K. M. (2000). Conversion motifs among British converts to Islam. *The International Journal for the Psychology of Religion, 10,* 101–110.

Kosmin, B. A., & Keysar, A. (Eds.). (2007). *Secularism & secularity: Contemporary international perspectives.* Hartford, CT: ISSSC.

Kuner, W. (1983). *Soziogenese der Mitgliedschaft in drei Neuen Religiösen Bewegungen.* Frankfurt, Germany: Lang.

Lakhdar, M., Vinsonneau, G., Apter, M. J., & Mullet, E. (2007). Conversion to Islam among French adolescents and adults: A systematic inventory of motives. *The International Journal for the Psychology of Religion, 17*(1), 1–15.

Leibniz Institute for the Social Sciences. (2010). *International Social Survey Programme 2008: Religion III* Retrieved from *http://zacat.gesis.org/webview/index.jsp?object=http://zacat.gesis.org/obj/study/ZA4950.*

Levine, S. V. (1984). *Radical departures: Desperate detours to growing up.* New York: Harcourt Brace Jovanovich.

Lewin, K. (1936). *Principles of topological psychology.* New York: McGraw-Hill.

Maslim, A. A., & Bjorck, J. P. (2009). Reasons for conversion to Islam among women in the United States. *Psychology of Religion and Spirituality, 1,* 97–111.

Murken, S. (2009). *Neue religiöse Bewegungen aus religionspsychologischer Sicht.* Marburg, Germany: Diagonal.

Murken, S., & Namini, S. (2007). Childhood familial experiences as antecedents of adult membership in new religious movements: A literature review. *Nova Religio, 10,* 17–37.

Namini, S. (2009). *Selbst gewählte Mitgliedschaft in neuen religiösen Bewegungen—eine Frage der Passung?: Empirische Befunde und kritische Überlegungen.* Marburg, Germany: Tectum.

Namini, S., Appel, C., Jürgensen, R., & Murken, S. (2010). How is well-being related to membership in new religious movements?: An application of person–environment fit theory. *Applied Psychology: An International Review, 59,* 181–201.

Namini, S., & Murken, S. (2008). Familial antecedents and the choice of a new religious movement. Which person in which religious group? *Nova Religio, 11,* 83–103.

National Opinion Research Center. (2009). *General Social Survey 1972–2008.* Chicago: Roper Center for Public Opinion Research, University of Connecticut.

Paloutzian, R. F. (2005). Religious conversion and spiritual transformation: A meaning-system analysis. In R. F. Paloutzian & C. L. Park (Eds.), *Handbook of the psychology of religion and spirituality* (pp. 331–347). New York: Guilford Press.

Paloutzian, R. F. (in press). Psychology of religious conversion and spiritual transformation. In L. Rambo & C. Farhadian (Eds.), *Oxford handbook of religious conversion.* Oxford, UK: Oxford University Press.

Paloutzian, R. F., & Lowe, D. A. (2012). Spiritual transformation and engagement in workplace culture. In P. C. Hill & B. Dik (Eds.), *Psychology of religion and workplace spirituality* (pp. 179–199). Charlotte, NC: Information Age.

Paloutzian, R. F., & Park, C. L. (2005). Integrative themes in the current science of the psychology of religion. In R. F. Paloutzian & C. L. Park (Eds.), *Handbook of the psychology of religion and spirituality* (pp. 3–20). New York: Guilford Press.

Paloutzian, R. F., Richardson, J. T., & Rambo, L. R. (1999). Religious conversion and personality change. *Journal of Personality, 67,* 1047–1079.

Pargament, K. I., Johnson, S. M., Echemendia, R. J., & Silverman, W. H. (1985). The limits of fit: Examining the implications of person–environment congruence within different religious settings. *Journal of Community Psychology, 13,* 20–30.

Pargament, K. I., Tyler, F. B., & Steele, R. E. (1979). Is fit it?: The relationship between church/synagogue member fit and the psychosocial competence of the member. *Journal of Community Psychology, 7,* 243–252.

Park, C. L. (2005). Religion and meaning. In R. F. Paloutzian & C. L. Park (Eds.), *Handbook of the psychology of religion and spirituality* (pp. 295–314). New York: Guilford Press.

Park, C. L. (2010). Making sense of the meaning literature: An integrative review of meaning making and its effects on adjustment to stressful life events. *Psychological Bulletin, 136,* 257–301.

Pirutinsky, S. (2009). Conversion and attachment insecurity among Orthodox Jews. *The International Journal for the Psychology of Religion, 19,* 200–206.

Poling, T. H., & Kenney, J. F. (1986). *The Hare Krishna character type: A study of the sensate personality.* Lewiston, NY: Mellen.

Rambo, L. R. (1993). *Understanding religious conversion.* New Haven, CT: Yale University Press.

Rambo, L., & Farhadian, C. (Eds.). (in press). *Oxford handbook of religious conversion.* Oxford, UK: Oxford University Press.

Richardson, J. T. (Ed.). (1978). *Conversion careers: In and out of the new religions.* Beverly Hills, CA: Sage.

Richardson, J. T. (1985a). Psychological and psychiatric studies of new religions. In L. B. Brown (Ed.), *Advances in the psychology of religion* (pp. 209–223). Oxford, UK: Pergamon Press.

Richardson, J. T. (1985b). The active vs. passive convert: Paradigm conflict in conversion/recruitment research. *Journal for the Scientific Study of Religion, 24,* 163–179.

Richardson, J. T. (1995). Clinical and personality assessment of participants in new religions. *The International Journal for the Psychology of Religion, 5,* 145–170.

Richardson, J. T., & Stewart, M. (1977). Conversion process models and the Jesus movement. *American Behavioral Scientist, 20,* 819–838.

Richardson, J. T., Stewart, M. W., & Simmonds, R. B. (1979). *Organized miracles: A study of a contemporary, youth, communal, fundamentalist organization.* New Brunswick, NJ: Transaction.

Richter, P., & Francis, L. J. (1998). *Gone but not forgotten: Church leaving and returning.* London: Darton, Longman, Todd.

Ryff, C. D., & Singer, B. H. (1996). Psychological well-being: Meaning, measurement, and implications for psychotherapy research. *Psychotherapy and Psychosomatics, 65,* 14–23.

Ryff, C. D., & Singer, B. H. (1998). The role of purpose in life and growth in positive human health. In P. T. P. Wong & P. S. Fry (Eds.), *The human quest for meaning: Handbook of psychological research and clinical applications* (pp. 213–235). Mahwah, NJ: Erlbaum.

Silberman, I. (2005). Religion as a meaning-system: Implications for the new millennium. *Journal of Social Issues, 61,* 641–664.

Skonovd, L. N. (1981). *Apostasy: The process of defection from religious totalism.* Unpublished doctoral dissertation, University of California, Davis.

Streib, H. (1999). Sub-project on 'Biographies in Christian Fundamentalist Milieus and Organizations.' In Deutscher Bundestag, Referat Öffentlichkeitsarbeit (Ed.), *Final Report of the Enquête Commission on 'So-called Sects and Psychogroups. New religious and ideological communities and psychogroups in the Federal Republic of Germany* (pp. 402–414). Bonn, Germany: Deutscher Bundestag. Retrieved from *http://repositories.ub.uni-bielefeld.de/biprints/volltexte/2009/3220/pdf/Streib1999Enquete_Final_Report.pdf.*

Streib, H. (2000). *Biographies in Christian fundamentalist milieus and organizations: Report to the Enquete Commission of the 13th German Parliament on "So-called sects and psychogroups"* (CIRRuS Research Reports, No. 1). Bielefeld, Germany: University of Bielefeld. Retrieved from *http://repositories.ub.uni-bielefeld.de/biprints/volltexte/2009/2134.*

Streib, H. (2008). More spiritual than religious: Changes in the religious field require new approaches. In H. Streib, A. Dinter, & K. Söderblom (Eds.), *Lived religion—Conceptual, empirical and practical-theological approaches* (pp. 53–67). Leiden, The Netherlands: Brill.

Streib, H. (in press). Deconversion. In. L. Rambo & C. Farhadian (Eds.), *Oxford handbook of religious conversion.* Oxford, UK: Oxford University Press.

Streib, H., Hood, R. W., Keller, B., Csöff, R.-M., & Silver, C. (2009). *Deconversion: Qualitative and quantitative results from cross-cultural research in Germany and the United States of America* (Research in Contemporary Religion 5). Göttingen, Germany: Vandenhoeck & Ruprecht.

Streib, H., Hood, R. W., & Klein, C. (2010). The Religious Schema Scale: Construction and initial validation of a quantitative measure for religious styles. *The International Journal for the Psychology of Religion, 20*(1), 151–172.

Streib, H., & Keller, B. (2004). The variety of deconversion experiences: Contours of a concept in respect to empirical research. *Archive for the Psychology of Religion, 26*(1), 181–200.

Streib, H., & Klein, C. (2013). Atheists, agnostics, and apostates. In K. I. Pargament, J. J. Exline & J. W. Jones (Eds), *APA handbook of psychology, religion and spirituality (Vol 1): Context, theory, and research.* Washington, DC: American Psychological Association.

Tashakkori, A., & Teddlie, C. (2003). The past and future of mixed methods research: From data triangulation to mixed model designs. In A. Tashakkori & C. Teddlie (Eds.), *Handbook on mixed methods in the behavioral and social sciences* (pp. 671–701). Thousand Oaks, CA: Sage.

van der Lans, J., & Derks, F. (1986). Premies versus sannyasins. *Update: A Quarterly Journal on New Religious Movements, 10,* 19–27.

Van Harrison, R. (1978). Person-environment fit and job stress. In C. L. Cooper & R. Payne (Eds.), *Stress at work* (pp. 175–205). Chichester, UK: Wiley.

Vermeer, P., Janssen, J., & Scheepers, P. (2012). Authoritative parenting and the transmission of religion in the Netherlands: A panel study. *The International Journal for the Psychology of Religion, 22,* 42–59.

Wright, S. A. (1987). *Leaving cults: The dynamics of defection.* Washington, DC: Society for the Scientific Study of Religion.

Wright, S. A. (in press). Disengagement and apostasy in new religious movements. In. L. Rambo & C. Farhadian (Eds.), *Oxford handbook of religious conversion.* Oxford, UK: Oxford University Press.

Yang, F., & Abel, A. (in press). Sociology of conversion. In L. Rambo & C. Farhadian (Eds.), *Oxford handbook of religious conversion.* Oxford, UK: Oxford University Press.

21

Mystical, Spiritual, and Religious Experiences

Ralph W. Hood, Jr., and Zhuo Chen

There probably is no area in the psychology of religion that addresses the call for a new *multilevel interdisciplinary paradigm* (MIP) first proposed by Emmons and Paloutzian (2003) and referenced throughout the first edition of this *Handbook* (see Paloutzian & Park, Chapter 1, this volume) than in research on the psychology of religious and spiritual experience. The one undisputed classic in the field of psychology of religion is *The Varieties of Religious Experience* (James, 1902/1985), a text that Miller and Thorensen (1999, p. 7) suggest might be titled *The Varieties of Spiritual Experience* if published today. Importantly, its subtitle is *A Study in Human Nature*. This implies that psychologists ought to be interested in mystical, spiritual, and religious experiences insofar as they are part of human nature. Precisely what that nature is requires interdisciplinary considerations integral to the MIP. Reviews have been published on the literature on mysticism (Hood, 2008) and on religious and spiritual experience (Hood, 2009). Therefore, this chapter is selective in focusing our evaluation on the literature on mystical, religious, and spiritual experiences and on research that either anticipated the MIP or is illustrative of it in practice.

THE RELIGION–SPIRITUALITY DEBATE

A dominant theme within the psychology of religion is whether religion and spirituality can or ought to be differentiated (Hood, 2003; see Oman, Chapter 2, this volume). There is consensus that scientific definitions of both spirituality and religion must include a sense of, a belief in, or a search for what is implicitly or explicitly taken to be transcendent (Hill et al., 2000). However, a continuing debate is whether the transcendent is vertical, implying a sense of or search for the divine, essentially a code expression for a supernatural being or beings, or whether it is horizontal and need not imply any claim to the supernatural (Hood, 2008; Keysar & Kosmin, 2008). While most religious persons define themselves as spiritual, there is an emerging group of people in America, India, and Europe who define themselves as spiritual but not religious (Hood, 2003; Keysar & Kosmin, 2008; Streib, Hood, Keller, Csöff, & Silver, 2008, Chapter 2). Some psychologists have argued that the diversity of belief and experiences of these people make spirituality a "fuzzy" concept (Zinnbauer, et al., 1999). We explore this claim shortly, but for now it is worth noting that when religion is defined so broadly as to exclude the necessity for a sense of the divine, the term loses its analytic power, as both psychologists (Beit-Hallahmi, 2003) and sociologists (Stark, 2001) have argued.

If religion is defined to necessitate the supernatural, the psychological consequence is that those who identify themselves as both religious and spiritual will have to define experiences within the linguistic forms of a particular faith tradition. One experiences the realities of his or her faith, labeled or constructed accordingly. Even mystical experiences will be faith specific (Katz, 1977). One can empirically identify the ways in which religious beliefs contribute to both the identification and the interpretation of experiences that are deemed religious (Taves, 2009).

Experiences of Being Both Religious and Spiritual

The majority of people in the West identify themselves as *both* religious and spiritual (Hood, 2003; Streib et al., 2008). For these persons, being spiritual identifies a largely experiential component of their faith (Zinnbauer et al., 1999). Field studies have been particularly useful in providing thick descriptions of normative constraints and social support that legitimate particular religious experiences. For instance, Apolito (1998) has used direct testimony to explore how complex social and psychological processes interacted to result in the acceptance of the apparition of the Virgin Mary that appeared to children at Oliveto Citra, Spain. Likewise, Carroll (1986) has provided an empirically based interpretation of psychodynamics involved in Marian apparitions based largely upon classical oedipal theory applied to historical data. Quasi-experimental techniques support Carroll's thesis among Protestant males unfamiliar with the Catholic tradition (Hood, Morris, & Watson, 1991). Thus, congruent with the MIP, a consistent theme emerges from questionnaire, interview, field, and experimental studies revealing how spiritual experiences become meaningful when sanctioned with religious systems.

Adding another dimension to the MIP, Hufford (1982, p. xv) has proposed the useful term "phenomenography" paralleling ethnography to demand that social scientists pay careful attention to the richness of experience to see precisely what aspects of experience their theories can and cannot explain. His own empirical work on the Old Hag phenomenon common in Scandinavian culture and Wiebe's (1997) phenomenological studies of historical and contemporary visions of Christ indicate that no single methodological approach is sufficient to explain such experiences. Lundmark (2010) has shown how narrative psychology can be used to illuminate Christic visions in his single-case study of a woman who had Christic visions during radiotherapy. These studies reveal that the MIP is useful in focusing on the way in which varying theoretical explanations and different methodological approaches can be used to complement one another to provide a more complete understanding of what can variously be seen as apparitions, visions, or hallucinations, each with different ontological consequences (Hood, 2012; Park, Chapter 18, this volume).

Consistent with the new paradigm are a series of studies using both field and quasi-experimental methods to understand the conditions under which sectarian forms of experiencing religion occur. A term gaining acceptance that unites all these approaches is "reflexive ethnography" (Davies, 1999), which tends to focus on lived religion of everyday experience. For instance, Poloma's (1989) participant observation study of the Assemblies of God documents the shift in Pentecostalism from an emphasis on glossolalia to other gifts of the spirit (such as holy laughter) that serve to revitalize religious feelings suppressed by institutionalization. Poloma and Hood (2008) conducted a participant observation study of a Pentecostal cult in Atlanta whose self-proclaimed visionary prophet led to a schism, the dynamics of which were documented over a 4-year period. Likewise, Hood and his colleagues have used a wide variety of methodologies to explore the contemporary serpent handlers of Appalachia (see Hood & Belzen, Chapter 4, this volume). Historical, narrative, ethnographic, and quasi-experimental studies supplement one another to provide an enhanced understanding of less normatively accepted religious practices.

Experiences of Being Spiritual but Not Religious

The persistent finding that about 25 to 30% of individuals in Western cultures identify themselves as spiritual but not religious has been usefully explored in depth by qualitative methods (Hood, 2003). Studies by both psychologists (Day, 1994) and sociologists (Roof, 1993) indicate that this minority is likely to be vociferously antireligious. For some, spirituality is a fierce rejection of religion but not necessarily indicative of atheism or nonbelief (Day, 1994; Pasquale, 2007). Furthermore, the effort to empirically identify characteristics of these spiritual but not religious persons is hampered by the overlap between measures of spirituality and of purely secular views of mental health (Koenig, 2008).

The discovery by psychologists of spirituality opposed to religion is really a rediscovery. Vernon (1968) noted over a quarter-century ago that those who answered "none" to questions of religious preference nevertheless had experiences that those with religious preference would identify as religious. Reviews of the empirical literature indicate that those who identify themselves as spiritual but not religious have high rates of spiritual experiences, including mystical (Hood, 2003; Zinnbauer et al., 1999). However, they are reluctant to describe these experiences in explicitly religious language. Thus, the social construction of experience for "spiritual but not religious" persons is not framed within the language of a specific faith tradition nor is it constrained by a more or less explicit set of beliefs.

Another issue in the "spiritual but not religious" worldview is the possibility noted previously that transcendence can be horizontal as opposed to vertical. For instance, the sociologist Mathew's (2003) typology of the sacred explicitly excludes restricting the sacred to the supernatural. Likewise, the psychologist Elkins (2001) has proposed a humanistic model of the sacred focusing on its more secular (horizontal) psychological expressions. The psychologist Emmons (1999) allows for both a vertical and a horizontal axis of spiritual striving. Finally, McClenon (1994), working from an experience-centered approach that is quite akin to reflexive ethnography, reminds us that what he terms "wondrous events" can occur in cultures and traditions that have no term for the supernatural (such as Tibetan Buddhism). Thus, while wondrous events may stimulate religious explanations, they need not do so. Hufford (1982) and Spickard (1993) make the same claim for paranormal experiences. Let us briefly explore three controversial but persistently identified areas of paranormal experiences that are more often identified as spiritual but not religious experiences: the report of alien abductions, experiences triggered by specific chemicals, and near-death experiences.

ANOMALOUS EXPERIENCES VIEWED AS RELIGIOUS OR SPIRITUAL

Psychologists of religion have avoided the study of paranormal experiences, tending to classify them as neither religious nor spiritual. Earlier investigators labeled paranormal experiences as anomalous, attributing them to simply erroneous ("magical") thinking (Zusne & Jones, 1989). However, more recent work keeps open the possibility of non-reductionist views of even the more extreme among anomalous experiences. The edited work published by the American Psychological Association (APA) identifies anomalous experiences as those that, although common, are nevertheless believed to deviate from ordinary experience or from the usually accepted definitions of reality (Cardeña, Lynn, & Krippner, 2000, p. 4). Examples include hallucinations, near-death, past-life, mystical, and paranormal experiences. Porpora (2006) has applauded this work as indicative of the rejection of a methodological atheism in favor of an agnosticism that leaves ontological questions open and frames the way in which research is conducted. Hood (2012) has defended this in light of the MIP as methodological agnosticism, which is of particular usefulness in the study of what Taves (2009) refers to as not necessarily religious, but special experiences.

The religious and spiritual relevance of these experiences is that they often gain added meaning when they are embedded in sectarian discourse, religious or scientific, which both explains and legitimates them in opposition to more culturally accepted knowledge systems (Cardeña et al., 2000; McClenon, 1994). As Truzzi (1971) noted, anomalous experiences contradict institutionalized knowledge, both scientific and religious. Persons who endorse the ontological claims implied in anomalous experiences often are self-identified as spiritual but not religious (Hood & Chen, 2013). It is likely that the specific presence or absence of the term "God" in survey items showing an association between reports of paranormal and various religious experiences produces different results, in that persons committed to a mainstream religion are most likely to respond to religious language and to make distinctions among various experiences based on religious knowledge (Hood, Hill, & Spilka, 2009, pp. 347–350).

UFOs and Alien Abductions

Jung (1958/1964, p. 315) referred to the sighting of UFOs as "visionary" and cautioned that psychology alone could not exhaust their explanation. Investigators such as Strassman (2001) have suggested that certain chemicals that affect receptors for serotonin may elicit awareness of dimensions of reality in which reports of alien abduction become possible as actual events. However, as with many religious experiences, psychologists are more likely to be comfortable with explanations that are within the mainstream of realities psychologists accept. For instance, Skal (1998) has noted that the term "flying saucer" came into vogue only after newspaper headlines in June 1947, when a Boise, Idaho pilot named Kenneth Arnold described nine strange objects flying near Mt. Rainer as moving "like a saucer if you skipped it across the water" (p. 204). Newspaper headlines reported "flying saucers," and only then did individuals begin to report sightings of them. Thus, cultural expectations based upon journalistic headlines that actually were in error might have played a role in shaping what have become common sightings of UFOs. Instead of moving "like saucers," they became identified as flying saucers. This social construction became the template for perception of flying saucers within American culture.

Alien abduction experiences are beginning to gain significant subcultural support, granting believers a form of social legitimization that refutes the claim that these experiences are delusional (Appelle, Lynn, & Newman, 2000; Skal, 1998; Williams & Fallconer, 1994). They are often associated with paranormal claims, which, as we shall see, several research methodologies reveal are differentially linked to spiritual and specific religiously identified experiences. Walach, Kohlls, von Stillfried, Hinterberger, and Schmidt (2009) have argued that research on spirituality is the legacy of previous research on parapsychology. Some define paranormal events in a fashion to deny them religious importance (Spickard, 1993). However, as Kelsey (1972, p. 21) notes, "The Bible is a mine of information on ESP or psi phenomena. Nearly every book of the Bible shows the belief that human beings have contact with more than just the physical world and that there are ways of influencing the world and people besides the physical senses." Poloma (1989) created a Charismatic Experience Index—praying in tongues, receiving answers to prayers, prophecy, being slain in the spirit, and receiving personal confirmation of scriptural truths—that she defines as paranormal powers commonly experienced by many Pentecostals. Based upon her participant observation study of the Assemblies of God tradition, Poloma's (1989) data are consistent with Kelsey's claim. For many Pentecostals, the experience of the paranormal is normal. However, even among religious groups that accept paranormal claims, like apparitions, they must conform to a particular meaning system to be deemed religious (Taves, 2009).

Apparently even less plausible than the existence of UFOs are claims to alien abduction experiences (AAEs), which include being captured and taken aboard a UFO and being subjected to physical, mental, and spiritual examinations before being returned to Earth (Bullard, 1987). Other more extreme claims may include the taking of tissue samples, body implants, and even the birth of alien-hybrid babies (Jacobs, 1992). As fantastic as these claims appear, explanations must include the fact that the reports of such experiences are no more frequent among the mentally ill than among normal individuals (Jacobson & Bruno, 1994). Thus, pathological processes cannot explain the experience, however curious, nor is the experience necessarily delusional (Williams & Fallconer, 1994).

Among the most plausible and least controversial explanations for these reports are fantasy proneness or boundary deficits using culturally available scenarios derived from film and other media sources, confusing subjective experiences with objectively real events, suggestibility and hypnosis (especially when such reports are "recovered" in therapeutic encounters using hypnosis), sleep disorders, and various possible psychoses in at least a minority of cases (Appelle et al., 2000). However, the fact that often AAEs contain theophanies (the receipt of explicit religious or spiritual messages) links AAEs to other experiences more common within mainstream faith traditions. Lest skeptics too quickly consider these experiences to be simply bizarre manifestations exhaustively explainable by the social sciences, they might be cautioned that those who have studied these experiences in depth have found that the dismissal of their veridicality, as with many claims to more mainstream religious experiences, is more difficult than one might at first think (Skal, 1998; Strassman, 2001).

The fact that psychology of religion is confronted with the power of alien abduction claims in such groups as Heaven's Gate is but a recent example. Despite the popular press descriptions of a suicide cult, the cult's own framing of their acts was in religious terms. For instance, the cult's official website *(www.wave.net/upg/gate)* referred to the "willful leaving of the body." It noted the sacrifices of the Jews at Masada in 73AD and claimed the willingness of the cult members to avoid "true suicide" by not refusing to prepare to enter the Kingdom of Heaven by means of the Hale-Bopp Comet. The linking of images of inhabitants of the Kingdom of Heaven with aliens associated with UFOs aided Heaven's Gate claims to religious legitimacy. Bader (2003) has empirically documented that the demographics of members of Heaven's Gate parallels those for members attracted to new religious movements that mix the therapeutic and the spiritual. Finally, Zeller (2003) notes how the cult opposed both the supernatural claims of religion as well as purely natural scientific epistemologies in favor of its own "scientific religion." It has been more than a half-century since Jung said of UFOs (much less AAEs), "If military authorities have felt compelled to set up bureaus for collecting and evaluating UFO reports, then psychology, too, has not only the right but also the duty to do what it can to shed light on this dark problem" (1958/1964, p. 416). The new MIP is ideally suited to explore these experiences and has been anticipated by research in this area.

Psychedelics or Entheogens

A controversial area of empirical research is that of entheogens, a term preferred by those who argue drugs can facilitate spiritual and religious experiences (Forte, 1997). It has long been recognized that many religions have employed various naturally occurring and synthetic substances in their religious rituals. However, until the discovery of psychedelic drugs, it was rather arrogantly assumed that concern with the facilitation of experience by drugs was the domain of anthropology and sister disciplines concerned with less "advanced" religions. In a new and controversial discipline by the cumbersome name *archaeopsychopharmacology*, ancient texts and artifacts are combined with contemporary cross-cultural studies of the use of naturally occurring psychedelic substances to speculate on the origins of religions (see Hood et al., 2009, pp. 323–324). While the speculative theories of achaeopsychopharmacology cannot be easily empirically confirmed, they have raised a crucial question for the social scientific study of religion: Can entheogens facilitate or produce religious or spiritual experiences?

Very few studies have been conducted using religious variables or directly assessing the religious importance of entheogens. The lack of research attention is curious since it has long been noted that there is an obvious similarity between various religious experiences and chemically facilitated experiences. Before the turn of this century, this similarity was used by Leuba (1896) as evidence to argue that religious experience in advanced traditions was to be invalidated as it was similar to experiences in less advanced traditions and to those induced by drugs. The essence of Leuba's argument was advanced by

Zaehner (1957), who argued that if a mystical experience is drug induced, it cannot be genuinely religious, as are those that occur spontaneously or by means of disciplined religious practice. These largely conceptually based debates do little to advance a scientific understanding of the possible religious importance of psychedelic drugs. Since James's (1902/1985, pp. 20–21) discussion of "medical materialism," it is obvious that one can no more invalidate an experience because its physiology is known than one can invalidate physiology because its biochemistry has been identified. As Weil (1986) has emphasized, the similarity of psychedelic substances found within plants, animals, and the human brain suggests that any simple distinction between natural and artificially induced brain states is arbitrary. Empirical studies indicate that more dogmatic persons will reject as "genuine" religious experiences triggered by drugs (Hood, 1980). However, outside of mainstream religious, one of the most commonly cited triggers of mystical experience is entheogens (Hood, 2002).

For well-established physiological reasons, entheogens can be expected to produce reliable alterations in visual and imagery phenomena, which to informed and stable participants are interesting objects of conscious exploration (Shanon, 2002; Strassman, 2001). Meaningful images that occur under these substances with eyes closed are not typically attributed to the object expected to exist in the world as physical reality. Likewise, with eyes open, alterations in perception of objects are noted as perceptual alterations of real existing objects, not changes in the actual physical objects or the perception of objects in fact not real. However, the ability to interpret perceptions in terms of a meaningful frame can transform one's perception of the world. With an appropriate religious set and setting, psychedelic drugs can facilitate religious experiences insofar as one under the influence of these drugs may for the first time see the world in terms appropriate to a particular system of meaning.

The frequent report of religious imagery is likely to be a function of set and setting, long known to be major determinants of the content of imagery elicited by entheogens (Barr, Langs, Holt, Goldberger, & Klein, 1972; Hood, 2008). It would be naïve to claim that religious experiences are drug-specific effects. Rather, the power of entheogens to facilitate religious experience is the extent to which states of consciousness, altered by chemical substances, are seen as relevant in religious or spiritual terms. Without a sense of what might be called ontological wonder, drug-elicited experiences become rather trivial.

Grof (1980) has argued that the therapeutic use of entheogens often provides a set and setting that encourage the reporting of religious and spiritual experiences, many interpreted in terms of Jungian theory. Jungian theory is particularly favorable to describing religious imagery and has been ignored by measurement-oriented psychologists. Leary (1964) demonstrated that religious imagery in LSD psychotherapy sessions is common and increases if the set and setting are made even more explicitly religious—for instance, by having religious symbols in the therapeutic room. Furthermore, Leary, Metzner, and Alpert (1964) were the first to utilize a religious classic (*Tibetan Book of the Dead*) as a cartography for psychedelic-induced mental states. More recently, the Dali Lama has favored Thurman's translation of this classic text, *The Tibetan Book of Liberation through Understanding in the Between* (1994). The term "in the between" focuses upon states of consciousness and not death. Once it is recognized that reincarnation is taken for granted in Tibetan culture, the ontological relevance of states of consciousness, drug-facilitated or not, meshes nicely with the MIP for the psychology of religion.

Stevens (1987) has documented the history of the original psychedelic movement, and its failure to have psychedelic drugs accepted for sacramental use within a religious frame. Two exceptions are the Native American Church in the United States (LaBarre, 1969) and the Church of Santo Daime in Brazil (Shanon, 2002). Both of these churches have a history of the sacramental use of entheogens, demonstrating that drugs can be incorporated into religious frameworks and used to facilitate experiences whose meaning is accepted as religious (LaBarre, 1969).

The cultural bias against entheogens has not only affected serious study of these chemicals, but also made it difficult to have a balanced view of the range of their effects (Forte, 1997). Furthermore, several reviewers have argued that typical double-blind studies are particularly inappropriate to investigate entheogens, especially since those who are in the control conditions are likely to be immediately aware of this fact (Yensen, 1990). Many researchers have supported the view that ingestion of psychedelic substances on the part of researchers is a valid and, some claim, necessary method of study. Experimental studies in the Good Friday tradition, using psilocybin to facilitate mystical experiences, have used both guides who have and guides who have not ingested psilocybin (see Hood & Belzen, Chapter 4, this volume).

Some psychologists have returned to the tradition common in early laboratory studies of serving as their own subjects (Danzinger, 1990). Exemplary is the provocative study of ayahuasca (a psychoactive brew consumed throughout the upper Amazon region) by the cognitive psychologist Benny Shanon (2002). He carefully compared his own numerous experiences with this brew with those reported by others to develop a nonreductive assessment of the phenomenology of the ayahuasca experience. Interestingly, ayahuasca-elicited experience has been both incorporated into a religious tradition (the Church of Santo Daime, a mixture of indigenous traditions with Catholicism) and cultivated by those who refuse to interpret the experience in specific religious language. The examples cited previously suggest that truly multilevel interdisciplinary approaches extend the range of material that psychologists must consider as they explore the conditions under which individuals experience their religion or spirituality.

Near-Death Experience

Probably no research illustrates the complexity of the MIP better than that on near-death experiences (NDEs). The history of NDE research illuminates serious conceptual issues that determine how one is to evaluate various research strategies and findings of what is a common human experience (Gallup & Procter, 1982). The process of dying is a complex one, and many of the phenomena experienced when one is near death have been attributed to a toxic psychosis generated by a dying brain (Rodin, 1980; Sabon, 1982). However, as Blose (1981) noted, the hypothesis of survival of bodily death is empirically testable, but only asymmetrically. "Allowing its truth, should it be true, but not its falsity, should it be false, to be learnt" (p. 59).

If death is a final declaration that nothing more can be done to resuscitate a person, then being near death is partly defined by approaching that limit. Several investigators have noted the immense value of having medical (physiological) indicators of organ states effectively monitored to indicate that death is near (Rodin, 1980; Sabon, 1982). Others have relied upon human anticipation of death, noting that NDEs can occur in the face of intense fear (Noyes & Kletti, 1976). However, it is not necessarily the case that being near death produces the thematic structure associated with NDEs (Greyson, 1990).

Moody (1975) identified 15 criteria common among NDEs. Unfortunately, these criteria mix phenomena occurring during the NDE (such as a panoramic life review) with consequences or effects of the NDE (such as a reduced fear of death). In a sequel, Moody (1977) added an additional four criteria of NDE. The NDE thematic narrative includes going through a dark tunnel, typically toward a luminous white light; a panoramic review of one's life; the return to one's body if the NDE included an out-of-body experience; and images of spiritual beings identified by the nearly deceased's own faith tradition (Moody, 1975, 1977). Moody's criteria have been used as "checklists" to measure the extent to which a reported NDE fits the phenomenological template identified by Moody. Importantly, no experience reported by any of Moody's subjects fulfilled all 19 criteria.

A more rigorous approach has been proposed by Greyson (1983) and has resulted in a scale to measure NDEs. Greyson's scale includes items familiar to NDE researchers and partisans following Moody's checklist approach, but in ways that are less doctrinaire. Greyson's NDE scale takes the phenomenology of NDEs seriously. It identifies cognitive, affective, paranormal, and transcendental dimensions that are conceptually open to empirical refinement (e.g., via factor analysis).

Zaleski (1987) has explored NDEs in the context of a religious imagination that has been fostered throughout Western culture. Her comparative study of medieval and contemporary NDEs is expanded to include "other-worldly journeys" that reveal variations in social construction over time. To cite but one example, the gradual minimization, if not elimination, of experienced journeys to an underworld or hell (common in medieval traditions) are all but excluded from NDEs in reports from contemporary Western persons. The rare citings of a negative phenomenology or of negative aftereffects (Greyson, 1990) are largely lost in narratives of NDEs, which are uniformly positive and with positive transformative effects. Segal's (2004) massive study of experiences of "life after death" argues that NDEs are a function of a religious imagination created in the interplay between a socially constructed image of an afterlife that becomes incorporated into individual experience that it helps shape, if not create.

To the extent that NDEs are solely intrapsychic phenomena, the claim to have transcended death is a delusion. Thus, the partisan claims of having empirical verification for life after death, for particular religious worldviews, and for other dimensions of reality are simply ignored; evolutionary and physiological psychology becomes the explanatory limits psychologists can use to explore NDEs. Ontological issues are ignored, or at best certain ontological possibilities such as consciousness surviving bodily death are simply denied without any genuine scientific warrant (Blose, 1981; Greyson, 2010).

However, in two volumes of APA Division 36's recently founded journal *Psychology of Religion and Spirituality*, a special section edited by Miller (2010) has called for a postmaterialistic psychology. In the initial volume, Greyson (2010) reviewed the ontological implications of NDEs. Rather than dismiss the possibility of actual survival of bodily death, he acknowledged the possibility that consciousness can exist independent of matter. In terms of the new MIP, this acknowledgment allows the engagement of NDE research with a claim common in many religious traditions, that persons have died and seen another dimension or world in which the ontological commitments of a scientific worldview are found to be merely limits to be transcended (Zaleski, 1987; Segal, 2004). Rather than discredit the ontological claims, experimentally oriented researches have placed phrases in surgical rooms likely to involve patients near death, hoping to see if the recovered patient "looking down" can report not only the standard visions of medical care persons but the secret and unexpected word or phrase as well (Fenwick & Fenwick, 1995). While some accept the methodological soundness of such research designs, others see this as curious pandering to a suspect ontology that places NDE research in the domain of pseudoscience (Alcock, 1981). Whatever one's private commitments are, it is clear that research on NDE will influence discussion on the MIP, as its research trajectories illustrated the new paradigm even before the MIP phrase was coined.

NUMINOUS AND MYSTICAL EXPERIENCES

Spickard (1993) has identified different approaches, constructionist and labeling models, to the study of religious experiences, which he notes sociologists (and we add psychologists) have not comprehended well. Both of these approaches emphasize the role of language and social process in identifying experiences of religion, spirituality, or mysticism within the confines of language, tradition, and culture. Spickard also identifies a Jamesian "overbelief" model (1993, p. 111), where the distinction between experience and interpretation is maintained but the focus is on experience and not the language in which it is expressed ("overbelief"). While there may be no religious experience that is not as deemed so (Taves, 2009), some experiences (mysticism is the best contender) are not reducible to sensory or linguistic terms and transcend culture (Hick, 1989; Hood, 2008). As we focus upon mystical, religious, and spiritual experiences, it behooves us to define such experiences as including recognition of and response to what might be inherently sacred realities. Two candidates are the numinous and the mystical.

Numinous Experience

Many scholars have contrasted numinous experience to mystical experience. A numinous experience is an awareness of a holy other beyond nature with which one is felt to be in communion. More typically, this experience is identified with the classic work of Otto (1917/1958), whose phenomenological analysis illuminates the human response to the transcendent. Elkins's (2001, p. 208) humanistic model also includes a response to the numinous, meaning there is a divine component to his model. Thus, introducing the numinous back into empirical psychology is congruent with the nonreductive nature of MIP.

Otto's translator noted that the emphasis on a response to the divine that characterizes numinous consciousness is the sensing of a "beyond" that gradually is realized "within" whether obscurely or clearly (Harvey, 1958, p. xv). This goes far to correct Schleiermacher's emphasis on a primary feeling of dependence that Proudfoot (1985) criticized as demanding a cognitive framework to experience. Obviously, religious traditions assert the reality of this object, refusing to accept reductive interpretations of the numinous. As social scientists, we can study the response to the numinous, noting that from the believer's perspective it is a response to a transcendent object experienced as real.

The numinous consciousness is both compelled to seek out and explore this transcendent object (*mysterium fascinans*) and to be repelled in the face of the majesty and awfulness of this object in whose presence one's creatureness is accentuated (*mysterium tremendum*). Mystical experiences of unity (variously expressed) can be numinous as well, eliciting the mysterium fascinans when the object is experienced in impersonal terms and the mysterium tremendum when the object is experienced in personal terms. Hick (1989, pp. 252–296) articulated this duality as the *personae* and *impersonae* of the real. Hood (2002) emphasized that William James accepted both impersonal (the absolute) and personal (God) interpretations as compatible with the facts of mystical experience. Empirical studies use measurements that tend to either emphasize experiences of a sense of presence favoring numinous experiences or a sense of unity favoring mystical experiences.

The empirical study of numinous experiences has largely focused on responses to surveys and questionnaires. Pafford (1973) had university and grammar school students read selections from an autobiography that described a numinous experience and then write about an experience of their own similar to the one read. He found that the most common word to describe such experiences was "awesome." He further suggested that children have an innate capacity to experience the numinous that is gradually dissipated as they matriculate in a more secular world. Glock and Stark (1965) found, in a survey sample of almost 3,000, that 72% answered "yes" to the question, "Have you ever as an adult had the feeling that you were somehow in the presence of God?" Using this question in a longitudinal study of Scandinavian youth (dropping "as an adult"), Tamminen (1991) showed a gradual decline of affirmative responses across grade level. Thus, in more secular cultures, one could argue that an innate ability to experience the numinous is possible but is likely to decline without cultural support. Hoffman's (1992) collection of spiritual and inspirational experiences in childhood also supports this claim (see Richert & Granqvist, Chapter 8, this volume). Also in support of this claim are numerous survey studies conducted in Australia, the United States, and Great Britain asking respondents if they have ever had an experience that easily in our classification is a numinous one.

Reviews of these studies show consistent high rates of endorsement of numinous experiences despite variations in the wording of questions (see Hood et al., 2009, pp. 343–347). Hence, the empirical point is simply that both children and adults report numinous experiences whether they identify themselves as religious and spiritual or simply spiritual but not religious. The former fact is inferred from religious identification and the latter from the fact noted previously that even people whose religious self-identification is "none" report such experiences. The fact that such experiences are so readily reported means that psychologists who take the MIP seriously should construct measures compatible with the already considerable phenomenological and survey work illuminating the nature of such experiences. Keitner and Haidt (2003) created a measure of awe that may, but need not, reference a vertical dimension. The cautionary note here is that measures that do no include explicit indices of the transcendent miss connecting to the large literatures in phenomenology and religious studies (Sundararajan, 2002). They also are less likely to empirically identify additional unique variance explained by measures that are explicitly linked to a sense of divine.

Mystical Experiences

James claimed that the "root and centre" of personal religion is in mystical states of consciousness (1902/1985, p. 301). Mysticism is a common phenomenon across the faith traditions within which it is given a specified religious interpretation, and also common outside faith traditions among those who accept it as a less specific but still meaningful spiritual experience (Hood, 2006). We focus on research linked to three different measures of mysticism, each with different linkages to the MIP.

Hood (1975) based his Mysticism Scale (M Scale) on the phenomenological work of Stace (1960). Reviews of this work are readily available (e.g., Hood, 2006). The M Scale conceptually demands three factors: introvertive (experiencing an undifferentiated unity through dissolution of selfhood), exrtrovertive (achieve a unified vision of multiplicity of the world), and interpretative factors. Hood argues that the common unity factors are possibly inherent in the nature of the experience (and perhaps reality) while the interpretation factor (whether noetic, religious, etc.) can vary.

Quantitative studies using the M Scale have empirically supported the common core thesis and the three-factor structure using subjects from various religious and cultural backgrounds. The three-factor structure has been replicated in American Protestants, Iranian Muslims, Israeli Jews, and Tibetan Buddhists (see Chen, Yang, Hood, & Watson, 2011b). A recent study reveals that both Christians and self-identified nonreligious people in a secular society—China—reported mystical experience that can form into the phenomenological three factors (Chen, Zhang, Hood, & Watson, 2011c). Christians scored higher on the interpretative factor than religious nones, while both groups scored comparably on the introvertive and extrovertive experience factors. These results echo our discussion that mystical experiences can and do appear in those without a systemized religious framework, and the phenomenology of experience remains comparable regardless of interpretive constructions imposed on by religious or spiritual beliefs.

While most extant studies involving the M Scale and Stace's conceptual work are quantitative in design, Chen, Qi, Hood, and Ralph (2011a) recently adapted the scale to semistructured interview questions and applied this interview protocol to 139 Chinese Pure Land and Chan monks and nuns. They coded the monks' and nuns' responses into themes and compared these themes with both Buddhist doctrines and the mystical facets and factors laid out in the M Scale. Furthermore, they coded their experience into binary data, which were subject to confirmatory factor analysis. Their results strongly supported the three-factor structure, while at the same time these themes fit neatly into the Mahayana Buddhist doctrinal systems which the participants frame their experience in. Research associated with testing the M Scale and the phenomenological structure of mystical experience in various cultural contexts using mixed methods are highly exemplary of the MIP. On the one hand, researchers of mysticism could test the generalizability of their theory in a different population; on the other hand, different methods could complement each other by exposing limitations of any single approach.

Francis and Louden (2000) constructed a measure of mysticism based upon Happold's (1963) conceptualization of mysticism. Happold adopted James's four well-known criteria of mysticism—its ineffable and noetic quality that is both passive and transient (James, 1902/1985, pp. 302–303). Happold then added three additional criteria:

consciousness of the oneness of everything, a sense of timelessness and true ego, and the conviction that the phenomenal ego is not the real I (1963, p. 48). Francis and Louden (2000) developed three items to access each of Happold's seven criteria to form a unidimensional Mysticism Orientation Scale (MOS). While at this stage of development the MOS is a single-factor scale, many of the items are similar to M Scale items, and given the history of research with the M Scale, the MOS may also yield separate factors identifying at least some clustering to Happold's seven criteria.

Much of the research with both the M Scale and the MOS has been correlational. Francis focused on the relationship of mysticism and personality, using measures related to Eysenck's well-known three-factor model and to an alternative model based on Jung's notion of psychological types (see Hood et al., 2009, pp. 368–370). Correlational research with both the M Scale and the MOS consistently failed to relate mysticism to measures of psychopathology but relate it to healthy indices of personality and adjustment (Hood & Byrom, 2010). Mysticism also consistently differently correlates with the report of a variety of paranormal experiences, depending on the spiritual/religious options discussed previously (Hood, 2008). The MIP should help overcome the lack of conversation among the various disciplines that study mysticism, which, in McGinn's (1991, p. 343) words, have been "equally at fault in this unrealized conversation."

Thalbourne and his colleagues have long championed the concept of *transliminality* as a concept to describe the ability, likely genetically based, to attend to inner psychological states and processes (e.g., Thalbourne & Delin, 1999). Lange and Thalbourne (2007) have also developed a single-factor measure of mysticism that is more restricted than the transliminal domain, but is similar to James's treatment of mysticism in *The Varieties of Religious Experience* as it allows for interval scaling of intensity of experiences as an empirical mystical ladder of sorts. However, at the empirical level, transliminality is a measure that links such phenomena as schizotypy, magical ideation, creativity, and paranormal experiences as interrelated because of the single factor of transliminality. Their scale heavily correlates with Hood's measure.

Much of Thalbourne's work has been published in journals of parapsychology often ignored by mainstream psychologists. However, it is significant for two reasons. First, it counters Hood's view that the phenomenology of mysticism developed by Stace is, in fact, likely an experience central to both religion (when interpreted within a specific faith tradition) and spirituality (when interpreted outside the claims of any dogma). Hood's claim that mysticism is a universal experience with ontological ramifications is countered by the research agenda of Thalbourne suggesting that mysticism is part of a purely natural psychology rooted in the tendency to be sensitive to internally generated states of consciousness, including a tendency to pathology. Thalbourne has noted that it remains to be seen if transliminality is "nothing more than schizotypy" (Thalbourne, Bartemucci, Delin, Fox, & Nofi, 1997, p. 327). Given that schizotypy is related to Hood's M Scale, the relationship between schizotypy and mysticism remains a crucial conceptual as well as empirical issue in need of clarification from the MIP (Hood & Byrom, 2010). Still, Thalbourne is willing to consider that not only does the eruption into consciousness produced by high transliminality appear to some to be miraculous or to derive from the Godhead, but in fact it may (Thalbourne & Delin, 1999, p. 59).

Second, it has not been stated as forcefully as it should, but it is clear that, however mystical experiences are assessed, they are associated with reports of paranormal phenomena. The frequency of reports of paranormal phenomena in survey studies parallels that of the reports of mystical and numinous experiences, and predictors of the reports of mystical experience are the same as those associated with reports of paranormal phenomena (Fox, 1992; Yamane, 2000). For instance, using survey data from Canadians, Orenstein (2003) found that, controlling for unconventional religious beliefs, church attendance is strongly associated with lower paranormal belief. Using the same data set, McKinnon (2002) suggested that belief in the paranormal and church attendance are correlated only for those who do not attend church regularly. Thus, mainstream religion tends to counter belief in the paranormal while those outside mainstream religions, including sectarian forms of religion that remain "spiritual but not religious," likely account for the substantial proportion of believers. Targ, Schiltz, and Irwin (2002) concluded that paranormal experiences are reported by over half the population in all countries where samples have been taken.

CONCLUSION

If we have reviewed experiences often ignored in mainstream psychology, it documents that the field of the psychology of religion has a tumultuous history. This history can serve to remind us of the state of the field when it began. As Coon (1992) noted, North American psychologists fought hard to differentiate the methodologically sound, scientific psychology from the popular supported psychology and thought the latter validated spiritual (as in spiritualism) and psychic phenomena. Perhaps the study of mystical, spiritual, and religious experiences within the spirit of the MIP will begin not only to allow the psychology of religion and spirituality to integrate with mainstream psychology, but to encourage mainstream psychology to adopt the spirit of MIP and to open itself to issues and methods long of concern to those who are interested in religious issues.

REFERENCES

Alcock, J. E. (1981). Pseudo-science and the soul. *Essence: Issues in the Study of Ageing, Dying, and Death, 5*, 65–76.

Apolito, P. (1998). *Apparitions of the Madona at Oliveto Citra: Local visions and cosmic drama* (W. Christian, Jr., Trans.). University Park: University of Pennsylvania Press.

Appelle, S., Lynn, S. J., & Newman, L. (2000). Alien abduction experiences. In E. Cardeña, S. J. Lynn, & S. Krippner (Eds.), *Varieties of anomalous experience* (pp. 253–282). Washington, DC: American Psychological Association.

Bader, C. D. (2003). Supernatural support groups: Who are the UFO abductees and ritual-abuse survivors? *Journal for the Scientific Study of Religion, 42*, 669–678.

Barr, H. L., Langs, R. J., Holt, R. R., Goldberger, L., & Klein, C. S. (1972). *LSD, personality and experience*. New York: Wiley.

Beit-Hallahmi, B. (2003). In debt to William James: The varieties as inspiration and blueprint. In H.M. P. Roelfsma, J. M. T. Corveleyn, & J. W. van Saane (Eds), *One hundred years of psychology and religion: Issues and trends in a century long quest* (pp. 83–104). Amsterdam, The Netherlands: VU University Press.

Blose, B. L. (1981). Materialism and disembodied minds. *Philosophy and Phenomenological Research, 42*, 59–74.

Bullard, T. E. (1987). *UFO abductions: The measure of a mystery*. Mount Rainer, MD: Fund for UFO Research.

Cardeña, E., Lynn, S. J., & Krippner, S. (2000). *Varieties of anomalous experience*. Washington, DC: American Psychological Association.

Carroll, M. P. (1986). *The cult of the Virgin Mary: Psychological origins*. Princeton, NJ: Princeton University press.

Chen, Z., Qi, W., Hood, R. W., Jr., & Watson, P. J. (2011a). Common core thesis and qualitative and quantitative study of Chinese Buddhist monks and nuns. *Journal for the Scientific Study of Religion, 50*, 654–670.

Chen, Z., Yang, L., Hood, R. W., Jr., & Watson, P. J. (2011b). Mystical experience in Tibetan Buddhists: Common core thesis revisited. *Journal for the Scientific Study of Religion, 50*(2), 328–338.

Chen, Z., Zhang, Y., Hood, R. W., Jr., & Watson, P. (2011c). *Mysticism in Chinese Christians and non-Christians: Measurement invariance of the Mysticism Scale and implications for the mean differences*. Manuscript submitted for publication.

Coon, D. J. (1992). Testing the limits of sense and science: American experimental psychologists combat spiritualism, 1880–1920. *American Psychologist, 47*, 143–151.

Dalai Lama, H. H., the. (1994). Foreword. In R. A. F. Thurman (Trans.), *The Tibetan Book of the Dead* (pp. xxi–xxii). New York: New York: Doubleday Dell.

Danzinger, K. (1990). *Constructing the subject: Historical origins of psychological research*. Cambridge, UK: Cambridge University Press.

Davies, C. A. (1999). *Reflexive ethnography: A guide to researching ourselves*. New York: Routledge.

Day, J. M. (1994). Moral development, belief and unbelief: Young adults account of religion in the process of moral growth. In J. Corveleyn & D. Hustebaut (Eds.), *Belief and unbelief: Psychological perspectives* (pp. 155–173). Amsterdam, The Netherlands: Rodopi.

Elkins, D. N. (2001). Beyond religions: Toward a humanist spirituality. In K. J. Schneider, J. T. Bugental, & J. F. Pierson (Eds.), *The handbook of humanistic psychology: Leading edges in theory, research, and practice* (pp. 201–212). Thousand Oaks, CA: Sage.

Emmons, R. A. (1999). *The psychology of ultimate concerns: Motivation and spirituality in personality*. New York: Guilford Press.

Emmons, R. A., & Paloutzian, R. F. (2003). The psychology of religion. *Annual Review of Psychology, 54*, 377–402.

Fenwick, P., & Fenwick, E. (1995). *The truth in the light*. London: Headline.

Forte, R. (1997). *Entheogens and the future of religion*. San Francisco: Council on Spiritual Practices.

Fox, J. W. (1992). The structure, stability, and social antecedents of reported paranormal experiences. *Sociological Analysis, 53*, 417–431.

Francis, L. J., & Louden, S. H. (2000). The Francis-Louden Mystical Orientation Scale (MOS): A study among Roman Catholic priests. *Research in the Social Scientific Study of Religion, 11*, 99–116.

Gallup, G., & Procter, W. (1982). *Adventures in immortality: A look beyond the threshold of death*. New York: McGraw-Hill.

Glock, C. Y., & Stark, R. (1965). *Religion and society in tension*. Chicago: Rand McNally.

Greyson, B. (1983). The near-death experience scale: Construction, reliability, and validity. *Journal of Nervous and Mental Disease, 171*, 369–375.

Greyson, B. (1990). Near-death encounters with and without near-death experiences: Comparative NDE profiles. *Journal of Near-Death Studies, 8*, 151–161.

Greyson, B. (2010). Implications of near-death experiences for a post materialist psychology. *Psychology of Religion and Spirituality, 2*, 37–45.

Grof, S. (1980). *LSD psychotherapy*. Pomona, CA: Hunter House.

Happold, F. C. (1963). *Mysticism: A study and an anthology*. Harmondsworth, UK: Penguin.

Harvey, J. W. (1958). Translator's preface (pp. ix–xix). In R. Otto, *The idea of the holy*. London: Oxford University Press.

Hick, J. (1989). *An interpretation of religion*. New Haven, CT: Yale University Press.

Hill, P. C., Pargament, K. I., Hood, R. W., Jr., McCullough, M. E., Sawyers, J. P., Larson, D. B., et al. (2000). Conceptualizing religiosity and spirituality: Points of commonality, points of departure. *Journal for the Theory of Social behavior, 30*, 50–77.

Hoffman, E. (1992). *Visions of innocence: Spiritual and inspirational experiences of childhood*. Boston: Shambhala.

Hood, R. W., Jr. (1975). The construction and preliminary validation of a measure of reported mystical experience. *Journal for the Scientific Study of Religion, 14*(1), 29–41.

Hood, R. W., Jr. (1980). Social legitimacy, dogmatism, and the evaluation of intense experiences. *Review of Religious Research, 21*, 184–194.

Hood, R. W., Jr. (2002). The mystical self: Lost and found. *The International Journal for the Psychology of Religion, 12*, 1–14.

Hood, R. W., Jr. (2003). The relationship between religion and spirituality. In A. L. Griel & D. G. Bromley (Eds.), *Defining religion: Investigating the boundaries between the sacred and the secular* (pp. 241–264). Oxford, UK: Elsevier Science.

Hood, R. W., Jr. (2006). The common core thesis in the study of mysticism. In P. McNamar (Ed.), *Where God and science meet* (Vol. 3, pp. 119–138). Westport, CT: Praeger.

Hood, R. W., Jr. (2008). Mysticism and the paranormal. In J. Harold Ellens (Ed.), *Miracles: God, science, and psychology in the paranormal* (Vol 3, pp. 16–37). Westport, CT: Praeger.

Hood, R. W., Jr. (2009). Spirituality and religion. In P. B. Clarke & P. Beyer (Eds.), *The world's religions* (pp. 675–689). New York: Routledge.

Hood, R. W., Jr. (2012). Methodological agnosticism for thr social sciences: Lessons from Sorokin's and James's allusions to psychoanalysis, mysticism, and Godly love. In M. T. Lee & A. Yong (Eds.), *The science and theology of Godly love* (pp. 121–140). DeKalb, IL: NIU Press.

Hood, R. W., Jr., & Byrom, G. (2010). Mysticism, madness, and mental health. In J. H. Ellens (Ed.), *The healing power of spirituality: Vol. 3. Psychodynamics* (pp. 171–191). Westport, CT: Praeger.

Hood, R. W., Jr., & Chen, Z. (2013). The social scientific study of Christian mysticism. In J. A. Lamm (Ed.), *The Wiley–Blackwell companion to Christian mysticism* (pp. 577–591). Chichester, UK: Wiley.

Hood, R. W., Jr., Hill, P. C., & Spilka, B. (2009). *The psychology of religion: An empirical approach* (4th ed.). New York: Guilford Press.

Hood, R. W., Jr., Morris, R. J., & Watson, P. J. (1991). Male commitment to the cult of the Virgin Mary and the passion of Christ as a function of early maternal bonding. *The International Journal for the Psychology of Religion, 1*, 221–231.

Hufford, D. (1982). *The terror that comes in the night. An experience centered study of supernatural assault traditions*. Philadelphia: University of Pennsylvania Press.

Jacobs, D. M. (1992). *Secret life: First-hand accounts of UFO abductions*. New York: Simon & Schuster.

Jacobson, E., & Bruno, J. (1994). Narrative variants and major psychiatric illnesses in close encounter and abduction narrators. In A. Pritchard, D. E. Prichard, J. E. Mack, P. Kasey, & C. Yapp (Eds.), *Alien discussions: Proceedings of the Abduction Study Conference, MIT* (pp. 304–309). Cambridge, MA: North Cambridge Press.

James (1985). *The varieties of religious experience*. Cambridge, MA: Harvard University Press. (Original work published 1902)

Jung, C. G. (1964). Flying saucers: A modern myth of things seen in the skies. *The collected works of C. G. Jung* (2nd ed., Vol. 10, pp. 309–433). Princeton, NJ: Princeton University Press. (Original work published 1958)

Katz, S. (1977). *Mysticism and philosophical analysis*. New York: Oxford University Press.

Keitner, D., & Haidt, J. (2003). Approaching awe, a moral, spiritual, and aesthetic emotion. *Cognition and Emotion, 17*, 297–314.

Kelsey, M. T. (1972). *Encounter with God*. Minneapolis, MN: Bethany Fellowship.

Keysar, A., & Kosmin, B. A. (2008). *International Survey: Worldviews and opinions of scientists. India 2007–08 summary report*. Hartford, CT: Institute for the Study of Secularism in Society and Culture.

Koenig, H. G. (2008). Concerns about measuring "spirituality" in research. *Journal of Nervous and Mental Disease, 196*, 349–355.

LaBarre, W. (1969). *The peyote cult*. New York: Schoken.

Lange, R., & Thalbourne, M. A. (2007). The Rasch scaling of mystical experiences: Construct validity and correlates. *The International Journal for the Psychology of Religion, 17*, 121–140.

Leary, T. (1964). Religious experience: Its production and interpretation. *Psychedelic Review, 1*, 324–346.

Leary, T., Metzner, R., & Alpert, R. (1964). *The psychedelic experience: A manual based on the Tibetan book of the dead*. New York: Citadel Press.

Leuba, J. (1896). A study on the psychology of religious phenomena. *American Journal of Psychology, 7*, 309–385.

Lundmark, M. (2010). When Mrs B met Jesus during radiotherapy: A single case study of a Christic vision: Psychological prerequisites and function and consideration on narrative methodology. *Archive for the Psychology of Religion, 32*, 27–68.

Mathew, T. E. (2003). The sacred: Differentiating, clarifying, and extending concepts. *Review of Religious Research, 45*, 32–47.

McClenon, J. (1994). *Wondrous events: Foundations of religious belief*. Philadelphia: University of Pennsylvania Press.

McGinn, B. (1991). *The foundations of Christian mysticism*. New York: Crossroads.

McKinnon, A. M. (2003). The religious, the paranormal, and church attendance: A response to Orenstein. *Journal for the Scientific Study of Religion, 42*, 299–303.

Miller, L. (Ed.). (2010). Watching for the light: Spiritual psychology beyond materialism. *Psychology of Religion and Spirituality, 2*, 35–66.

Miller, W. R., & Thorensen, L. E. (1999). Spirituality and health. In W. R. Miller (Ed.). *Integrating spirituality into treatment* (pp. 3–18). Washington, DC: American Psychological Association.

Moody, R. A. (1975). *Life after life*. Covington, GA: Mockingbird Books.

Moody, R. A. (1977). *Reflections on life after life*. Atlanta, GA: Mockingbird Books.

Noyes, R., Jr., & Kletti, R. (1976). Depersonalization in the face of life-threatening danger: An interpretation. *Omega, 7*, 103–114.

Orenstein, A. (2002). Religion and paranormal belief. *Journal for the Scientific Study of Religion, 41*, 301–311.

Otto, R. (1958). *The idea of the holy* (J. W. Harvey, Trans.). London: Oxford University Press. (Original work published 1917)

Pafford, M. (1973). *Inglorious wordsworths: A study in some transcendental experiences in childhood and adolescence*. London: Hodder & Stoughton.

Pasquale, F. (2007). The "nonreligious" in the American northwest. In B. A. Kosamin & Keysar (Eds.), *Secularism and secularity: Contemporary international perspectives* (pp. 41–58). Hartford, CT: Institute for the Study of Secularism in Society and Culture.

Poloma, M. M. (1989). *The Assemblies of God at the crossroads*. Knoxville: University of Tennessee Press.

Poloma, M. M., & Hood, R. W., Jr. (2008). *Blood and fire: Godly love in a Pentecostal emerging church*. New York: New York University Press.

Porpora, D. V. (2006). Methodological atheism, methodological agnosticism and religious experience. *Journal for the Theory of Social Behavior, 36*, 57–75.

Proudfoot, W. (1985). *Religious experience.* Berkeley: University of California Press.

Rodin, E. A. (1980). The reality of near death experiences: A personal perspective. *Journal of Nervous and Mental Disease, 168,* 259–263.

Roof, W. C. (1993). *A generation of seekers: The spiritual journeys of the boon generation.* San Francisco: Harper.

Sabon, M. B. (1982). *Recollections of death: A medical investigation.* New York: Harper & Row.

Segal, A. F. (2004). *Life after death: A history of the afterlife in Western religion.* New York: Doubleday.

Shanon, B. (2002). *The antipodes of the mind: Charting the phenomenology of the Ayahuasca experience.* New York: Oxford University Press.

Skal, D. J. (1998). *Screams of reason.* New York: Norton.

Spickard, J. V. (1993). For a sociology of religious experience. In W. H. Swatos, Jr. (Ed.), *A future for religion?: New paradigms for social analysis* (pp. 109–127). Thousand Oaks, CA: Sage.

Stace, W. (1960). *Mysticism and philosophy.* Phildelphia, PA: Lippincott.

Stark, R. (2001). Reconceptualizing religion, magic, and science. *Review of Religious Research, 43,* 101–120.

Stevens, J. (1987). *Storming heaven: LSD and the American dream.* New York: Harper & Row.

Strassman, R. (2001). *DMT: The spirit molecule.* Rochester, VT: Park Street Press.

Streib, H., Hood, R. W., Jr., Keller, B., Csöff, R.-M., & Silver, C. (2008). *Deconversion: Qualitative and quantitative results from cross-cultural research in Germany and the United States* (Research in Contemporary Religion, Vol. 4). Göttingen, Germany: Vandenhoeck & Ruprecht.

Sundararajan, L. (2002). Religious awe: Potential contributions of negative theology to psychology, "positive" or otherwise. *Journal of Theoretical and Philosophical Psychology, 22,* 174–197.

Tamminen, K. (1991). *Religious development in childhood and youth: An empirical study.* Helsinki: Soumalainen Tiedeakatemia.

Targ, E., Schlitz, M., & Irwin, H. J. (2002). Psi-related experiences. In E. Cardeña, S. J. Lynn, & S. Krippner (Eds.), *Varieties of anomalous experience: Examining the scientific evidence* (pp. 219–252). Washington, DC: American Psychological Association.

Taves, A. (2009). *Religious experiences reconsidered: A building block approach to the study of religion and other special things.* Princeton, NJ: Princeton University Press.

Thalbourne, M. A., Bartemucci, L., Delin, P. S., Fox, B., & Nofi, O. (1997). Transliminality: Its nature and correlates. *Journal of the American Society for Psychical Research, 91,* 305–331.

Thalbourne, M. A., & Delin, P. S. (1999). Transliminality: Its relation to dream life, religiosity, and mystical experience. *The International Journal for the Psychology of Religion, 91,* 45–61.

Truzzi, M. (1971). Definition and dimensions of the occult: Toward a sociological perspective. *Journal of Popular Culture, 5,* 635–646.

Vernon, G. M. (1968). The religious "nones": A neglected category. *Journal for the Scientific Study of Religion, 7,* 219–229.

Walach, H., Kohlls, N., von Stillfried, N., Hinterberger, T., & Schmidt, S. (2009). Spirituality: The legacy of parapsychology. *Archive for the Psychology of Religion, 31,* 277–308.

Weil, A. (1986). *The natural mind* (rev. ed.). Boston: Houghton Mifflin.

Wiebe, P. H. (1997). *Visions of Jesus: Direct encounter from the New Testament to today.* New York: Oxford University Press.

Williams, R. N., & Fallconer, J. E. (1994). Religion and mental health: A hermeneutical consideration. *Review of Religious Research, 35,* 335–349.

Yamane, D. (2000). Narrative and religious experience. *Sociology of Religion, 61,* 171–189.

Yensen, R. (1990). LSD and psychotherapy. *Journal of Psychoactive Drugs, 17,* 267–277.

Zaehner, R. C. (1957). *Mysticism, sacred and profane: An inquiry into some varieties of praenatural experience.* London: Oxford University Press.

Zaleski, C. (1987). *Other-world journeys: Accounts of near-death experience in medieval and modern times.* New York: Oxford University Press.

Zeller, B. (2003, November). *Gatekeepers of (Ir) religion: The scientific religion of Heaven's Gate.* Paper presented at the annual meeting of the American Academy of Religion, Atlanta, GA.

Zinnbauer, B. J., Pargament, K. I., Cole, B., Rye, M. S., Butter, E. M., Belavich, T. G., et al. (1999). Religion and spirituality: Unfuzzying the fuzzy. *Journal for the Scientific Study of Religion, 36,* 549–584.

Zusne, L., & Jones, W. H. (1989). *Anomalistic thinking: A study of magical thinking* (2nd ed.). Hillsdale, NJ: Erlbaum.

22

Ritual and Prayer

Forms, Functions, and Relationships

Kevin L. Ladd and Bernard Spilka

On the level of description, "ritual" refers to patterned behavior that is commonly repeated with minimal variation in content. Despite the simplicity of this characterization, ritual is integral to human life and pervades virtually every aspect of our daily existence. It is organized and as situationally pertinent responsivity may include any possibility from the most elemental movement to highly complex actions. Our culture provides virtually uncountable means for defining, shaping, focusing, and limiting rituals. In essence, however, these support communication and understanding on all levels from the personal and interpersonal to the sociocultural.

Theories regarding the formation, nature, and utilization of rituals range from psychology and psychoanalysis through anthropology to biogenetics (Bell, 1997; Karecki, 1997). While a wealth of information exists within "ritual studies," it is only possible for us to offer enough to whet the reader's appetite.

Grimes (1995) essentially identifies the study of ritual with understanding religion. His position is widely though not universally supported by historical and contemporary scholars. Further specification emphasizes religious rituals such as worship and prayer. Our purpose in this chapter, therefore, is to provide an overview of the psychology of ritual largely relative to its expression through the practice of prayer.

With this in mind, this chapter explores the use of ritual in a wide variety of situations, primarily religious. We see, therefore, that for adaptive purposes a ritual such as prayer is manifest in many forms, develops over time, and is applicable to a broad spectrum of psychosocial coping and health circumstances. We explore such possibilities in the following pages.

When scholars call ritual "the single most important characteristic of any living religiousness" (Pilgrim, 1978, p. 64) or note the "great attraction of humans to ritual experience" (Roberts, 1984, p. 100), we realize that understanding ritual is critical to comprehending human belief and behavior in some usually undefined way. But what is it that we're struggling to define? This leads us to questions of origin, purpose, and meaning.

FRAMEWORKS FOR UNDERSTANDING RITUAL

Some Fundamental Considerations

A Brief Incursion into Early History

Despite the fact that ritual is found throughout history and that there are some very scholarly treatments of the topic, there does not appear to be any universal or overall history of it per se. Literature and Internet searches by the authors found appeals by researchers to readers for such writings. Efforts are confined either to circumscribed historical periods or to specific, narrowly defined rituals. To demonstrate early concerns with the character and expression of ritual, we offer this very concise foray into the area during ancient times.

Eliade (1978) takes us back to Paleolithic carvings and cave paintings that he believes represent social rituals. In ancient Greece ritual, drama, and play were linked (Neale & Parr, 2002). Harrison (1974) cites ritual dance in Greek tragedy regarding relationships among the gods. This fits well with Greek intentions to employ physical actions to present ideas and concepts that are difficult to articulate in a solely linguistic fashion. Religious content is endemic in most of these efforts. Similar work is available for any historical period, though Christian symbolism, myth, and ritual soon took over. Anthropologist Roy Rappaport's (2004) definitive work, *Ritual and Religion in the Making of Humanity* even claims that "religion's major conceptual and experiential constituents . . . are creations of ritual" (p. 3). Prayer is one such creation.

Ritual in Biological Perspective

Looking to more basic sources, namely evolutionary and genetic possibilities, there are apparently no known cultures without ritual in some form (Helman, 1994). In addition, the literal omnipresence of ritual in a broad spectrum of animals, invertebrates and vertebrates in addition to humans, is well illustrated by Huxley (1966) and Laughlin and McManus (1979). Lorenz asserts that "human rituals serve the same function as animal ritualization—communicating" (cited by Wulff, 1997, p. 155). This does not constitute definitive proof of evolutionary or genetic origins, but it does suggest a potentially useful research direction (Mead, 1966/1972). Since an evolutionary basis for ritual is likely, Bell (1997) suggests a shaping via "genetic propensities" (p. 31), a view widely accepted among ethologists. Although no direct research seems to have found genetic indicators for ritual, considering its association with religion, we should note a fair amount of supportive twin-study work demonstrating a genetic component in religion (D'Onofrio, Eaves, Murrelle, Maes, & Spilka, 1999). Specifically what this component refers to is unknown, but the possibility of genetic overlap between ritual and religion cannot be ruled out. Since the understanding of ritual in biology has been extended into the realm of neurobiology, genetic factors may be operative here (d'Aquili & Laughlin, 1982).

Ritual in Psychological and Psychoanalytic Perspective

Like history, psychology can take us into many domains relevant to the study of ritual. A sampling suggests motivational, cognitive, coping and adjustment approaches. Starting with Freud, ritual became a significant concern, almost always strongly focused on religious practices (Gay, 1979). Theodor Reik (1946) devoted an entire volume to psychoanalytic studies on ritual, again primarily of a religious nature. Pruyser's (1983) psychoanalytic formulation identifies three realms of thinking that frame how we view ritual communicative functions. The first two, he argues, are Freudian by-products. An autistic (inner) form consists of behaviors the usefulness of which is limited to the individual performer. Ritualistic activity is here restricted to phenomenological description. A realistic (outer) approach encompasses both internal and external actions, making it more amenable to sharing with others. This also means that ideas are available for greater collective scrutiny employing scientific (and other) methods. The inner and outer orientations represent poles on a continuum. In between, Pruyser suggests, is an illusionistic option that reflects the work of Winnicott concerning transitional phenomena. This is where creativity of expression resides, mixing fantasy and fact to develop novel, playful responses to situational challenges to the meaning of ritual.

Becker (1973) believes that "the thing that has to be explained in human relations is precisely the fascination of the person who holds or symbolizes power" (p. 127). This "fascination" (p. 128) possesses a shamanic quality, which Freud and other analytic thinkers assert "has the elements of an intense love affair" (p. 128–129) that affects both sexes equally. These expressions include the features of religious experiences: sublime feelings, mystification, and identification with ultimate power; they are also linked to perceptions of gaining primary control over difficult personal situations. For Becker, this is religion; common explanatory and justifying beliefs and myths that represent a religious perspective. The central figure in the production of such a system is the shaman, who occupies a very privileged place in society. In modern society, clergy may play similar roles.

Multidimensional Perspectives

The foregoing brings us to our first main point with regard to ritual, namely that it is multidimensional. Each of Pruyser's three realms has room for its own subforms and interpretations. In the autistic realm, the activity in question should be of importance primarily to the self, and individuals will probably vary in their understanding of what occurs. Ritual from the realistic approach could be identified by its public nature in conjunction with systematic, repeatable characteristics. Greater agreement as to its meaning is likely to be present. The illusionistic style would have a loosely structured core, capable of meeting situational demands. These perspectives may offer information about the relative importance of the behaviors within the community. For instance, the most rigorous instructions might be associated with events socially deemed more powerful and personally of great significance. Over the course of a life span, individuals are likely to embrace rituals that fit each of these descriptions.

Pruyser (1968) personally favored the realistic understanding of ritual acts relative to religious ceremonies: "They are measured, precise, specified in great detail, highly stereotyped, and often very repetitive" (p. 185). He further stresses that ritual counters spontaneity; "it distrusts impulsivity. It capitalizes on inhibition, delay, and various other control devices" (p. 186). Although this makes ritual amenable to scientific study, and recognizes its habitual character, he desires to keep intention in the picture. One major question is the extent to which behaviors that look similar on the surface are driven by conscious intention and planning. Ashdown (2003), for instance, argues that rituals in general, and religious rituals in particular, are only truly identifiable in linguistic contexts where they are explicitly differentiated from acts that are both nonritual and nonreligious ritual. Goldsmith (2000) further highlights the importance of language as a tool that helps to solidify behavioral patterns. When practiced frequently across the life span, well-learned, ritualized actions can serve as substitutes for language.

Thus far, we have implied that ritual is a multidimensional form of communication that, while often heavily based on language, also moves beyond linguistics to feelings and emotions among other possibilities. This latter position, at least in the case of humans, has explicit links to Otto's (1923) notion concerning encounters with the numinous. While many such encounters are initially spontaneous, rituals may represent attempts to re-create the original experience. In other words, rituals are not solely about pragmatically solving logical puzzles, they are equally, if not more so, about (re-)creating sensations (cf. the writings on magic by Ortiz, 1994, as well as Burger & Neale, 1995). Watts and Williams (1988) characterize these as forms of knowing and experiencing alternatively driven by either the head or the heart. When these coalesce, the result is a combining of certainty and faith that yields conviction (Wonder & Minch, 1996). Whether public or private, the most powerful rituals are those that do not just encourage participants to suspend doubts and disbelief, but rather to radically transform skeptics into believers (Hass, 2007).

The breadth of both psychology and ritual has brought these two areas together in other ways. The cognitive science approach articulates how the human mind naturally processes information (Barrett, 2004; Chapter 12, this volume) and how that processing can be seen in action as ritual. McManus (1979) extends this orientation to social cognition. Peacock (1975) treats the consciousness aspect of cognition, while Jacobs (1992) discusses religious ritual in relation to mental health. In other words, this brief sampling can be easily expanded.

What Does Ritual Do?

As is often true, the attempt to define ritual places it in a variety of contexts that begin to explain its functions. Ritual clearly extends communicative options. It entails repetitive behaviors, with varying degrees of flexibility. At its most persuasive, it moves people toward or strengthens their belief in a particular system of thinking. A Navajo physician describes the purposes of Navaho ritual as one of building community: "Ceremony invites change, it prays for growth, harmony, order, balance" (Alvord, 1999, p. 12). In like manner, a fictional account outlines how a personally constructed ritual brought family members together following the death of a mother. One states that "it wasn't so much participating in the rituals themselves as it was the feeling of being part of a tribe, of feeling for the first time that I was involved in something authentic . . . This was my place. These were my people. My culture" (Ragen, 1998, p. 278).

Collectively, these observations suggest that a primary function of ritual is the provision of social cohesion or stability, especially in moments of elevated threat or ambiguity (Ladd, 2007; McIntosh, 1995; Sosis & Alcorta, 2003). This is especially appropriate for religious rituals. Individualistically, this translates into a sense of well-being and security.

For many, the stability and structure of rituals may segue into experiences of meaning, and control (Lorenz, 1963, 1966; Pruyser, 1968), enhancing social organization and strengthening a sense of community (Lorenz, 1963). Rituals function in this fashion during times of peace as well as times of disruption. It is during moments of upheaval, however, that most is expected from rituals. Virtually all rituals can be construed as connoting some level of control of self and/or environment, whether this control is actively directed toward specific situations or emotional states and interpretations (Fiske, Morling, & Stevens, 1996; Rothbaum, Weisz, & Snyder, 1982). Psychologically, they can reduce anxiety and uncertainty (Benson & Stark, 1996; Hinde, 1999; Pruyser, 1968). Erikson (1966) avers that "the overcoming of ambivalence as well as of ambiguity is one of the prime functions of ritualization" (p. 339).

By convincing people to care, rituals also lay a foundation upon which meaning can be constructed. Emphasizing the discrepancy between reality and ideal over which one frequently lacks control, Smith (1982/1996) claims that ritual indicates the way things ought to be. Ceremonial participation confirms the individual's identification with the ideal, that which is hoped for. It provides a basis for personal mastery and increasing one's sense of safety and security (Erikson, 1966). For some this enhances meaning and reduces stress, anxiety, and impulsivity. Such developments facilitate social bonding by channeling destructive and extreme emotions into controllable forms (Benson & Stark, 1996; Pargament, 1997; Pruyser, 1968).

RELIGION AND RITUAL

When Is It Religion and When Is It Magic?

Across time and traditions, there is much variability concerning the extent to which religious rituals are considered synonymous with "magic" (Faber, 2002). Versnel (1991) argues against simply equating the two. Instead, he finds great utility in Goode's (1949) articulation of the two concepts as existing along a continuum. Although a thorough exploration of this topic is beyond the scope of this chapter, it is helpful to note that this structure considers magic as possessing the following qualities: instrumental, manipulative, mechanical and nonpersonal, coercive, along with goals that are short term, concrete, and individualistic (Versnel, 1991, p. 186). All are pertinent to ritual.

Septimus (2012) follows a similar path, demonstrating how this approach can be useful in understanding prayers that are part of Jewish rituals. In particular, he shows how prayers can display actions that are either more or less magical in nature since they possess most if not all of the qualities just cited. The picture becomes more complex as he relates how the evaluation of any specific prayer may be altered by the context in which it is employed and whether or not the addressee of the prayer is divine. From the perspective of the practicing rabbis, the rituals and prayers embedded in them, regardless of subtle changes, remain firmly within a religious domain. Meanings, however, may be quite elusive as they tap personal motives and hopes plus circumstantial limitations that we are often aware of but aspire to overcome.

This is a very difficult area to parse, and even some of the best materials available (e.g., Sørensen, 2007) cannot address the breadth of the field. At present, we simply conclude that whether a ritual is more magical, religious, or spiritual in nature is highly dependent on a plethora of factors. The practitioner's intention, the context, and the format of presentation play critical roles in how the action is to be understood and personalized. We see this clearly when ritual is expressed through faith.

As a final coordinating perspective, Tremmel (1984) identifies three major functions for religious ritual: a metatechnological function in which ritual brings supernatural power into the natural world via magic, miracles, or forces designed to support people in everyday life. A second role is termed "sacramental." Divine power is called upon to help the individual buttress self-control and to offer protection against death and threats to life. The third, or, experiential function, fosters identification with one's God, and insinuates divine power into life; the person is renewed and reborn. Relative to this last function, Pruyser (1968) claims that the purpose of ritual worship is to stimulate religious experience.

The cognitive-structural approach to religious ritual offered by Lawson and McCauley (1990) is primarily concerned with the symbolic organization and significance of ritual. These scholars stress the themes of control, power, and change. We read that "religious rituals always do something to some thing or somebody . . . Participants perform rituals in order to bring about changes in the religious world" (p. 125). This is largely a way station to effect alterations in the real world. In other words, power and control needs are a fundamental source of ritual.

Clearly, ritual involves reification, and animism is one outcome of this process. Von Bertalanffy connotes such action as a primeval but beneficial effort to achieve environmental control (LaViolette, 1981). One can easily argue that religious ritual is a mechanism for enhancing mastery over oneself and one's personal world. Its use is strengthened by reinforcement, particularly of a social nature.

Ritual Expression through Religion

Ritual and Prayer

The Problem of Definition. As has already been intimated, ritual has historically and contemporaneously been thoroughly studied in both institutional and private religion. The former is largely evidenced in formal worship, which has also been termed "corporate prayer." It is mainly a public phenomenon, yet it does overlap with individual practices. Personal faith reflects how people distinctively utilize prayer, which has received more attention from psychologists of religion than worship. Here, however, we primarily emphasize the process of prayer as a form of "individualized ritual" (Janssen, de Hart, & den Draak, 1990, p. 72) and "self-generated ritual" (Hine, 1981, p. 404). Such an analysis readily displays the complexity, flexibility, and richness that prayer manifests in everyday life. Just as a primary role for ritual is communication, so prayer shares aspects of communication (Baesler, 2003). The variety of ways prayer does this almost defies definition. For example, Puglisi (1929) speaks of eudaemonistic prayer, which is fundamentally petitionary, but also denotes variants like aesthetic, noetic, and ethical types. He expands his list to include "prayers of invocation, of lamentation, of appeal, of petition, of sacrifice, of offering, of persuasion, of trust, of devotion, of submission, of dependence, of thanksgiving etc." (p. 150). Quite daunting is the work of Richards and Hildebrand (1990), who detail over 100 categories of prayer. In a more manageable analysis, Foster (1992) denotes 21 different kinds of prayer, which can be hierarchically organized into three purposeful directions: inward, outward, and upward. Prayer thus becomes communication with oneself, with others, and, in its upward forms, with what Lawson and McCauley (1990) and McCauley and Lawson (2002) term "culturally postulated superhuman agents (CPS)". Generally and popularly, the aim of those who pray has traditionally been to contact, identify with, and/or influence the CPS. When the rite in question has been completed, the sequence of enabling actions ends. This means that the next step must be taken by the CPS. Additional thought and analysis recognize the inward (personal) and outward (social) courses. All three have yielded to a more rigorous psychological treatment (Ladd & Spilka, 2002, 2006).

Another prayer dimension should be highlighted. Though discussed relative to Judaism and worship, Ehrlich and Ordan (2004) note that prayer has a nonverbal facet. Brown (1994) also speaks of gesture and posture. Physical movement is part of this "body language." Prayers clearly regard actions such as hand placement, resting on one's knees, eyes closed, and other responses as significant in prayer. Given that the difficulty of providing a broadly satisfactory definition of prayer is amply testified to by Brown (1994), we simply cite it as a kind of ritual and recognize this simplification with the circumscribing factors we discuss here.

A final appreciation of the problem of definition may be seen in its widespread use. Variety and prevalence are likely to parallel each other. National poll data inform us that approximately 90% of Americans claim to pray and 60% assert they pray daily (Poloma & Gallup, 1991). The General Social Survey's findings from 1972–2006 suggest that the percentage of pray-ers overall may be as high as 97% (National Opinion Research Center, 2007).

Worship: A Brief Overview. The usually public nature of most forms of worship connotes ritual that depends on objectified cultural signs and symbols that convey common meanings to large numbers of people. Participants are offered collective meanings that can weld those present into a community of worshippers (Whitley, 1964). This is ritual performing its well-accepted function of strengthening the group and committing individuals to their common faith. Since attitudes and belief often follow behavior as its justification, so worship, especially repetitive forms, must be convincingly explained. Cognitive dissonance is thus reduced (Festinger, 1957). Whether it is the five-times-daily experience of Muslim worship or the specific expectations of the Judeo-Christian traditions, ritualistic participation, with its supportive theologies, subjectively validates the approved kinds of observance.

The Complexity of Individual Prayer. Just as Foster's (1992) religious/theological analysis of prayer suggested 21 types of prayer that might be assessed, psychologists and sociologists of religion have applied sophisticated methods to creating multidimensional frameworks for the evaluation of prayer (Hood, Morris, & Watson, 1987; Ladd & Spilka, 2002, 2006; Poloma & Gallup, 1990). As a rule, these result in four to eight forms. We close this question of the number of kinds of prayer by noting that at least one form seems to elicit much agreement popularly, theologically, and research-wise: namely petitionary prayer. According to Capps (1982), "The heart of the psychology of religion is the psychology of prayer, especially petitionary prayer" (p. 130). Heiler (1932) declared that "the free spontaneous petitionary prayer of the natural man exhibits the prototype of all prayer" (p. 1). This is evidenced in both its character and frequency. Here we have a personally meaningful private ritual act of great personal importance that manifests much individual variation.

Despite the many studies identifying different kinds of prayer, we know surprisingly little about the contexts that motivate such efforts and how individuals conceptualize these endeavors regarding both themselves and the deity to whom prayers are directed. Psychosocial considerations that seem relevant only to prayer may also be appropriate to the understanding of ritual effects in general.

Meaning and Utility in Ritual and Prayer. Earlier we noted how Lorenz (1963) and Pruyser (1968) associated ritual with increased personal control. Nowhere is this tie stronger than with petitionary prayer. Jackson and Bergeman (2011) demonstrate a tie between religious practices, including prayer and worship, with a sense of control that eventuates in heightened well-being. In sum, when other behavioral alternatives have been exhausted, the supplicant identifies with and seeks supernatural agents, deities, and so on, for aid. By calling on such referents, as previously discussed, dissonance resulting from the individual's response is reduced and a sense of control is increased. This may be analogized to Pargament et al.'s (1988) treatment of the role of faith in the problem-solving process. We discuss this further shortly.

The Utility of Prayer

Prayer, Coping, and Adjustment. In one form or another, we are suggesting that ritual per se and worship and prayer as religious rituals help the individual to cope with personal and social issues and problems. One possible consideration is that practicing such established and approved rituals means conformity and "normality." Rappaport (2004) thus speaks of "meanings and effects from ritual's universal form" (p. 30). The literature on prayer and coping with life's problems is immense. We sample this here so that readers may gain some direction for further work in this area.

Pargament (1997) indicates that this holds true for both desirable and undesirable possibilities. Prayer and worship correlate positively with personal control, which leads to heightened well-being (Jackson & Bergeman, 2011). Poloma and Gallup (1991) similarly claimed that prayer's importance is largely due to its "improving a sense of well-being" (p. 5). Measures of related concepts such as purpose in life, self-esteem, and self-satisfaction have consistently confirmed these relationships (Maltby, Lewis, & Day, 1999; McCullough & Larson, 1999; Meraviglia, 1999).

The problem-solving scheme of Pargament et al. (1988) is especially appropriate for understanding how prayer is used. These authors speak of "three distinctive approaches to responsibility and control in coping" (Pargament, 1997, p. 182). In essence, these appropriately describe how pray-ers may conceive of their relationship to God during prayer. First, those employing a "self-directive" mode are essentially saying that despite their appeal, they are responsible for handling the task they confront. A second orientation is termed "collaborative" in which the individual and the deity work together. Last, a "deferring" method implies that whatever is to be done is fully in the hands of God. A number of research studies indicate that "the collaborative and self-directive modes involve more of an internal locus of control which research has shown to be generally beneficial" (Hood, Hill, & Spilka, 2009, p. 462).

The most frequent religious response to the stresses of old age is prayer (Manfredi & Pickett, 1987). Unfortunately, the results of research do not consistently show the often hypothesized positive associations. As a rule, either no significant correlations have been observed or questions of confounding with other variables and influencing factors imply doubts about the studies conducted (Krause, 2003, 2004; Levin & Markides, 1986; Markides, 1983; Markides, Levin, & Ray, 1987).

Moving beyond global well-being, seeking God's assistance relates negatively to trait anxiety (Harris, Schoneman, & Carrera, 2005). As might have been expected, a stress avoiding/deferring prayer style meant less anxiety control. Bradshaw, Ellison, and Flannelly (2008) found a weak negative association between prayer and depression. Another study reported that 56% of a sample of individuals experiencing depression felt prayer was effective while only 1% thought it was ineffective (Parker & Brown, 1982).

Other research directed at prayer and alcoholism reveals consistently constructive negative associations (Harris et al., 2010). Similar findings are reported relative to drug use (Hood, Hill, & Spilka, 2009).

Shifting from the individual to social situations, prayer again shows its constructive potential as a ritual for marital conflict resolution (Butler & Harper, 1994; Butler, Stout, & Gardner, 2002). A number of studies further confirm ties of prayer to relationship satisfaction and enrichment (Beach et al., 2011; Ellison, Burdette, & Wilcox, 2010; Fincham, Beach, Lambert, Stillman, & Braithwaite, 2008; Fincham, Lambert, & Beach, 2010). The next step may be to assess associations between prayer and larger group and community possibilities.

Ritual control in social life has also been called "a practical instrument of ethics" that serves to "coalesce the individual into the group which would be fragmented by his uncurbed impulses . . . When effective it not only curbs, but also helps to create the desire to serve the community in an extension of the service that ritual calls for" (Ostow & Scharfstein, 1954, pp. 100–101). In other words, ritual is a conservative cultural force that preserves the status quo (Sørensen, 2007). Ritual, therefore, supports expectations of how others will or should react. This pattern extends into religion, suggesting that our responses ought to elicit certain actions on the part of the deity to whom appeals are made.

Prayer and Health. People offer more prayers for health than for anything else (Bader et al., 2006; Bell et al., 2005; Eisenberg et al., 1993; MCaffrey, Eisenberg, Legedza, Davis, & Phillips, 2004; Wachholz & Sambamamoorthi, 2011). Two major distinctions categorize this literature: (1) whether prayers are for the self or others and (2) the extent to which findings are subjective (how the pray-er feels) or objective (actual physical or mental change). Despite much argument, the best case can be made for subjective effects. Because of weaknesses in physiological measurement and data analysis, this has become a highly controversial area with much questionable research (Spilka & Ladd, 2013; Sloan, 2006; Sloan & Bagiella, 2002).

Explaining why prayer should objectively work has resulted in arguments that either religious/spiritual intervention has occurred or paranormal forces have been operative. When changes occur or are claimed, Breslin and Lewis (2008) believe these may be explained by (1) placebo effects, (2) differences in healthy lifestyles between those who seemed to benefit and those who do not, (3) prayer as a diversion that allows expectations to be claimed, (4) actual stimulation of immune function, and (5) social support that helps the ill to cope better with their problems. To this list add the observation that the presence of Type 1 and 2 statistical errors coupled with persistent reporting of trivial and borderline significant correlations arouse considerable doubt. There is a strong need for cross-validation by others than the original researchers.

Serious backers of what has become known as "complementary and alternative medicine" (CAM), which includes prayer, express concern with data being faked, and instances of such practices have been exposed. Still, one national study revealed that 40% of patients resorted to CAM methods in 2008 (Barnes, Bloom, & Nahin, 2008). Minorities who sponsor their own forms of folk medicine are also inclined to use prayer and other CAM procedures (Arredondo-Holden, 1978). Stein (2006) noted the existence of "healing rooms," in which spiritual healing via prayer is sought. Patients who pray tend to be satisfied with the process and are more likely to be actively involved in health decisions than those who do not pray (O'Connor, Pronk, Tan, & Whitehead, 2005). Over half of those surveyed who resort to prayer believe that God's intervention will occur and be effective after a physician's negative prognosis (Stein, 2006). In addition, prayer-for-healing groups tend to create a sense of power in their members, which counters anxiety and generate hope (McGuire, 1988).

Health problems often either are the result of stress or produce it. This can affect both the pray-er and the patient; hence, the question may be posed whether prayer might mitigate the undesirable aspects of the physiology of stress and possibly reduce adverse symptomatology. Initial work on prayer relative to the "stress hormone" cortisol reports both positive and negative findings (Dedert et al., 2004; Katz, Weiner, Gallagher, & Hellman, 1970; Tartaro, Luecken, & Gunn, 2005). More exacting research in this area is merited.

We have tried to provide entrée to the major parameters of research on how prayer as a ritual expression relates to health. Because of the massive number of research studies on prayer relative to various medical conditions, we suggest that readers begin their search by examining the handbook compiled by Koenig, King, and Carson (2012). Works by Spilka and Ladd (2013) and Ladd and Spilka (2013) provide additional direction.

The Dark Side of Religious Ritual

Unhappily, the positive and constructive roles of ceremony have their counterparts in a pathology of ritual. Normal uses of ritual can shade into obsession, compulsivity, and a dogmatic rigidity that takes over one's daily life. One tragic manifestation is an excessive preoccupation with sin. The disorder of scrupulosity is an extreme example in which the individual suffers from severe doubts as to whether one has sinned or not (Hood et al., 2009). Rituals are developed to counter such thoughts and also to atone for possible sinning. St. Ignatius of Loyola, who had such concerns, created a substitute set of rituals to offset his obsessions (Gomez, 2001). Similar difficulties apparently affected a number of saints, often resulting in highly unconventional attempts to treat personal problems (McGinley, 1969).

Another negative connotation for religious ritual has come from the association of this concept with the notion of "ritual child abuse" (Victor, 1992). While the extent of such practices is hard to estimate, it is clear that a variety of forms of violence and abuse are often justified by perpetrators in the name of certain faith traditions (Ellens, 2004).

SOME FINAL CONSIDERATIONS: HOW IS RITUAL TO BE STUDIED?

We have argued that ritual, religion, spirituality, and prayer are multidimensional in nature. These realms increasingly require transdisciplinary models, a strategy that has been widely sidestepped in America since the early 1920s (Sumner, 2003). In addition, recognition of the complexity of patterned interdependencies necessitates multivariate methodologies. Consumers of research are also adopting holistic perspectives that reject restrictive disciplinary limitations (Hesse-Biber, 2010; Jaccard & Jacoby, 2010). With regard to ritual and religion, this means that scholars currently theorize and seek data ranging from evolutionary and genetic levels to the psychological (e.g., cognitive, physiological, social). For example, Medicus (2000, 2003) has shown how the same phenomenon (e.g., ritual dance) can be examined simultaneously from different intellectual angles.

The functions of prayer mirror those associated with ritual in general. Theories and models of prayer as communication that deal with relatedness to a deity and oneself have been proposed and to some degree discussed here (Baesler, 2003; Benson, 1960; Childs, 1983; Crocker, 1984; Ellens, 1977; Foster, 1992). Integral to all of this is the highly complex issue of meaning, which connects the individual to a network of factors ranging from personal experience and biology through group and subcultural levels to the overall culture itself. Such analysis is well beyond what can be accomplished here. In opening a door to the rich world of ritual as central to religion, we have very briefly sampled the significance of prayer in a number of areas. There remains, however, an enormous amount of room for scholars wishing to document further the importance and complexity of these aspects of human existence.

REFERENCES

Alvord, L. (1999, December). New beginnings. *Dartmouth Alumni Magazine*, p. 12.

Arredondo-Holden, J. (1978, December). *La salud mental de la raza: Curanderas and mental health centers in two-Mexican-American communities*. Unpublished doctoral dissertation, University of Denver, Denver, CO.

Ashdown, L. (2003). Religion without speech? *Ars Disputandi*, 3(3), 1–12. Retrieved from *www.arsdisputandi.org*.

Bader, C., Dougherty, K., Froese, P., Johnson, B., Mencken, F. C., Park, J. Z., et al. (2006). *American piety in the 21st century: New insights to the depth and complexity of religion in the US*. Waco, TX: Baylor Institute for the Study of Religion.

Baesler, E. J. (2003). *Theoretical explorations and empirical investigations of communication and prayer*. Lewistown, NY: Edwin Mellen Press.

Barnes, P. M., Bloom, B., & Nahin, R. L. (2008). Complementary and alternative medicine use among adults and children: United States, 2007. *National Health Statistics Reports.* Retrieved from *www.cdc.gov/nchs/data/nhsr/nhsr012.pdf.*

Barrett, J. L. (2004). *Why would anyone believe in God?* Walnut Creek, CA: AltaMira.

Beach, S. R. H., Hurt, T. R., Fincham, F. D., Franklin, K. J., McNair, L. M., & Stanley, S. S. (2011). Enhancing marital enrichment through spirituality: Efficacy data for prayer focused relationship enhancement. *Psychology of Religion and Spirituality, 3,* 201–216.

Becker, E. (1973). *The denial of death.* New York: Free Press.

Bell, C. (1997). *Ritual: Perspectives and dimensions.* New York: Oxford University Press.

Bell, R. A., Suerken, C., Quandt, S. A., Grzyacz, J. G., Lang, W., & Acury, T. A. (2005). Prayer for health among U.S. adults. *Complementary Health Practices Review, 10,* 175–188.

Benson, H., & Stark, M. (1996). *Timeless healing: The power and biology of belief.* New York: Scribner.

Benson, P. H. (1960). *Religion in contemporary culture.* New York: Harper.

Bradshaw, M., Ellison, C. G., & Flannelly, K. J. (2008). Prayer, God imagery, and symptoms of psychopathology. *Journal for the Scientific Study of Religion, 47,* 644–659.

Breslin, M. J., & Lewis, C. (2008). Theoretical models of the nature of prayer and health: A review. *Mental Health, Religion and Culture, 11*(1), 9–21.

Brown, L. B. (1994). *The human side of prayer.* Birmingham, AL: Religious Education Press.

Burger, E., & Neale, R. E. (1995). *Magic and meaning.* Seattle, WA: Hermetic Press.

Butler, M. H., & Harper, J. M. (1994). The divine *triangle*: Deity in the marital system of religious couples. *Family Process, 33,* 277–286.

Butler, M. H., Stout, J. A., & Gardner, B. C. (2002). Prayer as a conflict resolution ritual: Clinical implications of a religious couple's report of relationship softening, healing perspective, and change responsibility. *American Journal of Family Therapy, 30,* 19–37.

Capps, D. (1982). The psychology of petitionary prayer. *Theology Today, 39,* 130–141.

Childs, B. H. (1983). The possible connection between "private speech" and prayer. *Pastoral Psychology, 32,* 24–33.

Crocker, S. F. (1984). Prayer as a model of communication. *Pastoral Psychology, 33,* 83–92.

D'Aquili, E. G, & Laughlin, C. D., Jr. (1982). The neurobiology of ritual studies. In R. L. Grimes (Ed.), *Readings in ritual studies* (pp. 132–146). Saddle River, NJ: Prentice Hall.

Dedert, E. A., Studts, J. L., Weissbeckera, I., Salmon, P. G., Banis, P. L, & Sephton, S. E. (2004). Religion may help preserve the cortisol rhythm in women with stress-related illness. *International Journal of Psychiatry in Medicine, 34,* 61–77.

D'Onofrio, B., Eaves, L. J., Murrelle, L., Maes, H. H., & Spilka, B. (1999). Understanding biological and social influences on religious affiliation, attitudes, and behaviors: A behavior-genetic perspective. *Journal of Personality, 67,* 953–984.

Ehrlich, U., & Ordan, D. (2004). *Nonverbal language in prayer: A new approach to Jewish liturgy.* Tübingen, Germany: Mohr Siebeck.

Eisenberg, D. M., Kessler, R. C., Foster, C., Norlock, F. E., Calkins, D. R., & Delbanco, T. L. (1993). Unconventional medicine in the United Sates—Prevalence, costs, and patterns of use. *New England Journal of Medicine, 328*(4), 246–252.

Eliade, M. (1978). *A history of religious ideas.* Chicago: University of Chicago Press.

Ellens, J. H. (1977). Communication theory and petitionary prayer. *Journal of Psychology and Theology, 5,* 48–54.

Ellens, J. H. (Ed.). (2004). *The destructive power of religion: Violence in Judaism, Christianity, and Islam, Vol. 1–4.* Westport, CT: Praeger/Greenwood.

Ellison, C. G., Burdette, A. M., & Wilcox, W. B. (2010). The couple that prays together: Race, ethnicity, religion, and relationship quality among working-age adults. *Journal of Marriage and Family, 72,* 963–975.

Erikson, E. H. (1966). Ontogeny of ritualization in man. In J. Huxley (Ed.), A discussion on ritualization of behavior in animals and man. *Philosophical Transactions of the Royal Society of London: Series B. Biological Sciences, 251,* 337–349.

Faber, M. D. (2002). *The magic of prayer.* Westport, CT: Praeger.

Festinger, L. (1957). *A theory of cognitive dissonance.* Stanford, CA: Stanford University Press.

Fincham, F. D., Beach, S. R. H., Lambert, N. M., Stillman, T., & Braithwaite, S. R. (2008). Spiritual behaviors and relationship satisfaction: A critical analysis of the role of prayer. *Journal of Social and Clinical Psychology, 27,* 362–388.

Fincham, F. D., Lambert, N. M., & Beach, S. R. H. (2010). Faith and unfaithfulness: Can praying for your partner reduce infidelity? *Journal of Personality and Social Psychology, 99,* 649–659.

Fiske, S. T., Morling, B., & Stevens, L. E. (1996). Controlling self and others: A theory of anxiety, mental control, and social control. *Personality and Social Psychology Bulletin, 22,* 115–123.

Foster, R. J. (1992). *Prayer: Finding the heart's true home.* San Francisco, CA: Harper.

Gay, V. P. (1979). *Freud on ritual: Reconstruction and critique.* Missoula, MT: Scholars Press.

Goldsmith, M. (2000). When words are no longer necessary: The gift of ritual. *Journal of Religious Gerontology, 12*(3/4), 139.

Gomez, L. O. (2001). When is religion a mental disorder? The disease of ritual. In D. Jonte-Pace & W. B. Parsons (Eds.), *Religion and psychology: Mapping the terrain* (pp. 202–226). New York: Routledge.

Goode, W. J. (1949). Magic and religion: A continuum. *Ethnos, 14,* 172–182.

Grimes, R. L. (1995). *Beginnings in ritual studies* (Rev. Ed.). Columbia: University of South Carolina Press.

Harris, J. I., Erbes, C. R., Engdahl, B. E., Tedeschi, D. G., Olson, R. H., Ann, M. M., et al. (2010). Coping functions of prayer and posttraumatic growth. *The International Journal for the Psychology of Religion, 20,* 26–38.

Harris, J. I., Schoneman, S. W., & Carrera, S. R. (2005). Preferred prayer styles and anxiety control. *Journal of Religion and Health, 44,* 403–412.

Harrison, J. E. (1974, 1912). *Themis.* Gloucester, MA: Peter Smith.

Hass, L. (2007). *Transformation: Creating magic out of tricks.* Sherman, TX: Theory of Art and Magic Press.

Heiler, F. (1932). *Prayer: A study in the history and psychology of religion.* New York: Oxford University Press.

Helman, C. G. (1994). *Culture, health and illness* (3rd Ed.). Oxford, UK: Butterworth Heineman.

Hesse-Biber, S. N. (2010). *Mixed methods research.* New York: Guilford Press.

Hinde, R. A. (1999). *Why Gods persist: A scientific approach to religion.* London: Routledge.

Hine, V. H. (1981). Self-generated ritual: Trend or fad. *Worship, 55,* 404–419.

Hood, R. W., Jr., Hill, P. C., & Spilka, B. (2009). *The psychology of religion: An empirical approach* (4th ed.). New York: Guilford Press.

Hood, R. W., Jr., Morris, R. J., & Watson, P. J. (1987). Religious orientation and prayer experience. *Psychological Reports, 60,* 1201–1202.

Huxley, J. (1966). A discussion on ritualization of behavior in animals and man: Introduction. *Philosophical Transactions of the Royal Society of London: Series B. Biological Sciences, 251,* 249–272.

Jaccard, J., & Jacoby, J. (2010). *Theory construction and model-building skills.* New York: Guilford Press.

Jackson, B. R., & Bergeman, C. S. (2011). How does religiosity enhance well-being? The role of perceived control. *Psychology of Religion and Spirituality, 3,* 149–161.

Jacobs, J. L. (1992). Religious ritual and mental health. In J. F. Schumaker (Ed.), *Religion and mental health* (pp. 291–299). New York: Oxford University Press.

Janssen, J., de Hart, J., & den Draak, C. (1990). Praying as individualized ritual. In H.-G. Heimbrock & H. B. Boudewijnse (Eds.), *Current studies on rituals: Perspectives for the psychology of religion* (pp. 71–85). Amsterdam, the Netherlands: Rodopi.

Karecki, M. (1997). Discovering the roots of ritual. *Missionalia, 25*(2), 169–177.

Katz, J., Weiner, H., Gallagher, T., & Hellman, I. (1970). Stress, distress, and ego defenses. *Archives of General Psychiatry, 23,* 131–142.

Koenig, H. G., King, D. E., & Carson, V. B. (2012). *Handbook of religion and health* (2nd edition). New York: Oxford University Press.

Krause, N. (2003). Religious meaning and subjective well-being in late life. *Journals of Gerontology Series B: Psychological Sciences and Social Sciences, 58,* S160–S170.

Krause, N. L. (2004). Assessing the relationships among prayer expectancies, race, and self-esteem in late life. *Journal for the Scientific Study of Religion, 43,* 395–408.

Ladd, K. L. (2007). Religiosity, the need for structure, death attitudes, and funeral preferences. *Mental Health, Religion & Culture, 10*(5), 451–472.

Ladd, K. L., & Spilka, B. (2002). Inward, outward, upward: Cognitive aspects of prayer. *Journal for the Scientific Study of Religion, 41*(3), 475–484.

Ladd, K. L., & Spilka, B. (2006). Inward, outward, upward prayer: Scale reliability and validation. *Journal for the Scientific Study of Religion, 45*(2), 233–251.

Ladd, K. L, & Spilka, B. (2013). Prayer: A review of the empirical literature. In K. Pargament, J. Exline, & J. Jones (Eds.), *APA handbook of psychology, religion, and spirituality: (Vol. 1): Context, theory, and research.* Washington, DC: American Psychological Association.

Laughlin, C. D., Jr., & McManus, J. M. (1979). Mammalian ritual. In E. G. d'Aquili, C. D. Laughlin, Jr., & J. M. Manus (Eds.), *The spectrum of ritual: A biogenetic structural analysis* (pp. 80–116). New York: Columbia University Press.

LaViolette, P. A. (Ed.). (1981). *A systems view of man: Ludwig von Bertalanffy.* Boulder, CO: Westview.

Lawson, E. T., & McCauley, R. N. (1990). *Rethinking religion: Connecting cognition and culture.* Cambridge, UK: Cambridge University Press.

Levin, J. S., & Markides, K. S. (1986). Religious attendance and subjective health. *Journal of Religion and Health, 25,* 31–39.

Lorenz, K. (1963). *On aggression.* New York: Harcourt, Brace & World.

Lorenz, K. S. (1966). Evolution of ritualization in the biological and cultural spheres. In J. Huxley (Ed.), A discussion on ritualization of behavior in animals and man. *Philosophical transactions of the Royal Society of London, Series B., Biological Sciences, 251,* 273–284.

Maltby, J., Lewis, C. A., & Day, L. (1999). Religious orientation and psychological well-being: The role of the frequency of personal prayer. *British Journal of Health Psychology, 4,* 363–378.

Manfredi, C., & Pickett, M. (1987). Perceived stressful situations and coping strategies utilized by the elderly. *Journal of Community Mental Health Nursing, 4,* 99–110.

Markides, K. S. (1983). Aging, religiosity, and adjustment: A longitudinal analysis. *Journal of Gerontology, 38,* 621–625.

Markides, K. S., Levin, J. S., & Ray, L. A. (1987). Religion, aging, and life satisfaction: An eight year, three wave longitudinal study. *The Gerontologist, 27,* 660–665.

McCaffrey, A. M., Eisenberg, D. M., Legedza, A. T. R., Davis, R. B., & Phillips, R. S. (2004). Prayer for health concerns: Results of a national survey on prevalence and patterns of use. *Archives of Internal Medicine, 164,* 858–862.

McCauley, R. N., & Lawson, E. T. (2002). *Bringing ritual to mind.* Cambridge, UK: Cambridge University Press.

McCullough, M. E., & Larson, D. B. (1999). Prayer. In W. R. Miller (Ed.), *Integrating spirituality into treatment* (pp. 85–110). Washington, DC: American Psychological Association.

McGinley, P. (1969). *Saint-watching.* New York: Viking.

McGuire, M. (1988). *Ritual healing in suburban America.* New Brunswick, NJ: Rutgers University Press.

McIntosh, D. N. (1995). Religion as schema: Implications for the relation between religion and coping. *The International Journal for the Psychology of Religion, 5*(1), 1–16.

McManus, J. (1979). Ritual and human social cognition. In E. G. d'Aquili, C. D. Laughlin, Jr., &

J. M. Manus (Eds.), *The spectrum of ritual: A biogenetic structural analysis* (pp. 216–248). New York: Columbia University Press.

Mead, M. (1966). Ritual expression of the cosmic sense. In M. Mead (Ed.), *Twentieth century faith* (pp. 153–170). New York: Harper & Row. (Original work 1972)

Medicus, G. (2000). Fragen zur Geschlechterdifferenz—eine verhaltensbiologische Annäherung. *Wiener Medizinische Wochenschrift, 150*(10), 217–224.

Medicus, G. (2003). Orientierungsrahmen für Interdisziplinarität in den Humanwissenschaften. *Wiener Medizinische Wochenschrift, 153*(7–8), 183–185.

Meraviglia, M. G. (1999). Critical analysis of spirituality and its empirical indicators: Prayer and meaning in life. *Journal of Holistic Nursing, 17,* 18–33.

National Opinion Research Center. (2007). General Social Survey. *GSS cumulative datafile 1972–2006.* Chicago: Author. Retrieved from *www3.norc.org/GSS/website/Data/Analysis.*

Neale, R. E., & Parr, D. L. (2002). *The magic mirror.* Seattle, WA: Hermetic Press.

O'Connor, P. J., Pronk, N. P., Tan, A., & Whitehead, R. R. (2005). Characteristics of adults who use prayer as an alternative therapy. *American Journal of Health Promotion, 19,* 369–375.

Ortiz, D. (1994). *Strong magic.* Silver Spring, MD: Kaufman & Greenberg.

Ostow, M., & Scharfstein, B.-A. (1954). *The need to believe.* New York: International Universities Press.

Otto, R. (1923). *The idea of the holy.* New York: Oxford University Press.

Pargament, K. I. (1997). *The psychology of religion and coping.* New York: Guilford Press.

Pargament, K. I., Kennell, J., Hathaway, W., Grevengoed, N., Newman, J., & Jones, W. (1988). Religion and the problem-solving process: Three styles of coping. *Journal for the Scientific Study of Religion, 27,* 90–104.

Parker, G. B., & Brown, L. B. (1982). Coping behaviors that mediate between life events and depression. *Archives of General Psychiatry, 39,* 1386–1391.

Peacock, J. L. (1975). *Consciousness and change.* New York: Wiley.

Pilgrim, R. B. (1978). Ritual. In T. W. Hall (Ed.), *Introduction to the study of religion* (pp. 64–84). New York: Harper & Row.

Poloma, M. M., & Gallup, G. H., Jr. (1990, November). *Religiosity, forgiveness and life satisfaction: An exploratory study.* Paper presented at the convention of the Society for the Scientific Study of Religion, Virginia Beach, VA.

Poloma, M. M., & Gallup, G. H., Jr. (1991). *Varieties of prayer: A survey report.* Philadelphia, PA: Trinity Press International.

Pruyser, P. (1968). *A dynamic psychology of religion.* New York: Harper & Row.

Pruyser, P. (1983). *The play of the imagination: Toward a psychoanalysis of culture.* New York: International Universities Press.

Puglisi, M. (1929). *Prayer.* New York: Macmillan.

Ragen, N. (1998). *The ghost of Hannah Mendes.* New York: Simon & Schuster.

Rappaport, R. A. (2004). *Ritual and religion in the making of humanity.* New York: Cambridge University Press.

Reik, T. (1946). *Ritual: Psychoanalytic studies.* New York: Farrar Strauss.

Richards, C., & Hildebrand, L. (1990). *Prayes that prevail.* Tulsa, OK: Victory House.

Roberts, K. A. (1984). *Religion in sociological perspective.* Homewood, IL: Dorsey.

Rothbaum, F., Weisz, T. R., & Snyder, S. S. (1982). Changing the world and changing the self: A two-process model of perceived control. *Journal of Personality & Social Psychology, 42,* 5–37.

Septimus, Y. (2012). *On the boundaries of prayer.* Tübingen, Germany: Mohr Siebeck.

Sloan, R. P. (2006). *Blind faith.* New York: St. Martin's Press.

Sloan, R. P., & Bagiella, E. (2002). Claims about religious involvement and health outcomes. *Annals of Behavioral Medicine, 24,* 14–21.

Smith, J. Z. (1996). The bare facts of ritual. In R. L. Grimes (Ed.), *Readings in ritual studies* (pp. 473–483). Upper Saddle River, NJ: Prentice Hall. (Original work published 1982)

Sørensen, J. (2007). *A cognitive theory of magic*. New York: AltaMira.

Sosis, S., & Alcorta, C. (2003). Signaling, solidarity and the sacred: The evolution of religious behavior. *Evolutionary Anthropology, 12*, 264–274.

Spilka, B., & Ladd, K. L. (2013). *The psychology of prayer: A scientific approach*. New York: Guilford Press.

Stein, R. (2006, March 24). Researchers look at prayer and healing. *Washington Post*. Retrieved from *www.washingtonpost.com/wp-dyn/content/article/2006/03/23/AR2006032302177.html*.

Sumner, J. (2003). Relations of suspicion: Critical theory and interdisciplinary relations. *History of Intellectual Culture, 3*(1), 1–12.

Tartaro, J., Luecken, L. J., & Gunn, H. E. (2005). Exploring heart and soul: Effects of religiosity/spirituality and gender on blood pressure and cortisol stress responses. *Journal of Health Psychology, 10*, 753–766.

Tremmel, W. C. (1984). *Religion: What is it?* New York: Holt, Rinehart & Winston.

Versnel, H. S. (1991). Some reflections on the relationship magic-religion. *Numen, 38*(2), 177–197.

Victor, J. S. (1992). Ritual abuse and the moral crusade against satanism. *Journal of Psychology and Theology, 20*, 248–253.

Wachholtz, A., & Sambamoorthi, U. (2011). National trends in prayer use as a coping mechanism for health concerns: Changes from 2002 to 2007. *Journal of Religion and Spirituality, 3*, 67–77.

Watts, F., & Williams, M. (1988). *The psychology of religious knowing*. Cambridge, UK: Cambridge University Press.

Whitley, R. (1964). *Religious behavior*. Englewood Cliffs, NJ: Prentice Hall.

Wonder, T., & Minch, S. (1996). *The books of Wonder*. (Vols. 1–2). Seattle, WA: Hermetic Press.

Wulff, D. (1997). *Psychology of religion: Classic and contemporary views* (2nd ed.). New York: Wiley.

23

Religious Fundamentalism, Right-Wing Authoritarianism, and Prejudice

Insights from Meta-Analyses, Implicit Social Cognition, and Social Neuroscience

Wade C. Rowatt, Megan Johnson Shen, Jordan P. LaBouff, and Alfredo Gonzalez

Religious fundamentalism (RF) and right-wing authoritarianism (RWA) are widely studied psychological dimensions (cf. Altemeyer & Hunsberger, 2005) that predict and explain a range of social, cognitive, and behavioral processes, including but not limited to evaluative reactions to political processes (McFarland, 2010), decisions about medical treatment (Vess, Arndt, Cox, Routledge, & Goldenberg, 2009), social attitudes (McCleary, Quillivan, Foster, & Williams, 2011; Johnson et al., 2011), and many social behaviors (see Nielsen, Donahue, & Hatton, Chapter 16, this volume). Since Altemeyer and Hunsberger's chapter in the first edition of this *Handbook*, several theoretical, methodological, and statistical advances have aided in the understanding of RF and RWA. The present chapter reviews many of these advances as well as recent research on RF, RWA, and *prejudice*—a negative evaluation or attitude toward a group or toward members of a group (Stangor, 2009). Given strengths of a multilevel interdisciplinary paradigm and limits of a solely personality or individual difference approach to understanding prejudice (see Brown, 2010, pp. 18–20; Mavor, Louis, & Laythe, 2011), we also broaden our review to include individual studies that used (1) implicit measures of religiosity or prejudice, in part to circumvent issues with the self-report of socially sensitive attitudes; (2) mediation path analysis to remedy limits of multiple regression; or (3) priming techniques that leverage the power of experimental methods. Finally, we look forward to what advances in social neuroscience offer the psychology of religion, RF, RWA, and prejudice.

RF AND RWA OPERATIONALLY DEFINED

From a social-personality psychological perspective, RF includes "the belief that there is one set of religious teachings that clearly contain the . . . essential inerrant truth about humanity and the deity" (Altemeyer & Hunsberger, 1992, p. 118). RF is most frequently measured using brief self-report scales designed to be noncreedal (Altemeyer & Hunsberger, 1992, 2004), meaning religious fundamentalists from virtually any religious tradition should score high on the scale (Hunsberger, 1996; Paloutzian, 1999a). Example RF scale items include "To lead the best, most meaningful life, one must belong to the one, fundamentally true religion" and reverse-keyed "Scriptures may contain general truths, but they should NOT be considered completely, literally true from beginning to end" (Altemeyer & Hunsberger, 2004, p. 52). Previous RF measures, which included explicit references to Christ and the Bible (Waller, Kojetin, Bouchard, Lykken, & Tellegen, 1990; Wiggins, 1966), are most appropriate for samples composed entirely of Christians. For readers interested in the history of Protestant fundamentalism or religious fundamentalism among other faith traditions (e.g., Amish, Pentecostal, Islam), we highly recommend Hood, Hill, and Williamson (2005).

RWA is a blend of three related facets: conventionalism, submission to authority, and authoritarian use of aggression (Altemeyer, 1996; Duckitt, Bizumic, Krauss, & Heled, 2010; Mavor, Louis, & Sibley, 2010; Paloutzian, 1999b). Right-wing authoritarians agree that people should adhere to social conventions and submit to legitimate authorities. Right-wing authoritarians also condone the use of aggression against people they perceive to disobey authorities, violate laws, or deviate from social conventions.

RWA is most often measured with a 30-item scale (Altemeyer & Hunsberger, 1992), but 10-item (Mavor et al., 2010; Smith & Winter, 2002), 18-item, and 36-item RWA scales are also available (Duckitt et al., 2010). Although RWA is often treated as a unitary construct, a three-component model (conventionalism, submission to authority, and authoritarian use of aggression) has provided better fit than a one-component model (Mavor et al., 2010). Examples on Smith and Winter's (2002) 10-item scale include "What our country really needs is a strong, determined leader who will crush evil, and take us back to our true path" (RWA aggression), "What our country needs most is discipline, with everyone following our leader in unity" (RWA submission), and reverse-scored "Everyone should have their own lifestyle, religious beliefs, and sexual preferences, even if it makes them different from everyone else" (RWA conventionalism). Duckitt et al. (2010) also found a three-component model of RWA fit better than one- or two-dimensional models. Duckitt and his colleagues interpret the three dimensions as conservatism (i.e., RWA submission), traditionalism (i.e., RWA conventionalism), and authoritarianism (i.e., RWA aggression). They also conceptualize RWA more as a social attitude than a personality trait.

Another major recent advance was the discovery by Mavor, Macleod, Boal, and Louis (2009) that a widely used measure of RF was confounded with RWA conventionalism. Removal of the statistical confound revealed RF and prejudice were positively correlated (not negatively or unrelated as other researchers had reported). In the mediation section later in this chapter, we review additional research that has used this tripartite conceptualization of RWA to disentangle RWA from RF. Next, however, we briefly discuss evolutionary and personality theoretical perspectives on relationships between RWA, RF, and prejudice.

THEORETICAL FOUNDATION FOR RELATIONSHIPS BETWEEN RWA, RF, AND PREJUDICE

Some clues about why RF, RWA, and prejudices are related can be found in psychological theories about the evolution of religion more broadly (see Kirkpatrick, Chapter 6, this volume; Norenzayan & Shariff, 2008), dual-process models of personality (see Sibley & Duckitt, 2008), and social-psychological theories about terror management, realistic group conflict, and social identity (see Brown, 2010). From an evolutionary perspective, Kirkpatrick (2005), for example, posits religiousness is a by-product of other adaptive psychological mechanisms, such as those that support the formation and maintenance of alliances that lead to cooperation among persons with shared beliefs (Kirkpatrick, 2005; Wilson, 1978). For humans and other social animals, the formation and maintenance of strong coalitions and alliances usually increases personal, familial, and group success. However, as alliances form, the potential for within- and between-group conflict increases, especially if resources are limited or groups do not have shared beliefs or goals. According to Kirkpatrick (2005, p. 265), "Fundamentalism is largely about establishing and defending a particular set of beliefs and practices that define an in-group; those failing to accept and live by these particular standards are assigned to the out-group." Kirkpatrick (2005, p. 259) theorized that "our evolved psychology appears to contain a suite of mechanisms for distinguishing the good guys from the bad guys, or the in-group from the out-group, and then giving preferential treatment to the good guys."

That people form social groups based in part on religious beliefs has beneficial and detrimental social consequences. For example, religious fundamentalism correlates positively with helping in-group members (Blogowska & Saroglou, 2011; Gribbins & Vandeberg, 2011). But RF and RWA also correlate positively with out-group derogation, prejudice (Johnson, Rowatt, LaBouff, Patock-Peckham, & Carlisle, 2012; Rowatt, LaBouff, Johnson, Froese, & Tsang, 2009), and aggression (Vincent, Parrott, & Peterson, 2011). RWA even predicts support for a military attack (McFarland, 2005).

From a personality perspective, one finds metaphorical roots of RF, RWA, and prejudice in higher order personality traits such as openness to experience, which has also been interpreted as culture or intellect (John, Naumann, & Soto, 2008). RF and openness to experience were inversely related across nine samples (effect size = −0.21, N = 1,894; Saroglou, 2010). Sibley and Duckitt (2008) found low openness to experience underlies RWA and that effects of openness on prejudice were mediated by RWA (Sibley & Duckitt, 2008). Something about RF, RWA, and low openness may reduce intergroup contact or desire to interact prosocially with persons perceived to violate worldview claims. For example, across a 6-month period, RWA predicted general prejudice toward dangerous groups (criminals, drug dealers) and dissident groups (atheists, prostitutes, gay rights activists; Asbrock, Sibley, & Duckitt, 2010). Religious openness (i.e., quest), on the other hand, was negatively correlated with racial, sexual, and religious prejudices (Leak & Finken, 2011). The broader point here is that RF and RWA predict attitudes toward many groups, and these processes make theoretical sense from social evolutionary and social-personality perspectives.

RF, RWA, AND PREJUDICE: META-ANALYTIC FINDINGS

Dozens of empirical studies document connections between RF, RWA, and prejudices. Instead of reviewing the individual studies separately, we summarize three fairly recent meta-analytic studies that combined results of similar individual studies (Hall, Matz, & Wood, 2010; McCleary et al., 2011; Whitley, 2009). McCleary et al.'s (2011) meta-analysis of 28 studies revealed moderate to large weighted mean effect sizes (shown in parenthesis) for the relationships between RF and authoritarianism (.89), ethnocentrism (.55), militarism (.33), and prejudice (.45).

With regard to racial prejudice more specifically (i.e., attitudes toward African-Americans), Hall et al. (2010) found an average correlation of .41 between authoritarianism and racial prejudice across eight studies. The magnitude of the RF–racial prejudice relationship was smaller ($r = .13$; Hall et al., 2010) across 14 studies about racial prejudice. RF and racial prejudice were somewhat more strongly related in samples that included only religious participants and in studies published before 1986 (Hall et al., 2010). Across eight studies, when RWA was statistically controlled, the average RF–racial prejudice partial correlation was actually *negative* ($r = -.11$; see Hall et al., 2010, Table 5).

Before concluding that RF and racial prejudice are inversely related or unrelated, it is critical to remove statistical overlap between RF and RWA, because both scales include items about conventionalism with regard to sexual attitudes and religiosity (Mavor et al., 2009). Most empirical studies before 2009 did not remove this confound. When the conventionalism confound between RF and RWA was removed, the association between RF and racial prejudice was *positive* ($r = .15$; Mavor et al., 2009). Taken together, findings from both meta-analytic studies and Mavor et al. (2009) indicate a small, positive correlation between RF and racial prejudice.

Several studies also reveal connections between RF, RWA, and negative attitudes toward gay men and lesbians (i.e., sexual prejudice). Across 17 independent samples ($N = 5,237$), Whitley (2009) found a large mean effect size for the relation between RF and sexual prejudice ($d = -0.995$). This effect size corresponds to a correlation of $-.45$. Note that in this meta-analysis, as RF increases, attitudes toward gay men and lesbians become more negative; RF was not associated with a decrease in sexual prejudice. Mavor et al. (2009) also found a strong relationship between RF and sexual prejudice ($\beta = .68$) when RWA aggression was statistically controlled. Among men, there appears to be a particularly strong relationship between RWA and reported condemnation of gay men and lesbians (Stefurak, Taylor, & Mehta, 2010). This fits with Whitley's (2009) meta-analytic finding that the religiosity–sexual prejudice relationship is slightly larger among men than women.

Most studies about relationships between RF, RWA, and prejudice include only self-report measures. Much can be learned from these studies. However, a commonly noted limit of the self-report method is that responses to scale items are fairly easy to control. If motivated, one could easily evaluate an individual or group more positively to create an appearance of being less biased. Some researchers include measures of socially desirable responding as a statistical control. Some use implicit measures that are more difficult to fake (see Jonathan, 2008; Rowatt & Franklin, 2004). There are also limits of the correlational approach used in most studies of RF, RWA, and prejudice. In the next four sections, we integrate findings from individual studies that refined or extended what is known about the psychology of religion, RF, RWA, and prejudice by using implicit measures, advanced mediation analyses, or quasi-experimental social-psychological approaches informed by terror management theory (TMT) or priming religion.

IMPLICIT MEASURES OF BIAS/PREJUDICE AND RELIGIOUSNESS–SPIRITUALITY

The use of alternative measurement approaches has been a fairly recent advance in the study of RF, RWA, and prejudice. Implicit attitude measures, for example, often rely on reaction times to associate targets (blacks, whites) and attributes (pleasant, unpleasant) instead of deliberate responses on a self-report scale, which makes implicit measures more difficult to fake than self-report measures (Teige-Mocigemba, Klauer, & Sherman, 2010). LaBouff, Rowatt, Johnson, Thedford, and Tsang (2010) developed and validated an implicit measure of religiousness-spirituality that accounted for unique variability in self-reported attitudes toward gay men and lesbians even when self-reported RF and RWA aggression were statistically controlled.

Researchers have also examined how self-reported RF and RWA associated with measures of implicit racial and sexual prejudice. Somewhat weak associations were found between RF and both implicit racial ($r = .10$; Rowatt & Franklin, 2004) and implicit sexual ($r = .23$; Rowatt et al., 2006) prejudice. RWA, on the other hand, remained a strong correlate of implicit racial prejudice (Rowatt & Franklin, 2004) and implicit sexual prejudice (Jonathan, 2008) when RF and Christian orthodoxy were statistically controlled in regression models. Before concluding that RF and implicit prejudice are weakly linked, however (cf. Laythe, Finkel, & Kirkpatrick, 2001; Rowatt & Franklin, 2004), recall Mavor's critique that the conventionalism artifact between RF and RWA conceals the positive relationship between RF and prejudices (Mavor et al., 2009, 2011). Reexamining these relationships after removing the overlap between RF and RWA may reveal that RF is more strongly linked to implicit prejudice than previously believed.

Mediation path analysis using structural equation modeling (SEM) provides a better test of these relationships than multiple regression, in part because the mediation approach takes into account measurement error and allows for estimating confidence intervals of mediators in the relationship between an independent and dependent variable (see MacKinnon, 2008; MacKinnon, Lockwood, & Williams, 2004; Schumacker & Lomax, 2004). See Leak and Finken (2011) for an SEM study of how different dimensions of religiousness associate with racial, sexual, and religious prejudices. Next we discuss several studies that identified mediators between RF, RWA, and prejudices.

MEDIATION STUDIES OF RF, RWA, AND PREJUDICE

Several mediators of the RF–prejudice relationship have been hypothesized, such as RWA (Johnson et al., 2012; Laythe et al., 2001; Rowatt & Franklin, 2004) and social-cognitive variables (Hill, Cohen, Terrell, & Nagoshi, 2010). Given the strong positive relationship between RF and RWA, it makes sense to determine whether the RF–prejudice relationship weakens when RWA components are statistically controlled. However, the patterns are different when predicting prejudices that are proscribed (e.g., racial) and nonproscribed (e.g., sexual). RWA aggression mediated the relationship between RF and prejudice toward Arabs and African Americans (Johnson et al., 2012). In a methodologically similar study, RF was a stronger predictor of sexual prejudice than RWA aggression or RWA submission (Johnson, Rowatt, & LaBouff, 2011). Johnson et al. (2012) concluded that RWA aggression underlies societally prohibited racial prejudices and RF underlies prejudice toward perceived value violators.

Several researchers have found differences in how religious fundamentalists and right-wing authoritarians think about knowledge, the self, and others (i.e., social-cognitive style). In general, RF and RWA are associated with a relatively inflexible social-cognitive style (Hunsberger, Pratt, & Pancer, 1994; Hunsberger, Alisat, Pancer, & Pratt, 1996). Two research teams used SEM to examine specific social-cognitive mediators of the RF–prejudice relationship (Brandt & Reyna, 2010; Hill et al., 2010). Eric Hill and his colleagues (2010), for example, found persons high in need for structure and low in fear of invalidity had higher scores on measures of both RF and prejudices. Preference for consistency (PFC) partially mediated the relationship between RF and a proscribed prejudice (i.e., hostile sexism). PFC represents a cognitively rigid way of thinking that supports prejudices generally discouraged in the host culture (Hill et al., 2010). Need for cognition, on the other hand, partially mediated the relationship between RF and nonproscribed sexual prejudice and benevolent sexism. Cognitively elaborating on arguments is a strong tendency of persons with high need for cognition. Hill et al. (2010) suggest that increased critical thinking by RFs could reduce the expression of sexual prejudice or benevolent sexism.

Using data from the General Social Survey, Brandt and Reyna (2010) confirmed that need for closure partially mediated a RF–sexual prejudice relationship. Closed-mindedness and preference for order also partially mediated the relationship between RF and "seven items culled from Altemeyer's RWA scale expressing the desire to protect society from immoral or deviant groups" (Brandt & Reyna, 2010, p. 720). Taken together, these studies indicate there are different social-cognitive pathways between RF and proscribed versus nonproscribed prejudices.

One study examined how personal beliefs about knowledge influenced the RF–RWA relationship (Hathcoat & Barnes, 2010). Personal epistemology partially mediated the RF–RWA relationship. That is, RF and RWA correlated very strongly ($r = .81$), but the relationship weakened significantly when facets of beliefs about knowledge were included in the model (Hathcoat & Barnes, 2010). Preference for simple, absolute, certain knowledge or laws could make it difficult for religious fundamentalists or authoritarians to integrate information about the world that is often complex, contradictory, or inconsistent.

Several other psychological variables likely contribute to expression of prejudice or tolerance too, such as empathy or morality (Mavor & Gallois, 2008; McFarland, 2010), support for the status quo (Jost, 2011; Jost, Banaji, & Nosek, 2004), and perhaps aspects of political ideology (Cohen et al., 2009; Jost, Glaser, Kruglanski, & Sulloway, 2003). Jost et al. (2003), for example, reviewed several studies that reported positive correlations between RWA and personal need for structure, perception of the world as a dangerous place, and persuasive impact of threatening messages. Jackson and Esses (1997) theorized and found the degree of threat to values posed by a group and ascription of responsibility for a problem affected whether religious fundamentalists would help and the type of help offered.

Connections between RF, less integrative or cognitive complexity, and reactions to worldview threats are also found in studies from a TMT perspective. Friedman (2008), for example, found that RF was associated with responses to mortality salience that were "less cognitively complex, contained more positive emotion, and were more future and socially oriented" (p. 216). As reviewed in Hood and Chen (Chapter 21, this volume) and in the next section, how people cognitively interpret threats (like reminders of death) interacts with religiousness to affect social evaluations and behavior.

RF, TMT, AND WORLDVIEW DEFENSE

According to terror management theorists, existential concerns and death anxiety are managed, in part, by immersion in a cultural worldview that provides a sense of meaning, purpose, and standards for behavior (Greenberg, Landau, Losloff, & Solomon, 2009; Greenberg, Solomon, & Pyszczynski, 1997). When participants are reminded about the inevitability of death, they often engage in more worldview defense by derogating persons in outgroups more than participants who are in nonmortality-salience comparison conditions. For example, in mortality-salience conditions (compared with exam anxiety or dental pain comparison conditions), people are much more punitive toward value-violating persons. For example, across 277 independent effects, the average mortality salience effect size was moderate (.35; Burke, Martens, & Faucher, 2010).

Religiosity is very important to consider in the terror management process because most religions include concepts that presumably buffer existential anxiety about death among believers (e.g., soul, heaven, afterlife). For example, a verse in the Christian New Testament simply reads, "Whosoever believes in Him shall not perish but have everlasting life" (John 3:16). For RFs, who prefer simple and certain knowledge and interpret scripture like this to be true and without error, this verse provides great hope and promise. People with religious doubts, however, might be more concerned about death or experience negative affect when mortality becomes salient. Content analyses of self-reported religious doubts indicated that low RFs had questions about religion/God, whereas high RFs' religious doubts centered on anxiety that others were falling short of religious ideals (Hunsberger et al., 1996). Another classic study tested whether "scaring people to death" would lead to stronger belief in an afterlife. Believers made more aware of death reported increased belief in afterlife (Osarchuk & Tatz, 1973).

Although there are hundreds of TMT experiments, we focus on the handful that included measures of religiousness or RF. A main prediction across studies is that degree of religiousness or RF buffers effects of mortality salience on evaluations of people perceived to violate their worldview. Affirming participants' religious beliefs also strengthens this defense. When mortality was salient, intrinsically religious persons experienced less death-thought accessibility when their religious beliefs were affirmed than did less intrinsically religious persons (Jonas & Fischer, 2006). Death reminders also appeared to motivate religious fundamentalists to rely more on faith alone for medical treatment (Vess et al., 2009). Confronting fundamentalists with inconsistencies or contradictions in the scripture they believe to be without error could weaken their religion-based psychological defenses and allow thoughts of death to creep in. For example, after reading New Testament scripture passages containing inconsistencies or contradictions, accessibility of death-related thoughts increased among fundamentalist Christians but not among Christians low in fundamentalism (Friedman & Rholes, 2007).

Other nonreligious aspects of the self are critical to understanding the terror management process. For example, perceptions of the self as a person of worth (i.e., self-esteem; Harmon-Jones et al., 1997) and secure attachment (Mikulincer & Florian, 2000) also moderated mortality salience effects in TMT experiments. Friedman and Rholes (2009) found that how people construe the self in relation to others (i.e., independent or interdependent self-construal) interacts with RF in the terror management process. For persons with lower RF scores, interdependent self-construal was negatively correlated with death awareness. Perhaps people lower in RF rely more on social connections to find meaning or to cope with existential concerns. Among those with higher RF scores (who presumably already have sufficient defenses), there was no relationship between self-construal and death thought accessibility (Friedman & Rholes, 2009).

The effects of religious belief and mortality salience occur across religions and cultures. Iranian college students in a mortality-salience condition, for example, expressed more anti-Western sentiment than those in a dental pain-salience condition (Rothschild, Abdollahi, & Pyszczynski, 2009). This effect was "softened" somewhat when an aspect of benevolent religion was primed. That is, when exposed to compassionate Islamic values, those in a mortality-salience condition responded with less anti-Western sentiment than those in the dental pain-salience condition. Among American college students with high RF scores primed with biblical compassion (e.g., "Love your neighbor as yourself"), those in a mortality-salience condition expressed less support for extreme military action against an outgroup than low RFs (Rothschild et al., 2009). In a series of similar experiments, Schumann, Nash, McGregor, and Ross (2011) also found that a simple religious prime (i.e., asking the participant "Which religious belief system do you most identify with?") increased compassionate responses among participants in mortality-salience conditions but not among participants not primed with a question about their religious identification.

Given findings that priming with religion increases compassion or decreases antagonism when threatened, we share the hope of some that aspects of religion could be used to build bridges and facilitate cooperation and peace among individuals and perhaps even groups or nations. However, it appears that most people (including RFs) must be reminded that their religion teaches compassion or love of neighbor for this to occur. Without such reminders about positive religious values, mortality salience alone increased Americans' support for a conservative American political leader and his counterterrorism policies relative to a more liberal American politician (Landau et al., 2004). Furthermore, when sacred texts were perceived to sanction violence, participants across cultures behaved more aggressively (Bushman, Ridge, Das, Key, & Busath, 2007). There may even be a connection between a coalitional component of religious participation and support for suicide attacks (Ginges, Hansen, & Norenzayan, 2009). In sum, increasing awareness of death affects how people think and behave, in very subtle ways, and intrinsic religiousness, RF, and priming religion above awareness moderate the relationship between mortality salience and these outcomes.

PRIMING COMPONENTS OF RELIGION

Several other researchers have primed participants with religious concepts, below or slightly above awareness, to determine how priming religion affects attitudes and behavior. Johnson, LaBouff, and Rowatt (2010) investigated whether priming religion increased trait RF, RWA, or trait or state spirituality and found that it did not. However, priming components of religion is advantageous in part because it makes use of strong experimental designs from which causality can be inferred (Preston, Ritter, & Hernandez, 2010). In essence, priming involves "the temporary activation of an individual's mental representation by the environment and the effect of this activation on various psychological phenomena" (Bargh & Chartrand, 2000, p. 256). Priming produces powerful effects on goals (Fishbach, Friedman, & Kruglanski, 2003; Moskowitz, Gollwitzer, Wasel, & Shaal, 1999), emotions (Lerner, Small, & Loewenstein, 2004), and a variety of norms and behaviors. For example, college students primed with old-age-stereotypical words walked slower down a hall after the experiment than those primed with "young-person" words (Bargh, Chen, & Burrows, 1996; but see Doyen, Klein, Pichon, & Cleeremans, 2012). People primed with the goal to visit a library spoke more quietly and demonstrated increased accessibility of silence concepts (Aarts & Dijksterhuis, 2003).

Bargh and Chartrand (2000) provide procedural and theoretical specifics about how priming is thought to work. Although there are usually small variations in methodology, subtle presentations of religious stimuli influence a wide variety of attitudes and behaviors. Priming religious concepts increased helping (Pichon, Boccato, & Saroglou, 2007; Pichon & Saroglou, 2009), generosity (Shariff & Norenzayan, 2007), honesty (Randolph-Seng & Nielsen, 2007), self-control (Fishbach et al., 2003, Study 2), and submission to authority (Saroglou, Corneille, & Van Cappellen, 2009) and decreased moral hypocrisy (Carpenter & Marshall, 2009) and antagonism (Schumann et al., 2011). However, priming religion also increased positive attitudes toward a religious extremist (Ginges et al., 2009) and increased expression of racial and sexual prejudices (Johnson, Rowatt, & LaBouff, 2010, 2011). LaBouff (2011) found that participants in religious settings displayed more implicit sexual prejudice than participants tested in neutral settings.

Some scholars have noticed that priming religious concepts affects both prosociality and prejudice, which appears somewhat paradoxical. To address this apparently contradictory pattern, Preston, Ritter, and Hernandez (2010) posit that supernatural primes like "God" activate goals to live up to standards of supernatural agents (e.g., helping, honesty), whereas religion primes like "Bible" or "church" activate goals to protect ingroup values. Future experiments are needed to investigate the effects of priming religious agents, religious institutions, or spiritual concepts in the same series of studies, to examine whether RF and RWA can be primed, to determine whether priming concepts from world religions other than Christianity replicate effects, and to identify the underlying mechanism(s).

Given the complications of disentangling how priming various components of religion affect attitudes and behaviors, a social-neuroscience approach could help scholars better understand how priming religion affects neural processes that also underlie social evaluations. Inzlicht and Tullet (2010) found that religious believers primed with religion experienced reduced electrical activity in an area of the brain thought to operate like a cortical alarm (i.e., anterior cingulate cortex) when making simple errors. To better understand RF, RWA, and prejudice, many more studies are needed like that of Inzlicht and colleagues (Inzlicht, McGregor, Hirsh, & Nash, 2009; Inzlicht & Tallett, 2010) and others that incorporate social-neuroscience methods such as electroencephalograph (EEG), facial electromyography (EMG), or functional magnetic resonance imaging (fMRI) (Amodio & Lieberman, 2009; Harmon-Jones & Beer, 2009).

SOCIAL NEUROSCIENCE AND RELIGION

At present, the fields of psychology of religion and social neuroscience (Harmon-Jones & Winkielman, 2007) are progressing relatively independent of each other. Notable exceptions include Inzlicht and colleagues' research (2009; Inzlicht & Tullett, 2010), EEG and fMRI studies of Carmelite nuns during mystical experience (Beauregard & Paquette, 2006, 2008), a preliminary single photon emission computed tomography study of meditators (Newberg et al., 2001), fMRI studies of different dimensions of religious belief (Kapogiannis et al., 2009) and self-referential processing (Han et al., 2008), and others reviewed in McNamara and Butler (Chapter 11, this volume). Asp, Ramchandran, and Tranel (2012) discovered that patients with damage to the ventromedial prefrontal cortex (vmPFC) reported higher levels of RWA and RF than neurological and medical comparison patients. They also implicated the vmPFC in psychological doubting (Asp et al., 2012). Additional social-neuroscience research is needed to make better sense of RF and RWA processes as well.

Clearly complex activity occurs beneath the skin (in brain and body) when RFs or RWAs confront someone who deviates from their interpretation of scripture or other aspects of their worldview. Much more can be learned from measuring electrical activity in the brain or facial muscles as people make judgments or evaluate others. Inzlicht et al. (2009) found religious zeal was associated with less neural activity after making errors on a Stroop task, but not following correct responses. Items on the religious zeal scale overlap somewhat with RF (i.e., religious zeal = "I aspire to live and act according to my religious beliefs; My religious beliefs are grounded in objective truth; I would support a war that defended my religious beliefs"). Inzlicht et al. (2009) also found that greater belief in God was associated with less event-related negativity (ERN) following errors on the Stroop task. The ERN component of an EEG peaks at about 50 to 80 m after a response and is typically larger for incorrect than correct responses (Bartholow & Amodio, 2009). Belief in God was assessed with a single reverse-keyed item (1 = certain God exists; 5 = certain God does not exist). Inzlicht et al. (2009) suggested that the source of the ERN may be the anterior cingulate cortex, which in another study was implicated in conflict monitoring (Amodio, Devine, & Harmon-Jones, 2007, pp. 356–357). Future research could investigate whether RF is associated with less ERN activity following errors on a more difficult perceptual task on which more errors occur, such as the flanker task (Amodio, Devine, & Harmon-Jones, 2008; Eriksen & Schultz, 1979; Ochsner, 2007).

In addition to EEG, facial EMG methods could be very useful in RF prejudice research. One possibility is to measure electrical activity caused by facial muscle contractions in response to stimuli that evoke an affective or emotional response. It is known that startle eyeblink responses are amplified very shortly after the onset of negative affective stimuli and inhibited very soon after positive stimuli are presented (Lang, Bradley, & Cuthbert, 1990). As such, the startle eyeblink response can be used to determine degree of race or sexual orientation bias (Amodio, Harmon-Jones, & Devine, 2003; Mahaffey, Bryan, & Hutchison, 2005; Vanman, Saltz, Nathan, & Warren, 2004). If a person has positive feelings toward gay men or lesbians, the magnitude of his or her startle response to images of gay men or lesbians would be less than that of a person who has negative feelings toward gay men or lesbians.

In order to more fully understand RF, RWA, and prejudice, it may also be important to consider different motivations to control personal prejudices. Internal or external motivations to control prejudice (Plant & Devine, 1998), for example, moderate startle eyeblink modulation (Amodio et al., 2003) and connections between RF and prejudice (Ford, Brignall, VanValey, & Macaluso, 2009). Most people have an automatic race bias (Payne, 2001), but some are more motivated or able to regulate or inhibit the expression of bias after becoming aware of the negative response (Amodio et al., 2004; Amodio et al., 2008). Startle eyeblink modulation in response to African American faces, for example, was lower among persons with high internal and low external motivation to control racial prejudice (when contrasted with those with low external and high internal motivation to respond without prejudice; Amodio et al., 2003). It is possible that some religious fundamentalists, especially those with low motivation to respond without prejudice, will display more automatic race bias or experience more startle eyeblink modulation in response to photos representing individuals in historically disadvantaged groups (e.g., gay men and lesbians). It is also possible that those with high RF or RWA scale scores are simply less motivated to respond without prejudice, which would mean they would be less concerned about expressing prejudice.

In light of these and other social-neuroscience findings, our best guess is that race and sexual orientation biases (and perhaps others based on religious disbelief or worldview inconsistencies) occur very early in the stream of perceptual processing, and that some people (e.g., those who internalize religious values) are more motivated and able to control the expression of bias. We suspect that religious fundamentalists and right-wing authoritarians are less internally or externally motivated to overcome automatic biases and, therefore, experience less anxiety when making errors, and this may lead some to report more prejudice toward persons, dislike of value-violating behaviors, and support for potentially unfair or discriminatory policies. The startle eyeblink methodology and other social-neuroscience methods hold great promise for better understanding these relationships.

ROOTS OF RF AND RWA: CLUES FROM BEHAVIORAL GENETICS

Before concluding, it is important to touch on factors that contribute to variability in RF or RWA within persons and populations, such as genetic dissimilarity or nonshared environment. Certainly, there are strong socialization influences on personal religion, specific religious beliefs, RF, and authoritarianism (Altemeyer, 2003). Parent and child religiousness often correlate positively (which leads some to give more weight to common environment when explaining how RF or RWA develops). However, genetic and environmental influences are confounded within biological families. Behavioral genetic techniques are used to tease apart genetic and environmental influences on many traits, and often show that nonshared environmental influences are as important as or more important than common/shared environment (Plomin, DeFries, McClearn, & Rutter, 1997). Waller et al. (1990) found that about 46% of the variability in Wiggins's (1966) RF scale scores was attributable to genetic similarity and 54% to environmental factors. Waller et al. (1990, p. 141) concluded that "social scientists will have to discard the a priori assumption that individual differences in religious and other social attitudes are solely influenced by environmental factors." McCourt, Bouchard, Lykken, Tellegen, and Keyes (1999) also found that genetic influence and unshared environment accounted for more observed variance in RWA (50% and 35%, respectively) than shared environment. A strong correlation between RWA scale scores was found among genetically identical twins reared in different environments but not among fraternal twins reared apart.

Both genetic and environmental factors contribute to variability in RF and RWA in a population, not environment alone. As scholars continue to think about how RF and RWA develop within persons and populations, we can certainly look to family (for both genetic and common-environment contributions). However, we should not discount the powerful roles of nonshared influences in making people different and the socialization process, which may increase attitudinal similarity. For example, in a clever longitudinal study of peers' ideology and prejudices, Poteat, and Spanierman (2010) found friends' ideological beliefs predicted the prejudiced attitudes of the individuals with whom they affiliate. Usually social scientists study a sample of unrelated individuals to understand RF, RWA, and prejudices. There could be value in studying genetically related individuals and members of groups bound by ideology as well. For it is in the context of family, peers, and relatively small groups that RF, RWA, and prejudicial attitudes likely develop.

CONCLUSION

We are encouraged that so many researchers are embracing rigorous methodological and statistical techniques (e.g., meta-analysis, mediation path analyses with SEM, priming, behavioral genetic models) to investigate RF, RWA, and important social, cognitive, and behavioral processes. However, much is yet to be learned, especially about the social neuroscience of RF, RWA, and prejudice. We encourage the continued use of measures of RF and RWA in psychology of religion research in large part because the constructs account for unique variability in important psychological processes and outcomes. However, we urge researchers to remove the RWA-conventionalism facet in models than include RWA and RF to predict prejudice or other outcomes (Johnson et al., 2012; Mavor et al., 2009). Also, although RWA and RF are important variables, evaluative, behavioral, and social reactions cannot be understood solely from a personality/individual difference perspective. Broader social-psychological (Brown, 2010) or social-neuroscience perspectives (Amodio et al., 2004) will likely be needed.

In closing, although RF and RWA appear to be moderately related to prejudices, as other chapters in this handbook detail, the same religions that some fundamentalists believe to be true and without error also teach forgivingness, tolerance, and virtuous self-control—positive processes many religious people around the world strive to cultivate and practice. Our hope is that people can draw strength and virtues from their religion, or other personal beliefs and traditions, and put those virtues into action in relationships at home and abroad.

REFERENCES

Aarts, H., & Dijksterhuis, A. (2003). The silence of the library: Environment, situational norm and social behavior. *Journal of Personality and Social Psychology, 84,* 18–28.

Altemeyer, B. (1996). *The authoritarian specter.* Cambridge, MA: Harvard University Press.

Altemeyer, B. (2003). Why do religious fundamentalists tend to be prejudiced? *The International Journal for the Psychology of Religion, 13,* 17–28.

Altemeyer, B., & Hunsberger, B. (1992). Authoritarianism, religious fundamentalism, quest, and prejudice. *The International Journal for the Psychology of Religion, 2,* 113–133.

Altemeyer, B., & Hunsberger, B. (2004). A revised religious fundamentalism scale: The short and sweet of it. *The International Journal for the Psychology of Religion, 14,* 47–54.

Altemeyer, B., & Hunsberger, B. (2005). Fundamentalism and authoritarianism. In R. F. Paloutzian & C. L. Park (Eds.), *Handbook of the psychology of religion and spirituality* (pp. 378–393). New York: Guilford Press.

Amodio, D. M., Devine, P. G., & Harmon-Jones, E. (2007). Mechanisms for the regulation of intergroup responses: Insights from a social neuroscience approach. In E. Harmon-Jones & P. Winkielman (Eds.), *Social neuroscience: Integrating biological and psychological explanations of social behavior* (pp. 353–375). New York: Guilford Press.

Amodio, D. M., Devine, P. G., & Harmon-Jones, E. (2008). Individual differences in the regulation of intergroup bias: The role of conflict monitoring and neural signals for control. *Journal of Personality and Social Psychology, 94,* 60–74.

Amodio, D. M., Devine, P. G., Harmon-Jones, E., Curtin, J. J., Hartley, S. L., & Covert, A. E. (2004). Neural signals for the detection of unintentional race bias. *Psychological Science, 15,* 88–93.

Amodio, D. M., Harmon-Jones, E., & Devine, P. G. (2003). Individual differences in the activation and control of affective race bias as assessed by startle eyeblink response and self-report. *Journal of Personality and Social Psychology, 84,* 738–753.

Amodio, D. M., & Lieberman, M. D. (2009). Pictures in our heads: Contributions of fMRI to the study of prejudice and stereotyping. In T. Nelson (Ed.), *Handbook of prejudice, stereotyping, and discrimination* (pp. 347–365). New York: Psychology Press.

Asbrock, F., Sibley, C. G., & Duckitt, J. (2010). Right-wing authoritarianism and social dominance orientation and the dimensions of generalized prejudice: A longitudinal test. *European Journal of Personality, 24,* 324–340.

Asp, E., Ramchandran, K., & Tranel, D. (2012). Authoritarianism, religious fundamentalism, and the human prefrontal cortex. *Neuropsychology, 26,* 414–421.

Bargh, J. A., & Chartrand, T. L. (2000). The mind in the middle: A practical guide to priming and automaticity research. In H. T. Reis & C. M. Judd (Eds.), *Handbook of research methods in social and personality psychology* (pp. 253–285). New York: Cambridge University Press.

Bargh, J. A., Chen, M., & Burrows, L. (1996). Automaticity of social behavior: Direct effects of trait construct and stereotype activation on action. *Journal of Personality and Social Psychology, 71,* 230–244.

Bartholow, B. D., & Amodio, D. M. (2009). Using event-related brain potentials in social psychology research: A brief tutorial and review. In E. Harmon-Jones & J. Beer (Eds.), *Methods in social neuroscience* (pp. 198–232). New York: Guilford Press.

Beauregard, M., & Paquette, V. (2006). Neural correlates of a mystical experience in Carmelite nuns. *Neuroscience Letters, 405,* 186–190.

Beauregard, M., & Paquette, V. (2008). EEG activity in Carmelite nuns during a mystical experience. *Neuroscience Letters, 444,* 1–4.

Blogowska, J., & Saroglou, V. (2011). Religious fundamentalism and limited prosociality as a function of the target. *Journal for the Scientific Study of Religion, 50,* 44–60.

Brandt, M. J., & Reyna, C. (2010). The role of prejudice and the need for closure in religious fundamentalism. *Personality and Social Psychology Bulletin, 36,* 715–725.

Brown, R. (2010). *Prejudice: Its social psychology* (2nd ed.). Malden, MA: Wiley-Blackwell.

Burke, B. L., Martens, A., & Faucher, E. H. (2010). Two decades of terror management theory: A meta-analysis of morality salience research. *Personality and Social Psychology Review, 14,* 155–195.

Bushman, B. J., Ridge, R. D., Das, E., Key, C. W., & Busath, G. L. (2007). When God sanctions killing: Effects of scriptural violence on aggression. *Psychological Science, 18,* 204–207.

Carpenter, T. P., & Marshall, M. A. (2009). An examination of religious priming: An intrinsic religious motivation in the moral hypocrisy paradigm. *Journal for the Scientific Study of Religion, 48,* 386–393.

Cohen, A. B., Malka, A., Hill, E. D., Thoemmes, F., Hill, P. C., & Sundie, J. M. (2009). Race as a moderator of the relationship between religiosity and political alignment. *Personality and Social Psychology Bulletin, 35,* 271–282.

Doyen, S., Klein, O., Pichon, C.-L., & Cleeremans, A. (2012). Behavioral priming: It's all in the mind, but whose mind? *PLoS One, 7,* 1–7.

Duckitt, J., Bizumic, B., Krauss, S. W., & Heled, E. (2010). A tripartite approach to right-wing authoritarianism: The authoritarian–conservatism–traditionalism model. *Political Psychology, 31,* 685–715.

Eriksen, C. W., & Schultz, D. W. (1979). Information processing in visual search: A continuous flow conception and experimental results. *Perception & Psychophysics, 25,* 249–263.

Fishbach, A., Friedman, R. S., & Kruglanski, A. W. (2003). Leading us not into temptation: Momentary allurements elicit overriding goal activation. *Journal of Personality and Social Psychology, 84,* 296–309.

Ford, T. E., Brignall, T., VanValey, T. L., & Macaluso, M. J. (2009). The unmaking a prejudice: How Christian beliefs related to attitudes toward homosexuals. *Journal for the Scientific Study of Religion, 48,* 146–160.

Friedman, M. (2008). Religious fundamentalism and responses to mortality salience: A quantitative text analysis. *The International Journal for the Psychology of Religion, 18,* 216–237.

Friedman, M., & Rholes, W. S. (2007). Successfully challenging fundamentalist beliefs results in increased death awareness. *Journal of Experimental Social Psychology, 43,* 794–801.

Friedman, M., & Rholes, W. S (2009). Religious fundamentalism and terror management: Differences by interdependent and independent self-construal. *Self and Identity, 8,* 24–44.

Ginges, J., Hansen, I., & Norenzayan, A. (2009). Religion and support for suicide attacks. *Psychological Science, 20,* 224–230.

Greenberg, J., Landau, M., Losloff, S., & Solomon, S. (2009). How our dreams of death transcendence breed prejudice, stereotyping, and conflict: Terror-management theory. In T. Nelson (Ed.), *Handbook of prejudice, stereotyping, and discrimination* (pp. 309–332). New York: Psychology Press.

Greenberg, J., Solomon, S., & Pyszczynski, T. (1997). Terror management theory of self-esteem and social behavior: Empirical assessments and conceptual refinements. In M. P. Zanna (Ed.), *Advances in experimental social psychology* (Vol. 29, pp. 61–139). New York: Academic Press.

Gribbins, T., & Vandeberg, B. (2011). Religious fundamentalism, the need for cognitive closure, and helping. *The International Journal for the Psychology of Religion, 21,* 106–114.

Hall, D. L., Matz, D. C., & Wood, W. (2010). Why don't we practice what we preach?: A meta-analytic review of religious racism. *Personality and Social Psychology Review, 14,* 126–139.

Han, S., Mao, L., Gu, X., Zhu, Y., Ge, J., & Ma, Y. (2008). Neural consequences of religious belief on self-referential processing. *Social Neuroscience, 3,* 1–15.

Harmon-Jones, E., & Beer, J. S. (2009). *Methods in social neuroscience.* New York: Guilford Press.

Harmon-Jones, E., Simon, L., Greenberg, J., Pyszczynski, T., Solomon, S., & McGregor, H. (1997). Terror management theory and self-esteem: Does self-esteem attenuate or intensify mortality salience effects? *Journal of Personality and Social Psychology, 72,* 24–36.

Harmon-Jones, E., & Winkielman, P. (2007). *Social neuroscience: Integrating biological and psychological explanations of social behavior.* New York: Guilford Press.

Hathcoat, J., & Barnes, L. (2010). Explaining the relationship among fundamentalism and authoritarianism: An epistemic connection. *The International Journal for the Psychology of Religion, 20,* 73–84.

Hill, E. D., Cohen, A. B., Terrell, H. K., & Nagoshi, C. T. (2010). The role of social cognition in the religious fundamentalism-prejudice relationship. *Journal for the Scientific Study of Religion, 49,* 724–739.

Hood, R. W., Hill, P. C., & Williamson, W. P. (2005). *The psychology of religious fundamentalism.* New York: Guilford Press.

Hunsberger, B. (1996). Religious fundamentalism, right-wing authoritarianism, and hostility toward homosexuals in non-Christian religious groups. *The International Journal for the Psychology of Religion, 6,* 39–49.

Hunsberger, B., Alisat, S., Pancer, M. S., & Pratt, M. (1996). Religious fundamentalism and religious doubts: Content, connections, and complexity of thinking. *The International Journal for the Psychology of Religion, 6,* 201–220.

Hunsberger, B., Pratt, M., & Pancer, M. S. (1994). Religious fundamentalism and integrative complexity of thought: A relationship for existential content only? *Journal for the Scientific Study of Religion, 33,* 335–346.

Inzlicht, M., McGregor, I., Hirsh, J. B., & Nash, K. (2009). Neural markers of religious conviction. *Psychological Science, 20,* 385–392.

Inzlicht, M., & Tullett, A. M. (2010). Reflecting on God: Religious primes can reduce neurophysiological response to errors. *Psychological Science, 21,* 1184–1190.

Jackson, L. M., & Esses, V. M. (1997). Of scripture and ascription: The relation between religious fundamentalism and intergroup helping. *Personality and Social Psychology Bulletin, 23,* 893–906.

John, O. P., Naumann, L. P., & Soto, C. J. (2008). Paradigm shift to the integrative Big Five trait taxonomy: History, measurement, and conceptual issues. In O. P. John, R. W. Robins, & L. A. Pervin (Eds.), *Handbook of personality: Theory and research* (pp. 114–158). New York: Guilford Press.

Johnson, M. K., LaBouff, J., & Rowatt, W. C. (2010). [*Priming religion's effects on religiousness and spirituality measures*]. Unpublished raw data.

Johnson, M. K., Rowatt, W. C., Bernard-Brak, L. M., Patock-Peckham, J. A., LaBouff, J. P., & Carlisle, R. D. (2011). A meditational analysis of the role of right-wing authoritarianism and religious fundamentalism in the religiosity-prejudice link. *Personality and Individual Differences, 50,* 851–856.

Johnson, M. K., Rowatt, W. C., & LaBouff, J. (2010). Priming Christian religious concepts increases racial prejudice. *Social Psychological and Personality Science, 1,* 119–126.

Johnson, M. K., Rowatt, W. C., & LaBouff, J. (2011). Religion and prejudice revisited: In-group favoritism, out-group derogation, or both? *Psychology of Religion and Spirituality, 4,* 154–168.

Johnson, M. K., Rowatt, W. C., LaBouff, J., Patock-Peckham, J., & Carlisle, R. D. (2012). Facets of right-wing authoritarianism mediate the relationship between religious fundamentalism and attitudes toward Arabs and African-Americans. *Journal for the Scientific Study of Religion, 51,* 128–142.

Jonas, E., & Fischer, P. (2006). Terror management and religion: Evidence that intrinsic religiousness mitigates worldview defense following mortality salience. *Journal of Personality and Social Psychology, 91,* 553–567.

Jonathan, E. (2008). The influence of religious fundamentalism, right-wing authoritarianism, and Christian orthodoxy on explicit and implicit measures of attitudes toward homosexuals. *The International Journal for the Psychology of Religion, 18,* 316–329.

Jost, J. T. (2011). System justification theory as compliment, complement, and corrective to theories of social identification and social dominance. In D. Dunning (Ed.), *Social motivation* (pp. 223–263). New York: Psychology Press.

Jost, J. T., Banaji, M. R., & Nosek, B. A. (2004). A decade of system justification theory: Accumulated evidence of conscious and unconscious bolstering of the status quo. *Political Psychology, 25,* 881–919.

Jost, J. T., Glaser, J., Kruglanski, A. W., & Sulloway, F. J. (2003). Political conservatism as motivated social cognition. *Psychological Bulletin, 129,* 339–375.

Kapogiannis, D., Barbey, A. K., Su, M., Zamboni, G., Krueger, F., & Grafman, J. (2009). Cognitive and neural foundations of religious belief. *Proceedings of the National Academy of Sciences USA, 106,* 4876–4881.

Kirkpatrick, L. A. (2005). *Attachment, evolution, and the psychology of religion.* New York: Guilford Press.

LaBouff, J. P. (2011). *The ecological validity of priming religiousness: Context and culture.* Unpublished doctoral dissertation, Baylor University.

LaBouff, J. P., Rowatt, W. C., Johnson, M. K., Thedford, M., & Tsang, J. (2010). Development and initial validation of an implicit measure of religiousness–spirituality. *Journal for the Scientific Study of Religion, 49,* 439–455.

Landau, M. J., Solomon, S., Greenberg, J., Cohen, F., Pyszczynski, T., Arndt, J., et al. (2004). Deliver us from evil: The effects of mortality salience and reminders of 9/11 on support for President George W. Bush. *Personality and Social Psychology Bulletin, 30,* 1136–1150.

Lang, P. J., Bradley, M. M., & Cuthbert, B. N. (1990). Emotion, attention, and the startle reflex. *Psychological Review, 97,* 377–395.

Laythe, B., Finkel, D. G., & Kirkpatrick, L. A. (2001). Predicting prejudice from religious fundamentalism and right-wing authoritarianism: A multiple-regression approach. *Journal for the Scientific Study of Religion, 40,* 1–10.

Leak, G. K., & Finken, L. L. (2011). The relationship between the constructs of religiousness and prejudice: A structural equation model analysis. *The International Journal for the Psychology of Religion, 21,* 43–62.

Lerner, J. S., Small, D. A., & Loewenstein, G. (2004) Heart strings and purse strings: Carryover effects of emotions on economic decisions. *Psychological Science, 15,* 337–341.

MacKinnon, D. P. (2008). *Introduction to statistical mediational analysis.* Mahwah, NJ: Erlbaum.

MacKinnon, D. P., Lockwood, C. M., & Williams, J. (2004). Confidence limits for the indirect effects: Distribution of the product and resampling methods. *Multivariate Behavioral Research, 39,* 99–128.

Mahaffey, A. L., Bryan, A., & Hutchison, K. E. (2005). Using startle eye blink to measure the affective component of antigay bias. *Basic and Applied Social Psychology, 27,* 37–45.

Mavor, K. I., & Gallois, C. (2008). Social group and moral orientation factors as mediators of religiosity and multiple attitude targets. *Journal for the Scientific Study of Religion, 47,* 361–377.

Mavor, K. I., Louis, W. R., & Laythe, B. (2011). Religion, prejudice, and authoritarianism: Is RWA a boon or bane to the psychology of religion? *Journal for the Scientific Study of Religion, 50,* 22–43.

Mavor, K. I., Louis, W. R., & Sibley, C. G. (2010). A bias-corrected exploratory and confirmatory factor analysis of right-wing authoritarianism: Support for a three-factor structure. *Personality and Individual Differences, 48,* 28–33.

Mavor, K. I., Macleod, C. J., Boal, M. J., & Louis, W. R. (2009). Right-wing authoritarianism, fundamentalism and prejudice revisited: Removing suppression and statistical artefact. *Personality and Individual Differences, 46,* 592–597.

McCleary, D. F., Quillivan, C. C., Foster, L. N., & Williams, R. L. (2011). Meta-analysis of correlational relationships between perspectives of truth in religion and major psychological constructs. *Psychology of Religion and Spirituality, 3*(3), 163–180.

McCourt, K., Bouchard, T. J., Lykken, D. T., Tellegen, A., & Keyes, M. (1999). Authoritarianism revisited: Genetic and environmental influences examined in twins reared apart and together. *Personality and Individual Differences, 27,* 985–1014.

McFarland, S. G. (2005). On the eve of war: Authoritarianism, social dominance and American students' attitudes toward attacking Iraq. *Personality and Social Psychology Bulletin, 31,* 360–367.

McFarland, S. (2010). Authoritarianism, social dominance, and other roots of generalized prejudice. *Political Psychology, 31,* 453–477.

Mikulincer, M., & Florian, V. (2000). Exploring individual differences in reactions to mortality salience: Does attachment style regulate terror management mechanisms? *Journal of Personality and Social Psychology, 79,* 260–273.

Moskowitz, G. B., Gollwitzer, P. M., Wasel, W., & Schaal, B. (1999). Preconscious control of stereotype activation through chronic egalitarian goals. *Journal of Personality and Social Psychology, 77,* 167–184.

Newberg, A. B., Alavi, A., Baime, M., Pourdehnad, M., Santanna, J., & d'Aquili, E. G. (2001). The measurement of regional cerebral blood flow during the complex cognitive task of meditation: A preliminary SPECT study. *Psychiatry Research Neuroimaging, 106,* 113–122.

Norenzayan, A., & Shariff, A. F. (2008). The origin and evolution of religious prosociality. *Science, 322,* 58–62.

Ochsner, K. N. (2007). How thinking controls feeling: A social cognitive neuroscience approach. In E. Harmon-Jones & P. Winkielman (Eds.), *Social neuroscience: Integrating biological and psychological explanations of social behavior* (pp. 106–133). New York: Guilford Press.

Osarchuk, M., & Tatz, S. J. (1973). Effect of induced fear of death on belief in an afterlife. *Journal of Personality and Social Psychology, 27,* 256–260.

Paloutzian, R. F. (1999a). Religious fundamentalism scale. In P. Hill & R. Hood (Eds.), *Measures of religiosity* (pp. 422–425). Birmingham, AL: Religious Education Press.

Paloutzian, R. F. (1999b). The right-wing authoritarianism scale. In P. Hill & R. Hood (Eds.), *Measures of religiosity* (pp. 517–521). Birmingham, AL: Religious Education Press.

Payne, B. K. (2001). Prejudice and perception: The role of automatic and controlled processes in misperceiving a weapon. *Journal of Personality and Social Psychology, 81,* 181–192.

Pichon, I., Boccato, G., & Saroglou, V. (2007). Nonconscious influences of religion on prosociality: A priming study. *European Journal of Social Psychology, 37,* 1032–1045.

Pichon, I., & Saroglou, V. (2009). Religion and helping: The impact of target thinking styles and just-world beliefs. *Archive for the Psychology of Religion, 31,* 215–236.

Plant, E. A., & Devine, P. G. (1998). Internal and external motivation to respond without prejudice. *Journal of Personality and Social Psychology, 75,* 811–832.

Plomin, R., DeFries, J. C., McClearn, G. E., & Rutter, M. (1997). *Behavioral genetics* (3rd ed.). New York: Freeman.

Poteat, V. P., & Spanierman, L. B. (2010). Do the ideological beliefs of peers predict the prejudiced attitudes of other individuals in the group. *Group Processes and Interpersonal Relations, 13,* 495–514.

Preston, J. L., Ritter, R. S., & Hernandez, J. I. (2010). Principles of religious prosociality: A review and reformulation. *Social and Personality Compass, 4,* 574–590.

Randolph-Seng, B., & Nielsen, M. E. (2007). Honesty: One effect of primed religious representations. *The International Journal for the Psychology of Religion, 17*, 303–315.

Rothschild, Z. K., Abdollahi, A., & Pyszczynski, T. (2009). Does peace have a prayer?: The effect of mortality salience, compassionate values, and religious fundamentalism on hostility toward out-groups. *Journal of Experimental Social Psychology, 45*, 816–827.

Rowatt, W. C., & Franklin, L. (2004). Christian orthodoxy, religious fundamentalism, and right-wing authoritarianism as predictors of implicit racial prejudice. *The International Journal for the Psychology of Religion, 14*, 125–138.

Rowatt, W. C., LaBouff, J. P., Johnson, M., Froese, P., & Tsang, J. (2009). Associations among religiousness, social attitudes, and prejudice in a national sample of American adults. *Psychology of Religion and Spirituality, 1*, 14–24.

Rowatt, W. C., Tsang, J., Kelly, J., LaMartina, B., McCullers, M., & McKinley, A. (2006). Associations between religious personality dimensions and implicit homosexual prejudice. *Journal for the Scientific Study of Religion, 45*, 397–406.

Saroglou, V. (2010). Religiousness as a culture adaption of basic traits: A five-factor model perspective. *Personality and Social Psychology Review, 14*, 108–125.

Saroglou, V., Corneille, O., & Van Cappellen, P. (2009). "Speak, Lord, your servant is listening": Religious priming activates submissive thoughts and behaviors. *The International Journal for the Psychology of Religion, 19*, 143–154.

Schumacker, R. E., & Lomax, R. G. (2004). *A beginner's guide to structural equation modeling.* Mahwah, NJ: Erlbaum.

Schumann, K., Nash, K. A., McGregor, I., & Ross, M. (2012). *Religious magnanimity: Religion primes supplant antagonism with more compassionate reactions to threat.* Manuscript in preparation.

Shariff, A. F., & Norenzayan, A. (2007). God is watching you: Priming God concepts increases prosocial behavior in an anonymous economic game. *Psychological Science, 18*, 803–809.

Sibley, C. G., & Duckitt, J. (2008). Personality and prejudice: A meta-analysis and theoretical review. *Personality and Social Psychology Review, 12*, 248–279.

Smith, A. G., & Winter, D. G. (2002). Right-wing authoritarianism, party identification, and attitudes toward feminism in student evaluations of the Clinton-Lewinsky story. *Political Psychology, 23*, 355–383.

Stangor, C. (2009). The study of stereotyping, prejudice, and discrimination within social psychology: A quick history of theory and research. In T. Nelson (Ed.), *Handbook of prejudice, stereotyping, and discrimination* (pp. 2–22). New York: Psychology Press.

Stefurak, T., Taylor, C., & Mehta, S. (2010). Gender-specific models of homosexual prejudice: Religiosity, authoritarianism, and gender roles. *Psychology of Religion and Spirituality, 2*, 247–261.

Teige-Mocigemba, S., Klauer, K. C., & Sherman, J. W. (2010). A practical guide to implicit association tests and related tasks. In B. Gawronski & B. K. Payne (Eds.), *Handbook of implicit social cognition: Measurement, theory, and application* (pp. 117–139). New York: Guilford Press.

Vanman, E. J., Saltz, J. L., Nathan, L. R., & Warren, J. A. (2004). Racial discrimination by low-prejudiced whites: Facial movements as implicit measures of attitudes related to behavior. *Psychological Science, 15*, 711–714.

Vess, M., Arndt, J., Cox, C. R., Routledge, C., & Goldenberg, J. L. (2009). Exploring the existential function of religion: The effect of religious fundamentalism on mortality salience on faith-based medical refusals. *Journal of Personality and Social Psychology, 97*, 334–350.

Vincent, W., Parrott, D. J., & Peterson, J. L. (2011). Effects of traditional gender role norms and religious fundamentalism on self-identified heterosexual men's attitudes, anger, and aggression toward gay men and lesbians. *Psychology of Men & Masculinity, 12*(4), 383–400.

Waller, N. G., Kojetin, B. A., Bouchard, T. J., Lykken, D. T., & Tellegen, A. (1990). Genetic and environmental influences on religious interests, attitudes and values: A study of twins reared apart and together. *Psychological Science, 1,* 138–142.

Whitley, B. E., Jr. (2009). Religiosity and attitudes toward lesbians and gay men: A meta-analysis. *The International Journal for the Psychology of Religion, 19,* 21–38.

Wiggins, J. S. (1966). Substantive dimensions of self-report in the MMPI item pool. *Psychological Monographs: General and Applied, 80*(22, Whole No. 630).

Wilson, E. O. (1978). *On human nature.* Cambridge, MA: Harvard University Press.

24

Religion, Spirituality, and Forgiveness

Everett L. Worthington, Jr., Don E. Davis, Joshua N. Hook,
Daryl R. Van Tongeren, Aubrey L. Gartner,
David J. Jennings II, Chelsea L. Greer, and Yin Lin

In the previous edition of the *Handbook of Religion and Spirituality*, McCullough, Bono, and Root (2005) noted the increased interest in research on religion and forgiveness from the late 1990s to 2004, and summarized the status of this research. They also discussed the religion–forgiveness discrepancy (McCullough & Worthington, 1999), which is the tendency for religious individuals to report they are more forgiving across time and situations, but not be more forgiving of a specific offense (also see Tsang, McCullough, & Hoyt, 2005). They concluded that this effect was real but small—and was the result of theoretical (e.g., many religions have doctrines that support forgiveness as well as justice) and methodological (e.g., measuring religion and forgiveness at different levels, social desirability, or recall bias) reasons. They also suggested reasons why religious individuals might be more forgiving than non-religious individuals. Namely, many religious meaning systems (see Park, Chapter 18, this volume) prescribe forgiveness as a valued behavior; encourage emotions (see Tsai, Koopmann-Holm, Miyazaki, & Ochs, Chapter 14, this volume) that facilitate forgiveness such as sympathy, compassion, and love; have scriptures and rituals that promote forgiveness; and provide exemplars from religious traditions who model virtuous behavior through forgiveness. In the present chapter, we suggest that those religious and spiritual meaning systems can differ, and that the differences need to be taken seriously. Furthermore, McCullough et al. outlined an evolutionary account for the relationship between religion and forgiveness (see also Kirkpatrick, Chapter 6, this volume). They hypothesized that evolutionary survival might depend on a culture developing a moralizing god (see Zell & Baumeister, Chapter 25, this volume), who (1) punishes sinners (i.e., moral norm breakers) through justice and (2) rehabilitates them through forgiveness. The study of religion and spirituality and their relationship to forgiveness has cut across disciplinary and subdisciplinary lines, with evolutionary scientists (Kirkpatrick, 2005; McCullough, 2008), neuroeconomists (Fehr & Gächter, 2002), and others studying the topic.

Since the writing of the McCullough et al. 2005 chapter, much has occurred in the field on the relationship between religion/spirituality and forgiveness. Two meta-analyses have been conducted that help to organize the empirical findings on these relationships. Fehr, Gelfand, and Nag (2010), in a general meta-analysis of forgiveness, reported a moderator effect size of 0.19 for the correlation between religion/spirituality and forgiveness of a specific offense. Davis, Worthington, Hook, and Hill (in press) conducted meta-analyses with an explicit focus on the relationships between religion/spirituality and trait forgivingness ($k = 64$ studies; $N = 99{,}117$), state forgiveness ($k = 50$ studies; $N = 8{,}932$), and self-forgivingness ($k = 23$; $N = 4{,}000$). The effect size for religion/spirituality and trait forgivingness, state forgiveness, and self-forgivingness were 0.29, 0.14, and 0.12, respectively. They also examined several moderators and found that the relationship between religion/spirituality and state forgiveness was stronger when religion/spirituality was also measured as a state ($r = .33$) compared with when it was measured as a trait ($r = .10$). Additionally, the relationship between religion/spirituality and self-forgivingness was stronger when a measure of attachment to God was used to assess religion/spirituality ($r = .21$) than when a general measure of religiosity was used ($r = .10$). These meta-analytic reviews together summarized a vast number of studies on religion/spirituality and forgiveness.

Thus, our primary aim in the present chapter is not to review what has already been studied on this topic, although we do provide a brief review of the status of the literature. Rather, our eye is toward the future of this field. We highlight the areas that, after nearly 20 years of research, are still underdeveloped. In addition, we introduce theoretical precision that will clarify questions and help researchers address the gaps in this field.

We address three key themes that we believe will help spur the field forward. First, greater precision is needed in conceptualizing religion/spirituality (Kapuscinski & Masters, 2010). Prior research has emphasized the relationship between religion and forgiveness. Researchers also must now consider how *spirituality* influences forgiveness and expand upon the similarities and differences of these relationships. Researchers must also shift from studying religion/spirituality as a static personal characteristic (e.g., comparing people who are more religious with those who are less religious). Although such constructs need not be abandoned, more research is needed on how different spiritual experiences, which may change within a person over time, can influence forgiveness. Accordingly, we describe four types of spirituality and emphasize the importance of considering these in parallel with religiosity.

Second, the field must accommodate advances in conceptualizing forgiveness. Almost all research in this area has studied the religion/spirituality and forgiveness from the victim's perspective. For a complete picture, forgiveness must be considered from viewpoints of both the victim and the offender. We discuss seeking forgiveness, spiritual struggle (see Exline & Rose, Chapter 19, this volume), self-forgiveness, decisional and emotional forgiveness, and forgiveness by God, whose relationship to religion/spirituality has been rarely studied.

Third, we provide a theoretical model for organizing past and future research on religion/spirituality and forgiveness. Davis, Hook, and Worthington (2008) extended Shults and Sandage's (2006) theory of relational spirituality to the study of forgiveness. In the current chapter, we seek to consolidate current understanding within this theory, present an overview of the theory, and use it to address new questions that need empirical investigation.

In order to accomplish these goals, the present chapter is organized as follows. First, as a working definition, we define religion and spirituality. Second, we discuss constructs related to the victim's and the offender's perspective of forgiveness. Third, we present and elaborate on a model of relational spirituality and forgiveness. We use it to organize prior research and identify important gaps in the field that require additional inquiry.

DEFINING RELIGION AND SPIRITUALITY

Religion has been defined in many ways. We adopt Hill et al.'s (2000) definition of religion as one's adherence to a belief system and practices associated with a tradition and community in which there is general agreement about what is believed and practiced in a faith community. *Spirituality*, in contrast, can be defined as a more individual feeling of closeness and connectedness to objects one believes to be sacred. What one views as sacred is often a socially influenced perception of either (1) a divine being or object or (2) a sense of ultimate reality or truth (Hill et al., 2000). Many people experience their spirituality in the context of religion (i.e., religious spirituality), but not all do. *Religious spirituality* involves a sense of closeness and connection to God or a higher power, experienced through the practice of a particular religion (e.g., Christianity, Islam, Buddhism). Three other types of spirituality have been identified on the basis of the type of sacred object that is valued (Davis et al., 2008; Worthington, 2009). First, *humanistic spirituality* involves a sense of closeness and connection to humankind. This type of spirituality develops a sense of connection to a group of people, often involving feelings of love, altruism, or reflection. Second, *nature spirituality* involves a sense of closeness and connection to the environment or to nature. For example, one might experience wonder and awe by taking in a sunset, experiencing a natural wonder such as the Grand Canyon, or having a general sense of connection with the natural environment. Third, *transcendent spirituality* involves a sense of closeness and connection with the whole of creation or the natural order. This type of spirituality might be experienced by meditating on the magnificence of creation, contemplating the vastness of physical existence, or looking into the night sky and having a sense of connection with all natural objects.

A profile approach may prove the best way of describing a person's spirituality. Researchers could ask individuals the extent to which each of the four types of spirituality comprises an individual's spiritual experience. For example, religious individuals may derive their primary sense of spirituality from a close relationship to a divine being— understanding closeness to humanity as taught by the religion (e.g., God commands honor of humans, of nature, and of creation). Individuals with nonreligious spirituality may treat nature spirituality and humanistic spirituality as embedded within transcendent spirituality. Many current studies on spirituality fail to distinguish religious and nonreligious spirituality. Many people who are religious also consider themselves to be spiritual. Although one approach might be to strategically sample nonreligious individuals, we believe it is also important to develop measures that can assess these distinctions within religiously and spiritually heterogeneous samples.

WIDENING THE PERSPECTIVE: FORGIVENESS ACCORDING TO THE VICTIM AND OFFENDER

The Victim's Perspective on Forgiveness

Events, Relationships, and Traits

The bulk of research on forgiveness has examined the experience from the victim's perspective (see Table 24.1 for variables related to forgiving another person). Forgiveness refers to a victim reducing negative thoughts, emotions, and motivations toward an offender as well as the promotion of positive thoughts, emotions, and motivations (see Worthington, 2005, for a review of definitions). Forgiveness of others has been measured as both a trait (called forgivingness) and a state. *Forgivingness* refers to the degree to which a person tends to forgive across time and situations, whereas *state forgiveness* refers to a person's forgiveness of a specific offense. *Unforgiveness* is not merely the lack of forgiveness; it can manifest as grudge-holding or vengeful motives and feelings. Unforgiveness is a combination of negative emotions (i.e., resentment, hatred, bitterness, anger, fear) that the working memory labels as feeling negatively toward an offender (with negative motivations often being associated with those negative emotions). Forgiveness or unforgiveness can also generalize to a particular person such as forgiveness of a marriage partner (Paleari, Regalia, & Fincham, 2009).

Forgiveness as Change over Time

McCullough and his colleagues have argued that forgiveness should be conceptualized as change in motivations and emotions over time to more prosocial (or less antagonistic) emotions or motives (McCullough, Fincham, & Tsang, 2003; McCullough & Root, 2005). They argued that amounts of unforgiveness at the time of offense might differ. Person *A* might hold high unforgiveness and person *B* low. If person *A* reduced unforgiveness to the same level as person *B* and person *B* did not change, then person *A* forgave (but not person *B*); thus, forgiveness should be considered as a change over time. They defined three types of forgiveness: forbearance, trend forgiveness, and temporary forgiveness. *Forbearance* is the initial reduction of unforgiveness from the point that a transgression is experienced until it is measured initially. *Trend forgiveness* involves the rate of change in unforgiveness or forgiveness over time (the true measure of forgiveness according to McCullough et al., 2003). *Temporary forgiveness* involves daily fluctuations in unforgiveness or forgiveness levels, which might occur as a result of mood, or measurement fluctuation. Those are treated as measurement error.

We suggest that McCullough and colleagues' theorizing might profitably be extended to consider the effects of transgressions not just extending through a time period but also contextualized within time. That is, consider a transgression that occurs at some point in time (T1) and the average person's unforgiveness decays exponentially until some point in the future (T2). We plot a hypothetical curve in Figure 24.1. The initial unforgiveness was D as a result of the offense. The unforgiveness decays over time, and eventually approaches some asymptote, leaving a residual unforgiveness (noted as Δ). For some hurts, essentially $\Delta = 0$, but other hurts leave virtually permanent residual of unforgiveness and Δ can be large or small, likely depending on the hurt and forgivingness of the

TABLE 24.1. Variables Hypothesized to Predict Forgiveness from the Victim's and Offender's Perspective Using the Model Relating Relational Spirituality and Forgiveness

Victim's perspective	Variables hypothesized to predict forgiveness	Offender's perspective	Variables hypothesized to predict seeking forgiveness [reverse-scored]
V^V (victim's perspective, self-appraisal of traits related to forgiving)	Agreeableness / [Neuroticism] / Conscientiousness / Extraversion / Openness to experience / Trait forgivingness / [Trait vengefulness] / [Trait rumination] / [Trait anger] / [Trait anxiety] / [Depression] / [Narcissism] / Altruism / [Pride] · Humility / [Justice orientation high in value among the virtues] / Love orientation high in value among the virtues / Trait love / Trait compassion / Trait sympathy / Trait empathy / Virtue orientation / Self-control / [Ego-depletion] / Trait gratitude / Trait mercy	V^O (offender's perspective of characteristics of the victim that predict seeking forgiveness)	Needy / [Antagonistic] / [Weak and will permit being taken advantage of] / [Punitiveness] / [Vengeful] / [Vindictive] / Merciful / Humble / Compassionate / Loving / Generous
O^V (victim's perspective of the offender's characteristics related to forgiving)	[Unrepentant] / Repentant / [Hard-hearted] / Vulnerable / [Aggressive] / [Hate filled] / Virtue orientation toward being responsible / Responsible / Trustworthiness · Innocence / Vulnerable / [Provocative] / [Aggressive] / [Hate filled] / [Self-condemning] / Self-forgiving / Caring / [Loving]	O^O (offender's perspective of the offender's own characteristics that predict seeking forgiveness)	Shame prone / Guilt prone / [Narcissistic] / [Was right in inflicting the hurt] / [Justified] / [Self-righteous] / [Excusable] / [Defenses self-justify the behavior] / Wrongdoing admitted
T^V (victim's perspective of the transgression)	[Severe] / [Hurtful] / [Intentional] vs. accidental · [Ongoing] vs. on-off / [Stable and negative causal attributions]	T^O (offender's perspective of characteristics of the transgression that predict seeking forgiveness)	Serious / Hurtful / [Intentional] / Accidental / Easy to get over / [Long-lasting harm]

Variable		
VO^V (victim's perspective of the relationship between the victim and the offender)	Liking Loving Committed Satisfied Invested Affiliative Friendly Close Intimate	Permanent relationship Ongoing relationship Positively valenced relationship Type of relationship (lover ≥ parent > sibling ≥ friend = coworker > acquaintance > third-party observer)
VT^V (victim's perspective of the relationship between the victim and the transgression)	Deserved the wrong Justified	
OT^V (victim's perspective of the relationship between the offender and the transgression)	Remorse Contrition [Intention to repeat] Available good excuses	
S^V (victim's perspective of the characteristics of the sacred that could affect forgiving)	Just Loving All-knowing All-powerful Various religious beliefs about the nature of the sacred and its relationship to life	
VO^O (offender's perspective of characteristics of the relationship between the victim and offender that predict seeking forgiveness)	Liking Loving Committed Satisfied Invested Affiliative Friendly Close Intimate	Permanent relationship Ongoing relationship Positively valenced relationship Type of relationship (lover ≥ parent > sibling ≥ friend = coworker > acquaintance > third-party observer) [Competitive]
VT^O (offender's perspective of characteristics of the relationship between the victim and the transgression that predict seeking forgiveness)	[Deserved the consequences] [Had harmed the offender recently]	[Had "asked for it"] [Only giving just desserts]
OT^O (offender's perspective of characteristics of the relationship between the offender and the transgression that predict seeking forgiveness)	[Justified] [Excused]	
S^O (offender's perspective of the characteristics of the sacred that predict seeking forgiveness)	Tolerant Not actively condemning of misbehavior No belief in afterlife Common humanity All are part of nature	Brothers and sisters in the cosmos Transcendent ultimate being Belief in karma Belief in dharma [Justified as part of samarra (wheel of suffering)]

(continued)

481

TABLE 24.1. (*continued*)

Victim's perspective	Variables hypothesized to predict forgiveness	Offender's perspective	Variables hypothesized to predict seeking forgiveness	Variables hypothesized to predict seeking forgiveness [reverse-scored]
SVV (victim's own perspective of the relationship between the sacred and the victim)	What is sacred (God, humans, nature, cosmos); Closeness to the sacred (religious spirituality); Attachment to God; Religious commitment; Intrinsic religious motivation; Anger at God; Religious attitudes; Religious satisfaction; Investment in religion; Satisfaction with alternatives to religion; Valence and strength of relationship	SVO (offender's perspective of characteristics of the relationship between the sacred and the victim that predict seeking forgiveness)	Similarity of the offender's spirituality to the victim's; Judgment of the closeness of the victim to the sacred	Similarity of choice of what is sacred; Similarity of religious variables (e.g., denomination, beliefs, values, worldview)
SOV (victim's own perspective of the relationship between the sacred and the offender in terms of similarity or difference from the victim's own relationship)	Similarity of the Offender's Spirituality to One's Own; Judgment of the closeness of the Offender to the sacred; Similarity of choice of what is sacred; Similarity of religious variables (e.g., denomination, beliefs, values, worldview)	SOO (offender's own perspective of his or her own relationship between the sacred and the offender that predict seeking forgiveness)	What is sacred (God, humans, nature, cosmos); Closeness to the Sacred (religious spirituality); Attachment to God; Religious commitment; Intrinsic religious motivation	Anger at God; Religious attitudes; Religious satisfaction; Investment in religion; Satisfaction with alternatives to religion; Valence of relationship; Strength of relationship
STV (victim's own perspective of the relationship between the sacred and the transgression)	[Desecration]; [Sacred loss]; Nonsacred involvement	STO (offender's own perspective of the relationship between the sacred and the transgression that predict seeking forgiveness)	[Desecration]; [Sacred loss]; Nonsacred involvement	

Note. Variables in brackets are hypothesized to have an inverse relationship.

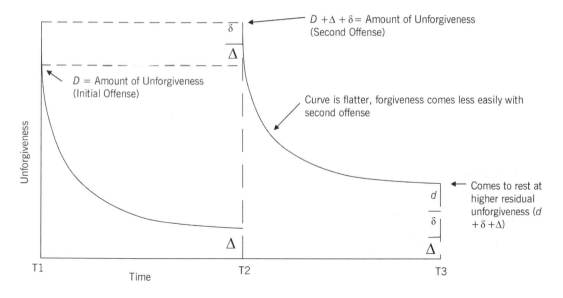

$D + \Delta + \delta =$ Amount of Unforgiveness
(Second Offense)

$D =$ Amount of Unforgiveness
(Initial Offense)

Curve is flatter, forgiveness comes less easily with second offense

Comes to rest at higher residual unforgiveness ($d + \delta + \Delta$)

Unforgiveness

Time

T1   T2   T3

FIGURE 24.1. Repeated offenses from the same offender result in increased initial unforgiveness, a slower reduction in unforgiveness, and greater residual unforgiveness.

victim. Suppose, in extending theorizing by McCullough, Luna, Berry, Tobak, and Bono (2010), the same offender perpetrates essentially the same hurt again at T2 (see Figure 24.1). The magnitude of unforgiveness felt by the victim as a result of the second hurt will be $D + \Delta$. That is, it will usually be greater than the original D because of the residual unforgiveness. A second hurt, however, will typically be felt to be a more severe betrayal (the exception might be if the victim distanced from the offender in order to decrease future hurts) because there is a history of hurt in the relationship. This adds an increment, δ. The new level of unforgiveness toward the offender is $D + \Delta + \delta$. Furthermore, because the relationship has a past and the second transgression demonstrates that the offender is not as trustworthy as expected after recovering from the T1 hurt, two things will happen. First, the rate of decline of unforgiveness will be slower. Second, the residual unforgiveness (when and if equilibrium is reached) will be higher than $\Delta + d$ by an increment of δ (thus, it will level out at $\Delta + d + \delta$). From the standpoint of religion and spirituality, we might speculate that religions and spiritualities will affect the magnitudes of D, d, Δ, and δ differentially (e.g., religious teachings to forgive).

The vast majority of research examining the relationship between religion/spirituality and forgiveness has treated both religion/spirituality and forgiveness as static variables. For example, a study might examine the correlation between an individual's level of religious commitment and the forgiveness of a specific offense. McCullough and colleagues have argued persuasively that forgiveness be studied as change over time, and we believe that the field of religion/spirituality and forgiveness must follow their lead, not only by examining forgiveness over time but also evaluating religious and spiritual constructs that may also change over time. These advances are considerable, and future research is certainly needed in this area. However, these approaches currently face methodological limitations. For example, static measures of forgiveness are not able to detect the degree to which one experienced forgiveness by reducing unforgiveness—they only provide information regarding current level of unforgiveness or forgiveness. Two identical scores on a measure of unforgiveness do not explain how much unforgiveness was reduced (e.g., it is possible that person A scored a 30 because he reduced his initial unforgiveness by 5 points [from 35] over 3 weeks, whereas person B scored a 30 because she reduced her initial unforgiveness by 20 [from 50] over 3 weeks). Without precision in measurement, valuable information regarding the *process* of forgiveness is lost. Recent studies are beginning to measure the relationship between religion and forgiveness across time (e.g., Davis, Hook, Van Tongeren, & Worthington, 2012).

Forbearance

We define forbearance differently than McCullough et al. (2003) because their definition may obscure important findings in the psychology of religion and spirituality. We define *forbearance* as the effortful suppression of the *expression of negative behavior* (not necessarily including or being limited to emotions or motivations) toward an offender. What McCullough et al. call forbearance we consider more akin to Gross's (1998) concept of *emotional suppression* (Srivastava, Tamir, McGonigal, John, & Gross, 2009), which is trying to suppress the experience of emotion. They focus on initial measured levels of unforgiveness—an intrapersonal experience—which are influenced by (1) personality traits, such as mercy, compassion, and humility; (2) situational factors, such as whether the offender apologized, offered excuses, or became arrogant; and (3) efforts to suppress the internal experience of unforgiveness and the external expression of unforgiving responses. On the other hand, we believe that when people forbear, they may be experiencing considerable emotional unforgiveness, but they try not to let it show. They suppress their expression of their experienced negative unforgiveness.

Forbearance may be more likely in collectivistic cultures (Hook, Worthington, & Utsey, 2009; Hook, Worthington, Utsey, Davis, & Burnette, 2012). Individuals may forbear conflict or forbear expression of experienced emotion to maintain group harmony. Religious or spiritual beliefs and values may also influence forbearance. Within a broader culture (e.g., an entire country), various groups may be more or less collectivistic than the general population. Religious individuals tend to be more collectivistic than people in matched secular environments because religion, by definition, involves identification with a religious group that adopts a collective set of shared beliefs and values. At a minimum, group identity provides a collectivistic motive to forgive other ingroup members (but perhaps not outgroup members). Thus, we hypothesize that religious individuals show greater forbearance toward ingroup members than to outgroup members.

Decisional and Emotional Forgiveness

Worthington (2006) argued that there are two types of forgiveness. They are related but distinct. *Decisional forgiveness* is a behavioral intention statement to forgo revenge and to treat the offender as a person of value. One could make a decision to forgive and still have negative vengeful motives and unforgiving emotions such as resentment, bitterness, hostility, hatred, anger, and fear toward the offender (e.g., unforgiveness). Accordingly, *emotional forgiveness* is the replacement of negative unforgiving emotions with positive other-oriented emotions of empathy, sympathy, compassion, and love.

Religions differ in the degree to which they emphasize decisional or emotional forgiveness (Worthington, 2009). For example, Christianity mandates decisional forgiveness, as seen in what Christians call the Lord's prayer: "Forgive us our debts as we forgive our debtors…For if you do not forgive the person who sins against you, your heavenly father will not forgive you your sins, but if you do forgive, your Father will forgive you your sins" (Mt 6:12, 14-5). Some strains of Buddhism value compassion, which engenders emotional forgiveness; other strains of Buddhism value detachment, which engenders decisional forgiveness. Humanistic spiritualities might value both emotional and decisional forgiveness, whereas transcendental spiritualities might value internalized experience (i.e., emotional forgiveness). Thus, differentiating decisional and emotional forgiveness should lead to a more nuanced understanding of how religion and spirituality may influence forgiveness.

"Forgiving God" or Anger at God

Exline and her colleagues have studied anger at God. Some find it theologically offensive to say "forgiving God" because it implies that God sits under human judgment (Exline, Park, Smyth, & Carey, 2011; Wood et al., 2010; see also Exline & Rose, Chapter 19, this volume). Those who are angry at God may believe that God has (1) not lived up to their expectations or (2) allowed or even caused evil to happen. As was shown repeatedly during the Holocaust, many individuals gave up their faith in God because of their perception of God's unwillingness or inability to stop the atrocities committed by Nazi Germany.

Exline et al. (2011) found that factors that predicted unforgiveness toward a human offender also predicted anger at God (e.g., holding God responsible for severe harm, seeing oneself as a victim, making attributions of cruelty by God, and having difficulty finding meaning from events). Individuals often reported feeling anger toward God after negative events, although positive feelings predominated. Anger and positive feelings toward God were moderately and negatively correlated. More religious and older people expressed less anger toward God. Some groups, such as Protestants and African Americans, reported lower anger at God than did other groups. Some atheists and agnostics reported they were angry with God because of past experiences or were angry with images of a hypothetical God. Anger toward God was related to poorer adjustment following bereavement and cancer, especially if anger lasted more than a year, which could put people at risk for stress-related disorders on top of bereavement.

The Offender's Perspective on Forgiveness

Almost all research on forgiveness in general (and the relationship between religion/spirituality and forgiveness in particular) has focused on the perspective of the victim. This is problematic for the study of religion/spirituality and forgiveness because many of the beliefs, norms, and rituals that promote forgiveness and reconciliation involve the offender, such as the tasks required of the offender to receive divine forgiveness and restoration within the religious or spiritual community.

The little research that has emerged on offenders' forgiveness has focused on variables affecting their seeking of forgiveness (for a summary of potential variables, see Table 24.1). Forgiveness for offenders and victims differs for many obvious reasons. First, the goal is usually different—to forgive if one is the victim or to seek forgiveness if one is the offender. Second, the emotional states are different for the offender and victim. The offender's emotional state is usually dominated by feelings of guilt, shame, or self-justification, whereas the victim's emotional state is usually centered on emotions such as anger, fear, hurt, resentment, hostility, or hatred. Those emotional states lead to different motivations (see Emmons & Schnitker, Chapter 13, this volume) and strategies for relational repair. Third, the offender and the victim will perceive the event differently simply because they are in different roles. Baumeister, Stillwell, and Wotman (1990) provided evidence that victims and offenders tend to remember transgressions that applied most directly to themselves. For example, victims might remember how much they suffered but not how hard it was for the offender to make an apology; offenders tend to remember the opposite.

Seeking Forgiveness

Building on Zechmeister and Romero's (2002) qualitative study of seeking forgiveness, early research examined reproaches for offenses, accounts, causal attributions, and confessions. Subjective experiences of guilt, remorse, and shame have been studied as well as individual's physiological responses to seeking forgiveness. Little research has studied the religious context of seeking forgiveness (see Witvliet, Ludwig, & Bauer, 2002).

McCullough, Bono, and Root (2005) hypothesized that higher levels of humility in an offender might make an offender more likely to seek forgiveness for wrongdoing, but little research has tested this hypothesis. Coming from a personality judgment perspective, Davis et al. (2010) studied *relational humility* (i.e., the victim's judgment of the offender's degree of humility) and *spiritual humility* (i.e., the victim's judgment of the offender's humility before God). They identified some connections of each to granting and experiencing forgiveness. However, the offender's judgment of the victim's degree of humility, and humility before God, and its relation to seeking and receiving forgiveness have not yet been studied.

Communicating about Transgressions

Fairly recent work has examined the processes of communicating about transgressions. For example, Waldron and Kelly (2008) summarized existing research on social interactions surrounding the forgiveness process (e.g., making reproaches and giving accounts of various types). Others have expanded research on interactions around transgressions. For example, Jennings (2010) studied various ways that offenders may respond to different offers of forgiveness (e.g., I forgive you; I forgive you, but I need time for my emotions to heal; I want to forgive you, but I need more time; I will not forgive you). Gartner (2009) studied the degree to which offenders accept or reject an offer of forgiveness. Indeed, offers of forgiveness also assume that the offender did something wrong. Offenders may reject forgiveness in order to deny such an accusation. To date, we are aware of no studies that have examined the various ways that religion and spirituality can influence the communication of forgiveness. Future research should address this glaring gap in the literature.

Self-Forgiveness

Self-forgiveness has been more difficult to define and study empirically than forgiveness of others. Complicating the conceptualization of forgiveness is that the forgiver is also the offender. Worthington (2006) conceptualized self-condemnation within a stress-and-coping model. Self-condemnation was conceptualized as a stressor that might be experienced intermittently or chronically. It may occur for two reasons: (1) doing wrong to another person or (2) falling short of one's moral standards or personal expectations. As such, one can feel self-condemnation even if no moral wrong has been committed, especially if one's expectations are unrealistic or illogical. Furthermore, self-forgiveness is one of many coping mechanisms to deal with the stress of self-condemnation (others include accepting and letting go; letting oneself off the hook; justifying, condoning, or trying to atone for one's behavior).

Worthington (2006) presented a model of the steps that are usually involved in forgiving oneself. First, the individual realizes that he or she has committed an offense against another individual or the sacred (e.g., God, humanity, nature) and tries to make amends to those harmed. Second, the individual seeks integrity between his or her behavior and moral standards, either by adopting more realistic standards or changing his or her behavior. Third, the individual grants decisional forgiveness to him- or herself and commits to work toward emotional forgiveness of the self. Fourth, the individual seeks self-acceptance for wrongdoing or failure to achieve moral standards. Fifth, the individual commits anew to virtuous living. Sixth, the individual acknowledges human limitations and allows space to fail.

Hall and Fincham (2005) advanced a model of self-forgiveness that involves seeking reconciliation for the wrongdoing with a higher purpose or being, making amends, and forgiving the self in light of the relationship with the person who might have been harmed. They also tested this model over time (Hall & Fincham, 2008) and found that self-forgiveness increased linearly over time. Increases in self-forgiveness were found to be related to decreases in guilt, perceived severity of the offense, and conciliatory behavior toward a higher power (e.g., prayer). Increases in perceived forgiveness from the victim and the higher power as well as conciliatory behavior toward the victim were also related to increases in self-forgiveness.

Divine Forgiveness

Divine forgiveness refers to people's sense of being forgiven by the deity they consider to be sacred. For religions and spiritualities in which other objects are treated as sacred, such as humans, nature, or transcendence of the cosmos, divine forgiveness might involve reaching a sense of adequate peace with what is considered sacred. The importance of divine forgiveness varies by population and type of problem (Webb & Brewer, 2010). In a national probability survey of 965 adults at least 67 years of age, feeling unforgiven by God was related to depressive symptoms, and this relationship was fully explained by self-forgiveness and rumination (Ingersoll-Dayton, Torges, & Krause, 2010).

Summary

In the past decade, much research has accumulated regarding varieties of forgiveness. Despite the vast number of studies on religion/spirituality and forgiveness, most research simply used religion or (less often) spirituality as a static person variable. It is clear, however, that religion and spirituality are more dynamic than a mere person variable. As people struggle with transgressions, their religiousness or spirituality might change—especially spirituality (the degree of perceived closeness to something they consider sacred). Thus, the field needs an organizing model that connects religion/spirituality with forgiveness. Next, we draw on an integration of theology and psychology by Shults and Sandage (2006) involving relational spirituality (i.e., ways of relating to the sacred) to propose a model for how relational spirituality influences forgiveness.

A MODEL OF RELATIONAL SPIRITUALITY AND FORGIVENESS

Shults and Sandage (2006) described a model of relational spirituality that focuses on the *relationship* between an individual and what he or she considers to be sacred. It is useful with myriad religions and nonreligious spiritualities. Davis et al. (2008) and Worthington (2009) applied this model of relational spirituality to forgiveness, describing relationships between what one considers to be sacred and (1) the offender, (2) the victim, and (3) the transgression. However, they described the model primarily within the context of religious spirituality. We present the model in the following, extending prior theorizing to also address nonreligious types of spiritual experience, such as closeness and connection with humanity, nature, and the transcendent.

The Secular Part of the Model

In Figure 24.2, we depict the model of relational spirituality and forgiveness as a pyramid (reprinted with permission, see Davis et al., 2008). The model can take the perspective of either the victim (V) or the offender (O). The subscripts designate the viewpoint (i.e., victim or offender). In Table 24.1, we describe how the various spiritual constructs are hypothesized to influence the likelihood that (1) the victim will forgive the offender or that (2) the offender will offend or seek forgiveness (if offenses have already been perpetrated). The base of the triangle refers to the secular context of forgiveness, including the victim, offender, transgression (T), and relationships among them, and hence are little related to religion or spirituality. The model, however, incorporates a vertical dimension, which represents the spiritual context in which the transgression occurs. This vertical dimension describes how views of the sacred, as well as the relationships between what one considers to be sacred and (1) victim, (2) offender, and (3) transgression, might affect forgiveness. The chief components of the model, which can be considered from either the

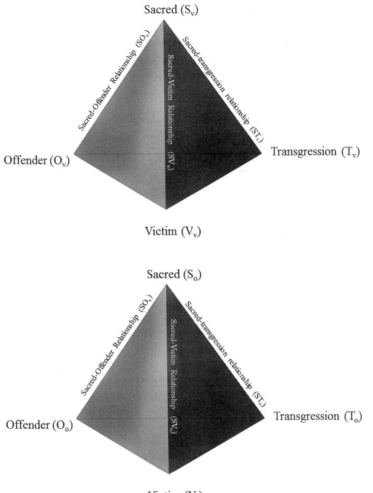

FIGURE 24.2. Model of forgiveness and relational spirituality. From Davis, Hook, and Worthington (2008). Reprinted by permission.

victim's or the offender's perspective, are described next. The V, O, and T variables and the VO, VT, and OT relationships have little connection to religion or spirituality (unless noted), but they are included for completeness.

The Victim (V)

A variety of dispositional variables have been found to predict whether people will forgive an offender. Mullet, Neto, and Rivière (2005) summarized 10 years of research on personality and forgiveness. They found that strong predictors of forgiveness included high levels of several traits: agreeableness, forgivingness, love, compassion, sympathy, empathy, self-control, and virtue orientation (see Zell & Baumeister, Chapter 25, this volume). Weaker predictors of forgiveness included high conscientiousness, extraversion, and openness. Conversely, *unforgiveness* was strongly predicted by narcissism, justice orientation, vengefulness, trait anger, trait fear, and trait anxiety.

Many of these personality and dispositional variables are highly related to religion or spirituality. In a recent review of personality and religion/spirituality, Miller and Worthington (2012) found that religion and spirituality were related to different images of God, to different types of attachment to God, and to low psychoticism. They also found that religious constructs are consistently related to high agreeableness, conscientiousness, and extraversion as well as low neuroticism. Spiritual constructs are related to high openness, agreeableness, and conscientiousness and to low neuroticism.

In addition, event-related variables associated with the victim can affect the likelihood of forgiveness. For example, an individual's humility may affect whether a person can forgive (Rowatt et al., 2006). If events trigger a sense of shame, the victim might feel the need to respond aggressively or vengefully to protect a fragile ego. For example, Kernis, Lakey, and Heppner (2008) reported that individuals who have fragile senses of self-esteem (as opposed to secure senses of self-esteem) are easily challenged or provoked to defend their ego. Those people are the most prone to angry outbursts and violence. Cultural differences may also exist, and culture can be intertwined with religion and spirituality. Collectivistic forgiveness may be less strongly related to internal personality variables such as self-esteem and more strongly related to societal variables such as the importance of social harmony (for a review of theory and research, see Hook et al., 2009; for empirical test, see Hook, Worthington, Utsey, Davis, & Burnette, 2012).

The Offender (O)

The offender can also influence forgiveness. Indeed, some individuals are easier to forgive than are others. For example, victims have trouble forgiving offenders who are arrogant and narcissistic (Exline, Baumeister, Bushman, Campbell, & Finkel, 2004). Religion or spirituality of the offender as a personality variable has not been investigated.

The Transgression (T)

Many aspects of transgressions affect likelihood of forgiveness. For example, forgiveness is more difficult to grant or experience if a transgression is evaluated as severe, hurtful, intentional, resulting in long-lasting or permanent harm, or avoidable (Zechmeister & Romero, 2002). When a transgression hurts people's feelings (besides being a wrong or an offense), then they are particularly unlikely to forgive (Leary & Leder, 2009). Exline, Baumeister, Zell, Kraft, and Witvliet (2008) have shown that people are more likely to forgive if they are induced to recall their own past wrongdoing. This is especially predictive of forgiving if the wrong they committed was similar to the one they received. Research has not often studied religious transgressions. Sutton and his colleagues have studied forgiveness of pastors' moral failures by members of their congregation (Thomas,

White, & Sutton, 2008). When pastors fall, those moral transgressions are particularly unlikely to be forgiven.

The Victim–Offender Relationship (VO)

Psychologists have long studied human–human relationships. Those relationships—and whether relationships are even valued—are affected by religious and spiritual variables. Those need investigation as they pertain to forgiveness.

The Victim–Transgression Relationship (VT)

Victims may be sensitive to certain transgressions. For example, a woman with a history of physical abuse from an alcoholic father may feel especially hurt if her husband lies to her about alcohol use or her son gets in trouble for underage drinking. Clinical psychologists can qualitatively understand how deep hurts during a client's childhood may surface in adult relationships. Forgiveness researchers have yet to incorporate information about the victim's history to predict the victim's reaction to and likelihood of forgiving an offense.

The Offender–Transgression Relationship (OT)

Offenders also may be tied to certain transgressions. If an offender, for example, is perceived as being in the throes of an inescapable pattern of hurtful behavior—such as alcoholism, eating disorder, or sexual addiction—the victim might discount the hurtfulness of the offender's behavior. On the other hand, repeated offenses are especially difficult to forgive: Each seems to gain hurtfulness from past transgressions. This relationship has not been scientifically studied, so very little is known about how the offender's history of transgressions (as viewed by both the victim and the offender), especially as it unfolds over time, affects the likelihood of forgiveness. More research is certainly needed.

The Aspects of the Model Connecting to What Is Perceived to Be Sacred

The Sacred (S)

The way individuals understand the nature or character of the sacred may influence the likelihood of forgiveness. As discussed earlier, Exline et al. (2011) has shown that a variety of ways that people perceive the sacred (S^v) affect whether they become angry with God (SV^v) and whether they will forgive. For instance, if a victim sees God as active and intervening, then that victim might be more likely to turn a transgression over to God than if one sees God as passive and inactive. If a person views God as a just God who repays evil, then the person might be more willing to forgive, trusting that God will take care of establishing justice.

In addition to the victim's perceptions of what God is like, the victim's religious/ spiritual beliefs about forgiveness can play a role in the aftermath of a transgression. Cohen, Malka, Rozin, and Cherfas (2006) showed that beliefs that one should forgive unconditionally predicted differences in forgiveness between Christians and Jews. Perhaps believing that God demands decisional forgiveness may encourage some victims to grant decisional forgiveness quickly. On the other hand, believing that the sacred incorporates *samsaric circularity* (a wheel of suffering) that is driven by *karma* (unrelenting justice) and *dharma* (holy duty) might make some indifferent to suffering (as in Hinduism; see Rye et al., 2000). Others might believe that forgiveness is a benevolent act that moves a person closer to *anatta* (release from suffering), which might increase the likeliness of forgiving. Furthermore, some religious/spiritual communities conflate forgiveness and reconciliation, which can make forgiveness difficult if the victim does not think reconciliation is appropriate (e.g., relationships with physical abuse).

Little research has examined the influence of nonreligious spiritual beliefs on forgiveness. Almost nothing is known about how humanistic, nature, and transcendent spiritualities may affect forgiveness. It might be helpful for researchers to develop measures—based on theory—to describe differences (between groups as well as individuals within those groups) in spiritual beliefs and values regarding forgiveness.

The Sacred–Victim Relationship (SV)

This relationship refers to the victim's moment-by-moment experience of relationship with the sacred. By conceptualizing spirituality in relational terms, we open up parallels between theories describing human–human relationships and those describing a relationship between a victim and what he or she considers to be sacred. Thus, for example, attachment toward God (Rowatt & Kirkpatrick, 2002) describes the relationship between a person and the person's God. This has been shown to relate to forgiveness. The more securely attached one feels toward God, the more likely one is to extend beneficence toward an offender (Davis et al., 2008). Other relational theories could also be used to investigate aspects of a person's relationship to whatever he or she considers sacred. For example, the interpersonal circle (Leary, 1957) characterizes relationships along the dimensions of affiliation (e.g., closeness, satisfaction, stability) and power (e.g., influence, power, dominance–submission). That could be used to characterize one's relationship with the sacred and predict extent of forgiveness. Rusbult developed an investment model of commitment (Rusbult, Drigotas, & Verette, 1994), in which commitment is described as a function of satisfaction with a current relationship minus satisfaction with alternatives plus investment in the relationship. That also could be used. Gottman (1993) identified a ratio of 5 to 1 positive to negative interactions to explain the likelihood of divorce, and that could be used to characterize relationship with what one considers sacred. These theories should be used to test hypotheses regarding how one's relationship with the sacred can affect a person's motivations and ability to forgive. For example, we predict that viewing one's relationship with the sacred as intimate (e.g., someone who is a devout member of a religious ingroup) enhances the salience of victims' religious/spiritual beliefs and values regarding forgiveness. Conversely, feeling less close to the sacred may evoke guilt in some victims, motivating them try to repair their relationship with the sacred, whereas in other victims it may evoke shame, motivating them to disengage from religious/spiritual community in order to cope. The offender's view of the victim's relationship with the sacred (VSO) may also affect his or her experience of forgiveness. For example, an offender who receives a conditional offer of forgiveness (e.g., "I'll forgive you if you make it up to me") from someone whom he or she views as a convicted Christian (whose faith expects them to forgive unconditionally) may react differently than if the offer was put forth by someone the offender views as an atheist (who may, therefore, assume no religious/ spiritual values of forgiveness).

A limitation of prior theory and research is that it has typically focused on religious spirituality, in which individuals typically view the sacred as a personal being (e.g., with thoughts, emotions, and intentions). It is less clear how these theories may need to be adapted to conceptualize humanistic, nature, and transcendent spiritualities.

The Sacred–Offender Relationship (SO)

This relationship refers to an offender's relationship to what is perceived to be sacred. For example, from the victim's perception (SO^v), the similarity of the victim's and the offender's spirituality may affect forgiveness. Wohl and colleagues (Wohl & Branscombe, 2005; Wohl, Branscombe, & Reysen, 2010) showed that the more similar the offender and victim are in group identity, the more hurt the victim feels by betrayal. Worthington (2006) has hypothesized that even though similarities in spirituality may lead to more hurt, similarities also increase the likelihood that the victim will forgive the offender (Davis et al., 2009). Wohl and Branscomb (2005) have also shown that characterizing offenders as humans rather than according to group identity enhanced forgiveness; these effects were enhanced by threats to the group's survival (Wohl et al., 2010).

No research has considered this relationship within the context of nonreligious spirituality. For instance, Haidt's five moral foundations (Haidt & Graham, 2007) could be extrapolated to have the victim (or offender) describe the degree of difference in sacred values. Differences on these sacred dimensions may even be important when only one person is religious or spiritual, such as when one partner is religiously committed but the other is atheist.

The Sacred–Transgression Relationship

This relationship refers to ways that the victim or offender may imbue the offense with spiritual meaning, which often intensifies hurtfulness or other emotions (see Davis, Hook, Worthington, Van Tongeren, Gartner, et al., 2011). For example, some individuals may view a marital affair as not just a personal betrayal but a desecration of something holy as well as an act that caused a breach in their own relationship with God (Pargament, Magyar, Benore, & Mahoney, 2005). A person may treat a variety of objects as sacred, such as the body, parenting, marriage, country, and sexuality. Viewing a transgression as a desecration has been found to be particularly hurtful (Pargament & Mahoney, 2005) and difficult to forgive (Davis et al., 2008). Forgiveness researchers have not considered ways that spiritual meaning may enhance the likelihood of forgiveness, such as viewing the sacred as relatively merciful toward a certain behavior.

This relationship has primarily been studied within the context of religious spirituality. It is important to explore analogous experiences of those from other types of spirituality. For example, individuals with humanistic spirituality may view certain transgressions (e.g., racism or intolerance) as being a desecration to humanity and the bonds that tie people together.

CONCLUSION

The study of forgiveness continues to grow rapidly, especially that focusing on religion/ spirituality and forgiveness. However, in order for the field to advance, more theoretical precision is needed. Importantly, there are different types of forgiveness, not simply one forgiveness response, and measurement approaches need to capture how forgiveness changes over time. We must differentiate internal experiences of emotional and decisional forgiveness from communication about forgiveness. Moreover, future research must continue to widen the perspective of forgiveness research by investigating the offender's experience. Also, religious beliefs and spiritual experiences, especially when seen from the viewpoint of a relationship with the sacred, can affect the likelihood of forgiveness. The relationships discussed in our model, however, are not simple. Religion and spirituality are multilevel meaning-making systems, and thus the aspects interact in complicated ways with forgiveness. They depend on people's (1) commitment to religion or spirituality, (2) ways of seeing the offender, (3) ways of seeing the victim, and (4) ways the transgression is conceptualized and experienced. All of those factors likely influence the way responses to a transgression unfold over time. Forgiveness happens within relational and cultural contexts. Cultural variables, such as individualism and collectivism, can affect whether a person might forbear or experience, and perhaps communicate, emotional and decisional forgiveness. Although forgiving and forbearing occur within individuals, people develop their identities within a wider context.

Religion and spirituality are two vital elements of that context. They are capable of motivating freedom and terrorism, great good and great evil. Religion and spirituality vary with individuals and groups, yet carry with them some of the strongest worldviews and motives in human experience. Forgiveness is indeed highly affected by those contexts, and the results can lead to world wars or world peace. The choices are up to us.

ACKNOWLEDGMENTS

Preparation of portions of this chapter was supported by Grant No. 2266, "Forgiveness and Relational Spirituality," from the Fetzer Institute to Everett L. Worthington, Jr.

REFERENCES

Baumeister, R. F., Stillwell, A. M., & Wotman, S. R. (1990). Victim and perpetrator accounts of interpersonal conflict: Autobiographical narratives about anger. *Journal of Personality and Social Psychology, 59,* 994–1005.

Cohen, A. B., Malka, A., Rozin, P., & Cherfas, L. (2006). Religion and unforgivable offenses. *Journal of Personality, 74,* 85–117.

Davis, D. E., Hook, J. N., Van Tongeren, D. R., & Worthington, E. L., Jr. (2012). Sanctification of forgiveness. *Psychology of Religion and Spirituality, 4,* 31–39.

Davis, D. E., Hook, J. N., & Worthington, E. L., Jr. (2008). Relational spirituality and forgiveness: The roles of attachment to God, religious coping, and viewing the transgression as a desecration. *Journal of Psychology and Christianity, 27,* 293–301.

Davis, D. E., Hook, J. N., Worthington, E. L., Jr., Van Tongeren, D. R., Gartner, A. L., & Jennings,

D. J., II. (2010). Relational spirituality and forgiveness: Development of the Spiritual Humility Scale (SHS). *Journal of Psychology and Theology, 38,* 91–100.

Davis, D. E., Hook, J. N., Worthington, E. L., Jr., Van Tongeren, D. R., Gartner, A. L., Jennings, D. J., II., et al. (2011). Relational humility: Conceptualizing and measuring humility as a personality judgment. *Journal of Personality Assessment, 93,* 225–234.

Davis, D. E., Worthington, E. L., Jr., Hook, J. N., & Hill, P. C. (in press). Research on forgiveness and religion/spirituality: A meta-analytic review. *Psychology of Religion and Spirituality.*

Davis, D. E., Worthington, E. L., Jr., Hook, J. N., Van Tongeren, D. R., Green, J. D., & Jennings, D. J., II. (2009). Relational spirituality and the development of the Similarity of the Offender's Spirituality (SOS) scale. *Psychology of Religion and Spirituality, 1,* 249–262.

Exline, J. J., Baumeister, R. F., Bushman, B. J., Campbell, W. K., & Finkel, E. J., (2004). Too proud to let go: Narcissistic entitlement as a barrier to forgiveness. *Journal of Personality and Social Psychology, 87,* 894–912.

Exline, J. J., Baumeister, R. F., Zell, A. L., Kraft, A. J., & Witvliet, C. V. O. (2008). Not so innocent: Does seeing one's own capability for wrongdoing predict forgiveness? *Journal of Personality and Social Psychology, 94,* 495–515.

Exline, J. J., Park, C. L., Smyth, J. M., & Carey, M. P. (2011). Anger toward God: Social-cognitive predictors, prevalence, and links with adjustment to bereavement and cancer. *Journal of Personality and Social Psychology, 100,* 129–148.

Fehr, E., & Gächter, S. (2002). Altruistic punishment in humans. *Nature, 415,* 137–140.

Fehr, R., Gelfand, M. J., & Nag, M. (2010). The road to forgiveness: A meta-analytic synthesis of its situational and dispositional correlates. *Psychological Bulletin, 136,* 894–914.

Gartner, A. L. (2009). *The acceptance of a communicated offer of forgiveness in romantic relationships.* Unpublished master's thesis, Virginia Commonwealth University, Richmond.

Gottman, J. M. (1993). A theory of marital dissolution and stability. *Journal of Family Psychology, 7,* 57–75.

Gross, J. J. (1998). The emerging field of emotion regulation: An integrative review. *Review of General Psychology, 2,* 271–299.

Haidt, J., & Graham, J. (2007). When morality opposes justice: Conservatives have moral intuitions that liberals may not recognize. *Social Justice Research, 20,* 98–116.

Hall, J. H., & Fincham, F. D. (2005). Self-forgiveness: The stepchild of forgiveness research. *Journal of Social and Clinical Psychology, 24,* 621–637.

Hall, J. H., & Fincham, F. D. (2008). The temporal course of self-forgiveness. *Journal of Social and Clinical Psychology, 27,* 174–202.

Hill, P. C., Pargament, K. I., Hood, R. W., Jr., McCullough, M. E., Swyers, J. P., Larson, D. B., et al. (2000). Conceptualizing religion and spirituality: Points of commonality, points of departure. *Journal for the Theory of Social Behaviour, 30,* 51–77.

Hook, J. N., Worthington, E. L., Jr., & Utsey, S. O. (2009). Collectivism, forgiveness, and social harmony. *Counseling Psychologist, 37,* 786–820.

Hook, J. N., Worthington, E. L., Jr., Utsey, S. O., Davis, D. E., & Burnette, J. L. (2012). Collectivistic self-construal and forgiveness. *Counseling and Values, 57,* 109–124.

Ingersoll-Dayton, B., Torges, C., & Krause, N. (2010). Unforgiveness, rumination, and depressive symptoms among older adults. *Aging and Mental Health, 14,* 439–449.

Jennings, D. J., II. (2010). *The transgressor's response to a rejected request for forgiveness.* Unpublished master's thesis, Virginia Commonwealth University, Richmond.

Kapuscinski, A. N., & Masters, K. S. (2010). The current status of measures of spirituality: A critical review of scale development. *Psychology of Religion and Spirituality, 2,* 191–205.

Kernis, M. H., Lakey, C. E., & Heppner, W. L. (2008). Secure versus fragile high self-esteem as a predictor of verbal defensiveness: Converging findings across three different markers. *Journal of Personality, 76,* 477–512.

Kirkpatrick, L. A. (2005). *Attachment, evolution, and the psychology of religion.* New York: Guilford Press.

Leary, M. R., & Leder, S. (2009). The nature of hurt feelings: Emotional experience and cognitive appraisals. In A. L. Vangelisti (Ed.), *Feeling hurt in close relationships* (Advances in personal relationships series) (pp. 15–33). New York: Cambridge University Press.

Leary, T. (1957). *Interpersonal diagnosis of personality.* New York: Ronald.

McCullough, M. E. (2008). *Beyond revenge: The evolution of the forgiveness instinct.* San Francisco: Jossey-Bass.

McCullough, M. E., Bono, G., & Root, L. M. (2005). Religion and forgiveness. In R. F. Paloutzian & C. L. Park (Eds.), *Handbook of the psychology of religion and spirituality* (pp. 394–411). New York: Guilford Press.

McCullough, M. E., Fincham, F. D., & Tsang, J.-A. (2003). Forgiveness, forbearance, and time: The temporal unfolding of transgression-related interpersonal motivations. *Journal of Personality and Social Psychology, 84,* 540–557.

McCullough, M. E., Luna, L. R., Berry, J. W., Tabak, B. A., & Bono, G. (2010). On the form and function of forgiving: Modeling the time-forgiveness relationship and testing the valuable relationships hypothesis. *Emotion, 10,* 358–376.

McCullough, M. E., & Root, L. M. (2005). Forgiveness as change. In E. L. Worthington, Jr. (Ed.), *Handbook of forgiveness* (pp. 91–107). New York: Brunner-Routledge.

McCullough, M. E., & Worthington, E. L., Jr. (1999). Religion and the forgiving personality. *Journal of Personality, 67,* 1141–1164.

Miller, A. J., & Worthington, E. L., Jr. (2012). Connection between personality and religion and spirituality. In J. D. Aten, K. A. O'Grady, & E. L. Worthington, Jr. (Eds.), *The psychology of religion and spirituality for clinicians: Using research in your practice* (pp. 101–130). New York: Brunner-Routledge.

Mullet, E., Neto, F., & Rivière, S. (2005). Personality and its effects on resentment, revenge, forgiveness, and self-forgiveness. In E. L. Worthington, Jr. (Ed.), *Handbook of forgiveness* (pp. 159–181). New York: Brunner-Routledge.

Paleari, F. G., Regalia, C., & Fincham, F. D. (2009). Measuring offence-specific forgiveness in marriage: The Marital Offence-Specific Forgiveness Scale (MOFS). *Psychological Assessment, 21,* 194–209.

Pargament, K. I., Magyar, G. M., Benore, E., & Mahoney, A. (2005). Sacrilege: A study of sacred loss and desecration and their implications for health and well-being in a community sample. *Journal for the Scientific Study of Religion, 44,* 59–78.

Pargament, K. I., & Mahoney, A. (2005). Sacred matters: Sanctification as a vital topic for the psychology of religion. *The International Journal for the Psychology of Religion, 15,* 179–198.

Rowatt, W. C., & Kirkpatrick, L. A. (2002). Two dimensions of attachment to God and their relations to affect, religiosity, and personality. *Journal for the Scientific Study of Religion, 41,* 637–651.

Rowatt, W. C., Powers, C., Targhetta, V., Comer, J., Kennedy, S., & Labouff, J. (2006). Development and initial validation of an implicit measure of humility relative to arrogance. *Journal of Positive Psychology, 1,* 198–211.

Rusbult, C. E., Drigotas, S. M., & Verette, J. (1994). The investment model: An interdependence analysis of commitment processes and relationship maintenance phenomena. In D. J. Canary & L. Stafford (Eds.), *Communication and relational maintenance* (pp. 115–139). San Diego: Academic Press.

Rye, M. S., Pargament, K. I., Ali, M. A., Beck, G. L., Dorff, E. N., Hallisey, C., Narayanan, V., & Williams, J. G. (2000). Religious perspectives on forgiveness. In M. E. McCullough, K. I. Pargament, & C. E. Thoresen (Eds.), *Forgiveness: Theory, research, and practice* (pp.17–40). New York: Guilford Press.

Shults, F. L., & Sandage, S. J. (2006). *Transforming spirituality: Integrating theology and psychology.* Grand Rapids, MI: Baker Academic.

Srivastava, S., Tamir, M., McGonigal, K. M., John, O. P., & Gross, J. J. (2009). The social costs of emotional suppression: A prospective study of the transition to college. *Journal of Personality and Social Psychology, 96,* 883–897.

Thomas, E. K., White, K., & Sutton, G. W. (2008). Clergy apologies following abuse: What makes a difference?: Exploring forgiveness, apology, responsibility-taking, gender, and restoration. *Journal of Psychology and Christianity, 27*(1), 16–29.

Tsang, J.-A., McCullough, M. E., & Hoyt, W. T. (2005). Psychometric and rationalization accounts for the religion-forgiveness discrepancy. *Journal of Social Issues, 61,* 785–805.

Waldron, V. R., & Kelley, D. L. (2008). *Communicating forgiveness.* Thousand Oaks, CA: Sage.

Webb, J. R., & Brewer, K. (2010). Forgiveness, health, and problematic drinking among college students in Southern Appalachia. *Journal of Health Psychology, 15,* 1257–1266.

Witvliet, C. V. O., Ludwig, T. E., & Bauer, D. J. (2002). Please forgive me: Transgressors' emotions and physiology during imagery of seeking forgiveness and victim responses. *Journal of Psychology and Christianity, 21,* 219–233.

Wohl, M. J., & Branscombe, N. R. (2005). Forgiveness and collective guilt assignment to historical perpetrator groups depend on level of social category inclusiveness. *Journal of Personality and Social Psychology, 88,* 288–303.

Wohl, M. J., Branscombe, N. R., & Reysen, S. (2010). Perceiving your group's future to be in jeopardy: Extinction threat induces collective angst and the desire to strengthen the ingroup. *Personality and Social Psychology Bulletin, 36,* 898–910.

Wood, B. T., Worthington, E. L., Jr., Exline, J. J., Yali, A. M., Aten, J. D., & McMinn, M. R. (2010). Development, refinement, and psychometric properties of the Attitudes Toward God Scale (ATGS-9). *Psychology of Religion and Spirituality, 2,* 148–167.

Worthington, E. L., Jr. (Ed.). (2005). *Handbook of forgiveness.* New York: Brunner-Routledge.

Worthington, E. L., Jr. (2006). *Forgiveness and reconciliation: Theory and application.* New York: Brunner-Routledge.

Worthington, E. L., Jr. (2009). *A just forgiveness: Responsible healing without excusing injustice.* Downers Grove, IL: InterVarsity Press.

Zechmeister, J. S., & Romero, C. (2002). Victim and offender accounts of interpersonal conflict: Autobiographical narratives of forgiveness and unforgiveness. *Journal of Personality and Social Psychology, 82,* 675–686.

25

How Religion Can Support Self-Control and Moral Behavior

Anne L. Zell and Roy F. Baumeister

One important way humans differ from other animals is in their extensive use of culture (Baumeister, 2005). Living in culture brings human beings tremendous social, economic, and other benefits. In order for culture to function, though, its members must adhere to certain rules. From a social-functionalist perspective, moral rules help society to function successfully and enable people to live together harmoniously (Baumeister, 2005; Baumeister & Boden, 1998; Hogan, 1973). These moral rules generally condemn selfish, impulsive, short-sighted actions and instead promote acts that are good for society as a whole or bring long-term gains. However, people are full of selfish desires and short-sighted urges whose fulfillment would be disruptive to the cultural system. People who consistently act on their first impulses are more likely to become criminals than pillars of the community. This means that to adapt to culture humans need the capacity to restrain their impulses and control their actions and bring them in line with meaningful rules and standards. In other words, living in a cultured society requires self-control. Most likely, human evolution increased the capacity for self-control to adapt to the increasing demands of human social life (see Kirkpatrick, Chapter 6, this volume, for more on the benefits of grounding psychology in evolutionary theory). The glass remains half empty, however: Human powers of self-control are partial. Probably everyone has occasionally failed to live up to his or her moral ideals, and most people experience such failures throughout life. Self-control thus needs help.

In this chapter, we examine the power of religion to promote morally virtuous behavior by means of improving self-control. More precisely, the goal of this chapter is to discuss how religion affects people's ability to be self-controlled. As a foundation, we present evidence that self-control is important for avoiding vice and enacting virtue, and we review theory and research about how self-control operates. Then we explore how religion might contribute to people's attempts to control themselves and pursue virtue. Stretching the reach of analysis from the individual to the culture, as we are doing in this chapter (see also Baumeister, 2005) automatically invokes the multilevel interdisciplinary paradigm (see Paloutzian & Park, Chapter 1, this volume). The perspective presented in this chapter is also consistent with the idea of religion as a meaning system (see Park, Chapter 18, this volume).

THE IMPORTANCE OF SELF-CONTROL FOR MORAL BEHAVIOR

Self-control (also self-regulation) refers to the capacity to override one incipient response, thereby permitting an (often unspecified) alternative. One example of exercising self-control would be overriding the urge to take a desirable bicycle out of a neighbor's garage and instead saving up money to purchase one. Using self-control, one may resist temptation, refocus attention, alter a mood or emotional state, overcome fatigue, or in other ways change one's state or actions. As a capacity for altering responses, self-control contributes greatly to the flexibility and diversity of human behavior. If people did not have the capacity to alter their behavior, moral rules would be useless. At best, such rules might make people realize the wrongness of their actions, but they would be powerless to change those actions. When self-interest and the common good conflict, self-control enables the individual to sacrifice his or her interest for the good of society.

Baumeister and Exline (1999, 2000) described self-control as a master virtue, in the sense that self-control seems necessary for people to be able to avoid many vices or sins and behave virtuously. They noted, for example, that failures of self-regulation are implicated in the seven deadly sins of medieval Christian theology: gluttony, sloth, lust, anger, and so on (e.g., Lyman, 1978). Consistent with this analysis, empirical evidence suggests that low or reduced/impaired self-control is associated with aggressive behavior (DeWall, Baumeister, Stillman, & Gailliot, 2007; Ronen, Rahav, & Moldawsky, 2007), intimate partner violence (Finkel, DeWall, Slotter, Oaten, & Foshee, 2009), dishonesty/cheating (Mead, Baumeister, Gino, Schweitzer, & Ariely, 2009; Muraven, Pogarsky, & Shmueli, 2006), greater alcohol consumption (Ostafin, Marlatt, & Greenwald, 2008), and unrestrained sexual behavior (Gailliot & Baumeister, 2007). Similarly, many virtues seem to hinge upon the ability to control oneself (Baumeister & Exline, 1999, 2000). For example, it would be difficult to realize Thomas Aquinas's cardinal virtues of prudence, temperance, or fortitude (Rickaby, 1896) without self-control.

To summarize, participation in culture requires that people be able to override their initial impulses and conform to moral rules. When people have low or temporarily impaired self-control, their impulses or automatic attitudes predict their behavior (Friese & Hofmann, 2009; Hofmann, Rauch, & Gawronski, 2007). Self-control can break the link from impulse to behavior, enabling people to override automatic, selfish, or short-sighted responses and to behave virtuously.

OPERATION OF SELF-CONTROL

To understand how religion might support self-control, we first need to consider how self-control operates. Thus far, researchers have identified four main elements in the operation of self-control: standards, monitoring, willpower, and motivation (Baumeister & Heatherton, 1996; Baumeister, Heatherton, & Tice, 1994; Baumeister & Vohs, 2007).

Standards

First, for self-control to be possible, people must have a standard, a conception of what they ought to do, to give direction to their self-control efforts. Problems can arise when a person either lacks standards or has conflicting standards, such as in a moral dilemma. In the face of conflicting standards, people may feel frustrated and confused.

Monitoring

Second, people must monitor their own behavior. Self-control is more likely to fail when people are not paying attention to their behavior and how it compares with standards. Thus, factors that reduce self-awareness should also reduce self-control. In a state of deindividuation, for example, people are more likely to steal or lie (e.g., Diener, Fraser, Beaman, & Kalem, 1976). Similarly, consumption of alcohol, which impairs self-relevant cognitive processing (Hull, 1981), is associated with sexual misbehavior and violence (Baumeister, 1997; Baumeister et al., 1994). By contrast, factors that increase self-awareness should also enhance self-control. For example, people are less likely to cheat when in the presence of a mirror (Diener & Wallbom, 1976).

Willpower

Standards and monitoring are useless unless people have the power to change their own behavior and make themselves adhere to the standards. Thus, the third element involves the actual operations that alter the self.

The Limited Resource Model and Its Evidence

A substantial body of evidence is consistent with the theory that self-control operates somewhat like a muscle (e.g., Baumeister, Bratslavsky, Muraven, & Tice, 1998; Schmeichel, 2007). This muscle, or limited-resource, model of self-control proposes that operations that alter the self all consume a single resource or energy supply, which is limited but renewable. Any time a person exercises self-control, overrides an impulse, or makes a conscious choice, the store of this resource is drawn upon. When the resource has been depleted, a person may attempt to conserve the limited remaining stores (Muraven, Shmueli, & Burkley, 2006). Thus, using self-control will deplete this resource, impairing subsequent self-control efforts. This depletion is analogous to a temporary state of muscle fatigue.

The results of many studies have generally conformed to the pattern predicted by the limited-resource model. For example, participants who were first asked to regulate their emotional response to an upsetting video subsequently performed worse on a handgrip task than participants who watched an upsetting video without regulating their emotional response (Muraven, Tice, & Baumeister, 1998). Participants who first had to eat radishes while resisting the temptation to sample some freshly baked chocolate cookies subsequently persisted for a shorter time on a different task (Baumeister et al., 1998). In these studies, the effect of depletion has been found to carry across strikingly different domains of self-control, including regulating task performance, suppressing thoughts, and regulating emotional responses, as well as acts of conscious choice (Baumeister et al., 1998), consistent with the assumption that various forms of self-control all draw from the same limited resource. Performing a depleting task also produces subsequent performance decrements on complex cognitive tasks such as logic and reasoning (Schmeichel, Vohs, & Baumeister, 2003). Thus, when thinking requires effortful volition, it too is degraded under conditions of ego depletion, such as resulting from a recent act of self-control.

Implications of the Limited-Resource Model

If all acts of volition, including self-control, conscious choice, and effortful reasoning, place demands upon the same limited resource, this would directly affect the degree of success people experience in their self-control efforts. For example, it implies that self-control is likely to break down in multiple areas at once (Baumeister & Exline, 1999). Gottfredson and Hirshi (1990) reported that most criminals show this pattern, being arrested repeatedly but for different types of crimes. Criminals are also more likely to smoke, drink, contribute to unplanned pregnancies, and have erratic attendance at school and work, all of which reflect chronically low self-control. A related implication is that attempting too many different self-control projects at the same time (e.g., ambitious lists of "New Year's resolutions") or starting new self-control projects during times of great stress may be unwise (Baumeister & Exline, 1999, 2000; Glass, Singer, & Friedman, 1969).

Because making conscious choices depletes the self's resources (Vohs et al., 2008), when depleted, people may find it easier to exercise self-control in areas that will not require numerous decisions. Partly for this reason, the formation of good habits may ease self-control efforts. Controlled processes that are repeated can eventually become at least somewhat automatic. Automatic processes deplete the self's resources less than controlled processes do (Bargh, 1982). If people regularly perform *virtuous behaviors*, eventually they will no longer have to make a decision each time about whether to perform the virtuous behavior, and they will have formed a *virtuous habit*. To the extent that people can automatize virtuous behavior in that way, their self-control should be less likely to suffer decrements during states of ego depletion (Baumeister, Muraven, & Tice, 2000).

An implication of the finding that effortful thought can be impaired by depletion is that moral reasoning is likely to be impaired under ego depletion, even though automatic moral responses such as gut reactions would not be affected. When the self's resources have been expended, a person may be less able to carry out reasoning processes so as to resolve moral dilemmas in mature, sophisticated ways. Simple, deeply rooted moral reactions, such as revulsion against incest, would however most likely remain intact.

The muscle analogy also implies that exercise may increase or build up people's self-control strength, making people less vulnerable to depletion effects (see Baumeister, Gailliot, DeWall, & Oaten, 2006, for review). For example, Muraven, Baumeister, and Tice (1999) found that participants who were instructed to perform self-control exercises for 2 weeks subsequently in the lab showed less of a performance decrement when asked to do two different depleting tasks in a row. Regular, long-term exercise may reduce a person's vulnerability to becoming quickly depleted and consequently experiencing decreased self-control.

Motivation

The fourth element of self-regulation is motivation (Baumeister & Vohs, 2007). Clear standards are unlikely to produce self-regulation unless people care about reaching those standards. Muraven and Slessareva (2003) found that depletion impaired the performance of participants low in motivation but not of participants high in motivation, suggesting that when people are more highly motivated they are able and willing to expend more of the self's resources. Thus, motivation may help people to circumvent lapses of self-control.

Summary: Operation of Self-Control

To understand how self-control functions, we must consider at least four basic ingredients: standards, monitoring, operations that alter the self, and motivation. Self-control and other acts of volition seem to draw upon a limited resource or energy supply. After using self-control, subsequent uses of self-control are impaired temporarily, as if self-control were a muscle that had become tired from exertion. This model has many practical implications. For example, initiating too many new self-control projects at the same time sets oneself up for failure. Regular exercise of self-control should decrease one's vulnerability to becoming rapidly depleted by exertions of self-control. Automatizing behaviors, or forming virtuous habits, can conserve the self's resource and make it easier to maintain virtuous behavior when one is depleted.

RELIGION AND SELF-CONTROL

Existing research is consistent with the idea that religion can facilitate self-control. For example, McCullough and Willoughby (2009) reviewed evidence that religion is associated with self-control, noting that religious people tend to score higher on measures of self-control and to have children who are more self-controlled. Toburen and Meier (2010) also found that participants who had been primed with God-related concepts versus neutral concepts subsequently persisted longer on an unsolvable anagram task. We turn next to an exploration of specific ways that religion might support self-control. We do not, of course, intend to imply anything either positive or negative about the possibility of religion providing supernatural help to self-control. Instead, our goal is to consider how particular religious beliefs and behaviors may be helpful to people trying to exercise self-control.

Religion and Standards

Clarity of Moral Standards

The first way religion can facilitate self-control is by providing clear standards about right and wrong. Religious traditions provide direct commands about what people ought to do and instructions on how people ought to live, such as the Ten Commandments in the Judeo-Christian tradition, the Eightfold Path of Buddhism, or the Five Pillars in Islam. Religious traditions also include moral exemplars for people to emulate, such as

Muhammed, Sri Krishna, Jesus, the Buddha, or Mother Theresa (as noted by Oman & Thoresen, 2003). However, Baumeister and Exline (1999) noted that certain cultural changes may hamper the ability of religion to set forth clear standards.

One such cultural change is the adoption of a capitalist economy (Baumeister & Exline, 1999). Historically, virtue meant sacrificing self-interest for the sake of society. However, in a capitalist economy, if a person tries to make as much profit for him- or herself as possible, this theoretically should benefit the economy as a whole. Thus, under this economic system there is no longer a simple, clear distinction between what is good for the individual and what is good for society. This shift is also reflected in the changed moral sensibilities of the Christian church: Whereas the early Christian church had taught that trying to make money qualified as the sin of greed, today most Christians have no moral qualms about seeking to maximize a profit (Baumeister & Exline, 1999).

A second cultural change is the elevation of selfhood into a value base (Baumeister, 1991; Baumeister & Exline, 1999). Habermas (1973) posited that society needs to have sources of value (such as tradition, or God's will) that do not derive their value from any outside source, but rather are sources of value for other things. Baumeister (1991) suggested that society has turned to the self and elevated it into a value base in order to fill the value gap caused by modernization. It is now considered acceptable, and perhaps even morally obligatory, to act in the best interest of one's self, whereas, traditionally, morality and religion have sought to restrain self-interested behavior. This means a near reversal of some moral norms. For example, in the past, society put pressure upon women to be willing to sacrifice a great deal for the sake of a marriage, whereas now women are often made to feel as though they have an obligation to leave a marriage that does not satisfy them fully or allow them to pursue their own potential (Zube, 1972).

Now people must find a way to reconcile historical conceptions of morality as intended to restrain the self with the recent formulation of the self as a source of value with inherently authoritative claims (Baumeister, 1991). Society may compromise between traditional morality and the newly elevated status of the self by, for example, approving a person's selfish actions except in those cases where the person deliberately tries to hurt someone else (Baumeister & Exline, 1999). Both of these cultural changes have contributed to the obscuring of moral standards and the lack of consensus on moral issues, which may pose problems for society (Haidt, Rosenberg, & Hom, 2003).

As one of culture's foremost promulgators of moral standards, religion can scarcely escape this cultural evolution unscathed. In response, some religious groups shift their moral stance to be more in line with the broader culture or increase their attention to values and services that are "friendly" to the self, such as positive self-worth, mental health, or recreation (Baumeister, 1991). Although such adaptations may help religious groups to meet the felt needs of people in society, they may do so at the cost of being able to provide clear standards for morally confused people. Religious groups that do not make such concession to cultural change may face their own resulting challenges. Although an unwavering moral stance has the benefit of providing clear guidance, people may find it difficult to adhere to religious teachings that diverge sharply from the practices of the surrounding culture. When unmarried Christians have sex (e.g., Charles, 2011), for example, or when Catholics use birth control, their cognitive dissonance regarding disobeying their religion's clear moral rules (e.g., Antonovsky, Shoham, Kavenocki, Modan, & Lancet, 1978) may erode their commitment to religion as their moral authority. Thus, problems may also arise when the moral standards provided by religion do not also allow for the flexibility or complexity necessary to comprehend the evolution of culture.

In summary, religion is an important source of moral standards for many people. However, religion's standard-setting role is accompanied by additional challenges and complications as a result of cultural shifts that may be producing conflict or confusion about moral standards or undermining the moral authority of religion.

Accountability to Moral Standards

Whether people think it is possible to control themselves affects how hard they try to maintain control. As Baumeister et al. (1994) argued, although the evidence suggests that people generally acquiesce in their own loss of control, cultural trends may be leading people to believe that aggressive impulses, drug addictions, and so on are impossible to resist. If people believe they are helpless to resist, they may feel less accountable for their actions and reduce their efforts to resist, resulting in an increase in undesirable behavior. Similarly, people who are led to disbelieve in free will become more aggressive, less helpful, and more willing to cheat on a test to get money (Baumeister, Masicampo, & DeWall, 2009; Vohs & Schooler, 2008). Thus, cultural trends that support the belief that people cannot control, and therefore cannot be held accountable for, their actions may actually detract from people's success at self-control.

Countering these cultural trends, religious beliefs may increase people's sense of being accountable for meeting moral standards. One way religion may strengthen people's sense of personal responsibility is by promoting belief in free will. The idea that God will judge people based on their behavior presupposes that people have some freedom to choose how to behave (Baumeister, Bauer, & Lloyd, 2010). Likewise, a belief that karma determines one's station in the next reincarnate life presupposes this same freedom of action. Another way religion may encourage people to hold themselves to high moral standards is by increasing their sense of self-efficacy (Fearer, 2007). Research finds that when people perceive themselves to be depleted, they perform worse on subsequent self-control tasks (Clarkson, Hirt, Jia, & Alexander, 2010), presumably because they are withdrawing effort to conserve self-control strength. However, we speculate that religious beliefs that God is aiding or strengthening one's self-control attempts (e.g., Galatians 5:22–23) could lead a person to continue to exert rather than conserve self-control strength. In summary, religious people may take divine commands as implying that obedience is possible and expected. If religious beliefs lead people to think they can regulate themselves, they are more likely to try; and if they try, they're more likely to succeed.

However, limits must be acknowledged: It may be counterproductive for people to believe they have control over things they cannot actually control, such as impulses. Baumeister et al. (1994) argued that most impulses cannot be directly controlled (although one can control the behavior that might stem from the impulse). Some religious authorities have voiced similar opinions. The Jewish sages taught that the "evil inclination" was created by God, and thus it was not in man's power to completely uproot, although it was in man's power to rule (Urbach, 1994). Christian ascetics of the fourth century concurred. In the stories of the desert fathers, when a hermit claimed to have succeeded in "killing" sinful passion—even one who had "fasted valiantly for fifty years"—that person was corrected or warned by the others. They viewed such claims as indication of self-deception or lack of insight, and even considered that the person's seemingly passion-less state could be spiritually harmful (Merton, 1960).

Religion and Monitoring

Third, religion can facilitate people's monitoring of their behavior. Monitoring is often crucial to the success of self-control efforts (e.g., Michie, Abraham, Whittington, McAteer, & Gupta, 2009). Many religious groups have instituted periodic times for self-examination, for example, as part of regular religious meetings, sweat lodges, the Catholic rite of confession, or daily prayer or journaling. Some religions remind adherents that God is also monitoring their behavior; for example, a Jewish saying counsels, "Consider three things and you will not fall into the grip of sin. Know what is above you: a seeing eye and a hearing ear, and that all your deeds are recorded in The Book" (Hirsch, 1989). In light of research findings that people behave more morally when in the presence of images of eyes (Bateson, Nettle, & Roberts, 2006; Haley & Fessler, 2005), that seems like a particularly apt reminder!

Religion and Limited Self-Regulatory Resources

We earlier presented the theory that self-control and other acts of volition draw upon a single limited resource. Religion may help people to use their self-regulatory resource more optimally in two ways. First, evidence suggests that practicing self-control can increase self-control capacity (e.g., Muraven, 2010). Religions ask their adherents to practice self-control by engaging in moral behavior, refraining from indulging in vices, and carrying out religious practices that require self-discipline, such as fasting during Ramadan, meditating, or giving money (McCullough & Willoughby, 2009). Consequently, religious people may build up greater self-control strength over time.

Religion may also help people to avoid ego-depleting conditions. For example, the biblical advice to "flee" from temptation (e.g., 2 Timothy 2:22) is consistent with the limited-resource model's suggestion that resisting temptation depletes one's self-regulatory resources. Muraven and Shmueli (2006), for example, found that just sniffing alcohol caused people high in temptation to drink to perform worse on unrelated self-control tasks. Furthermore, people have a tendency to overestimate their ability to control themselves (Nordgren, van Harreveld, & van der Pligt, 2009) and to underestimate how strong tempting urges can be (Nordgren, van der Pligt, & van Harreveld, 2007). In light of these empirical findings, the advice to flee temptation seems wise indeed. Religion may also help people to avoid becoming depleted by telling them what to do. Since making choices is depleting (Baumeister et al., 1998), people may feel relieved to be able to defer automatically to their religious authority's moral rulings.

Religion and Temptations

How people behave reflects not only their level of self-control but also the intensity of their urges (Baumeister, 2005). Is it possible to eradicate or reduce sinful impulses or desires? After all, it would be easier for people to be good if they didn't want so badly to be bad. Baumeister et al. (1994) suggested that it is probably futile to try to stop feeling a nonvirtuous desire through sheer force of will. They described nonvirtuous desires and impulses as arising from a combination of a latent motivation and an activating cue. People have a variety of latent motivations (or wants and needs) that may be more or less automatic or biologically programmed. At any given time, these motivations, although present, may not be felt consciously if there is no activating cue or stimulus—either in the environment or naturally arising in the person (such as hunger). However, in the presence of the appropriate cue, the impulse to satisfy a particular latent motivation will automatically arise whether a person wants it to or not. Following this framework, we propose ways that religion might help people to avoid sinful urges or reduce their appeal.

Avoiding Activating Cues

One especially effective target of self-control may be the environment: By purging one's environment of activating cues, one may be able to prevent an impulse from arising. In dealing with inappropriate desires, attention is the place to begin (Baumeister et al., 1994). The safest way to ensure that a cue does not capture one's attention may be to remove the cue from one's environment, such as removing cigarettes and lighters from one's home if one is trying to quit smoking.

Being a member of a religious group permits even greater control over the tempting stimuli in the environment, because people can surround themselves with others who share similar moral standards. For example, some religious groups and orders seek to promote celibacy as a way of life. To avoid activating sexual thoughts, they remove people from contact with sexually suggestive stimuli. Living in a cave or desert is one option. Another is to have the members live in same-gender groups with unflattering haircuts and concealing, unfashionable clothing. In contrast, if one is close to people who like to indulge in pleasures that one is trying to resist, motivation to abstain from those pleasures is likely to be undermined (Leander, Shah, & Chartrand, 2009). An additional benefit of being a member of a religious community is that one might be surrounded by exemplars of high self-control. Oman and Thoresen (2003) pointed out that family and community members can serve as helpful spiritual models, raising people's estimations of the level of virtue that is possible for them to attain and increasing their motivation. This idea is consistent with recent findings that thinking about people who have good self-control can increase people's state self-control (vanDellen & Hoyle, 2010).

Modifying Latent Motivations

A secondary and less certain target of control may be the latent motivations themselves. Motivations that are mainly biologically programmed would resist change, but it is possible that other motivations that are more a product of learning may be somewhat amenable to being unlearned. Religion may facilitate this kind of reeducation. Religion sometimes entails beliefs about what will and what will not make people happy, satisfied, or fulfilled. A person's religion may teach that engaging in a certain sin will not truly produce the satisfaction or positive emotion that she or he is seeking. To the extent that the person is convinced that this is true, she or he might be less likely to desire those sinful indulgences or to turn to them in order to regulate her or his affect. (Again, however, latent motivations that are biologically programmed are not likely to be greatly affected, no matter how fervent a person's beliefs might be.) We also speculate that people's cravings for sinful pleasures may fade slightly with disuse. Baumeister (2005) argued that indulging a craving may reinforce it, whereas abstinence may lead to the desire being weakened over time. Accordingly, we speculate that after not indulging in a sin for a period of time, people may gradually begin to forget how much they had once enjoyed that sinful activity, especially if they are motivated to remember their past in a negative light.

Handling Sinful Urges

Last, when an activating cue does slip through a person's net and triggers an inappropriate latent motivation, how can he or she deal with the nonvirtuous impulse that arises? Strategies such as distraction or reconstrual may help people to manage tempting impulses, and religion is well equipped to capitalize on these strategies.

Distraction is an important aid to management of inappropriate desires. In a classic study, Wegner, Schneider, Carter, and White (1987) demonstrated that asking people to try not to think about a white bear led to an ironic rebound effect such that, after the prohibition against white bear thoughts was lifted, people thought about white bears even more. However, providing participants with a distraction—in this case, instructing them to think about a red Volkswagen instead of a white bear—enabled them to be much more successful at avoiding thinking about the white bear (Wegner et al., 1987). The effectiveness of distraction has been noted in research on delay of gratification as well (Mischel, 1974; Rodriguez, Mischel, & Shoda, 1989). Children who succeeded in waiting for the delayed larger reward commonly found a way, such as playing games with their feet, singing, covering their eyes, or trying to sleep, to occupy their attention with something other than the temptingly available smaller prize (Mischel, 1974).

Religion can supply people with multiple avenues for distraction from temptation. Religious conversion is often accompanied by new goals and motives (Paloutzian, Richardson, & Rambo, 1999). The force of these newly acquired goals may overpower the person's old, inappropriate desires. For example, someone who used to go to wild parties on the weekend may, after a religious conversion, prefer to attend a religious meeting.

The way people construe a situation can also affect the likelihood that they will maintain self-control. For example, higher level (i.e., more abstract, connected to a broader perspective or longer time frame) construals facilitate self-control (Fujita & Han, 2009; Schmeichel & Vohs, 2009), as does construing a task as a test of willpower (Magen & Gross, 2007). Both of these types of construals apparently reduce the temptation's appeal. Religion is uniquely suited for promoting high level construals because it connects to the highest levels of meaning and the longest time frames (Baumeister, 1991). Religion can also be a source of helpful reconstruals, such as viewing a desired indulgence as representing a spiritual test or even battle.

Religion and Motivation

An important way in which religion can contribute to self-control efforts is by supplying motivation. Religion provides an array of compelling reasons for moral conduct. The belief that God wants you to behave in a certain way is the ultimate reason to do so (Baumeister, 1991; Emmons, 1999). Particularly motivating may be religious beliefs about salvation or enlightenment (Baumeister, 1991). Many religious people associate moral virtue with positive outcomes after death, such as with beliefs that moral behavior will guarantee salvation or lead closer to nirvana. Thinking about this ultimate goal (i.e., salvation or enlightenment) can help people to transcend their immediate stimulus environment (Baumeister et al., 1994). Rather than focusing on everything around them that makes them want to quit being good, they can remind themselves of their higher level goals and base their behavior upon those.

Some religious people also associate immoral behavior with negative outcomes after death. For example, the story is told about a fourth-century "desert father" (i.e., an ascetic Christian who lived as a hermit), that a woman arrived at his cell one night and begged for shelter. Determined to restrain his sexual desire, the hermit thought about "the judgment of God." When that thought alone failed to quench his burning lust, he reportedly said to himself, "Well, let's see whether you will be able to bear the flames of hell," and put his fingers into the flame of the lamp, burning them one by one until morning came and he could finally send the woman on her way (Merton, 1960). Thus, whereas the promise of ultimate fulfillment may motivate some people, others may be inspired to virtue more effectively by their desire to avoid the ultimate negative outcome. People may perceive fear to be helpful when they are pursuing avoidance goals (Tamir & Ford, 2009).

Religion can provide other motivations for virtuous behavior, aside from concerns about what will happen after death. Religiously based motivations for moral behavior may also include desires to show gratitude to God, to promote one's religion to others, or to accomplish other goals. In general, because religion allows people to base their everyday behavior upon high-level principles, it can sanctify and imbue the most mundane of activities with meaning and importance (McCullough & Willoughby, 2009). The ability to view one's activity in a larger meaningful context has been found to help people to persist on aversive or dull tasks (Sansone, Weir, Harpster, & Morgan, 1992).

People may also be more likely to reach their self-control goals when their motivation is autonomous (i.e., because they "want to") rather than forced or obligated (i.e., because they "should") (Berg, Janoff-Bulman, & Cotter, 2001; Mata et al., 2009; Williams, Niemiec, Patrick, Ryan, & Deci, 2009). Furthermore, exerting self-control for autonomous reasons apparently depletes people less than does exerting self-control for extrinsic/controlled reasons (e.g., Muraven, 2008; Muraven, Gagné, & Rosman, 2008; Muraven, Rosman, & Gagné, 2007). Religious beliefs give people multiple angles for transforming externally imposed moral rules into intrinsically motivated personal values.

The desire to avoid guilt may be one of the most powerful motivators for moral behavior. The moral emotion of guilt arises when people fail to behave in a virtuous way or when people hurt another (Tangney, 1991, 1992). Guilt motivates people to try to restore or maintain relationships, such as by making amends for wrongs they have committed, apologizing to people they have hurt, and trying not to commit the same offense again in the future (Baumeister, Stillwell, & Heatherton, 1994). Because the feeling of guilt is experienced as aversive, guilt also teaches people the lesson that they should not do again what they had done to arouse the guilt (Baumeister, Stillwell, & Heatherton, 1995).

Cultural changes may have slightly weakened guilt's efficacy at spurring people to be virtuous (Baumeister & Exline, 1999). Over time, social relationships have become less stable. During the Middle Ages, a typical person might have lived in proximity to the same few dozen people for his or her whole life (Shorter, 1975). People now are more mobile. They can easily move to a different geographical location or move from one level of society or economic class to another. As a result, people have fewer long-term, stable relationships. Because people are most likely to feel guilty about harm done to someone with whom they have a stable long-term relationship (see Baumeister et al., 1994, for a review), a reduction in long-term relationships diminishes guilt's power to enforce morality. Friedman's (2002) history of American law notes that laws and morals often use similar rules to promote similar behaviors, but insofar as morality depends on reputation and long-term relationship contexts to provide its force, it loses effectiveness in promoting prosocial behavior between strangers. Therefore, as society changes to increase the amount of dealings people have with relative strangers, they increasingly rely more on law than on morality to ensure fair treatment.

Religiousness, on the other hand, is associated with increased experience of guilt (e.g., Albertsen, O'Connor, & Berry, 2006). We suspect that religion may reinforce the power of guilt for promoting prosocial behavior in several ways. First, religion puts forth clear moral standards, which enables people to know clearly when they have failed to meet those standards. Second, religious traditions may emphasize the moral accountability of the individual. Third, membership in close-knit religious groups sometimes entails a certain degree of accountability to shared moral standards. Members of such groups sometimes feel entitled or obligated to inform or confront each other when they perceive each other as falling short of virtue. In addition to helping to monitor each others' behavior, religious groups may reward virtuous behavior with acceptance or status, while punishing sinful behavior with ostracism or public shame. Fourth, religion may supply an additional relationship about which to feel guilty. Some Christians, for example, consider themselves to have a personal relationship with God and believe that their sin offends or hurts God.

In short, religion offers people a range of potent motivations for moral behavior. Foremost among the religious motivations may be the pursuit of ultimate fulfillment in the form of religious salvation. Without the framework of religion, people are often hard put to come up with compelling motivations for good behavior (Baumeister & Exline, 1999; MacIntyre, 1981). Religion also supports guilt, which makes people less likely to commit the same failures of self-control or interpersonal transgressions again in the future.

Religion and Affect

Emotional distress may function like an activating cue for people to engage in vices. Tice, Bratslavsky, and Baumeister (2001) found that when people are emotionally distressed, they indulge their immediate impulses in an attempt to make themselves feel better, sacrificing their self-control goals in order to boost their mood. Prioritizing the goal of affect regulation over other self-control goals is a common cause of self-control failures. For example, if a person who is in a bad mood believes that buying new clothes will make her feel better, she may choose to go shopping, even if that causes her to fail in her goal of saving money (Baumeister, 2002).

Emotional distress is an internal cue that is not easily controlled. In general, people don't have direct control over whether they are going to be in a bad mood. However, some beliefs commonly associated with religion may reduce people's emotional distress during experiences of misfortune, discomfort, or suffering. Christian beliefs that God is sovereign and benevolent are a tremendous resource for people who are coping with distressing events because they imply that the difficulty is not meaningless but rather has some good (even if unknown) purpose (see Park, Chapter 18, this volume). The Hindu belief that life is an illusion could also alleviate distress during difficult times. Furthermore, if religious beliefs actually increase positive affect, this may promote self-regulation. A positive mood induction has been found to eliminate the depletion effect, possibly because when people are in a good mood they are more willing to expend their self-regulatory resources (Tice, Baumeister, Shmueli, & Muraven, 2007).

Belief in ultimate religious salvation can also be helpful to people's self-control efforts. First, it may alleviate any fears about death, perhaps especially among those with an intrinsic religious orientation (e.g., Jonas & Fischer, 2006). Dealing with threatening thoughts about death is depleting (Gailliot, Schmeichel, & Baumeister, 2006). Religious beliefs that a happy future awaits after death may free up self-regulatory resources for use at self-control efforts. Second, religious teachings sometimes assure people that the coming happiness will more than compensate for their present tribulations (e.g., Romans 8:18), which may enable people to endure more trouble than they otherwise would. Although we are not aware of any controlled tests of this hypothesis, it seems consistent with the example of religious martyrs.

Religion can also promote a sense of belonging and connection to God, to other members of the religious community, and to religious culture (see Saroglou & Cohen, Chapter 17, this volume). In doing so, religion may protect people from suffering social exclusion. Baumeister et al. (2010) argue that social rejection can undermine people's motivation to self-regulate because a major reason people self-regulate is so that they can belong to society. They posit that religious traditions that offer unconditional acceptance may further support people's self-regulation.

Thus, religious beliefs may supply people with motivation, hope, and meaning, which can allow them to maintain virtuous behavior, even when to do so is painful or difficult. Furthermore, religious beliefs may reduce people's emotional distress when experiencing difficulties, may help people to be less threatened by the thought of their mortality, and may cause people to be less likely to suffer feelings of rejection and isolation. If religion helps people to feel less negative affect, they may be less tempted to indulge in vices in order to repair their mood. Finally, religious beliefs may provide people with positive affect, which may lead to greater self-regulatory exertion. In summary, helping people to regulate their affect is an important way that religion may support people's successful self-control.

Summary: Religion and Self-Control

Religiousness can affect self-control efforts in multiple ways—most of them positive. The evolution of a capitalist economy and the elevation of the self into a value base have complicated the moral landscape. Nevertheless, religion remains an important source of moral standards to guide people's self-control endeavors. There is also a disturbing trend for American culture to support people's belief that they are sometimes incapable of controlling their actions. We are generally skeptical of people's efforts to abnegate personal responsibility for losses of self-control and their ensuing misdeeds. Thus, we suggest that another important way in which religion supports self-control is by reinforcing people's belief in free will and in their ability to control themselves. Religion gives people standards and encourages people to hold themselves to those standards.

An abundance of empirical evidence tells us that if one wishes to regulate a behavior, it helps to keep track of it. Religious organizations have in place helpful traditions and practices that facilitate people's self-monitoring. Certain religious teachings and practices also seem to mesh well with findings that self-control depends upon a limited resource. For example, the advice to flee temptation is eminently sensible in light of research findings that exposure to temptation temporarily depletes people's self-control strength. Religious people also have regular opportunities to practice self-control, which may increase their self-control strength.

People may try to use a variety of strategies to deal with inappropriate or immoral desires. Preventing tempting stimuli from coming to one's attention by controlling one's environment can be an effective way to stay on the path of virtue. When a tempting stimulus does catch a person's eye, distraction has been shown to be very helpful. Changing the way one thinks about a nonvirtuous impulse (e.g., thinking of it as a temptation from the devil) may also make it less appealing.

As a source of motivation for moral behavior, religion is unparalleled. Religion can sanctify any endeavor, imbuing it with significance (Emmons, 1999), as well as offer the ultimate incentives. Despite the great mobility of people in contemporary society, religion continues to make good use of guilt, which is one of the most important motivators for moral behavior. The religious groups to which people belong are often excellent at supplying guilt for people who do not meet moral standards. It is important to keep in mind that some types of religious motivation, such as autonomous motivation, are likely to be more helpful than others. McCullough and Willoughby (2009) cautioned that introjected or extrinsically motivated religiosity may not be associated with greater self-control or other positive outcomes. Thus, future researchers may find it productive to take into account the nature and not merely the intensity of people's religious motivation.

People's bad moods and emotional distress can lead them to try to remedy their mood by indulging in some vice or allowing their other self-control goals to fail. Religion often helps people to cope with negative situations. Therefore, religious people may escape some of the self-control failures that occur as a result of people's immediate affect-regulation goals taking precedence over their normal self-control goals.

CONCLUSION

There can be a dark side to religion and to self-control. Sometimes religious beliefs lead people to pursue goals that harm others, as in the case of suicide bombings (see Moghaddam, Warren, & Love, Chapter 32, this volume). Sometimes religion may encourage people to lose control, as when religious practices deindividuate participants (but see also Leary, Adams, & Tate, 2006). Sometimes people use self-control to pursue selfish ends at the expense of society. While these are important phenomena and worthy of examination (for a different chapter!), we suspect that they are a smaller part of the story about religion and self-control. We believe that, on balance, religion and self-control offer many benefits, both to individuals and to society as a whole (e.g., Tangney, Baumeister, & Boone, 2004). This assumption is consistent with an analysis of moral rules as functioning to enable humans to live in culture and of self-control as enabling humans to adhere to moral rules.

Self-control is likely one large indirect means by which the benefits of religion are obtained (see McCullough & Willoughby, 2009, for a review). By offering a framework that supports self-control, religion promotes a trait that enables people to do what is morally and pragmatically best for society and that also helps them do what best serves their own long-term, enlightened self-interest. We have proposed that self-control is vital for moral action and for living successfully in culture. However, people's ability to control themselves is limited. We have suggested that religion offers crucial support for self-control in a variety of ways.

At present, psychology has a better understanding of how self-control works than of how religiosity promotes self-control, and so our discussion of the latter has necessarily been largely speculative. Religion may promote self-control by upholding specific moral standards, by motivating people to want to be good, by exploiting the prosocial power of guilt, by linking the religious individual into a stable network of relationships to other believers and to God, by promoting character strength through regular exercise of the moral muscle, by fostering self-criticism, and by making people feel that their good and bad deeds are being observed and recorded. Probably there are other ways as well. As knowledge continues to accumulate, it seems likely that self-control will continue to loom large in accounting for the earthly benefits of religion.

ACKNOWLEDGMENTS

Preparation of this chapter was supported by an Augustana Research and Artists Fund grant from Augustana College to Anne Zell.

REFERENCES

Albertsen, E. J., O'Connor, L. E., & Berry, J. W. (2006). Religion and interpersonal guilt: Variations across ethnicity and spirituality. *Mental Health, Religion & Culture, 9*, 67–84.

Antonovsky, H. F., Shoham, I., Kavenocki, S., Modan, B., & Lancet, M. (1978). Sexual attitude-behavior discrepancy among Israeli adolescent girls. *Journal of Sex Research, 14*, 260–272.

Bargh, J. (1982). Attention and automaticity in the processing of self-relevant information. *Journal of Personality and Social Psychology, 43*, 425–436.

Bateson, M., Nettle, D., & Roberts, G. (2006). Cues of being watched enhance cooperation in a real-world setting. *Biology Letters, 2*, 412–414.

Baumeister, R. F. (1991). *Meanings of life.* New York: Guilford Press.

Baumeister, R. F. (1997). *Evil: Inside human violence and cruelty.* New York: W.H. Freeman.

Baumeister, R. F. (2002). Yielding to temptation: Self-control failure, impulsive purchasing, and consumer behavior. *Journal of Consumer Research, 28*, 670–676.

Baumeister, R. F. (2005). *The cultural animal: Human nature, meaning, and social life.* New York: Oxford University Press.

Baumeister, R. F., Bauer, I. M., & Lloyd, S. A. (2010). Choice, free will, and religion. *Psychology of Religion and Spirituality, 2*, 67–82.

Baumeister, R. F., & Boden, J. M. (1998). Aggression and the self: High self-esteem, low self-control, and ego threat. In R. G. Geen & E. Donnerstein (Eds.), *Human aggression: Theories, research, and implications for social policy* (pp. 111–137). San Diego, CA: Academic Press.

Baumeister, R. F., Bratslavsky, E., Muraven, M., & Tice, D. M. (1998). Ego depletion: Is the active self a limited resource? *Journal of Personality and Social Psychology, 74*, 1252–1265.

Baumeister, R. F., & Exline, J. J. (1999). Virtue, personality, and social relations: Self-control as the moral muscle. *Journal of Personality, 67*, 1165–1194.

Baumeister, R. F., & Exline, J. J. (2000). Self-control, morality, and human strength. *Journal of Social and Clinical Psychology, 19*, 29–42.

Baumeister, R. F., Gailliot, M., DeWall, C. N., & Oaten, M. (2006). Self-regulation and personality: How interventions increase regulatory success, and how depletion moderates the effects of traits on behavior. *Journal of Personality, 74*, 1773–1801.

Baumeister, R. F., & Heatherton, T. F. (1996). Self-regulation failure: An overview. *Psychological Inquiry, 7*, 1–15.

Baumeister, R. F., Heatherton, T. F., & Tice, D. M. (1994). *Losing control: How and why people fail at self-regulation*. San Diego: Academic Press.

Baumeister, R. F., Masicampo, E. J., & DeWall, C. N. (2009). Prosocial benefits of feeling free: Disbelief in free will increases aggression and reduces helpfulness. *Personality and Social Psychology Bulletin, 35*, 260–268.

Baumeister, R. F., Muraven, M., & Tice, D. M. (2000). Ego depletion: A resource model of volition, self-regulation, and controlled processing. *Social Cognition, 18*, 130–150.

Baumeister, R. F., Stillwell, A. M., & Heatherton, T. F. (1994). Guilt: An interpersonal approach. *Psychological Bulletin, 115*, 243–267.

Baumeister, R. F., Stillwell, A. M., & Heatherton, T. F. (1995). Personal narratives about guilt: Role in action control and interpersonal relationships. *Basic and Applied Social Psychology, 17*, 173–198.

Baumeister, R. F., & Vohs, K. D. (2007). Self-regulation, ego depletion, and motivation. *Social and Personality Psychology Compass, 1*, 115–128.

Berg, M. B., Janoff-Bulman, R., & Cotter, J. (2001). Perceiving value in obligations and goals: Wanting to do what should be done. *Personality and Social Psychology Bulletin, 27*, 982–995.

Charles, T. (2011). (Almost) everyone's doing it. *Relevant Magazine, 53*, 65–69.

Clarkson, J. J., Hirt, E. R., Jia, L., & Alexander, M. B. (2010). When perception is more than reality: The effects of perceived versus actual resource depletion on self-regulatory behavior. *Journal of Personality and Social Psychology, 98*, 29–46.

Dewall, C. N., Baumeister, R. F., Stillman, T. F., & Gailliot, M. T. (2007). Violence restrained: Effects of self-regulation and its depletion on aggression. *Journal of Experimental Social Psychology, 43*, 62–76.

Diener, E., Fraser, S. C., Beaman, A. L., & Kelem, R. T. (1976). Effects of deindividuation variables on stealing among Halloween trick-or-treaters. *Journal of Personality and Social Psychology, 33*, 178–183.

Diener, E., & Wallbom, M. (1976). Effects of self-awareness on antinormative behavior. *Journal of Research in Personality, 10*, 107–111.

Emmons, R. A. (1999). *The psychology of ultimate concerns: Motivation and spirituality in personality*. New York: Guilford Press.

Fearer, S. A. (2007). Examining the role of social cognitive constructs in religion's effect on alcohol use. *Dissertation Abstracts International: Section B: The Sciences and Engineering, 68*(3-B), 1923.

Finkel, E. J., DeWall, C. N., Slotter, E. B., Oaten, M., & Foshee, V. A. (2009). Self-regulatory failure and intimate partner violence perpetration. *Journal of Personality and Social Psychology, 97*, 483–499.

Friedman, L. M. (2002). *Law in America: A short history*. New York: Random House.

Friese, M., & Hofmann, W. (2009). Control me or I will control you: Impulses, trait self-control, and the guidance of behavior. *Journal of Research in Personality, 43,* 795–805.

Fujita, K., & Han, H. A. (2009). Moving beyond deliberative control of impulses: The effect of construal levels on evaluative associations in self-control conflicts. *Psychological Science, 20,* 799–804.

Gailliot, M. T., & Baumeister, R. F. (2007). Self-regulation and sexual restraint: Dispositionally and temporarily poor self-regulatory abilities contribute to failures at restraining sexual behavior. *Personality and Social Psychology Bulletin, 33,* 173–186.

Gailliot, M. T., Schmeichel, B. J., & Baumeister, R. F. (2006). Self-regulatory processes defend against the threat of death: Effects of self-control depletion and trait self-control on thoughts and fears of dying. *Journal of Personality and Social Psychology, 91,* 49–62.

Glass, D. C., Singer, J. E., & Friedman, L. N. (1969). Psychic cost of adaptation to an environmental stressor. *Journal of Personality and Social Psychology, 12,* 200–210.

Gottfredson, M. R., & Hirschi, T. (1990). *A general theory of crime.* Stanford, CA: Stanford University Press.

Habermas, J. (1973). *Legitimation crisis* (T. McCarthy, trans.). Boston: Beacon.

Haidt, J., Rosenberg, E., & Hom, H. (2003). Differentiating diversities: Moral diversity is not like other kinds. *Journal of Applied Social Psychology, 33,* 1–36.

Haley, K. J., & Fessler, D. M. T. (2005). Nobody's watching?: Subtle cues affect generosity in an anonymous economic game. *Evolution and Human Behavior, 26,* 245–256.

Hirsch, S. R. (Trans.). (1989). *Chapters of the fathers.* Jerusalem: Feldheim.

Hofmann, W., Rauch, W., & Gawronski, B. (2007). And deplete us not into temptation: Automatic attitudes, dietary restraint, and self-regulatory resources as determinants of eating behavior. *Journal of Experimental Social Psychology, 43,* 497–504.

Hogan, R. (1973). Moral conduct and moral character: A psychological perspective. *Psychological Bulletin, 79,* 217–232.

Hull, J. G. (1981). A self-awareness model of the causes and effects of alcohol consumption. *Journal of Abnormal Psychology, 90,* 586–600.

Jonas, E., & Fischer, P. (2006). Terror management and religion: Evidence that intrinsic religiousness mitigates worldview defense following mortality salience. *Journal of Personality and Social Psychology, 91,* 553–567.

Leander, N. P., Shah, J. Y., & Chartrand, T. L. (2009). Moments of weakness: The implicit context dependencies of temptations. *Personality and Social Psychology Bulletin, 35,* 853–866.

Leary, M. R., Adams, C. E., & Tate, E. B. (2006). Hypo-egoic self-regulation: Exercising self-control by diminishing the influence of the self. *Journal of Personality, 74,* 1803–1831.

Lyman, S. (1978). *The seven deadly sins: Society and evil.* New York: St. Martin's.

MacIntyre, A. (1981). *After virtue.* Notre Dame, IN: University of Notre Dame Press.

Magen, E., & Gross, J. J. (2007). Harnessing the need for immediate gratification: Cognitive reconstrual modulates the reward value of temptations. *Emotion, 7,* 415–428.

Mata, J., Silva, M. N., Vieira, P. N., Carraça, E. V., Andrade, A. M., Coutinho, S. R., et al. (2009). Motivational "spill-over" during weight control: Increased self-determination and exercise intrinsic motivation predict eating self-regulation. *Health Psychology, 28,* 709–716.

McCullough, M. E., & Willoughby, B. L. B. (2009). Religion, self-regulation, and self-control: Associations, explanations, and implications. *Psychological Bulletin, 135,* 69–93.

Mead, N. L., Baumeister, R. F., Gino, F., Schweitzer, M. E., & Ariely, D. (2009). Too tired to tell the truth: Self-control resource depletion and dishonesty. *Journal of Experimental Social Psychology, 45,* 594–597.

Merton, T. (1960). *The wisdom of the desert.* New York: New Directions.

Michie, S., Abraham, C., Whittington, C., McAteer, J., & Gupta, S. (2009). Effective techniques in healthy eating and physical activity interventions: A meta-regression. *Health Psychology, 28,* 690–701.

Mischel, W. (1974). Processes in delay of gratification. In L. Berkowitz (Ed.), *Advances in experimental social psychology* (Vol. 7, pp. 249–292). New York: Academic Press.

Mischel, W., Shoda, Y., & Peake, P. K. (1988). Delay of gratification in children. *Science, 244,* 933–938.

Muraven, M. (2008). Autonomous self-control is less depleting. *Journal of Research in Personality, 42*(3), 763–770.

Muraven, M. (2010). Building self-control strength: Practicing self-control leads to improved self-control performance. *Journal of Experimental Social Psychology, 46,* 465–468.

Muraven, M., Baumeister, R. F., & Tice, D. M. (1999). Longitudinal improvement of self-regulation through practice: Building self-control through repeated exercise. *Journal of Social Psychology, 139,* 446–457.

Muraven, M., Gagné, M., & Rosman, H. (2008). Helpful self-control: Autonomy support, vitality, and depletion. *Journal of Experimental Social Psychology, 44*(3), 573–585.

Muraven, M., Pogarsky, G., & Shmueli, D. (2006). Self-control depletion and the general theory of crime. *Journal of Quantitative Criminology, 22,* 263–277.

Muraven, M., Rosman, H., & Gagné, M. (2007). Lack of autonomy and self-control: Performance contingent rewards lead to greater depletion. *Motivation and Emotion, 31*(4), 322–330.

Muraven, M., & Shmueli, D. (2006). The self-control costs of fighting the temptation to drink. *Psychology of Addictive Behaviors, 20,* 154–160.

Muraven, M., Shmueli, D., & Burkley, E. (2006). Conserving self-control strength. *Journal of Personality and Social Psychology, 91,* 524–537.

Muraven, M., & Slessareva, E. (2003). Mechanism of self-control failure: Motivation and limited resources. *Personality and Social Psychology Bulletin, 29,* 894–906.

Muraven, M., Tice, D. M., & Baumeister, R. F. (1998). Self-control as limited resource: Regulatory depletion patterns. *Journal of Personality and Social Psychology, 74,* 774–789.

Nordgren, L. F., van der Pligt, J., & van Harreveld, F. (2007). Evaluating eve: Visceral states influence the evaluation of impulsive behavior. *Journal of Personality and Social Psychology, 93,* 75–84.

Nordgren, L. F., van Harreveld, F., & van der Pligt, J. (2009). The restraint bias: How the illusion of self-restraint promotes impulsive behavior. *Psychological Science, 20,* 1523–1528.

Oman, D., & Thoresen, C. E. (2003). The many frontiers of spiritual modeling: Reply. *The International Journal for the Psychology of Religion, 13,* 187–213.

Ostafin, B. D., Marlatt, G. A., & Greenwald, A. G. (2008). Drinking without thinking: An implicit measure of alcohol motivation predicts failure to control alcohol use. *Behaviour Research and Therapy, 46,* 1210–1219.

Paloutzian, R. F., Richardson, J. T., & Rambo, L. R. (1999). Religious conversion and personality change. *Journal of Personality, 67,* 1047–1079.

Rickaby, J. (1896). *Aquinas ethicus: The moral teaching of St. Thomas.* London: Burns and Oates.

Rodriguez, M. L., Mischel, W., & Shoda, Y. (1989). Cognitive person variables in the delay of gratification of older children at risk. *Journal of Personality and Social Psychology, 57,* 358–367.

Ronen, T., Rahav, G., & Moldawsky, A. (2007). Aggressive behavior among Israeli elementary school students and associated emotional/behavioral problems and self-control. *School Psychology Quarterly, 22,* 407–431.

Sansone, C., Weir, C., Harpster, L., & Morgan, C. (1992). Once a boring task, always a boring task?: Interest as a self-regulatory mechanism. *Journal of Personality and Social Psychology, 63,* 379–390.

Schmeichel, B. J. (2007). Attention control, memory updating, and emotion regulation temporarily reduce the capacity for executive control. *Journal of Experimental Psychology: General, 136,* 241–255.

Schmeichel, B. J., & Vohs, K. (2009). Self-affirmation and self-control: Affirming core values counteracts ego depletion. *Journal of Personality and Social Psychology, 96,* 770–782.

Schmeichel, B. J., Vohs, K. D., & Baumeister, R. F. (2003). Intellectual performance and ego depletion: Role of the self in logical reasoning and other information processing. *Journal of Personality and Social Psychology, 85,* 33–46.

Shorter, E. (1975). *The making of the modern family.* New York: Basic Books.

Tamir, M., & Ford, B. Q. (2009). Choosing to be afraid: Preferences for fear as a function of goal pursuit. *Emotion, 9,* 488–497.

Tangney, J. P. (1991). Moral affect: The good, the bad, and the ugly. *Journal of Personality and Social Psychology, 61,* 598–607.

Tangney, J. P. (1992). Situational determinants of shame and guilt in young adulthood. *Personality and Social Psychology Bulletin, 18,* 199–206.

Tangney, J. P., Baumeister, R. F., & Boone, A. L. (2004). High self-control predicts good adjustment, less pathology, better grades, and interpersonal success. *Journal of Personality, 72,* 271–322.

Tice, D. M., Baumeister, R. F., Shmueli, D., & Muraven, M. (2007). Restoring the self: Positive affect helps improve self-regulation following ego depletion. *Journal of Experimental Social Psychology, 43*(3), 379–384.

Tice, D. M., Bratslavsky, E., & Baumeister, R. F. (2001). Emotional distress regulation takes precedence over impulse control: If you feel bad, do it! *Journal of Personality and Social Psychology, 80,* 53–67.

Toburen, T., & Meier, B. P. (2010). Priming God-related concepts increases anxiety and task persistence. *Journal of Social and Clinical Psychology, 29,* 127–143.

Urbach, E. E. (1994). *The sages: Their concepts and beliefs* (I. Abrahams, trans.). Cambridge, MA: Harvard University Press.

vanDellen, M. R., & Hoyle, R. H. (2010). Regulatory accessibility and social influences on state self-control. *Personality and Social Psychology Bulletin, 36,* 251–263.

Vohs, K. D., Baumeister, R. F., Schmeichel, B. J., Twenge, J. M., Nelson, N. M., & Tice, D. M. (2008). Making choices impairs subsequent self-control: A limited-resource account of decision making, self-regulation, and active initiative. *Journal of Personality and Social Psychology, 94,* 883–898.

Vohs, K. D., & Schooler, J. W. (2008). The value of believing in free will: Encouraging a belief in determinism increases cheating. *Psychological Science, 19,* 49–54.

Wegner, D. M., Schneider, D. J., Carter, S. R., & White, T. L. (1987). Paradoxical effects of thought suppression. *Journal of Personality and Social Psychology, 53,* 5–13.

Williams, G. C., Niemiec, C. P., Patrick, H., Ryan, R. M., & Deci, E. L. (2009). The importance of supporting autonomy and perceived competence in facilitating long-term tobacco abstinence. *Annals of Behavioral Medicine, 37,* 315–324.

Zube, M. J. (1972). Changing concepts of morality: 1948–1969. *Social Forces, 50,* 385–393.

Part V

THE PSYCHOLOGY OF RELIGION AND APPLIED AREAS

26

Religion, Spirituality, and Health

Kevin S. Masters and Stephanie A. Hooker

The first edition of this *Handbook* featured an excellent chapter by Doug Oman and Carl Thoresen (2005) investigating the question of whether religion and spirituality (R/S) influence physical health. The authors also offered an informative account of historical development in this area and focused much of their chapter on examining the ways R/S may affect health. They specifically attended to health relevant lifestyle behaviors, coping skills, social support, positive psychological/emotional states, utilization of health services, meditation, forgiveness, service to others, virtues, and distant healing all within the context of R/S. The authors concluded with a discussion of areas within R/S–health research where more work was needed, and cautioned that, although there was persuasive evidence of a link between R/S and health, the empirical data supporting R/S as a causal factor in health outcomes remained limited.

We are honored to write the sequel to their chapter, and as a first order of business, we highly recommend that the interested reader review that earlier work before proceeding through our chapter, the reason being that the previous chapter provides an excellent background within which to consider the current material. Thus, in this chapter, our goal is not to repeat what Oman and Thoresen presented but rather to update the literature in two areas—(1) definitional and measurement issues and (2) R/S and overall mortality—by discussing studies published subsequent to the previous chapter. We then center our discussion on R/S as related to cardiovascular disease and cancer. We chose to focus on these diseases for two primary reasons. First, as is well known, they are by far the major causes of mortality and morbidity in the United States and many countries throughout the world. In 2007, the most recent year for which final data are available, the Centers for Disease Control and Prevention (CDC) study by Xu, Kochanek, Murphy, and Tejada-Vera reported that the top cause of death in the United States was heart disease, followed by cancer and stroke (or cerebrovascular disease, in many cases a form of cardiovascular illness). Second, substantive research investigating the links between R/S and these diseases has been conducted. As in the previous edition, this chapter focuses somewhat arbitrarily on what we are considering to be physical, as differentiated from mental, health.

Readers interested in R/S as related to mental health and psychopathology are referred to Park and Slattery (Chapter 27, this volume).

DEFINITIONAL AND MEASUREMENT CONCERNS

Research on R/S and health has increased notably in recent times. Masters (2007) found that from 1975 to 1979 fewer than 100 articles—less than 20 per year—were published that scientifically investigated this topic. In the 7 years between 2000 and 2006, more than 650 were identified, or approximately 93 per year. These data also demonstrate a greater rate of increase for published studies investigating spirituality and health than for religion and health. The central constructs of religiousness and spirituality were discussed in detail in Oman (Chapter 2, this volume). What is clear from a focused review of the literature on R/S and health, however, is that definitions of religion and spirituality, and measures based on these definitions, vary widely. These variations are even more pronounced when the multidimensional nature of the constructs is considered and investigators attempt to delineate and measure particular aspects of religion or spirituality. Kapuscinski and Masters (2010) reviewed measures of spirituality with particular emphasis on scale development. They noted that scales are often constructed by researchers who fail to adequately consider popular usage and who likely view R/S in ways that differ from those of lay individuals or believers. The importance of using definitions (and measures based on these definitions) of R/S that are not only conceptually grounded but also in accord with popular usage was noted by Oman and Thoresen (2005) and remains a concern.

This is important because if measures of R/S employed in health research are incongruent with everyday understanding of R/S by study participants, then measurement error will increase and limit the degree of relationship that can be assessed. One common way health researchers have sidestepped this issue is by using a very basic measure: religious service attendance. This has been the "workhorse" of R/S and health research and has been instrumental in large epidemiological studies that have established relations between service attendance (i.e., R/S) and health. Although attendance is free from conceptual confusion, it suffers from other difficulties, most importantly the failure to enlighten regarding the psychological factors hidden in, and not identified by, service attendance. There is little explanatory power in the observation that entering a house of worship with regularity is associated with better health. Consequently, investigators are interested in learning much more about the psychological aspects of R/S. This is a formidable challenge that is exacerbated by the reality that many health researchers and epidemiologists are not particularly well versed in the R/S literature.

Kapuscinski and Masters (2010) presented several suggestions for how to proceed. First, health investigators should carefully deliberate when choosing a measure of R/S to be confident that it is congruent with the definition of R/S they intend to employ. Second, there is a need for measures of R/S (and specific dimensions) that are developed based on extensive qualitative research within the population of interest. Third, researchers must consider the extent to which the chosen measure of R/S may be conceptually confounded with characteristics of health. This is an important concern because measures of spirituality seem to often contain items that are confounded with mental and physical health, thus potentially inflating observed relations between spirituality and health. Fourth, the use of multiple informants may provide crucial data. Finally, behavioral measures of spirituality are rarely used but are important in establishing health relationships; thus, they are recommended.

R/S AND MORTALITY

Oman and Thoresen (2005) briefly reviewed the literature relating R/S with mortality, and concluded that there was persuasive evidence that religious service attendance was associated with reduced mortality in population-based studies, supported by the review by Powell, Shahabi, and Thoresen (2003) and the meta-analysis by McCullough, Hoyt, Larson, Koenig, and Thoreson (2000). Our presentation focuses on the R/S and mortality literature that has been published since 2003.

The most notable empirical review of R/S and mortality published subsequent to the first edition of this *Handbook* was by Chida, Steptoe, and Powell (2009). They investigated primary studies of both healthy (i.e., not having a chronic life-threatening or life-limiting disease) and initially diseased populations. Sixty-nine studies of healthy populations were located; of these, 27 found a significant protective effect of R/S on mortality. Only three studies of healthy populations showed a harmful effect of R/S on mortality and 39 had null findings. Overall results for the healthy populations demonstrated a significant protective effect for R/S. The protective effect of R/S in healthy populations was only partly accounted for by behavioral factors (smoking, drinking alcohol, exercising, and socioeconomic status), negative affect, or social support, suggesting that R/S may directly affect mortality. The authors further analyzed the data by investigating specific aspects of R/S. They found that in healthy populations both organizational activity and multidimensional aspects (i.e., measures that included more than one of the following: organizational activity, religious social support, nonorganizational activity [e.g., prayer, sacred book study], intrinsic R/S, and R/S-based coping) had stronger associations with decreased mortality than found for the overall effect. The effects were also stronger in healthy population studies with older people (i.e., ≥ 60 years old) and for women.

In studies of initially diseased populations, 22.7% demonstrated a protective effect for R/S, whereas null effects were observed in 77.3% of the studies. Overall, R/S was unrelated to mortality in the diseased populations, and there are several possible explanations for this. Most obvious, R/S may be a more important factor in preventing disease and encouraging health maintenance than in impacting existing disease. This seems likely given the relationships between R/S and various health-relevant behaviors, including moderate alcohol consumption and decreased cigarette smoking in healthy populations. McCullough and Willoughby (2009) reported on ways that religiousness may influence and strengthen self-control, self-regulation, and goal selection and attainment, important factors that influence engagement in health enhancing or risky behaviors. These ideas deserve greater exploration regarding their roles as possible mechanisms in the R/S–health relationship via both controlled laboratory studies and investigations of individuals in their natural environments.

Two methodological issues, however, must also be considered to account for the non-findings with diseased populations. First, the studies of diseased populations generally did not investigate organizational activity, including religious service attendance, which demonstrated some of the strongest effects in the healthy populations. The likely reason that organizational activity is less often studied in diseased populations is that the effects of disease may severely limit one's ability to attend religious services, reducing variability in the measure of attendance. Thus, reduced service attendance may be caused by poor health, not vice versa. Nevertheless, studying attendance, with appropriate controls for health status, may shed light on this relationship. Second, studies of diseased populations tended to be of lower quality than those with healthy populations. However, when Chida and colleagues (2009) looked deeper, they found that, even in the diseased populations, multidimensional aspects of R/S demonstrated a protective effect on risk for mortality. These results must be interpreted cautiously because they are based on a small number of studies, but the suggestion that greater involvement in many aspects of R/S (e.g., prayer, R/S-based coping, religious social support) may be beneficial for both healthy and diseased populations warrants further investigation.

We now turn our focus on primary studies of R/S and mortality that have been published subsequent to the 2005 *Handbook*. One particularly encouraging finding regarding this literature as a whole is the international and ethnic diversity found in these studies. Zhang (2008) reported on a sample of elderly Chinese in the Chinese Longitudinal Healthy Longevity Survey. This investigation included numerous controls and revealed the somewhat surprising finding, given that evidence for a protective religious effect is strongest for healthy populations, that religious participation (i.e., involvement in religious activities) predicted lower risk of mortality for the *oldest* women and for individuals in *poor* health. The author notes that religious participation in this study is a combination of public attendance and private religious practice (e.g., home prayer) and suggests that it be further dissected to uncover more precise delineation of its effective aspects. Also in Asia, Yeager, Glei, Au, Lin, Sloan, and Weinstein (2006) studied a nationally representative sample of older Taiwanese, and found that religious attendance, compared with religious affiliation, beliefs, and religious practices, showed the most consistent beneficial association with health outcome variables, including self-report (overall health status, mobility limitations, depressive symptoms, cognitive function) and clinical (systolic and diastolic blood pressure, serum interleukin-6, 12-hour urinary cortisol, 4-year mortality) measures. When controls for health behaviors, social networks, and prior self-assessed health status were included, only religious attendance remained significantly associated with lower mortality.

Two additional studies were published in Europe. In the first, La Cour, Avlund, and Schultz-Larsen (2006) studied community-dwelling Danes who were 70 years old at study entry and were monitored over 20 years. They described their sample as living in a secular culture, and they were interested in determining whether religious variables (i.e., importance of religious affiliation, church attendance, listening to religious media) would predict survival in this environment. Initial results demonstrated significant positive associations between the importance of religious affiliation and church attendance with survival. When controls for gender, education, mental and physical health, social support, and several health behaviors were included, only church attendance still predicted survival. These effects were stronger for women than men. O'Reilly and Rosato (2008) studied religious affiliation and mortality in Northern Ireland. This census-based longitudinal study covered a 6-year period and divided the population into six religious affiliation groups: Catholics, Presbyterians, Church of Ireland, Methodists, other (mostly fundamentalist) Christians, and other/not stated. It demonstrated advantages in survival for non-Catholic groups that largely disappeared when socioeconomic status was controlled. Perhaps most interesting was the variability that was observed among the non-Catholic groups. For many years research in Northern Ireland has compared Catholics and non-Catholics, essentially assuming that both groups are homogeneous. This study demonstrated that the non-Catholic group is, in fact, quite heterogeneous pertaining to religious affiliation relations with mortality. The Church of Ireland group, for example, had markedly higher rates of fully adjusted mortality compared with the other Christians, who had the lowest mortality rates.

Sullivan (2010) recently conducted a study of religious affiliation, attendance, and mortality in the United States using data from the Health and Retirement Study (HRS), a representative, longitudinal investigation of Americans over age 50, to compare mainline Protestants, Jews, Catholics, Evangelical Protestants, black Protestants, and those with no religious preference with controls on health behaviors (smoking, drinking) and sociodemographic composition (gender, race/ethnicity, marital status, foreign born, and socioeconomic status). Across religious groups, attendance was related to a reduced risk for mortality. However, this effect also differed based on religious affiliation. Black Protestants had approximately a 29% higher risk of mortality than mainline Protestants. The effect of attendance did not differ much based on religious affiliation, although mortality rates were higher among Evangelical Protestants who never or rarely attended services than mainline Protestants who never attended. Finally, health behaviors only mediated the relationship between attendance and mortality for the Evangelical Protestants.

Two other studies from the United States are notable. Hill, Angel, Ellison, and Angel (2005) accessed mortality data over an 8-year period for elderly Mexican Americans living in the Southwest. They found that weekly religious attendance was a robust predictor of decreased mortality after controlling for many relevant health and sociodemographic factors. It was interesting, and perhaps surprising, that social support, drinking alcohol, and smoking were essentially unrelated to risk of mortality and explained only a small amount of the association between religious attendance and mortality.

Finally, the Women's Health Initiative Observational Study (Schnall et al., 2010) reported on postmenopausal women over a 7.7-year period. After controlling for demographic, socioeconomic, and prior health variables, self-reported religious affiliation, frequent religious service attendance, and level of strength and comfort provided by religion were all associated with decreased mortality. Particularly strong effects were found for those who attended religious services at least once per week. These results held when those with a history of myocardial infarction or stroke were removed from the sample, suggesting that service attendance is prospectively related with reduced mortality rather than that experiencing disease encourages religious behavior.

When we consider these studies in light of their predecessors cited in the previous edition of this *Handbook*, it seems quite unlikely that the positive association of R/S (particularly religious service attendance) with survival is artifactual or spurious. Data have continued to accumulate from diverse regions of the world suggesting a protective effect for R/S on mortality. The size of this effect varies depending on the particular statistical model and covariates that are tested as well as the age and gender compositions of the sample. Overall, it appears that the risk reduction in mortality associated with R/S involvement ranges from 10 to 40%, with an overall average point estimate of about 30%. These figures are based on an expanding research body that has established a relatively consistent and nontrivial association for R/S. A few large investigations have employed measures of R/S beyond religious service attendance that advance understanding and clarity regarding the psychological and behavioral aspects of R/S involvement that may confer a survival advantage. We hope and predict that the growing trend of research in this area will continue.

R/S AND CARDIOVASCULAR DISEASE

There has been an abiding interest in the possible connection between R/S and the heart. The Christian Bible notes, "Hope deferred maketh the heart sick" (Proverbs 13:12; King James Version [KJV]) and "Wait on the Lord: be of good courage, and he shall strengthen thine heart" (Psalm 27:14; KJV). Indeed, the heart has historically been viewed as the center of emotional well-being and spiritual functioning, both metaphorically and literally. But is there an empirically observable relationship between R/S and cardiovascular functioning and disease?

R/S and Cardiovascular Mortality

In their meta-analysis, Chida et al. (2009) investigated the relationship between R/S and cardiovascular disease (CVD) mortality. This was the first quantitative review of the empirical literature to determine that R/S was associated with a reduced risk for cardiovascular mortality in healthy population studies.

Although the aggregated data across studies suggests a beneficial association for R/S relevant to CVD mortality, not all primary studies are concordant with this finding. For example, data from the Women's Health Initiative Observational Study (Schnall et al., 2010) did not find specific effects related to CVD mortality. Religious variables were generally not associated with risk specific to CVD events, and in some adjusted models, gaining greater comfort and strength from religion was actually associated with increased risk. The authors hypothesized that cardiac patients who were most ill may have been most likely to turn to religion for support.

The two most notable studies of representative samples that investigated CVD mortality and R/S are those of Hummer, Rogers, Nam, and Ellison (1999) and Oman, Kurata, Strawbridge, and Cohen (2002). Hummer et al. found those who never attended religious services, compared with those who attended more than once a week, were at 1.57 times the risk of CVD mortality after controlling for demographic and health variables.

Oman et al. (2002) reported prospective findings relating religious attendance and death over 31 years among a representative sample of adults in the Alameda County Study. In models controlling for age, sex, sociodemographics, health status, health behaviors, and social connections, death by CVD for infrequent (less than weekly) attendees was significantly higher than for weekly attendees. Health behaviors accounted for only part of this relationship.

Other studies utilizing nonrepresentative samples demonstrated similar findings. Overall it appears that (1) regular involvement in healthy behaviors accounts for some but not all of the beneficial association between R/S and CVD mortality; (2) the effects of R/S on CVD mortality are not as strong among older adults and perhaps males; and (3) religious service attendance has been the measure that has produced the most consistent results.

R/S and Cardiovascular Morbidity

A number of studies have investigated R/S variables and their relations with and effects on CVD morbidity. Many of these recent studies examine the effects of R/S in samples of patients who have suffered a myocardial infarction or undergone cardiac surgery.

Myocardial Infarction

Blumenthal and colleagues (2007) prospectively investigated a subset of patients from the Enhancing Recovery in Coronary Heart Disease (ENRICHD) trial to determine whether R/S predicted death or recurrent nonfatal myocardial infarction (MI). Over 18 months, R/S measures failed to predict CVD morbidity. Those who never attended church tended (not statistically significant) to have a higher event rate than weekly attendees but a *lower* event rate than those who attended several times per month. Similarly, there was a trend for those who had more daily spiritual experiences to have a *higher* probability of an event. R/S was not related to recurrent MI or death. The ENRICHD cohort is, however, a unique sample of patients who had previously experienced an acute MI and were at risk for a subsequent cardiac event because of their high levels of depression and low social support. Thus, sample composition is key in considering these results.

Cardiac Surgery

Several studies have investigated patients recovering from cardiac surgery. Ai and colleagues (e.g., Ai, Park, Huang, Rodgers, & Tice, 2007; Ai, Peterson, et al., 2007) published a series of studies in this area. They used different designs and investigated numerous R/S variables with patients recovering from cardiac surgery. They found that prayer was commonly used by patients recovering from coronary artery bypass grafting (CABG) and that it predicted decreases in both depressive symptoms and general distress. They also published several studies utilizing the same sample of patients who were undergoing a variety of cardiac surgeries. Several aspects of faith-based coping were investigated as predictors of postsurgery outcomes that included depression, global functioning, fatigue, and distress. In general, they found that positive religious coping predicted better psychological and functional outcomes, whereas negative religious coping predicted worse results. They also found that (1) the effects of positive religious coping were mediated by hope, optimism, and social support; and (2) cross-sectional analyses indicated a relationship between prayer and poorer overall functioning but longitudinal analysis showed that prayer predicted better functioning.

Two publications by Contrada and colleagues (2004, 2008) investigated patients undergoing elective CABG or cardiac valve surgery. In the first, they found that stronger presurgical religious beliefs predicted fewer postsurgery complications and shorter length of hospital stay, with complications mediating the effect on length of stay. Religious attendance was, however, associated with *longer* hospital stay and frequency of prayer did not predict outcomes. The authors discuss attendance in light of the possible influence of negative religious coping strategies. The study also found that relationships were stronger among women than men, and prayer and attendance tended to be less related than beliefs to psychosocial variables (optimism, hostility, depression, social support). Contrada et al. also observed longer hospital stays for individuals whose frequency of religious attendance exceeded what would be predicted by the strength of their beliefs compared with those whose attendance was less frequent than would be expected based on their beliefs. These findings suggest a behaviorally based self-report measure of extrinsic and intrinsic religiousness, with extrinsic exemplified by those who attended more than their beliefs would predict. In the second study of elective cardiac surgery patients, the effect of religious involvement on length of stay was mediated by perceived social support and sense of purpose was mediated by reduced depressive symptoms.

Congestive Heart Failure

A generally overlooked cardiac population consists of those suffering from congestive heart failure (CHF). Because it is less widely understood than other heart conditions, we briefly describe the illness. CHF is a chronic, progressive, life-limiting disease with a high mortality rate. Within 5 years of diagnosis, approximately 50% of patients will die (Roger et al., 2011). By way of demonstrating its prevalence, in the United States in 2007 (Xu et al., 2010), more people died from CHF than any single type of cancer except lung cancer. The deteriorating course of the disease is predictable over the long term, but on a daily basis the symptom profile can vary widely, leaving patients with uncertainty and the inability to plan activities. In many ways, CHF presents a model disease in which R/S concerns are likely to be salient, because patients must cope with declining functionality and increasing symptoms over time as well as the knowledge that their heart cannot be fixed. Park and colleagues (e.g., Edmondson, Park, Chaudoir, & Wortmann, 2008; Park, 2008; Park, Brooks, & Sussman, 2009; Park, Malone, Suresh, Bliss, & Rosen, 2008; Park, Moehl, Fenster, Suresh, & Bliss, 2008) conducted a series of studies investigating various aspects of R/S with different CHF patient outcomes. First, Park (2008) demonstrated that as individuals with CHF perceive the approach of death, they become more concerned about spiritual issues. Park, Moehl, et al. (2008) examined religious support, commitment, and positive and negative religious coping as predictors of treatment adherence in patients afflicted with CHF. The most prominent finding was that religious commitment predicted greater treatment adherence over 6 months. In a separate study (Park, Malone, et al., 2008), they determined that religious coping among CHF patients predicted increased sense of meaning in life and suggested that religious coping could be important for posttraumatic growth.

Positive religious coping and support appear to have generally beneficial effects, but other studies in this line of investigation point to the problematic roles of religious struggle and negative religious coping. Park, Brooks, et al. (2009) studied CHF patients at two time intervals 6 months apart. They found that negative religious coping was the R/S variable most consistently associated with outcomes; it predicted increases in depressive symptoms and decreases in self-efficacy and growth. On the other hand, only religious support predicted lessened depression, only daily spiritual experiences predicted increased self-efficacy, and only private religious practices predicted increased stress-related growth. Edmondson et al. (2008) found that religious struggle was related to greater depression in CHF patients through increased concern with personal mortality. For other patients belief in an afterlife was related to religious comfort. Finally, Fitchett's research team (2004) studied religious struggle among patients suffering from CHF, diabetes, or cancer. Although overall rates of religious struggle were low in all three groups, they found comparatively higher levels of both religious struggle, and negative religious coping for CHF patients. Those with higher rates of religious service attendance had lower levels of religious struggle but frequent use of positive religious coping did not rule out concurrent use of negative religious coping.

Hypertension

Hypertension (HTN) is a particularly important form of cardiovascular morbidity because it is a major risk factor for premature death, MI, stroke, CHF, vision loss, and erectile dysfunction and is a leading cause of kidney failure (Roger et al., 2011). Because psychological stress is associated with HTN and it is believed that R/S may help individuals better cope with stress, it has been hypothesized that R/S will associate with reduced rates of HTN. The evidence on this is generally supportive though far from complete. Although many studies use cross-sectional designs and nonrepresentative samples, a reasonable body of literature has emerged.

A number of studies (e.g., Hixson, Gruchow, & Morgan, 1998; Koenig et al., 1998; Masters, Hill, Kircher, Lensegrav Benson, & Fallon, 2004; Sethness et al., 2005; Steffen, Hinderliter, Blumenthal, & Sherwood, 2001; Timio et al., 1997) found positive relations for R/S constructs, including service attendance, intrinsic religiousness, prayer, reading spiritual material, considering spirituality important, and positive religious coping with better blood pressure (BP). These findings have been observed among several racial/ethnic groups, including older whites, African Americans, young American Latino/as, and Italian nuns.

Two studies suggest, however, that these relations may be complex. Fitchett and Powell (2009) found that daily spiritual experiences did not protect against 3-year increases in systolic BP or HTN status. Buck, Williams, Musick, and Sternthal (2009) observed a complex pattern of results wherein religious service attendance did not relate to BP or HTN, belief in the social benefits of attendance (similar to extrinsic religiousness) predicted increased systolic BP, and meaning and forgiveness were associated with decreased diastolic BP and HTN. Clearly, continued research in this area is justified.

R/S and Cardiovascular Function

A small number of studies have addressed the question of whether R/S phenomena have associations with the functioning of the cardiovascular system. Several investigations utilized the cardiovascular reactivity/stress paradigm. Masters et al. (2004) found that older extrinsically religious adults displayed exaggerated BP reactivity across both cognitive and interpersonal stressors, whereas older intrinsically religious adults demonstrated healthier reactivity profiles similar to individuals 40 to 50 years younger. Recently, Masters and Knestel (2011) found dampened reactivity for proreligious participants compared with intrinsic or nonreligious individuals, though these findings were difficult to interpret because of a number of unusual characteristics of the proreligious sample. Lawler and Younger (2002) found benefits for intrinsic religiousness for diastolic BP reactivity among younger and middle-aged adults. Tartaro, Luecken, and Gunn (2005) obtained lower BP and cortisol reactivity measures among those who had a greater composite R/S scale score. Finally, Edmondson's group (2008) determined that higher levels of religious well-being predicted smaller systolic BP reactivity, whereas higher levels of spiritual and existential well-being predicted lower heart rate reactivity.

Probably the most impressive study to date in this area was conducted by Berntson, Norman, Hawkley, and Cacioppo (2008). They investigated R/S and autonomic cardiac control in a representative sample of middle-aged adults. R/S was construed as either religious attendance or as a composite of spiritual well-being and closeness to God. Only the R/S composite was positively related to cardiac autonomic regulation, parasympathetic cardiac control, and sympathetic cardiac control, but it was not related to cardiac autonomic balance. The relationships held after control for demographic, health behavior, and personality variables. Further, the effects could not be accounted for by psychological characteristics such as loneliness, perceived stress, social support, hostility, depression, or general satisfaction with others. R/S was negatively related to myocardial infarction, and the relationship between R/S and infarction was mediated by autonomic regulation. Although the study was cross-sectional, it appears that R/S may contribute to cardiac health through a high level of cardiac autonomic regulatory capacity that may signify enhanced neuroregulatory control of the heart.

Conclusions for R/S and CVD

There is reliable meta-level evidence of a beneficial relationship between R/S and CVD mortality that cannot be accounted for by variables such as previous health status or demographics, and there may be a direct relationship between R/S and CVD mortality. It is not clear which aspects of R/S are the important predictors, and it appears that the salient aspects of R/S may differ depending on the demographics of the population. Studies from patient populations are less clear. Although they generally indicate R/S is beneficial, the findings are far from uniform and are likely influenced by a number of factors, including the aspects of R/S under consideration, type and demographics of patient population, and study design. The aspects of R/S that are the strongest candidates as factors influencing the R/S–CVD relationship are health-related behavioral practices and social support, but religious coping (positive, negative) and religious motivation (intrinsic, extrinsic) are also notable. A handful of studies have investigated R/S and cardiovascular functioning and suggest relevant physiological processes that might be influenced by R/S phenomena. More controlled work of this type is likely to illuminate which dimensions of, and how, R/S relates to cardiovascular functioning.

R/S AND CANCER

There has been a recent surge of attention to the relationship between R/S and cancer. Researchers have become increasingly interested in whether and how R/S variables influence risk factors for cancer and psychosocial adjustment after a cancer diagnosis. Three recent reviews (Stefanek, McDonald, & Hess, 2005; Thuné-Boyle, Stygall, Keshtgar, & Newman, 2006; Visser, Garssen, & Vingerhoets, 2010) have been conducted. Stefanek et al. (2005) noted that previously little attention had been paid to the relationship between R/S and cancer, and thus no conclusions could be drawn about how R/S relates to cancer. However, since the first edition of this *Handbook,* a number of studies have been published addressing these concerns.

R/S and Risk for Cancer

It is well known that individuals who engage in healthy behaviors (e.g., not smoking, moderate or no alcohol) decrease their risk of developing cancer and other diseases, including CVD. It is also known that individuals high in R/S tend to consume less tobacco and alcohol. To the extent that healthy behaviors are developed and maintained because of R/S factors such as particular beliefs, values, and the presence of a supportive community, these can be properly interpreted as effects of R/S on health. We do not, however, focus on these topics because they are relatively well known and accepted. However, R/S-related behaviors that influence risk of breast cancer have not been as widely discussed or understood, and we briefly focus on this area.

Two studies demonstrated that R/S factors relate to lower likelihood of having risk factors for breast cancer. In the first, Daniels, Merrill, Lyon, Stanford, and White (2004) were interested in identifying reasons why women in Utah, and specifically women who were members of the Church of Jesus Christ of Latter-Day Saints (LDS; Mormon) had lower rates of breast cancer than the U.S. population. They surveyed Utah women about risk factors for breast cancer, religious preference (LDS vs. non-LDS), and religious activity level. They found that active LDS women were more likely to have breastfed, spent more years breastfeeding, and had more pregnancies than less active LDS women or women of other religions regardless of activity level. In another study, Gillum and Williams (2009) analyzed the National Survey of Family Growth data to see whether attendance at religious services and current religious affiliation were related to breast cancer risk factors. They found that women who attended services weekly were more likely to have children and less likely to report using oral contraceptives than those who never attended. Moreover, women who never attended were seven times more likely to report having four or more risk factors than women who attended weekly or more. Women with no religious affiliation were twice as likely to report having four or more risk factors. These studies provide evidence that R/S factors relate to a reduced likelihood of having breast cancer risk factors.

Another breast cancer study investigated whether R/S factors influenced time to seek medical treatment. Gullatte, Brawley, Kinney, Powe, and Mooney (2010) noted that African American women are more likely to receive a later stage breast cancer diagnosis than other racial groups and that they tend to hold strong R/S beliefs that influence health-related decision making. Gullatte et al. surveyed African American women diagnosed with breast cancer within the last 12 months. Religious problem solving and spiritual coping were not associated with time to seek medical care, whereas having a higher income and telling someone about symptoms were related to shorter time to seek medical care. They concluded that R/S may not play a role in time to seek medical care in this specific group.

R/S and Adjustment to Cancer

The area that has received the most attention in the R/S and cancer literature is the relationship between R/S and psychosocial adjustment to a cancer diagnosis. Many studies examined how spirituality measures or measures of religious coping are related to adjustment (e.g., lower levels of depression, greater well-being). Other studies looked at how R/S factors are related to making health behavior changes after a diagnosis.

Visser et al. (2010) reviewed 27 studies concerning relations between spirituality (defined as "one's striving for and experience of a connection with the essence of life" [p. 565]; note that studies using measures of religion, i.e., questions relating to God or prayer, were excluded) and well-being in cancer patients and 13 studies of relations between meaning in life and well-being in cancer patients. Twenty-three of the cross-sectional studies suggested that more spiritual involvement is associated with greater well-being; however, the lone longitudinal study found that spirituality was cross-sectionally associated with decreased hopelessness but did not predict hopelessness 1 year later. Of the 11 cross-sectional studies on meaning and well-being in cancer patients, nine found that meaning was associated with increased well-being. These results suggest a cross-sectional relationship between meaning and spirituality with well-being but this relationship may not sustain longitudinally. Visser et al. posit this may be due to the few (only four of the 40 studies reviewed) longitudinal studies and their several methodological weaknesses.

There is often a positive relationship between the Functional Assessment of Chronic Illness Therapy—Spiritual Well-Being Scale (FACIT-Sp; Peterman, Fitchett, Brady, Hernandez, & Cella, 2002) dimensions of meaning/peace or faith and psychosocial adjustment to cancer. In gastrointestinal cancer patients, older age was related to lower rates of depressive symptoms, and spiritual well-being (i.e., FACIT-Sp meaning/peace and faith) mediated this effect (Lo et al., 2009). In a sample of men with metastatic prostate cancer, Zavala, Maliski, Kwan, Fink, and Litwin (2009) found that spiritual well-being was associated with higher health-related quality of life (HRQOL) and psychosocial functioning. Moreover, the meaning/peace domain, but not faith, was positively associated with scores in several HRQOL and psychosocial domains. However, spiritual well-being may vary across cancer groups. For instance, Clay, Talley, and Young (2010) found that lung cancer survivors reported lower levels of meaning/peace than colorectal cancer survivors. It is important to note that some of the FACIT-Sp items may be confounded with items on mental health scales. For example, the FACIT-Sp refers to feeling peaceful, having "peace of mind," and being able to "reach down deep . . . for comfort" (Peterman et al., 2002). Some have argued that the FACIT-Sp is a measure of well-being (e.g., Visser et al., 2010); thus, correlating it with other measures of well-being does not provide important new information.

In a sample of prostate cancer patients, Nelson et al. (2009) tested the relationship between religiosity (measured by intrinsic/extrinsic religious motivation) and depression. They found that intrinsic religiosity was negatively associated with depression scores but there was no relationship between extrinsic religiosity and depression. They were also interested in the possible mediating role of spirituality (i.e., faith and meaning/peace). Meaning/peace, but not faith, significantly and negatively related to depression. Further, meaning/peace significantly mediated the relationship between intrinsic religiousness and depression. The authors suggested that whether through organized religion or one's own means, feeling a sense of meaning/peace is more important than faith or religiousness in buffering against depressive symptoms.

It may be useful to employ case–control studies of people with and without cancer to better understand the influence of spirituality on well-being. Costanzo, Ryff, and Singer (2009) examined psychosocial impairment, resilience, and thriving among cancer survivors ages 25–74 years (mean = 63 for females and 37 for males) in the general population compared with controls matched on age, gender, and education level. Cancer survivors had higher depression, anxiety, and negative affect and lower positive affect, environmental mastery, positive relations with others, and self-acceptance. However, there were no differences on social well-being or spirituality. Both cancer survivors and controls showed increased religious identification and spirituality from Time 1 to Time 2 (10 years), but cancer survivors reported slightly less strong identification than the controls. These results seem to suggest that a cancer diagnosis may not predict subsequent greater spirituality than what is found simply through aging.

R/S beliefs may, however, play an important role in adjustment to cancer. In one study, breast cancer patients were divided into high-, medium-, and low-religious-strength groups. Patients in the high-religiosity group had lower prevalence of depression than those in the medium or low groups (Aukst-Margetic, Jakovljevic, Margetic, Biscan, & Samija, 2005). Howsepian and Merluzzi (2009) tested a path model to explain how religious beliefs could be related to cancer adjustment. They found that religious beliefs were positively related to perceived social support, which was positively related to coping self-efficacy. In turn, coping self-efficacy was positively related to psychosocial adjustment to cancer. However, the relationship between R/S beliefs and well-being is not always consistent. For instance, patients living with incurable cancer reported mild levels of hopelessness, mild to moderate depressive symptoms, and high pain intensity that interfered with their general activity, mood, work, and enjoyment of life. Spiritual beliefs, practices, applications (practicing forgiveness and humility), and existential beliefs were not related to hopelessness, depressive symptoms, pain, or cognitive functioning in these cancer patients (Mystakidou et al., 2007). The authors noted that their findings contrasted with much of the literature on cancer patients. Notably, their sample was composed of patients with incurable forms of cancer (e.g., gastrointestinal, lung, urogenital) housed in palliative care units, whereas many of the studies of cancer patients have involved either those who were recently diagnosed or who were cancer survivors.

Few longitudinal studies examined relations between spirituality and adjustment in cancer patients. Yanez et al. (2009) examined data from two longitudinal studies. Among breast cancer patients, meaning/peace at baseline was related to lower levels of depressive symptoms and greater vitality at 6- and 12-month follow-up. Baseline faith was not related to depressive symptoms or vitality but rather to posttraumatic growth. In their second study, among a group of cancer survivors, meaning/peace was related to better mental health and lower cancer-related distress and, again, faith was related to growth.

Gall and colleagues (Gall, Guirguis-Younger, Charbonneau, & Florack, 2009; Gall, Kristjansson, Charbonneau, & Florack, 2009) conducted a longitudinal study of adjustment to cancer diagnosis. Women receiving biopsies on breast tumors were recruited. Participants were divided into benign and cancer groups. The cancer group was assessed prior to biopsy, 1 week presurgery, and four more times over the next 2 years, whereas the benign group was assessed prior to biopsy and two more times postdiagnosis to coincide with the surgery dates of the cancer group. In the first study, a longitudinal path model exploring positive and negative images of God and religious salience presurgery on positive attitude and social well-being at 6 months postsurgery and emotional distress at 1 year post-surgery was tested. Women who had a more negative image of God presurgery had a less positive attitude 6 months postsurgery and were more distressed prediagnosis and 1 year postsurgery. In the second study, women with both benign and cancer diagnoses, reported religious coping efforts increased from presurgery to 3 months postdiagnosis (with the exception of benevolent reappraisal). However, this mobilization of religious coping resources seemed to be short lived; levels of religious coping returned to baseline levels at 14 months post diagnosis.

Thuné-Boyle et al. (2006) conducted a systematic review of the relations between R/S coping strategies and psychosocial adjustment to cancer. Seven of the 17 studies showed a positive relationship between religious coping and psychological well-being. Three found religious coping to be negatively related to well-being and seven found no relation. Thune-Boyle et al. concluded that the studies that found negative relations were mainly those that measured negative forms of religious coping and those that found no relation did not differentiate between different forms of religious coping (i.e., they used the religious items from the Brief COPE [Carver, 1997] instead of a specific religious coping measure). Subsequently, other studies investigated the relations between R/S coping and adjustment. In a sample of patients coping with cancer, greater use of positive religious coping was related to better overall quality of life (QoL) as well as better scores on the existential and support dimensions of QoL. Conversely, negative religious coping was negatively related to overall QoL and to scores of psychological and existential well-being (Tarakeshwar et al., 2006). Similarly, German breast cancer patients who reported higher negative religious coping also reported higher levels of anxiety (Zwingmann, Muller, Körber, & Murken, 2008). Positive R/S coping (effectively using spiritual beliefs and social support from a R/S community) was also positively correlated with dimensions of HRQOL in a group of Latina breast cancer patients (Wildes, Miller, San Miguel de Majors, & Ramirez, 2009). Thus, it appears positive R/S coping is related to greater well-being in cancer patients, whereas negative R/S coping is related to poorer well-being (see in this volume Exline & Rose, Chapter 19, and Pargament, Falb, Ano, & Wachholtz, Chapter 28, for more discussion).

Two longitudinal studies were designed to investigate the effect of religious coping in cancer patients. Hebert, Zdaniuk, Schulz, and Scheier (2009) found that negative religious coping measured 1 month after beginning cancer treatment predicted worse overall mental health, more depression, and less life satisfaction. Further, changes in negative religious coping predicted worse mental health, increases in depressive symptoms, and decreases in life satisfaction 8 to 12 months after study entry. Positive religious coping was not associated with well-being. Well-being is not the only outcome studied in relation to R/S coping in cancer patients. In a unique study of those with advanced cancer, Phelps et al. (2009) examined the responses of patients who died after completing baseline questionnaires. Nearly 80% of patients reported that religion helped them cope "to a moderate extent" or more. High positive religious coping at baseline was associated with receipt of mechanical ventilation and intensive life-prolonging care. This suggests that religious coping may contribute to receiving aggressive medical care near death.

Receiving a cancer diagnosis may also be related to health behavior change. In a group of young cancer survivors, Park, Edmondson, Hale-Smith, and Blank (2009) examined the relations between R/S and various health behaviors. Religious service attendance was unrelated to health behavior, whereas daily spiritual experiences (DSE) and religious struggle were related to multiple health behaviors. DSE were related to having more days of eating five or more servings of fruits and vegetables and getting moderate to vigorous physical exercise as well as adhering to doctors' orders. Religious struggle was related to poor adherence to doctors' advice and medication adherence and marginally related to greater alcohol use. The relations between religious struggle and health behaviors were mediated by guilt, whereas the relations between DSE and health behaviors were mediated by self-assurance. Another study investigated behavior change after a cancer diagnosis. Hawkins et al. (2010) found that participants who reported making a positive behavior change after diagnosis also reported greater faith and meaning/peace. This suggests that spirituality may be related to health-promoting behaviors after a cancer diagnosis, whereas a religious struggle could be related to risky health behaviors.

R/S Interventions in Cancer Patients

Some authors noted that the significant relationship between meaning and psychosocial adjustment to cancer could be used in interventions to help patients cope with cancer (Breitbart, 2005; Nelson et al., 2009). Kaplar, Wachholtz, and O'Brien (2004) conducted a meta-analysis on the effect of R/S interventions on cancer patients and included eight studies, of which only four had a control group. Although the effect sizes on biological, psychological, and social outcome measures were moderate to large, Kaplar et al. noted that there were many methodological problems and limitations and that more methodologically rigorous studies of R/S interventions were needed. One group (Breitbart et al., 2010) conducted a randomized controlled trial of meaning-centered group therapy (MCGP) compared with a standard supportive-group therapy (SGP) for cancer patients. The MCGP was designed to help patients find and/or sustain a sense of meaning or purpose in their lives in the face of death. Participants were randomly assigned to an 8-week MCGP therapy or SGP therapy. At the end of treatment, compared with pretreatment, the MCGP group had greater spiritual well-being, meaning/peace, and optimism as well as lower psychosocial distress, whereas the SGP group did not change. Both groups had a reduced desire for death from pretreatment to 2-month follow-up. These results suggest that MCGP therapy may be efficacious for helping patients adjust to a cancer diagnosis.

Conclusions for R/S and Cancer

R/S and cancer research is a burgeoning field within the R/S and health literature that focuses on two main areas: (1) risk for cancer and (2) psychosocial adjustment to cancer diagnosis. Evidence suggests that R/S factors may be related to having fewer risk factors for developing cancer; however, this evidence comes from cross-sectional studies that do not relate R/S factors to actual development of cancer. Positive R/S factors are related to greater psychosocial adjustment to cancer diagnosis, whereas negative R/S factors (e.g., negative God) tend to be related to poorer psychosocial adjustment. The positive and negative R/S relations also exist in healthy populations. Thus, the unique relations of R/S to psychosocial factors in cancer patients are not well understood or identified. Although the number of published studies has grown in recent years, significant methodological limitations remain. Cross-sectional research designs make it difficult to know if having greater R/S helps one adjust after the cancer diagnosis, if R/S changes in response to a cancer diagnosis, or if better adjustment in general is related to higher R/S. More studies like the two by Gall's team that are longitudinal and assess patients before and after they receive a cancer diagnosis are needed to understand how R/S variables are related to cancer adjustment.

CONCLUDING COMMENTS

Investigators who venture into the area of R/S and health must know that they are entering extremely difficult terrain. Neither construct is easily, perhaps even capably, defined and consequently measures of both present serious concerns. Whatever R/S and heath may be, there is agreement that both are multidimensional and, therefore, create an enormous number of possible associations to be investigated. To further complicate the matter, the manifestation of these multidimensional constructs is the result of multiple causal factors that may exist prior to birth (genes) and impinge on individuals to varying degrees throughout life. Finally, there are serious research design concerns that must be addressed. Controlled laboratory studies are very difficult and limited by both ethical concerns and properties inherent in the phenomena. Consequently, much of the research is observational, with the best studies including carefully considered longitudinal measures of R/S and health along with adequate controls in large samples. All of this must be done with precious little availability of both government and foundation funding. The work is daunting.

In spite of these obstacles, patterns of findings are emerging. The literature suggests that R/S factors, particularly attendance, have a consistent protective relationship with risk for mortality in healthy populations. However, as Chida et al.'s (2009) meta-analysis demonstrated, this effect may not be found in already diseased populations. Consequently, it appears that R/S factors may help prevent disease, and though the precise mechanisms are not fully articulated, establishing health maintenance behaviors, generating greater social support, and/or strengthening self-regulation are reasonable candidates in addition to the everyday use of effective religious coping strategies and the presence of intrinsic religious motivation. The more inconsistent results in diseased population studies may be the result of methodological limitations, the use of many different measures of R/S with different disease populations, and the difficulty of truly understanding the phenomenological experience of individuals engaging in R/S practices in the face of serious disease. For example, among patients with severe disease, is engagement in greater frequency of prayer the act of a desperate person wishing for a miracle, or is it an indicator of greater comfort found in communicating with the Almighty? Without this level of examination, we can expect conflicting findings regarding, in this case, the relations between prayer frequency and health.

Religious service attendance is well established as predicting better health outcomes. Although it is a simple construct, it may also be one of the more difficult R/S variables to interpret. What is it about attending religious services that predicts protective health effects? Perhaps it is the social support gained from the religious community, the sense of connection to something greater than oneself, or simply having a stable and predictable routine that provides comfort and leads to health benefits. We simply do not know.

There are many future directions that would be beneficial to this area of research. First, prospective, longitudinal designs are needed to better understand how R/S factors influence disease morbidity and mortality over time. Determining whether R/S factors play a role in development of diseases relies on this type of design. Second, though randomized experimental studies are difficult to conduct in this area, they are not impossible and may be more capably carried out if investigators attend to our next recommendation: the incorporation of culturally sensitive and specific R/S measures, designs, and research questions. For example, we recently completed a not-yet-published laboratory cardiovascular reactivity study that compared Christian devotional prayer, secular meditation based on the same content found in the prayer condition but void of any religious reference, and a control condition among Christians who were exposed to a religiously themed social confrontation. Both the stressor and the experimental task were specifically designed to be relevant to Christian populations. This same type of work should be conducted with other religious and spiritual groups. The field has also been moving toward greater investigation of specific R/S factors that may influence physical health. This is a positive step but one that has the potential to fragment the literature, resulting in small numbers of studies, each investigating unique R/S constructs. This is not unusual in psychological research; many areas of investigation have gone through or are in this stage of development. Nevertheless, it would be good if investigators gave careful consideration to the likely impact that their work will have on the overall field of R/S and health and determined *a priori* whether it was most advantageous to the field to launch a new area of investigation or carefully follow-up and improve the depth of already existing lines of research.

Finally, we have a few thoughts about R/S intervention studies. The argument is sometimes made that R/S–health research should not receive funding because even if it is demonstrated that R/S has beneficial, even causal, relations with improved health, there is no practical advantage to these findings because it is unethical to promote R/S interventions. Although we recognize the delicate ethical concerns that this topic raises, a blanket prohibition against R/S interventions is, we believe, mistaken. First, it is possible to design interventions with R/S topics integrated in ways that are not sectarian or promote any particular R/S perspective but that encourage patients to explore their own R/S and seek, for example, meaning, purpose, or forgiveness within whatever R/S tradition they choose. Second, in the United States, somewhere between 20 and 40% of the population, depending on how the data are collected, attend religious services weekly (Hadaway & Marler, 2005; Presser & Chaves, 2007). This presents a large and captive audience that is receptive to religious messages that potentially influence their behavioral and emotional lives. Having a better understanding of how R/S dimensions influence or predict health would allow investigators to work with clergy to design religious and culturally sensitive interventions to be delivered in the context of the religious community. This is really no different than designing any other culturally sensitive intervention for use with particular groups.

We are encouraged by the work in the area of R/S and health that has been conducted since the first edition of this *Handbook*. Although problems and obstacles abound, investigators have continued to develop productive lines of research. There are many more areas to be examined; we hope that both the investigators and the funding agencies that support them will engage in this effort in greater numbers.

REFERENCES

Ai, A. L., Park, C. L., Huang, B., Rodgers, W., & Tice, T. N. (2007). Psychosocial mediation of religious coping styles: A study of short-term psychological distress following cardiac surgery. *Personality and Social Psychology Bulletin, 33*, 867–882.

Ai, A. L., Peterson, C., Tice, T. N., Huang, B., Rodgers, W., & Bolling, S. F. (2007). The influence of prayer coping on mental health among cardiac surgery patients: The role of optimism and acute distress. *Journal of Health Psychology, 12*, 580–596.

Aukst-Margetic, B., Jakovljevic, M., Margetic, B., Biscan, M., & Samija, M. (2005). Religiosity, depression and pain in patients with breast cancer. *General Hospital Psychiatry, 27*, 250–255.

Berntson, G. G., Norman, G. J., Hawkley, L. C., & Cacioppo, J. T. (2008). Spirituality and autonomic cardiac control. *Annals of Behavioral Medicine, 35*, 198–208.

Blumenthal, J. A., Babyak, M. A., Ironson, G., Thoresen, C., Powell, L., Czajkowski, S., et al. (2007). Spirituality, religion, and clinical outcomes in patients recovering from an acute myocardial infarction. *Psychosomatic Medicine, 69*, 501–508.

Breitbart, W. (2005). Spirituality and meaning in cancer. *Revue Francophone de Psycho-Oncologie, 4*, 237–240.

Breitbart, W., Rosenfeld, B., Gibson, C., Pessin, H., Poppito, S., Nelson, C., et al. (2010). Meaning-centered group psychotherapy for patients with advanced cancer: A pilot randomized controlled trial. *Psycho-Oncology, 19*, 21–28.

Buck, A. C., Williams, D. R., Musick, M. A., & Sternthal, M. J. (2009). An examination of the relationship between multiple dimensions of religiosity, blood pressure, and hypertension. *Social Science & Medicine, 68*, 314–322.

Carver, C. S. (1997). You want to measure coping but your protocol is too long: Consider the brief COPE. *International Journal of Behavioural Medicine, 4*, 92–100.

Chida, Y., Steptoe, A., & Powell, L. H. (2009). Religiosity/spirituality and mortality. *Psychotherapy and Psychosomatics, 78*, 81–90.

Clay, K., Talley, C., & Young, K. (2010). Exploring spiritual well-being among survivors of colorectal and lung cancer. *Journal of Religion & Spirituality in Social Work, 29*, 14–32.

Contrada, R. J., Boulifard, D. A., Hekler, E. B., Idler, E. L., Spruill, T. M., Labouvie, E. W., et al. (2008). Psychosocial factors in heart surgery: Presurgical vulnerability and postsurgical recovery. *Health Psychology, 27*, 309–319.

Contrada, R. J., Goyal, T. M., Cather, C., Rafalson, L., Idler, E. L., & Krause, T. J. (2004). Psychosocial factors in outcomes of heart surgery: The impact of religious involvement and depressive symptoms. *Health Psychology, 23*, 227–238.

Costanzo, E., Ryff, C., & Singer, B. (2009). Psychosocial adjustment among cancer survivors: Findings from a national survey of health and well-being. *Health Psychology, 28*, 147–156.

Daniels, M., Merrill, R., Lyon, J., Stanford, J. B., & White, G. L., Jr. (2004). Associations between breast cancer risk factors and religious practices in Utah. *Preventive Medicine, 38*, 28–38.

Edmondson, D., Park, C. L., Chaudoir, S. R., & Wortmann, J. H. (2008). Death without God: Religious struggle, death concerns, and depression in the terminally ill. *Psychological Science, 19*, 754–758.

Fitchett, G., Murphy, P. E., Kim, J., Gibbons, J., Cameron, J. R., & Davis, J. A. (2004). Religious struggle: Prevalence, correlates, and mental health risks in diabetic, congestive heart failure, and oncology patients. *International Journal of Psychiatry in Medicine, 34*, 179–196.

Fitchett, G., & Powell, L. H. (2009). Daily spiritual experiences, systolic blood pressure, and hypertension among midlife women in SWAN. *Annals of Behavioral Medicine, 37*, 257–267.

Gall, T., Guirguis-Younger, M., Charbonneau, C., & Florack, P. (2009). The trajectory of religious coping across time in response to the diagnosis of breast cancer. *Psycho-Oncology, 18,* 1165–1178.

Gall, T., Kristjansson, E., Charbonneau, C., & Florack, P. (2009). A longitudinal study on the role of spirituality in response to the diagnosis and treatment of breast cancer. *Journal of Behavioral Medicine, 32,* 174–186.

Gillum, F., & Williams, C. (2009). Associations between breast cancer risk factors and religiousness in American women in a national health survey. *Journal of Religion and Health, 48,* 178–188.

Gullatte, M., Brawley, O., Kinney, A., Powe, B., & Mooney, K. (2010). Religiosity, spirituality, and cancer fatalism beliefs on delay in breast cancer diagnosis in African American women. *Journal of Religion and Health, 49,* 62–72.

Hadaway, C. K., & Marler, P. L. (2005). How many Americans attend worship each week?: An alternative approach to measurement. *Journal for the Scientific Study of Religion, 44,* 307–322.

Hawkins, N., Smith, T., Zhao, L., Rodriguez, J., Berkowitz, Z., & Stein, K. D. (2010). Health-related behavior change after cancer: Results of the American Cancer Society's studies of cancer survivors (SCS). *Journal of Cancer Survivorship: Research and Practice, 4,* 20–32.

Hebert, R., Zdaniuk, B., Schulz, R., & Scheier, M. (2009). Positive and negative religious coping and well-being in women with breast cancer. *Journal of Palliative Medicine, 12,* 537–545.

Hill, T. D., Angel, J. L., Ellison, C. G., & Angel, R. J. (2005). Religious attendance and mortality: An 8–year follow-up of older Mexican Americans. *The Journals of Gerontology: Series B: Psychological Sciences and Social Sciences, 60,* S102–S109.

Hixson, K. A., Gruchow, H. W., & Morgan, D. W. (1998). The relation between religiosity, selected health behaviors, and blood pressure among adult females. *Preventive Medicine, 27,* 545–552.

Howsepian, B., & Merluzzi, T. (2009). Religious beliefs, social support, self-efficacy and adjustment to cancer. *Psycho-Oncology, 18,* 1069–1079.

Hummer, R. A., Rogers, R. G., Nam, C. B., & Ellison, C. G. (1999). Religious involvement and U. S. adult mortality. *Demography, 36,* 273–285.

Kaplar, M., Wachholtz, A., & O'Brien, W. (2004). The effect of religious and spiritual interventions on the biological, psychological, and spiritual outcomes of oncology patients: A meta-analytic review. *Journal of Psychosocial Oncology, 22,* 39–49.

Kapuscinski, A. N., & Masters, K. S. (2010). The current status of measures of spirituality: A critical review of scale development. *Psychology of Religion and Spirituality, 2,* 191–205.

Koenig, H. G., George, L. K., Hays, J. C., Larson, D. B., Cohen, H. J., & Blazer, D. G. (1998). The relationship between religious activities and blood pressure in older adults. *International Journal of Psychiatry in Medicine, 28,* 189–213.

La Cour, P., Avlund, K., & Schultz-Larsen, K. (2006). Religion and survival in a secular region: A twenty year follow-up of 734 Danish adults born in 1914. *Social Science & Medicine, 62,* 157–164.

Lawler, K. A., & Younger, J. W. (2002). Theobiology: An analysis of spirituality, cardiovascular responses, stress, mood, and physical health. *Journal of Religion and Health, 41,* 347–362.

Lo, C., Lin, J., Gagliese, L., Zimmermann, C., Mikulincer, M., & Rodin, G. (2009). Age and depression in patients with metastatic cancer: The protective effects of attachment security and spiritual well-being. *Ageing and Society, 30,* 325–336.

Masters, K. S. (2007). Religiosity/spirituality and behavioral medicine: Investigations concerning the integration of spirit with body. *Journal of Behavioral Medicine, 30,* 287–289.

Masters, K. S., Hill, R. D., Kircher, J. C., Lensegrav Benson, T. L., & Fallon, J. A. (2004). Religious orientation, aging, and blood pressure reactivity to interpersonal and cognitive stressors. *Annals of Behavioral Medicine, 28,* 171–178.

Masters, K. S., & Knestel, A. (2011). Religious motivation and cardiovascular reactivity among middle aged adults: Is being pro-religious really that good for you? *Journal of Behavioral Medicine, 34,* 449–461.

McCullough, M. E., Hoyt, W. T., Larson, D. B., Koenig, H. G., & Thoresen, C. (2000). Religious involvement and mortality: A meta-analytic review. *Health Psychology, 19,* 211–222.

McCullough, M. E., & Willoughby, B. L. B. (2009). Religion, self-regulation, and self-control: Associations, explanations, and implications. *Psychological Bulletin, 135,* 69–73.

Mystakidou, K., Tsilika, E., Parpa, E., Pathiaki, M., Patiriaki, M., Galanos, A., et al. (2007). Exploring the relationships between depression, hopelessness, cognitive status, pain, and spirituality in patients with advanced cancer. *Archives of Psychiatric Nursing, 21,* 150–161.

Nelson, C., Jacobson, C., Weinberger, M., Bhaskaran, V., Rosenfeld, B., Breitbart, W., et al. (2009). The role of spirituality in the relationship between religiosity and depression in prostate cancer patients. *Annals of Behavioral Medicine, 38,* 105–114.

Oman, D., Kurata, J. H., Strawbridge, W. J., & Cohen, R. D. (2002). Religious attendance and cause of death over 31 years. *International Journal of Psychiatry in Medicine, 32,* 69–89.

Oman, D., & Thoresen, C. E. (2005). Do religion and spirituality influence health? In R. F. Paloutzian & C. L. Park (Eds.), *Handbook of the Psychology of Religion and Spirituality* (pp. 435–459). New York: Guilford Press.

O'Reilly, D., & Rosato, M. (2008). Religious affiliation and mortality in Northern Ireland: Beyond Catholic and Protestant. *Social Science & Medicine, 66,* 1637–1645.

Park, C. L. (2008). Estimated longevity and changes in spirituality in the context of advanced congestive heart failure. *Palliative and Supportive Care, 6,* 3–11.

Park, C. L., Brooks, M. A., & Sussman, J. (2009). Dimensions of religion and spirituality in psychological adjustment in older adults living with congestive heart failure. In A. Ai & M. Ardelt (Eds.), *The role of faith in the well-being of older adults: Linking theories with evidence in an interdisciplinary inquiry* (pp. 112–134). Hauppauge, NY: Nova Science.

Park, C., Edmondson, D., Hale-Smith, A., & Blank, T. O. (2009). Religiousness/spirituality and health behaviors in younger adult cancer survivors: Does faith promote a healthier lifestyle? *Journal of Behavioral Medicine, 32,* 582–591.

Park, C. L., Malone, M. R., Suresh, D. P., Bliss, D., & Rosen, R. I. (2008). Coping, meaning in life, and quality of life in congestive heart failure patients. *Quality of Life Research, 17,* 21–26.

Park, C. L., Moehl, B., Fenster, J. R., Suresh, D. P., & Bliss, D. (2008). Religiousness and treatment adherence in congestive heart failure patients. *Journal of Religion, Spirituality & Aging, 20,* 249–266.

Peterman, A. H., Fitchett, G., Brady, M. J., Hernandez, L., & Cella, D. (2002). Measuring spiritual well-being in people with cancer: The Functional Assessment of Chronic Illness Therapy—Spiritual Well-Being Scale (FACIT-Sp). *Annals of Behavioral Medicine, 24,* 49–58.

Phelps, A., Maciejewski, P., Nilsson, M., Balboni, T. A., Wright, A. A., Paulk, M. E., et al. (2009). Religious coping and use of intensive life-prolonging care near death in patients with advanced cancer. *Journal of the American Medical Association, 301,* 1140–1147.

Powell, L. H., Shahabi, L., & Thoresen, C. E. (2003). Religion and spirituality: Linkages to physical health. *American Psychologist, 58,* 36–52.

Presser, S., & Chaves, M. (2007). Is religious service attendance declining? *Journal for the Scientific Study of Religion, 46,* 417–423.

Roger, V. L., Go, A. S., Lloyd-Jones, D. M., Adams, R. J., Berry, J. D., Brown, T. M., et al. (2011). Heart disease and stroke statistics—2011 update: A report from the American Heart Association. *Circulation, 123,* e18–e209.

Schnall, E., Wassertheil-Smoller, S., Swencionis, C., Zemon, V., Tinker, L., O'Sullivan, M. J., et al. (2010). The relationship between religion and cardiovascular outcomes and all-cause mortality in the women's health initiative observational study. *Psychology & Health, 25,* 249–263.

Sethness, R., Rauschhuber, M., Etnyre, A., Gilliland, I., Lowry, J., & Jones, M. E. (2005). Cardiac health: Relationships among hostility, spirituality, and health risk. *Journal of Nursing Care Quality, 20,* 81–99.

Stefanek, M., McDonald, P., & Hess, S. (2005). Religion, spirituality and cancer: Current status and methodological challenges. *Psycho-Oncology, 14,* 450–463.

Steffen, P. R., Hinderliter, A. I.., Blumenthal, J. A., & Sherwood, A. (2001). Religious coping, ethnicity, and ambulatory blood pressure. *Psychosomatic Medicine, 63,* 523–530.

Sullivan, A. R. (2010). Mortality differentials and religion in the United States: Religious affiliation and attendance. *Journal for the Scientific Study of Religion, 49,* 740–753.

Tarakeshwar, N., Wanderwerker, L. C., Paulk, E., Pearce, M. J., Kasl, S. V., & Prigerson, H. G. (2006). Religious coping is associated with the quality of life of patients with advanced cancer. *Journal of Palliative Medicine, 9,* 646–657.

Tartaro, J., Luecken, L. J., & Gunn, H. E. (2005). Exploring heart and soul: Effects of religiosity/spirituality and gender on blood pressure and cortisol stress responses. *Journal of Health Psychology, 10,* 753–766.

Thuné-Boyle, I. C., Stygall, J. A., Keshtgar, M. R., & Newman, S. P. (2006). Do religious/spiritual coping strategies affect illness adjustment in patients with cancer?: A systematic review of the literature. *Social Science & Medicine, 63,* 151–164.

Timio, M., Lippi, G., Venanzi, S., Gentill, S., Quintaliani, G., Verdura, C., et al. (1997). Blood pressure trend and cardiovascular events in nuns in a secluded order: A 30–year follow-up study. *Blood Pressure, 6,* 81–87.

Visser, A., Garssen, B., & Vingerhoets, A. (2010). Spirituality and well-being in cancer patients: A review. *Psycho-Oncology, 19,* 565–572.

Wildes, K., Miller, A., San Miguel de Majors, S., & Ramirez, A. G. (2009). The religiosity/spirituality of Latina breast cancer survivors and influence on health-related quality of life. *Psycho-Oncology, 18,* 831–840.

Xu, J., Kochanek, K. D., Murphy, S. L., & Tejada-Vera, B. (2010, May 20). Deaths: Final data for 2007. *National Vital Statistics Report, 58*(19). Retrieved from *www.cdc.gov/NCHS/data/nvsr/nvsr58/nvsr58_19.pdf.*

Yanez, B., Edmondson, D., Stanton, A., Park, C., Kwan, L., Ganz, P. A., et al. (2009). Facets of spirituality as predictors of adjustment to cancer: Relative contributions of having faith and finding meaning. *Journal of Consulting and Clinical Psychology, 77,* 730–741.

Yeager, D. M., Glei, D. A., Au, M., Lin, H., Sloan, R. P., & Weinstein, M. (2006). Religious involvement and health outcomes among older persons in Taiwan. *Social Science & Medicine, 63,* 2228–2241.

Zavala, M. W., Maliski, S. L., Kwan, L., Fink, A., & Litwin, M. S. (2009). Spirituality and quality of life in low-income men with metastatic prostate cancer. *Psycho-Oncology, 18,* 753–761.

Zhang, W. (2008). Religious participation and mortality risk among the oldest old in China. *The Journals of Gerontology: Series B. Psychological Sciences and Social Sciences, 63,* S293–S297.

Zwingmann, C., Muller, C., Körber, J., & Murken, S. (2008). Religious commitment, religious coping and anxiety: A study in German patients with breast cancer. *European Journal of Cancer Care, 17,* 361–370.

27

Religion, Spirituality, and Mental Health

Crystal L. Park and Jeanne M. Slattery

Religious suffering is, at the same time, the expression of real suffering and a protest against real suffering. Religion is the sigh of the oppressed creature, the heart of a heartless world, and the soul of soulless conditions. It is the opium of the people.
—KARL MARX

Religion becomes a state of mind achievable in almost any activity of life, if this activity is raised to a suitable level of perfection.
—ABRAHAM MASLOW

As these quotes illustrate, the relationship between religiousness and spirituality, on the one hand, and mental health, on the other, evokes strong interest, passion, and contradictory perspectives. Is religion a positive, growth-oriented striving or an indication of pathology? This issue is an important one, on which writers have opined with limited information. For example, Ellis (1980) observed that "devout, orthodox, or dogmatic religion (or what might be called religiosity) is significantly correlated with emotional disturbance," and concluded that the "elegant therapeutic solution to emotional problems is to be quite unreligious" (p. 637). Similar comments are still made (e.g., Watters, 2007); nonetheless, the research generally shows positive relations between religion and mental health (cf. Baetz, Bowen, Jones, & Koru-Sengul, 2006; Koenig, McCullough, & Larson, 2001; Koenig, 2009).

Historically, many such conclusions were drawn in the absence of empirical data on the relationship between religiousness/spirituality and mental health. Further, much research has focused on religion's association with *negative* aspects of mental health (e.g., religion and depression) rather than also considering its possible relationships with positive functioning, flourishing, and thriving. In this chapter, we first examine the research on the relationships between religion and mental health, in terms of both psychopathology and well-being, flourishing, and thriving. We also discuss moderating variables and potential mechanisms of these relationships as well as the limitations of the data currently available.

RELATIONSHIPS BETWEEN RELIGIOUSNESS/SPIRITUALITY AND MENTAL HEALTH

Research on the relationships between religion and mental health suffers from severe limitations that make the data difficult to interpret (see Shreve-Neiger & Edelstein, 2004, for a review). Very few studies are experimental in nature; almost all of the research is correlational, cross-sectional, and contaminated by confounding factors. Without, at minimum, longitudinal research on the relationships between religious variables and mental health outcomes, accurate interpretation of these correlations is difficult. Furthermore, religion and spirituality can be measured in many different ways (see Hill, Chapter 3, this volume), with important and contradictory implications for conclusions about their relations with mental health (cf. Baetz et al., 2006; Zinnbauer & Pargament, 2005), yet most studies examine a narrow range of religious dimensions. Much of the research has been conducted with healthy populations, assessing differences on continua (e.g., number of depressive symptoms) rather than examining diagnostic criteria for mental disorders. In addition, self-reported religious behavior can differ in important ways from actual behavior (Marler & Hadaway, 1999). Finally, researchers do not agree on what mental health is, although there appears to be significant consensus that it is more than an absence of symptoms (Miller & Kelley, 2005). These limitations should be kept in mind when interpreting the literature.

Affective Symptoms and Disorders

Probably the religiousness/spirituality–mental health link that has received the most empirical attention is that of affective symptoms and disorders, particularly depression. Several large-scale meta-analyses and reviews concluded that religiousness and spirituality are generally reliably, but modestly, inversely related to depressive symptoms. One meta-analysis of 147 studies found a statistically reliable relationship of modest effect size (similar to the association between gender and depressive symptoms), with religious involvement associated with fewer depressive symptoms (Smith, McCullough, & Poll, 2003). In a review of 115 cross-sectional and longitudinal studies, 64% reported that religiousness was related to fewer depressive symptoms, with the majority of the rest reporting no effect (Koenig et al., 2001).

Not all studies have reported positive relationships between religion/spirituality and affective disorders or symptoms, however. Only 24% of the studies reviewed by Dew et al. (2008) found uniformly positive relationships between religiousness and lower levels of depression, while 42% reported mixed positive and nonsignificant findings, 15% reported nonsignificant findings and the remaining 19% reported only negative ones. For example, a large-scale interview-based study of 37,000 Canadians using World Health Organization diagnostic criteria and controlling for demographic variables found that although religious service *attendance* was related to lower lifetime and current incidence of depression and mania, the extent to which people placed *value* on their spirituality was *positively* related to lifetime and current depression and mania (Baetz et al., 2006).

Although affective disorders are a significant risk factor for suicide (Hillbrand, 2001), there are other risk factors as well. Nonetheless, in a review of 68 studies, religiousness and spirituality generally predicted more negative attitudes toward suicidality and lower suicide rates among both adolescents and adults across many world religions (Koenig et al., 2001).

Religion and spirituality have been inversely associated with depressive symptoms in a wide variety of groups: African Americans (Randolph-Seng, Nielsen, Bottoms, & Filipas, 2008; Utsey, Hook, & Stanard, 2007), Turkish adolescents (Eskin, 2004), veterans with a history of traumatic brain injury (Brenner, Homaifar, Adler, Wolfman, & Kemp, 2009), Aboriginals and non-Aboriginals in a Canadian forensic psychiatric hospital population (Mela et al., 2008), and adolescent single parents and their children (Carothers, Borkowski, Lefever, & Whitman, 2005).

Anxiety Symptoms and Disorders

Research on relations between religiousness/spirituality and anxiety has been mixed (see Koenig, 2009; Shreve-Neiger & Edelstein, 2004, for reviews). One review of 69 cross-sectional correlational studies addressing this issue found that 51% reported significantly less anxiety/stress/fear among the more religious; however, 35% reported no association with anxiety and 14% reported greater anxiety, stress, or fear (Koenig et al., 2001).

Different dimensions of religion and spirituality may correlate differently with different dimensions of anxiety. For example, in the just-mentioned large-scale Canadian study, greater frequency of worship was related to lower rates of panic disorder and social phobia, but higher valuing of spirituality was related to higher rates of both panic disorder and social phobia (Baetz et al., 2006). A further example is a study of female college students with histories of panic disorder who reported more religious conflict than did students in general psychotherapy or healthy control groups (Trenholm, Trent, & Compton, 1998).

Clearer results emerge with obsessiveness/compulsivity. Religiousness has been shown to relate positively to levels of obsessive symptoms, compulsive washing, and thought–action fusion (i.e., the belief that thoughts are morally equivalent to the related acts) (Abramowitz, Deacon, Woods, & Tolin, 2004) and greater fear of God and of sinful thoughts (Abramowitz, Huppert, Cohen, Tolin, & Cahill, 2002). All of these studies were conducted in the United States, although similar findings were reported in an Italian sample (Sica, Novara, & Sanavio, 2002). Differences in obsessive and compulsive symptoms across religious groups (with Christians reporting more symptoms than Jews) are related to thought–action fusion, with especially religious Christians being much more likely to equate immoral thoughts and immoral actions (Siev & Cohen, 2007).

The reported relationship between religiousness/spirituality and anxiety is smaller and less consistent than that for depression or mania, but interpreting it is made difficult by heavy reliance on correlational and cross-sectional designs. People who are more anxious may be more religious (perhaps to cope with anxiety), although those who are religious are not necessarily more susceptible to anxiety (Koenig, 2009). Furthermore, strong religious beliefs may protect people from existential issues and anxiety, while a search for meaning or spiritual struggle may lead to increased anxiety, at least in the short term (Baetz et al., 2006; see Exline & Rose, Chapter 19, this volume).

Posttraumatic Stress Symptoms and Posttraumatic Stress Disorder

A review of 11 studies investigating the relationship between religiousness/spirituality and posttraumatic stress disorder (PTSD) and associated symptoms reported inconsistent findings (i.e., three inverse, four positive, three mixed, and one nonassociated) (Chen & Koenig, 2006). Chen and Koenig attributed these mixed results to the overly simplistic approaches many studies took to assess the complex constructs of religiousness/spirituality, the different populations and traumas studied, and the use of cross-sectional designs and self-report measures. At present, it would be premature to draw conclusions; more and better research is needed.

More recent studies suggest that religion may protect some people from posttraumatic stress symptoms (PTSS) (e.g., Walker, Reid, O'Neill, & Brown, 2009). Religion's ability to protect people from PTSS seems to depend on the types of trauma and religious coping strategies used. A study of Wesleyan missionaries found that they reported very high levels of exposures to trauma in the field (94%, with 83% being exposed to multiple incidents) but unexpectedly low rates of PTSS, even when describing their most distressed period (probably immediately after the trauma) (Bagley, 2003). No missionary met diagnostic criteria for PTSD when interviewed. Of course, missionaries likely differ from other groups in other ways, too, making conclusions tentative. Nonetheless, a study of Iranian veterans (all Muslims) found that those who were more religious reported better general health and fewer symptoms of PTSD than did less religious veterans, effects primarily mediated by religious coping (Aflakseir & Coleman, 2009).

Schizophrenia and Psychotic Disorders

Koenig et al. (2001) identified 10 cross-sectional studies of the relationship between religion and psychosis. The results across studies were mixed (four with less psychosis for people who were more religious, three with no association, and two with findings that varied across dependent measures). Koenig's (2009) review concluded that other kinds of religious involvement (other than religious delusions) may improve long-term prognosis for patients diagnosed with psychotic disorders. People diagnosed with schizophrenia were more likely than the general population to identify religion as central to their lives, although fewer were actively involved with a religious group compared with the general population (Mohr, Gillieron, Borras, Brandt, & Huguelet, 2007). Another study found that people diagnosed with schizophrenia reported that religion (in most cases Christianity) helped them develop a sense of meaning that fostered their acceptance of symptoms and use of positive religious coping strategies while decreasing substance use and abuse, willingness to act on suicidal ideation, and impact of their symptoms (Huguelet, Mohr, & Borras, 2009). A small percentage, however, reported negative consequences from religious coping and increased despair and suicidality. People with a religious affiliation, especially Protestants, were first treated and first hospitalized later and had longer periods of untreated symptoms relative to those without an affiliation (Moss, Fleck, & Strakowski, 2006). Although treatment outcomes were not specifically reported, delaying treatment is generally related to poorer outcomes.

A study of people with delusions found that those reporting religious delusions had lower levels of functioning and were more likely to describe themselves as religious (especially taking an orthodox orientation), report hallucinations, and be prescribed higher levels of antipsychotics than those who had nonreligious delusions (Siddle, Haddock, Tarrier, & Faragher, 2002). People with religious delusions were less likely to seek treatment and more likely to perceive a conflict between their religion and psychiatric treatment; further, their religion tended to contribute to a negative sense of self and increased symptoms (Mohr et al., 2010). In their qualitative study of religious delusions, Drinnan and Lavender (2006) suggested that delusions and other religious beliefs were often strategies for understanding difficult family experiences and finding meaning (e.g., their relationship with God provided guidance and protection). The content of delusions and hallucinations seems to be sensitive to and influenced by the person's familial, cultural, political, and religious context, although religious upbringing and beliefs did not appear to play a significant role in schizophrenia's etiology (Miller & Kelley, 2005; Wilson, 1998).

Substance Abuse

In a review of 138 studies examining relations between substance abuse and religion, 90% of these studies indicated that more religious people had lower use of substances and were less likely to abuse them (Koenig et al., 2001). Another review of the literature on religiousness and various aspects of adolescent mental health reported that the most favorable relationships were with substance use (Dew et al., 2008). In the Canadian study of 37,000 people, higher reported frequencies of worship and stronger spiritual values were related to lower rates of current alcohol or drug dependency (Baetz et al., 2006). Similar findings have been reported in a wide range of populations. Religion and spirituality may provide one area of vulnerability regarding substance abuse, however, Koenig (2009) observed that when people from religions that promote complete abstinence from substances begin using alcohol or drugs, "substance use can become severe and recalcitrant" (p. 289), presumably because in going against religious proscriptions, they withdraw from religious involvement, become more isolated, and feel more guilt and shame.

Stress-Related/Posttraumatic Growth

Most people report perceiving positive life changes following adversity, commonly referred to as stress-related or posttraumatic growth (PTG) (Linley & Joseph, 2004). In their review of the literature, Linley and Joseph found that growth was related to numerous aspects of religiousness and spirituality, including positive religious coping, existential openness, intrinsic religiousness, and religious participation. These findings have been reported in many different samples, including older adults whose personal and public religiousness and religious coping were especially related to perceiving themselves as having made meaning following a stressful event (Park, 2006), adults who reported more PTG after multiple traumas when they sought spiritual support (Harris et al., 2008), and women with breast cancer who were more likely to perceive cancer-related growth when they had higher levels of religious faith (Yanez et al., 2009).

Psychological Well-Being

Most studies suggest that religiousness and spirituality are associated with increased levels of happiness, life satisfaction, and well-being (see Koenig et al., 2001, for a review).

A meta-analysis of 35 studies examining the relationship between type of religiousness (i.e., institutional religion, ideological religion, and personal devotion) and mental health (i.e., psychological distress, life satisfaction, self-actualization) found that mental health was modestly related to institutional religiousness and, fairly strongly related to ideological religion and personal devotion. Both ideological religion and personal devotion were more strongly correlated with life satisfaction and self-actualization than with measures of distress (Hackney & Sanders, 2003). Similarly, a meta-analysis of 59 studies yielded a reliable and positive moderate-sized relationship between spirituality and quality of life (Sawatzky, Ratner, & Chiu, 2005).

Although most of the studies included in these meta-analyses were conducted with Caucasian, female, U.S.-born Christian young adults, similar positive relationships between religiousness/spirituality and well-being have been reported with Algerian Muslims (Tiliouine, Cummins, & Davern, 2009), older African Americans (Frazier, Mintz, & Mobley, 2005), Aboriginals and nonAboriginals in a Canadian forensic psychiatric center (Mela et al., 2008), and older men (Koenig & Vaillant, 2009).

Summary

Religiousness/spirituality appear to have a consistent relationship with low levels of substance abuse and dependence; a weaker, although reliable, salutary association with affective disorders, suicide, and well-being; and a less consistent pattern of associations for schizophrenia, anxiety, and reactions to trauma (PTSD, PTSS, and perceived growth) (e.g., Baetz et al., 2006; Koenig, 2009). These relationships can be difficult to interpret because of the limitations of research designs used (mostly cross-sectional, with many confounding variables). To some degree, these differences may be attributable to the ways that people use religion/spirituality to handle difficult experiences (e.g., thought–action fusion, negative relationships with God). Further, as discussed in the next section, in some cases, the associations may depend on characteristics such as gender, race, and denomination.

MODERATORS OF THE RELATIONSHIP BETWEEN RELIGIOUSNESS/SPIRITUALITY AND MENTAL HEALTH

The effect of a given dimension of religion/spirituality on mental health can vary based on some other characteristic that functions as a moderator. Relatively few studies, however, have examined the role that moderator variables play in the relationships between religiousness/spirituality and mental health, yet studies attending to moderating variables have yielded important findings.

Demographic characteristics are commonly suggested as moderating factors. For example, some studies have found that links between religion and mental health are stronger for women (e.g., Ellison, Finch, Ryan, & Salinas, 2009; Maselko & Buka, 2008), African Americans (Hackney & Sanders, 2003; Randolph-Seng et al., 2008), Asian Americans (Randolph-Seng et al., 2008), and Latinos (Ellison, Finch, et al., 2009).

Gender may also be a moderator. One study found that women who made changes in their religious activity (mostly becoming less active) were more than twice as likely to have met criteria for a lifetime diagnosis of generalized anxiety disorder, substance abuse, or substance dependence as those who maintained childhood levels of religious activity (Maselko & Buka, 2008). However, men who changed their religious activity were only half as likely to have met criteria for lifetime diagnosis with an affective disorder as men who hadn't changed. In a national sample of older adults, feeling grateful to God had stronger stress-buffering effects against the chronic stresses of aging for women than for men (Krause, 2006).

Such findings regarding race and gender are inconsistent across studies, however. For example, Musick (2000) observed that beliefs that the world was full of sin were strongly inversely related to life satisfaction for European Americans but unrelated for African Americans. But in a meta-analysis of 147 studies, Smith et al. (2003) found no evidence that gender or race moderated the relationship between religion and depression.

Denomination appears to moderate relationships between religion and mental health. In one study, both religious beliefs and religious practices were related to lower levels of depressive symptoms and anxiety for Orthodox Jews but not for non-Orthodox Jews (Rosmarin, Pirutinsky, Pargament, & Krumrei, 2009). Christians also report more obsessive and compulsive symptoms than Jews (Siev & Cohen, 2007). In a sample of college students, intrinsic religiousness buffered the effects of uncontrollable life stress on depressive and anxiety symptoms for Protestants and controllable life events for Catholics (Park, Cohen, & Herb, 1990). In a sample of older adults, Protestants reported better morale, less death anxiety, and greater levels of social satisfaction than Jews (Cohen & Hall, 2009). These relationships have been inconsistent, however, as no denominational differences in distress were reported by Rosmarin, Krumrei, and Andersson (2009). Denominational differences probably reflect doctrine-specific beliefs and cultural values (e.g., Abramowitz et al., 2002, 2004; Siev & Cohen, 2007; see Saroglou & Cohen, Chapter 17, this volume).

Age and income are sociodemographic characteristics worth additional investigation as moderators. For example, in one study, religious doubt was associated with a wide variety of psychological symptoms (e.g., depression, anxiety, hostility), but the strength of this effect was smaller for older than younger adults (Galek, Krause, Ellison, Kudler, & Flannelly, 2007). In a study of maternal caregivers of ill children, prayer was associated with better quality of life only for less educated and less affluent caregivers (Banthia, Moskowitz, Acree, & Folkman, 2007).

Finally, level of stress may serve as a moderator. In some cases, the relationships between religiousness/spirituality and mental health are stronger at higher levels of stress (Smith et al., 2003), although this may depend on the type of stressors encountered (Ellison, Finch, et al., 2009).

POTENTIAL PATHWAYS THROUGH WHICH RELIGIOUSNESS/SPIRITUALITY INFLUENCE MENTAL HEALTH

Although the results are not entirely consistent, the preponderance of evidence suggests that some aspects of religiousness and spirituality are related to some aspects of mental health. To account for these relationships, we developed a bidirectional model of the mediational pathways through which various dimensions of religiousness/spirituality may help or hinder mental health and vice versa (see Figure 27.1). In this section, we describe these pathways and the evidence regarding them. Many are presumed to be positive pathways—for example, religious life often provides social support, which is related to better psychological well-being (Carothers et al., 2005; Cohen, Yoon, & Johnstone, 2009; Contrada et al., 2008; Ellison, Finch, et al., 2009). However, other aspects of religiousness or spirituality may lead to poorer mental health. It is important to note that many studies have linked these proposed mediators with religion and mental health, but few have explicitly tested them these linkages.

How Religiousness/Spirituality May Facilitate Mental Health

Social Support

One of the most obvious benefits to those involved in organized religion is the social support that comes with that involvement. Individuals regularly involved with a congregation have larger social networks, interact with network members more frequently, receive more diverse types of support, and find their support networks more satisfying and more

FIGURE 27.1 Model of proposed relationship between religious and spiritual dimensions and mental health, with proposed mediators (left, right).

reliable than those who do not attend services regularly (Carothers et al., 2005; Cohen et al., 2009; Contrada et al., 2008; Ellison, Zhang, Krause, & Marcum, 2009). Further, the social support people gain through their religious involvement may be qualitatively different than secular social support (Hayward & Elliott, 2009; Krause, 2006). Religious social support reinforces and is reinforced by a collective framework of ultimate meaning, belongingness, and cohesion in ways that may not be matched by secular groups (Ladd & McIntosh, 2008; Smith, 2003; Ysseldyk, Matheson, & Hymie, 2010). Given that social support has long been demonstrated to promote mental health and buffer stress (Taylor, 2007), the link between religiousness/spirituality and mental health may in large part be mediated through social support.

Social Identity

One potent pathway through which religiousness may influence mental health is through the strong social identity that religion can offer, which goes beyond social support. Although many groups offer a sense of social identity, it has been claimed that religion "offers a distinctive 'sacred' worldview and 'eternal' group membership, unmatched by identification with other social groups" (Ysseldyk et al., 2010, p. 60).

Guidelines for Living

Another route through which religion and spirituality may lead to better mental health outcomes is the provision of prescriptions, proscriptions, guidelines, and limits for many areas of life, most of which lead to healthier lifestyles and avoidance of deviant and problematic behavior. For example, many religions forbid the use of alcohol or other intoxicants. For adherents of those religions, substance abuse is far less likely, and comorbid conditions, such as depression, may be less likely as well (Smith et al., 2003). Proscriptions against suicide may protect more religious people from taking their own lives (e.g., Eskin, 2004; Huguelet et al., 2009), and other proscriptions may prevent adolescents from making risky decisions (Smith, 2003).

Forgiveness

Religiousness and spirituality appear to encourage forgiveness and more benevolent attitudes about others after significant interpersonal transgressions (Schultz, Tallman, & Altmaier, 2010), and people who are more religious tend to score higher on measures of forgiveness (Worthington & Scherer, 2004). Forgiveness has been related to better psychological well-being in many studies. For example, in a study of older adults, forgiveness (by God, of themselves, or of others) partially or completely mediated healthy relationships between religion and both depressive symptoms and subjective well-being (Lawler-Row, 2010).

Positive Relationship with God/Sense of Divine or Transcendent

Religious or spiritual individuals may be more likely to experience subjective feelings of closeness to God, positive views of God and God's role in one's life, and a sense of the divine in daily life (Ellison & Fan, 2008). These subjective religious/spiritual experiences have been favorably related to mental health in a variety of samples, including a group with heterogeneous medical problems (Cohen et al., 2009), people with chronic pain (Rippentrop, Altmaier, Chen, Found, & Keffala, 2005), and a large sample representative of the U.S. population (Bradshaw, Ellison, & Flannelly, 2008). However, these effects may be substantially due to confounds such as demographic factors. For example, in the Cohen et al. (2009) study of rehabilitation patients, when statistically controlling for income, correlations between subjective religious experiences and mental health disappeared.

Religious Coping Resources and Strategies

Religiousness and spirituality may promote mental health by providing beliefs that lead to more benign interpretations of situations, which in turn minimize exposure to negative affect. Thus, benign religious beliefs can protect people against the daily wear and tear of stressors as well as help them face highly stressful or traumatic situations. A meta-analysis of 31 studies examining variables predicting reports of posttraumatic growth found a strong effect of religious coping (Prati & Pietrantoni, 2009). Positive types of religious coping (e.g., making benevolent religious reappraisals, seeking spiritual support) tend to be correlated with indices of positive mental health, although negative religious coping tends to be associated with poorer adjustment (Ano & Vasconcelles, 2005; Harris et al., 2008; see Pargament, Ano, & Wachholtz, Chapter 28, this volume).

Religious Practices

Religious and spiritual life presents a panoply of religious practices and rituals in which adherents can engage, many of which may facilitate mental health. One of the most common of these is prayer. It is important to note, however, that the nature of prayer varies dramatically (see Ladd & Spilka, Chapter 22, this volume). Some types of prayer may lead to increased feelings of peace and support or to more productive ways of viewing a problem, while other types may cause increased distress (Masters & Spielmans, 2007). Consistent with this perspective, Ellison and his colleagues (Bradshaw et al., 2008; Ellison, Finch, et al., 2009) observed that prayer was related to poorer mental health for people with a negative God image and unrelated to mental health for people with a positive God image. In their summary of the literature, Masters and Spielmans (2007) also observed that many people use prayer when problems are severe and unresponsive to other treatments, which may mean that they are more likely to pray when they are distressed rather than distressed because they pray.

Positive Affect

Positive affect is often associated with higher levels of religion and spirituality (Ellison & Fan, 2008; Saroglou, Buxant, & Tilquin, 2008; see Lewis & Cruise, 2006), and religions often explicitly promote spiritually relevant positive emotions (Steffen & Masters, 2005; Krause, 2002; see Tsai, Koopmann-Holm, Miyazaki, & Ochs, Chapter 14, this volume). Positive affect is increasingly documented to favorably affect physical health as well as emotional well-being (see Pressman & Cohen, 2005; Park & Slattery, 2012, for reviews). Thus, positive affect is a potentially important pathway through which religion and spirituality may influence health and well-being (Fredrickson, 2002).

Sense of Meaning

Religion often serves as a core aspect of individuals' ultimate sense of meaning or purpose (e.g., Emmons, 2005; Park, 2010; Steger & Frazier, 2005) and, as such, seems likely to be an important pathway protecting individuals against distress and psychopathology as well as promoting positive mental health and well-being (see Park, Chapter 18, this volume).

Emotional Regulation

Another pathway through which religion may exert salutary effects on mental health is the provision of avenues for regulating emotions. Emotional regulation is receiving increasing attention as an important factor in emotional health and well-being (e.g., Gross & Barrett, 2011). Religion and spirituality provide many ways to regulate emotions, some of which may be considered coping, as discussed previously (Watts, 2007), but others of which are better considered aspects of a more general religious or spiritual life. For example, contemplative and meditative practices have been shown to decrease emotional reactivity (Chopko & Schwartz, 2009; Watts, 2007). Even the presence of religious imagery dampens not only the expression but the experience of negative emotions (Koole, McCullough, Kuhl, & Roelofsma, 2010). A related but somewhat separate literature has linked religion to behavioral self-control (e.g., avoiding temptations, regulating impulses), which may also lead to better emotional well-being (see Zell & Baumeister, Chapter 25, this volume).

Afterlife Beliefs

Most major religions offer some perspective on an afterlife (Slattery & Park, 2012), which may provide a comforting perspective on trials experienced during earthly life and thus protect against psychological distress. For example, in a national U.S. sample, belief in life after death was inversely related to a variety of psychiatric symptoms (i.e., anxiety, depression, obsession–compulsion, paranoia, phobia, and somatization), relationships that remained even after controlling for demographic and other variables such as stress and social support (Flannelly, Koenig, Ellison, Galek, & Krause, 2006). Positive views of the afterlife (e.g., peace and reunion with loved ones) were strongly related to fewer reported symptoms (Flannelly, Ellison, Galek, & Koenig, 2008).

How Religiousness/Spirituality May Harm Mental Health

Negative Religious Attributions/Interpretations

Copious research has demonstrated the negative effects of negative religious coping and spiritual struggle on many aspects of psychological well-being. For example, a meta-analysis of 49 studies examining relations between religious coping and adjustment identified a modest but reliable positive association between negative religious coping (e.g., spiritual discontent, demonic and punishing-God appraisals) and negative adjustment (e.g., depression, anxiety, distress) (Ano & Vasconcelles, 2005). In a nationwide survey, religious doubt was inversely related to various measures of mental distress, including depression, anxiety, interpersonal sensitivity, phobic anxiety, obsessive–compulsive symptoms, somatization, paranoid ideation, and hostility (Galek et al., 2007; see Exline & Rose, Chapter 19, and Pargament et al., Chapter 28, this volume).

Negative Social Interactions

Although social support is a common benefit of religious involvement, negative religious social interactions with fellow congregants and religious leaders can include disapproval and criticism or excessive demands, which can be quite distressing (Exline, 2002). In a nationwide sample of Presbyterians, for example, negative interactions with fellow church members were correlated with higher levels of depressive symptoms and a lower sense of well-being (Krause, Ellison, & Wulff, 1998), effects that held across time (Ellison, Zhang, et al., 2009). In addition, in a national sample of older adults, negative interactions with clergy members were related to lower levels of self-esteem (Krause, 2003).

Negative Affect

Some types of religion can lead to negative emotions such as hatred, fear, and guilt, increasing the risk of coping difficulties and depression (Albertsen, O'Connor, & Berry, 2006; Williams & Sternthal, 2007; see Nielsen, Hatton, & Donahue, Chapter 16, this volume). Further, some religious and spiritual traditions may be linked with negative affect through their emphasis on the sinful nature of humans and the resulting inner conflicts over issues such as sexuality, sexual identity, or selfishness (Slattery & Park, 2012).

Perceptions of Treatment as Contraindicated by Religion

People may perceive medical advice as conflicting with their religious beliefs (Miller & Kelley, 2005; Mitchell & Romans, 2003; Moss et al., 2006). For example, as cited previously, Moss and colleagues (2006) found that when people with schizophrenia perceived religious and medical advice as conflicting, they had longer periods to first diagnosis and treatment. Similarly, people with bipolar disorder who were more religious tended to be less compliant with their medications (Mitchell & Romans, 2003). When they perceived treatment as inconsistent with their religious beliefs, they were less likely to report that their religious beliefs helped them manage symptoms.

HOW MENTAL HEALTH MAY INFLUENCE RELIGIOUSNESS/SPIRITUALITY

Fewer pathways have been proposed for how mental health may influence religion or spirituality, but one very strong and long-standing theory is that distress or stress pushes people toward a stronger reliance on or embrace of religion. One version of this is the

Stark-Bainbridge model of religion as compensation, a sociological model explaining positive associations of religion and socioeconomic disenfranchisement (Flynn & Kunkel, 1987). A variant of this model, the emotional compensation theory, holds that people turn to religion for comfort when experiencing psychological distress (Brown, Nesse, House, & Utz, 2004). People in stress or distress may turn to religion to access a variety of important coping resources, such as social support, structure, comfort, sense of meaning, or control of undesirable aspects.

Although these models (Brown et al., 2004; Flynn & Kunkel, 1987) are compelling, empirical tests are sparse and findings inconsistent. Some people in poor mental or physical health or who are experiencing greater distress turn to religion, while others turn away (Maselko & Buka, 2008; Pargament, Desai, & McConnell, 2006). Further, such changes may be short lived. In the aftermath of the 9/11 terrorist attacks, a national survey found reports of increased church attendance (Schuster et al., 2001), but attendance quickly returned to pre-9/11 levels (Barna Group, 2001). Finally, high stress levels are often reported (retrospectively) in cases of religious conversion (see Paloutzian, Murken, Streib, & Roßler-Namini, Chapter 20, this volume). The ways that poor mental health or trauma exposure affect religiousness and spirituality may depend on many individual characteristics, including preexisting religiousness or spirituality and the extent to which individuals' religious and spiritual needs are being met (e.g., Walker et al., 2009).

The positive associations between religiousness/spirituality and mental health can also be explained in terms of psychological resources available to engage in activities fostering a sense of transcendence. People in good mental health may be more expansive and have more mental energy for religious and spiritual engagement (e.g., Hackney & Sanders, 2003). On the other hand, poorer mental health may decrease resources available to engage in meaningful activities, lead to greater spiritual struggle, and increase reliance on negative religious coping (see Exline & Rose, Chapter 19, this volume), all of which may increase spiritual alienation.

LIMITATIONS

Although religiousness/spirituality and mental health are clearly related, this relationship is not simple and is likely bidirectional. Research in this field must acknowledge this complexity. Religiousness and spirituality can have both positive and negative effects on mental health, at both the individual and group level. These differences may be related to other factors, including hardiness, the rigidity with which religious beliefs are held, and the ability to assimilate trauma without being shaken to the core (Kelley, 2007; Maddi, Brow, Khoshaba, & Vaitkus, 2006). People may experience distress during periods of spiritual struggle, PTG, or otherwise adaptive coping processes, which may reflect short-term problems incurred in the process of long-term growth (Warner, Mahoney, & Krumrei, 2009). Therefore, a one-time measure of church attendance or beliefs is unlikely to have much predictive validity over the long term. Nor are single or limited measures of religiousness and spirituality—or mental health—likely to be able to assess the rich and complicated interactions between these two realms.

Much of the research on the relationships between beliefs and mental health outcomes is plausible, yet speculative, as it has been based on self-reports and is correlational and cross-sectional in design (e.g., Hackney & Sanders, 2003; Rosmarin, Pirutinsky, et al., 2009). Findings from studies using such designs cannot determine whether relationships are causal and, if so, their direction. Group and denominational differences are difficult to interpret, as they may be better related to differences in willingness to report mental health problems than mental health per se (Cohen & Hall, 2009). In some cases, correlations might be a proxy for another variable (e.g., church attendance being a proxy for functional health) (Koenig & Vaillant, 2009). Performing analyses solely at the group level also obscures individual differences in connections between religiousness and spirituality and mental health, such that religiousness and spirituality can be helpful or protective for some people, hurtful for others, and make little difference for still others (Rosmarin, Pirutinsky, et al., 2009).

Finally, much of the research on the relationship between religiousness and spirituality and mental health has used self-report measures of behavior, which are often inaccurate: People respond according to social desirability biases and sometimes significantly overestimate their tithing and church attendance (e.g., Marler & Hadaway, 1999). Further, religiousness and spirituality are multidimensional variables; outcomes depend on the specific behaviors and beliefs assessed. Other more ecologically valid strategies for assessing beliefs, attitudes, and behavior (e.g., children's drawings of God, narrative responses about coping with stressors and trauma, observations of religious behavior) may further clarify the relationships between religiousness, spirituality, and mental health (Hill & Pargament, 2003).

FUTURE RESEARCH

Research on relationships between religiousness/spirituality and mental health has focused on a narrow segment of the world population, largely neglecting Buddhists, Muslims, Hindus, and other groups. More empirical research is needed on the roles of global religions, culture, level of acculturation, gender and age, and the interactions among these factors on mental health. Religion appears to be more helpful for some groups under some conditions and less helpful for others (cf. Ellison, Finch, et al., 2009; Ellison, Zhang, et al., 2009; Rosmarin, Pirutinsky, et al., 2009). Like other cultural factors, religion may influence not only a person's risk of mental illness but also the manifestations of that illness (e.g., the form of obsessions or delusions) (Miller & Kelley, 2005). Some of these differences may be related to the nature of the religious and spiritual attributions drawn (Lawler-Row, 2010; Warner et al., 2009). For example, identifying the degree to which people who are depressed feel that God has abandoned them, have lost their faith that God is omnipotent and good, or believe that they are unforgivable may help identify mediating pathways between mental health and religiousness/spirituality.

Although religiousness and spirituality appear to provide some level of protection against mental health problems, especially substance abuse and depression, researchers should also pay attention to happy and healthy nonbelievers, those who are able to thrive *without* reference to the divine or the spiritual (Maddi et al., 2006; Miller & Kelley, 2005). Do they take a different path to mental health and well-being, or do they hold secular beliefs and practices that are similar to those that are helpful for more religious and spiritual people? For example, many atheists and agnostics also believe that one should show compassion to those in need, forgive oneself and others, and care for the well-being of the planet and its inhabitants. Many hold a sense of meaning and purpose that informs their daily life. To what degree are religious and spiritual beliefs and rituals a systematized description of how to live well, find happiness and love, and create fairness and justice? To what degree does having a sense of meaning and peace, of finding a way of forgiving wrongs—with or without spiritual or religious beliefs—lead to positive outcomes (Maddi et al., 2006; Schultz et al., 2010; Yanez et al., 2009)?

Although many issues remain, it is clear that we have a stronger understanding of the linkages between mental health and religion/spirituality than we did even 8 years ago. The questions being asked are more sophisticated, the comparisons across groups are becoming more nuanced, and the directions for future progress are better illuminated.

REFERENCES

Abramowitz, J., Deacon, B., Woods, C., & Tolin, D. (2004). Association between Protestant religiosity and obsessive–compulsive symptoms and cognitions. *Depression and Anxiety, 20,* 70–76.

Abramowitz, J., Huppert, J., Cohen, A., Tolin, D., & Cahill, S. (2002). Religious obsessions and compulsions in a non-clinical sample: The Penn Inventory of Scrupulosity (PIOS). *Behaviour Research and Therapy, 40,* 824–838.

Aflakseir, A., & Coleman, P. (2009). The influence of religious coping on the mental health of disabled Iranian war veterans. *Mental Health, Religion & Culture, 12,* 175–190.

Albertsen, E. J., O'Connor, L. E., & Berry, J. W. (2006). Religion and interpersonal guilt: Variations across ethnicity and spirituality. *Mental Health, Religion & Culture, 9,* 67–84.

Ano, G. G., & Vasconcelles, E. B. (2005). Religious coping and psychological adjustment to stress: A meta-analysis. *Journal of Clinical Psychology, 61,* 461–480.

Baetz, M., Bowen, R., Jones, G., & Koru-Sengul, T. (2006). How spiritual values and worship attendance relate to psychiatric disorders in the Canadian population. *Canadian Journal of Psychiatry, 51,* 654–661.

Bagley, R. (2003). Trauma and traumatic stress among missionaries. *Journal of Psychology and Theology, 31,* 97–112.

Banthia, R., Moskowitz, J. T., Acree, M., & Folkman, S. (2007). Socioeconomic differences in the effects of prayer on physical symptoms and quality of life. *Journal of Health Psychology, 12,* 249–260.

Barna Group. (2001, November 26). *How America's faith has changed since 9–11.* Retrieved from *www.barna.org/barna-update/article/5-barna-update/63-how-americas-faith-has-changed-since-9-11.*

Bradshaw, M., Ellison, C., & Flannelly, K. (2008). Prayer, God imagery, and symptoms of psychopathology. *Journal for the Scientific Study of Religion, 47,* 644–659.

Brenner, L. A., Homaifar, B. Y., Adler, L. E., Wolfman, J. H., & Kemp, J. (2009). Suicidality and veterans with a history of traumatic brain injury: Precipitating events, protective factors, and prevention strategies. *Rehabilitation Psychology, 54,* 390–397.

Brown, S. L., Nesse, R. M., House, J. S., & Utz, R. L. (2004). Religion and emotional compensation: Results from a prospective study of widowhood. *Personality and Social Psychology Bulletin, 30,* 1165–1174.

Carothers, S. S., Borkowski, J. G., Lefever, J. B., & Whitman, T. L. (2005). Religiosity and the socioemotional adjustment of adolescent mothers and their children. *Journal of Family Psychology, 19,* 263–275.

Chen, Y. Y., & Koenig, H. G. (2006). Traumatic stress and religion: Is there a relationship?: A review of empirical findings. *Journal of Religion and Health, 45*, 371–381.

Chopko, B. A., & Schwartz, R. C. (2009). The relation between mindfulness and posttraumatic growth: A study of first responders to trauma-inducing incidents. *Journal of Mental Health Counseling, 31*, 363–376.

Cohen, A., & Hall, D. (2009). Existential beliefs, social satisfaction, and well-being among Catholic, Jewish, and Protestant older adults. *The International Journal for the Psychology of Religion, 19*, 39–54.

Cohen, D., Yoon, D. P., & Johnstone, B. (2009). Differentiating the impact of spiritual experiences, religious practices, and congregational support on the mental health of individuals with heterogeneous medical disorders. *The International Journal for the Psychology of Religion, 19*, 121–138.

Contrada, R. J., Boulifard, D. A., Hekler, E. B., Idler, E. L., Spruill, T. M., Labouvie, E. W., et al. (2008). Psychosocial factors in heart surgery: Presurgical vulnerability and postsurgical recovery. *Health Psychology, 27*, 309–319.

Dew, R. E., Daniel, S. S., Armstrong, T. D., Goldston, D. B., Triplett, M. F., & Koenig, H. G. (2008). Religion/spirituality and adolescent psychiatric symptoms: A review. *Child Psychiatry and Human Development, 39*, 381–398.

Drinnan, A., & Lavender, T. (2006). Deconstructing delusions: A qualitative study examining the relationship between religious beliefs and religious delusions. *Mental Health, Religion & Culture, 9*, 317–331.

Ellis, A. (1980). Psychotherapy and atheistic values: A response to A. E. Bergin's "psychotherapy and religious values." *Journal of Consulting and Clinical Psychology, 48*, 635–639.

Ellison, C., Zhang, W., Krause, N., & Marcum, J. (2009). Does negative interaction in the church increase psychological distress?: Longitudinal findings from the Presbyterian Panel Survey. *Sociology of Religion, 70*, 409–431.

Ellison, C. G., & Fan, D. (2008). Daily spiritual experiences and psychological well-being among US adults. *Social Indicators Research, 88*, 247–271.

Ellison, C. G., Finch, B. K., Ryan, D. N., & Salinas, J. J. (2009). Religious involvement and depressive symptoms among Mexican-origin adults in California. *Journal of Community Psychology, 37*, 171–193.

Emmons, R. A. (2005). Striving for the sacred: Personal goals, life meaning, and religion. *Journal of Social Issues, 61*, 731–745.

Eskin, M. (2004). The effects of religious versus secular education on suicide ideation and suicidal attitudes in adolescents in Turkey. *Social Psychiatry and Psychiatric Epidemiology, 39*, 536–542.

Exline, J. J. (2002). The picture is getting clearer, but is the scope too limited?: Three overlooked questions in the psychology of religion. *Psychological Inquiry, 13*, 245–247.

Flannelly, K. J., Ellison, C., Galek, K., & Koenig, H. (2008). Beliefs about life-after-death, psychiatric symptomology and cognitive theories of psychopathology. *Journal of Psychology and Theology, 36*, 94–103.

Flannelly, K. J., Koenig, H. G., Ellison, C. G., Galek, K., & Krause, N. (2006). Belief in life after death and mental health: Findings from a national survey. *Journal of Nervous and Mental Disease, 194*, 524–529.

Flynn, C. P., & Kunkel, S. R. (1987). Deprivation, compensation, and conceptions of an afterlife. *Sociological Analysis, 48*, 58–72.

Frazier, C., Mintz, L. B., & Mobley, M. (2005). A multidimensional look at religious involvement and psychological well-being among urban elderly African Americans. *Journal of Counseling Psychology, 52*, 583–590.

Fredrickson, B. L. (2002). How does religion benefit health and well-being?: Are positive emotions active ingredients? *Psychological Inquiry, 13*, 209–213.

Galek, K., Krause, N., Ellison, C., Kudler, T., & Flannelly, K. (2007). Religious doubt and mental health across the lifespan. *Journal of Adult Development, 14,* 16–25.

Gross, J. J., & Barrett, L. F. (2011). Emotion generation and emotion regulation: One or two depends on your point of view. *Emotion Review, 3,* 8–16.

Hackney, C., & Sanders, G. (2003). Religiosity and mental health: A meta-analysis of recent studies. *Journal for the Scientific Study of Religion, 42,* 43–55.

Harris, J. I., Erbes, C. R., Engdahl, B. E., Olson, R. H. A., Winskowski, A. M., & McMahill, J. (2008). Christian religious functioning and trauma outcomes. *Journal of Clinical Psychology, 64,* 17–29.

Hayward, R. D., & Elliott, M. (2009). Fitting in with the flock: Social attractiveness as a mechanism for well-being in religious groups. *European Journal of Social Psychology, 39,* 592–607.

Hill, P. C., & Pargament, K. I. (2003). Advances in the conceptualization and measurement of religion and spirituality: Implications for physical and mental health research. *American Psychologist, 58,* 64–74.

Hillbrand, M. (2001). Homicide–suicide and other forms of co-occurring aggression against self and against others. *Professional Psychology: Research and Practice, 32,* 626–635.

Huguelet, P., Mohr, S., & Borras, L. (2009). Recovery, spirituality and religiousness in schizophrenia. *Clinical Schizophrenia and Related Psychoses, 2,* 307–316.

Kelley, T. A. (2007). The role of religion, spirituality, and faith-based community in coping with acts of terrorism. In B. Bongar, L. M. Brown, L. E. Beutler, J. N. Breckenridge, & P. G. Zimbardo (Eds.), *Psychology of terrorism* (pp. 137–152). New York: Oxford University Press.

Koenig, H. G. (2009). Research on religion, spirituality, and mental health: A review. *Canadian Journal of Psychiatry, 54,* 283–291.

Koenig H. G., McCullough M. E., & Larson D. B. (2001). *Handbook of religion and health.* New York: Oxford University Press.

Koenig, L. B., & Vaillant, G. E. (2009). A prospective study of church attendance and health over the lifespan. *Health Psychology, 28,* 117–124.

Koole, S. L., McCullough, M. E., Kuhl, J., & Roelofsma, P. H. M. P. (2010). Why religion's burdens are light: From religiosity to implicit self-regulation. *Personality and Social Psychology Review, 14,* 95–107.

Krause, N. (2002). Church-based social support and health in old age: Exploring variations by race. *Journals of Gerontology: Series B. Psychological Sciences and Social Sciences, 57B,* S332–S347.

Krause, N. (2003). Exploring race differences in the relationship between social interaction with clergy and feelings of self-worth in late life. *Sociology of Religion, 64,* 183–205.

Krause, N. (2006). Exploring the stress-buffering effects of church-based and secular social support on self-rated health in late life. *Journals of Gerontology: Series B. Psychological Sciences and Social Sciences, 61B,* 533–543.

Krause, N., Ellison, C. G., & Wulff, K. H. (1998). Church-based emotional support, negative interaction, and psychological well-being: Findings from a national sample of Presbyterians. *Journal for the Scientific Study of Religion, 37,* 725–741.

Ladd, K. L., & McIntosh, D. N. (2008). Meaning, God, and prayer: Physical and metaphysical aspects of social support. *Mental Health, Religion & Culture, 11,* 23–38.

Lawler-Row, K. A. (2010). Forgiveness as a mediator of the religiosity—health relationship. *Psychology of Religion and Spirituality, 2,* 1–16.

Lewis, C. A., & Cruise, S. M. (2006). Religion and happiness: Consensus, contradictions, comments and concerns. *Mental Health, Religion & Culture, 9,* 213–225.

Linley, P. A., & Joseph, S. (2004). Positive change following trauma and adversity: A review. *Journal of Traumatic Stress, 17,* 11–21.

Maddi, S. R., Brow, M., Khoshaba, D. M., & Vaitkus, M. (2006). Relationship of hardiness and religiousness to depression and anger. *Consulting Psychology Journal: Practice and Research, 58,* 148–161.

Marler, P. L., & Hadaway, C. K. (1999). Testing the attendance gap in a conservative church. *Sociology of Religion, 6*, 175–186.

Maselko, J., & Buka, S. (2008). Religious activity and lifetime prevalence of psychiatric disorder. *Social Psychiatry and Psychiatric Epidemiology, 43*, 18–24.

Masters, K., & Spielmans, G. (2007). Prayer and health: Review, meta-analysis, and research agenda. *Journal of Behavioral Medicine, 30*, 329–338.

Mela, M., Marcoux, E., Baetz, M., Griffin, R., Angelski, C., & Deqiang, G. (2008). The effect of religiosity and spirituality on psychological well-being among forensic psychiatric patients in Canada. *Mental Health, Religion & Culture, 11*, 517–532.

Miller, L., & Kelley, B. S. (2005). Relationships of religiosity and spirituality with mental health and psychopathology. In R. F. Paloutzian & C. L. Park (Eds.), *Handbook of the psychology of religion and spirituality* (pp. 460–478). New York: Guilford Press.

Mitchell, L., & Romans, S. (2003). Spiritual beliefs in bipolar affective disorder: Their relevance for illness management. *Journal of Affective Disorders, 75*, 247–257.

Mohr, S., Borras, L., Betrisey, C., Pierre-Yves, B., Gilliéron, C., & Huguelet, P. (2010). Delusions with religious content in patients with psychosis: How they interact with spiritual coping. *Psychiatry: Interpersonal and Biological Processes, 73*, 158–172.

Mohr, S., Gillieron, C., Borras, L., Brandt, P., & Huguelet, P. (2007). The assessment of spirituality and religiousness in schizophrenia. *Journal of Nervous and Mental Disease, 195*, 247–253.

Moss, Q., Fleck, D. E., & Strakowski, S. M. (2006). The influence of religious affiliation on time to first treatment and hospitalization. *Schizophrenia Research, 84*, 421–426.

Musick, M. A. (2000). Theodicy and life satisfaction among Black and White Americans. *Sociology of Religion, 61*, 267–287.

Pargament, K. I., Desai, K. M., & McConnell, K. M. (2006). Spirituality: A pathway to posttraumatic growth or decline? In L. G. Calhoun & R. G. Tedeschi (Eds.), *Handbook of posttraumatic growth: Research and practice* (pp. 121–137). London: Erlbaum.

Park, C. L. (2006). Exploring relations among religiousness, meaning, and adjustment to lifetime and current stressful encounters in later life. *Anxiety, Stress and Coping, 19*, 33–45.

Park, C. L. (2010). Making sense of the meaning literature: An integrative review of meaning making and its effects on adjustment to stressful life events. *Psychological Bulletin, 136*, 257–301.

Park, C. L., Cohen, L. H., & Herb, L. (1990). Intrinsic religiousness and religious coping as life stress moderators for Catholics versus Protestants. *Journal of Personality and Social Psychology, 52*, 562–574.

Park, C. L., & Slattery, J. M. (2012). Spirituality, emotions, and physical health. In L. Miller (Ed.), *The Oxford handbook of the psychology of spirituality and consciousness* (pp. 379–387). New York: Oxford University Press.

Prati, G., & Pietrantoni, L. (2009). Optimism, social support, and coping strategies as factors contributing to posttraumatic growth: A meta-analysis. *Journal of Loss and Trauma, 14*, 364–388.

Pressman, S. D., & Cohen, S. (2005). Does positive affect influence health? *Psychological Bulletin, 131*, 925–971.

Randolph-Seng, B., Nielsen, M. E., Bottoms, B., & Filipas, H. (2008). The relationship between ethnicity, Christian orthodoxy, and mental health. *Mental Health, Religion & Culture, 11*, 795–805.

Rippentrop, E. A., Altmaier, E. M., Chen, J. J., Found, E. M., & Keffala, V. J. (2005). The relationship between religion/spirituality and physical health, mental health, and pain in a chronic pain population. *Pain, 116*, 311–321.

Rosmarin, D. H., Krumrei, E., & Andersson, G. (2009). Religion as a predictor of psychological distress in two religious communities. *Cognitive Behaviour Therapy, 38*, 54–64.

Rosmarin, D. H., Pirutinsky, S., Pargament, K. I., & Krumrei, E. J. (2009). Are religious beliefs relevant to mental health among Jews? *Psychology of Religion and Spirituality, 1*, 180–190.

Saroglou, V., Buxant, C., & Tilquin, J. (2008). Positive emotions as leading to religion and spirituality. *Journal of Positive Psychology, 3,* 165–173.

Sawatzky, R., Ratner, P., & Chiu, L. (2005). A meta-analysis of the relationship between spirituality and quality of life. *Social Indicators Research, 72,* 153–188.

Schultz, J. M., Tallman, B. A., & Altmaier, E. M. (2010). Pathways to posttraumatic growth: The contributions of forgiveness and importance of religion and spirituality. *Psychology of Religion and Spirituality, 2,* 104–114.

Schuster, M. A., Stein, B. D., Jaycox, L., Collins, R. L., Marshall, G. N., Elliott, M. N., et al. (2001). A national survey of stress reactions after the September 11, 2001, terrorist attacks. *New England Journal of Medicine, 345,* 1507–1512.

Shreve-Neiger, A. K., & Edelstein, B. A. (2004). Religion and anxiety: A critical review of the literature. *Clinical Psychology Review, 24,* 379–397.

Sica, C., Novara, C., & Sanavio, E. (2002). Religiousness and obsessive–compulsive cognitions and symptoms in an Italian population. *Behaviour Research and Therapy, 40,* 813–823.

Siddle, R., Haddock, G., Tarrier, N., & Faragher, E. (2002). Religious delusions in patients admitted to hospital with schizophrenia. *Social Psychiatry and Psychiatric Epidemiology, 37,* 130–138.

Siev, J., & Cohen, A. B. (2007). Is thought–action fusion related to religiosity?: Differences between Christians and Jews. *Behaviour Research and Therapy, 45,* 829–837.

Slattery, J. M., & Park, C. L. (2012). Religious and spiritual beliefs in psychotherapy: A meaning perspective. In J. Aten, K. O'Grady, & E. V. Worthington (Eds.), *The psychology of religion and spirituality for clinicians: Using research in your practice* (pp. 189–216). New York: Routledge.

Smith, C. (2003). Theorizing religious effects among American adolescents. *Journal for the Scientific Study of Religion, 42,* 17–30.

Smith, T. B., McCullough, M. E., & Poll, J. (2003). Religiousness and depression: Evidence for a main effect and the moderating influence of stressful life events. *Psychological Bulletin, 129,* 614–636.

Steffen, P. R., & Masters, K. S. (2005). Does compassion mediate the intrinsic religion-health relationship? *Annals of Behavioral Medicine, 30,* 217–224.

Steger, M. F., & Frazier, P. (2005). Meaning in life: One link in the chain from religion to well-being. *Journal of Counseling Psychology, 52,* 574–582.

Taylor, S. E. (2007). Social support. In H. S. Friedman & R. C. Silver (Eds.), *Foundations of health psychology* (pp. 145–171). New York: Oxford University Press.

Tiliouine, H., Cummins, R., & Davern, M. (2009). Islamic religiosity, subjective well-being, and health. *Mental Health, Religion & Culture, 12,* 55–74.

Trenholm, P., Trent, J., & Compton, W. C. (1998). Negative religious conflict as a predictor of panic disorder. *Journal of Clinical Psychology, 54,* 59–65.

Utsey, S., Hook, J., & Stanard, P. (2007). A re-examination of cultural factors that mitigate risk and promote resilience in relation to African American suicide: A review of the literature and recommendations for future research. *Death Studies, 31,* 399–416.

Walker, D. F., Reid, H. W., O'Neill, T., & Brown, L. (2009). Changes in personal religion/spirituality during and after childhood abuse: A review and synthesis. *Psychological Trauma: Theory, Research, Practice, and Policy, 1,* 130–145.

Warner, H. L., Mahoney, A., & Krumrei, E. J. (2009). When parents break sacred vows: The role of spiritual appraisals, coping, and struggles in young adults' adjustment to parental divorce. *Psychology of Religion and Spirituality, 1,* 233–248.

Watters, W. W. (2007). Re: How spiritual values and worship attendance relate to psychiatric disorders in the Canadian population. *Canadian Journal of Psychiatry, 52,* 406.

Watts, F. (2007). Emotion regulation and religion, In J. J. Gross (Ed.), *Handbook of emotion regulation* (pp. 504–520). New York: Guilford Press.

Williams, D. R., & Sternthal, M. J. (2007). Spirituality, religion and health: Evidence and research directions. *Medical Journal of Australia, 186,* S47–S50.

Wilson, W. P. (1998). Religion and psychoses. In H. G. Koenig (Ed.), *Handbook of religion and mental health* (pp. 161–173). San Diego: Academic Press.

Worthington, E. L., & Scherer, M. (2004). Forgiveness is an emotion-focused coping strategy that can reduce health risks and promote health resilience: Theory, review, and hypotheses. *Psychology and Health, 19,* 385–405.

Yanez, B., Edmondson, D., Stanton, A. L., Park, C. L., Kwan, L., Ganz, P. A., et al. (2009). Facets of spirituality as predictors of adjustment to cancer: Relative contributions of having faith and finding meaning. *Journal of Consulting and Clinical Psychology, 77,* 730–741.

Ysseldyk, R., Matheson, K., & Hymie, A. (2010). Religiosity as identity: Toward an understanding of religion from a social identity perspective. *Personality and Social Psychology Review, 14,* 60–71.

Zinnbauer, B., & Pargament, K. I. (2005). Religiousness and spirituality. In R. F. Paloutzian & C. L. Park (Eds.), *Handbook of the psychology of religion and spirituality* (pp. 21–42). New York: Guilford Press.

28

The Religious Dimension of Coping

Advances in Theory, Research, and Practice

Kenneth I. Pargament, Melissa D. Falb,
Gene G. Ano, and Amy B. Wachholtz

Major life events touch people spiritually as well as emotionally, socially, and physically. Crises can be viewed through a spiritual lens as threats, challenges, losses, or opportunities for growth of whatever the individual may hold sacred. In coming to terms with trauma and tragedy, people can draw on a number of resources prescribed by the religions of the world for thousands of years. Yet it is also true that religion can be a source of burden and struggle for people facing difficult life situations, adding another dimension to the pain and hardship of coping.

Perhaps then, it should come as no surprise that where we find crisis and tragedy, we often find religion. "In times of crisis," psychologist Paul Johnson (1959, p. 82) once wrote, "religion usually comes to the foreground." For example, in a survey of Americans shortly after the 9/11 attacks, Schuster et al. (2001) found that 90% reportedly turned to religion for solace and support. As singular an event as 9/11 was, people's responses to it were not unusual. Other groups experiencing traumatic life events also frequently draw on their religion to cope. For example, national surveys show that the use of prayer to cope with health issues has increased dramatically from 13.7% in 1999 (Ni, Simile, & Hardy, 2002) to 48% in 2007 (Wachholtz & Sambamoorthi, 2011).

Historically, researchers and theorists have neglected the role of religion in coping or viewed it from a critical perspective. More recently, however, this picture has begun to change. Over the past several decades, there has been a sharp increase in the number of studies of religion and coping by researchers in the social sciences and health (see Harrison, Koenig, Hays, Eme-Akwari, & Pargament, 2001; Gall & Guirguis-Younger, 2013; Pargament, 1997, 2011). In this chapter, we review the current theoretical and empirical status of the psychology of religion and coping, the practical interventions that have grown out of this body of work, and future directions for research and practice to advance this exciting area of study further.

WHAT WE KNOW ABOUT RELIGION AND COPING

Freud (1927/1961) argued that religion is rooted in the child's sense of helplessness in the face of a world filled with dangerous and uncontrollable forces. By transforming the natural into the supernatural, he maintained, the child is able to defend against threats posed by the external environment. He wrote: "If the elements have passions that rage as they do in our own souls, if death itself is not something spontaneous but the violent act of an evil Will, if everywhere in nature there are Beings around us of a kind that we know in our own society, then we can breathe freely, can feel at home in the uncanny and can deal by psychical means with our senseless anxiety" (p. 20). For Freud, religion was defensive in nature, designed to allay anxiety and avoid confrontation with reality. This perspective is still widely held within psychology. It is, however, a stereotype that oversimplifies religious life and is inconsistent with an emerging literature on religion and coping (see Pargament & Park, 1995, for review).

Religion Is More Than a Defense

Like most stereotypes, there is a grain of truth to the "religion as defense" view. Many people, in fact, turn to their faith to reduce anxiety and gain solace and support in times of stress. Shrimali and Broota (1987) captured this defensive process at work in a study comparing Indian patients undergoing major surgery with patients receiving minor surgery and a control group. Before surgery, patients facing major surgery reported higher levels of anxiety, superstitious beliefs, and beliefs in God than the other groups. After surgery, however, levels of anxiety and religious beliefs declined significantly among those experiencing serious procedures, but remained constant in the other two groups. More recently, terror management theory studies point to links between death-related fears and heightened signs of religiousness (Vail et al., 2010). Other studies have shown that people are more likely to turn to religious beliefs and practices in time of greater uncertainty (Hogg, Adelman, & Blagg, 2010).

Nevertheless, several lines of study suggest that religion is more than defensive in nature. First, religion has been linked theoretically and empirically to coping functions that go beyond anxiety reduction, including meaning making (Paloutzian, 1981; Park, 2010, see Park, Chapter 18, this volume), intimacy (Johnson & Mullins, 1989), stress-related growth (Park, Edmondson, & Blank, 2009), self-regulation (McCullough & Willoughby, 2009), and the search for something deemed sacred (Dein & Pargament, 2012; Pargament, Magyar, & Murray-Swank, 2005; Pargament, 2013). These motivations are not mutually exclusive; in fact, part of the power of religion lies in its ability to serve a variety of needs among its adherents (see Emmons & Schnitker, Chapter 13, this volume).

Second, empirical studies indicate that religion is not generally linked with blanket denial of a situation. Most religious traditions provide their members with rites of passage that encourage them to acknowledge and mark difficult life transitions (e.g., funerals) rather than deny their reality. Rather than encouraging denial, religion promotes reinterpretations of negative events through a sacred lens. Thus, a major life crisis can be viewed as an opportunity for spiritual growth, a crisis can be attributed to a loving God trying to teach the individual a valuable lesson, and a tragedy can be perceived as part of a larger, mysterious, but ultimately benevolent plan. Certainly, these benevolent views may make pain more bearable, but people do not necessarily "shut down" emotionally to reach this point.

Third, although religion has been accused of passivity in response to critical life events, empirical studies suggest otherwise. Various studies have shown that measures of religiousness are more consistently linked to active coping than to passive coping (see Pargament & Park, 1995, for review). Pargament et al. (1988) distinguished among active and passive ways in which religion can be involved in the search for control in the problem-solving process: a deferring approach in which the individual relinquishes responsibility for problem solving to God; a self-directing approach in which the individual perceives God giving him/her the skills and resources to solve problems independently; and a collaborative approach in which the individual perceives God to be a partner who shares in the responsibility for problem solving.

Although deferring styles have been associated with negative outcomes, including physical disability and anxiety (Burker, Evon, Sedway, & Egan, 2004), more active strategies such as collaborative problem solving have been shown to contribute to positive outcomes. For example, Yangarber-Hicks (2004) found that individuals with serious mental illness who engaged in collaborative coping with God experienced greater empowerment in the recovery process. Moreover, in some instances, a deferring style may not be problematic. In a structural equation modeling study, Schottenbauer, Rodriguez, Glass, and Arnkoff (2006) found that passive religious deferral loaded onto negative religious coping for individuals in high-control situations, such as interpersonal or practical problems, but not for those in low-control situations, such as personal illness or death of a loved one, suggesting that deferring styles of coping may be adaptive in situations in which individuals have limited control.

In sum, the accumulating evidence indicates that the idea that religion is merely a defense oversimplifies and stereotypes religious life. Empirical studies of people grappling with life crises reveal a much richer, multidimensional picture of religious coping.

Religion Expresses Itself in Many Ways in Coping

When religion has been examined within the general coping literature, it has usually been assessed by only one or two items. For example, in the widely used Ways of Coping Scale by Lazarus and Folkman (1984), religiousness is measured by two items: "found new faith" and "I prayed." This approach offers only the smallest window into religious life. Religiousness is neither simple nor uniform, but a complex process consisting of cognitive, behavioral, emotional, interpersonal, and physiological dimensions. Empirical investigations have repeatedly revealed multidimensionality in religious life. For example, in an extensive review of the literature, Hill and Hood (1999) identified 125 measures of religiousness representing 17 different categories (e.g., beliefs, congregational involvement, attitudes, religious orientations).

Religious coping represents a rich phenomenon in and of itself. Religious coping could be defined and measured in terms of the degree to which religion is a part of the process of understanding and dealing with critical life events. However, it is important to consider not only *how much* religion is involved in coping, but also *how* religion is involved in coping; specifically the *who* (e.g., clergy, congregation members, God), the *what* (e.g., prayer, Bible reading, ritual), the *when* (e.g., acute stressors, chronic stressors), the *where* (e.g., congregation, privately), and the *why* (e.g., to find meaning, to gain control) of coping.

In perhaps the most comprehensive effort to date to identify various religious coping methods, Pargament, Koenig, and Perez (2000) developed a 105-item measure of 21 types of religious coping, the RCOPE. The coping methods encompass active, passive, and interactive strategies; emotion-focused and problem-focused approaches; and cognitive, behavioral, interpersonal, and spiritual domains. Table 28.1 shows that religious coping activities represent five key religious functions: the search for meaning, the search for mastery and control, the search for comfort and closeness to God, the search for intimacy and closeness to God, and the search for life transformation. As comprehensive as this measure is, it still does not capture many religious coping methods specific to various religious traditions (e.g., karma, spiritual healing, pilgrimage). Clearly, religion can express itself in a variety of ways in the coping process.

To digress for a moment, the transformational role of religion in coping is particularly noteworthy (see Pargament, 1997; Park, Chapter 18, this volume). Generally, religion has been viewed as a conservational force: an attempt to sustain meaning, control, comfort, intimacy, or spiritual connection in crisis. Sometimes, however, conservation is no longer possible. Internal changes, developmental transitions, or external life events may result in the loss of goals and strivings that have given an individual's life direction. At these times, transformational religious coping (e.g., religious conversion, seeking religious direction, forgiveness) is available to assist in the process of acknowledging loss, letting go of old goals and values, and moving toward new sources of significance, purpose, and meaning (Park & Folkman, 1997). Cole, Hopkins, Tisak, Steel, and Carr (2008) developed a spiritual transformation scale to assess the profound changes that may grow out of such coping in cancer patients. In their study, two subscales—spiritual growth and spiritual decline—were both predictive of adjustment to a cancer diagnosis above and beyond related constructs such as religiousness, spiritual coping, and posttraumatic growth.

Religious Coping Methods Can Be Helpful or Harmful

In the past, macroanalytic studies that investigated religiousness as a global, dispositional variable yielded mixed results. Thus, the efficacy of religious coping for people undergoing stressful events remained unclear. However, advances in measuring religious coping have led to microanalytic studies that clarify the efficacy of religious coping by focusing on the relationships of specific religious coping strategies to the outcomes of stressful situations. The results show that religious coping can be helpful or harmful, depending on the strategies employed.

While some studies have examined religious coping in fine detail, higher order factor analyses of the RCOPE have revealed that religious coping methods can be grouped into two overarching categories: positive and negative religious coping (Pargament, Smith, Koenig, & Perez, 1998). Positive religious coping strategies reflect a secure relationship with God and a sense of spiritual connectedness with others. Negative religious coping methods reflect a struggle within oneself, with others, or with God around sacred matters. The most often used measure of these two patterns is the 14-item Brief RCOPE

TABLE 28.1. The Many Methods of Religious Coping

Religious methods of coping to find meaning

- *Benevolent religious reappraisal*—redefining the stressor through religion as potentially beneficial
- *Punishing God reappraisal*—redefining the stressor as a punishment from God for the individual's sins
- *Demonic reappraisal*—redefining the stressor as an act of the Devil
- *Reappraisal of God's powers*—redefining God's power to influence the stressful situation

Religious methods of coping to gain mastery and control

- *Collaborative religious coping*—seeking control through a partnership with God in problem solving
- *Passive religious deferral*—passive waiting for God to control the situation
- *Active religious surrender*—active giving up of control to God in coping
- *Pleading for direct intercession*—seeking control indirectly by pleading to God for a miracle or divine intervention
- *Self-directing religious coping*—seeking control through individual initiative rather than help from God

Religious methods of coping to gain comfort and closeness to God

- *Seeking spiritual support*—searching for comfort and reassurance through God's love and care
- *Religious focus*—engaging in religious activities to shift focus from the stressor
- *Religious purification*—searching for spiritual cleansing through religious actions
- *Spiritual connection*—seeking a sense of connectedness with forces that transcend the self
- *Spiritual discontent*—expressing confusion and dissatisfaction with God' relationship to the individual in the stressful situation
- *Marking religious boundaries*—clearly demarcating acceptable from unacceptable religious behavior and remaining within religious boundaries

Religious methods of coping to gain intimacy with others and closeness to God

- *Seeking support from clergy or members*—searching for intimacy and reassurance through the love and care of congregation members and clergy
- *Religious helping*—attempting to provide spiritual support and comfort to others
- *Interpersonal religious discontent*—expressing confusion and dissatisfaction with the relationship of clergy or members to the individual in the stressful situation

Religious methods of coping to achieve a life transformation

- *Seeking religious direction*—looking to religion for assistance in finding a new direction for living
- *Religious conversion*—looking to religion for a radical change in life
- *Religious forgiving*—looking to religion for help in shifting from anger, hurt, and fear associated with an offense to peace

(Pargament, Feuille, & Burdzy, 2011), which consists of seven items each for positive and negative categories of religious coping.

Positive religious coping strategies tend to be more beneficial. For example, in a meta-analytic review of research on religious coping and psychological adjustment to stress, positive religious coping strategies (e.g., spiritual connectedness, benevolent religious reappraisals, collaborative religious coping, and seeking spiritual support) were positively associated with positive outcomes and negatively associated with negative outcomes among various populations dealing with a variety of life stressors (Ano & Vasconcelles, 2005). Specifically, positive religious coping methods have been associated with indices of better physical health in a number of studies (see Koenig, King, & Carson,

2012, for a review; Masters & Hooker, Chapter 26, this volume). For example, in a study using a spiritually focused treatment, Cole (2005) found that positive religious coping was related to reduced pain severity and greater physical well-being in patients with cancer. Likewise, in a study of older patients undergoing cardiac surgery, Ai, Peterson, Bolling, and Rodgers (2006) reported a salutary relationship between preoperative positive religious coping and short-term postoperative global functioning (including measures of daily activities such as bathing, ambulation, and light housework).

Positive religious coping has been found to contribute to posttraumatic growth in survivors of a range of distressing events as well, including natural disasters, sudden death of a loved one, sexual harassment, childhood sexual abuse, and life-threatening accidents, assaults, and injuries (Harris et al., 2008). Relationships between various aspects of religious coping and growth have also been found in young adults living with serious mental illness (Phillips & Stein, 2007) and in children (Benore, Pargament, & Pendleton, 2008).

In contrast, negative religious coping methods are generally more maladaptive (see Exline & Rose, Chapter 19, this volume). For example, in their meta-analysis, Ano and Vasconcelles (2005) found that negative religious coping strategies, or "spiritual struggles," such as spiritual discontent, punishing God reappraisals, reappraisals of God's powers, demonic reappraisals, and interpersonal religious discontent were linked with negative psychological outcomes such as depression, anxiety, callousness, posttraumatic stress disorder symptoms, and spiritual injury among samples coping with a range of negative life events. Similarly, in a nationally representative sample, McConnell, Pargament, Ellison, and Flannelly (2006) found that, even after controlling for demographic and religious variables, spiritual struggles were significantly related to multiple forms of psychopathology, particularly among individuals suffering from a recent physical illness.

Negative religious coping also has harmful implications for physical functioning. In a longitudinal study of religious coping among ill elderly patients, spiritual discontent and demonic reappraisals at baseline were associated with a 19–28% increased mortality risk 2 years later, even after controlling for demographic and predictor variables, such as illness severity and mental health status (Pargament, Koenig, Tarakeshwar, & Hahn, 2001). Additional analyses suggested that patients with consistently high levels of spiritual struggle over 2 years were at greatest risk for declines in physical and mental health. In a sample of HIV/AIDS patients, Trevino et al. (2010) found that spiritual struggle was related to negative outcomes, including detectable viral load, lower quality of life, and increased HIV and depressive symptoms. In addition, individuals experiencing spiritual struggles showed declines over time in a range of variables. Ai, Seymour, Tice, Kronfol, and Bolling (2009) found that spiritual struggles had a negative effect on the inflammation-immune system, as indicated by excess plasma interleuken-6 in patients undergoing cardiac surgery. These studies make an important point. Religious coping is not automatically beneficial and some types are more harmful than others.

Although most studies looking at religious coping focus on Christian samples, findings appear robust for other populations as well. Measures of positive and negative religious coping, often derived from the RCOPE and Brief RCOPE, have been validated across cultures and religions. For example, Tarakeshwar, Pargament, and Mahoney (2003), using their Hindu coping scale, found that positive religious coping was related to better mental health among U.S. Hindus. Likewise, several measures have been developed to assess how Muslims cope with stress, including, for example, the Psychological Measure of Islamic Religiousness (Raiya, Pargament, Mahoney, & Stein, 2008). Rosmarin, Pargament, Krumrei, and Flannelly (2009) constructed the Jewish RCOPE and found that positive and negative religious coping were tied in predictable ways to psychological distress in Jews. These studies and others point to the value of studying religious coping strategies across religious and ethnic groups.

Three additional points are important here. First, the existing literature has shown religious coping to be related not only to psychological indicators of adjustment but also to measures of social, spiritual, and physical well-being (e.g., Cummings & Pargament, 2010; Pearce, Singer, & Prigerson, 2006). Second, the relationships between religious coping and adjustment remain significant after adjusting for the effects of demographic variables and nonreligious coping measures. Findings such as these suggest that religious coping represents a distinctive resource that cannot be "explained away" in terms of presumably more basic phenomena (Pargament, 2002). Third, some religious coping studies have reported nonsignificant, contradictory, or complex findings (Culver, Arena, Antoni, & Carver, 2002; VanNess & Larson, 2002). Differences in samples, stressors, and measures may partly account for these discrepancies. It is also possible that some forms of religious coping have mixed rather than exclusively positive or negative implications. Consider a few examples. Groups that respond to threats by marking boundaries (i.e., sharply distinguishing between insiders and outsiders) may preserve the integrity and well-being of the group (e.g., Seth & Seligman, 1993), but at the cost of prejudice toward outsiders (Altemeyer & Hunsberger, 1992). Positive religious coping at the end of life in patients with advanced cancer has been associated with less advance care planning and more intensive life-prolonging care (Phelps et al., 2009); whether these findings speak to the "fighting spirit" of positive religious copers and/or their refusal to face the reality of their deaths is unclear. Finally, although cross-sectional studies sometimes show correlations between overall religious coping and poor outcomes, this trend often disappears in longitudinal studies. This pattern of findings may be the result of a "mobilization effect" in which high levels of distress or illness trigger religious coping strategies that help people deal with their stressors (Pargament, 1997).

People Draw on a General Orienting System in Religious Coping

Research examining the nature of religious coping has shown that people do not come to coping empty-handed. They enter the coping process with a general orienting system of resources and burdens that influences how they interpret and handle stressful situations. The orienting system is a general disposition that involves beliefs, feelings, relationships, and practices embedded in religious, personality, and social domains (Pargament, 1997). In specific situations, people draw on coping methods that are part of their general orienting system. Path analytic studies have shown that elements of the general orienting system, such as religious orientation (Roesch & Ano, 2003), church attendance and prayer (Nooney & Woodrum, 2002), and attachment to God (Belavich & Pargament, 2002) differentially relate to the religious coping strategies employed to deal with stressful events. In these studies, religious coping mediated the relationship between these general religious orienting variables and the outcomes of stressful events. Banziger, van Uden, and Janssen (2008) elaborated some of the complexities of the relationships between different types of prayer and styles of coping. Specifically, religious prayer (emphasizing communion with God) was related to collaborative and deferring coping, whereas meditative prayer (focused on the self rather than God) was related to receptive coping, which assumes a more impersonal God and acceptance toward situations one cannot control.

Thus, as a general disposition, the orienting system may influence the types of religious coping strategies employed in specific situations. General resources (e.g., intrinsic religious orientation, secure attachment to God, church attendance) lead to more positive religious coping strategies, whereas general burdens (e.g, insecure attachment to God, neuroticism) lead to more negative religious coping methods. However, it is important to stress that specific religious coping methods are related more directly to the resolution of critical situations.

Effects of Religious Coping Are Moderated by Different Factors

Religious coping does not occur in a vacuum. It is employed by particular people, in particular contexts, in response to particular stressful situations. As such, different factors have been identified that moderate the links between religious coping and outcomes to stressful events. Generally, religious coping is more salient and helpful under two conditions: when it is more available to people and when it is more compelling to people.

First, religious coping appears to be more helpful to those for whom religion is more available, including those who are more religious and thus have greater access to and familiarity with religious resources. In two studies of religious coping among a sample of Presbyterian members, elders, and clergy in the United States, religious coping was more strongly associated with adjustment for those who were more religious (i.e., clergy vs. elders and elders vs. members) (Krause, Ellison, & Wulff, 1998; Pargament, Tasakeshwar, Ellison, & Wulff, 2001). Specifically, among the more religious, positive religious coping and church-based emotional support were more strongly related to positive affect and less depression, whereas negative religious coping and interpersonal conflicts in the church were more strongly associated with less positive affect and depression. Similarly, in a study of Jewish and Christian clergy, Proffitt, Cann, Calhoun, and Tedeschi (2007) found that, unlike nonclergy, clergy members experienced higher levels of posttraumatic growth when using either positive or negative coping methods.

Second, religious coping appears to be more helpful when it is more compelling to the individual. Taxing situations that push people to the edge and beyond their limitations and deplete their personal and social resources are likely to be particularly compelling. For example, in a study of religious coping of parents dealing with the loss of a child, spiritual support was more strongly associated with lower levels of depression among those who were more distressed (i.e., recently bereaved parents) than for those who were less distressed (i.e., parents who lost a child more than 2 years ago) (Maton, 1989).

It is also worth noting that religious coping has differential effects for people from different religious affiliations. A few studies have shown religious coping to be more helpful for Protestants than for Catholics. Tix and Frazier (1998) found that religious coping was related to greater life satisfaction and less distress for Protestant kidney transplant patients but not for Catholics. In a study of Hispanic breast cancer patients, higher levels of religious coping were related to less distress among Evangelicals but greater distress among Catholics (Alferi, Culver, Carver, Arena, & Antoni, 1999). These findings do not necessarily mean Protestants are "better off" than Catholics. In a study of parochial school adolescents, religious doubts were more strongly associated with distress among Protestants than Catholics (Kooistra & Pargament, 1999). Additionally, Braam et al. (2008) found a stronger relationship between religious discontent and depressive symptoms among Protestants than Catholics. Thus, religious affiliation moderates the effects of religious coping, but in complex ways (see Park, Cohen, & Herb, 1990).

FROM RESEARCH TO PRACTICE

Building on the growing body of research that has demonstrated empirical links between religious coping and adjustment, researchers and practitioners have begun to develop and evaluate therapeutic methods that draw on religious coping resources or address religious struggles in counseling (Pargament, 2007; Pargament, Mahoney, Shafranske, Exline, & Jones, 2013; Shafranske, Chapter 30, this volume). Although empirical evidence for the efficacy of spiritually integrated therapies is just beginning to emerge, the results are encouraging. In one meta-analysis, McCullough (1999) reviewed five studies comparing a Christian-accommodative form of cognitive-behavioral therapy (CBT), which emphasized religious imagery, prayer, and biblical perspectives, with standard CBT. While both treatments produced positive outcomes, the two treatments did not differ in efficacy. However, the results suggested that religiously oriented approaches may be the treatment of choice for Christian clients. In another review, Smith, Bartz, and Richards (2007) assessed 31 outcome studies of spiritual therapies. Spiritually oriented psychotherapy approaches were beneficial to individuals with problems including depression, anxiety, eating disorders, and stress. They found a moderate effect size of 0.56 for spiritual therapies, with a similar effect size of 0.51 when comparing spiritual interventions with those without a spiritual component. Spiritual therapies seemed particularly effective when evaluated by measures of overall quality of life and well-being. Additionally, a meta-analysis on religious and spiritual interventions for cancer patients observed small to moderate positive effect sizes across psychological, spiritual, and biological outcomes (Kaplar, Wachholtz, & O'Brien, 2004). More research is needed and the jury is still out, but spiritually based therapies deserve ongoing attention.

A number of studies have demonstrated the positive effects of meditation on health and well-being as well. Wachholtz and Pargament (2008) conducted a study that underscores the potential value of an explicitly spiritual form of meditation. They compared spiritual meditation (using mantras such as "God is love") with internally focused meditation ("I am good"), externally focused meditation ("Sand is soft"), and progressive muscle relaxation in individuals with migraines. Spiritual meditators showed greater improvements in many areas, including migraine frequency, anxiety, negative affect, pain tolerance, and existential well-being. The findings suggest spiritual meditation may be a distinctive therapeutic resource that might improve patients' lives without the financial expense and negative side effects of medication.

Researchers have also evaluated the effects of prayer as an intervention. However, prayer is a global resource that can encompass many types of religious coping. For example, Rajagopal, Mackenzie, Bailey, and Lavizzo-Mourey (2002) studied the effects of using a prayer wheel on anxiety and depression among an elderly population. The prayer wheel embodied several types of prayer and coping, such as requests for spiritual protection and guidance, forgiveness of self and others, and offering spiritual support to others. Participants who used the prayer wheel reported significant decreases in anxiety and, to a lesser degree, depression.

Several researchers have developed and tested psychospiritual interventions that use religious and spiritual resources to facilitate the health and well-being of patients with physical and mental illnesses. In women with breast cancer, Targ and Levine (2002) compared the effects of two types of intervention: (1) a mind–body–spirit group intervention—using meditation, imagery, ritual, and affirmation and (2) a support group. All participants showed positive changes in quality of life, depression, anxiety, and spiritual well-being, but the spiritual group showed greater increases in spiritual integration and less avoidance than the support group. However, the support group showed more declines in confusion and helplessness/hopelessness. Similarly, Reavley, Pallant, and Sali (2009) conducted a 10-day residential program for cancer patients, incorporating stillness and visualization meditations, as well as psychosocial and lifestyle interventions. The program had beneficial effects on adjustment and quality of life. Finally, Beitel et al. (2007) created a manualized therapy (spiritual self schema [3-S]) based on Buddhist principals to treat addiction and HIV risk behaviors in American non-Buddhists. A preliminary study of the therapy (Margolin et al., 2007) found that 3-S patients showed greater decreases in impulsivity and intoxicant use than patients in a comparison condition. In addition, 3-S patients reported greater increases in spiritual practices as well as motivation for abstinence, medication adherence, and HIV prevention.

A number of studies have evaluated the effects of religious coping interventions specific to particular religious traditions. For instance, religious support, encouragement, and guidance have been shown to be helpful to Malaysian Muslim religious patients coping with bereavement (Azhar & Varma, 1995) and generalized anxiety disorder (Azhar, Varma, & Dharap, 1994). In these studies, patients who were encouraged to pray, discuss religious issues, and read from the Qu'ran reported greater and more rapid improvement than support group patients. In another program, Gruner (1984) evaluated a residential drug rehabilitation program for adolescents administered through the Assemblies of God church. The program sought to help participants challenge feelings of meaninglessness, hopelessness, and alienation and overcome addiction through a reprioritization of values and new dedication of their lives to God. Retention and rehabilitation rates in this program were higher than those reported by other comparable, secular programs.

Finally, a few researchers have begun to examine the impact of spiritually oriented interventions on people encountering spiritual struggles. Murray-Swank and Pargament (2005) developed and evaluated an 8-week manualized intervention that drew on spiritual resources to help women who had experienced childhood sexual abuse. Following the intervention and at 1-month follow-up, 80% of the women reported reductions in psychological and spiritual distress. Similarly, Phillips, Lakin, and Pargament (2002) implemented a psychospiritual intervention designed for individuals with serious mental illness (SMI). This 7-week intervention provided group members a chance to share their religious journeys and discuss spiritual topics such as strivings, struggles, forgiveness, and hope. In contrast to concerns about raising spiritual matters among people with SMI, the group did not trigger serious psychological disturbances. In fact, the participants asked the leaders to continue the group over the next year.

Such interventions show potential for use in nonclinical populations. In an intervention with college students, Oman et al. (2007) utilized two meditation-based programs (Passage Meditation and Mindfulness-Based Stress Reduction) to assess changes in religious coping and perceptions of God as loving versus controlling. Participants in both groups showed a significant reduction in negative religious coping and negative images of God. In addition, in a study of spiritual struggles in college students, Gear et al. (2008) assessed a 9-week spiritually sensitive manualized group intervention. Participants showed significant improvements on measures including psychological distress, emotion regulation, congruence between spiritual values and personal behaviors, and spiritual struggles. Finally, Pargament and Sweeney (2011) have developed an online program to foster spiritual resilience and reduce spiritual struggles among U.S. Army soldiers as part of a Comprehensive Soldier Fitness program. The effectiveness of the program has not been evaluated as yet.

Overall, this body of research suggests religious coping resources may offer valuable adjuncts to the treatment process. As yet, however, we do not know which specific religious coping methods are most helpful in the therapeutic process. Additional studies are still needed to pinpoint and evaluate the efficacy of promoting specific religious coping methods in treatment.

FUTURE DIRECTIONS FOR RESEARCH AND PRACTICE

In the past quarter-century, the psychology of religion has reemerged as a significant area of scientific inquiry (see Emmons & Paloutzian, 2003). Within this context, there has also been a dramatic rise in studies of religion and coping even since the publication of the first edition of this *Handbook*. Some researchers (Hill & Gibson, 2008) have suggested this field of study has reached maturity; however, we believe coping research still has a way to go. We conclude this chapter by pointing to several important directions for future research and practice.

First, studies of religion and coping are primarily designed, implemented, and interpreted by researchers within the scientific study of religion. Given its significance for the physical, psychological, social, and spiritual well-being of people, research in the domain of religion and coping should be more fully integrated into mainstream research and practice within the applied health professions and the social and health sciences. Meditation research provides a case in point. While mindfulness and meditation studies have become more mainstream in recent years, many researchers deliberately remove spiritual concepts from their programs. Preliminary research indicates that these omissions may lessen the potential efficacy of such interventions (Wachholtz & Pargament, 2008). Researchers in the area of religion and coping should also draw more fully upon theory and research from other disciplines and make more concerted efforts to disseminate their findings to the wider applied and scientific community.

Second, although empirical advances in the psychology of religion and coping have yielded a reasonable base of established findings, most research has been conducted with Caucasian/European American samples. An increasing number of studies have examined religious coping among African Americans (Dilworth-Anderson, Boswell, & Cohen, 2007; Molock, Puri, Matlin, & Barksdale, 2006), and studies comparing religious coping *across* ethnicities have increased (Chatters, Taylor, Jackson, & Lincoln, 2008; Lee, Czaja, & Schultz, 2010). However, research including minorities such as Asians and Native Americans remains sparse. Drawing from research on multicultural psychology, it would be interesting to examine the nature and prevalence of religious coping strategies in these groups, given the value they place on collectivism compared with Caucasian/European Americans.

In terms of religious diversity, the majority of studies of religious coping has been conducted with Christians, with the exception of a few recent studies examining religious coping among Hindus (Tarakeshwar et al., 2003), Jews (Rosmarin et al., 2009), Muslims (Ai, Peterson, & Huang, 2003; Raiya, Pargament, Mahoney, & Stein, 2008), and Buddhists (Phillips et al., 2009). Future studies should examine religious coping in Eastern and nontheistic religions to identify other forms of religious coping, understand how other religious beliefs and practices might contribute to the coping process, and examine the relationships between religious coping and psychological and health outcomes. In addition, studies have not parsed out differences between coping methods used by various Christian denominations, with a few exceptions (Krause, 2010).

Third, there is a need for more longitudinal studies of religious coping, though researchers have begun to clarify temporal relationships between stressors, religious coping, and adjustment as well as the longer term impact of religious coping (e.g, McConnell et al., 2006; Pargament, Koenig, Tarakeshwar, & Hahn, 2004). Longitudinal studies are also needed to examine fluctuations in religious coping and their implications for adjustment. In this vein, Keefe et al. (2001) conducted a diary study of religious coping in rheumatoid arthritis patients and found significant variations in day-to-day religious coping over 30 consecutive days, indicating that religious coping was a dynamic process. Several studies have assessed longitudinal changes in religious coping among patients with HIV/AIDS (Cotton et al., 2006), psychosis (Huguelet, Mohr, Gilliéron, Brandt, & Borras, 2010), and alcoholism (Robinson, Cranford, Webb, & Brower, 2007). Further studies are needed to increase our understanding of longitudinal changes and effects of religious coping with respect to other psychological and physical conditions.

Fourth, future studies should investigate religious coping among relatively neglected groups, such as people with serious mental illness. Several studies (Borras et al., 2007; Phillips & Stein, 2007) have found high levels of religious coping and positive relationships with outcomes in individuals with persistent mental illness. Given the prevalence of religious coping among this population and the seeming benefits, future research should continue to examine the unique implications that religious coping might have for those with serious mental illness.

Another relatively neglected group in the religious coping literature is children (Benore et al., 2008; Molock et al., 2006), even though many studies have examined parents' religious coping. The recent publication of an Adolescent Religious Coping Scale (Bjorck, Braese, Tadie, & Gililland, 2010) should foster this research. Future investigations might assess how children's religious coping evolves across the life span. This research should explore how cognitive development influences religious coping, drawing on and, in turn, informing cognitive developmental psychology. Such interdisciplinary approaches would allow the psychology of religion to be influenced by and simultaneously impact mainstream psychology and advance the multilevel interdisciplinary paradigm articulated in this *Handbook*.

Fifth, there is a need for studies of specific religious coping methods. For example, while a number of studies have examined forgiveness (see Worthington et al., Chapter 24, this volume), particularly from the perspective of victims, few studies have examined its flipside—confession (see Murray-Swank, 2003), which may have unique and important implications for social psychology, since most transgressions are interpersonal. Religious rites of passage (e.g., confirmations, funerals, and bar/bat mitzvah) are another type of religious coping that involves ceremonial rituals to signify the passing from one stage of spiritual identity to the next (Pargament, Poloma, & Tarakeshwar, 2001). These rites of passage can be imbued with deep emotions and significance, and thus represent rich targets for studies of the affective basis of spirituality. These studies, in turn, may hold important implications for psychological theories of emotion. Finally, researchers should pay closer attention to situations that could be perceived as a threat to what people hold sacred. Several studies have shown that perceptions of divorce or romantic offense as a sacred violation (i.e., desecration) have a negative impact on health and well-being (Krumrei, Mahoney, & Pargament, 2009). In addition, Pargament, Magyar, Benore, and Mahoney (2005) found that individuals who described the most significant negative event in their recent past as a sacred violation reported increased anger, more intrusive thoughts, and reduced posttraumatic growth compared with those who did not consider such events desecrations.

Sixth, future research should incorporate both quantitative and qualitative methods of studying religious coping. In this vein, Ganzevoort (1998) conducted a qualitative study of religious coping by examining people's life narratives and weaving religious storylines together with other prominent life themes. Ganzevoort (2001) then integrated quantitative methods by conducting cluster analyses of story themes and examining their intercorrelations. Similarly, Ahmadi (2006) conducted a qualitative study of religious coping based on semi-structured interviews with Swedish cancer patients. She tape-recorded, transcribed, and analyzed interviews for themes, using a qualitative data analysis program to create networks of consistent themes. These types of innovative methodologies allow for fine-grained analyses of complex constructs, providing a richly informative picture of religious coping.

Seventh, because religious coping has implications for people across domains, there is a need for studies including multiple criteria of well-being. Most religious coping research has been conducted by psychologists interested in mental health (see Park & Slattery, Chapter 27, this volume). Consistent with the multilevel interdisciplinary paradigm, an increasing number of studies have looked at the relationship between religious coping and physical health outcomes; however, additional studies are needed that consider the implications of religious coping for social and spiritual dimensions. For example, with respect to the social dimension, Mahoney et al. (2002) found that college students who perceived the 9/11 attacks as desecrations adopted more severe retaliatory attitudes toward the perpetrators. In addition, studies of religious attitudes found that Christians who view members of other religions as desecrators of Christianity show more severe anti-Muslim (Raiya, Pargament, Mahoney, & Trevino, 2008) and anti-Semitic (Pargament, Trevino, Mahoney, & Silberman, 2007) attitudes. From a sociological perspective, such findings could help explain the perpetuation and exacerbation of tensions between societies, cultures, and nations that perceive the other as desecrating their own sacred objects, lands, values, and ideals.

Finally, although researchers and practitioners have begun to develop and evaluate religiously oriented treatments, additional experimental studies are needed to compare them with secular interventions. For example, Rye and Pargament (2002) developed a religiously oriented group forgiveness intervention for college women hurt in a romantic relationship and compared it with a secular forgiveness group and a no-treatment condition. Although both treatment groups were more effective than the control, there was no difference between the religious and secular interventions. However, post hoc analyses revealed that secular group participants reported drawing on religious resources, even though spiritual techniques were not integrated in the intervention. More controlled experimental studies that distinguish between religious and secular interventions are needed to examine the unique contributions psychospiritual techniques make toward well-being. Furthermore, most psychospiritual interventions augment traditional approaches to treating psychological problems. Additional studies are needed to develop and evaluate spiritually based interventions that address religious problems. For example, Ano (2005) developed and evaluated a manualized group intervention for church members experiencing spiritual struggles between vice and virtue. The treatment program consisted of four sessions organized around various themes related to religious problems: "The Value of Virtue," "The Problem with Perfection," "Growth and God's Grace," and "Relapse, Reconciliation, and Repentance." Compared with participants in a waitlist control group, those who completed the treatment showed improvements in anxiety, stress, scrupulosity, spiritual development, self-control, spiritual motivation, and their ability to cultivate specific virtues and resist particular vices. These improvements were also maintained at 4-week follow-up.

There is no shortage of basic or applied questions about the roles of religion in coping. Investigations of religious coping in a variety of domains continue to grow rapidly, especially across disciplinary lines, suggesting that this is a promising area of study with vast potential to foster integrative research and theory. Further work in this area can significantly increase our ability to help people come to terms with the most profound problems of their lives.

REFERENCES

Ahmadi, F. (2006). *Culture, religion, and spirituality in coping: The example of cancer patients in Sweden*. Uppsala: Acta Universitatis Upsaliensis.

Ai, A. L., Peterson, C., Bolling, S. F., & Rodgers, W. (2006). Depression, faith-based coping, and short-term postoperative global functioning in adult and older patients undergoing cardiac surgery. *Journal of Psychosomatic Research, 60*, 21–28.

Ai, A. L., Peterson, C., & Huang, B. (2003). The effect of religious spiritual coping on positive attitudes of adult Muslim refugees from Kosovo and Bosnia. *The International Journal for the Psychology of Religion, 12*, 29–47.

Ai, A. L., Seymour, E. M., Tice, T. N., Kronfol, Z., & Bolling, S. F. (2009). Spiritual struggle related to plasma interleukin-6 prior to cardiac surgery. *Psychology of Religion and Spirituality, 1*, 112–128.

Alferi, S. M., Culver, J. L., Carver, C. S., Arena, P. L., & Antoni, M. H. (1999). Religiosity, religious coping, and distress: A prospective study of Catholic and Evangelical Hispanic women in treatment for early-stage breast cancer. *Journal of Health Psychology, 4*, 343–356.

Altemeyer, B., & Hunsberger, B. (1992). Authoritarianism, religious fundamentalism, quest, and prejudice. *The International Journal for the Psychology of Religion, 2*, 113–133.

Ano, G. G. (2005). *Spiritual struggles between vice and virtue: A brief psychospiritual intervention.* Unpublished doctoral dissertation. Bowling Green State University, Bowling Green, OH.

Ano, G. G., & Vasconcelles, E. B. (2005). Religious coping and psychological adjustment to stress: A meta-analysis. *Journal of Clinical Psychology, 61,* 461–480.

Azhar, M. Z., & Varma, S. L. (1995). Religious psychotherapy as management of bereavement. *Acta Psychiatric Scandinavica, 91,* 233–235.

Azhar, M. Z., Varma, S. L., & Dharap, A. S. (1994). Religious psychotherapy in anxiety disorder patients. *Acta Psychiatrica Scandinavica, 90,* 1–3.

Banziger, S., van Uden, M., & Janssen, J. (2008). Praying and coping: The relation between varieties of praying and religious coping styles. *Mental Health, Religion & Culture, 11,* 101–118.

Beitel, M., Genova, M., Schuman-Olivier, Z., Arnold, R., Avants, S. K., & Margolin, A. (2007). Reflections by inner-city drug users on a Buddhist-based spirituality-focused therapy: A qualitative study. *American Journal of Orthopsychiatry, 77,* 1–9.

Belavich, T. G., & Pargament, K. I. (2002). The role of attachment in predicting spiritual coping with a loved one in surgery. *Journal of Adult Development, 9,* 13–29.

Benore, E., Pargament, K., & Pendleton, S. (2008). An examination of religious coping in children with asthma. *The International Journal for the Psychology of Religion, 18,* 267–290.

Bjorck, J. P., Braese, R. W., Tadie, J. T., & Gililland, D. D. (2010). The adolescent religious coping scale: Development, validation, and cross-validation. *Journal of Child and Family Studies, 19,* 343–359.

Borras, L., Mohr, S., Brandt, P. Y., Gillieron, C., Eytan, A., & Huguelet, P. (2007). Religious beliefs in schizophrenia: Their relevance for adherence to treatment. *Schizophrenia Bulletin, 33,* 1238–1246.

Braam, A. W., Schaap-Jonker, H., Mooi, B., de Ritter, D., Beekman, A. T. F., & Deeg, D. J. H. (2008). God image and mood in old age: Results from a community-based pilot study in the Netherlands. *Mental Health, Religion & Culture, 11,* 221–237.

Burker, E. J., Evon, D. M., Sedway, J. A., & Egan, T. (2004). Religious coping, psychological distress and disability among patients with end-stage pulmonary disease. *Journal of Clinical Psychology in Medical Settings, 11,* 179–193. Retrieved from *www.springerlink.com.*

Chatters, L. M., Taylor, R. J., Jackson, J. S., & Lincoln, K. D. (2008). Religious coping among African Americans, Caribbean blacks and non-Hispanic Whites. *Journal of Community Psychology, 36,* 371–386.

Cole, B. S. (2005). Spiritually-focused psychotherapy for people diagnosed with cancer: A pilot outcome study. *Mental Health, Religion & Culture, 8,* 217–226.

Cole, B. S., Hopkins, C. M., Tisak, J., Steel, J. L., & Carr, B. I. (2008). Assessing spiritual growth and spiritual decline following a diagnosis of cancer: Reliability and validity of the spiritual transformation scale. *Psycho-Oncology, 17,* 112–121.

Cotton, S., Puchalski, C. M., Sherman, S. N., Mrus, J. M., Peterman, A. H., Feinberg, J., et al. (2006). Spirituality and religion in patients with HIV/AID. *Journal of General Internal Medicine, 21,* S5–S13.

Culver, J. L., Arena, P. L., Antoni, M. H., & Carver, C. S. (2002). Coping and distress among women under treatment for early stage breast cancer: Comparing African Americans, Hispanics, and non-Hispanic whites. *Psycho-Oncology, 11,* 495–504.

Cummings, J. P., & Pargament, K. I. (2010). Medicine for the spirit: Religious coping in individuals with medical conditions. *Religions, 1,* 28–53.

Dein, S., & Pargament, K. I. (2012). On not praying for the return of an amputated limb: Conserving a relationship with God as the primary function of prayer. *Bulletin of the Menninger Clinic, 76,* 235–259.

Dilworth-Anderson, P., Boswell, G., & Cohen, M. D. (2007). Spiritual and religious coping values and beliefs among African American caregivers: A qualitative study. *Journal of Applied Gerontology, 26,* 355–369.

Emmons, R. A., & Paloutzian, R. F. (2003). The psychology of religion. *Annual Review of Psychology, 54*, 377–402.

Freud, S. (1961). *The future of an illusion*. New York: Norton. (Original work published 1927)

Gall, T. L., & Guirguis-Younger, M. (2013). Religious and spiritual coping: Current theory and research. In K. I. Pargament, J. J. Exline & J. W. Jones (Eds.), *APA handbook of psychology, religion, and spirituality (Vol. 1): Context, theory, and research* (pp. 349–364). Washington, DC: American Psychological Association.

Ganzevoort, R. R. (1998). Religious coping reconsidered: Part two. A narrative reformulation. *Journal of Psychology and Theology, 26*, 276–286.

Ganzevoort, R. R. (2001). Religion in rewriting the story: Case study of a sexually abused man. *The International Journal for the Psychology of Religion, 11*, 45–62.

Gear, M. R., Faigin, C. A., Gibbel, M. R., Krumrei, E., Oemig, C., McCarthy, S. K., et al. (2008). The winding road: A promising approach to addressing the spiritual struggles of college students. *Spirituality in Higher Education Newsletter, 4*(4), 1–8.

Gruner, L. (1984). Heroin, hashish, and hallelujah: The search for meaning. *Review of Religious Research, 26*, 176–186.

Harris, J. I., Erbes, C. R., Engdahl, B. E., Olson, R. H. A., Winskowski, A. M., & McMahill, J. (2008). Christian religious functioning and trauma outcomes. *Journal of Clinical Psychology, 64*, 17–29.

Harrison, M. O., Koenig, H. G., Hays, J. C., Eme-Akwari, A. G., & Pargament, K. I. (2001). The epidemiology of religious coping: A review of recent literature. *International Review of Psychiatry, 13*, 86–93.

Hill, P. C., & Gibson, N. J. S. (2008). Whither the roots?: Achieving conceptual depth in psychology of religion. *Archive for the Psychology of Religion, 30*, 19–35.

Hill, P. C., & Hood, R. W., Jr. (Eds.). (1999). *Measures of religiosity*. Birmingham, AL: Religious Education Press.

Hogg, M. A., Adelman, J. R., & Blagg, R. D. (2010). Religion in the face of uncertainty: An uncertainty-identity theory account of religiousness. *Personality and Social Psychology Review, 14*, 72–83.

Huguelet, P., Mohr, S., Gilliéron, C., Brandt, P. Y. & Borras, L. (2010). Religious explanatory models in patients with psychosis: A three-year follow-up study. *Psychopathology, 43*, 230–239.

Johnson, D. P., & Mullins, L. C. (1989). Religiosity and loneliness among the elderly. *Journal of Applied Gerontology, 9*, 110–131.

Johnson, P. E. (1959). *Psychology of religion*. Nashville, TN: Abingdon Press.

Kaplar, M. E., Wachholtz, A. B., & O'Brien, W. H. (2004). The effect of religious and spiritual interventions on the biological, psychological, and spiritual outcomes of oncology patients. *Journal of Psychosocial Oncology, 22*, 39–49.

Keefe, F. J., Affleck, G., Lefebvre, J., Underwood, L., Caldwell, D. S., Drew, J., et al. (2001). Living with rheumatoid arthritis: The role of daily spirituality and daily religious and spiritual coping. *Journal of Pain, 2*, 101–110.

Koenig, H. G., King, D. E., & Carson, V. B. (2012). *Handbook of religion and health* (2nd ed.). New York: Oxford University Press.

Kooistra, W. P., & Pargament, K. I. (1999). Religious doubting in parochial school adolescents. *Journal of Psychology and Theology, 27*, 33–42.

Krause, N. (2010). Assessing coping responses within specific faith traditions: Suffering in silence, stress, and depressive symptoms among older Catholics. *Mental Health, Religion & Culture, 13*, 513–529.

Krause, N., Ellison, C. G., & Wulff, K. M. (1998). Church-based emotional support, negative interaction, and psychological well-being: Findings from a national sample of Presbyterians. *Journal for the Scientific Study of Religion, 37*, 725–741.

Krumrei, E. J., Mahoney, A., & Pargament, K. I. (2009). Divorce and the divine: The role of spirituality in adjustment to divorce. *Journal of Marriage and the Family, 71*, 373–383.

Lazarus, R. S., & Folkman, S. (1984). *Stress, appraisal, and coping.* New York: Springer.

Lee, C. C., Czaja, S. J., & Schulz, R. (2010). The moderating influence of demographic characteristics, social support, and religious coping on the effectiveness of a multicomponent psychosocial caregiver intervention in three racial ethnic groups. *Journal of Gerontology, 65,* 185–194.

Mahoney, A. M., Pargament, K. I., Ano, G. G., Lynn, Q., Magyar, G. M., McCarthy, S., et al. (2002, August). *The devil made them do it: Demonization and desecration of the 9/11 terrorist attacks.* Paper presented at the 110th Annual Convention of the American Psychological Association, Chicago.

Margolin, A., Schuman-Olivier, Z., Beitel, M., Arnold, R. M., Fulwiler, C. E., & Avants, S. K. (2007). A preliminary study of spiritual self-schema (3-S(+)) therapy for reducing impulsivity in HIV-positive drug users. *Journal of Clinical Psychology, 63,* 979–999.

Maton, K. I. (1989). The stress-buffering role of spiritual support: Cross-sectional and prospective investigations. *Journal for the Scientific Study of Religion, 28,* 310–323.

McConnell, K. M., Pargament, K. I., Ellison, C. G., & Flannelly, K. J. (2006). Examining the links between spiritual struggles and symptoms of psychopathology in a national sample. *Journal of Clinical Psychology, 62,* 1469–1484.

McCullough, M. E. (1999). Research on religion-accommodative counseling: Review and meta-analysis. *Journal of Counseling Psychology, 46,* 92–98.

McCullough, M. E., & Willoughby, B. L. B. (2009). Religion, self-regulation, and self-control: Associations, explanations, and implications. *Psychological Bulletin, 135,* 69–93.

Molock, S. D., Puri, R., Matlin, S., & Barksdale, C. (2006). Relationship between religious coping and suicidal behaviors among African American adolescents. *Journal of Black Psychology, 32,* 366–389.

Murray-Swank, A. (2003). *Exploring spiritual confession: A theoretical synthesis and experimental study.* Unpublished doctoral dissertation. Bowling Green State University, Bowling Green, OH.

Murray-Swank, N. A., & Pargament, K. I. (2003). God, where are you?: Evaluating a spiritually integrated intervention for sexual abuse. *Mental Health, Religion & Culture, 8,* 191–204.

Ni, H., Simile, C., & Hardy, A. M. (2002). Utilization of complementary and alternative medicine by United States adults: Results from the 1999 National Health Interview Survey. *Medical Care, 40,* 353–358.

Nooney, J., & Woodrum, E. (2002). Religious coping and church-based social support as predictors of mental health outcomes: Testing a conceptual model. *Journal for the Scientific Study of Religion, 4,* 359–368.

Oman, D., Shapiro, S. L., Thoresen, C. E., Flinders, T., Driskill, J. D., & Plante, T. G. (2007). Learning from spiritual models and meditation: A randomized evaluation of a college course. *Pastoral Psychology, 55,* 473–493.

Paloutzian, R. F. (1981). Purpose in life and value changes following conversion. *Journal of Personality and Social Psychology, 41,* 1153–1160.

Pargament, K. I. (1997). *The psychology of religion and coping: Theory, research, practice.* New York: Guilford Press.

Pargament, K. I. (2002). Is religion nothing but . . . ?: Explaining religion versus explaining religion away. *Psychological Inquiry, 13,* 239–244.

Pargament, K. I. (2007). *Spiritually integrated psychotherapy: Understanding and addressing the sacred.* New York: Guilford Press.

Pargament, K. I. (2011). Religion and coping: The current state of knowledge. In S. Folkman (Ed.), *The Oxford handbook of stress, health, and coping* (pp. 269–288). New York: Oxford University Press.

Pargament, K. I. (2013). Searching for the sacred: Toward a nonreductionistic theory of spirituality. In K. I. Pargament, J. J. Exline, & J. W. Jones (Eds.), *APA handbook of psychology, religion, and spirituality (Vol. 1): Context, theory, and research* (pp. 257–274). Washington, DC: American Psychological Association.

Pargament, K. I., Feuille, M., & Burdzy, D. (2011). The Brief RCOPE: Current psychometric status of a short measure of religious coping. *Religions, 2,* 51–76.

Pargament, K. I., Kennell, J., Hathaway, W., Grevengoed, N., Newman, J., & Jones, W. (1988). Religion and the problem-solving process: Three styles of coping. *Journal for the Scientific Study of Religion, 27,* 90–104.

Pargament, K. I., Koenig, H. G., & Perez, L. (2000). The many methods of religious coping: Development and initial validation of the RCOPE. *Journal of Clinical Psychology, 56,* 519–543.

Pargament, K. I., Koenig, H. G., Tarakeshwar, N., & Hahn, J. (2001). Religious struggle as a predictor of mortality among medically ill elderly patients: A two-year longitudinal study. *Archives of Internal Medicine, 161,* 1881–1885.

Pargament, K. I., Koenig, H. G., Tarakeshwar, N., & Hahn, J. (2004). Religious coping methods as predictors of psychological, physical, and spiritual outcomes among medically ill elderly patients: A two-year longitudinal study. *Journal of Health Psychology, 9,* 713–730.

Pargament, K. I., Magyar, G. M., Benore, E., & Mahoney, A. (2005). Sacrilege: A study of sacred loss and desecration and their implications for health and well-being in a community sample. *Journal for the Scientific Study of Religion, 44,* 59–78.

Pargament, K. I., Magyar, G. M., & Murray-Swank, N. (2005). The sacred and the search for significance: Religion as a unique process. *Journal of Social Issues, 61,* 665–687.

Pargament, K. I., Mahoney, A., Shafranske, E., Exline, J. J., & Jones, J. (in press). From research to practice: Towards an applied psychology of religion and spirituality. In K. I. Pargament, A. Mahoney, & E. Shafranske (Eds.), *APA handbook of psychology, religion, and spirituality (Vol. 2): An applied psychology of religion and spirituality* (pp. 3–22). Washington, DC: American Psychological Association.

Pargament, K. I., & Park, C. L. (1995). Merely a defense?: The variety of religious means and ends. *Journal of Social Issues, 51,* 13–32.

Pargament, K. I., Poloma, M., & Tarakeshwar, N. (2001). Spiritual healing, karma, and the Bar Mitzvah: Methods of coping from the religions of the world. In C. R. Snyder (Ed.), *Coping and copers: Adaptive processes and people* (pp. 259–284). New York: Oxford University Press.

Pargament, K. I., Smith, B. W., Koenig, H. G., & Perez, L. (1998). Patterns of positive and negative religious coping with major life stressors. *Journal for the Scientific Study of Religion, 37,* 710–724.

Pargament, K. I., & Sweeney, P. J. (2011). Building spiritual fitness in the Army: An innovative approach to human development. *American Psychologist, 66,* 58–64.

Pargament, K. I., Tarakeshwar, N., Ellison, C., & Wulff, K. (2001). Religious coping among the religious: The relationships among religious coping and well-being in a national sample of Presbyterian clergy elders and members. *Journal for the Scientific Study of Religion, 40,* 497–513.

Pargament, K. I., Trevino, K., Mahoney, A., & Silberman, I. (2007). They killed our Lord: The perception of Jews as desecrators of Christianity as a predictor of anti-Semitism. *Journal for the Scientific Study of Religion, 46,* 143–158.

Park, C. L. (2010). Making sense of the meaning literature: An integrative review of meaning making and its effects on adjustment to stressful life events. *Psychological Bulletin, 136,* 257–301.

Park, C. L., Cohen, L. H., & Herb, L. (1990). Intrinsic religiousness and religious coping as life stress moderators for Catholics vs. Protestants. *Journal of Personality and Social Psychology, 59,* 562–574.

Park, C. L., Edmondson, D., & Blank, T. O. (2009). Religious and non-religious pathways to stress-related growth in cancer survivors. *Applied Psychology, Health and Well-Being, 1,* 321–335.

Park, C. L., & Folkman, S. (1997). Meaning in the context of stress and coping. *Review of General Psychology, 1,* 115–144.

Pearce, M. J., Singer, J. L., & Prigerson, H. G. (2006). Religious coping among caregivers of terminally ill cancer patients: Main effects and psychosocial mediators. *Journal of Health Psychology, 11,* 743–759.

Phelps, A. C., Maciejewski, P. K., Nilsson, M., Balboni, T. A., Wright, A. A., Paulk, M. E., et al. (2009). Religious coping and use of intensive life prolonging care near death in patients with advanced cancer. *Journal of American Medical Association, 301,* 1140–1147.

Phillips, R. E., III, Cheng, C. M., Pargament, K. I., Oemig, C., Colvin, S. D., Abarr, A. N., et al. (2009). Spiritual coping in American Buddhists: An exploratory study. *The International Journal for the Psychology of Religion, 19,* 231–243.

Phillips, R. E., III, Lakin, R., & Pargament, K. I. (2002). Development and implementation of a spiritual issues psychoeducational group for those with serious mental illness. *Community Mental Health Journal, 38,* 487–495.

Phillips, R. E., III, & Stein, C. H. (2007). God's will, God's punishment, or God's limitations?: Religious coping strategies reported by young adults living with serious mental illness. *Journal of Clinical Psychology, 63,* 529–540.

Proffitt, D., Cann, A., Calhoun, G., & Tedeschi, R. G. (2007). Judeo-Christian clergy and personal crisis: Religion, posttraumatic growth and well-being. *Journal of Religion and Health, 46,* 219–231.

Raiya, H. A., Pargament, K. I., Mahoney, A., & Stein, C. (2008). A psychological measure of Islamic religiousness: Development and evidence for reliability and validity. *The International Journal for the Psychology of Religion, 18,* 291–315.

Raiya, H. A., Pargament, K. I., Mahoney, A., & Trevino, K. (2008). When Muslims are perceived as a religious threat: Examining the connection between desecration, religious coping, and anti-Muslim attitudes. *Basic and Applied Social Psychology, 30,* 311–325.

Rajagopal, D., Mackenzie, E., Bailey, C., & Lavizzo-Mourey, R. (2002). The effectiveness of a spiritually-based intervention to alleviate subsyndromal anxiety and minor depression among older adults. *Journal of Religion and Health, 41,* 153–166.

Reavley, N., Pallant, J. F., & Sali, A. (2009). Evaluation of the effects of a psychosocial intervention on mood, coping, and quality of life in cancer patients. *Integrative Cancer Therapies, 8,* 47–55.

Robinson, E. A. R., Cranford, J. A., Webb, J. R., & Brower, K. J. (2007). Six-month changes in spirituality, religiousness, and heavy drinking in a treatment-seeking sample. *Journal of Studies on Alcohol and Drugs, 68,* 282–290.

Roesch, S. C., & Ano, G. (2003). Testing an attribution and coping model of stress: Religion as an orienting system. *Journal of Psychology and Christianity, 22,* 197–209.

Rosmarin, D. H., Pargament, K. I., Krumrei, E. J., & Flannelly, K. J. (2009). Religious coping among Jews: Development and initial validation of the JCOPE. *Journal of Clinical Psychology, 65,* 670–683.

Rye, M. S., & Pargament, K. I. (2002). Forgiveness and romantic relationships in college: Can it heal the wounded heart? *Journal of Clinical Psychology, 58,* 419–441.

Schottenbauer, M. A., Rodriguez, B. F., Glass, C. R., & Arnkoff, D. B. (2006). Religious coping research and contemporary personality theory: An explanation of Endler's (1997) integrative personality theory. *British Journal of Psychology, 97,* 499–519.

Schuster, M. A., Stein, B. D., Jaycox, L. H., Collins, R. L., Marshall, G. N., Elliott, M. N., et al. (2001). A national survey of stress reactions after the September 11, 2001, terrorist attacks. *New England Journal of Medicine, 345,* 1507–1512.

Seth, S., & Seligman, M. E. P. (1993). Optimism and fundamentalism. *Psychological Science, 4,* 256–259.

Shrimali, S., & Broota, K. D. (1987). Effect of surgical stress on beliefs in God and superstition: An in situ investigation. *Journal of Personality and Clinical Studies, 3,* 135–138.

Smith, T. B., Bartz, J., & Richards, P. S. (2007). Outcomes of religious and spiritual adaptations to psychotherapy: A meta-analytic review. *Psychotherapy Research, 17,* 643–655.

Tarakeshwar, N., Pargament, K. I., & Mahoney, A. (2003). Initial development of a measure of religious coping among Hindus. *Journal of Community Psychology, 31,* 607–628.

Targ, E. F., & Levine, E. G. (2002). The efficacy of a mind–body–spirit group for women with breast cancer: A randomized controlled trial. *General Hospital Psychiatry, 24,* 238–248.

Tix, A. P., & Frazier, P. A. (1998). The use of religious coping during stressful life events: Main effects, moderation, and mediation. *Journal of Consulting and Clinical Psychology, 66,* 411–422.

Trevino, K. M., Pargament, K. I., Cotton, S., Leonard, A. C., Hahn, J., Caprini-Faigin, C. A., et al. (2010). Religious coping and physiological, psychological, social, and spiritual outcomes in patients with HIV/AIDS: Cross-sectional and longitudinal findings. *AIDS and Behavior, 14,* 379–389.

Vail, K. E., III, Rothschild, Z. K., Weise, D. R., Solomon, S., Pyszczynski, T., & Greenberg, J. (2010). A terror management analysis of the psychological functions of religion. *Personality and Social Psychology Review, 14,* 84–94.

VanNess, P. H., & Larson, D. B. (2002). Religion, senescence, and mental health: The end of life is not the end of hope. *American Journal of Geriatric Psychiatry, 10,* 386–397.

Wachholtz, A., & Sambamoorthi, U. (2011). National trends in prayer use as a coping mechanism for health concerns: Changes from 2002 to 2007. *Psychology of Religion and Spirituality, 3,* 67–77.

Wachholtz, A. B., & Pargament, K. I. (2008). Migraines and meditation: Does spirituality matter? *Journal of Behavioral Medicine, 31,* 351–366.

Yangarber-Hicks, N. (2004). Religious coping styles and recovery from serious mental illness. *Journal of Psychology and Theology, 32,* 305–317.

29

Mindfulness in Psychology and Religion

Michael R. Levenson and Carolyn M. Aldwin

In the past 30 years, the construct of mindfulness has played an increasingly important role in psychology. Kornfield (2008) reported that there have been almost 1,000 scientific studies on mindfulness. A recent check (2012) of PsycINFO yielded 2,932 entries, including 1,865 journal articles, most of which are focused on clinical interventions. There is even a journal devoted to the topic: *Mindfulness.* Obviously, it is not possible to review all of this work here (see Hofman, Sawyer, Witt, & Oh, 2010; Shapiro & Carlson, 2009). Rather, we briefly provide an overview of the construct and use of mindfulness in contemporary psychology and adult development. Then we examine mindfulness in the context of religion, especially contemplative practice. While mindfulness is most often associated with Buddhism, we review material showing that it is also central to Christian and Islamic contemplative traditions. Finally, we examine the role of mindfulness in ethics.

MINDFULNESS IN CONTEMPORARY PSYCHOLOGY

Mindfulness has been imported from Buddhism into the field of psychology as a therapeutic method. Practitioners have sought to employ it to relieve specific kinds of suffering. Many studies have documented the benefits of cultivating mindfulness on those seeking relief from specific sources of distress. (For reviews, see Grossman, Niemann, Schmidt, & Wallach, 2004; Hofman et al., 2010; Shapiro & Carlson, 2009; Shapiro, Oman, Thoresen, Plant, & Flinders, 2008.)

For present purposes, we can think of this as *utilitarian mindfulness.* That is, it is not mindfulness as a spiritual practice but as a means to solve or cope with a specific problem. Psychologists have applied mindfulness in a secular context as "present-centered awareness" and openness to the experience that arises in the present moment (Bishop, Lau, Shapiro, Carlson, Anderson, et al., 2007). Mindfulness practice has been employed in the treatment of chronic pain (McCracken, Gauntlett-Gilbert, & Vowles,

2007), depression and anxiety disorders (Fjorback, Arendt, Ørnbøl, Fink, & Walach, 2011; Kiken & Shook, 2012), and even basic biological aging processes such as telomere length (Jacobs, Epel, Lin, Blackburn, Wolkowitz, et al., 2011).

Mindfulness in clinical practice can be summarized as self-regulation by self-observation. In clinical practice, for example, mindfulness may be applied to the experience of anxiety. First, people are instructed to simply dwell in the awareness of the anxiety they are experiencing without judging whether it is "good" or "bad" or due to some influence on which our minds might then elaborate. That is, one should not dwell on the source of anxiety but just be present to the anxiety. When practitioners "catch" their minds elaborating, they are instructed simply to bring the attention back to the experience of anxiety itself.

Next, the practitioner begins to be aware of what thoughts and memories are setting the anxiety process in motion. Again, these states of mind are not to be judged but simply accepted and not elaborated. Once again, the practitioner needs to return gently to the pure experience of anxiety, and then generalize this nonjudgmental stance to everyday activity. As time goes by, we may find that our anxiety becomes less "raw" and less easily triggered. However, the point is not to eliminate the feeling of anxiety but to cease identifying with it.

This use of mindfulness is consistent with Buddhist teaching inasmuch as the latter places its emphasis on the removal of suffering by eliminating the causes of suffering. However, the Buddhist concept of suffering—and mindfulness—is much broader.

The development of mindfulness scales has been useful in expanding the range of mindfulness research in psychology, including measures by Brown and Ryan (2003), Feldman, Hayes, Kumar, Greeson, and Laurenceau (2007), and Lau, Bishop, Segal, Buis, Andersson, et al. (2006), among others. However, the development of these self-report measures has not been without controversy. (For a debate on the construct validity of mindfulness scales, see Brown, Ryan, Loverich, Biegel, & West, 2011; Grossman, 2011.) We would add that mindfulness is a subtle refinement of experience that can be measured only somewhat crudely. Nonetheless, psychometric development has allowed for more in-depth investigations into the correlates and consequences of mindfulness in everyday life.

For example, research has sought to link mindfulness with personality traits. In general, mindfulness meditators are higher in traits such as such as openness to experience and extraversion, and they are lower in neuroticism (van den Hurk et al., 2011). However, mindfulness is not really a personality characteristic, but has been linked more explicitly to attentional processes (Jensen, Vangkilde, Frokjaer, & Hasselbalch, 2012; Mrazek, Smallwood, & Schooler, 2002) and emotion regulation (Hill & Updegraff, 2012). As such, one could argue that it is a characteristic reflecting developmental processes.

MINDFULNESS IN ADULT DEVELOPMENT

Although mindfulness is an inherently developmental construct, there has been little or no direct research on how mindfulness changes with age. To our knowledge, not even cross-sectional studies have been conducted. Indirectly, there is good evidence that emotion regulation improves with age (Charles, 2010), which suggests that mindfulness may as well. In contrast, openness to experience may decline slightly with age (Roberts & Mroczek, 2008; but see Noftle & Fleeson, 2010). It is likely that there are individual differences in mindfulness trajectories in adulthood.

Ellen Langer and her colleagues (1989, 1998; Langer & Moldoveanu, 2000) have presented a theoretical foundation for a developmental psychology that centrally involves mindfulness. Langer is careful to distinguish her approach from mindfulness as it is practiced in Buddhism per se, yet, as she acknowledged, there are some striking similarities. She pointed out the extent to which "objectivity" is governed by fixed categories that prove to be largely arbitrary habits of thought. Released from such habits, our minds reveal a world of shifting meanings and provisional categorical boundaries. We learn to discard categories that are no longer useful and that can limit our developmental potential. This can lead to a freeing of the mind from the bondage of fixed categories, automatism, and the tyranny of a single perspective, the defining features of mindlessness in Langer's exposition. Langer's approach leads from the "objective" to the subjective, restoring the legitimacy of the subjective in psychology (see also Lazarus & Folkman, 1984) and establishes much evidence for the untenable status of the dualism of "objective" and "subjective."

This approach moves beyond utilitarian mindfulness to mindfulness as a wellspring of human psychological development generally. Mindfulness is a *practice* that frees the mind from constraint (Langer, 1989; Levenson & Crumpler, 1996; Rosch, 2008). We have argued elsewhere that this "liberative approach" of freeing the mind from biosocial conditioning is the basis of the development of wisdom (Levenson & Crumpler, 1996). Such a process would rely on increasing openness to experience and a decrease in neuroticism and self-focus. Much of Langer's work has concentrated on the importance of mindfulness as a protective factor in physical, cognitive, and psychological aging (e.g., Alexander, Langer, Newman, Chandler, & Davies, 1989), and we would extend that to wisdom as well.

Curnow (1999) noted that most of the religious and philosophical systems of the world address wisdom in remarkably similar ways. In his review, Western and Eastern theories of wisdom share very similar characteristics. In many ways, his argument is quite similar to ours, in that he focused on the *practices*, universally, across religious and philosophical systems, which are thought to result in wisdom. At the heart of all of these practices is the cultivation of mindfulness. He identified the aspects of wisdom as self knowledge, detachment, integration, and transcendence.

Self-Knowledge

Knowledge about the self can be attained in several ways. For psychoanalysis and analytic psychology, self-knowledge is accomplished by bringing to consciousness hidden aspects of the self, while for humanistic and transpersonal psychology self-knowledge is an uncovering of the highest self. The religious traditions employ mindfulness meditative techniques that systematically undermine the empirical self by observing the nonidentity of oneself with the objects of thoughts and feelings and, finally, nonidentity with the thoughts and feelings themselves. For Buddhist meditators, this ideally results in an experiencing of the self as an ever-changing flow. Rather than an entity on its own, it is experienced as continuously created by a process rooted in attraction and aversion, as

James (1981) also recognized. Hindu Advaita Vedantists, on the other hand, experience the self as pure awareness (Forman, 1990).

Social psychology has a long tradition of understanding the constructed nature of the self, largely through understanding illusions (Aronson, 2012). With notable exceptions (e.g., Langer's 1989 previously cited work on mindfulness), social psychology does not describe how to overcome the tendency to create illusions. However, this is described in great detail by the contemplative psychologies, beginning with detachment.

Detachment

Contemplative traditions advocate detachment or, more properly, nonattachment, which does not necessarily imply aloofness or lack of concern. Nonattachment is the recognition that one's thoughts and feelings are not essential to one's self but are merely phenomena, just as those experienced in the rest of the environment (Forman, 1998). As we have seen earlier, mindfulness meditation techniques are the bases of the development of nonattachment. Consistent with McKee and Barber's (1999) approach to wisdom, all of the versions of detachment can be organized around the theme of "seeing through illusion," with detachment understood to refer to a disempowering, through insight, of the multifarious sources of self-deception. However, detachment by itself runs the risk of being confused with aloofness by novice practitioners, unless it is accompanied by integration.

Integration

Curnow (1999) characterizes integration as the "other side" of detachment. Citing Neo-Confucian Wang Yang-ming, Curnow observed that, "For Wang, being distracted by the things of the world undermines the integration of the individual" (Curnow, 1999, p. 208). Helminski (1992, p. 86) said, "We are forever in parts and yet wish to be whole. We are distracted and yet wish to concentrate; we are scattered and yet wish to be gathered."

Modern psychology understands integration as a harmonious relationship among the various aspects of psyche or self, which entails self-knowledge. Only the self that has been made conscious can be integrated. It would seem, moreover, that the greater one's self-knowledge, the lesser one's need for defense mechanisms such as projection and reaction formation. Illusion stems from an attachment to one's own assumptions and desires; detachment from these promotes self-knowledge. These insights, however, need to be integrated back into one's self. From a Jungian perspective, this would be equivalent to understanding one's shadow self, and then integrating the shadow into one's conscious self in a nondestructive way (Jung, 1968). Self-knowledge, detachment, and integration thus set the stage for self-transcendence.

Transcendence

Transcendence is often understood as referring to a deity existing beyond or above created things, distinct from an immanent divine. However, transcendent *experience*, Curnow (1999) observed, unites the immanent and the transcendent. Such experience transcends ordinarily fragmented (disintegrated) human experience. Understood in this way, transcendence is transcendence of self, the limited and limiting confinement of experience based on biosocial conditioning as discussed in connection with the liberative model of development (Levenson & Crumpler, 1996). Experience becomes nondual, that is, the subject (self)–object (non-self) distinction is experienced as a provisional construction rather than constitutive of "objective reality" (cf. Loy, 1988).

This conceptualization is consistent with Piedmont's (1999) description of spiritual transcendence, which is characterized by transcendence of "the immediacy of our own individual consciousness that binds all things into a more unitive harmony" (p. 988), which he believes is characteristic of all religious traditions.

Thus, mindfulness not only is a means to ending suffering, but also forms the basis for both self-knowledge and nonattachment, which in turn sets the stage for integration and, ultimately, self-transcendence.

MINDFULNESS WITHIN RELIGIONS

In this section, we address mindfulness in terms of *practice* and *function* across religions. In so doing, we hope to show that practice and function are much more similar than different across traditions that might, at first, appear very different. The contemplative traditions we have chosen as examples—Buddhism, Sufism, and contemplative Christianity—are by no means exhaustive (see Michaelson, 2007, for a discussion of mindfulness in the Kabala and Judaism). However, we chose to focus on these religions as they have the most substantive literatures on mindfulness.

Each contemplative tradition is situated in a religious context and often uses language specific to a religious tradition. However, in all of these traditions, mindfulness is remembrance or the process of being aware. The elementary foundation of contemplative traditions is the experienced difference between our sensations, thoughts, and feelings on the one hand and *who we are* on the other. In Sanskrit, the foundational Indo-European language, mindfulness is *smirti*, or, in the closely related Pali language of relatively early Buddhist texts it is *sati*. In Sufism, mindfulness is practiced in the context of *zhikr*. All three terms refer to "remembrance," and so it is still defined in contemporary English (OED, 1993, pp. 1778–1779).

When we are mindful, we "remember" by gathering our attention from a scattered and distracted state. Mindfulness is *not* thinking, but thinking can be mindful when thought is no longer an automatic process but, rather, when thought proceeds from the expanded awareness of mindfulness. Tenzin Palmo (2002) observed that *being* mindful is defeated by thinking that one is being mindful. The very thought of "being mindful" is a distraction. Keating, writing from the Christian contemplative tradition, cited a remark by Anthony of Egypt: "Perfect prayer is not to know that you are praying" (Keating, 1986, p. 91). Palmo also drew attention to mindfulness as remembrance, taking note of the presence of "recollection" in the Christian contemplative tradition. When we refer to "collecting ourselves" after being distressed or excited, we are referring to reestablishing a level of mindfulness. Thinking mindfully means that our thinking begins with a lack of bias and with panoramic awareness that takes in "forest" and "trees." When we turn mindfulness inward toward ourselves, we approach mindfulness as religious practice or as a clarification of consciousness.

Similarities across Religions

The term "mindfulness" is best known from its usage in Buddhism. Kornfield (2008) defines it as "attention" (p. 96), but not just *any* attention. "It is a non-judging and respectful awareness" (Kornfield, 2008, p. 96) in which one is present to bodily states, sensations, the thinking mind itself, and the experiences that comprise the objects of the mind. This is panoramic awareness (Palmo, 2002). Gunaratana (1994, p. 151) defined mindfulness as "mirror thought." It reflects only what is presently happening and in exactly the way it is happening. There are no biases.

As the contemporary Sufi, Kabir Helminski (1992, p. viii), wrote, "In certain teachings, such as Buddhism, the practice of mindful presence is the central fact. In Islam, remembrance is the qualifier of all activity." Helminski referred to mindfulness as "presence" and defines it as "the quality of *consciously being here*" (Helminski, 1992, p. viii, italics added).

Thomas Keating spoke of the spiritual journey as composed of two great questions, "*Where* are you?" (Keating, 1999, p. 7, italics added) and "*Who* are you?" (Keating, 1999, p. 29) We know by being present, by remembering. It is noteworthy that Keating (1999) used a Sufi story to illustrate the spiritual search and a story from the life of Buddha to illustrate the unity of all of reality. Keating included issues in life span development and the importance of unconscious processes in the dynamic process of contemplative practice. We cannot know who or where we are—we cannot be fully present to being—if our perception is guided by unconscious processes. One of the major functions of contemplative practice is to free us from the automatisms of such processes.

One way of understanding mindfulness across contemplative traditions is in terms of a dialectic between *presence* and *absence*. When we are fully present, we experience our absence as our sensations, thoughts, and feelings. As noted earlier, mindfulness can be understood both as *practice* and as *function*. We return to this theme later.

Mindfulness in Buddhism

As noted earlier, mindfulness is best known from its presentation in Buddhist literature, teaching, and meditation. The elementary teaching of Buddha is expressed in the teaching on Right View (Nanamoli & Bodhi, 1995) as the Four Noble Truths that suffering exists, that it has a cause, that suffering can cease, and that there is a method to bring about its cessation. The method for causing the cessation of suffering is summarized in the Noble Eightfold Path consisting of right view, right intention, right speech, right action, right livelihood, right effort, right mindfulness, and right concentration (Nanamoli & Bodhi, 1995, see pp. 1097–1101 for the full sutta). In this chapter, we are concerned with "right mindfulness" and its connection to "right concentration."

In Buddhism, mindfulness offers a release from suffering by correcting a wrong view of our experiences as definitive of ourselves. Here the term "suffering" denotes much more than it does in contemporary ordinary language. Pleasant experiences to which we are attached are suffering in that they inevitably end and our attachment to them—our craving or longing for them—causes us pain. Thus, the root cause of suffering is attachment and its psychological correlate, craving. One can even be attached to feelings of sadness, victimization, or to diagnostic labels. According to Buddhist teaching, ceasing to identify ourselves with attributes is powerfully liberating because attributes are inherently transitory.

In Buddhism, an "object" of mindfulness may be an aspect of one's body (such as breathing or walking), feelings, the mind itself, or "mind objects." In the context of awareness of this experience, we begin also to experience the arising and subsiding of sensations, thoughts, and feelings and the practice of "letting them be." That is, we do not try to stop them and we do not elaborate upon them or "follow" them. We observe them and let them go.

The larger purpose of mindfulness in Buddhism is clear awareness. One can think of the tangle of sensations, thoughts, and feelings as a storm. As the storm abates, there is, quite naturally, a clearing of the sky—the "torment" ceases. In meditation, we become aware of the storm in what we call "ourselves." In so doing, we can have an effect on our "inner weather" simply by observing it in detail. As we see that it is not ourselves, we can accept its impermanence and let it dissipate. This kind of insight, or *vipassana*, is the central feature of mindfulness in Buddhist practice. The insight opens the mind. Its result is what Suzuki (1970) called "Big Mind." In Buddhism this is more conventionally called "emptiness," but Suzuki, a truly bicultural Zen teacher, was wise enough to realize that this word is misunderstood by Western people to mean a sort of unthinking blankness of mind, which is far from its actual meaning of complete openness to experience.

The Context of Mindfulness Teaching

As noted earlier in this chapter, *Sati* is the Pali word that translates the Sanskrit word *smirti* or "remembrance." But what is remembered? Continuing with the theme of pure awareness, what is remembered is to bring one's attention back to the object of contemplation. There are potentially countless objects of contemplation. In *vipassana* meditation, the object of contemplation is usually the breath. One does not *control* the breath or manipulate it in any way. One simply *observes* it (Gunaratana, 1994).

The *function* of contemplation is *purification or clarification of consciousness*, that is, through full awareness, to experience insight into impermanence and "not self" and thus to solve the problem of the existence of suffering that is the first of the Four Noble Truths. The second is that suffering has causes, usually negative emotions, thoughts, and desires. However, these can seem to be positive thoughts and emotions such as desires that our culture deems acceptable or laudable, such as desires for wealth, celebrity, and possessions. The third is that suffering can cease, especially when we stop grasping for objects of desire. The fourth is that there is a path to the cessation of suffering. The practice of mindfulness and the cultivation of the Noble Eightfold Path (cf. Nanamoli & Bodhi, 1995) constitute the methods that are collectively called the path to the cessation of suffering. The Buddha's message concerns the method by which we can control attention sufficiently to sustain pure awareness, the ultimate stage of mindfulness. The method of the purification of consciousness was presented by Buddhaghosa (Nanamoli, 1975) and by Goleman (1988). It is important to recognize that the benefit of this practice in no way depends on an adherence to the literal doctrine of "no self," which, like "emptiness," has caused needless confusion. Mindfulness is practice, not doctrine.

"Original" Buddhism, if it is even possible to make this attribution on the evidence available, is nontheistic in the sense of not acknowledging a creator god who (which) rules the cosmos. Of course, inasmuch as Buddha's teaching is, in part, a reaction against caste-ridden Brahmanism, gods appear frequently in the Buddha's discourses, and they are beings who inhabit more refined realms of being yet they do not possess the Buddha's complete wakefulness. Indeed, "Buddha" is translated as "the awakened one."

Concentration and Contemplation

In order to practice mindfulness, we must be able to concentrate our minds. Yet, as Gunaratana (1994) pointed out, concentration is a capacity of mind that must be fully in the service of mindfulness itself rather some extrinsic goal in order to be helpful. Thus, mindfulness and concentration form a dynamic process in which mindfulness governs concentration. One way to determine the "honesty" of concentration in the service of mindfulness is to "check" ourselves to make certain that we are free from intention in concentration. That is, our concentration is simply an openness, or *receptivity* without *reactivity* to what is happening, with nothing added.

Both concentration and contemplation have been described in great detail in Buddhist literature. Presenting this level of detail would be untenable in a brief chapter and would be distracting in an overview that attempts to present mindfulness from the perspectives of several different traditions. However, it is important to bear in mind that concentration is increasing absorption of attention and a tranquility of one's emotional state that serves as a basis for insight. This synergy can happen as a result of years of practice, but it can also happen spontaneously. We can all remember moments when a state of calm, alert, undistracted presence has led to "seeing through" a problem without effort. What distinguishes concentration and contemplation as religious or spiritual practice is that they allow us to see our states of mind clearly as merely states of mind as distinct from ourselves. We can cease to identify with our sensations, thoughts, and emotions. All contemplative traditions hold that this cessation provides freedom to access the "vertical," or transcendent, dimension of consciousness. This emphasis on the vertical dimension is especially emphasized in Sufism.

Mindfulness in Sufism

Sufism is widely regarded as "Islamic mysticism." Sufi *practice* involves mindfulness. Helminski (1992), defined mindfulness as "presence" or simply being where we are. We are in the moment, and from the Sufi (and the Augustinian Christian) perspectives, that moment is contained in being such that all moments are facets of the same moment (cf. Izutsu, 1977).

Mindfulness is not an end in itself. If there is an end in itself, it is awareness or wakefulness. The various contemplative psychologies provide words that describe what we are thought to experience in awakening. In Sufism, the mantra practice of *zikr*, remembrance of God, is said to awaken us in the "unity of being," or, in Arabic, *wahdat-al-wujud*.

If we return to the basic question of the function of the practice of mindfulness, we are presented with a way of framing the question, "What does mindfulness *do* in contemplative practice?' One answer is that mindfulness practice works to remove whatever stands between the experiencer and the experience itself. How does mindfulness do this?

Sufism describes the process in the metaphor "polishing the mirror of the heart" attributed to the Prophet Muhammad, who said that the "polish" is the remembrance of God (Helminski, 1992), or *zikr*.

The mirror metaphor arises also in Gunaratana's (1994) description of Buddhist mindfulness. This kind of practice is also very apparent in Tantric Buddhism, wherein one polishes away one's self and what remains is the deity. It is an excellent metaphor for practice that clears the heart of all contents that cloud the consciousness and prevent the experience of the Real. In his 13th-century *Rose Garden of Mystery*, the Sufi Mahmud Shabistari employs another cleaning metaphor: "Go you, and sweep out the house of the heart/mind" (Levenson & Khilwati, 1999, p. 253; Darr, 2007). In this sweeping we find existence itself as the basis of our specific experiences. Mindfulness is, therefore, a practice that functions to provide a direct experience of unity of being or, put another way, of nonseparation.

Sufism, like all theistic religions, emphasizes that "pure" mindfulness is not enough for the *religious* practice of mindfulness. Rather, mind and heart, artificially separated in the Greek model of mind and in modern and postmodern usage, are reunited. This idea is certainly not foreign to Buddhism even though early Buddhism emphasized analysis of one's thoughts and feelings. As the Buddhist teacher Gunaratana remarked, "Mindfulness is objective, but it is not cold or unfeeling" (Gunaratana, 1994, p. 154). In the theistic religions, "heart" or affect is actually fuel for the practice of mindfulness, hence the great importance of the love poetry written by some of the most celebrated Sufis, such as Ibn 'Arabi (Sells, 2000), Rumi (Ergin & Johnson, 2006), and Hafez (Gray, 1995).

Mindfulness in Contemplative Christianity

Keating has been a key figure in restoring the mantram to a position of daily practice in contemplative Christianity. Like *zikr*, *centering prayer* is the silent repetition of a sacred word that opens one to the working of the divine in one's self. "Jesus said, 'watch and pray.' This is what we are doing in centering prayer. Watching is just enough activity to stay alert. Praying is opening to God" (Keating, 1986, p. 39). Keating makes it clear that the function of centering prayer is not to *produce* mystical experience or paranormal phenomena. However, it does open the mind to the vertical, or transcendent, dimension of experience. Experience has levels of refinement that can include extraordinary experience (cf. Steinbock, 2007). Mindfulness itself is extraordinary because it shows us that that we are not the contents of our minds, a seemingly prosaic but actually quite illuminating experience.

Contemplative practice is at the heart of Christianity, not just monastic Christianity (Keating, 1986). Wallace (2009) traced the meditative practice of mindfulness back to the Desert Fathers, citing a seventh-century manuscript by Hesychios the priest entitled *On Watchfulness and Holiness*. In this meditation manual, Hesychios speaks of ways of developing the "heart's stillness" which is "unbroken" by any thought. These techniques were preserved by Greek Orthodox monks.

In Western Christianity, the practice of *lectio divina* or divine reading or listening has been the preferred method of contemplative practice for many centuries (Keating, 1986). However, there is a long tradition of more personal meditation as expressed in

The Cloud of Unknowing by an unknown author of 14th-century England who inspired other great contemplatives such as St. Teresa of Jesus and St. John of the Cross in Spain. He wrote that "everything you dwell upon during this work becomes an obstacle to union with God. For if your mind is cluttered with these concerns there is no room for him. Of course, it is laudable to reflect upon God's kindness and to love and praise him for it; yet it is far better to let your mind rest in the awareness of him in his naked existence and to love and praise him for what he is in himself" (Johnston, 1973, p. 54). It seems to us that it is this practice that centering prayer restores. Nonattachment appears to be as central in contemplative Christianity as it is in Buddhism. Keating (1999), speaking from a Christian contemplative perspective, commented on Jesus's advice to "bring oneself to nothing" (Matthew 10:38). He said that "to bring oneself to nothing—no thing—is to cease to identify with the tyranny of our emotional programs for happiness and the limitations of our cultural conditioning. They are so strong in our culture that even our language reflects them. We say 'I am angry.' But *you* are not angry; you just have angry feelings. You may say, 'I am depressed.' No, *you* are not depressed; you have feelings of depression" (Keating, 1999, p. 42). It is *identifying* with these feelings that causes suffering, which is very similar to the Buddhist construct.

Mindfulness across Contemplative Traditions

As noted above, contemplative traditions in all religions are centrally concerned with mindfulness. All such traditions begin with the practice of mindfulness as sustained pure awareness. However, other traditions may appear to differ from Buddhism in the *object* of mindfulness. As we shall see, the objects of attention in practice may be different, but the *objective* of practice may be the same or, at least, very similar.

Buddhism seems strikingly different from the theistic traditions of South Asia (e.g., Vedanta) and the Abrahamic religions. However, if mindfulness is found in all contemplative traditions and if such traditions are central to all religions, these religions may be more similar than it might at first appear. To reiterate, it is useful to approach the comparative study of contemplative psychologies by treating them as *practices* and to recognize that practices have *functions*. The practice that is central to the development of mindfulness in all traditions is mantra.

Mantra as Practice

Concentration and contemplation are blended together in the mantram (the singular form of mantra). Most contemplative traditions contain a mantra practice. It involves the remembrance of a deity (e.g., Jesus), a sacred phrase (e.g., *om mani padme hum*, which translates as "the jewel in the lotus"), a phrase from a scripture, such as *La illaha il'Allah*, the affirmation by Muslims that "there is no God but God," or a prayer, such as centering prayer, in which a sacred name or phrase in Christianity is remembered.

A very interesting and useful synthesis of mantra practice was presented by Easwaran (2008), who found in his own teaching practice that the key to a successful mantram is that the one repeating it and many others regard it as sacred. Easwaran observed that mantra have the distinct advantage that they do not require that any specific place or time be set aside for their practice, although they certainly can and sometimes should be given a time and place of their own. However, when circumstances do not permit that, a mantram can be repeated anywhere or anytime. Easwaran also makes very clear the correctness of treating mantra practice as mindfulness practice by translating mantram as having a sacred name or phrase in mind, the more conventional translation, but also as derived from the Sanskrit roots "*man*, 'the mind,' and *tri*, 'to cross'" (Easwaran, 2008, p. 43).

Mantra practice crosses fortified religious boundaries without being touched by weighty theological issues. Indeed, a lightness of heart is the hallmark of mindfulness practice in general and of mantra specifically. In the context of centering prayer, one of Keating's students remarked that "during prayer, I sometimes have a happy-go lucky feeling that I find most enjoyable." Keating replied, "You should not take prayer too seriously. There is something playful about God" (Keating, 1986, p. 61).

It might appear that religions differ in their relative emphases on practice or belief (Armstrong, 2006). Islam could be regarded as a religion of practice while Christianity may appear to be a religion of belief. On the surface, this seems to make sense. In Islam one must only make the profession of faith that "there is no God but God and Muhammad is his prophet." After that, the central practice of the Islamic religious life is prayer five times per day and observing the fast of Ramadan, tithing (giving to those in need), and making the pilgrimage to Mecca at least once in one's life, if possible. One is also expected to observe certain prohibitions, including abstention from intoxicants and, interestingly, abstention from violence except under the most severe threat of harm. Christianity, on the other hand, presumably requires belief in the Holy Trinity and the divinity of Christ. That belief seems to define Christianity.

On closer inspection, this distinction breaks down. In Islam, one would not practice absent belief in the uniqueness of God or the mission of the Prophet. In Christianity, there is growing evidence that the belief in the unique divinity of Christ is *one* interpretation based on the politics of scriptural competition and the suppression of scriptures that would have us all, not only Jesus, carrying the spark of divinity (cf. Pagels, 2003). This would make Jesus a prophet in the same sense as Muhammad, a claim that is part of Islamic faith, in which Jesus is held in great reverence.

If mindfulness releases us from identification with the contents of mind, it releases us *into* a larger mind, as Suzuki (1970) taught. Basically, "God" is a way of talking about a "big mind" that we cannot really talk about because our talk is forever from "small mind"—our sensations, thoughts, and emotions. Thus, it is important to emphasize that to the mindful contemplative, God is not a "thing." This is the key connection between the function mindfulness in the different traditions and is well expressed by Meister Eckhart (Forman, 1991).

Summary

Mindfulness is at the heart of all of the contemplative religions. The construct of mindfulness is remarkably similar, whether it is called *sati*, *zhikr*, or centering prayer. It is remarkable that all of these constructs translate into "remembrance." Further, both the practice and function of mindfulness are markedly similar across religions. Our understanding of the function of mindfulness is self-transcendence—whether that means being in the presence of God for Muslims and Christians or resting in nonduality for Buddhists.

Thus, underlying this is the fundamental notion of the interconnected of all beings. This interconnectedness has profound implications for ethics.

MINDFULNESS AND ETHICS

One of the leading thinkers in the contemporary Catholic Benedictine tradition observed that "awareness of the sacred in life is what holds the world together and the lack of awareness and sacred care is what is tearing it apart" (Chittister, 1990, p. 69). From a Buddhist perspective, Gunaratana (1994, p. 42) asserted that "we ignore our inherent connectedness to all other beings and we decide that "I" have to get more for "me;" then we marvel at how greedy and insensitive human beings are. And on it goes. Every evil deed, every example of heartlessness in the world stems directly from this false sense of "me" as distinct from all else that is out there." In Buddhism, it is said that the dharma runs on two wheels: mindfulness and compassion.

Curnow (1999) argued that self-transcendence is the basis of ethnical intuition. Indeed, Kohlberg and Ryncarz (1990) developed an eighth stage of moral development based largely on self-transcendence. However, self-transcendence—the ability to put larger interests ahead of one's own—is in itself not sufficient for an ethical life. Recent historical events are replete with instances of individuals submerging their own identities in larger organizations that can be massively destructive, like the Nazi party. Rather, self-transcendence must be paired with compassion.

Leary, Tipsord, and Tate (2008) proposed that increasing inclusivity or connect-edness with others, and also the natural world, is also at the heart of many religions. "Some traditions maintain that construing oneself in relation to the rest of existence is a central characteristic of an adjusted, moral, and fully functioning individual, and some even identify it as a feature of self-realization or enlightenment" (Leary et al., 2008, p. 145). Thus, mindfulness not only has implications for individual development, but, when paired with compassion, also has larger, prosocial implications (McAdams, 2008). Quieting the mind and experiencing the connectedness between all beings can form the basis of an ethical relationship to others. In the words of one Sufi writer, "Whatever you do, you do to yourself" (Bayman, 2001, p. 92). In Christianity, Jesus is reported to have said, "Whatever you do to the least of these, you do to me" (Matthew 25: 31–46). Thus, the practice of mindfulness opens the door to remembering our interconnectedness with all life, and thus may help to develop compassion. Taken together, these form the basis of an experiential or intuitive ethics that go well beyond individual well-being.

CONCLUSION

In psychology, mindfulness practice has been used to alleviate suffering such as anxiety or chronic pain. However, the examination of the psychology within religion suggests that utilitarianism is only part the function of mindfulness. As we have seen, mindfulness is an important component of both adult development and ethics. Psychological research on mindfulness should investigate these additional functions, taking very seriously the transcendent function of spiritual practice.

ACKNOWLEDGMENTS

Preparation of this chapter was supported by Grant No. 21733 from the John Templeton Foundation to Carolyn M. Aldwin.

REFERENCES

Alexander, C. N., Langer, E. J., Newman, R. I., Chandler, H. M., & Davies, J. L. (1989). Transcendental meditation, mindfulness, and longevity: An experimental study with the elderly. *Journal of Personal and Social Psychology, 57*, 950–964.

Aronson, E. (2012). *The social animal* (11th ed.). New York: Worth.

Bayman, H. (2001). *The station of no station: Open secrets of the Sufi.* Berkeley, CA: North Atlantic Books.

Bishop, S. R., Lau, M., Shapiro, S., Carlson, L., Anderson, N. D., Carmody, J., et al. (2004). Mindfulness: A proposed operational definition. *Clinical Psychology: Science & Practice, 11*, 230–241.

Brown, K. W., & Ryan, R. M. (2003). The benefits of being present: Mindfulness and its role in psychological well-being. *Journal of Personality and Social Psychology, 84*, 822–848.

Brown, K., W., Ryan, R. M., & Creswell, J. (2007). Mindfulness: Theoretical foundations and evidence for its salutary effects. *Psychological Inquiry, 18*, 211–237.

Brown, K. W., Ryan, R. M., Loverich, T. M., Biegel, G. M., & West, A. M. (2011). Out of the armchair and into the streets: Measuring mindfulness advances knowledge and improves interventions: Reply to Grossman (2011). *Psychological Assessment, 23*, 1041–1046.

Charles, S. T. (2010). Strength and vulnerability integration: A model of emotional well-being across adulthood. *Psychological Bulletin, 136*, 1068–1091.

Chittister, J. (1990). *Wisdom distilled from the daily: Living the rule of St. Benedict today.* New York: Harper.

Darr, R. (2007). *Garden of mystery: The* Gulshan-e-Raz *of Mahmoud Shabistari.* Cambridge, UK: Archetype.

Easwaran, E. (2008). *The mantram handbook.* Tomales, CA: Nilgiri Press.

Ergin, N. O., & Johnson, W. (2006). *The forbidden Rumi: The suppressed poems of Rumi on love, heresy, and intoxication.* Rochester, VT: Inner Traditions.

Feldman, G. C., Hayes, A. M., Kumar, S. M., Greeson, J. M., & Laurenceau, J. P. (2007). Mindfulness and emotion regulation: The development and initial validation of the Cognitive and Affective Mindfulness Scale—Revised (CAMS-R). *Journal of Psychopathology and Behavioral Assessment, 29*, 177–190.

Fjorback, L. O., Arendt, M., Ørnbøl, E., Fink, P., & Walach, H. (2011). Mindfulness-based stress reduction and mindfulness-based cognitive therapy—A systematic review of randomized controlled trials. *Acta Psychiatrica Scandinavica, 124*, 102–119.

Forman, R. K. C. (1990). *The problem of pure consciousness: Mysticism and philosophy.* New York: Oxford University Press.

Forman, R. K. C. (1991). *Meister Eckhart: Mystic as theologian.* Rockport, MA: Element.

Forman, R. K. C. (1998). What does mysticism have to teach us about consciousness? *Journal of Consciousness Studies, 5*, 185–201.

Goleman, D. (1988). *The meditative mind: The varieties of meditative experience.* New York: Tarcher/Putnam.

Gray, E. T., Jr. (1995). *Hafez: The green sea of heaven. 50 Ghazals from the Diwan-i-Hafez.* Ashland, OR: White Cloud Press.

Grossman, P. (2011). Defining mindfulness by how poorly I think I pay attention during everyday awareness and other intractable problems for psychology's (re)invention of mindfulness: Comment on Brown et al. (2011). *Psychological Assessment, 23*, 1034 –1040.

Grossman, P., Niemann, L., Schmidt, S., & Wallach, H. (2004). Mindfulness-based stress reduction and health benefits: A meta-analysis. *Journal of Psychosomatic Research, 57*, 35–43.

Gunaratana, H. (1994). *Mindfulness in plain English.* Boston: Wisdom.

Helminski, K. E. (1992). *Living presence: A Sufi way to mindfulness & the essential self.* New York: Tarcher/Putnam.

Hill, C. L. M., & Updegraff, J. A. (2012). Mindfulness and its relationship to emotional regulation. *Emotion, 12*(1), 81–90.

Hofman, S. G., Sawyer, A. T., Witt, A. A., & Oh, D. (2010). The effect of mindfulness-based therapy on anxiety and depression: A meta-analytic review. *Journal of Clinical and Consulting Psychology, 78*, 169–183.

Izutsu, T. (1977). *Creation and the timeless order of things.* Ashland, OR: White Cloud Press.

Jacobs, T. L., Epel, E. S., Lin, J., Blackburn, E. H., Wolkowitz, O. M., Bridwell, D. A., et al. (2011). Intensive meditation training, immune cell telomerase activity, and psychological mediators. *Psychoneuroendocrinology, 36*, 664–681.

James, W. (1981). *The principles of psychology.* Cambridge, MA: Harvard University Press.

Jensen, C. G., Vangkilde, S., Frokjaer, V., & Hasselbalch, S. G. (2012). Mindfulness training affects attention—Or is it attentional effort? *Journal of Experimental Psychology: General, 141*, 106–123.

Johnston, W. (Ed.). (1973). *The cloud of unknowing and the book of privy counseling.* New York: Image Books.

Keating, T. (1986). *Open mind, open heart: The contemplative dimension of the Gospel.* New York: Continuum.

Keating, T. (1999). *The human condition: Contemplation and transformation.* Mahwah, NJ: Paulist Press.

Kiken, L. G., & Shook, N. J. (2012). Mindfulness and emotional distress: The role of negatively biased cognition. *Personality and Individual Differences, 52*, 329–333.

Kohlberg, L., & Ryncarz, R. A. (1990). Beyond justice reasoning: Moral development and consideration of a seventh stage. In C. Alexander & E. J. Langer (Eds.), *Higher stages of human development* (pp. 191–207). New York: Oxford University Press.

Kornfield, J. (2008). *The wise heart: A guide to the universal teachings of Buddhist psychology.* New York: Bantam.

Langer, E. J. (1989). *Mindfulness.* Cambridge, MA: Perseus Books.

Langer, E. J. (1998). *The power of mindful learning.* Cambridge, MA: Perseus Books.

Langer, E. J., & Moldoveanu, M. (2000). The construct of mindfulness. *Journal of Social Issues, 56*, 1–9.

Lazarus, R. S., & Folkman, S. (1984). *Stress, appraisal, and coping.* New York: Springer.

Leary, M. R., Tipsord, J. M., & Tate, E. B. (2008). Allo-inclusive identity: Incorporating the social and natural worlds into one's sense of self. In H. A. Wayment & J. J. Bauer (Eds.), *Transcending self-interest: Psychological explorations of the quiet ego* (pp. 137–148). Washington, DC: American Psychological Association.

Levenson, M. R., & Crumpler, C. A. (1996). Three models of adult development. *Human Development, 39*, 135–149.

Levenson, M. R., & Khilwati, A. H. (1999). Mystical self-annihilation: Method and meaning. *The International Journal for the Psychology of Religion, 9*, 251–258.

Loy, D. (1988). *Nonduality: A study in comparative philosophy.* New Haven, CT: Yale University Press.

McAdams, D. P. (2008). Generative, the redemptive self, and the problems of a noisy ego in American life. In H. A. Wayment & J. J. Bauer (Eds.), *Transcending self-interest: Psychological explorations of the quiet ego* (pp. 125–242). Washington, DC: American Psychological Association.

McCracken, L., Gauntlett-Gilbert, J., & Vowles, K. E. (2007). The role of mindfulness in a contextual-cognitive-behavioral analysis of chronic pain-related suffering and disability. *Pain, 131*(1), 63–69.

McKee, P., & Barber, C. (1999). On defining wisdom. *International Journal of Aging and Human Development, 49*, 149–164.

Michaelson, J. (2007). *God in your body: Kabbalah, mindfulness, and embodied spirituality.* Woodstock, VT: Jewish Lights.

Miller, J., Fletcher, K., & Kabat-Zinn, J. (1995). Three-year follow-up and clinical implications of a mindfulness-based stress reduction intervention in treatment of anxiety disorders. *General Hospital Psychiatry, 17*, 192–200.

Nanamoli, B., & Bodhi, B. (1995). *The middle-length discourses of the Buddha: A new translation of the Majjhima Nikaya.* Boston: Wisdom.

Noftle, E. E., & Fleeson, W. (2010). Age differences in Big Five behavior averages and variabilities across the adult life span: Moving beyond retrospective, global summary accounts of personality. *Psychology and Aging, 25*, 95–107.

Nanamoli, B. (1975). *The path of purification.* Kandy, Sri Lanka: Buddhist.

Pagels, E. (2003). *Beyond belief: The secret gospel of Thomas.* New York: Random House.

Palmo, A. T. (2002). *Reflections on a mountain lake: Teachings on practical Buddhism.* Ithaca, NY: Snow Lion.

Piedmont, R. L. (1999). Does spirituality represent the sixth factor of personality?: Spiritual transcendence and the five-factor model. *Journal of Personality, 67*, 985–1013.

Roberts, B., & Mroczek, D. (2008). Personality trait change in adulthood. *Current Directions in Psychological Science, 17*, 31–35.

Rosch, E. (2008). Beginner's mind: Paths to the wisdom that is not learned. In M. Ferrari & G. Potworowski (Eds.), *Teaching for wisdom: Cross-cultural perspectives on fostering wisdom* (pp. 135–162). New York: Springer.

Sells, M. A. (2000). *Stations of desire: Love elegies from Ibn 'Arabi and new poems.* Jerusalem: Ibis Editions.

Shapiro, S. L., & Carlson, L. E. (2009). *The art and science of mindfulness: Integrating mindfulness into psychology and the helping professions.* Washington, DC: American Psychological Association.

Shapiro, S. L., Oman, D., Thoresen, C. E., Plante, T. G., & Flinders, T. (2008). Cultivating mindfulness: Effects on well-being. *Journal of Clinical Psychology, 64*, 840–862.

Steinbock, A. J. (2007). *Phenomenology and mysticism: The verticality of religious experience.* Bloomington: Indiana University Press.

Suzuki, S. (1970). *Zen mind, beginner's mind: Informal talks on Zen meditation and practice.* New York: Weatherhill.

van den Hurk, P. A. M., Wingens, T., Giommi, F., Barendregt, H. P., Speckens, A. E. M., & van Schie, H. T. (2011). On the relationship between the practice of mindfulness meditation and personality—An exploratory analysis of the mediating role of mindfulness skills. *Mindfulness, 2*, 194–200.

Wallace, B. A. (2009). *Mind in the balance: Meditation in science, Buddhism, and Christianity.* New York: Columbia University Press.

30

Addressing Religiousness and Spirituality in Psychotherapy

Advancing Evidence-Based Practice

Edward P. Shafranske

With the adoption in 2005 of evidence-based professional practice as the standard in healthcare (American Psychological Association [APA] Presidential Task Force on Evidence-Based Practice, 2006), psychologists are duty-bound to integrate the "best available research with clinical expertise in the context of patient characteristics, culture, and preferences" (p. 273). Psychologists must not only understand and apply science-informed knowledge, but do so in a way that is responsive to a client's multicultural identities, context, and preferences. For many clients (but not all), spirituality is integral to the means by which they establish personal meaning, cope with adversity, and understand their psychological difficulties. This chapter presents theory and research drawn from the psychology of religion and spirituality to establish a foundational clinical approach that is sensitive to clients for whom spirituality is personally salient. Implementation of such an approach requires an intentional focus that is grounded in science-derived knowledge and training rather than rooted in the clinician's personal faith commitments.

By adopting an *intentional orientation,* clinicians are better prepared to understand the contributions of religion/spirituality (R/S) to the client's worldview and as clinical variables relevant to the client's psychological treatment. Such an approach does not minimize appreciation of the other psychological, behavioral, or biological contributions to mental health or compete with or replace other forms of help (Pargament, 2007, p. 21); rather, it aims for a more comprehensive and holistic approach (Shafranske & Sperry, 2005).

A FOUNDATIONAL STANCE TO RELIGIOUSNESS AND SPIRITUALITY AS CLINICAL VARIABLES

Professional competence involves not only knowledge and skills but also attitudes and values. This is particularly important when addressing R/S in the clinical setting. Respecting clients' prerogative in determining what is sacred for them is an essential value. Also, drawing from multicultural psychology, we find that developing awareness of one's personal beliefs (and their possible impacts on clinical understanding and treatment) is fundamental to competently integrate R/S in treatment (Sue, Arredondo, & McDavis, 1992).

Therapists and clients alike strive to make meaning in their lives; however, the pathways and foundational beliefs upon which they construct global meaning often differ (Park, Chapter 18, this volume; Slattery & Park, 2011). Even in cases in which similarities exist (e.g., members of the same religion), individual differences likely occur when R/S beliefs are applied to real-life situations. Also, when therapists and clients share cultural borderlines (areas of overlap between individuals; see Falicov, 1995), the psychologist's sense of connection with the client may unwittingly foreclose meaningful exploration of the client's religiousness or spirituality and empathy may be hindered (Morrison & Borgen, 2010). Therefore, clinicians should actively seek to understand the client's spiritual orientation rather than making assumptions or using religious stereotypes.

Careful consideration of client experience is particularly important given the findings of survey research suggesting that psychologists as a group differ markedly in their general orientation to religion and spirituality and the beliefs they hold compared with the general population. Shafranske and Cummings (2013) examined the body of survey data and concluded that psychologists and psychiatrists are substantially less likely to consider religion personally salient and, although differences appear to close when psychologists are asked about the salience of spirituality, striking differences nevertheless exist, particularly in respect to affiliation with and participation in religion. Therefore, psychologists and other mental health professionals need to be mindful of the likely differences in spiritual orientation and religious preference between themselves and their clients and consider the impacts such differences may make in understanding clients' R/S, in the therapeutic relationship, and on the treatment itself.

In addition to the normative challenges faced when encountering differences in spiritual perspective, Pargament (2007) identified two types of "spiritual dis-integration" that are particularly dangerous: spiritual intolerance and spiritual illiteracy (p. 187). Spiritual intolerance is reflected in forms of rejectionism and exclusivism. In the former, a therapist assumes that spirituality is inherently problematic and a source of pathology to be addressed. While outright antagonism would likely not be expressed by a therapist, more subtle forms of insensitivity or devaluation (reflecting a lack of respect) collapses any useful consideration of R/S and may likely threaten the therapeutic alliance. Such a situation is at variance with professional ethics, which require respectful consideration of multicultural factors such as religion. Spiritual exclusivism rests on "the assumption that there is a single absolute truth and a single best way to approach it" (Pargament, 2007, p. 188). This belief can lead to faulty assumptions about the client's spiritual worldview and obscure important nuances in their expression of faith. Also, potentially valuable resources and perspectives unique to the client's faith tradition may be overlooked. Similar to "colorblindness" as related to race, spiritual blindness can occur when a well-intentioned therapist looks beyond actual differences in beliefs and practices and reaches for or assumes a commonality in spirituality (e.g., "We are all spiritual beings"). Rather than fostering understanding, spiritual blindness disrespects the unique spiritual and/or religious commitments and identity of the client.

Spiritual illiteracy concerns the lack of knowledge about spirituality, including familiarity with the major world religions and spiritual traditions, and knowledge of the theoretical and empirical literature in the psychology of religion and spirituality, especially the contributions relevant to clinical practice. A recent survey found that, on average, Americans correctly answered just 50% of questions on religious knowledge (Pew Research Center's Forum on Religion & Public Life, 2010, p. 6). This finding suggests that without additional education, psychologists (similar to the general population) may be ill informed regarding many of the faith traditions with which their clients affiliate. Such spiritual illiteracy limits the clinician's preparedness to appreciate in a sophisticated way the contributions of R/S to a client's life, difficulties, and solutions. Adopting an intentional orientation requires respectful interest in the client's experience, cultural humility, and a willingness to be taught by the client about his or her religion or spirituality.

Aligned with the objectives of multicultural competence, clinicians are encouraged to consider R/S not in isolation but rather as participating with other cultural identities to form a rich backdrop of individual and collective influences that contribute to a client's meaning making, identity, and affiliations. Building upon a foundation of attitudes and values that promotes respect and offers genuine interest in the client's worldview, knowledge and skills can be developed that prepare the clinician to address R/S in clinical practice.

DOMAINS OF KNOWLEDGE

The study of R/S is a field in itself, and the practicing clinician is not expected to become an expert in that academic discipline; however, therapists should familiarize themselves with scholarship in the psychology of religion and spirituality. They should develop a basic understanding of the nature and functions of R/S, its expressions within the culture in which they practice, the empirical findings concerning R/S and health (Masters & Hooker, Chapter 26, this volume), religious coping (Pargament, Falb, Ano, & Wachholtz, Chapter 28, this volume), and spiritual struggles (Exline & Rose, Chapter 19, this volume).

Religion and Spirituality

No single definition adequately captures the complexity of religion or spirituality, nor does a consensus exist among believers (or clinicians) as to the use of the terms (Oman, Chapter 2, this volume). No matter the precise definitions that are adopted for these constructs, religion and spirituality are best understood as multidimensional constructs, serving multiple purposes, holding multiple consequences (Pargament, Exline, Jones, Mahoney, & Shafranske, 2013; see also Paloutzian & Park, Chapter 1, this volume). Religious or spiritual experience cannot be divorced from institutional, collective, or cultural settings; cognitive beliefs cannot be separated from emotional experiences; ritual participation cannot be disentangled from social support and affiliation; and sources of coping and resilience are not immune from spiritual struggles. Such a perspective challenges the practicing clinician to resist any tendencies toward a simplistic, reductionistic appraisal of R/S in a client's life (Zinnbauer et al., 1997).

The Demographics of Religious Commitment

Demographic research points to a broad landscape of religious and spiritual beliefs and involvement in many countries. For example, 92% of participants in a poll conducted in the United States reported belief in God (Gallup, 2011), and in response to the question, "How important would you say religion is in your own life?" 53% reported "Very Important," 26% "Fairly Important," and 20% "Not Very" (Gallup, 2010b). While these figures suggest strong endorsement of religion, a trend is emerging, particularly within younger cohorts, which forecasts declining involvement and participation in religion. For example, seven in 10 Americans say religion is losing its influence (Gallup, 2010a), and a steep rise has been reported in the number of persons who are "unaffiliated" with religion (16.1%) (Pew Research Center's Forum on Religion & Public Life, 2010). Also, about half of Americans leave the religion in which they were raised at some point in their lives (Pew Research Center's Forum on Religion & Public Life, 2009), reflecting a flux in religious affiliation and involvement. These findings point to the importance of carefully assessing a client's religiousness and spirituality, including changes in affiliation. Also, leaving a faith tradition may reflect a past spiritual struggle in which doctrinal beliefs were no longer held or spiritual needs were unfulfilled. Particularly for the unaffiliated, a void in faith or religious support may result, initiating a pursuit of other sources of meaning or social support, including psychotherapy (Shafranske & Sperry, 2005).

R/S and Mental Health

Religiousness and spirituality are increasingly being studied as clinical factors affecting health (Koenig, 2004, 2008; Masters & Hooker, Chapter 26, this volume), and systematic reviews of the empirical literature have identified clinically relevant associations between R/S and mental health (Koenig, King, & Carson, 2012; Park & Slattery, Chapter 27, this volume). R/S beliefs and practices on the whole appear to be associated with less depression and anxiety (Koenig, 2009, 2010); provide comfort to people when they are experiencing threat or anxiety (Shreve-Neiger & Edelstein, 2004); and religion, however assessed, is a generally protective factor for mental illness (Levin, 2010).

R/S and Coping

Theoretical and empirical research, as well as everyday observation, point to the role of religion and spirituality in coping (Pargament et al., Chapter 28, this volume). Research has found that individuals who used religious coping strategies "typically experience more stress-related growth, spiritual growth, positive affect, and had higher self esteem" (Ano & Vasconcelles, 2005, p. 473) as well as less depression, anxiety, and distress (p. 474). However, not all forms of religious coping are associated with positive gains or support. The use of negative religious coping (e.g., people who felt God was punishing them for their sins) was associated with poorer psychological adjustment, and for some people involvement in religion or spirituality may prompt spiritual struggles, which may undermine their health and well-being (Exline & Rose, Chapter 19, this volume). Clinicians should, therefore, be alert to the presence of signs of spiritual struggle. The nature, use, and effectiveness of religious coping is complex (Gall et al., 2005; Pargament et al., Chapter 28, this volume), and although a full discussion of the topic is beyond the scope of this chapter, the following points (drawn also from Pargament, 2002, 2007) are important for clinicians to consider.

- Religious coping, such as the use of prayer (Masters & Spielmans, 2007), is often turned to when facing extreme situations and psychological and other resources are exhausted.
- The efficacy of religion (and religious coping) is associated with the degree to which it is internalized, intrinsically motivated, well integrated, and based on a secure relationship with God.
- There are advantages and disadvantages to even controversial forms of religion, and the use and effectiveness of religious coping is highly contextual based on the severity of the stressor, individual subjective experience, as well as on social and situational factors, such as the culture's valuation of religion (Gebauer, Sedikides, & Neberich, 2012).
- The use of religious coping does not always lead to healthy adjustment. Certain forms of religious coping (i.e., negative religious coping) are associated with poorer outcomes and spiritual struggles may negatively impact a client's psychological adjustment and emotional well-being.

In keeping with the spirit of evidence-based practice, psychologists should develop familiarity with the theoretical, empirical, and applied/clinical literature in the psychology of religion and spirituality. Fortunately, there is a large and growing body of scholarship and resources to draw upon, including publications in scientific journals, volumes (such as this *Handbook*), clinical applied texts, and training videos (see References for selected resources, indicated by an asterisk following the reference).

ADDRESSING R/S IN THE CLINICAL SETTING

No matter whether the therapeutic approach is named spiritually oriented psychotherapy (Sperry & Shafranske, 2005; Sperry, 2012), theistic psychotherapy (Richards & Bergin, 2005), spiritually integrated psychotherapy (Pargament, 2007), spiritually directive care (Saunders, Miller, & Bright, 2010), or religiously accommodative interventions (Worthington, Hook, Davis, & McDaniel, 2011), clinicians should adopt an intentional, evidence-based orientation in order to offer spiritually conscious care (Saunders et al., 2010). It is important for clinicians to thoughtfully consider this recommendation, since it is necessary to assess whether a client's R/S contributes to his or her presenting difficulties, may impact treatment (involving attitudes, preferences, and barriers to treatment), or offers resources to enhance coping and support the therapeutic process. While not every psychotherapist may feel comfortable or be fully prepared to conduct such an assessment, efforts should be taken to develop the knowledge, skills, and attitudes/values required to enable the clinician to formulate a culturally sensitive, comprehensive understanding of his or her client, which includes his or her R/S.

ASSESSING R/S AS RELEVANT CLINICAL FACTORS

The overarching goal in assessing a client's religiousness and spirituality is to obtain a clinically meaningful understanding of the role R/S plays in their orienting system (i.e., worldview/global life meaning), their use of religious coping and spiritual resources, and the potential impacts of the client's R/S on treatment. The following content areas, drawn from the literature, constitute the foci of a comprehensive R/S assessment:

1. *Salience.* How important is religion and/or spirituality in the life of the client from the client's perspective?
2. *Integration.* In what ways and to what extent does R/S impact the daily life of the client (e.g., influence on values, decision making, and behavior)?
3. *R/S experiences, beliefs, values, affiliations, and practices.* How does the client experience sacredness? What are his or her core beliefs and values? What is the nature of his or her R/S involvement and its impact?
4. *Coping.* To what extent does the client use religious and spiritual sources of coping, and how effective are these resources in enhancing coping and psychological adjustment?
5. *Struggles/conflict.* Are the client's present difficulties related to R/S conflicts or spiritual struggles? (See Exline & Rose, Chapter 19, this volume.) Does the client believe that R/S is a cause of his or her distress? Does the client use negative religious coping, or does the client's thinking include "red flags," such as anger toward God? (See Pargament, 1997, p. 181; Pargament et al., Chapter 28, this volume.) Does the client's psychiatric condition impair his or her use of religious resources (i.e., clinically significant religious impairment)? (See Hathaway, 2003.)
6. *Potential impact on treatment.* Does the client believe that there is a R/S cause for his or her psychological difficulties/distress? Does the client believe that spiritual healing is necessary or plays an important role in his or her treatment? Does the R/S background of the clinician affect the client's participation in treatment? If religiously affiliated, does the client's faith community support mental health treatment?

Given the importance that many people place on religion, engaging the client in a sensitive and respectful inquiry of his or her R/S beliefs, practices, and struggles provides an opportunity for the therapist to demonstrate genuine interest in the client as a whole person, which may also enhance rapport and strengthen the therapeutic alliance. However, for some clients, inquiry into personal beliefs is off-putting, as they may consider such questioning to be irrelevant, intrusive, or unprofessional. Some clients might not have considered that R/S might play a role in their difficulties or offer resources.

Therefore, clinicians should initiate discussion with sensitivity and respect, paying close attention to clients' reactions and level of comfort and should never be performed as a perfunctory information-seeking activity. Any inclusion of R/S in assessment and treatment, beyond the initial inquiry regarding salience, requires clients' formal consent.

Conducting an R/S Assessment

The assessment of clients' religiousness and spirituality is conducted for the purpose of gaining understanding relevant to their psychological treatment. Practically speaking, this means that inquiry into clients' R/S beliefs, practices, religious affiliation, religious history, and so on must be *explicitly* linked to client care and be tailored to the salience of R/S to them. For clients for whom R/S plays a minor role in their lives, a brief assessment is usually sufficient; however, clinicians should remain attuned and "turn on their 'spiritual radars'" (Pargament, 2007, p. 218) to client experiences that reflect forms of implicit spirituality in which sacred qualities may be ascribed to aspects of life, without the use of explicit R/S language or constructs (Pargament & Krumrei, 2009). A comprehensive assessment should be undertaken with clients for whom R/S is integral to their daily lives and in clinical circumstances in which R/S plays a role in their present difficulties or models of coping. While initiated in the intake phase, assessment is a *process* that is ongoing over the course of treatment (Pargament & Krumrei, 2009). The assessment process is of critical importance, since clinicians must make a series of decisions about the nature and the degree to which R/S will be directly integrated in treatment. As presented in Figure 30.1, a logical sequence based on the principles of evidence-based practice is proposed. Commencing with an initial assessment of salience (Stage 1), decisions are made that govern the extent to which further assessment is conducted (Stage 2), which then lead to decisions about the integration of R/S in treatment (Stage 3) and its implementation and evaluation (Stage 4).

Stage 1: Assessment of Salience of R/S

A two-stage approach is recommended in conducting a R/S assessment (Pargament & Krumrei, 2009; Richards & Bergin, 2005; Shafranske, 2005b). The first stage aims to identify the salience of R/S and should be a routine part of intake for all clients. Open-ended questions (e.g., "I was wondering how important is religion or spirituality to you?") are asked to assess the importance the client places on R/S. It important to use inclusive language and mention both religion and spirituality and, following clients' reply, to use their preferred terms. Follow-up questions are offered to better assess the degree of integration in clients' orienting system and daily life (e.g., participation in religion or in R/S observances). Usually clients who are outliers (no R/S involvement or high R/S involvement/integration) spontaneously describe their level of or lack of involvement when asked about salience. For the large group of clients for whom R/S salience is somewhat unclear, prompts may be offered to encourage self-reflection and to make explicit the nature of their R/S involvement. Clients may be asked to discuss previous challenges and difficulties and the means by which they coped with these challenges. These self-reports provide historical snapshots of clients' use of R/S beliefs, attributions, and resources and their effects on coping. The outcome of this initial stage of assessment

Initial Assessment

Preparation for Integration of R/S Interventions

Continuous Assessment

Integration of R/S Interventions

	Stage 1: Assessment of Salience of Religion and Spirituality (R/S)	Stage 2: In-depth Assessment of Contributions of Religiousness and Spirituality (R/S)	Stage 3: Decision Making Regarding the Use of R/S Interventions in Psychological Treatment	Stage 4: Use of R/S Interventions in Psychological Treatment and Assessment of Effectiveness
TASKS	Obtain client self-report of salience of R/S	Conduct assessment of contributions of R/S to orienting system	Assess salience (high salience is required for the integration of R/S interventions in treatment)	Implement the integration of R/S interventions in treatment
	Conduct preliminary assessment of client use of R/S coping/resources	Identify client's use of R/S coping	Identify client preference regarding the integration of R/S interventions in treatment	Assess the impact and effectiveness of R/S interventions
	Conduct preliminary assessment of degree of R/S involvement in orienting system	Identify client's R/S beliefs, affiliations, practices, and involvement in faith community	Assess therapeutic alliance (strong therapeutic alliance is required for the integration of R/S interventions in treatment)	Elicit client feedback
	Identify impairment in R/S functioning or spiritual struggles	Identify client's God concept, God representations,* R/S experiences	Review the best available scientific knowledge on R/S interventions specific to the client's difficulties	Monitor therapeutic alliance
		Identify client's R/S moral proscriptions/prescriptions		

Obtain information about client's R/S, education/developmental milestones/family involvement and its salience	Consider the appropriateness of integrating R/S interventions in light of the goals and tasks of treatment and psychotherapy orientation Clinician self-assessment of expertise in integrating R/S interventions in treatment Assess possible use of consultation, collaboration, or referral Determine integration approach: implicit–explicit, including religious accommodative treatments Obtain explicit client consent to integrate R/S interventions in treatment		Tailor use of R/S interventions in treatment based on client feedback
CRITERIA FOR USE Perform Stage 1 with all clients	Perform Stage 2 with clients for whom R/S has high salience	Perform Stage 3 with clients for whom R/S has high salience and who express a preference for inclusion of R/S in treatment	Perform Stage 4 with clients who have given explicit consent to integrate R/S interventions in treatment

FIGURE 30.1. A model for the integration of religious and spiritual interventions in psychological treatment.

*In theistic R/S traditions.

is the clear understanding of the importance of R/S for the clients and the extent to which R/S is integrated into their daily lives.

Stage 2: In-Depth Assessment of Contributions of R/S

A second stage of assessment is recommended when R/S (1) figures prominently in clients' worldview, (2) is involved in their coping, or (3) presents the potential to serve as a resource or a barrier to the therapeutic process, (4) when R/S problems are themselves the focus of clinical attention (American Psychiatric Association, 2013), or (5) when clients' psychological or psychiatric difficulties trigger spiritual crises or impair their involvement in religion or the use of religious or spiritual resources (Hathaway, 2003). Additionally, further assessment is warranted when psychological crisis has led to a strain, change, or loss in spiritual orientation, particularly for those for whom R/S had previously played a significant role (Pargament, 2007), and when R/S problems, including spiritual struggles (Exline & Rose, Chapter 19, this volume), are identified. Such problems include religious rigidity, histories in which clients have felt victimized by their religious traditions or by their religious leaders, and feeling one has been damaged by one's religious traditions (e.g., nonacceptance of sexual orientation), or holding religious viewpoints that are damaging to themselves or others (Plante, 2011).

While a consensus on a universally accepted structured interview for R/S assessment has not been achieved, the content areas for assessment can be readily been culled from the literature (see Hodge, 2013; Pargament & Krumrei, 2009). Plante (2009) enumerates categories that are widely accepted as areas for inquiry: metaphysical worldview, religious affiliation, religious orthodoxy, religious problem-solving style, spiritual identity, God image, value–lifestyle congruence, doctrinal knowledge, and religious and spiritual health and maturity.

A combination of open-ended and closed questions, reflection, and empathy may be used to facilitate a collaborative inquiry with the client to explore the role of R/S. The clinician should follow the client's lead as his or her spiritual narrative unfolds while keeping in mind the clinical aim of the assessment, which includes consideration of the role of R/S in the client's problems as well as potentially as resources in healing. Assessment is, for the most part, transtheoretical in approach; however, theoretical orientation may influence the particular focus or emphasis taken. For example, within cognitive-behavioral therapy, inquiry may be directed on assessing cognitive distortions, dysfunctional schemas, and the client's *style* of thinking about his or her relationship with God (cf. Nielson, Johnson, & Ellis, 2001, p. 113) that may contribute to the development or alleviation of symptoms (Tan, 2013; Tan & Johnson, 2005). Alternatively, psychoanalysts have greater interest in the nature and function of God representations and in the role R/S plays in intrapsychic conflict and compromise formation (Rizzuto, 2005; Rizzuto & Shafranske, 2013; Shafranske, 2005a, 2009). The client's expressed relationship with God may provide a window into the client's relational capacities and attachment style (Kirkpatrick, Chapter 6, this volume).

In addition to the clinical interview, spiritual and religious life maps can provide clients with a process that incorporates recollection, reflection and depiction of the significant events making up their R/S journey (Hodge, 2005, 2013; Wiggins, 2009). The procedure serves as both a therapeutic and an assessment tool, since clients actively reflect on their life experience, situate their present difficulties within a broad context of their lives (as illustrated in the life map), and may gain insight into the role of R/S in their lives when creating the life map. Similarly, the use of a R/S genogram provides a means to depict the individuals who played a role in the clients' R/S history and to explore the role and functions of religion and spirituality as well as divergences, and problems can be explored from intergenerational and systems perspectives (Frame, 2003; Hodge, 2001). These approaches should not be routinely used in assessment but rather are available for use with clients who are comfortable with such visual modes of expression. Also, emphasis is placed on the processes of reflection and insight rather than simply on the information that is depicted.

Instruments developed within the psychology of R/S may also be used to supplement interview data, although few have been systematically evaluated for their application in clinical practice and, more to the point, challenges exist as a result of imprecision in the definition of the constructs measured (see Hill, Chapter 3, this volume; Kapuscinski & Masters, 2010, for discussion of the current status of measures of spirituality). Pargament and Krumrei (2009) identified 14 instruments relevant to assessing spirituality in psychotherapy, among them the National Institute on Aging/Fetzer Short Form for the Measurement of Religiousness and Spirituality (Idler et al., 2003) and the Religious Comfort Scale (Exline, Yali, & Sanderson, 2000). Measures developed by Pargament and colleagues provide valuable empirically supported approaches to assess religious coping (see Pargament et al., Chapter 28, this volume).

INTEGRATING SPIRITUALITY IN PSYCHOLOGICAL TREATMENT

Information obtained during the assessment process informs clinical decision making regarding the incorporation of R/S in treatment. The use of an *intentional orientation* promotes congruence between the salience of R/S for the client and the inclusion of R/S perspectives and resources in treatment. The decision to integrate R/S into treatment should not be based on the psychotherapist's personal faith orientation; rather, it should correspond to the salience and function of R/S in the client's life and with the client's explicit consent. Such decisions, consistent with the principles of evidence-based practice, draw upon the best available scientific knowledge, taking into consideration the scope of the clinician's competence and tailored to the mutually defined goals and tasks of the treatment and client preferences.

Stage 3: Decision Making Regarding the Use of R/S Interventions in Psychological Treatment

Tan (1996) proposed a model that presents two distinct forms of integration, which exist on a continuum. *Implicit integration* refers to "a more covert approach that does not initiate the discussion of religious or spiritual issues and does not openly, directly, or systematically use spiritual resources like prayer and Scripture or other sacred texts in therapy . . . [and] *Explicit integration,* a more overt approach that directly and systematically deals with spiritual or religious issues in therapy, and uses spiritual resources like prayer, Scripture or sacred texts, referrals to church or other religious groups or lay counselors, and other religious practices" (cf. p. 368). Plante (2009) identified 13 tools originating in religious and spiritual traditions that can be incorporated into psychological treatment: prayer; meditation; meaning, purpose, and calling in life; bibliotherapy; attendance in community services and rituals; volunteerism; ethical values and behavior; forgiveness, gratitude, and kindness; social justice; learning from spiritual models; acceptance of self and others (even with faults); being part of something larger than oneself; and appreciating the sacredness of life.

In addition to salience, the psychotherapy approach also prescribes the nature of integration and delimits the kinds of religious or spiritual interventions to be employed. In cognitive-behavioral psychotherapy, for example, explicit forms of integration may be readily assimilated, such as collaboratively examining with the client his or her use of Scripture in making attributions about behavior. Psychodynamic and other insight-oriented approaches usually employ implicit integration, in which religious content is addressed through exploration and interpretation consistent with the clinician's usual mode of activity. A comprehensive discussion of the ways in which each therapeutic modality may approach integration is beyond the scope of this chapter. However, there are a number of clinical texts that contain exemplar clinical illustrations of integration (e.g., Sperry & Shafranske, 2005).

These approaches place emphasis on integrating R/S as clinically relevant dimensions into existing secular therapeutic frameworks and do not challenge the implicit epistemic, values-based foundations of the therapeutic modalities or require accommodation to a spiritual worldview. Worthington, Hook, Davis, and McDaniel (2011) refer to treatments that modify an existing secular treatment to include methods and goals that are religious in nature or psychological treatments created specifically for use with specific religious or spiritual people as *religiously accommodative treatments*.

Models have also been developed that draw more liberally from an integration of psychological and religious-spiritual worldviews (see, e.g., the use of the Eight-Point Program empirically studied by Oman, Hedberg, & Thorsen, 2006). Clinical models have been developed (although relatively few have been scientifically evaluated or presented within mainstream clinical training) that integrate secular and religious viewpoints (e.g., Buddhist, Christian, Jewish, and Muslim) beliefs, traditions, and healing practices (Richards & Bergin, 2000, 2004, 2005). There are also approaches, such as Alcoholics Anonymous programs, that offer a spiritual perspective without being situated within particular religious traditions. Although many questions remain concerning the functional contributions of spirituality (Tonigan, Toscova, & Connors, 1999), 12-step programs illustrate the potential benefits of integrating a spiritual dimension.

There are also clinical models that involve integration at the most fundamental level and are based on a theistic, spiritual view of human nature and of the world (Richards & Bergin, 2005; Richards, 2005). Such approaches bring directly into the therapeutic relationship the faith commitments of both the client and the clinician, belief in the healing power of God, consideration of a theistic moral framework, and the explicit use of spiritual inventions, such as prayer, scripture, spiritual direction, or meditation practices (Richards, 2005). In such approaches, psychological and spiritual dimensions may be viewed as distinct, parallel, and complementary trajectories, as interwoven, or in which the psychological is subsumed into the spiritual (Sperry & Shafranske, 2005; Sperry, 2012). Such forms of explicit integration challenge assumptions about therapeutic neutrality and call into question the boundary between professional practices that appropriately bring R/S into treatment and conduct that skirts professional standards. Thoughtful consideration of ethics and clinical decision making based on the best available theoretical and empirical literature provide safeguards against unprofessional and unethical practice. Fortunately, an emerging body of empirical research can be drawn upon to inform decisions about integration.

Evidence-Based Practice and Empirically Supported Treatment

Evidence-based practice is the standard for professional practice in psychology and requires that "the best available research" be considered, together with client preferences and clinical expertise, when making clinical decisions (APA Presidential Task Force on Evidence-Based Practice, 2006). Therefore, treatments that have received empirical support for their efficacy should be carefully considered when making treatment decisions. Reviews of the empirical literature (Hook et al., 2010; Post & Wade, 2009; Smith, Bartz, & Richards, 2007; Wade, Worthington, & Vogel, 2007; Walker, Gorsuch, & Tan, 2004) point to the effectiveness of religiously accommodative treatments. For example, Christian accommodative cognitive-behavior therapy for depression and 12-step facilitation for alcoholism were deemed efficacious, and two R/S treatments for depression and for anxiety were found to be efficacious when combined with medication (Hook et al., 2010). While religious accommodative treatments have been found to work as well as secular treatments, there is insufficient evidence to establish that such treatments work better (Worthington et al., 2013). Such treatments offer religious clients alternatives to secular treatments and are responsive to their preferences.

Client Preference and the Integration of R/S Interventions and Resources

Client preference plays an essential role in determining whether or not R/S is addressed in treatment. Many clients, when seeking healthcare, prefer physicians and other providers to be mindful of their spirituality. For example, MacLean et al. (2003) reported that one-third of medical patients wanted to be asked about their religious beliefs and two-thirds felt that physicians should be aware of their beliefs (p. 38). According to a national survey of 1,000 likely voters conducted by Greenberg Quinlan Research (American Association of Pastoral Counselors Samaritan Institute, 2000), 83% of respondents said they thought there was a relationship between spiritual faith/religious beliefs and mental and emotional health, and 75% stated it was important to see a professional counselor who would consider and integrate their values and beliefs into the counseling process (see also Rose, Westefeld, & Ansley, 2001).

Integrating R/S Interventions and Resources in Professional Practice

In addition to client preference, surveys of psychotherapists indicate that R/S issues often are involved in treatment (Delaney, Miller, & Bisonó, 2007; Frazier & Hansen, 2009; Shafranske & Cummings, 2013). For example, respondents to an online survey of over 200 psychologists, employing a real-time behavior sampling (RTBS) methodology, reported that spirituality contributed to the solution in 37% of the cases and were involved in both problem and solution in 26% (American Psychological Association Practice Directorate, 2003).

While it appears that the majority of psychologists believe that R/S is clinically relevant, there is not a clear consensus as to how such integration should be accomplished. A range of interventions, reflecting varying degrees of explicit integration of R/S perspectives and practices, are available. For example, Richards and Bergin (2005, pp. 234–235) identified 19 examples of R/S interventions that could be applied within explicit integration, including therapist prayer, teaching scriptural concepts, reference to scripture, spiritual self-disclosure, spiritual confrontation, spiritual assessment, religious relaxation or imagery, therapist and client prayer, blessing by therapist, encouragement for forgiveness, use of religious community, client prayer, encouragement of client confession, referral for blessing, religious journal writing, spiritual meditation, religious bibliotherapy, Scripture memorization, and dream interpretation. Most psychologists say they address R/S at least sometimes through general, basic therapy behaviors, such as assessing their clients' R/S beliefs and practices (Delaney et al., 2007); however, it appears less common for psychologists to use active interventions that deal with R/S more explicitly, such as prayer and citing religious texts (Frazier & Hansen, 2009; Shafranske, 1996, 2001), and relatively little is known about the actual "in-the-moment" decision-making processes clinicians employ. Reviews of the literature (Worthington, Kurusu, McCullough, & Sandage, 1996; Worthington & Sandage, 2001, 2002) suggest that the use of R/S interventions (1) does not appear to be consistent or systematic across clinicians; (2) is influenced by the personal commitments of the clinicians; and (3) varies according to the degree of involvement of the clinician in the performance of explicit R/S behavior (Shafranske, 1996, 2000; Shafranske & Cummings, 2013). Inconsistencies appear to exist between espoused beliefs and attitudes and actual professional practices. For example, according to Hathaway, Scott, and Garver (2004), over 80% of respondents in their national survey of psychologists believe that "religious/spiritual functioning is a significant and important domain in human adjustment," yet "over half reported asking about client religiousness or spirituality 50% of the time or less" and 12% and 18% reported that they never asked "about client religiousness or spirituality, respectively, during assessment" (p. 100). This inconsistency may suggest that clinicians are uncertain as to how far to go in integrating R/S in treatment.

Personal R/S commitment of the clinician appears to play a significant role in the psychologist's practice of integration: The more clinicians self-identify as religious, the more likely they are to integrate R/S interventions in treatment (Shafranske & Cummings, 2013). Also, as the intervention becomes more active and requires direct clinician participation (e.g., prayer), endorsement and performance of the intervention decrease (Shafranske, 1996, 2000, 2001). Interestingly, clients may also hesitate when R/S interventions more directly involve the participation of the clinician. Whereas 33% of patients endorsed discussion of spiritual issues with their physicians, only 19% agreed that the doctor should pray with a patient (MacLean et al., 2003).

A guiding principle, when considering the use of R/S interventions in professional practice, is to first identify the naturally occurring use of spiritual resources by the client. The clinician then discusses with the client possible inclusion of such resources into treatment. The aim of spiritually oriented approaches in psychotherapy is to develop a place in the therapeutic process for the *client's* spirituality and to support his or her use of these personal R/S resources. Clinicians should approach decision making and the process of integration with sensitivity and deep respect for client autonomy and with a foundation of knowledge and training. Therapists should also consider whether the consultation, collaboration with or referral to a religious professional (e.g., rabbi, minister, imam) or pastoral counselor is appropriate.

Stage 4: Use of R/S Interventions in Psychological Treatment and Assessment of Effectiveness

Clinicians should initiate the use of R/S interventions only after conducting a thorough R/S assessment (Stages 1 and 2), evaluating the appropriateness of the inclusion of such interventions in light of the scientific literature, treatment plan, client preferences, and therapist expertise and following discussion with the client and obtaining his or her consent. Even though formal consent has been obtained, it is important to elicit input and consent when introducing specific interventions (e.g., prayer). Also, it is important to continuously monitor the impact of the interventions on the therapeutic alliance and to engage the client in collaborative inquiry about his or her level of comfort as well as the usefulness of the interventions. Client feedback should then be used to tailor the interventions to the client's level of comfort and self-report of usefulness. Clinicians should commit to self-assessment regarding their ability to competently integrate R/S resources in treatment or to implement religious accommodative treatment with fidelity to the protocol, draw upon the clinical literature for guidance, and seek consultation as appropriate to ensure client welfare and effective treatment.

EDUCATION AND TRAINING

Historically, most psychologists and other mental health professionals have received minimal or no education and training in assessing R/S as clinical variables or in the use of R/S interventions (Frazier & Hansen, 2009; Hage, Hopson, Siegel, Payton, & DeFanti, 2006; Shafranske & Cummings, 2013). While there is some evidence of increases in coverage, although minimal, in graduate coursework and in supervision, recent survey data suggest no systematic improvement in the preparation psychologists receive to address client R/S in professional practice (Schafer, Handal, Brawer, & Ubinger, 2011). This finding is consistent with earlier studies of counseling, clinical, and psychology and counseling programs accredited by the Council for Accreditation of Counseling and Related Educational Programs (CACREP) (Brawer, Handal, Fabricatore, Roberts, & Wajda-Johnston, 2002; Schulte, Skinner, & Claiborn, 2002; Young, Cashwell, Wiggins-Frame, & Belaire, 2002). Although the groundswell of research as well as continued efforts to ensure diversity competence may prompt increased attention to R/S as relevant to clinical practice, at present there is no evidence to suggest significant curricular investment to ensure systematic and comprehensive education and training in this area. Doctoral programs that have as their mission the explicit integration of a faith dimension will continue to train psychologists to employ R/S approaches consistent with their faith tradition. Clinical supervision provides additional opportunities to assist novice clinicians to become sensitive and effective in addressing R/S issues (Miller, Korinek, & Ivey, 2004; Polanski, 2003;

Shafranske & Vargas, in press). The development of competence in understanding the contributions of R/S to mental health as well as in the applied psychology of religion, in the near term, is likely to rest on unique training experiences rather than on systematic attention throughout all levels of graduate education and clinical training. Personal faith commitment of the clinician will continue to serve as the primary source of motivation in obtaining training in this competency area.

ETHICS

Guidelines exist regarding the requirement of taking R/S into consideration as a feature of diversity (APA 2002a, 2002b), including a 2007 resolution of the APA Council of Representatives addressing religious prejudice (APA Presidential Working Group, 2008). However, psychologists face a number of ethical challenges when addressing client beliefs and values and integrating R/S interventions and resources in psychological treatment. While a comprehensive review of the relevant literature (e.g., Gonsiorek, Richards, Pargament, & McMinn, 2009; Hathaway, 2011) is beyond the scope of this chapter, ethical challenges commonly described include professional competence (in light of the minimal education and clinical training generally offered as described by Shafranske and Cummings, 2013); dual-role and boundary conflicts (imposing personal beliefs/values or displacing or usurping R/S authority); bias/prejudice or spiritual intolerance; failure to obtain informed consent; and failure to seek appropriate consultation, collaboration, or referral (McMinn, Aikins, & Lish, 2003). Richards (Gonsiorek et al., 2009, p. 389) poses four questions to stimulate self-reflection and facilitate metacompetence:

1. Do I have the ability to create a spiritually safe and affirming therapeutic environment for my clients?
2. Do I have the ability to conduct an effective religious and spiritual assessment of my clients?
3. Do I have the ability to use or encourage religious and spiritual interventions, if indicated, in order to help clients access the resources of their faith and spirituality during treatment and recovery?
4. Do I have the ability to effectively consult and collaborate with, and when needed, refer to clergy and other pastoral professionals?

Reflection on these questions, review of the preliminary practice guidelines proposed by APA Division 36 (Hathaway, 2011), as well as application of the principles set forth in the Code of Ethics (APA, 2002a) and the policy on evidence-based practice (APA Presidential Task Force on Evidence-Based Practice, 2006) provide a foundation for ethical practice.

CONCLUSION

Evidence-based professional practice (APA Presidential Task Force on Evidence-Based Practice, 2006) requires consideration of client characteristics, culture, and preferences as well as knowledge of and application of the best available research evidence, together with clinical expertise. The application of knowledge and skills, drawing in part from the psychology of R/S and informed by respectful appreciation of the pathways by which clients make meaning and relate to whatever they consider sacred, prepares psychologists and other mental health professionals to respond more fully to the clinical needs of clients. Continuing advances in applied scholarship and enhanced education and training will set the stage for increased consideration of religiousness and spirituality as clinical factors and the appropriate integration of R/S resources in psychological treatment.

REFERENCES

Note: Resources that are specifically intended to assist clinicians to develop competence in the use of R/S interventions in psychological treatment are indicated by an asterisk (*) following the reference, and resources that are also cited in the chapter are indicated by two asterisks (**).

American Association of Pastoral Counselors Samaritan Institute. (2000). Report. *www.google. com/search?ix=ucb&sourceid=chrome&ie=UTF-8&q=American+Association+of+Pastoral +Counselors+Samaritan+Institute+Report+2000*

American Psychiatric Association. (2013). *Diagnostic and statistical manual of mental disorders* (5th ed.). Washington, DC: Author.

American Psychological Association. (2002a). *Ethical principles of psychologists and code of conduct 2002*. Retrieved May 1, 2003, from *www.apa.org/ethics/code2002.html*.

American Psychological Association. (2002b). *Guidelines for multicultural education, training, research, practice, and organizational change for psychologists*. Washington, DC: Author.

American Psychological Association. (2004–2011). *The American Psychological Association spirituality video series*. Washington, DC: Author. (*)

American Psychological Association Practice Directorate. (2003). *PracticeNet survey: Clinical practice patterns*. Retrieved December 1, 2004, from *www.apapracticenet.net/results/Summer2003/2.asp*.

American Psychological Association Presidential Task Force on Evidence-Based Practice. (2006). Evidence-based practice in psychology. *American Psychologist, 61*(4), 271–285.

American Psychological Association Presidential Working Group. (2008). Resolution on religious, religion-based, and/or religion-derived prejudice. *American Psychologist, 63*, 431–434.

Ano, G. G., & Vasconcelles, E. B. (2005). Religious coping and psychological adjustment to stress: A meta-analysis. *Journal of Clinical Psychology, 61*, 461–480.

Aten, J. D., & Leach, M. M. (Eds.). (2008). *Spirituality and the therapeutic process: A comprehensive resource from intake to termination*. Washington, DC: American Psychological Association. (*)

Aten, J. D., McMinn, M. R., & Worthington, E. L., Jr. (2011). *Spiritually oriented interventions for counseling and psychotherapy*. Washington, DC: American Psychological Association. (*)

Brawer, P. A., Handal, P. J., Fabricatore, A. N., Roberts, R., & Wajda-Johnston, V. A. (2002). Training and education in religion/spirituality within APA-accredited clinical psychology programs. *Professional Psychology: Research and Practice, 33*, 203–206.

Cashwell, C. S., & Young, J. S. (2011). *Integrating spirituality and religion into counseling*. Alexandria, VA: American Counseling Association. (*)

Delaney, H. D., Miller, W. R., & Bisonó, A. M. (2007). Religiosity and spirituality among psychologists: A survey of clinician members of the American Psychological Association. *Professional Psychology: Research and Practice, 38*, 538–546.

Exline, J. J., Yali, A. M., & Sanderson, W. C. (2000). Guilt, discord, and alienation: The role of religious strain in depression and suicidality. *Journal of Clinical Psychology, 56*, 1481–1496.

Falicov, C. J. (1995). Training to think culturally: A multidimensional comparative framework. *Family Process, 34*, 373–388.

Frame, M. W. (2003). *Integrating religion and spirituality into counseling.* Pacific Grove, CA: Thomson Brooks/Cole. (**)

Frazier, R. E., & Hansen, N. (2009). Religious/spiritual psychotherapy behaviors: Do we do what we believe to be important? *Professional Psychology: Research and Practice, 40*, 81–87.

Fukuyama, M. A., & Sevig, T. D. (1999). *Integrating spirituality into multicultural counseling.* Thousand Oaks, CA: Sage. (*)

Gall, T. L., Charbonneau, C., Clarke, N., Grant, K., Joseph, A., & Shouldice, L. (2005). Understanding the nature and role of spirituality in relation to coping and health: A conceptual framework. *Canadian Psychology/Psychologie Canadienne, 46*, 88–104.

Gallup. (2010a). *Near-record high see religion losing influence in America.* Retrieved January 5, 2012, from *www.gallup.com/poll/145409/Near-record-high-religion-losing-influence-america.aspx.*

Gallup. (2010b). *USA Today/Gallup Poll, December wave 1.* Retrieved October 1, 2011, from *http://cnsnews.com/sites/default/files/documents/GALLUP-MOST%20ADMIRED-2011.pdf.*

Gallup. (2011). *More than 9 in 10 Americans continue to believe in God.* Retrieved October 1, 2011, from *www.gallup.com/poll/147887/Americans-Continue-Believe-God.aspx.*

Gebauer, J. E., Sedikides, C., & Neberich, W. (2012). Religiosity, social self-esteem, and psychological adjustment: On the cross-cultural specificity of the psychological benefits of religiosity. *Psychological Science, 23*(2), 158–160.

Gonsiorek, J. C., Richards, P., Pargament, K. I., & McMinn, M. R. (2009). Ethical challenges and opportunities at the edge: Incorporating spirituality and religion into psychotherapy. *Professional Psychology: Research and Practice, 40*, 385–395. (**)

Hage, S. M., Hopson, A., Siegel, M., Payton, G., & Defanti, E. (2006). Multicultural training in spirituality: An interdisciplinary review. *Counseling & Values, 50*, 217–234.

Hathaway, W. L. (2003). Clinically significant religious impairment. *Mental Health, Religion & Culture, 6*, 39–55.

Hathaway, W. L. (2011). Ethical guidelines for using spiritually oriented interventions. In J. D. Aten, M. R. McMinn, & E. R. Worthington (Eds.), *Spiritually oriented interventions for counseling and psychotherapy* (pp. 65–81). Washington, DC: American Psychological Association. (**)

Hathaway, W. L., Scott, S. Y., & Garver, S. A. (2004). Assessing religious/spiritual functioning: A neglected domain in clinical practice. *Professional Psychology: Research and Practice, 35*, 97–104. (**)

Hodge, D. R. (2001). Spiritual assessment: A review of major qualitative methods and a new framework for assessing spirituality. *Social Work, 46*, 203–214. (**)

Hodge, D. R. (2005). Spiritual life maps: A client-centered pictorial instrument for spiritual assessment, planning, and intervention. *Social Work, 50*, 77–87. (**)

Hodge, D. R. (2013) Assessing spirituality and religion in the context of counseling and psychotherapy. In K. Pargament, A. Mahoney & E. Shafranske (Eds.), *APA handbook of psychology, religion, and spirituality: Volume 2* (pp. 93–123). Washington, DC: American Psychological Association. (**)

Hook, J. N., Worthington, E. R., Davis, D. E., Jennings, D., Gartner, A. L., & Hook, J. P. (2010). Empirically supported religious and spiritual therapies. *Journal of Clinical Psychology, 66*, 46–72. (**)

Idler, E. L., Musick, M. A., Ellison, C. G., George, L. K., Krause, N., Ory, M. G., et al. (2003). Measuring multiple dimensions of religion and spirituality for health research: Conceptual background and findings from the 1998 General Social Survey. *Research on Aging, 25*, 327–365.

Kapuscinski, A. N., & Masters, K. S. (2010). The current status of measures of spirituality: A critical review of scale development. *Psychology of Religion and Spirituality, 2,* 191–205.

Koenig, H. G. (2004). Religion, spirituality, and medicine: Research findings and implications for Clinical Practice. *Southern Medical Journal, 97*(12), 1194–1200.

Koenig, H. G. (2008). *Medicine, religion, and health: Where science and spirituality meet.* West Conshohocken, PA: Templeton Foundation Press.

Koenig, H. G. (2009). Research on religion, spirituality, and mental health: A review. *Canadian Journal of Psychiatry, 54,* 283–291.

Koenig, H. G. (2010). Spirituality and mental health. *International Journal of Applied Psychoanalytic Studies, 7,* 116–122.

Koenig, H. G., King, D. E., & Carson, V. B. (2012). *Handbook of religion and health* (2nd ed.). New York: Oxford University Press.

Levin, J. (2010). Religion and mental health: Theory and research. *International Journal of Applied Psychoanalytic Studies, 7,* 102–115.

MacLean, C. D., Susa, B., Phifer, N., Bynum, D., Franco, M., Klioze, A., et al. (2003). Patient preference for physician discussion and practice of spirituality: Results from a multicenter patient survey. *Journal of General Internal Medicine, 18,* 38–43.

Masters, K. S., & Spielmans, G. I. (2007). Prayer and health: Review, meta-analysis, and research agenda. *Journal of Behavioral Medicine, 30,* 329–338.

McMinn, M. R., Aikins, D. C., & Lish, R. A. (2003). Basic and advanced competence in collaborating with clergy. *Professional Psychology: Research and Practice, 34*(2), 197–202. (**)

Miller, G. A. (2003). *Incorporating spirituality in counseling and psychotherapy.* New York: Wiley. (*)

Miller, M., Korinek, A. W., & Ivey, D. C. (2004). Integrating spirituality into training: The Spiritual Issues in Supervision Scale. *American Journal of Family Therapy, 34,* 355–372.

Miller, W. R. (1999). *Integrating spirituality into treatment: Resources for practitioners.* Washington, DC: American Psychological Association. (*)

Morrison, M., & Borgen, W. A. (2010). How Christian spiritual and religious beliefs help and hinder counselors' empathy toward clients. *Counseling & Values, 55(1),* 25–45.

Nielson, S. L., Johnson, W. B., & Ellis, A. (2001). *Counseling and psychotherapy with religious persons: A rational emotive behavior therapy approach.* Mahwah, NJ: Erlbaum. (**)

Oman, D., Hedberg, J., & Thoresen, C. E. (2006). Passage meditation reduces perceived stress in health professionals: A randomized, controlled trial. *Journal of Consulting and Clinical Psychology, 74,* 714–719.

Pargament, K. I. (1997). *The psychology of religion and coping.* New York: Guilford Press. (**)

Pargament, K. I. (2002). The bitter and the sweet: An evaluation of the costs and benefits of religiousness. *Psychological Inquiry, 13,* 168–181.

Pargament, K. I. (2007). *Spiritually integrated psychotherapy: Understanding and addressing the sacred.* New York: Guilford Press. (**)

Pargament, K. I., & Krumrei, E. J. (2009). Clinical assessment of clients' spirituality. In J. D. Aten, M. M. Leach, J. D. Aten, M. M. Leach (Eds.), *Spirituality and the therapeutic process: A comprehensive resource from intake to termination* (pp. 93–120). Washington, DC: American Psychological Association. (**)

Pargament, K. I., Mahoney, A., Exline, J. J., Jones, J. W., & Shafranske, E. P. (2013). Envisioning an integrative paradigm for the psychology of religion and spirituality. In K. I. Pargament, J. J. Exline, & J. W. Jones (Eds.), *APA handbook of psychology, religion, and spirituality (Vol. 1): Context, theory, and research* (pp. 3–19). Washington, DC: American Psychological Association.

Pargament, K. I., Mahoney, A., & Shafranske, E. (2013). *APA handbook of psychology, religion, and spirituality: Volume 2.* Washington, DC: American Psychological Association. (*)

Peteet, J., Lu, F., & Narrow, W. (Eds.). (2011). *Religious and spiritual issues in psychiatric diagnosis: A research agenda for DSM V.* Washington, DC: American Psychiatric Publishing. (*)

Pew Research Center's Forum on Religion & Public Life. (2009). *Faith in flux*. Retrieved March 1, 2011, from *www.pewforum.org/newassets/images/reports/flux/fullreport.pdf*.

Pew Research Center's Forum on Religion & Public Life. (2010). *U.S. religious knowledge survey*. Retrieved October 1, 2011, from *www.pewforum.org/U-S-Religious-Knowledge-Survey-Who-Knows-What-About-Religion.aspx*.

Plante, T. G. (2009). *Spiritual practices in psychotherapy: Thirteen tools for enhancing psychological health*. Washington, DC: American Psychological Association. (**)

Plante, T. G. (2011). Addressing problematic spirituality in therapy. In J. D. Aten, M. R. McMinn, & E. R. Worthington (Eds.), *Spiritually oriented interventions for counseling and psychotherapy* (pp. 83–106). Washington, DC: American Psychological Association. (**)

Polanski, P. J. (2003). Spirituality in supervision. *Counseling & Values, 47*, 131–141.

Post, B. C., & Wade, N. G. (2009). Religion and spirituality in psychotherapy: A practice-friendly review of research. *Journal of Clinical Psychology, 65*, 131–146. (**)

Richards, P. S. (2005). Theistic psychotherapy approach. In L. Sperry & E. P. Shafranske (Eds.), *Spiritually oriented psychotherapy* (pp. 259–285). Washington, DC: American Psychological Association. (**)

Richards, P. S., & Bergin, A. E. (Eds.). (2000). *Handbook of psychotherapy and religious diversity*. Washington, DC: American Psychological Association. (**)

Richards, S., & Bergin, A. E. (Eds.). (2004). *Religion and psychotherapy: A casebook*. Washington, DC: American Psychological Association. (**)

Richards, P., & Bergin, A. E. (2005). *A spiritual strategy for counseling and psychotherapy* (2nd ed.). Washington, DC: American Psychological Association. (**)

Richards, P. S., Hardman, R. K., & Berrett, M. E. (2007). *Spiritual approaches in the treatment of women with eating disorders*. Washington, DC: American Psychological Association. (*)

Rizzuto, A.-M. (2005). Psychoanalytic considerations about spiritually psychotherapy. In L. Sperry & E. P. Shafranske (Eds.), *Spiritually oriented psychotherapy* (pp. 31–50). Washington, DC: American Psychological Association. (**)

Rizutto, A.-M., & Shafranske, E. P. (2013). Addressing religion and spirituality in treatment from a psychodynamic perspective. In K. Pargament, A. Mahoney, & E. Shafranske (Eds.), *APA handbook of psychology, religion, and spirituality: Volume 2* (pp. 125–146). Washington, DC: American Psychological Association. (**)

Rose, E. M., Westefeld, J. S., & Ansley, T. N. (2001). Spiritual issues in counseling: Clients' beliefs and preferences. *Journal of Counseling Psychology, 48*, 61–71.

Saunders, S. M., Miller, M. L., & Bright, M. M. (2010). Spiritually conscious psychological care. *Professional Psychology: Research and Practice, 41*, 355–362. (**)

Schafer, R., Handal, P., Brawer, P., & Ubinger, M. (2011). Training and education in religion/spirituality within APA-accredited clinical psychology programs: 8 years later. *Journal of Religion and Health, 50*, 32–39.

Schulte, D. L., Skinner, T. A., & Claiborn, C. D. (2002). Religious and spiritual issues in counseling psychology training. *The Counseling Psychologist, 30*, 118–134.

Shafranske, E. P. (1996). Religious beliefs, affiliations, and practices of clinical psychologists. In E. Shafranske (Ed.), *Religion and the clinical practice of psychology* (pp. 149–162). Washington, DC: American Psychological Association.

Shafranske, E. P. (2000). Religious involvement and professional practices of psychiatrists and other mental health professionals. *Psychiatric Annals, 30*(8), 1–8.

Shafranske, E. P. (2001). The religious dimension of patient care within rehabilitation medicine. The role of religious beliefs, attitudes, and personal and professional practices. In T. G. Plante & A. C. Sherman (Eds.), *Faith and health: Psychological perspectives* (pp. 311–335). New York: Guilford Press.

Shafranske, E. P. (2005a). Psychoanalytic approach. In L. Sperry & E. P. Shafranske (Eds.), *Spiritually oriented psychotherapy* (pp. 105–130). Washington, DC: American Psychological Association. (**)

Shafranske, E. P. (2005b). Psychology of religion in clinical and counseling psychology. In R. Paloutzian & C. Park (Eds.), *Handbook of the psychology of religion* (pp. 496–514). New York: Guilford Press. (**)

Shafranske, E. P. (2009). Spiritually oriented psychodynamic psychotherapy. *Journal of Clinical Psychology: In Session, 65*, 147–157. (**)

Shafranske, E. P., & Cummings, J. P. (2013). Religious and spiritual beliefs, affiliations, and practices of psychologists. In K. Pargament, A. Mahoney, & E. Shafranske (Eds.), *APA handbook of psychology, religion, and spirituality: Volume 2* (pp. 23–41). Washington, DC: American Psychological Association.

Shafranske, E. P., & Sperry, L. (2005). Addressing the spiritual dimension in psychotherapy: Introduction and overview. In L. Sperry & E. P. Shafranske (Eds.), *Spiritually oriented psychotherapy* (pp. 11–29). Washington, DC: American Psychological Association. (**)

Shafranske, E. P., & Vargas, L. (in press). Addressing spirituality in clinical supervision. In C. A. Falender, E. P. Shafranske, & C. J. Falicov (Eds.), *Diversity and multiculturalism in clinical supervision: Foundation and praxis*. Washington, DC: American Psychological Association (**)

Shreve-Neiger, A. K., & Edelstein, B. A. (2004). Religion and anxiety: A critical review of the literature. *Clinical Psychology Review, 24*(4), 379–397.

Slattery, J. M., & Park, C. L. (2011). Meaning making and spiritually oriented interventions. In J. D. Aten, M. R. McMinn, & E. R. Worthington (Eds.), *Spiritually oriented interventions for counseling and psychotherapy* (pp. 15–40). Washington, DC: American Psychological Association.

Smith, T. B., Bartz, J., & Richards, P. (2007). Outcomes of religious and spiritual adaptations to psychotherapy: A meta-analytic review. *Psychotherapy Research, 17*(6), 643–655.

Sperry, L. (2012). *Spirituality in clinical practice: Theory and practice of spiritually oriented psychotherapy* (2nd ed.). New York: Routledge/Taylor & Francis. (**)

Sperry, L., & Shafranske, E. P. (Eds.). (2005). *Spiritually oriented psychotherapy*. Washington, DC: American Psychological Association. (**)

Sue, D. W., Arredondo, P., & McDavis, R. J. (1992). Multicultural counseling competencies and standards: A call to the profession. *Journal of Counseling & Development, 70*, 477–486.

Tan, S.-Y. (1996). Religion in clinical practice: Implicit and explicit integration. In E. P. Shafranske (Ed.), *Religion and the clinical practice of psychology* (pp. 365–387). Washington, DC: American Psychological Association. (**)

Tan, S.-Y. (2013). Addressing religion and spirituality from a cognitive behavioral perspective. In K. Pargament, A. Mahoney, & E. Shafranske (Eds.), *APA handbook of psychology, religion, and spirituality: Volume 2* (pp. 169–187). Washington, DC: American Psychological Association. (**)

Tan, S.-Y., & Johnson, W. B. (2005). Spiritually-oriented cognitive-behavioral approach. In L. Sperry & E. P. Shafranske (Eds.), *Spiritually oriented psychotherapy* (pp. 77–103). Washington, DC: American Psychological Association. (**)

Tonigan, J. S., Toscova, R. T., & Connors, G. J. (1999). Spirituality and the 12–step programs: A guide for clinicians. In W. R. Miller (Ed.), *Integrating spirituality into treatment* (pp. 111–131). Washington, DC: American Psychological Association. (**)

Wade, N. G., Worthington, E. R., & Vogel, D. L. (2007). Effectiveness of religiously tailored interventions in Christian therapy. *Psychotherapy Research, 17*, 91–105.

Walker, D. F., Gorsuch, R. L., & Tan, S. (2004). Therapists' integration of religion and spirituality in counseling: A meta-analysis. *Counseling And Values, 49*(1), 69–80.

Wiggins, M. I. (2009). Therapist self-awareness of spirituality. In J. D. Aten & M. M. Leach (Eds.), *Spirituality and the therapeutic process: A comprehensive resource from intake to termination* (pp. 53–74). Washington, DC: American Psychological Association. (**)

Worthington, E. L., Jr., Hook, J. N., Davis, D. E., Gartner, A. L., Jennings, D. J., II, Gibson, J. S. J. (2013). Conducting empirical research on religiously accommodative treatments. In K.

Pargament, A. Mahoney, & E. Shafranske (Eds.), *APA handbook of psychology, religion, and spirituality: Volume 2* (pp. 651–669). Washington, DC: American Psychological Association. (**)

Worthington, E. L., Jr., Hook, J. N., Davis, D. E., & McDaniel, M. A. (2011). Religion and spirituality. *Journal of Clinical Psychology, 67*(2), 204–214. (**)

Worthington, E. L., Jr., Kurusu, T. A., McCullough, M. E., & Sandage, S. J. (1996). Empirical research on religion and counseling: A ten-year update and prospectus. *Psychological Bulletin, 119,* 448–487.

Worthington, E. L., Jr., & Sandage, S. J. (2001). Religion and spirituality. *Psychotherapy, 38,* 473–478. (**)

Worthington, E. L., Jr., & Sandage, S. J. (2002). Religion and spirituality. In J. C. Norcross (Ed.), *Psychotherapy relationships that work: Therapist contributions and responsiveness to patients* (pp. 383–399). New York: Oxford University Press. (**)

Young, J. S., Cashwell, C., Wiggins-Frame, M., & Belaire, C. (2002). Spiritual and religious competencies: A national survey of CACREP-Accredited programs. *Counseling and Values, 47,* 22–33.

Zinnbauer, B. J., Pargament, K. I., Cole, B., Rye, M. S., Butter, E. M., Belavich, T. G., et al. (1997). Religion and spirituality: Unfuzzying the fuzzy. *Journal for the Scientific Study of Religion, 36,* 549–564.

31

From Concept to Science

Continuing Steps in Workplace Spirituality Research

Peter C. Hill, Carole L. Jurkiewicz,
Robert A. Giacalone, and Louis W. Fry

The organizational sciences are not immune to our culture's burgeoning interest in religion and spirituality, and such interest is taxing the capacity of scholars to keep pace both theoretically and methodologically. Elementary attempts at understanding workplace spirituality began in the early 1990s as evidenced in books, articles, and special journal issues or sections (e.g., *Journal of Managerial Psychology*, *Journal of Management Inquiry*, *Journal of Management Education*, *Organization*, and *Journal of Organizational Change Management*). However, much of this early work emerged in the form of theoretical advocacy and organizational case study rather than through empirical investigation, and it became increasingly clear that systematic scientific study to address this salient aspect of organizational life was necessary.

PROGRESS IN THE STUDY OF WORKPLACE SPIRITUALITY

Such recognition has spurred scientific efforts, resulting in a growing empirical literature and conceptual sophistication. A formal interest group with a primary focus on the intersection of management, spirituality, and religion was founded in the Academy of Management, the professional organization for scholars in business management. The *Handbook of Workplace Spirituality and Organizational Performance* (Giacalone & Jurkiewicz, 2003), a 32-chapter landmark publication, established a new paradigm for the field. A second edition of the handbook, an indication in itself of the strong interest in workplace spirituality as well as an increasing acceptance of its scientific legitimacy, was published in 2010.

The charge in both editions of the *Handbook of Workplace Spirituality and Organizational Performance* (Giacalone & Jurkiewicz, 2003, 2010b) was clear: a scientific, data-based approach to workplace spirituality. While conceptual development was important, the editors and the contributors maintained that the study of workplace spirituality also needs to demonstrate *effects* in order for it to be seen as a legitimate discipline in the field of organizational science. While the potentially constructive benefits of spiritual pursuits have been lauded effectively in psychological (Koenig, 1998) and medical (Koenig, McCullough, & Larson, 2001) writing, the organizational treatises prior to the first handbook focused on the normative, humanistic necessity of workplace spirituality. Indeed, if for no other reason, these scholars served an important function in introducing the concept to organizational leaders. But organizations, by their very nature, are far less interested in ideologies concerned with normative necessities and ultimately more entrenched in outcomes. Legitimizing workplace spirituality, therefore, required a demonstrable positive impact of spiritual variables on workplace-related functioning. Without this demonstration, the topic of workplace spirituality would be marginalized as a philosophical and impractical pursuit.

Defining and Conceptualizing Workplace Spirituality

Among the numerous definitions of workplace spirituality, three dimensions are frequently identified: (1) an inner life that is brought to the workplace; (2) the desire to find work purposeful and meaningful; and (3) a sense of connectedness and community often exemplified through commitment, sharing, and mutual obligation (Badrinarayanan & Madhavaram, 2008; Fry, 2005a). Definitions frequently used in the workplace spirituality literature include the following as examples:

- "The recognition that employees have an inner life that nourishes and is nourished by meaningful work that takes place in the context of community" (Ashmos & Duchon, 2000, p. 137)
- The recognition "that people have both a mind and a spirit, seek to find meaning and purpose in their work, and desire to connect with other human beings and be part of a community" (Robbins, 2003, p. 542)
- "Aspects of the workplace, either in the individual, the group, or the organization, that promote individual feelings of satisfaction through transcendence" (Giacalone & Jurkiewicz, 2010b, p. 13).

What is clear in these definitions is that spirituality has a clear interior focus—an inner, subjective experience that reflects core values—but one that is integrated with and facilitated by an organizational milieu.

Just as psychologists of religion and spirituality have grappled with and differed on the conceptual relationship between religion and spirituality (see Oman, Chapter 2, this volume), so too have workplace spirituality researchers shown considerable variability on the extent to which they see these two constructs related. For example, in their review of 87 scholarly articles Dent, Higgins, and Wharff (2005) found that 29% of the articles defined spirituality only as a religious construct, 17% made no reference to religion in defining spirituality, and 21% defined spirituality as both a religious and nonreligious construct. The remaining one-third of the articles made no mention of the relationship of spirituality to religion. For scientific study to advance, researchers in this field must clarify the degree to which spirituality in the workplace should be connected to or independent of religion. One issue, repeatedly stressed throughout this chapter, that may help clarify the relationship spirituality should have with religion is whether workplace spirituality is being conceptualized at the individual or the organizational level.

At the individual level, what is clear is that the focus of workplace spirituality should be the private realm of the interior life, which is now commonly designated by the term "spirituality." However, for many, the spiritual life is made explicit through doctrinal teachings of religion and should be respected as such. Thus, a major challenge for workplace researchers is to be able to conceptualize and measure a spirituality that for some is independent of religion (and for some of these, religion may even have a negative connotation), yet for others is best captured through codified beliefs. From this perspective, spirituality is necessary for religion but religion is not necessary for spirituality. Workplace spirituality can, therefore, be inclusive or exclusive of religious theory and practice. However, for a thorough understanding, both a religious and nonreligious spirituality must be investigated.

However, at the organizational level, workplace spirituality should be distinguished from religion unless, of course, religion is directly related to the organization's mission (e.g., mosques, churches, or synagogues; some mission organizations; religiously affiliated educational institutions). Conceptualizing workplace spirituality through the lens of religious traditions and practice is potentially divisive in that, to the extent the religious tradition is exclusivist (i.e., it views its teachings as the only source of spiritual truth), there will be those who do not share in the tradition (Cavanaugh, 1999). Furthermore, religious practices often conflict with the social, legal, and ethical foundations of business, law, and public and nonprofit administration (Nadesan, 1999). Imbuing religion into workplace spirituality has the potential to foster zealotry at the expense of organizational goals, offend constituents and customers, and decrease morale and employee well-being (Giacalone & Jurkiewicz, 2010b).

Nevertheless, a general agreement with the broad definitional and scientific parameters introduced in the two editions of Giacalone and Jurkiewicz's (2003, 2010a) handbook have successfully provided a foundation for the study of workplace spirituality upon which many avenues of inquiry, though some still in infancy, have blossomed. We review some of this literature later in this chapter. However, in a nascent field that has undergone enormous change, where theoretical advocacy and organizational case study are increasingly being supplanted by scientific data, the question of direction continues to loom large. What are the variables of interest? What conceptual distinctions are appropriate? What should the focus of measurement be? It is to these questions that researchers have turned in moving the study of workplace spirituality from advocacy to science. It is also to these same questions that workplace spirituality and the psychology of religion and spirituality become intertwined and to which scholars in the latter field have much to offer to a conceptual and empirical grounding for the former. For researchers in the psychology of religion and spirituality, this is yet another example of putting into practice Emmons and Paloutzian's (2003) call for a *multilevel interdisciplinary paradigm,* which "recognizes the value of data at multiple levels of analysis while making nonreductive assumptions concerning the value of spiritual and religious phenomena" (p. 395).

The Psychology of Religion and Workplace Spirituality

While many may have expected workplace spirituality to emerge from research on the psychology of religion and spirituality, this is not at all the case. Largely for the purposes of scientific credibility, the field of workplace spirituality was born of organizational and social psychology, ethics, and management. The disconnection between these fields can be best understood if we consider that the psychology of religion, particularly over the past 40 years, has been characterized by data gathering, while the study of workplace spirituality, as already noted, emerged through theoretical advocacy and organizational case study.

However, there are discernible indicators that cross-fertilization between the two fields is occurring. First, the existence of this chapter in both the first and now the second edition of this volume represents the recognition of workplace spirituality as an important application of the psychology of religion and spirituality. In fact, even our authorship team, with the addition of the first author (a psychologist of religion and spirituality, whereas the other authors all come from the field of management) to this second edition chapter, is a sure sign that these two disciplines can (and should) work together. Second, a recent edited volume (Hill & Dik, 2012a) has been published with the expressed purpose of drawing on the strengths of the scholarly literature in the psychology of religion and spirituality to help provide scientific moorings for the emerging discipline of workplace spirituality. The Hill and Dik volume is the first of an interdisciplinary series titled *Advances in Workplace Spirituality: Theory, Research and Application*. The purpose of the series is to "draw from a wide variety of stakeholder disciplines to promote integrative thinking with the broad goal of adding to the value of workplace spirituality theory, research, and its application" (p. vii), to which the editors of the first volume rhetorically respond, "What better place to ground this emerging field than in the psychology of religion and spirituality?" (Hill & Dik, 2012a, p. vii). Perhaps a fruitful relationship has only begun.

A Meaning-Making Approach

Just as meaning holds promise as a central and unifying construct to the psychological study of religion (Paloutzian & Park, Chapter 1, this volume), so too it provides a framework for understanding workplace spirituality. People often consider the "big picture" kinds of questions (e.g., "What makes life worth living?" "What are my deepest held values?") in terms of their work. Such considerations may also include how the answers to those questions line up with the organizational mission and culture. For example, when a colleague of one of the authors was asked why he left his lucrative position as a computer programmer at a successful customized t-shirt company to go to graduate school (and eventually earn a considerably lesser income in an academic position), he replied that, quite simply, he did not want to make t-shirts for the rest of his life. In essence, his spiritual strivings would not be fulfilled.

At the Individual Level

Later in this chapter, we more thoroughly discuss the distinction between individual and organizational workplace spirituality. For now, it is sufficient to point out that meaning can be made at both levels. At the individual level, Park (2012; also Chapter 18, this volume) persuasively contends that religion and spirituality are major players in both global meaning systems (beliefs, goals, values, and sense of purpose) as well as how meaning is made in specific contexts that arc oftcn strcssful in nature. Park's (2012) review of the workplace literature suggests that spiritually based meaning systems can influence such aspects of the workplace as career choice and development, on-the-job conduct, work-related stress and coping, as well as work-related well-being.

At the Organizational Level

Spirituality is often predicated on shared beliefs, visions, and values such that, though few organizations may think of themselves as spiritual entities, there is frequently a certain organization identity that reflects at least implicit (and sometimes explicit) values and norms from which individuals may experience a sense of connection and personal growth (Jurkiewicz & Giacalone, 2004; Kolodinsky, Giacalone, & Jurkiewicz, 2008). Ashforth and Pratt (2010) point out that various types of organizations (among those at least somewhat receptive to spirituality) will likely exert different levels of control. For example, some organizations, especially those that may be explicit in describing their spiritual orientation, can be described as spiritually *directing* in that the organization itself has an explicit cosmology that is directly connected to its mission and practices, including some that may be imposed on individual employees. Examples of spiritually directive organizations include ServiceMaster, Chick-fil-A, and some network marketing organizations such as Amway or Mary Kay. This need not necessarily imply that individuals have to be forced to adopt the organizational culture; few of such organizations require wholesale adoption, and, regardless, in many cases individuals self-select to be part of that culture. Pointing out both the benefits (e.g., the facilitation of spiritual community and personal fulfillment, an enhanced sense or organizational unity, the potential for greater likelihood of organization goal achievement) and liabilities (e.g., conformity pressure, the possibility of limited diversity and adaptability, an unhealthy resistance to change) of spiritually directing organizations, Ashforth and Pratt characterize such organizations as having "strong cultures that provide clear and often distinctive hooks for spiritual strivings" (p. 49).

Other organizations, according to Ashforth and Pratt (2010), are spiritually *enabling* in that they allow individuals "to discover their own idiosyncratic transcendence, whether through prayer groups, meditation, yoga, journaling, spiritual retreats, or other means" (p. 47), the primary benefit of which is a personalized ownership of one's spiritual journey. An enabling approach, too, has its advantages (e.g., increased personal commitment, enhanced diversity and possible creativity, worker satisfaction) and disadvantages (e.g., potentially highlighting individual differences that may weaken organizational unity, sanctioning unusual and potentially divisive practices). Between the extremes of spiritually directing and enabling organizations are what the authors call *partnering* organizations that involve a mix of the benefits and liabilities of the other two approaches.

Regardless of organizational characteristics, the spiritually attuned organization as an entity can play a key role in facilitating a sense of meaning and purpose beyond bottom-line results or simply drawing a paycheck. The extent to which such meaning-making influences workplace functioning, at both the individual and the organizational level, is a topic fertile for further research.

CRITICAL ISSUES IN ADVANCING THE SCIENCE OF WORKPLACE SPIRITUALITY

In calling for a scientific inquiry into workplace spirituality, Giacalone and Jurkiewicz, (2010b) identify four major weaknesses that must addressed if this newly emerging paradigm is to achieve acceptance within the scientific community: (1) the lack of an accepted, conceptual definition; (2) inadequate measurement tools; (3) limited theoretical development; and (4) legal concerns. To attend to these weaknesses and to advance a workplace spirituality paradigm rooted in science, three critical issues, all of which lie at the heart of scientific inquiry, including the theory-building and testing process central to it (Dubin, 1978), need to be addressed: levels of conceptual analysis; conceptual distinctions and measurement foci; and clarification of the relationship between criterion variables. Though considerable progress has been made regarding each issue since we first identified them in the first edition of this volume, these three critical issues require ongoing attention if we are to advance a scientifically based workplace spirituality paradigm.

Level of Conceptual Analysis

Individual Spirituality

As repeatedly noted, workplace spirituality can be conceptualized at both the individual and the organizational level of analysis. At the individual level, workplace spirituality refers to a personal set of values that promote the experience of transcendence through the work process, thereby facilitating a sense of connectedness to others in a way that provides feelings of completeness and joy (Giacalone & Jurkiewicz, 2010b; Heaton, Schmidt-Wilk, & Travis, 2004). When employees bring their spirituality and related values to work, such spirituality might be considered an *integrative* spirituality in which personal spirituality is woven into various facets of the job. Conversely, when employees fail to bring their spirituality into work, it would be defined as a *segmented* spirituality. Segmented spirituality may be the result of the individual's unwillingness to bring spiritual beliefs to work (don't want to share this part of one's life, fear of reprisal), or it may be a function of the individual's inability to enact his or her spiritual beliefs (don't know how to integrate such beliefs into one's work). Thus, in understanding workplace spirituality at the individual level, we must determine not only the level of spirituality but also the level or integration of that spirituality into the organizational environment. Of course, some employees may sense that spirituality should not be carried into the work environment at all.

Those factors that predict the extent to which employees bring spiritual values into the workplace have not been determined. Surely some factors may be at the dispositional level, such as level of spiritual commitment, spiritual well-being, or spiritual intelligence. For example, Paloutzian, Emmons, and Keortge (2010) suggest that the need for transcendence or a healthy sense of well-being applies to life on the job in much the same way as functioning in society as a whole. They also contend that Emmons's (2000) concept of *spiritual intelligence*—that ability to experience transcendent states of consciousness, to maintain overarching spiritual strivings through which other life pursuits are organized and integrated, and to regulate one's behavior virtuously (such as showing compassion, granting forgiveness, expressing gratitude, and behaving humbly)—will likely impact the degree to which spiritual values are brought to the workplace setting. Similarly, Hill and Dik (2012b) recommend that workplace researchers employ Allport's (1950) notion of intrinsic and extrinsic religious motivation, which also can be conceptualized and measured in spiritual but nonreligious ways, to better understand how spirituality is carried to the workplace.

Organizational Spirituality

At the organizational or strategic level, workplace spirituality is a descriptor of the organization as an entity, including such characteristics as organizational values, human resource systems, and organizational plans for the future (Milliman, Ferguson, Trickett, & Condemi, 1999). In this sense, workplace spirituality can be thought of as a framework of organizational values evidenced in the culture that promote employees' experience of organizational transcendence through the work process, and facilitates their sense of being connected to others in a way that provides feelings of completeness and joy (Giacalone & Jurkiewicz, 2010b). As such, workplace spirituality at this level can be considered both in terms of vision and cultural values, and both approaches are of value in understanding workplace spirituality (Pawar, 2008).

The Interaction of Individual and Organizational Spirituality

Kolodinsky et al. (2008) found that workers' positive attitudinal outcomes often depend on a person–organization (P-O) fit; that is, the match between workers' spiritual values and their perceptions of the spiritual values exuded by the organization (e.g., stressing openness, connection, truth, personal development and growth, work-related meaning and purpose, servant leadership, and sharing). In general, shared P-O values have been documented to indicate strong P-O fit and positive work attitudes (Balazas, 1990), operating unit performance (Enz & Schwenk, 1991), and both job satisfaction and lower turnover rates (O'Reilly, Chatman, & Caldwell, 1991). Across five separate cross-sectional samples, Kolodinsky et al. found that especially perceptions of organizational spirituality positively predicted organizational identification, job involvement, and satisfaction with work rewards and negatively predicted work frustration. Somewhat surprisingly, personal spirituality appeared to be a less robust predictor of the outcomes studied. Their results suggest that even if the workers themselves are not personally spiritual, they desire workplaces perceived as exhibiting spiritual values, causing the researchers to conclude that "the establishment of a spiritual climate through modeling servant leadership, open communication, and valuing individual differences will go a long way to affecting worker perceptions and attitudes" (p. 476). Still much work needs to be done with regard to understanding the effect of organizational spirituality on workers—questions such as how perceptions of organizational spirituality are formed, how such perceptions are transferred to individuals, what specific spiritual attributes are valued by prospective employees, and what spiritual values help predict positive worker outcomes, remain largely unexplored.

Conceptual Distinctions and Measurement Focus

Conceptually, there are aspects of workplace spirituality, particularly at the individual level, that are theoretically and empirically connected to other areas, notably those behaviors and dispositional traits identified in the areas of positive psychology (Snyder

& Lopez, 2002) and character ethics (Lickona, 1991). While the work of Fry (2005b), Emmons (2003), Emmons and Paloutzian (2003), Giacalone and Jurkiewicz (2010a), Giacalone, Jurkiewicz, and Dunn (2005), and Jurkiewicz and Giacalone (2004) have identified the core values, attitudes, and behavior of ethical and spiritual well-being, their approach integrates and envelopes other frameworks, theories, and concepts. For example, both Fry (2005b) and Giacalone and Jurkiewicz (2010a) use conceptualizations that are mainstays in social psychology and political science.

Among other issues, such conceptual overlaps raise concerns over measurement. With many good treatises written on spiritual and religious measurement (see Hill, Chapter 3, this volume; Hill & Hood, 1999; Hill & Pargament, 2003; Hill & Edwards, 2013; MacDonald, Friedman, & Kuentzel, 1999; MacDonald, Kuentzel, & Friedman, 1999), none has confronted the complexity of firmly distinguishing among these conceptual overlaps, nor have they addressed whether such conceptualizations can be aggregated at a macro (organizational) level. Getting to the root of this complexity is critical if workplace spirituality is to develop as a scientific area of inquiry. We know from related research on postmaterialist values (Inglehart, 1990) that conceptual ambiguities, when coupled with measurement problems, create voluminous research output that focuses on conceptual problems rather than theoretical advances. In the case of postmaterialist values, for example, the assessment problems have embroiled researchers in trying to determine the number of dimensions involved, the level at which responses can be aggregated, and the theoretically appropriate way to determine how a hypothesis might be tested (e.g., Davis & Davenport, 1999). Another example, familiar to many psychologists of religion and spirituality, is the conceptual and measurement ambiguity surrounding Allport's (1950) theory of intrinsic–extrinsic religious motivation (see Hill & Edwards, 2013, for further discussion). Such difficulties have caused Kirkpatrick and Hood (1990) to suggest that the emphasis by psychologists of religion on Allport's theory has actually worked against the field's theoretical advance.

Workplace spirituality research is now in a similarly difficult stage of development. The lack of conceptual clarity related to level of analysis makes measurement questionable. Whether we assess at the individual or the organizational level depends on one's conceptualization, but since there is no agreement on the level of analysis, researchers must decide for themselves. Such decisions are pivotal in developing foundations for further research. This lack of clarity is an example of unrationalized categorization at the theoretical level (Fry & Smith, 1987; Stanfield, 1976) and, like the research on postmaterialist values and religious intrinsic–extrinsic motivation, could result in a hodgepodge of empirical studies that, even though reliable and valid, will serve to diffuse rather than solidify theory building on workplace spirituality.

Establishing Clear Relationships with Criterion Variables

Even if spirituality's normative sense of goodness is acknowledged (e.g., employee completeness and joy as integral parts of the organizational culture, the incorporation of humanitarian concerns and outcomes), organizations (especially the power elite) are likely to remain disinterested in creating spiritual workplaces without a demonstrable, bottom-line (though not necessarily financial) type of outcome associated with it. Therefore, creating spiritual workplaces will require demonstrating that workplace spirituality is aligned to organizational goals (Fry & Slocum, 2008; Fry, Matherly, & Ouimet, 2010).

The legitimacy of this association has been discussed by Fry (2003, 2008), who notes that, by understanding the vision of the organization and being empowered with the autonomy to act as they see fit, participants have an experience of competence in that, through their work, they are making a positive difference in other people's lives, which in turn enriches their own. It is such outcomes, ultimately based in the satisfactions that result from work performed as if it were a calling (Dik & Duffy, 2009; Dik, Duffy, & Eldridge, 2009; Dik, Duffy, & Tix, 2012), that will result in higher levels of organizational commitment, productivity, and reduced stress—the same organizational goals most often reported as affective outcomes of organizational research. Conceptually, organizations would be interested in workplace spirituality if it demonstrated either a positive relationship with desirable outcomes or an inverse relationship with undesirable outcomes. These relationships need not be directly tied to a financial outcome (such as increased individual productivity or decreased theft), but could be tied indirectly to financially related outcomes such as associations with positive employee attitudes (yielding lower turnover), lowered rates of illness (reducing healthcare costs and absenteeism), or improved public image (yielding more interest in the company).

One possible line of research is to examine the role that perceived organizational spirituality has in relation to commitment to the organization. For example, research (e.g., Randall & O'Driscoll, 1997) has identified two dimensions of commitment to an organization: calculative commitment and affective commitment. Calculative commitment reflects an exchange relationship orientation whereby commitment to an organization is contingent upon perceived benefits in relation to costs. In contrast, affective commitment involves identification and involvement with the organization on the basis of perceptions of similar values and goals. Thus, employees who remain with an organization because of a calculative commitment may feel that they have no choice but to remain (an extrinsic motivation), whereas those whose stay is affective based remain with the company because they want to (an intrinsic motivation). Research has shown affective (calculative) commitment is positively (negatively) related to supervisor ratings of overall job performance and promotability of their subordinates (Meyer, Paunonen, Gellatly, Goffin, & Jackson, 1989) as well as to positive work-related attitudes such as satisfaction with supervisors and coworkers, job involvement, and overall job satisfaction (Mathieu & Zajac, 1990). The extent to which an organization with a perceived spiritual climate might facilitate an affective commitment and its attendant benefits is ripe for empirical research.

FURTHER ADVANCING WORKPLACE SPIRITUALITY: THE EXAMPLE OF SPIRITUAL LEADERSHIP THEORY

We now discuss a conceptualization of spiritual leadership, proposed by Fry (2003, 2005b, 2008; Fry et al., 2010), that we believe addresses the three critical issues just discussed (level of conceptual analysis, conceptual distinctions, and clarification of relationship between criterion variables) and, therefore, is an example of the types of theories necessary for further advancing the empirical study of workplace spirituality. Fry's causal theory of spiritual leadership is developed within an intrinsic motivation model that incorporates inner life, vision, hope/faith, and altruistic love, theories of workplace spirituality, and spiritual well-being through calling and membership. The purpose of spiritual leadership is to tap into the fundamental needs of both leader and follower to create vision and value congruence across the strategic, empowered team, and individual levels. Ultimately, the goal of spiritual leadership is to foster higher levels of ethical, spiritual, and psychological well-being, positive human health, life satisfaction, organizational commitment and productivity, corporate social responsibility, and financial performance.

As indicated at the top of Figure 31.1, spiritual leadership is defined as comprising the values, attitudes, and behaviors that are necessary to intrinsically motivate one's self and others so that they have a sense of spiritual well-being through calling and membership, which, in turn, enhances individual and organizational outcomes. This entails:

1. Creating a vision wherein organization members experience a sense of calling in that their life has meaning and makes a difference;
2. Establishing a social/organizational culture based on altruistic love whereby leaders and followers have genuine care, concern, and appreciation for *both* self and others, thereby producing a sense of membership that promotes feelings of being understood and appreciated.

The foundation of spiritual leadership, as indicated toward the left side of Figure 31.1, begins with an acknowledgment of the importance of an inner life, frequently involving a spiritual practice (e.g., spending time in nature, prayer, meditation, reading inspirational literature, yoga, observing religious traditions, or writing in a journal) that relates to the worker's fundamental sense of individual and social identity. As further suggested in Figure 31.1, organizational cultures that support their members' inner life have employees who are more likely to develop the values of altruistic love in pursuit of a transcendent vision and the hope/faith to achieve the vision that ultimately produces the worker trust, intrinsic motivation, and spiritual well-being necessary to optimize important individual and organizational outcomes. "Doing what it takes" through hope and faith in the organization's vision keeps followers looking forward to the future and provides the desire and positive expectation that fuels effort through intrinsic motivation. In pursuing the vision, an organizational culture based in the values of altruistic love is also received by followers. This drives out and removes fears associated with worry, anger, jealousy, selfishness, failure, and guilt and gives one a sense of membership—that part of spiritual well-being that gives one an awareness of being understood and appreciated. This is, of course, one of the most fundamentally motivating factors in the workplace overall. This intrinsic motivation cycle results in an increase in one's sense of spiritual well-being (e.g., calling and membership) and ultimately in positive personal, group, and organizational outcomes such as increased ethical and spiritual well-being, life satisfaction, organizational commitment and productivity, corporate social responsibility, and financial performance.

To date, the theory has been tested in a diverse range of organizations, including schools, military units, city governments, police, and for-profit organizations. These studies have found support for the spiritual leadership causal model and the general reliability and validity of its measures. Initial findings include a significant positive influence of spiritual leadership on employee life satisfaction, organizational commitment and productivity, sales growth, and other unit performance outcomes (Fry, Hanna, Noel, & Walumbwa, 2011; Fry et al., 2010; Fry, Nisiewicz, & Vitucci, 2007; Fry, Nisiewicz, Vitucci, & Cedillo, 2007; Fry & Slocum, 2008; Fry, Vitucci, & Cedillo, 2005).

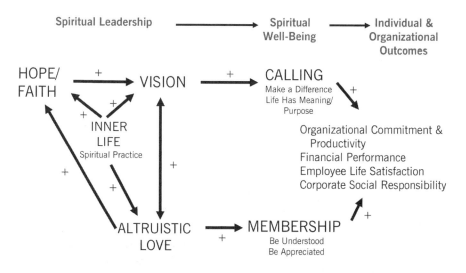

FIGURE 31.1. Model of spiritual leadership.

Still, however, research on several fronts is necessary to establish the validity of spiritual leadership theory before it should be widely applied as a model of organizational and professional development toward the end of fostering systemic change and transformation. For example, outcomes across levels (e.g., ethical and spiritual well-being; joy, peace, and serenity; corporate social responsibility, financial performance) hypothesized to be affected by spiritual leadership (Fry, 2005a; Fry & Slocum, 2008; Fry et al., 2010) need to be validated. Additional longitudinal studies are needed to test for changes in key variables over time, particularly as relating to performance. Studies, too, are needed that incorporate more objective performance measures from multiple sources (Podsakoff, MacKenzie, Podsakoff, & Lee, 2003). Also, the conceptual distinction between spiritual leadership theory variables and other leadership theories, such as authentic leadership, ethical leadership, and servant leadership in relation to workplace spirituality, should be refined (Fry, 2003; Fry, Matherly, Whittington, & Winston, 2007; Fry & Whittington, 2005). Further, research might investigate whether these theories are perhaps mutually reinforcing or serve to moderate the effects of one another. Finally, further conceptual refinement between spiritual leadership theory variables and other workplace spirituality and workplace religion theories and constructs is needed in order to advance this key new paradigm in organizational studies. This kind of research fertility is precisely why the theory is so valuable and why it is put forward here as the type that will advance the study of workplace spirituality.

FUTURE DIRECTIONS FOR WORKPLACE SPIRITUALITY RESEARCH

Although important research in workplace spirituality has been conducted and considerable advancement has been made since the first edition of this *Handbook* was published in 2005, our claim then that workplace spirituality research is in the initial concept/ elaboration stage of development (Hunt, 1999; Reichers & Schneider, 1990) still applies.

It, therefore, follows that the four components viewed as necessary and sufficient conditions for the development of any theoretical model (Dubin, 1978) continue to remain important to the study of workplace spirituality at this point in time: (1) identifiable units or variables of interest to the researcher; (2) congruence as defined by the laws of relationship among units of the model that specify how they are associated; (3) boundaries within which the laws of relationships are expected to operate; and (4) contingency effects that specify system states within which the units of the theory take on characteristic values that are deterministic and have a persistence through time (see also Fry & Smith, 1987). It is toward fulfilling these components that scholarship in workplace spirituality must continue to focus.

Drawing upon the expertise of psychologists of religion and spirituality is crucial to the development of the science of workplace spirituality. The fact that psychologists of religion and spirituality have produced a volume (Hill & Dik, 2012a) devoted specifically to the workplace will no doubt be an invaluable aid in furthering the discipline.

Finally, it is likely that research in workplace spirituality will continue to expand in the years ahead. Promising topical areas for theoretical development and empirical research in workplace spirituality include the nonprofit sector (Alexander, 2010), crisis and disaster management (Cigler, 2010; Jurkiewicz, 2010), and politics and leadership (Bowen, Ferris, & Kolodinsky, 2010), each of which attest to the relevancy and vibrancy of this area of research and the breadth toward which future research can be directed.

REFERENCES

Alexander, J. (2010). Spirituality of work in nonprofit organizations. In R. A. Giacalone & C. L. Jurkiewicz (Eds.), *The handbook of workplace spirituality and organizational performance* (2nd ed., pp. 291–305). New York: Sharpe.

Allport, G. W. (1950). *The individual and his religion.* New York: Macmillan.

Ashforth, B. E., & Pratt, M. G. (2010). Institutionalized spirituality: An oxymoron? In R. A. Giacalone & C. L. Jurkiewicz (Eds.), *Handbook of workplace spirituality and organizational performance* (2nd ed., pp. 44–58). New York: Sharpe.

Ashmos, D. P., & Duchon, D. (2000). Spirituality at work: A conceptualization and measure. *Journal of Management Inquiry, 9,* 134–145.

Badrinarayanan, V., & Madhavaram, S. (2008). Workplace spirituality and the selling organization: A conceptual framework and research propositions. *Journal of Personal Selling & Sales Management, 28,* 421–434.

Balazas, A. L. (1990). Value congruency: The case of the socially responsible firm. *Journal of Business Research, 20,* 171–181.

Bowen, M. G., Ferris, G. R., & Kolodinsky, R. W. (2010). Political skill, servant leadership, and workplace spirituality in the creation of effective work environments. In R. A. Giacalone & C. L. Jurkiewicz (Eds.), *Handbook of workplace spirituality and organizational performance* (2nd ed., pp. 126–142). New York: Sharpe.

Cavanagh, G. F. (1999). Spirituality for managers: Context and critique. *Journal of Organizational Change Management, 12,* 186–199.

Cigler, B. A. (2010). Spirituality in crisis and disaster management: The case of Hurricane Katrina. In R. A. Giacalone & C. L. Jurkiewicz (Eds.), *The handbook of workplace spirituality and organizational performance* (2nd ed., pp. 306–320). New York: Sharpe.

Davis, D. W., & Davenport, C. (1999). Assessing the validity of the postmaterialism index. *American Political Science Review, 93,* 649–664.

Dent, E. B., Higgins, M. E., & Wharff, D. M. (2005). Spirituality and leadership: An empirical review of definitions, distinctions, and embedded assumptions. *Leadership Quarterly, 16,* 625–653.

Dik, B. J., & Duffy, R. D. (2009). Calling and vocation at work: Definitions and prospects for research and practice. *The Counseling Psychologist, 37,* 424–450.

Dik, B. J., Duffy, R. D., & Eldridge, B. M. (2009). Calling and vocation in career counseling: Recommendations for promoting meaningful work. *Professional Psychology: Research and Practice, 40,* 625–632.

Dik, B. J., Duffy, R. D., & Tix, A. P. (2012). Religion, spirituality, and a sense of calling in the workplace. In P. C. Hill & B. J. Dik (Eds.), *Psychology of religion and workplace spirituality* (pp. 113–133). Charlotte, NC: Information Age.

Dubin, R. (1978). *Theory building.* New York: Free Press.

Emmons, R. A. (2000). Is spirituality an intelligence?: Motivation, cognition, and the psychology of ultimate concern. *The International Journal for the Psychology of Religion, 10,* 3–26.

Emmons, R. A. (2003). Acts of gratitude in organizations. In K. S. Cameron, J. E. Dutton, & R. E. Quinn (Eds.), *Positive organizational scholarship: Foundations of a new discipline.* San Francisco: Berrett-Koelher.

Emmons, R. A., & Paloutzian, R. F. (2003). The psychology of religion. *Annual Review of Psychology, 54,* 377–402.

Enz, C. A., & Schwenk, C. R. (1991). The performance edge: Strategic and value dissensus. *Employee Responsibilities and Rights Journal, 4,* 75–85.

Fry, L., Hanna, S., Noel, M., & Walumbwa, F. (2011). Impact of spiritual leadership on unit performance. *The Leadership Quarterly, 22,* 259–270.

Fry, L., & Matherly, L., & Ouimet, R. (2010). The spiritual leadership balanced scorecard business model: The case of the Cordon Bleu-Tomasso Corporation. *Journal of Management, Spirituality and Religion, 7,* 283–314.

Fry, L. W. (2003). Toward a theory of spiritual leadership. *The Leadership Quarterly, 14,* 693–727.

Fry, L. W. (2005a). Toward a paradigm of spiritual leadership. *The Leadership Quarterly, 16,* 619–622.

Fry, L. W. (2005b). Toward a theory of ethical and spiritual well-being, and corporate social responsibility through spiritual leadership. In R. A. Giacalone, C. L. Jurkiewicz, & C. Dunn (Eds.), *Positive psychology in business ethics and corporate responsibility* (pp. 47–83). Greenwich, CT: Information Age.

Fry, L. W. (2008). Spiritual leadership: State-of-the-art and future directions for theory, research, and practice. In J. Biberman & L. Tishman (Eds.), *Spirituality in business: Theory, practice, and future directions* (pp. 106–124). New York: Palgrave.

Fry, L. W., Matherly, L. L., Whittington, J. L., & Winston, B. (2007). Spiritual leadership as an integrating paradigm for servant leadership. In S. A. Singh-Sengupta & D. Fields (Eds.), *Integrating spirituality and organizational leadership* (pp. 70–82). Deli: Macmillan India.

Fry, L. W., Nisiewicz, M., & Vitucci, S. (2007, August). *Transforming police organizations through spiritual leadership: Measurement and establishing a baseline.* Paper presented at the national meeting of the Academy of Management, Philadelphia.

Fry, L. W., Nisiewicz, M., Vitucci, S., & Cedillo, M. (2007). *Transforming city government through spiritual leadership: Measurement and establishing a baseline.* Paper presented at the National Meeting of the academy of management, Philadelphia, Pennsylvania.

Fry, L. W., & Slocum, J. (2008). Maximizing the triple bottom line through spiritual leadership. *Organizational Dynamics, 37,* 86–96.

Fry, L. W., & Smith, D. A. (1987) Congruence, contingency, and theory building. *Academy of Management Review, 12,* 117–132.

Fry, L. W., Vitucci, S., & Cedillo, M. (2005). Spiritual leadership and Army transformation: Theory, measurement, and establishing a baseline. *The Leadership Quarterly, 16,* 835–862.

Fry, L. W., & Whittington, J. L. (2005). In search of authenticity: Spiritual leadership theory as a source for future theory, research, and practice on authentic leadership. In B. Avolio, W. Gardner, & F. O. Walumbwa (Eds.), *Authentic leadership: Origins, development and effects: Monographs in Leadership and Management* (pp. 183–200). New York: Elsevier.

Giacalone, R. A., & Jurkiewicz, C. L. (Eds.). (2003). *Handbook of workplace spirituality and organizational performance.* Armonk, NY: Sharpe.

Giacalone, R. A., & Jurkiewicz, C. L. (Eds.). (2010a). *Handbook of workplace spirituality and organizational performance* (2nd ed.). Armonk, NY: Sharpe.

Giacalone, R. A., & Jurkiewicz, C. L. (2010b). The science of workplace spirituyality. In R. A. Giacalone & C. L. Jurkiewicz (Eds.), *Handbook of workplace spirituality and organizational performance* (2nd ed., pp. 3–26). Armonk, NY: Sharpe.

Giacalone, R. A., Jurkiewicz, C. L., & Dunn, C. (Eds.). (2005). *Positive psychology in business ethics and corporate responsibility.* Greenwich, CT: Information Age Publishing.

Heaton, D. P., Schmidt-Wilk, J., & Travis, F. (2004). Constructs, methods, and measures for researching spirituality in organizations. *Journal of Organizational Change Management, 17,* 62–82.

Hill, P. C., & Dik, B. J. (Eds.). (2012a). *Psychology of religion and workplace spirituality.* Charlotte, NC: Information Age.

Hill, P. C., & Dik, B. J. (2012b). Toward a science of workplace spirituality: Contributions from the psychology of religion and spirituality. In P. C. Hill & B. J. Dik (Eds.), *Psychology of religion and workplace spirituality* (pp. 3–24). Charlotte, NC: Information Age.

Hill, P. C., & Edwards, E. (2013). Measurement in the psychology of religiousness and spirituality: Existing measures and new frontiers. In K. I. Pargament, J. J. Exline, & J. W. Jones (Eds.), *APA handbook of psychology, religion, and spirituality (Vol. 1): Context, theory, and research* (pp. 51–77). Washington, DC: American Psychological Association.

Hill, P. C., & Hood, R. W., Jr. (1999). *Measures of religiosity.* Birmingham, AL: Religious Education Press.

Hill, P. C., & Pargament, K. I. (2003). Advances in the conceptualization and measurement of religion and spirituality. *American Psychologist, 58,* 64–74.

Hunt, J. G. (1999). Transformational/charismatic leadership's transformation of the field: An historical essay. *Leadership Quarterly, 10,* 129–143.

Inglehart, R. (1990). *Culture shift in advanced industrial society.* Princeton, NJ: Princeton University Press.

Jurkiewicz, C. L. (2010). Ethics and spirituality in crisis. In R. A. Giacalone & C. L. Jurkiewicz (Eds.), *The handbook of workplace spirituality and organizational performance* (2nd ed., pp. 87–98). New York: Sharpe.

Jurkiewicz, C. L., & Giacalone, R. A. (2004). A values framework for measuring the impact of workplace spirituality on organizational performance. *Journal of Business Ethics, 49,* 129–142.

Kirkpatrick, L. A., & Hood, R. W., Jr. (1990). Intrinsic-extrinsic religious orientation: The boon or bane of contemporary psychology of religion? *Journal for the Scientific Study of Religion, 29,* 442–462.

Koenig, H. (1998). *The handbook of religion and mental health.* San Diego: Academic Press.

Koenig, H. G., McCullough, M. E., & Larson, D. B. (2001). *Handbook of religion and health.* Oxford, UK: Oxford University Press.

Kolodinsky, R. W., Giacalone, R. A., & Jurkiewicz, C. L. (2008). Workplace values and outcome: Exploring personal, organizational, and interactive workplace spirituality. *Journal of Business Ethics, 81,* 465–480.

Lickona, T. (1991). *Educating for character: How our schools can teach respect and responsibility.* New York: Bantam.

MacDonald, D. A., Friedman, H. L., & Kuentzel, J. G. (1999). A survey of measures of spiritual and transpersonal constructs: Part one. Research update. *Journal of Transpersonal Psychology, 31,* 137–154.

MacDonald, D. A., Kuentzel, J. G., & Friedman, H. L. (1999). A survey of measures of spiritual and transpersonal constructs: Part two. Additional instruments. *Journal of Transpersonal Psychology, 31,* 155–177.

Mathieu, J. E., & Zajac, D. M. (1990). A review and meta-analysis of the antecedents, correlates, and consequences of organizational commitment. *Psychological Bulletin, 108,* 171–194.

Meyer, J. P., Paunonen, S. V., Gellatly, I. R., Goffin, R. D., & Jackson, D. N. (1989). Organizational commitment and job performance: It's the nature of the commitment that counts. *Journal of Applied Psychology, 74,* 152–156.

Milliman, J., Ferguson, J., Trickett, D., & Condemi, B. (1999). Spirit and community at Southwest Airlines. *Journal of Organizational Change Management, 12,* 211–233.

Nadesan, M. H. (1999). The discourses of corporate spiritualism and evangelical capitalism. *Management Communication Quarterly, 13,* 3–42.

O'Reilly, C., Chatman, J., & Caldwell, D. (1991). People and organizational culture: A profile comparison approach to assessing person–organization fit. *Academy of Management Journal, 34,* 487–516.

Paloutzian, R. F., Emmons, R. A., & Keortge, S. G. (2010). Spiritual well-being, spiritual intelligence, and healthy workplace policy. In R. A. Giacalone & C. L. Jurkiewicz (Eds.), *The handbook of workplace spirituality and organizational performance* (2nd ed., pp. 73–86). New York: Sharpe.

Park, C. L. (2012). Religious and spiritual aspects of meaning in the context of work life. In P. C. Hill & B. J. Dik (Eds.), *Psychology of religion and workplace spirituality* (pp. 25–41). Charlotte, NC; Information Age Publishing.

Pawar, B. S. (2008). Two approaches to workplace spirituality facilitation: A comparison and implications. *Leadership and Organization Development Journal, 29,* 544–567.

Podsakoff, P. M., MacKenzie, S. B., Podsakoff, N. P., & Lee, J. Y. (2003). The mismeasure of man(agement) and its implications for leadership research. *The Leadership Quarterly, 14,* 615–656.

Randall, D. M., & O'Driscoll, M. P. (1997). Affective versus calculative commitment: Human resource implications. *Journal of Social Psychology, 137,* 606–617.

Reichers, A. E., & Schneider, B. (1990). Climate and culture: An evolution of constructs. In B. Schneider (Ed.), *Organizational climate and culture* (pp. 5–39). San Francisco: Jossey-Bass.

Robbins, S. P. (2003). *Organizational behavior* (10th ed.). Upper Saddle River, NJ: Prentice Hall.

Snyder, C. R., & Lopez, S. J. (Eds.). (2002). *Handbook of positive psychology.* New York: Oxford University Press.

Stanfield, G. (1976). Technology and structure as theoretical categories. *Administrative Science Quarterly, 21,* 489–493.

32

Religion and the Staircase to Terrorism

Fathali M. Moghaddam, Zachary Warren,
and Karen Love

Particularly since 9/11, the Western mass media has reinforced a popular association between "religious fanatics" and "terrorism" (Al-Khattar, 2003). *Terrorism* refers to politically motivated violence, perpetrated by individuals, groups, or state-sponsored agents, intended to bring about feelings of terror and helplessness in a population in order to influence decision making and to change behavior (Moghaddam, 2005b, p. 161). This increased salience of the relationship between religion and terrorism appears in public policy and law enforcement discourse as well. For example, in 1980, the U.S. State Department's list of Foreign Terrorist Organizations (FTOs) scarcely listed religious organizations. Today, more than 60% of those organizations are religious (*www.state. gov/j/ct/rls/other/des/123085.htm*). In this chapter, we provide a psychological exploration of the relationship between religion and terrorism. Those who seek social science theories to explain the relationship between religion and terrorism will not be disappointed in the number of theories available (see Brown & Gaertner, 2001; Taylor & Moghaddam, 1994), but they may be disappointed in the explanatory power of each theory independent of other theories. The dilemma can only be resolved, we argue, by turning to a broader context and focusing on the relationship between this macrocontext and identity processes.

Identity is central to the most important psychological processes involved in terrorism (Moghaddam, 2006, 2008a). By this we do not refer to the question of "Who am I?" We can answer the question of "Who am I?" by looking at our birth certificates or passports. Unless a person is suffering memory loss, she or he knows who she or he is. By identity, we mean "the sort of person I am." We argue that the motivation to achieve and defend a certain sort of collective identity (such as *salafist*, or a group wed to "pure" Islam) is central to the process of becoming a terrorist. But to understand this process and why the collective identity of certain groups is perceived to be threatened, it is necessary to look outward, to the macro, long-term changes taking place at the global level.

In the first major part of this chapter, we outline the presence of threats to particular collective identities from contemporary globalization. Globalization is best understood in relation to *catastrophic evolution* (Moghaddam, 2006a), a rapid and often fatal decline in a life form following sudden contact with another life form without sufficient preadaptation (see also the discussion of religious identity in evolutionary psychology in Kirkpatrick, 2005, Chapter 6, this volume). In the second major part of the chapter, we use a *staircase metaphor* (Moghaddam, 2005b) for terrorism to illustrate how individuals who react to these macrochanges by using violence are, in a psychological sense, intentional actors responding to increasingly limited degrees of freedom in their social environment.

A focus on context is a deviation from mainstream psychology, which has tended to view the relationship between religion and terrorism through a prism of dispositional, "intrapersonal" factors such as personality traits embodied by the Big Five (see Moghaddam, 2005a, for further discussion). The failure of this approach, we argue, is twofold: First, it commits the *fundamental attribution error* (Heider, 1958) by ignoring the corpus of literature documenting the overwhelming power of situations to influence individual behavior (e.g., Asch, 1956; Festinger & Carlsmith, 1959; Milgram, 1963; Sherif, 1956; Zimbardo, 2007); second, it ignores the justifications given by those who actually commit terrorist acts, that is, the collective meaning making of religiously motivated groups (also see the discussion of religion and meaning by Park, Chapter 18, this volume).

REDUCTIONISM AND FOCUS ON LEADERSHIP

The reductionism of the traditional approach to understanding the relationship between religion and terrorism is also reflected in a focus on individual leaders rather than the context from which such leadership emerges. Particularly after 9/11, Islamic leaders, rather than the contexts from which they arise, have become uniquely associated in Western popular media with terrorism. Indeed, "Islamic terrorism" was a centerpiece of the 9/11 Commission Report (National Commission on Terrorist Attacks upon the United States, 2004), which highlights "terrorist entrepreneurs" (p. 145) and focuses on the rise of Osama bin Ladin and Al-Qaeda (p. 55). The report notes that bin Ladin "appeals to people disoriented by cyclonic change as they confront modernity and globalization" (p. 48). However, the report's discussion of globalization and macrolevel influences stops there, and we see this as a major shortcoming.

Why is it tempting to overvalue the role of individual leaders and undervalue situational factors? No doubt the explanation arises in part from the individualism and reductionism of mainstream psychology (Moghaddam, 2005a). Much has been written on this topic (Harré & Moghaddam, 2012), and we do not review this debate here. But perhaps the explanation is also in part evolutionary and not specific to any cultural group. In early childhood, infants who anticipate threats through their mother's fear were more likely to be alert for possible dangers. In the earliest months and years of life, faces are the primary way we distinguish between caretakers and strangers or potential threats (see Nelson, 2001). When considering macrolevel threats, perhaps it is human instinct to "put a face on it"—that is, to reframe macrothreats into microforms: a person, a face, a name. Thus, Osama bin Ladin, Saddam Hussein, or Iranian President Mahmoud Ahmadinejad become the "face of terror," the terror of the democratically elected Nazi Reich is reduced to the face of Adolf Hitler, and so on. Systemic threats become person-centered threats.

However, the context of contemporary globalization has changed the nature of perceived threats in two significant ways. First, the majority of threats to human existence today, such as environmental destruction and global economic crises, are no longer encountered mainly through direct experience. Rather, they are mediated by technology and third-party reports that instantaneously communicate "eyewitness accounts" of events around the world. News of threat is no longer limited to the speed of Paul Revere's horse. Second, terror networks in the 21st century are increasingly characterized as "leaderless" (Sageman, 2008). Psychological processes can help explain the situational factors for religiously motivated terrorism without focusing on individual leaders. However, it is important to understand how the situational constraints of contemporary globalization are in significant ways different from globalization of previous eras.

Whereas personality theories think in terms of a few "bad apples," a contextualized approach considers the "bad barrel." The "barrel" includes historical, social, political, and cultural factors that influence the "mind" of an individual agent. In this approach, all decision making and the exercise of "free will" can be understood as operating within the restrictions of a broader context. We argue that the contemporary "religious resurgence" (Robertson & Chirico, 1985) can be understood as a reaction to contemporary globalization. Religion is a source of societal stability and social identity, functioning in a psychological sense as a vessel to weather the storm of catastrophic evolution and fractured globalization.

Thus, our approach is situational, but the "situation" we are considering is far more expansive than the laboratory contexts typically considered in psychological research. We believe that psychologists should broaden their approach, and particularly focus on macroprocesses such as globalization. Despite the central place of globalization in everyday discourse and also the mass media, there is very little attention to the psychology of globalization and how globalization processes are impacting human behavior psychologically (Moghaddam, 2010).

THE EVOLUTIONARY AND GLOBAL CONTEXT

We have entered an era of accelerating globalization that is in important respects unprecedented (Moghaddam, 2010). Consider, for instance, the globalization of the 19th century, when the British Empire reached its zenith. Trade and communications routes were developed to such an extent that it became a truism that "the sun never sets on the British Empire." The reach of British power seemed global. However, there are at least three monumental differences between 21st century globalization and what came before.

Present Globalization Compared to the Past

1. *Technology-driven change and multiplier effects: The case of cyber-jihad.* Twenty-first-century globalization is fast paced and driven in large part by technology. Technological changes in the 21st century have a number of new characteristics: They take place with unprecedented speed, have global reach and impact, and are in some key

respects unpredictable both in how they develop and how they influence social life. For example, consider the tremendous pace and reach of computer changes over the last few decades. Who would have predicted that "cyber-jihad" would develop? Today, a radical preacher in Yemen or Pakistan has opportunities to persuade young individuals in America to become home-grown terrorists. Cyber-jihadists can influence disaffected youth in the West to identify with the radical Muslim cause and to see themselves as part of an effort to "defend Islam." The key to understanding "home-grown terrorism" is identification of Muslim youth with the treatment of Muslims, particularly identification with what they perceive as the "plight of the Palestinians" at the hands of the Israeli military with its U.S. backers (Cook, 2010).

2. *Interconnectedness and the global economy.* Increasing specialization in the production of many goods has resulted in greater interdependence. For example, a single car can be assembled using parts manufactured in many different countries. Lack of production by one of the specialized manufacturers would result in slowdown or even stoppage in the production of the final product, as can happen during labor management disputes in factories that produce a car component. The level of interdependence achieved in the 21st century, and the interpenetration of economies into one another, is on a scale greater than in any previous century in human history.

3. *Magnified global inequalities.* The "new" globalization can be considered fractured because it is characterized by expanding inequality between the rich and poor (Moghaddam, 2008a). For example, while over half of the world's population still lives on less than $2.00 a day, the number of billionaires has been growing; one of these billionaires can now hire several million of the world's poor (Homer-Dixon, 2006). In this sense, we have returned to the age of the pharoahs. However, the list of global billionaires today is dominated by private individuals rather than state heads and religious leaders, a testament to the power of a global market economy.

But an even more important set of contradictions concern change: Globalization involves pushing individuals to be part of larger and larger units, whereas from an evolutionary perspective almost all of our time on earth as humans has involved living in small groups numbering a few hundred (Moghaddam, 2008b, p. 12). Human social skills evolved in small groups, and our identifications were in the context of relatively small groups. Now we are required to identify not with a village or town but with units as large as the European Union or even with all of "humanity" and the "global village."

The new characteristics of globalization have created on the one hand a global village based on interdependence but on the other hand a place in which some groups feel seriously threatened. Indeed, from some perspectives, globalization has fueled a fierce competition for survival among groups, a topic we turn to next.

Catastrophic Evolution

From our earliest experiences with bipedalism about 5 million years ago, human populations were on the move and came to occupy all of the major land masses by about 10,000 years ago, as documented by genetic studies tracing the patterns of human movements around the globe (Cavalli-Sforza, Menozzi, & Piazza, 1994). The movements of humans into new territories necessarily took place fairly slowly, and this meant that human groups had relatively more time to adapt to new environmental conditions as well as to new animals, plants, and also other groups of humans. As human groups dispersed to find vacant spaces, their characteristics changed to fit environmental conditions and variations across groups increased. This dispersion and adaptation to different environmental conditions resulted in widely different variations in behavior. For example, in the domain of collective aggression, the traditional Tiwi of northern Australia had little experience of collective aggression (Hart, Pilling, & Goodale, 2000), whereas the Yanamamo, who live in the Amazon jungles of Brazil and Venezuela, routinely participated in collective aggression (Chagnon, 1997).

Sudden contact is made possible by far more efficient transportation and communications systems. Modern ships, aircraft, trains, automobiles, and so on enable hundreds of millions of people to move around the world at a rapid pace every year. Of course, during the height of the Chinese, Egyptian, and Roman empires of the ancient world, there was extensive international trade, but this did not involve the movement of people (1) in such enormous numbers and (2) at such rapid speeds. Also, in the premodern world, most of the movement of people around the world consisted of the slave trade. Thus, a new feature of globalization in the 21st century is the rapid speed with which large populations can be voluntarily transported and put into contact with other groups with which they previously had little or no contact. This has important implications when life forms have not previously had opportunities to develop the characteristics for survival in contact with particular other life forms, as discussed next.

Preadaptiveness

All life forms have a given level of preadaptiveness (after Ehrlich, 2000), which indicates their level of evolutionary success in a given environment and in contact with other competitors. High preadaptiveness in a given environment and in contact with other competitors means that a life form will increase in numbers; low preadaptiveness means the life form will decline in numbers and perhaps even become extinct.

An important aspect of coping with change for all life forms is postcontact adaptation speed, how quickly they can adapt to new environmental conditions, including contact with new life forms, which serve as their competitors. While traditional Darwinian approaches to evolution give attention to long-term change processes, more recent scholarship has also focused on rapid change, particularly evolutionary change associated with human activities (e.g., Palumbi, 2001). The evolutionary history of human cultures and languages demonstrates considerable variation across groups in postcontact adaptation speed, so that some groups are in greater danger of experiencing decline and extinction as a result of sudden contact.

Numerous groups in Africa, Asia, and the Americas experienced rapid decline and even extinction after sudden contact with Europeans during the centuries of colonization by Western powers. Prior to the arrival of Europeans, the population of Africa is estimated to have been around 50 million (e.g., Caldwell, 1985) and that of the Americas to have been up to 100 million (e.g., Mann, 2006), but enormous numbers of these natives were killed (often through disease) in the centuries immediately after the arrival of European colonists. In some cases, entire populations seem to have been wiped out.

What made sudden contact between European colonists and African, Asian, and American natives extremely dangerous for the natives was the strong sense of superiority among many Europeans. There was a general tendency for Europeans, and later Americans, to take at face value the idea of the white man's burden, as the poet Rudyard Kipling described it, with the implication that white Europeans have a moral duty to guide the lives of "natives" whether they wanted outside intervention or not. An essential part of this guidance was forced conversion to Christianity. Thus, from the point of view of non-Western people, historically it is Christianity that is associated with violence and "terror."

Rethinking Contact

There is a long history of social-psychological research on intergroup contact, reflecting two different traditions (Moghaddam, 2008b). Underlying the first tradition is the idea that intergroup contact leads to more positive intergroup attitudes. Allport (1954) had stipulated a number of conditions that avowedly had to be met in order for intergroup contact to result in positive outcomes, such as the idea that the two groups should enjoy equal status. However, in meta-analytic reviews of the research literature on the contact hypothesis, Pettigrew and colleagues (e.g., Pettigrew & Tropp, 2006) concluded that irrespective of the conditions in which intergroup contact takes place, contact has positive outcomes. This optimistic view of intergroup contact is opposed by terror management theory (Pyszczynski, Solomon, & Greenberg, 2004), which postulates that contact with dissimilar outgroups can raise mortality salience and result in increased feelings of threat among ingroup members.

Catastrophic evolution is more in line with terror management theory, in that intergroup contact is depicted as potentially associated with the perception of outgroup threat. According to catastrophic evolution, under certain conditions groups can achieve the preadaptation necessary to overcome the challenges raised by sudden contact. One such condition is that the two groups coming into contact should be fairly equal in power and resources. This is not presently the case in contact between Muslims and Christians in much of the world: Muslims have relatively less military, economic, and political power. Consequently, at the global level Muslims are a power minority in this relationship. This power and resource disparity, and the minority status of Muslims at the global level, must be kept in mind in order to better understand the emergence of Islamic radicalization and terrorism.

Thus, catastrophic evolution constitutes the macrocontext in which some groups experience threatened collective identities. We now turn to a staircase metaphor to discuss the paths followed by individuals to commit acts of terror. Again, our focus is on context rather than dispositional characteristics. Our argument is that under certain conditions there inevitably will be individuals who emerge to commit acts of terror: tactics such as psychological profiling do not solve root problems, because every terrorist "taken out" is simply replaced by others moving up the staircase to terrorism. The long-term solution to terrorism is to understand and act to change the context from which terrorists arise. However, this does not negate the need for short-term solutions as well: individuals who climb all the way up the staircase to terrorism have to be dealt with through short-term solutions (Moghaddam, 2006b).

MOVING UP THE STAIRCASE TO TERRORISM: PSYCHOLOGICAL PROCESSES

Imagine a narrowing staircase in a tall building, leading an individual higher and higher to the final floor where the terrorist act is undertaken. The vitally important feature of the situation is how individuals subjectively perceive the staircase, the different floors, and the doors and spaces that are open or closed to them. Thought and action on each floor is characterized by particular psychological processes, but a theme that continues all the way up the staircase is the primacy of identity and the perception of threatened collective identity. All individuals start on the ground floor—there are over a billion Muslims at the bottom of the staircase. The vast majority of these Muslims never leave the ground floor, and never think about stepping onto the staircase to terrorism. But a tiny minority does move up to higher floors, and as they climb their choices become fewer and fewer, because the variety of choices available to them are perceived to be narrower.

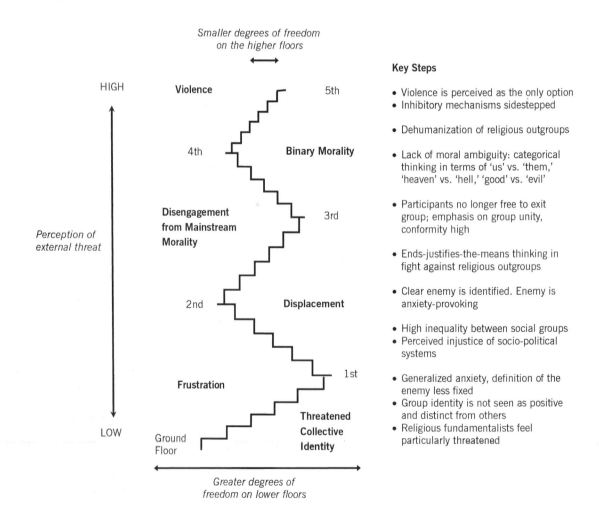

FIGURE 32.1. The staircase to terrorism with associated psychological processes on each floor.

Degrees of Freedom and the Staircase to Terrorism

A key assumption behind theories of social influence, such as theories of obedience, conditioning, revenge, or victimization, is that human agency operates within situational constraints. The fewer the degrees of freedom in a given situation, the less important is the role of personality in explaining behavior. In contexts with low degrees of freedom, such as Catholic mass or performing *namaz* at mosque, the who/what/how/when of behavior is restricted, as situational constraints allow for only a narrow range of physical and spoken behaviors. Contexts with high degrees of freedom, such as an informal social party, allow for a wide range of behaviors. Using a "big picture" approach, these constraints extend to cultural and historical situations.

First, though, let us consider a microcontext of situational constraint: a trial in a courtroom. All actors are appointed to arrive on a fixed day and time. If a person is a witness, he or she is sworn in by a court official and required to abide by a strict set of rules for conduct. The person is not permitted to speak aloud at whim, nor move from the witness stand and walk about freely. If the person notices something humorous about the jury or the judge, and recalls a funny joke from a friend, the person is not allowed to share this comical insight aloud. On the stand, the person is obligated to listen to questions asked by lawyers and the judge and to answer these honestly and directly. Failure to do so may constitute breaking the law and the person can be punished. From the moment an actor steps into the court until the moment he or she leaves, behavior is bounded by the situational context.

By contrast, consider celebratory traditions such as Saturnalia, *el Dia de Los Muertos,* and *Mardi Gras.* These appear to have no rule but the absence of rules, including in some cases the freedom to invert social norms: men dress as women, commoners dress as royalty, and so on (see Cox, 1969). In a typical county fair, parade, or festival, one can show up in the beginning, middle, or even the end: Time is not fixed. A person can walk freely, choosing where to stand, and can shout and voice opinions openly. Clowning and joking are permitted. These have a high degree of freedom, meaning that the power of the context to determine behavior is relatively weak and the power of personal choice is strong. A court of law, on the other hand, is a situation with low degrees of freedom, meaning that the power of the context on behavior is strong and personal choice is weak.

Importantly, the power of social context to restrict degrees of freedom extends to broader cultural, political, and religious contexts. For example, in Afghanistan (where one of us has carried out extensive fieldwork), it is legally permissible for a person to have a love marriage instead of an arranged one, but the informal social consequences of doing so when one's family or tribe is opposed may be so great that love marriage is not a viable option. Similarly, children raised in traditional religious families in various societies may face social obligations to marry a partner of the same religion, attend regular worship at church, temple, mosque, or meetinghouse, and raise progeny to be "good" members of their religious tribe. The formal and informal pressures may be such that significant behavioral "choices" are largely removed from the realm of individual personality or preference.

The Paradox of Choice and the Ground Floor

They [Westerners] imported their half-naked women into these regions, together with their liquors, their theatres, their dance halls, their amusements, their stories, their newspapers, their novels, their whims, their silly games, and their vices. Here they countenanced crimes they did not tolerate in their own countries, and decked out this frivolous strident world, reeking with sin and redolent with vice, to the eyes of the deluded, unsophisticated Muslims of wealth and prestige, and to those of rank and authority.—Hasan al-Banna (1906–1949), founder of the Muslim Brotherhood (al-Banna, 1979, pp. 49–50)

On the surface, the degrees of freedom available for individual action on the ground floor seem to be increased through economic and technological changes. Individuals seem to have more choices available to them, not only in terms of food and material things but also friends and social connections through electronic communications. However, in a profound way, individuals on the ground floor also have fewer choices. Globalization threatens diversity, even as it increases exposure to difference.

Consider, for example, the general concern in many parts of the world about declining diversity among animals and plants, a concern clearly reflected in academic publications, in the global mass media, in political discussions, and in the growing strength of the "green" environmentalist movement (Ehrlich & Ehrlich, 2008). Concepts of environmental pollution, invasive species, and endangered species lists are readily applied to plants and animals (e.g., Baskin, 2002; Ruiz & Carlton, 2004) but not to human societies. Despite documented declines in diversity among human cultures and languages (Crystal, 2003), contemporary globalization conveys an illusion of free choice.

Gergen (1991) describes the effect of increasing choices but declining agency in terms of the "saturated self." Inundated with a "sensory assault" of external information, such as a barrage of electronic messages and increased choices in consumption and relationships, the individual develops feelings of insecurity about self-identity. The individual's instinct is to react with fight-or-flight mechanisms rather than introspection. There are general feelings of discomfort, without a clear direction or object for blame, and the search for a secure identity can result in acts of displaced aggression.

A similar pattern can be used to describe groups. At the group level, globalization creates accelerated change and brings diverse social identities into contact and competition, often at tremendous speed. Presented with an avalanche of foreign identities, many groups, particularly minorities, feel a sense of insecurity. Often, groups react by forming an *oppositional identity* to whatever is perceived as external or foreign to their social identity (Ogbu, 1978). This can take the shape of religious and national identity. For example, the anti-Christian movement in China during the 1920s emerged as a reaction to rapid change and modernization, drawing upon public associations between Christianity and previous invasions of China by Western countries (Lutz, 1988; Hodous, 1930).

In many countries, religion and/or nationalism are primary sources for this oppositional identity (Moghaddam, 2008c). For example, anti-Western Islamic revivalism appears in the wake of postcolonial independence for countries like Lebanon, Syria, Egypt, and Saudi Arabia (Lapidus, 2002). These correspond with the need for a new, positive, and original identity, separate from the yoke of Western influence. Religious leaders such as al-Banna, quoted previously, regard the importation of Western culture, through trade, technology, colonialism, and neo-colonialism, as a central threat to Islamic identity. For al-Banna, Islam is perceived as alternative—rather than complementary—to Western culture.

In some cases, Islamic leaders rose to popularity primarily on the basis of anti-Western political and social platforms. For example, negative public opinion toward the Western-backed regime of the Shah of Iran contributed directly to the rise of Ayatollah Rohullah Khomeini (1902–1989) and the Islamic regime in Iran. A relationship between religion and nationalism emerged within a framework of oppositional identity, best summarized by the motto of the Revolutionary Guard itself: "Neither East Nor West—Islamic Republic!" (Ramazani, 1989). Lapidus (2002) argues that Islamic revivalism in various post-colonial countries, such as 1970s Egypt, "appealed especially to segments of the population that have lost out in the drive to modernization" (p. 530). In Egypt, many students and professionals from conservative and rural backgrounds felt a sense of insecurity in response to modern social changes, including changes in gender roles, urbanization, and frustrations about social class and corruption. Despite having access to professional skills, "socially they felt oppressed and frustrated" and had not undergone "a deep process of social or cultural adjustment" (p. 530).

Not surprisingly, many religious groups draw upon imagery of "golden ages" or call for a return to traditional values as an alternative to modern social changes. In his book *Milestones (Ma'alim fil Tariq)*, Egyptian author Sayyed Qutb (1964) describes the history of Islam as a short golden age under the Prophet Muhammad and Rashidun Caliphs, followed by constant decay. He calls for radical renewal *(tajdid)* by a return to the "pure" sources of Qu'ran and hadith, an approach that influenced many Islamic extremists, including Osama bin Ladin (Burke, 2007). Whereas global influences are associated with rapid change and uncertainty, religious identity enables a feeling of stability through connection to the past, whether or not that past is real or imagined, such as Qutb's vision of a golden era or fundamentalist Christian accounts of creationism as a viable alternative to evolution. However, not all collective identity insecurity leads to terrorist acts. The difference lies in a series of psychological steps.

Restraint Reduction, Suggestibility, and Social Identity Theory

A dispositional, leader-centered approach to understanding religiously motivated terrorism fails to understand not only the origin of terrorism but also the way that terrorism spreads. As noted in the *9/11 Commission Report*, anti-Western leadership meets broad appeal, particularly in developing regions of the world (see the discussion of the Ahmadinejad effect; Moghaddam, 2011). Yet of the many individuals who share this anti-Western sentiment, only a small minority join anti-Western organizations. Of those who join anti-Western organizations, only a small minority become violent. Important questions are "What stops the rest?" "Why do only a few become violent?" We argue that those who do become violent are influenced by *restraint reduction*, after ascending a "staircase" of decreasing degrees of freedom.

Restraint reduction refers to the removal of a restraint that otherwise prevents an individual from acting on an existing impulse or desire. *Suggestibility* refers to "the readiness of the individual to rely on others for psychological patterning when experiencing uncertainty, suspense, or anxiety" (Turner & Killian, 1987, p. 23). In a classic study on restraint reduction, Stephenson and Fielding (1971) examined the impact of a person leaving the room during a boring task on a subject paid to complete the same task. American female undergraduates were presented with the tedious task to construct as many words as possible using the letters of a given word (e.g., "stream" and "dinosaur").

The dependent variable was how long the participants stayed in the situational task before leaving. The independent variable was whether there was a confederate present who always left the situation after a short time. Once the confederate left the situation, participants tended to spend less time on the boring task. When multiple participants were grouped with one confederate, the same result occurred: Once one group member left, other group members followed more quickly and in a clustered fashion compared with the control group. Variations of the experiment have changed the task, confederate role (whether presented as a task peer vs. nonpeer), and degree to which the researcher emphasizes the rules. A "contagion effect" from rule violation behavior has also been observed in teenage smoking (Ritter & Holmes, 1969; Rowe, Chassin, Presson, Edwards, & Sherman, 1992), substance abuse (Ennett, Flewellin, Lindrooth, & Norton, 1997), delinquency (Jones, 1998), and youth sex (Rodgers & Rowe, 1993).

There also appears to be a key interaction effect between restraint reduction and categorical thinking. When restraints are lifted by someone perceived as similar, and when that similar person models aggressive behavior, the likelihood that aggressive behavior is mimicked increases. For example, Wheeler and Levine (1967) explored restraint reduction among U.S. Navy members using aggression models and tape-recorded conversations with confederates who expressed socially undesirable opinions. Researchers measured perceived similarity or difference to the confederate in terms of age, family size, home state, religion, race, and marital status. When participants were paired with confederates perceived (by the participant) to be socially similar, the participants were significantly more likely to model the aggressive response. Nearly a decade later, Goethals and Perlstein (1978) replicated this study on "contagious" aggressive behavior and found similar results: Contagion increased along categories of race, age, and marital status. Not coincidentally, terrorist organizations do not draw attention to likenesses between Islamic and Western societies. Instead, however, their messages are characterized by an emphasis on categorical differences with whatever is perceived to be the "superpower" (e.g., Islam in opposition to "the West"). What drives this tendency toward oppositional identity?

According to social identity theory (Tajfel & Turner, 1986), individuals strive to achieve positive and distinct identities which they derive from group membership. If an individual perceives that his or her group's traditions, values, and goals are both positive and distinct from those of other groups, this individual will likely have a positive and distinct identity. In contrast, if a person perceives that his or her group does not have a positive and distinct identity, he or she may challenge rival outgroups in an attempt to create an authentic identity.

Many young Muslims, including those living in the West, suffer from a lack of authentic identity, which may lead them to challenge Western culture. The Muslim community is undergoing a collective identity crisis (Moghaddam, 2006b), which trickles down to youth. Islamic group identity is not authentic but instead is dominated by imported Western ideals and cultural systems. The strategy of "copying the West" in some cases leads to the good copy problem, which arises when an "ideal identity" is adopted by individuals who can, at best, become good copies of the original and who are condemned to lack authenticity (Moghaddam, 2006b, pp. 36–38). Given the avalanche of Western cultural products, the best many young Muslims can hope for is to be a good copy of a Westernized individual but never "as good or better than the original Western models." However, many young Muslims who experience a lack of authentic identity see "pure" Islam as a viable alternative. In fundamentalist forms, it is expressed through alternative rules for dress, speech, interaction with women, marriage, finance and banking, diet, facial hair and hygiene, and other codes for social identity. Nonetheless, of those who use religion as a source of positive, alternative social identity, only a minority turn to violence: How? We contend that there is no single answer. Rather, the answer lies in a set of complex psychological processes related to decreasing degrees of freedom.

Beyond the Ground Floor

On climbing to the first floor, individuals are primarily concerned about mobility: improving their lives and moving up the system. They try different doors and spaces to find a path to improve their positions, given the severe political, economic, and social restrictions they suffer (Mostyn, 2002). Mobility is at the heart of modern ideas about fairness and justice: The popularity of the American dream attests to this. However, in ancient eras as well, Plato (see 1987, Book III, 415b, c, d) is among the important thinkers who endorsed the idea that there should be room for upward and downward circulation of individuals based on talent. The popularity of the American Dream—the notion that anyone who works hard and has talent can make it in America—attests to the continued popularity of individual social mobility. Unfortunately, in many Islamic societies, paths to social mobility based on merit are closed, and mobility depends on family connections and corruption.

Experiences on the first floor leave some individuals highly dissatisfied. The people who have climbed to this floor are not a large group in terms of the total population, but they are extremely angry and frustrated by the situation of their home countries and the threat that globalization poses for Muslim identity. On the second floor, these individuals find ways to vent their frustration—through displacement.

Displacement is a mechanism that plays a vital role in Freud's psychology and continues to be given attention in contemporary research (Miller, Pederson, Earlywine, & Pollock, 2003). Through displacement of negative sentiments onto outgroup targets, groups are able to achieve greater cohesion. Also, group leaders who focus group attention on external threats often benefit from stronger support themselves. This is well known in politics: In times of danger, citizens show stronger support for the ingroup leader and more authoritarian policies (e.g., Huddy, Feldman & Weber, 2007). Of course, in Islamic societies, much of the rhetoric from the leadership and the mass media helps to displace aggression onto two groups that represent the two major "rival" religions: Christianity, as represented by the United States, and Judaism, as represented by Israel (Moghaddam, 2006b).

The individuals who continue to move up the staircase experience a shift in moral thinking on the third floor. This shift involves disengagement from the morality of mainstream society, which judges terrorism to be immoral. Second, the individual engages strongly with a morality that endorses terrorism and the view that "the ends justify the means." The outcome is that those leaving the third floor to move to the fourth floor have already taken on a moral viewpoint that agrees: "Our enemy is evil and against God, and every means available to us must be used to win the war of good against evil. If innocent people are killed as a result of this war, they will go to heaven, and if they are guilty they will go to hell." Of those who adopt this moral system, some move further up the staircase.

Those who reach the fourth floor of the staircase to terrorism take on even more rigid categorical thinking, in a world they see to be divided into "us" and "them," good and bad, the godly and the godless, with no in-between. The adoption of this categorical thinking moves individuals a step further toward carrying out acts of terrorism. But a final set of steps have to be taken to the fifth floor, where the training of individuals results in a sidestepping of inhibitory mechanisms, behavioral signals that make it difficult for one human (or animal) to kill another (Lorenz, 1966). Would-be terrorists sidestep inhibitory mechanisms by coming to see potential victims as "against God," "deserving to die," "in league with Satan," and the like (Moghaddam, 2006b).

Thus, the journey up the staircase to terrorism is motored by perceived threats of globalization and Westernization to social identity, by a deep unhappiness about the regimes in power in many Muslim societies (regimes that are seen to be manipulated by Western and particularly American governments), and by various contributing psychological processes, each decreasing the degrees of freedom. Where the United States is seen as a driver of the global economy, and a military force backing many dictatorial regimes, such as in Saudi Arabia, anti-Western sentiment is often expressed through anti-American sentiment. The outcome is a displacement of aggression onto the United States and on the country perceived to be its ally in "Muslim" territory: Israel.

CONCLUSION

The challenges of globalization and social identity, of preadaptation and sudden contact, would not exist if religiously motivated terrorism were trait based. Personality and intrapersonal theories do little to explain the rise of Islamic terrorist groups, for example, or the role of collective, categorical meaning making by the Tutsi and the Hutu, or by members of the Islamic Brotherhood. Psychological theory can help explain the contemporary relationship between religion and terrorism when situational and macrolevel factors are taken into context. As the power of situational factors increases, the degrees of freedom decrease, and theories that emphasize the power of context should be given high priority.

However, this presents a dilemma for modern psychology. While situational constraints are major determinants of behavior, they are often perceived as "outside" mainstream psychology because they cannot be isolated in an experimental context. Psychology assumes that human actions are causally determined (Wegner, 2002), and the traditional experimental model in psychology involves manipulating independent variables, assumed causes, to determine their impact on dependent variables, assumed effects (see Moghaddam, 2005a, Chapter 2). Of course, intentionality and some measure of free will has to be assumed in the world outside the laboratory, such as in the law courts; otherwise, everyday life would become impossible as we know it. The major religions would also become nonsensical, because if human behavior is causally determined, then ideas such as sin, guilt, and personal responsibility go out of the window.

Traditional texts in psychology (e.g., Kalat, 2008) present the causal model as the only valid "scientific" paradigm for psychological inquiry and research. Not surprisingly, studies such as the Stanford Prison Experiment, Zimbardo's research on the power of situational factors to influence behavior, are often criticized as unscientific because they lack the traditional markers of an experiment: a control group and independent variables to be manipulated. However, in research contexts outside the laboratory, where the power of situational determinants is great, it is often impossible to isolate such variables. To study the relationship between religion and terrorism in a psychology laboratory, using the traditional experimental model, is as impractical as trying to understand bird migration patterns by unleashing a gaggle of geese in an auditorium. In the pursuit of bite-size simplicity, one misses the big picture.

Why do some religious individuals become violent, while others do not? For those who have reached the highest level of the staircase, the answer is relatively straightforward: Violence is seen as the only option. At the top of the staircase, there is no room for complexity. Dichotomous categorical thinking dominates: "us versus them," "Islam versus the West," "heaven versus hell." Not surprisingly, the convictions of those who commit terrorist acts must be very strong. Wavering, questioning, or engaging in ambiguity is not a social option. As Chris Hedges (2003) explains in his book *War is a Force that Gives Us Meaning,* violent acts are saturated with collective meaning. The act of killing another human being requires a tremendous amount of social training, including narratives that make killing the rational choice. Indeed, state-sanctioned militaries spend millions of dollars to socialize soldiers to obey orders and override inhibitory mechanisms (Grossman, 1995). In state-sanctioned violence, the language is binary (e.g., "You are either with us or against us"), and the collective narrative is based on patriotism. In religiously motivated terrorism, the language is binary and the narratives are based on religion. Both depend on training camps to ensure transmission. However, it is easy to lose sight of the big picture. Terrorism is not the result of a handful of psychopaths, or even a few training camps in this or that country. Rather, it is the result of a series of psychological processes driven by an unprecedented globalization and catastrophic evolution.

If our analysis is correct, then we should see terrorism arise not just in the Islamic world but also in other communities where collective ingroup identity is perceived to be threatened, and experiences of humiliation and fear arise in association with global trends (Moisi, 2009; also see the discussion of emotion and religion by Tsai, Koopmann-Holm, Miyazaki, & Ochs, Chapter 14, this volume). A closer examination of terrorist acts, such as the terrible events in Norway on July 22, 2011, demonstrate this to be the case. Collective identity threat was experienced by the 32-year-old white Norwegian male who detonated a car bomb outside the offices of the Norwegian prime minister and attacked youth attending a summer camp on a small island off the coast of Norway, killing 77 people and seriously injuring hundreds more. This Norwegian terrorist justified his acts as a way to defend Christian Norway and Europe against the "Islamic colonization" that he saw to be ongoing (Murphy, 2011). Sudden intergroup contact is likely to bring to the forefront collective identity threats, and extremists from many different groups, including religious ones, are likely to feel compelled to defend their ingroup collective identities. In this way, there will continue to be an association between religious extremism and terrorism, because of the important role that religion plays in the group life of 21st-century humans—but not because religion per se causes terrorism.

REFERENCES

al-Banna, Hasan. (1979). *Five tracts of Hasan al-Banna: A selection from majmu'at rasail al imam al shahid hasan al-banna* (C, Wendell, Trans.). Berkeley: University of California Press.

Al-Khattar, A. M. (2003). *Religion and terrorism: An interfaith perspective.* Westport, CT: Praeger.

Allport, G. (1954). *The nature of prejudice*. Cambridge, MA: Addison-Wesley.

Asch, S. E. (1956). Studies of independence and conformity: A minority of one against a unanimous majority. *Psychological Monographs, 70*(9, Whole No. 416).

Baskin, Y. (2002). *A plague of rats and rubber vines*. Washington, DC: Island Press.

Brown, R., & Gaertner, S. L. (Eds.). (2001). *Blackwell handbook of social psychology: Intergroup processes*. Oxford, UK: Blackwell.

Burke, J. (2007). *Al Qaeda*. London: Penguin Books.

Caldwell, J. C. (1985). The social repercussions of colonial rule: Demographic aspects. *UNESCO, 7*, 458–486.

Cavalli-Sforza, L. C., Menozzi, P., & Piazza, A. (1994). *The history and geography of human genes*. Princeton, NJ: Princeton University Press.

Chagnon, N. (1997). *Yanomamo*. New York: Harcourt Brace Jovanovich.

Cook, W. (2010). *The plight of the Palestinians: A long history of destruction*. London: Palgrave Macmillan.

Cox, H. (1969). *The feast of fools: A theological essay on festivity and fantasy*. Cambridge, MA: Harvard University Press.

Crystal, D. (2003). *Language death*. Cambridge, UK: Cambridge University Press.

Ehrlich, P. R. (2000). *Human natures: Genes, cultures, and the human prospect*. Washington, DC: Island Press.

Ehrlich, P. R., & Ehrlich, A. H. (2008). *The dominant animal: Human evolution and the environment*. Washington, DC: Island Press.

Ennett, S. T., Flewelling, R. L., Lindrooth, R. C., & Norton, E. C. (1997). School and neighborhood characteristics associated with school rates of alcohol, cigarette, and marijuana use. *Journal of Health and Social Behavior, 38*, 55–71.

Festinger, L., & Carlsmith, J. M. (1959). Cognitive consequences of forced compliance. *Journal of Abnormal and Social Psychology, 58*(2), 203–210.

Gergen, D. (1991). *The saturated self: Dilemmas of identity in contemporary life*. New York: Basic Books.

Goethals, G. R., & Perlstein, A. L. (1978). Level of instigation and model similarity as determinants of aggressive behavior. *Aggressive Behavior, 4*, 115–124.

Grossman, D. (1995). *On killing: The psychological cost of learning to kill in war and society*. New York: Little, Brown.

Harré, R., & Moghaddam, F. M. (Eds.). (2012). *Psychology for the third millennium*. London: Sage.

Hart, C. W. M., Pilling, A. R., & Goodale, J. C. (2011). *The Tiwi of Northern Australia* (3rd ed.). Mason, OH: Cengage Learning.

Hedges, C. (2003). *War is a force that gives us meaning*. New York: Anchor.

Heider, F. (1958). *The psychology of interpersonal relations*. New York: Wiley.

Hodous, L. (1930) The Anti-Christian Movement in China. *Journal of Religion, 10*(4), 487–494.

Homer-Dixon, T. (2006). *The upside of down: Catastrophe, creativity, and the renewal of civilization*. Washington, DC: Island Press.

Huddy, L., Feldman, S., & Weber, C. (2007). The political consequences of perceived threat and felt insecurity. *Annals of the American Academy of Political and Social Sciences, 614*, 131–153.

Jones, M. B. (1998). Behavioral contagion and official delinquency: Epidemic course in adolescence. *Social Biology, 45*, 134–142.

Kalat, J. W. (2008). *Introduction to psychology* (8th ed.). Pacific Grove, CA: Wadsworth.

Kirkpatrick, L. A. (2005). *Attachment, evolution, and the psychology of religion*. New York: Guilford Press.

Lapidus, I. M. (2002). *A history of Islamic societies*. Cambridge, UK: Cambridge University Press.

Lorenz, K. (1966). *On aggression* (M. Wilson, Trans.). New York: Harcourt, Brace & World.

Lutz, J. G. (1988). *Chinese politics and Christian missions: The anti-Christian movements of 1920–28*. Notre Dame, IN: Cross Cultural.

Mann, C. C. (2006). *1491: New revelations of the Americas before Columbus*. New York: Knopf.

Milgram, S. (1963). Behavioral study of obedience. *Journal of Abnormal and Social Psychology*. 67(4), 371–378.

Miller, N., Pederson, W. C., Earlywine, M., & Pollock, V. E. (2003). A theoretical model of triggered displaced aggression. *Personality and Social Psychology Review, 7*, 75–97.

Moghaddam, F. M. (2005a). *Great ideas in psychology: A cultural and historical introduction*. Oxford, UK: Oneworld.

Moghaddam, F. M. (2005b). The staircase to terrorism: A psychological exploration. *American Psychologist, 60*, 161–169.

Moghaddam, F. M. (2006a). Catastrophic evolution, culture, and diversity management policy. *Culture & Psychology, 12*, 415–434.

Moghaddam, F. M. (2006b). *From the terrorists' point of view: What they experience and why they come to destroy*. Westport, CT: Praeger.

Moghaddam, F. M. (2008a). *How globalization spurs terrorism*. Westport, CT.: Praeger.

Moghaddam, F. M. (2008b). *Multiculturalism and intergroup relations*. Washington, DC: American Psychological Association.

Moghaddam, F. M. (2008c). Religion and regional planning: The case of the emerging Shi'a region. In N. Slocum-Bradley (Ed.), *How identity constructions promote peace or conflict* (pp. 165–181). London: Ashgate.

Moghaddam, F. M. (2010). *The new global insecurity*. Santa Barbara, CA: Praeger.

Moghaddam, F. M. (2011). The 'Ahmadinejad effect' and 'pre-emptive' rights and duties. *Culture & Psychology, 17*, 297–301.

Moisi, D. (2009). *The geopolitics of emotion: How cultures of fear, humiliation, and fear are reshaping our world*. New York: Doubleday.

Mostyn, T. (2002). *Censorship in Islamic societies*. London: Saqi Books.

Murphy, D. (2011, July 25). Norwegian terrorist stirs multiculturalism opponents. *The Christian Science Monitor*. Retrieved December 8, 2011, from *www.csmonitor.com/World/Backchannels/2011/0725/Norwegian-terrorist-stirs-multicultural-opponents*.

National Commission on Terrorist Attacks upon the United States. (2004). *The 9/11 commission report*. Washington, DC: U.S. Government Printing Office.

Nelson, C. A. (2001). The development and neural bases of face recognition. *Infant and Child Development, 10*(1–2), 3–18.

Ogbu, J. U. (1978). *Minority education and caste: The American system in cross-cultural perspective*. San Diego: Academic Press.

Palumbi, S. R. (2001). *The evolution explosion: How humans cause rapid evolutionary change*. New York: Norton.

Pettigrew, T. F., & Tropp, L. R. (2006). A meta-analytic test of intergroup contact theory. *Journal of Personality and Social Psychology, 90*, 751–783.

Plato. (1987). *The republic* (D. Lee, Trans.). Harmondsworth, UK: Penguin.

Pyszczynski, T., Solomon, S., & Greenberg, J. (2004). *In the wake of 9/11: The psychology of terror*. Washington, DC: American Psychological Association.

Qutb, S. (1964). *Milestones*. Beirut: Holy Koran Publishing House.

Ramazani, R. K. (1989). Iran's foreign policy: Contending orientations. *Middle East Journal*. 43(2), 202–217.

Ritter, E. H., & Holmes, D. S. (1969). Behavioral contagion: Its occurrence as a function of different restraint reduction. *Journal of Experimental Research in Personality, 3*, 242–246.

Robertson, R., & Chirico, J. (1985). Humanity, globalization, and worldwide religious resurgence: A theoretical exploration. *Sociology of Religion, 46*(3), 219–242.

Rogers, J. L., & Rowe, D. C. (1993). Social contagion and adolescent sexual behavior—A developmental EMOSA model. *Psychological Review, 100*, 479–510.

Rowe, D. C., Chassin, L., Presson, C., Edwards, D., & Sherman, S. J. (1992). An epidemic model of adolescent cigarette-smoking. *Journal of Applied Social Psychology, 22*, 261–285.

Ruiz, G. M., & Carlton, J. T. (Eds.). (2004). *Invasive species: Vectors and management strategies.* Washington, DC: Island Press.

Sageman, M. (2008). *Leaderless Jihad: Terrorist networks in the 21st century.* Philadelphia: University of Pennsylvania Press.

Sherif, M. (1956). Experiments in group conflict. *Scientific American, 195,* 54–58.

Stephenson, G. M., & Fielding, G. T. (1971). An experimental study of the contagion of leaving behavior in small gatherings. *Journal of Social Psychology, 84,* 81–91.

Tajfel, H., & Turner, J. C. (1986). The social identity theory of intergroup behavior. In S. Worchel & W. G. Austin (Eds.), *Psychology of intergroup relations* (pp. 7–24). Chicago: Nelson-Hall.

Taylor, D. M., & Moghaddam, F. M. (1994). *Theories of intergroup relations: International social psychological perspectives.* Westport, CT: Praeger.

Turner, R. H., & Killian, L. M. (1987). *Collective behavior* (3rd ed.). Englewood Cliffs, NJ: Prentice-Hall.

Wegner, D. M. (2002). *The illusion of conscious will.* Cambridge, MA: MIT Press.

Wheeler, L., & Levine, L. (1967). Observer–model similarity in the contagion of aggression. *Sociometry, 30,* 41–49.

Zimbardo, P. (2007). *The Lucifer effect: Understanding how good people turn evil.* New York: Random House.

Part VI

CONCLUSION AND FUTURE DIRECTIONS

33

Directions for the Future of the Psychology of Religion and Spirituality

Research Advances in Methodology and Meaning Systems

Crystal L. Park and Raymond F. Paloutzian

The increasing interest in the psychology of religion and spirituality among researchers and clinicians (Paloutzian & Park, Chapter 1, this volume) raises many questions about the directions in which the field is headed. We are optimistic about the continued growth and sophistication in our understanding of the ways in which religion and spirituality comprise critical aspects of human experience. We also believe that this increased understanding will be influenced by the changes and trends occurring in the larger culture and must be understood within this context. In this chapter, we present our vision of the psychology of religion and spirituality in the coming years and provide suggestions for scholars in this area, including important directions for future research along with some caveats. To provide structure, these suggestions are presented according to our (slightly modified) integrative thematic framework. However, to complement our emphases in Chapter 1, we highlight two foci in this chapter. First, we discuss the unfolding of research and theory on meaning making. Second, we present exemplary research that illustrates how studies can be done in different contexts and various creative ways in which researchers can craft designs, procedures, and measures to yield new knowledge to feed a multilevel interdisciplinary paradigm. These two major sections are preceded by a shorter section on theory and followed by information about possible future paths and roles of this field.

THE CONTINUING SEARCH FOR THEORY IN THE PSYCHOLOGY OF RELIGION

The lack of strong theory in the psychology of religion has been noted for many years (see Paloutzian & Park, 2005, for a detailed discussion). Our discussion of theoretical issues in Chapter 1 did not attempt to assess the ideas actually put forth as psychological theories of religion. Before such an evaluation of theory can be made, we must first settle the question of what such a theory would have to accomplish and for specifically what phenomena it would have to do so. A successful theory cannot emerge until scholars of the psychology of religion settle this point. Until then, it is fine to explore the depth of the ideas that have been offered–attachment theory, psychoanalytic theory, Jungian psychology of religion, various minimodels—and generate additional ones, but none would be likely to become the major, overarching explanation of religion because, given the field's present discourse, there is not enough common ground regarding the proper focus of a theory of religion. Whatever shape our combined thinking eventually takes, we propose that in order to succeed, it will have to rest heavily on the model of religion as a meaning system.

RELIGIOUS MEANING SYSTEMS

Issues of meaning and meaning making are increasingly regarded as central to many domains of functioning and well-being (see Park, 2010, for a review). We anticipate that work highlighting meaning will increase in both quantity and sophistication in coming years, and as it does, the relationship between meaning systems and religion and spirituality will be increasingly illuminated. Park (2011; Chapter 18, this volume) argued that although religion/spirituality is not explicitly present in all meaning systems, all meaning systems are built on some fundamental assumptions regarding epistemology, cosmology, and theology: Even hard-core atheists' global (i.e., overarching) meaning systems take a perspective, whether explicit or implicit, on who we are, how we got here, and what our responsibilities in this life are, if any.

Implicit Religion

A related line of thought is apparent in the notion of "implicit religion." Implicit religion refers to "those aspects of ordinary life which seem to contain an inherently religious element within them—whether or not they are expressed in ways that are traditionally described as "religious" (Centre for the Study of Implicit Religion and Contemporary Spirituality [CSIRCS], 2012). According to this view, the core defining features of religion, whether implicit or explicit (traditional), involve some kind of commitment, regardless of the characteristics or degree of that commitment or the extent to which it deals with sacrality or moral values (Bailey, 2010). To further characterize implicit religion, Schnell (2003) introduced the Tripartite Model of the elements that all things commonly identified as religions share: myth, ritual, and the experience of transcendence. These elements are similar to some of the five dimensions of religious commitment identified by Glock (1962) (i.e., ideology, ritual, and experience) and can be viewed as patterns of thinking (myth), acting (rituals), and feeling (in particular, experiences of transcendence). Schnell (2003) argued that these three elements underlie all kinds of religions, implicit and explicit, and are common elements independent of their particular content. However, she went further, stating that for a phenomenon to constitute a religion for someone requires that these myths, rituals, and experiences be personally meaningful. Thus, a particular set of myths, rituals, and experiences constitute religion only if the contents have personal referents and significance: "They turn into 'personal myth', 'personal rituals' and subjectively accessible transcendent experiences" (Schnell, 2003).

There are pros and cons to this idea of implicit religion. On the positive side, it specifies human commonalities as central to religion. However, there seem to be at least two difficulties with this notion. One is that just as anything can be sacred to someone, so also can anyone be committed to anything. Therefore, the logic of this way of solving the problem of defining religion is the same as the problem of defining "the sacred." The second difficulty surfaces in that, by default, this concept says that "everybody is religious," which does not provide a deep explanation. Obviously, *something* is implicit to humans, but religion may not be the most useful, or accurate, word for it.

Specific Personal Beliefs

The prior discussion leads to an important notion that we feel has not yet taken center stage but we believe will receive increased attention in coming years: the *specific* content of individuals' religious meanings. Very little work has taken seriously the need to focus on the specifics of one's belief system. Instead, studies have commonly used the term "beliefs" to refer to various and sundry aspects of religiousness or spirituality, such as behavior or emotions or identifications, rather than core beliefs (Park, 2012a). Further, even studies that have examined beliefs have tended to be based not on theological views or other religions doctrines but rather often combine different beliefs into omnibus "strength of belief" measures (Park, 2012a). Recent research suggests that the specifics of religious beliefs may powerfully affect general health and well-being as well as the types of meaning made from stressful and traumatic situations. For example, a study that went beyond inquiring about belief in an afterlife to inquiring about specific beliefs regarding the afterlife found that pleasant afterlife beliefs (e.g., a life of peace and tranquility) were associated with better mental health, but unpleasant beliefs about the afterlife were associated with poorer mental health (Flannelly, Ellison, Galek, & Koenig, 2008).

Attachment and Cognition

In addition to explicitly fleshing out the theory and specific workings of religious meaning systems, many lines of research within the psychology of religion and spirituality are incorporating religious and spiritual meaning system frameworks within their theoretical views. For example, Richert and Granqvist (Chapter 8, this volume) noted that much remains to be learned about children's religious and spiritual development, particularly the timing and processes through which children begin to question and reflect on their religious beliefs and how religion and spiritual meanings develop. Researchers are likely to pay increasing attention to the influences that shape religous and spiritual meaning systems not only in childhood but across the life span (McFadden, Chapter 10, this volume), an issue made increasingly salient with the aging of the baby boomers.

Cognitive aspects of religiousness and spirituality are also being profitably explored through a meaning framework. For example, Richert and Granqvist (Chapter 8, this volume) discussed the increasing recognition of dual cognitive processing models. Emerging research into the architecture of thought processes indicates that individuals process information at two different levels: an implicit/intuitive level and an abstract/rational level (Watts, 2007). People tend to combine these types of reasoning in idiosyncratic ways to in order to make meaning in accord with the needs of particular situations. Future research tracking these processes more closely will provide important insights into cognition about religious and spiritual things.

Self-Regulation and Control

Self-regulation (McCullough & Willoughby, 2009), also known as self-control (Zell & Baumeister, Chapter 25, this volume), is an emerging area of psychological inquiry that could usefully incorporate a focus on religious meaning systems, although it has yet to do so. As Zell and Baumeister (Chapter 25, this volume) note, the ways in which religion and spirituality promote self-control is poorly understood. They note that religion promotes self-control by upholding specific moral standards, by motivating people to want to be good, by exploiting the prosocial power of guilt, by linking the religious individual into a stable network of relationships to other believers and to God, by promoting character strength through regular exercise of the moral muscle, by fostering self-criticism, and by making people feel that their good and bad deeds are being observed and recorded. Religious meanings may be central in providing the specific moral standards to which people compare their behavior as well as the motivation to adhere to those standards. In addition, self-regulation can in large part be understood as efforts to maintain a relatively coherent overarching meaning system and to make meaning of encounters with the environment. Determining the links between religious meaning systems and self-regulation awaits future research.

Religion as Culture

Another emerging area within the psychology of religion and spirituality that can profitably incorporate a religious meaning-systems framework is that of religion as culture. As Saroglou and Cohen (Chapter 17, this volume) have discussed, there is great utility in thinking about religion as culture. Using a meaning-systems perspective can be helpful in understanding both the universalities and the idiosyncrasies in how each aspect of religiousness and spirituality (e.g., beliefs and thought processes regarding supernatural agents, moral rules and practices, collective and personal rituals and emotions, and identity) is transmitted from the cultural environment to the meaning system of the individual under study.

Healthcare

As a final example of religious meaning system frameworks being applied to a substantive area, consider health care. Mental health service providers are increasingly recognizing the importance of religious meaning systems to their clients, and increasingly attending to religious and spiritual issues at assessment and throughout the course of treatment (Shafranske, Chapter 30, this volume; Park & Slattery, 2009). Such recognition of the importance of religious and spiritual meaning systems to clients and patients will continue to spread through the healthcare system. Much of this expansion is due to the accumulating research demonstrating important links between religiousness or spirituality and physical health. The potential for religiousness and spirituality to affect hard endpoints such as morbidity and mortality (see Park, 2012b, and Masters & Hooker, Chapter 26, this volume) as well as medical decision making (e.g., Phelps et al., 2009) is increasingly demonstrated. With this increasing research, we believe the notion that knowledgeable and competent healthcare treatment must take religious meaning systems into account will be increasingly evident (Puchalski & Ferrell, 2010).

Some investigators have raised ethical questions regarding the promotion of religiousness and spirituality by healthcare professionals (see Mills, 2002). That is, if religiousness and spirituality are related to better health, should physicians and others in the healthcare system promote it? For example, Powell, Shahabi, and Thoresen (2003) argued, "When one considers that attending religious services is an inexpensive but widely available resource in the community, this could be a very cost-effective way to maintain the health of elderly people with disability or chronic diseases (p. 49). Hall (2006) noted that the cardiovascular benefits of Lipitor were comparable to those of service attendance vis-à-vis mortality in the general population. While he cautioned that there are "ethical, theological, and methodological problems with this instrumental approach" (p. 107), he nonetheless suggested that the associations between attendance and other aspects of religiousness and spirituality may have implications for medical practice in terms of providing an inexpensive and easily implementable intervention. Researchers asking questions about religious and spiritual meaning systems and physical and mental health should also take on the tough questions of the implications of their research for real-life practice and provide input into the broader discussion of ethics and policy in this regard (see Masters & Hooker, Chapter 26, this volume, for one approach).

In the long run, the broadening reach of meaning systems may give rise to the emergence of a new area of psychology called the "psychology of meaning processes." If so, it would be an umbrella that covers far more than just religiousness and spirituality, but the area called psychology of religion and spirituality may be a central part of it.

MULTILEVEL METHODOLOGICAL TRENDS

The recent past has seen an increase in the variety of ways that researchers have tried to answer psychology of religion questions. They look like an interesting mix of methods—some particularly clever—that enable us to explore the degree to which complementary methods yield consistent findings about the same phenomenon. If such findings are consistent, then the principles on which they rest can be considered more robust. For example, studies have combined two diverse methods (e.g., in-depth interviews plus controlled laboratory manipulations and measurements) or focused on a particularly unusual phenomenon of study. Together, they cover the range of psychological methods from so-called qualitative to quantitative, questionnaire administration to in-depth interviews, and physiological recording to simple stimulus presentation and response recording in the laboratory and the field. We now summarize illustrative examples and encourage their expansive and creative application in future work.

Questionnaires

The mainstay of procedures for research in the psychology of religion and spirituality has been the questionnaire. Questionnaires remain the most widely used tool, especially given the many scales developed to measure myriad aspects of religiousness and spirituality, including, among others, religious orientation or motivation, belief strength, degree of doubt, transcendence, religious social support, spiritual struggle, religious affect, sense of purpose, and fundamentalism (see Hill, Chapter 3, this volume). We expect that use of questionnaires in research on the psychology of religion and spirituality will have a long life. However, we anticipate that, concomitant with the continued development and refinement of other methods, some of which we describe here, questionnaire findings will increasingly be combined with those of other methods. Through triangulation, the questionnaire data and data obtained by other means can be brought together to jointly assess the meaning and reliability of the results and add to the richness of the findings.

Priming

A prominently used technique at present involves priming a subject with a religiously relevant stimulus (above or below sensory threshold) and examining the effect of that stimulus on a range of attitudinal, emotional, or behavioral dependent variables compared with a no-stimulus control group and/or a neutral-stimulus control group. Experiments of this sort are seen frequently now (see, e.g., Randolph-Seng & Nielsen, 2007; Saroglou, Corneille, & Van Cappellen, 2009; Shariff & Norenzayan, 2007; Van Cappellen, Corneille, Cols, & Saroglou, 2011), and we expect this trend to continue.

Especially promising for purposes of external validity, researchers have also demonstrated that the priming technique can be successfully used in the context of a field experiment, under ordinary "real-life" circumstances. For example, in a clever study, LaBouff, Rowatt, Johnson, and Finkle (2012) studied people who were walking by either a religious landmark (e.g., a historic church building) or an equivalent nonreligious landmark, in order to assess whether effects on attitudes toward outgroups would differ according to the contexts. When walking by the religious landmark, the prime increased the participants' self-reported political conservatism, negative opinions of outgroups, and personal religiosity compared with those walking by a nonreligious landmark; the differences were not related to personal belief in God. This field experiment is a fine example of how to derive hypotheses from laboratory studies and test them in real-life field settings.

Qualitative Methods

Qualitative methods are a set of techniques whose aim is to dig deep into the thought processes of a subject in order to discover the deeper psychological meanings that may underlie the person's speech. As such, qualitative approaches may be particularly useful when the aim of a study is to dig deep into the specifics of a person's stated beliefs. The procedure includes an open-ended or guided interview that is recorded and transcribed. The transcriptions are then closely examined, ideally by independent coders who do not know the hypotheses of the study, whose codings are then examined relative to one other in order to establish scoring reliability. Grounded theory is a frequently used procedure for analyzing the transcriptions (Glaser & Strauss, 1999; Strauss & Corbin, 1998).

Because it is a labor-intensive procedure, such studies typically include data from a relatively small number of participants, which some might consider a drawback relative to quantitative methods because the representativeness of the sample is necessarily minimal. For example, a study of this sort might report data from as few as three but often about 12–20 participants, whereas questionnaire data can be collected from hundreds or thousands of people, especially using technology such as Amazon Mechanical Turk or other Internet modalities. One fine exception to the small sample size typical of qualitative studies was by Streib, Hood, Keller, Csöff, and Silver (2009; see also Paloutzian, Murken, Streib, & Rößler-Namini, Chapter 20, this volume). The research team conducted in-depth interviews with 99 deconverts and 177 in-tradition religious believers, an unusually large sample for such methods. A single datum, however, was expensive in terms of labor; it took the researchers 3 years to collect these data. Two fine small-scale examples, more typical of such methods, are in Jindra's (2008) study of religions conversion and Gockel's (2009) study of spirituality and healing.

Social Neuroscience

The multilevel field of social neuroscience has become prominent in recent years. This is partly because new tools allow for ever-more-precise brain imaging and partly because our conceptualization of what the brain is and does is undergoing change. The emerging understanding of the brain is that it is an organ that interacts with the body but also with culture and the world; it proactively regulates what the human sees, does, and feels in relation to the environment, while at the same time it is determined, shaped, and molded by it (Kitayama & Park, 2010; Todorov, Fiske, & Prentice, 2011). Thus, the human brain and the social and cultural context in which the person is submerged are an inseparable interacting unit. For overviews of research, see McNamara (2009; McNamara & Butler, Chapter 11, this volume); for well-executed experimental investigations and analyses, see a study in which participants' brains were scanned when reading biblical Psalm 23 (Azari, 2006; Azari, Missimer, & Seitz, 2005; Azari & Slors, 2007) and a study in which charismatic Christians' brains were scanned while speaking in tongues (Schjødt, Stødkilde-Jørgensen, Geertz, Lund, & Roepstorff, 2011). Brain-scanning techniques seem likely to be increasingly used in future psychology of religion and spirituality studies.

In the Wild

The phrase "in the wild" connotes studying religiousness in all its manifestations—belief, feeling, knowledge, practice, consequences (Glock, 1962)—as it is naturally occurring "out there in real ordinary life," rather than as it is reflected by a response to a manipulated stimulus cue, a mark on a questionnaire, words confided to an interviewer, or with one's head in a brain scan machine. It is not that experiments, questionnaires, interviews, and neuroscientific data are of no use, but that if our goal is to understand religiousness as it occurs in people's ordinary lives, then sooner or later ideas derived from other methods need to be tested out there, "in the wild" so to speak. We briefly describe four examples of field studies selected to illustrate various ways that research in this area can be done.

One strategy is to take the laboratory to the field. Many people perform rituals as part of their religious expression. Most rituals do not seem particularly intense or dangerous, although they might be uniquely intense for a particular person. But some rituals are intense and dangerous by their very nature. In some countries, such as Greece, fire-walking rituals may have a fundamentally religious character (Xygalatas, 2012). In the small Spanish village of San Pedro Manrique (population 600), however, the fire walking itself is not explicitly religious, but the Catholic religion carries "tremendous importance for the locals" (Xygalatas, Konvalinka, Roepstorff, & Bulbulia, 2011, p. 735). Xygalatas studied fire walking in this village. Before a crowd of 3,000 onlookers (five times the size of the village), the participants walked across a bed of hot, glowing coals while holding another person, usually a loved one, on their shoulders. Xygalatas measured participants' heart rate during and after the walking, had participants rate their degree of pain sensation, took photographs of their faces as they had their bare feet on the coals, and assessed their perceptions of their sensations several months later. Many interesting findings emerge from this research, but one of them gleaned from interview data was "a strong social desire in the participants to appear calm," which was "further supported by anthropological data showing a popular opinion that getting burned was an indication of weakness or lack of divine protection" (Schjødt et al., 2013).

Another strategy is to combine methods, using each for its particular strength but joining the ideas that drive them as well as evaluating their findings in combination in order to gain a more whole understanding of the phenomena of concern. An excellent example of combining methods is Luhrmann (2012) plus Luhrmann, Nusbaum, and Thisted (2013). Luhrmann's 2012 book documents a multiyear in-depth interview and behavioral observation examination of the nature of prayer in a set of Evangelical Christians, members of the Vineyard Church, who engage in "lite" speaking in tongues. These believers also say that prayer means talking with God, and that a relationship with God can include having a cup of coffee with God (such that a cup is poured for God as well as for oneself), going on a date with God, and other similar behaviors for which the capability to vividly imagine God as a live person in the here and now suggests that the individuals have a special proclivity to be able to become fully absorbed in the mental and "social" processes with God. The interviews suggested a research hypothesis to Luhrmann, that such persons, who would in particular engage in kataphatic (imagination-based) prayer, would, in a laboratory situation, show more vividness in mental imagery, use mental imagery more than others, show more attention to specific objects, and report more unusual sensory experience and religious experience—all manifestations of differences in the nature of cognitive processes between persons who engage in such imagery and those who do not. The study by Luhrmann (2012) is a multiyear interview study; that by Luhrmann et al. (2013) is an experimental investigation of a group of "gently" charismatic Evangelicals. The results that emerge from these two very different methods converge; they map well upon each other and support the notion that intentional immersion in a worldview influences perception of reality. This series of studies illustrates how findings are more robust when they are supported by data from multiple methods.

Another strategy is to take well-known tools, such as questionnaires, to the field. Chilcott (2012) did this in order to examine the degree to which religious practice within a single tradition played a role in how much people explicitly and implicitly tended to anthropomorphize divine agents. His study exemplified ethnographic quasi-experimental research, testing ideas that extend findings from Western psychology laboratories but for which, to determine their external validity out in the "real world," there was no substitute but to go collect data in the field. This took Chilcott (2012) to the area of West Bengal, India, to focus on the Gaudiya Vaishnava tradition for whom the supreme diety and exclusive object of devotion is Krishna. In a sample of 206 indigenous participants who either ritually or self-identified as Gaudiya practitioners, Chilcott measured the extent to which individuals *explicitly* attributed anthropomorphic properties to the deity Krishna and administered a set of narrative comprehension tasks to measure the extent to which each *implicitly* attributed anthropomorphic properties to Krishna. A multiple regression procedure showed that the more a person was engaged in exoteric[1] practices, the less he or she would explicitly as well as implicitly attribute anthropomorphic properties to Krishna. This project can be seen as a small tip of a big iceberg of possible research in the field across global and local religions, whose results bear upon questions of how deities are perceived and what they, or relations with them, mean to humans.

The study by LaBouff et al. (2012) noted previously in the discussion on priming is an excellent example of combining methods. LaBouff skillfully adapted the priming technique developed in the laboratory to the field setting. He was thus able to test a laboratory-derived hypothesis "in the wild," confirm it, and add to the robustness of the principle.

Integrative Thread of Meaning

In the context of this broad menu of methodological options, we highlight a core conceptual thread that can link findings from one to the other: the notion of meaning processes. Whether the study involves in-depth interviews with interpretations to get at the root of what people mean when they talk, observing behavior in naturally occurring circumstances, rating strength of belief or frequency of a practice, documenting the relationships between social context and neural events, or recording a response triggered by a religiously laden cue, the key to our generating a theory capable of accounting for them is to integrate them within the framework of meaning making. This approach is useful for conceptualizing a wide array of processes through which people behave, think, feel, perceive, and decide. As illustrated in Chapter 1, this statement holds at the microlevel of neural processing of information, intermediate levels such as perception and learning, and more complex levels such as social and religious behaviors, attitudes, and decisions. We need to collect the data and connect the data points that integrate findings at these various levels.

CONTINUING TO WIDEN THE RELIGION/SPIRITUALITY RESEARCH PATH

As we noted in Chapter 1, research in the psychology of religion and spirituality has developed along a number of new pathways, and we anticipate that advances in these new directions will continue. Three such directions suggest an array of research possibilities that seems wide open.

Technology and Religion

One pathway likely to receive additional research attention in coming years is the intersection of religion and spirituality, with the changes occurring in society at large wrought by the ever-increasing incursion of technology into modern life. The world is interconnected in ways that would have been unimaginable just a few decades ago, and the rapid pace of change poses constant challenges to adjust. People are—or can be—wired in 24/7, instantly connected with friends and family—or complete strangers—any time, any place. The accumulated knowledge of the world is literally at our fingertips. Research is needed to understand the effects of these lifestyle changes on our religious and spiritual lives. For example, how does the constant temptation to multitask affect an individual's inner spiritual life? As more of life is lived online, how does that virtual life affect one's sense of connection to others sharing similar beliefs and one's participation in traditional congregational life? These issues are being actively pursued by researchers from many disciplines (e.g., Campbell, 2012; Kale, 2004; Lundby, 2011), but to date few psychologists have contributed to this inquiry.

Globalization

Globalization is another pathway of increasing importance in the future of the psychology of religion and spirituality. Although the world is becoming increasingly interconnected and seemingly smaller, modern psychology is still primarily a Western enterprise, and the majority of research in the psychology of religion and spirituality has been conducted in Western countries. Research across a greater span of the globe is needed. Without it, our understanding of the commonalities and variations of the meanings of religion and spirituality across different groups is hindered (Saroglou & Cohen, Chapter 17, this volume). However, this situation is changing as researchers in the Middle East, Far East, and other regions of the world increasingly take on aspects of the psychology of religion and spirituality (for examples, see recent issues of *Mental Health, Religion & Culture* and *The International Journal for the Psychology of Religion*). And we anticipate that researchers will increasingly turn to broader samples, attending more closely to the issues of religion as culture (Saroglou & Cohen, Chapter 17, this volume) as well as the extent to which culture shapes religious expressions.

Secularization

At least in the United States and Europe, researchers have noted a trend toward secularization. This trend is reflected by the increasing numbers of people reporting that they do not identify with any religious affiliation as well as the number of people reporting that they are atheist or agnostic. Recent polls in the United States have indicated that 19% of Americans claim "none" as their religion, up from 8% in 1990 (Kosmin/*USA Today*, 7/20/12), and that 10% of Americans refer to themselves as "atheist" and an additional 9% as "agnostic" (Zuckerman, 2011). There is a new discipline of secular studies, with college programs as well as its own journal *(www.secularismandnonreligion.org)*. We anticipate that this trend toward secularization will receive increasing research attention, and will bring renewed attention to the focus on atheism and apostacy/deconversion, which have been areas of research concern within the psychology of religion and spirituality for many years (see in this volume Rowatt, Johnson, LaBouff, & Gonzalez, Chapter 23, and Paloutzian et al., Chapter 20).

WHAT ADDITIONAL ROLES MIGHT THE PSYCHOLOGY OF RELIGION AND SPIRITUALITY PLAY?

More Diffuse and Distinct

The field of the psychology of religion and spirituality is becoming more diffuse. Research is increasingly undertaken not only by psychologists who identify as specialists in this particular domain, but by many psychologists, sociologists, healthcare researchers, anthropologists, cognitive neuroscientists, and others. Further, applications of religiousness and spirituality to clinical settings have become fairly commonplace, particularly as adjuncts to other types of empirically validated treatments (Shafranske, Chapter 30, this volume). In addition, many of the so-called "third-wave therapies" integrate a good dose of mindfulness, much of it borrowed from Buddhism (e.g., Churchill et al., 2010), thus bringing spirituality into manual-based empirically supported treatments through the back door.

As research and applications in the psychology of religion and spirituality become more common and mainstream, the question naturally arises, "Will the psychology of religion and spirituality as a subdiscipline disappear, becoming so thoroughly integrated into the broader field of psychology and taken up by so many other disciplines that its distinct character disappears?"

We believe that the answer to this question is "No." Psychologists from other subdisciplines and researchers from other disciplines have long been studying religiousness and spirituality, and while this multidisciplinary attention is likely to continue, this work, when focused on psychological aspects, will likely to contribute to the corpus of research in the psychology of religion and spirituality, regardless of the title or training of the researchers conducting the studies. In addition, it is important that work done by researchers who do not have a strong background in the psychology of religion and spirituality and only minimal knowledge of religiousness and spirituality draws strongly from this corpus of theory and empirical study in designing and interpreting results; otherwise, it is easy to mischaracterize religious or areligious people, misinterpret results, and perpetuate stereotypes.

Research Funding

There is a trend opposite that of the increasing interest in and proliferation of research in the psychology of religion that is apparent in the U.S. National Institutes of Health (NIH). The National Center for Complementary and Alternative Medicine (NCCAM), part of NIH, has completely moved away from not only religion but spirituality in terms of a focus of information or funding opportunities. Previously, NCCAM considered prayer as an aspect of CAM, but no longer does (Park, in press). Although there has been some controversy about whether prayer should be considered CAM (Tippens, Marsman, & Zwickey, 2009), Americans are increasing their use of prayer as healthcare (Wachholtz

& Sambamoorthi, 2011). Given this increased use, along with the accumulating research showing the impact of religious and spiritual factors on physical health (e.g., see Masters & Hooker, Chapter 26, this volume), it is surprising that NIH now devotes virtually no funding for research on religion/spirituality and health, aside from an occasional grant focused on minority health issues. In fact, a search of NIH websites, of which there are hundreds, yields almost no mention of religious or spiritual issues (cf. *www.cancer.gov/ cancertopics/pdq/supportivecare/spirituality/Patient/page3*). This silence on the part of the federal organization most prominent in research on the health of U.S. citizens speaks loudly. In terms of a funded research area, the psychology of religion and spirituality appears to be dropping off the radar as a mainstream topic. On the other hand, some funds from private sources appear to be increasing along with influencing the topics of research. For example, the Templeton Foundation supports research in the psychology of religion and spirituality along lines in keeping with its mission. The long-term implications of this changing funding landscape are not yet clear. We think it is better for intellectual work in this field to be supported by a variety of funding sources.

Politics and Religion

Politics in the United States and around the world greatly interact with and are concerned with religion-related issues. In the United States, abortion and gay rights continue to garner an arguably disproportionately large share of attention and controversy relative to other issues of greater impact on citizen's lives, such as the economy or involvement in military conflicts. One recent issue draws upon the First Amendment, invoking the terminology of religious freedom in issues of reproductive health. For example, some religious organizations have cited personal religious commitments as a reason to be released from professional obligations to dispense birth control measures to patients who ask for them (Shah, Franck, & Farr, 2012). Perhaps our increased understanding of the psychology of religion and spirituality can shed some light on these issues. We hope to see more political decisions informed by the science of the psychology of religion and spirituality in the future.

In closing, research ideas such as those presented here take us to a new place that may be uncomfortable for those who desire a clearly bounded subdiscipline, but it does not mean that there is no center or ground to it. It does mean that it has to be approached with more flexibility, so we in the psychology of religion and spirituality see ourselves playing a part with companions to see how people work out their questions of meaning. As with the 2005 *Handbook*, we think that this area of scientific research is among the most important that can be studied. It is to the good of this world that we hope that this second edition contributes.

NOTE

1. Mental and behavioral practices that serve the two-fold purpose of regulating, modifying, and orienting one's thoughts and behavior away from the mundane world and toward Krishna and for becoming steeped in understanding of Krishna in both his anthropomorphic and nonanthropomorphic dimensions.

REFERENCES

Azari, N. P. (2006). Neuroimaging studies of religious experience: A critical review. In P. McNamara (Ed.), *The psychology of religious experience: Where God and science meet* (Vol. 3, pp. 33–54). Westport, CT: Praeger.

Azari, N. P., Missimer, J., & Seitz, R. J. (2005). Religious experience and emotion: Evidence for distinctive cognitive neural patterns. *The International Journal for the Psychology of Religion, 15*, 263–281.

Azari, N. P., & Slors, M. (2007). From brain imaging religious experience to explaining religion: A critique. *Archive for the Psychology of Religion, 29*, 67–85.

Bailey, E. (2010). Implicit religion. *Religion, 40*, 271–278.

Campbell, H. A. (2012). Understanding the relationship between religion online and offline in a networked society. *Journal of the American Academy of Religion, 80*, 64–93.

Centre for the Study of Implicit Religion and Contemporary Spirituality. (2012). *Implicit religion.* Retrieved August 10, 2012, from *www.equinoxjournals.com/IR/index*

Chilcott, T. (2012, October). *Religious practices, frequencies of engagement, and anthropomorphic attribution: An experimental ethnographic study on the cognitive effects of Bengal Vaishnava practices.* Paper presented at the conference on Homo Experimentalis: Experimental Approaches in the Study of Religion, Brno, Czech Republic.

Churchill, R., Moore, T. H. M., Davies, P., Caldwell, D., Jones, H., Lewis, G., et al. (2010). Mindfulness-based 'third wave' cognitive and behavioural therapies versus treatment as usual for depression (protocol). *Cochrane Database of Systematic Reviews*, Issue 9. Art. No.: CD008705.

Flannelly, K., Ellison, C., Galek, K., & Koenig, H. (2008). Beliefs about life-after-death, psychiatric symptomology and cognitive theories of psychopathology. *Journal of Psychology and Theology, 36*, 94–103.

Glaser, B., & Strauss, A. (1999). *The discovery of grounded theory: Strategies for qualitative research.* New York: DeGruyter.

Glock, C. Y. (1962). On the study of religious commitment: Review of recent research bearing on religious character formation. *Religious Education, 42*(Suppl.), 98–110.

Gockel, A. (2009). Spirituality and the process of healing: A narrative study. *The International Journal for the Psychology of Religion, 19*, 201–230.

Hall, D. E. (2006). Religious attendance: More cost-effective than Lipitor? *Journal of the American Boa rd of Family Medicine, 19*, 103–109.

Jindra, I. W. (2008). Religious stage development among converts to different religious groups. *The International Journal for the Psychology of Religion, 18*, 195–215.

Kale, S. K. (2004). Spirituality, religion, and globalization. *Journal of Macromarketing, 24*, 92–107.

Kitayama, S., & Park, J. (2010). *Cultural neuroscience of the self: Understanding the social grounding of the brain.* New York: Oxford University Press.

Kosmin/USA Today, 7/20/12. Retrieved from *www.usatoday.com/USCP/PNI/Nation/World/2012–07–22–NORELIGION_ST_U.htm.*

LaBouff, J. P., Rowatt, W. C., Johnson, M. K., & Finkle, C. (2012). Differences in attitudes towards outgroups in religious and non-religious contexts in a multi-national sample: A situational context priming study. *The International Journal for the Psychology of Religion, 22*, 1–9.

Luhrmann T. A. (2012). *When God talks back: Understanding the American Evangelical relations with God.* New York: Knopf.

Luhrmann, T. A., Nusbaum, H., & Thisted, R. (2013). "Lord, teach us to pray": Prayer practice affects cognitive processing. *Journal of Cognition and Culture, 13*, 159–177.

Lundby, K. (2011). Patterns of belonging in online/offline interfaces of religion. *Information, Communication & Society, 14*, 1219–1235.

McCullough, M. E., & Willoughby, B. L. B. (2009). Religion, self-regulation, and self-control: Associations, explanations, and implications. *Psychological Bulletin, 135,* 69–93.

McNamara, P. (2009). *The neuroscience of religious experience.* New York: Cambridge University Press.

Mills, P. J. (2002). Spirituality, religiousness, and health: From research to clinical practice. *Annals of Behavioral Medicine, 24,* 1–2.

Paloutzian, R. F., & Park, C. L. (2005). Integrative themes in the current science of the psychology of religion. In R. F. Paloutzian & C. L. Park (Eds.), *Handbook of the psychology of religion and spirituality* (pp. 3–20). New York: Guilford Press.

Park, C. L. (2010). Making sense of the meaning literature: An integrative review of meaning making and its effects on adjustment to stressful life events. *Psychological Bulletin, 136,* 257–301.

Park, C. L. (2011). Implicit religion and the meaning making model. *Implicit Religion, 14,* 405–420.

Park, C. L. (2012a). Attending to the construct of beliefs in research on religion/spirituality and health: Commentary on 'beyond belief.' *Journal of Health Psychology, 17*(7), 969–973.

Park, C. L. (2012b). Viewing atheism as an individual-difference variable: Suggestions for advancing research. *Religion, Brain, and Behavior, 2,* 35–38.

Park, C. L. (in press). Mind–body CAM interventions: Current status and considerations for integration into clinical health psychology. *Journal of Clinical Psychology.*

Park, C. L., & Slattery, J. M. (2009). Spirituality and case conceptualizations: A meaning system approach. In J. Aten & M. Leach (Eds.), *Spirituality and the therapeutic process: A guide for mental health professionals* (pp. 121–142). Washington, DC: American Psychological Association.

Phelps, A. C., Maciejewski, P. K., Nilsson M., Balboni, T. A., Wright, A. A., Paulk, M. E., et al. (2009). Religious coping and use of intensive life-prolonging care near death in patients with advanced cancer. *Journal of the American Medical Association, 301,* 1140–1147.

Powell, L. H., Shahabi, L., & Thoresen, C. E. (2005). Religion and spirituality: Linkages to physical health. *American Psychologist, 58,* 36–52.

Puchalski, C., & Ferrell, B. (2010). *Making health care whole: Integrating spirituality into patient Care.* West Conshohocken, PA: Templeton Press.

Randolph-Seng, B., & Nielsen, M. E. (2007). Honesty: One effect of primed religious representations. *The International Journal for the Psychology of Religion, 17,* 303–315.

Saroglou, V., Corneille, O., & Van Cappellen, P. (2009). "Speak, Lord, your servant is listening": Religious priming activates submissive thoughts and behaviors. *The International Journal for the Psychology of Religion, 19,* 143–154.

Schjødt, U., Sørensen, J., Nielbo, K., Xygalatas, D., Mitkidis, P., & Bulbulia, J. (2013). Cognitive resource depletion in religious interactions. *Religion, Brain, and Behaviour, 3*(1), 39–55.

Schjødt, U., Stødkilde-Jørgensen, H., Geertz, A. W., Lund, T. E., & Roepstorff, A. (2011). The power of charisma: Perceived charisma inhibits the frontal executive network of believers in intercessory prayer. *Social Cognitive and Affective Neuroscience, 6,* 119–127.

Schnell, T. (2003). A framework for the study of implicit religion: The psychological theory of implicit religiosity. *Implicit Religion, 6,* 86–104.

Shah, T. S., Franck, M. J., & Farr, T. F. (2012). *Religious freedom: Why now? Defending an embattled human right.* Princeton, NJ: Witherspoon Institute.

Shariff, A., & Norenzayan, A. (2007). God is watching you: Priming God concepts increases prosocial behavior in an anonymous economic game. *Psychological Science, 18,* 803–809.

Strauss. A., & Corbin. J. (1998). *Basics of qualitative research: Techniques and procedures for developing grounded theory* (2nd ed). Thousand Oaks, CA: Sage.

Streib, H., Hood, R. W., Jr., Keller, B., Csöff, R.-M., & Silver, C. (2009). *Deconversion: Qualitative and quantitative results from cross-cultural research in Germany and the United States of America* (Research in Contemporary Religion). Göttingen, Germany: Vandenhoeck & Ruprecht.

Tippens, K., Marsman, K., & Zwickey, H. (2009). Is prayer CAM? *Journal of Alternative and Complementary Medicine, 15*, 435–438.

Todorov, A., Fiske, S., & Prentice, D. (2011). *Social neuroscience: Toward understanding the underpinnings of the social mind*. New York: Oxford University Press.

Van Cappellen, P., Corneille, O., Cols, S., & Saroglou, V. (2011). Beyond mere compliance to authoritative figures: Religious priming increases conformity to informational influence among submissive people. *The International Journal for the Psychology of Religion, 21*, 97–105.

Wachholtz, A., & Sambamoorthi, U. (2011). National trends in prayer use as a coping mechanism for health concerns: Changes from 2002 to 2007. *Psychology of Religion and Spirituality, 3*, 67–77.

Watts, F. (2007). Emotion regulation and religion. In J. J. Gross (Ed.), *Handbook of emotion regulation* (pp. 504–520). New York: Guilford Press.

Xygalatas, D. (Ed.). (2012). *The burning saints: Cognition and culture in the fire-walking rituals of the Anastenaria*. Sheffield, UK: Equinox.

Xygalatas, D., Konvalinka, I., Roepstorff, A., & Bulbulia, J. (2011). Quantifying collective effervescence: Heart-rate dynamics at a fire-walking ritual. *Communicative & Integrative Biology, 4*(6), 735–738.

Zuckerman, P. (2011). *Faith no more: Why people reject religion*. New York: Oxford University Press.

Author Index

Aardema, F., 151
Aarts, H., 465
Abdel-Khalek, A. M., 334
Abdollahi, A., 464
Abel, A., 404
Abraído-Lanza, A. F., 343
Abraham, C., 505
Abramowitz, J., 337, 391, 542, 546
Abu Raiya, H., 330
Abu-Rayya, H. M., 342, 344
Abu-Zeid, H. A. H., 335
Acree, M., 546
Acton, C., 387
Adams, C. E., 511
Adams, D., 132
Adelman, J. R., 315, 357, 415, 561
Adherents.com, 274
Adler, A., 294
Adler, L. E., 542
Adorno, T. W., 84
Aflakseir, A., 543
Aglioti, S. M., 224
Ahadi, S., 280
Ahmad, A., 63, 321
Ahmadi, F., 572
Ai, A. L., 53, 340, 383, 384, 525, 565, 571
Aikins, D. C., 610
Ainsworth, M. D. S., 133, 170, 171
al-Banna, H., 640
Albertsen, E. J., 509, 551
Albrecht, S. L., 61
Alcock, J. E., 431
Alcorta, C., 445
Aldwin, C. M., 5, 18, 50, 99, 165, 296, 372, 373
Aletti, M., 105
Alexander, C., 582
Alexander, J., 628
Alexander, J. C., 11, 14
Alexander, M. B., 504

Alferi, S. M., 567
Alisat, S., 462
Al-Khattar, A. M., 632
Allen, R. O., 127
Allport, G. W., 49, 54, 60, 63, 67, 132, 257, 258, 263, 264, 294, 298, 312, 313, 320, 387, 622, 624, 637
Alpert, R., 428
Altemeyer, B., 63, 67, 84, 322, 387, 400, 410, 415, 457, 458, 467, 566
Altmaier, E. M., 372, 548, 549
Alvord, L., 444
Alzayed, A., 389
Amer, M. M., 334, 344
American Association of Pastoral Counselors Samaritan Institute, 607
American Psychiatric Association, 604
American Psychological Association, 610
American Psychological Association Practice Directorate, 608
American Psychological Association Presidential Task Force on Evidence-Based Practice, 595, 607, 610
American Psychological Association Presidential Working Group, 610
Amodio, D. M., 466, 467, 468
Anaissie, E. J., 382
Anderson, E. Z., 388
Anderson, J. W., 94
Anderson, N. D., 580, 581
Andersson, G., 546
Andrée, B., 226
Angel, J. L., 207, 523
Angel, R. J., 207, 523
Anisman, H., 324, 357

Ano, G. G., 50, 63, 148, 274, 369, 380, 381, 382, 383, 385, 390, 532, 549, 551, 564, 565, 566, 597, 598
Ansley, T. N., 607
Anthony, F.-V., 54, 333
Antoni, M. H., 566, 567
Antonovsky, A., 64, 67
Antonovsky, H. F., 503
Anttonen, V., 30
Apolito, P., 423
Appel, C., 403
Appel, H., 384
Appelle, S., 426
Apter, M. J., 415
Ardelt, M., 364, 365
Arena, P. L., 566, 567
Arendt, M., 581
Argyle, M., 27, 35, 110
Ariely, D., 499
Ariyabuddhiphongs, V., 334
Armel, K. C., 230
Armstrong, K., 194, 590
Arndt, J., 457
Arnett, J., 184, 185, 189
Arnkoff, D. B., 562
Aronson, E., 83, 583
Arredondo, P., 596
Arredondo-Holden, J., 450
Arthurs, O. J., 218
Asbrock, F., 459
Asch, S., 633
Ashdown, L., 444
Ashforth, B. E., 621
Ashmos, D. P., 618
Ashton, M. C., 299
Asp, E., 466
Astuti, R., 169, 247
Atchley, R. C., 42, 201
Aten, J. D., 64
Atran, S., 123, 144, 151, 166, 167, 238, 240, 241, 275, 281, 322, 330, 345
Au, A. K. M., 317

Au, M., 522
Au, P., 133
Auerbach, J. S., 105
Aukst-Margetic, B., 531
Au-Yeung, F. S. W., 54
Aviles, J., 79
Avlund, K., 522
Awad, G. H., 318
Awad, J. H., 344
Aydin, N., 340
Azar, F., 338
Azari, N. P., 11, 227, 657
Azhar, M. Z., 569

B

Bachrach, B., 82
Bader, C., 427, 449
Badrinarayanan, V., 618
Baer, L., 223
Baesler, E. J., 446, 451
Baetz, M., 540, 541, 542, 544, 545
Bagary, M. S., 222
Bagiella, E., 108, 449
Bagley, R., 543
Bailey, C., 568
Bailey, E., 358, 652
Baillet, S., 219
Baird, R. D., 152
Baker, J. O., 208
Baker, K. M. 76
Baker, W. E., 336
Balazas, A. L., 623
Ball, C. T., 52
Banaji, M. R., 462
Bandura, A., 35, 38
Banthia, R., 546
Banziger, S., 566
Barbas, H., 229
Barber, C., 583
Barbour, J. D., 408, 409
Bargh, J., 260, 465, 465, 501
Barker, E., 403
Barker, R. A., 225
Barksdale, C., 570
Barna Group, 552
Barnes, C. D., 260
Barnes, L., 462
Barnes, P. M., 78, 450
Barr, H. L., 428
Barrett, H. C., 168
Barrett, J. L., 5, 14, 15, 16, 17, 35, 50, 119, 123, 124, 131, 144, 146, 154, 166, 167, 168, 236, 238, 240, 241, 242, 243, 244, 245, 246, 247, 248, 365, 389, 444
Barrett, L. F. 550
Barro, R., 415
Barron, C. R., 368
Bartemucci, L., 434
Bartholow, B. D., 466
Bartkowski, J. P., 316

Bartlett, M. Y., 283
Bartoli, E., 107
Bartz, J., 568, 607
Baskin, Y., 640
Bassett, R. L., 52, 61, 391
Bastida, E., 372
Bateson, M., 505
Batson, C. D., 27, 36, 52, 63, 67, 81, 84, 101, 130, 132, 313, 314, 358, 387
Bauer, D. J., 486
Bauer, I. M., 293, 504
Bauer, J., 194
Bauer, J. A., 391
Baumeister, R. F., 9, 11, 206, 293, 357, 358, 362, 363, 364, 365, 366, 367, 370, 476, 486, 490, 498, 499, 500, 501, 502, 503, 504, 505, 506, 507, 508, 509, 510, 550, 654
Baxendale, S., 389
Bayman, H., 591
Beach, S. R. H., 449
Beaman, A. L., 500
Bear, D. M., 215, 219, 221, 222, 230
Bearman, P., 319
Beard, A. W., 215, 219, 220
Beauregard, M., 228, 466
Beck, R., 61, 66, 386, 387, 388, 389
Becker, E., 443
Beckford, J. A., 403
Bedard, C., 371
Beedie, C. J., 147
Beer, J. S., 466
Beeson, W. L., 335
Behne, T., 168
Beitel, M., 104, 569
Beit-Hallahmi, B., 27, 94, 95, 100, 110, 111, 317, 415, 423
Beitman, J. A., 382
Belaire, C., 609
Belavich, T. G., 566
Bell, C., 441, 442, 449
Bellah, R., 27, 148, 151, 152, 157
Belot, C., 341
Belzen, J. A., 16, 17, 54, 75, 76, 81, 82, 89, 94, 97, 99, 101, 103, 199, 227, 330, 332, 346, 429
Bem, D. J., 80
Benedetti, F., 147
Benet-Martinez, V., 282
Benore, E. R., 385, 368, 493, 565, 571, 572
Benson, H., 67, 78, 445, 451
Benson, P. L., 4, 38, 60, 66
Berg, M. B., 508
Bergeman, C. S., 448
Bergin, A. E., 337, 599, 601, 606, 608

Berman, M., 372
Bering, J. M., 166, 168, 174, 176, 226, 239, 247
Bernhardt, W. H., 366
Bernstein, D. P., 415
Berntson, G. G., 528
Berry, J. W., 332, 334, 336, 483, 509, 551
Biegel, G. M., 581
Bierman, A., 343
Billiet, J., 341
Billig, M. G., 155
Bilsky, W., 363
Binau, B., 80
Biscan, M., 531
Bishop, C. T., 335
Bishop, S. R., 581, 605
Bisonó, A. M., 607
Bittner, D., 226
Bizumic, B., 458
Bjorck, J. P., 61, 66, 415, 571
Bjorkland, D. F., 247
Bjorklund, D. F., 168
Black, D. M., 99
Black, H. K., 51
Blackburn, E. H., 581
Blackwell, D. L., 319
Blagg, R. D., 315, 357, 415, 561
Blakeslee, S., 221
Blank, T. O., 372, 533, 561
Blasi, A. J., 337
Blasi, C. H., 168
Blass, R. B., 96, 97, 100
Blatt, S. J., 101, 105
Blehar, M. C., 133, 170
Blender, J. A., 207
Bleske, A. L., 121
Blieszner, R., 207
Bliss, D., 526
Blogowska, J., 459
Bloom, B., 450
Bloom, P., 5, 146, 174, 246, 247, 251
Blose, B. L., 429, 430
Blum, L. S., 388
Blumenthal, J. A., 525, 527
Blumer, H., 42
Boal, M. J., 458
Boccaccini, M. T., 59
Boccato, G., 465
Bockian, M. J., 415
Boden, J. M., 498
Bodhi, B., 585
Bolling, S. F., 384, 565
Bond, K., 30
Boniface, S., 218
Bonner, G., 283
Bono, G., 371, 476, 483, 486
Boone, A. L., 512
Booth, R. J., 79, 278
Borg, J., 226
Borgen, W. A., 596
Borkowski, J. G., 542
Bornstein, B. H., 316

Borras, L., 222, 543, 571
Boswell, G., 570
Bottoms, B., 322, 542
Bouchard, T. J., 458, 468
Bourhis, R. Y., 344
Bowdle, B. F., 322
Bowen, M. G., 628
Bowen, R., 540
Bowlby, J., 170, 171, 175, 176
Bowlin, P., 60, 66
Bowman, E. S., 382, 386
Boyatt, E., 314
Boyatzis, C. J., 165, 166, 206, 296
Boyd, R., 129, 134
Boyer, P., 123, 131, 144, 146, 151, 166, 235, 236, 238, 241, 242, 244, 247, 251
Braam, A. W., 568
Bradley, R., 383
Bradley, M. M., 467
Bradshaw, M., 549
Brady, M. J., 59, 530
Braese, R. W., 571
Braithwaite, S. R., 449
Braithwaite, V. A., 51
Branch, P. S., 66
Bradshaw, M., 449
Brandt, M. J., 462
Brandt, P. Y., 222, 543, 571
Brandt, P.-Y., 415
Branscombe, N. R., 344, 493
Bransford, J. D., 243
Brant, C. R., 367
Brashears, M. E., 208
Bratslavsky, E., 500, 509
Brawer, P., 609
Brawley, O., 529
Brayne, C. E. G., 225
Bréchon, P., 335, 341
Breen, W. E., 266
Brefczynski-Lewis, J., 283
Breitbart, W., 533
Brelsford, G. M., 206, 319
Brenner, L. A., 542
Brenner, P. S., 324
Breslin, M. J., 450
Bretherton, I., 171
Breugelmans, S. M., 276, 332
Brewer, K., 487
Brewer, M. B., 83
Bridwell, D. A., 581
Bright, M. M., 599
Brignall, T., 467
Brion, S., 297
Brockman, J. M., 362
Broen, W. E., Jr., 132
Brokaw, B. F., 105
Brooks, M. A., 382, 385, 526
Broota, K. D., 561
Brow, M., 552, 553, 554
Brower, K. J., 571
Brown, A., 225
Brown, C. G., 79

Brown, D. E., 216
Brown, K. W., 581
Brown, L., 543
Brown, L. B., 367, 447, 449
Brown, R., 457, 459, 468, 632
Brown, S. L., 552
Brown, W. P., 260
Brückner, H., 319
Brundin, P., 225
Bruner, J., 11, 175
Bruno, J., 426
Bryan, A., 467
Bucher, A., 190
Buck, A. C., 527
Bucklin, M. A., 28, 38
Bufford, R. K., 38, 53
Buis, T., 581
Buka, S., 545, 546, 552
Bulbulia, J., 242, 658
Bull, D. L., 388
Bullard, T. E., 426
Bundy, R. P., 155
Burdette, A. M., 207, 449
Burdett, E. R., 241, 247
Burdzy, D., 564
Bures, R., 319, 334
Burger, E., 444
Burghardt, G. M., 151
Burke, B. L., 463
Burke, J. 641
Burker, E. J., 562
Burkley, E., 500
Burnette, J. L., 484, 490
Burns, J. E., 65
Burnside, C., 149
Burris, C. T., 62, 344, 410
Burris, J. P., 9, 138, 139
Burrows, L., 465
Burrus, J., 339
Burton, T., 88
Busath, G. L., 260, 322, 392, 464
Busath, G. W., 283
Bushman, B. J., 260, 283, 322, 392, 464, 490
Buss, D. M., 119, 121, 122, 132, 301
Buswell, R. E., 141
Butter, E. M., 382
Buxant, C., 344, 404, 549
Butler, M. H., 449
Butler P. M., 6, 15, 16, 17, 78, 122, 217, 225, 315, 466, 657
Byng, M. D., 344
Byrne, P., 26
Byrom, G., 434

C

Cable, D. M., 407
Cacioppo, J. T., 528
Cadge, W., 342
Cahill, S., 337, 542

Caldwell, A. E., 286
Caldwell, D., 623
Caldwell-Harris, C., 226
Calhoun, L., 385, 567
Callaghan, T., 167
Camerer, C., 154
Camic, P. M., 103
Campbell, H. A., 660
Campbell, N. J., 260
Campbell, W. K., 490
Campiche, R. J., 341
Cann, A., 567
Caplan, R. D., 405
Capps, D., 98, 448
Capra, F., 281
Cardeña, E., 425
Carey, M. P., 380, 485
Carlino, E., 147
Carlisle, R. D., 459
Carlo, G., 340
Carlsmith, J. M., 633
Carlson, L., 580
Carlson, S. M., 167
Carlton, J. T., 640
Carmody, J., 580
Carothers, S. S., 542, 547, 548,
Carpenter, M., 238
Carpenter, T. P., 465
Carr, B. I., 64, 372, 382, 563
Carrera, S. R., 449
Carroll, J. S., 319
Carroll, M. P., 87, 423
Carson, V. B., 32, 450, 564, 598
Carter, S. R., 507
Carvalho J. J., IV, 361
Carver, C. S., 532, 566, 567
Casalfiore, S., 404
Casalone, C., 108
Cashwell, C., 609
Casler, K., 239
Cassibba, R., 172, 173
Cassidy, J., 171
Castel, P.-H., 98
Cavalli-Sforza, L. C., 635
Cavanaugh, G. F., 619
Cavilli, K. S., 52
Cecero, J. C., 104
Cella, D., 59, 530
Central Intelligence Agency, 274
Chagnon, N., 636
Chaminade, T., 283
Champagne, E., 296
Chandler, H. M., 582
Charbonneau, C., 387, 531
Charland, K., 172
Charles, S. T., 581
Charles, T., 503
Chartrand, T. L., 465, 506
Chasiotis, A., 332
Chassin, L. 642
Chatman, J., 623
Chatters, L. M., 51, 203, 571
Chau, A. Y., 188
Chaudoir, S. R., 383, 526

Chave, E. J., 61, 66
Chaves, M. A., 391, 535
Cheek, N. H., Jr., 133
Chen, J. J., 549
Chen, M., 465
Chen, T. P., 306
Chen, X., 332
Chen, Y. Y., 542
Chen, Z., 54, 55, 78, 103, 226, 333, 425, 433, 463
Chentsova-Dutton, Y., 276
Cheong, J. W., 279
Cherfas, L., 275, 338, 491
Cherry, C., 183
Cheung, C., 264
Chida, Y., 521, 522, 524, 534
Chilcott, T., 658, 659
Childs, B. H., 451
Chim, L., 281, 286
Chirico, J., 634
Chittister, J., 591
Chiu, C., 342
Chiu, L., 545
Choi, N. W., 335
Chomsky, N., 129
Chopko, B. A., 550
Christians, L.-L., 404
Churchill, R., 661
Ciarrocchi, J., 206, 296, 303
Ciccetti, D., 207
Ciciolla, L., 296
Cigler, B. A., 628
Cimbolic, P., 104
Cirignotta, F., 220
Claiborn, C. D., 609
Clare, L., 199
Clark, A., 334
Clark, W. H., 64
Clarkson, J. J., 504
Cleeremans, A., 465
Clobert, M., 339
Cloninger, C. R., 224
Cohen, A., 542
Cohen, A. B., 5, 6, 15, 17, 18, 25, 52, 55, 129, 139, 202, 204, 275, 284, 285, 286, 293, 323, 330, 331, 333, 335, 337, 338, 339, 340, 364, 369, 371, 389, 399, 462, 491, 510, 542, 546, 654, 660
Cohen, D., 322, 338, 346, 547
Cohen, E., 246, 247, 248, 249
Cohen, H. J., 337
Cohen, L. H., 542, 568
Cohen, M. D., 570
Cohen, M. S., 228
Cohen, R. D., 524
Cohen, S., 550
Colby, P. M., 263, 371
Cole, B. S., 64, 67, 372, 382, 563, 565
Cole, R., 176

Coleman, P. G., 202, 205, 206, 207, 209, 306, 543
Cols, S. 656
Colzato, L. S., 338, 366
Compton, W. C., 542
Condemi, B., 623
Condon, P., 283
Connors, G. J., 62, 66, 606
Contrada, R. J., 525, 526, 547, 548,
Cook, S., 335
Cook, W., 635
Coon, D. J., 435
Corbin, J. 657
Corneille, O., 283, 465, 656
Cornille, C., 41
Cornwall, M., 61
Corveleyn, J., 7, 87, 94, 98, 99, 101, 103, 104, 105, 107, 108, 110, 294
Cosmides, L., 119, 120, 129, 132
Costa, P. T., 280, 294, 295, 301
Costantini, A., 172
Costanzo, E., 531
Cothran, D. L., 314
Cotter, J., 508
Cowan, D. E., 404
Cox, C. R., 457
Cox, E., 133
Cox, H., 639
Coyle, A., 5
Cragun, R. T., 318, 320
Cranford, J. A., 571
Crocker, S. F., 451
Cronbach, L., 57
Cross, D., 167
Cruise, S. M., 549
Crumbaugh, J. C., 64, 67
Crumpler, C. A., 192, 194, 283, 582, 584
Crystal, D., 640
Csöff, R.-M., 85, 400, 423, 657
Cukur, C. S., 340
Cullen, F. T., 316
Culver, J. L., 566, 567
Cummings, J. P., 566, 596, 607, 608, 609, 610
Cummins, R., 545
Cunningham, P. H., 61
Curnow, T., 582, 583, 591
Cuthbert, B. N., 467
Cutler, H. C., 277
Czaja, S. J., 571

D

Dalai Lama, H. H. the, 277
Dalby, P., 301
Daley, D., 207
Damisch, L., 148
Dannefer, D., 205
Danziger, K., 78
Danzinger, K., 429
d'Aquili, E., 52, 87, 230, 442

Darr, R., 588
Das, E., 260, 283, 322, 392, 464
Dauer, W., 225
Daugherty, T. K., 362
Davenport, C., 624
Davern, M., 545
Davidson, R. J., 282, 283, 284
Davies, J. L., 582
Davies, C. A., 424
Davis, C. G., 360, 370
Davis, D. E., 477, 478, 484, 486, 488, 489, 490, 492, 493, 599, 606
Davis, D. W., 624
Davis, L. J., 388
Davis, R. B., 449
Davis, W., 14
Dawson, L. L., 185, 186
Day, J. M., 424
Day, L., 448
Deacon, B., 391, 542
DeBerg, B. A., 183
Debiec, J., 13
de Certeau, M., 98
Decety, J., 283
Deci, E. L., 364, 365, 508
Dedert, E. A., 450
Defanti, E., 609
DeFries, J. C., 468
de Guzman, M. R. T., 340
de Hart, J., 446
Deile, A. J., 323
Dein, S., 82, 561
DeJong, G. F., 61
Delamontagne, R. G., 322
Delaney, H. D., 314, 608
Delin, P. S., 434
Delpierre, V., 279, 333, 365
DeMarco, G. A., 384
Demoulin, S., 345
den Draak, C., 446
DeNeve, K., 265
Dennett, D. C., 251
Dent, E. B., 618
Denton, M. L., 317
Denzin, N. K., 102, 417
Derks, F., 404
Dernelle, R., 279, 320, 333, 365
De Roos, S. A., 172, 173, 174
Desai, K. M., 385, 552
de Souza, M., 4
DeSteno, D., 283
Devereux, G., 95
Devine, P. G., 466, 467
Devinsky, O., 220, 222, 230
Devisch, R., 95
Devos, T., 335
Dew, R. E., 382, 541, 544
Dewall, C. N., 499, 501, 504
Dewhurst, K., 215, 219, 220
Dezutter, J., 7, 87, 103, 105, 294, 367, 373
Dharap, A. S., 569
Dickie, J. R., 171, 172, 173

Diener, E., 276, 278, 280, 283, 337, 415, 500
Diesendruck, G., 168
Digman, J., 132, 295
Dijksterhuis, A., 465
Dijkstra, M., 306
Dik, B., 620, 622, 625, 628
Dillon, M., 188, 205, 296, 297, 301
Dilworth-Anderson, P., 570
DiMaggio, P., 185
Kinney, A., 529
Dissanayake, E., 144
Dittes, J. E., 49
DiYanni, C., 239
Doblin, R., 77, 89
Dollahite, D. C., 27
Dolto, F., 98
Donahue, M., 19, 60, 66, 274, 313, 314, 315, 324, 332, 364, 457, 551
D'Onofrio, B., 58, 442
Dowling, E. M., 4
Downs, D. L. 131
Doyen, S., 465
Doyle, D., 28, 36
Dreisenga, A., 167
Dreyfus, G., 43
Driesenga, A., 240
Drigotas, S. M., 492
Drinnan, A., 544
Driskel, R. L., 323
Driskell, R., 317
Dubin, N., 226
Dubin, R., 622, 628
Duchon, D., 618
Duckitt, J., 458, 459
Dumont, L., 148, 149, 150
Dunn, C., 624
Dupuis, D. R., 344
Dupuis, J., 278
Duriez, B., 283, 342
Durkheim, E., 9, 27, 32, 36, 140, 141, 142, 143, 144, 145, 148, 149, 150, 151, 154, 156, 157, 335
Durso, R., 217, 225
Dutton, K., 283
Dy-Liacco, G. S., 206, 303, 305, 333, 340
Dynes, R. R., 66
Dzokoto, V., 280

E

Eagle, D. E., 317
Earlywine, M., 643
Easwaran, E., 191, 589, 590
Eaves, L. J., 58, 224, 295, 442
Eccles, J. S., 190, 193, 194
Echemendia, R., 66, 406
Echevarria, S., 316
Ecklund, E. H., 342
Edelstein, B. A., 541, 542, 598

Edmondson, D., 10, 14, 66, 357, 360, 361, 362, 372, 383, 526, 527, 528, 533, 561
Edwards, D., 642
Edwards, E., 55, 624
Edwards, J. R., 405, 407
Edwards, K., 241
Edwards, K. J., 60, 66, 105, 314, 333, 382, 385, 387, 388
Egan, T., 562
Ehrlich, A. H., 640
Ehrlich, P. R., 636, 640
Ehrlich, U., 447
Eid, S., 389
Eisen, J. L., 223
Eisenberg, D. M., 449
Ekstrom, A., 218
Elder, G. H., 183
El-Geledi, S., 344
Eliade, M., 142, 143, 154, 442
Eliason, G., 364
Elkind, D., 166, 240
Elkins, D. N., 67, 424, 431
Ellens, J. H., 451
Elliot, A. J., 256, 266
Elliott, M., 337, 548
Elliott, R., 102
Ellis, A., 108, 131, 540, 604
Ellison, C. G., 51, 199, 206, 316, 343, 368, 382, 391, 449, 523, 524, 545, 546, 547, 548, 549, 550, 551, 553, 565, 567, 653
Ellison, C. W., 53, 59, 65
El Mouden, C., 134
Emavardhana, T., 60, 66
Emblen, J. D., 36
Embry, E., 317
Eme-Akwari, A. G., 560
Emmons, R. A., 5, 6, 13, 14, 15, 23, 26, 38, 48, 50, 53, 75, 84, 94, 102, 126, 132, 152, 191, 256, 258, 259, 260, 263, 264, 265, 266, 270, 271, 274, 275, 277, 278, 283, 284, 285, 292, 323, 360, 363, 364, 365, 366, 371, 380, 400, 422, 424, 486, 508, 511, 550, 561, 570, 620, 622
Enders, C. K., 297
Ennett, S. T., 642
Enz, C. A., 623
Epel, E. S., 581
Epley, N., 361
Ergin, N. O., 588
Erickson, J. A., 60, 66
Eriksen, C. W., 466
Erikson, E. H., 98, 99, 192, 293, 445
Ervin, F. R., 129
Eshleman, A. K., 172, 173
Eskin, M., 542, 548
Esses, V. M., 463

Eurelings-Bontekoe, E., 104
Evans, E. M., 167, 168, 177, 239
Everson-Rose, S. A., 391
Evon, D. M., 562
Exline, J. J., 4, 13, 38, 64, 67, 362, 363, 371, 372, 373, 380, 381, 382, 383, 386, 387, 388, 389, 390, 391, 392, 477, 485, 490, 491, 499, 501, 503, 508, 509, 532, 542, 551, 552, 565, 597, 599, 600, 604, 605

F

Fabbro, F., 224
Faber, M. D., 445
Fabricatore, A. N., 609
Fahlberg, L. A., 28
Fahlberg, L. H., 28
Falb, M. D., 50, 63, 148, 274, 369, 381, 532, 597
Fales, E., 361
Falicov, C. J., 596
Fallconer, J. E., 426
Fallon, A. E., 149
Fallon, J. A., 527
Fan, D., 549
Faragher, E., 544
Farde, L., 226
Farhadian, C., 323, 402
Faris, R., 317
Farrell, J., 199
Farrugia, G., 27
Faucher, E. H., 463
Faulkner, J., 241
Faulkner, J. E., 61
Fearer, S. A., 504
Fedio, P., 215, 219, 221, 222, 230
Fehr, E., 476, 477
Feldman, D. H., 193
Feldman, S., 581, 543, 643
Feldman Barrett, L., 276
Fenster, J. R., 372, 526
Fenwick, E., 431
Fenwick, P., 431
Ferguson, J., 623
Ferguson, M. J., 260
Ferré, F., 152
Ferrell, B., 655
Ferris, G. R., 628
Fessler, D. M. T., 505
Festinger, L., 81, 447, 633
Feuille, M., 564
Fiala, W. E., 61, 66
Fialkowski, G. M., 303
Fielding, G. T., 641
Figueredo, A. J., 360
Filipas, H., 322, 542
Filius, R., 389
Filipp, S.-H., 366
Finch, B. K., 343, 545, 546, 547, 549, 553

Fincham, F. D., 30, 449, 479, 487
Fink, A., 530
Fink, P., 581
Finke, R., 318
Finkel, D. G., 461
Finkel, E. J., 490, 499
Finken, L. L., 459, 461
Finkle, C., 656
Fiorito, B., 266
Fischer, C. T., 102
Fischer, J. D., 59
Fischer, P., 322, 340, 463, 510
Fish, S. B., 60, 66
Fishbach, A., 465
Fisher, L. A., 296
Fiske, A. P., 331
Fiske, S. T., 445, 657
Fitchett, G., 59, 382, 384, 527, 530
Fitzsimmons, G. M., 270
Fjorback, L. O., 581
Flament, C., 155
Flanagan, O., 14
Flannelly, K. J., 54, 201, 368, 382, 449, 546, 549, 550, 565, 653, 566
Flannelly, L. T., 201
Flavell, J. H., 167
Fleck, D. E., 543
Fleeson, W., 582
Flere, S., 314, 333
Fletcher-Brokaw, B., 105
Flewelling, R. L., 642
Flinders, T., 38, 43, 580
Florack, P., 387, 531
Florian, V., 464
Flynn, C. P., 552
Folkman, S., 12, 358, 360, 368, 546, 562, 563, 582
Foltynie, T., 225
Fonagy, P., 101, 105
Fong, T. C. T., 54
Fontaine, D., 223
Ford, B. Q., 508
Ford, T. E., 467
Forman, R. K. C., 583, 590
Forte, R., 184, 427, 429
Forum, P., 41
Foshee, V. A., 499
Foster, L. N., 457
Foster, R. J., 128, 447, 451
Found, E. M., 549
Fournier, C.-A., 416
Fox, B., 434, 435
Fowler, J., 60, 66, 192, 193, 417
Frame, M. W., 605
Francis, L. J., 4, 60, 61, 66, 313, 314, 364, 365, 410, 433, 434
Francis, M. E., 79, 80, 278
Franck, M. J., 662
Frankl, V., 293, 298
Fraser, S. C., 500

Frazier, C., 545
Frazier, P., 364, 365, 372, 550
Frazier, P. A., 258, 262, 567
Frazier, R. E., 607, 608, 609
Frankl, V., 11, 294, 357
Franklin, L., 461
Franklin, M. D., 363
Frankfurter, D., 388
Frantz, C. M., 361
Fredrickson, B. L., 550
Freeman, A., 220
Freeman, R. D., 218
Frenkel-Brunswik, E., 84
Freud, E. L., 109
Freud, S., 94, 95, 96, 97, 98, 109, 294, 561
Frey, D., 340
Friedman, E. H., 335
Friedman, H. L., 624
Friedman, L. M., 509
Friedman, L. N., 501
Friedman, M., 343, 463, 464
Friedman, R., 67
Friedman, R. S., 266, 465
Friere-Bebau, L. H., 276
Friese, M., 499
Friesen, C. K., 389
Frisby, C. L., 51
Frith, 11
Froehlich, J. P., 303
Froese, P., 459
Frokjaer, V., 581
Fry, L., 6, 18, 618, 624, 625, 626, 627, 628
Fryer, J. W., 256
Fujikawa, A., 386, 388
Fujita, K., 507
Fullerton, J. T., 60, 66
Funder, D. C., 303
Fung, H. H., 277, 286
Fung, H. L., 281
Furnham, A., 323, 367

G

Gaanzevoort, R. R., 315
Gächter, S., 476
Gaertner, S. L., 632
Gagné, M., 508
Gailliot, M. T., 499, 501, 510
Gala, G. G., 78
Galand, P., 341, 343, 344
Galanter, M., 130
Galek, K., 368, 546, 550, 551, 653
Galen, L., 321
Galen, L. W., 5, 19
Gall, T. L., 387, 531, 560, 599
Gallagher, T., 450
Gallois, C., 462
Gallup, 598
Gallup, G, 85, 128, 283, 429, 447, 448

Gallup Center for Muslim Studies, 319, 320
Gane, B., 314
Ganzevoort, R. R., 389, 572
Garagher, E. B., 222
Garbarino, J., 371
Garcia, J., 129
Gardner, A., 134
Gardner, B. C., 449
Gardner, H., 132
Gardner, W. L., 256, 257
Garnero, L., 219
Garssen, B., 529
Gartner, A. L., 486, 493
Garver, S. A., 608
Gashghaei, H. T., 229
Gastaut, H., 221
Gaucher, D., 275, 357
Gauntlett-Gilbert, J., 580
Gaur, S. D., 322
Gauvain, M., 175
Gawronski, B., 499
Gay, P., 96
Gay, V. P., 443
Gear, M. R., 383, 570
Gearing, R. E., 222
Gebauer, J. E., 279, 361, 599
Geertz, A. W., 11, 16, 95, 228, 657
Geertz, C., 148, 151, 275
Geisinger, K. F., 51
Gelfand, M. J., 477
Gelman, S. A., 157, 251
Genia, V., 61, 63, 66, 67
Georgas, J., 334, 336
George, L. K., 66, 206, 207, 281
Gerard, S. M., 104
Gergen, D., 640
Gergen, K. J., 88
Gergen, M. M., 88
Gervais, W. M., 318, 320
Geschwind, N., 215, 220, 221, 230
Geyer, A. L., 206
Ghofrani, J., 217, 225
Ghorbani, N., 54
Ghorpade, J., 342
Ghramaleki, A. F., 54
Giacalone, R. A., 6, 18, 38, 617, 618, 619, 621, 622, 623, 624
Gibson, N. J. S., 570
Gijsberts, M., 343
Gilillland, D. D., 571
Gillespie, V. B., 314
Gilliéron, C., 222, 543, 571
Gillies, J., 368
Gillum, F., 529
Gimello, R. M., 141
Giménez Dasí, M., 167, 168, 169
Ginges, J., 322, 464, 465
Gino, F., 499
Giordano, J., 147
Glaser, B., 657

Glaser, J., 462
Glass, C. R., 562
Glass, D. C., 501
Glei, D. A., 522
Glenwick, D. S., 415
Glicksman, A., 201, 202, 203, 204
Glock, C. Y., 65, 127, 409, 432, 652, 657
Gmunder, P., 192, 193
Gockel, A., 657
Goethals, G. R., 642
Goldberg, L. R., 295, 299
Goldberger, L., 428
Goldblatt, V., 335
Goldenberg, J. L., 457
Goldman, R. G., 166, 240
Goldsmith, M., 444
Goldstein, E. B., 407
Goldstein, J., 191
Goldstein, M., 281
Goldstein, S., 108
Goldwyn, R., 173
Goleman, D., 586
Gollwitzer, P. M., 465
Gomez, L. O., 450
Gonce, L. O., 241
Gonsiorek, J. C., 610
Gonzalez, A., 6, 333, 661
Good, B., 276
Good, G., 11
Goodale, J. C., 636
Goode, W. J., 445
Gorsuch, R. L., 5, 28, 48, 49, 51, 53, 55, 56, 61, 63, 65, 66, 67, 75, 78, 100, 217, 269, 313, 333, 365, 607
Gorvine, B. J., 335
Gorvine, H., 335
Gottfredson, M. R., 501
Gottman, J. M., 492
Gould, S. J., 121
Gow, K. M., 389
Graetz, J. E., 226
Graetz Simmons, J., 107
Graham, J., 144, 149, 206, 493
Graham, J. E., 76
Graham, S. M. 30
Granqvist, P., 17, 50, 99, 105, 133, 166, 169, 170, 171, 172, 173, 174, 176, 296, 318, 345, 404, 407, 415, 432, 653
Grant H., 256, 257
Gray, E. T., Jr., 588
Gray, K., 357, 366, 368
Gray, M. J., 360, 371
Greenberg, D., 223, 224
Greenberg, J., 12, 463, 637
Greenberg, R. P., 101, 105
Greenfield, E. A., 190
Greenwald, A. G., 499
Greeson, J. M., 581
Gregory, J., 241, 242

Greider, K. J., 202
Greiling, H., 132
Greitemeyer, T., 322
Greteman, A. J., 265
Grevengoed, N., 67
Greyson, B., 430
Gribbins, T., 459
Gries, P., 41
Griffiths, R. R., 77
Grimes, R. L., 441
Grof, S., 428
Gross, J. J., 276, 280, 283, 484, 507, 550
Gross, R., 319
Grossman, D., 645
Grossman, P., 580, 581
Grossoehme, D. H., 80
Grubbs, J. B., 386, 387
Gruber, J., 285
Gruchow, H. W., 527
Gruner, L., 569
Guenther, M., 25
Guerrero, S., 167
Guest, A. M., 318
Guilliford, L., 283
Guirguis-Younger, M., 531
Guiso, L., 336
Gullatte, M., 529
Gunaratana, H., 585, 586, 587, 588, 591
Gunn, H. E., 450, 528
Gupta, S., 505
Gurney, A. G., 108
Guthrie, S. E., 235, 237, 238, 239
Guthrie, S. G., 123, 131

H

Haber, L., 168
Habermas, J., 503
Hackney, C., 545, 552, 553
Hadaway, C. K., 37, 541, 535, 553
Haddock, G., 222, 544
Hage, S. M., 609
Hager, J., 129
Hahn, J., 204, 371, 382, 384, 565, 571
Haidt, J., 144, 149, 206, 285, 432, 493, 503
Halama, P., 415
Hale-Smith, A., 10, 66, 357, 361, 362, 533
Haley, K. J., 505
Halifax, R. J., 368
Hall, D. E., 202, 203, 204, 275, 314, 315, 333, 335, 552, 553, 655
Hall, D. L., 460
Hall, J. H., 487
Hall, M. E. L., 362
Hall, T. W., 60, 66, 87, 94, 96, 99, 105, 206, 382, 385, 386, 387, 388

Halman, L., 335
Ham, B.-J., 226
Hamilton, W. D., 121
Hammer, J. H., 320
Hammond, P. E., 340
Han, H. A., 507
Han, S., 466
Handal, P., 609
Hanique, B., 341, 343
Hansen, I. G., 281, 464
Hansen, N., 607, 608, 609, 610
Happold, F. C., 433, 434
Hardy, A. M., 560
Harmon-Jones, E., 219, 464, 466, 467
Harper, F. W. K., 360
Harper, J. M., 449
Harpster, L., 508
Harré, R., 633
Harrington, A., 284
Harris, A. H., 79
Harris, E., 225
Harris, J. I., 449, 544, 549, 565
Harris, P. L., 151, 167, 168, 169, 175, 176, 177, 247
Harris, S., 228
Harrison, J. E., 442
Harrison, M. O., 560
Hart, C. W., 95
Hart, C. W. M., 636
Hart, K. H., 262, 263
Hart, T., 28
Hartog, K., 389
Harvey, D. K., 128
Harvey, J. W., 431
Haselton, M. G., 121
Haslam, S. A., 340
Hass, L., 444
Hassanein, K., 198
Hasselbalch, S. G., 581
Hathaway, W., 67, 600, 604, 610
Hathcoat, J., 462
Hatton, A. T., 19, 332, 457, 551
Hauser, D. J., 389
Hawkins, N., 533
Hawkley, L. C., 528
Hayes, A. M., 581
Hayford, S. R., 317
Hays, J. C., 66, 337, 560
Hayward, R. D., 316, 334, 337, 347, 548
Hazan, C., 133
Head, M., 198
Heath, A. C., 295
Heatherton, T. F., 499, 508
Heaton, D. P., 622
Heaven, P. C. L., 296
Hebert, R., 532
Hedberg, J., 606
Hedden, K., 389
Hedges, C., 645
Hedges, D. W., 390
Hedstrom, L. J., 67
Heider, F., 633

Heiler, F., 448
Heine, S. I., 338, 346
Heine, S. J., 11, 12, 14, 94, 332, 345
Heled, E., 458
Heller, D., 171
Hellerstein, H. K., 335
Hellman, I., 450
Helman, C. G., 442
Helminski, K. E., 583, 585, 587, 588
Henderson, R. C., 322, 343
Henrich, J., 338
Henry, J., 80
Heppner, W. L., 490
Herb, L., 568
Hermans, C. A. M., 54, 333
Herman, J. L., 368
Hernandez, J. I., 465
Hernandez, L., 59, 530
Hernández-Blasi, C., 247
Hertz, R., 148, 149
Hess, J. A., 316
Hess, S., 529
Hesse, C., 317
Hesse, E., 173
Hesse-Biber, S. N., 451
Hick, J., 431, 432
Hicks, J. A., 365
Higgins, M. E., 618
Highfield, M. E., 27, 36, 38
Hildebrand, L., 447
Hilgetag, C. C., 229
Hill, C. L. M., 581
Hill, E. D., 462
Hill, P. C., 6, 12, 28, 32, 33, 39, 43, 48, 49, 51, 52, 53, 55, 60, 62, 63, 76, 89, 94, 141, 184, 199, 201, 217, 259, 275, 305, 313, 315, 333, 338, 339, 340, 346, 360, 361, 380, 422, 425, 449, 458, 477, 478, 541, 553, 562, 570, 620, 622, 624, 628, 656
Hill, T. D., 207, 523, 527
Hillbrand, M., 542
Hills, P. R., 364
Hilty, D. M., 61, 65, 66
Hinderliter, A. L., 527
Hine, V. H., 445, 446
Hinterberger, T., 81, 426
Hipp, K. M., 367
Hirsch, S. R., 505
Hirschi, T., 501
Hirsh, J. B., 466
Hirstein, W. S., 230
Hirt, E. R., 504
Hixson, K. A., 527
Ho, Y., 281
Hodge, D. R., 79, 604, 605
Hodous, L., 640
Hofer, S. M., 205
Hoff, E. V., 171

Hoffman, E., 432
Hoffman, M., 386, 388
Hoffmann, J. P., 316
Hofman, S. G., 580
Hofmann, W., 499
Hogan, R., 498
Hoge, D. R., 313
Hogg, M. A., 315, 324, 357, 415, 561
Holden, G. W., 332
Holland, J. C., 50, 60, 66
Holmes, D. S., 642
Holt, R. R., 101, 428
Hom, H., 503
Homaifar, B. Y., 542
Homer-Dixon, T., 635
Hong, J., 281
Hong, Y., 342
Honorton, C., 80
Hood, R. W., Jr., 12, 16, 49, 51, 52, 54, 55, 58, 60, 63, 65, 67, 75, 76, 77, 78, 79, 80, 81, 82, 83, 84, 85, 86, 87, 88, 89, 94, 100, 101, 103, 128, 146, 184, 199, 226, 227, 269, 313, 314, 315, 333, 334, 346, 360, 361, 364, 365, 366, 400, 412, 422, 423, 424, 425, 427, 428, 429, 431, 432, 433, 434, 447, 449, 450, 458, 463, 562, 624, 657
Hooghe, M., 341
Hook, J. N., 477, 484, 489, 490, 493, 558, 599, 606, 607
Hooker S. A., 75, 282, 334, 565, 597, 598, 655, 662
Hopkins, C. M., 64, 372, 382, 563
Hopson, A., 609
Hornsby-Smith, P., 336
Horváth-Szabó, K., 259, 306, 363
Hough, J. C., Jr., 66
House, J. S., 552
Houskamp, B. M., 296
Hover, M., 108
Hovey, J. D., 344
Hovi, T., 87
Howard, A. H., 286
Howsepian, B., 531
Hoyle, R. H., 506
Hoyt, W. T., 283, 476, 521
Huang, B., 53, 383, 525, 571
Huang, H. S., 225
Hubert, H., 145
Huddy, L., 643
Hufford, D. J., 28, 35, 38, 423, 425
Hughes, J. R., 220
Hughes, L. L., 67
Huguelet, P., 222, 543, 548, 571
Huismans, S., 278, 279, 364
Hull, J. G., 500

Hummer, R. A., 524
Hunsberger, B., 60, 63, 66, 67, 100, 132, 269, 333, 365, 387, 400, 410, 415, 457, 458, 462, 463, 566
Hunt, R. A., 132
Hunt, S. J., 403
Huppert, J. D., 223, 337, 391, 542
Huprich, S. K., 101, 105
Hurford, J. R., 14
Husaini, B. A., 337
Hutcherson, C. A., 283
Hutchinson, G. T., 279
Hutchison, K. E., 467
Hutsebaut, D., 342
Hutz, A., 104
Huxley, J., 442
Hvithamar, A., 340
Hwang, J., 415

I

Iannaccone, L. R., 318
Idinopulos, T. A., 142
Idler, E. L., 200, 605
Iedema, J., 172, 174
Igarashi, H., 50, 99, 165, 296, 373
Imada, S., 149
Ingersoll-Dayton, B., 41, 488
Inglehart, R., 331, 336, 624
Inzlicht, M., 11, 282, 315, 466
Iragui, V., 230
Ironson, G., 65, 363
Irwin, H. J., 435
Ito, S., 286
Ittzés, A., 306
Ivey, D. C., 609
Izutsu, T., 587

J

Jaccard, J., 451
Jackson, B. R., 448
Jackson, C. J., 364
Jackson, J. S., 203, 571
Jackson, L. M., 333, 344, 463
Jacobs, D. M., 426
Jacobs, J. L. 410, 444
Jacobs, T. L., 581
Jacobsen, B. A., 340
Jacobson, E., 426
Jacoby, J., 451
Jain, A. R., 297
Jakovljevic, M., 531
James, W., 27, 81, 120, 264, 294, 583
Jamieson, A., 410
Jana-Masri, A., 53
Janoff-Bulman, R., 358, 360, 361, 508
Janosova, P., 300, 303, 306
Janssen, J., 415, 446, 566
Janus, M.-D., 80

Jarusawad, O., 53
Jarvis, G. K., 335
Jenike, M. A., 223
Jenkins, D. D., 319
Jennings, D. J., II., 486
Jensen, C. G., 581
Jensen, L. A., 389
Jesse, R., 77
Jessor, R., 65
Jewell, A., 365
Jia, L., 504
Jindra, I., 415, 657
Jobes, D., 104
John, O. P., 459, 484
Johnson, C. N., 151, 174, 176
Johnson, D. P., 561
Johnson, E. L., 362
Johnson, M., 140, 141, 148, 172, 173
Johnson, M. K., 260, 457, 459, 461, 462, 465, 468, 656
Johnson, M. W., 77
Johnson, P. E., 263, 560
Johnson, S., 316
Johnson, S. M., 66, 406
Johnson, W., 588
Johnson, W. B., 108, 604
Johnson Shen, M., 6, 333, 661
Johnston, W., 589
Johnstone, B., 547
Johnstone, T., 283
Jonas, E., 463, 510
Jonas, W. B., 147
Jonathan, E., 461
Jones, C., 104
Jones, G., 540
Jones, H. B., 323
Jones, J., 4
Jones, J. W., 94, 97, 100, 568, 597
Jones, M. B., 642
Jones, W., 67
Jones, W. H., 425
Joseph, C., 149
Joseph, S., 372, 544
Jost, J. T., 462
Juergensmeyer, M., 322
Juhl, J., 14
Julian, T., 266
Jung, C. G., 294, 425, 427, 583
Jürgensen, R., 403
Jurkiewicz, C. L., 6, 18, 38, 617, 618, 619, 621, 622, 623, 624, 628

K

Kagitçibasi, C., 334
Kahneman, D., 236
Kahoe, R. D., 373
Kaiser, H. A., 263, 371
Kakar, S., 97, 100
Kalat, J. W., 644
Kalayjian, A., 106

Kale, S. K., 660
Kaler, M., 365
Kalkstein, S., 62
Kalmijn, M., 341
Kaplan, K. J., 386, 387
Kaplan, N., 171
Kaplan, T. J., 42
Kaplar, M. E., 533, 568
Kapleau, P., 189
Kapogiannis, D., 228, 229, 466
Kaptchuk, T. J., 147, 157
Kapuscinski, A. N., 50, 55, 75, 301, 303, 305, 477, 520, 605
Karecki, M., 441
Karoly, P., 256, 258, 358
Karyotis, G., 342
Kashdan, J. B., 266
Kaslow, N. J., 383
Kass, J. D., 67
Kasser, T., 260
Kastenmuller, A., 322
Katz, J., 450
Katz, S., 423
Katz, Y. J., 60, 61, 66
Kaufmann, E., 344
Kavenocki, S., 503
Kay, A. C., 275, 279, 281, 357, 362
Kazyak, E., 320
Kearns, J. N., 30
Keating, T., 191, 584, 585, 588, 598, 590
Keefe, F. J., 571
Keffala, V. J., 549
Keil, F. C., 243
Keitner, D., 432
Kelem, R. T., 500
Kelemen, D., 168, 174, 239, 250
Keller, B., 85, 400, 408, 409, 417, 423, 657
Keller, J., 315
Kelley, B. S., 108, 541, 544, 551, 553
Kelley, D. L., 486
Kelley, T. A., 552
Kelley-Moore, J. A., 205
Kelsey, M. T., 426
Keltner, D., 85, 285
Kemmelmeier, M., 334, 347
Kemp, J., 542
Kendler, K. S., 295
Kennell, J., 67
Kenney, J. F., 403
Keortge, S., 622
Kernberg, O. F., 96
Kernis, M. H., 490
Keshtgar, M. R., 381, 529
Kessler, R. C., 295
Ketelaar, T., 280
Kettell, S., 323
Key, C. W., 260, 283, 322, 392, 464
Keyes, M., 468
Keysar, A., 320, 410, 423

Kézdy, A., 259, 363
Khan, Z. H., 54, 314
Khilwati, A. H., 588
Khoshaba, D. M., 552, 553, 554
Kieschnick, J., 279
Kiken, L. G., 581
Killian, L. M., 641
Kilpatrick, S. D., 284
Kim, H. S., 282, 337, 339
Kim-Prieto, C., 278, 283
King, D. E., 32, 450, 564, 598
King, K., 67
King, L. A., 263, 365
King, M. B., 58, 60, 66, 132
King, P. E., 4, 38
Kinzler, K. D., 246
Kirby, S. E., 207
Kircher, J. C., 527
Kirk, K. M., 224
Kirkpatrick, L. A., 8, 10, 11, 12, 49, 61, 63, 66, 85, 86, 105, 123, 125, 130, 131, 133, 144, 151, 166, 169, 170, 172, 244, 269, 313, 315, 318, 345, 361, 380, 386, 388, 404, 407, 415, 459, 461, 476, 492, 498, 604, 624, 633
Kitayama, S., 338, 339, 657
Kivisto, P., 340, 342, 343
Klanjšek, R., 314, 333
Klauer, K. C., 461
Klein, C., 408, 412
Klein, C. S., 428
Klein, O., 465
Kleinman, A., 276
Kletti, R., 430
Klinger, E., 358
Klosinski, G., 403
Kluckhohn, C., 275
Kneezel, T. T., 267, 270
Knestel, A., 527
Knight, N., 167, 240, 247
Knott, K., 149
Knowles, E. D., 335
Knutson, B., 277, 281
Koelling, R. A., 129
Koenig, H. G., 27, 32, 35, 36, 40, 43, 54, 63, 67, 201, 202, 203, 204, 217, 281, 282, 304, 313, 314, 333, 337, 368, 369, 371, 380, 381, 382, 384, 386, 424, 450, 521, 527, 540, 541, 542, 543, 544, 545, 550, 553, 560, 563, 564, 565, 571, 598, 618, 653
Kohlberg, L., 591
Kohlls, N., 426
Kohls, N., 81, 147
Kojetin, B. A., 458
Kolligian, J., 101
Kolodinsky, R. W., 621, 623, 628
Koltko-Rivera, M. E., 358, 361

Konvalinka, J., 658
Koo, M., 286
Kooistra, W. P., 568
Koole, S. L., 357, 365, 550
Koopman, C., 382
Koopmann-Holm, B., 6, 50, 279, 281, 284, 285, 476, 549, 645
Kopytoff, I., 143
Körber, J., 383, 532
Korinek, A. W., 609
Kornfield, J., 580, 585
Koropeckyj-Cox, T., 204
Koru-Sengul, T., 540
Köse, A., 415
Kosmin, B. A., 320, 410, 423, 660
Koss, M. P., 360
Kraft, A. J., 490
Krause, N., 41, 64, 66, 67, 199, 201, 203, 205, 206, 208, 364, 372, 373, 391, 449, 488, 546, 548, 549, 550, 551, 567, 571
Krauss, S. W., 458
Kravetz, S., 333
Kremer, H., 363
Kremer, K. E., 251
Kripal, J. J., 87
Krippner, S., 425
Krishnan, L., 339
Kristeva, J., 98, 103
Kristjansson, E., 387, 531
Kroeber, A. L., 275
Kroll, J., 82
Kronfol, Z., 384, 565
Kruger, A. C., 175
Kruglanski, A. W., 263, 462, 465
Krumrei, E. J., 54, 368, 382, 383, 385, 386, 388, 546, 552, 566, 572, 601, 604, 605
Krysinska, K., 104, 105
Kuchan, K. L., 108
Kudler, T., 546
Kuentzel, J. G., 624
Kuhl, J., 357, 550
Kuhn, T. S., 48
Kumar, M., 581
Kuner, W., 404
Kunkel, S. R., 552
Kunovich, R. M., 341
Kuras, L., 361
Kurata, J. H., 524
Kurusu, T. A., 108, 608
Kurzban, R., 132
Kushner, H. S., 362, 371
Kuzma, J. W., 335
Kwan, L., 530

L

LaBarre, W., 81, 429
LaBouff, J. P., 6, 260, 333, 459, 461, 462, 465, 656, 659, 661

Lackritz, J. R., 342
Lacna, M., 415
La Cour, P., 522
Ladd, K. L., 62, 66, 78, 128, 445, 447, 450, 548, 549
Lai, G., 220, 222, 230
Laidlaw, J. A., 246
Lakey, C. E., 490
Lakhdar, M., 415
Lakin, R., 569
Lakoff, G., 140
Lambert, N. M., 30, 449
Lamkaddem, B., 344
Landau, M., 463, 464
Lancet, M., 503
Lane, J. D., 167, 177
Lang, P. J., 467
Lange, R., 434
Langer, E. J., 582
Langs, R. J., 428
Lanham, J. A., 131
Lapidus, I. M., 640, 641
Larson, D. B., 79, 284, 304, 448, 521, 540, 566, 618
Larson, J., 370
Larsen, R. J., 276
Latif, U., 382
Lau, M., 580, 581
Laufer, A., 372
Laughlin, C. D., Jr., 442, 442
Laurenceau, J. P., 581
Lavender, T., 544
LaViolette, P. A., 446
Lavizzo-Mourey, R., 568
Law, S. K. W., 54
Lawler, K. A., 528
Lawler-Row, K. A., 391, 548, 553
Lawrence, R. T., 303
Lawson, E. T., 148, 235, 237, 243, 244, 249, 251, 446, 447
Lawson, R. B., 76
Lawton, L., 319, 334
Laythe, B., 457, 461
Lazar, A., 333
Lazarus, R. S., 562, 582
Leach, M. M., 53, 300, 334
Leaf, J. A., 67
Leak, G. K., 60, 66, 265, 459, 461
Leander, N. P., 506
Leary, M. R., 131, 490, 511, 591
Leary, T., 428, 492
Ledbetter, M. F., 59
Leder, S., 490
LeDoux, J. E., 13
Lee, A., 363
Lee, C. C., 571
Lee, K., 167, 299
Lee, M., 335
Lee, M. T., 79
Lee, T. L., 188
Lefever, J. B., 542

Legare, C. H., 177
Legedza, A. T. R., 449
Lehman, D. R., 360
Leibniz Institute for the Social Sciences, 410
Lekh, S. K., 222
Lelkes, O., 334
Lelkes, Y., 323
Lens, W., 364
Lensegrav Benson, T. L., 527
Lerner, J. S., 465
Lerner, M. J., 361
Leserman, J., 67
Leslie, A. M., 151
Lester, D., 283
Leuba, J., 26, 152, 427
Levasseur, M., 403
Levenson, M. R., 5, 18, 50, 99, 165, 192, 193, 194, 296, 373, 582, 584, 588
Levenson, R. W., 276
Levin, J., 598
Levin, J. S., 449
Levine, E. G., 569
Levine, L., 642
Levine, S. V., 405, 410
Levine, S. Z., 372
Levinson, D. J., 84
Levy, K. N., 105
Lewicka, M., 276
Lewis, C., 450
Lewis, C. A., 332, 364, 448, 549
Lewis, R. J., 344
Lewontin, R. C., 121
Liang, J., 41
Lichter, D. L., 319
Lickona, T., 624
Lieberman, M. D., 466
Liénard, P., 244
Lietaer, H., 98, 107
Lin, H., 522
Lin, J., 581
Lincoln, K. D., 51, 571
Lincoln, Y. S., 102
Lindahl, J., 141
Lindberg, 14
Lindeman, M., 146, 155
Lindgren, T., 87
Lindrooth, R. C., 642
Linley, P. A., 372, 544
Liu, E. Y., 338
Ljungdahl, C., 172
Lisdorf, A., 241
Lish, R. A., 610
Listhaug, O., 341, 344
Little, B. R., 267, 358
Litwin, M. S., 530
Litz, B. T., 360
Lloyd, S. A., 293, 504
Lo, C., 530
Lobel, M., 387
Lockwood, C. M., 461
Loewenstein, G., 465

Loewenthal, K. M., 335, 337, 415
Lohr, J. M., 391
Lomax, R. G., 461
Long, J., 372
Longest, K., 183
Lopez, S. J., 623, 624
Lorenz, K., 445, 448, 644
Lorenzi, C., 226
Losloff, S., 463
Lotharius, J., 225
Lotz, T., 335
Loucks, A. A., 60, 66
Louden, S. H., 433, 434
Louis, W. R., 457, 458
Love, K., 6, 15, 323, 363, 381, 511
Lovejoy, A. O., 32
Loverich, T. M., 581
Lowdermilk, C., 286
Lowe, D. A., 399
Lowery, L., 149
Loy, D., 584
Lubbers, M., 343
Lucas, R., 280
Lucas, V., 361
Ludwig, T. E., 486
Luecken, L. J., 450, 528
Lugaresi, E., 220
Luhrmann, T. A., 15, 658
Luna, L. R., 483
Lund, T. E., 657
Lundby, K., 660
Lundmark, M., 423
Luquis, R., 319
Lutz, A., 283
Lutz, C. A., 276
Lutz, J. G., 640
Lutzky, H., 33, 42-43
Luyten, P., 7, 87, 94, 101, 102, 103, 294, 342
Lykken, D., 280, 458, 468
Lyman, S., 499
Lynn, S. J., 425, 426
Lyon, J. L., 335
Lyon, L., 317, 323
Lyons, E., 5
Lytle, J. A., 199

M

Macaluso, M. J., 467
MacDonald, D. A., 300, 624
Machado, A., 76
MacIntyre, A., 509
Macleod, C. J., 458
Mackenzie, E., 568
MacKinnon, D. P., 461
MacLean, C. D., 607, 608
MacLeod, A. K., 335
Maddi, S. R., 552, 553, 554
Madhavaram, S., 618
Maes, H. H., 58, 442
Magen, E., 507

Maguen, S., 360
Magyar, G. M., 380, 385, 392, 493, 561, 572
Magyar-Russell, G. M., 126, 141, 274, 363
Mahaffey, A. L., 466
Maholick, L. T., 64, 67
Mahoney, A., 4, 9, 33, 34, 38, 53, 54, 141, 142, 261, 263, 278, 363, 366, 368, 382, 385, 392, 493, 566, 568, 571, 572, 597
Main, M., 170, 171, 173, 175, 176
Maini, K. K., 335
Maître, J., 98
Makris, N., 167
Maliepaard, M., 343
Maliski, S. L., 530
Malka, A., 275, 323, 338, 491
Malkwitz, L., 94, 108
Malley, B., 244, 249
Malone, M. R., 526
Malony, H. N., 100
Maltby, J., 448
Manfredi, C., 449
Mann, C. C., 636
Mann, N., 268
Manzo, P. A., 223
Mapa, A. T., 300
Mapel, T., 319
Marcum, J., 548
Marett, R. R., 145
Margetic, B., 531
Margolin, A., 569
Marinelli, S., 206
Markides, K. S., 334, 449
Markman, 14
Marks, N. E., 190
Markus, H. R., 278, 339
Marlatt, G. A., 499
Marler, P. L., 37, 541, 535, 553
Marmon, T. S., 104
Marmor, G. S., 298
Marshall, M. A., 465
Marsman, K., 661
Martens, A., 463
Martin, A., 386, 391
Martin, L. H., 246
Martin, N. C., 102
Martin, N. G., 224
Martos, T., 259, 306, 363
Maselko, J., 545, 546, 552
Masicampo, E. J., 504
Maslim, A. A., 415
Maslow, A. H., 293, 294, 298, 358
Masters, K. S., 50, 55, 75, 282, 301, 303, 305, 334, 477, 520, 527, 549, 565, 597, 598, 599, 605, 655, 662
Mata, J., 508
Mataix-Cols, D., 223
Matheson, K., 324, 357

Mathew, T. E., 424
Mathijsen, F., 341, 343
Matlin, S., 570
Maton, K. I., 567
Matsumoto, D., 346
Mattei, V., 223
Matz, D. C., 460
Maugans, T. A., 66
Mauss, M., 143, 145
Mavor, K. I., 457, 458, 460, 461, 462, 468
Maxwell, S. E., 314
Mayes, P., 101
Mayne, T. J., 80
McAdams, D. P., 258, 260, 591
McAteer, J., 505
McCaffrey, A. M., 449
McCann, U. D., 77
McCarrell, N. S., 243
McCauley, R. N., 144, 146, 148, 149, 235, 237, 241, 244, 246, 249, 251, 446, 447
McClearn, G. E., 468
McCleary, D. F., 457, 460
McCleary, R., 415
McClenon, J., 424, 425
McClymond, M. J., 79
McConahay, J. B., 66
McConnell, K. M., 382, 385, 552, 565, 571
McCourt, K., 468
McCracken, L., 580
McCrae, R. R., 280, 294, 295, 301, 303
McCullough, M. E., 55, 58, 79, 108, 259, 275, 279, 281, 283, 284, 297, 334, 357, 371, 382, 448, 476, 477, 479, 483, 484, 486, 502, 505, 508, 511, 512, 521, 540, 541, 550, 561, 568, 608, 618, 654
McDaniel, M. A., 599, 606
McDargh, J., 104, 105, 110
McDavis, R. J., 596
McDonald, A., 386, 388
McDonald, D. A., 61, 66, 80
McDonald, P., 529
McFadden, J. T., 207
McFadden, S. H., 50, 198, 201, 207, 653
McFann, K., 78
McFarland, S., 457, 459, 462
McFarlane, E. A., 314
McGinley, P., 451
McGinn, B., 434
McGregor, I., 264, 268, 275, 357, 358, 464, 466
McGonigal, K. M., 484
McGuire, M., 318, 450
McIntosh, D. N., 361, 366, 368, 369, 373, 445, 548
McKee, P., 583
McKinnon, A. M., 435

McKown, C., 341
McLeod, K., 247
McManus, J., 442, 444
McMinn, M. R., 64, 610
McNamara, P., 6, 11, 15, 16, 17, 78, 122, 217, 221, 225, 226, 315, 466, 657
McPherson, M., 208
McPherson, S. E., 63, 67, 217, 313
McWilliams, N., 97, 106
Mead, M., 442
Mead, N. L., 499
Meador, K. G., 63, 66, 79, 202, 203, 204, 217, 313, 314, 333
Medicus, G., 451
Medin, D., 322
Mehta, S., 460
Meier, A. M., 319
Meier, B. P., 389, 502
Meissner, W. W., 94, 96, 99, 100, 107, 110
Mela, M., 542, 545
Meng, H., 109
Menozzi, P., 635
Merasco, D. M., 172, 173
Meraviglia, M. G., 448
Mercer, J. A., 296
Merino, S. M., 318
Merluzzi, T., 531
Merton, T., 505, 508
Mesquita, B., 276
Metzner, R., 428
Meuleman, B., 341
Meyer, D. E., 306
Miao, F., 277, 286, 339
Michael, S. T., 360
Michaelson, J., 584
Michie, S., 505
Mickley, J. R., 367
Miedema, S., 172, 174
Mikkelson, A. C., 317
Mikulas, W., 43
Mikulincer, M., 14, 170, 345, 464
Milevsky, A., 319
Milgram, S., 633
Miller, A., 532
Miller, A. J., 490
Miller, A. S., 338
Miller, C. H., 390
Miller, D. T., 323
Miller, L, 4, 105, 108, 430, 541, 544, 551, 553
Miller, M., 609
Miller, M. K., 316
Miller, M. L., 599
Miller, N., 643
Miller, O., 337
Miller, W. R., 33, 36, 49, 62, 66, 422, 607
Milliman, J., 623
Mills, M., 14, 360

Mills, P. J., 655
Milton, J., 80
Minch, S., 444
Mintz, L. B., 545
Mischel, W., 507
Missimer, J. 657
Mitchell, L., 551
Miyakawa, T., 220
Miyazaki, M., 6, 50, 476, 549, 645
Mobley, M., 545
Moehl, B., 503, 522
Modan, B., 503
Moerman, D. E., 147
Moghaddam, F. M., 6, 15, 18, 323, 363, 381, 392, 511, 632, 633, 634, 635, 637, 640, 641, 642, 643, 644
Mohr, S., 222, 543, 544, 571
Moisi, D., 645
Moldawsky, A., 499
Moldoveanu, M., 582
Molendijk, A. L., 23, 25
Molock, S. D., 570, 571
Montague, P. R., 154
Montana, S., 104
Montemayor, R., 298
Moody, R. A., 430
Moon, A., 281
Mooney, K., 529
Morales, C., 157
Moreno-Jiménez, B., 306
Morgan, C., 508
Morgan, D., 227, 527
Morgan, R., 238
Morgan, R. L., 61, 65, 66
Moriarty, G., 386, 388
Morling, B., 445
Morris, M. W., 339, 362
Morris, P., 340
Morris, R. J., 54, 85, 88, 128, 314, 423, 447
Morrison, M., 596
Morgenthaler, C., 202
Mory, S. C., 79
Moses, L. J., 167
Moskowitz, G. B., 256, 257, 465
Moskowitz, J. T., 546
Moss, Q., 542, 551
Mostyn, T. 643
Moyaert, P., 98
Mrazek, M. D., 581
Mroczek, D., 582
Müller, C., 383, 532
Mullet, E., 283, 338, 415, 489
Mullins, L. C., 561
Muñoz-García, A., 333, 341, 364
Musgrave, C. F., 314
Muraven, M., 499, 500, 501, 502, 505, 508, 510
Murdock, G. P., 216
Murken, S., 13, 18, 82, 106,

371, 383, 403, 404, 405, 406, 532, 552, 657
Murphy, D., 645
Murray, K., 303
Murray, R., 322
Murray-Swank, A., 572
Murray-Swank, N., 126, 141, 274, 303, 319, 333, 363, 380, 381, 383, 392, 561, 569
Murrelle, L., 58, 442
Musick, M. A., 304, 337, 343, 391, 527, 546
Mussweiler, T., 148
Myers, D., 5, 19, 321, 337, 415
Myers, J. E., 28, 35

N

Nader, K., 13
Nadesan, M. H., 619
Nag, M., 477
Nagoshi, C. T., 279, 462
Nahin, R. L., 78, 450
Nam, C. B., 524
Namini, S., 403, 404, 405, 406, 408
Nanamoli, B., 585, 586
Nash, K., 268, 275, 357, 464, 466
Nasr, S., 52
Nathan, L. R., 467
National Commission on Terrorist Attacks upon the United States, 633
National Opinion Research Center, 410, 447
Naumann, L. P., 459
Nauta, W. J., 229
Neale, M. C., 295
Neale, R. E., 442, 444
Neberich, W., 336, 599
Neimeyer, R. A., 368
Nelsen, H. M., 133
Nelson, C., 530, 533
Nelson, C. A., 633
Nelson, E. A., 391
Nelson, J. M., 192, 202
Nelson, L. J., 319
Nelson, N. A., 335
Nemeroff, C., 337
Nesse, R. M., 552
Neto, F., 489
Nettle, D., 505
Neuhauser, L., 38
Nevo, B., 415
Newberg, A., 11, 52, 87, 227, 230, 466
Newman, R. I., 582
Newman, J., 67
Newman, L., 426
Newman, R., 167, 240
Newman, S. P., 381, 529
Newton, A. T., 368

Neyrinck, B., 364
Ng, S., 54
Ni, H., 560
Nicholas, J. J., 384
Nicki, R., 53
Nielsen, M. E., 19, 52, 274, 313, 315, 316, 318, 320, 321, 332, 457, 465, 542, 551, 656
Nielsen, N. S., 335
Nielsen, S. L., 108
Nielson, S. L., 604
Niemann, L., 580
Niemiec, C. P., 508
Nijran, K. S., 222
Nillson, K. W., 226
Nimen, D. S., 319
Nisbett, R. E., 322
Nitt, T., 276
No, S., 342
Nofi, O., 434
Noftle, E. E., 582
Nolen-Hoeksema, S., 370
Nooney, J., 566
Nordgren, L. F., 505
Norenzayan, A., 241, 275, 281, 318, 320, 321, 332, 338, 345, 363, 459, 464, 465, 656
Norman, G. J., 528
Norris, P., 331
Norton, E. C., 642
Norton, M., 11
Nosek, B. A., 462
Noth, I., 202
Novak, P., 43
Novara, C., 542
Novotni, M., 387
Novotny, C. M., 101
Noyes, R., Jr., 430
Nusbaum, H., 658
Nyhof, M., 241

O

Oaten, M., 499, 501
O'Brien, W. H., 533, 568
Ochs, C., 6, 50, 279, 284, 476, 549, 645
Ochsner, K. N., 221, 276, 466
O'Collins, G., 27
O'Connor, K. P., 151
O'Connor, L. E., 509, 551
O'Connor, P. J., 450
O'Connor, S., 337
Offenbächer, M., 147
Ogata, A., 220
Ogbu, J. H., 343
Ogbu, J. U., 640
Oh, D., 580
O'Higgins-Norman, J., 4
Oishi, S., 280, 282, 286, 365
Olanow, C. W., 225
Olatunji, B. O., 391

O'Leary, D., 228
Olsman, E., 315
Oman, D., 7, 9, 15, 29, 33, 38, 40, 43, 86, 96, 103, 143, 166, 190, 191, 201, 202, 203, 208, 319, 380, 402, 416, 422, 503, 506, 519, 520, 521, 524, 570, 580, 597, 606, 618
O'Neill, T., 543
Ordan, D., 447
O'Reilly, C., 623
O'Reilly, D., 447522
Orenstein, A., 435
Ørnbøl, E., 581
Ortigues, E., 95
Ortigues, M.-C., 95
Ortiz, D., 444
Osarchuk, M., 463
Oser, F., 190, 192, 193
Ostafin, B. D., 499
Osteen, J., 277
Ostow, M., 449
Otto, R., 32, 142, 143, 292, 431, 444
Oud, J. H. L., 298
Owsianiecki, L., 241
Oxman, T. E., 78
Ozer, D. J., 282
Ozorak, E. W., 235, 365, 366

P

Padilla-Walker, L. M., 319
Pafford, M., 432
Pagels, E., 590
Pahnke, W. N., 76, 77
Paleari, F. G., 479
Palesh, O., 382
Pallant, J.F., 569
Palmo, A. T., 584, 585
Paloutzian, R. F., 3, 5, 9, 13, 15, 18, 23, 38, 48, 53, 59, 64, 65, 75, 82, 84, 89, 94, 106, 174, 176, 199, 202, 256, 271, 292, 346, 371, 373, 380, 399, 400, 401, 402, 407, 409, 415, 416, 422, 458, 499, 507, 552, 561, 570, 620, 622, 624, 651, 657, 661
Palumbi, S. R., 636
Pancer, S. M., 387, 462
Paquette, V., 228, 466
Pargament, K. I., 4, 7, 9, 10, 26, 27, 32-39, 43, 48, 50, 51, 52, 53, 54, 62, 63, 66, 67, 126, 140, 141, 142, 143, 144, 148, 156, 199, 201, 204, 205, 259, 260, 261, 263, 264, 265, 270, 274, 285, 304, 330, 361, 362, 363, 366, 367, 369, 370, 371, 380, 381, 382, 383,

384, 385, 386, 387, 389, 392, 406, 445, 448, 493, 532, 541, 546, 549, 551, 552, 553, 560, 561, 562, 563, 564, 565, 566, 567, 568, 569, 570, 571, 572, 573, 595, 596, 597, 598, 599, 600, 601, 604, 605, 610, 624
Park, C. L., 3, 9, 10, 11, 12, 14, 15, 18, 36, 64, 66, 75, 103, 104, 174, 176, 199, 202, 239, 249, 256, 259, 274, 275, 282, 315, 324, 331, 332, 334, 346, 357, 358, 360, 361, 362, 366, 367, 368, 369, 371, 372, 373, 380, 381, 382, 383, 385, 390, 399, 400, 401, 402, 407, 409, 422, 423, 476, 485, 499, 510, 520, 525, 526, 533, 544, 546, 550, 551, 561, 562, 563, 568, 572, 595, 596, 597, 598, 599, 600, 601, 604, 605, 610, 620, 621, 624, 633, 651, 652, 653, 654, 655, 662
Park, J., 657
Parker, B. D., 176
Parker, G. B., 449
Parkerson, G., 217, 313
Parkin, R., 149, 150
Parr, D. L., 442
Parrott, D. J., 459
Pasquale, F., 424
Patock-Peckham, J. A., 279, 459
Patrick, H., 508
Patrick, K., 387
Patrikios, S., 342
Patterson, G. R., 63
Paul, G., 347
Pawar, B. S., 623
Payne, B. K., 467
Payton, G., 609
Peacock, J. L., 444
Pearce, M. J., 383, 566
Peck, M. S., 388
Pederson, W. C., 643
Pendleton, B. F., 66, 128
Pendleton, S., 52, 565
Pennebaker, J. W., 79, 80, 278
Perez, L., 36, 54, 63, 369, 380, 381, 386, 563
Perlstein, A. L., 642
Persinger, M. A., 230
Peteet, J. R., 27
Peterman, A. H., 59, 64, 65, 67, 530
Petersen, R., 387
Peterson, C., 53, 201, 525, 565, 571
Peterson, C. K., 219
Peterson, J. L., 459

Petrovich, O., 167, 251
Pettigrew, T. F., 637
Pew Research Center, 319, 597, 598
Pfister, O., 96
Pfeifer, S., 65
Phelps A. C., 532, 566, 655
Phillips, R. E., III, 385, 565, 569, 571
Phillips, R. L., 335
Phillips, R. S., 449
Phills, C. E., 268
Piaget, J., 171, 240
Piccinin, A. M., 205
Pichon, C.-L., 465
Pichon, I., 320, 465
Pickering, W. S. F., 142
Pickett, M., 449
Piedmont, R. L., 50, 53, 58, 65, 126, 206, 293, 294, 295, 300, 301, 302, 303, 304, 306, 332, 333, 382, 584
Pietrantoni, L., 549
Pike, P., 105
Pilgrim, R. B., 441
Pilling, A. R., 636
Pine, F., 97, 98
Pinker, S., 119, 251
Pirutinsky, S., 415, 546, 553
Pisante, J., 224
Pitcher, B. L., 61
Pitts, R. C., 30, 37
Plakun, E. M., 388
Plant, E. A., 467
Plante, T. G., 43, 59, 66, 382, 580, 604, 606
Plato, 643
Platvoet, J., 26, 31
Plomin, R., 468
Plüss, C., 342, 343
Pnevmatikos, D., 167
Pogarsky, G., 499
Poland, W. S., 108
Polanski, P. J., 609
Poling, D. A., 168
Poling, T. H., 403
Polio, H. R., 88
Poll, E., 172
Poll, J., 382, 541
Pollo, A., 147
Pollock, V. E., 643
Poloma, M. M., 66, 79, 85, 128, 283, 424, 426, 447, 448, 572
Poortinga, Y. H., 332, 334
Popper, K., 23
Porpora, D. V., 425
Porr, M., 363
Porter, T. J., 241
Porterfield, A., 183
Post, B. C., 607
Powe, B., 529
Powell, L. H., 521, 527, 655
Poteat, V. P., 468

Powell-Griner, E., 78
Prati, G., 549
Pratt, J. B., 27, 35
Pratt, M., 387, 462
Pratt, M. G., 621
Prentice, D., 657
Prentice, M., 268
Presser, S., 535
Pressman, S. D., 550
Presson, C., 642
Preston, J., 361, 465
Previc, F. H., 226
Prez, J. E., 382
Priester, P. E., 53
Prigerson, H. G., 383, 566
Procter, M., 336
Procter, W., 429
Proffitt, D., 567
Pronk, N. P., 450
Proudfoot, W., 431
Proulx, T., 11, 12, 14
Pruyser, P., 100, 443, 445, 446, 448
Przedborski, S., 225
Przymus, D., 276
Puchalski, C., 28, 36, 40, 655
Puglisi, M., 446
Puri, B. K., 222
Puri, R., 570
Purzycki, B. G., 11
Pyszczynski, T., 12, 463, 464, 637
Pyysiäinen, I., 144, 251

Q

Qatar, K. Z., 384
Qi, W., 433
Quay, S., 223
Quillivan, C. C., 457
Quin, R., 199
Quintana, S. M., 341
Qutb, S., 641

R

Raab, A., 319
Radhakrishnan, P., 280
Ragen, N., 444
Rahav, G., 499
Raiya, H. A., 53, 382, 386, 566, 571, 572
Rajagopal, D., 568
Rakoczy, H., 151
Ramchandran, K., 466
Ramachandran, V. S., 221, 230
Ramazani, R. K., 641
Ramble, C., 241
Rambo, L. R., 38, 399, 400, 402, 403, 507
Ramirez, A. G., 532
Ramos-Grenier, J., 51
Ramsey, J. L., 207
Randolph-Seng, B., 316, 321, 465, 542, 545, 656

Rangel, A., 154
Rappaport, R. A., 442, 448
Ratner, H. H., 175
Ratner, P., 545
Rauch, S. L., 223
Rauch, W., 499
Rause, V., 52, 87
Ray, L. A., 449
Read, J. G., 317
Reavley, N., 569
Redden, E. K., 410
Reeskens, T., 341
Regalia, C., 479
Regmi M. P., 339
Regnerus, M. D., 191, 317, 319
Reichbart, R., 388
Reid, H. W., 543
Reik, T., 443
Reiss, S., 269
Reker, G. T., 358
Rennie, B., 152
Rennie, D. L., 102
Reyna, C., 462
Reysen, S., 493
Rhodes, J. E., 103
Rholes, W. S., 464
Rican, P., 300, 303, 306
Rice, E., 96
Richards, C., 447
Richards, P. S., 337, 568, 599, 601, 606, 607, 608, 610
Richards, W. A., 77
Richardson, A. J., 222
Richardson, J. T., 399, 403, 414, 507
Richerson, P. J., 129, 134
Richert, R. A., 17, 50, 99, 166, 167, 168, 169, 175, 240, 296, 318, 407, 410, 432, 653
Rickaby, J., 499
Ricoeur, P., 149
Ridge, R. D., 260, 283, 322, 392, 464
Riecken, H.W., 81
Riesebrodt, M., 145
Rigby, S., 67
Riis, O., 335
Rippentrop, E. A., 549
Risk, J. L., 382
Ritter, E. H., 642
Ritter, R. S., 465
Ritzler, B. A., 104
Rivière, S., 489
Rizzuto, A.-M., 94, 96, 99, 100, 104, 105, 110, 171, 172, 294, 604
Robbins, M., 364, 365
Robbins, S. P., 618
Robbins, T. W., 225
Roberts, B., 261, 582
Roberts, G., 505
Roberts, K. A., 441
Roberts, P. H., 223

Roberts, R., 609
Robertson, R., 634
Robins, R. W., 261
Robinson, E. A. R., 571
Robinson, M. D., 389
Roccas, S., 336, 363
Rochat, P., 238
Rodgers, W., 383, 525, 565
Rodgerson, T. E., 303, 333
Rodin, E. A., 429
Rodriguez, B. F., 562
Rodriguez, C. M., 322
Rodriguez, M. L., 507
Rodríguez-Carvajal, R., 306
Roehlkapartain, E. C., 4, 38, 39
Roelofsma, P. H. M. P., 357, 550
Roepstorff, A., 11, 228, 657, 658
Roesch, S. C., 566
Roger, V. L., 526, 527
Rogers, J. L., 642
Rogers, R. G., 524
Rogers, S. A., 108
Rohner, R. P., 133
Rohrbaugh, J., 65
Rokeach, M., 84, 284
Romans, S., 551
Romero, C., 486, 490
Ronen, T., 499
Roof, W. C., 424
Root, L. M., 371, 476, 479, 486
Rosato, M., 522
Rosch, E., 24, 29, 30, 582
Rose, E. D., 13, 38, 64, 363, 371, 373, 380, 381, 386, 388, 389, 390, 391, 392, 477, 485, 532, 542, 565, 597, 599, 600, 604
Rose, E. M., 607
Rosen, R. I., 526
Rosenberg, E., 503
Rosenberg, S. D., 78
Rosengren, K. S., 151, 177
Roskam, I., 342
Rosman, H., 508
Rosmarin, D. H., 54, 382, 386, 546, 553, 566, 571
Ross, J. M., 54, 63, 67, 132, 133
Ross, L. D., 323
Ross, M., 464
Rosset, E., 168, 239
Rößler-Namini, S., 13, 18, 82, 106, 371, 552, 657
Rothbard, N. P., 405
Rothbaum, F., 362, 445
Rothman, A., 281
Rothschild, Z. K., 464
Routledge, C., 14, 457
Rowatt, W. C., 6, 61, 66, 260, 320, 321, 333, 341, 386, 388, 459, 461, 462, 465, 490, 492, 656, 661
Rowe, D. C., 642
Rowlands, J. M., 199

Rozin, P., 149, 275, 337, 338, 340, 491
Rózycka, J., 306
Ruckmick, C. A., 300
Rueb, J. D., 316
Ruffle, B. J., 320
Ruiz, G. M., 640
Rümke, H. C., 109
Rusbult, C. E., 492
Ruskin, R., 388
Russell, A. G., 323
Russell, J. A., 276
Rutter, M., 468
Ryan, D. N., 343, 545
Ryan, K. R., 266
Ryan, R. M., 67, 260, 334, 364, 365, 508, 581
Rybarczyk, B. D., 384
Rye, M. S., 492, 573
Ryff, C., 411, 531
Ryncarz, R. A., 591

S

Sabbagh, M. A., 167
Sabon, M. B., 429
Sachdeva, S., 322
Sadiq, M., 63
Safdar, S., 344
Saffady, W., 94
Sageman, M., 634
Saha, S., 97
Salas, O., 321
Saler, B., 24, 29, 31, 37, 42
Sali, A., 569
Salinas, J. J., 343
Saltz, J. L., 467
Sam, D., 332
Samanez-Larkin, G., 277
Sambamoorthi, U., 449, 560, 662
Samija, M., 531
Samuels, P. A., 283
Sanavio, E., 542
Sanchez-Burks, J., 286, 335
Sandage, S. J., 108, 477, 488, 608
Sanders, G., 545, 552, 553
Sanderson, W. C., 64, 382, 605
Sandoval, J. H., 51
Sanford, R. N., 84
San Miguel de Majors, S., 532
Sansone, C., 508
Sapienza, P., 336
Sapp, S., 201
Saroglou, V., 4, 5, 6, 15, 17, 18, 19, 25, 55, 129, 139, 204, 275, 278, 280, 282, 283, 286, 293, 295, 296, 298, 302, 315, 320, 321, 330, 331, 332, 333, 334, 339, 341, 342, 343, 344, 345, 364, 365, 399, 404, 459, 465, 510, 546, 549, 654, 656, 660

Sasaki, J. Y., 282, 337, 339
Saucier, G., 299, 300
Sauer, S., 147
Saunders, C., 67
Saunders, S. M., 361, 599
Sawatzky, R., 545
Sawyer, A. T., 580
Scarlett, W. G., 4, 190
Scarpa, C., 5
Schaal, B., 465
Schaap-Jonker, H., 104
Schachter, S., 81
Schafer, R., 609
Schaffer, H. R., 166, 170
Schak, D., 41
Schaler, J. A., 60, 66
Schaller, M., 241
Scharfstein, B.-A., 449
Scheepers, P., 415
Scheers, N. J., 303
Scheier, M., 532
Scherer, K., 276, 548
Scheuneman, J. D., 51
Schiaffino, K. M., 319
Schimmack, U., 280, 282
Schjeldahl, K., 389
Schjødt, U., 11, 228, 657
Schlitz, M., 435
Schlundt, D. G., 363
Schmeichel, B. J., 500, 501, 507, 510
Schmida, M., 60
Schmidt, S., 81, 426, 580
Schmidt-Wilk, J., 622
Schnall, E., 253, 524
Schneider, D. J., 507
Schneiders, S. M., 26, 28, 35, 37
Schnell, T., 652, 653
Schnitker, S. A., 6, 13, 50, 267, 364, 366, 486, 561
Schnurr, P. P., 78
Schoenrade, P. A., 27, 36, 52, 63, 81, 130, 387
Scholl, B., 238
Schoneman, S. W., 449
Schooler, J. W., 504, 581
Schottenbauer, M. A., 562
Schulte, D. L., 609
Schultz, A., 151
Schultz, D. W., 466
Schultz, J. M., 372, 548, 554
Schultz-Larsen, K., 522
Schulz, L., 168
Schulz, R., 532, 571
Schuster, M. A., 560
Schumacker, R. E., 461
Schumann, K., 464, 465
Schvaneveldt, R. W., 306
Schwartz, A. C., 383
Schwartz, B., 263
Schwartz, G. E., 283
Schwarz, N., 322
Schwartz, R. C., 550
Schwartz, S., 88

Schwartz, S. H., 278, 279, 335, 336, 363, 364
Schweitzer, M. E., 499
Schwenk, C. R., 623
Scollon, C. N., 286
Scott, A. B., 32, 382
Scott, D. G., 4
Scott, S. Y., 608
Scott, W. A., 51
Sears, D., 84
Sechrest, L., 303
Sedikides, C., 5, 279, 361, 599
Sedway, J. A., 562
Segal, A. F., 430, 431
Segal, R. A., 95
Segal, Z. V., 581
Seitz, R. J. 657
Seligman, M., 129
Seligman, M. E. P., 201, 566
Sells, M. A., 588
Seol, K. O., 286
Seppala, E., 277, 283, 339
Septimus, Y., 445
Seth, S., 566
Sethness, R., 527
Settersten, R. A., Jr., 200
Séverin, G., 98
Seymour, E. M., 384, 565
Shackelford, T. K., 121, 247
Shafranske, E., 4, 6, 18, 28, 108, 110, 282, 337, 568, 595, 596, 597, 598, 599, 601, 604, 606, 607, 608, 609, 610, 654, 661
Shah, I., 191
Shah, J. Y., 256, 257, 263, 270, 506
Shah, T. S., 662
Shahabi, L., 521, 655
Shanahan, M. J., 183
Shanon, B., 77, 78, 428, 429
Shapiro, S. L., 43, 283, 580
Shariff, A. F., 52, 275, 318, 320, 321, 459, 465, 656
Shaver, P. R., 14, 61, 66, 130, 133, 170, 345, 361
Shaw, A., 372
Shedler, J., 102
Sheldon, K. M., 334
Sheldrake, P., 26, 27, 28, 29, 38
Shepard, A., 172
Shepherd, B. C., 391
Sherif, M., 633
Sherman, A. C., 59, 382, 384
Sherman, J. W., 461
Sherman, M. F., 303, 333
Sherman, S. J., 642
Sherwood, A., 527
Sheth, S. A., 228
Shettleworth, S. J., 357
Shmueli, D., 499, 500, 505, 510
Shoda, Y., 507
Shoham, I., 503
Shook, N. J., 581

Shorter, E., 509
Shreve-Neiger, A. K., 541, 542, 598
Shrimali, S., 561
Shtulman, A., 167, 168, 389
Shults, F. L., 477, 488
Shuman, J., 79
Shweder, R., 278
Sibley, C. G., 458, 459
Sica, C., 542
Siddle, R., 222, 544
Siegel, J. I., 338
Siegel, M., 609
Siev, J., 337, 542, 546
Silberman, I., 278, 361, 365, 392, 400, 401, 407, 572
Silva, F. J., 76
Silver, C., 85, 400, 423, 657
Silver, R. C., 360, 366
Silverman, W. H., 66, 406
Simile, C., 560
Simmonds, R. B., 403
Simonton, S., 382
Sims, T., 277, 281
Singer, B., 531
Singer, B. H., 411
Singer, J. A., 265
Singer, J. D., 102
Singer, J. E., 501
Singer, J. L., 101, 383, 566
Singh, G., 342
Sirin, S. R., 343
Skaggs, B. G., 368
Skal, D. J., 425, 426, 427
Skinner, T. A., 609
Skonovd, L. N., 410
Skrap, M., 224
Skrzypinska, K., 300
Slattery, J. M., 282, 332, 333, 361, 381, 390, 520, 550, 551, 572, 596, 598, 654
Slessareva, E., 502
Slingerland, E., 18, 141, 156
Sloan, R. P., 108, 449, 522
Slone, D. J., 154, 241, 243, 243
Slors, M., 657
Slotter, E. B., 499
Small, D. A., 465
Smallwood, J., 581
Smart, N., 33
Smith, A. G., 458
Smith, B., 208, 316
Smith, B. W., 54, 369, 381, 385, 386, 389, 563
Smith, C., 76, 183, 184, 186, 187, 188, 189, 190, 191, 317, 548
Smith, D. A., 624
Smith, E. I., 166, 168, 175
Smith, H., 26, 32, 43, 184, 274
Smith, J. Z., 152, 445
Smith, L. A., 59
Smith, P., 11

Smith, T. B., 382, 541, 546, 548, 568, 607
Smith, T. W., 188, 189
Smith, W. C., 190
Smith-Lovin, L., 208
Smyth, J. M., 380, 485
Snauwaert, B., 342
Snell, P., 183, 184, 186, 187, 188, 189, 190, 191
Snibbe, A. C., 278
Snyder, C. R., 360, 623, 624
Snyder, S., 66
Snyder, S. S., 362, 445
Sober, E., 134
Soderstrom, H., 226
Soenens, B., 364
Solomon, J., 170
Solomon, S., 12, 463, 637
Solomon, Z., 372
Sørensen, J., 146, 148, 446, 449
Sorenson, R. L., 87, 89, 94
Sosis, R., 11, 242
Sosis, R. H., 320
Sosis, S., 445
Soto, C. J., 323, 459
Sousa, P., 167, 240
Spanierman, L. B., 468
Spelke, E. S., 246
Spence, D. P., 101, 102
Sperber, D., 129, 235, 236, 251
Sperry, L., 293, 595, 598, 599, 606
Spickard, J. V., 425, 426, 431
Spielmans, G. I., 549, 599
Spilka, B., 12, 58, 62, 66, 76, 78, 94, 100, 106, 127, 128, 130, 184, 269, 315, 360, 361, 365, 368, 370, 371, 425, 442, 447, 449, 450, 549
Spini, D., 335
Spiro, M. E., 144
Srivastava, S., 484
Sroufe, L. A., 171
Stace, W. T., 54, 77, 433, 434
Stanard, P., 542
Stangor, C., 457
Stanovich, K. E., 236
Stanton, J., 330
Stark, M., 445
Stark, R., 65, 81, 84, 318, 339, 423, 432
Steel, J. L., 64, 372, 382, 563
Steele, R. E., 406
Stefanek, M., 529
Steffen, P. R., 527, 549
Stefurak, T., 460
Steger, M. F., 11, 364, 365, 372, 550
Stein, C., 53, 382
Stein, C. H., 369, 385, 565, 566, 571
Stein, R., 450
Steinbock, A. J., 588

Steketee, G., 223
Stephenson, G. M., 641
Steptoe, A., 521
Sterkens, C., 54, 333
Sternthal, M. J., 527, 551
Stetz, K., 389
Stevens, J., 429
Stevens, L. E., 445
Stewart, M. W., 403
Stillman, T. F., 11, 449, 499
Stillwell, A. M., 486, 508
Stoberock, B., 148
Stocks, E. L., 358
Stødkilde-Jørgensen, H., 11, 228, 657
Storch, E. A., 60
Storm, I., 208
Storr, A., 82
Stout, J. A., 449
Strabac, Z., 341, 344
Strakowski, S. M., 543
Strassman, R., 425, 427, 428
Strauss, A., 657
Strawbridge, W. J., 524
Strean, H. S., 109
Strelan, P., 387
Streib, H., 13, 18, 82, 85, 106, 371, 400, 408, 409, 410, 411, 412, 413, 417, 423, 552, 657
Strock, A. L., 201
Stuber, M. L., 296
Stygall, J. A., 381, 529
Su, J., 41
Subbotsky, E., 146
Sue, D. W., 596
Sugisawa, H., 41
Sullivan, A. R., 523
Sulloway, F. J., 462
Sumner, J., 451
Sundararajan, L., 432
Suresh, D. P., 526
Sussman, J., 382, 385, 526
Sutton, G. W., 491
Sutton, S., 280
Suzuki, S., 586, 590
Swedholm, A. M., 146, 155
Sweeney, P. J., 260, 570
Symons, D., 120
Szabó, T., 306
Sze, J., 279, 284

T

Tabak, B. A., 483
Tadie, J. T., 571
Tajfel, H., 155, 642
Talley, C., 530
Tallman, B. A., 372, 548
Tamayo, A., 98, 99
Tamir, M., 484, 508
Tamminen, K., 172, 177, 432
Tan, A., 450
Tan, S.-Y., 604, 605, 607

Tangney, J. P., 508, 512
Tapanya, S., 53
Tarakeshwar, N., 53, 54, 204, 330, 371, 382, 384, 532, 565, 567, 571, 572
Targ, E., 435
Targ, E. F., 569
Target, M., 101, 105
Tarrier, N., 222, 544
Tart, C. T., 28
Tartaro, J., 450, 528
Tashakkori, A., 417
Tashiro, T., 372
Tate, E. B., 511, 591
Tatton, W. G., 225
Tatz, S. J., 463
Taves, A., 6, 9, 15, 18, 19, 25, 32, 33, 78, 79, 81, 89, 95, 103, 125, 139, 141, 143, 144, 145, 148, 154, 157, 293, 331, 402, 423, 425, 426, 431
Tay, L., 337, 415
Taylor, C., 460
Taylor, D. M., 632
Taylor, R. J., 51, 203, 571
Taylor, S., 389
Tecoma, E., 230
Teddlie, C., 417
Tedeschi, R. G., 385, 567
Tehrani, K., 264
Teige-Mocigemba, S., 461
Tellegen, A., 276, 280, 458, 468
Templeton, J. L., 190, 193, 194
Teresi, J. A., 54, 62
Terrell, H. K., 462
Thalbourne, M. A., 434
Thayer, R. E., 276
Thedford, M., 461
Thisted, R., 658
Thomas, E., 281
Thomas, E. K., 490
Thompson-Brenner, H., 101
Thorensen, L. E., 422
Thoresen, C. E., 29, 33, 36, 38, 43, 79, 191, 208, 503, 506, 208, 503, 506, 519, 520, 521, 580, 606, 655
Thoresen, D. E., 190
Thuné-Boyle, I. C., 381, 532, 529, 532
Thurstone, L. L., 61, 66
Tice, D. M., 499, 500, 501, 509, 510
Tice, T. N., 383, 384, 525, 565
Tiliouine, H., 545
Tillich, P., 143, 152, 263
Tilquin, J., 549
Timio, M., 527
Tippens, K., 661
Tipsord, J. M., 591
Tisak, J., 64, 372, 382, 563
Tisdale, T. C., 60

Titus, P., 281
Tix, A. P., 258, 262, 567
Toburen, T., 502
Todesco, C. V., 220
Todorov, A., 657
Tolin, D. F., 337, 391, 542
Tomasello, M., 175
Tomcsányi, T., 306
Tomer, A., 364
Tonigan, J. S., 62, 66, 606
Tooby, J., 119, 120, 129, 132
Torges, C., 488
Tori, C. D., 60, 66
Toscova, R. T., 606
Toussaint, L. L., 391
Tower, R. B., 62
Tracy, A., 296
Tranel, D., 466
Traphagan, J. W., 304
Traunmüller, R., 335
Travis, F., 622
Tremmel, W. C., 446
Tremoulet, P. D., 238
Trenholm, P., 542
Trent, J., 542
Trevino, K. M., 384, 392, 565, 572
Triandis, H. C., 339
Trickett, D., 623
Trimble, M., 220, 230
Trinitapoli, J., 317
Trommsdorff, G., 332
Trompette, L., 320
Tropp, L. R., 637
Trout, D., 257
Truzzi, M., 425
Tsai, J. L., 6, 50, 274, 276, 277, 278, 279, 280, 281, 284, 285, 286, 339, 476, 549, 645
Tsang, J., 55, 58, 283, 297, 459, 461, 476, 479
Tsui, E. Y. L., 54
Tucker, G. J., 78
Tullet, A. M., 11, 282, 315, 466
Tummala-Narra, P., 108
Tumminia, D., 82
Turner, J. C., 642
Turner, R. H., 641
Tweney, R. D., 241
Tyler, F. B., 406
Tylor, E. B., 143, 144, 145, 146, 151

U

Ubinger, M., 609
Uecker, J. E., 191
Underwood, L. G., 54, 62, 66
Unnever, J. D., 316
Upal, M. A., 241, 242
Updegraff, J. A., 581
Urbach, E. E., 504
Urgesi, C., 224

Utsey, S., 484, 490, 542
Utz, R. L., 552

V

Vaaler, M. L., 191
Vail, K. E., 357, 361, 561
Vaillant, G. E., 190, 545, 553
Vaitkus, M., 552, 553, 554
Vallaeys, C. L., 59
Van Cappellen, P., 283, 465, 656
Vandeberg, B., 459
VandeCreek, L., 80, 108
vanDellen, M. R., 506
Vandenberg, B., 337
van den Hurk, P. A. M., 581
van der Laan, M., 315
van der Lans, J., 404
Van der Leeuw, G., 145, 154
van der Pligt, J., 505
Van der Straten Waillet, N., 342
VanderWilt, M., 173
van de Vijver, F. J. R., 334, 336, 346
Van de Vliert, E., 347
van Dierendonck, D., 306
Vangkilde, S., 581
van Harreveld, F., 505
Van Harrison, R., 405
Van Hoesen, G. W., 229
van IJzendoorn, M. H., 173
Vanman, E. J., 467
VanNess, P. H., 566
VanOrman, B., 243
Van Pachterbeke, M., 315, 344, 345
Vansteenkiste, M., 364
Van Tongeren, D. R., 484, 493
van Uden, M., 566
VanValey, T. L., 467
van Wicklin, J. F., 301
Vargas, L., 610
Varma, S. L., 569
Vasconcelles, E. B., 381, 382, 385, 549, 551, 564, 565, 598
Vaughan, F., 28
Vazsonyi, A. T., 319
Vehling, S., 14
Venable, D. G.
Venable, G. D., 53, 313
Ventis, W. L., 27, 36, 52, 81, 130, 313, 314
Verbit, M. F., 127
Verette, J., 492
Vergote, A., 95, 96, 97, 98, 99, 103, 104, 106, 107
Verhagen, P. J., 104
Verkuyten, M., 343
Vermeer, P., 415
Vernon, G. M., 424

Verschueren, M., 320
Versnel, H. S., 445
Vess, M., 457, 464
Victor, J. S., 451
Viggiano, C., 52
Viladrich, A., 343
Vincent, W., 459
Vingerhoets, A., 529
Vinsonneau, G., 415
Visser, A., 529, 530
Viswanathan, A., 218
Vittrup, B., 332
Vogel, D. L., 607
Vohs, K. D., 12, 366, 499, 501, 502, 504, 507
Voicu, M., 317
von Balthasar, H. U., 28
von Stillfried, N., 81, 426
Vosler-Hunter, W. L., 59
Vowles, K. E., 580
Vygotsky, L. S., 167, 175

W

Wachholtz, A. B., 50, 63, 104, 105, 148, 274, 369, 381, 449, 532, 533, 560, 568, 570, 597, 661
Wade, N. G., 607
Waelty, U., 65
Wagener, L. M., 4, 38
Wagner, N., 198
Wajda-Johnston, V. A., 609
Wakefield, G. S., 28
Wakefield, J. C., 121
Walach, H., 81, 581
Waldman, M. R., 11, 227
Waldron, V. R., 486
Walker, D. F., 543, 552, 607
Walker, L. J., 30, 37
Walker, S., 166
Wall, S., 133, 170
Wallace, B. A., 43, 588
Wallach, H., 580
Wallbom, M., 500
Waller, N. G., 458, 468
Wallerstein, R. S., 97
Wallston, K. A., 59, 363
Wan, C., 342
Warburg, M., 340
Warland, R. H., 61
Warner, H. L., 368, 552, 553
Warner, K., 340
Warnock, C. J., 38
Warren, J. A., 467
Warren, Z., 6, 15, 323, 363, 381, 511
Wasel, W., 465
Waters, E., 133, 170, 171
Watson, D., 276
Watson, J., 167
Watson, P. J., 54, 314, 333, 423, 433, 447
Watters, W. W., 540

Watts, F., 283, 285, 444, 550, 654
Waxman, S. G., 215, 220, 230
Wayment, H. A., 194, 391
Weaver, A. J., 201, 205
Webb, J. R., 487, 571
Webb, M., 389
Weber, C., 643
Weber, M., 145, 157
Webster, D. G., 52
Wegner, D. M., 357, 367, 368, 507, 644
Weil, A., 428
Weiner, H., 450
Weinstein, M., 522
Weir, C., 508
Weisz, J. R., 362
Weisz, T. R., 445
Wellman, H. M., 167, 171, 174
Wenger, J. L., 52
West, A. M., 362, 581
West, R. F., 236
West, S. A., 134
Westefeld, J. S., 607
Westen, D., 101, 102, 105
Wharff, D. M., 618
Wheeler, L., 642
White, D., 315, 316
White, F. A., 344
White, T. L., 507
White, K., 223, 491
White, O. K., 316
Whitehead, R. R., 450
Whitehouse, H., 148, 235, 237, 245, 246, 251
Whiteside, S. P., 391
Whitley, B. E., Jr., 460
Whitley, R., 447
Whitman, T. L., 542
Whittington, C., 505
Wiebe, P. H., 423
Wiggins, J. S., 458
Wiggins, M. I., 604
Wiggins-Frame, M., 609
Wilcox, P. C., 303
Wilcox, W. B., 449
Wildes, K., 532
Wildman, A. J., 38, 53
Wilkins, T. A., 50, 294, 332
Willett, J. B., 102
Williams, C., 529
Williams, D. R., 391, 527, 551
Williams, G. C., 508
Williams, J., 316, 461
Williams, J. E. G., 300, 303
Williams, M., 444
Williams, M. C., 362
Williams, R., 79
Williams, R. L., 457
Williams, R. N., 426
Williams-Gray, C. H., 225
Williamson, W. P., 63, 67, 79, 82, 88, 89, 361, 458
Williard, K., 28, 35

Willoughby, B. L. B., 275, 259, 279, 281, 334, 502, 505, 508, 511, 512, 521, 561, 654
Wilson, D. S., 134, 151
Wilson, E. O., 118, 459
Wilson, T. D., 83
Wilson, W. P., 544
Winer, J. A., 94
Wink, P., 205, 296, 297, 298, 301
Winkielman, P., 466
Winnicott, D., 100
Winter, D. G., 458
Wintering, N. A., 227
Wirtz, M., 383
Wiseman, R., 80
Witt, A. A., 580
Witvliet, C. V. O., 486, 490
Witztum, E., 224
Wohl, M. J., 493
Wolfe, A., 275
Wolfman, J. H., 542
Wolkowitz, O. M., 581
Wonder, T., 444
Wong, P. T. P., 14, 358
Wood, B. T., 64, 66, 382, 386, 387, 485
Wood, W., 460
Woodrum, E., 566
Woods, C., 542
Woodworth, R. S., 300
Woolley, J. D., 176
Worthington, E. L. Jr., 59, 64, 66, 108, 283, 323, 476, 477, 478, 479, 484, 485, 487, 488, 489, 490, 493, 548, 572, 599, 606, 607, 608
Wortman, C. B., 360, 366
Wortmann, J. H., 383, 526
Wotman, S. R., 486
Wright, P. J., 317
Wright, S. A., 410
Wulff, D. M., 26, 38, 61, 94, 96, 100, 442
Wulff, K. M., 206, 551, 567
Wuthnow, R., 28, 38, 40, 41, 183, 185, 186, 187, 189, 190, 191, 208

X

Xu, F., 167
Xu, J., 282, 337, 519, 526
Xygalatas, D., 658

Y

Yali, A. M., 64, 382, 387, 605
Yamane, D., 435
Yancey, G., 320
Yanez, B., 531, 544, 554
Yang, F., 404
Yang, L., 54, 333, 433
Yangarber-Hicks, N., 562
Yardley, L., 103
Yeager, D. M., 522
Yensen, R., 429
Yildiz, A. A., 343
Yin, R., 102

Yonan, E. A., 142
Yoon, D. P., 547
Young, J. S., 609
Young, K., 530
Young, M. J., 339, 362
Younger, J. W., 528
Ysseldyk, R., 324, 357, 361, 373, 548

Z

Zaehner, R. C., 428
Zaleski, E. M., 319, 430, 431
Zavala, M. W., 530
Zdaniuk, B., 532
Zechmeister, J. S., 486, 490
Zell, A. L., 365, 476, 490, 550, 654
Zeller, B., 427
Zerowin, J., 382
Zhang, W., 522, 548, 551, 553
Zhang, Y., 433
Zimbardo, P. G., 633
Zingales, L., 336
Zinnbauer, B. J., 7, 9, 26, 32, 33, 35, 36, 37, 86, 141, 142, 201, 264, 304, 371, 380, 382, 423, 424, 541, 598
Zock, H., 99, 104
Zube, M. J., 503
Zuckerman, P., 660
Zusne, L., 425
Zuttermeister, P. C., 67
Zwickey, H., 661
Zwingmann, C., 383, 532

Subject Index

Note. *t* = tables; *f* = figures; *n* = note.

Abortion, social attitudes, 316
Affect valuation theory (AVT), 274–287
    actual affect, 277–281, 286, 287
    attitude towards death and suffering, 275, 281, 285
    avoided affect, 279
    cross-cultural issues, 275, 276–280, 282, 286–287
    and emotional well-being, 280–283
    high-arousal positive states (HAP), 276, 278, 280, 281, 283
    ideal affect, 277–281, 286, 287
    low-arousal positive states (LAP), 276, 278, 280
    and meaning systems, 275, 285–286
    and meditation, 275, 279, 280, 283, 284
    overview, 277–281, 287
    prosocial emotions, 283–285
    and religious emotions, 285–286
    and religious rituals, 275
    religious culture perspective, 275–276, 277–280, 282, 286–287
    and sacrality, 275, 278, 285
    temperamental factors, 280–281, 286, 294
African Americans and religiousness, 51, 317, 337, 342, 343, 485, 570

and gerontology, 203–205, 364
and health, 523, 527, 529, 545
and mental health, 542, 545, 546
and racial prejudice, 460, 462, 467
Afterlife beliefs, 168–169, 177, 238–239, 246, 247–248, 250, 361, 368, 428, 430, 508, 509, 510, 527, 550, 653
Aggression, 283
Alcoholics Anonymous (AA), 262, 263, 606
Alcoholism, 262, 334, 347, 499, 500, 505, 571, 607
Anger toward God, 384–388, 392, 485, 491
    see also Forgiveness; Religious and spiritual struggles
Asian Americans and religiousness, 339, 342, 545
Atheism, 131, 208, 226, 281, 306, 315, 318, 320, 322, 333, 341, 387, 485, 493, 652, 660
    and religious deconversion, 400, 408, 410, 413, 415
    and mystical experiences, 424, 425
Authoritarianism, 84–85, 185
    see also Religious fundamentalism; Right-wing authoritarianism

Autobiography, 78, 408–409, 432
Ayahuasca, 77–78, 429

B

Behavior, see Social psychology
Big Five personality dimensions, 58, 132, 266, 292, 294–302, 305, 411, 414, 633
Buddhism, 31, 43*n*, 141, 189, 194, 274, 319, 372, 388, 424, 428, 433, 485, 502, 569, 571, 661
    and affect valuation theory, 275, 277, 278, 279, 280, 283, 284, 285
    and cross-cultural psychology of religion, 331, 333, 334, 338, 339, 345
    and mindfulness, 580, 581, 582, 584–591

C

Capital punishment, social attitudes, 316
Catholicism, 168–169, 189, 503, 505, 523, 546, 567, 568, 639
    and Affect valuation theory, 279
    and cross-cultural psychology of religion, 331, 334, 335, 336, 338, 339, 340, 341
    and social psychology, 316, 318, 319

Centers for Disease Control and Prevention (CDC), 519

Chinese religion and spirituality, 167, 168, 306, 317, 388, 433, 522, 640
measurement, 54, 188, 522

Christianity, 26, 31, 32, 149, 227, 362, 372, 389, 433, 485, 491, 523, 535, 542, 543, 546, 551, 567, 607, 657
and affect valuation theory, 276, 277, 278, 279, 283, 287
and cross-cultural psychology of religion, 333, 334, 335, 338, 339, 341, 342, 344, 346
and mindfulness, 580, 584, 588–591
and moral behavior, 499, 502, 503, 504, 509, 510
and religious coping, 568, 571, 572
and religious fundamentalism (RF), 458, 461, 463, 464
and social psychology, 316, 317, 318, 319, 322
and terrorism, 637, 641

Christina the Astonishing, 389–390

Chomsky, Noam, 244

Cicero (106–46 B.C.E.), 26

Clinical practice, see Psychotherapy

Cognitive dissonance, 447, 503
and research methods, 81–82

Cognitive priming, 322, 323, 465–466, 656, 659

Cognitive science of religion (CSR), 17, 145–146, 148, 154, 234–251, 389, 412, 444, 446, 462, 568, 604, 606, 653–654
anthropomorphism theory, 237–238, 240, 243
and belief in afterlife, 237, 246, 247, 250
doctrinal mode of religiosity, 246
and dualism, 246
hyperactive agency detection device (HADD), 14, 238–239, 249

imagistic mode of religiosity, 245–246
and meaning systems, 14, 238–239, 412
minimal counterintuitiveness (MCI), 241–242, 243, 247, 249
overview, 235–237
'promiscuous teleology', 239–240, 249
and religious rituals, 237, 242, 243–246, 251n
'theological correctness' (TC), 242–243, 245
two-systems approach, 236, 241–243, 247
see also Developmental psychology, Evolutionary psychology; Hyperactive agency detection device (HADD); Theory of mind

Conformity, 30, 278, 321, 324, 338
see also Authoritarianism; Right-wing authoritarianism

Confucianism, 54, 336, 338, 583

Conversion, see Religious conversion; Religious deconversion; Spiritual transformation

Coping, see Religious coping

Cross-cultural psychology of religion, 17, 32–33, 41, 53–55, 138–139, 154–156, 330–347, 364, 427, 433, 570
and affective valuation theory (AVT), 275, 276–280, 282, 286–287
cultural factors as moderating religion, 335–340, 343–347
differences across religious and cultural groups, 332, 334, 335, 336–340, 345–347
differences between Western and Eastern religions, 331, 338–339, 345, 346
differences within monotheistic traditions, 337–338
and ethnicity, 340–342
and health behaviors, 335, 336, 343

and immigrant acculturation, 342–344
individualism and collectivism, 339–340, 345–347
and mental health, 334, 335, 336, 343–344
overview, 330–331, 345–347
and parental roles, 334
and personality psychology, 293, 295, 300, 305, 306–307, 333–334
political context, 336, 344
and religious conversion and deconversion, 399, 411–414, 415
and religious expression, 235, 236, 244, 245, 247–248
and sexuality, 334, 336
similarities across religious and cultural groups, 332, 333, 336–340, 345–347
socioeconomic relations, 336
see also Cognitive science of religion; Social psychology

C

Daoism, 54, 339

Deconversion, see Religious deconversion; Religious conversion; Spiritual transformation

Definitional issues of religion and spirituality (R/S), 23–25, 29–31, 30f, 32–42, 216, 274–275, 380, 422–423, 478, 520, 597, 618–619
cross-cultural definitions, 32–33, 41, 237, 332
derivative R/S constructs, 38–39
Religion and spirituality distinctions, 32–33, 95–96, 110n, 184, 189–190, 201–202, 300, 333, 412, 422–423, 477, 478, 488, 618–619
and evolutionary psychology, 125–127
histories of R/S meanings, 25–29
intrinsic and extrinsic dimensions of R/S, 33–35, 49
pragmatics, 25, 31, 42
prototype phenomena, 30–31,

Definitional issues of religion and spirituality (R/S) (*continued*)

and religion, 26, 27t, 31, 32–37, 40–42, 138–141, 143–152, 154–156, 157n, 166, 201–202, 216, 237, 251n, 332

and sacrality, 139–141, 143, 146, 148–149, 154–155, 166, 332

as search process, 39

and spirituality, 26–29, 28t, 31, 32–42, 138–141, 143–152, 154–156, 157n, 166, 201–202, 478, 530

and supernatural agent, 216

see also Measurement assessment in religion and spirituality (R/S); Sacrality

Demonic possession, *see* Supernatural evil

Developmental psychology, 99, 165–166, 217, 240–241, 341, 404, 561, 571, 582, 633, 653

attachment theory, 169–174, 175, 177, 407

changes in religiousness in adolescents, 186–188, 189

children's concept of God, 167, 172–174, 176

children's concept of origins, 167–168, 177

children's concept of soul and afterlife, 168–169, 177

cognitive development, 166–167, 170–171, 174–175, 177, 191–192, 194, 207, 217, 238–240, 244, 250, 412, 571

compensation hypothesis, 172–174, 175, 407

correspondence hypothesis, 172–174, 175, 407

and evolutionary psychology, 166, 170, 175

and independence, 184–185, 191

and Internet use, 185–186, 190, 194, 198–199

intuitive and explicit concepts, 174–177

and parental involvement in religiousness, 184, 187, 191

representation of supernatural agents, 166

religious and spiritual development from adolescence to adulthood, 183–195

religious and spiritual development in childhood, 165–178, 404, 407, 432

religious and spiritual development in old persons, 198–209

and religious conversion and deconversion, 404–405, 407, 412, 415

and religious influence, 184–186, 190

and religious meaning systems (RMS), 176–177, 191–192

and religious rituals, 169, 175, 203, 206

and religious socialization, 184–186, 190

and R/S distinctions, 184, 189–190, 191, 201–202

and sacrality, 146, 151–152, 155

social cognition, 166

stages of development, 192–194

symbolic thinking, 171, 174, 177

theory of mind, 166–167

see also Evolutionary psychology; Gerontology and R/S

Diagnostic and Statistical Manual of Mental Disorders, 82

Diversity in religiousness and spirituality, 183–184, 186–190, 191; *see also* Affect valuation theory (AVT); Cross-cultural psychology of religion

Divine, belief in, *see* Sacrality

Dogmatism, 84–85, 86, 190, 265, 314, 540

see also Authoritarianism; Religious fundamentalism

Dostoyevsky, Fyodor, 220

E

Electroencephalography (EEG), 218–219, 220, 228, 466

Emotion, *see* Affect valuation theory (AVT)

Entheogens (drugs), 76–78, 184, 217, 226–227, 425, 427–429

European values study (EVS), 336, 341

Evangelicalism, 186, 266, 316, 319, 415, 523, 567, 658, 523, 567, 658

Evolutionary psychology (EP), 8, 118–134, 151–152, 154, 442, 476

adaptation theory, 119–123, 127–128, 130, 132, 152, 166, 298, 345

by-product theory, 119–123, 127–128, 130, 132, 151–152, 166, 298

and cognitive science of religion, 119, 124–125, 129, 131, 132, 238–239, 244, 246, 247

and defining religion, 125–127, 151

and developmental psychology, 166

evolutionary psychology of religion (EPR), 118–119, 122–123, 126–128, 129–134, 244

and functionality, 127–134

and group cohesion, 123, 125, 134n

and motivational science, 269–270

and natural selection, 119–122, 132, 170, 239, 242, 269

overview, 118–122, 133–134

and pervasiveness of religion, 128–130

and religious fundamentalism (RF), 459–460, 467–468

and religious motivation, 130–132

and standard social science model (SSSM), 120, 124, 130

and terrorism, 633–636, 637, 645

and transcendence, 10

and variability of religion, 132–133

see also Cognitive science of religion (CSR)

Existential concerns, 12, 36, 59, 63, 200, 202, 247, 250, 262, 294, 296, 315, 357, 358, 368, 463, 528, 532, 542, 544

F

Facebook, 198, 199, 320
Fetzer Institute/National Institute of Aging Working Group, 58, 65, 217, 605
Fetzer Institute/National Institute of Health Brief Multidimensional Measure of Religiousness/ Spirituality (BMMRS), 302, 605
Forgiveness, 30, 33, 106, 283, 284, 302, 321, 323, 338, 371, 476–494, 527, 548, 606
    anger toward God, 485, 491
    forbearance, 484
    offender, 480–482t, 483f, 485–488, 489f, 490, 491, 493
    overview, 476–478, 479, 480–482t, 494
    and personality, 489–490
    relational spirituality and forgiveness, 488–493, 489f
    religion and spirituality distinctions, 477, 478, 488
    and sacrality, 487–488, 491–493, 494
    self-forgiveness, 390–391, 392, 487, 488
    transgression, 483, 486, 488, 489f, 490–491, 493, 494
    unforgiveness, 479, 480–482t, 483f, 483, 484, 490
    victim, 479, 480–482t, 483f, 483–485, 486, 489f, 489–493
    see also Moral concern; Religious and spiritual struggles
Freud, Sigmund, 7, 240, 443, 561, 643
    approaches to religion and spirituality, 94–97, 100, 107–110, 561
    and religious neutrality, 108–110

and research methods, 100–101, 110, 110–111n
    see also Lacan, Jacques; Psychoanalysis
Functional magnetic resonance imaging (fMRI), 217–219, 228, 229, 466
Fundamentalist thinking, see Authoritarianism; Religious fundamentalism

G

Gandhi, Mahatma, 98–99
Gender distinctions and R/S, 99, 133, 297, 317, 390–391, 403, 526, 545–546
General Social Surveys (GSS), 50, 65, 185, 186, 187, 324, 410, 447, 462
Gerontology and religion and spirituality, 198–209, 364
    and African Americans, 203–205, 364
    church attendance, 203, 206
    cognitive decline, 207
    commonalities, 200, 202–204
    and dementia, 199, 207
    and Internet use, 198–199, 207–209
    multidimensional measures, 199–201, 202, 205, 209
    religious coping, 204–205
    resilience, 207
    social connectivity, 198–199, 203–205, 206–209
    and 'unmoored spirituality', 201
    see also Developmental psychology
Gestalt psychology, 405
Ghosts, belief in, 126, 238–239, 246, 247, 248
    see also Spirit possession; Supernatural agents
Glossolalia, 227, 424
Goal theory and religion and spirituality, 256–271, 409
    and adaptive problems, 269–270
    approach and avoidance motivation, 266–267, 268
    goal conflict, 263–264
    goal integration, 263–264
    goal language, 259
    and intrinsic religiousness, 262

and meaning systems, 256–257, 267
    and moral behavior, 502, 506, 507–509, 510, 511, 512
    overview, 256–258, 270–271
    personal projects, 267–268
    personal strivings, 258–265, 268
    reactive approach motivation (RAM), 268
    religious and spiritual motivation, 257, 258–260, 268–270, 271
    sanctification, 261–265, 267, 268
    search for the sacred, 259, 261–265, 267, 268–270
    spiritual strivings, 258–265, 268–270, 424
    spiritual striving questionnaire (SSQ), 265–266
    and ultimate concerns, 256–257, 259, 263–265, 550
    see also Evolutionary psychology; Motivational science
Gratitude, 199, 201, 202, 206, 283, 284, 300, 508, 606, 622

H

Hallucinations, 87, 106, 220, 423, 425, 544
    see also Mystical experiences
Health and religion and spirituality, 519–535, 597, 654–655, 661
    blood pressure, 527, 528
    cancer, 519, 528–534
    cardiovascular disease (CVD), 519, 524–528, 529
    cardiovascular disease morbidity, 525–527, 535
    cardiovascular disease mortality, 524–525, 528, 535
    and church service attendance, 520, 522, 523, 524, 525, 527, 529, 533, 534, 535
    health-related quality of life (HRQOL), 530, 532
    and intrinsic and extrinsic religiousness, 526, 527, 528, 530, 534

Health and religion and
    spirituality (*continued*)
    longitudinal studies, 522,
        523, 524, 525, 530, 531,
        532, 534, 535
    mortality and R/S, 521–524,
        525, 528, 534, 535, 655
    multidimensional aspects,
        520, 521, 522, 534
    negative religious coping,
        526, 527, 532, 533
    overview, 519–521, 534–
        535
    psychosocial adjustment to
        cancer, 530, 531, 532,
        533, 534
    and prayer, 525, 527, 534,
        535
    religious coping, 526, 527,
        528, 531
    religious struggle, 526, 527,
        533
    see also Mental Health,
        Religious coping
Hedonism, 261, 279, 333, 363,
    364, 365
Hinduism, 26, 43*n*, 53, 141,
    149, 189, 244, 283, 322,
    492, 510, 565, 571, 583,
    659, 662*n*
    and cross-cultural psychol-
        ogy of religion, 331, 333,
        336, 338, 339
HIV/AIDS, 363, 384, 565,
    569, 571
Homosexuality, 87, 315, 320,
    333
Hyperactive agency detection
    device (HADD), 238–239,
    249
    and meaning systems, 14,
        239
    see also Cognitive science of
        religion
Hyperreligiosity, 221–224

I

Ignatius of Loyola, 99, 450
Immigration, *see* Cross-cultural
    psychology of religion
Institute of Human
    Development (IHD),
    205
International Social Survey
    Programme, 410, 415
Internet, 185–186, 190,
    198–199, 207–209

Intrinsic and extrinsic
    dimensions of R/S, 33–35,
        132, 174–177, 225, 258,
        312–315, 318, 320, 323,
        544, 546, 567, 599, 601,
        652–653
    and cross-cultural psychol-
        ogy of religion, 340, 343,
        344
    current research, 313–314
    fourfold approach, 314
    and health, 526, 527, 528,
        530, 534
    and meaning systems (MS),
        358, 364, 365, 372, 417*n*,
        652–653
    and moral behavior, 508,
        510, 511
    and prejudice, 313, 319–
        320, 324
    and quest, 314–315, 320,
        333
    and workplace spirituality,
        623–626
    see also Social psychology
Islam, 53, 54, 191, 244, 259,
    278, 283, 382, 386, 433,
    502, 543, 545, 566, 569,
    571
    and cross-cultural psychol-
        ogy of religion, 333, 334,
        336, 339, 340, 341, 342,
        343, 344, 346, 415
    and Islamophobia, 344,
        572
    and mindfulness (Sufism),
        580, 584, 585, 587–591
    and religious fundamental-
        ism (RF), 464
    and social psychology, 314,
        317, 318, 319, 322
    and terrorism, 632–635,
        637–645

J

Japanese religion and
    spirituality, 41, 331
Jeanne des Anges of Loudun,
    98
Jehovah's Witnesses, (JW),
    403, 405, 406, 415
Judaism, 31, 96, 149, 203–
    204, 244, 372, 382, 386,
    433, 445, 491, 523, 542,
    546, 566, 571, 572
    and affect valuation theory,
        283, 284

and cross-cultural psychol-
    ogy of religion, 333, 335,
    336, 338, 340, 341, 343,
    344, 415
and moral behavior, 502,
    504, 505
and social psychology, 314,
    319
and terrorism, 635, 643,
    644

K

Karma, 60, 243, 362, 388,
    492, 504
Kohlberg, Lawrence, 193

L

Lacan, Jacques, 98
Luther, Martin, 98
Lutheran theology, 207

M

Meaning systems (MS), 6–7,
    10, 11–14, 16, 176–177,
    230, 239, 249, 331,
    357–373, 359*f*, 476, 494,
    564*t*, 596–598, 606, 651,
    652–655, 659, 661–662
    accommodation, 360
    appraised meaning, 358,
        359*f*, 360, 367–368, 370
    assimilation, 360
    definition, 11–12, 358–360
    and desecration, 368
    discrepancies, 368–373
    examples, 13–14, 357, 358,
        360, 373
    global religious goals and
        beliefs, 358–364, 359*f*,
        366
    global meaning, 358–365,
        359*f*, 366–373
    identity construction, 361,
        373
    intrinsic and extrinsic
        constructs, 358, 364, 365,
        372
    meaning appraisal and con-
        struction, 12, 256, 275,
        285–286, 293–294, 300,
        306–307
    meaning making, 10, 11–14,
        58–65, 75–76, 103, 106,
        139, 154–156, 177,
        358–373, 359*f*, 544, 550,
        562, 570–573

meaning-related needs, 357–358

and memory, 13

and moral behavior, 361, 363–364, 499, 508, 509, 510

and motivational science, 256–257, 267, 363–364, 366

multilevel analysis, 11–12, 13, 16, 18, 75–76, 78, 89, 146, 154–156, 305, 345–347, 361

and mystical experiences, 423, 426, 428

negative interpretations, 370, 371

and operant conditioning, 13

overview, 11–14, 357–360, 359f, 372–373, 651, 652–655, 659, 661–662

and pain, 362, 366–367, 371, 372, 373

reappraised meaning, 369–373

and religious coping, 562, 570–573

and religious conversion, 399, 400, 401, 407, 416

and religious deconversion, 408, 409, 412–414, 416, 416n

and sacrality, 360, 363, 366, 368, 369

and sanctification, 363, 366

situational meaning, 358, 359f, 360, 365–373

and trauma, 360, 366–367, 368–373

and ultimate concerns, 357, 358, 361–364, 365, 366

and workplace spirituality, 618–619, 620, 621, 627–628

see also Multilevel interdisciplinary paradigm (MIP); Religious meaning systems (RMS); Social structure and psychological meaning

Measurement assessment in religion and spirituality (R/S), 55–58, 56t, 58–67, 75–76, 520, 605

Assessment of Spirituality and Religious Sentiments Scale (ASPIRES), 300, 302, 304, 306, 382

cross-cultural dimensions, 53–55, 364

evaluation criteria, 55–58, 56t

and meaning making, 75–76

measures of dispositional R/S, 58–62, 65–66

measures of functional R/S, 62–65, 67

overview, 48–52, 65–67

problems with existing measures, 49–52

and psychotherapy, 605

RCOPE, 53, 54, 63, 204, 369, 382, 386, 388, 389, 563, 565, 566, 576

and religious coping, 562–563

Religious Schema Scale (RSS), 412, 413, 417n

R/S scales, 301–303

and representation, 50–51, 57

and self-reporting, 52

and translation, 53–54

see also Research methods

Meditation, 30, 37, 60, 78, 108, 185, 186, 189, 190, 194, 227, 275, 279, 280, 283, 284, 346, 535, 550, 606, 608, 626

and mindfulness, 582, 586

and religious coping, 567, 568, 570

Mental health, 62, 105–107, 108, 200, 202, 266, 296, 333–337, 343, 382–384, 388–390, 406, 411–413, 424, 540–554, 547f, 598, 653

affective disorders, 541–542, 545, 546

anxiety disorders, 542, 545

overview, 540–541, 545–546, 547f, 552–554

psychopathology, 540, 543–544,

and religious coping, 543, 544, 549–551, 552, 565, 568–570, 571, 572, 598

schizophrenia, 543–544, 545, 551

spiritual struggles, 550, 552

stress, 546, 549, 553

substance abuse, 544, 545, 548

suicide, 542, 543, 548

trauma, 543, 545, 552, 553

well-being, 540, 544–545, 565, 568–570, 572

see also Religious and spiritual struggles

Mexican Americans, 343, 372, 523

Mindfulness, 43n, 191, 280, 284, 391, 580–591, 661

and adult development, 581–584, 591

and Buddhism, 580, 581, 582, 584–591

and Christianity, 580, 584, 588–591

detachment, 582, 583, 584

and ethics, 591

Four Noble Truths, 585, 586

integration, 582, 583, 584

and Islam (Sufism), 580, 584, 585, 587–591

mantra, 587, 589–590

meditation, 582, 586

Noble Eightfold Path, 585, 586

openness to experience, 582, 586

overview, 580–581, 590–591

and personality, 581

as practice and function, 582, 584–591

and prayer, 588, 590

sacrality, 589–591

self-knowledge, 582–583, 584

self-transcendence, 584, 590, 591

and suffering, 580, 584, 585–586, 591

transcendence, 582, 583, 584, 588, 590, 591

Moral concern and behavior, 193–194, 242, 278, 414, 462, 498–512, 591, 643, 652, 654

automatic processes, 501, 502, 511

and capitalist economy, 503, 510

and cross-cultural psychology of religion, 332, 335, 338, 339

distraction, 507

Moral concern and behavior
(*continued*)
emotional distress, 509–510
and elevation of selfhood,
503, 510
'Expanding Circle Morality'
(ECM), 194
and forgiveness, 476, 487
guilt, 508–509, 511, 512
latent motivation, 506, 507
limited-resource model,
500–502, 505, 511
and meaning systems (MS),
361, 363–364, 499, 508,
509, 510, 654
monitoring, 500, 502, 505,
511
and motivation, 502, 506,
507–509, 510, 511, 512
overview, 498–499, 510–512
and religious and spiritual
struggles, 386, 390
and self-control, 489–512,
654
and social concerns, 498,
509, 510, 512
standards, 500, 502–505
willpower, 500, 502
see also Affective valuation theory; Goal theory;
Motivational science
Mormonism, 318, 319, 335,
529
Mortality, *see* Health
Motivational science, 256–258,
260, 264, 268–271
approach and avoidance
motivation, 266–267
and moral behavior, 502,
506, 507–509, 510, 511,
512
and personality psychology,
296, 298, 299–301, 305
see also Evolutionary psychology; Goal theory
Multilevel interdisciplinary
paradigm (MIP), 6–7, 11,
15–18, 23, 48, 75–76, 78,
89, 124, 138–139,
154–156, 174, 199, 248,
271, 287, 292, 345–347,
380, 393, 457, 498–499,
520, 572, 597–598, 619
applications and develop-
ments of, 17–18, 53,
199–201, 202, 205, 209,
229, 572

and meaning systems, 16,
18, 139, 235, 305, 331,
494, 619, 655–659,
661–662
and mystical experiences,
422, 423, 425, 427–435
overview, 15, 651, 655–659,
661–662
and religious conversion and
deconversion, 400, 401,
407–408, 414, 416
and research methods,
75–76, 78, 81–82, 89,
655–659
Mystical experiences, 220,
227, 228, 234, 333, 342,
422–435, 443, 466
alien abduction experiences
(AAE), 425–427
apparitions, 423
archaeopsychopharmacol-
ogy, 427
entheogens, 425, 427–429
hallucinations, 423, 425
and meaning systems, 423,
426, 428
and multilevel interdisciplinary paradigm (MIP), 422,
423, 425, 427–435
Mysticism Scale (M Scale),
433, 434
near death experiences
(NDEs), 425, 429–431
numinous experiences,
431–432
paranormal experiences,
425–427, 434, 435
phenomenography, 423
reflexive ethnography, 424
and religion and spirituality
distinctions, 422–425
and research methods,
85–86, 87
and sacrality, 422–423, 424,
431
and supernatural agents,
422, 423, 424
transliminality, 434
and transcendence, 422,
424, 431
see also Sacrality
Myth, 25, 442, 443, 652, 653

N

Near death experiences (NDE),
425, 429–431
see also Mystical experiences

Negative religious coping,
see Health; Religious
and spiritual struggles;
Religious coping
Neuroeconomics, 154, 155,
476
Neurological functioning, 122,
155, 277, 282, 385, 657
and meaning systems, 11,
13, 16, 407
and research methods, 87
Neurology of religiosity,
215–230, 657
autism spectrum disorder,
226
decreases in religiosity,
225–226
Geschwind syndrome, 221
increases in religiosity,
219–225
Klüver–Bucy syndrome, 221
neuroanatomical sites, 215,
220–225, 229–230
neuroimaging and modeling,
217–219
neurotransmitters, 217,
226–227, 228
obsessive–compulsive disorder (OCD), 223–224, 244
overview, 229–230
parietal lobe excision, 224
Parkinson's disease, 225–226
and religious ecstasy, 220,
222, 225, 227
and religious experiences,
220–225, 227
and religious fundamentalism, 465, 466–468
schizophrenia, 222–223
temporal lobe epilepsy
(TLE), 215, 219–222,
223, 224, 230
see also Cognitive science of
religion (CSI); Religious
fundamentalism
New Apostolic Church (NAC),
403, 405, 406
Numinous experiences, 292,
295, 301, 302, 305–307,
431–432, 444

O

Obsessive–compulsive disorder
(OCD), 337
Orthodoxy, 51, 52, 60, 65,
84–85, 246, 279, 299,
314, 319

and cross-cultural psychology, 333, 334, 336, 341
Oxytocin, 282

P

Pain, 260, 274, 284, 285, 492, 526–527, 540, 565
  and meaning systems (MS), 362, 366–367, 371, 372, 373
  and mindfulness, 580, 581, 584, 585–586, 591
  and religious and spiritual struggles, 380, 386, 388–390
  Theodicy, 362
  Views of Suffering Scale, 362
  see also Stress; Trauma
Paranormal experiences, 425–427, 434, 435, 450
  see also Mystical experiences; Parapsychology
Parapsychology, 80–81, 426, 434, 426, 434
Pentecostalism, 79, 88, 389, 424, 426
  Pentecostal parish (PP), 403, 405, 406
Personality psychology, 292–307, 459–460, 581
  and cross-cultural psychology, 293, 295, 300, 305, 306–307, 333–334
  and developmental psychology, 293, 296–298, 301
  five-factor model of personality (FFM), 58, 132, 266, 292, 294–302, 305, 411, 414, 633
  and forgiveness, 489–490
  gender distinctions, 297
  genetic basis, 295
  longitudinal studies, 296, 297, 305
  and meaning systems, 293–294, 300, 306–307
  and R/S motivation, 296, 298, 299–301, 305
  numinous constructs, 292, 295, 301, 302, 305–307
  psychoticism, 297
  and religious conversion and deconversion, 400, 401, 403, 406, 407, 411, 414, 415
  religious temperament, 294, 300

and R/S constructs, 293–296, 298–307
  R/S construct independence, 298–303, 306–307
  and R/S definitional issues, 293, 300, 301–302, 304
  and R/S scales, 301–303
  and sacrality, 292, 293, 296
  structural equation modeling (SEM), 304, 305
  see also Affect valuation theory; Motivational science
Piaget, Jean, 99, 166, 171–172, 192–193, 240, 251n
Priming, see Cognitive priming
Positive psychology, 199, 201, 623
Positron emission tomography (PET), 218, 226, 227
Posttraumatic growth (PTG), 385, 414, 526, 531, 544, 549, 565, 567, 572
Prayer, 30, 176, 187, 189, 228, 237, 242, 245, 251n, 275, 362, 441–442, 445, 446–451, 626, 658, 661
  and complimentary and alternative medicine (CAM), 450
  and religious coping, 448–449, 546, 560, 566–567, 568
  definition, 446–447
  and health, 449–450, 525, 527, 534, 535, 546
  and mindfulness, 588, 590
  and psychotherapy, 599, 605, 606, 608
  and research methodology, 78–80
  and evolutionary psychology, 128
  see also Religious rituals
Prejudice, 313, 319–320, 324, 457–464, 467, 468, 566
  racial and sexual prejudice, 460–462, 467
  see also Intrinsic and Extrinsic dimensions; Religious fundamentalism; Right-wing authoritarianism; Social psychology
Prosocial behavior, 19, 217, 277, 283–285, 296, 298, 303, 320–322, 323, 333,

459, 465, 479, 509, 512, 591, 654
  see also Cross-cultural psychology of religion; Social psychology
Protestantism, 51, 55, 433, 458, 485, 523, 543, 546, 567, 568
  and affect valuation theory, 279, 284
  and cross-cultural psychology, 331, 333, 334, 335, 336, 338, 339, 340, 341, 346, 347
  and social psychology, 316
Psilocybin, 76–77, 429
Psychoanalysis, 94–110, 294, 389, 443, 568, 604
  Freudian approaches to religion and spirituality, 94–97, 100, 107–110
  and cultural or personal distinctions, 95–96, 100–101
  and drive psychology, 98
  and ego psychology, 98–99
  and meaning making, 103
  and mental health, 105–107
  and object relational psychology, 99–100
  and psychodynamics, 97, 105, 106, 110n
  and religious experience, 103–104, 176
  and religious neutrality, 108–110
  and representations of God, 99–100, 104–105
  and research methods, 86–87, 89, 100–105, 110–111n
  see also Freud, Sigmund; Lacan, Jacques; Psychopathology; Psychotherapy
Psychology of religion, 3–19, 651–662
  and globalization, 660
  implicit religion, 652–653
  integrative themes, 3, 6–7, 89, 118, 146–147, 293, 651, 654, 657–659, 661–662
  meaning systems (MS), 10, 11–12, 103, 154–156, 293, 651, 652–655, 659, 661–662
  measures of R/S, 58–67, 75–76

Psychology of religion
(*continued*)
methodologies, 16–17,
75–76, 81–89, 100–105,
110–111*n*, 655–659,
661–662
multilevel interdisciplinary
paradigm (MIP), 6–7,
11, 15–18, 75–76,78, 89,
124, 138–139, 154–156,
271, 346, 651, 655–659,
661–662
overview, contributions, and
recent progress, 3–7, 14,
18–19, 651, 657–659,
661–662
and politics, 662
professional organizations,
5, 17, 19
professional publications,
4–5, 23, 24*f*, 75, 165,
193, 580, 618
and research funding,
661–662
and secularization, 660
and technology, 660
and workplace spirituality,
620
see also Meaning systems
(MS); Measurement
assessment; Multilevel
interdisciplinary paradigm
(MIP); Religion; Spiritu-
ality
Psychological well-being, *see*
Mental health
Psychopathology, 82, 99,
106–107, 222, 296–297,
382, 540, 543–544, 565,
571
see also Mental health
Psychophysics, 219
Psychotherapy, 38, 95,
107–108, 428, 542, 568,
595–611, 602–603*f*, 661
client preference, 607
evidence-based practice,
595–611
intentional orientation, 595,
600, 605
and meaning systems, 596,
606
overview, 595–597,
602–603*f*, 610–611
prayer, 599, 605, 606, 608
R/S assessment, 601–609
R/S as clinical variables,

596–597, 600–609,
602–603*f*
R/S integration, 599–601,
602–603*f*, 604–609
R/S intervention, 602–603*f*,
605–609, 610
R/S measurement, 605
R/S salience, 600, 601, 605,
606
religious coping, 597,
598–599, 600, 604
sacrality, 596, 600, 606,
611
spiritual illiteracy, 596–597
spiritual intolerance,
596–597
spiritual struggles, 597, 599,
600, 604
training, 609–610
see also Psychoanalysis;
Religious and spiritual
struggles; Religious coping

Q

Quest, 387, 459
see also Intrinsic and Extrinsic dimensions

R

Religion
and chemical facilitation of
R/S experiences, 76–78
as cultural and personal,
95–96, 151–152
definitions, 26, 27*t*, 31,
32–37, 40–42, 95–96,
110*n*, 138–141, 143–152,
154–156, 157*n*, 166, 184,
201–202, 216, 237, 251*n*,
274–275, 300, 478
derivative religion and spirituality (R/S) constructs,
38–39, 189–190
distinctive features of R/S,
32–33, 86–87, 184,
189–190, 201–202, 300,
333, 422–423, 477, 478,
488, 618–619
histories of meanings, 25–
29
measures of R/S, 58–67
and motivational science,
257, 258–260, 268–270,
271
professional organizations,
24*f*
and uniqueness, 8–9

see also Meaning systems
(MS); Psychology of reli-
gion; Sacrality; Spirituality
Religious and spiritual
struggles, 380–393, 526,
527, 533, 550, 552
anger toward God, 384–
388, 392
gender distinctions, 390–391
demonic appraisal and
supernatural evil, 380–
381, 388–390, 392, 565
and emotional distress,
381–384, 387–390
interpersonal conflicts, 381,
391–392
and mental health, 382–384,
388–390
overview, 380–381, 392–393
physical symptoms, 384–
385, 387, 388–390
and psychotherapy, 597,
599, 600, 604
and religious coping, 565,
569–570
and R/S growth, 385–386
and sacrality, 380, 391–392
scrupulosity, 390–391
self-forgiveness, 390–391,
392
and stress, 381, 383,
388–390
and trauma, 383, 388–
390
see also Meaning systems
(MS); Mental Health;
Pain; Religious violence;
Stress; Trauma
Religious cognition, 216,
226–227, 229–230
Religious conversion, 215,
399–408, 414–416, 416*n*,
444, 507, 552, 657
and childhood familial experiences, 404–405, 415
cross-cultural comparisons,
399
and gender distinctions,
403
individual and group variables, 402–408
and meaning systems, 13,
371, 399, 400, 401, 407,
416
and multilevel interdisciplinary paradigm (MIP), 400,
401, 407–408, 416

and new religious movements (NRMs), 402, 403, 404, 415
overview, 399–402, 414–416
and personality traits, 400, 401, 403, 406, 407, 415
person–environment fit model, 405–408
person–religion fit model, 402–408
psychosocial patterns, 402, 406
qualitative and quantitative research, 400, 415
and research methods, 82
and trauma, 404
see also Religious deconversion; Spiritual transformation
Religious coping, 204–205, 448–449, 526, 527, 528, 531, 560–573, 564t
active and passive coping, 562
general orienting system, 566–568
meditation, 567, 568, 570
and mental health, 543, 544, 549–551, 552, 565, 568–570, 571, 572
multidimensional aspects, 562, 570–573
negative religious coping, 384–388, 392, 526, 527, 532, 533, 549–551, 563–568, 570, 599
overview, 560–562, 564t
positive religious coping, 563–568
prayer, 560, 566–567, 568
RCOPE, 53, 54, 63, 204, 369, 382, 386, 388, 389, 563, 565, 566, 576
and sacrality, 560, 561, 572
and stress, 561, 563, 564, 566, 567
and cancer patients, 563, 565, 568, 569, 572
therapeutic methods, 568–573
and trauma, 560, 565
and well-being, 565, 568–570, 572
see also Health; Mental health; Posttraumatic growth (PTG); Religious and spiritual struggles

Religious culture perspective, 275–276, 277–280, 282, 286–287
see also Affect valuation theory (AVT)
Religious deconversion, 399–400, 408–414, 410t, 416n, 417n, 657, 660
apostasy, 400, 408
atheism, 400, 408, 410, 413, 415
cross-cultural comparisons, 411–414
five criteria of deconversion, 409
and goal theory, 409
individual and group variables, 412–414
and meaning systems, 408, 409, 412–414, 416, 416n
and multilevel interdisciplinary paradigm (MIP), 408, 414, 416
and new religious movements (NRMs), 402, 403, 404, 410
overview, 399–402, 414–416
and personality traits, 411, 414
person–environment fit model, 408–414
person–religion fit model, 408–414
and psychological well-being, 411–413
psychosocial patterns, 413, 414
qualitative and quantitative research, 408, 411, 414, 415, 417n
and religious styles, 411–414
and trauma, 408, 409, 413–414
see also Religious conversion; Spiritual transformation
Religious fundamentalism (RF), 84–85, 132, 265, 316, 320, 333, 341, 411, 414, 457–468, 643
definition, 458
event-related negativity (ERN), 466
and evolutionary perspective, 459–460
and genetics, 467–468
implicit measures, 461

and mortality salience, 463–465
neuroimaging and modeling, 466
overview, 457
and personality, 459–460
and prejudice, 457–464, 467, 468
priming, 465–466
racial prejudice, 460–462, 467
and right-wing authoritarianism (RWA) mediation, 459, 461–463, 467–468
sexual prejudice, 460–462, 467
and social neuroscience, 465, 466–468
structural equation modeling (SEM), 461, 462, 468
terror management theory (TMT), 461, 463–465, 561
see also Authoritarianism; Right-wing authoritarianism
Religious judgment, 193–194
Religious meaning systems (RMS), 6–7, 8, 14, 476, 564t, 652–655
and cognitive science of religion, 249–250
and developmental psychology, 176–177
religion and global meaning, 360–373, 407, 414
religion and situational meaning, 365–373
research on, 14
see also Meaning systems (MS)
Religious rituals, 169, 175, 203, 206, 237, 242, 243–246, 251n, 332, 333, 441–451, 572, 606, 652–653, 658
history, 442
biological perspective, 442
and church service attendance, 520, 522–525, 527, 529, 533–535, 541, 606
complimentary and alternative medicine (CAM), 450
and coping, 448–449
and health, 449–450
and 'magic', 445, 446

Religious rituals (*continued*)
    multidimensional perspective, 443–444, 451
    and pathology, 450–451
    and prayer, 441–442, 445, 446–451
    and psychoanalysis, 443
    and social stability, 445
    see also Prayer
Religious studies, 138–140
Religious violence, 322, 392
    see also Religious and spiritual struggles
Research methods in religion and spirituality (R/S), 16–17, 75–89, 100–105, 110–111n, 655–659, 661–662
    and chemical facilitation of R/S experiences, 76–78
    and cognitive dissonance, 81–82
    correlational and survey studies, 84–86
    field studies, 83–84
    and intercessory prayer, 78–80
    longitudinal research, 86, 104, 105, 133, 177, 183, 186–188, 194, 204–206, 296, 297, 305, 317, 372, 382–386, 389, 392, 403, 432, 468, 522, 523, 524, 525, 530, 531, 532, 534, 535, 541, 565, 566, 571, 627
    and multilevel interdisciplinary paradigm (MIP), 75–76, 78, 81–82, 89, 154–156, 345–347
    and mystical experience, 85–86, 87
    overview, 75–76, 89, 138–140, 655–659, 661–662
    and parapsychology, 80–81
    and psychoanalysis, 86–87, 89, 100–105, 110–111n
    psychometric measures, 75
    and psychotherapy, 605
    qualitative methodology, 16, 78, 88, 102, 187, 220, 269, 296, 339, 400, 408, 411, 414, 415, 417n, 424, 486, 491, 520, 544, 548, 572, 655, 656–657
    quantitative methodology, 77, 78, 88, 138, 218–219, 228, 296, 342, 400, 408, 411, 414, 415, 417n, 433, 524, 572, 655
    and sacralities, 147–148, 154–156
    see also Measurement assessment in R/S
Right-wing authoritarianism (RWA), 52, 63, 84, 411
    definition, 458
    event-related negativity (ERN), 466
    and evolutionary perspective, 459–460
    and genetics, 467–468
    implicit measures, 461
    and mortality salience, 463–465
    neuroimaging and modeling, 466
    overview, 457
    and personality, 459–460
    and prejudice, 457–464, 467, 468
    priming, 465–466
    racial prejudice, 460–462, 467
    and religious fundamentalism (RF) mediation, 459, 461–463, 467–468
    RWA aggression, submission, and conventionalism, 458
    sexual prejudice, 460–462, 467
    and social neuroscience, 465, 466–468
    structural equation modeling (SEM), 461, 462, 468
    terror management theory (TMT), 461, 463–465
    see also Authoritarianism; Religious fundamentalism

S

Sacrality, 30, 139–156, 201, 245, 322, 331, 380, 391–392, 446, 560, 561, 572, 652–653, 659
    and affective valuation theory (AVT), 275, 278, 285
    animistic and preanimistic approaches, 144–147, 157n
    and art, 189
    defilement and desecration, 149–150, 368, 392, 572
    and definitions of R/S, 34–37, 39, 138–141, 143–152, 154–156, 157n, 166, 274–275, 478
    as divine, 142–143
    and forgiveness, 487–488, 491–493, 494
    and 'magic', 145–147, 150, 155, 156n, 157n
    and meaning making, 9, 139, 154–156, 360, 363, 366, 368, 369
    and mindfulness, 589–591
    and motivational science, 259, 261–265, 267, 268–270
    and mystical experiences, 422–423, 424, 431
    and 'nonordinary powers', 144–148, 150, 152, 155
    and 'nonordinary worlds', 148–152, 155
    and oppositions, 148–150
    overview, 8, 9, 139–142
    and placebo effects, 147–148, 155, 157n
    as prohibition and taboo, 142
    and psychotherapy, 596, 600, 606, 611
    and R/S as composites, 139–141, 143–144, 149–152, 154–156
    and singularity, 8, 32–33, 141–142, 143–144, 154, 155
    valuation, 152–154, 155, 156
    see also Definitional issues; Meaning systems (MS); Psychology of Religion; Religion; Religious studies; Spirituality
Sanctification, 32, 33, 34, 38, 39, 261–265, 267, 268, 278, 363, 366, 392, 508, 511
    see also Goal theory; Meaning systems (MS)
Satan, *see* Supernatural evil
Schizophrenia, 222–223, 543–544, 545, 551
Secular trends in religion and spirituality, 183–190
    secularization theory, 188

Self-control, *see* Moral concern and behavior
Serpent handling, 87, 88, 424
Sexual practices, 87, 121, 220, 221, 223–224, 315, 318–319, 293, 323, 324, 334, 336, 499, 500, 506
see also Homosexuality
Sex differences in religiosity, *see* Gender distinctions
Shamanism, 25, 184, 443
Single photon emission computed tomography (SPECT), 218, 222, 227
Social psychology and religiousness, 312–324, 373, 583
and aggression, 322
gender distinctions, 317
and honesty, 321–322, 323
identity construction, 315–316, 323–324
intrinsic and extrinsic constructs, 312–315, 318, 320, 323
and moral behavior, 498, 509, 510, 512
and politics, 323
prejudice, 319–320
prosocial behavior, 320–322, 323
quest, 314–315, 320
and sexuality, 318–319, 323, 324
social attitudes, 316–317, 323–324
social influence, 317–318, 323–324
see also Cross-cultural psychology of religion; Goal theory; Motivational science; Social structure
Social structure and psychological meaning, 183–186, 190, 191, 315–318, 335–340, 343–347, 639
see also Cross-cultural psychology of religion; Religious conversion; Religious deconversion; Social psychology; Terrorism
Spirit possession, 246, 247–248, 250, 251*n*, 388–390
see also Ghosts; Supernatural agents

Spiritual transformation, 13, 64, 86, 266, 371, 399–417
and religious conversion, 399–408, 414–416
and religious deconversion, 408–414
see also Religious conversion; Religious deconversion
Spirituality,
and chemical facilitation of R/S experiences, 76–78
definitions, 26–29, 28*t*, 31, 32–42, 95–96, 110*n*, 138–141, 143–152, 154–156, 157*n*, 166, 184, 201–202, 274–275, 300, 478, 530
derivative religion and spirituality (R/S) constructs, 38–39, 478
distinctive features of R/S, 32–33, 86–87, 184, 189–190, 201–202, 300, 333, 422–423, 477, 478, 488, 618–619
histories of meanings, 25–29
intrinsic and extrinsic dimensions of R/S, 33–35, 174–177
measures of R/S, 58–67
and motivational science, 258–265, 268–270
professional organizations, 24*f*
as search process, 39
social dimension, 37–38, 40
see also Meaning systems (MS); Mystical experiences; Psychology of religion; Religion; Sacrality
Stanford Prison Experiment, 644
Stem cell research, social attitudes, 316
St. John of the Cross, 589
St. Teresa of Jesus, 589
Stress, 63, 83, 85, 86, 106, 128, 172, 173, 175, 204, 263, 264, 296, 343, 487, 653
and meaning systems (MS), 358, 360, 362, 365–373
and mental health, 546, 549, 553

and moral behavior, 509–510
and religious and spiritual struggles, 381, 383, 388–390
and religious coping, 561, 563, 564, 566, 567
see also Pain; Trauma
Suffering, *see* Pain
Supernatural agents, 32, 40, 123, 131, 146, 148, 166, 174, 175, 216, 221, 237, 238–242, 247, 275, 281, 282, 380, 422, 423, 424, 446, 448
see also Ghosts; Mystical experiences; Spirit possession; Supernatural evil
Supernatural evil, 149, 371, 511, 564*t*
and religious and spiritual struggles, 380–381, 388–390, 392

T
Tanquerey, Adolphe-Alfred, 42*n*
Taoism, *see* Daoism
Terror management theory (TMT), 461, 463–465, 561, 637
Terrorism, 344, 511, 632–645, 638*f*
and 9/11, 344, 552, 560, 572, 632, 633, 641
catastrophic evolution, 633–636, 637, 645
and Christianity, 637, 641
and colonization, 636–637
cyber-jihad, 634–635
evolutionary psychology, 633–636, 637, 645
globalization, 633–635, 640, 644–645
intergroup contact, 637, 645
and Islam, 632–635, 637–645
and Israel, 635, 643, 644
overview, 632–634, 638*f*, 644–645
and Palestine, 635
personality psychology, 633
preadaptiveness, 636–637
social identity theory, 632, 634, 638, 640, 641–644, 645

Terrorism (*continued*)
staircase to terrorism, 633, 637, 638*f*, 641, 644
see also Religious fundamentalism
Theodicy, 362
see also Pain
Theory of mind, 166–167, 216, 228, 229, 239, 247, 250
Therapy, *see* Psychotherapy
Theresa of Avila, 98
Transcendence, 32, 50, 189, 193, 201, 259, 267, 268, 293, 345, 331, 548–549, 552, 652–653
and meaning systems (MS), 357, 361, 363, 366, 652–653
and mindfulness, 582, 583, 584, 588, 590, 591
and mystical experiences, 422, 424, 431
overview, 9–10
self-transcendence, 224, 296, 345, 366, 584, 590, 591
and workplace spirituality, 618, 622, 623, 626
Trauma, 64, 79, 104, 316, 360, 366–367, 368–373, 404, 653

and mental health, 543, 545, 552, 553, 560, 565
posttraumatic stress disorder (PTSD), 543, 545, 565
and religious and spiritual struggles, 383, 388–390
and Religious deconversion, 408, 409, 413–414
see also Mental health; Pain; Posttraumatic growth (PTG); Stress

V

Voting, social attitudes, 316, 323

W

Winnicott, Donald, 100, 443
Wittgenstein, Ludwig, 42*n*
Women's Health Initiative Observational Study, 523, 524
Workplace spirituality, 18, 38, 617–628
definitional issues, 618–619, 622
individual levels, 618–619, 620–621, 622–623, 624, 625, 626

integrative spirituality, 622
intrinsic and extrinsic motivation, 623–626
meaning systems, 618–619, 620, 621, 627–628
measurement, 623–624
organizational goals, 624–625
organizational levels, 618, 619, 621, 623, 624
overview, 617–619, 622, 627–628
person–organization (P-O) fit, 623
postmaterialist values, 624
professional publications, 617–619, 621
and psychology of religion, 620
spiritual intelligence, 622
spiritual leadership theory, 625–627, 627*f*
transcendence, 618, 622, 623, 626
World values study (WVS), 336, 337, 415

Y

Yoga, 37, 53, 108, 621, 626